The
Amphibians
and Reptiles
of the
Yucatán Peninsula

Agalychnis callidryas, Chiapas, Mexico, 15 km S Palenque

Theories pass. The frog remains.
—Jean Rostand, *The Substance of Man*

Drawings by Julian C. Lee

The Amphibians and Reptiles of the Yucatán Peninsula

JULIAN C. LEE

Department of Biology, The University of Miami
Coral Gables, Florida

Comstock Publishing Associates

a division of **Cornell University Press**

ITHACA AND LONDON

For Elena, William, and Edward

Copyright © 1996 by Cornell University
Jacket painting © 1996 by Christopher R. Mills

First published 1996 by Cornell University Press.

Library of Congress Cataloging-in-Publication Data
Lee, Julian C.
    The amphibians and reptiles of the Yucatán Peninsula / Julian C.
Lee ; drawings by Julian C. Lee.
        p. cm.
    English and Spanish.
    Includes bibliographical references (p.   ) and indexes.
    ISBN 0-8014-2450-X (cloth : alk. paper)
    1. Amphibians—Yucatán Peninsula—Identification.   2. Reptiles—
Yucatán Peninsula—Identification.   I. Title.
    QL655.L424   1996
    597.6'0972'65—dc20   95-20413

Printed in the United States of America.
Color plates printed in Hong Kong.

⊛ The paper in this book meets the minimum requirements of the
American National Standard for Information Sciences—Permanence
of Paper for Printed Library Materials, ANSI Z39.48–1984.

Contents

SPECIES ACCOUNTS

The color figures follow pages 20 and 436

Preface

In 1989 Wake and Johnson published the description of a new species of salamander from the cloud forests of Chiapas, Mexico. So distinctive that the authors erected a new genus to accommodate it, the salamander was named *Ixalotriton niger*, "black bounding salamander." It is apparently restricted to a small patch of forest, and the authors cautioned that the genus might very well become extinct in the near future. Similarly, J. A. Campbell et al. (1989), in describing a new species of lizard from the cloud forests of Hidalgo, Mexico, noted that the vegetation at the type locality had been nearly completely removed by 1987. They, too, warned that their new species was at risk of extinction. It is entirely possible that these two novel forms have, or shortly will, become extinct before the details of their biology can be ascertained.

Such examples are by no means unique to Mexico, of course, or to amphibians and reptiles. Yet they illustrate why studies of biotic diversity in the New World tropics are presently conducted with a sense of urgency, and they underscore the need for baseline biological inventories and surveys. Because even the most elementary information is lacking for many groups in many parts of the Neotropics, floral and faunal surveys and basic taxonomic studies are critical.

From an ecological perspective, no more fundamental biological questions can be asked than, How many species occur here? or To what species does this specimen belong? What does it eat? How does it reproduce? and What is its distribution? Our knowledge of many Neotropical organisms is too rudimentary to allow answers to even these basic questions. Yet, sufficient information is now available for the amphibians and reptiles of the Yucatán Peninsula to be treated comprehensively. Indeed, for no other area of comparable size in the New World tropics is the herpetofauna so well known in terms of distribution and taxonomic composition. In 1980 I summarized information on the distributions of amphibians and reptiles in the Yucatán Peninsula, and I noted that taxonomic problems were particularly apparent for members of the genera *Sphaerodactylus*, *Eleutherodactylus*, *Elaphe*, *Micrurus*, *Tantilla*, and *Pliocercus* (J. C. Lee, 1980a). In the ensuing sixteen years, the status of the lizards of the genus *Sphaerodactylus* was clarified by Harris and Kluge (1984), and certain of the *Eleutherodactylus* were treated by Savage (1987). Problems within the genus *Elaphe* have been resolved by Dowling and Fries (1987). Savage and Crother (1989) treated *Pliocercus*, J. M. Savage and J. Slowinski (pers. comm.) revised *Scaphiodontophis*, and L. D. Wilson (1982a) clarified the status of the species of *Tantilla*. Additionally, problems within the *Anolis sericeus* complex were resolved by me (J. C. Lee, 1980b). Thus, we now have the opportunity—rare with regard to Neotropical flora and fauna—to move to the next, more synthetic stage in the development of knowledge.

The immediate purpose of this book is to provide a guide that anyone—specialist or nonspecialist—can use to identify any species of amphibian or reptile encountered in the Yucatán Peninsula. After determining the specimen's identity, the user has access to information on the species' distribution, both throughout its range and within the Yucatán

Peninsula, and its natural history, including habitat, behavior, reproduction, and diet. This summary of biological information is something of a benchmark, a measure of how much is known and how much there is yet to know about the biology of the amphibians and reptiles of the Yucatán Peninsula. It is my hope that this treatment of the Yucatecan herpetofauna will contribute to the larger purpose of furthering knowledge and understanding of tropical biodiversity and will instill a greater appreciation for these fascinating animals and for their rapidly diminishing habitats.

Many people have assisted with various phases of my work in the Yucatán Peninsula over the past twenty-four years, and I am pleased to extend to them a heartfelt, though inadequate, thanks. For loan of specimens, answers to my written queries, and provision of working space, I am grateful to the following individuals and their institutions: John E. Cadle, Academy of Natural Sciences, Philadelphia; C. J. Cole, D. Frost, Charles W. Myers, Richard G. Zweifel, Margaret Arnold, Philip Damiani, and Carol Townsend, American Museum of Natural History; Howard Hunt, Atlanta Zoo; Barry Clarke and P. J. Stafford, British Museum (Natural History); Robert C. Drews, Alan E. Leviton, and Jens V. Vindum, California Academy of Sciences; Ellen Censky and the late Clarence J. McCoy, Carnegie Museum; Hobart M. Smith, University of Colorado; Shi-Kuei Wu, University of Colorado Museum; Kraig Adler, Cornell University; John B. Iverson, Earlham College; Robert F. Inger, Hymen Marx, Alan Resetar, and Harold K. Voris, Field Museum of Natural History; Walter Auffenberg and David L. Auth, Florida Museum of Natural History; John W. Wright and Robert L. Bezy, Los Angeles County Museum; Max Nickerson and Robert W. Henderson, Milwaukee Public Museum; M. C. Carmen-Pozo and Humberto Bahena Basave, Museo de Zoología, Centro de Investigaciones de Quintana Roo; Ernest E. Williams and José P. Rosado, Museum of Comparative Zoology, Harvard University; David B. Wake and Harry W. Greene, Museum of Vertebrate Zoology, University of California, Berkeley; Douglas A. Rossman, Museum of Zoology, Louisiana State University; Arnold G. Kluge, Ronald A. Nussbaum, and Greg Schneider, Museum of Zoology, University of Michigan; George R. Zug, W. Ronald Heyer, Roy McDiarmid, and Ronald I. Crombie, National Museum of Natural History; Robert W. Murphy and Ross MacCulloch, Royal Ontario Museum; Gregory K. Pregill, San Diego Museum of Natural History; James R. Dixon, Texas Cooperative Wildlife Collection, Texas A & M University; David C. Cannatella, Texas Memorial Museum, University of Texas; Harold A. Dundee, Tulane University; Thomas J. Uzzel, University of Illinois Museum of Natural History; William E. Duellman and John Simmons, University of Kansas; Jonathan A. Campbell, University of Texas, Arlington; Tod Reeder, University of Texas, Austin; Robert G. Webb, University of Texas, El Paso; and Eric Richart and John Legler, University of Utah. Ernest A. Liner, James Knight, and John Iverson supplied data and loaned specimens from their private collections. Tommy Allison provided many locality data for specimens from Quintana Roo, Mexico. William F. Pyburn kindly supplied field notes pertaining to his collections from Belize. Jay M. Savage provided data on *Scaphiodontophis*, allowed me to examine specimens in his possession, and was helpful in *Eleutherodactylus* identification.

For permission to publish their own photographs or photographs under their care I am grateful to Robert L. Bezy, Los Angeles County Museum of Natural History; Jonathan A. Campbell, University of Texas, Arlington; Frederick Dodd, International Zoological Expeditions; Carol Farneti; Anne Heimann; Jeffrey Himmelstein; John B. Iverson; William W. Lamar; Robert A. Lubeck; the late Clarence J. McCoy, Carnegie Museum of Natural History; James R. McCranie; Roy McDiarmid, National Museum of Natural History; Jacob A. Marlin; Sharon Matola, the Belize Zoo; Carolyn M. Miller; Paul Moler; Norman J. Scott; Tom Smoyer, Harbor Branch Oceanographic Institute; Stephen G. Tilley; R. Wayne Van Devender; and Richard C. Vogt, Estación de Biología Tropical "Los Tuxtlas." John W. Wright kindly supplied living specimens of *Cnemidophorus* to be photographed. All uncredited photographs were taken by me.

I thank Gordon Browning, Elena M. de Jongh, Marian Demos, Oscar Flores-Villela, Irene Goyenechea, and Benjamin D. Webb for their assistance with language translations.

Portions of this book were reviewed by specialists whose knowledge of certain taxonomic groups far exceeds my own. Their invaluable comments improved the species accounts considerably. Reviewers and the taxa on which they commented are: Aaron Bauer (*Aristelliger*), Robert L. Bezy (*Lepidophyma*), David C. Cannatella (*Physalaemus pustulosus*), Roger Conant (*Agkistrodon bilineatus*,

Nerodia rhombifer), Brian I. Crother (*Urotheca*), Kevin de Queiroz (*Ctenosaura, Iguana*), James Dixon (*Phyllodactylus*), C. Kenneth Dodd (*Caretta*), Herndon G. Dowling (*Elaphe, Senticolis*), Arther C. Echternacht (*Ameiva*), Carl H. Ernst (*Terrapene, Rhinoclemmys*), Marc P. Hayes (Centrolenidae), Laurence M. Hardy (*Ficimia*), W. Ronald Heyer (*Leptodactylus*), Jerry D. Johnson (*Masticophis, Stenorrhina*), Carl S. Lieb (*Anolis*), Andrew Ross (Crocodylidae), Jack W. Sites, Jr., (*Sceloporus cozumelae, S. chrysostictus, S. teapensis*), Jaime Villa (*Tretanorhinus*), David B. Wake (*Bolitoglossa, Oedipina*), Marvalee H. Wake (*Dermophis, Gymnopis*), Steven Werman (*Atropoides*). Jerry D. Johnson reviewed the distribution maps of species occurring in Chiapas, Mexico. Hobart M. Smith reviewed the chapter on the historical development of herpetological knowledge in the Yucatán Peninsula, provided advice concerning etymologies, and responded patiently to my many written queries. Elizabeth P. Benson, Sylvia Scudder, and Elizabeth S. Wing reviewed the section on ethnoherpetology. Alan H. Savitzky informed me of several important references; he also carefully reviewed the glossary and made numerous useful suggestions for its improvement.

Through the years, a host of Belizeans, Yucatecos, and Guatemaltecos—many of them children whose collecting prowess often exceeded my own—assisted with specimen acquisition or facilitated my fieldwork in other ways. In many cases I never knew their names, but I carry with me the memory of their kindness, generosity, and enthusiasm. I remember especially the children at Río Lagartos who made a game of catching *Sphaerodatylus argus* and selling them to me for a few pesos, never realizing of course that their specimens constituted the first record of that species for Mexico; the young boy at Uaxactún who brought me a magnificent specimen of *Lampropeltis triangulum*, which he believed was the deadly venomous coralillo, and which, although dead, had not a single blemish; the Maya woman on the road to El Seibal who told me how to remove the botfly larvae from my leg; the pilot of the single-engine Cessna with the door held in place with rope who cursed his temperamental plane but was nonetheless able to set down on the tiny landing strip at Yaxchilán—on the third try; the elderly man on the outskirts of Muna who offered me a gift of fresh oranges to augment my steady diet of oatmeal, tuna, and macaroni and cheese; the "veterinarian" at Felipe Carrillo Puerto who did all that he could for my seriously injured German shepherd; and the woman who towed me and my disabled van behind her truck, at frightening speed, to Chiquilá. Each of these persons, and countless others, contributed materially to the successful completion of this book and forever shaped my attitude toward the people of Middle America.

I am grateful to Sharon Matola, Director of the Belize Zoo, for placing the facilities of the zoo at my disposal, for helping to arrange collecting permits, and for logistical support of my fieldwork in Belize. I owe a special debt of gratitude to the late L. C. Stuart. "Don Pancho" provided accommodations at Panajachél, Guatemala, shared with me his unparalleled knowledge of Middle American herpetology, and smoothed the way for me in many other ways.

For companionship and assistance with fieldwork, I thank Brady Barr, Elena M. de Jongh, Tony Garel, Emilio Reyner Gil, Bruce Grayson, the late Richard Lacer, Janet M. Lee, Peter Luykx, Michael V. Plummer, Tony Rath, Mark Salzburg, Alan H. Savitzky, Thomas R. Sharp, Dawn S. Wilson, and Karen Zachow. Brenda and Roberto Colli, of Mérida, Yucatán, and Emilio and Ileana Reyner, of Cancún, opened their homes to me and provided both friendship and logistical support.

I am indebted to Dr. Beatriz Mateos López, of the Centro de Salud, Pueblo Nuevo X-Can, Quintana Roo, who successfully treated me for snakebite.

Collecting permits were graciously issued by E. O. Bradley, Oscar Rosado, and E. D. Green, of the Ministry of Trade and Industry, Belize; and by Antonio Landazuri Ortiz and Manual G. Gonzales E., Dirección General de la Fauna Silvestre, Mexico.

My work in the Yucatán Peninsula has been supported by the National Science Foundation (DEB 7609303, BSR 9024738), the American Philosophical Society (Penrose Fund), the Southern Regional Education Board, the National Institutes of Health (Biomedical Research Grant administered through the University of Miami), and by award of an Orovitz Summer Research Fellowship from the University of Miami.

I thank the staff of Cornell University Press for their encouragement, support, and patience as I repeatedly defaulted on submission deadlines. In particular I thank Robb Reavill, science editor, for initially suggesting that I undertake this project. To Mindy Conner fell the unenviable task of copyediting the manuscript and transforming the academese of my early drafts into something accessible to nonherpetologists. In this she has largely succeeded, but any remaining deficiencies are mine, for I do not always recognize—much less accept—good advice. Helene Maddux, senior manuscript editor, oversaw production of this book, responded cheerfully to my queries, and was enthusiastic in her support of this project.

Finally, I am especially grateful to Elena M. de Jongh for her transcriptions and translations of tape-recorded interviews, for providing companionship in the field, sometimes under difficult circumstances, and for reading and rereading many sections of this manuscript. Her assistance, encouragement, and support have been invaluable.

JULIAN C. LEE

Coral Gables, Florida

Introduction

Like a hitchhiker's thumb, the Yucatán Peninsula juts north-northeast into the Gulf of Mexico and the Caribbean Sea (Map 1). Bounded to the north, east, and west by water, and to the south and southwest by the highlands of Guatemala and the Meseta Central of Chiapas, Mexico, the peninsula is a distinct natural area of approximately 240,000 km². From the perspective of political geography, this peninsula marks the point where North America and Central America join. From an anthropological point of view, the Yucatán Peninsula is part of Meso-America—that portion of southern Mexico and northern Central America whose indigenous peoples shared several cultural attributes such as hieroglyphic writing, a game played in special courts with a rubber ball, an emphasis on human sacrifice and ritual bloodletting, and a complex pantheon of deities inhabiting a multilevel heaven and underworld. It was in the Yucatán Peninsula that the Maya civilization attained its greatest florescence, and even today the Maya constitute the largest more or less homogeneous population of native Americans north of Peru.

The Yucatán Peninsula is an area rich in endemic species of plants and animals. The uniqueness of the Yucatecan biota has long been appreciated by naturalists, who have often treated the peninsula as a distinct biotic province (e.g., Barrera, 1963; Goldman and Moore, 1945). Moreover, the Yucatán Peninsula has served as a notable center of vertebrate differentiation and, perhaps, dispersal (P. Müller, 1973). Finally, powerful north-south gradients in the amount and seasonality of precipitation exist

there and are not seriously confounded by topographic relief. The Yucatán Peninsula thus offers excellent opportunities to study patterns of geographic distribution and to evaluate hypotheses concerning the factors believed to be important in setting distributional limits and controlling the numbers of co-occurring species (J. C. Lee, 1980a).

Defined on the basis of physiographic considerations rather than on geopolitical criteria, the Yucatán Peninsula spans nearly six degrees of tropical latitude and contains in their entirety the Mexican states of Campeche, Quintana Roo, and Yucatán, the Lacandón region of Chiapas, eastern Tabasco, the republic of Belize, and the Guatemalan Department of El Petén (Map 1).

For the purposes of this work, I take the 600-m contour in northern Alta Verapaz, Guatemala, and Chiapas, Mexico, as the southern and southwestern boundaries of the peninsula, respectively. This is not an altogether arbitrary delineation, for it approximates the upper limit of the Lower Tropical Zone, an elevation at which a rather distinct biotic break occurs, especially for amphibians and reptiles (Stuart, 1948:14–15). To the north, the highlands of Chiapas gradually give way to the Gulf coastal plain, a vast wetland formed by the anastomosis of the Río Grijalva, the Usumacinta, and their tributaries. At this point, delineation of the westernmost extent of the Yucatán Peninsula is entirely arbitrary. I include the lowlands of northern Chiapas and Tabasco east of an imaginary line extending north-northwest from Palenque, Chiapas, to Frontera, Tabasco, near where the Río Grijalva enters the

MAP 1. The Yucatán Peninsula showing political subdivisions and major topographic features. Area above 600 m is shaded. Stippled area is the Sierrita de Ticul of Yucatán and Campeche.

Gulf of Mexico. Thus, my definition of the Yucatán Peninsula is somewhat more inclusive than that usually given. It would not be acceptable to a political geographer, and the people of Belize, northern Guatemala, and northern Chiapas certainly do not consider themselves residents of the Yucatán Peninsula. But for the naturalist, this definition is defensible, even desirable, for it circumscribes the peninsula on the basis of biologically relevant natural features that constitute a barrier to the dispersal of the terrestrial fauna.

How to Use This Book

This book is, first and foremost, an identification guide. With it one should be able to identify any species of amphibian or reptile encountered in the Yucatán Peninsula, with the possible exception of tadpoles in their early stages of development and the hatchlings of some species of *Anolis* lizards. Identification can be accomplished in several ways.

The majority of the species of amphibians and reptiles in the Yucatán Peninsula are so distinctive in terms of size, shape, color, and color pattern that identification can often be accomplished by simply comparing the specimen in question with the photographs and drawings. If identification is still uncertain, one should read the descriptions of the species that resemble the specimen at hand, together with the sections on similar species. In addition, the distribution maps should be consulted, for some species may be eliminated from further consideration on geographical grounds. Taken together, the illustrations, descriptions, and distribution maps will allow correct identification of many of the most commonly encountered species.

In a minority of cases identification will require attention to anatomical detail and the use of identification keys. The keys (given in both English and Spanish) are dichotomous, meaning that they consist of pairs of alternative, contrasting statements. In effect, one proceeds by a process of elimination, until all but one of the possible alternatives have been eliminated. The herpetological jargon used in the species descriptions and in the identification keys can be daunting to nonspecialists, but it is easily mastered by anyone willing to take a little time to learn the anatomical terms. The introduction to each major group of amphibians and reptiles includes a brief comment on identification, noting which characters are most useful and explaining basic terminology. Moreover, distinguishing characters are virtually always illustrated, and they are defined in the Glossary.

Organization of the Species Accounts

The species accounts are arranged alphabetically by species within genera, and the genera are listed alphabetically within families. Each family and genus is introduced by a brief description that characterizes the salient biological features of the taxon, its distribution, and its taxonomic diversity, thereby placing its Yucatecan representatives into perspective.

Each species account begins with the currently accepted scientific name and the author of the name, followed by reference to the original description, type specimen, and type locality. In deciding which names to accept, I have generally followed the recommendations of the author who has most recently examined the taxon comprehensively. Next, the species' common names are presented. The English common name or names appear first, if an acceptable one exists, followed by the vernacular names applied to the species in Belize, Guatemala, and Mexico. Maya names are given wherever possible, and these are identified as to dialect. Throughout most of the Yucatán Peninsula, the dominant Maya dialect is Yucatec, and a variant of this is spoken by the Lacandón Maya of northeastern Chiapas. The Mopan Maya of Belize also speak a dialect similar to Yucatec, whereas the Kekchi of Belize and of Alta Verapaz, Guatemala, speak a language quite different from that of the Yucatec, Lacandón, and Mopan speakers. On the fringes of the Yucatán Peninsula, in the vicinity of Palenque, in northern Chiapas, the Maya dialect is Chol, whereas in adjacent Tabasco, Chontal is spoken. For some species there will be no entry for a particular language because no common name exists in that language or the name is unknown to me. Variant spellings exist for many Maya words, including place names and the names of amphibians and reptiles.

Attempts to establish a standard orthography are presently under way in the highlands of Guatemala, where Maya writing and language groups, in cooperation with the Academia de Lenguas Mayas de Guatemala and the Proyecto Lingüístico Francisco Marroquín, have adopted a uniform alphabet (Freidel et al. 1993:16). A comparable effort, using a very similar alphabet, is under way in the Mexican portions of the Yucatán Peninsula. In this system, such familiar place names as *Uaxactún* and *Yucatán* become *Waxaktun* and *Yukatan*, respectively, and the Yucatec (= Yukatek) word for "snake," *can*, becomes *kan*. After careful consideration I have decided not to adopt the new, standard orthography in this book. To do so, I believe, would unnecessarily confuse and hinder, rather than promote, the dissemination of information about the Yucatecan herpetofauna. Virtually all maps and gazetteers in circulation contain the earlier, familiar spellings of Maya place names. Moreover, the locality data recorded on museum specimen tags and on jar labels, data that also reside in museum catalogs and databases, almost without exception use the earlier spellings. My decision not to use the standard alphabet is simply a concession to reality, for I agree completely with Freidel et al. (1993:17) that "the Maya have the right to decide how their own languages should be written."

The description section of each species account emphasizes the features that characterize that form and distinguish it from other species. The descriptions are based on adult specimens, but in those cases where pronounced ontogenetic variation exists, this is described. For those species of anurans with free-living aquatic larvae, the tadpole is described. The size and shape of tadpoles varies depending on the developmental stage, as does the extent to which the mouthparts are fully formed. Consequently, the descriptions of tadpoles are generally based on specimens at or beyond Gosner (1960) stage 30, by which time mouthparts are fully developed and the length of the hindlimb bud is about twice its diameter. For species exhibiting sexual dimorphism or dichromatism, the distinctions between the sexes are noted. With respect to size it is important to realize that many, perhaps even most, amphibians and reptiles exhibit indeterminate growth, meaning that they grow throughout their lives, albeit more slowly after reaching reproductive maturity. Thus one may occasionally find old individuals that greatly exceed the average size for the species. Moreover, differential mortality and collecting biases will result in real or apparent geographic variation in size within the Yucatán Peninsula.

A description of the most characteristic vocalization is given for species that vocalize. For anurans this is generally the advertisement call emitted by males. A graphical representation of that call is usually provided, consisting of a sonogram, a plot of frequency against time that also displays the relative strengths of the component frequencies. Subtending the sonogram is a representation of the waveform of the sound, which plots amplitude (strength) against time. Finally, a spectrogram is included that plots amplitude against frequency.

Next, the section on similar species contrasts the species under consideration with others with which it might be confused. This is followed by a brief statement giving the full distribution of the species and its distribution in the Yucatán Peninsula. In characterizing distributions, I follow Stuart (1963: 11) in defining *low elevations* as those below about 600 m, *moderate elevations* as those between 600 and 1,500 m, and *intermediate elevations* as those between 1,500 and 2,700 m. I use the term *Atlantic slope* to include the Gulf and Caribbean coastal plains and foothills of Mexico and Central America. The term *Pacific slope* applies to the Pacific coastal plain and foothills of Mexico and Central America. The distribution of each species within the Yucatán Peninsula is illustrated by a map on which are plotted the localities of reliable reports. The localities are based primarily on museum specimens, but some records are from published sources, and a few are based on photographs, sight records, or acoustic records. The estimated geographical distribution of each species is indicated by shading on the map. My estimates of the distribution are conservative and serve to emphasize areas where additional collecting efforts can be profitably focused. The estimates are quite subjective, but documentation is provided for each locality plotted; readers are thus free to draw their own inferences concerning geographical distribution.

The section dealing with natural history contains information about habitat, behavior, diet, and reproduction, and also includes a statement concerning the abundance of the species. The coverage in this section is not intended to be exhaustive, although for the rarer species it may very nearly be so; rather, my intent is to provide an introduction to the biology of each form and an entry into the literature on that species. Wherever possible, I have drawn on sources dealing with the species in the Yucatán Peninsula or areas immediately adjacent. So little is known of the basic biology of many Yucatecan species, however, that I frequently have had to rely on the results of studies conducted elsewhere, especially in southern Veracruz, Costa Rica, and Panama. Readers should be aware that geographic variation in natural history attributes is certain to exist, and characterization of Yucatecan species on the basis of extrapeninsular studies should be interpreted cautiously.

Each species is usually characterized as abundant, common, uncommon, or rare, sometimes with qualifiers. These are necessarily subjective designations based largely on my field experience. A species is considered *abundant* if, under the proper conditions and in the appropriate environment, one can always expect to find individuals of that species. During the rainy season in suitable habitat, for example, *Smilisca baudinii* and *Hyla microcephala* are abundant. Similarly, the small, terrestrial *Sceloporus*, such as *S. chrysostictus* and *S. cozumelae*, are abundant lizards. A species is *common* if, under suitable conditions, one can often, but not always, find individuals. *Agalychnis callidryas* and *Phrynohyas venulosa* are examples of common species. A species is *uncommon* if one cannot expect to find specimens even under the most suitable circumstances. Examples of uncommon species include the two species of *Laemanctus* and the two of *Corytophanes*. Finally, a species is *rare* if it is known from only a few specimens or if finding it can never be anticipated. *Agkistrodon bilineatus* and *Amastridium veliferum* are examples of rare species. These designations are very rough approximations and are subject to errors of many kinds. For example, the abundance of any species will vary geographically, and its real and apparent abundance will also vary seasonally. Moreover, the application of these categories to the occupants of different trophic levels is problematic: as top carnivores, many snakes must occur at low densities relative to species at lower trophic levels, such as lizards and frogs. Thus, it is doubtful that any of the snakes in the Yucatán Peninsula can be properly characterized as abundant. The number of peninsular localities from which a species is known can be approximated by examining its distribution map, which shows most (resolution is inadequate to plot all nearby records) of the known peninsular localities. To the extent that the maps reflect the distribution and abundance of the animals, rather than the activities of collectors, they provide an index of abundance. Finally, the number of specimens of each species collected in the Yucatán Peninsula can be roughly calculated from the number of museum specimens listed in the locality records. The list underestimates the actual number of museum specimens, however, for some museums catalog more than a single specimen under a single museum number, especially if the specimens are tadpoles.

If subspecies have been recognized by previous workers, those occurring within the Yucatán Peninsula are usually indicated in the subspecies section. This inclusion does not mean that I uncritically accept the utility of the subspecific category, or the desirability of conferring formal nomenclatural recognition on geographical segments of any species of amphibian or reptile in the Yucatán Peninsula. Listing subspecies does, however, indicate the extent to which geographical variation in the elements of the Yucatecan herpetofauna has been detected.

The Greek or Latin derivation of the specific name is given in the section on etymology, as is the meaning intended by the author of the name, if known. Usually the original description contains no such indication, in which case I venture a conjecture as to the probable meaning of the scientific name.

Some accounts contain a comments section, in which various issues, often nomenclatural or taxonomic, are briefly discussed. Here reference is usually made to the most recent taxonomic treatment for the species. If the species is considered endangered under the United States Endangered Species Act, or if it is listed in the appendixes of the Convention on International Trade in Endangered Species of Wild Fauna and Flora (CITES), its conservation status is indicated here. In the CITES system, a species listed in Appendix 1 is considered endangered and may not be traded among party nations "for primarily commercial purposes." Species listed in Appendix 2 are those which, although not presently endangered, could become so if trade is not regulated.

Finally, a listing of locality records concludes each species account. The records are based primarily on museum specimens but also include literature citations and photographs. In a few cases, localities are based on my sight records, and a few anuran localities are based on my records of vocalizations. The locality records are arranged alphabetically by country, and, within countries, alphabetically by political subdivision (Mexican state,

Guatemalan department, Belizean district). Within these subdivisions, the records are alphabetized by locality, and, for the same locality, by museum code. The codes are generally those recommended by Leviton et al. (1985). The codes and other abbreviations are as follows:

AMNH	American Museum of Natural History
ANSP	Academy of Natural Sciences, Philadelphia
ASU	Arizona State University
BCB	Collection of Bryce C. Brown at the Strecker Museum, Baylor University
BMNH	British Museum of Natural History
CAS	California Academy of Sciences
CF photo	Kodachrome by Carol Farneti, Belize Zoo, Belize
CM	Carnegie Museum
CMM photo	Kodachrome in the collection of Carolyn M. Miller, Gallon Jug, Belize
COHECERN	Colección Herpetológica del Centro de Estudios para la Conservación de los Recursos Naturales, San Cristóbal de las Casas, Chiapas, Mexico
EAL	private collection of Ernest Liner, Houma, Louisiana
FAU	Florida Atlantic University
FD photo	Frederick Dodd, Sherborn, Massachusetts
FMNH	Field Museum of Natural History
IHNHERP	Colección Herpetológica del Instituto de Historia Natural, San Cristóbal de las Casas, Chiapas, Mexico
INIRB	Instituto Nacional de Investigaciones sobre Recursos Bióticos, Chiapas, Mexico
JAM photo	Jacob A. Marlin, Belize
JBI	private collection of John B. Iverson, Earlham College
JBI photo	Kodachrome in the collection of John B. Iverson
JCL audio	tape-recorded vocalization in the collection of J. C. Lee, Miami, Florida
JCL photo	Kodachrome in the collection of Julian C. Lee
JCL sight record	unequivocal field identification by J. C. Lee
JCL	specimens secured by J. C. Lee in 1987 in Quintana Roo, Mexico, and deposited with the Centro de Investigaciones de Quintana Roo in August of that year, apparently now lost, ac-

	cording to M. C. Carmen Pozo (in litt.)
JLK	private collection of James L. Knight
JRB	Kodachrome in the collection of James R. Buskirk, Oakland, California
JRM	Kodachrome in the collection of James R. McCranie, Miami, Florida
KU	Museum of Natural History, University of Kansas
LACM	Los Angeles County Museum of Natural History
LSUMZ	Museum of Zoology, Louisiana State University
MCZ	Museum of Comparative Zoology, Harvard University
MNHNP	Museum National d'Histoire Naturelle, Paris, France
MPM	Milwaukee Public Museum
MSU	Michigan State University
MVZ	Museum of Vertebrate Zoology, University of California, Berkeley
MZCIQRO	Museo de Zoología, Centro de Investigaciones de Quintana Roo
MZFC	Museo de Zoología, Facultad de Ciencias, Universidad Nacional Autónoma de México, Mexico City
NMSU	New Mexico State University
NRM	Naturhistoriska Riksmuseet, Stockholm
RAL photo	Kodachrome in the collection of Robert A. Lubeck, Ava, New York
RMNH	Rijksmuseum van Natuurlijke Historie, Leiden
ROM	Royal Ontario Museum
RWV photo	Kodachrome in the collection of Robert Wayne Van Devender, Boone, North Carolina
SDSNH	San Diego Natural History Museum
SGT photo	Kodachrome in the collection of Stephen G. Tilley, Smith College
SM	Strecker Museum, Baylor University
SMF	Forschungsinstitut und Natur-Museum Senckenberg, Frankfurt am Main, Germany
TCWC	Texas Cooperative Wildlife Collection, Texas A & M University
TLB	private collection of T. L. Brown
TNHC	Texas Memorial Museum, University of Texas
TU	Tulane University

UAYX	Universidad Autónoma de Yucatán, Campus Xmatkuil, Mérida, Yucatán, Mexico
UAZ	University of Arizona
UCM	Museum of Natural History, University of Colorado
UF	Florida Museum of Natural History, University of Florida
UIMNH	Museum of Natural History, University of Illinois
UMMZ	Museum of Zoology, University of Michigan
UMRC	University of Miami Reference Collection
USNM	National Museum of Natural History
UTA	University of Texas, Arlington
UTEP	University of Texas, El Paso
UU	University of Utah
UWZH	Zoological Museum, University of Wisconsin
ZFMK	Universität Göttingen, Zoologisches Museum, Göttingen, Germany
ZMB	Universität Humboldt, Zoologisches Museum, Berlin
ZMUP	Museo Zoológico, Università di Padova, Italy
ZSM	Zoologisches Sammlung des Bayerischen Staates, Munich, Germany.

Color photographs are provided for 80 percent of the species treated in this book. Species that exhibit pronounced ontogenetic, sexual, or geographic variation are sometimes represented by more than one photograph to illustrate the range of variation. The photographs are usually, but not always, of Yucatecan specimens. For a minority of species I have had to use photographs of specimens from outside the Yucatán Peninsula, but in such cases the specimens illustrated are from populations that do not differ notably from those in the Yucatán Peninsula. In addition to the photographs, many species, including most of those for which photographs were unavailable, are illustrated with pen-and-ink drawings. Thus, 97 percent of the 182 species treated in this book are illustrated by color photographs, drawings, or both. As with the photographs, the drawings are usually based on specimens from the Yucatán Peninsula.

The Environment of the Yucatán Peninsula

Physiography

The Yucatán Peninsula is essentially a broad, relatively flat limestone platform extending north-northeast into the Gulf of Mexico and the Caribbean Sea. The northern third of the peninsula is devoid of major topographic relief. Only the Sierrita de Ticul breaks the monotony of the countryside, which is as flat as the ocean that covered it repeatedly during the Pleistocene (see Map 1 and the Gazetteer and associated maps for the locations of place names). The Sierrita—a low range of hills in western Yucatán and northern Campeche—attains an elevation of no more than 270 m. To the south, the peninsula rises gradually to a maximum elevation of about 350 m in southeastern Campeche and southwestern Quintana Roo. Commencing in northeastern El Petén and continuing eastward through northern Belize and into southern Quintana Roo is a series of faults that have formed low limestone ridges and intervening swampy areas. South of parallel 17° N, in central and southern El Petén, a series of folded limestone ridges known as the La Libertad Arch runs east-west and thence northwest into Chiapas and Tabasco, producing a more varied topography. To the south and southwest these ridges gradually give way to foothills and, eventually, to the highlands of Alta Verapaz, Guatemala, and Chiapas, Mexico.

The most conspicuous topographic feature of the peninsula is the ancient uplifted south-central portion of Belize known as the Maya Mountains. These consist of granitic, metamorphic, and volcanic rocks and include the oldest rocks in the Yucatán Peninsula. Oriented along a northeast-southwest axis, the Maya Mountains arise rather abruptly from the narrow coastal plain, but they slope away gradually to the northwest, where they are continuous with the Vaca Plateau and the Mountain Pine Ridge. Much of the area lies between the 600- and 800-m contour lines, and several peaks exceed 1,000 m in elevation. An eastward-projecting spur, the Cockscomb Range, includes Victoria Peak, which, with an elevation of 1,120 m, is generally considered the highest point in Belize—and thus the highest point in the Yucatán Peninsula. Miller and Miller (1992:18), however, gave an elevation of 1,160 m for a point in the Maya Mountains of southern Cayo District at approximately 16° 30' N, 89° 00' W.

The surface of much of the peninsula consists of eroded and thoroughly karsted limestone. Caves, caverns, and subterranean waterways abound, especially in the north, where the porosity of the limestone precludes much accumulation of surface water. Lakes are uncommon and rivers are virtually absent from the northern third of the peninsula. Throughout much of this area, natural wells called *cenotes* (from the Mayan word *dzonot*), which result from the collapse of the limestone roofing of subterranean chambers, are important sources of fresh water and support a mesophilic biota.

Scattered throughout the peninsula are depressions called *bajos* that fill with water during the rainy months but are frequently dry at other times. A belt of lakes extends across southern Campeche and through southern Quintana Roo. From west to east these are Laguna Silvituc, Zoh Laguna, Laguna Chacanbacab, Laguna Om, and Lago Bacalar. Farther south, at approximately 17° N, a chain of lakes lies in a major east-west fault. Among these are Laguna Perdida, Lago Macanché, Laguna Yaxhá, and Lago Petén Itzá; the latter is the largest and deepest lake in the peninsula, with a depth in excess of 32 m and a surface area of 567 km^2.

The northernmost river of any consequence is the Río Champotón, which drains portions of west-central Campeche and enters the Gulf of Mexico at the town of Champotón. In southwestern Campeche several rivers flow in a northerly direction into Laguna de Términos, a large bay that is nearly cut off from the Gulf of Mexico by Isla del Carmen. Among these rivers are the Río Candelaria, which originates in northwestern El Petén, and the Ríos Chumpán and Palizada. By far the largest and most important river in the Yucatán Peninsula is the Usumacinta, which originates in the Departments of Huehuetenango and Alta Verapaz and flows northwestward onto the Tabasco lowlands, where it joins the Río Grijalva before entering the Gulf of Mexico. Its major tributaries—the Río Salinas (or Río Chixoy), the Lacantún, the Río de la Pasión, and the Río San Pedro—drain much of the Lacandón region of Chiapas and El Petén.

The northernmost river with Caribbean drainage is the Río Hondo, whose headwaters drain northeastern El Petén and southeastern Campeche, where the river is known as the Río Azul. The Río Hondo forms the international boundary between Belize and Mexico as it courses northeastward, finally entering Bahía Chetumal. Most of north-central Belize is drained by the Belize and Sibun Rivers, and the southern third of the country is dissected by numerous rivers and streams, principal among which are the Deep and Monkey Rivers, Golden Stream, and the Río Grande. Farther south, the Río Sarstoon forms the southern boundary of Belize as it flows eastward into the Bahía de Amatique.

Narrow sandy beaches characterize much of the west coast of the Yucatán Peninsula. These are occasionally interrupted by low cliffs and rocky areas, as in the vicinity of the town of Campeche. Paralleling much of the northern margin of the peninsula from Celestún, Yucatán, to the vicinity of Chiquilá, Quintana Roo, is a sandy barrier beach, behind which lies a series of swamps, marshes, salt flats, and shallow lagoons. Along portions of the east coast of Quintana Roo limestone outcrops form sea cliffs and headlands, which alternate with small, sandy beaches, as at Tulum. Halfway down the east coast of Quintana Roo are the large shallow bays known as Bahía de la Ascensión and Bahía del Espíritu Santo. Farther south lies Bahía Chetumal, which marks the coastal boundary between Belize and Mexico.

To the north and west of the peninsula the Campeche Banks extend up to 250 km offshore, contrasting with the east side of the peninsula, where the continental shelf is narrow. Immediately off the northeast coast of Quintana Roo lie several small, sandy islands, possibly the remnants of barrier bars. These include Islas Contoy and Blanca, and, farther south, Cancún and Mujeres. Still farther south, at approximately 20° 30' N, the much larger Isla Cozumel lies 10 to 15 km off the coast. Beginning at the northeast corner of the peninsula and extending discontinuously southward for roughly 650 km to the Gulf of Honduras lies the longest coral barrier reef in the Atlantic tropics. Hundreds of tiny islets, atolls, and cays dot the reef, especially off the coast of Belize. The protected shallow lagoon behind the reef contains numerous small mangrove islands.

Climate

Owing to its tropical setting, low elevation, and strong maritime influences, the temperatures of the Yucatán Peninsula are warm and relatively homogeneous, with only slight fluctuations in mean temperature from one locality to another, and from season to season. Frost and freezing temperatures are unknown here. The mean annual temperature generally ranges from about 25 to 26°C, and the annual range of mean monthly temperatures is about 4 to 6°C. Within a single month, however, temperature extremes can be considerable, especially during winter, when "northers" occasionally sweep across the peninsula, producing extremes of 22 and 28°C. The annual pattern of monthly mean temperatures is similar throughout the peninsula, with January and May being usually the coldest and warmest months, respectively.

The amount of rainfall varies considerably throughout the peninsula, and from year to year at any one locality. In general, rainfall is greatest at the base of the peninsula and decreases to the north and, especially, to the northwest. As little as 500 mm of rain may fall annually along the northwest coast of the peninsula, whereas southern El Petén may receive in excess of 1,700 mm, and southern Belize, where the Maya Mountains intercept the moisture-bearing trade winds, receives upward of 4,000 mm of rain annually. Complicating this general north-south gradient in annual precipitation is an area of unusually high rainfall in northern Quintana Roo where 1,200 to 1,500 mm of rain may fall in a year.

As is the case elsewhere in Middle America, summer is the rainy season, with most of the rain falling from May to October, generally with peaks in June and September separated by a relatively dry July. The percentage of total annual rainfall occurring from May to October—a measure of seasonality—increases from south to northwest. Some 80 to 90 percent of the annual precipitation in western Yucatán and northern Campeche falls during that six-month period, whereas in El Petén the corresponding figures are about 60 to 70 percent. As elsewhere in the lowland tropics, there is a strong negative association between the amount and the seasonality of precipitation: areas that receive the most rainfall also exhibit the least seasonal rainfall pattern.

In summary, the climate of the Yucatán Peninsula is thoroughly tropical with uniformly high temperatures and seasonal rainfall. Annual rainfall is greatest in the south and east portions of the peninsula, and least in the northwest corner. Seasonality of precipitation exhibits an opposite pattern and is greatest in the northwest sector.

Vegetation

No system of vegetation classification or vegetation map can adequately reflect the complex mosaic that is the vegetation of the Yucatán Peninsula. Vegetation types grade subtly and imperceptibly into one another or interdigitate in intricate ways. Slope, aspect, elevation, drainage, and edaphic factors combine to produce a heterogeneous vegetation even within limited areas. Add to this the effects of climate and several millennia of human disturbance, and the result is a vegetation so complex as to defy simple generalization. Nonetheless, it cannot be denied that both the height and the luxuriance of the forest diminish dramatically from south to north. From a structurally complex, multi-layered mesophytic forest in southern El Petén and southern Belize, the vegetation gives way gradually to a low, scrubby xerophytic thorn forest at the north end of the peninsula. The following major

vegetation types can be recognized, and their approximate areal extent is depicted in Map 2.

Tropical Rainforest Northern Alta Verapaz and southern El Petén, southern Belize, and much of the Lacandón region of Chiapas support a structurally complex, luxuriant, mesophytic forest in which giants such as the ceiba (*Ceiba pentandra*) and the mahogany (*Swietenia macrophylla*) may reach heights of 40 m. Many trees attain heights in excess of 30 m and have interlocking crowns that produce a closed canopy through which little light penetrates to the forest floor. Lianas, bromeliads, and orchids are abundant, and members of the genus *Piper* are common understory plants. Palms are common, especially the cohune palm, *Orbignya cohune*, which in some areas forms a near monoculture (Fig. 1).

Montane Forest At higher elevations in the Maya and Cockscomb Mountains of Belize, especially on the windward slopes, is a lush, wet forest of pines (*Pinus oocarpa*), palms (*Euterpe macrospadix*), and tree ferns (*Alsophila mysuroides*). At lower elevations on the Vaca Plateau and on the western slopes of the Maya Mountains a somewhat drier forest type occurs, with oak (*Quercus*), pines (*Pinus oocarpa*), and cypress (*Podocarpus guatemalensis*) the dominant tree species.

Tropical Evergreen Forest Over much of northern El Petén, northern Belize, southern Campeche, and Quintana Roo is a medium-high forest with a canopy that averages perhaps 25 to 30 m (Fig. 2). Characteristic tree species include the ramón (*Brosimum alicastrum*), the sapodilla (*Manilkara zapota*), and the Mexican cedar (*Cedrela mexicana*). Palms such as the escoba palm (*Chrysophila argentea*) and *Sabal* sp. may be locally common and rare at other localities. Epiphytes are present, but generally less abundantly than in rainforest. In some areas the canopy is sufficiently open to allow penetration of considerable light, whereas in others the canopy is partly closed and the understory is a dense tangle of small vines and shrubs. This vegetation type has been termed *quasi rainforest* by some authors (e.g., Duellman, 1965a).

Tropical Deciduous Forest Much of southern Yucatán supports (or, more accurately, once supported) a forest that on average is lower than tropical evergreen forest and contains fewer palms and a higher proportion of deciduous trees, especially var-

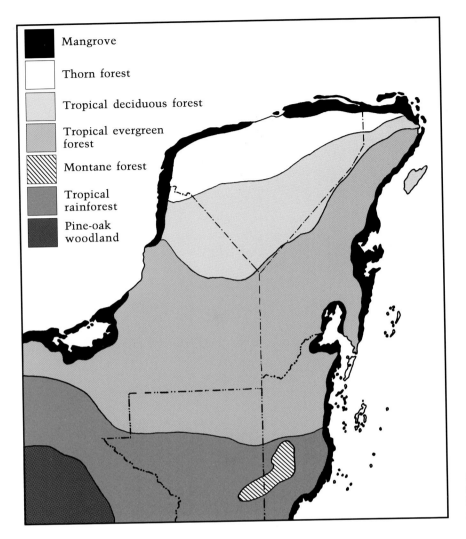

Legend:
- Mangrove
- Thorn forest
- Tropical deciduous forest
- Tropical evergreen forest
- Montane forest
- Tropical rainforest
- Pine-oak woodland

MAP 2. Generalized vegetation map of the Yucatán Peninsula showing approximate distribution of major vegetation types.

ious leguminous species. Epiphytes may be locally common, especially in low, swampy areas, but elsewhere they are rare or absent. *Bursera simaruba* and *Manilkara zapota* are common trees, and they typically attain a height of perhaps 20 m (Fig. 3).

Thorn Forest The northern and northwesternmost portions of the Yucatán Peninsula support a low, dense forest dominated by deciduous species of small, leguminous, thorny trees such as *Lysiloma sabicu* and *Mimosa albida*. Species characteristic of more mesic vegetation associations do occur, but in a somewhat stunted form (e.g., *Bursera simaruba* and *Cedrela mexicana*). Thorn forest attains a height of perhaps 5 to 7 m. In some areas there is little understory, but more typically the vegetation forms a dense tangle that is nearly impenetrable (Fig. 4).

Habitats of Amphibians and Reptiles
in the Yucatán Peninsula

The absence of major topographic relief in the Yucatán Peninsula precludes the existence of certain kinds of tropical habitats. There are, for example, no true cloud forests (although something like that vegetation type occurs at high elevations in the Maya Mountains of Belize) and no rain-shadow deserts. Nonetheless, the steep peninsular gradient in the amount and seasonality of precipitation exerts a powerful influence on the structure and floristic composition of the vegetation, which in turn greatly affects the nature of local habitats and thus the composition of the herpetofauna. At a finer level, subtle differences in soils, slope, and aspect combine to produce a complex ecological mosaic within which the local distribution and abundance of amphibians and reptiles are expressed.

What follows is a somewhat arbitrary delineation and characterization of major habitat types in the Yucatán Peninsula, often defined on the basis of vegetation. Habitats frequently grade imperceptibly into one another, producing transition areas—ecotones—that may support an especially diverse herpetofauna. In many cases, however, the habitat boundaries are quite abrupt—as, for example, the sudden transition from tropical forest to savanna in northern Guatemala.

Coastal Habitats

Coastal Strand A sandy barrier beach extends along much of the north coast of the peninsula. Sandy beaches also characterize much of the east coast and occur intermittently along the west coast as well. Dunes immediately behind the beach support low xerophytic shrubs, agaves, and cactus. Common species of reptiles in this habitat are *Sceloporus cozumelae, Conophis lineatus,* and *Cnemidophorus angusticeps* (Fig. 5).

Rocky Coastline Along the west coast, beach habitats are interrupted by stretches of rocky coastline, as, for example, in the vicinity of Seybaplaya, Campeche. *Ctenosaura similis* is a common and conspicuous inhabitant of these rocky coastlines (Fig. 6).

Mangrove Swamp In the low, swampy areas of La Ciénaga along the north coast, and along much of the west and east coasts of the peninsula, extensive stands of mangroves line the shore and may extend inland for many kilometers (see Map 2). The more salt-tolerant red mangroves (*Rhizophora mangle*) extend into the shallow stretches of bays, lagoons, and flats. Behind these, much taller black mangroves (*Avicennia germinans*) form nearly impenetrable forests. *Coniophanes quinquevittatus, Drymarchon corais,* and *Crocodylus acutus* are characteristic inhabitants of mangrove swamp (Fig. 7).

Agricultural Habitats

Human activity has long influenced the vegetation of the peninsula, and its impact has been profound.

Current and past agricultural practices have produced a variety of anthropogenic habitats, principal among which are the following.

Coconut Plantations Groves of coconut palms (*Cocos nucifera*) dot the sandy areas of the coasts on all sides of the peninsula. Coconut plantations provide a semishaded habitat with substantial surface debris in the form of decaying palm fronds. Common species in this habitat are *Sceloporus chrysostictus*, *Cnemidophorus angusticeps*, *Sphaerodactylus glaucus*, and *Ameiva undulata* (Fig. 8).

Cacao Plantations Prized by the ancient Maya, who used the beans as a form of currency, cacao (*Theobroma cacao*) is grown today in limited quantities, primarily in central and southern Belize (Fig. 9). Old cacao groves provide a rather open, yet shaded habitat for amphibians and reptiles. Various forest-inhabiting lizards such as *Anolis lemurinus* and *A. uniformis* are common inhabitants of cacao plantations.

Henequén Plantations Although less extensive than in the past, large areas of northern and northwestern Yucatán are still devoted to the production of henequén, a plant cultivated for its tough fibers, which are used in the manufacture of rope and twine. Henequén fields are generally established on rocky soils, and, when abandoned, quickly revert to thorn forest. Tracts of henequén provide an open habitat for amphibians and reptiles, and the abandoned fields provide a patchwork of vegetation plots in various stages of secondary succession. Henequén fields are usually bordered by limestone rock walls, which are often inhabited by such species as *Ctenosaura similis*, *Sceloporus serrifer*, and *Mabuya unimarginata* (Fig. 10).

Citrus Groves Although the yard of virtually every Maya home has several citrus trees, citrus is grown as a commercial crop mainly in the Puuc region of Yucatán (e.g., in the vicinity of Oxkutzcab) and, especially, in the Stann Creek Valley in central Belize, where extensive citrus groves provide a shaded habitat with an open understory. The snakes *Drymobius margaritiferus* and *Leptophis mexicanus* are common citrus grove denizens (Fig. 11).

Sugarcane Fields Extensive areas of northern Belize are devoted to sugarcane (*Saccharum officinarum*) production, as are smaller areas in Campeche and Yucatán. Sugarcane forms a dense monoculture and is generally unsuitable for heliothermic reptiles, although it provides a shaded, humid environment for various species of frogs such as *Bufo marinus*, *Scinax staufferi*, and *Hyla microcephala* (Fig. 12).

Milpas Many present-day Maya farmers practice the slash-and-burn agricultural methods of their ancestors in which sections of forest are cleared and burned, and crops, principally corn, are planted (Fig. 13). The nutrient-poor soil is exhausted within a few years, after which the milpa is abandoned and the cycle is repeated elsewhere. Although ephemeral, active and abandoned milpas provide open habitats and forest edge situations for forest-avoiding species such as *Sceloporus chrysostictus*, *Ameiva undulata*, and *Anolis sericeus*.

Pastures Large tracts once covered with lush tropical forest today serve as cattle pastures, as in the vicinity of Tizimín, Yucatán. Occasional giants such as the ceiba (*Ceiba pentandra*) still dot the countryside, remnants of the lost forest (Fig. 14). During the rainy season several species of frogs, including *Hyla microcephala*, *H. picta*, and *Scinax staufferi*, breed in flooded pastures. Forest-avoiding lizards such as *Anolis sericeus* can be found in pastures as well.

Freshwater Habitats

Lakes Lakes are uncommon in the northern third of the Yucatán Peninsula, where the porous limestone substrate often precludes the accumulation of surface water. Notable exceptions are the cluster of lakes at Cobá and at Punta Laguna in Quintana Roo, and Laguna Chichancanab in southern Yucatán. Farther south, lakes are more numerous, especially in central Petén, where a series of them lie in an east-west fault: Lago Petén Itzá, Lago Macanché, and Lago Yaxhá, as well as many smaller bodies of water. Several species of turtles, especially *Trachemys scripta* and various *Kinosternon*, inhabit freshwater lakes, as does *Crocodylus moreletii* (Fig. 15).

Cenotes These natural wells result from the collapse of the limestone roofing of subterranean chambers. Throughout much of the arid northwest portion of the Yucatán Peninsula cenotes are an important source of fresh water, and they support a mesophilic biota in an otherwise xeric environment

(Fig. 16). Turtles of several species, as well as the lizards *Basiliscus* and *Ctenosaura*, are common reptilian inhabitants of cenotes or their vegetation-covered rock walls. *Rana berlandieri* is also common, and the Yucatecan endemics *Eleutherodactylus yucatanensis* and *Bolitoglossa yucatana* have been found in cenotes.

Rivers and Streams Only the southern half of the Yucatán Peninsula is drained by surface rivers. Rivers and streams are especially plentiful in Belize, the Petén of Guatemala, and in Tabasco and southwestern Campeche (Fig. 17). The meanders and oxbows of rivers are inhabited by turtles, especially *Dermatemys mawii* and *Staurotypus triporcatus*, and by *Crocodylus moreletii*. Iguanas are common in the trees overhanging the riverbanks.

The northwest flanks of the Maya Mountains of Belize are drained by numerous small streams (Fig. 18). Clear and swift-moving, these provide habitat for *Rana juliani* and *R. berlandieri*, among others.

Aguadas Aguadas are more or less permanent bodies of water in forested areas. Various species of turtles, especially *Kinosternon*, and *Crocodylus moreletii* are typical aguada inhabitants. *Basiliscus vittatus* commonly occurs in the vicinity of aguadas, and *Leptodactylus melanonotus* and *L. labialis* are common amphibian inhabitants (Fig. 19).

Bajos Called *akalche* by the Maya, bajos are low areas in forested regions that fill with water during the rainy season but are otherwise dry. They are important breeding habitats for many species of frogs, and when filled with water they are often inhabited by species of *Kinosternon* (Fig. 20).

Wetlands The Río Grijalva–Usumacinta floodplain of Tabasco and southwestern Campeche (Fig. 21) forms an extensive wetland that supports numerous species of turtles (e.g., *Claudius angustatus*, *Staurotypus triporcatus*), amphibians (*Rana berlandieri*, *Hyla loquax*), and semiaquatic snakes (*Nerodia rhombifer* and *Coniophanes quinquevittatus*).

Forest Habitats

Much of the southern and central Yucatán Peninsula is covered by vast tropical forests of various types, although the extent of these forests is rapidly diminishing as a result of human activity. Lundell

(1934:265) doubted that any truly pristine forest remained anywhere in the Yucatán Peninsula, owing to deforestation by the Classic Maya, whom, he believed, brought virtually all of the peninsula under cultivation. Nonetheless, something approaching climax forest has long characterized extensive areas of the peninsula, and these forests support the greatest diversity of amphibians and reptiles. The major forest types in the Yucatán Peninsula were briefly characterized above. Within them a distinction can be made between primary forest and secondary forest.

Primary Forest

Primary forest is a stable, essentially undisturbed climax association (Fig. 1). The number of species of amphibians and reptiles is generally higher in primary forest than in earlier successional stages, and some species are restricted to primary forests. *Anolis uniformis* and *Ameiva festiva*, for example, tend to occur only in primary forest.

Secondary Forest

Secondary forest exists as the result of disturbance, usually deforestation associated with agriculture or logging but occasionally caused by natural events such as hurricanes or fires. Known as *acahuales* by the Maya, secondary forest may consist of any of a series of subclimax successional stages in which the forest is lower and the canopy is more open than in primary forest (Fig. 22). Many species of amphibians and reptiles, especially those that avoid the deep shade of primary forests, inhabit secondary forests. *Ameiva undulata*, *Anolis rodriguezii*, and *Leptophis mexicanus* are common reptiles in secondary forests, and the frogs *Hyla microcephala*, *Scinax staufferi*, and *Smilisca baudinii* commonly occur there as well.

Some forest habitats are so dominated by one or a few tree species that distinctive habitats can be recognized within the larger forest types described above.

Corozal

Embedded within the luxurious mesophytic forests that cloak much of the base of the Yucatán Peninsula are stands of the cohune or corozo palm (*Orbignya cohune*). These large palms generally form a closed-canopy monoculture beneath which only a sparse understory can persist. The forest floor is littered with huge decomposing palm fronds. *Micrurus diastema, Lepidophyma flavimaculatum, Anolis lemurinus,* and *Ninia diademata* are among the corozal inhabitants.

Ramonal

Dense stands of ramón (*Brosimum alicastrum*) are scattered throughout the southern half of the Yucatán Peninsula, especially in the vicinity of archaeological sites, suggesting that it may have been cultivated, or its growth at least encouraged, by the ancient Maya (Lundell, 1934:271). Ramón forests provide a rather open habitat within which lizards such as *Anolis lemurinus* and *Ameiva festiva* are commonly encountered.

Savanna Habitats

Pine Savanna   In southeastern El Petén and southern and central Belize there are extensive flat, open, grassy situations where *Pinus caribaea* is the dominant woody plant and scattered shrubs and small broadleaf trees dot the landscape (Fig. 23). The Mountain Pine Ridge of Belize supports a similar vegetation, but it lies at a higher elevation and has a much more rugged topography (Fig. 18). Characteristic pine savanna species include *Anolis sericeus, Ameiva undulata, Bufo marinus,* and *Crotalus durissus.*

Nanze Savanna South and southwest of Lago Petén Itzá in central El Petén lies a series of grassy savannas scattered with low, scrubby trees, especially the nanze (*Byrsonima crassifolia*). These savannas represent islands of open habitat in a region that is otherwise largely forested (Fig. 24). *Cnemidophorus angusticeps, Coluber constrictor, Anolis sericeus,* and *Pseustes poecilonotus* are typical nanze savanna species. During the rainy season, *Rhinophrynus dorsalis* and *Triprion petasatus* are among the common breeding frogs.

Composition of the Herpetofauna

As presently understood, the herpetofauna of the Yucatán Peninsula consists of 182 species representing 101 genera and 33 families (Table 1). Included in this count is a species of lizard, *Anolis cristatellus*, whose presence in the Yucatán Peninsula is based on a single specimen collected on Isla Cozumel in 1899. Also included is one species of snake, *Storeria dekayi*, for which there are no definite locality records within the Yucatán Peninsula. The type locality for *Storeria tropica* (= *Storeria dekayi tropica*) is Petén, Guatemala (Cope, 1885a: 175), however, and Stuart (1963:117) considered the species to be present in the Department of El Petén. Several other species that barely enter the Yucatán Peninsula are included. Among these are *Nerodia rhombifer*, which reaches its southern distributional limit in eastern Tabasco and southwestern Campeche, and *Geophis carinosus*, which is gener-

ally restricted to elevations of 1,000 to 1,500 m, but which has been taken at Palenque, Chiapas.

In comparison with other tropical areas, the herpetofauna of the Yucatán Peninsula is remarkably depauperate (J. D. Johnson, 1989:20). This is largely owing to the relatively homogeneous topography of the peninsula, which results in lower habitat diversity and thus fewer species. For example, the Mexican state of Michoacán, which has only about 25 percent of the area, has 164 species, only 16 fewer than the Yucatán Peninsula (Duellman, 1965b). Similarly, San Luis Potosí, also about 25 percent of the size of the Yucatán Peninsula, has 148 species (82 percent) (J. D. Johnson, 1989:20). Comparisons with lower Central America and Amazonia are even less favorable. Costa Rica, with 21 percent of the area of the Yucatán Peninsula, has substantially more than twice the number of species of amphibians and reptiles (Savage and Villa, 1986:1); and a 3-km² area of Ecuadorian rainforest is known to support 173 species of amphibians and reptiles (Duellman, 1978).

Although not especially rich in numbers of species, the herpetofauna of the Yucatán Peninsula is nonetheless noteworthy for the relatively large number of endemic species that occur there. About 14 percent of the Yucatecan herpetofauna is endemic, a figure that compares favorably with that for Nuclear Central America—the area centered on the highlands of southern Mexico, Guatemala, and Honduras—where 13 percent of the herpetofauna is endemic (J. D. Johnson, 1989:19).

TABLE 1

Taxonomic composition of the herpetofauna of the Yucatán Peninsula

Group	Families	Genera	Species
Caecilians	1	2	2
Salamanders	1	2	6
Frogs and toads	7	15	35
Crocodiles	1	1	2
Turtles	6	13	16
Lizards	11	20	48
Snakes	6	48	73
TOTAL	33	101	182

A Brief History of Herpetology in the Yucatán Peninsula

The following account of the history of herpetology in the Yucatán Peninsula represents one small chapter in a much larger story—one that traces the history of biological investigation in Middle America. With characteristic European ethnocentrism, this chapter treats that history as a series of post-Columbian activities conducted by and for Europeans and their descendants. In reality, a sophisticated civilization—the Maya—flourished in the Yucatán Peninsula for many centuries before the Europeans arrived. The archaeological record, much of it written by the Maya themselves on palace and temple walls, in codices, on funerary ceramics, and carved on stone monuments, indicates clearly that the pre-Columbian inhabitants of the Yucatán Peninsula possessed a substantial body of knowledge concerning the natural world, and that amphibians and reptiles were important in Maya life, both from a practical perspective and in terms of mythology and religious practice. The Maya compendium of herpetological knowledge is treated later in this volume, in the chapter entitled "Ethnoherpetology in the Yucatán Peninsula."

Pre-Linnaean Contributions

The study of the amphibians and reptiles of the New World began as an essentially descriptive endeavor. Early workers were concerned principally with describing, classifying, and cataloging new species. Perhaps the earliest attempt to summarize information on amphibians and reptiles in Middle America

was the *Rerum medicarum novae hispaniae thesaurus seu plantarum animalium mineralium mexicanorum* of Francisco Hernández, for whom the lizard *Corytophanes hernandezii* was named. Hernández traveled in Mexico from 1570 to 1577, but his great work was not published until 1648, in Rome, some 61 years after his death. In 1889 Alfredo Dugès, a French immigrant to Mexico who is often considered the father of Mexican herpetology, identified 29 of Hernández's herpetological names, which were given in Nahuatl, and descriptions, which were in Latin. H. M. Smith (1969) associated many of the remaining names with known species. Hernández worked in central Mexico, but several of his descriptions clearly apply to species that also occur in the Yucatán Peninsula, including such common forms as the boa constrictor (*Boa constrictor*), the marine toad (*Bufo marinus*), and the tropical rattlesnake (*Crotalus durissus*). Thus, the systematic accumulation of knowledge of the amphibians and reptiles of Mexico—and, indirectly, of the Yucatán Peninsula—began with the appearance of Hernández's work, although his names and descriptions have no nomenclatural significance in the modern classification system.

Linnaeus and the Eighteenth Century

The application of scientific names dates formally from 1758, the year Carolus Linnaeus, a Swedish botanist, published the 10th edition of *Systema naturae*. That volume, which established a consistent binomial nomenclature and is the basis for nomenclatural priority, contains the original descriptions of 15 species of amphibians and reptiles now known to occur in the Yucatán Peninsula or in immediately adjacent waters. Three years later the leatherback turtle (*Dermochelys coriacea*) was named by Vandelli. The 12th edition of *Systema naturae*, published in 1766, describes an additional Yucatecan species, the turtle *Eretmochelys imbricata*. For his descriptions Linnaeus drew on a number of sources, in particular the illustrations in Seba, 1734–1765, Catesby's studies of the natural history of the southeastern United States (1743, 1754), and the 1756 account by Gronovius. The type localities of many of Linnaeus's names were vague (e.g., "insulas Americanas"), and it is doubtful that any of his descriptions were based on material actually collected in the Yucatán Peninsula, although Schmidt (1953: 106) restricted the type locality of Linnaeus's *Eretmochelys imbricata* to Belize.

The remainder of the eighteenth century saw little progress in Middle American herpetology, and a mere four additional valid species now known to occur in the Yucatán Peninsula were named between 1766 and the end of the century: the treefrog *Phrynohyas venulosa*, described by Laurenti in 1768; Houttuyn's 1782 description of the gecko *Thecadactylus rapicauda*; the description of the snake *Lampropeltis triangulum* by Lacépède in 1788; and Schoepf's *Trachemys scripta*, a turtle, described in 1792. Again, none of the descriptions were based on material from the Yucatán Peninsula, an area that at the close of the eighteenth century was virtually unknown herpetologically.

European Dominance

During the first half of the nineteenth century, the development of Middle American herpetology was largely a French, German, and, to a lesser extent, English enterprise. In 1803 François Marie Daudin authored two names that apply to species in the Yucatán Peninsula and are still in use today: the snakes *Clelia clelia* and *Oxybelis fulgidus*, both probably first collected in Surinam. Four years later, Cuvier named the American crocodile, *Crocodylus acutus*, based on material possibly from Haiti.

Three German collectors, Christian Schiede, Graf von Sack, and Ferdinand Deppe (whose name is perpetuated in several patronyms, e.g., *Cnemi-*

dophorus deppii), collected amphibians and reptiles in Mexico during the 1820s and 1830s. As these men were in the employ of Berlin and Vienna museums, much of their material went to those institutions, where it served as an impetus for the production of the *Herpetologia Mexicana*, published in 1834 by Arend Friedrich August Wiegmann. This work contains descriptions of four species of lizards that occur in the Yucatán Peninsula: *Ameiva undulata*, *Anolis biporcatus*, *Cnemidophorus deppii*, and *Laemanctus longipes*, although none were described on the basis of material from the Yucatán Peninsula.

Also in the 1820s and 1830s, John Edward Gray, keeper of zoology at the British Museum (Natural History), initiated the publication of catalogs based on the museum's collections with descriptions of new species of amphibians and reptiles from Middle America, including species found in the Yucatán Peninsula. Among them is the original description of the mud turtle *Kinosternon acutum*, published by Gray in 1831, possibly the first description of a species based on material from the Yucatán Peninsula (probably Belize, *fide* Schmidt, 1941:488). In that same year Gray named the spiny-tailed iguana, *Ctenosaura similis*. In 1845 he described the gecko *Coleonyx elegans* on the basis of material from Belize, and in 1847 he described the river turtle, *Dermatemys mawii*, whose type locality was restricted by H. M. Smith and Taylor (1950b:346) to Alvarado, Veracruz. But Gray's influence on the subsequent course of herpetological investigation in Middle America extended far beyond his own publications, which span an impressive 50 years (1825–1874) and number more than 1,162 titles. In 1857 Gray appointed Albert Günther, a young German physician and ordained Lutheran minister, as his assistant in the divisions of herpetology and ichthyology. Günther, ultimately Gray's successor as keeper of zoology, was quickly put to work cataloging the museum's fishes, amphibians, and reptiles. The next year, 1858, Günther's *Catalogue of Colubrine Snakes in the British Museum* appeared. This work contains the original descriptions of five Yucatecan snakes, including two (*Pseustes poecilonotus* and *Coniophanes bipunctatus*) believed by Schmidt (1941:499, 504, respectively) to have been based on material from Belize, and one (*Sibon fasciata*) whose type locality was restricted by H. M. Smith and Taylor (1950b:352) to Chichén Itzá, Yucatán.

Five years later, in 1863, Günther named two more Yucatecan snakes: *Tantilla moesta*, based on material from El Petén; and the distinctive *Agkistrodon bilineatus*, from the Pacific coast of Guatemala.

In 1881, Günther hired a young Belgian zoologist named George A. Boulenger and placed him in charge of the collections of fishes, amphibians, and reptiles in the British Museum. Boulenger was soon at work preparing a new edition of the catalog of the museum's amphibians and reptiles. This enormous project, which eventually treated 8,469 species, was published in nine volumes between 1882 and 1896. Volume 1 contains the description of the frog *Gastrophryne elegans*, based on material from Veracruz. Considered by some the leading taxonomic herpetologist of his day (Adler, 1989:55), Boulenger published several books in addition to the catalog, and hundreds of papers, including the original description of the frog *Eleutherodactylus alfredi*, which appeared in 1898 based on material from Veracruz.

Unquestionably Günther's most enduring endowment to Middle American herpetology was his contribution of the sections on amphibians and reptiles in the *Biología Centrali-Americana*. Subtitled "Contributions to the Knowledge of the Fauna and Flora of México and Central America," the *Biología Centrali-Americana* was the undertaking of two British naturalists, Osbert Salvin and Frederick DuCane Godman. Issued irregularly from 1879 to 1915, the work ultimately numbered 67 volumes. Günther's treatment of the amphibians and reptiles appeared over the period 1885–1902 and contains numerous records for the Yucatán Peninsula, based largely on material in the British Museum collected by G. F. Gaumer in Yucatán and Isla Cozumel. Only one Yucatecan species was described as new, however; the original description of *Hyla picta* appeared in part 166, issued in September 1901.

The French claim to preeminence in herpetology during the nineteenth century rests primarily on the work of André-Marie-Constant Duméril and Gabriel Bibron of the National Museum in Paris. Between 1834 and 1854, Duméril and Bibron published the nine-volume *Erpétologie générale, ou Histoire naturelle complète des reptiles*, described by Schmidt (1955:592) as "the crowning work of a century of herpetological studies." Auguste-Henri-André Duméril, son of the senior author, assisted his father with the production of volumes 7 and 9 after Bibron died in 1848. Contained within the volumes of this great work are the original descriptions of no fewer than 14 species of amphibians and

reptiles that occur in the Yucatán Peninsula. Several of these descriptions were based on specimens obtained by Marie Arthur Morelet, for whom *Crocodylus moreletii* and *Agalychnis moreletii* are named. Morelet traveled through southern Mexico and Guatemala, including the Yucatán Peninsula, in 1847 and 1848, and his herpetological material, much of it from El Petén, was deposited at the National Museum in Paris. Yucatecan amphibians and reptiles whose original descriptions appear in the *Erpétologie générale* include two anoles (*Anolis cristatellus* and *A. sagrei*) in volume 4, one snake (*Leptotyphlops goudotii*) in volume 6, eight snakes (*Coniophanes quinquevittatus, Conophis lineatus, Leptophis mexicanus, Masticophis mentovarius, Ninia sebae, Scaphiodontophis annulatus, Stenorrhina freminvillei*, and *Micrurus diastema*) in volume 7, two frogs (*Rhinophrynus dorsalis* and *Smilisca baudinii*) in volume 8, and a salamander (*Bolitoglossa mexicana*) in volume 9. Only one of these names, however, the snake *Coniophanes quinquevittatus*, might be based on type material from the Yucatán Peninsula (El Petén) (Stuart, 1963:92).

While the last volumes of the *Erpétologie générale* were in production, A. M. C. and A. H. A. Duméril published the *Catalogue methodique de la collection des reptiles du Muséum d'Histoire Naturelle de Paris*, which appeared in 1851. This work contains three original descriptions of reptiles occurring in the Yucatán Peninsula. The turtle *Rhinoclemmys areolata* was named by Duméril and Duméril on the basis of material from El Petén. The crocodile *Crocodylus moreletii* and the turtle *Kinosternon leucostomum* were named by Duméril and Bibron, the former based on material from El Petén. The latter was believed by Schmidt (1941:488) to be based on material from the Río Usumacinta in El Petén, although its type locality was restricted by H. M. Smith and Taylor (1950b:347) to Cosamaloapam, Veracruz.

In that same volume the younger Duméril named *Lepidophyma flavimaculatum* from El Petén (restricted by H. M. Smith and Taylor [1950b:318] to the Río de la Pasión, El Petén), and two years later he named two new frogs, *Agalychnis moreletii* and *Eleutherodactylus laticeps*, both probably based on material from Alta Verapaz.

The German contribution to the herpetology of Middle America initiated by Wiegmann continued through the studies of Wilhelm Carl Hartwig Peters, a professor at the University of Berlin and the director of the Zoological Museum there. Between

1861 and 1882 he described five species of amphibians and reptiles found in the Yucatán Peninsula: the lizards *Anolis capito* and *A. tropidonotus*, the snakes *Dendrophidion nuchale* and *Micrurus hippocrepis*, and the salamander *Bolitoglossa yucatana*. Only the latter, described by Peters the year before his death, was based on type material collected in the Yucatán Peninsula.

Georg Jan, director of the Museum of Natural History in Milan, is best known for the *Iconographie générale des ophidiens*, an ambitious attempt to illustrate all the species of snakes in the world. Portions of that work, illustrated by Ferdinand Sordelli, appeared between 1860 and 1881. In 1862 Jan described the Yucatecan snake *Adelphicos quadrivirgatus* based on material from Mexico.

In 1864 Marie-Firmin Bocourt, whose association with the National Museum in Paris began in 1834 when he was 15, was placed in charge of the Mission Scientifique. This undertaking, sponsored by the French government, was essentially an adjunct to the attempt by Napoleon III to establish a Mexican empire under the titular rule of Maximilian. With the collapse of that effort and continuing political instability in Mexico, the directors of the mission found it expedient to send Bocourt to neighboring Guatemala. Departing France in late 1864, he visited Belize briefly before arriving in Guatemala in early 1865, where he collected until June 1866 (Stuart, 1948:8). Bocourt's collections formed the basis for the *Mission scientifique au Mexique et dans l'Amérique Centrale*, the first part of which was published by A. H. A. Duméril in 1870, the last year of his life. The remaining portions dealing with reptiles were completed by Angel, Mocquard, and Vaillant, and were published irregularly over the next 39 years. The amphibian section of the *Mission scientifique* was published by Brocchi between 1881 and 1883. Among the herpetological novelties contained in Bocourt's collections was a species of Yucatecan frog, *Rana vaillanti*, which was described by Brocchi in 1877 based on material from Belize.

The Emergence of Herpetology in North America

The first attempt at a synthesis and comprehensive treatment of the amphibians and reptiles of America north of Mexico was John Edwards Holbrook's *North American Herpetology*, which first appeared as four volumes issued between 1836 and 1840. In this great work, Holbrook sought to describe and illustrate every species known to occur in the United States. The work contains the original descriptions of many common reptiles and amphibians, including one species, *Storeria dekayi*, that probably enters the Yucatán Peninsula in southern El Petén.

Biological investigation in North America received a major impetus in 1846 when the United States Congress passed a bill establishing the Smithsonian Institution, financed initially through an endowment from the estate of the Englishman James Smithson. Spencer Fullerton Baird, who was appointed assistant secretary (effectively the director) of the institution in 1850, initiated the accumulation of natural history materials. Baird and his chief assistant, a young Frenchman named Charles Girard, undertook to coauthor a series of volumes cataloging the reptiles in the Smithsonian Museum. Only the first catalog, on snakes, actually appeared, this in 1853. It contains the original descriptions of two species occurring in the Yucatán Peninsula: *Ninia diademata* and *Thamnophis marcianus*. A year later, Girard named the coral snake *Micrurus nigrocinctus* based on material from Panama.

While Baird and Girard studied the extensive collections arriving at the Smithsonian from the various government surveying expeditions in western North America, a precocious eighteen-year-old volunteer at the Academy of Natural Sciences in Philadelphia was busy reorganizing the herpetological collections in the academy's museum. Edward Drinker Cope later spent the winters of 1861–1863 at the Smithsonian, where he came under the influence of Baird. Thus began the career of one of North America's most illustrious herpetologists. Over the course of a relatively short professional life (he died at age 57), Cope published 1,395 works, including about 170 dealing with Recent amphibians and reptiles. The original descriptions of many Yucatecan amphibians and reptiles are contained within this prodigious outpouring, and some 40 species are considered valid today. Seven of these were described in a single publication (Cope, 1866): the lizards *Ctenosaura defensor*, *Sceloporus chrysostictus*, and *S. serrifer*; and the snakes *Typhlops microstomus*, *Ficimia publia*, *Dipsas brevifacies*, and *Senticolis triaspis*. Cope was responsible for naming more than 22 percent of the species of amphibians and reptiles known to occur in the Yucatán Peninsula. Unlike most of his contemporaries, Cope was an accomplished field biologist, although he focused on paleontology in his fieldwork. He is perhaps best known for his work on the dinosaurs of the North American West. He generally left it to others to supply the tropical specimens that he described as new species. Much of the material that formed the basis for Cope's descriptions of Yucatecan novelties was secured by Arthur Schott, a naturalist for the Comisión Científica de Yucatán who collected in the northern portions of the peninsula in the early 1860s. Schott's specimens were deposited in the Smithsonian Institution, the United States National Museum (now the National Museum of Natural History), and in the collections of the Academy of Natural Sciences of Philadelphia.

An expedition by the Academy of Natural Sciences under the leadership of Angelo Heilprin visited northern Yucatán in February and March 1890 at the height of the dry season. J. E. Ives, a member of that expedition, reported on the 14 species of amphibians and reptiles obtained there (Ives, 1891), which were deposited at the academy in Philadelphia.

During the last decade of the nineteenth century, Alfonso Luis Velasco produced a multivolume series titled *Geografía y estadística de la República Mexicana*, with each volume devoted to a particular Mexican state. Not all the states were treated, but volumes 16 and 20 deal with Campeche and Chiapas, respectively, and include listings of the amphibians and reptiles from those areas together with their vernacular names.

At about this time a major contribution to the natural history of Mexico was initiated by Edward William Nelson and Edward Alfonso Goldman, of the United States Bureau of Biological Survey. Nelson and Goldman conducted biological explorations throughout Mexico from 1892 to 1906, including visits to various points in the Yucatán Peninsula in 1900–1901. Although their focus was primarily on birds and mammals, they also accumulated substantial collections of herpetological specimens, which went to the National Museum of Natural History. An account of the Nelson-Goldman investigations is presented in Goldman, 1951.

The Twentieth Century

By the turn of the century, some 90 percent of the species of amphibians and reptiles occurring in the Yucatán Peninsula had been formally described (see Fig. 25), although relatively few of the descriptions were based on material collected in the peninsula, and the actual composition of the Yucatecan herpetofauna was very imperfectly known. Political complications in Mexico and the First World War prevented extensive herpetological investigations in the early decades of the twentieth century, and only a few species were added to the Yucatecan faunal list during this time, most notably the parthenogenetic *Cnemidophorus cozumela*, described in 1906 by Hans Gadow as a subspecies of *C. deppii*.

Anthropological Exploration

At the close of the nineteenth century and during the first decade of the twentieth, some herpetological materials were accumulated incidental to archaeological studies of Maya ruins. Edward H. Thompson, archaeologist and United States consul in Yucatán from 1885 to 1909, obtained some specimens of amphibians and reptiles from the vicinity of Chichén Itzá, and in 1904 he actually purchased that famous site. Thompson's specimens and those collected by Leon J. Cole in Yucatán, most of them now at the Museum of Comparative Zoology at Harvard University, were among those reported by Barbour and Cole (1906). Thompson deposited a few additional specimens from the ruins of Chichén Itzá at the Philadelphia Academy of Natural Sciences, and these were reported by Fowler (1913).

By the 1920s a resurgence of biological investigation was under way in the Yucatán Peninsula, stimulated in large measure by the accelerating pace of archaeological exploration. The next three decades saw the initiation of large-scale archaeological projects throughout much of the lowland Maya area. These projects, especially those sponsored by the Carnegie Institute of Washington, often involved biologists who studied the flora and fauna of the Maya area with the ultimate objective of obtaining an ecological perspective on the rise, florescence, and decline of the Maya. In one of those biotic surveys, A. S. Pearse of Duke University and his coworkers collected amphibians and reptiles in and around the caves in the vicinity of Oxkutzcab, Yucatán (summarized in Pearse et al., 1938). Much of their herpetological material now resides at the Museum of Zoology at the University of Michigan. A partial listing of amphibians and reptiles from the state of Yucatán appears in Pearse, 1945.

In 1929, and again in 1947, Robert T. Hatt of the Cranbrook Institute of Science excavated the caves

Fig. 1. Tropical rainforest, near Dolores, Toledo District, Belize.

Fig. 2. Tropical evergreen forest, near X-Kanhá, Campeche, Mexico.

Fig. 3. Tropical deciduous forest, near Santa Rosa, Yucatán, Mexico.

Fig. 4. Thorn forest, 1.5 mi N Kabah Ruins, Yucatán, Mexico.

Fig. 5. Sandy coastline, 10 km S Champotón, Campeche, Mexico.

Fig. 6. Rocky coastline, near Seybaplaya, Campeche, Mexico.

Fig. 7. Mangrove swamp, 8 km S La Arena, Campeche, Mexico.

Fig. 8. Coconut plantation, Celestún, Yucatán, Mexico.

Fig. 9. Recently established cacao grove near the Hummingbird Highway, Cayo District, Belize.

Fig. 10. Henequén plantation, near Ticopó, Yucatán, Mexico.

Fig. 11. Citrus groves, Stann Creek Valley, Stann Creek District, Belize. Photo by Tony Rath.

Fig. 12. Sugarcane cultivation, 7 km W Sihochac, Campeche, Mexico.

Fig. 13. A milpa along the Hummingbird Highway, Stann Creek District, Belize.

Fig. 14. A pasture in what was formerly tropical evergreen forest, 6.4 km W Colonia Yucatán, Yucatán, Mexico. The tree in the foreground is *Ceiba pentandra*.

Fig. 15. Lago Cobá, a lake situated in tropical evergreen forest in northern Quintana Roo, Mexico.

Fig. 16. Cenote Tahmek, Yucatán, Mexico.

Fig. 17. Upper Raspaculo River, Cayo District, Belize. Photo by Sharon Matola.

Fig. 18. Little Vaqueros Creek, Mountain Pine Ridge, Cayo District, Belize.

Fig. 19. A forest aguada between Felipe Carrillo Puerto and Vigía Chico, Quintana Roo, Mexico.

Fig. 20. A bajo in tropical evergreen forest, 18.4 km NE Felipe Carrillo Puerto, Quintana Roo, Mexico.

Fig. 21. Wetlands of the Usumacinta floodplain, 16.6 km NE Campeche-Tabasco border, Hwy. 186, Campeche, Mexico.

Fig. 22. Secondary forest, 16.5 km S Cancún, Quintana Roo, Mexico.

Fig. 23. Pine savanna in Toledo District, Belize.

Fig. 24. Nanze savanna, near La Libertad, El Petén, Guatemala.

of western Yucatán. The first expedition sought to trace sequential changes in the terrestrial vertebrate fauna of Yucatán. The 1947 effort sought to correlate this faunal evidence with the history of human occupation of the Yucatán Peninsula. The herpetological materials obtained by the Hatt expeditions are at the American Museum of Natural History and at the Museum of Zoology at Michigan. Langebartel (1953) published an account of the fossil material from the caves.

In 1924 the Carnegie Institution began excavating and restoring Chichén Itzá, a project that was to continue until 1933. Most of the herpetological materials accumulated during the course of the archaeological work there are in the collections of the Museum of Comparative Zoology and the Field Museum of Natural History in Chicago, although the small collections secured by F. M. Gaige and K. MacKay in the early 1930s at Chichén Itzá are at the University of Michigan. Edwin Creaser, of the United States Biological Survey, and A. S. Pearse, working for the Carnegie Institute, collected amphibians and reptiles in Yucatán in June, July, and August 1932, focusing especially on Chichén Itzá, Mérida, and Progreso, in Yucatán, and Champotón, Campeche. Their specimens are also at the University of Michigan, including the type specimen of the mud turtle *Kinosternon creaseri*, named in honor of Edwin Creaser by Norman Hartweg in 1934. In 1932, the botanist Cyrus L. Lundell collected amphibians and reptiles in southern Campeche in the vicinity of Tuxpeña, and his specimens, too, are at the University of Michigan. In the early 1930s Eunice Blackburn, of the Colegio Americano in Mérida, assembled a collection of herpetological specimens from the vicinity of Mérida. These were deposited at Field Museum in 1934. In their report on the snakes in these Yucatán collections, K. P. Schmidt and E. W. Andrews IV (1936) described the Yucatecan endemic *Coniophanes meridanus*. Andrews, an archaeologist, collected additional herpetological specimens at Chichén Itzá and at Cobá in 1937. These specimens, now at the Field Museum, formed the basis for a report on the snakes by E. W. Andrews (1937), and on the collection as a whole by H. M. Smith (1939a).

To the south, in the Department of El Petén, a gradual accumulation of herpetological materials was under way. H. F. Loomis of the United States Department of Agriculture visited the archaeological site at Uaxactún in 1922, in connection with an agricultural survey of northern Guatemala, and collected several specimens that are now in the National Museum of Natural History. The following year, Harry Malleis, of the United States Biological Survey, collected specimens at various points in El Petén. His collection, also deposited at the National Museum of Natural History, includes over 338 specimens and was included in Stuart's 1934 report on the Petén herpetofauna. Major archaeological excavation was begun at Uaxactún in 1928, also under the auspices of the Carnegie Institute, and work there continued until 1938. In connection with that effort, Oliver G. Ricketson, Jr., the director of the first phase of the Uaxactún project, collected several snakes, now in the Museum of Comparative Zoology. A small collection of 60 specimens of amphibians and reptiles made by Josselyn Van Tyne and Adolph Murie at Uaxactún in 1931 was deposited at the Museum of Zoology at the University of Michigan. In 1929, the University of Pennsylvania initiated archaeological work at Piedras Negras, El Petén, a site that was to be an important collecting station for Hobart M. Smith some ten years later. In the winter and spring of 1935, Carl Hubbs and Henry van der Schalie, of the University of Michigan, collected in the central Petén region. Fishes and mollusks were the focus of their work, but they also secured approximately 300 specimens of amphibians and reptiles. These specimens were reported by Stuart (1937) and are now in the Museum of Zoology in Ann Arbor. Julian Steyermark, a member of the Field Museum's 1942 expedition to Guatemala, collected amphibians and reptiles in the Department of El Petén, as did Tom Larson four years later. Their specimens are at the Field Museum. Ken Gosner collected in the Uaxactún area in 1947 and 1949 and deposited his specimens in the American Museum of Natural History. Frank B. Smithe, an ornithologist, collected specimens at Tikal that are in the Museum of Comparative Zoology.

A third major project undertaken by the Carnegie Institute was the excavation of the ruins at Mayapán, Yucatán, which commenced in the early 1950s and continued until 1958. The herpetological specimens secured in connection with the work there are on deposit at the Field Museum.

Perhaps the most ambitious archaeological venture of all was the Tikal project. Initiated in 1956 as a joint undertaking by the government of Guatemala and the University of Pennsylvania, the project continued into the early 1970s. L. C. Stuart, of the University of Michigan, worked at Tikal during the first field season in 1956 and secured 775 herpetological specimens as the ruins were cleared. These are in the Museum of Zoology at Michigan and were reported by Stuart (1958). In 1960–1961, Anne Meachem Rick, then a graduate student of anthropology at the University of Florida, assembled approximately 175 specimens of reptiles collected at Tikal. These were deposited at the Florida Museum of Natural History.

Contemporary with the Tikal project was the excavation of Dzibilchaltún in northern Yucatán. That project, under the direction of E. W. Andrews IV, was sponsored by the Middle American Research Institute of Tulane University and the National Geographic Society. The substantial herpetological materials obtained incidental to the archaeological work were deposited at the Field Museum. Andrews also directed archaeological research at Becan, in southeastern Campeche, in 1969 and 1970. The small collection of reptiles and amphibians (about 68 specimens of 24 species) obtained there are now at the University of Wisconsin, Madison.

The fusion of Darwinian natural selection theory with population genetics theory in the 1930s profoundly affected the course of evolutionary biology and led to an enhanced appreciation of the role of population differentiation in the evolutionary process. Consequently, systematists placed greater emphasis on documenting geographical distributions and establishing the existence—and describing the nature—of geographic variation within species. In the Yucatán Peninsula, where most of the species of amphibians and reptiles were already known to science, herpetological research began to focus on refining the knowledge of geographic distributions, on formally recognizing geographic variants as subspecies, and on erecting higher classifications.

The Smith-Taylor Era of Mexican Herpetology

In 1932 Edward H. Taylor, of the University of Kansas, and his student, Hobart M. Smith, initiated an ambitious program of field and laboratory work on the herpetofauna of Mexico. In 1936 Smith collected briefly in Yucatán, chiefly at Chichén Itzá, Mérida, and Progreso, and then more extensively at several sites in southwestern Campeche near Laguna de Términos. In Campeche, Smith's host was John Martin, the owner of several ranches in southwestern Campeche, who accompanied Smith on

several collecting trips. The results of this work, including a treatment of a small collection from various archaeological sites in southeastern Campeche secured by Mrs. J. H. Denison, Jr., were published by Smith in 1938. Smith's materials became part of the Edward H. Taylor–Hobart M. Smith collection, roughly half of which was deposited at the Museum of Natural History at the University of Illinois. In 1959, most of the remainder was deposited at the Field Museum. In 1937, a year after Smith's early fieldwork in Campeche, Martin assembled a small collection of herpetological specimens from southwestern Campeche that are now at the University of Michigan.

In 1938, under the auspices of a three-year Walter Rathbone Bacon Traveling Scholarship, Smith and his wife, Rozella, collected amphibians and reptiles throughout much of mainland Mexico. Their itinerary included brief visits to several sites at the margins of the Yucatán Peninsula. In May 1939 they traveled to Tenosique, Tabasco, via riverboat from Ciudad del Carmen. From there they went to the archaeological site of Piedras Negras in El Petén, where they obtained the type material of the frog *Smilisca cyanosticta* (as *Hyla phaeota cyanosticta*) and the snakes *Dendrophidion vinitor* and *Tantillita lintoni*, all new species named by Hobart Smith. The Smiths then collected in the vicinity of the village and the ruins of Palenque from early July to 6 August 1939. There Rozella collected the type specimen of the lizard that bears her name, *Celestus rozellae*. In all, the Smiths accumulated some 22,000 specimens of amphibians and reptiles during Hobart's tenure as a Bacon scholar. They were deposited at the National Museum of Natural History and the Field Museum, and information on the amphibian material was reported by Taylor and Smith (1945). Three additional Yucatecan endemics were named by Smith during this time: the lizard *Sceloporus lundelli* and the snake *Tantilla cuniculator* (as *T. moesta cuniculator*), both named in 1939, and the small hog-nosed viper, *Porthidium yucatanicum*, named in 1941.

The importance of Smith's and Taylor's contributions to Mexican herpetology can scarcely be overstated. Over a span of 17 years, some 50,000 specimens of amphibians and reptiles were secured through their indefatigable efforts. This material provided the basis for Smith and Taylor's annotated checklists of snakes (1945), amphibians (1948), and reptiles exclusive of snakes (1950a). A generation of herpetologists carried the checklists with them to

Mexico, and they remain indispensable to any serious student of Mexican herpetology. The checklists are, however, in the process of being superseded by the Smiths' very ambitious *Synopsis of the Herpetofauna of Mexico*, a comprehensive multivolume treatment of the biology of the amphibians and reptiles of Mexico that summarizes the voluminous literature and includes synonymies, identification keys, and distribution maps. At this writing, seven volumes have appeared (H. M. Smith and Smith, 1971, 1973, 1976a,b, 1977, 1979, 1993), covering the amphisbaenians, crocodilians, turtles, and lizards.

Laurence C. Stuart and Guatemalan Herpetology

While Smith and Taylor were conducting their work in Mexico, Laurence C. Stuart, of the University of Michigan, initiated his studies on the Guatemalan herpetofauna. The studies continued for the next forty years and established "Don Pancho" as the preeminent authority on the herpetofauna of northern Central America. With coauthor Helen Gaige, Stuart named the distinctive hylid frog *Hyla loquax* in 1934, based on material from El Petén collected by Stuart the year before. That collection, deposited at the University of Michigan, formed the basis of two reports (Stuart, 1934, 1935) on the herpetofauna of El Petén. In 1941 Stuart described the snake *Geophis carinatus*, a form that enters the Yucatán Peninsula in the vicinity of Palenque, and in 1942 he named the teiid lizard *Ameiva chaitzami*. Although he undertook several important revisions of Guatemalan reptiles, Stuart's most enduring contributions are his biogeographical treatments of various physiographic regions of Guatemala. His 1963 checklist of the herpetofauna of Guatemala summarizes thirty years of work and serves today as an important adjunct to Smith and Taylor's checklists for adjacent Mexico. In 1969 Stuart retired to Panajachél, Sololá, Guatemala, where he served as a congenial contact person and opened his home to numerous naturalists working in northern Central America.

Karl P. Schmidt in Belize

Stuart's early work in Guatemala was complemented by studies in neighboring Belize (then British Honduras) by Karl P. Schmidt of the Field Museum. Schmidt visited Belize in 1923 as a participant in the Marshall Field Expedition to Central America. He collected principally in the vicinity of Middlesex, but also secured a few specimens in and around Belize City, as well as in the environs of Stann Creek (now Dangriga) and on Tom Owen Cay. Schmidt's collection totaled 441 specimens, all of which he placed in the Field Museum. One especially notable outcome of Schmidt's work was the rediscovery of *Crocodylus moreletii*, a form whose specific status had been held in doubt (Schmidt, 1924).

Schmidt's material augmented a small collection made in June 1905 by B. H. Bailey at Manatee, and a more substantial collection assembled by the missionary priest W. A. Stanton, S.J., of St. John's College, Belize City. Both collections eventually found their way to the Field Museum. In the 1930s additional small collections of amphibians and reptiles were made in Belize by field parties from the University of Michigan in connection with fieldwork in neighboring Petén. The specimens secured by Van Tyne and Murie, L. C. Stuart, and C. L. Lundell are mostly at the University of Michigan, including the type of *Sceloporus lundelli*, named by Hobart Smith (H. M. Smith, 1939b), but a few specimens are in the Field Museum. In 1935 the ornithologists E. R. Blake and C. T. Agostini collected birds in the Cockscomb Mountains and incidentally secured 182 specimens of amphibians and reptiles, which are now in the Carnegie Museum. Under the auspices of the 1940 Mandel Caribbean Expedition of the Field Museum, Rudyard Boulton and D. Dwight Davis collected reptiles on Half Moon Cay, Glover's Reef, and in the Turneffe Islands off the Belizean coast. Their 122 specimens, now at the Field Museum, include a series of *Phyllodactylus* from Half Moon Cay that would be named *Phyllodactylus insularis* by James Dixon some 20 years later. In 1940 the explorer and novelist Ivan T. Sanderson visited Belize and Yucatán and assembled 513 herpetological specimens that he deposited at the Field Museum. Sanderson published a popular account of his travels in 1941. The collections described above provided the basis for Schmidt's 1941 paper on the herpetofauna of Belize, the first comprehensive treatment of the amphibians and reptiles of the country.

Post–World War II

E. Ross Allen visited Belize briefly in 1937 and secured a few herpetological specimens that were "variously distributed" (W. T. Neill and Allen, 1959c:1). He returned in 1957 to collect in the vicinity of Belize City, at Cayo (now San Ignacio), and in eastern Petén, Guatemala. In 1959 he was joined by Wilfred T. Neill, and together they initiated comprehensive studies on the herpetofauna of Belize. They were assisted by Anthony Wolffsohn, of the British Honduras Forestry Department, who had been collecting herpetological specimens in the colony since the early 1950s. Some of Wolffsohn's specimens are now at the Field Museum. The results of these herpetological investigations appeared in a series of papers (W. T. Neill and Allen, 1959a,b,c), and much of the material Neill and Allen accumulated eventually found its way to the American Museum of Natural History.

In 1958 Charles M. Fugler, a student at A & M College of Texas, visited Belize to assess the feasibility of conducting biogeographic work there. Between 14 June and 7 July he collected several hundred specimens of amphibians and reptiles, including a number of species and genera previously unreported from Belize, which he retained in his personal collection. In 1960 Fugler published a report on these specimens plus Belizean material accumulated by George H. Lowery and his field parties from Louisiana State University.

During July and August 1960, Peter H. Litchfield, an undergraduate student at the University of Michigan, collected amphibians and reptiles in Tabasco, Campeche, and Belize, which he placed in the University of Michigan's museum. Two years later Thomas P. C. Monath and friends collected amphibians and reptiles in Belize that were deposited at the Museum of Comparative Zoology. Wilfred T. Neill (1965) published an account of the material secured by the Monath party. In 1962 Neill and Allen reported on a small collection of amphibians and reptiles that were accumulated by the Cambridge Expedition to Belize, under the patronage of Prince Philip, Duke of Edinburgh. The expedition was primarily concerned with archaeological investigation at Xunantunich, botanical surveys of the pine savannas and the Maya Mountains, and studies of the reefs fringing the coast, but some herpetological materials were secured, and these are now at the Museum of Comparative Zoology.

Herpetological exploration at the southwest periphery of the Yucatán Peninsula was materially enhanced with the arrival in Chiapas of Miguel Alvarez del Toro, formerly of Colima, Mexico, in 1942. Alvarez del Toro became the director of the Institute of Natural History of Chiapas and the state's preeminent naturalist. His *Los reptiles de Chiapas* (1960; 2nd ed., 1973; 3rd ed., 1983) constitutes the first attempt to deal comprehensively with the reptiles of that Mexican state. Also important is his 1974 book *Los Crocodylia de México*, which contains a wealth of information on the three species of crocodilians found in Mexico.

During the late 1940s a small but important collection of snakes and lizards from the vicinity of Felipe Carrillo Puerto, Quintana Roo, was assembled by Mauro Cárdenas Figueroa of the Instituto Politécnico de México. At that time the herpetofauna of the eastern half of the Yucatán Peninsula was very imperfectly known, and many of the specimens represented first records for the area. This material was deposited at the Museum of Zoology at the University of Michigan, and the specimens were reported by J. A. Peters (1953).

The dramatic expansion of tourism in the 1960s and 1970s—particularly that associated with archaeological sites and the coastal areas of Quintana Roo—resulted in the construction of many new roads, especially in the Mexican portion of the peninsula. Commercial airline service to the area was expanded, and areas previously reached only with great difficulty became easily accessible. To the south, efforts by the government of Guatemala to develop the sparsely populated Department of El Petén opened new areas to biological exploration. Research on the herpetofauna of the Yucatán Peninsula proliferated accordingly, and the amount of herpetological material in museums increased substantially.

In early 1960, William E. Duellman, of the University of Kansas, assisted by J. Knox Jones and John Wellman, collected amphibians and reptiles in the tall forests at the Alta Verapaz–El Petén border and on the savannas of central El Petén. These specimens were reported by Duellman in 1963 and are now in the Museum of Natural History at the University of Kansas.

In the summer of 1962 Duellman and students from the University of Kansas collected amphibians and reptiles throughout the Mexican portion of the Yucatán Peninsula. Percy L. Clifton, a collector for the university's museum, made additional collections there in the winter of 1962–1963 (Duellman, 1965a).

In June 1964, Bryce Brown of Baylor University and members of his family collected amphibians and reptiles in Belize and in the Mexican portions of the Yucatán Peninsula. These specimens are at the Strecker Museum at Baylor University. In 1965, Frederick G. Thompson, at the time a graduate student in the Mollusc Division at the Museum of Zoology at the University of Michigan, collected amphibians and reptiles in Chiapas, Tabasco, and Campeche. His specimens are in the Museum of Zoology.

An interest in parthenogenetic species of the genus *Cnemidophorus* attracted T. Paul Maslin, of the University of Colorado, to the Yucatán Peninsula, first in the summer of 1959, when he collected in the vicinity of Pisté, Yucatán, and again in 1960, when he and his associates collected on Cozumel, at that time one of the few known localities for the all-female *Cnemidophorus cozumela*. In 1961 he headed a field party from the University of Colorado that collected generally throughout the Mexican portion of the peninsula, though always with an emphasis on *Cnemidophorus*. The results of that fieldwork are reported in Maslin, 1963a; information on the tadpoles of some anurans from Yucatán is in Maslin, 1963b. *Cnemidophrus cozumela rodecki* was named in 1962 by Maslin and his graduate student, C. J. McCoy, on the basis of material obtained in 1961 in Quintana Roo. These specimens are on deposit at the Colorado Museum. In 1964 McCoy, together with Maslin and others from Colorado, returned to Yucatán to collect generally, but with a focus on *Cnemidophorus angusticeps*. Those specimens, too, are at the University of Colorado museum. *Cnemidophorus angusticeps petenensis*, named by Beargie and McCoy (1964), was based in part on the material obtained during the 1964 field season.

In Mérida, in 1961, McCoy met Edward Welling, a lepidopterist and professional collector of biological materials. Welling, who spoke Mayan, paid local collectors in Yucatán, Belize, and Guatemala to assemble collections of herpetological specimens. These were purchased by McCoy, who forwarded them to the Colorado Museum and, later, to the Carnegie Museum, where he assumed the position of curator of herpetology in 1965. A large collection of snakes secured by Welling at Middlesex, Belize, was reported by McCoy (1970c). The collections secured by Welling are especially notable for the very large series of snakes from the vicinity of Pisté and X-Can, Yucatán, and Nuevo X-Can, Quintana Roo. These served as the basis for a report by Henderson (1982) on the diet of *Oxybelis*, a paper by Censky and McCoy (1988) on reproductive cycles in

several species of snakes, and a paper summarizing information on the biology of the endemic Yucatecan pitviper, *Porthidium yucatanicum* (McCoy and Censky, 1992).

McCoy and his co-workers, especially Ellen Censky, continued their herpetological investigations in the Yucatán Peninsula, focusing on the herpetofauna of Belize. In 1982 and 1984, Laurie J. Vitt and associates collected amphibians and reptiles throughout Belize under the auspices of the Carnegie Museum. Those specimens, together with material accumulated as a result of several Carnegie Museum expeditions to Belize, have refined understanding of herpetofaunal distribution patterns in that country (McCoy, 1986, 1990; McCoy et al. 1986).

Additional work on the parthenogenetic *Cnemidophorus* of the Yucatán Peninsula was conducted in the late 1960s by Thomas Fritts, then a graduate student at the University of Illinois. Along with his wife, Pat, Fritts collected at several localities in Campeche and Yucatán, with special emphasis on the coastal localities of southwestern Campeche. His specimens were deposited at the Museum of Natural History at the University of Illinois. Fritts's studies led him to elevate *Cnemidophorus cozumela rodecki* to the rank of full species and further showed that *C. cozumela* very likely arose as a result of hybridization between *C. deppii* and *C. angusticeps* (Fritts, 1969).

In the early 1970s, Robert W. Henderson, at that time a Peace Corp volunteer assigned to Belize, made one of the first serious attempts to conduct sustained studies of the ecology of the Belizean herpetofauna. Henderson published several ecological studies of common Belizean reptiles, and in 1975 he coauthored, with Leo G. Hoevers, a checklist of the amphibians and reptiles of Belize. Hoevers, then a resident of Orange Walk District, also collaborated with Henderson on several taxonomic and ecological studies of Belizean amphibians and reptiles. Henderson's early collections were deposited at the Museum of Natural History, University of Kansas. His later collections, and Hoevers', were deposited primarily at the Milwaukee Public Museum, although some of Hoevers' specimens went to the National Museum of Natural History.

Also in the early 1970s, John Hudson, a forestry officer at Augustine, Cayo District, assembled a herpetological collection, primarily of snakes, from the vicinity of the Mountain Pine Ridge. The distributional records represented by those specimens are included in J. C. Lee, 1980a, but the present whereabouts of the collection is uncertain. According to E. D. Green, who served as the forestry officer at Augustine in the late 1980s, the specimens were lost, although Tony Garel of the Belize Zoo believes that the collection was deposited at St. John's College in Belize City, where a herpetological collection had been established by Father Leonard Dieckmann, S.J. Father Dieckmann also supplied the specimens of *Anolis sagrei* used in studies of reproduction by K. M. Brown and Sexton (1973; Sexton and Brown, 1977).

In 1966 and again in 1971, Ernest Liner and his associates collected amphibians and reptiles throughout the Mexican portion of the Yucatán Peninsula. Their specimens are in Liner's private collection at Houma, Louisiana. In 1974, Larry David Wilson, Randy McCranie, and Louis Porras also collected in that area, and their specimens are at the Museum of Zoology at Louisiana State University, where they augment the collection made by Richard Blaney in 1974–1976 and 1978.

I first came to the Yucatán Peninsula in 1972, and my herpetological work there began in 1974. During the next three years I accumulated approximately 2,000 specimens, representing 103 species. Those specimens are now at the Museum of Natural History at the University of Kansas, and the results of a distributional study based in part on that material appeared in J. C. Lee, 1980a. In subsequent years I made smaller collections at various points in the peninsula, and these are in the University of Miami Reference Collection.

In the mid-1980s, Harold Dundee and associates collected amphibians and reptiles in the Mexican portion of the Yucatán Peninsula, with special emphasis on the western section. Noteworthy specimens are reported in their 1986 publication, and the specimens are on deposit at Tulane University.

Jerry D. Johnson worked at the western periphery of the peninsula while he was a graduate student at Texas A & M University. His dissertation on the biogeography of amphibians and reptiles of Chiapas is an important addition to the literature (Johnson, 1989). Much of the material he assembled during the course of his fieldwork is at the University of Texas, El Paso.

A welcome addition to the herpetological literature of Mexico was the illustrated key to the genera, families, suborders, and orders of Mexican amphibians and reptiles, by Gustavo Casas-Andreu and C. J. McCoy, that appeared in its first edition in 1979 and was reprinted in 1987.

Beginning in 1973, the Mexican government, through what was then the Secretaría de Desarrollo Urbano y Ecología (SEDUE), began establishing field stations to study and protect the five species of sea turtles known to nest on the beaches of the Yucatán Peninsula. Today a number of federal, state, and local agencies, together with several nongovernment organizations, are involved with research and conservation of sea turtles in the peninsula (Frazier and Rodríguez, 1992:45). The results of work conducted at Río Lagartos and on Islas Holbox and Contoy were reported by Nájera (1990:29–33).

Contemporary Herpetology in the Yucatán Peninsula

A number of important herpetological studies are presently under way or have been recently concluded. Marco Lazcano studied the herpetofauna of the *petenes* region of the northwestern portion of the peninsula and the crocodiles of the Sian Ka'an Biosphere Reserve in Quintana Roo. García Téllez and Golubov Figueroa (1992) published on the nesting success of sea turtles in Sian Ka'an, and Kenneth Towle (1989) studied the status of *Crocodylus acutus* there. The vertebrates in the vicinity of Dzilám Bravo, Yucatán, are presently being surveyed by biologists from the Universidad Autónoma de Yucatán under the direction of M. C. Silvia Hernández Betancourt. Carlos Alberto López-Gonzales, of the Instituto de Ecología, Veracruz, studied the vertebrate fauna of coastal northern Quintana Roo and Cozumel (López-Gonzales, 1991). The Centro de Investigaciones de Quintana Roo (CIQRO) established a museum of zoology in Chetumal, where Humberto Bahena-Basave is establishing a herpetological collection and has recently completed a thesis on the distribution and ecology of the reptiles of southern Quintana Roo. Richard Vogt, of the Estación Biología de Los Tuxtlas, and his associates have been studying the biology of several species of turtles in the Lacandón region of Chiapas. The parthenogenetic *Cnemidophorus* of the Yucatán Peninsula continue to receive attention from biologists, including Harry L. Taylor of Regis University, who is studying the systematics of Yucatecan *Cnemidophorus*. Oscar Flores-Villela is presently working with Jack Sites on a study of the evolution of certain lizards of the genus *Sceloporus*, including species endemic to the Yucatán Peninsula. In addition, he published an annotated checklist of the amphibians and reptiles of Mexico that includes a summary of recent taxonomic changes (Flores-Villela, 1993).

In Guatemala, Enrique Pérez Cruz surveyed the herpetofauna of Tikal National Park. Together with J. P. Vannini, Jonathan Campbell (1989) published a distributional analysis of the amphibians and reptiles of Guatemala and Belize. Campbell and his students are presently working on various taxonomic problems involving Guatemalan amphibians and reptiles, in preparation for writing a comprehensive book dealing with the entire herpetofauna of that country.

In recent years a small collection of amphibians and reptiles has accumulated incidental to archaeological work at Lamanai, Orange Walk District, Belize, and these are deposited at the Royal Ontario Museum, Canada. At the time of this writing, Steven Platt is studying the breeding biology and feeding ecology of *Crocodylus moreletii* in Belize, and Bruce Means is undertaking herpetofaunal surveys in the Mountain Pine Ridge. The Iguana Project administered by the Belize Zoo under the direction of Anthony Garel succeeded in releasing hundreds of young green iguanas into habitats where that species has been hunted to near extinction. In 1989 and 1990 John Polisar, of the University of Florida, studied the reproductive biology and the exploitation of the turtle *Dermatemys mawii* in Belize (Polisar, 1992). Jan C. Meerman conducted herpetological inventories at the Shipstern Nature Reserve in Corozal District, and in 1993 published a checklist of the amphibians and reptiles of the reserve. A useful addition to the popular herpetological literature of Belize is the account of the common snakes of Belize by Dora Weyer (1990). A popular guide to the common snakes of Belize by Tony Garel and Sharon Matola is in production.

Although the composition and distribution of the herpetofauna of the Yucatán Peninsula is now comparatively well known, new information continues to accumulate. For example, in 1991 a joint expedition to Belize involving staff from the British Museum (Natural History) and the British Forces of Belize provided the first confirmed record of the caecilian *Gymnopis syntrema* from the Yucatán Peninsula (Stafford, 1991:12). Even more recently, in 1992, a field party from the National Museum of Natural History, with support from Conservation International, discovered a new species of *Eleutherodactylus* in southern Belize, as well as two species of frogs (*Hyla valancifer* and *H. bromeliacia*) new to the Yucatán Peninsula (Parker et al., 1993).

Prospects for Future Research

There remain a few undescribed species of amphibians and reptiles in the Yucatán Peninsula, but the facts of taxonomic composition and geographical distribution have been reasonably well established. Additional fieldwork can be expected to refine our knowledge of distribution patterns, but major contributions in the future are likely to be less and less concerned with the details of alpha taxonomy and distribution, important as those details may be. Nonetheless, the relatively high level of endemism in the Yucatecan herpetofauna ensures that Yucatecan species will play an important role in phylogeny reconstruction and historical biogeographical analysis.

Surprisingly little is known about the basic natural history of many amphibians and reptiles in the Yucatán Peninsula. Time and time again in the species accounts I have had to rely on information derived from populations to the north or south of the peninsula. Careful, detailed studies of the ecology of Yucatecan species, conducted within the peninsula, are very much to be desired for purposes of comparison.

Several exotic species of lizards are well established within the Yucatán Peninsula (e.g., *Hemidactylus frenatus*, *Sphaerodactylus argus*) and appear to be expanding their ranges there. These species offer excellent opportunities to study competitive interactions between resident species and colonizing ones. Similarly, the geographic distribution of *Anolis sagrei* is expanding rapidly through human transport, and that species may be expected to compete with other anoles of similar size (e.g., *A. lemurinus*, *A. tropidonotus*). The steep north-south gradients in the amount and seasonality of precipitation that characterize the Yucatán Peninsula, and the fact that these gradients are largely unconfounded by major topographic relief, provide a unique setting for gradient analyses involving geographic variation in morphology (e.g., J. C. Lee, 1993), physiology, ecology, and behavior.

Five species of marine turtles occur in the waters of the Yucatán Peninsula, and all breed on beaches within the peninsula. All are endangered, and their Yucatecan populations will likely continue to be the focus of intense research activity and conservation efforts (e.g., Frazier, 1993). Similarly, the two species of crocodiles that occur in the Yucatán Peninsula are endangered. Sizable populations persist in some areas of the peninsula, however, and afford excellent opportunities for ecological and behavioral studies.

Summary and Conclusions

Our knowledge of the amphibians and reptiles of the Yucatán Peninsula accumulated gradually over a span of about 400 years, punctuated by bursts of intense research activity. Until the middle of the nineteenth century, herpetology in Middle America was essentially the domain of museum-based European biologists who described and classified specimens supplied by field collectors but had little or no appreciation for the living animals or the habitats from which they came. Nonetheless, to judge by the numbers of species described, the decades of the 1850s and 1860s constituted something of a golden age in Middle American herpetology, as French and British workers, together with their counterparts in the United States, described and named 73 (41 percent) of the species of amphibians and reptiles found in the Yucatán Peninsula (Fig. 25).

From the middle of the nineteenth century onward, Europeans' contributions to knowledge of the herpetofauna of the Yucatán Peninsula waned markedly while North American workers increased their efforts. After about 1910, the activity of describing and naming the amphibians and reptiles of the Yucatán Peninsula became exclusively the province of North American biologists (Fig. 26).

As evidenced by the naming of new species, a second pulse of herpetological research occurred in the 1930s and 1940s (Fig. 25), primarily through the activities of Hobart M. Smith, Karl P. Schmidt, and Laurence C. Stuart, all accomplished field biologists who secured many specimens through their own fieldwork, often under difficult, even dangerous, conditions. These men and other herpetologists working in the Yucatán Peninsula at this time benefited greatly from the surge of large-scale anthropological exploration in the lowland Maya area. The field camps of archaeologists, often situated in remote areas, served as bases for herpetological work as well.

The 1930s and 1940s saw the integration of Darwinian evolutionary theory with advances in the nascent field of population genetics. As a result, the role of populations in the evolutionary process was seen to be of paramount importance, and the tasks of describing patterns of geographic variation and naming subspecies became a major preoccupation for herpetologists working in the Yucatán Peninsula.

By the 1960s the taxonomic composition of the herpetofauna of the Yucatán Peninsula was well established, at least in broad outline, and the major patterns of distribution were apparent. With few herpetological novelties left to describe, the emphasis began to shift from taxonomy to ecology and life history studies, including studies on diet and reproduction, behavior, and biogeographic analyses that sought to explain large-scale patterns of distribution, species diversity, and endemism.

Today herpetological research in the Yucatán

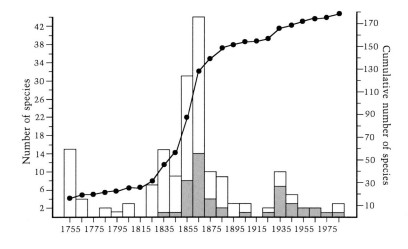

Fig. 25. Rates of discovery of amphibians and reptiles in the Yucatán Peninsula. Open bars represent the numbers of valid species named in 10-year intervals; shaded bars represent the numbers of valid species named based on type material known or presumed to have originated in the Yucatán Peninsula. The curve represents the cumulative number of valid species named from 1758 through 1988.

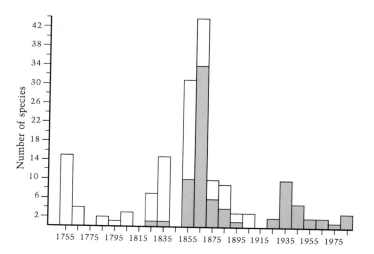

Fig. 26. North Americans' contributions to the discovery of amphibian and reptile species in the Yucatán Peninsula. Symbols as in Fig. 25 except that shaded bars represent the numbers of valid species named by North American workers.

Peninsula is progressing on many fronts, ranging from biochemical studies of lizards intended to improve our understanding of evolutionary relationships to field studies on crocodile ecology that will provide the information necessary for wise conservation and management decisions. But unlike the situation in previous decades, many of today's research projects are being designed and conducted by dedicated and capable Belizean, Guatemalan, and Mexican biologists, many of them leaders of the conservation movements in their countries. The task confronting these biologists is nonetheless daunting, for much still remains to be learned about the biology of amphibians and reptiles in the Yucatán Peninsula. Given the pace of environmental deterioration, it is difficult to remain sanguine concerning the future of biological investigation in the Yucatán Peninsula. There are some encouraging signs, however, and a basis for guarded optimism. Substantial portions of the Yucatán Peninsula have now been set aside and given varying degrees of official protection by the governments of Belize, Guatemala, and Mexico. In Belize, for example, several areas have been designated as protectorates,

including the wildlife sanctuaries of the Cockscomb Basin and Crooked Tree, the Río Bravo Conservation Area, the Shipstern Nature Reserve, and Caracol and Half Moon Cay National Monuments. In Mexico, several coastal areas of Yucatán are now protected as national parks, among them the Celestún, San Felipe, and Río Largartos National Parks. In Quintana Roo, some of the finest remaining forest is contained within the 528,147-hectare Sian Ka'an Biosphere Reserve. In Campeche, the Calakmul Biosphere Reserve encompasses nearly 23 percent of the state and is contiguous with the Maya Biosphere Reserve in neighboring Guatemala. The latter reserve includes roughly a third of the Department of El Petén. Thus, some restrictions on development and deforestation are in place. It still remains to be seen whether governments have the will and the capacity to resist the pressures being exerted by burgeoning populations and powerful economic interests. Given that uncertainty, it would be prudent to learn as much as we can, as quickly as we can, about the biota of this rapidly changing area.

SPECIES ACCOUNTS

Class **Amphibia** (Amphibians)

The class Amphibia comprises about 400 species of salamanders (order Caudata), 3,967 species of frogs and toads (order Anura), and about 155 species of caecilians (order Gymnophiona). Amphibians typically have smooth, moist, glandular skin. Most species lay their eggs in water. The eggs hatch into aquatic larvae that undergo metamorphosis to produce terrestrial juveniles and then adults. Amphibians are found everywhere in the world except Antarctica and many oceanic islands, and are most numerous and diverse in the tropics. In the Yucatán Peninsula, 43 species of amphibians (belonging to 19 genera and 9 families) are known or presumed to occur (see Table 1).

Key to the Orders of Amphibia

1. Limbs absent 2
   Limbs present. 3
2. Eyes degenerate; body attenuate; skin with deep annular grooves; tail absent; terrestrial or semiaquatic . . . . Gymnophiona
   Eyes not degenerate; skin without deep annular grooves; tail present; aquatic . . . . Anura (larvae)
3. Tail absent. . . . . Anura (larvae)
   Tail present . . . . Anura
   4
4. Tail strongly compressed laterally; dorsal and ventral caudal fins present; aquatic . . . . Anura (larvae)
   Tail not strongly compressed laterally; no caudal fins; terrestrial. . . . . Caudata

Clave para los Ordenes de Anfibios

1. Sin extremidades. 2
   Con extremidades 3
2. Ojos vestigiales; cuerpo alargado; la piel con pliegues anulares; sin cola; organismos terrestres o semiacuáticos. . . . . Gymnophiona
   Ojos bien desarrollados; piel sin pliegues anulares; cola presente; organismos acuáticos . . . . Anura (larvas)
3. Organismos con cola. 4
   Organismos sin cola . . . . Anura

4. Organismos con la cola muy comprimida; con una aleta dorsal y ventral; acuáticos . . . .
. . . . Anura (larvas)
Organismos con cola, pero no muy comprimida; sin aleta caudal; terrestres . . . . Caudata

 ## Order Gymnophiona (Caecilians)

Caecilians are blind, limbless, burrowing or aquatic amphibians that inhabit the lowland tropics of the New and Old Worlds. They superficially resemble giant earthworms because their extremely long bodies are distinctly segmented by deep annular grooves. The tiny eyes are covered with skin or with skin and bone. A sensory tentacle is present on the side of the face, posterior to the nostril. Many caecilians are oviparous, but some exhibit aplacental viviparity. Taylor (1968) provided a monographic treatment of the Gymnophiona. Nussbaum and Wilkinson (1989), in the most recent comprehensive treatment of the higher classification of caecilians, recognized 6 families, one of which (Typhlonectidae) was subsequently synonymized within Caeciliaidae by Hedges et al. (1993) on the basis of gene sequence data. One family of caecilians occurs in the Yucatán Peninsula.

IDENTIFICATION   The absence or reduction of many external morphological features can make identification of caecilians difficult. In the Yucatán Peninsula, however, the two species of caecilians known or suspected to occur there are easily distinguished on the basis of obvious external features.

The number of primary (completely encircling the body) and secondary (incompletely encircling the body) annuli is an important distinguishing feature. The extent to which the eye is covered by bone also helps to distinguish the two species, and the position of the tentacular aperture relative to the eye and nostril is an especially useful character.

Family Caeciliaidae

This most widely distributed of caecilian families occurs throughout the lowland tropics of Middle and South America, sub-Saharan Africa, India, and the Seychelle Islands. Members of the Caeciliaidae have a countersunk lower jaw and no tail. The family contains 101 living species grouped into 27 genera. One genus is known to occur in the Yucatán Peninsula, and one additional caeciliaid genus may occur there.

Although the family name was long spelled Caeciliidae, the International Commission on Zoological Nomenclature (see Bull. Zool. Nomencl., 1987: 263, opinion no. 1462) decided the name should be rendered Caeciliaidae (see discussion in Nussbaum and Wilkinson, 1989:32).

Key to the Genera of Caeciliaids Known or Presumed to Occur in the Yucatán Peninsula

Primary annuli fewer than 120; the eye covered with skin, visible externally; tentacular opening approximately equidistant between nostril and eye. . . . . *Dermophis*

Primary annuli more than 120; eye covered with bone and skin, not visible externally; tentacular opening much closer to eye than to nostril . . . . *Gymnopis*

Clave para los Géneros de Gymnophiona Conocidos o de Probable Ocurrencia en la Península de Yucatán

Menos de 120 anillos primarios en el cuerpo; el ojo está cubierto por piel; abertura tentacular más o menos equidistante entre el nostrilo y el ojo . . . . *Dermophis*

Más de 120 anillos primarios en el cuerpo; el ojo está cubierto por hueso y piel; abertura tentacular situada más cerca del ojo que del nostrilo. . . . . *Gymnopis*

Genus *Dermophis*

This small genus of Neotropical caecilians contains three species, one of which may occur in the Yucatán Peninsula, although its presence there is not yet confirmed. Savage and Wake (1972) studied the distribution and geographic variation in members of this genus, whose representatives range from southern Mexico to Colombia. *Dermophis* is from the Greek *derma*, "skin" or "leather," and *ophis*, "snake" or "serpent," in reference to the smooth integument of this superficially serpentlike amphibian.

Dermophis mexicanus (Duméril and Bibron)
(Fig. 218; Map 3)

Siphonops mexicanus A. M. C. Duméril and Bibron, 1841:284. HOLOTYPE: MNHNP 4275. TYPE LOCALITY: Mexique; restricted by H. M. Smith and Taylor (1950b:347) to Cuatotolapam, Veracruz, Mexico.

Mexican caecilian; culebra de dos cabezas, dos cabezas (Guatemala, Mexico); barretilla (Mexico).

DESCRIPTION This relatively large, thick-bodied caecilian attains a maximum total length of about 600 mm. The head is roughly triangular in dorsal aspect, and the head and body are similar in diameter (Fig. 218). The snout is very bluntly rounded, the tentacle exits at a point approximately equidistant between the eye and the nostril, and the eyes are covered by skin but visible externally. There is no tail. The body is distinctly segmented with folds, or annuli. The number of primary annuli varies with the location of the populations; among populations along the Atlantic slope in Mexico and Honduras, the range is 104 to 107; the number of secondary annuli ranges from 51 to 72 (Savage and Wake, 1972). Small dermal scales are present in the annuli.

The dorsal coloration is dark gray, purple, or black, and the venter is light gray or creamy white.

SIMILAR SPECIES In the Yucatán Peninsula *D. mexicanus* can be confused only with *Gymnopis syntrema*, which differs in having more primary (128–132) and secondary (63–93) annuli than *D. mexicanus* from the Atlantic slope of Mexico. *Gymnopis syntrema* is further distinguished from *D. mexicanus* by the presence of yellow, cream, or white pigment in the annular grooves.

DISTRIBUTION The Mexican caecilian occurs at low elevations on the Atlantic slope from southern Veracruz to Costa Rica and on the Pacific slope from Oaxaca to Panama. Its occurrence in the Yucatán Peninsula is probable but not yet confirmed (Map 3). See Comment.

NATURAL HISTORY This burrowing amphibian commonly occurs in loose moist soil, beneath surface litter, in the soil of stream banks, and beneath rotting logs. Individuals have also been found under banana leaves, coffee hulls, and garbage piles, and in piles of old stable manure. *Dermophis mexicanus* feeds predominantly on earthworms, and local population densities may be influenced by the worms' distribution and abundance (M. H. Wake, 1980:245). E. O. Moll and Smith (1967:1) reported a lizard, *Ameiva undulata*, in the stomach of *D. mexicanus*.

Dermophis mexicanus is viviparous. After examining specimens from northwestern Guatemala, M. H. Wake (1980) concluded that gametogenesis begins at about one year of age in both sexes, although males may not reproduce until they are two years old, whereas females may breed at the beginning of their second year. Copulation apparently occurs in May and June. The gestation period is about one year, and parturition occurs the following May and June. The brood size ranges from 4 to 12, with a mean of 7.

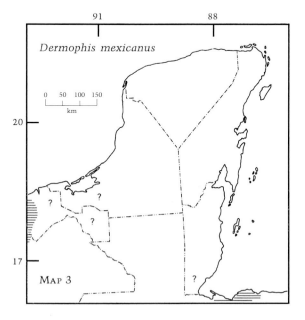

Thurow and Gould (1977:234–235) reported sounds produced by this species (as *D. septentrionalis*) as consisting of soft yelps, squawks, or squeaks. They also described an almost inaudible soft, lip-smacking sound as well as a series of soft clicks. They suggested that the clicks may aid in orientation but were unable to determine how the sounds are produced.

ETYMOLOGY   The specific name, *mexicanus*, is a toponym that refers to Mexico, where the type material originated.

SUBSPECIES   Taylor (1968) recognized two subspecies of *D. mexicanus*—the nominate subspecies and *D. m. clarkii*—either of which might occur in the Yucatán Peninsula. Savage and Wake (1972), however, declined to recognize subspecies, owing to their analysis of morphological variation throughout the range of the species.

COMMENT   Velasco (1895:38) listed this species (as *Siphonops mexicanus*) as present in the state of Campeche, and H. M. Smith and Smith (1976b: G-11) included it in their state lists for Campeche and Yucatán. Moreover, although Smith and Smith (1976b:G-3) asserted that caecilians (presumably *D. mexicanus*) "certainly occur" in Quintana Roo, the only confirmed record for any caecilian in the Yucatán Peninsula as here defined are two specimens of *Gymnopis syntrema* from southern Belize. Nonetheless, *D. mexicanus* could conceivably occur within the peninsula. Duellman (1963:246) reported that the natives of Chinajá, at the Alta Verapaz–El Petén border, were familiar with caecilians, suggesting the occurrence of this species (or of *G. syntrema*) in southernmost Petén. In addition, *D. mexicanus* is known from the lower Motagua Valley of Guatemala (D. R. Frost, 1985:626) and can thus be expected to occur in the very wet portions of southern Belize. It is definitely known to approach the westernmost limits of the Yucatán Peninsula in eastern Tabasco and may very well occur in the Río Grijalva–Usumacinta floodplain in westernmost Campeche.

Locality Records   Mexico: Campeche: no specific locality (H. M. Smith and Smith, 1976b:G-11; Velasco, 1895:38); Yucatán: no specific locality (H. M. Smith and Smith, 1976b:G-11).

Genus *Gymnopis*

This small genus of caecilians is apparently restricted to Central America, where it occurs from central Guatemala to Panama. Two species are currently recognized, one of which occurs in the Yucatán Peninsula. *Gymnopis* is derived from the Greek *gymnos*, "naked" or "lightly clad," and *opsis*, "aspect" or "view," possibly in reference to the smooth integument, which lacks obvious scales.

Gymnopis syntrema (Cope)
(Map 4)

Siphonops syntremus Cope, 1866. HOLOTYPE: probably USNM 25187, *fide* Nussbaum, 1988:927. TYPE LOCALITY: the neighboring [to Belize] region of Honduras; presumably the northern coastal region of Honduras, as suggested by Taylor (1968:597).

Dos cabezas (Guatemala).

DESCRIPTION   The adults of this moderately small, rather slender caecilian average about 272 mm in total length and may reach a maximum of 307 mm. A specimen from the Yucatán Peninsula has a total length of 144 mm (Stafford, 1994). The maximum body width is about 9 mm, and the head is about 7 to 9 mm long. The eyes are hidden in some specimens but are visible as spots in others. The tentacular aperture is much closer to the eye than to the nostril. The head and body are of approximately equal width; the snout is rounded in dorsal aspect and projects beyond the mouth. There is no tail, and the terminus of the body is bluntly pointed. The number of primary annuli ranges from 128 to 132, with an average of 130. The number of secondary annuli ranges from 63 to 93, with an average of about 75. Small scales are present in the primary and secondary annuli; these are larger and more numerous posteriorly.

In preservative the body is dark gray or black; the head is lighter gray with a light patch of skin surrounding the tentacular aperture. The annular grooves are lighter. Living animals are brownish gray (M. H. Wake and Campbell, 1983:858) and their annular grooves are "vividly outlined in white or cream" (Nussbaum, 1988:922). Cope (1866:9) described this species as "dark plumbeous, annuli yellow lined; head yellowish brown."

SIMILAR SPECIES The only other caecilian that might occur in the Yucatán Peninsula is *Dermophis mexicanus*, a larger, more robust animal that has fewer than 120 primary annuli. In addition, the tentacular aperture is approximately equidistant between the eye and the nostril in *Dermophis*, whereas in *Gymnopis* it lies very close to the eye.

DISTRIBUTION *Gymnopis syntrema* occurs at low and moderate elevations in central and eastern Guatemala, in Belize, and possibly in northern Honduras. In the Yucatán Peninsula the species is known with certainty from a single specimen collected in Cayo District, Belize (Map 4), and there is a recent unconfirmed record (P. J. Stafford, in litt.) of a second specimen from Cayo District.

NATURAL HISTORY Little is known of the natural history of this uncommon caecilian. It appears to inhabit humid forests at moderate elevations, although Stuart (1948:18) reported a specimen from Alta Verapaz brought to him by an Indian "who found it in the dust near his hut at 900 meters." A specimen from Belize was found dead beneath a partially protruding tree root (P. J. Stafford, in litt.) in moist tropical forest at an elevation of about 440 m (Stafford, 1991:12, 1994). M. H. Wake and Campbell (1983:859) described specimens taken in soft soil near a stream in undisturbed wet forest in the Department of Izabal, Guatemala. Thus, *Gymnopis syntrema* burrows in loose soil in moist forests, where it presumably feeds on earthworms and perhaps other soil invertebrates.

Nothing is known about reproduction in this species. *Gymnopis multiplicata*, the other member of the genus—and *syntrema*'s presumed closest relative—exhibits aplacental viviparity (M. H. Wake, 1977:89).

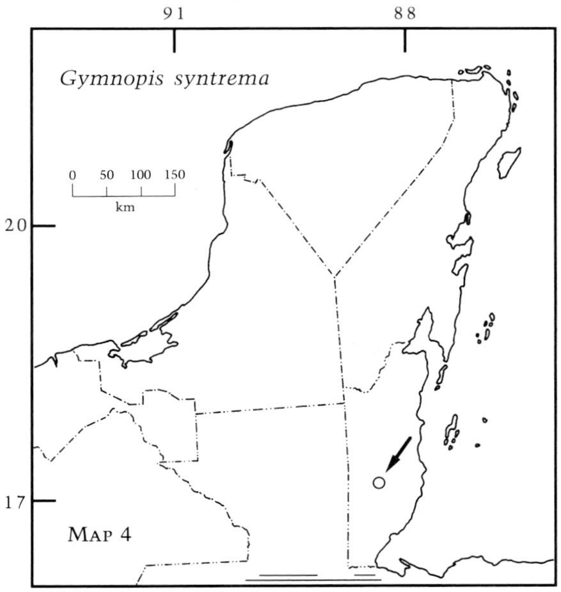

ETYMOLOGY The specific name, *syntrema*, comes from the Greek prefix *syn-*, "together," and *trema*, "hole," perhaps referring to the fact that the tentacular aperture lies close to the orbit.

COMMENT Nussbaum (1988) reviewed the highly confusing taxonomic literature pertaining to this species and concluded that *Gymnopis oligozona* and *Minascaecilia sartoria* are junior synonyms of *G. syntrema*, and that the genera *Copeotyphlinus* Taylor and *Minascaecilia* Wake and Campbell are junior synonyms of *Gymnopis* Peters. In addition, Nussbaum (1988:927) argued that the types of *G. syntrema* (Cope) and *G. oligozona* (Cope) are one and the same specimen, USNM 25187.

Locality Records Belize: Cayo: upper Raspaculo River basin (Stafford, 1991:12; Stafford, 1994:277).

 Order Caudata (Salamanders)

Salamanders are generally quadrupedal, tailed amphibians that have a predominantly Northern Hemispheric distribution. Some species are strictly aquatic and undergo incomplete metamorphosis. Some are fossorial, many are semiaquatic or terrestrial, and some are arboreal. Most species have internal fertilization and aquatic larvae, but a few reproduce by external fertilization. Most salamanders in the New World tropics do not have free-living aquatic larvae. Instead, the eggs are laid in moist terrestrial situations and hatch into miniature replicas of the adults.

The approximately 400 species of living salamanders are grouped into 62 genera representing 10 families. One salamander family occurs in the Yucatán Peninsula.

IDENTIFICATION The six species of salamanders found in the Yucatán Peninsula can usually be distinguished on the basis of their external mor-

Map 4

Gymnopis syntrema

0 50 100 150
km

MAP 4

phology and geographical distribution. If comparison with the photographs and illustrations provided here does not result in conclusive identification, use the key to identify the animal. Note the overall size and robustness of the specimen. Size in salamanders is indexed as snout-vent length (SVL), the straight-line distance from the tip of the snout to the posterior margin of the vent (Fig. 27). This measurement is sometimes termed *standard length* to distinguish it from the snout-vent length measurement applied to snakes and lizards. Is the animal slender and delicate, or is it robust and thick bodied? Note the relative length of the tail. Is it longer or shorter than the snout-vent length? Count the number of costal grooves between the axilla and the groin, including one each in the axilla and the groin (Fig. 27). Also count the number of costal grooves that lie between the forelimbs and hind limbs when they are folded against the side of the body (adpressed). It may be necessary to examine the number and pattern of the teeth, in which case magnification will be necessary. Note whether or not the animal has maxillary teeth. Also look at the teeth borne on the vomer in the roof of the mouth (Fig. 28). Count the number of these vomerine teeth and

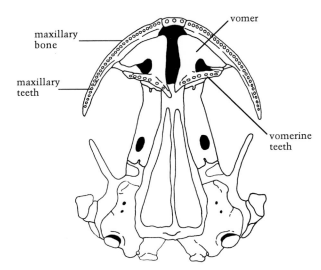

Fig. 28. Palatal view of the skull of a salamander showing vomerine and maxillary teeth.

determine whether they are arranged in discrete patches or in a continuous series.

Family Plethodontidae
(Lungless Salamanders)

Members of this family, the largest and most successful family of salamanders, are characterized by the complete absence of lungs. Gas exchange is accomplished through cutaneous and buccopharyngeal respiration. All metamorphosed and direct-developing plethodontids have a small groove running from the margin of the upper lip to each nostril. This nasolabial groove apparently serves an olfactory function. Some lungless salamanders are permanently aquatic, some are burrowers, others are terrestrial, and still others are arboreal. One group of plethodontids has become established in the New World tropics, and its members have evolved to occupy a variety of niches. These Neotropical species have direct development, meaning that there is no free-living aquatic larval stage. Instead, the eggs are deposited in moist terrestrial situations. The larvae complete their development within the egg and hatch into miniature replicas of the adults. Lungless salamanders occur throughout much of the United States, southern Canada, central and southern Mexico, and south through Central America and Amazonian South America. One genus occurs in southern Europe. About 28 genera and 246 living species are presently recognized. Two genera and 6 species occur in the Yucatán Peninsula.

Fig. 27. Dorsal (*left*) and ventral (*right*) views of a salamander showing characters useful in identification.

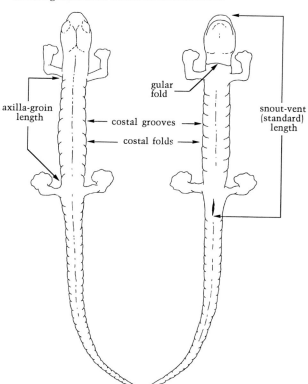

Key to the Genera of the Family Plethodontidae

Slender, elongate salamanders with tiny limbs and tail much longer than SVL; more than 16 costal grooves; sublingual fold present . . . . *Oedipina*

Moderate to robust salamanders with well-developed limbs; tail less than or about equal to SVL; costal grooves fewer than 16; sublingual fold absent . . . . *Bolitoglossa*

Clave para los Géneros de la Familia Plethodontidae

Salamandras con el cuerpo elongado y delgado, con extremidades pequeñas (reducidas), la longitud de la cola mayor a la longitud hocico-cloaca (LHC); más de 16 pliegues costales; un pliegue sublingual presente . . . . *Oedipina*

Salamandras con cuerpo moderadamente robusto, con extremidades bien desarrolladas; la longitud de la cola más o menos igual a la LHC; menos de 16 pliegues costales; sin pliegue sublingual . . . . *Bolitoglossa*

Genus *Bolitoglossa*

This is the largest genus of salamanders. D. B. Wake and Elias (1983:9) referred 64 species to this genus, several more species have since been described, and a number of unnamed forms await description. Five species occur in the Yucatán Peninsula. Members of this genus are distinguished from all other tropical salamander genera by the absence of a sublingual fold. These salamanders are morphologically diverse, ranging in size from small to very large, and from delicate and attenuate to stout and robust forms. The hands and feet are partially to fully webbed. The genus ranges from the lowlands of eastern San Luis Potosí south through Central America to the Amazonian lowlands of southern Peru and to Bolivia and Brazil. *Bolitoglossa* is from the Greek *bolites*, a kind of mushroom, and *glossa*, "tongue," presumably in reference to the shape of the projectile tongue.

Key to the Species of the Genus *Bolitoglossa*

1. Moderate to very large salamanders, adult SVL greater than 40 mm; tail about equal to or greater than SVL; maxillary teeth present 2
   Small salamanders, adult SVL less than 40 mm; tail short, conspicuously shorter than SVL; maxillary teeth absent . . . . *Bolitoglossa rufescens*

2. Medium-sized salamanders, adult SVL less than 85 mm; three to five costal grooves between adpressed limbs 3
   Very large, robust salamanders, adult SVL exceeding 85 mm; two or three costal grooves between adpressed limbs . . . . *Bolitoglossa dofleini*

3. Vomerine teeth arranged in a continuous series; base and northeast corner of the Yucatán Peninsula (Maps 6 and 7) 4
   Vomerine teeth arranged in several series; northern half of the Yucatán Peninsula only (Map 9) . . . . *Bolitoglossa yucatana*

4. Light pigment present on head anterior to the eyes; base and northeast corner of Yucatán Peninsula (Map 6) . . . . *Bolitoglossa mexicana*
   Little if any light pigment on head anterior to the eyes; Lacandón of Chiapas and southern El Petén only (Map 7) . . . . *Bolitoglossa mulleri*

Clave para las Especies del Género *Bolitoglossa*

1. Salamandras de tamaño grande, los adultos con una LHC mayor a 40 mm; la longitud de la cola igual o mayor que la LHC; dientes maxilares presentes 2

Salamandras de tamaño pequeño, los adultos con una LHC menor a 40 mm; cola corta, notoriamente más corta que la LHC; dientes maxilares ausentes . . . . . *Bolitoglossa rufescens*

2. Salamandras de tamaño mediano, los adultos no exceden los 85 mm de LHC; de tres a cinco pliegues costales entre los miembros cuando estos se pliegan sobre el cuerpo 3
Salamandras con cuerpo robusto y muy grandes, los adultos exceden los 85 mm de LHC; de dos a tres pliegues costales entre los miembros cuando estos se pliegan sobre el cuerpo . . . . . .
. . . . *Bolitoglossa dofleini*

3. Dientes vomerinos arreglados en series continuas; organismos que habitan en la base y porción noreste de la Península de Yucatán (Mapas 6 y 7) 4
Dientes vomerinos arreglados en varias series; organismos que solamente habitan en la mitad norte de la Península de Yucatán (Mapa 9) . . . . *Bolitoglossa yucatana*

4. Pigmentación clara presente en la parte de la cabeza anterior a los ojos; base y porción noreste de la Península de Yucatán (Mapa 6) . . . . *Bolitoglossa mexicana*
Poco o nada de pigmentación clara en la parte de la cabeza anterior a los ojos; solamente habitan en el área Lacandona de Chiapas y en el sur de El Petén (Mapa 7) . . . .
. . . . *Bolitoglossa mulleri*

Bolitoglossa dofleini (Werner)
(Fig. 219; Map 5)

Spelerpes dofleini Werner, 1903:352. HOLOTYPE: originally in ZSM, now lost. TYPE LOCALITY: Guatemala (possibly Alta Verapaz, *fide* Stuart, 1963:17).

Doflein's salamander.

DESCRIPTION   This very large, robust salamander is probably the most massive member of its genus, although some specimens of *B. schmidti* from Honduras may exceed *B. dofleini* in size—if, in fact, the two forms are considered heterospecific (Fig. 219). The adults of *B. dofleini* commonly reach 100 mm in snout-vent length. There are 13 costal grooves, 2 or 3 of which lie between the adpressed limbs. The tail length is about equal to or slightly shorter than the head and body. The limbs are well developed, and the hands and feet are fully webbed. Duellman (1963:219) described a specimen from Chinajá, near the Alta Verapaz–El Petén border: "The dorsum was rusty brown with irregular black and orange spots and streaks. The flanks were bluish gray with black in the costal grooves and creamy tan flecks along the ventral edge of the flank. The belly and underside of the tail were yellowish tan with dark brown spots laterally. The limbs were orange proximally and black distally; the pads of the feet were bluish black. The dorsal and lateral surfaces of the tail were yellowish orange with black spots. The iris was grayish yellow."

SIMILAR SPECIES   No other salamander in the Yucatán Peninsula approaches *B. dofleini* in size.

Bolitoglossa yucatana has three to five costal grooves between the adpressed toes rather than two or three, and it does not overlap geographically with *B. dofleini* (cf. Maps 5 and 9). *Bolitoglossa mexicana* has fewer vomerine teeth (12–13 vs. 35–38); and *B. rufescens* is much smaller, has a tail conspicuously shorter than the length of the head and body, and lacks maxillary teeth.

DISTRIBUTION   This giant salamander occurs at low and moderate elevations on the Caribbean slope of northern Guatemala, Belize, and Honduras. In the Yucatán Peninsula it is known only from northernmost Alta Verapaz and adjacent Belize (Map 5).

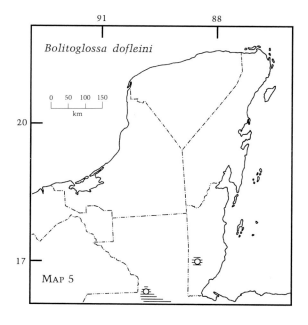

NATURAL HISTORY   Little is known of the habits of this salamander, which, although locally common, seems to be generally rare in the Yucatán Peninsula. Stuart (1943a:18, 1948:18) suggested that *B. dofleini* inhabits decaying vegetation on the ground in lowland forests, which accords with the terrestrial habits of the other members of the *dofleini* group (*B. schmidti*, *B. yucatana*). McCoy (1990:165) reported a specimen from Belize found beneath a rotten log in rainforest; D. B. Wake (in litt.) reported specimens beneath surface debris on coffee plantations; and Duellman (1963:220) secured a specimen from the water-filled axil of an elephant ear. Stuart (1943a:18) described these salamanders as extremely sluggish.

Doflein's salamander presumably preys on invertebrates and is in turn eaten by the false coral snake, *Urotheca elapoides* (Stuart, 1948:18). *Bolitoglossa dofleini* is presumably oviparous, with direct development. A female from Alta Verapaz obtained in August had small ovarian eggs, and another collected in March also contained minute ovarian eggs (Duellman, 1963:219).

ETYMOLOGY   The specific name, *dofleini*, is a patronym that honors Franz J. Theodor Doflein, a German biologist of the late nineteenth and early twentieth centuries who studied amphibian parasites and served as director of the Zoologisches Staatssammlung in Munich in the early part of the twentieth century.

Locality Records   Belize: Cayo: Chiquibul Branch of Macal River, S Granos de Oro Camp (CM 112124). *Guatemala*: Alta Verapaz: Chinajá (Duellman, 1963: 219).

Bolitoglossa mexicana
Duméril, Bibron, and Duméril
(Figs. 220, 221; Map 6)

Bolitoglossa mexicana A. M. C. Duméril, Bibron, and Duméril, 1854:96. SYNTYPES: MNHNP 4747 (two syntypes). TYPE LOCALITY: Province d'Oaxaca au Mexique and Vera Crux; questionably restricted by H. M. Smith and Taylor (1950b:339) to San Felipe Cerro, 15 km northeast of Oaxaca, Mexico.

Galliwasp (Belize); salamanquesa (Mexico).

DESCRIPTION   This medium-sized, moderately robust salamander has large, fully webbed hands and feet (Fig. 220). The adults probably average between 55 and 70 mm in snout-vent length, but specimens with a snout-vent length of 80 mm are known. The tail is approximately as long as the head and body. The head is moderately broad and slightly distinct from the neck in dorsal view. The eyes are rather small and protruding (Fig. 221). There are 13 costal grooves, 3 to 5 of which lie between the adpressed limbs.

This species is highly variable in color and pattern, but there is always some indication of longitudinal bands or stripes on the dorsum. The lateral surfaces of the body and tail are often chocolate brown, whereas the dorsal surfaces may be reddish brown or red-orange, usually with irregular spots and blotches of dark brown, tan, and cream. In some specimens the light dorsal coloration forms a broad, irregular dorsal band extending from the base of the head onto the tail. Often a pair of irregular light dorsolateral stripes run the length of the body. The limbs are generally dark brown with a few scattered light flecks and small blotches.

SIMILAR SPECIES   The smaller *B. rufescens* has a tail that is conspicuously shorter than the head and body, and it lacks maxillary teeth. *Bolitoglossa yucatana* is less robust, and its vomerine teeth are arranged in patches rather than in a continuous series; *B. dofleini* is much larger, has more vomerine teeth (35–38 vs. 12–13), and has two or three, rather than three to five, costal grooves between the adpressed limbs.

DISTRIBUTION   This species occurs at low, moderate, and intermediate elevations (to 1,700 m) on the Atlantic slope from southern Veracruz to Honduras. It occurs through the base of the Yucatán Peninsula, and there is an apparently isolated population at the outer end of the peninsula (Map 6).

NATURAL HISTORY   *Bolitoglossa mexicana* inhabits humid lowland and premontane forests, where it is both arboreal and terrestrial. Individuals of this uncommon species have been found beneath surface debris (Stuart, 1958:16), on roads at night (D. B. Wake and Lynch, 1976:20), and in bromeliads (W. T. Neill and Allen, 1959c:20; Taylor and Smith, 1945:548). Himmelstein (1980:23) reported a specimen found beneath a limestone rock in tropical evergreen forest, and J. R. McCranie (pers. comm.) found a specimen beneath surface debris in a sawmill. Stuart (1935:35) reported three specimens col-

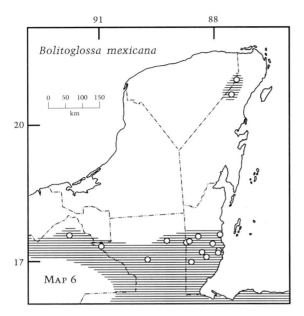

91   88

Bolitoglossa mexicana

0 50 100 150
km

20

17

MAP 6

lected at an aguada near La Libertad, El Petén. I encountered a specimen at night on low vegetation in a citrus grove in Belize. A specimen found beneath a log in open pine woods in Chiapas had a body temperature of 20.5C (Feder et al., 1982:2). Terrestrial activity is probably restricted to the rainy season, at least in the more arid parts of the range. During the dry season these salamanders most likely inhabit bromeliads and other water-retaining epiphytes.

Nothing is known of the diet, but it almost certainly consists predominantly of small invertebrates. In turn, these salamanders are preyed on by the false coral snake, *Urotheca elapoides*, for Duellman (1963:242) found a *B. mexicana* in the stomach of one from southern El Petén.

Bolitoglossa mexicana is oviparous. Duellman (1963:220) reported a specimen from the El Petén–Alta Verapaz border of Guatemala that contained 63 large eggs. As is the case for other species of the genus *Bolitoglossa*, the eggs of this species are deposited in moist terrestrial situations, and the larvae develop within the egg.

ETYMOLOGY   The specific name, *mexicana*, is a toponym referring to Mexico, where the type material originated.

Locality Records   Belize: Belize: Cayo: Benque Viejo (USNM 65131), 0.5 mi W Camalot (CM 105764), Caracol (CMM photo), upper Raspaculo River basin (Stafford, 1991:12), Xunantunich (W. T. Neill and Allen, 1959c:20), no specific locality (RAL photo); Manatee

(FMNH 3237–38); Stann Creek: Cockscomb Wildlife Sanctuary (CF photo), Middlesex (FMNH 4268, 4270), Silk Grass (FMNH 49099), 5.7 mi S Silk Grass (KU 156297), Stann Creek Valley (Schmidt, 1941:481). *Guatemala*: El Petén: near La Libertad (UMMZ 75453–55), Piedras Negras (USNM 116070), Tikal (UF 13475; UMMZ 117990). *Mexico*: Chiapas: Palenque (FMNH 91455, 91457, 98727, 179609–10, 179731–48, 190591; UCM 22125–26; UIMNH 11287, 13571–73, 13576–88, 49090, 67081; USNM 116071–98); Quintana Roo: Cobá (Himmelstein, 1980:23), near Pueblo Nuevo X-Can (JRM photo).

Bolitoglossa mulleri (Brocchi)
(Map 7)

Spelerpes mulleri Brocchi, 1883:116. SYNTYPES: MNHNP 6395 (four syntypes). TYPE LOCALITY: several localities in Alta Verapaz, Guatemala; restricted by Stuart (1943:12) to "les montagnes qui dominent Cobán."

Müller's salamander; salamanquesa (Mexico).

DESCRIPTION   This rather large, moderately robust salamander may attain a snout-vent length slightly in excess of 80 mm, although most specimens probably range between 60 and 70 mm. Adult specimens from the base of the Yucatán Peninsula measured 56.5 and 80 mm in snout-vent length (Duellman, 1963:220; Lazcano-Barrero, 1992a:316). The head is somewhat depressed, and the snout is truncate in dorsal view. The tail is constricted at the base and about 130 percent of the snout-vent length. The limbs are stout and well developed, and the digits are fully webbed. There are 13 costal grooves, 3 or 4 of which lie between the adpressed limbs. Maxillary teeth are present, and there is a continuous series of vomerine teeth, about 10 to 13 in number.

The ground color of *B. mulleri* is dark gray to nearly black on both the dorsal and ventral surfaces. Typically, a broad yellow middorsal stripe extends onto the tail, where it breaks up into a series of irregular spots. The dorsal surfaces of the head and limbs bear small spots and flecks of yellow pigment, but light pigment is generally absent on the head anterior to the eyes. On the lateral surfaces of the head there is usually an indistinct yellowish stripe or line that extends from behind the eye posteriorly onto the neck, where it joins the middorsal stripe.

SIMILAR SPECIES *Bolitoglossa mulleri* most closely resembles *B. mexicana*, to which it is probably closely related, but differs in having little or no yellow pigment on the head anterior to the eyes, and in having a single broad yellow middorsal stripe rather than the irregular blotches or indistinct light stripes of *B. mexicana*. *Bolitoglossa dofleini* is much larger and has more vomerine teeth (35–38 vs. 10–13), and *B. rufescens* is much smaller, lacks maxillary teeth, and has a tail distinctly shorter than the snout-vent length.

DISTRIBUTION *Bolitoglossa mulleri* ranges from northeastern Chiapas eastward through north-central Guatemala. In the Yucatán Peninsula it is known from a single specimen taken in the Lacandón region of northeastern Chiapas and from the Alta Verapaz–El Petén border of Guatemala (Map 7).

NATURAL HISTORY This species lives predominantly at moderate elevations on the Atlantic slope of Guatemala. Stuart (1943:13, 1948:19) characterized *B. mulleri* as a pine belt species but suggested that it might occur in cloud forest at higher elevations. It is now known from rainforest at lower elevations as well. Although Brocchi (1883:116) stated that the specimens collected by Bocourt came from beneath stones, most specimens have been taken from bromeliads (Schmidt, 1936:151; Stuart, 1943:13), including one from the Lacandón of Chiapas at a height of 5 m (Lazcano-Barrero, 1992a:316). Duellman (1963:220) found specimens

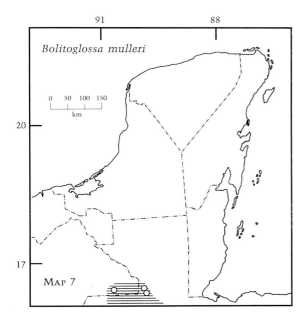

Bolitoglossa mulleri

0 50 100 150
km

20

17

MAP 7

beneath logs in southern El Petén, however, and suggested that habitat utilization may vary seasonally.

Little is known of the diet or reproductive biology. Presumably these salamanders feed on small invertebrates and produce terrestrial eggs that undergo direct development. Duellman (1963:220) removed a specimen of *B. mulleri* from the stomach of a false coral snake (*Urotheca elapoides*) collected in southern El Petén.

ETYMOLOGY The specific name, *mulleri*, is a patronym honoring Friedrich Müller, a nineteenth-century Swiss physician and zoologist whose catalogue of the amphibians and reptiles in the Basel Museum, published in 1878, contained the original descriptions of many new species of amphibians and reptiles.

COMMENT Lazcano-Barrero (1992b) summarized the available information on *B. mulleri*.

Locality Records Guatemala: Alta Verapaz: Chinajá (Duellman, 1963:220); El Petén: 16 km NNW Chinajá (Duellman, 1963:220). *Mexico*: Chiapas: Boca de Chajul (INIRB 161).

Bolitoglossa rufescens (Cope)
(Fig. 222; Map 8)

Oedipus rufescens Cope, 1869:104. HOLOTYPE: USNM 6886 (lost, *fide* Stuart, 1963:19). TYPE LOCALITY: Orizava (= Orizaba), Veracruz, Mexico; considered erroneous by Schmidt (1936:152).

Rufescent salamander; galliwasp (Belize).

DESCRIPTION This is the smallest *Bolitoglossa* in the Yucatán Peninsula. The adults average about 28 to 33 mm in snout-vent length, and the tail is shorter than the head and body (Fig. 222). The head is somewhat depressed and slightly distinct from the neck in dorsal view. The eyes are large, with horizontally elliptical pupils and golden irises. There is a conspicuous gular fold. In males, each nasolabial groove traverses a downward fleshy projection of the upper lip. These delicate, moderately slender salamanders have 13 costal grooves, 3 or 4 of which lie between the adpressed limbs. The hands and feet are fully webbed.

Bolitoglossa rufescens is highly variable in color and pattern. Many specimens have a brown or reddish brown dorsum that contrasts with the darker brown or black on the sides of the body and the venter. In these, the limbs are generally dark with irregular darker blotches. Other specimens are light tan above and below, with small dark flecks.

SIMILAR SPECIES The small size, short tail, and lack of maxillary teeth distinguish this species from all other *Bolitoglossa* in the Yucatán Peninsula. *Oedipina elongata* is much more elongate, has more than 16 costal grooves, and its tail is substantially longer than the snout-vent length (Fig. 29).

DISTRIBUTION The rufescent salamander occurs at low and moderate elevations to about 1,500 m on the Atlantic slope from San Luis Potosí, Veracruz, and northern Chiapas through northern Guatemala and southern Belize to northern Honduras. It is restricted to the base of the Yucatán Peninsula (Map 8).

NATURAL HISTORY Stuart (1948:20) characterized *B. rufescens* as the most abundant and widespread salamander in Alta Verapaz, but in the Yucatán Peninsula it is an uncommon inhabitant of lowland and premontane forests. It is nocturnal and largely arboreal. In Mexico, H. M. Smith (1941e:37) found *B. rufescens* to be a common inhabitant of bromeliads, and in Guatemala, Stuart (1948:20) found it only in the leaf axils of bromeliads and bananas, as did Schmidt (1936:151). Feder et al. (1982:3) reported a range of body temperatures of 17.0 to 27.6C for specimens found in banana plants in Veracruz.

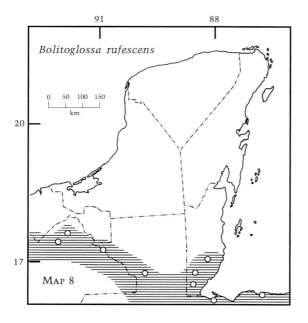

MAP 8

Bolitoglossa rufescens exhibits an antipredator defensive behavior involving elevation and undulation of the tail. Like many other species, this salamander is capable of caudal autotomy, but the tail is unusually delicate and easily lost in this species (Ducey et al. 1993:346).

Nothing is known of reproduction in this species. It is presumably oviparous, with direct development, like the other members of its genus.

ETYMOLOGY The specific name, *rufescens*, is the Latin present participle of *rufesco*, "to become reddish or tawny," alluding to the reddish dorsum of many individuals.

COMMENT *Bolitoglossa rufescens* is very similar morphologically to *B. occidentalis*, which occurs primarily on the Pacific slope from Oaxaca to Honduras, but differs in lacking maxillary teeth. Although D. B. Wake and Lynch (1976:19) expressed doubt that the two forms are separate species, A. Larson (1983) documented substantial molecular divergence among the various populations assigned to *B. rufescens* and *B. occidentalis*, and suggested that several cryptic species may be involved, a view shared by D. B. Wake (pers. comm.).

Locality Records   *Belize*: Cayo: Doyle's Delight (UMRC 89-44); Stann Creek: Cockscomb Basin Jaguar Preserve (CM photo 34040.2); Toledo: Blue Creek Village (MVZ 191636–37; RWV photo). *Guatemala*: El Petén: Piedras Negras (USNM 117400–6), Sayaxché (UCM 22139). *Mexico*: Chiapas: Palenque (USNM 117407).

Bolitoglossa yucatana (Peters)
(Fig. 223; Map 9)

Spelerpes yucatanus W. C. Peters, 1882:137. HOLOTYPE: ZMB 10231. TYPE LOCALITY: Yucatán, Mexico.

Yucatán salamander; salamandra de Yucatán, salamanquesa (Mexico).

DESCRIPTION This is a medium-sized, somewhat attenuate salamander. The adults average about 53 mm in snout-vent length (Fig. 223). The tail is approximately as long as the head and body and is sometimes swollen with massive fat deposits, perhaps an adaptation to the prolonged dry season throughout much of its range (D. B. Wake and Lynch, 1976:20). The head is moderately depressed and is distinct from the neck in dorsal view. In males, the nasolabial groove traverses a fleshy downgrowth of the upper lip, and a mental gland is present. There is a distinct gular fold. Thirteen costal grooves lie between the axilla and the groin, three to five of which lie between the adpressed limbs. The fingers and toes are completely webbed.

The dorsal coloration is predominantly gray, brown, or reddish brown, with an irregular mottling of cream or light tan. The lighter pigment is sometimes arranged to form indistinct dorsolateral stripes that originate on the head and fade posteriorly. The lateral surfaces of the body are generally a uniform dark brown. The ventral surfaces of the throat and body are a uniform brown or tan.

SIMILAR SPECIES   *Bolitoglossa rufescens* is smaller, lacks maxillary teeth, and has a tail conspicuously shorter than its head and body length; *B. mexicana* is often reddish or reddish brown in color, and its vomerine teeth are arranged in a continuous series rather than in patches, as in *B. yucatana*. *Bolitoglossa dofleini*, a much larger animal, is restricted to the base of the Yucatán Peninsula (cf. Maps 5 and 9).

DISTRIBUTION   This species is endemic to the Yucatán Peninsula, where it is known from several localities in the states of Campeche, Quintana Roo, and Yucatán. There is a population in northern Belize that is apparently isolated from the Mexican populations (Map 9).

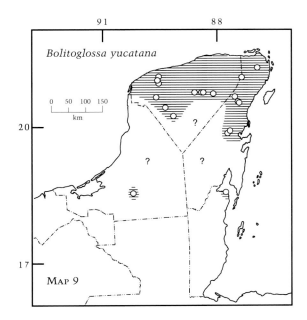

MAP 9

NATURAL HISTORY   Although a large series was obtained at an aguada near Yaxcopoil, Yucatán, by collectors from the Carnegie Museum, this is an uncommon salamander, or at least an infrequently encountered one. In spite of its fully webbed feet, *B. yucatana* is apparently terrestrial. Specimens have been found beneath surface debris in thorn forest, and I have taken them in tropical evergreen forest on roads at night following heavy rains. Dunn (1926:415) recorded two large adults "dredged from the Sacred Cenote at Chichén Itzá." At Ticul, Yucatán, a specimen was found in shallow soil at the base of a tree stump (P. E. Moler, pers. comm.), and Duellman (1965:586) reported a specimen (as *B. mexicana*) found beneath a log at the edge of a cenote in Yucatán. Surface activity is likely restricted to the rainy season. At other times these salamanders probably sequester themselves deep within the recesses of the karsted limestone that abounds throughout their range.

A specimen taken from a small mammal trap in Quintana Roo had ants in its mouth (P. Tucker, in litt.), but beyond that nothing is known concerning the diet of these salamanders, which probably feed on a variety of small invertebrates.

Reproduction has not been investigated in detail, but the first report of reproduction in any Neotropical salamander was Barbour and Cole's (1906:155) description of a *B. yucatana* "taken, together with a single egg, in the damp earth near a watering trough on March 7" at Chichén Itzá. Thus, like other *Bolitoglossa*, this species produces terrestrial eggs, and the embryos undergo direct development. This lone observation suggests that oviposition may occur during the dry season and that the female may attend the eggs, as some other members of the genus do (McDiarmid and Worthington, 1970:66). The interpretation of this observation is clouded, however, by Dunn's (1926:415) assertion that the specimen in question (MCZ 2431) is not an adult.

ETYMOLOGY   The specific name, *yucatana*, is a toponym that refers to Yucatán, the general area where the type specimen originated.

Locality Records   Belize: Corozal: 0.5 mi W Sarteneja Village (UMRC 92-20, 92-21). *Mexico*: Campeche: 24 km E and 20 km S Escárcega (LACM 116544); Quintana Roo: near Cobá (JCL photo), 14.6 km SE Cobá (UMRC 79-250), 13 to 19 km SE Cobá (MVZ 197507–16, 207628, 207639, 207789–90, 208379), 20.2 km SE Cobá (UMRC 79-251), 5.4 km NE Felipe Carrillo Puerto on rd. to Vigía Chico (MVZ 194945), 8 mi NNE

Felipe Carrillo Puerto (P. Tucker, in litt.), Reserva El Edén (COHECERN uncat.); Yucatán: Actun Sabaca, 6 km S Tekax (MVZ 128364), Chichén Itzá (FMNH 36599–600; MCZ 2431, 2773, 14792), 2 km E Chichén Itzá (KU 71591), Dzibilchaltún (FMNH 154569–71; UMMZ 124024), 1.5 mi S Libre Unión (UCM 18173), near Mérida (FMNH 124499), 5 mi N Mérida (TU 19781), Tekom (FMNH 49100), Ticul (JCL photo), 16.2 km S Yaxcopoil (CM 45203–24).

Genus *Oedipina*

These slender, elongate salamanders are found in Middle America and northern South America. Their extreme attenuation suggests adaptation for a burrowing existence, and individuals have been found within and beneath rotting logs, under slabs of bark, and in mats of wet moss in humid lowland forests. Representatives of the genus occur at low and moderate elevations from eastern Chiapas southward through Central America to western Colombia and central Ecuador. Sixteen species are recognized, of which only one occurs in the Yucatán Peninsula. Brame (1968) provided the most recent review of this genus, and Brodie and Campbell (1993) discussed the four Guatemalan species. *Oedipina* is named after Oedipus, a hero of Greek mythology; *-ina* is a suffix denoting "likeness." The name literally means "swollen footed," referring to the wounds sustained by Oedipus as a child and describing the swollen appearance of the feet of members of this genus caused by the extensive webbing that encloses the digits.

Oedipina elongata (Schmidt)
(Fig. 29; Map 10)

Oedipus elongatus Schmidt, 1936:165. HOLO-TYPE: FMNH 20059. TYPE LOCALITY: Escobas, the site of the water supply for Puerto Barrios, Izabal, Guatemala.

Galliwasp (Belize).

DESCRIPTION This extremely elongate, worm-like salamander has small, delicate limbs and a long tail (Fig. 29). It is robust for an *Oedipina*, however, and the adults have an average snout-vent length of about 55 mm. Too few specimens have been collected to allow an assessment of possible sexual size dimorphism. There are 17 costal grooves, and the

Fig. 29. *Oedipina elongata*, ca. 52 mm SVL; Monte Libano, Chiapas, Mexico. Redrawn from Brame, 1968:12, by permission of the Society for the Study of Amphibians and Reptiles.

tail exceeds the snout-vent length by about 30 percent. The head is slightly distinct from the neck in dorsal aspect, and the snout is bluntly rounded. The digits are extensively webbed and pointed at their tips. The dorsal coloration is dark bluish gray with lighter gray stippling, and there are spots and patches of white on the head.

SIMILAR SPECIES The attenuate form and extremely long tail immediately distinguish *O. elongata* from all other salamanders in the Yucatán Peninsula. Moreover, no other salamander there has more than 15 costal grooves between the axilla and groin.

DISTRIBUTION The geographical distribution of *O. elongata* is poorly known. It has been recorded from low and moderate elevations in northern Chiapas, from eastern Guatemala, and from central Belize. There are no records from El Petén, although its occurrence there is probable (Map 10).

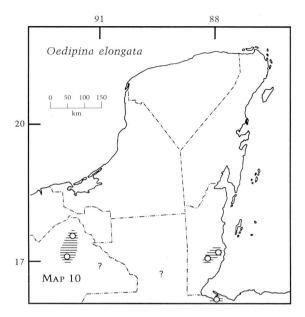

Oedipina elongata

Map 10

NATURAL HISTORY Very little is known about the natural history of this seemingly rare species. According to Brame (1968:59), these salamanders live within rotting logs and beneath slabs of bark on fallen logs, where they probably feed on small invertebrates. A specimen was found beneath a rock in a parking lot at Palenque, Chiapas (D. B. Wake, pers. comm.). Sanderson (1941:155), who claimed that *O. elongata* is cannibalistic, related an incident in which a recently collected specimen regurgitated the remains of two smaller individuals of its own kind. I have examined the specimens in question and find Sanderson's account highly improbable. Presumably *O. elongata* lays terrestrial eggs that undergo direct development.

ETYMOLOGY The specific name, *elongata*, is Latin for "elongate," in reference to the attenuate form.

Locality Records *Belize*: Stann Creek: Bokowina (Schmidt, 1941:481), Double Falls (FMNH 49098). *Mexico*: Chiapas: Finca Monte Libano (UIMNH 59182–83); Palenque (D. B. Wake, pers. comm.).

 Order Anura (Frogs and Toads)

Frogs and toads are tailless (as adults) amphibians with a vertebral column that consists of no more than nine presacral vertebrae and elongate hind limbs specialized for jumping. Anurans are by far the most successful group of living amphibians, with 3,967 living species recognized and many new forms described each year. Twenty-one to 23 living families are generally recognized, and about 300 genera. Anurans occur worldwide except at Arctic and Antarctic latitudes and on some oceanic islands. Fertilization is usually external, although internal fertilization occurs in a few species. The eggs are typically deposited in water, hatch into aquatic larvae, and subsequently metamorphose into small replicas of the adults. There are many departures from this general mode of reproduction, however, especially among tropical anurans. Some species deposit their eggs in foam nests, others deposit eggs on vegetation overhanging water, and still others lay eggs in moist terrestrial situations, where they undergo direct development without a free-living aquatic larval stage. Some species exhibit parental care in which the eggs are attended or transported by a parent. Seven families, 15 genera, and 35 species of anurans are known to occur in the Yucatán Peninsula (see Table 1).

IDENTIFICATION The frogs and toads of the Yucatán Peninsula can often be identified by comparing the specimens with the illustrations provided here for most species. Reference to the species accounts, especially the section describing similar species, will help to confirm or reject a tentative identification. The location where a specimen was found is important. Some species can be eliminated from consideration based on their geographical distribution. In a minority of cases it may be necessary to resort to the identification keys. The keys rely almost exclusively on external morphological characters, most of which are illustrated and defined in the Glossary.

The texture of the skin is an important feature. Many species have smooth skin, but in some species the skin may be rough to the touch, owing to the presence of numerous integumentary denticles. In this case the skin is said to be *shagreen*. When the skin is highly wrinkled it is termed *rugose*. In some species, such as *Physalaemus pustulosus*, the skin is covered with many small, distinct, blisterlike pustules, and the skin is termed *pustulate*. The skin is said to bear warts if the glands of the integument are concentrated into distinct wartlike structures, as is the case in members of the genus *Bufo*. The size, shape, and position of these structures can be useful in identification. In some species integumentary glands may form glandular ridges, or they may

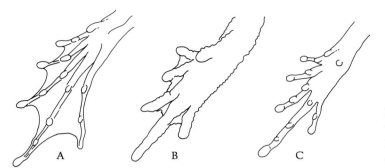

Fig. 30. Feet of anurans. A, *Rana berlandieri* with digits fully webbed. B, *Bufo valliceps* with digits slightly webbed. C, *Eleutherodactylus chac* with digits unwebbed.

be generally distributed through the integument, producing a marbled effect that may simply be described as *glandular*, as in *Phrynohyas venulosa*.

The hands and feet of anurans bear many useful identifying characters. The presence, absence, and extent of webbing between the digits can be important. In some species the digits are devoid of webbing, in others digits are webbed only at their bases, and in still other species the digits are extensively webbed (Fig. 30). The tips of the digits may be expanded or not. If expanded, they may form rounded disks (Fig. 69) or they may terminate as T-shaped or heart-shaped structures (Fig. 41). A fold of skin

along the tarsus, the *tarsal fold*, is present in some species, and a *tarsal tubercle* may or may not be present (Fig. 31). The tubercles immediately beneath the joints of the digits are termed *subarticular tubercles* (Fig. 31). The extent to which these tubercles are developed may be a useful feature, and the same is true of the *supernumerary tubercles*, which lie between the subarticular tubercles (Fig. 31).

Color pattern is sometimes species-specific and

Fig. 31. Plantar view of the foot of an anuran showing features important in the identification of frogs and toads.

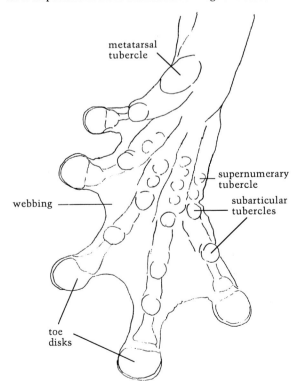

metatarsal tubercle

supernumerary tubercle

webbing

subarticular tubercles

toe disks

Fig. 32. Dorsal view of the pectoral region of *Hyla loquax* showing the extensive axillary membrane (*arrow*).

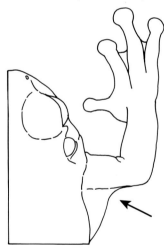

Fig. 33. Dorsal surface of the head of *Hypopachus variolosus* showing transverse fold of skin behind the eyes (*arrow*).

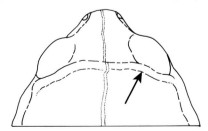

thus may be a useful character. In some cases the color of the iris is distinctive, as in the red-eyed treefrog, *Agalychnis callidryas*. Some species of frogs have a thin sheet of skin in the axillary region (Fig. 32) called the *axillary membrane*. This may be extensive (as in *Hyla loquax*), weakly developed, or absent. The size of the eye relative to the tympanic membrane may aid in identification, and the shape of the pupil (round, horizontally elliptical, or vertically elliptical) is also a useful character.

The adult males of most anurans in the Yucatán Peninsula possess vocal sacs whose number, shape, and position may be distinguishing features. A few species apparently lack vocal sacs, and a few others (e.g., *Rhinophrynus dorsalis*) have internal vocal sacs, but most species have external vocal sacs. The sacs may be paired or unpaired. Unpaired vocal sacs are *subgular*, meaning that they lie in the throat region (e.g., in *Bufo valliceps*, Fig. 237). Paired vocal sacs may be subgular (e.g., in *Smilisca baudinii*, Fig. 249) or *lateral* in position; that is, they lie posterior to the angle of the jaws (e.g., in *Phrynohyas venulosa*, Fig. 246).

Key to the Families of Anura

1. Enlarged gland present at nape of the neck 2
    No enlarged gland at nape of the neck. 3

2. Cranial crests present; adult SVL greater than 45 mm . . . . Bufonidae
    Cranial crests absent; adult SVL less than 45 mm . . . . Leptodactylidae (part)

3. Tips of the digits distinctly expanded into round or heart-shaped disks (Figs. 41, 69) 4
    Tips of the digits not distinctly expanded 5

4. Toes extensively webbed (Fig. 30A). . . . . Hylidae
    Toes webbed only basally or not at all (Fig. 30B,C) . . . . Leptodactylidae (part)

5. Five digits on foot; no enlarged digging tubercles present on foot. 6
    Four digits on foot; pair of enlarged digging tubercles present on foot . . . . Rhinophrynidae

6. A transverse fold of skin crosses the head posterior to the eyes (Fig. 33); snout pointed . . . . . .
    . . . . Microhylidae
    No transverse fold of skin present; snout rounded or truncated 7

7. Color and size variable; venter opaque 8
    Diminutive green frogs; viscera visible through the transparent venter . . . . Centrolenidae

8. Toes extensively webbed. . . . . Ranidae
    Toes webbed only slightly or not at all . . . . Leptodactylidae (part)

Clave para las Familias de Anura

1. Con una glándula alargada en la parte posterior del cuello. 2
    Sin una glándula alargada en la parte posterior del cuello. 3

2. Crestas craneales presentes; adultos miden más de 45 mm de LHC . . . . Bufonidae
    Crestas craneales ausentes; adultos miden menos de 45 mm de LHC . . . .
    . . . . Leptodactylidae (en parte)

3. Puntas de los dedos distintivamente expandidas a manera de discos redondeados o en forma de corazón (Figs. 41, 69) 4
    Puntas de los dedos no distintivamente expandidas 5

4. Dedos de los pies con membranas interdigitales amplias (Fig. 30A) . . . . Hylidae
    Dedos de los pies con membranas interdigitales en la base de los dedos o sin membranas (Fig. 30B,C). . . . . Leptodactylidae (en parte)

5. Con cinco dedos en los pies; sin un par de tubérculos alargados en los pies que le sirven para excavar. 6
    Con cuatro dedos en los pies; un par de tubérculos alargados en los pies que le sirven para excavar. . . . . Rhinophrynidae

6. Sin un pliegue transversal de la piel cruzando la cabeza por detrás de los ojos; punta del hocico roma redondadea 7
   Con un pliegue transversal de la piel cruzando la cabeza por detrás de los ojos (Fig. 33); punta del hocico aguda . . . . Microhylidae

7. Ranas de color y tamaño variable, vientre opaco 8
   Ranas muy pequeñas de color verde; las vísceras se observan a través del vientre translúcido
   . . . . Centrolenidae

8. Dedos de los pies ampliamente enembranados . . . . Ranidae
   Dedos de los pies con una leve membrana interdigital o sin membranas . . . .
   . . . . Leptodactylidae (en parte)

Tadpoles

Twenty-four of the 33 species of anurans in the Yucatán Peninsula have free-living aquatic larvae (tadpoles). The 8 *Eleutherodactylus* species are known or presumed to have terrestrial eggs and direct development, and thus to lack a free-living aquatic larval stage. The tadpole of *Hyla valancifer* is unknown, and the *H. loquax* tadpole described by Duellman (1970:362) actually belongs to another species (R. W. McDiarmid, pers. comm.).

IDENTIFICATION   A few of the anurans in the Yucatán Peninsula have tadpoles so distinctive in morphology and coloration that they can be identi-

fied easily from the illustrations included with the species accounts. For most species, however, identification of tadpoles requires attention to anatomical detail. Duellman (1970) discussed the characters most useful in the identification of hylid treefrog tadpoles, and Altig (1970) helped standardize the terminology of tadpole morphology. Altig and Brandon (1971) provided a generic key to the free-living amphibian larvae of Mexican amphibians, and Altig (1987) published a key to the species of Mexican tadpoles. In general, the following treatment uses the terminology developed by those authors. All terms are defined in the Glossary, and most are illustrated in the accompanying figures or in the figures that accompany the species accounts.

The number and position of the spiracles is an important character. Spiracles are usually single, but one Yucatecan species has two spiracles, and these are situated ventrally. In species with a single

Fig. 34. Position of spiracles in tadpoles. A, *Bufo valliceps* with lateral spiracle. B, *Agalychnis callidryas* with ventrolateral spiracle. C, *Hypopachus variolosus* with ventral spiracle.

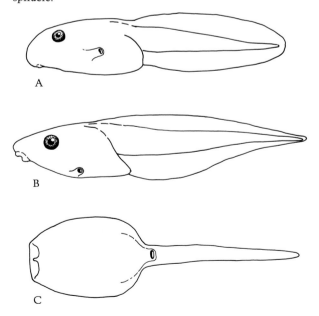

Fig. 35. Oral disk of a tadpole showing position and configuration of mouthparts. Adapted from Duellman, 1970, by permission of William E. Duellman.

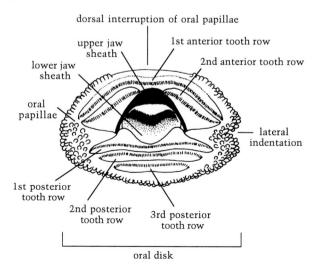

dorsal interruption of oral papillae

upper jaw sheath

1st anterior tooth row

2nd anterior tooth row

lower jaw sheath

oral papillae

lateral indentation

1st posterior tooth row

2nd posterior tooth row

3rd posterior tooth row

oral disk

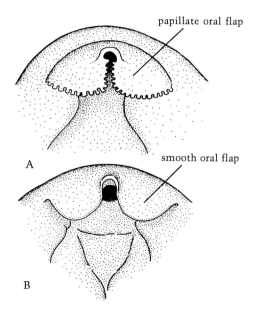

papillate oral flap

A

smooth oral flap

B

Fig. 36. Mouthparts of microhylid tadpoles. A, *Hypopachus variolosus* showing papillate oral flaps. B, *Gastrophryne elegans* showing smooth oral flaps.

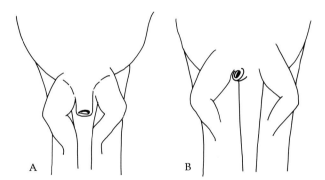

A   B

Fig. 37. The position of the vent tubes in tadpoles. A, medial tube. B, dextral tube.

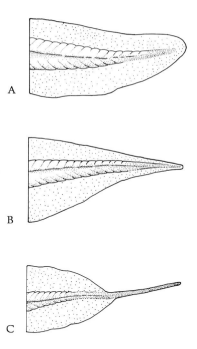

A

B

C

Fig. 38. Configuration of tadpole tails. A, bluntly rounded. B, acuminate. C, xiphicercal.

spiracle the opening is generally on the left side of the body (sinistral), where it may be lateral or ventrolateral. In a few species the spiracle is ventral in position (Fig. 34). The opening of the vent tube is usually to the right of the caudal fin (dextral), but it may open along the ventral midline, in which case it is said to be medial (Fig. 37).

The mouthparts are especially important in tadpole identification. Some species have keratinized sheaths (beaks) covering the upper and lower jaws (Fig. 35). Keratinized denticles ("teeth"), are present in many species. The number of rows of teeth above and below the jaw sheaths is often a distinguishing feature.

The mouthparts are generally enclosed by fleshy lips that constitute an oral disk. The oral disk may be indented laterally (Fig. 35) and is often surrounded by small, fleshy protuberances called *oral papillae*. These may be continuous around the oral disk, or they may be interrupted dorsally, ventrally, or both (Fig. 35).

The overall configuration of the body may vary from globose to depressed. The eyes may be small, medium, or large, and they may be situated laterally, dorsolaterally, or dorsally. The mouth may open at the end of the head, in which case it is said to be *terminal*. More often the mouth opens forward and downward, in which case it is *anteroventral*. Occasionally the mouth opens downward and is said to be *ventral* in position.

The size and configuration of the tail can also distinguish different species (Fig. 38). The length and depth of the tail relative to the body and the relative depth of the dorsal and ventral fins are useful characters. The extent to which the dorsal fin extends onto the body of the tadpole can help in identification, as can the shape of the tip of the tail. The tail may be rounded at its terminus, or it may be pointed, in which case it is termed *acuminate*. In a few species the tip of the tail is drawn out as a thin filament and is called *xiphicercal*.

Key to the Tadpoles

1. Keratinized "teeth" (denticles) absent 2
   Keratinized "teeth" (denticles) present (Fig. 35) 6
2. Jaws without keratinized sheaths (beaks) 3
   Jaws with keratinized sheaths (beaks) (Fig. 35) 5
3. Barbels present (Fig. 39); spiracles paired .... *Rhinophrynus dorsalis*
   Barbels absent; spiracle single 4
4. Oral flaps papillate or scalloped (Fig. 36A) .... *Hypopachus variolosus*
   Oral flaps smooth (Fig. 36B) .... *Gastrophryne elegans*
5. Vent tube dextral (Fig. 37B); no papillae under mouth; tail terminates as a thin filament
   (Fig. 38C) .... *Hyla microcephala*
   Vent tube medial (Fig. 37A); a single row of papillae under mouth; tail does not terminate as
   a thin filament (Fig. 38A,B) .... *Hyla ebraccata*
6. Two anterior and three posterior rows of teeth.. 7
   Anterior or posterior rows of teeth not as above..................................... 14
7. Oral disk indented laterally (Fig. 35).. 8
   Oral disk not indented laterally (Fig. 35) 11
8. Oral papillae incomplete dorsally and ventrally (Fig. 35) 9
   Oral papillae incomplete dorsally, complete ventrally (Fig. 35) 10
9. Caudal musculature with white spots dorsally......................... *Bufo valliceps*
   Tail and body uniform brown or black................................... *Bufo marinus*
10. Small tadpoles, generally less than 25 mm total length at Gosner stage 30 or beyond; dorsal
    fin extends onto body to level of the spiracle.................... *Physalaemus pustulosus*
    Larger tadpoles, generally greater than 25 mm total length at Gosner state 30 or beyond;
    dorsal fin does not extend onto body to level of spiracle............ *Rana berlandieri* (part)
11. Vent tube medial (Fig. 37A)... 12
    Vent tube dextral (Fig. 37B) 18
12. Body vermiform; body and tail red in life.............. *Hyalinobatrachium fleischmanni*
    Body globose; body and tail not red 13
13. Tail with dark spots and blotches; eyes relatively large (Fig. 46) ..... *Leptodactylus labialis*
    Tail uniformly dark or with a few light spots; eyes relatively small (Fig. 49) ....
    .... *Leptodactylus melanonotus*
14. Vent tube dextral (Fig. 37B).. 15
    Vent tube medial (Fig. 37A) .... *Phrynohyas venulosa*
15. Tail long, about three times body length; caudal fins low, essentially clear ....
    .... *Hyla bromeliacia*
    Tail shorter, less than three times body length; caudal fins moderately high, pigmented ... 16
16. Five or six posterior tooth rows; Maya Mountains of Belize................. *Rana juliani*
    Fewer than five posterior tooth rows 17
17. Four posterior tooth rows; southern half of Yucatán Peninsula (Map 42)..... *Rana vaillanti*
    Three posterior tooth rows; pan-peninsular (Map 40) .... *Rana berlandieri* (part)
18. Spiracle ventolateral (Fig. 34B).. 19
    Spiracle lateral (Fig. 34A)... 20
19. Ventral fin conspicuously deeper than dorsal fin (Fig. 60) .... *Agalychnis callidryas*
    Ventral and dorsal fins subequal (Fig. 63)........................ *Agalychnis moreletii*
20. Tail bluntly rounded at tip (Fig. 38A)........................... *Triprion petasatus*
    Tail pointed at tip (Fig. 38B) 21
21. Maximum depth of tail greater than two-thirds body length 22
    Maximum depth of the tail less than two-thirds body length........................ 23

22. Dark stripe runs from snout to eye. . . . . *Hyla picta*
    No dark stripe from snout to eye. . . . . *Scinax staufferi*

23. Tip of tail rounded or bluntly pointed (Fig. 38A), not acuminate; posterior half of fins not uniform dark gray 24
    Tip of tail acuminate (Fig. 38B); posterior half of fins uniform dark gray (Fig. 70) . . . .
    . . . . *Hyla loquax*

24. Maximum tail depth greater than one-half body length (Fig. 84); pan-peninsular . . . .
    . . . . *Smilisca baudinii*
    Maximum tail depth less than one-half body length (Fig. 86); base of Yucatán Peninsula (Map 35). . . . . *Smilisca cyanosticta*

Clave para los Renacuajos

1. Dientes (dentículos) queratinizados ausentes. 2
   Dientes (dentículos) queratinizados presentes (Fig. 35) 6

2. La mandíbula sin vainas queratinizadas. 3
   La mandíbula con vainas queratinizadas (Fig. 35) 5

3. Barbillas ausentes; espiráculo único en posición ventromedial 4
   Barbillas presentes (Fig. 39); espiráculos pareados en posición ventral . . . .
   . . . . *Rhinophrynus dorsalis*

4. Pliegues orales papilados u ondulados (Fig. 36A). . . . . *Hypopachus variolosus*
   Pliegues orales lisos (Fig. 36B). . . . . *Gastrophryne elegans*

5. Tubo anal en posición dextral (Fig. 37B); sin papilas debajo de la boca; la cola termina en forma de un filamento fino (Fig. 38C) . . . . *Hyla microcephala*
   Tubo anal en posición media (Fig. 37A); una hilera única de papilas debajo de la boca; la cola no termina en forma de un filamento fino (Fig. 38A,B) . . . . *Hyla ebraccata*

6. Dos hileras anteriores y tres posteriores de dentículos 7
   Las hileras anteriores y posteriores de dentículos no como las descritas 14

7. El disco oral indentado lateralmente (Fig. 35). 8
   El disco oral no indentado lateralmente (Fig. 35) 11

8. Papilas orales incompletas dorsal y ventralmente (Fig. 35) 9
   Papilas orales incompletas dorsalmente y completas ventralmente (Fig. 35) 10

9. La porción dorsal de la musculatura caudal con puntos blancos. . . . . *Bufo valliceps*
   Cuerpo y cola de color uniformemente pardo o negro . . . . *Bufo marinus*

10. Renacuajos pequeños, generalmente menos de 25 mm de longitud total en la etapa Gosner 30 o en etapas más avanzadas; aleta dorsal se extiende en el cuerpo al nivel del espiráculo
    . . . . *Physalaemus pustulosus*
    Renacuajos más grandes, generalmente más de 25 mm de longitud total en la etapa Gosner 30 o en etapas más avanzadas; aleta dorsal no se extiende en el cuerpo al nivel del espiráculo
    . . . . *Rana berlandieri* (en parte)

11. Tubo anal medial (Fig. 37A) 12
    Tubo anal dextral (Fig. 37B). 18

12. Cuerpo globoso; cuerpo y cola de cualquier color menos rojo en vida. 13
    Cuerpo vermiforme; cuerpo y cola rojos en vida . . . . *Hyalinobatrachium fleischmanni*

13. La cola con puntos y manchas oscuros; ojos relativamente grandes (Fig. 46) . . . .
    . . . . *Leptodactylus labialis*
    La cola uniformemente oscura, o con algunos puntos claros; ojos relativamente pequeños (Fig. 49). . . . . *Leptodactylus melanonotus*

14. Tubo anal dextral (Fig. 37B). 15
    Tubo anal medial (Fig. 37A). . . . . *Phrynohyas venulosa*

15. Cola corta, menos de tres veces la longitud del cuerpo; aletas caudales moderadamente altas, y pigmentadas 16
    Cola larga, más o menos tres veces la longitud del cuerpo; aletas caudales bajas, y transparentes . . . . *Hyla bromeliacia*

16. Menos de cinco hileras posteriores de dientes 17
    Cinco o seis hileras posteriores de dientes; habitan las Montañas Maya de Belice . . . .
    . . . . *Rana juliani*

17. Cuatro hileras posteriores de dientes; habitan en la mitad sur de la península de Yucatán (Mapa 42) . . . . *Rana vaillanti*
    Tres hileras posteriores de dientes; organismos pan-peninsulares . . . .
    . . . . *Rana berlandieri* (en parte)

18. Espiráculo en posición ventrolateral (Fig. 34B) 19
    Espiráculo en posición lateral (Fig. 34A) 20

19. La aleta ventral conspicuamente más ancha que la dorsal (Fig. 60) . . . *Agalychnis callidryas*
    Aletas ventral y dorsal más o menos del mismo ancho (Fig. 63) . . . . *Agalychnis moreletii*

20. Punta de la cola aguda (Fig. 38) 21
    Punta de la cola roma, redondeada (Fig. 38) . . . . *Triprion petasatus*

21. El ancho máximo de la cola mayor a dos tercios de la longitud del cuerpo 22
    El ancho máximo de la cola menor a dos tercios de la longitud del cuerpo 23

22. Una línea oscura que va del hocico al ojo . . . . *Hyla picta*
    No hay una línea oscura que va del hocico al ojo . . . . *Scinax staufferi*

23. Punta de la cola redondeada o bruscamente apuntada, no agudamente apuntada; mitad posterior de las aletas sin color pardo oscuro uniforme 24
    Punta de la cola agudamente apuntada; mitad posterior de las aletas con color pardo oscuro uniforme . . . . *Hyla loquax*

24. El ancho máximo de la cola mayor a la mitad de la longitud del cuerpo (Fig. 84); organismos pan-peninsulares . . . . *Smilisca baudinii*
    El ancho máximo de la cola menor a la mitad de la longitud del cuerpo (Fig. 86); habitan en la base de la Península de Yucatán (Mapa 35) . . . . *Smilisca cyanosticta*

Family Rhinophrynidae

This primitive family contains a single living species, the curious Mexican burrowing toad, *Rhinophrynus dorsalis*, of southern Mexico and Central America.

Genus *Rhinophrynus*

Rhinophrynus, is from the Greek *rhinos*, "nose," and *phrynos*, "toad."

Rhinophrynus dorsalis Duméril and Bibron
(Figs. 39, 40, 224; Map 11)

Rhinophrynus dorsalis A. M. C. Duméril and Bibron, 1841:758. HOLOTYPE: MNHNP 693. TYPE LOCALITY: Vera Cruz, Mexico.

Mexican burrowing toad; sapo borracho (Guatemala, Mexico); ranita boquita (Mexico); uo (Lacandón Maya, Yucatec Maya); uo much (Yucatec Maya).

DESCRIPTION These moderately large toads are unmistakable. The adults average about 60 to 65 mm in snout-vent length, and the females are substantially larger than the males. The body is globose, flaccid, and covered with loose skin (Fig. 224). The head is tiny and pointed; the snout is truncated in dorsal and lateral views and covered with sensory tubercles. The eyes are very small. There is no semblance of a neck and no visible tympanum. The limbs are short, stout, and muscular. The fingers bear only a trace of webbing at their bases, and there are only four digits on the foot; these are short and extensively webbed, and there are two enlarged digging "spades" on the inner surface of the metatarsus. The vent is surrounded by low tubercles. The males have paired internal vocal sacs.

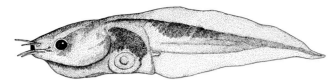

Fig. 39. Tadpole of *Rhinophrynus dorsalis* (UMRC 93-7), TL 34 mm; Suc Tuc, Campeche, Mexico.

The dorsal coloration is dark brown to nearly black, with scattered blotches and spots of yellow, yellow-orange, or reddish orange, especially on the lateral surfaces of the body. A light vertebral stripe extends from the head to above the vent. The venter is generally dark brown or gray with little or no pattern.

TADPOLE *Rhinophrynus* tadpoles are distinctive in several respects. The head is broad and flat, and the mouth is wide and slitlike. The eyes are small, widely spaced, and lateral in position. The tail is about 1.5 times the length of the body, the dorsal fin extends onto the posterior third of the body, and the dorsal and ventral fins are of approximately equal depth (Fig. 39). There are no keratinized mouthparts, but the mouth is bordered by a series of delicate barbels. The spiracles are paired and situated ventrally. The dorsum is generally dark gray or black, and the venter is iridescent silver. The extent of pigmentation may exhibit a diel cycle, for at night the head and body are often translucent.

VOCALIZATION The advertisement call of *Rhinophrynus* is a loud, protracted, ascending whoop, perhaps best described as *uooooooooo*. R. E. Etheridge (pers. comm.) likened the call to the sound of human

Fig. 40. Advertisement call of *Rhinophrynus dorsalis*, recorded 20 June 1962, 18.4 mi N Monterrey, Nuevo León, Mexico.

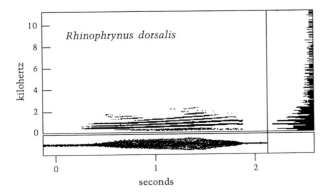

regurgitation. The Maya name for this species, *uo*, is an onomatopoeic rendering of the call. Porter (1962: 171) showed that the rising pitch of the call results from the addition of higher frequencies near the end of the call rather than from an overall upward inflection of all frequencies. I analyzed recordings of frogs from southern Campeche, El Petén, and southern Texas and found the note repetition rate to be about 15 to 20 per minute; the average note duration is 1.4 sec. The call is generally well modulated and has a distinct harmonic structure. The fundamental frequency is around 250 Hz. The dominant frequency lies at about 500 Hz, with several additional harmonics emphasized at about 750, 1,000, and 1,250 Hz (Fig. 40).

SIMILAR SPECIES The much smaller *Hypopachus variolosus* and *Gastrophryne elegans* superficially resemble *Rhinophrynus* in possessing triangle-shaped bodies with small, pointed heads, but both lack the paired digging spade on the heel and have a transverse fold of skin on the dorsal surface of the head behind the eyes.

DISTRIBUTION *Rhinophrynus dorsalis* occurs at low elevations from southern Texas to Guatemala on the Atlantic slope, and from Guerrero to Costa Rica on the Pacific slope. In the Yucatán Peninsula the species is probably pan-peninsular, although it has yet to be recorded from southern Yucatán and central Quintana Roo (Map 11).

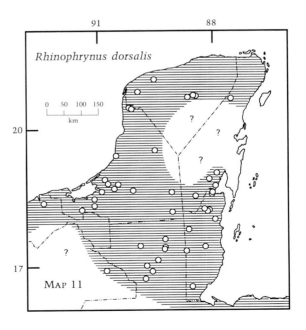

NATURAL HISTORY Throughout its extensive range in the lowlands of Middle America, this common fossorial frog is generally found on savannas and in seasonally dry forests (Duellman, 1971a:55). Surface activity is largely restricted to the beginning of the rainy season, when large choruses of males call from temporary bodies of water such as flooded pastures, roadside ditches, and savanna aguadas. I found tadpoles at Gosner stage 25 (Gosner, 1960) in early October in Campeche, however, indicating that reproduction may also occur late in the rainy season. The distinctive call is unusually loud and can be heard over great distances. Males generally call from the surface of the water. Their internal vocal sacs become enormously distended, causing the body to rotate in the water during vocalization. Fouquette and Rossman (1963:186) reported that in Guerrero, the female initiates contact with the calling male by bumping her snout against his throat or chest, and the male then clasps her in inguinal amplexus. The females produce several thousand eggs, which they release into the water singly or in small groups. These sink to the bottom and hatch within a few days. Stuart (1961) observed aggregation behavior in tadpoles in the aguadas at Tikal, El Petén, in which groups of 50 or more tadpoles swam in coordinated fashion. I saw the same behavior in Campeche. The aggregations varied in size from approximately 10 cm in diameter and a few hundred individuals to over a meter in diameter and many thousands of tadpoles. All the individuals were similar in size, and tadpoles that were displaced from one aggregation were readily integrated into others.

Stuart (1961) showed that these tadpoles are predominantly filter feeders on algae, and he found no evidence of the cannibalism reported for this species in Tehauntepec, Oaxaca, by Starrett (1960:8). Transformed individuals use the enlarged tubercles on the heel to burrow backward into soft substrates. They feed on insects, especially ants and termites (McCoy, 1966:306), and they pass the dry season beneath the surface of the ground in a subterranean chamber of their own construction (Foster and McDiarmid, 1983:420). Within these chambers the frogs are able to endure long periods of drought and can withstand tremendous desiccation, for Fouquette and Rossman (1963:187) reported a captive that burrowed into the soil of its terrarium and survived for nearly two years without food or water.

ETYMOLOGY The specific name, *dorsalis*, is Modern Latin meaning "pertaining to the back."

COMMENT Fouquette (1969) reviewed *R. dorsalis*.

Locality Records   *Belize*: Belize: Rockstone Pond (AMNH 83597–98; UU 9352–61); Cayo: 15 mi S Belmopan (MCZ 82899, 82902), Benque Viejo (W. T. Neill, 1965:80), 1.5 mi SE Mountain Cow (CM 112171–75), 1 mi E Mountain Cow (CM 112199); Corozal: S edge Corozal Town (JLK 422), 3 mi N Corozal Town (JLK 423–24); Orange Walk: 10 km E Carmelita (CM 107440), Gallon Jug (LSUMZ 6420–21), 20 mi SE Orange Walk (BCB 12433), 17.3 to 23.2 mi SE Orange Walk (NMSU 3086), Tower Hill (USNM 167474). *Guatemala*: El Petén: Flores (UMMZ 79012), La Libertad (UMMZ 90645; USNM 71335–58, 71431–35, 101831, 220175–76), vicinity La Libertad (UMMZ 75287–96), N La Libertad (CAS 2231, 84163; MCZ 21464), 15 km SE La Libertad (KU 58895), Paso Caballos (MCZ 19936), Sacluc (USNM 25134–36), Sayaxché (UCM 22140–42), Tikal (AMNH 62920; UF 13372–76; UMMZ 129640–41, 129646–48), 1 km SW Tikal (UMMZ 120484, 129640–48), Uaxactún (AMNH 55114–18; CM 4032; KU 156298); no specific locality (USNM 71797). *Mexico*: Campeche: Champotón (UMMZ 73143), Dzibalchén (KU 75198), 79.9 km NE Emiliano Zapata (EAL 2919), Encarnación (FMNH 105709), 5 mi W Escárcega (UCM 28084–85), 5 km N Escárcega (KU 717201–2), 7.5 km W Escárcega (KU 70974–85), bet. Escárcega and Champotón (UMRC 78-4), 56.6 km SW Mamantel (EAL 2920), Plan de Ayala (JCL photo), 8 to 9 mi S Río Chumpán on Hwy. 261 (LACM 114371), Suc Tuc (UMRC 93-7), Tankuche–El Remate, 4 km (IHNHERP 161–62), Tuxpeña Camp (UMMZ 73240), 6.5 km S Xpujil (KU 75007), 21 km N Hwy. 186 on rd. to Sabancuy (JCL sight record); Chiapas: vicinity of Bonampak (MZFC 1207); Quintana Roo: 10 mi W Bacalar (LSUMZ 32980–3009), Cobá (JCL photo), Chetumal (MZCIQRO 57), 13 mi NW Chetumal (BCB 12435), 15 mi NW Chetumal (BCB 12424), Kohunlich ruins (LSUMZ 33382, 40586), 13.4 mi SW Limones (KU 157684; UMRC 81-5), Xcopen (MCZ 2856); Tabasco: 4–6 mi S Frontera (CM 40078; UCM 28086–91); Yucatán: 5.4 km E Bella Flor (UMRC 79-255), Chichén Itzá (MVZ 14791; UMMZ 83917), Dzibilchaltún (FMNH 153417), 1.5 mi S Libre Unión (UCM 18174–76, 28092–93), Pisté (UMMZ 80449).

Family Leptodactylidae

This is a large and diverse family of New World frogs. Some species are squat, toadlike, and terrestrial or fossorial. The arboreal species have expanded toe pads. The semiaquatic species are streamlined and have smooth skin. Members of this family exhibit a variety of reproductive modes. Some have lost the aquatic larval stage and instead deposit their eggs in moist terrestrial situations where the embryos undergo direct development. Other species construct foam nests for their eggs. Members of this family occur from the southern United States and the West Indies south through Mexico, Central America, and virtually all of South America. There are approximately 710 species assigned to 51 genera. Three genera and 10 species are found in the Yucatán Peninsula. The most recent comprehensive taxonomic treatment of leptodactylid frogs is Lynch, 1971.

Key to the Genera of the Family Leptodactylidae

1. Enlarged gland at nape of neck; dorsum rough, pustulate . . . . *Physalaemus*
   No enlarged gland at nape of neck; dorsum smooth or granular, not pustulate 2
2. Toes not webbed; tips of the digits not or only slightly expanded (Figs. 45, 48); legs short, the length of the thigh plus shank less than the distance from the posterior margin of the eye to the vent . . . . *Leptodactylus*
   Toes slightly webbed at the base; tips of the digits slightly or distinctly expanded (Fig. 41); legs longer, the length of the thigh plus shank greater than the distance from the posterior margin of the eye to the vent . . . . *Eleutherodactylus*

Clave para los Géneros de la Familia Leptodactylidae

1. Una glándula alargada en el dorso del cuello; dorso del cuerpo rugoso, pustulado . . . .
   . . . . *Physalaemus*
   Sin una glándula alargada en el dorso del cuello; dorso del cuerpo liso o granular, no pustulado
   2
2. Dedos de los pies sin membranas interdigitales; la punta de los dedos sin expandir o ligeramente expandidas (Figs. 45, 48); ancas cortas, la longitud del muslo y la espinilla es menos que la distancia entre el margen posterior del ojo y la cloaca . . . . *Leptodactylus*
   Dedos de los pies ligeramente con membranas interdigitales en la base; la punta de los dedos ligeramente expandidas o muy expandida (Fig. 41); ancas más largas, la longitud del muslo y la espinilla es mayor que la distancia entre el margen posterior del ojo a la cloaca . . . .
   . . . . *Eleutherodactylus*

Genus *Eleutherodactylus*

This strictly New World genus is the largest of all vertebrate genera. More than 500 species are known, and new species are being discovered at the rate of several per year. All members of the genus have circumvented the aquatic larval stage; most deposit their eggs in moist terrestrial situations, and the eggs hatch into miniatures of the adults. One species is viviparous, and at least two species have internal fertilization. The genus is found at low and moderate elevations on the Atlantic slope from Tamaulipas and the Pacific slope from Sinaloa, south and eastward through Middle America to northern Argentina and southern Brazil. *Eleutherodactylus* species are present on many West Indian islands and have been introduced into southern Florida and Louisiana. At least eight (several undescribed) species occur in the Yucatán Peninsula. *Eleutherodactylus* derives from the Greek *eleutheros*, "free, not bound," and *daktylos*, "finger" or "toe," in reference to the lack of webbing between the digits of most members of the genus.

Key to the Species of the Genus *Eleutherodactylus*

1. Dorsum smooth or slightly granular 2
   Dorsum rugose and strongly granular . . . . *Eleutherodactylus rugulosus*

2. No inner tarsal tubercle at the middle of the tarsus; at least a vestige of a tarsal fold is present
....3
Inner tarsal tubercle present at the middle of the tarsus; no tarsal fold ....
.... *Eleutherodactylus rhodopis*

3. Tips of the digits distinctly expanded, heart shaped (Fig. 41)...........................4
Tips of the digits rounded and only slightly expanded 5

4. Few or no tubercles on the sole; supratympanic fold present; base of the Yucatán Peninsula
(Map 12) .... *Eleutherodactylus alfredi*
Numerous small tubercles present on the sole; supratympanic fold absent; northern half of
the Yucatán Peninsula (Map 18) .... *Eleutherodactylus yucatanensis*

5. No dark seat patch..6
Dark seat patch present .... *Eleutherodactylus chac*

6. Small frogs, adult SVL less than 30 mm; no dark facial mask; dorsal pattern of dark spots or
reticulations against a lighter background...................... *Eleutherodactylus leprus*
Larger frogs, adult SVL larger than 30 mm; dark facial mask usually present; dorsal pattern
not as above .... *Eleutherodactylus laticeps*

Clave para las Especies del Género *Eleutherodactylus*

1. Dorso liso o ligeramente granular 2
Dorso rugoso y muy granular............................... *Eleutherodactylus rugulosus*

2. Sin un tubérculo tarsal presente a mitad del tarso; por lo menos un vestigio de un pliegue
tarsal..3
Con un tubérculo tarsal presente a mitad del tarso; sin un pliegue tarsal ....
.... *Eleutherodactylus rhodopis*

3. Puntas de los dedos fuertemente expandidas, en forma de corazón (Fig. 41)..............4
Puntas de los dedos redondeadas y solo ligeramente expandidas 5

4. Muy pocos o ningún tubérculo pequeño en la planta del pie; con un pliegue supratimpánico;
organismos que se distribuyen en la base de la Península de Yucatán (Mapa 12) ....
.... *Eleutherodactylus alfredi*
Varios tubérculos pequeños en la planta del pie; sin un pliegue supratimpánico; organismos
que se distribuyen en la mitad norte de la Península de Yucatán (Mapa 18) ....
.... *Eleutherodactylus yucatanensis*

5. Sin un parche oscuro alrededor de la cloaca..6
Con un parche oscuro alrededor de la cloaca .... *Eleutherodactylus chac*

6. Ranas de tamaño pequeño, adultos menores a 30 mm de LHC; sin una mancha oscura como
máscara; patrón de coloración dorsal consiste de puntos oscuros o reticulaciones sobre un
fondo más claro .... *Eleutherodactylus leprus*
Ranas de mayor tamaño, adultos mayores a 30 mm de LHC; con una mancha oscura como
máscara usualmente presente; patrón de coloración dorsal no como el descrito ....
.... *Eleutherodactylus laticeps*

Eleutherodactylus alfredi (Boulenger)
(Figs. 41, 225; Map 12)

Hylodes alfredi Boulenger, 1898:480. SYNTYPES:
BMNH 1947.2.15.54, 1947.2.14.55 (two syntypes).
TYPE LOCALITY: Atoyac, state of Vera Cruz, Mexico.

Alfredo's rainfrog.

DESCRIPTION The adults of this medium-sized
Eleutherodactylus average between 30 and 40 mm
in snout-vent length (Fig. 225). The head is broad,
moderately depressed, and approximately as wide
as the body. The snout is truncated in dorsal view
and rounded in lateral profile. The eyes are large and
protruding, and the interorbital distance is about
equal to the maximum diameter of the eye. The
pupils are horizontally elliptical. The canthus rostralis is rounded, and the loreal region is slightly
concave. The tympanum is distinct, with a diameter about one-half that of the eye. The supratympanic fold is weakly developed. The skin of the

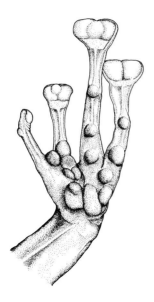

Fig. 41. Palmar view of the hand of *Eleutherodactylus alfredi* (EAL 3329) showing heart-shaped toe pads and lack of webbing between the digits; Palenque, Chiapas, Mexico.

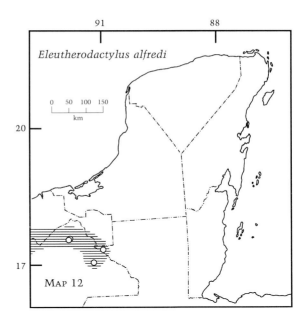

dorsum is weakly granular, that of the lateral surfaces of the body is more strongly granular, and there are a few scattered tubercles on the forelimbs and surrounding the tympanum. The skin of the venter is smooth. The fingers are long, thin, and devoid of webbing, and they bear well-developed, projecting subarticular tubercles. The tips of the digits are expanded to form broad, heart-shaped adhesive disks (Fig. 41); those on the fingers are nearly twice the width of those on the toes.

The dorsal ground color is light tan, brown, or grayish brown with a few small, irregular light tan spots. The appendages are light tan with scattered dark brown spots and irregular bands and blotches.

SIMILAR SPECIES   This species is most similar to *E. yucatanensis*, its presumed closest relative and the only other member of the *E. alfredi* group in the Yucatán Peninsula. It differs from *E. yucatanensis*, with which it does not co-occur, in lacking supernumerary tubercles on the sole of the foot.

DISTRIBUTION   *Eleutherodactylus alfredi* occurs at low and intermediate elevations on the Atlantic slope from central Veracruz to western El Petén (Map 12).

NATURAL HISTORY   Seemingly uncommon in the Yucatán Peninsula, this frog inhabits moist lowland forests, where individuals have been found beneath surface debris and under the leaf sheaths of red banana plants (R. W. McDiarmid, pers. comm.).

Fugler and Webb (1957:105) reported finding *E. alfredi* among large boulders at the edge of a forest clearing in Oaxaca.

Virtually nothing is known of the natural history of *E. alfredi*. These frogs certainly prey on invertebrates, especially insects. Presumably they lay terrestrial eggs and the larvae undergo direct development.

SUBSPECIES   Shreve (1957:247) applied the name *E. alfredi conspicuus* to the frogs from western El Petén and the Lacandón of Chiapas, believing them to be subspecifically distinct from the nominate form to the west. Duellman (1960:54), however, found little justification for recognizing subspecies of *E. alfredi*.

ETYMOLOGY   The specific name, *alfredi*, is a patronym in honor of Alfredo Dugès, the famous nineteenth-century herpetologist from Guanajuato, Mexico, who supplied Boulenger with the type material.

Locality Records Guatemala: El Petén: Piedras Negras (FMNH 126318, 178281; USNM 116506–11). *Mexico*: Chiapas: Laguna Ocotal (MCZ 28224), Palenque (FMNH 68041–42), Palenque ruins (EAL 3329; UIMNH 11300, 62397).

Eleutherodactylus chac Savage
(Fig. 226; Map 13)

Eleutherodactylus chac Savage, 1987:31. HOLOTYPE: KU 186243. TYPE LOCALITY: 12.6 km west of Santo Tomás, Izabel, Guatemala, at 774 m.

Chac's rainfrog.

DESCRIPTION This frog is the smallest of the *E. gollmeri* group. The males average about 23 to 25 mm in snout-vent length, the females average 35 to 37 mm. These are moderately slender frogs with fairly long limbs (Fig. 226). The tips of the digits are rounded and slightly expanded, and the toes are slightly webbed at their bases. In dorsal aspect the head is rather narrow, and the snout is rounded (females) or elliptical (males). The dorsum is weakly granular, and most specimens have several enlarged, often paired, dorsal tubercles. There are several weak pustules on the heel and a row of pustules on the outer edge of the tarsus.

Coloration is variable. The dorsal ground color is yellowish, tan, brown, or gray, with darker markings on the back that may have an hourglass shape. A very thin, light vertebral stripe is generally present. Often there are dark eye and supratympanic stripes. A dark, triangular seat patch is usually present. The limbs usually have a series of dark bands against a lighter background. The venter is immaculate white, cream, or gray. The iris is reddish orange.

VOCALIZATION Stafford (1991:12) described the vocalization of *Eleutherodactylus*, probably *E. chac*, from Belize. The call consisted of "a series of usually four sharp croaks rising gradually in pitch." More recently, Stafford (in litt.) described the vocalization as "a series of 4–9 soft, short, duck-like 'quacks.'" These are the only reports of vocalization in this species, and they require confirmation.

SIMILAR SPECIES Of the *Eleutherodactylus* that co-occur with *E. chac*, *E. rugulosus* and *E. laticeps* are much larger; *E. rhodopis* has neither toe webbing nor a metatarsal fold, and it has a bronze iris (versus reddish orange in *E. chac*).

DISTRIBUTION *Eleutherodactylus chac* is found at low and moderate elevations from Alta Verapaz and Izabal, Guatamala, through central and southern Belize to northern Honduras. In the Yucatán Peninsula it is known only from southern Belize and from the vicinity of Chinajá, near the Alta Verapaz–El Petén border (Map 13).

NATURAL HISTORY This frog is a moderately common terrestrial inhabitant of premontane and lowland forests. In the Yucatán Peninsula, individ-

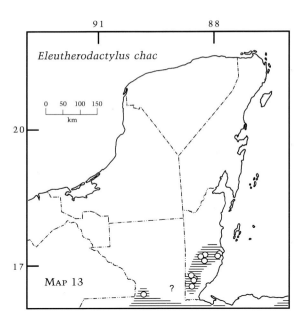

uals have been found in the wet broadleaf forests of the Maya Mountains of Belize, where they were abroad by day on the forest floor. In southern El Petén, Duellman (1963:222) found this species (reported as *E. rostralis*) to be common on the forest floor by day; he found one specimen on the forest floor at night. I found this species abroad by day on the forest floor in southern Belize.

Nothing is known about reproduction in *E. chac*. Presumably the eggs are deposited in moist terrestrial situations and direct development ensues, as is the case with other members of the genus *Eleutherodactylus*.

ETYMOLOGY The specific name is that of the Maya deity Chac, a god associated with rain.

COMMENT Savage (1987) considered this species a small lowland relative of *E. rostralis*, with which it is sometimes confused. Savage also traced the history of the names *E. rhodopis* and *E. loki*, which are sometimes inappropriately applied to *E. chac*.

Locality Records Belize: Cayo: Doyle's Delight (UMRC 93-4), upper Raspaculo River basin (Stafford, 1991:12); Stann Creek: Bokowina (FMNH 49039–40), Cockscomb Basin (UMRC 93-3), Double Falls (FMNH 49041–44), Silk Grass (FMNH 49045); Toledo: Blue Creek (Savage, 1987:32), 2 km N Blue Creek Village (UF 87174), Gloria Camp, Columbia River Forest Reserve (USNM 319782–83), SW end Little Quartz Ridge

(W. F. Pyburn, in litt.). *Guatemala*: Alta Verapaz: Chinajá (Savage, 1987:32).

Eleutherodactylus laticeps (Duméril)
(Fig. 42; Map 14)

Hylodes laticeps A. H. A. Duméril, 1853:178. HOLOTYPE: MNHNP 509. TYPE LOCALITY: Yucatán, Mexico; restricted by Firschein (1951:268) to Champotón, Campeche; but Savage (1987:17) suggested that the type locality is probably near Cobán, Alta Verapaz, Guatemala.

Broad-headed rainfrog; rana cavernícola de cabeza ancha (Mexico).

DESCRIPTION   This is a large *Eleutherodactylus* with a broad head and a rounded, rather squat body in dorsal aspect (Fig. 42). The males average about 38 to 40 mm in snout-vent length, and the females are much larger, averaging 67 to 70 mm. The canthus rostralis is rounded, and the loreal region is concave. The tympanum is about two-thirds the diameter of the eye, and a supratympanic fold is present. There is a ventral dermal disk, which is hypertrophied in large females. The limbs are rather short and stout, and the digits terminate in slightly expanded disks. The fingers are devoid of webbing, and the toes are slightly webbed at their bases. The dorsum is covered with fine granulation, and there is usually a distinct dorsolateral glandular ridge. A

transverse scapular fold is usually present but may be obscure in preserved specimens.

Color and pattern are highly variable in *E. laticeps*. Usually a dark face mask extends from the snout, through the eye, to (and often including) the tympanum. The dorsum is often a uniform dark brown, but some specimens have a thin, distinct pale vertebral stripe, and many have a series of dark spots or bars, sometimes arranged in an hourglass shape. The dorsal surfaces of the limbs may be uniform brown or strongly marked with dark bars. There is usually a dark stripe extending from the knee to the heel along the outer surface of the shank. The venter is generally immaculate white, cream, or light tan.

SIMILAR SPECIES   In the Yucatán Peninsula *E. laticeps* is approached in size only by *E. rugulosus*, which differs in having a strongly rugose dorsum and strongly contrasting light spots against a dark background on the posterior surface of the thighs (Fig. 44).

DISTRIBUTION   *Eleutherodactylus laticeps* occurs at low, moderate, and intermediate elevations on the Atlantic slope from southern Veracruz to northern Honduras. The species is restricted to the base of the Yucatán Peninsula (Map 14).

NATURAL HISTORY   This frog is an uncommon inhabitant of lowland and premontane tropical forests, where individuals have been collected on the

Fig. 42. Dorsal view of *Eleutherodactylus laticeps* (UIMNH 11301), 71.4 mm SVL; Palenque, Chiapas, Mexico. Note the transverse scapular fold. Adapted from Firschein, 1951.

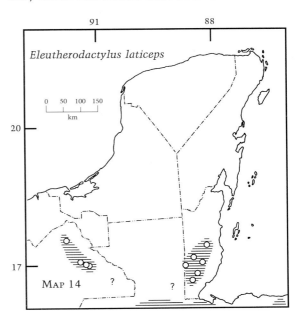

forest floor at night—although W. T. Neill (1965:83) reported finding a specimen in grass in a roadside puddle during the day. Neill (1965:85) also noted that a specimen from Cayo District had swallowed a large katydid, so the diet certainly includes insects.

Presumably *E. laticeps*, like other members of the genus, lays its eggs in terrestrial situations, and the larvae undergo direct development.

ETYMOLOGY The specific name, *laticeps*, is from the Latin *latus*, "wide," and *ceps*, "head"—hence, "wide headed."

COMMENT Schmidt (1941:483) proposed the name *E. stantoni* for specimens of a broad-headed form of *Eleutherodactylus* from Belize. W. T. Neill (1965:85) considered *E. stantoni* a junior synonym of *E. laticeps*, a view confirmed by Savage (1987), who also clarified the confused nomenclatural history of these frogs and suggested that the type locality of *E. laticeps* is most likely near Cobán, Alta Verapaz.

Locality Records *Belize*: Cayo: 13.5 mi SE Belmopan (UF 732909), Doyle's Delight (UMRC 93-1), 5 mi N Millionario (MCZ 38000), Valentine (UMMZ 80672–73); Stann Creek: Double Falls (FMNH 49046–48, now apparently lost); Toledo: Gloria Camp, Columbia River Forest Reserve (USNM 319784–85). *Mexico*: Chiapas: Laguna Ocotal (MCZ 28225–29), bet. Laguna Ocotal and El Censo (MCZ 28245–46), Monte Libano (MCZ 28220), Palenque ruins (UIMNH 11301).

Eleutherodactylus leprus (Cope)
(Fig. 43; Map 15)

Syrrhophus leprus Cope, 1879:268. HOLOTYPE: USNM 10040. TYPE LOCALITY: Santa Efigenia, Oaxaca, Mexico.

Leprus chirping frog, ranita leprosa (Mexico).

DESCRIPTION The males attain a maximum snout-vent length of about 27 mm, the slightly larger females reach about 29 mm. The head is about as wide as the body and moderately depressed

Fig. 43. *Eleutherodactylus leprus*, from Teapa, Tabasco, Mexico. A, dorsal view (UMMZ 113800), 19.4 mm SVL. B, lateral view of the head (UMMZ 113799), 20.2 mm SVL. C, palmar view of the hand (UMMZ 113799), 20.2 mm SVL.

(Fig. 43A). The snout is truncated to rounded in dorsal aspect and bluntly rounded in lateral view. The eyes are large, and the pupils are horizontally elliptical. The tympanum is well developed but conspicuously smaller in diameter than the eye, and there is no supratympanic fold (Fig. 43B). The tips of the digits are rounded and slightly but distinctly expanded. The fingers and toes are unwebbed (Fig. 43C).

The dorsum is green or yellowish green with dark brown spots or reticulations. Some specimens have a dark interorbital bar. The venter is yellow, cream, or gray. According to Sumichrast, who collected the type specimen, "the dorsal spots are yellow in life" (quoted in Cope, 1879:269).

VOCALIZATION   The males possess vocal slits and thus presumably emit an advertisement call, but vocalization has not been described in *E. leprus*. Closely related species produce calls that have been described variously as chirps, peeps, trills, and short whistles.

SIMILAR SPECIES   In the Yucatán Peninsula *E. leprus* most closely resembles the other *Eleutherodactylus* species. The small size of adults distinguishes this species from *E. rugulosus* and *E. laticeps*. *Eleutherodactylus alfredi* and *E. yucatanensis* have distinctly enlarged, heart-shaped disks at the tips of the fingers, whereas in *E. leprus* the tips of the fingers are rounded and only slightly expanded. *Eleutherodactylus leprus* differs from *E. rhodopis* in lacking a tubercle at the middle of the tarsus and a dark facial stripe from the snout through the eye to the tympanum, and it differs from *E. chac* in lacking a dark seat patch.

DISTRIBUTION   This species occurs at low elevations on the Atlantic slope from central Veracruz and the Pacific slope from the Isthmus of Tehauntepec, eastward through northern Guatemala and Belize. In the Yucatán Peninsula the species is known from the Departments of Alta Verapaz and El Petén, and Toledo District (Map 15).

NATURAL HISTORY   Little is known of the natural history of this uncommon frog. It apparently inhabits humid lowland forests and is active on the forest floor, probably hunting for small invertebrates. In the forests of southern El Petén, Duellman (1963:223) reported finding a specimen out on the forest floor during the day and two others be-

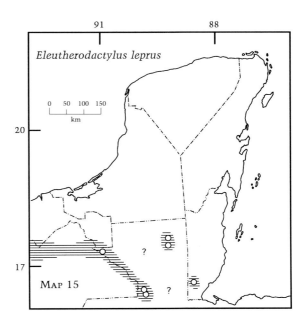

Eleutherodactylus leprus

MAP 15

neath rocks. W. T. Neill (1965:86) found specimens abroad at night on dirt roads in a well-forested area of Toledo District.

Presumably this species lays terrestrial eggs and exhibits direct development, as do other members of the subgenus *Syrrhophus* (see Comment).

SUBSPECIES   W. T. Neill (1965) described *Syrrhophus leprus cholorum* from Belize, but Lynch (1970a:20) concluded that the form was not distinct from other specimens collected throughout the range of the species.

ETYMOLOGY   The specific name, *leprus*, is from the Greek *lepra*, meaning "leprosy," and refers to the vermiculate or mottled dorsal color pattern.

COMMENT   This species and its close allies were long placed in the genus *Syrrhophus*. Hedges (1989:318) combined *Syrrhophus* and three other genera with *Eleutherodactylus*, thereby adding 26 species to *Eleutherodactylus* and reducing the paraphyly of that genus. Although this action has not been universally accepted, I follow Lynch (1991:1138) in accepting the placement of *Syrrhophus* within *Eleutherodactylus*. Lynch (1970) reviewed *E. leprus* as part of his revision of the genus *Syrrhophus*.

Locality Records   Belize: Toledo: Columbia Branch Camp (W. T. Neill, 1965:86), 3.9 mi N San Antonio (W. T. Neill, 1965:85). *Guatemala*: Alta Verapaz: Chinajá (KU 55961–62); El Petén: 15 km NW Chinajá

(KU 55963), Piedras Negras (FMNH 113752, 113754; USNM 114085–92), Tikal (UMMZ 117035), Uaxactún (AMNH 55121–22).

Eleutherodactylus rhodopis (Cope)
(Fig. 227; Map 16)

Lithodytes rhodopis Cope, 1867:323. LECTOTYPE: USNM 16558. TYPE LOCALITY: Vera Cruz, at Orizava and Cordoba; restricted to the vicinity of Orizaba, Veracruz, Mexico, by H. M. Smith and Taylor (1948:67).

Ranita (Guatemala, Mexico).

DESCRIPTION   The males of this medium-sized, moderately stout *Eleutherodactylus* attain a snout-vent length of approximately 30 mm. The females are substantially larger, up to about 40 mm. The head is about equal to the body in maximum width. The snout is rather pointed in dorsal view and rounded in lateral profile (Fig. 227). The eyes are moderately large, and the interorbital distance is about 1.5 times the maximum diameter of the eye. The distinct tympanum is about two-thirds the diameter of the eye. The pupil is horizontally elliptical. The canthus rostralis is indistinct and rounded, and the loreal region is slightly concave. The skin on the dorsum is smooth or very weakly granular with a few scattered tubercles. The skin on the venter is smooth, but on the ventral and posterior surfaces of the thighs it is granular. The limbs are relatively short and stout. The fingers are slender and devoid of webbing, and their subarticular tubercles are well developed and projecting. The tips of the fingers are rounded and only very slightly expanded, if at all. The toes are long, slender, and unwebbed. The subarticular tubercles are well developed and projecting. Low, rounded supernumerary tubercles are present, and there is a low tarsal tubercle at about the middle of the tarsus.

The dorsum is brown, often with a pair of small, dark rectangular marks on the middle of the back. There is often a narrow, light vertebral stripe. Most specimens have a dark facial stripe extending from the nostril, through the dorsal half of the eye, and over the dorsal margin of the tympanum. A dark, triangular seat patch is generally present. The appendages are tan with indistinct dark brown bands and spots. The soles of the feet and the inferior surfaces of the tarsus are dark brown.

SIMILAR SPECIES   In the Yucatán Peninsula *E. rhodopis* differs from others of its genus in possessing a tubercle at the middle of the tarsus. In addition, *E. rugulosus* and *E. laticeps* are much larger, *E. leprus* lacks a dark facial stripe, and *E. chac* possesses at least a vestige of a tarsal fold. *Eleutherodactylus alfredi* and *E. yucatanensis* have large, heart-shaped disks at the tips of their fingers (Fig. 41).

DISTRIBUTION   This species occurs at low and moderate elevations on the Atlantic slope from San Luis Potosí and Veracruz south and eastward through Oaxaca and Chiapas to El Petén, Belize, and northern Honduras. On the Pacific slope it occurs from Oaxaca and Chiapas to El Salvador. In the Yucatán Peninsula it is known from Chiapas, El Petén, and Belize (Map 16).

NATURAL HISTORY   *Eleutherodactylus rhodopis* is a terrestrial inhabitant of humid lowland forests. It is so characteristic of that vegetation type that Stuart (1948:24) considered it an index species for virgin lowland forest in Alta Verapaz. In El Petén, Stuart (1934:7) found *E. rhodopis* at night hopping on the ground near a small aguada, and by day he found specimens hopping on the forest floor (Stuart, 1935:37).

Little else is known of the natural history of this species. It must surely prey on small invertebrates, especially insects, and it presumably lays terrestrial

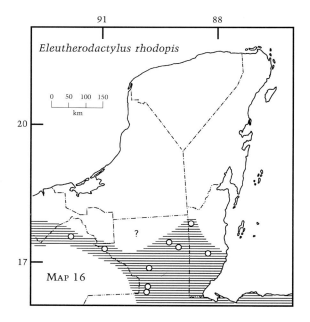

eggs within which the larvae undergo direct development.

ETYMOLOGY The specific name, *rhodopis*, is from the Greek *rhodon*, "rose," hence "red," and *opsis*, "aspect," "view," or "appearance," a reference to the reddish appearance of some specimens.

COMMENT There is some uncertainty concerning the application of *E. rhodopis* to frogs in the Yucatán Peninsula. Savage (1987) believed that two superficially similar but distinct species, *E. rhodopis* and *E. chac*, occur together throughout much of northern Guatemala and Belize. J. A. Campbell and Vannini (1989:6), however, considered *E. rhodopis* absent from the Caribbean slope of Guatemala and Belize, and Campbell (pers. comm.) favored the view that only *E. chac* occurs at the base of the Yucatán Peninsula. Pending thorough study of this issue, I provisionally follow Savage (1989) in recognizing *E. rhodopis* as present in the Yucatán Peninsula.

Locality Records Belize: Orange Walk: 2 mi N Gallon Jug (MCZ 37847); Stann Creek: N slope Cockscomb Mts. (CM 9872). *Guatemala*: Alta Verapaz: Chinajá (KU 55928–29, 58686–88), 5 km NE Chinajá (KU 55927); El Petén: Piedras Negras (FMNH 94204–7, 108574, 123062–68, 123070–95, 123097–130, 125700–9, 190634; UIMNH 14585–653, 14710–32; USNM 116889–90), Santa Cruz (UMMZ 75378), Santa Teresa (UMMZ 75377), Tikal (UMMZ 117991). *Mexico*: Chiapas: Palenque (USNM 116901), Palenque ruins (UIMNH 11287, 11289–90).

Eleutherodactylus rugulosus (Cope)
(Figs. 44, 228, 229; Map 17)

Liyla rugulosa Cope, 1870:160. LECTOTYPE: USNM 29971. TYPE LOCALITY: Tehuantepec, Oaxaca, Mexico, by lectotype designation of Savage (1975).

Rugulose rainfrog.

DESCRIPTION This medium to large *Eleutherodactylus* exhibits enormous sexual dimorphism in size. The males average about 35 to 40 mm in snout-vent length and attain a maximum of about 50 mm, whereas the females may grow to 90 mm. These are moderately robust, rather squat frogs with stout limbs (Figs. 228, 229). The snout is

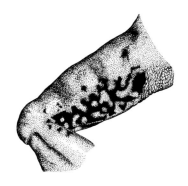

Fig. 44. Posterior view of the thigh of *Eleutherodactylus rugulosus* (UMRC 93-5) showing pattern of light spots and reticulations against a dark background; Cockscomb Wildlife Sanctuary, Stann Creek, Belize.

bluntly rounded in dorsal and lateral aspects, the canthus rostralis is rounded, and the loreal region is slightly concave. The tympanum is much smaller than the eye, and there is a supratympanic fold. The tips of the fingers and toes form expanded disks, the toes are moderately webbed at their bases, and there is a conspicuous tarsal fold. The males lack vocal slits and nuptial pads. The dorsum is granular with a few to many enlarged pustules.

Coloration is variable, but the dorsum is generally dark gray, brown, or reddish brown, usually with indistinct darker spots and blotches. Some specimens have a narrow, light vertebral stripe. The venter is white, cream, or yellow, and the throat is often suffused with dark pigment. Some individuals have a series of dark bars on the lips. The posterior surfaces of the thighs are boldly marked with light spots against a dark background (Fig. 44), although these may be obscure in preserved specimens.

VOCALIZATION Stafford (1991:12) described the vocalization of this species in Belize as "a short, but unbroken soft warble." Vocalization in *E. rugulosus* in the Yucatán Peninsula is otherwise unknown, and Stafford's description requires confirmation.

SIMILAR SPECIES *Eleutherodactylus laticeps*, which is similar to *E. rugulosus* in size, lacks a coarse, granular dorsum, possesses a ventral disk, and lacks bold markings on the posterior surface of the thigh.

DISTRIBUTION This wide-ranging species occurs at low to moderate elevations (to 1,200 m) from southern San Luis Potosí on the Atlantic slope and

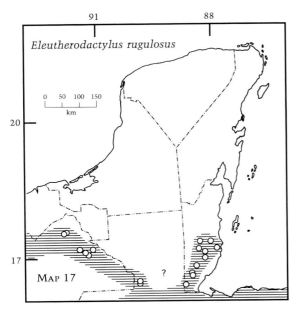

Eleutherodactylus rugulosus

91   88

20

17

MAP 17

central Guerrero on the Pacific slope, east and southward through Central America to western Panama. It is found throughout the base of the Yucatán Peninsula from the vicinity of Palenque, Chiapas, to central Belize (Map 17).

NATURAL HISTORY   This common rainfrog prefers rocky streams, particularly in forested areas. Individuals may be found at night perched on rocks in and adjacent to the water, as well as on the forest floor nearby. I have occasionally found juveniles perching low on vegetation near water. Although this frog seems to be generally nocturnal, Duellman (1963:223) found it on the forest floor by day in southern El Petén. The diet consists primarily of invertebrates, especially insects. Noble (1918:328) found grasshoppers among the stomach contents of specimens from Nicaragua.

Eleutherodactylus rugulosus is oviparous. Large females collected in Guerrero in mid-June by W. B. Davis and Dixon (1964:227) bore large-yolked eggs. The eggs are laid in moist, terrestrial situations and undergo direct development.

SUBSPECIES   Savage (1975) noted that populations from lower Central America were distinct from Mexican and Central American populations, but he declined to accord them formal nomenclatural recognition. No subspecies are currently recognized (but see Comment).

ETYMOLOGY   The specific name, *rugulosus*, is the diminutive of the Latin *rugosus*, "wrinkled," in

reference to the rough surface of the skin on the dorsum.

COMMENT   The biosystematics of the *E. rugulosus* group in Mexico and northern Central America was reviewed by Lynch in 1965, and Savage (1975) later reviewed the group throughout its geographical range. Miyamoto (1983) evaluated cladistic relationships within and among members of the group using morphological, biochemical, and karyological data.

Despite the attention that the *E. rugulosus* group has received from systematists, the status of several nominal forms is uncertain. Campbell et al. (1994) recently described *Eleutherodactylus psephosypharus*, known from montane forest habitats in northern Guatemala and Belize. It differs from *E. rugulosus* in having a strongly tuberculate dorsum and in lacking pale spots, blotches, or mottling on the posterior surfaces of the thighs. Ultimately, as many as three species of *rugulosus*-group frogs may be shown to occur in Belize and neighboring El Petén, none of which may be *E. rugulosus*. Jonathan A. Campbell and Jay M. Savage are preparing a revision of the *rugulosus* group, to include descriptions of additional species.

Locality Records Belize: Cayo: head of Roaring Creek (USNM 319790–92), upper Raspaculo River basin (Stafford, 1991:12); Stann Creek: Bokowina (FMNH 49021–31), N slope Cockscomb Mts. (CM 9873), Cockscomb Basin Wildlife Sanctuary (UMRC 93-5), Double Falls (FMNH 49032–37), Middlesex (FMNH 4407); Toledo: Columbia Branch Camp (W. T. Neill, 1965:82), Gloria Camp, Columbia River Forest Reserve (USNM 319768), Union Camp, Columbia River Forest Reserve (USNM 319766–67), Dolores (UMRC 93-2), Doyle's Delight (UMRC 93-6). *Guatemala*: El Petén: 6 km NW Chinajá (KU 55930), 15 km NW Chinajá (KU 55931–33, 58587). *Mexico*: Chiapas: 6.7 mi SE Cristóbal Colón (J. C. Lee, 1980a:50), bet. El Censo and Monte Libano (MCZ 28258), Laguna Ocotal (MCZ 28222–23), bet. Laguna Ocotal and El Censo (MCZ 28247–50), Monte Libano (MCZ 28221), Palenque ruins (UIMNH 11292–99; JCL photo), 6.5 km SW Palenque (UTEP 12259), 7.5 km SW Palenque (UTEP 12134), San Juanito (UIMNH 49223).

Eleutherodactylus yucatanensis Lynch
(Fig. 230; Map 18)

Eleutherodactylus yucatanensis Lynch, 1965a: 249. HOLOTYPE: KU 71094. TYPE LOCALITY: 1.5 km south and 1 km east of Pueblo Nuevo X-Can, Quintana Roo, Mexico.

Yucatán rainfrog.

DESCRIPTION   This is a rather squat, medium-sized frog (Fig. 230). The type series (four females) averages about 34 mm in snout-vent length. The head is moderately depressed and slightly broader than long. The canthus rostralis is rounded, and the loreal region is flat. There is an indistinct supratympanic fold. The limbs are moderately robust, and the tips of the fingers and toes are expanded slightly to form disks, which are slightly emarginate. There is virtually no webbing between the toes. A tarsal fold is present for about one-third the length of the tarsus. The distinct tympanum is much smaller than the eye, which is large and protruding. The dorsum, sides, and venter are smooth, and there is an obscure ventral disk.

The dorsal coloration is olive brown to gray, sometimes with a pinkish cast, with darker mottling. The iris is golden gray. The venter is largely devoid of pigment and is thus nearly transparent.

VOCALIZATION   The call of this species is unknown; it may be mute. Lynch (1965a:249) claimed that E. yucatanensis lacks vocal slits and sacs, but his type series consists solely of females.

SIMILAR SPECIES   Eleutherodactylus yucatanensis is very similar to E. alfredi, to which Lynch (1965a:249) considered it most closely related, and from which it differs in having numerous small tubercles on the soles. This is the only Eleutherodactylus in the northern half of the Yucatán Peninsula; so far as is known, it does not occur in sympatry with any of its congeners.

DISTRIBUTION   This apparently rather rare frog is endemic to the Yucatán Peninsula, where it is known from several localities in Yucatán and northern Quintana Roo (Map 18).

NATURAL HISTORY   The biology of this uncommon rainfrog is poorly understood. The type specimen was collected in a cave, suggesting that these frogs may inhabit cenotes and caverns. They are presumably terrestrial and nocturnal, for specimens have been found abroad at night in forested areas.

Lynch (1965a:251) reported that three of the specimens of the type series, collected in June and July,

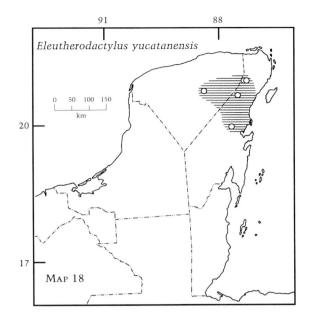

Eleutherodactylus yucatanensis

MAP 18

contained large yellow ova. Presumably this species oviposits in moist, terrestrial situations and the larvae undergo direct development.

ETYMOLOGY   The specific name, yucatanensis, is a toponym referring to the Yucatán Peninsula (not the state of that name), where the type material originated.

Locality Records   Mexico: Quintana Roo: Cobá (JCL photo), 25.4 km NE Felipe Carrillo Puerto (KU 171210), 1.5 km S, 1 km E Pueblo Nuevo X-Can (KU 71094), 1.5 km S, 7 km E Pueblo Nuevo X-Can (KU 71095–96), Yucatán: Chichén Itzá (LSUMZ 28253), near Chichén Itzá (CM 36444), Chichén Itzá, Cenote Xtolok (LACM 114253), Cueva de Sabaca Teca (FMNH 191785).

Genus *Leptodactylus*

This New World genus has many species, most of which are rather uniform morphologically, although they range in body size from small to very large. These frogs are semiaquatic to terrestrial, and most species are somewhat streamlined and smooth skinned. Males often possess keratinized spines on the thumbs, chest, or both. Some species exhibit direct development, and some others deposit their eggs in foam nests. The genus contains approximately 50 living species distributed from southern Texas and Sonora southward through Middle America to coastal Peru and Argentina. The genus also occurs in the Lesser Antilles, Hispaniola, Puerto Rico, and the Virgin Islands. Two species occur within the Yucatán Peninsula. The genus *Leptodactylus* was redefined by Heyer (1969a), who reviewed the *L. melanonotus* group in 1970, the *L. marmoratus* group in 1973, the *L. fuscus* group in 1978, and the *L. pentadactylus* group in 1979.

Leptodactylus is from the Greek *leptos*, "slender" or "thin," and *daktylos*, "finger."

Key to the Species of the Genus *Leptodactylus*

Dermal fringes present on toes; males with black keratinized spines on thumbs (Fig. 48); ventral dermal disk poorly defined; no conspicuous white labial stripe . . . . *Leptodactylus melanonotus*

No dermal fringes on toes; males without keratinized spines on thumbs (Fig. 45); ventral dermal disk well defined; conspicuous white labial stripe . . . . *Leptodactylus labialis*

Clave para las Especies del Género *Leptodactylus*

Un fleco dermal presente en los dedos de los pies; los machos poseen una espina oscura queratinizada en la base del dedo interno de las manos (Fig. 48); un disco ventral dérmico pobremente definido; una línea blanca pobremente definida sobre el labio . . . . *Leptodactylus melanonotus*

Sin un fleco dermal presente en los dedos de los pies; los machos sin una espina oscura queratinizada en la base del dedo interno de las manos (Fig. 45); un disco ventral dérmico bien definido; una línea blanca conspicuamente definida sobre el labio . . . . . . *Leptodactylus labialis*

Leptodactylus labialis (Cope)
(Figs. 45–47, 231, 232; Map 19)

Cystignathus labialis Cope, 1877:90. HOLOTYPE: USNM 31302. TYPE LOCALITY: uncertain, but "probably a part of Sumichrast's Mexican collection" (Cope, 1877:90); restricted by H. M. Smith and Taylor (1950b:350) to Potrero Viejo, Veracruz, Mexico; but D. M. Cochran (1961:40) stated that the type locality was probably Tehuantepec, Oaxaca, Mexico.

White-lipped frog; ranita (Guatemala); ranita hojarasca (Mexico).

DESCRIPTION This medium-sized frog averages about 35 mm in snout-vent length and apparently exhibits no sexual size dimorphism (Heyer, 1978:47). The skin is rather smooth, the head is relatively narrow, and the appendages are moderately long (Figs. 231, 232). The snout is rather pointed in dorsal and lateral views. The canthus rostralus is weakly developed, and the loreal region is slightly concave. The tympanum is distinct, about two-thirds the diameter of the eye, and covered by a supratympanic fold at its dorsal margin. The toes and fingers are slender, have slightly expanded tips, and bear a trace of webbing at their bases (Fig. 45). A distinct ventral dermal disk is present. Some specimens have indistinct dorsolateral folds. Most have white tubercles covering the dorsal surface of the tibia, the posterior surface of the tarsus, and the sole of the foot.

The dorsal color pattern is variable but generally consists of dark brown, tan, or gray spots or blotches against a lighter background (Fig. 231). In some specimens the dorsum has a reddish cast (Fig. 232). The dorsal surfaces of the appendages bear dark spots or transverse bands. Most animals have a conspicuous white labial stripe, although it may be obscure in preserved specimens. The venter and the

Fig. 45. Hand of *Leptodactylus labialis* (UMRC 79-254); 5.9 km N Dzibalchén, Campeche, Mexico.

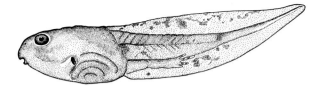

Fig. 46. Tadpole of *Leptodactylus labialis* (USNM 321154), TL 29 mm; Cañas, Guanacaste, Costa Rica.

ventral surfaces of the appendages are usually immaculate cream or gray.

TADPOLE   The body is globose in dorsal aspect; the snout is bluntly rounded in both dorsal and lateral views (Fig. 46). The body length is slightly less than twice the maximum body depth. The eyes are relatively large, close together, and directed laterally. The mouth is anteroventral. The oral disk is not indented laterally, and its surrounding labial papillae are discontinuous dorsally. The keratinized jaw sheaths bear fine serrations, and there are two anterior and three posterior rows of denticles. The sinistral spiracle is lateral and slightly below the midline. The vent tube is medial. The acuminate tail is about 1.8 times the body length, and its maximum depth is approximately equal to that of the body. The dorsal and caudal fins are subequal in depth, and the dorsal fin extends onto the posterior surface of the body. This is a predominantly brown tadpole, darker above than below, with darker spots, blotches, and mottling on the tail.

VOCALIZATION   The advertisement call of *L. labialis* consists of a long series of simple notes, perhaps best described as *wheet wheet wheet*. The note repetition rate is variable, but in my experience it averages between 120 and 150 per minute. The

Fig. 47. Advertisement call of *Leptodactylus labialis*, recorded 2 June 1989, near Burrell Boom, Belize, Belize.

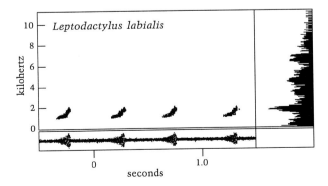

average note duration is approximately 160 msec. The dominant frequency of each note ascends in frequency from about 1,000 to 2,000 Hz, producing a clearly audible upward inflection to each note (Fig. 47).

SIMILAR SPECIES   The other *Leptodactylus* in the Yucatán Peninsula, *L. melanonotus*, lacks a well-developed ventral dermal disk and possesses dermal fringes on the toes, and the males have keratinized spines on the base of each thumb (Fig. 48). Frogs of the genus *Rana* may superficially resemble *Leptodactylus*, but the former all have extensively webbed toes.

DISTRIBUTION   *Leptodactylus labialis* occurs from southern Texas on the Gulf slope and from at least Sinaloa on the Pacific slope, south through Central America to Venezuela and Colombia. It is found throughout the Yucatán Peninsula (Map 19).

NATURAL HISTORY   This widespread and common species occurs in a variety of habitats, especially areas with permanent water such as marshes and aguadas. Individuals are often encountered on roads at night during or following rains. They breed throughout the rainy season. Males, which call during the day as well as at night, vocalize from the edges of temporary or permanent bodies of water in forests or savannas, usually from hiding places at the bases of grass tufts or sequestered within burrows in the mud. Amplexus is axillary. The amplectant frogs use their hind legs to whip their secre-

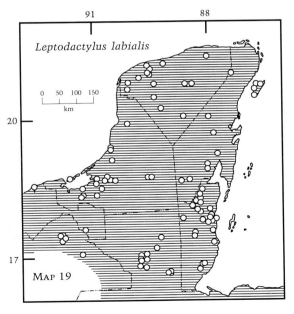

tions into a foam nest. The eggs are deposited in the foam nest, and the larvae undergo early development there. Foam nests are usually placed in terrestrial situations subject to flooding, ensuring the release of the larvae from the nest.

ETYMOLOGY The specific name, *labialis*, is Latin for "pertaining to the lips," presumably in reference to the light labial stripe, which Cope (1877:90) described as a "brilliant white band."

COMMENT Between 1978 and 1992 this species was known as *L. fragilis*. Dubois and Heyer (1992: 584), however, concluded that *Cystignathus labialis* Cope 1877 has priority over *C. fragilis* Brocchi 1877 and restored the name *labialis*.

The literature on *L. labialis* was summarized by Heyer (1971), who also evaluated the taxonomic status of the species (as *L. fragilis*) as part of his review of the *L. fuscus* group (Heyer, 1978).

Locality Records Belize: Belize: Belize City (FMNH 4392, 4398, 4732; UMMZ 124744), 10 mi NW Belize City (CM 105750), 10 mi W Belize City (UF 24533–35), 13.5 mi NW Belize City (KU 156303–7), 30 mi W Belize City (BCB 12110), 39 mi W Belize City (BCB 12111), Burrell Boom (RWV photo; JCL audio record), Burrell Boom Rd. at Belize River (CM 105787–91), Crooked Tree (CM 111931), 11 km SW Hattieville (CM 90909), bet. Ladyville and Sandhill (CM 90939–45, 90950), due W Maskall (CM 105749–50), Manatee (FMNH 4263); Cayo: 2 mi W Belmopan (CM 105771–74), Cocquercot (UMMZ 75359), 0.5 mi S Georgeville (CM 105697), 3 mi S Georgeville (CM 91021, 91025), 4 mi S Georgeville (CM 105700–6); Corozal: Buena Vista (USNM 211459–71); Orange Walk: August Pine Ridge (USNM 194931), 10 mi E Carmelita (TU 20910), Gallon Jug (LSUMZ 6418; MCZ 37863), Guinea Grass Rd., 4 mi S Northern Hwy. (CM 105714–21), Kate's Lagoon (FMNH 49060), Lamanai (ROM H12742–44), Orange Walk Town (USNM 211472–510), 45 mi SE Orange Walk (BCB 12109), Otro Benque (USNM 194891–99), San Felipe (USNM 211511–23), Tower Hill (USNM 167739, 194081–83); Stann Creek: 1 mi S Kendall (CM 105843), 4 mi S Waha Leaf Creek (MCZ 37864–66); Toledo: Bladen Branch of Monkey River (CM 105924–27), 14.5 mi NE Golden Stream (KU 156299), Monkey River (MCZ 37867–72), 4.1 mi W Monkey River (KU 156301), 2.5 mi S Swasey Bridge (CM 105929–30), 4 mi S Swasey Bridge (CM 105932–33). *Guatemala*: El Petén: 11 mi SW Flores (KU 156312), 23.5 mi SW Flores (KU 156313–15), vicinity La Libertad (UMMZ 75360–66), N La Libertad (CM 13020; MCZ 21455), 4.9 km SW La Libertad (KU 171208), 15 km SE La Libertad (KU 58950–51), Pacomon (USNM 71333), Poptún (UMMZ

117989, 120484, 130005), 1 km S Poptún (UMMZ 120483), 2 km E Poptún (UMMZ 124377–80), 2 mi N Poptún (KU 156311), 4 mi N Poptún (KU 156308–10), 9.9 mi N Río de la Pasión (KU 156316), 1 mi W Ruinas Seibal (KU 156317), Tikal (UF 13418–37; UMMZ 117988; UTA A-26019), 2 to 3 km SW Tikal (UMMZ 120482). *Mexico*: Campeche: Actun Chen, Chumpich (KU 159615), Balchacaj (FMNH 108273, 108276, 108279–80, 108282–87, 108289–91, 108298–301, 108306, 108310–11, 108315–16, 108319, 108322–27, 108329–30, 108333–35, 108337, 108340–41, 108344, 108355, 108357, 108362, 108364–71, 108376, 108380–81, 108385, 108388, 108390–92, 108395–98, 108401, 108408, 108410–11, 108413–15, 108422, 108423–24, 108426), 21 mi E Campeche (UIMNH 86636), 7.8 km SE Hwy. 186 on rd. to Candelaria (KU 171224), Champotón (MCZ 21452; UMMZ 73149), 3.5 mi S Champotón (UCM 18192–93), Chuina (KU 75009–12, 75014), Ciudad del Carmen (UMMZ 83550), 5.9 km N Dzibalchén (UMRC 79-254), 30.8 mi NE Emiliano Zapata (EAL 1646), Encarnación (FMNH 106351, 108272, 108274–75, 108278, 108281, 108292–97, 108302–5, 108307, 108309, 108313–14, 108317–18, 108321, 108328, 108331–32, 108336, 108338–39, 108342–43, 108345–47, 108349–51, 108353–54, 108356, 108358–60, 108363, 108372, 108374–75, 108377–79, 108382, 108384, 108386–87, 108389, 108393–94, 108399–400, 108402–7, 108412, 108416–20, 108425, 108456), 5 mi W Escárcega (UCM 27558–67, 40106–7, 45839–40), 6 km W Escárcega (KU 71101), 7.5 km W Escárcega (KU 71098–100), 13 km W, 1 km N Escárcega (KU 71097), Laguna Silvituc (KU 75015–16), Matamoros (FMNH 38588), Pital (FMNH 108271, 108312, 108348, 108352, 108361, 108373, 108383, 108409, 108421), Tres Brazos (FMNH 108288, 108320), Tuxpeña Camp (UMMZ 73237), 32.1 km NE Xpujil (KU 171223); Chiapas: 1 km S, 3 km E Palenque (UTEP 6937–39), 10 to 15 mi S Palenque (LSUMZ 33748), 10 km S Palenque ruins (USNM 114219), 19.1 to 28.5 km N Pueblo Palenque (EAL 2906), rd. bet. Palenque and Palenque ruins (EAL 3322), San José Carpizo (UMMZ 99880), San Juanito (USNM 114220–24); Quintana Roo: 10 mi W Bacalar (LSUMZ 33749–53), 9.9 mi S Felipe Carrillo Puerto (KU 156319), S end Isla Cozumel (UMMZ 78545), Cozumel, San Miguel (UMMZ 78547–49), Cozumel, 6 mi E San Miguel (UMMZ 78546), Cozumel, 9 km S San Miguel (UCM 12332), Cozumel, 2 km E San Miguel (UCM 20530–33), Cozumel, 6 km S San Miguel (UCM 20534–35), Cozumel, 3.5 km N San Miguel (KU 71102–5), near Circuito Benito (MCZ 89759), 4.6 km N Kohunlich ruins (KU 171205), Laguna Chacanbacab (CM 45231–32), 3.5 mi N Limones (KU 156320), Pueblo Nuevo X-Can (UCM 27616), 2.3 mi S, 1.9 mi E Santa Rosa (KU 156322–32), Sian Ka'an Reserve (MZCIQRO 34–35), 31.8 mi S Tepich (KU 156321), 13 km N jct. Hwys. 307 and 186 (KU 171203–4); Tabasco: 4–6 mi W Frontera (UCM 27568–74), Tenosique (USNM

114217–18); Yucatán: Chichén Itzá (UMMZ 73147, 83111–12, 83919), 3 mi E Chichén Itzá (UMMZ 73150), 13.8 km N Chunchucmíl (TU 19816–20), 22.5 km N Chunchucmíl (TU 19810), Dzibilchaltún (CM 45230; FMNH 153416; UCM 18191), Kinchil (JCL photo), 10 mi SW Kinchil (KU 156333), Laguna Chichancanab (UMRC 78-37), Lol-Tun (MZFC 3174), Mérida (UMMZ 73152), 1 mi N Mérida (UMMZ 73148), Pisté (UCM 12333–50, 15589), pools N of Pisté (UMMZ 73198), 3 mi S Progreso (UCM 39079), near Tekantó (Ives, 1891:461), 3 mi N Telchac (UCM 28098), 31.8 mi S Tepich (JCL sight record), 12 mi N Tizimín (UCM 27575–615), 3 mi S Yokat (AMNH 33306), Yuncu (Gaige, 1936:291).

Leptodactylus melanonotus (Hallowell)
(Figs. 48–50, 233; Map 20)

Cystignathus melanonotus Hallowell, 1861:485. HOLOTYPE: USNM 6264 (lost, *fide* Heyer, 1970:9). TYPE LOCALITY: Nicaragua; restricted by H. M. Smith and Taylor (1950b:320) to Recero, Nicaragua.

Black-backed frog; ranita hojarasca (Mexico).

DESCRIPTION These are medium-sized, semi-aquatic frogs. The males average about 36 mm in snout-vent length, and the females are 3 to 5 mm longer. The head is broad, the snout is bluntly rounded in both dorsal and lateral aspects, and the trunk is short and stocky (Fig. 233). The canthus rostralis is indistinct, and the loreal region is slightly concave. The eyes are moderately large, the pupils are horizontally elliptical, and the interorbital distance is about two-thirds the diameter of the eye. The tympanum is distinct and slightly less than the eye in diameter. There is no supratympanic fold. The limbs are relatively short, and the fingers and toes have only a trace of webbing at their bases. Dermal fringes are present on the digits (Fig. 48) and are especially well developed on the toes. The males are unique among the frogs in the Yucatán Peninsula in possessing dark, keratinized spines at the bases of their thumbs (Fig. 48). The dorsal surfaces of the head, trunk, and appendages are covered with tiny pustulations. The integument of the venter is smooth, and a ventral dermal disk is absent or poorly developed.

These frogs are generally dark brown, gray, or nearly black above, often with indistinct darker markings and a triangular interorbital spot. The ventral coloration is highly variable but generally involves a dark reticulum against a lighter back-

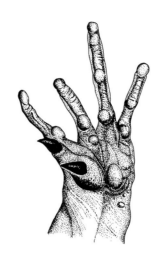

Fig. 48. Hand of *Leptodactylus melanonotus* male (UMRC 78-38) showing dermal fringes on the digits and keratinized spines on the thumb; Belize City, Belize, Belize.

ground, often with a yellowish cast. The throat and chin are generally dark brown, gray, or nearly black.

TADPOLE The body is approximately half as wide as long, and the snout is bluntly rounded in dorsal aspect. The eyes are small, rather closely spaced, and high on the head (Fig. 49). The tail is about twice the length of the body, and its greatest depth slightly exceeds that of the body. The dorsal fin extends onto the posterior portion of the body, and its depth is approximately equal to that of the ventral fin. The mouth is ventral. The oral disk is not indented laterally, and the labial papillae are discontinuous dorsally. There are two anterior and three posterior rows of denticles, and the keratinized jaw sheaths are finely serrated. The vent tube is medial. The spiracle is sinistral and lies slightly below the midline. The general color is brown, somewhat darker above than below. The caudal fins are lighter than the caudal musculature and may bear indistinct light spots and flecks.

VOCALIZATION The advertisement call of *L. melanonotus* is a simple but well-modulated *tuc, tuc, tuc-tuc* given in sequences that may last sev-

Fig. 49. Tadpole of *Leptodactylus melanonotus* (KU 60061), 24 mm TL; 8 km ENE Rio Hondo, Zacapa, Guatemala.

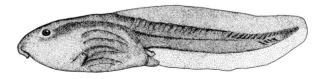

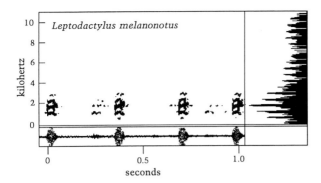

Fig. 50. Advertisement call of *Leptodactylus melanonotus*, recorded 11 October 1988, Río Lagartos, Yucatán, Mexico.

eral minutes. The note repetition rate is quite variable, ranging from 240 to perhaps 300 per minute, and note duration is approximately 110 msec. The dominant frequency is about 1,800 Hz (Fig. 50).

SIMILAR SPECIES *Leptodactylus labialis* has a well-developed ventral dermal disk and a narrower, more pointed head. It lacks dermal fringes on the toes, and the males lack spines on the thumbs (cf. Figs. 45, 48). Ranid frogs have extensive webbing between the toes, and all the *Eleutherodactylus* species have digits with expanded tips.

DISTRIBUTION *Leptodactylus melanonotus* occurs at low and moderate elevations on both the Pacific and Gulf slopes of Mexico from Sonora and Tamaulipas, respectively, throughout Central

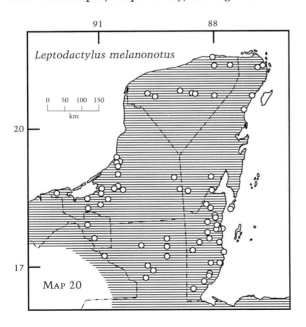

America and into South America west of the Andes to Ecuador. In the Yucatán Peninsula the species is pan-peninsular (Map 20).

NATURAL HISTORY *Leptodactylus melanonotus* is a common frog. It occurs in virtually all peninsular habitats that do not have brackish water. Males call from the ground at the edges of temporary or permanent ponds, flooded pastures, bajos, or aguadas, often in close association with human habitations. Calling individuals are difficult to locate because they sequester themselves at the bases of tufts of grass or within burrows in the mud. These frogs are terrestrial and largely nocturnal, although males frequently call during the day as well as at night. During or shortly after rains they may appear on roads in large numbers.

Breeding occurs during the rainy season. The males possess keratinized spines on their thumbs that may aid them in clasping females or may function in male-male aggressive interactions. Amplexus is axillary. The eggs are deposited in foam nests constructed on or at the edge of water. The eggs hatch into aquatic larvae, which pass a variable amount of time in the nest before entering the water to complete their development.

ETYMOLOGY The specific name, *melanonotus*, is from the Greek *melas*, "black," and *notos*, "back," presumably in reference to the dark dorsum of many individuals.

COMMENT The biosystematics of this species was treated by Heyer (1970) as part of his revision of the *L. melanonotus* group.

Locality Records   Belize: Belize: Belize City (CM 111930; FMNH 4389–91, 4393–97, 4399–405; UMRC 78-38), near Belize City (UF 84501), 7.8 km W Belize City (CM 90985–86), 10.3 mi W Belize City (NMSU 3096), 11.7 mi W Belize City (KU 156335–38), 13 mi NW Belize City (UMMZ 124741), Crooked Tree Village (CM 112090–93), Hummingbird Hershey Farm (CM 105826–28), bet. Ladyville and Sandhill (CM 90946–47), Manatee (FMNH 4262), 8.5 mi W, 7.5 mi N Maskalls (W. T. Neill and Allen, 1959c:24), Rockstone Pond (UU 9329–32); no specific locality (LSUMZ 10275); Cayo: 15 mi E Belmopan (CM 112093), Cocquercot (UMMZ 75368), 3.1 mi W Mountain Pine Ridge Rd. on Belize-Cayo Rd. (UMMZ 124740), Privassion Creek (W. T. Neill and Allen, 1961a; Corozal: Ambergris Cay, 17 km N, 6.5 km E San Pedro (CM 91102), 5 km NNE San Pedro (CM 91124), 3 mi N

Corozal Town (JLK 449–53); Orange Walk: 0.5 mi N Gallon Jug (MCZ 37873–74), Kate's Lagoon (FMNH 49058–59, 49061), Otro Benque (USNM 194890); Stann Creek: Dangriga (RWV photo), Mango Creek (MCZ 37884), 4 mi S Waha Leaf Creek (MCZ 37877–78), 2 mi S Waha Leaf Creek (MCZ 37880–83); Toledo: Bladen Branch of Monkey River (CM 105910–11), 3 mi S Bladen Branch (LSUMZ 9611), 2.7 mi NE Golden Stream (KU 156300), 3.5 mi E, 2.5 mi S San Antonio (W. T. Neill and Allen, 1961a; no specific locality (USNM 57763, 59939). *Guatemala*: El Petén: La Libertad (MCZ 21454), N La Libertad (UMMZ 75367), vicinity La Libertad (UMMZ 75369–71, 75373–76), 15 km SE La Libertad (KU 58959), Paso de los Caballos (Stuart, 1937:68), 5 mi S Piedras Negras (USNM 114391), Remate (UMMZ 75372), Sayaxché (KU 55947), Tikal (UF 13438–54; UMMZ 117987, 126452, 130053; UTA A-26028–29), Uaxactún (KU 156339–40). *Mexico*: Campeche: Balchacaj (FMNH 102450, 102475–76, 102511, 102521, 102523–24, 102527, 102529, 102551, 102567, 102575, 102582, 102598, 102607, 102614, 102619, 102629, 102647, 102649, 102660, 102662–63, 108308, 108419, 117522–24), 53 mi SW Campeche (EAL 1197), 7.9 km SE Hwy. 186 on rd. to Candelaria (KU 171226), Champotón (MCZ 21453; UMMZ 73153–54, 73156), 3.5 mi S Champotón (UCM 18194–220), 5 km S Champotón (KU 71106–12), 10.5 km S Champotón (KU 71113), 14.6 mi S Champotón (EAL 1656), Chuina (KU 75013, 75017–31), 30.8 mi NE Emiliano Zapata (EAL 1647), Encarnación (FMNH 102431, 102435–36, 102445, 102467, 102469, 102478, 102484, 102493–94, 102497, 102507–8, 102513–14, 102516–17, 102530, 102533–34, 102542, 102562, 102573, 102587, 102589, 102595, 102597, 102601, 102620, 102639, 102655–56, 102658, 102668), 5 km N Escárcega (KU 171225), 13 km W, 1 km N Escárcega (KU 71114–16, 75032), E edge Ingenio La Joya (KU 156341), Matamoros (FMNH 36568), Pacaitún on Río Candelaria (FMNH 36569, 36578–79, 36581), Pital (FMNH 102512), 17 km S Sabancuy (JCL photo), 1–2 km W San Antonio Cárdenas (UTEP 13994–95), San José Carpizo (UMMZ 99881), Tres Brazos (FMNH 102477, 102540, 117521, 117525–26, 190629), 18 km ENE Zoh Laguna (CM 45244–51); Chiapas: 8 mi E Emiliano Zapata (EAL 1641); Quintana Roo: 10 mi W Bacalar (LSUMZ 33745–47), 3 km E Caobas (KU 75033), Laguna Chacanbacab (CM 45252–57), 17.1 mi SW Playa del Carmen (KU 156342–43), 26 km SSW Puerto Juárez (LSUMZ 28271), 4 km WSW Puerto Juárez (KU 41117–18); Tabasco: Tenosique (USNM 114264–71); Yucatán: 12.5 km N Colonia Yucatán (JCL sight record), 12 mi S Izamal (UMMZ 80887), 1.5 mi S Libre Unión (UCM 15594–97), 45 km SW Mérida (UMMZ 73155), pools N of Pisté (UMMZ 73200), Río Lagartos (JCL audio record), 12 mi N Tizimín (CM 40108–10), 16.2 km S Yaxcopoil (CM 45233–41, 45243).

Genus *Physalaemus*

This is a moderately large genus of small Neotropical frogs found from southern Mexico to Bolivia, Brazil, and Argentina. Of the 37 species, only one occurs in the Yucatán Peninsula. Lynch (1970b) redefined the genus and its species groups, and Duellman and Cannatella (1984) reviewed the *pustulosus* group. *Physalaemus* is from the Greek *physa*, "bellows" or "bubble," and *laemus*, "throat," perhaps in allusion to the distended vocal sac of calling males.

Physalaemus pustulosus (Cope)
(Figs. 51–53, 234; Map 21)

Paludicola pustulosa Cope, 1864:180. HOLOTYPE: USNM or ANSP 4339 (lost, *fide* H. M. Smith and Taylor, 1948:47). TYPE LOCALITY: New Granada on the River Truando, Colombia.

Tungara frog.

DESCRIPTION This is a small frog, although moderately large for a *Physalaemus*. The males attain a snout-vent length of about 33 mm, the females reach about 35 mm. The body is rather globose, and the head is much narrower than the body. The snout is pointed in dorsal aspect, the eyes are moderately large, and the pupils are horizontally elliptical. There is a large parotoid gland at the nape of the neck. The appendages are slender and delicate. The toes and fingers are rounded at their tips and lack webbing. The dorsal surfaces of the head, body, and appendages are densely covered with warts and tubercles, thus justifying the specific name, *pustulosus* (Fig. 234). The tympanum is likewise covered with warts and tubercles and is indistinguishable externally. The males have a large subgular vocal sac.

These predominantly gray, brown, or tan frogs have a few to many reddish brown and black spots arranged irregularly on the dorsum. The venter is gray with a few to many dark spots. In most specimens a light midgular stripe contrasts with the darker pigment of the throat.

TADPOLE The body of the *P. pustulosus* tadpole is globose in dorsal aspect, and its width is equal to about two-thirds of its length (Fig. 51). The snout is bluntly rounded. The rather widely spaced eyes are situated high on the head. The short tail is approximately 1.3 times the length of the body. The mouth

Fig. 51. Tadpole of *Physalaemus pustulosus* (KU 87689), 17 mm TL; 5 km N, 14 km E Condega, Estelí, Nicaragua.

is ventral, the oral disk is indented laterally, and the labial papillae are discontinuous anteriorly. There are two anterior and three posterior rows of denticles and finely serrated jaw sheaths. The vent tube is medial. The spiracle is sinistral and lies well below the level of the midline. The dorsal fin extends onto the posterior surface of the body; its depth is approximately equal to that of the ventral fin. The dorsum and caudal musculature are brown. The caudal fins bear indistinct brown mottling.

VOCALIZATION The advertisement call of *P. pustulosus* is unique among the frogs of the Yucatán Peninsula because it exhibits a pronounced downward frequency modulation. The call can best be described as *pow*, a whine whose dominant frequency begins at about 900 Hz and sweeps downward to about 400 Hz. In Campeche, the duration of the whine is about 250 to 400 msec, and the call is typically given at a rate of about 45 to 60 per minute (Fig. 52), although in Panama the mean is about 30 calls per minute (M. J. Ryan, pers. comm.). In lower Central America and in Venezuela the calls of this species vary in complexity depending on the social and, perhaps, ecological context. Males calling in large choruses may increase the complexity of their calls by adding one to several secondary notes known as chucks. Ryan (1985) showed that females are preferentially attracted to complex calls con-

Fig. 52. Advertisement call of *Physalaemus pustulosus*, recorded 2 October 1991, 6.7 km S Chekubúl, Campeche, Mexico.

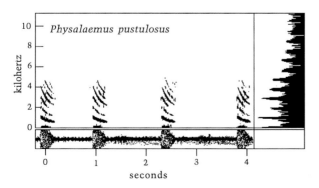

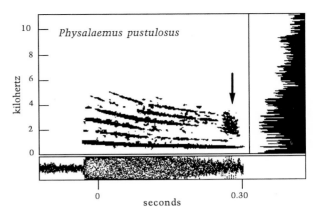

Fig. 53. Advertisement call of *Physalaemus pustulosus* showing the whine component plus a single chuck (*arrow*), recorded 2 October 1991, 6.7 km S Chekubúl, Campeche, Mexico.

taining chucks, but complex calls also attract predators, such as the bat *Trachops cirrhosus*. When calling singly or in small groups, frogs from the Yucatán Peninsula typically give simple calls consisting of the whine component alone (Fig. 52). In playback experiments in the field I was able to elicit complex calls that incorporated at least one chuck component (Fig. 53).

SIMILAR SPECIES The extremely pustulate texture of the skin distinguishes this frog from all others in the Yucatán Peninsula, with the possible exception of the toads *Bufo marinus* and *B. valliceps*, both of which are much larger, possess a series of cranial crests on the dorsal surface of the head, and lack a tarsal tubercle.

DISTRIBUTION *Physalaemus pustulosus* occurs at low and moderate elevations from southern Oaxaca and southern Veracruz south through Central America to northern Colombia, Venezuela, Trinidad, and Guyana. In the Yucatán Peninsula the species is known from several localities in eastern Tabasco, southern Campeche, southern Quintana Roo, and northern Belize (Map 21).

NATURAL HISTORY This species, which is moderately common in the Yucatán Peninsula, has been the subject of intensive study in Panama (Rand and Ryan, 1981; Ryan, 1985). Throughout its range *P. pustulosus* is primarily an inhabitant of savannas and deciduous forests. It is terrestrial, nocturnal, and rarely encountered except at the breeding congregations that form during the rainy season. Breeding can occur in almost any temporary body of wa-

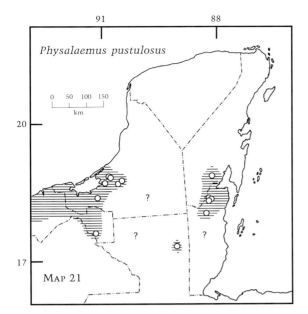

MAP 21

This species was long placed in the genus *Engystomops*, and much of the earlier literature on the species will be found under that name. *Physalaemus pustulosus* was reviewed by Duellman and Cannatella (1984) as part of their review of the *pustulosus* group.

Locality Records Belize: Orange Walk: near Lamanai (ROM H12710–14), NW Orange Walk Town (KU 156356–65), Otro Benque (USNM 194090–95), Tower Hill (USNM 167740–41), near Tower Hill (UF 84502). *Guatemala*: El Petén: N shore Lake Yaxhá (UTEP 6015–16). *Mexico*: Campeche: 6.8 km S Chekubúl (JCL photo), Encarnación (FMNH 111389–404), 79.9 km NE Emiliano Zapata (EAL 2912), 4.4 mi N Escárcega (KU 156366–68), 5 mi W Escárcega (CM 40104–5; UCM 28069–83), Plan de Ayala (JCL photo); Quintana Roo: 10 mi W Bacalar (LSUMZ 33743); Tabasco: Tenosique (H. M. Smith and Taylor, 1948:47).

ter, including roadside ditches, flooded pastures, small puddles, and even in hoofprints made by cattle and horses. Males typically call from the surface of the water. The females approach the calling males, which initiate amplexus. Amplexus is axillary, and 200 to 300 eggs are deposited in a foam nest in shallow water that is formed when the amplectant male kicks the egg jelly into a foam with his hind legs (Heyer and Rand, 1977). The foam nest affords protection against both desiccation (Heyer, 1969b) and predation. Ryan (1985:47) reported predation by tadpoles of *Agalychnis callidryas* on *P. pustulosus* tadpoles whose nest had been broken apart by heavy rain. Downie (1988, 1990) showed experimentally that the foam protects eggs from drying and that it may protect eggs from predation by invertebrates and tadpoles of other species. The females may produce multiple clutches during the breeding season (Rand, 1983:413). Females in captivity with unlimited food produced clutches at intervals of about six weeks (Davidson and Hough, 1969).

ETYMOLOGY The specific name, *pustulosus*, is Latin for "covered with pimples," a reference to the dense warts and tubercles on the dorsum.

Family Bufonidae (True Toads)

Members of this large and cosmopolitan family of primarily terrestrial anurans generally have thick, glandular, often wart-covered skin. Many bufonids have enlarged parotoid glands on the neck, and most have a rather squat, rounded body with short limbs. The family occurs worldwide except in the Australian region (where *Bufo marinus* has been introduced), Saharan Africa, and the high latitudes of the Holoarctic region. Duellman (1993) recognized 365 species in 31 genera. In the Yucatán Peninsula the family is represented by a single genus and 2 species.

Genus *Bufo*

The distribution of this genus is essentially that of the family. Of the approximately 200 species presently recognized, 3 occur in the Yucatán Peninsula. Blair (1972) summarized the available information on the genus. *Bufo* is Latin for "toad."

Key to the Species of the Genus *Bufo*

Large toads with relatively enormous parotoid glands with a maximum length at least twice the diameter of the eye (Fig. 54A); distinct tarsal fold.............................*Bufo marinus*

Smaller toads with relatively small parotoid glands with a maximum length less than twice the diameter of the eye (Fig. 54B); no tarsal fold.................................*Bufo valliceps*

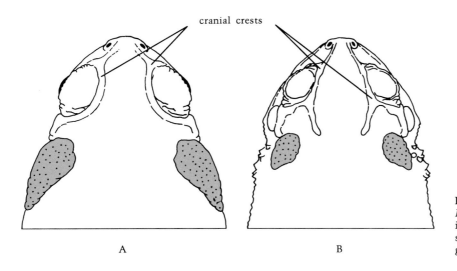

cranial crests

Fig. 54. Dorsal view of the head of (A) *Bufo marinus* and (B) *B. valliceps* showing arrangement of cranial crests and size and configuration of the parotoid glands (*shaded*).

A   B

Clave para las Especies del Género *Bufo*

Sapos de gran tamaño con glándulas parotoides muy grandes, la longitud máxima de las parotoides es por lo menos el doble del diámetro del ojo (Fig. 54A); un pliegue tarsal distintivo .... *Bufo marinus*

Sapos de tamaño pequeño con glándulas parotoides relativamente pequeñas, la longitud máxima de las parotoides es menor al diámetro del ojo (Fig. 54B); sin pliegue tarsal .... *Bufo valliceps*

Bufo marinus (Linnaeus)
(Figs. 54A, 55, 56, 235; Map 22)

Rana marina Linnaeus, 1758:211. HOLOTYPE: apparently a specimen that appeared as figure 1 of plate 76 in volume 1 of Seba, 1734 (Kellogg, 1932: 54). TYPE LOCALITY: America; restricted to Surinam by L. Müller and Hellmich (1936:14).

Marine toad; sapo gigante, sapo grande, sapo marino (Mexico); nim li compopó (Kekchi Maya); v'op (Lacandón Maya); much, bezmuch, totmuch (Yucatec Maya).

DESCRIPTION   This enormous toad is by far the largest anuran in the Yucatán Peninsula, and one of the largest in the world. The females, which substantially exceed the males in size, may attain a snout-vent length in excess of 200 mm, although most are less then 150 mm long. The body is squat, rounded, and somewhat dorsoventrally compressed (Fig. 235). The limbs are short and robust. Warts are scattered irregularly over the dorsum. In sexually active males the dorsal warts bear small, keratinized spines and the thumbs support a dark nuptial

pad. The large, ovate parotoid glands extend posteriorly onto the shoulder (Fig. 54A). Cranial crests are well developed. The fingers and toes are short with rounded tips. The fingers are devoid of webbing, whereas the toes are slightly webbed at their bases. There is a distinct tarsal fold, and males have a subgular vocal sac.

This species exhibits sexual dichromatism. The males are generally tan above and on the flanks, with scattered light spots, whereas the females have a darker mottled pattern on the dorsum and the flanks. The pupil is horizontally elliptical and flecked with silver and gold.

TADPOLE   The body of the tadpole of *B. marinus* is globose in dorsal aspect and somewhat depressed in lateral view, with a bluntly rounded snout (Fig. 55). The eyes are small, close together, and dorsal. The mouth is ventral, and the oral disk is indented laterally. Fringing labial papillae are present but interrupted both dorsally and ventrally. Finely serrated cornified jaw sheaths are present, and there are two anterior and three posterior rows of denticles. The vent tube is dextral. The spiracle is sinistral and lies well below the midline. The dorsal

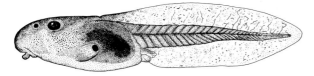

Fig. 55. Tadpole of *Bufo marinus* (KU 104115), 13 mm TL; Santa Cruz Barillas, Huehuetenango, Guatemala.

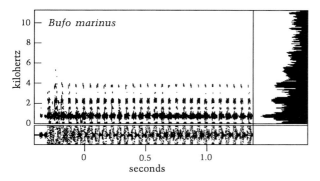

Fig. 56. Advertisement call of *Bufo marinus*, recorded 15 July 1992, Cobá, Quintana Roo, Mexico.

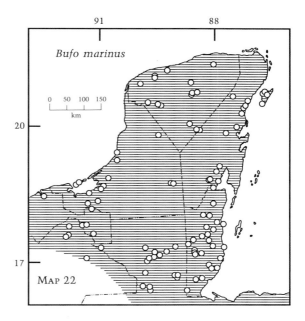

MAP 22

and ventral fins are of approximately equal depth, and the former extends onto the posterior surface of the body. The length of the body is about 2.5 times the maximum depth of the tail. The dorsum, venter, and caudal musculature are all uniform brown or black. The caudal fins are tan or gray.

VOCALIZATION   The advertisement call of *B. marinus* is a protracted, low-pitched trill with a dominant frequency of between 650 and 800 Hz and a pulse rate of about 15 to 20 per second. The call is given at irregular intervals, and the duration of the call may vary from 2 to many seconds (Fig. 56).

SIMILAR SPECIES   The much smaller *B. valliceps* has a small parotoid gland—less than twice the diameter of the eye (Fig. 54A,B)—possesses a posterolateral row of enlarged warts, and lacks a distinct tarsal fold.

DISTRIBUTION   *Bufo marinus* occurs at low to moderate elevations on the Atlantic slope from southern Texas and the Pacific slope from southern Sonora, south through Mexico and Central America to central Brazil. This species has been introduced into southern Florida, many islands in the West Indies, Oahu, the Philippines, Papua–New Guinea, and Australia. In the Yucatán Peninsula the species is pan-peninsular (Map 22).

NATURAL HISTORY   This is primarily a toad of open habitats such as savannas and secondary forests; it is uncommon in or completely absent from closed-canopy forests. Over much of its range *B. marinus* has become a human commensal, and it is now very abundant in and around human habitations. Throughout the Yucatán Peninsula these toads congregate beneath streetlights and feed on the insects attracted to the lights. They are often seen on roads at night, especially following rains, and can easily be mistaken for small boulders.

Marine toads are nocturnal, and they consume a wide variety of invertebrate and vertebrate prey. Virtually any animal that can be taken into the mouth can become a prey item, including small conspecifics. In Nicaragua, Noble (1918:333) found mostly cockroaches in the stomachs of individuals collected in villages. In southern Florida the diet of *B. marinus* includes canned pet food, overripe avocados, and broccoli (Alexander, 1964). Zug et al. (1975) reported that in Papua–New Guinea this species consumes plant material when animal prey is unavailable.

Zug and Zug (1979) studied the natural history of *B. marinus* in Panama and summarized information on other native populations. The females in Panama become reproductively mature at a snout-vent length of about 90 to 100 mm; the males are mature at about 85 to 95 mm. Most Middle American populations of *B. marinus* exhibit a bimodal reproductive pattern, with peaks in the dry season and the wet season. Barbour and Cole (1906:154) found the species breeding in February at Chichén Itzá, and Stuart (1935:36) found tadpoles and juveniles in central El Petén in early May. Schmidt (1941:481) reported that marine toads breed in February in Belize, and Duellman (1963:221) found breeding toads in March and July at Chinajá, Alta Verapaz. I have heard calling males throughout the rainy season, including a chorus on Isla Cozumel in October. A protracted, perhaps bimodal or continuous, pattern of breeding is thus indicated. The males call from the edges of temporary or permanent bodies of water. Male-male competition for females can be intense and may involve attempts by competing males to supplant amplectant males (J. C. Lee, 1986:208). Amplexus is axillary. The females produce many thousands of eggs, which they deposit in the water as long strings. The eggs hatch in one and a half to four days, and the larvae complete metamorphosis in one to two months (Zug and Zug, 1979:11).

The skin of this species is particularly well supplied with granular poison glands. The parotoid glands produce a toxic secretion with digitalis-like pharmacological properties. Dogs have been known to die from biting these toads, and Dodds (1923:6) reported that the natives of eastern Sinaloa used the skin secretions to poison their arrow tips. W. T. Allen and Neill (1956) recorded instances in which handling *B. marinus*, or even being near them, brought on headaches, nausea, and even vomiting in humans; and Dioscoro (1952:282) reported that a man died after eating three toads that he mistook for edible frogs. See "Ethnoherpetology in the Yucatán Peninsula" (in this volume) for a discussion of the psychoactive properties of the secretions of *B. marinus* and their possible ritual use by the ancient Maya.

ETYMOLOGY   The specific name, *marinus*, Latin for "of the sea," reflects Linnaeus's erroneous belief that this species lived both on the land and in the sea.

COMMENT   For many years the name *B. horribilis* was applied to Mexican populations, and some of the early literature will be found under that name. Although the Mexican populations have been treated as subspecifically distinct—and the name *B. m. horribilis* applied to them—Easteal (1986) concluded that no subspecies should be recognized.

Locality Records   Belize: Belize: Belize City (FMNH 4286–302, 4307–16, 4388, 4536–37; USNM 57599),
Crooked Tree Village (CM 112094), 11 km SW Hattieville (CM 90908), bet. Ladyville and Sandhill (CM 90936), 19.2 mi E Roaring Creek (KU 156372); Cayo: bet. Augustine and 12.7 mi S Cayo (UMMZ 129722–23), Belmopan (RWV photo), Cayo (UMMZ 70400, 75401, 75420–21), 36 mi S Cayo on Mountain Pine Ridge Rd. (UMMZ 129725–26), Cocquercot (UMMZ 75424, 75426), Georgeville (CM 91029–32, 91061–68), Mountain Pine Ridge (MCZ 37907–12), San Ignacio (UMMZ 75401, 75420–21; USNM 71244–45), San Luis (KU 156369–70), Sibun River at Hummingbird Hwy. (FMNH 203739–40), upper Raspaculo River basin (Stafford, 1991:12); Corozal: Corozal (MCZ 37903), S edge Corozal (CM 105969); Orange Walk: Hill Bank (MCZ 37904–6), Kate's Lagoon (FMNH 49017–19), Lamanai (ROM H12739, H12748); Stann Creek: All Pines (CM 9875), Mango Creek (MCZ 37913–14), near Monkey River, ca. 10 mi S Stann Creek (UMMZ 129729), Middlesex (FMNH 4271, 4273, 4303–6; UCM 25728, 25758–62, 25765–68, 45049–53, 45381–92, 48025–29), Stann Creek (UMMZ 129727); Toledo: Bladen Branch of Monkey River (CM 105912–14), Dolores (JCL sight record), 7.3 mi SW Golden Stream (KU 156371), 14 mi W Mango Creek (LSUMZ 11446–47), San Pedro Columbia (MCZ 37915–19), Union Camp, Columbia River Forest Reserve (USNM 319760–61). *Guatemala*: El Petén: 10 km NNW Chinajá (KU 55871), 11 km NNW Chinajá (KU 55870), near Flores (UMMZ 79044), Lago Petén Itzá, near San Benito (UMMZ 79049), E end Lago Petén Itzá (KU 156374; UMMZ 79034), Laguna Eckixil (UMMZ 79048), Laguna Perdida (UMMZ 79045), Laguna Rompido (AMNH 78270), La Libertad (UMMZ 75418; USNM 71246–56, 71260–77, 71436–44, 71446–60, 71462–66, 71469, 71471–73), near La Libertad (UMMZ 75457), 1 mi S La Libertad (UMMZ 79047), 5 mi NW La Libertad (UMMZ 79046), Pacomon (USNM 71325–29), Piedras Negras (USNM 116524–35), Poptún (UMMZ 117971), 1 km S Poptún (UMMZ 120473), 7 km NW Poptún (UMMZ 124386), 2 mi N Poptún (KU 156373), Remate (UMMZ 75419; USNM 220100), Río de la Pasión at San Diego (UMMZ 79038, 79043), Río de la Pasión at Río Santa Amelia (UMMZ 79040), Río de la Pasión at Tres Islas (UMMZ 90206), Río de la Pasión near Alta Verapaz border (UMMZ 79042), San Andrés (UMMZ 75402), Santa Ana Rd., S Flores (UMMZ 79039), Sayaxché (AMNH 78269), Sayaxché Arroyo (UMMZ 79037), Yaxhá (UMMZ 75417, 75425). *Mexico*: Campeche: Balchacaj (FMNH 112188, 112261–63, 112265–76, 112278–79, 112282, 115913; UIMNH 24786–92), near Chekubúl (JCL photo), Champotón (UMMZ 73138–41), 15 mi S Champotón (UMMZ 73144), Ciudad del Carmen (FMNH 112280–81, 112283–88, 112290, 118477; UIMNH 24783–84, 24793, 24795), 5 km ENE Ciudad del Carmen (KU 70986), 40 mi NE Emiliano Zapata (UTA A-2223–24, A-2226–27, A-2229–30), Encarna-

ción (H. M. Smith, 1938:10), Pacaitún (FMNH 36563), Pital (H. M. Smith, 1938:10), Santa Rosa Xtampak (JCL photo), Tres Brazos (FMNH 112183; UIMNH 24794, 24796), 3.3 mi W Xpujil (KU 156376–77), 5.2 km W Xpujil (EAL 2892); Chiapas: Monte Libano (MCZ 28212), Palenque (USNM 116518–22), 19.1 to 28.5 km N Pueblo Palenque (EAL 2903), 4 km SW Palenque (EAL 3317), rd. bet. Palenque and Palenque ruins (EAL 3321, 3333), San Juanito (FMNH 196086); Quintana Roo: 15.4 km N Akumal (EAL 2872), Bacalar (MZCIQRO 29), Lake Bacalar (LSUMZ 34038), Chetumal (FMNH 49020), 35 mi NE Chetumal (UMMZ 129724), Chunyaxché (Himmelstein, 1980:24), Cobá (JCL sight and acoustic records; MCZ 92551–61), 3 mi E Esmeralda (LACM 113897–98), 4 km NNE Felipe Carrillo Puerto (KU 70987), Hacienda Santa Rosa (UMMZ 113555), Isla Cozumel (CM 27582–94; UMMZ 76172; USNM 13907, 47571), S end Cozumel (UMMZ 87551–53), Cozumel, Chancanah (UIMNH 11304), Cozumel, San Miguel (UCM 15687–88; UMMZ 78554–55), Cozumel, 3.5 km N San Miguel (KU 70988), Cozumel, 14 to 14.5 km E San Miguel (CM 55812), 1.5 mi SE Presumida (UCM 45835), Tulum (Himmelstein, 1980: 24; UIMNH 11305–7), 5 mi inland from Vigía Chico (UMMZ 78556), 3.5 mi E jct. Hwys. 186 and 307 (KU 156378), 6.3 mi W jct. Hwys. 186 and 307 (KU 156379); Tabasco: Emiliano Zapata (EAL 1638; LSUMZ 44033–35), 8 km E Emiliano Zapata (EAL 1642), 4 to 6 mi S Frontera (UCM 27436–37), Tenosique (USNM 116523); Yucatán: Aguada Sayucil, 2.5 km S Libre Unión (CM 45225; UCM 15722–24), Bella Flor (MZFC 1801–2), Calcehtok (AMNH 33256; UMMZ 113554), Chichén Itzá (AMNH 33251, 33257–58; FMNH 36545, 36594, 115914; KU 70990; LACM 87748; MCZ 2624, 35765; UIMNH 24779; UMMZ 73133–35, 73203–6, 80890–95), Dzibilchaltún (FMNH 153406, 153418), 1.5–2.5 mi S Libre Unión (UCM 27445), 8 mi N Mérida (UMMZ 73142), Pisté (UMMZ 73136–37), 3.9 mi W Telchac (UMMZ 76173), Ticul (Ives, 1891: 461), 12 mi N Tizimín (UCM 48024), Tunkás (KU 156380), Yokat (AMNH 33252–55); no specific locality (FMNH 549; USNM 12288, 19280).

Bufo valliceps Wiegmann
(Figs. 54B, 57, 58, 236, 237; Map 23)

Bufo valliceps Wiegmann, 1833:657. SYNTYPES: ZMB 3525–27, 3532 (eight syntypes). TYPE LOCALITY: Mexico and Vera Cruz, Mexico; restricted to Veracruz, Veracruz, Mexico, by H. M. Smith and Taylor (1950b:351).

Gulf Coast toad; sapo, sapo común (Guatemala, Mexico); compopó (Kekchi Maya); chunte' (Lacandón Maya); much (Yucatec Maya).

DESCRIPTION   The males of this medium-sized toad reach an average snout-vent length of about 73 mm; the females are about 84 mm long (Fig. 236). The head is moderately depressed and scarcely distinct from the body in dorsal aspect. The limbs are short, and the forearm musculature is robust, especially in males. The fingers are devoid of webbing, whereas the toes are webbed at their bases. There is no tarsal fold. The tips of the digits are not expanded. A series of conspicuous cranial crests is present on the dorsal surface of the head, and the parotoid glands are relatively small, approximately the size of the eye (Fig. 54B). The dorsum is rough and covered with warts. A row of enlarged, pointed warts extends from the posterior margin of the parotoid gland posterolaterally to the groin region. The males have a single subgular vocal sac (Fig. 237).

These toads are highly variable in coloration. Some have a reddish ground color, others are predominantly gray, while still others are deep brown. Most have a light vertebral stripe and indistinct darker mottling on the lateral surfaces of the body and on the limbs. Usually a broad, indistinct light stripe extends from the posterior margin of the parotoid gland posterolaterally to the groin. The venter is light tan or gray, sometimes with dark spots and bars. In males the vocal sac is generally darker than the adjacent tissue.

TADPOLE   The body is globose in dorsal view and somewhat depressed in lateral aspect (Fig. 57). The snout is bluntly rounded, and the mouth is ventral. The close-set eyes are situated high on the head. There are finely serrated cornified jaw sheaths and two anterior and three posterior rows of denticles. The oral disk is indented laterally, and the fringing labial papillae are incomplete both dorsally and ventrally. The vent tube is dextral; the spiracle is sinistral and lies slightly below the level of the midline. The tail is slightly longer than the body, and the dorsal fin is noticeably deeper than the ventral fin and extends onto the posterior surface of the body. The body length is about 2.2 times the max-

Fig. 57. Tadpole of *Bufo valliceps* (UMRC 93-9), 22 mm TL; Suc Tuc, Campeche, Mexico.

imum tail depth. The dorsum is dark brown or black. The ventral surface of the body is lighter. The caudal musculature is dark brown or black with irregular light spots along the ventral margin. The caudal fins, especially the dorsal fin, are mottled with dark pigment.

VOCALIZATION   The males of *B. valliceps* emit a moderately high-pitched trill with a dominant frequency between 1,800 and 2,000 Hz and a pulse rate of about 40 to 50 per second. The calls are intermittent and average between 2 and 5 sec in duration (Fig. 58).

SIMILAR SPECIES   Size alone will distinguish adults of *B. valliceps* from the other toad in the Yucatán Peninsula, the much larger *B. marinus*, which also has a relatively enormous parotoid gland (Fig. 54A,B) and a distinct tarsal fold. *Physalaemus pustulosus* is much smaller, lacks cranial crests, and has a densely pustulate dorsum.

DISTRIBUTION   *Bufo valliceps* occurs at low and moderate elevations on the Atlantic slope from Louisiana and Texas south through the Gulf and Caribbean lowlands to Nicaragua, across the Isthmus of Tehauntepec to Oaxaca and Chiapas, and to Guatemala on the Pacific slope. It occurs throughout the Yucatán Peninsula (Map 23).

NATURAL HISTORY   This abundant toad occurs in virtually all habitats within the Yucatán Peninsula,

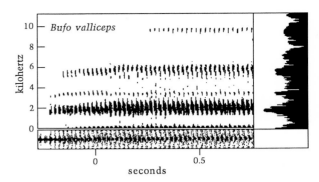

Fig. 58. Advertisement call of *Bufo valliceps*, recorded 2 June 1989, Maskall, Belize, Belize.

although it seems most common in open, nonforested situations. It commonly occurs in disturbed areas and in association with human habitations, but it is also frequently encountered at night on the floor of primary forest. W. E. Neill and Grubb (1971) reported that toads in central Texas, although predominantly terrestrial, were adept at climbing, and some individuals habitually used tree hollows 3 to 5 m above the ground as daytime retreats. Gulf Coast toads are nocturnal and feed largely on insects.

Despite their presumably noxious skin secretions, *Bufo valliceps* are common items in the diet of many snakes (e.g., *Drymobius margaritiferus*, *Xenodon rabdocephalus*). At Tikal, this species is preyed on by the great black hawk, *Buteogallus urubitinga* (Gerhardt et al. 1993:350).

Reproduction may occur throughout the summer but tends to coincide with the first heavy rains at the onset of the rainy season; however, Barbour and Cole (1906:154) reported breeding in February at Chichén Itzá, Yucatán. As is the case for many species of toads, reproduction in *B. valliceps* is "explosive" (Wells, 1977) in the sense that reproductive activity may be intense but restricted to one or a few nights. Large choruses of calling males establish themselves at the edges of temporary bodies of water. Amplexus is axillary, and males will indiscriminately clasp almost any moving object. Homosexual pairings are thus common. Eggs are released in long strings into the water, where they hatch and the tadpoles complete their development. J. C. Lee and Salzburg (1989) found evidence of a large-male mating advantage in *B. valliceps* at Chichén Itzá that they attributed to female choice. Wagner and Sullivan (1992) studied populations of this species in south-central Texas and concluded that the potential for sexual selection driven by female choice was high.

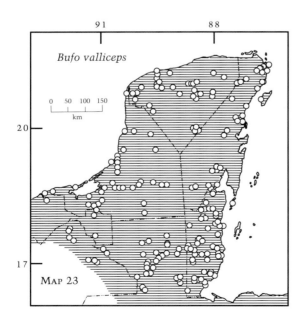

SUBSPECIES Subspecific status has been conferred on several geographical segments of *B. valliceps*, but Porter (1970:94.2) concluded that recognition of subspecies was unjustified (see Comment).

ETYMOLOGY The specific name, *valliceps*, is from the Latin *vallis*, "valley" or "hollow," and *ceps*, "head," presumably in reference to the deep depression between the cranial crests on the dorsal surface of the head.

COMMENT The literature on *B. valliceps* was reviewed by Porter (1970), who erroneously included specimens of *B. leutkenii* from southeastern Guatemala, El Salvador, western Nicaragua, and northwestern Costa Rica in his account (Savage, in D. R. Frost, 1985:52). Mendelson (1993) analyzed the morphology of populations from throughout Mexico and Central America and suggested that several species may be combined under the name *B. valliceps*. In 1994 Mendelson described *B. campbelli*, which is said to occur sympatrically with *B. valliceps* in southern Belize and in the vicinity of Chinajá, Guatemala.

Locality Records   *Belize*: Belize: Altun Ha (CM 105824; USNM 194953), Belize City (CM 9319, 90918, 111926–28; FMNH 4317–41, 49001–6; UMMZ 75427; KU 144918; USNM 26067, 59938), 7.8 km W Belize City (CM 90968–75), 10 mi NW Belize City (CM 105781), Burrell Boom Rd. at Belize River (CM 105786), Yarbourough Cemetery (USNM 204800–1), bet. Ladyville and Sandhill (CM 90934–35, 90937–38), Manatee (FMNH 3019), near Maskall (JCL photo), due W Maskall (CM 105751), 2.7 mi N Maskall (KU 156383), Rockstone Pond (AMNH 83599–600; UU 9301–15); Cayo: Augustine (MCZ 37956; UMMZ 80734), Belize-Cayo Rd., 0.25 mi W Mountain Pine Ridge Rd. (UMMZ 124702), 0.5 mi W Camalot (CM 105767), Cayo (FMNH 195629; UMMZ 70393), 4 mi S Cayo (MCZ 37955), 4 mi SW Cayo (UMMZ 124706), Chiquibul Branch, S Granos de Oro Camp (CM 112123), Cocquercot (UMMZ 75439), Cohune Ridge (UMMZ 80733), Georgetown (CM 90999–1000), 4 mi S Georgeville (CM 105707), Macal River at Guacamillo Bridge (CM 112143), 36 mi S Belize-Cayo Rd. on Mountain Pine Ridge Rd. (UMMZ 124701), bet. 36 and 49 mi S Belize-Cayo Rd. on Mountain Pine Ridge Rd. (UMMZ 124703), 50 mi S Belize-Cayo Rd. on Mountain Pine Ridge Rd. (UMMZ 124705), W side Mountain Pine Ridge (MCZ 37957–58), Río On (KU 157685), Roaring Creek (CM 112088), 6.6 mi SE Roaring Creek (KU 156382), San Ignacio (UMMZ 75428; USNM 71278), 5 mi N San Luis (KU 156381), 0.5 mi S San Luis

(CM 105753), upper Raspaculo River basin (Stafford, 1991:12); Corozal: Ambergris Cay, 17 km N, 6.5 km E San Pedro (CM 91101), Ambergris Cay, Mariah Reef (CM 91122–23), 3 mi S Chan Chen (JLK 426), Corozal (MCZ 37920–22), 3 mi S Corozal (MCZ 37923); Orange Walk: August Pine Ridge (USNM 194928), Gallon Jug (LSUMZ 9319–20; MCZ 37924–25, 37945–54), Guinea Grass Rd., 4 mi S Northern Hwy. (CM 105736–37, 105739), Hill Bank (MCZ 37943–44), Kate's Lagoon (FMNH 49010–13), Lamanai (ROM H12746–47, H12749–51), 14.3 mi NW Maskall (KU 156384–86), Orange Walk Town (KU 156387–89), Otro Benque (USNM 194088–89, 194110–13, 194950), Tower Hill (USNM 194834–37); Stann Creek: 2 mi SE Big Falls, Río Grand (CM 105895), Bokowina (FMNH 49007), N slope Cockscomb Mountains (CM 9874), Double Falls (FMNH 49009), Freetown (CM 9876–77), 5 mi SW Mango Creek (MCZ 37979), Melinda Forest Station (UU 9444), Middlesex (FMNH 4343–53; UCM 25763–64, 25906–7, 45054–55, 45393, 48030–32), Silk Grass (FMNH 49008), Southern Hwy. 7 mi S Hummingbird Hwy. (UMMZ 124704), Southern Hwy. 10 mi S Hummingbird Hwy. (UMMZ 124707), Twelve-Mile Station on Stann Creek Railroad (FMNH 4342), 3 mi S Waha Leaf Creek (MCZ 37959–66), 4 mi S Waha Leaf Creek (MCZ 37967–78); Toledo: 3 mi S Bladen Branch (LSUMZ 9321–22), Blue Creek (RWV photo), Columbia Branch Camp (W. T. Neill, 1965:81), Columbia Forest Reserve (CM 105856, 105858), Columbia River Forest Reserve (USNM 319760–61), Dolores (JCL sight record), Old Toledo Settlement (W. T. Neill, 1965:81), Punta Gorda (W. T. Neill, 1965:81), jct. Río Grand and Southern Hwy. (MCZ 93258), San Pedro Columbia (MCZ 37991–99), 2 mi W Swasey Branch (MCZ 37980–82), 3 mi W Swasey Branch (MCZ 37983), bet. Swasey Branch and Bladen Branch (MCZ 37984–90). *Guatemala*: El Petén: Altar de Sacrificios (AMNH 78275–76), Arroyo San Martin (UMMZ 79028), Chuntuquí (USNM 71279–81), 8 km NNW Chinajá (KU 55873–86), 10 km NNW Chinajá (KU 55887–90), 11 km NNW Chinajá (KU 55891–99), 16 km NNW Chinajá (KU 55900–16), 20 km NNW Chinajá (KU 58377–86), 30 km NNW Chinajá (KU 58376), 15 km NW Chinajá (KU 55917–18), 8.6 mi W El Cruce (KU 156415), 34.6 mi E El Cruce (KU 156422), El Paso de Caballo (UMMZ 79030), 1.7 mi SW Flores (KU 156404–5), Isla de Pato (AMNH 78277), E end Lago Petén Itzá (KU 156421), Laguna Rompido (AMNH 78271–73), Laguneta Ixcoche (AMNH 78274), N shore Lake Yaxhá (UTEP 6017), La Libertad (USNM 71284–324), vicinity La Libertad (UMMZ 75430–31), near La Libertad (UMMZ 75432–33), 1.9 mi S La Libertad (KU 156409–13), 15 km SE La Libertad (KU 55919–20, 58387–95), Las Cañas (CM 58227–30), Pacomon (USNM 71282), Paso Caballos (MCZ 21440–41), Piedras Negras (FMNH 122468, 122470, 122472, 122476, 179152; UIMNH 14372–78; USNM 116973–80), 5 mi

S Piedras Negras (USNM 11681–83), Poptún (UMMZ 120471, 130054), 1 km W Poptún (UMMZ 120472), 1 km E Poptún (UMMZ 124383), 7 km NW Poptún (UMMZ 124384), 10 km NW Poptún (UMMZ 124385), 4 mi N Poptún (KU 156396–403), Remate (USNM 71283), 13.7 mi N Río de la Pasión (KU 156406), Río de la Pasión, 13 mi above Sayaxché (UMMZ 79027), Río de la Pasión at Tres Islas (UMMZ 79029), 1 mi W Ruinas Seibal (KU 156407–8), Sacluc (USNM 25138), San Andrés (UMMZ 75432), Santa Cruz (UMMZ 75429), Sayaxché (KU 57142–43; UCM 22143–58), Tikal (AMNH uncat.; FMNH 109778–80; UF 13403–17, 24562–70, 24572–76; UIMNH 52521–23; UMMZ 117972–74, 120468, 120470, 126453, 130053), 2–3 km SW Tikal (UMMZ 120469), 3 mi S Tikal (KU 156416–20), Uaxactún (AMNH 53588–93; KU 156390–95; UMMZ 70394–99; UMRC 78-35), Yalpemech (FMNH 40933), Zotz (UMMZ 75438). *Mexico*: Campeche: Aguada Mocu (FMNH 36564), Balchacaj (UIMNH 25251–63), Becan (UMMZ 76114–15; UWZH 20523, 20529, 20535), Campeche (H. M. Smith, 1938:11), 21 mi E Campeche (UIMNH 86275–313), 53 mi SW Campeche (EAL 1196), Champotón (UMMZ 73127, 73129–30), 5 km S Champotón (KU 70991–71002), 14 km S Champotón (KU 71003), 35.8 mi S Champotón (EAL 1652), 37.6 mi S Champotón (EAL 1650), Chuina (KU 75038–44), Ciudad del Carmen (UCM 15811, 18178–86, 20516–29; UIMNH 25265–67, 56440–41; UMMZ 83549), 13 km N Concepción (KU 75035), Dzibalchén (KU 75234–37), 30.8 mi NE Emiliano Zapata (EAL 1645), 40 mi NE Emiliano Zapata (UTA A-2225, A-2228, A-2231), 65.9 km NE Emiliano Zapata (EAL 2911), 79.9 km NE Emiliano Zapata (EAL 2913), Encarnación (UIMNH 25242–50), 7.5 km W Escárcega (KU 71004–21), 1 km W Escárcega (KU 71022–33), 5 mi W Escárcega (UCM 27446–51, 27453–65, 27478–80), 13 km W, 1 km N Escárcega (KU 71034–35), 3 km E Escárcega (KU 75008), 46 mi E Escárcega (UCM 27470–77), 54 mi E Escárcega (UCM 27466–69), 3 km N Hopelchén (KU 75231–33), Laguna Chumpich (KU 75036–37), Laguna Silvituc (KU 75045–56), 10 km E Laguna Silvituc (KU 75034), 56.6 km SW Mamantel (EAL 2925), Matamoros (FMNH 36565), Pital (UIMNH 25241), San José Carpizo (UMMZ 99868), 46 mi E Silvituc (CM 40087–88) Suc Tuc (UMRC 93-9), Tres Brazos (UIMNH 25264), 11.4 mi W Xpujil (KU 156423–24); Chiapas: El Censo (MCZ 28251), bet. El Censo and Monte Libano (MCZ 28259–63), bet. Laguna Ocotal and El Censo (MCZ 28240–44), Monte Libano (MCZ 28213–16), Palenque (FMNH 122483; MZFC 1209–11; USNM 116960–64, 116966–72), 13 mi SE Palenque (LSUMZ 36323–27), 19.1 to 28.5 km N Pueblo Palenque (EAL 2904), Palenque–Pueblo Palenque Rd. (EAL 3332, 3340), Palenque ruins (EAL 3640; UIMNH 11308–21, 14381–88), San Juanito (FMNH 122469, 122484; UIMNH 14389–92, 49106–8); Quintana Roo: 5.2 km N Akumal (EAL 2874), 6.8 mi N Bacalar (KU 156425), 10 mi N Bacalar (LSUMZ 33253–57), 10 mi W Bacalar (LSUMZ 33258–70), Cancún (Himmelstein, 1980:24), 40 to 70 km S Cancún on Hwy. 307 (UTA A-23525–26), 3 km E Caobas (KU 75058), Chetumal (CM 45226), 86 km W Chetumal (KU 75057), Chunyaxché (Himmelstein, 1980:24; MZFC 3393, 3415), Cobá (FMNH 26959), Estero Franco, rd. to Río Hondo (MZCIQRO 51–54), 4 km NNE Felipe Carrillo Puerto (KU 71054–55), 5 km NNE Felipe Carrillo Puerto (KU 71056), 10 km NNE Felipe Carrillo Puerto (KU 71057–58), 88.9 km NE Felipe Carrillo Puerto (EAL 2877), Isla Cozumel, 12 km SW San Miguel (CM 41315), Isla Mujeres (UMMZ 78550), 4 mi S Las Palmas (UCM 39067–74), 5 mi S Las Palmas (UCM 39075), 12.2 km SW Leona Vicario (EAL 2849), 13.4 mi SW Limones (KU 156426–28), 1.5 mi E Presumida (UCM 27483–84), Pueblo Nuevo X-Can (KU 71036–50), 9–10 mi E Pueblo Nuevo X-Can (UCM 27485–86, 27488–90), Puerto Juárez (Himmelstein, 1980:24), 4 km WSW Puerto Juárez (KU 71051), 7 km W Puerto Juárez (KU 71052), 8 km W Puerto Juárez (KU 71053), 17 km S Puerto Juárez (EAL 2855), 22 km SW Puerto Juárez (EAL 2870), 25 km SW Puerto Juárez (EAL 2852), Puerto Morelos (Himmelstein, 1980:24), 1 km W Puerto Morelos (UCM 39064–66), 5 mi W, 10 mi S Puerto Morelos (UU 9274), Punta Herrero (MZCIQRO 39), Tulum (LSUMZ 33271), 25.8 mi SW Tulum (KU 156429), 27.3 km NE X-Can (EAL 2848), 6.8 mi W jct. Hwys. 186 and 307 (KU 156431); Tabasco: Frontera (USNM 37747), 4 to 6 mi S Frontera (UCM 27502–4), 10 mi E Frontera (UIMNH 86265–66), Tenosique (UIMNH 10006, 14379–80; USNM 116986); Yucatán: Bella Flor (MZFC 1799–1800), 5.4 km E Bella Flor (JCL photo), 20 km W Bella Flor (TU 19812), Calcehtok (UMMZ 153618), Celestún (KU 156445–54), Chichén Itzá (FMNH 26956–58, 36593; KU 71059–61; MCZ 2511, 14790; UMMZ 73126; UIMNH 25216, 73128, 73201, 83110; UMRC 85-19; UU 9270–73), 5 mi S Chichén Itzá (UMMZ 73125), 12 km E Chichén Itzá (KU 71062), Chunchucmíl (MZFC 1795–96), 18.4 km N Chunchucmíl (TU 19813), Culuba, 28 km E Sucopo (FMNH 36566), Dzibilchaltún (FMNH 153405, 153407–9), 5 km E Dziuché (CM 45261), 3 mi E Esmeralda (LACM 114013–17), 12.3 mi E Izamal (KU 156439, 156441), 16.8 mi E Izamal (KU 156441), 1.5 mi S Libre Unión (UCM 15826–27, 28096), 1.2 to 2 mi S Libre Unión (UCM 27532–37), Mérida (FMNH 26951–52, 40653–58; TNHC 33224; UCM 39076; USNM 12292), 2 mi S Mérida (AMNH 73364), 14 km SE Mérida (UMMZ 73131), 14 km N, 2 km E Mérida (UMMZ 73202), Pisté (KU 71063; UCM 15828; UMMZ 73124), 1.8 km W Pisté (KU 71064), 4.5 km W Pisté (KU 71065), 17 km N Pisté (KU 75195), Progreso (FMNH 99350, 110848; UIMNH 25207–15, 25217–24), 3 mi S Progreso (UCM 39077), 2.3 mi S, 1.9 mi E Santa Rosa (KU 156431–34), near Tekantó (Ives, 1891:461), Tekom (FMNH 49015–16), 3 mi N Telchac (UCM

27507–8), 12 mi N Tizimín (UCM 27509–27), 12.25 mi N Tizimín (UCM 27528–31), 6.5 mi W Tunkás (KU 156438), 7.1 mi W Tunkás (KU 156442), Uxmal (UCM 18177; USNM 238378), Valladolid (FMNH 26953–55), Xocchel (KU 156435–37), 4.5 km E Yokdzonot (KU 71066); no specific locality (FMNH 49014).

Family Hylidae (Treefrogs)

Representatives of this very large and heterogeneous family occur throughout much of North, Central, and South America, the West Indies, the Australo-Papuan region, North Africa, and Eurasia. Hylid frogs typically have rounded, expanded adhesive disks at the tips of their digits, an intercalary cartilage between the penultimate and terminal phalanges, smooth skin, and moderately long limbs. Amplexus is generally axillary. Most hylids are arboreal, although some are terrestrial and a few are fossorial. Duellman (1993) recognized 719 species in 39 genera. Eleven species of treefrogs belonging to 6 genera occur in the Yucatán Peninsula. All are more or less arboreal. The most recent comprehensive work on hylid frogs of Middle America is by Duellman (1970).

Key to the Genera of the Family Hylidae

1. Iris red, pupil vertically elliptical; palpebral membrane reticulate (Fig. 59); dorsum usually green (blue in preservative)..*Agalychnis*
   Iris not red, pupil horizontally elliptical; palpebral membrane clear; dorsal coloration variable 2

2. Prenasal and maxillary bones expanded to form a conspicuous labial shelf (Fig. 88) ....
   ....*Triprion*
   Prenasal and maxillary bones not expanded to form a labial shelf 3

3. Skin of dorsum glandular, males with paired vocal sacs situated behind angle of jaws ....
   ....*Phrynohyas*
   Skin of dorsum smooth; males with unpaired vocal sacs or, if paired, situated below and anterior to angle of jaws 4

4. Vocal sacs of males paired; adult SVL greater than 45 mm ....*Smilisca*
   Vocal sacs of males unpaired; adult SVL less than 45 mm 5

5. Head narrow, snout projecting shelflike beyond lower jaw (Fig. 80) ....*Scinax*
   Head broad, snout not projecting shelflike beyond lower jaw........................*Hyla*

Clave para los Géneros de la Familia Hylidae

1. Iris de color rojo, pupila verticalmente elíptica; membrana palpebral reticulada (Fig. 59); dorso usualmente de color verde (azul en conservador) ....*Agalychnis*
   Iris no de color rojo, pupila horizontalmente elíptica; membrana palpebral clara; coloración del dorso variable..2

2. Los huesos prenasal y maxilar expandidos formando una especie de espátula labial (Fig. 88)
   ....*Triprion*
   Los huesos prenasal y maxilar no están expandidos formando una especie de espátula labial
  3

3. La piel del dorso glandular; los machos con sacos gulares pareados situados por detrás del ángulo de la mandíbula..*Phrynohyas*
   La piel del dorso lisa; los machos sin sacos gulares pareados, o si están pareados, situados por abajo y anteriores al ángulo de la mandíbula 4

4. Sacos bucales pareados en los machos; los adultos mayores a 45 mm de LHC.......*Smilisca*
   Sacos bucales no pareados en los machos; los adultos menores a 45 mm de LHC..........5

5. Cabeza angosta, la punta de la maxila se proyecta hacia adelante de la mandíbula (Fig. 80)
   ....*Scinax*
   Cabeza ancha; la punta de la maxila no se proyecta hacia adelante de la mandíbula.....*Hyla*

Genus *Agalychnis* (Leaf Frogs)

These medium to large treefrogs are green above and have variously colored flanks. The iris is red, yellow, or orange, and the pupil is vertically elliptical. Leaf frogs are slender and rather delicate, with long, thin limbs and partially webbed hands and feet. The tips of the digits support expanded disks, and the thumb is opposable. Members of this genus typically inhabit forests at low and intermediate elevations from central Veracruz and Oaxaca through Central America to Ecuador. There are eight species in the genus; two occur in the Yucatán Peninsula. Funkhouser (1957) reviewed the species of *Agalychnis* as part of her review of the genus *Phyllomedusa*, Savage and Heyer (1967, 1969) treated the species of *Agalychnis* in Costa Rica, and Duellman (1970) provided comprehensive coverage of the Middle American species. *Agalychnis* is from the Greek *aga*, an intensive prefix, and *lychnis*, the name of a plant with scarlet flowers, in reference to the bright red eyes of some members of the genus.

Key to the Species of the Genus *Agalychnis*

Flanks purple or bluish with vertical light bars . . . . *Agalychnis callidryas*

Flanks orange, without vertical bars . . . . *Agalychnis moreletii*

Clave para las Especies del Género *Agalychnis*

Los flancos de color púrpura o azulado, con barras claras verticales . . . . . . *Agalychnis callidryas*

Los flancos de color anaranjado, sin barras verticales . . . . *Agalychnis moreletii*

Agalychnis callidryas (Cope)
(Figs. 59–62, 238; Map 24)

Hyla callidryas Cope, 1862b:359. HOLOTYPE: ANSP 2091. TYPE LOCALITY: Darien, Panama; corrected to Córdoba, Veracruz, Mexico, by H. M. Smith and Taylor (1950b:347), but that correction considered unjustified by Duellman (1970:102).

Red-eyed leaf frog (Belize); rana verde, rana arbórea (Guatemala, Mexico); t'zu pak (Lacandón Maya); quech yaax, yaxmuch (Yucatec Maya).

DESCRIPTION   These are slender, delicate treefrogs with long, thin appendages, partially webbed hands and feet, and expanded toe disks (Fig. 238). The males average about 45 to 55 mm in snout-vent length, and the females are about 10 mm longer. The head is somewhat depressed, the canthus rostralis is rounded, and the loreal region is flat. The tympanum is distinct and about half the diameter of the eye, and its dorsal and posterior margins are covered by a fold of skin. In dorsal aspect the snout is truncate; in lateral view it slopes forward to the upper margin of the jaw. The eyes are large and protruding, the pupil is vertically elliptical, and the palpebral membrane is reticulate (Fig. 59). The iris is bright red.

The dorsal surfaces of the head, body, forearms, and hind limbs are bright green. Many specimens have a few to many white spots scattered over the surface of the back. The venter is white or cream. The flanks are bluish or purplish with a series of yellow or cream vertical bars. The anterior and posterior surfaces of the limbs and the skin between the toes are yellowish or orange.

TADPOLE   The tadpole of *A. callidryas* is moderately streamlined and has a relatively low dorsal fin (Fig. 60). The body is 1.7 times longer than wide, and the tail is about twice the length of the body. The

Fig. 59. Lateral view of the head of *Agalychnis callidryas* (UMRC 79-257), 41 mm SVL, showing the vertically elliptical pupil and the reticulate palpebral membrane; 8 km N Felipe Carrillo Puerto, Quintana Roo, Mexico.

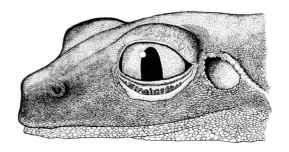

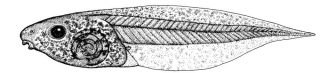

Fig. 60. Tadpole of *Agalychnis callidryas* (KU 60006), 29 mm TL; Toocog, El Petén, Guatemala.

snout is broadly rounded in dorsal view and truncate in lateral aspect. The eyes are relatively small, widely spaced, and directed laterally. The mouth is directed anteroventrally. The jaw sheaths are finely serrated, and there are two anterior and three posterior rows of denticles, although the third row may be abbreviated. The oral disk is not indented laterally, and the surrounding labial papillae are discontinuous dorsally. The vent tube is dextral to the caudal fin. The spiracle is sinistral and lies low on the body, well below the midline. The maximum depth of the body approximates that of the tail. The dorsal fin extends well onto the body, and its depth is conspicuously less than that of the ventral fin. The caudal musculature extends the length of the tail, which terminates as a fine point. The dorsal and lateral surfaces of the body are olive gray; those of the venter are lighter and may have golden flecks. The caudal musculature is tan, and the fins are variously translucent or reticulate with dark pigment.

VOCALIZATION The advertisement call, generally a single note described variously as *chock* (Duellman, 1970:108), *chack* (Pyburn, 1970:210), or a loud kiss, is given every 10 to 60 sec or so. Sometimes a double note—two notes given in rapid succession—is produced. The calls generally have a pulse rate of about 175 to 200 per second, and a note duration of approximately 40 msec. The fundamental frequency is about 180 Hz, and the dominant frequency averages between 1,700 and 1,900 Hz (Fig. 61).

SIMILAR SPECIES The only other frog in the Yucatán Peninsula with red eyes is *A. moreletii*, which has orange flanks without vertical light bars.

DISTRIBUTION The red-eyed treefrog occurs at low and moderate elevations from central Veracruz on the Caribbean slope and from Nicaragua on the Pacific slope south to eastern Panama. The species is distributed through the base of the Yucatán Peninsula. It extends northward in Quintana Roo and

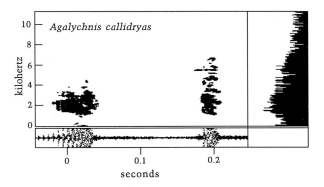

Fig. 61. Advertisement call of *Agalychnis callidryas*, recorded 18 October 1988, 8 km S Chekubúl, Campeche, Mexico.

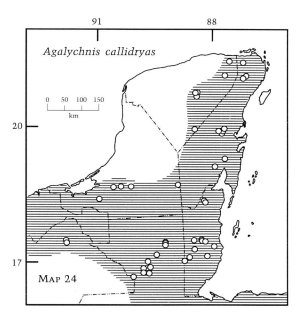

eastern Yucatán, but it is apparently absent from the arid northwest corner of the peninsula (Map 24).

NATURAL HISTORY These common and colorful frogs are nocturnal inhabitants of lowland tropical forests. They are arboreal and generally move through the vegetation using slow, graceful, hand-over-hand movements. During the dry season they hide in arboreal vegetation such as bromeliads and palm fronds (Stuart, 1958:18). Reproduction is initiated by the onset of the rainy season, and the males congregate in choruses of a few to hundreds and call from trees and shrubs surrounding temporary bodies of water. Calling generally begins about dusk, and the males usually sit perpendicular to the axis of the stem or twig from which they are calling. The fe-

Fig. 62. Egg clutch of *Agalychnis callidryas*; 8.2 km N Felipe Carrillo Puerto, Quintana Roo, Mexico.

males are attracted by the vocalizations and approach the males. During the breeding season, males and females are known to descend rapidly from high in trees to lower vegetation by "parachuting." The animal makes a controlled leap, holding the limbs, toe pads, and webbing parallel to the ground, and descends at an angle of up to 45° (Pyburn, 1964; Roberts, 1994:196). Amplexus is axillary, and the pale green eggs, about 20 to 50 per clutch, are deposited on vegetation overhanging the water (Fig. 62). Pyburn (1970:211) observed breeding in southern Veracruz and reported that amplectant females descend to the water and fill their bladders before ascending to oviposit. As eggs are deposited, they are hydrated by water released from the female's bladder. Females deposit multiple clutches, descending to fill the bladder before each oviposition. Pyburn (1970:212) observed male-male aggression in which nonamplectant males attempted to displace amplectant males. In some instances more than one male fertilized a single egg clutch. On hatching, the larvae drop into the water, where they complete their development. The tadpoles of *A. callidryas* are known to feed on the larvae of other species of frogs (Ryan, 1985:47).

SUBSPECIES Funkhouser (1957:34) used differences in size and proportions to distinguish two subspecies of *A. callidryas*, of which *A. c. taylori* occurs in the Yucatán Peninsula. Savage and Heyer (1967) argued against recognizing subspecies. Duellman (1970:111) noted that northern, central, and southern segments are recognizable within *A. callidryas* but declined to afford them nomen-

clatural recognition pending the acquisition of material from critical areas.

ETYMOLOGY The specific name, *callidryas*, is from the Greek *calli-*, a prefix meaning "beauty," and *dryas*, a deity or nymph of the woods.

Locality Records Belize: Cayo: 1 mi S Belmopan (CM 112153–55), 3 mi S Belmopan (CM 112178), Blue Hole (JCL photo), 2.8 mi W Blue Hole (KU 156456–57), Cohune Ridge (UMMZ 80743), 15.4 mi E Georgeville (KU 156455), Mountain Pine Ridge Rd., 36 to 49 mi S Belize-Cayo Rd. (UMMZ 124708–9), Valentin (UMMZ 80743); Orange Walk: Orange Walk Town (KU 156458–62), Otro Benque (USNM 194096–102, 194908); Stann Creek: Cockscomb Basin Wildlife Sanctuary (JCL photo), 19 mi W Stann Creek (JLK 429). *Guatemala*: El Petén: Altar de Sacrificios (AMNH 56240), 3 km SE La Libertad (KU 57905–11), 15 km SE La Libertad (KU 57892–904, 57920), 6.1 mi N Río de la Pasión (KU 156463), 1 mi W Ruinas Seibal (KU 156464), Santa Elena (UMRC 79-259), Sayaxché (UCM 22176), 5 km E Sayaxché (UMRC 79-260), Tikal (UF 24554; KU 144919–20; UMMZ 117986, 117997, 120481, 130048), 3.1 km S Tikal (UMRC 85-10–12), 3 mi S Tikal (KU 156469–81), 5.9 mi S Tikal (KU 156465–68). *Mexico*: Campeche: 7.5 km W Escárcega (KU 71327–31), Matamoros (FMNH 36556), Pacaitún (FMNH 36446), Tuxpeña Camp (UMMZ 73236); Chiapas: 15 km S Palenque (JCL photo), 10 to 15 mi S Palenque (LSUMZ 38165); Quintana Roo: 6 mi N Bacalar (KU 156482–85), 3.7 mi NE Felipe Carrillo Puerto (KU 156488–93), 5.9 km NE Felipe Carrillo Puerto (KU 171234–35), 6 to 8 km NE Felipe Carrillo Puerto (UMRC 79-257), 8.2 km N Felipe Carrillo Puerto (UMRC 79-258), 13.3 km NE Felipe Carrillo Puerto (KU 171236–42), Laguna Chacanbacab (CM 45262), 2 mi SW Leona Vicario (KU 156495), 8.9 mi NE Leona Vicario (KU 156494), 13.4 mi N Limones (KU 156486–87), 1.5 mi E Presumida (UCM 27635–40, 28111), 2.6 km S Solferino (UMRC 79-256); Tabasco: La Venta (USNM 117557–58); Yucatán: Chichén Itzá (FMNH 26925–28, 36553, 36555, 49069–70; UMMZ 73207), 1.5 mi E Chichén Itzá (UMMZ 73241), 6.5 mi S Chichén Itzá (UMMZ 73183–87, 80450), 12.5 km N Colonia Yucatán (JCL sight record), Culubá, 28 km E Sucopo (FMNH 36554).

Agalychnis moreletii (A. Duméril)
(Figs. 63, 64, 239; Map 25)

Hyla moreletii A. H. A. Duméril, 1853:169. SYNTYPES: MNHNP 428 (two syntypes). TYPE LOCALITY: Vera-Paz; restricted by H. M. Smith and Taylor (1950b:317) to Cobán, Alta Verapaz, Guatemala.

Morelet's leaf frog; escuerzo, rana arbórea (Mexico); quech yaax (Yucatec Maya).

DESCRIPTION The males of this moderately large *Agalychnis* average between 55 and 60 mm in snout-vent length, the females are about 70 to 80 mm long. These rather slender frogs are somewhat more robust than *A. callidryas* (Fig. 239). The head is moderately depressed, the canthus rostralis is rounded, and the loreal region is slightly concave. In lateral view the snout slopes forward to the margin of the upper jaw. The tympanum is distinct and slightly more than half the diameter of the eye; its dorsal and posterior margins are overlaid with skin. The limbs are long and slender. The fingers and toes are extensively webbed, and their tips are expanded into large adhesive disks. The eyes are large and protruding with dark red irises, and the pupils are vertically elliptical. The palpebral membrane is reticulate.

The dorsal surface of the head, body, and hind limbs ranges from dark to light green. Some specimens have scattered white flecks on the dorsal surface of the body. The flanks, inner surfaces of the appendages, and the webbing between the first three fingers and the first four toes are orange. The venter and throat are white, cream, or yellowish.

TADPOLE These are robust tadpoles with a body that is deeper than broad (Fig. 63). The tail is about 1.5 to 2 times the body length, and about half as deep as long. The caudal musculature is well developed, the tail is acuminate, and the dorsal fin does not extend onto the body. The spiracle is ventrolateral and sinistral, and the vent tube opens to the right of the caudal fin. The mouthparts are bordered by papillae, except on the dorsal surface of the upper lip, which is bare. The jaw sheaths are well developed with serrated margins. There are two upper and three lower rows of denticles. Stuart (1948:38) described tadpoles from Alta Verapaz as purplish brown in life, with tail fins clear or slightly darkened on the posterior half.

Fig. 63. Tadpole of *Agalychnis moreletii* (KU 68531), 54 mm TL; 1 km W Cobán, Alta Verapaz, Guatemala.

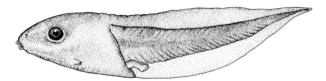

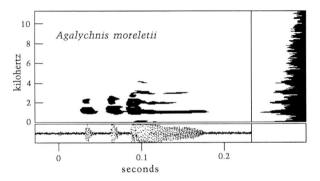

Fig. 64. Advertisement call of *Agalychnis moreletii*, recorded 18 July 1960, Finca Chicoyou, Alta Verapaz, Guatemala.

VOCALIZATION As described by Duellman (1970:115), the advertisement call of males is a single *wor-or-orp* given at intervals of one to several minutes, with a pulse rate of 55 to 61 per second, a fundamental frequency of 160 to 185 Hz, and a dominant frequency of 1,110 to 1,260 Hz (Fig. 64).

SIMILAR SPECIES The only other frog in the Yucatán Peninsula with a red iris, *A. callidryas*, has purple or blue flanks with light vertical bars.

DISTRIBUTION *Agalychnis moreletii* occurs at moderate elevations from central Veracruz on the Gulf slope and Guerrero on the Pacific slope eastward to Honduras and El Salvador. In the Yucatán Peninsula the species is known only from the vicinity of the Maya Mountains of Belize (Map 25).

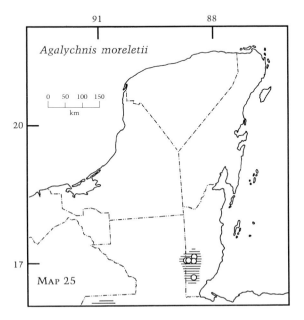

NATURAL HISTORY This uncommon frog is a strictly arboreal inhabitant of moist montane forests. Breeding occurs in ponds and temporary impoundments. According to Stuart (1948:36), in Alta Verapaz these frogs have a protracted breeding season during the summer months. Amplexus is axillary. The eggs, which bear a green pigment, are deposited in clutches of about 50 to 75 on vegetation or rocks overhanging water. On hatching the larvae drop into the water, where they complete their development. Presumably these frogs feed on invertebrates.

ETYMOLOGY The specific name, *moreletii*, is a patronym that honors Pierre-Marie Arthur Morelet, who collected amphibians and reptiles in southern Mexico and Guatemala in 1847 and 1848.

Locality Records Belize: Cayo: Caracol (CMM photo), Chiquibul Branch, S Granos de Oro Camp (CM 112125), 3 mi from Millionario Camp (UMMZ 124711–12), Valentin (UMMZ 80744–46); Toledo: Gloria Camp, Columbia River Forest Reserve (USNM 319786); no specific locality (FMNH 27105; MCZ 110463–66).

Genus *Hyla* (Treefrogs)

These are the familiar arboreal treefrogs with expanded toe disks. The genus ranges throughout much of the New World and the Greater Antilles but is most diverse in the tropics of Middle and South America. The genus also occurs in Eurasia and North Africa. Duellman (1993) recognized 281 living species, of which 6 occur in the Yucatán Peninsula. *Hyla* may derive from the Doric Greek *hyla*, "a wood"; however, Stejneger (1907:75) claimed that the name derives from the vocative of Hylas, a lost friend of Hercules.

Key to the Species of the Genus *Hyla*

1. Small frogs, SVL generally less than 35 mm 2
   Larger frogs, SVL generally greater than 35 mm 5

2. Thighs mostly unpigmented; SVL generally greater than 22 mm 3
   Posterior surfaces of thighs pigmented; tiny frogs, SVL generally less than 22 mm . . . .
   . . . . *Hyla picta*

3. Dorsum yellowish or orangish tan without large brown blotches on cream or light tan background 4
   Dorsal pattern of one to several large brown blotches on cream or light tan background . . . . .
   . . . . *Hyla ebraccata*

4. Dorsal pattern a reticulum of fine dark lines and flecks against yellow or tan background; single subgular vocal sac in males; widespread throughout Yucatán Peninsula (Map 29) . . . . .
   . . . . *Hyla microcephala*
   Dorsal pattern uniform yellowish, yellow-orange, tan, or brown, with scattered dark flecks; males with paired subgular vocal sacs; Maya Mountains of Belize only (Map 26) . . . .
   . . . . *Hyla bromeliacia*

5. Dermal fringes present on lateral surfaces of appendages (Fig. 76); Maya Mountains of Belize only . . . . *Hyla valancifer*
   No dermal fringes on lateral surfaces of appendages (Fig. 69); widespread in Yucatán Peninsula . . . . *Hyla loquax*

Clave para las Especies del Género *Hyla*

1. Ranas de tamaño pequeño, generalmente menores a 35 mm de LHC 2
   Ranas de mayor tamaño, generalmente mayores a 35 mm de LHC 5

2. Los muslos en general sin pigmentación; ranas mayores a 22 mm de LHC 3
   La superficie posterior de los muslos pigmentada; ranas de tamaño muy pequeño, generalmente menores a 22 mm de LHC . . . . *Hyla picta*

3. El patrón de coloración dorsal amarillento o anaranjado bronceado sin manchas de color pardo sobre un fondo bronceado crema o claro 4

El patrón de coloración dorsal consiste de una a varias manchas de color pardo sobre un fondo bronceado crema o claro. . . . . *Hyla ebraccata*

4. El patrón de coloración dorsal consiste de un reticulado de líneas oscuras finas y flecos sobre un fondo amarillo o broceado; un saco bucal subgular único en los machos; organismos que se distribuyen ampliamente en la Península de Yucatán (Mapa 29). . . . . *Hyla microcephala*
El patrón de coloración dorsal uniformemente amarillo, amarillo anaranjado, bronceado, o pardo, con flecos oscuros esparcidos; sacos bucales subgulares pareados en los machos; organismos que se distribuyen solamente en las Montañas Maya de Belice (Mapa 26) . . . .
. . . . *Hyla bromeliacia*

5. Bordes dermales presentes en las superficies laterales de las extremidades (Fig. 76); organismos que se distribuyen solamente en las Montañas Maya de Belice . . . . . . *Hyla valancifer*
Sin bordes dermales en las superficies laterales de las extremidades (Fig. 69); organismos que se distribuyen ampliamente en la Península de Yucatán . . . . *Hyla loquax*

Hyla bromeliacia Schmidt
(Figs. 65, 66; Map 26)

Hyla bromeliacia Schmidt, 1933:19. HOLOTYPE: FMNH 4718. TYPE LOCALITY: mountains west of San Pedro, Honduras.

Bromeliad treefrog.

DESCRIPTION *Hyla bromeliacia* is a moderately small treefrog. The males average 28 mm in snout-vent length, and the females are about 3 mm longer. The only known specimen from the Yucatán Peninsula, a female, measures 32.9 mm in snout-vent length. The head is moderately depressed and slightly narrower than the body (Fig. 65). The snout is bluntly rounded in dorsal view and truncate in lateral aspect. The eyes are large and somewhat protruding, and the pupil is horizontally elliptical. The interorbital distance is about 1.25 times the maximum diameter of the eye. The small, distinct tympanum is approximately one-third the diameter of the eye. The canthus rostralis is gently rounded, and the loreal region is not or only slightly concave. The skin on the dorsal surfaces of the body and appendages is smooth, on the ventral surfaces the skin is weakly granular. The limbs are moderately slender, and the tips of the digits are expanded to form adhesive disks, with those on the fingers distinctly larger than those on the toes. There is no axillary membrane. The fingers are slightly webbed; the toes are extensively webbed. Subarticular tubercles are present on the foot, and there are numerous small tubercles on the ventral surface of the metatarsus. There is no tarsal fold. The first subarticular tubercle on the fourth digit is distinctly bifid. The males possess paired subgular vocal sacs, and during the breeding season they have a velvety nuptial excrescence on the base of each thumb.

The head, body, and appendages are reddish brown or yellowish tan above with numerous small, dark flecks. There may be a suffusion of dark gray pigment on the anterior surface of the head, and the chin and throat are cream with a light suffusion of brown pigment. The abdomen is translu-

Fig. 65. Dorsal view of *Hyla bromeliacia* (USNM 319779), 32.9 mm SVL; Gloria Camp, Toledo, Belize.

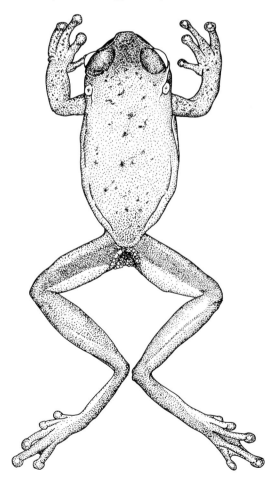

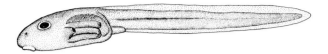

Fig. 66. Tadpole of *Hyla bromeliacia* (KU 59980), 27 mm TL; Finca Chicoyou, Alta Verapaz, Guatemala.

cent, and the viscera are clearly visible. The ventral surfaces of the appendages are cream with a peppering of dark brown, especially on the thighs. The posterior margins of the thighs are unpigmented, and a triangular patch of dark pigment surrounds the vent.

TADPOLE The *H. bromeliacia* tadpole exhibits distinctive morphological adaptations to the bromeliad environment within which it develops (Fig. 66). The body is very depressed, approximately half as deep as long. The tail is unusually long, about 2.5 times the body length, and low, its maximum depth approximately equal to that of the body. The dorsal fin is slightly deeper than the ventral fin and does not extend onto the body. The eyes are dorsolateral and directed upward. The spiracle is sinistral, lateral, and lies about two-thirds posteriorly on the body. The anus is dextral. The mouth is ventral, the oral disk is not indented laterally, and the oral papillae are discontinuous dorsally. The jaw sheaths are well developed and finely serrated. There are two anterior and four or five posterior rows of denticles. The overall color is cream or light tan, darker above than below. The body and the caudal musculature are finely spotted with dark brown, and the caudal fin is nearly devoid of pigment.

VOCALIZATION Schmidt (1933:20) described the vocalization of this species as "like isolated strokes on a small clear bell." According to Duellman (1970:432) the advertisement call "consists of five or six soft notes repeated at intervals of 45 to 70 seconds. The duration of each call group is approximately five seconds. The last note in each call group is double or triple in some calls." A single recording analyzed by Duellman (1970:432) indicated a note duration of about 140 msec, a pulse rate of 196 pulses per second, a fundamental frequency of 135 Hz, and a dominant frequency of 3,100 Hz.

SIMILAR SPECIES *Hyla loquax* most closely resembles *H. bromeliacia* but possesses a distinct axillary membrane, is somewhat larger, and occurs at lower elevations. The other small yellowish tree-

frogs in the Yucatán Peninsula—*H. ebraccata, H. microcephala,* and *H. picta*—are smaller, their males have single rather than paired vocal sacs, and they occur at lower elevations.

DISTRIBUTION This species occurs at moderate and intermediate elevations on the Atlantic slope in Guatemala, the Maya Mountains of southern Belize, and in northern Honduras. In the Yucatán Peninsula it is known only from southern Toledo District (Map 26).

NATURAL HISTORY *Hyla bromeliacia* is a nocturnal, arboreal inhabitant of wet montane and premontane forests. Individuals have been found in bromeliads and beneath the leaf-sheaths of bananas as well as on understory vegetation at night. The breeding season is apparently protracted, for Stuart (1943b:14) found gravid females, egg masses, tadpoles in all stages of development, and a fully transformed individual in Alta Verapaz on 29 July, and he found eggs and tadpoles in various stages of development in Alta Verapaz in April (1948:31). Amplexus is presumably axillary. The only known specimen from the Yucatán Peninsula, a gravid female from southern Toledo District, was collected on 11 April.

This species is eaten by the jumping viper, *Atropoides nummifer,* according to Stuart (1948:29), who removed a specimen of *H. bromeliacia* from the stomach of a snake in Alta Verapaz.

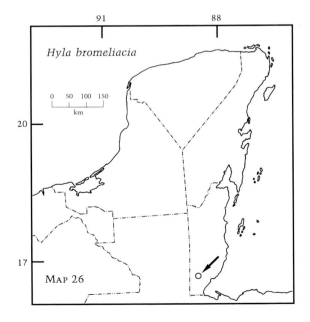

ETYMOLOGY   The specific name, *bromeliacia*, alludes to the fact that this species deposits its eggs in the water at the base of bromeliad leaves.

Locality Record   Belize: Toledo: Columbia River Forest Reserve, Gloria Camp (USNM 319779).

Hyla ebraccata Cope
(Figs. 67, 68, 240; Map 27)

Hyla ebraccata Cope, 1874:69. HOLOTYPE: ANSP 2079. TYPE LOCALITY: region of Nicaragua. Duellman (1970:227) indicated that the type specimen came from Machuca, Zelaya, Nicaragua.

Hourglass treefrog; ranita amarillenta (Mexico).

DESCRIPTION   The males of this small yellowish frog average about 25 mm in snout-vent length. The females generally exceed males by several millimeters. The head is rather broad, depressed, and approximately equal to the body in width. The snout is short and blunt in dorsal and lateral aspects (Fig. 240). The large, protruding eyes are two to three times the diameter of the tympanum, which is partly obscured by skin along its dorsal margin. The pupil is horizontally elliptical. The limbs are long and moderately slender, and the digits terminate in expanded adhesive disks. There is an extensive axillary membrane and extensive webbing between both the fingers and the toes. The skin on the dorsal surface of the body is smooth, and that on the venter is granular. Males have a single subgular vocal sac.

At night these frogs are predominantly yellowish orange above, usually with a single large, pale brown dorsal spot. In most specimens this dorsal spot is continuous with a broad, dark triangular mark on the head. A broad, dark brown stripe extends from the snout, through the eye, and onto the lateral surface of the body. The appendages generally have brown spots or bars, but the thighs are invariably clear yellow. The ventral surfaces of the body and appendages are yellowish orange. During the day, and also in preservative, the dark dorsal spot is rich chocolate brown, contrasting with the light tan or creamy white background.

TADPOLE   The tadpole of *H. ebraccata* is distinctive (Fig. 67). The body is rather elongate, about twice as long as wide. The snout is bluntly rounded in dorsal aspect but rather pointed in lateral view. The eyes are large, widely spaced, and directed lat-

Fig. 67. Tadpole of *Hyla ebraccata* (KU 59986), 14 mm TL; Toocog, El Petén, Guatemala.

erally. The mouth is terminal. The jaw sheaths are finely serrated, and there are no denticles. The oral disk is not indented laterally, and it is surrounded by a fleshy lobe bearing large papillae, except on the dorsal surface of the upper lip, which is bare. The vent tube is medial. The spiracle is sinistral and lies slightly below the midline of the body. The tail is slightly deeper than the body and about 1.8 times the body length. The dorsal fin extends well onto the body, and its depth is about equal to that of the ventral fin. The tip of the tail is acuminate. The dorsum is tan or yellowish with irregular brown markings. A white stripe generally extends from the snout, below the eye, and onto the lateral surfaces of the body and tail. The venter is light gray or white with indistinct gray markings on the sides. The caudal fin is strongly marked with spots of dark gray or black and red.

VOCALIZATION   The advertisement call consists of a single buzzlike primary note, described by Duellman (1970:232) as an insectlike *creek*, followed by zero to four secondary click notes. The primary note has a dominant frequency of about 2,300 to 2,700 Hz and a pulse rate of about 90 to 100 per second (Fig. 68). The males also emit aggressive calls, which also consist of a single primary note but with a much higher pulse rate—140 to 315 per sec-

Fig. 68. Advertisement call of *Hyla ebraccata*, recorded 12 June 1989, Blue Hole, Cayo, Belize.

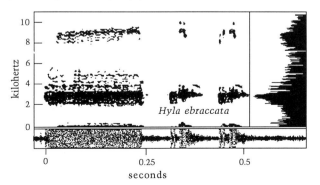

ond. The aggressive call may be followed by click notes. Wells and Greer (1981) showed that males modify their vocalizations depending on the social context, and they suggested that males are capable of transmitting separate acoustic messages to males and females simultaneously.

SIMILAR SPECIES   Of the other small yellowish frogs in the Yucatán Peninsula, *H. ebraccata* most closely resembles *H. microcephala*, but differs from it in being larger and in usually having distinct dark markings on the dorsal surface of the body and head. *Hyla picta* is much smaller than *H. ebraccata*, has a more pointed snout, and lacks extensive axillary webbing. *Hyla loquax* is much larger and is red-orange between the toes and fingers.

DISTRIBUTION   *Hyla ebraccata* occurs at low elevations on the Atlantic slope from southern Veracruz and northern Oaxaca eastward to Belize, and from Nicaragua to Costa Rica and Panama, where it occurs on both the Atlantic and Pacific slopes. It is found at the base of the Yucatán Peninsula, and an apparently isolated population occurs in central Quintana Roo (Map 27).

NATURAL HISTORY   This common treefrog lives primarily in forests and forest edges. During the rainy season breeding occurs in temporary forest ponds, and aggregations of up to several hundred males call from emergent vegetation or from shrubs and small trees overhanging the water. The males

defend their calling sites by emitting aggressive calls (see above) and occasionally by physical combat that involves grappling and pushing contests (Wells and Greer, 1981:616). Miyamoto and Cane (1980a,b) described the reproductive behavior of this species in Costa Rica as follows. A female attracted by a calling male approaches to within 6 to 30 cm of him and rotates her flanks toward him. The male jumps to a position parallel to her and then initiates axillary amplexus. Noncalling males may act as sexual parasites on calling males by intercepting and clasping females that are moving toward the vocalizing male. Egg masses of 20 to 80 eggs are generally deposited on the upper surfaces of leaves overhanging water. On hatching, the larvae fall into the water, where they complete their development.

ETYMOLOGY   The specific name, *ebraccata*, is from the Latin *bracatus*, "pants" or "trousers," and the prefix *e-*, "out" or "beyond." According to Duellman (1970:233) the name literally means "without trousers," in reference to Cope's (1874:69) observation that "the femur is entirely colorless."

Locality Records Belize: Cayo: 3 mi S Belmopan (CM 112162–64, 112180–81), near Blue Hole (JCL photo), Cohune Ridge (MCZ 24085), Hummingbird Hwy., 10 mi S Belize-Cayo Rd. (UMMZ 124713), Hummingbird Hwy. bet. Roaring Creek and Stann Creek (UMMZ 124716), 3 mi from Millionario Camp (UMMZ 124714–15); Toledo: Blue Creek Village (RWV photo); no specific locality (FMNH 27104). *Guatemala*: El Petén: 8 km S La Libertad (Duellman, 1970:700), 15 km SE La Libertad (KU 57250–305), Piedras Negras (FMNH 123473–74), 5 mi S Piedras Negras (USNM 111148–52), 4 mi N Río de la Pasión (KU 156499–502), 13.7 mi N Río de la Pasión (KU 156496–98), 7.4 mi W Ruinas Seibal (KU 156503–5), Sayaxché (UCM 22159), near Sayaxché (UMRC 77-6), 5 km E Sayaxché (UMRC 79-279), 3 mi S Tikal (KU 156506–16), near Yaxhá (UMMZ 75312). *Mexico*: Quintana Roo: 3.7 mi NE Felipe Carrillo Puerto (KU 156517–23), 8.2 km N Felipe Carrillo Puerto (UMRC 79-278; UF 84494), 13.3 km NE Felipe Carrillo Puerto, on rd. to Vigía Chico (KU 171304–7).

Hyla loquax Gaige and Stuart
(Figs. 32, 69–71, 241; Map 28)

Hyla loquax Gaige and Stuart, 1934:1. HOLOTYPE: UMMZ 75446. TYPE LOCALITY: Ixpuc Aguada, north of La Libertad, El Petén, Guatemala.

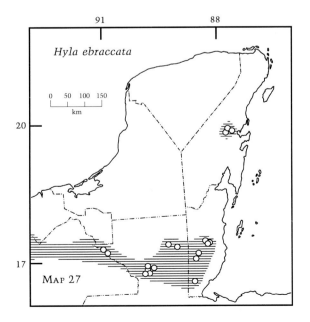

Hyla ebraccata

0 50 100 150
km

MAP 27

Loquacious treefrog; rana arborícola (Mexico).

DESCRIPTION This medium-sized treefrog is one of the largest hylas in the Yucatán Peninsula. Only *H. valancifer* is larger. Duellman (1970:360) reported a maximum snout-vent length for males of 44.7 mm and for females of 41.7 mm, suggesting that females are not generally larger than males, in contrast with the usual condition in anurans. In the Yucatán Peninsula both males and females average about 40 mm in snout-vent length. This is a relatively squat frog with a head that is broad and rounded in dorsal aspect (Fig. 241). In lateral view the snout is rounded or weakly truncate. The canthus rostralis is rounded, and the loreal region is flat or slightly convex. The large, protuberant eyes are two to three times the diameter of the tympanum and have horizontally elliptical pupils. A thick supratympanic fold is present. The appendages are moderately short and stout, the hands and feet are extensively webbed, and the tips of the digits are expanded, forming rounded disks (Fig. 69). There is an extensive axillary membrane (Fig. 32). The males have a single subgular vocal sac. The skin on the dorsal surface of the body is smooth or finely wrinkled, and that on the venter is coarsely granular.

At night these frogs are predominantly yellow, yellow-orange, or light tan with indistinct flecks or small spots of darker pigment; during the day the dorsal coloration is often light gray or cream. The dorsal surfaces of the appendages bear brown bars or spots. The ventral surfaces of the body and appendages are light yellow or cream. This is the only *Hyla* in the Yucatán Peninsula with red or red-orange webbing between the toes and fingers, and red or red-orange on the posterior surfaces of the thighs.

TADPOLE The snout is bluntly rounded in dorsal and lateral aspects, and the eyes are relatively large, widely spaced, and situated laterally (Fig. 70A,B). The nostril lies approximately equidistant between the eye and the tip of the snout. The body is globose, and its length is about 1.6 times its greatest depth. The tail is acuminate, and its maximum depth slightly exceeds that of the body. The dorsal fin is somewhat deeper than the ventral fin and extends onto the body to the level of the spiracle. The spiracle is sinistral and lateral, and the vent tube is dextral. The mouth is anteroventral. The oral disk is not indented laterally, and the surrounding oral papillae are discontinuous across the upper lip. There are two anterior rows of denticles; the first is complete, and the second is discontinuous medially. There are three posterior rows of denticles, of which row 2 is unusual in having a medial interruption. Row 3 is abbreviated. The jaws bear a dark, finely serrated sheath (Fig. 70C).

Fig. 70. Tadpole of *Hyla loquax* (UMRC 79-316), 45 mm TL. A, dorsal view. B, lateral view. C, mouthparts; 15.8 km N Panabá, Yucatán, Mexico.

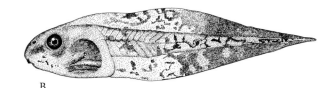

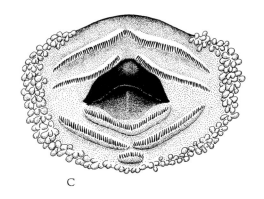

Fig. 69. Hand of *Hyla loquax* (UMRC 79-287) showing expanded toe disks and extensive webbing between the digits; 8.2 km N Felipe Carrillo Puerto, Quintana Roo, Mexico.

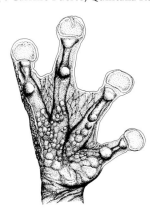

In formalin the head and body are predominantly translucent, but the dorsal surface of the head bears a dark gray spot between the eyes, and a pair of short, dark stripes originates on the anterodorsal surface of the head, converging on the snout. The caudal musculature bears dark variegations that are most distinct on the posterior two-thirds of the tail. The dorsal and ventral fins are mottled with dark pigment, becoming uniform gray over their posterior one-third. In life the ventral surfaces of the body are metallic silver or copper, the caudal musculature bears a silvery variegation, and the caudal fins are translucent anteriorly, becoming more or less uniformly gray posteriorly. The iris is orange.

VOCALIZATION   The advertisement call of *H. loquax* consists of a series of short, rather explosive notes described by Langebartel and Smith (1959:28) as a single *kaaack*, and by Duellman (1970:362) as like the honk of a goose, although to my ear the former description more accurately describes the call in the Yucatán Peninsula. The call is given irregularly at intervals of one to several seconds, and a call sequence is usually followed by a longer, drawn-out chattering note. The note duration is about 170 msec, and the duration of the chattering note is about 300 msec. The dominant frequency is approximately 3,000 Hz, and the fundamental frequency is at about 900 Hz (Fig. 71).

SIMILAR SPECIES   This distinctive frog is difficult to confuse with any other in the Yucatán Peninsula. Pale specimens of *Smilisca baudinii* and *Phrynohyas venulosa* may superficially resemble *H. loquax*, but they lack an extensive axillary membrane and red webbing between the fingers and toes. The other predominantly yellow frogs in the peninsula—*H. microcephala*, *H. picta*, *H. bromeliacia*,

Fig. 71. Advertisement call of *Hyla loquax*, recorded 18 October 1988, 6.7 km S Chekubúl, Campeche, Mexico.

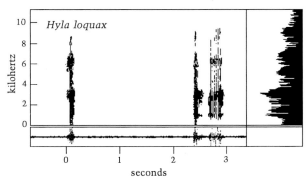

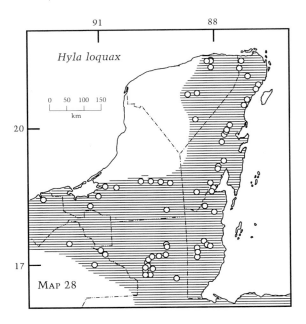

MAP 28

and *H. ebraccata*—are much smaller and lack red or red-orange webbing.

DISTRIBUTION   *Hyla loquax* occurs at low and moderate elevations on both sides of the Isthmus of Tehauntepec, east through much of the Yucatán Peninsula, and southward to Costa Rica. It ranges through the base of the Yucatán Peninsula and northward on the east side, apparently avoiding the dry northwest corner (Map 28).

NATURAL HISTORY   This predominantly arboreal frog is a common inhabitant of humid lowland forests and savannas. Reproduction occurs throughout the rainy season, and males can be found calling from emergent vegetation and from shrubs and small trees at the edges of temporary or permanent bodies of water. Breeding is generally restricted to relatively deep bodies of water, more so than is the case for the other hylas in the Yucatán Peninsula. Amplexus is axillary. The eggs are deposited in the water, and the larvae develop there. *Hyla loquax* preys on a variety of small invertebrates, especially insects.

ETYMOLOGY   The specific name, *loquax*, is Latin meaning "talkative" or "chattering," in reference to the "noisy song" of the male (Gaige and Stuart, 1934:1).

COMMENT   Duellman (1970) described and illustrated a tadpole that he believed to be *H. loquax*, but

R. G. Altig and R. W. McDiarmid (pers. comm.) pointed out that the tadpole described and illustrated by Duellman belongs to another species.

Locality Records   Belize: Cayo: Augustine (UMMZ 80740), 0.4 mi S Belmopan (KU 156524–25), 1 mi S Belmopan (CM 112156–57), 1.5 mi SW Cayo (UMMZ 124729), Hummingbird Hwy., 50 mi NW Stann Creek (UF 24544045), Hummingbird Hwy., 10 mi from Belize-Cayo Rd. (UMMZ 124728), 1.5 mi SE Mountain Cow (CM 112176), Mountain Pine Ridge Rd., 12.7 mi S Belize-Cayo Rd. (UMMZ 124726), Mountain Pine Ridge Rd., 36 to 49 mi S Belize-Cayo Rd. (UMMZ 124727); Corozal: 2.5 mi N Corozal Town (JLK 432), 5.3 mi SW Corozal Town (KU 156529–32); Orange Walk: 8 mi NW Maskall (KU 156526–28), Tower Hill (USNM 194936–37); no specific locality (UF 24543). *Guatemala*: El Petén: Ixpuc Aguada (FMNH 100156), E end Lago Petén Itzá (KU 156560–63), N side Lago Petén Itzá (JCL sight record), La Libertad (KU 57399–415), near La Libertad (UMMZ 75442–52), 2 mi N La Libertad (FMNH 100165; UIMNH 43483), 2 mi S La Libertad (USNM 941000), 15 km SE La Libertad (KU 57390–98), N La Libertad (MCZ 19754), Piedras Negras (FMNH 105191, 105302; UIMNH 28852), 5 mi S Piedras Negras (USNM 114609–41), 4 mi N Poptún (KU 156533–37, 157686), 8.4 mi N Río de la Pasión (KU 156552), 13.7 mi N Río de la Pasión (KU 156538–51), 1 mi W Ruinas Seibal (KU 156553–57), Santa Elena (UTA A-30252–53), Sayaxché (UCM 22160; UMRC 78-32), 5 km E Sayaxché (UMRC 79-285), Tikal (UF 13455; UMMZ 117979, 120467; UMRC 79-288; USNM 204802–3), 3 mi S Tikal (KU 156558–59). *Mexico*: Campeche: Encarnación (H. M. Smith, 1938:12), 5 mi W Escárcega (CM 40089–90; UCM 27809, 27823–29, 27872–75, 28111–12), 40.1 mi SW Escárcega (UTA A-2290), Laguna Alvarado (KU 75061–81), 10 km E Laguna Silvituc (KU 75059–60), 23.2 mi E Silvituc (KU 156564–68), 52 mi E Silvituc (Colonia López Mateos) (UCM 27876–90), Tres Brazos (FMNH 99021; UIMNH 28851), Xpujil (JCL sight record); Chiapas: Laguna Ocotal (MCZ 28238), 12 mi S Palenque (LSUMZ 38153–54, 38158); Quintana Roo: 6 mi N Bacalar (KU 156569), 7.6 mi N Bacalar (KU 156570), 3.7 mi NE Felipe Carrillo Puerto (KU 156580–85), 5.9 km NE Felipe Carrillo Puerto (KU 1712439–48), 8.2 km N Felipe Carrillo Puerto (UMRC 79-288), 9.2 mi S Felipe Carrillo Puerto (KU 156572–79), 10 mi S Felipe Carrillo Puerto (KU 156571), 13.2 km NE Felipe Carrillo Puerto (KU 171259–61), 31.2 mi NE Felipe Carrillo Puerto (KU 156586–90), 3.9 km N Kantunil Kin (KU 171262–67), 0.8 km N Kohunlich ruins (KU 171249–58), 2 mi SW Leona Vicario (KU 156596–98), 3.5 mi N Limones (KU 156602–3), 10.8 mi E Nicolas Bravo (KU 156604–7), 10.5 mi NE Playa del Carmen (KU 156593–95), 2.6 km S Solferino (UMRC 79-286), 5.5 mi NE Tulum (KU 156591), 15.1 mi NE Tulum (KU 156592), 8.1 mi SW Vicente Guerrero (KU 156599–601); Tabasco: 4 to 6 mi S Frontera (UCM 27821); Yucatán: Chichén Itzá (FMNH 36571), 1.5 mi S Libre Unión (UCM 28099–100), 15.8 km N Panabá (UMRC 79-316; USNM 321152), 9 mi S Río Lagartos (UCM 27810–20, 27891), 9.2 mi S Río Lagartos (KU 156608), 13.4 mi S Río Lagartos (JCL sight record), Santa Rosa (JCL sight record).

Hyla microcephala Cope
(Figs. 72, 73, 242; Map 29)

Hyla microcephala Cope, 1886:281. SYNTYPES: USNM 13473 (two syntypes; now lost, *fide* Duellman, 1970:211). TYPE LOCALITY: Chiriqui, Panama.

Small-headed treefrog; rana arborícola, ranita (Guatemala, Mexico); rerek (Lacandón Maya); quech (Yucatec Maya).

DESCRIPTION   This is a small, yellowish orange or tan frog. The males average about 23 mm in snout-vent length; females are a few millimeters longer. The head is slightly narrower than the body, and the snout is bluntly truncate in dorsal and lateral views (Fig. 242). The moderately large eyes have horizontally elliptical pupils. The limbs are moderately long and slender, the fingers and toes are extensively webbed, especially the toes, and the tips of the digits are expanded to form rounded disks. The males possess a single median vocal sac. The skin on the dorsal surface of the body is smooth; that on the venter is coarsely granular. The dorsum is grayish, yellowish tan, or orange, with irregular thin, dark markings, these often in the form of an H or an X at the level of the shoulders. Often a fine, dark ocular stripe, bordered above by white, extends from the rostrum, through the upper edge of the eye, and onto the lateral surface of the body. The dorsal surfaces of the forearms and shanks are tan with indistinct dark spots and bars, but the thighs are largely unpigmented. The ventral surface of the body is white or cream. The throat, including the vocal sac, and the undersurfaces of the appendages are yellow or yellow-orange.

TADPOLE   The tadpoles are distinctive in having a xiphicercal tail with a high dorsal fin roughly equal in width to the caudal musculature and ventral fin combined (Fig. 72). The dorsal fin extends onto the body. The snout is pointed, the eyes are relatively small, and the small terminal mouth lacks denticles and fringing labial papillae. Finely

Fig. 72. Tadpole of *Hyla microcephala* (UMRC 79-317), 31 mm TL; 15.8 km N Panabá, Yucatán, Mexico.

serrated jaw sheaths are present. The spiracle is sinistral, and the vent tube is dextral. The general coloration is yellowish tan with a dark stripe extending from the snout, through the eye, and onto the lateral surfaces of the body. The posterior portion of the tail is orange, whereas the more proximal portions are largely devoid of pigment. The posterior margins of the tail are dark brown or black. The venter is cream, white, or light gray.

VOCALIZATION   The advertisement call of *H. microcephala* generally consists of a single primary note, a short pause, and then several secondary notes given in rapid succession. Duellman (1970: 214) described the call as an insectlike *creeek-eek-eek*. Primary notes have a duration of about 180 msec, secondary notes last about 110 msec. Both primary and secondary notes are high-pitched, with harmonics at about 3,800 and 7,000 Hz (Fig. 73). J. J. Schwartz and Wells (1985:29) described an aggressive call that differs from the advertisement call in its longer duration and higher pulse rate. The acoustic characteristics of the advertisement and aggressive calls may be modified depending on the social context (J. J. Schwartz and Wells, 1985). In the presence of competing conspecifics, males may increase the complexity of their advertisement calls by adding notes, and they may increase the duration of their aggressive calls. In playback experiments, *H. microcephala* males increased their calling rate and the complexity of their calls in response to in-

Fig. 73. Advertisement call of *Hyla microcephala*, recorded 12 October 1988, 8 km SE Cobá, Quintana Roo, Mexico.

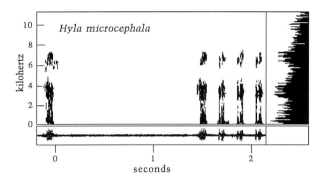

creases in the calling rate and complexity of stimulus calls (J. J. Schwartz, 1986). Females preferred higher calling rates and more complex calls.

SIMILAR SPECIES   In size and shape *H. microcephala* is most similar to *H. ebraccata*, but it lacks the distinct dark dorsal markings found in that species. *Hyla picta* is smaller and has pigmented thighs. *Hyla loquax* is larger and has pigmented thighs, a more extensive axillary membrane, and red or red-orange webbing between the toes and fingers.

DISTRIBUTION   *Hyla microcephala* is a common lowland species along the Gulf and Caribbean slopes from southern Veracruz eastward to northern Honduras, and on the Pacific slope from Nicaragua to Panama, Colombia, and the Amazon Basin. It occurs continuously throughout the Yucatán Peninsula with the exception of the northwest corner, where it is apparently restricted to an area known locally as "Los Petenes" (Map 29).

NATURAL HISTORY   In the Yucatán Peninsula this abundant frog is most frequently encountered in disturbed habitats, where large choruses of calling males form during the rainy season. The species is apparently uncommon or absent from deep primary forest. Instead, roadside ditches, puddles, and low, flooded areas in pastures are often used for breeding. These little frogs are nocturnal, insectivorous, and largely arboreal.

Males call from emergent vegetation and from

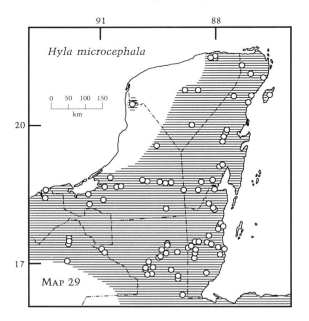

Hyla microcephala

MAP 29

shrubs and small trees adjacent to water. Enormous breeding aggregations are common, with many hundreds of males calling. Reproduction in the Yucatán Peninsula is closely tied to the rainy season, although elsewhere the species may breed throughout the year. Amplexus is axillary. The eggs are deposited directly into the water, where the eggs hatch and the larvae undergo development.

SUBSPECIES H. M. Smith (1951) considered the populations of this species in southern Mexico and Guatemala to be subspecifically distinct from those to the south and applied the name *H. m. martini* to them. Duellman and Fouquette (1968) argued that only a single subspecies occurs north of Costa Rica, and they placed *H. m. martini* in the synonymy of *H. m. underwoodi*, the subspecies found in the Yucatán Peninsula.

ETYMOLOGY The specific name, *microcephala*, is from the Greek *mikros*, "small," and *kephale*, "head," in reference to what Cope thought was an unusually small head in this species.

Locality Records Belize: Belize: 7.8 km W Belize City (CM 90976–84), 13 mi NW Belize City (UMMZ 124732), Burrell Boom Rd. at Belize River (CM 105792), 11 km SW Hattieville (CM 90963–64), Missionary Lake Rd. 4.3 mi E Northern Hwy. (CM 91072), 19.2 mi E Roaring Creek (KU 156621–22); Cayo: Belize-Cayo Hwy., 3.1 mi W Mountain Pine Ridge Rd. (UMMZ 124730), 15 mi E Belmopan (CM 112098–99), 3 mi SW Cayo (UMMZ 124734), Georgeville (CM 91033–34), 0.4 mi E Georgeville (KU 156610–11), 15.4 mi E Georgeville (KU 156609), Hummingbird Hwy., 10 mi S Belize-Cayo Rd. (UMMZ 124733), Macal River at Guacamallo Bridge (CM 112142), Mountain Pine Ridge Rd., 42 mi S Belize-Cayo Rd. (UMMZ 124731), 4 mi S San Ignacio (MCZ 37893–95), S edge San Luis (KU 156638); Corozal: 5.3 mi SW Corozal Town (KU 156633–37); Orange Walk: 8 mi NW Maskall (KU 156623–27), 14.3 mi NW Maskall (KU 156628–32), 17.3 to 23.2 mi SE Orange Walk (NMSU 3082), Otro Benque (USNM 194938–41); Stann Creek: 17.5 mi SE Blue Hole (KU 156612), Dangriga (CM 105836; FMNH 49068), 5.7 mi S Silk Grass (KU 156613–18), 19 mi W Stann Creek (JLK 430–31); Toledo: 7.4 mi NE Golden Stream (KU 156619–20). *Guatemala*: El Petén: 34.6 mi E El Cruce (KU 156678–81), 1 mi S Flores (KU 156664–71), E end Lago Petén Itzá (KU 156677), N side Lago Petén Itzá (JCL sight record), La Libertad (KU 57447–97), near La Libertad (UMMZ 75332–35), 15 km SE La Libertad (KU 57426–46), Piedras Negras (FMNH 113123; UIMNH 20966), 5 mi S Piedras Negras (USNM 114951–72), N edge Poptún (UMMZ 125889), 1 km S Poptún (UMMZ

120480), 4 mi N Poptún (KU 156639–44), 39.6 mi NW Poptún (KU 156645–57), 8.4 mi N Río de la Pasión (KU 156662), 13.7 mi N Río de la Pasión (KU 156658–61), 1 mi W Ruinas Seibal (KU 156663), Santa Elena (UMRC 79-282), 5 km E Sayaxché (UMRC 79-283), Tikal (UF 13456–57; UMMZ 117981, 120478–79, 130051, 130069; UMRC 79-284), 3 mi S Tikal (KU 156672–76), just N Río Sarstoon (UMRC 77-7); *Mexico*: Campeche: Balchacaj (FMNH 100406, 113094, 113099, 113101–2, 113110; UIMNH 20944–46), Carretera Tankuche–El Remate (IHNHERP 139–41), 10 km S Chekubúl (JCL audio record), 3.3 km N Dzibalchén (UMRC 79-280), Encarnación (FMNH 27069–70, 75784, 105307, 113081, 113085–96, 113098, 113100, 113103, 113106–9, 113111, 113113–14, 113118–19, 113121–22; MCZ 28360, 29637; TU 18814; UIMNH 20948–58, 20965; USNM 134264–65), 5 mi W Escárcega (UCM 27833–50), 7.5 km W Escárcega (KU 71229–43), Laguna Alvarado (KU 75084–89), Pacaitún (FMNH 83118–20), 5 mi E Silvituc (JCL sight record), 23.2 mi E Silvituc (KU 156682–86), 52 mi E Silvituc (Colonia López Mateos) (UCM 27892–93), Tres Brazos (FMNH 113104; UIMNH 20947), Xpujil (JCL sight record), 10 km W Xpujil (KU 75082–83); Chiapas: 7 km NE Ocosingo (UTEP 7693–97), Palenque (USNM 114973–79), 10 to 15 mi S Palenque (LSUMZ 38021, 38155–56), 8 mi S Palenque (LSUMZ 38083–85), San Juanito (UIMNH 49139–50); Quintana Roo: 6 mi N Bacalar (KU 156687–91), 7.4 mi W Chetumal (JCL sight record), Cobá (CAS 141865–66), 3.7 mi NE Felipe Carrillo Puerto (KU 156695), 10 mi S Felipe Carrillo Puerto (KU 156693–94), 16.3 mi NE Felipe Carrillo Puerto (KU 156696–97), E side Isla Cozumel (UF uncat.), 4.3 km N Kantunil Kin (KU 171278–86), 0.8 km N Kohunlich ruins (KU 171287–96), near Laguna Chicanbacab (McCoy, 1969: 848), 2 mi SW Leona Vicario (KU 156704–6), 13.4 mi SW Limones (KU 156692), 10.8 mi E Nicolas Bravo (KU 156707–9), 0.75 mi W Puerto Morelos (UF uncat.), 5.5 mi NE Tulum (KU 156698–99), 15.1 mi NE Tulum (KU 156700–3); Tabasco: 4 to 6 mi S Frontera (UCM 27851–52), 15 mi N Frontera (MCZ 35665–70); Yucatán: Chichén Itzá (Barbour and Cole, 1906:154), 1.5 mi S Libre Unión (UCM 28109–28110), 15.8 km N Panabá (UMRC 79-317), 11 mi S Río Lagartos (UCM 27830–32), 9 mi S Río Lagartos (UCM 27871), 9.2 mi S Río Lagartos (KU 156443–44), bet. Santa Rosa and Dzuiché (KU 171268–77; UMRC 79-281).

Hyla picta (Günther)
(Figs. 74, 75, 243; Map 30)

Hylella picta Günther, 1901:286. HOLOTYPE: BMNH 1947.2.22.62. TYPE LOCALITY: Mexico, Jalapa (Veracruz, Mexico).

Ranita, rana arborícola (Mexico); rerek (Lacandón Maya).

DESCRIPTION This is the smallest frog in the Yucatán Peninsula. The males average about 20 mm in snout-vent length, and females are about a millimeter longer. The head is approximately equal to the body in width. The snout is bluntly truncate in lateral view and rather pointed in dorsal aspect (Fig. 243). The eyes are large, protuberant, and about three times the diameter of the tympanum. The pupil is horizontally elliptical. The limbs are moderately long and delicate, and the tips of the digits are expanded to form rounded adhesive disks. The fingers are slightly webbed, the toes are about three quarters webbed. The skin on the dorsal surface of the body is smooth, and that on the venter is coarsely granular. The males possess a single subgular vocal sac.

These diminutive frogs are predominantly yellow or yellow-orange, with dark brown or reddish flecks and spots on the dorsum. A reddish, brown, or gray stripe originates on the snout and passes through the eye, over the tympanum, and onto the lateral surface of the body. A pair of white or cream dorsolateral stripes is generally apparent, although these may be obscure in preserved specimens.

TADPOLE The *H. picta* tadpole has a rather narrow, deep body and a snout that is bluntly rounded in both dorsal and lateral views (Fig. 74). The eyes are large, widely separated, and directed laterally. The mouth is anteroventral, and the keratinized jaw sheaths are finely serrated. There are two anterior and three posterior rows of denticles. The oral disk is not indented laterally, and the surrounding labial papillae are discontinuous anteriorly. The vent tube is dextral. The sinistral spiracle is lateral and lies slightly below the midline. The tail is approximately twice the length of the body and tapers to a point. The dorsal fin extends onto the body to the level of the spiracle, and the dorsal and ventral fins are approximately equal in depth. The depth of the tail noticeably exceeds that of the body.

The body and caudal musculature are tan. The caudal fins are clear with brown flecks and mot-

tling. A dark brown stripe extends from the tip of the snout to the eye and, in some specimens, onto the lateral surface of the body.

VOCALIZATION The advertisement call is a high-pitched, insectlike buzz. My analyses of recordings made in southern Campeche generally agree with Duellman's (1970:367) findings, except that the dominant frequency of calls made by frogs from Campeche usually lies between 5,200 and 5,300 Hz, much higher than the 1,676 to 3,320 Hz range reported by Duellman (but more nearly consistent with his plate 19, fig. 1). The pulse rate is about 55 to 60 per second, the note repetition rate is about 60 per minute, and the average note duration is approximately 400 msec (Fig. 75).

SIMILAR SPECIES The other two species of small yellowish treefrogs in the Yucatán Peninsula, *H. ebraccata* and *H. microcephala*, are larger and lack dorsolateral stripes.

DISTRIBUTION *Hyla picta* occurs at low and moderate elevations on the Atlantic slope from San Luis Potosí and Veracruz south and eastward through northern Guatemala and Belize to northern Honduras. It ranges through the base of the Yucatán Peninsula and then northward through Quintana Roo and westward to central Yucatán (Map 30).

NATURAL HISTORY This common species inhabits a variety of habitats in the Yucatán Peninsula, including tall forests, forest edges, savannas, and second-growth vegetation as well as edificarian situations. Breeding activity is correlated with the summer rains, and large numbers of males congregate at temporary bodies of water and call from

Fig. 75. Advertisement call of *Hyla picta*, recorded 18 October 1988, 8 km S Chekubúl, Campeche, Mexico.

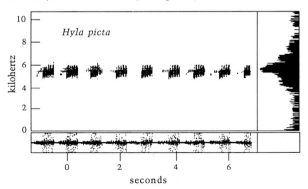

Fig. 74. Tadpole of *Hyla picta* (UMRC 93-8), 29 mm TL; Suc Tuc, Campeche, Mexico.

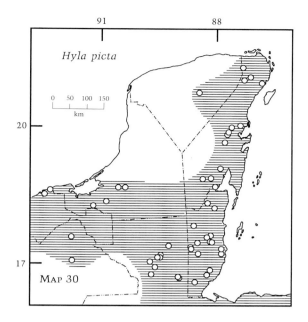

Hyla picta

MAP 30

emergent grasses and shrubs. Forest pools, grassy depressions in pastures, and roadside ditches are among the situations in which this species breeds. *Hyla picta* often breeds in association with *H. microcephala* and *Scinax staufferi*, but its vocalization is much weaker than theirs and its presence can thus be overlooked. Amplexus is axillary. The eggs are deposited in the water, where the larvae complete their development.

ETYMOLOGY   The specific name, *picta*, is Latin meaning "painted" or "embroidered," perhaps in reference to the flecks and spots on the dorsum.

Locality Records   Belize: Belize: 19.2 mi E Roaring Creek (KU 156747); Cayo: Belize-Cayo Rd. 3.1 mi W Mountain Pine Ridge Rd. (UMMZ 124735), near Blue Hole (JCL photo), Caracol (CMM photo), 3 mi SW Cayo (UMMZ 124737), 15.4 mi E Georgetown (KU 156730), 4 mi S San Ignacio (MCZ 37893–95), 5 mi N San Luis (KU 156725–29); Corozal: 1 mi N Corozal Town (JLK 432); Orange Walk: Gallon Jug (CMM photo), 17 mi NW Maskall (KU 156748), Tower Hill (USNM 167742); Stann Creek: 17.5 mi SW Blue Hole (KU 156731–35), 5.7 mi S Silk Grass (KU 156741–46), 6 mi E Stann Creek (UMMZ 124736); Toledo: Blue Creek Village (RWV photo), 0.25 mi SW Deep River (KU 156738–40), 2.9 mi NW Golden Stream (KU 156736–37). *Guatemala*: El Petén: Flores (UMRC 77-5), 1 mi S Flores (KU 156752–66), near La Libertad (UMMZ 75351–53), 15 km SE La Libertad (KU 57585–92), N edge Poptún (UMMZ 125888), 2 mi N Poptún (KU 156749), 4 mi N Poptún (KU 157688), 7.4 mi W Ruinas Seibal (KU 156750–51), Santa Elena (UMRC

79-293), 3 mi S Tikal (KU 156767–69). *Mexico*: Campeche: 7.5 km W Escárcega (KU 71245–60), Matamoros (FMNH 36590), Pacaitún (FMNH 36591–92), Suc Tuc (UMRC 93-8), Tres Brazos (Duellman, 1970: 708); Chiapas: 7 km NE Ocosingo (UTEP 7699–703), Palenque (Duellman, 1970:708); Quintana Roo: 6 mi N Bacalar (KU 156770–73), 3.7 mi NE Felipe Carrillo Puerto (KU 156779–83), 5.9 km N Felipe Carrillo Puerto (KU 171297–302), 10 mi S Felipe Carrillo Puerto (KU 156774–78), 29.1 mi NE Felipe Carrillo Puerto (KU 156784–85), 36.2 km NE Felipe Carrillo Puerto (KU 171400), 4.3 km N Kantunil Kin (KU 171748–57), 2 mi SW Leona Vicario (KU 156786–88), 10.8 mi E Nicolas Bravo (KU 156792–95), 19.3 mi E Nicolas Bravo (JCL sight record), 10 mi NE Playa del Carmen (JCL sight record), 8.1 mi SW Vicente Guerrero (KU 156789–91); Tabasco: Frontera (USNM 37739–46), 10 mi E Frontera (UIMNH 86349–50); Yucatán: Chichén Itzá (MCZ 2463).

Hyla valancifer Firschein and Smith
(Figs. 76, 244; Map 31)

Hyla valancifer Firschein and Smith, 1956:18.
HOLOTYPE: UIMNH 35398. TYPE LOCALITY: Volcán San Martín, Veracruz, Mexico.

Fringe-limbed treefrog.

DESCRIPTION   *Hyla valancifer* is a large treefrog. The adults attain a snout-vent length of 82 mm. Too few specimens are known to assess sexual size dimorphism reliably, but females appear to exceed males significantly in size. The head is somewhat depressed and broad, and its width is approximately equal to that of the body (Fig. 244). In dorsal view the snout is truncate and protrudes beyond the upper lip; in lateral profile it is bluntly rounded. The eyes are large and protruding, and the pupil is horizontally elliptical. The interorbital distance is about 1.3 times the diameter of the eye. The tympanum is distinct and has a diameter approximately two-thirds that of the eye. A distinct supratympanic fold covers the dorsal margin of the tympanum. The canthus rostralis is sharply angled anteriorly and gently rounded posteriorly, and the loreal region is distinctly concave. The limbs are robust, the fingers and toes are extensively webbed, and the digits terminate in expanded adhesive disks. The disks on the fingers are noticeably larger than those on the toes. The prepollex is elongate and flat. The lateral surface of each forelimb bears a conspicuous scalloped dermal fringe that is continuous with the lat-

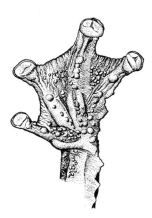

Fig. 76. Palmar view of the hand of *Hyla valancifer* (USNM 319780); Gloria Camp, Toledo, Belize.

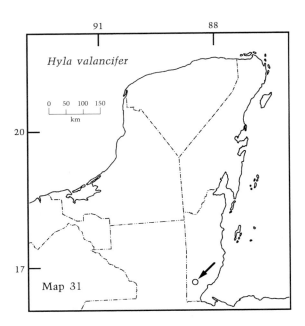

eral surface of digit 4 (Fig. 76). There is a cluster of pustules on each heel, and a distinct fold is present on each tarsus. On the hind limbs, a scalloped dermal fringe is present on the posterior margin of the tarsus and extends along the posterior margin of digit 5. The skin on the dorsal surface of the head, body, and appendages bears scattered pustules. The throat is weakly pustulate, and the ventral surface of the body and appendages is granular. The granular posteroventral surfaces of the thighs grade into a series of large pustules surrounding the vent.

The dorsum is reddish or purplish brown with numerous irregular dark brown, green, or black spots, flecks, and blotches. The pustules and the fringes on the appendages are light tan or cream. The dorsal surfaces of the appendages bear dark brown bands against a lighter brown background. Brown spots against a light brown background are present on the lateral and ventral surfaces of the body and on the ventral surfaces of the appendages. The iris is metallic gold with dark brown reticulations.

TADPOLE   The tadpole of *H. valancifer* is unknown.

VOCALIZATION   The vocalization of *H. valancifer* is unknown.

SIMILAR SPECIES   In the Yucatán Peninsula *Phrynohyas venulosa* most closely resembles *H. valancifer*, but it lacks dermal fringes on the appendages (cf. Figs. 76, 77) and has a glandular rather than a pustulate dorsum.

DISTRIBUTION   The distribution of *H. valancifer* is poorly understood. It is known from cloud forests in the Sierra de los Tuxtlas in southern Veracruz and from a single specimen collected in Toledo District (Map 31).

NATURAL HISTORY   This rare frog inhabits humid montane and cloud forests, and specimens have been found on vegetation several meters above the ground. The only known specimen from the Yucatán Peninsula was found at night on a palm frond 3 m above the ground at an elevation of about 680 m.

Nothing is known of reproduction in *H. valancifer*, but L. D. Wilson et al. (1985:149) published observations on the breeding biology of *H. salvaje*, a Honduran species of fringe-limbed treefrog that is presumably related to *H. valancifer* and may exhibit similar reproductive behavior. *Hyla salvaje* oviposits in water-filled cavities in tree trunks, and the tadpoles feed on the eggs of their own species.

ETYMOLOGY   The specific name, *valancifer*, comes from the English *valence*, "a short drapery or curtain," and the Latin suffix *-ifer*, "to bear" or "to carry," in reference to the fringe on the limbs.

COMMENT   Specimens previously assigned to *H. valancifer* from the Sierra de las Minas, Baja Verapaz, Guatemala, were described by L. D. Wilson et al. (1985:145) as *H. minera*, a species said to differ from *H. valancifer* in having cranial co-ossification and prepollical spines in males. The single known specimen of fringe-limbed *Hyla* from the Yucatán

Peninsula is a female from the Maya Mountains of Belize that lacks cranial co-ossification and was identified as *H. valancifer* on that basis. As *H. valancifer* is otherwise known only from southern Veracruz, the record for Belize is anomalous. The very similar *H. minera* is known from several localites in nearby northern Guatemala, however. J. A. Campbell examined the type material of both taxa and said (in litt.) that there is little to distinguish them.

Locality Record *Belize*: Toledo: Columbia River Forest Reserve, Gloria Camp (USNM 319780).

Genus *Phrynohyas*

The genus *Phrynohyas* includes a few species of large Neotropical treefrogs with thick glandular skin. The males are unusual in possessing paired lateral vocal sacs. Representatives of the genus occur from northern Mexico to Brazil and Argentina, but the genus is most diverse in South America, where four of the five known species are endemic. Only the large and widely distributed *P. venulosa* occurs in the Yucatán Peninsula. *Phrynohyas* derives from the Greek word *phrynos*, "toad," and Hylas, a mythical companion of Hercules. According to Duellman (1970:160), the name literally means "toad-treefrog." The most recent review of this genus is by Duellman (1971b).

Phrynohyas venulosa (Laurenti)
(Figs. 77–79, 245, 246; Map 32)

Rana venulosa Laurenti, 1768:1–214. HOLOTYPE: plate 72, figure 4, in volume 1 of Seba, 1734. TYPE LOCALITY: America.

Veined treefrog; rana arbórea, quech (Guatemala, Mexico).

DESCRIPTION   This is the largest treefrog in the Yucatán Peninsula. The males have an average snout-vent length of about 75 mm, and the females average about 4 mm longer. There is geographic variation in body size throughout the extensive range of this species (McDiarmid, 1968), and also within the Yucatán Peninsula, where specimens from El Petén are smaller than those from Yucatán (Duellman, 1970:165). The head is broad, somewhat depressed, and slightly narrower than the body (Fig. 245). The eyes are large and protuberant, and they exceed the tympanum in diameter. The pupil is horizontally elliptical, and the iris has gold flecks. The limbs are relatively short and robust, and the thick, fleshy fingers are webbed for about half their length. The toes are extensively webbed, and the digits terminate in large adhesive disks (Fig. 77). The skin on the dorsal and lateral surfaces of the body is thick and glandular; the venter is granular. The males of this species are unique among anurans in the Yucatán Peninsula in possessing paired lateral vocal sacs behind the angles of the jaw (Fig. 246).

The dorsum is predominantly light brown or tan with one or a few irregular dark brown blotches, these often edged with black. In many specimens the lateral surfaces of the body are suffused with creamy white with strongly contrasting brown spots. The dorsal surfaces of the appendages are tan with transverse dark bars, and the venter is yellowish tan or white and without dark markings. Zweifel (1964:205) described an ontogenetic change in the color pattern of this species. For the first few days following metamorphosis the newly transformed frogs have a dark longitudinal stripe on the hind legs and a monochromatic dorsum.

TADPOLE   The *P. venulosa* tadpole is rather streamlined, with a body slightly wider than deep and an acuminate tail that is approximately twice

Fig. 77. *Phrynohyas venulosa* (UMRC 78-22) (A) foot and (B) hand, showing expanded toe disks and extensive webbing between the digits. Note the bifid subarticular tubercle on digit 4 of the hand; Corozal, Corozal, Belize.

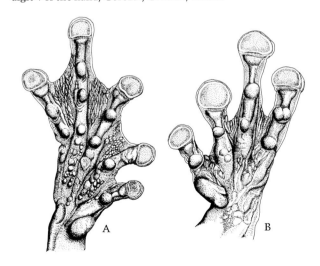

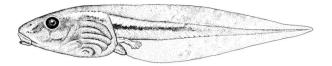

Fig. 78. Tadpole of *Phrynohyas venulosa* (USNM 321153), 44 mm TL; Cañas, Guanacaste, Costa Rica.

the length of the body (Fig. 78). The snout is bluntly rounded in dorsal aspect and somewhat pointed in lateral view. The eyes are moderately large and widely separated. The mouth is anteroventral. The jaw sheaths are finely serrated. There are three or four anterior rows of denticles, and five, six, or, occasionally, seven posterior rows. The oral disk is not indented laterally, and the surrounding labial papillae are discontinuous dorsally. The vent tube is medial. The sinistral spiracle lies well below the midline of the body. The depth of the tail slightly exceeds that of the body, and the dorsal fin extends well onto the body. The ventral fin is slightly deeper than the dorsal fin. The dorsal coloration is dark brown or olive, lighter below. The caudal musculature is light tan or yellowish, with a dark brown stripe. The caudal fins are clear with flecks of dark pigment.

VOCALIZATION   The advertisement call of *Phrynohyas* consists of a single note that has been described by Duellman (1970:168) as a loud growl, and by Dundee and Liner (1985b:109) as *grrraaack*. In my experience the call rate is about one per second, and the duration of the call is about 500 msec. The dominant frequency generally lies between 2,200 and 2,500 Hz (Fig. 79).

SIMILAR SPECIES   The two species of *Smilisca* resemble *Phrynohyas*, and W. T. Neill (1965:89)

Fig. 79. Advertisement call of *Phrynohyas venulosa*, recorded 21 June 1961, 4 km WNW Esparta, Puntarenas, Costa Rica.

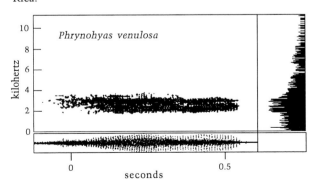

suggested that *S. baudinii* is a mimic of *P. venulosa*. The species of *Smilisca* are smaller, however, and lack a rough, glandular dorsum, and the males have paired subgular vocal sacs rather than the paired lateral vocal sacs of *Phrynohyas* males.

DISTRIBUTION   *Phrynohyas venulosa* has an extensive geographical distribution in the lowlands of Middle America. It occurs at low and moderate elevations from Tamaulipas on the Atlantic slope and from Sinaloa on the Pacific slope, south and eastward through Central America to Argentina and Brazil. This species very likely occurs throughout the Yucatán Peninsula, although there are no records from southern El Petén or southern Belize (Map 32).

NATURAL HISTORY   This is a common and widespread frog in the Yucatán Peninsula, where it can be found in most habitats other than those with brackish water. Individuals pass the dry season sequestered in a variety of retreats, including bromeliads (H. M. Smith, 1941e:38), leaf axils, tree crevices, and beneath the bark on standing trees.

As is the case for most anurans in the Yucatán Peninsula, *Phrynohyas* breeds in association with the summer rains, but this species seems especially dependent on heavy rains to initiate breeding. Large breeding aggregations form at temporary bodies of water, and males generally call from the surface of the water. Pyburn (1967:186) described oviposition in this species in Veracruz. Amplexus is axillary,

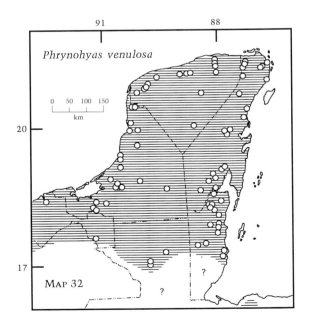

and a single amplectant pair will deposit several masses of eggs in an evening. The eggs are deposited as a surface film. The larvae complete metamorphosis in about 47 days, at which time the froglets are 13 to 16 mm in snout-vent length.

Phrynohyas venulosa feeds primarily on small invertebrates, especially insects, but its large size allows it to take small vertebrates as well, such as the *Hypopachus* that Dundee and Liner (1985a:109) found in the mouth of a specimen in northwestern Yucatán. Dundee and Liner (1985a:109) examined the stomach contents of 70 specimens from six Mexican states and concluded that *P. venulosa* feeds predominantly on insects, especially grasshoppers and crickets, beetles, flies, and bugs. At night individuals are sometimes seen clinging to the walls of buildings, where they prey on insects attracted to electric lights.

This species is particularly well suited for existence in areas with prolonged dry seasons. Frogs from areas with a pronounced dry season tend to be larger than those from wetter areas, perhaps because the smaller surface-to-volume ratio of large frogs confers an advantage in a desiccating environment (McDiarmid, 1968). The thick dermal glands on the dorsum are rich in granular poison glands, which are relatively much more numerous than mucous glands (Duellman, 1956:14). Glands in the integument produce a thick, sticky, milky secretion that is highly irritating to mucous membranes and can cause sneezing in humans, even without direct contact (Duellman, 1956:34; Janzen, 1962:651; H. M. Smith, 1941e:38). The secretion undoubtedly discourages predators, but it may also impede evaporative water loss (McDiarmid, 1968). In addition, Goeldi (1895:135) reported that *Phrynohyas* uses its integumentary secretions to line the interior of the tree cavities within which it seeks refuge.

ETYMOLOGY The specific name, *venulosa*, is from the Latin *venula*, "a small vein," and *-osa*, meaning "full of," "augmented," or "prone to," perhaps in reference to the rough, glandular dorsal integument.

Locality Records Belize: Belize: 18 mi W, 5.5 mi S Belize City (W. T. Neill and Allen, 1959b:235), 12 mi W, 11 mi N Belize City (W. T. Neill and Allen, 1959b:235), 20 mi WSW Belize City (UF 73287), 7 mi W Boom (W. T. Neill, 1965:88), Lemonal (MPM 7730), Maskalls (W. T. Neill and Allen, 1959b:235), Rabaurel Creek near Belize City (AMNH 55660); Cayo: 1.5 mi S Bel-

mopan (CM 112158–59), Georgeville (CM 91069), Corozal: Corozal Town (KU 156888; UMRC 78-22), S edge Corozal Town (CM 105967; JLK 435), 2 mi N Corozal Town (JLK 436), 2 mi S Corozal Town (MCZ 37899), 3.5 mi SW Corozal Town (KU 1568898); Orange Walk: Orange Walk (CM 112186–90), 20 mi SE Orange Walk (BCB 12552–56), Otro Benque (USNM 194886–89), Progresso Lagoon (USNM 194901), 0.5 km S San Juan Nuevo (UTA A-15875), Tower Hill (KU 156887; USNM 167743–49, 194904); Stann Creek: Melinda Forestry Station (Fugler, 1960:10; JLK 434), 5.7 mi S Silk Grass (KU 156884–86). *Guatemala*: El Petén: near Caoba (JCL audio record), La Libertad (MCZ 21457), vicinity La Libertad (UMMZ 75301–9, 75336), N La Libertad (FMNH 27083), NW La Libertad (FMNH 27082), Sacluc (USNM 25141–42). *Mexico*: Campeche: Becan (UMMZ 76116), Calikini-Tankuche (IHNHERP 120–21), 5 mi N Campeche (UCM 15829), S edge Campeche (KU 156890–91), 21 mi E Campeche (UIMNH 86483), Carretera Tankuche–El Remate (IHNHERP 150–51, 159), Champotón (UMMZ 73170), 5 km S Champotón (KU 71315–19), 33.9 mi S Champotón (EAL 1654), 43.5 mi NE Emiliano Zapata (UTA A-2292), 7.5 km W Escárcega (KU 71320–21), 2.5 km W Escárcega (KU 71322), 12 km W Escárcega (KU 71323), 13 km W, 1 km N Escárcega (KU 75095–97), Laguna Silvituc (KU 75098), 56.6 km SW Mamantel (EAL 2923), Pacaitún on Río Candelaria (FMNH 36574–75), Plan de Ayala (JCL photo), Ruinas Edzná (KU 101529), Tankuche (IHNHERP 166, 196), Tres Brazos (FMNH 113158; UIMNH 25373); Quintana Roo: 6.6 mi N Bacalar (KU 156892), 10 mi W Bacalar (LSUMZ 33113–41), 13 mi NW Chetumal (BCB 12549–51), Chunyaxché (Himmelstein, 1980:24), Cobá (JCL sight record), 4 km NNE Felipe Carrillo Puerto (KU 71326), 7.9 km N Felipe Carrillo Puerto (JCL photo), 21.8 km NE Felipe Carrillo Puerto (EAL 2882), 13.4 mi W jct. Hwys. 186 and 307 (KU 156893), 2.5 km N Kantunil Kin (KU 171342), 9.5 km S Kantunil Kin (KU 171343), 4.6 km N Kohunlich ruins (KU 171344), 8.9 mi S La Panteria (LSUMZ 38142–43), 13.4 mi SW Limones (KU 157690), 2.8 km W Nachi Cocom (EAL 2890), 5.1 mi E Nicholas Bravo (KU 156894–97), Puerto Juárez (Himmelstein, 1980:24), 8 km W Puerto Juárez (KU 71324), 13 km W Puerto Juárez (KU 71325), Puerto Morelos (Himmelstein, 1980:24), 17.25 km NW Hwy. 307 on rd. to Reforma (KU 171346), 7.2 km S Solferino (KU 171337), 30.3 km S Solferino (KU 171338), 32.7 km S Solferino (KU 171339), 34.6 km S Solferino (KU 171340), 36.2 km S Solferino (KU 171341), 8.3 mi N Tizimín (KU 156909), Tulum (Himmelstein, 1980:24), 6.3 km W Ucum (EAL 2889); Tabasco: 4 to 6 mi S Frontera (CM 40091–92; UCM 27627–34), 11 mi N Teapa (NMSU 3104), Tenosique (USNM 115009); Yucatán: Chichén Itzá (UMMZ 83914), 12.8 km N Chunchucmil (TU 19814), Dzibilchaltún (FMNH 153421, 153423–26), 5.5 mi NE Kinchil (KU 156910), 7.7 mi SW Kinchil (KU 156913), 8.6 mi SW Kinchil (KU 156911), 10.2 mi SW Kinchil (KU 156912), 9.5 mi S Río Lagartos (KU 156908), 20.6 km S Río Lagartos (KU 171334), 31.7 km S Río Lagartos (KU 171335), 2.3 mi S, 1.9 mi E Santa Rosa (KU 156898–901), 2.2 mi E Temax (KU 156907), 5.1 mi W Temax (KU 156906), 6.6 km E Temax (KU 171336).

Genus *Scinax*

This rather large assemblage of Neotropical tree-frogs ranges from southern Mexico to Argentina and Uruguay. Known formerly as the *Hyla rubra* group, these frogs were shown by Fouquette and Delahoussaye (1977) to constitute a monophyletic group on the basis of sperm morphology. About 76 small to moderately large species are referred to this genus, but only one occurs in the Yucatán Peninsula. Leon (1969) reviewed the Middle American species (as the *H. rubra* group), and Duellman and Wiens (1992) reviewed the genus as a whole and demonstrated that the name *Scinax* has priority over *Ololygon*. *Scinax* is derived from the Greek *skinax*, "quick, nimble," presumably in reference to the quick and agile movements of these frogs.

Scinax staufferi (Cope)
(Figs. 80–82, 247; Map 33)

Hyla staufferi Cope, 1865:195. HOLOTYPE: USNM 15317. TYPE LOCALITY: Orizaba, Veracruz, Mexico.

Stauffer's treefrog; ranita arborícola (Mexico).

DESCRIPTION The males of this small treefrog average about 25 mm in snout-vent length, and the females are about 2 mm longer. The head is flat and narrower than the body (Fig. 247). The snout is rather pointed and in lateral view projects shelflike beyond the lower jaw (Fig. 80). The canthus rostralis is gently rounded, and the loreal region is flat or slightly concave. The large and protuberant eyes are two to three times the diameter of the tympanum and have horizontally elliptical pupils. The males possess a single subgular vocal sac. The limbs are moderately long, and the tips of the digits bear rounded adhesive disks. The fingers bear only a trace of webbing at their bases, whereas the toes are webbed for about half their length. The skin on the dorsal surface of the body is weakly to moderately pustulate; the venter is coarsely granular.

Fig. 80. Lateral view of the head of *Scinax staufferi* (UMRC 79-291); between Santa Rosa and Dziuché, Yucatán, Mexico.

These frogs are generally gray or grayish brown above, with a few longitudinal dark brown or black bars or broken stripes. A dark interorbital spot or bar is usually present, and the limbs have indistinct transverse dark bars. The ventral surfaces of the body and the appendages are tan or gray, without dark markings.

TADPOLE The body of the tadpole of *S. staufferi* is ovoid in dorsal view and is approximately 1.4 times longer than wide (Fig. 81). The snout is broadly rounded in dorsal aspect but truncate in lateral view. The eyes are relatively large and widely spaced. The mouth is anteroventral. The jaw sheaths are finely serrated, and there are two anterior and three posterior rows of denticles. The oral disk is not indented laterally, and the labial papillae are discontinuous dorsally. The vent tube is dextral. The spiracle is sinistral and lies slightly below the midline. The tail is about 1.8 times the length of the body and tapers to a long point. The depth of the tail substantially exceeds that of the body, and the dorsal fin extends onto the body to the level of the spiracle. The dorsal fin is deeper than the ventral fin. Dorsally, the body is light brown; the venter is translucent. The caudal musculature is tan, and the fins are clear with indistinct brown spots and blotches and a fine brown reticulum.

Fig. 81. Tadpole of *Scinax staufferi* (KU 157690), 35 mm TL; 13.4 mi SW Limones, Quintana Roo, Mexico.

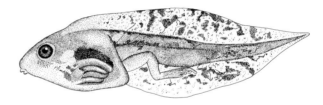

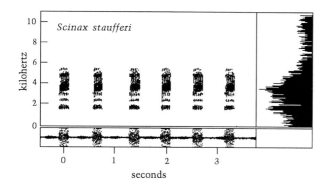

Fig. 82. Advertisement call of *Scinax staufferi*, recorded 3 June 1989, San Luis, Cayo, Belize.

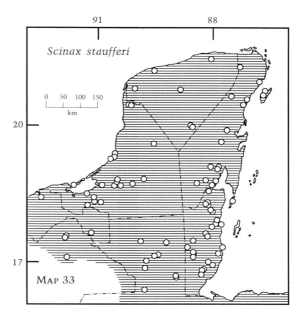

Map 33

VOCALIZATION   Duellman (1970:198) character-ized the advertisement call as a series of short, nasal notes that sound like *ah-ah-ah-ah*. My analysis of recordings from Belize, southern Campeche, Quin-tana Roo, and El Petén indicated that the note repe-tition rate is about 120 per minute, and notes have an average duration of about 120 to 130 msec (Fig. 82). Three harmonics are fairly equally emphasized: one at about 2,080 Hz, one at about 2,900, and one at about 3,900 Hz. The pulse rate is approximately 130 per second, slightly higher than that reported by Duellman (1970:198).

SIMILAR SPECIES   The other small hylids in the Yucatán Peninsula—*Hyla bromeliacia, H. ebrac-cata, H. microcephala,* and *H. picta*—are yellowish and lack the protruding snout of *Scinax staufferi.* *Triprion petasatus* has a protruding snout, but it is much larger, it is casque-headed and has a co-ossi-fied skull, and its males have paired subgular vocal sacs. The *Eleutherodactylus* and *Leptodactylus* found in the Yucatán Peninsula lack extensive web-bing between the toes.

DISTRIBUTION   *Scinax staufferi* occurs at low and moderate elevations on both the Atlantic and Pacific slopes from southern Tamaulipas and Guer-rero, respectively, south and eastward to Panama. This species occurs throughout the Yucatán Penin-sula but is relatively uncommon in the arid north-west, where it probably occurs discontinuously (Map 33).

NATURAL HISTORY   This abundant frog lives pri-marily in subhumid and xeric habitats; apparently it avoids deep forests. Duellman (1963:226) conjec-

tured that the specimen he obtained in the rain-forest at Chinajá may have been transported there from the nearby savannas of Toocog. Breeding is initiated by the onset of the summer rainy season, and males congregate at temporary bodies of water in pastures, on savannas, and at roadside ditches—often in association with *Hyla microcephala* and *H. picta*—where they call from low in the emergent vegetation or on the ground at the edge of the water. The calling sites are often well hidden in grasses or sedges, and the calling frog may be difficult to lo-cate. Amplexus is axillary, and the eggs are depos-ited in the water, where they hatch and the tadpoles complete their development. During the dry season these frogs sequester themselves beneath the bark on standing trees or within bromeliads (H. M. Smith, 1941e:38), where they can sometimes be found in considerable numbers.

SUBSPECIES   Leon (1969) recognized two sub-species, of which *S. s. staufferi* occurs in the Yuca-tán Peninsula.

ETYMOLOGY   No etymology was given by Cope, nor does the name Stauffer appear anywhere in the original description of this form. The species name is a patronym, but the identity of Stauffer is a mystery.

COMMENT   Before 1977 this species was placed in the genus *Hyla,* and much of the earlier literature will be found under that name. From 1977 to 1992 this species was placed in the genus *Ololygon*, but Duellman and Wiens (1992) showed that the name *Scinax* has priority.

Locality Records   Belize: Belize: Belize City (FMNH 4406), 11.7 mi W Belize City (KU 156826–27), 13.5 mi NW Belize City (KU 156828–32), 30 mi W Belize City (CM 105941), bet. Ladyville and Sandhill (CM 90948–49), Missionary Lake Rd., 4.3 mi E jct. Northern Hwy. (CM 91071), 8 mi NW Maskall (KU 156824–25), 19.2 mi E Roaring Creek (KU 156820–23); Cayo: Augustine (UMMZ 80741), Blancaneaux Lodge (CM 91027–28), 15 mi E Belmopan (CM 112100–1), Georgeville (CM 91037–53), 0.4 mi E Georgeville (KU 156802–3), 4 mi S San Ignacio (MCZ 37896–97), 5 mi N San Luis (KU 156804), bet. Roaring Creek and Stann Creek (UMMZ 125721); Corozal: Ambergris Cay, 22.5 km N, 14.5 km E San Pedro (CM 91113), 2.5 mi N Corozal Town (JLK 421), 5.3 mi SW Corozal Town (KU 156838–42); Orange Walk: 14.3 mi NW Maskall (KU 156833–37), 5.1 mi SE Orange Walk (NMSU 3092), Otro Benque (USNM 194942–48), Tower Hill (USNM 194932, 194957); Stann Creek: Dangriga (CM 105837–41), 5.7 mi S Silk Grass (KU 156810–19), Stann Creek (NMSU 3094), 6 mi E Stann Creek (UMMZ 125720); Toledo: 3 mi S Bladen Branch (LSUMZ 9612), 0.25 mi SW Deep River (KU 156806–9), 14.5 mi NE Golden Stream (KU 156805), 14 mi W Mango Creek (LSUMZ 10299), 3 mi S Waha Leaf Creek (MCZ 37898). *Guatemala*: Alta Verapaz: Chinajá (Duellman, 1963:226); El Petén: Flores (UMRC 78-33), 1 mi S Flores (KU 156844–52), La Libertad (KU 57770; USNM 94341–42), near La Libertad (UMMZ 75338–50), N La Libertad (FMNH 27096–97; MCZ 21459–60), Paso de los Caballos (UMMZ 79026), N edge Poptún (UMMZ 125887), 1 km S Poptún (UMMZ 120477), 2 mi N Poptún (KU 156843), Sacluc (USNM 25143), Santa Elena (UMRC 79-292; UTA A-33135), Tikal (UF 13458). *Mexico*: Campeche: Balchacaj (FMNH 108098, 108133, 108139, 108183, 108234, 108265; UIMNH 31406–10), Carretera Tankuche–El Remate (IHNHERP 214–15), Carretera Tankuche–El Remate, km 9 (IHNHERP 216), Champotón (MCZ 21448, 24075), 5 km S Champotón (KU 71296–97), 10 mi SW Champotón (UIMNH 86414), Ciudad del Carmen (FMNH 108117, 108137, 108201, 108209; UIMNH 31431), 3.3 km N Dzibalchén (UMRC 79-289), 79.9 km NE Emiliano Zapata (EAL 2915), Encarnación (FMNH 102923, 102925–27, 102929–30, 102932, 102936–37, 102939, 102942, 108086, 108092, 108102, 108106, 108111, 108118–19, 108121, 108124, 108130, 108135, 108142, 108151, 108155, 108158, 108161, 108165, 108172, 108186–88, 108194, 108211, 108215, 108221, 108223, 108230, 108235, 108239, 108241–42, 108245–46, 108255,

108260, 172100; UIMNH 30360, 31411–30), 5 mi W Escárcega (UCM 27853–59, 28113), 7.5 km W Escárcega (KU 71298–306), 6 km W Escárcega (KU 71307–8), 4.4 mi N Escárcega (KU 156854–56), 13 km W, 1 km N Escárcega (KU 71309–10, 75091–94), 56.6 km SW Mamantel (EAL 2921), Matamoros (FMNH 36572), Pacaitún (FMNH 36588–89), Potrero Viejo (FMNH 108202), 23.2 mi E Silvituc (KU 156853), Tuxpeña Camp (UMMZ 73238), Tres Brazos (FMNH 108085, 108120, 108196, 108203, 108263, 108267, 108270; UIMNH 31402–5); Chiapas: 7 km NE Ocosingo (UTEP 7691–92), Palenque (USNM 114902–25), rd. bet. Palenque and Palenque ruins (EAL 3336), San Juanito (UIMNH 49179–82); Quintana Roo: 6 mi N Bacalar (KU 156857–59), 10 mi W Bacalar (LSUMZ 38126–36), Chetumal (NMSU 3119), Cobá (UMMZ 83916), Cozumel, 3 mi N San Miguel (UCM 12327–31), Cozumel, 3.5 km N San Miguel (KU 71311, 71710–11), Cozumel, 3.5 km S San Miguel (Himmelstein, 1980:24), 10 mi S Felipe Carrillo Puerto (KU 156862–64), 16.3 mi NE Felipe Carrillo Puerto (KU 156865), 4.3 km N Kantunil Kin (KU 171324–33), 13.4 mi SE Limones (KU 156860–61), 10.8 mi E Nicolas Bravo (KU 156868), 10.5 mi NE Playa del Carmen (KU 156867), 5.5 mi NE Tulum (JCL sight record), 15.1 mi N Tulum (KU 156866); Tabasco: 4 to 6 mi S Frontera (UCM 27866–67), 10 mi E Frontera (UIMNH 86400–13), Tenosique (USNM 114950); Yucatán: 5.4 km E Bella Flor (UMRC 79-290), 1.5 mi S Libre Unión (UCM 28101–8), 3 mi S Progreso (UCM 39088–90), 13 mi S Río Lagartos (UCM 27860–64), 2.3 mi S, 1.9 mi E Santa Rosa (KU 156872–76), bet. Santa Rosa and Dzuiché (KU 171308–23; UMRC 79-292).

Genus *Smilisca*

All the known species of this rather small assemblage of treefrogs are found in Middle America. Representatives of the genus are distributed from southern Texas and Sonora to Colombia and Ecuador. Most species inhabit the lowlands of Mexico and Central America, but some occur at elevations of nearly 2,000 m. Six species of *Smilisca* are presently recognized, of which two occur in the Yucatán Peninsula. *Smilisca* is derived from the Greek *smile*, "carving knife, chisel," and the diminutive suffix *-iskos*, apparently a reference to the pointed process on the frontoparietal bone that is characteristic of members of this genus.

Duellman and Trueb (1966) and Duellman (1968a, 1970) reviewed the genus *Smilisca*.

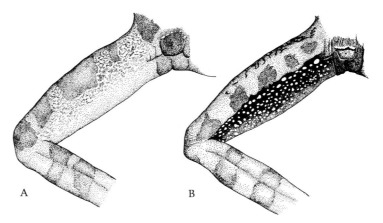

Fig. 83. Posterior views of the thighs of (A) *Smilisca baudinii* (UMRC 86-41), 7.4 km S Chekubúl, Campeche, Mexico; and (B) *S. cyanosticta* (USNM 319763), Union Camp, Columbia Forest Reserve, Toledo, Belize. Note the relatively unpatterned thigh of *S. baudinii* and the distinct light spots against a dark background in *S. cyanosticta*.

Key to the Species of the Genus *Smilisca*

Flanks and posterior surfaces of thighs of variable color but without blue spots (Fig. 83A); no white labial stripe; occurs throughout the Yucatán Peninsula (Map 34) . . . . . . *Smilisca baudinii*

Flanks and posterior surfaces of thighs with blue spots (white in preservative) (Fig. 83B); white labial stripe present; base of the Yucatán Peninsula (Map 35). . . . . *Smilisca cyanosticta*

Clave para las Especies del Género *Smilisca*

Los flancos y la superficie posterior de los muslos de color variable, pero sin puntos azules (Fig. 83A); sin una línea blanca en el labio; organismos que se distribuyen en la toda de la Península de Yucatán (Mapa 34) . . . . *Smilisca baudinii*

Los flancos y la superficie posterior de los muslos con puntos de color azul (blancos en conservador) (Fig. 83B); con una línea blanca en el labio; organismos que se distribuyen en la base de la Península de Yucatán (Mapa 35) . . . . *Smilisca cyanosticta*

Smilisca baudinii (Duméril and Bibron)
(Figs. 83A, 84, 85, 248, 249; Map 34)

Hyla baudinii A. M. C. Duméril and Bibron, 1841:564. HOLOTYPE: MNHNP 4798. TYPE LOCALITY: Mexique; restricted by H. M. Smith and Taylor (1950b:347) to Veracruz, Veracruz, Mexico.

Mexican treefrog; rana, rana arbórea, rana arborícola mexicana (Mexico); rerek (Lacandón Maya); quech (Yucatec Maya).

DESCRIPTION *Smilisca baudinii* is a medium to large, rather robust treefrog. The males average about 55 mm in snout-vent length. The females are significantly larger, exceeding the males by 10 mm on average (Fig. 248). There is significant geographical variation in the size of breeding males within the Yucatán Peninsula. Those from the base of the peninsula are generally much larger than those from the northwest (J. C. Lee, 1993). The head is relatively broad, flattened, and indistinct from the body. The snout is rounded in dorsal aspect and bluntly truncate in lateral view. The canthus rostralis is weakly angular, and the loreal region is concave. The eyes are large and prominent, with horizontally elliptical pupils and golden or silvery irises. The tympanum is distinct, and its diameter is about two-thirds that of the eye. The appendages are moderately long and robust, and the digits terminate in expanded adhesive disks, with those on the fingers larger than those on the toes. The fingers bear a trace of webbing at their bases, and the toes are extensively webbed. The males have paired subgular vocal sacs (Fig. 249). The skin on the dorsal surfaces of the body and appendages is smooth; that on the venter is granular.

Smilisca baudinii is extremely variable in color and pattern. In general, the ground color is tan, brown, olive, or green, with irregular darker spots and blotches, these often edged with black. The appendages usually bear a series of dark transverse bars (Fig. 83A). The flanks are lighter, often with dark variegations that produce a mottled or spotted appearance, especially in the groin. Most individuals have a dark interorbital bar, and there is usually a broad, dark stripe extending from the nostril, through the eye, over the tympanum, and onto the lateral surfaces of the body. A distinct dark spot is usually present on the upper lip immediately below the eye. This is bordered posteriorly by a white spot that lies just anterior to the tympanum. The ventral surfaces of the body and appendages are cream, yellowish, white, or gray and largely devoid of markings.

TADPOLE   The body of the tadpole of *S. baudinii* is ovoid in dorsal view, and the body length is approximately 1.7 times the greatest width (Fig. 84). The tail is rounded and about 1.5 times the body length. The eyes are relatively small and widely separated. The mouth is anteroventral. The jaw sheaths are serrated, and there are two anterior and three posterior rows of denticles. The oral disk is not indented laterally, and the fringing labial papillae are discontinuous dorsally. The vent tube is dextral to the ventral fin. The spiracle is sinistral and lies slightly below the midline. The dorsal fin extends well onto the body and is approximately equal to the ventral fin in depth. The maximum depth of the tail slightly exceeds that of the body. The dorsal coloration of the body is dark gray; the venter is light gray. The caudal musculature is peppered with dark pigment, and the fins are translucent with a fine, dark reticulum.

VOCALIZATION   The advertisement call consists of a series of loud notes best described as *wonk-wonk-wonk*. The number of notes in a call group may range from 3 to more than 12. The note repetition rate is about 300 to 350 per minute, note duration is about 60 msec, and the dominant frequency is approximately 2,400 Hz. At the initiation or ter-

Fig. 84. Tadpole of *Smilisca baudinii* (UMRC 93-19), 30 mm TL; Vaqueros Creek at San Luis, Cayo, Belize.

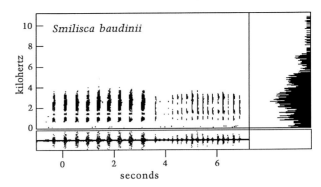

Fig. 85. Advertisement call of *Smilisca baudinii*, recorded 7 August 1989, Cobá, Quintana Roo, Mexico.

mination of a call sequence, individuals sometimes emit a series of cackling notes that have a much higher repetition rate than the advertisement call—about 650 per minute (Fig. 85).

SIMILAR SPECIES   The species of *Eleutherodactylus* in the Yucatán Peninsula lack webbing between the toes. *Phrynohyas* resembles *S. baudinii* in size and shape, but its dorsal integument is strongly glandular and the males have paired lateral (rather than subgular) vocal sacs. *Smilisca cyanosticta* has bluish spots on the flanks and posterior surfaces of the thighs (Fig. 83B) and a white labial stripe. Moreover, *S. cyanosticta* is restricted to the base of the Yucatán Peninsula, whereas *S. baudinii* is pan-peninsular (cf. Maps 34, 35). *Hyla loquax* is smaller, has an extensive axillary membrane (Fig. 32), and is red-orange between the fingers and toes.

DISTRIBUTION   This species is widely distributed at low and intermediate elevations from southern Texas on the Atlantic slope and Sonora on the Pacific slope, south and eastward throughout Mexico and Central America to Panama. It is found throughout the Yucatán Peninsula (Map 34).

NATURAL HISTORY   *Smilisca baudinii* is perhaps the most abundant and ubiquitous amphibian in the Yucatán Peninsula. On most any night during the rainy season, and in virtually every peninsular habitat, the distinctive *wonk-wonk-wonk* of calling males fills the air. Males typically call from shrubs, small trees, or at the edges of temporary bodies of water. Any temporary impoundment will suffice for breeding, including mud puddles, cattle tanks, and cisterns. Amplexus is axillary, and the females deposit masses of several hundred eggs as a film over the surface of the water. The larvae metamor-

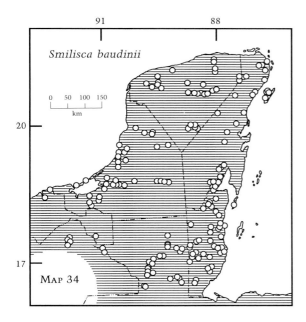

Smilisca baudinii

0   50 100 150
km

20

17

Map 34

phose into froglets averaging about 13 mm in snout-vent length (Duellman, 1970:598). At night, these frogs are often seen clinging to the sides of buildings near lights, and during and after rains they are often found on roads. During the day, and during the dry season, they seek refuge in bromeliads (H. M. Smith, 1941e:38), in the axils of aroids, beneath tree bark, and in various crevices and recesses in the substrate.

These frogs feed on invertebrates, especially insects and spiders. Noble (1918:342) found grasshoppers in the stomachs of specimens from Nicaragua.

ETYMOLOGY   The specific name, baudinii, is a patronym that honors the French commander Thomas Nicolas Baudin, who secured the type specimen while he was stationed in Mexico.

COMMENT   Duellman (1968b, 1970) summarized the available information on S. baudinii.

Locality Records Belize: Belize: Belize (CM 9321, 90917, 111921–25, 111929; FMNH 4153, 4384–87; UMMZ 75310), 11.7 mi W Belize City (KU 156924), 30 mi W Belize City (CM 105965), 11 km SW Hattieville (CM 90962), bet. Ladyville and Sandhill (CM 90933), Manatee (FMNH 4264–67), 0.8 mi N Maskall (KU 156925–26), Missionary Lake Rd. 4.3 mi E jct. Northern Hwy. (CM 91070), Rockstone Pond (UU 9362–63); Cayo: Augustine (UMMZ 80739), Belmopan (CM 105966), 4.5 mi SE Blue Hole (KU 156917–18), 1.5 mi SW Cayo (UMMZ 124724), Cocquercot (UMMZ 75331), Cohune Ridge (UMMZ 80738), Georgeville (CM 91035–36), 4 mi E Georgeville (KU 156914),

Hummingbird Hwy. bet. Roaring Creek and Stann Creek (UMMZ 124725), Macal River at Guacamallo Bridge (CM 112141), 3 mi from Millionario (UMMZ 124721, 124723), Mountain Pine Ridge (MCZ 37857–58), Mountain Pine Ridge Rd. 36 mi S Belize-Cayo Rd. (UMMZ 124720), Mountain Pine Ridge Rd. 36 to 49 mi S Belize-Cayo Rd. (UMMZ 124719), San Ignacio (UMMZ 75311), 4 mi S San Ignacio (MCZ 37856), 5 mi N San Luis (KU 156915–16), upper Raspaculo River basin (Stafford, 1991:12), Valentin (UMMZ 80735–37); Corozal: Ambergris Cay, 5 km NNE San Pedro (CM 91120–21), 3 mi S Chan Chen (JLK 437–38), S edge Corozal Town (CM 105968), 2 mi N Corozal Town (JLK 443); Orange Walk: August Pine Ridge (USNM 194929), Gallon Jug (MCZ 37848–55), 17.3 to 23.2 mi SE Orange Walk (NMSU 3076–82), 20 mi SE Orange Walk (BCB 12891–904), Otro Benque (USNM 194106–9), Progresso Lagoon (USNM 194900), 0.5 km S San Juan Nuevo (UTA A-15874), Tower Hill (KU 156927–29; USNM 167750–51, 194084–85, 194105, 194933–34); Stann Creek: Bokowina (FMNH 49064–65), Double Falls (FMNH 49066), Melinda Forestry Station (JLK 442), Middlesex (UCM 45104–10, 48033–38), Southern Hwy. 10 mi S Hummingbird Hwy. (UMMZ 124722), 5.7 mi S Stann Creek (KU 156919–20, 156923), 14 mi W Stann Creek (JLK 441), 19 mi W Stann Creek 439–40); Toledo: 3 mi S Bladen Branch (LSUMZ 11846–49), Blue Creek Village (RWV photo), 0.25 mi SW Deep River (KU 156921–22), San Pedro Columbia (MCZ 37860–62), 3 mi S Waha Leaf Creek (MCZ 37859); no specific locality (USNM 26065). Guatemala: El Petén: Asseradero Machaquila (UMMZ 124387), 16 km NNW Chinajá (KU 559420–46), 20 km NNW Chinajá (KU 57199–240), 8.6 mi W El Cruce (KU 156945–47), 26.8 mi E El Cruce (KU 156957), Dolores (UMMZ 125886), Flores (UMMZ 117985), 13.4 mi SW Flores (KU 156939), Lake Yaxhá, N shore (UTEP 6012–14), La Libertad (KU 60024–25), near La Libertad (UMMZ 75313–20, 75323–29), 3 km SE La Libertad (KU 57243–44), 8 mi S La Libertad (MCZ 21458), 15 km SE La Libertad (KU 57241–42), Las Cañas (CM 58231–32), Pacomon (USNM 71334), Piedras Negras (USNM 114469–71), 5 mi S Piedras Negras (USNM 114472), Poptún (UMMZ 120475, 124388), N edge Poptún (UMMZ 125886), 7 km NW Poptún (UMMZ 124387), 2 mi N Poptún (KU 156958–59), 4 mi N Poptún (KU 156938, 156960, 157470), Remate-Yaxhá trail (UMMZ 75321), 13.7 mi N Río de la Pasión (KU 156940), Río de la Pasión bet. Sayaxché and Subin (KU 57151), 1 mi W Ruinas Seibal (KU 156941–44), Sacluc (USNM 25137), Santa Elena (UTA A-33188–89), Sayaxché (KU 57144–45; UCM 22161–75), Tikal (AMNH uncat.; KU 157691; MCZ 81072; UF 13459–73, 24588–92; UMMZ 117983–84, 117993, 120474, 130049, 130070), 3 mi S Tikal (KU 156952–56), 5.9 mi S Tikal (KU 156948–51), Uaxactún (KU 156930–37; UMMZ 70401–3; UMRC 78-34), Yaxhá (UMMZ 75322), 12 mi E Yaxhá (UMMZ 75330); no specific locality (USNM 71794–95). *Mexico*: Campeche: Balchacaj (FMNH 102285, 102288, 102291, 102311, 110904–7, 110921, 110923, 110925, 110927, 110931–32, 110935–36, 110939–40, 110942–43, 110945, 110947, 110949–51, 110953–54, 110956, 110958–60, 110962–65, 110967, 110969, 110971–72, 110977; UIMNH 30711–22, 30726), bet. Becanchén and Dzibalchén (UMRC 79-297), 21 mi E Campeche (UIMNH 86578–91), Champotón (MCZ 21447; UMMZ 73172, 73180), 10 mi E Champotón (UMMZ 73181), 10.3 mi N Champotón (EAL 1660), 10.5 km S Champotón (KU 71365–66), 9 km S Champotón (KU 71367–68), 5 km S Champotón (KU 71369–75), 14 mi S Champotón (UMMZ 73177), 14.6 mi S Champotón (EAL 1657), 33.9 mi S Champotón (EAL 1653), 37.6 mi S Champotón (EAL 1651), Chekubúl (UMRC 86-41), Chuina (KU 75101–3), Ciudad del Carmen (FMNH 110914–18, 110922, 110924, 110929, 110934, 110941, 110944, 110957, 110975, 110981, 110983; UCM 18188–90, 20536–42; UIMNH 30703–8), Dzibalchén (KU 75413–31), 30.8 mi NE Emiliano Zapata (EAL 1644; LSUMZ 31835), 79.9 km NE Emiliano Zapata (EAL 2914), Encarnación (FMNH 102282, 102289, 102294–95, 102300, 102302, 102306–8, 102312, 102314, 102316–17, 102319, 102322, 110911–13, 110933, 110937–38, 110946, 110952, 110955, 110961, 110970, 110976, 110978, 110980, 110982, 110984; UIMNH 30727–40, 30836–37), 1 km W Escárcega (KU 71391–96), 6 km W Escárcega (KU 71397–403), 5 mi W Escárcega (UCM 27894–907, 41990), 7.5 km W Escárcega (KU 71376–89), 14 km W Escárcega (KU 71390), 13 km W, 1 km N Escárcega (KU 71404), 3 km N Hopelchén (KU 75410–11), 2 km NE Hopelchén (KU 75412), 10 mi W Hopelchén (AMNH 73371), 56.6 km SW Mamantel (EAL 2924), Matamoros (FMNH 36573), Pital (UIMNH 30741), 1 km SW Puerto Real (KU 71345–64), Ruinas Edzná (KU 101530), San José Carpizo (UMMZ 99879), 48 mi E Silvituc (CM 40093–94; UCM 27908–17), 52 mi E Silvituc (UCM 27918–19), Tres Brazos (FMNH 102284, 110920, 110968; UIMNH 30723–25), Tuxpeña Camp (UMMZ 73239), 3 mi W Xpujil (LSUMZ 33010), 11.4 mi W Xpujil (KU 156961), 2.8 mi W Xpujil (KU 156962); Chiapas: Palenque (USNM 114473–84), near Palenque (LSUMZ 33022–23), 1 km S, 3 km E Palenque (UTEP 7804), 4 km SW Palenque (EAL 3318–19), 6 km SW Palenque (EAL 3642), 6.5 km SW Palenque (UTEP 12261), 13 mi S Palenque (LSUMZ 33024–27), 10 to 15 mi S Palenque (LSUMZ 33028–35), 19.1 to 28.5 km N Pueblo Palenque (EAL 2905), rd. bet. Palenque and Palenque ruins (EAL 3320, 3334–35), San Juanito (UIMNH 49286); Quintana Roo: 6 mi N Bacalar (KU 156964), 10 mi N Bacalar (LSUMZ 33037–39), 10 mi W Bacalar (LSUMZ 33040–58), Chetumal (LACM 114042), 13 mi NW Chetumal (BCB 12890), 20.8 km W Chetumal (EAL 2888), Chunyaxché (Himmelstein, 1980:25), Cobá (FMNH 26937; Himmelstein, 1980:25; UMRC 84-98), Cozumel (Himmelstein, 1980:25), Cozumel, 2 km W Cedral (CM 55815), Cozumel, 2 mi W, 2 mi SW Cedral (CM 55807), Cozumel, San Miguel (UCM 15872–75; UMMZ 78542–44), Cozumel, 3.5 km N San Miguel (KU 71419–22), Cozumel, 6 mi E San Miguel (UMMZ 78541), Esmeralda (UMMZ 113551), Felipe Carrillo Puerto (MZFC 3390), 4 km NNE Felipe Carrillo Puerto (KU 71417–18), 4.1 km NE Felipe Carrillo Puerto (UMRC 81-9), 9.9 mi S Felipe Carrillo Puerto (KU 156966), 65.6 km NE Felipe Carrillo Puerto (EAL 2880), 4 mi S Las Palmas (UCM 39091–96), 5 mi S Las Palmas (UCM 39097–99), 13.4 mi SW Limones (KU 156965), 8.7 mi S Playa del Carmen (LSUMZ 33036), 12.7 mi SW Playa del Carmen (KU 156967), near Presumida (UCM 27920–27), 1.5 mi E Presumida (UCM 27928–31), 10 km ENE Pueblo Nuevo X-Can (KU 71406), 9 to 10 mi E Pueblo Nuevo X-Can (UCM 27932–33), Pueblo Nuevo X-Can (CM 40097–99; KU 71405; LSUMZ 28273–74; UCM 27933–50, 27973–76, 28115), Puerto Juárez (Himmelstein, 1980:25), 4 km WSW Puerto Juárez (KU 71407–11, 71721), 12 km W Puerto Juárez (KU 71412–13), 13 km W Puerto Juárez (KU 71414–16), 26 km SSE Puerto Juárez (LSUMZ 28270), Puerto Morelos (MZCIQRO 36–38, 48), 10.5 mi S Tepich (KU 156968), 13.5 mi W jct. Hwys. 186 and 307 (KU 156969); Tabasco: 4 to 6 mi S Frontera (UCM 27963–72), 10 mi E Frontera (UIMNH 86573–77), Tenosique (USNM 114505–7); Yucatán: Chichén Itzá (UCM 12355; MCZ 2478; UIMNH 30742–46; UMMZ 73173–75, 73178–79, 76171, 83107–9, 83915; USNM 72744; UU 9333–44), 3 km E Chichén Itzá (UCM 12389–92), 9 km E Chichén Itzá (KU 71438–39), 12 km E Chichén Itzá (KU 71440), Dzibilchaltún (FMNH 153410–11, 153422), Dzitás (UMRC 79-300), Dzuiché (UMRC 79-298), 0.6 km E Ebtún (LSUMZ 28288–91), 2.8 mi SW Hunucmá (KU 156977), 12.3 mi E Izamal (KU 157692), 1.5 mi S Libre Unión (UCM 28116–17), Mérida (CM 44461; MCZ 2240; UIMNH 30747–48; UMMZ 73182; UMRC 79-302), 2 mi S Mérida (AMNH 73372), 6 km S Mérida (KU 75194), Oxholom (JCL photo), Pisté (UCM 12356–88, 15876–901, 18187), 13.4 mi S Río Lagartos (KU 156975), 24.2 km S Río Lagartos (UMRC 79-301), 2.3 mi S, 1.9 mi E Santa Rosa (KU 156970–71), Telantunich (FMNH 26950), 1.7 km S Tecoh (UMRC 79-299), 3 mi N Telchac (UCM 27961–27962), 9 mi N Tizimín (KU 156976), 12 to 25 mi N Tizimín (UCM 27951–60), Valladolid (AMNH 88514), 2 km W X-Can (LSUMZ 28280), 3.5 mi E Yokdzonot (KU 71441–43, 71720); no specific locality (USNM 32298).

Smilisca cyanosticta (Smith)
(Figs. 83B, 86, 87, 250, 251; Map 35)

Hyla phaeota cyanosticta H. M. Smith, 1953:150. HOLOTYPE: USNM 111147. TYPE LOCALITY: Piedras Negras, Petén, Guatemala.

DESCRIPTION This is a moderately large tree-frog. The males attain a maximum snout-vent length of about 58 mm; females are substantially larger, reaching about 70 mm (Fig. 250). The head is broad, somewhat depressed, and slightly narrower than the body (Fig. 251). The snout is rounded in dorsal and lateral view, the canthus rostralis is angular, and the loreal region is distinctly concave. The eyes are larger than the tympanum and somewhat protruding, and the pupils are horizontally elliptical. The limbs are relatively long, the fingers and especially the toes are extensively webbed, and the digits terminate in expanded adhesive disks. The skin on the dorsal surface of the body and appendages is smooth; the ventral surface of the body is granular. Coloration is variable. Generally the adults are tan or light green above with irregular dark markings, although some are nearly uniform green or tan. The appendages usually bear dark bars against a lighter background. There is a light labial stripe and usually a broad, dark supratympanic stripe. The flanks and posterior surfaces of the thighs are tan or dark brown with numerous light blue or greenish blue spots (Fig. 83B). The venter is cream or light gray.

TADPOLE The tadpole of *S. cyanosticta* is moderately streamlined, with a body that is slightly wider than deep and a tail approximately 1.3 times the body length (Fig. 86). The snout is bluntly rounded in dorsal aspect and slightly pointed in lateral view. The relatively large eyes are widely separated. The mouth is anteroventral. The oral disk is not indented laterally, and it is surrounded by labial papillae that are discontinuous dorsally. The jaw sheaths are finely serrated, and there are two anterior and three posterior rows of denticles. The vent tube is dextral. The spiracle is sinistral and lies well below the midline of the body. The tail is acuminate, and its dorsal fin extends onto the posterior portion of the body. The depth of the tail only slightly exceeds that of the body, and the dorsal and ventral fins are subequal in depth. The dorsal surface of the body is brown, the ventral surface is

Fig. 86. Tadpole of *Smilisca cyanosticta* (KU 87651), 26 mm TL; 11 km N Vista Hermosa, Oaxaca, Mexico.

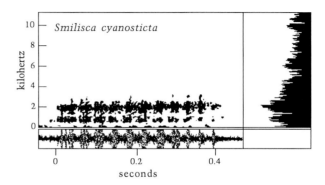

Fig. 87. Advertisement call of *Smilisca cyanosticta*, recorded 3 October 1991, 12.7 km S Palenque, Chiapas, Mexico.

translucent, and the caudal fins are clear with small clumps of brown pigment.

VOCALIZATION The advertisement call has been described as a short, rasping squawk (Pyburn, 1966:4) and as *wonk-wonk* (Duellman, 1970:602). To my ear, the former is the more accurate description. The call consists of one or two short notes, given intermittently, with pauses of up to several minutes in between. The note duration averages 340 msec, and the pulse rate is about 25 to 30 per second. Two harmonics are emphasized, one at about 800 Hz and another, the dominant frequency, at about 2,000 Hz (Fig. 87).

SIMILAR SPECIES *Smilisca cyanosticta* most closely resembles its congener, *S. baudinii*, from which it differs in having blue or greenish blue spots on its flanks and the posterior surface of its thighs (Fig. 83A,B). *Smilisca cyanosticta* also possesses a light labial stripe, and its snout is much less truncate in lateral view than that of *S. baudinii*. The species of *Agalychnis* have vertically elliptical pupils, and *Phrynohyas venulosa* has a glandular dorsum. *Hyla loquax* has red or red-orange webbing between the toes.

DISTRIBUTION This species has a restricted and discontinuous distribution. It is found at low and moderate elevations on the Atlantic slope of southern Mexico and northern Central America. In the Yucatán Peninsula it is known from northern Chiapas, northern Guatemala, and southern Belize (Map 35).

NATURAL HISTORY Uncommon in the Yucatán Peninsula, *S. cyanosticta* lives primarily in humid

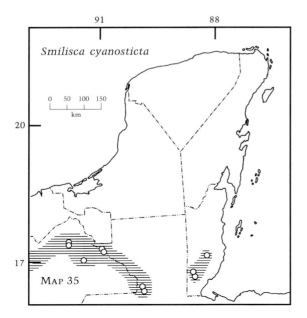

Smilisca cyanosticta

MAP 35

Genus *Triprion*

These casque-headed treefrogs are restricted to Mexico and northern Central America. They are so named because the skin on the dorsal surface of the head is fused (co-ossified) with the underlying cranial bones, which are expanded to produce a helmeted appearance. An unpaired prenasal bone is present, and it and the enlarged maxillary bones extend forward as a labial shelf. Of the two species recognized, one occurs in the Yucatán Peninsula. Trueb (1970) studied the development and evolution of casque-headed hylid frogs, including this genus. *Triprion* derives from the Greek *treis*, "three," and *prion*, "a saw." According to Duellman (1970:628), this is a reference to the serrated labial fringes found on both species.

Triprion petasatus (Cope)
(Figs. 88–90, 252; Map 36)

Pharyngodon petasatus Cope, 1865:193. HOLO-TYPE: USNM 12287. TYPE LOCALITY: Cenote Pamanche, on the new road to Progreso; restricted to Chichén Itzá, Yucatán, by H. M. Smith and Taylor (1950b:351); but that restriction rejected by Duellman and Klaas (1964:309), who argued that the type locality was probably Cenote Tamaché, 17 km north of Mérida, Yucatán, Mexico.

Yucatán casque-headed treefrog; rana arbórea (Mexico).

DESCRIPTION *Triprion petasatus* is a medium to large, moderately slender frog. The males average about 55 mm in snout-vent length, and the females are considerably larger, about 70 mm (Fig. 252). The limbs are long and rather slender. The fingers are scarcely webbed, but the toes have extensive webbing. The tips of the digits are expanded to form rounded disks. The head is covered with a large, bony casque, and the skin on the dorsal surface of the head is co-ossified with the underlying cranial bones. The unpaired prenasal bone and the maxillary bones are expanded to form a labial shelf such that the snout extends far beyond the lower jaw. A bony preorbital knob is present above each eye. Taken together, these features produce a bizarre and unique appearance (Fig. 88). The large, protruding eyes are about twice the diameter of the tympanum. The males have paired subgular vocal sacs.

The dorsal surface of the body and appendages is

premontane forests. According to Pyburn (1966:2), who studied the species in southern Veracruz, breeding probably continues throughout the rainy season. Pyburn found individuals breeding in shallow pools, in forks of trees, and in depressions in logs. The eggs were deposited as a thin surface film, and the clutch size ranged from about 500 to 2,000 eggs. A captive female produced nine clutches of eggs over a 13-month period, and metamorphosis occurred at a snout-vent length of 14 mm (Pyburn, 1966:5).

ETYMOLOGY The specific name, *cyanosticta*, is from the Greek *kyanos*, "dark blue," and *stiktos*, "spotted," in reference to the blue spots on the flanks and thighs.

COMMENT Duellman (1968c) reviewed the literature on *S. cyanosticta*, and the species is treated comprehensively in Duellman, 1970.

Locality Records Belize: Cayo: Puente Natural (CMM photo); Stann Creek: western Cockscomb Basin (UMRC 92-22; Toledo: Gloria Camp, Columbia River Forest Reserve (USNM 319765), Unión Camp, Columbia River Forest Reserve (USNM 319762–64). *Guatemala*: Alta Verapaz: Chinajá (Duellman, 1963:229); El Petén: 10 km NNW Chinajá (KU 55934), Piedras Negras (FMNH 99006-7; UIMNH 28853; USNM 111139–47), 5 mi S Piedras Negras (FMNH 99008). *Mexico*: Chiapas: Monte Libano (MCZ 28217–19), 8 mi S Palenque (LSUMZ 38081–82), 12 mi S Palenque (JCL audio record).

Fig. 88. Ventrolateral view of the head of *Triprion petasatus* (UMRC 79-306), 55 mm SVL; Tecoh, Yucatán, Mexico.

generally brown, olive, or gray, with indistinct darker spots and reticulations. The appendages bear dark spots or bars against a lighter background. The venter is light tan or gray.

TADPOLE   The body of the tadpole is ovoid in dorsal view, and the length is approximately 1.5 times the greatest width (Fig. 89). The tail is rounded at the tip, roughly 1.2 times the body length, and its greatest depth slightly exceeds that of the body. The eyes are relatively small and widely separated. The spiracle is sinistral and lies well below the level of the midline. The vent tube is dextral to the ventral fin. The mouth is anteroventral. The jaw sheaths bear coarse serrations, and there are two anterior and three posterior rows of denticles. The oral disk is not indented laterally, and the fringing labial papillae are incomplete dorsally. The dorsal fin extends well onto the body and is approximately equal in depth to the ventral fin. Dorsally the body is grayish brown; the venter is lighter brown. There is a brown reticulum on the caudal musculature, and the caudal fins are clear with a fine network of dark brown pigment.

VOCALIZATION   The advertisement call is a ducklike *quack-quack-quack*. My recordings from various localities in Yucatán and Quintana Roo indicate that the dominant frequency lies between 2,100 and 2,300 Hz, and the pulse rate averages

Fig. 89. Tadpole of *Triprion petasatus* (KU 71730), 31 mm TL; 3.5 km N Pisté, Yucatán, Mexico.

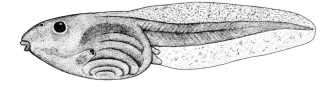

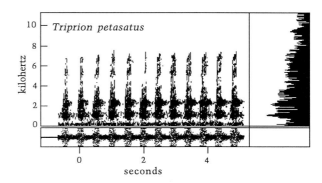

Fig. 90. Advertisement call of *Triprion petasatus*, recorded 7 August 1989, Cobá, Quintana Roo, Mexico.

between 75 and 90 per second. The note repetition rate is quite variable, ranging from about 40 to 105 per minute; the average note duration is approximately 350 msec (Fig. 90).

SIMILAR SPECIES   The unique configuration of the skull of *T. petasatus* distinguishes it from all other species in the Yucatán Peninsula. Moreover, no other treefrog in the peninsula exhibits cranial co-ossification. The two species of *Smilisca* lack supraorbital knobs and a labial shelf. *Scinax staufferi* possesses a modest labial shelf (Fig. 80) but is much smaller and lacks supraorbital knobs.

DISTRIBUTION   This species is very nearly restricted to the Yucatán Peninsula, where it occurs more or less continuously from central El Petén

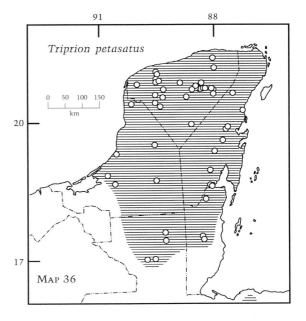

MAP 36

northward (Map 36). L. D. Wilson et al. (1986:4) reported an apparently disjunct population at Santa Elena, Cortes, Honduras.

NATURAL HISTORY These curious frogs generally inhabit seasonally dry forests and savannas. They are particularly abundant in the arid northwest portion of the peninsula, where the ducklike quacking of the males can be heard in the henequén fields and thorn forests on any rainy summer night. Males call from shrubs and small trees and from the edges of temporary bodies of water. Often several males chorus from small limestone solution pits no more than 10 or 15 cm in diameter. Females approaching the water are intercepted by males and clasped, often well before they reach the water. J. C. Lee and Crump (1980) documented male-male competition for females and a pattern of size-assortative mating in this species. Amplexus is axillary, and the eggs are deposited in the water, where the tadpoles complete their development.

Triprion is nocturnal, and its aboveground activity is restricted to the rainy season. During the day these frogs seek refuge in the recesses of tree trunks and in rock crevices. Stuart (1935:37) reported that at La Libertad, El Petén, individuals could be found during the day in holes in trees surrounding an aguada. The frogs plugged the openings with their heads and were nearly impossible to extract. This behavior, termed *phragmosis*, probably helps prevent desiccation. A reduction in cutaneous water loss across the co-ossified skull relative to other surfaces of the body has been demonstrated for certain other frogs with co-ossified skulls (Seibert et al., 1974). These frogs feed on a variety of invertebrates, and large females will eat other species of small frogs.

ETYMOLOGY The specific name, *petasatus*, is derived from the Greek *petasos*, a kind of broad-brimmed hat, and the Latin suffix *-atus*, meaning "provided with," in reference to the helmetlike casque.

COMMENT Duellman and Klaas (1964) summarized the biology of *T. petasatus*, and the species was treated comprehensively by Duellman (1970:628).

Locality Records Belize: Cayo: ca. 1.5 mi S Belmopan (CM 112160–61), ca. 5 mi S Belmopan (CM 112169–70); Corozal: 3 mi S Chan Chen (JLK 427), 0.5 mi N Corozal (JLK 428); Orange Walk: Orange Walk Town (Hoevers and Henderson, 1974:1). *Guatemala*: El Petén: La Libertad (CAS 2232; FMNH 27102–3; MCZ 21462; UMMZ 75300), San Francisco (UTA A-26016–18, A-26505–6), Tikal (KU 156982–89; UF 13474), Uaxactún (KU 156978–81; UMRC 77-1; UF 84491). *Mexico*: Campeche: Becan (UWZH 20512), Carretera Nunkini–Hacienda Santa Cruz, km 7 (IHNHERP 127, 134), 5 km S Champotón (KU 71444), 7.5 km S Chekubúl (UMRC 80-60), Dzibalchén (KU 75175–88), 7.5 km W Escárcega (KU 71445–48), 48 mi E Silvituc (CM 40100–3; UCM 27977–28006); Quintana Roo: 10 mi W Bacalar (LSUMZ 33273–88), Chunyaxché (Himmelstein, 1980:25), Cobá (JCL audio record), 6 to 8 km NE Felipe Carrillo Puerto (UMRC 79-313), 10 mi S Felipe Carrillo Puerto (LSUMZ 33272), 21.5 km NE Felipe Carrillo Puerto (KU 171358), 40 mi S Felipe Carrillo Puerto (UIMNH 79899–902), 1.5 mi E Presumida (UCM 28007–8); Yucatán: 5.4 km E Bella Flor (JCL photo), Cenote Pamanche 17 km N Mérida (USNM 12287), Chichén Itzá (FMNH 26921–23, 111002; MCZ 3559, 6835, 11633; UIMNH 30670; UMMZ 73188–92, 83106; USNM 118660–62), 2.5 km E Chichén Itzá (KU 71484–93, 71746), 9 km E Chichén Itzá (AMNH 23556, 69398; KU 71449–63, 71732–34, 71736, 92720; UU 9276–95), 12 km E Chichén Itzá (KU 71464–82, 71731, 71778–80, 89926–28), Dzibilchaltún (KU 75190–93; FMNH 153431), 3.6 km S Dzitás (UMRC 79-310), 0.6 km E Ebtún (LSUMZ 28275–79, 28287), Labná (MZFC 3175), Mama (KU 171351), vicinity Mérida (KU 92632–39; UMRC 77-3; UTA A-1120), 6 km S Mérida (KU 71735), 3 km S Muna (KU 171398), 7 km N Muna (KU 75189), Pisté (KU 71529–30, 71759–60; UCM 12393–401, 15830–39; UF 17550; UMMZ 80448), 2 mi N Pisté (UMMZ 143300), 5 km W Pisté (UTA A-20925), 24.2 km S Río Lagartos (UMRC 79-311), San Pedro Chimay̓ (KU 171353–57), 0.7 km S Sudzal (KU 171399), 0.7 km N Tahdzibichén (KU 171352), 1.7 km S Tecoh (UMRC 79-309), Tekom (FMNH 49071–86), 12 mi N Tizimín (UCM 28009), 3.6 km S Valladolid (UMRC 80-45), 3.5 km E Yokdzonot (KU 71494–528, 71724–30, 71744).

Family Centrolenidae

This is a moderately large family of predominantly tropical New World frogs. The family ranges from southern Mexico through Central America to northern Argentina and Bolivia. Most centrolenids are green above and have a transparent venter through which the viscera are visible. They oviposit on vegetation overhanging moving water. Three genera and in excess of 100 species of these small arboreal frogs are presently recognized, with many additional species awaiting description. One genus occurs in the Yucatán Peninsula.

Genus *Hyalinobatrachium*
(Glass Frogs)

This Neotropical genus is distributed from Guerrero on the Pacific slope and Veracruz on the Atlantic slope southward to Brazil, Bolivia, and northern Argentina. These diminutive frogs are arboreal inhabitants of humid tropical forests, where they are generally found in association with streams. Twenty-four species are presently recognized, and several undescribed South American species await formal description. One species occurs in the Yucatán Peninsula. The frogs now assigned to this genus were long considered members of the genus *Centrolenella*, but Ruiz-Carranza and Lynch (1991) erected the genus *Hyalinobatrachium* to accommodate the clade that included *C. fleischmanni*. *Hyalinobatrachium* is from the Greek *hyaleos*, "glassy," and *batrachion*, "small frog," in reference to the semitransparent and delicate appearance of these frogs.

Hyalinobatrachium fleischmanni (Boettger)
(Figs. 91–93, 253; Map 37)

Hylella fleischmanni Boettger, 1893:251. HOLO-TYPE: SMF 3760. TYPE LOCALITY: San José, Costa Rica.

Fleischmann's glass frog; ranita verde (Guatemala, Mexico).

DESCRIPTION *Hyalinobatrachium fleischmanni* is a tiny, delicate frog—so delicate, in fact, that individuals have been killed by the impact of a falling raindrop (Hayes, 1991:107). The males average about 25 mm in snout-vent length, and the females are about a millimeter longer. The head is broad and rounded in dorsal aspect, and the snout is truncate in lateral view (Fig. 253). The tympanum is small, inconspicuous, and less than half the diameter of the eye. The dorsal surface of the head and body is shagreened, and ventrally the skin is granular. The limbs are slender and delicate, and the tips of the digits are slightly expanded. The toes are exten-

Fig. 91. Palmar view of the hand of *Hyalinobatrachium fleischmanni* (UMRC 89-40) showing extensive webbing between digits 3 and 4; 3.6 km N San Luis, Cayo, Belize.

sively webbed, whereas the fingers bear extensive webbing only between digits 3 and 4 (Fig. 91). The eyes are large and protruding and face forward, permitting a high degree of binocular vision. The iris is gold, and the pupil is horizontally elliptical.

Dorsally, the head, body, and appendages are pale lime green, sometimes with a few small cream or yellow spots. The skin of the ventral surfaces is transparent, and the viscera are visible through the ventral skin.

TADPOLE   The tadpole has a broad, flat body that is noticeably wider than deep. The body length is about 1.7 times the greatest width, and the tail is remarkably long—more than twice the length of the body (Fig. 92). The snout is rounded in dorsal aspect and ovate in lateral view. The eyes are small, rather close-set, and situated high on the head. The dark pigmentation in the orbit and the position of the eyes give live tadpoles a planarian-like appearance when viewed from above. The mouth is directed ventrally. The keratinized jaw sheaths bear fine serrations, and there are two anterior and three posterior rows of denticles. The oral disk is not indented laterally, and it is surrounded by large, fleshy papillae that are discontinuous dorsally. The vent tube is medial. The spiracle is sinistral, lies slightly below the midline, and opens on the posterior third of the body. The depth of the tail only slightly exceeds that of the body. The dorsal and caudal fins

Fig. 92. Tadpole of *Hyalinobatrachium fleischmanni* (KU 68376), 22 mm TL; 4 km S Pavones, Cartago, Costa Rica.

are shallow and subequal, and the dorsal fin extends onto the posterior surface of the body. In life the body and caudal musculature are red. In preservative they are a pale pinkish, with indistinct tan pigmentation on the dorsal surface of the body and caudal musculature.

VOCALIZATION   The advertisement call consists of a single high-pitched note repeated at irregular intervals of several seconds to more than a minute. The call is a bell-like *tink* or *peep* (B. J. Greer and Wells, 1980:319). Starrett and Savage (1973:63) described the call as a short note and likened it to a rising whistled *wheet* lasting 400 to 500 msec. My analyses of calls from individuals in the Mountain Pine Ridge of Belize indicate a much shorter note duration, about 125 msec. Two harmonics are emphasized, the dominant one at about 4,400 Hz and another at about 9,000 Hz (Fig. 93). In addition to their advertisement call, males also emit an aggressive call during male-male agonistic interactions. It was described by McDiarmid and Adler (1974:75) as a medium- to low-pitched *preep*, and by B. J. Greer and Wells (1980:319) as a *mew*.

SIMILAR SPECIES   No other frog in the Yucatán Peninsula is lime green above and transparent below. Hylid frogs are occasionally green or greenish, but they lack the transparent venter and forward-facing eyes of *Hyalinobatrachium*.

DISTRIBUTION   *Hyalinobatrachium fleischmanni* is the most widely distributed member of its genus. It ranges from Guerrero and Veracruz to Ecuador, Colombia, Venezuela, and Surinam. It also has a wide elevational range, from sea level to above 1,600 m. In the Yucatán Peninsula the species oc-

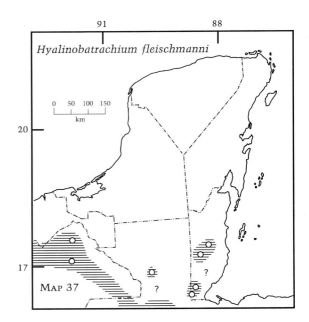

curs discontinuously in Belize, El Petén, and northern Chiapas (Map 37).

NATURAL HISTORY   These tiny, delicate frogs are restricted to the immediate vicinity of swift-flowing streams, at least during the breeding season, when they are most likely to be encountered. They are common in suitable habitat, but this is limited in the Yucatán Peninsula.

Except for the information recorded by Duellmen and Tulecke (1960), little is known of the biology in southeastern Mexico and northern Central America. The species has been the subject of several studies in lower Central America, however (Clark, 1981; B. J. Greer and Wells, 1980; Hayes, 1991; Jacobson, 1985), and it is from these that the following summary is mostly derived. Through most the rainy season, males vocalize from the undersides of leaves in vegetation overhanging water. The males are territorial, and male-male aggression sometimes escalates to include physical grappling (McDiarmid and Adler, 1974:75). The females approach calling males and initiate amplexus, which is axillary. Clutches of about 25 to 30 pale green eggs are deposited on the undersurfaces of leaves. At night males periodically attend their egg clutches and hydrate the eggs by ventral brooding (Hayes, 1991). Clutches deprived of their attendant males experience increased mortality from dessication (Hayes, 1991). *Hyalinobatrachium fleischmanni* larvae undergo initial development within the egg. Hatching typically occurs during a rain, and the larvae fall

Fig. 93. Advertisement call of *Hyalinobatrachium fleischmanni*, recorded 4 June 1989, 2.5 mi N San Luis, Cayo, Belize.

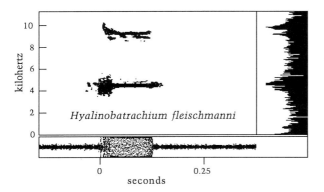

directly into the water, where they complete metamorphosis after about nine months.

The larvae of a drosophilid fly infest the gelatinous egg masses of this species and feed on the developing frog embryos, thereby decreasing embryonic survival (Villa, 1977, 1984).

ETYMOLOGY The specific name, *fleischmanni*, is a patronym honoring Carl Fleischmann, a German naturalist affiliated with the Senckenberg Museum who secured herpetological material in Costa Rica in the latter part of the nineteenth century.

COMMENT *Hyalinobatrachium fleischmanni* was placed in the genus *Centrolenella* until Ruiz-Carranza and Lynch (1991) erected a new genus on the basis of their cladistic analysis of morphological characters. *Hyalinobatrachium* contains *H. fleischmanni* and 23 other species formerly placed in *Centrolenella*. The name *C. viridissima* has often been applied to this form in Mexico. Starrett and Savage (1973:64) could find no basis for separating *C. viridissima* from *C. fleischmanni*, however, and they applied the latter name to the frogs in Mexico, including those in the Yucatán Peninsula.

Locality Records Belize: Cayo: 7.1 km SSE Belmopan (Olson, 1984:76), 2.2 mi N San Luis (KU 156990; UMRC 89-40); Toledo: Blue Creek Village (CM photos 33025.27–29), Dolores (JCL acoustic record). *Guatemala*: El Petén: Arroyo Subin at Santa Teresa (UMMZ 79025). *Mexico*: Chiapas: 6.9 km N Ocosingo (JCL photo), Palenque ruins (UIMNH 11302–3).

Family Microhylidae

The microhylids are a predominantly Southern Hemispheric group of frogs with diverse morphologies and habits. Some are squat and toadlike, others resemble treefrogs, and still others are slender and semiaquatic. Some species lack free-swimming larvae, instead producing larvae that undergo direct development within a terrestrial egg. In the New World, the family occurs from the southeastern United States south through Mexico and Central America to Argentina. In the Old World, the family is found in sub-Saharan Africa, Southeast Asia, and the Indo-Australian Archipelago. There are roughly 64 genera and 313 species, of which 2 genera and 2 species occur in the Yucatán Peninsula.

Key to the Genera of the Family Microhylidae

Adult SVL greater than 30 mm; dorsum brown or reddish brown with a thin vertebral stripe
. . . . *Hypopachus*

Adult SVL less than 30 mm; dorsum gray or tan, without a vertebral stripe . . . . . . *Gastrophryne*

Clave para los Géneros de la Familia Microhylidae

Adultos mayores a 30 mm de LHC; dorso de color pardo o pardo rojizo, con una línea vertebral delgada . . . . *Hypopachus*

Adultos menores a 30 mm de LHC; dorso de color gris o bronceado, sin una línea vertebral
. . . . *Gastrophryne*

Genus *Gastrophryne*
(Narrow-mouthed Toads)

This genus of small, toadlike frogs ranges from the central United States to Costa Rica. All five species are roughly triangular in dorsal aspect, with squat bodies and narrow, pointed heads. Only one species occurs in the Yucatán Peninsula. The most recent taxonomic treatments of *Gastrophryne* are by Nelson (1972a, 1973b). *Gastrophryne* is derived from the Greek *gaster*, "belly" or "stomach," and *phrynos*, "toad," presumably in reference to the squat, globose body form.

Gastrophryne elegans (Boulenger)
(Figs. 36B, 94, 254; Map 38)

Engystoma elegans Boulenger, 1882:162. HOLO-TYPE: BMNH 1947.2.11.86. TYPE LOCALITY: Cordoba (Córdoba), Veracruz, Mexico.

Elegant narrow-mouthed toad; sapito (Guatemala, Mexico).

DESCRIPTION The adult males attain an average snout-vent length of only about 24 mm; the females average about 27 mm. The body is squat, the head is small, and the snout is pointed (Fig. 254). Viewed from above, narrow-mouthed toads appear triangular. The appendages are short and stocky. The eyes are small, and there is a transverse fold of skin across the head behind the eyes, although this may be obscure or lacking in preserved specimens. The terminal phalanges on the outer toes are slightly dilated, and the toes bear traces of webbing at their bases.

The dorsal ground color is gray or tan with one or a few large, dark brown blotches, which are usually outlined with black. The appendages have dark brown bars, also outlined in black. A dark brown lateral stripe passes from the snout, through the eye, to the shoulder, and posteriorly to the groin. The dark brown lateral surfaces of the head and body contrast sharply with the lighter dorsum. Ventrally, the coloration consists of a dark brown ground color with numerous light spots, many of which coalesce to form extensive areas of light pigmentation. The undersurfaces of the appendages also bear numerous light spots.

TADPOLE The tadpole of *G. elegans* is poorly known. The following account is based on the description of a tadpole presumed to be *G. elegans* by Nelson and Altig (1972) and my examination of KU 145983 from Veracruz, Mexico (Fig. 94). The body length is approximately 1.2 times the greatest width. The eyes are small, widely spaced, and lie on the lateral edge of the body. The snout is truncate in lateral view, and the mouth is terminal. Keratinized mouthparts are lacking, and a pair of semicircular flaps encloses the mouth. The flaps are smooth, without papillae or scalloping (Fig. 36B). The spiracle lies in close association with the anal tube, near the ventral midline, and is deflected to the right. The vent tube is dextral. The tail is short—approximately 1.3 times the length of the body—and bluntly rounded at its tip. The dorsal and ventral fins are subequal in depth, and the dorsal fin extends only slightly onto the body. The maximum

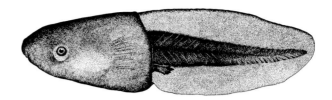

Fig. 94. Tadpole of *Gastrophryne elegans* (KU 145983), 25 mm TL; 2.6 km E. Tolome, Veracruz, Mexico.

depth of the caudal fin slightly exceeds that of the body. The body is uniformly black dorsally and ventrally, and there may be a light lateral stripe on the caudal musculature at the base of the tail.

VOCALIZATION The call of *G. elegans* is a high-pitched, rather nasal *naaaa*. Nelson (1972a:113) reported that males from Alta Verapaz produced calls that were 4 to 5 sec in duration and had a fundamental frequency of 200 Hz and a dominant frequency between 2,900 and 3,300 Hz.

SIMILAR SPECIES The larger *Hypopachus variolosus* is similar in habitus but is brick red above and has a narrow, light vertebral stripe.

DISTRIBUTION *Gastrophryne elegans* occurs at low elevations on the Atlantic slope from central Veracruz through northern Guatemala and Belize to northern Honduras. It occurs through the base of the Yucatán Peninsula as far north as central Campeche and northern Belize (Map 38).

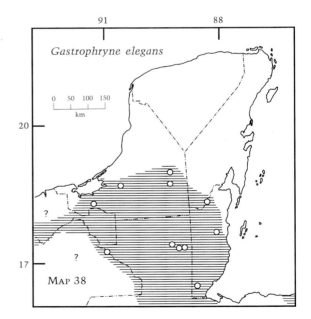

NATURAL HISTORY   This inconspicuous frog inhabits leaf litter in humid lowland forests. It is uncommon in the Yucatán Peninsula, although individuals are occasionally found on the forest floor at night. Duellman (1965a:589) reported a specimen taken from submerged grass roots in a marsh in southern Campeche. These diminutive frogs feed primarily on ants, as do most others of the genus *Gastrophryne* (Nelson, 1972a:123).

Reproduction occurs during the rainy season, and males call from the surface of temporary bodies of water, usually in forests. Amplexus is presumably axillary. The eggs are deposited directly into the water, where they hatch and the larvae complete their development.

ETYMOLOGY   The specific name, *elegans*, is Latin meaning "elegant" or "fine," presumably in reference to the attractive coloration.

COMMENT   *Gastrophryne elegans* was reviewed by Nelson (1972b).

Locality Records Belize: Belize: 30.5 mi WSW Belize City (CM 109027); Orange Walk: Albion Island (Henderson and Hoevers, 1975:16); Stann Creek: Cockscomb Jaguar Reserve (CM photo); Toledo: Blue Creek Village (ASU 10177; RWV photo). *Guatemala*: El Petén: 5 mi S Piedras Negras (USNM 116025), Tikal (UMMZ 117977; UMRC 79-253), near Yaxhá (UMMZ 77060), 12 mi E Yaxhá (UMMZ 75440). *Mexico*: Campeche: Becan (UMMZ 76118), 5 mi W Escárcega (UCM 28010–17), Tres Brazos (FMNH 103218), 20 km N Xpujil (KU 75099).

Genus *Hypopachus*

This genus of microhylid frogs, which contains but two species, ranges from southern Texas and Sonora to Costa Rica. Morphologically these frogs are larger versions of *Gastrophryne*, which they closely resemble in their squat bodies, small heads, and pointed snouts. *Hypopachus* is from the Greek *hypo*, meaning "under," "beneath," or "less than usual," and *pachys*, "thick." As an adjective *hypopachus* means "somewhat fat or thick." Nelson (1973a, 1974) provided the most recent taxonomic treatment of the genus.

Hypopachus variolosus (Cope)
(Figs. 33, 36A, 95, 96, 255; Map 39)

Engystoma variolosum Cope, 1866:131. HOLOTYPE: USNM 6486. TYPE LOCALITY: Arriba, Costa Rica (= uplands of Costa Rica?).

Sheep frog; rana manglera (Mexico); chacmuch (Yucatec Maya).

DESCRIPTION   These small, squat frogs have globose bodies and small, pointed heads (Fig. 255). The males average about 33 mm in snout-vent length, and females are about 38 mm long. The limbs are relatively short and stout. The fingers and toes are unwebbed, and their tips are not expanded. There are two enlarged, keratinized tubercles on the heel. There is a transverse fold of skin immediately behind the eyes (Fig. 33), although it may be indistinct, especially in preserved specimens. The skin is smooth.

The dorsum is predominantly brown or reddish brown with a series of dark brown or black markings on the sides, at the waist, and on the dorsal surfaces of the limbs. A thin yellow or cream line extends from the tip of the snout to just above the vent. The venter is light tan or gray with variegated darker markings. In many specimens a thin, light line extends from the chin onto the abdomen, and it may be joined at the midline by similar lines originating in the axillary regions.

TADPOLE   The body is oval in dorsal aspect, and the length is about 1.4 times the greatest width. The eyes are small and widely separated. In dorsal view the snout is bluntly rounded, although in lateral view it is rather pointed (Fig. 95). The tail is approximately 1.8 times the length of the body and has a maximum depth that slightly exceeds that of the body. The dorsal fin, which extends onto the posterior surface of the body, may slightly exceed the ventral fin in depth. There is a single median spiracle. Keratinized mouthparts are lacking, and the oral disk is covered by a pair of fleshy flaps that bear papillae (Fig. 36A). Dorsally the body is tan or brown; the venter is lighter tan. The caudal mus-

Fig. 95. Tadpole of *Hypopachus variolosus* (KU 104203), 25 mm TL; 24 km S Las Cruces, Chiapas, Mexico.

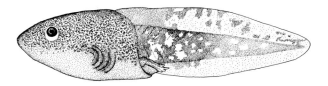

culature is brown with lighter spots, and the dorsal and caudal fins are mottled with brown.

VOCALIZATION As the English common name suggests, calling males emit a nasal, sheeplike bleat. This advertisement call consists of a single drawn-out note that lasts about 2.5 to 3 seconds. It is given at irregular intervals ranging from 10 to 15 seconds to up to several minutes in duration. The dominant frequency is approximately 2,750 Hz (Fig. 96).

SIMILAR SPECIES *Gastrophryne elegans* is smaller and lacks the reddish brown dorsum and vertebral stripe of *H. variolosus*. *Rhinophrynus dorsalis* is larger and lacks a transverse fold of skin behind the eyes.

DISTRIBUTION Sheep frogs occur at low and moderate elevations from southern Texas and Sonora south to Costa Rica. They probably occur throughout the Yucatán Peninsula, although there are no records from southern Belize (Map 39).

NATURAL HISTORY This terrestrial and fossorial frog is widespread and common in the Yucatán Peninsula in both forested and more open situations, although it is apparently most abundant in the latter. Individuals are commonly found in breeding congregations, which generally form at temporary bodies of water. Often sheep frogs can be found at night on roads after heavy rains; otherwise, they sequester themselves beneath surface debris and in burrows of other animals or of their own construction. They feed on invertebrates, especially ants (Dundee and Liner, 1985a:109) and termites.

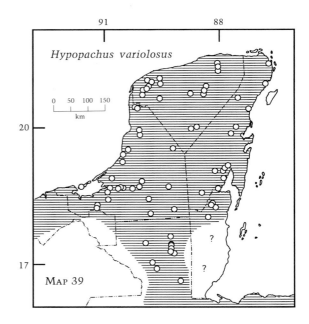

During the rainy season, males call from temporary bodies of water such as roadside ditches, flooded pastures, and limestone sinkholes, usually from the water's surface. Amplexus is axillary, and the eggs are deposited directly into the water, where the larvae develop. They occasionally oviposit in aboveground tree hollows, at least in Costa Rica, where McDiarmid and Foster (1975:264) found a single tadpole of *H. variolosus* in a hollow nearly a meter above the forest floor.

ETYMOLOGY The specific name, *variolosus*, is from the Latin *vario*, "to variegate" or "change," and *-osus*, a termination denoting "full of," "augmented," or "prone to," presumably in reference to the variegated pattern on the venter.

Locality Records   Belize: Corozal: 2 mi N Corozal Town (JLK 444–48); Orange Walk: Lamanai (ROM H12708, H12752–53), 20 mi SE Orange Walk (BCB 12942–50), Otro Benque (USNM 194114–18), Tower Hill (KU 156991). *Guatemala*: El Petén: 5.8 mi E El Cruce (KU 157003), Paso Caballos (MCZ 19937–38), vicinity La Libertad (UMMZ 75354–58), N La Libertad (MCZ 21463), 15 km SE La Libertad (KU 58962–63), 1 km W Poptún (UMMZ 128076), Tikal (UF 13394–402; UMMZ 117975–76), 3 mi S Tikal (KU 157000–2), 8.4 mi S Tikal (KU 156999), 14.2 mi S Tikal (KU 156998), Uaxactún (KU 156992–97; MCZ 12170). *Mexico*: Campeche: Balakbal (UMMZ 76117), Becan (UWZH 20494, 20496–501, 20504, 20508–10, 20522, 20524, 20528, 20532–34, 20537–39, 20542, 20552), bet. Be-

Fig. 96. Advertisement call of *Hypopachus variolosus*, recorded 9 June 1989, near Caobas, El Petén, Guatemala.

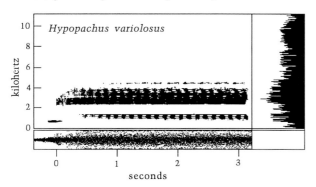

canchén and Dzibalchén (UMRC 79-266), 21 mi E Campeche (UIMNH 86744–47), Carretera Tankuche–El Remate (IHNHERP 147, 187, 191), Champotón (USNM 118656–57; UMMZ 73146), S Champotón (MCZ 19753, 21451), 24 km S Champotón (Nelson, 1974:263), Ciudad del Carmen (UMMZ 83551), 28 km N Concepción (KU 75104), 79.9 km NE Emiliano Zapata (CM 63198; EAL 2916), Encarnación (FMNH 100064, 127008–14, 127016–52, 127054–64; UIMNH 31244–72), 1 km W Escárcega (KU 71531–38), 4.5 km W Escárcega (KU 71539–40), 6 km W Escárcega (KU 71541–42), 7.5 km W Escárcega (KU 71543–55), 5 mi W Escárcega (CM 40111–17; UCM 28021–63), 11 km W Escárcega (KU 71556–58), 14 km W Escárcega (KU 71559–63), 15.5 km W Escárcega (KU 71564–66), 17.7 mi E Escárcega (LSUMZ 38005), Laguna Chumpich (KU 75105), Laguna Silvituc (KU 75106), 56.6 km SW Mamantel (EAL 2922), Plan de Ayala (JCL photo), Pital (FMNH 127053), San José Carpizo (UMMZ 99878), Tres Brazos (UIMNH 31242–43), Tuxpeña Camp (UMMZ 73235), km 143 on Hwy. 186 (UWZH 20530); Quintana Roo: Lake Bacalar (LSUMZ 33164–67), 6.7 mi N Bacalar (KU 157004), 10 mi W Bacalar (LSUMZ 33162–63, 33169–84), 15 mi NW Chetumal (BCB 12941), near Cobá (JCL photo), 4 km NNE Felipe Carrillo Puerto (KU 71567–68), 29.1 mi NE Felipe Carrillo Puerto (KU 157006), jct. Hwy. 186 and rd. to Kohunlich ruins (KU 171359), 13.4 mi SW Limones (KU 157005), Laguna Alvarado (Duellman, 1965a:589), 10.9 mi NE Playa del Carmen (KU 157007), Puerto Juárez (Duellman, 1965a:589), Tulum ruins (UMMZ 172760–61); Yucatán: 5.4 km E Bella Flor (UMRC 79-267), Chichén Itzá (AMNH 14297; UMMZ 83105, 83918), 12.8 km N Chunchucmil (TU 19815), 13.8 km N Chunchucmil (TU 19821–22), Dzibilchaltún (FMNH 153430), Dzitás (UMRC 79-264), 4.8 km S Dzitás (KU 71569), 10.5 mi NW Hunucmá (KU 157012), 5.3 mi SW Kinchil (KU 157010–11), 10.9 mi SW Kinchil (KU 157009), 1.5 mi S Libre Unión (UCM 28118), Mérida (UCM 39100–1), 14 km N, 2 km E Mérida (UMMZ 73197), 24.2 km S Río Lagartos (UMRC 79-265), 2.3 mi S, 1.9 mi E Santa Rosa (KU 157008), Telantunich (FMNH 26965), 15 mi N Tizimín (UCM 28064–69), 12 to 25 mi N Tizimín (UCM 28066–68), 16.2 km S Yaxcopoil (CM 45258–60).

Family Ranidae (True Frogs)

Members of this cosmopolitan family exhibit a wide variety of morphologies and habits. New World ranids are generally streamlined, smooth-skinned, semiaquatic frogs with powerful hind legs that allow them to jump great distances. Elsewhere in the world, ranids may be squat, toadlike, and fossorial, or treefrog-like and arboreal. Most ranids exhibit the generalized mode of reproduction in which eggs are deposited in the water and the larvae develop there, although a few species have direct development. This family occurs worldwide except for Saharan Africa, southern South America, and most of Australia. There are 44 genera and 625 species, including the world's largest anuran, *Conraua goliath* of West Africa, which attains a snout-vent length of 300 mm. One genus of ranid frogs occurs in the Yucatán Peninsula.

Genus *Rana*

This large genus is found everywhere in the world except Australia, Saharan Africa, and southern South America. These are semiaquatic frogs, generally streamlined and smooth skinned. The toes are usually extensively webbed, and the hind limbs are long and muscular, allowing most members of the genus to leap great distances. Approximately 222 living species are presently recognized, of which 3 occur in the Yucatán Peninsula. *Rana* is Latin for "frog."

Key to the Species of the Genus *Rana*

1. No conspicuous elongate glandular ridges between dorsolateral folds; dorsal pattern usually green or brown, without distinct brown spots 2
   Conspicuous elongate glandular ridges between dorsolateral folds; dorsal pattern usually a series of brown spots . . . . *Rana berlandieri*
2. Distinct supralabial stripe; posterior margins of thighs with dark variegations against a light background; Maya Mountains of Belize . . . . *Rana juliani*
   No distinct supralabial stripe; posterior margins of thighs without dark variegations; southern half of the Yucatán Peninsula . . . . *Rana vaillanti*

Clave para las Especies del Género *Rana*

1. Sin flecos glandulares conspicuos elongados entre los pliegues dorsolaterales; la coloración dorsal es verde o pardo sin series de puntos de color pardo. 2
   Con flecos glandulares conspicuos elongados entre los pliegues dorsolaterales; patrón de coloración dorsal consiste usualmente de series de puntos de color pardo . . . . *Rana berlandieri*

2. Línea supralabial distintiva; los márgenes posteriores de los muslos con jaspeaduras sobre un fondo claro; organismos que se distribuyen en las Montañas Maya de Belice. . . . *Rana juliani*
   Sin línea supralabial distintiva; los márgenes posteriores de los muslos sin jaspeaduras sobre un fondo claro; organismos que se distribuyen en la mitad sur de la Península de Yucatán . . .
   . . . . *Rana vaillanti*

Rana berlandieri Baird
(Figs. 97, 98, 256, 257; Map 40)

Rana berlandieri Baird, 1859:27. SYNTYPES: USNM 3293 (9 specimens); MCZ 155 (2 specimens); USNM 131513 designated the lectotype by Pace (1974:25). TYPE LOCALITY: southern Texas generally (specifically, Brownsville, Texas, by lectotype designation).

Río Grande leopard frog; rana leopardo (Mexico); chut'o t'iu' (Lacandón Maya).

DESCRIPTION   This is one of the larger anurans in the Yucatán Peninsula. The adults average between 65 and 80 mm in snout-vent length. They are rather slender, streamlined frogs with rather narrow, pointed heads. The moderately large eyes are roughly the diameter of the tympanum (Figs. 256, 257). The males have paired vocal sacs behind the angles of the jaw. Their long, robust hind limbs enable these frogs to leap considerable distances. The fingers are essentially devoid of webbing, but the toes are extensively webbed. The digits are not expanded at the tips. A pair of light-colored dorsolateral folds is present, and between them run parallel series of glandular ridges.

The color and pattern are highly variable (Figs. 256, 257). A few animals are very dark with little evident dorsal pattern. Most, however, are greenish, brown, or tan above with distinct dark brown spots. The dorsal surfaces of the limbs are usually marked with dark brown spots and bars, and the posterior surfaces of the thighs are boldly marked with dark reticulations against a light background. The throat, venter, and undersurfaces of the appendages are cream or yellowish.

TADPOLE   The body is ovoid in dorsal view and is approximately 1.8 times longer than wide. The eyes are moderately large and situated rather high on the head. The snout is rounded in both dorsal and lateral views, and the mouth is anteroventral (Fig. 97). There are normally two anterior and three posterior rows of denticles, but some specimens have an abbreviated third anterior row. The jaw sheaths are finely serrated, and the oral disk is indented laterally. The fringing labial papillae are discontinuous dorsally. The vent tube is dextral; the spiracle is sinistral and lies slightly below the midline of the body. The tail is about 1.4 times the length of the body and slightly exceeds it in depth. The dorsal fin extends onto the posterior portion of the body and is somewhat deeper than the ventral fin. The tadpoles are predominantly dark brown above, lighter below, and the caudal musculature and fins are distinctly spotted with brown.

VOCALIZATION   As described by Platz (1991:2), the advertisement call of *R. berlandieri* consists of a complex series of trills, grunts, and grinding sounds. In my experience trills are the most common vocal element, with each note containing 9 to 11 pulses, and a pulse rate of about 20 per second. The dominant frequency of the trill is around 500 to 600 Hz (Fig. 98).

SIMILAR SPECIES   The spotted dorsum usually distinguishes *R. berlandieri* from all other *Rana* in the Yucatán Peninsula. Very dark specimens could be confused with *R. vaillanti*, but that species lacks

Fig. 97. Tadpole of *Rana berlandieri* (UMRC 91-18), 50 mm TL; Vaqueros Creek at San Luis, Cayo, Belize.

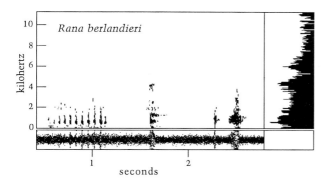

Fig. 98. Advertisement call of *Rana berlandieri*, recorded 14 August 1992, 6.1 km E La Cristalina, Campeche, Mexico.

elongate glandular ridges on the dorsum. *Rana juliani* lacks a spotted dorsum and possesses a distinct light labial stripe.

DISTRIBUTION   These frogs occur at low, moderate, and intermediate elevations on the Atlantic slope from central Texas and southeastern New Mexico south through eastern Mexico to northern Nicaragua. In Mexico this species also occurs on the Pacific slope in Oaxaca and Guerrero, and it has been introduced into the lower Colorado River in western Arizona (Platz, 1991:2). It is found throughout the Yucatán Peninsula (Map 40).

NATURAL HISTORY   This common frog can be found in virtually all freshwater habitats in the Yucatán Peninsula, although it seems to reach especially high densities in open, disturbed situations. It is a common inhabitant of cenotes in the northern third of the Yucatán Peninsula, and Duellman (1965a:590) reported a specimen from a cave in Quintana Roo. Individuals are also common in the ciénaga along the north coast, where the water is possibly brackish. These frogs are both nocturnal and diurnal. They are terrestrial and feed primarily on invertebrates, but they attain a size sufficient to allow them to prey on small vertebrates as well.

During the summer rainy season individuals may move long distances over land. In central El Petén, Stuart (1935:40) found specimens several miles from water soon after the rainy season had begun. Reproduction is associated with the summer rains, and males call from the surface of permanent or temporary bodies of water. Amplexus is axillary, and the eggs are deposited in the water, where they hatch and the larvae complete their development.

SUBSPECIES   Two subspecies of *R. berlandieri* occur within the Yucatán Peninsula (Sanders, 1973): *R. b. brownorum*, in southwestern Campeche, Tabasco, and southern Veracruz; and the nominate form, *R. b. berlandieri*, which occurs throughout the remainder of the peninsula. See Comment.

ETYMOLOGY   The specific name, *berlandieri*, is a patronym honoring Luis Berlandier, a nineteenth-century Swiss naturalist who lived for many years in Matamoros, Tamaulipas, and assembled a substantial collection of amphibians and reptiles from northern Mexico.

COMMENT   *Rana berlandieri brownorum* from Campeche is said to differ most notably from *R. b. berlandieri* in possessing narrow, elongate-ellipsoid markings on the dorsum rather than the rounded spots or blotches of the nominate form (Sanders, 1973:90). Hillis (1981:313) elevated this race to the rank of full species but provided no additional information beyond that in the original description. J. S. Frost (1982) commented on the distinctive appearance of Sanders's specimens but provisionally treated them as subspecifically distinct within *R. berlandieri*. Hillis et al. (1983:138) treated the specimens as members of a distinct species, as did Flores-Villela (1993:59). The relationship of this form to the other leopard frogs in the Yucatán Peninsula is presently unknown, and the geographical distribution of *brownorum* within the peninsula is not

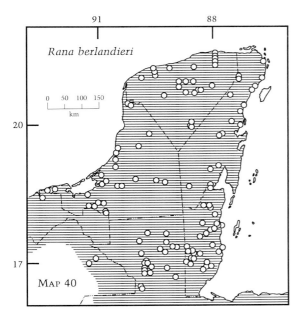

MAP 40

known with any certainty. Pending resolution of the taxonomic status of the leopard frogs in the Yucatán Peninsula, *brownorum* might best be treated as a subspecies of *R. berlandieri*, although Platz (1991) recognized no subspecies within that species.

Platz (1991) reviewed the biosystematics of *R. berlandieri* and summarized information on the species.

Locality Records   Belize: Belize: near Altun Ha (CM 107439), Belize City (FMNH 4410–21, 49087), near Belize City (UF uncat.), Botanic Garden on Belize River (FMNH 4423), 7.8 km W Belize City (CM 90967), 29.5 mi W Belize City (CM 112096), Burrell Boom (CM 105970), 11 km SW Hattieville (CM 90957–61), Lemonal (MPM 7723), Missonary Lake Rd., 5.3 mi E Northern Hwy. (CM 91059), 19.2 mi E Roaring Creek (KU 157031–32), Rockstone Pond (UU 9350–51); Cayo: Augustine (UMMZ 80730–32), ca. 2 mi W Belmopan (CM 105768–70), Blancaneaux Lodge (CM 91026), Caracol (CMM photo), 4 mi SW Cayo (UMMZ 124687), 12 mi S Cayo (UMMZ 70406–10), Macal River at Guacamallo Bridge (CM 112139), 3 mi from Millionario Camp (UMMZ 124685–86), Mountain Pine Ridge Rd., 36 mi S Belize-Cayo Rd. (UMMZ 124683), Mountain Pine Ridge Rd., 36 to 49 mi S Belize-Cayo Rd. (UMMZ 124684), Privassion Creek, Mountain Pine Ridge (W. T. Neill and Allen, 1959c:27), Queen Mary Lake (USNM 319793), San Ignacio (UMMZ 75384), San Luis (JCL photo), S edge San Luis (KU 157028–29), Succotz (W. T. Neill and Allen, 1959c:27), upper Raspaculo River basin (Stafford, 1991:12), Valentin (UMMZ 80728–29); Corozal: 3 mi S Chan Chen (JLK 425), 5.3 mi SW Corozal (KU 157034); Orange Walk: Guinea Grass Rd. ca. 4 mi S Northern Hwy. (CM 105723–33), 14.3 mi NW Maskall (KU 157033), 17.3 to 23.3 mi SE Orange Walk (NMSU 3084); Stann Creek: Dangriga (RWV photo), Middlesex (FMNH 4422, 4424; UCM 45112), 5.7 mi S Silk Grass (KU 157030), 3 mi S Waha Leaf Creek (MCZ 37902); Toledo: Bladen Branch of Monkey River (CM 105915–17), Columbia Branch Camp (W. T. Neill, 1965:89), Medina Bank (MPM 7618), Punta Gorda (W. T. Neill, 1965:89), 4 mi SE San Antonio (W. T. Neill, 1965:89), 2.5 mi S Swasey Bridge (CM 105931), mi 45 on Southern Hwy. (CM 105844). *Guatemala*: El Petén: 16 km NNW Chinajá (KU 55958), 20 km NNW Chinajá (KU 58887), Chuntuquí (USNM 71331), El Paso de Caballos (UMMZ 79008), E end Lago Petén Itzá (KU 157046–47; UMMZ 79009), N side Lago Petén Itzá (JCL sight record), La Libertad (UMMZ 75398), vicinity La Libertad (UMMZ 75386), 1 mi S La Libertad (UMMZ 75388), 3 mi SE La Libertad (UMMZ 75393), 3 mi S La Libertad (UMMZ 75399), 15 km SE La Libertad (KU 58889), Nuevo Aguada (USNM 71332), 4 mi N Poptún

(KU 157036–39), 41.2 mi NW Poptún (KU 157040), 8.4 mi N Río de la Pasión (KU 157042–44), 13.7 mi N Río de la Pasión (KU 157041), Río de la Pasión 13 mi above Sayaxché (UMMZ 79007), Santa Cruz (UMMZ 75385), Sayaxché (UCM 22177), 1 mi W Ruinas Seibal (KU 157045), Tikal (UF 13377–93; UMMZ 117970, 117995–96, 126454; UTA A-26075), Uaxactún (KU 157035), Zotz (UMMZ 75394, 79010). *Mexico*: Campeche: Balchacaj (FMNH 107751–52, 107755–58, 107760, 107763, 110784, 110786, 110795, 110872; UIMNH 32273–77), Calkini-Tankuche (IHNHERP 97–98, 123), 11.1 km S Candelaria (KU 171393–94), 12.5 km S Candelaria (KU 171395), Carretera Tankuche–Isla Arena, km 19 (IHNHERP 204–6), Champotón (UMMZ 73162–63), 15 mi S Champotón (UMMZ 73164), Chuina (KU 75108–9), ca. 6 km E La Cristalina (JCL acoustic record), 30.8 mi NE Emiliano Zapata (EAL 1648), 65.9 km NE Emiliano Zapata (EAL 2910), Encarnación (FMNH 107753–54, 107761–62; UIMNH 32279–82), near Escárcega (JCL photo), 2 km NE Hopelchén (KU 75441), E edge Ingenio La Joya (KU 157049), Laguna Silvituc (KU 75110–12), Matamoros (FMNH 36547–48), Pacaitún on Río Candelaria (FMNH 36550–52, 36580), 4.3 km W Pich (KU 171391), 5.3 km S Sabancuy (KU 171392), 1 to 2 km W San Antonio Cárdenas (UTEP 13993), 52 mi E Silvituc (Colonia López Mateos) (UCM 27539–41), Tankuche-El Remate (IHNHERP 163, 193, 195, 199), Tres Brazos (FMNH 107759, 110794; UIMNH 32278), 41 mi W Xicalango (BCB 12494–500), 4.4 mi W Xpujil (KU 157048); Chiapas: 6.7 mi SE Cristóbal Colón on rd. to Bonampak (JCL sight record), Laguna Ocotal (MCZ 28230–33), Quintana Roo: 10 mi W Bacalar (LSUMZ 33203–8), 6 mi N Bacalar (KU 157051), 3 km E Caobas (KU 75107), Chunyaxché (Himmelstein, 1980:24), Cobá (Himmelstein, 1980:24; UMMZ 83920), SE edge Cobá (KU 171360–61, 171367), 5 km E Dzuiché (CM 45227–29), 3 mi E Esmeralda (LACM 114020), 2 km NNE Felipe Carrillo Puerto (KU 71576), 42.8 km NE Felipe Carrillo Puerto (KU 171366), 10.3 km N jct. Hwys. 186 and 307 (KU 171368–69), 12.9 km S Kantunil Kin (KU 171362–64), 15.9 km S Kantunil Kin (KU 171365), 1.5 mi N Pamal (TNHC 49260, 49410), Playa del Carmen (Himmelstein, 1980:24), Puerto Juárez (Himmelstein, 1980:24), 4 km WSW Puerto Juárez (KU 71577–80), 0.5 km W Puerto Juárez (KU 171370–71), Puerto Morelos (AMNH 88515; MZCIQRO 40–41), 1 km W Puerto Morelos (UCM 39104–5), 5 mi W, 10 mi S Puerto Morelos (UU 9345–49), rd. to Reforma, 20.1 km NW Hwy. 307 (KU 171372), 2.3 mi S, 1.9 mi E Santa Rosa (KU 157052), Tulum Ruins (UMMZ 172757–59), Vigía Chico (MZCIQRO 45–46); Tabasco: 4 to 6 mi S Frontera (UCM 27556–27557), 10 mi E Frontera (UIMNH 86833); Yucatán: 14.6 km E Buctzotz (KU 171377), Chichén Itzá (CM 36445; KU 71581–82; MCZ 4060, 9712–14; UMMZ 73159–61, 73196, 80889), 3 km E Chichén Itzá (UCM 12351–54),

6.5 mi SW Chichén Itzá (UMMZ 73167), near Izamal (Ives, 1891:461), 12 mi S Izamal (UMMZ 80888), 12.2 mi E Izamal (KU 157054), 1.5 mi S Libre Unión (UCM 15572–82, 18221, 28094), Mayapán (UMRC 79-294), 8 mi N Mérida (UMMZ 73165), 14 km N Mérida (UMMZ 73168), 14 km N, 2 km E Mérida (UMMZ 73195), Progreso (MCZ 9710–11), 1.4 mi S Río Lagartos (UMMZ 142990), 6.1 km S Río Lagartos (KU 171381), 9.1 km S Río Lagartos (KU 171382), 11.5 km S Río Lagartos (KU 171383), 12.2 km S Río Lagartos (KU 171384), 12.7 km S Río Lagartos (KU 171385), 13 km S Río Lagartos (KU 171386), 13.2 km S Río Lagartos (KU 171387), 16.2 km S Río Lagartos (KU 171388), 21.9 km S Río Lagartos (KU 171389), 25.4 km S Río Lagartos (KU 171390), 9 mi S Río Lagartos (UCM 27552), 9.2 mi S Río Lagartos (KU 157053), 12.7 km S Río Lagartos (KU 171378), 11 mi S Río Lagartos (UCM 27548–27551), 26.8 km S Río Lagartos (KU 171379), 36.3 km S Río Lagartos (KU 171380), 4.6 mi SE Sisal (KU 157055), 3 mi N Telchac (UCM 27547), bet. Tunkás and Sitilpich (KU 171373), ca. 4 mi N Valladolid (UMMZ 138342).

Rana juliani Hillis and de Sa
(Figs. 99, 258; Map 41)

Rana juliani Hillis and de Sa, 1988:1–26. HOLO-TYPE: UTA A-9068. TYPE LOCALITY: Southwest end of Little Quartz Ridge, Maya Mountains, Toledo District, Belize.

DESCRIPTION   This medium-sized, rather streamlined frog has a narrow, pointed snout (Fig. 258). The body is slightly wider than the head. The eyes are large, exceeding the tympanum in diameter. The canthus rostralis is angulate, and the loreal region is distinctly concave. The males average about 70 mm in snout-vent length, and the females are presumably larger, although there are too few specimens to assess sexual size dimorphism. The limbs are moderately robust. The fingers are unwebbed and slightly expanded at their tips; the toes are extensively webbed.

This is a predominantly brown frog. The dorsum is more or less uniform light brown or grayish brown, sometimes with small spots and bars. The sides of the body and the flanks are darker brown separated from the dorsum by indistinct light dorsolateral stripes, which extend forward through the eye. The dorsal surfaces of the appendages are brown with indistinct dark bars. There is a conspicuous light labial stripe. The throat and chest are yellowish cream with brown or grayish variegations, and the abdomen is yellowish. The undersur-

Fig. 99. Tadpole of *Rana juliani* (UMRC 91-20), 71 mm TL; Vaqueros Creek at San Luis, Cayo, Belize.

faces of the appendages are yellowish, and the posterior surfaces of the thighs are boldly marked with dark brown variegation against a yellowish or cream background.

TADPOLE   The tadpole is robust (Fig. 99). Its body is somewhat depressed, with a length about 2.5 times the maximum depth. The snout is bluntly rounded in both lateral and dorsal profiles. The moderately large eyes are directed dorsolaterally. The mouth is anteroventral. The oral disk is indented laterally and surrounded by labial papillae that are discontinuous dorsally. The jaw sheaths are finely serrated. Although variable, the number of rows of denticles is unusually high in this species, with five the apparent minimum number of posterior rows in specimens at or beyond Gosner stage 30 (J. C. Lee, 1976:211). The spiracle is sinistral and lies slightly below the midline. The vent tube is dextral. The tail is about 1.8 times the length of the body, the caudal musculature is robust, and the depth of the tail is about one-third its length. The dorsal fin, which is slightly deeper than the ventral fin, does not extend onto the body. This is a predominantly brown or olive brown tadpole, darker above than below. The pigmentation on the tail and caudal fins is distinctive, consisting of several large, dark spots.

VOCALIZATION   Vocalization in *R. juliani* has not been described; the species may be mute.

SIMILAR SPECIES   *Rana juliani* differs from *R. vaillanti* in possessing a distinct light labial stripe. *Rana berlandieri* is generally spotted and has elongate glandular ridges between the dorsolateral folds. Frogs of the genus *Leptodactylus* lack extensive webbing between the toes.

DISTRIBUTION   This species is endemic to the Maya Mountains of Belize, where it is presently known from five localities (Map 41). These frogs can be expected in many of the swift-flowing rocky streams that drain the Mountain Pine Ridge of Belize.

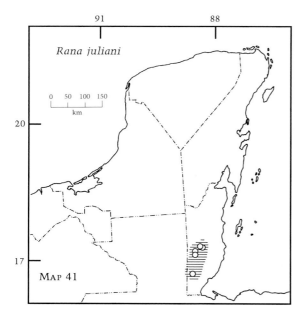

MAP 41

NATURAL HISTORY *Rana juliani* is common in the streams of Mountain Pine Ridge in the Maya Mountains, as well as in the vicinity of Little Quartz Ridge, Toledo. Individuals of this species are wary and difficult to capture. They leap into the water at the slightest disturbance. Concerning the type series, which was collected by W. F. Pyburn and associates at Little Quartz Ridge, Belize, Pyburn noted that they were "extremely shy and difficult to approach" (W. F. Pyburn, in litt.). Tadpoles have been taken from beneath the shrub-choked over-hanging banks of Vaqueros Creek at San Luis and at Little Vaqueros Creek (J. C. Lee, 1976:211). Little is known of reproduction in this species, but at Va-queros Creek, Cayo, I found tadpoles ranging from Gosner stages 26 to 33 in August, suggesting that breeding occurs during the summer rainy season. Tadpoles collected in mid-August metamorphosed in the laboratory in late September or early October.

ETYMOLOGY The specific name, *juliani*, is a pat-ronym that honors Julian C. Lee, who collected the first specimens.

COMMENT J. C. Lee (1976) reported the first known specimens as *R. maculata* but noted that the tadpoles were distinctive. Hillis and de Sa (1988) showed that the adult and larval morphology are distinctive enough to warrant specific status, and they concluded that this is the sister species of *R. maculata* + *R. sierramadrensis*.

The biosystematics of *R. juliani* was treated by

Hillis and de Sa (1988) as part of their revision of the *R. palmipes* group.

Locality Records Belize: Cayo: 23.2 km S Georgeville, Little Vaquero Creek (KU 157161–62), Hidden Valley (CMM photo), Mountain Pine Ridge, Tiger Creek (USNM 319796), San Luis (UMRC 91-20); Toledo: SW end Little Quartz Ridge (UTA A-9067–97).

Rana vaillanti Brocchi
(Figs. 100, 101, 259; Map 42)

Rana vaillanti Brocchi, 1877:175. HOLOTYPE: MNHNP 6328. TYPE LOCALITY: les rives de la rivière de Mullins pres de Belize (Honduras).

Vaillant's frog; rana (Guatemala, Mexico); rana verde (Mexico).

DESCRIPTION *Rana vaillanti* is a large, rather streamlined frog. The males average about 80 mm in snout-vent length, and the females are substan-tially larger, averaging about 100 mm. In dorsal as-pect the head is approximately as wide as the body, and the snout is rather pointed (Fig. 259). The can-thus rostralis is angulate, and the loreal region is distinctly concave. The eyes are moderately large, equal to or exceeding the diameter of the tympa-num. The limbs are well developed, the toes are ex-tensively webbed, and the tips of the digits are very slightly expanded. The skin is generally smooth, although in preserved specimens the dorsum may develop a sandpaper-like texture owing to the pres-ence of integumentary denticles (H. M. Smith, 1959:213). Dorsolateral folds extend from the pos-terior margin of the eye to beyond the sacral region, becoming indistinct posteriorly. Males generally, but not invariably, have vocal slits and sacs (Hillis and de Sa, 1988:13).

In general the dorsum is dark brown, tan, or olive gray with a few indistinct, irregular dark spots or bars. The dorsal surface of the head and the anterior portion of the body are often bright green. The ap-pendages usually have indistinct dark bars, espe-cially on the hind limbs, and the posterior surfaces of the thighs have inconspicuous light and dark reticulations. The ventral surfaces are light gray, tan, or cream.

TADPOLE The body of the tadpole is globose in dorsal view, and its length is about 1.5 times the maximum width. The tail is short—approximately 1 to 1.3 times the body length—and its depth

Fig. 100. Tadpole of *Rana vaillanti* (KU 200853), 43 mm TL; 15 km from Jalapa de Díaz, Oaxaca, Mexico.

slightly exceeds that of the body (Fig. 100). The dorsal fin extends onto the posterior surface of the body and is deeper than the ventral fin. The snout is rounded in dorsal view and somewhat pointed in lateral aspect. The spiracle is sinistral and lies below the level of the midline. The vent tube is dextral. There are generally four anterior and four posterior rows of denticles, and the jaw sheaths bear fine serrations. The oral disk is indented laterally, and the fringing labial papillae are discontinuous dorsally. The body is predominantly brown above and lighter below. The caudal musculature and fins are mottled or spotted with brown.

VOCALIZATION   Greding (1976:263) characterized the vocalization of *R. vaillanti* from Costa Rica as a series of grunts separated by intervals of 2 to 11 seconds. Each grunt consisted of five or six pulses, and the dominant frequency was about 1,000 Hz, approximately equal to that of the call illustrated here in Figure 101. H. M. Smith (1938:13) reported that when disturbed, these frogs simultaneously leap and emit a peculiar low croak.

SIMILAR SPECIES   *Rana berlandieri* has glandular ridges on the dorsum between the dorsolateral folds and a predominantly spotted dorsal pattern. *Rana juliani* has a distinct light labial stripe and is restricted to the Maya Mountains of Belize, where it

Fig. 101. Advertisement call of *Rana vaillanti*, recorded 17 May 1961, Los Diamontes, Limón, Costa Rica.

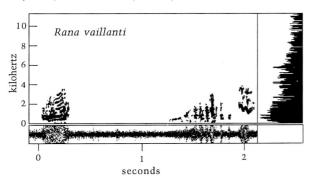

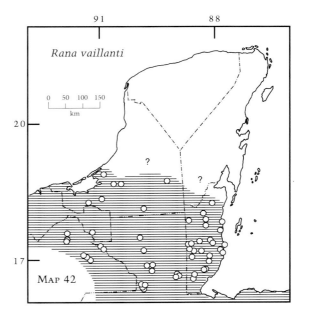

apparently does not co-occur with *R. vaillanti*. Peninsular species of *Leptodactylus* lack extensive webbing between the toes.

DISTRIBUTION   *Rana vaillanti* occurs at low and moderate elevations from Veracruz on the Atlantic slope and Oaxaca on the Pacific slope, south through Central America to the Pacific lowlands of Ecuador and Colombia. It is found throughout the base of the Yucatán Peninsula and north to southern Campeche and northern Belize (Map 42).

NATURAL HISTORY   In the Yucatán Peninsula this common species lives primarily in humid lowland forests, generally in association with lakes, aguadas, woodland pools, and the slower-moving stretches of streams and rivers. Individuals have also been found at night on the forest floor. These frogs feed primarily on invertebrates, but their large size allows them to consume small vertebrates, including fish and small conspecifics (Noble, 1918: 317).

Males call from the water's edge or surface throughout the summer rainy season. Amplexus is axillary, and eggs are deposited in the water. Duellman (1963:229) found a recently metamorphosed specimen in El Petén on 24 June.

COMMENT   This species was long known as *R. palmipes*, but Hillis and de Sa (1988) showed that that name properly applies to frogs of the *R. palmipes* complex that occur in northern South America east of the Andes, and that *R. vaillanti* applies to the populations from southern Mexico, Central America, and the Pacific slope of Ecuador and Colombia.

Hillis and de Sa (1988) reviewed the biosystematics of *R. vaillanti* as part of their revision of the *R. palmipes* group.

ETYMOLOGY The specific name, *vaillanti*, is a patronym that honors the nineteenth-century French ichthyologist and herpetologist Leon-Louis Vaillant, of the Museum National d'Histoire Naturelle at Paris.

Locality Records Belize: Belize: Belize (FMNH 4408–9), Belize River (UF uncat.), Lemonal (MPM 7719–22), Manatee (FMNH 6286–87); Cayo: Augustine (CM 105734), 12 mi S Cayo (UMMZ 70404–5), Cocquercot (UMMZ 75380), Macal River at Guacamallo Bridge (CM 112135–38), Mountain Pine Ridge (MCZ 37900), Mountain Pine Ridge Rd., 36 to 49 mi S Belize-Cayo Rd. (UMMZ 124681), San Ignacio (UMMZ 75379), Succotz (W. T. Neill and Allen, 1959c:27), Thousand Foot Falls (USNM 319794), upper Raspaculo River basin (Stafford, 1991:12); Orange Walk: near Gallon Jug (USNM 194907), Kate's Lagoon (FMNH 49096), Lamanai (ROM H12745); Stann Creek: 28 km SE Blue Hole (KU 157013–16), Bokowina (FMNH 49089–90), Cockscomb Basin Wildlife Sanctuary (JCL photo), Dangriga (RWV photo), Double Falls (FMNH 49091–95), Freetown (CM 9878–85), Middlesex (UCM 45111); Toledo: Bladen Branch of Monkey River (CM 105918–21), 3 mi S Bladen Branch (LSUMZ 11850), San Pedro Columbia (MCZ 37901), Unión Camp, Columbia River Forest Reserve (USNM 319769). *Guatemala*: Alta Verapaz: Chinajá (KU 55957–58); El Petén: 5 km NNW Chinajá (KU 55948–49), 8 km NNW Chinajá (KU 55959–60), 10 km NNW Chinajá (KU 55956), 11 km NNW Chinajá (KU 55951–54), 15 km NW Chinajá (KU 55955), 20 km NNW Chinajá (KU 55950), Laguna Yalac (UMMZ 79003), 15 km SE La Libertad (KU 58879), Paso de los Caballos (Stuart, 1937:68), 5 mi S Piedras Negras (USNM 113793), Piedras Negras (USNM 113794–95), 4 km N Poptún (KU 157017–21), 5 km SE Poptún (UMMZ 124392), 1 km E Poptún (UMMZ 124393), 1 mi W Ruinas Seibal (KU 157022–27; UMRC 80-6), Santa Terresa (UMMZ 75381–82), Zotz (UMMZ 75383). *Mexico*: Campeche: 5 mi W Escárcega (UCM 27542–43), Laguna Chumpich (KU 75100), Matamoros (FMNH 36576–77), Pacaitún on Río Candelaria (FMNH 36549), bet. Sabancuy and Chekubúl (JCL sight record), Tres Brazos (FMNH 102362, 107970, 107983; UIMNH 32396–97), Xpujil (UWZH 20505); Chiapas: El Censo (MCZ 28256), bet. El Censo and Laguna Ocotal (MCZ 28270), bet. El Censo and Monte Libano (MCZ 28257), Laguna Ocotal (MCZ 28234–37), Palenque, San Juanito (UIMNH 49238; USNM 113760–61), 10 to 15 mi S Palenque (LSUMZ 33199), 22 km S Palenque (UMRC 85-28); Tabasco: Tenosique (USNM 113752–59).

Class Reptilia (Reptiles)

Reptiles are vertebrates that possess epidermal scales and lack feathers or hair. The class includes approximately 5,300 living species placed in four orders: Testudines (turtles), Crocodylia (crocodiles, alligators, caimans, and gharials), Rhynchocephalia (tuataras), and Squamata (lizards and snakes). Many other species are known from fossils, including an enormous variety of diverse types such as dinosaurs, pterosaurs, and ichthyosaurs. Modern reptiles are found throughout the world, including on many oceanic islands, but they are generally absent from the higher latitudes. Only a few species are found above the Arctic Circle. Reptiles are most diverse and attain their greatest species richness in the tropics. The three orders of reptiles that occur in the Yucatán Peninsula are represented by 140 species belonging to 84 genera and 24 families.

Key to the Orders of Reptilia

1. Limbs present. 2
   Limbs absent . . . . Squamata (part)

2. Body encased in a shell; teeth absent. . . . . Testudines
   Body not encased in a shell; teeth present 3

3. Vent longitudinal; teeth set in sockets; tail strongly compressed laterally; adult SVL longer than 1,000 mm. . . . . Crocodylia
   Vent horizontal; teeth attached to sides of jaws; tail not strongly compressed laterally; adult SVL less than 1,000 mm . . . . Squamata (part)

Clave para los Ordenes de Reptiles

1. Con extremidades 2
   Sin extremidades . . . . Squamata (en parte)

2. Cuerpo no encerrado en una concha; con dientes. 3
   Cuerpo encerrado en una concha; sin dientes . . . . Testudines

3. Abertura cloacal longitudinal, dientes con raíz, en alveólos, cola robusta y comprimida lateralmete, adultos mayores a los 100 cm de LHC . . . . Crocodylia
   Abertura cloacal horizontal, dientes sobre los lados de las mandíbulas, no en alveólos; cola no comprimida lateralmente, adultos menores a los 100 cm de LHC . . . . Squamata (en parte)

Order Crocodylia (Crocodilians)

The crocodilians are large, quadrupedal, semi-aquatic reptiles with robust, muscular tails that are laterally compressed and provide propulsion for swimming. The well-developed limbs have five webbed fingers and four webbed toes. The head is depressed, the snout elongate. The eyes and external nares are elevated such that they alone may protrude from the water while the rest of the animal is submerged. The ear opening and the external nares are valvular, and there is a valve in the throat anterior to the internal nares that permits the animal to breathe while holding prey underwater in its jaws. All crocodilians are oviparous, and some species exhibit elaborate social behaviors, including sophisticated maternal care. Crocodilians are essentially circumtropical in distribution, although a few species range through the subtropics into temperate zones. Three living families are presently recognized, one of which occurs in the Yucatán Peninsula.

Family Crocodylidae
(Crocodiles, Dwarf Crocodiles, False Gharial)

With three living genera and 14 of the 23 living species, this is the largest family of crocodilians (King and Burke, 1989). Although essentially circumtropical, crocodylids range into subtropical latitudes in the extreme southeastern United States and are also found in southern Africa. In the Yucatán Peninsula the family is represented by one genus.

Crocodiles are almost universally feared as predators of humans, and several Old World species, especially the Nile crocodile (*Crocodylus niloticus*) and the Indopacific or estuarine crocodile (*C. porosus*), can be justly accused of including an occasional human in their diets. The other species of crocodiles are generally timid and inoffensive, although there are rare instances of attacks on humans by the two species that occur in the Yucatán Peninsula, *C. moreletii* and *C. acutus*.

Genus *Crocodylus* (Crocodiles)

This genus, the largest in the family Crocodylidae, includes the world's largest reptile, *C. porosus* of India and Southeast Asia, which attains a length in excess of 7 m and a mass greater than 1,000 kg. Members of the genus range through northern Australia and Southeast Asia, tropical India and Africa, southern Florida, the Greater Antilles, and Mexico south to northern South America. Twelve living species are currently recognized, of which two occur in the Yucatán Peninsula. *Crocodylus* is derived from *krokodeilus*, the Greek name for a kind of large lizard.

Both species of *Crocodylus* in the Yucatán Peninsula are seriously threatened by habitat destruction and overexploitation, primarily for leather goods made from the hide. In some areas crocodiles are used for food, and hatchling crocodiles frequently enter the pet trade (Lazcano-Barrero, 1984). Abercrombie et al. (1980) surveyed crocodile populations throughout Belize and reported that crocodiles were heavily exploited by hide hunters there. One dealer told them that he had sold about 125 skins in May 1978. Some of these were *C. moreletii*, although the majority may have been *C. acutus*. Juvenile *C. moreletii* were rather common in remote areas of Belize, but few specimens of breeding size were observed, suggesting overexploitation of adults. Commercial crocodile hunting is prohibited in Mexico, and the export of crocodile hides from Belize was banned in 1981. Nonetheless, the illegal harvest of crocodiles continues to threaten many local populations. Meerman (1992a:4) surveyed eastern Corozal District, Belize, and found that the two species of crocodiles were much less common than expected.

Fig. 102. Ventrolateral views of the tails of crocodiles. A, *Crocodylus acutus*. B, *C. moreletii* showing subcaudal whorls interrupted by irregular groups of small scales (*shaded*). Redrawn from Ross and Ross, 1974, by permission of the Biological Society of Washington.

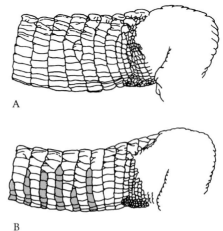

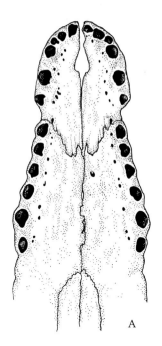
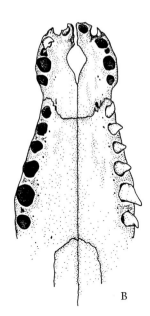

Fig. 103. Ventral views of the anterior portion of the skulls of crocodiles. A, *Crocodylus acutus* showing the V- or W-shaped premaxillary-maxillary suture. B, *Crocodylus moreletii* showing the transverse premaxillary-maxillary suture. B redrawn from Ross, 1987, by permission of the Society for the Study of Amphibians and Reptiles.

Platt (1992:7) discovered low densities of adult crocodiles in the vicinity of Belize City, although they were abundant in areas where they had received protection. Under no circumstances should either species of *Crocodylus* be harmed or disturbed.

IDENTIFICATION   Much confusion exists concerning proper identification of the crocodiles in the Yucatán Peninsula owing to variation in the characters commonly used to distinguish the two species (C. A. Ross, 1987:2). As a consequence, the geographical distributions of the two species are rather imperfectly known, and knowledgeable herpetologists disagree sharply concerning their distribution in the Yucatán Peninsula. C. A. Ross, for example (in litt.), was of the opinion that there are no verified records of *C. acutus* from the mainland of Quintana Roo, whereas Towle (1989) conducted the research for his master's thesis on what he believed to be *C. acutus* at several coastal localities in the Sian Ka'an Biosphere Reserve in Quintana Roo. F. D. Ross and Mayer (1983:318) suggested hybridization between the two species, and J. W. Wright (pers. comm.) took the extreme view that *C. more-*

letii and *C. acutus* may be conspecific, with the differences between the two forms simply a reflection of geographic variation related to marine or esturine (*acutus*) versus freshwater (*moreletii*) habitats. Nonetheless, at close range *C. moreletii* clearly has a broader snout than *C. acutus*. The ratio of snout length (measured from the tip of the snout to the anterior margin of the orbit) to snout width (maximum width at the anterior margin of the orbits) is about 1.5 in *C. moreletii*, and closer to 2 in *C. acutus* (Brazaitis, 1973). The whorls of caudal scales in *C. moreletii* are typically interrupted by groups of smaller scales, whereas *C. acutus* exhibits few if any such groups of irregular scales (C. A. Ross and Ross, 1974) (Fig. 102A,B). The skulls of the two species can usually be distinguished on the basis of the configuration of the suture between the premaxillary and maxillary bones (C. A. Ross, 1987; Schmidt, 1927) (Fig. 103). Finally, the number of enlarged scutes at the nape of the neck can assist in distinguishing between the two species: two to four in *C. acutus*, and four to seven in *C. moreletii* (C. A. Ross and Ross, 1987).

Key to the Species of the Genus *Crocodylus*

Subcaudal whorls of scales generally not interrupted by irregular groups of smaller scales (Fig. 102A); snout relatively slender, about twice as long as wide; premaxillary-maxillary suture W-shaped (Fig. 103A) . . . . *Crocodylus acutus*

Subcaudal whorls of scales interrupted by irregular groups of smaller scales (Fig. 102B); snout relatively broad, length about 1.5 times width; premaxillary-maxillary suture transverse (Fig. 103B) . . . . *Crocodylus moreletii*

Clave para las Especies del Género *Crocodylus*

Escamas subcaudales en verticilos generalmente sin interrumpción por grupos irregulares de escamas más pequeñas (Fig. 102A); hocico relativamente delgado, dos veces más largo que ancho; sutura premaxilar-maxilar en forma de W (Fig. 103A). . . . . *Crocodylus acutus*

Escamas subcaudales en verticilos interrumpidas por grupos irregulares de escamas más pequeñas (Fig. 102B); hocico relativamente ancho, 1.5 veces más largo que ancho; sutura premaxilar-maxilar transversal (Fig. 103B). . . . . *Crocodylus moreletii*

Crocodylus acutus Cuvier
(Figs. 102A, 103A, 260; Map 43)

Crocodilus acutus Cuvier, 1807:55. TYPE: originally in the MNHNP, now lost. TYPE LOCALITY: San Domingo; restricted to L'Etan Saumatre, Haiti, by Schmidt (1953:111).

American crocodile; alligator, agarei (Belize); cocodrilo amarillo, cocodrilo de río, lagarto (Mexico); ain, chiuan, kum ayim (Yucatec Maya).

DESCRIPTION *Crocodylus acutus* is a narrow-snouted crocodile that may attain a total length of up to 6 m, although most adults are substantially smaller than that, averaging perhaps 2.5 to 3 m in total length. Males tend to be larger than females (C. A. Ross and Magnusson, 1989:65) and to have more robust jaw musculature (Alvarez del Toro, 1974:16).

The adults are grayish green, grayish brown, or olive green above, with dark crossbands on the body and tail (Fig. 260). This dorsal pattern is most distinct in juveniles and may become obscure in older individuals. The venter is white, cream, or yellowish.

SIMILAR SPECIES This species differs from *C. moreletii* in its larger average size and narrower snout, and in possessing few if any groups of scales intercalated between the caudal whorls (Fig. 102A,B). Moreover, the premaxillary-maxillary suture is W-shaped in *C. acutus* and transverse in *C. moreletii* (Fig. 103A,B). Finally, in the Yucatán Peninsula *C. acutus* apparently favors coastal habitats and large rivers, while *C. moreletii* prefers lakes, ponds, aguadas, and swamps.

DISTRIBUTION This is the most widely distributed crocodile in the Americas. It ranges from extreme southern Florida, throughout many of the Antilles, and at low elevations from Sinaloa on the Pacific slope, and possibly from Campeche and islands off the coast of Belize, southward through Central America to Colombia and Venezuela. Its distribution in the Yucatán Peninsula is very uncertain owing to confusion with *C. moreletii* (C. A. Ross, 1987:2). In the Yucatán Peninsula *C. acutus* is known from the Ríos Grijalva and Usumacinta and their tributaries in Campeche and Chiapas, and the Petén of Guatemala, and from islands and cays off the coast of Quintana Roo and Belize. According to C. A. Ross (in litt.), substantial populations exist along the Usumacinta in the Lacandón of Chia-

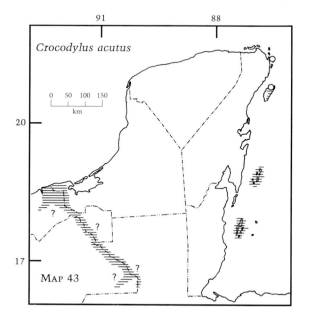

MAP 43

pas. There are several records for this species from coastal localities in mainland Quintana Roo, and one from Yucatán, but these may actually pertain to *C. moreletii* (Ross, in litt.) (Map 43).

NATURAL HISTORY *Crocodylus acutus* inhabits coastal situations such as mangrove swamps, estuaries, and coastal lagoons, as well as large rivers and lakes. Individuals penetrate into the interior for many kilometers along major rivers such as the Usumacinta and the Lacantún. Although large crocodiles are now rare, until the mid-1940s it was dangerous to bathe in the large rivers of northern Chiapas owing to the presence of large crocodiles, and as recently as 1955 individuals 5 to 6 m long were common (Alvarez del Toro, 1974:14). Diego de Landa reported what is surely the first European account of a human fatality caused by crocodile attack in Yucatán in his *Relación de las cosas de Yucatán*, written in 1566 (see "Ethnoherpetology in the Yucatán Peninsula," in this volume). Although Landa did not distinguish between the two species of *Crocodylus* in Yucatán, his descriptions of the nesting habits suggest *C. acutus*, even though there are apparently no confirmed records for that species from the state of Yucatán.

Crocodylus acutus feeds on a variety of aquatic invertebrate and vertebrate prey, and larger individuals are known to exhibit cannibalism. In Mexican populations, especially in Chiapas, small individuals eat insects, tadpoles, small fish, and crustaceans, and mammals, birds, and larger fish are incorporated into the diet as the animals grow older and larger (Alvarez del Toro, 1974:16). In northern Honduras, Schmidt (1924:91) found that small individuals fed predominantly on small fish, and larger animals consumed turtles, fish, a large mammal (probably a peccary), and smaller individuals of their own species. Thus, as an animal ages, its diet shifts from predominantly invertebrates to a more varied fare that includes larger vertebrates.

Crocodylus acutus is oviparous. In Chiapas, egg laying normally occurs in March, April, and May, although fresh nests have been found as early as February (Alvarez del Toro, 1974:18). In northern Honduras, egg laying begins in the first week of April (Schmidt, 1924:91). The female excavates a shallow nest, approximately 70 cm in diameter and 20 to 50 cm deep. Nests typically are constructed in sandy soil or gravel near the water's edge, but in the absence of ideal sites, nests may be excavated in, and covered over with, decomposing vegetation. The female deposits 20 to 60 oval, hard-shelled eggs and then covers the nest so skillfully that its location is difficult to discern. The period of incubation is approximately 70 to 80 days, during which the females are said to be territorial. Aguilar (1994) demonstrated temperature-dependent sex determination (TSD) in this species. A preponderance of females is produced at high and low incubation temperatures, whereas intermediate temperatures produce mostly males. When the eggs begin to hatch, the female opens the nest and transports the young to water (C. A. Ross and Magnusson, 1989:65).

ETYMOLOGY The specific name, *acutus*, is Latin for "sharp" or "pointed," in reference to the relatively tapered snout.

COMMENT H. M. Smith and Smith (1977) traced the complicated nomenclatural history of this species and summarized the literature pertaining to it.

The conservation status of *C. acutus* was reviewed by King et al. (1982), who considered the species endangered in Guatemala and Belize. It is listed as endangered in the Red Data Book of the International Union for the Conservation of Nature (IUCN) (Groombridge, 1982:319), and it is an endangered species under the United States Endangered Species Act. The Convention on International Trade in Endangered Species (CITES) lists this species in Appendix 1.

Locality Records Belize: no specific locality (FMNH 4156–57; USNM 59935); *Mexico*: Chiapas: Río Grijalva (Alvarez del Toro, 1974:13), Río Lacantún (Alvarez del Toro, 1974:13), Río Usumacinta (Alvarez del Toro, 1974:13); Quintana Roo: near Boca Paila (Towle, 1989:58), bet. Boca Paila and Chunyaxché (Towle, 1989:102), Cozumel (FMNH 23147), N end Isla Cozumel (UMMZ 78630), Isla Mujeres (H. M. Smith and Taylor, 1950a:211), Laguna Nixtchupte (Towle, 1989:103); Yucatán: Río Lagartos (Morfín, 1918).

Crocodylus moreletii Duméril and Bibron
(Figs. 102B, 103B, 261; Map 44)

Crocodilus moreletii A. M. C. Duméril and Bibron, 1851:28. HOLOTYPE: MNHNP 7520. TYPE LOCALITY: Laguna de Petén, El Petén, Guatemala.

Morelet's crocodile; agarei, alligator (Belize); cocodrilo de pantano, cocodrilo pardo, lagarto (Guatemala, Mexico); ayim (Lacandón Maya); ain, chiuan, kum ayim (Yucatec Maya).

DESCRIPTION   This is a relatively broad-snouted crocodile that attains a maximum total length of 4.1 m (Pérez-Higareda et al., 1991:35). Today in the Yucatán Peninsula a specimen 2.5 m long would be considered large. The dorsal surface of the head and body is heavily armored with bony scales (Fig. 261). The powerful tail is laterally compressed and has numerous groups of irregular small scales intercalated between the caudal whorls of scales (Fig. 102B). The maxillary-premaxillary suture is transverse (Fig. 103B).

The adults are uniformly dark brown or black above and lighter below. The juveniles have a lighter dorsum, tending toward yellowish, with transverse black bands on the body and tail.

SIMILAR SPECIES   *Crocodylus acutus* is larger (although less so than previously thought, according to Pérez-Higareda et al., 1990:36), has a narrower snout, and has few if any groups of small scales between the caudal whorls (Fig. 102A,B). The premaxillary-maxillary suture is transverse, not W-shaped, as in *C. acutus* (Fig. 103A,B).

DISTRIBUTION   Morelet's crocodile occurs at low elevations on the Gulf and Caribbean slopes from Tamaulipas and San Luis Potosí south and eastward through northern Guatemala, Belize, and the Yucatán Peninsula. H. M. Smith and Smith (1977:101) suggested that it might also occur in Lake Yojoa, Honduras, but L. D. Wilson et al. (1986:88) demonstrated that only *C. acutus* is known from Honduras. In the Yucatán Peninsula the species may be essentially pan-peninsular, although there are few records for the northern interior of the peninsula, nor are there verified records from southernmost Belize, although the species very likely occurs there (Map 44).

NATURAL HISTORY   This crocodile is primarily an inhabitant of freshwater lakes, rivers, and ponds, although individuals do enter brackish water, and Meerman (1992:4) claimed to have found one in Corozal Bay, Belize. Throughout its range, nearly every local aguada has (or had) its *lagarto*, which generally proves to be *C. moreletii*.

Crocodylus moreletii eats a variety of inverte-

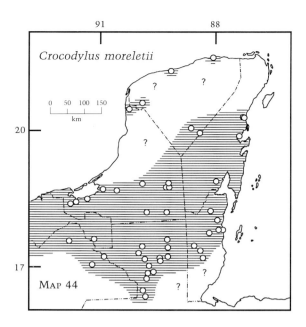

MAP 44

brate and vertebrate prey, and there is some indication of a size-related shift in diet. In Belize, Schmidt (1924:80–81) found that the stomachs of four small individuals contained only the remains of aquatic invertebrates, whereas two larger individuals contained a fish and mammal remains in addition to insects, mollusks, and crustaceans. Invertebrates predominate in the diet of juvenile and subadult specimens in Belize, although fishes, frogs, lizards, turtles, birds, and mammals are also eaten (S. Platt, unpubl. data). Shreve (1957:242) reported various species of turtles eaten by crocodiles in the Lacandón region of Chiapas. In Veracruz, *C. moreletii* feeds on a wide variety of fishes, reptiles, amphibians, birds, and mammals, including dogs and goats (Pérez-Higareda et al., 1989). According to the same report, *C. moreletii* exhibits necrophagy, often sequestering large prey for 24 hours or more, presumably because larger prey items are easier to dismember after decomposition sets in. Pooley et al. (1989:186), however, stated that such behavior is not usually characteristic of crocodiles.

Although these crocodiles are generally timid and retiring, large individuals occasionally attack humans. Shattuck (1933:18–19) reported that a young girl was attacked by a crocodile at Laguna Perdida, El Petén, "from which she was rescued just in time to save her life." A similar account, possibly based on the same incident, was given by Thompson (1963:263), who told of an attack on a young girl in El Petén who was seized and dragged down by a crocodile, but "her father attacked the beast and forced it to let go of the child, who, except for some bad cuts and scratches, was unharmed." Although the identity of the crocodile was not established, on distributional and ecological grounds it was likely *C. moreletii*. A case of human fatality attributable to this species appeared in an article published in the *Belize Reporter* on 13 April 1980. According to this account, a thirty-year-old man was spearfishing in waist-deep water in Honey Camp Lagoon, Orange Walk District (actually Kate's Lagoon in that district, *fide* R. H. Hunt, pers. comm.), when his two brothers, who had accompanied him, "heard a terrified scream and saw their brother's upraised hand descend into the water. At about 7 o'clock on Holy Sat. morning, friends and relatives came across his body badly mangled from the bites of a pair of giant jaws, hauled up on the mudbank at the edge of the lagoon. An autopsy performed at Orange Walk showed that the victim had died almost immediately from fatal bite wounds to his throat." That evening a crocodile measuring 8 feet was shot near where the body was recovered. When it was cut open, "they found a piece of his clothing and pieces of human flesh which allowed them a positive ID."

As described by Pérez-Higareda et al. (1989) for animals in southern Veracruz, courtship involves mutual head raising and neck rubbing accompanied by soft snorts. The male then snaps his jaws and slaps his tail against the water repeatedly. If the female is receptive, copulation lasting between one and two minutes occurs beneath the water. These authors also reported that courtship may involve a "sonorous roar" emitted by males, and that occasionally a female initiates courtship by emitting a short, loud roar while beating her head on the water.

Like all crocodilians, *C. moreletii* is oviparous. Schmidt (1924:81) conjectured that reproductive maturity is attained at a total length of about 1.5 m. In April, May, and June breeding females construct nests of decaying vegetation that average about 1.5 m in diameter and perhaps 1 m in height. The female deposits 20 to 40 smooth, hard-shelled eggs within the nest and remains to attend them during the 75 to 80 days of incubation (Alvarez del Toro, 1974:37–38). As is the case with the other species of *Crocodylus* that have been studied, this species exhibits temperature-dependent sex determination (TSD). High and low incubation temperatures produce a preponderance of females, whereas intermediate temperatures produce mostly males (Aguilar, 1994). Nests are generally situated on land near water, but Pérez-Higareda (1980:52) described a nest in southern Veracruz that was constructed over an accumulation of aquatic vegetation rather than on land. In Yucatán the eggs hatch in September (Brazaitis, 1973:73), suggesting oviposition in June or July. S. Platt (unpubl. data) found that nesting begins in mid-June in Belize and suggested that it continues throughout the rainy season. When hatching time arrives, the young crocodiles begin to grunt while still inside the eggs. Their grunting stimulates the attending female to open the nest with her front legs, and she carries the hatchlings to the water in her jaws, one or two at a time (Hunt, 1975:763). Females are generally aggressive toward other crocodiles that approach the nest or the hatchlings, and they respond protectively to hatchlings' distress grunts (Hunt, 1975:764). Adults in general show a strong protective response toward hatchlings, and they threaten or attack juvenile crocodiles, which may prey on the hatchlings (Hunt, 1977:199–200).

ETYMOLOGY The specific name, *moreletii*, is a patronym that honors Pierre-Marie Arthur Morelet, who collected amphibians and reptiles in southern Mexico and Guatemala in 1847–1848.

COMMENT *Crocodylus moreletii* is listed as endangered in the IUCN Red Data Book (Groombridge, 1982:341); it is considered endangered under the United States Endangered Species Act; and it is listed in Appendix 1 of the Convention on International Trade in Endangered Species. Although fully protected in the countries in which it occurs, Morelet's crocodile continues to be exploited, primarily as a source of leather (Groombridge, 1987), and its numbers continue to decline as a result of illegal hunting and habitat destruction (Thorbjarnarson, 1992). Information on *C. moreletii* was summarized by C. A. Ross (1987).

Locality Records Belize: Belize: Altun Ha (C. A. Ross, pers. comm.), Belize (FMNH 11041–44; W. T. Neill and Allen, 1961a:51; USNM 10288), ca. 5 mi W Belize City (W. T. Neill and Allen, 1959c:30), Old River (USNM 26068); Cayo: Central Farm (MCZ 71630–31), Coquercot (UMMZ 75032), Macal River (Stafford, 1991:14), upper Raspaculo River basin (Stafford, 1991:14); Orange Walk: Kate's Lagoon (FMNH 49369); no specific locality (FMNH 4430–36, 4438; MCZ 18856). *Guatemala*: Alta Verapaz: Chinajá (Duellman, 1963:229); El Petén: Arroyo Subin (UMMZ 79092), 16 km NNW Chinajá (Duellman, 1963:229), Lago Petén Itzá (MNHNP 7520), Laguna de Zotz (UMMZ 79089–91, 79097), Laguna Perdida (UMMZ 79096, 79099), Laguna

Petenxil (UMMZ 79898), Laguna Rompido, Río Salinas drainage (AMNH 99925–26), La Libertad (USNM 72343), near La Libertad (UMMZ 75030–31), 15 km SE La Libertad (KU 55981–82), Paso de Caballo (UMMZ 79093–95), 10 mi S Piedras Negras (USNM 115355), Remate (USNM 71428), Sayaxché (UCM 22191), Tikal (Stuart, 1958:29), Uaxactún (Stuart, 1958:29); no specific locality (USNM 71954–60). *Mexico*: Campeche: Balchacaj (H. M. Smith, 1938:21), Becan (UMMZ 76119), El Remate (Dundee et al., 1986:40), Encarnación (H. M. Smith, 1938:21), Laguna Chumpich (Duellman, 1965a:593), 10 km E Laguna Silvituc (KU 75124), Palizada (H. M. Smith and Smith, 1977:93), Panlao (H. M. Smith, 1938:22); Treinta y Seis (Duellman, 1965a:593), 65 km S Xpujil (KU 75123, 75125), Xpujil (Duellman, 1965a:593), Zoh Laguna (JCL sight record); Chiapas: Laguna Ocotal (MCZ 53860), Palenque, near San Juancito (USNM 115358–60); Quintana Roo: Bahía de la Ascensión (UF 29160), km 15 on Chetumal-Bacalar Hwy. (MZCIQRO 04), Chunyaxché (Himmelstein, 1980:26), 3 mi E Esmeralda (LACM 113909–10), Hacienda Santa Rosa (UMMZ 155300), Laguna Chunyaxché (UF 29160), Río Hondo District (MCZ 8047); Tabasco: Tenosique (USNM 115356–57); Yucatán: Helacho (N. P. Wright, 1973:91), Río Lagartos (H. M. Smith and Smith, 1977:94), Telchac Puerto (UMMZ 76157).

Order Testudines
(Turtles, Tortoises, and Terrapins)

Turtles today form only a small component of the world's reptile fauna, but they have a long and extensive fossil history extending back at least 200 million years. Turtles typically have a bony shell consisting of an upper component, the carapace, and a lower component, the plastron. They have solidly constructed skulls, and modern forms lack teeth. The ribs are usually incorporated into the shell, and the limb girdles lie within the rib cage, allowing most turtles to retract their limbs into the shell, at least to some extent. In addition, the neck is unusually flexible, and many turtles are capable of retracting the head and neck into the shell also. Turtles are found throughout the temperate and tropical latitudes of the world, including the oceans and on many oceanic islands. Although predominantly aquatic as a group, some are semiaquatic, others are terrestrial or semifossorial, and some live in deserts. At the other extreme are the sea turtles, which are strictly marine and normally come ashore only to lay eggs. Although all members of the order Testudines are immediately recogniz-

able as turtles, there is enormous variation within the order. Turtles range in size from the enormous leatherback (*Dermochelys coriacea*), which attains a carapace length of 1.8 m and is among the largest of all living reptiles, to tiny mud turtles (*Kinosternon*) no more than 8 to 10 cm long. The most recent checklist of turtles (Iverson, 1992) recognizes 12 living families containing 87 genera and 257 species. Six families, 13 genera, and 16 species of turtles occur in the Yucatán Peninsula and adjacent waters (see Table 1).

IDENTIFICATION Identifying the 16 species of turtles in the Yucatán Peninsula is a relatively straightforward matter that can usually be accomplished by comparing the specimen with the photographs and illustrations provided here, reading the descriptions in the species accounts, and referring to the section on similar species that appears in each account. Location can also assist in identification, for some species have restricted distributions that may eliminate them from consideration. It is important, therefore, to know the origin of the specimen. The habitat in which the specimen was found is also important. For example, the predominantly terrestrial *Terrapene carolina* would not be expected to occur in large bodies of water; nor would

Fig. 104. Dorsal view of a hatchling of *Caretta caretta* (UMRC 56-109), 46.9 mm carapace length; Miami Beach, Dade Co., Fla.

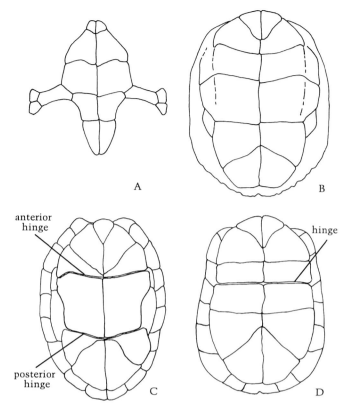

anterior
hinge

posterior
hinge

A

B

hinge

C

D

Fig. 105. Ventral views of the plastra of turtles. A, *Chelydra serpentina* showing reduced cruciform plastron. B, *Trachemys scripta* showing normal configuration and the plastron attached to the carapace by a bridge. C, *Kinosternon scorpioides* showing an anterior and posterior hinge and the plastron and carapace united by a bridge. D, *Terrepene carolina* with a single hinge and the plastron and carapace in direct contact, without a bridge.

Fig. 106. Lateral view of the tail of *Chelydra serpentina* showing rows of enlarged, sawtoothed scales.

any of the sea turtles normally be encountered on land.

The following identification keys rely on features of external morphology. The most important physical characters are defined in the Glossary and illustrated in the figures cited in the keys. First, note whether the forelimbs are paddle shaped and the extent to which the digits are webbed. The configuration of the carapace is a helpful characteristic. Is it relatively low and flat, or is it high and dome shaped? Is the carapace keeled, and if so, how many keels does it bear? Note the overall configuration of the plastron. In some species it is reduced and cross shaped (cruciform), whereas in others it is broad and well developed. Is the plastron hinged, or are the lobes of the plastron fixed and immovable? The number and arrangement of the epidermal scutes on the carapace and plastron are especially important characters.

The color of the shell may aid in identification, but the color and pattern of the skin on the soft parts (head, neck, limbs, and tail) are equally important.

Key to the Families of Turtles

1. Forelimbs modified as flippers (Fig. 104); no more than two claws present on hand; strictly marine, comes ashore only to lay eggs 2
Forelimbs not modified as flippers; more than two claws present on hand; terrestrial or freshwater aquatic, rarely marine 3

2. Carapace with leathery covering, lacking horny scutes; seven dorsal and five ventral longitudinal ridges on the carapace and plastron, respectively . . . . .Dermochelyidae
Carapace covered with horny scutes; fewer than seven dorsal and two ventral ridges on the carapace and plastron, respectively . . . . .Cheloniidae

3. Plastron reduced in size, cruciform in shape (Fig. 105A) 4
Plastron not reduced in size, not cruciform (Fig. 105B) 5

4. Dorsal surface of tail with rows of enlarged scales (Fig. 106) . . . . .Chelydridae
Dorsal surface of tail without rows of enlarged scales . . . . .Kinosternidae (part)

5. Plastral hinge present, anterior lobe movable 6
No plastral hinge, plastron fixed 7

6. Eleven plastral scutes; carapace and plastron connected by a bridge (Fig. 105C) . . . .
. . . . .Kinosternidae (part)

Twelve plastral scutes; carapace and plastron in direct contact, no bridge (Fig. 105D) . . . .
. . . . Emydidae (part)

7. Head and neck boldly marked with yellow, orange, or red stripes or spots; carapace with or
without light spots . . . . Emydidae (part)
No stripes or spots on head and neck; carapace uniform brown, olive, or gray . . . .
. . . . Dermatemydidae

Clave para las Familias de Tortugas

1. Miembros anteriores modificados como aletas (Fig. 104); no más de dos uñas presentes en la
mano; especies estrictamente marinas que se acercan a la costa sólo a desovar 2
Miembros anteriores no modificados como aletas; más de dos uñas presentes en la mano;
organismos de hábitos terrestres o dulceacuícolas, raramente marinos 3

2. Carapacho con cubierta de cuero (laúd), sin escudos córneos; siete crestas longitudinales
dorsales y cinco ventrales en el carapacho y plastrón, respectivamente . . . . . Dermochelyidae
Carapacho cubierto con escudos córneos; menos de siete crestas dorsales y dos ventrales en el
caparazón y plastrón, respectivamente. . . . . Cheloniidae

3. Plastrón reducido en tamaño, forma cruciforme (Fig. 105A) 4
Plastrón no reducido en tamaño, no cruciforme (Fig. 105B) 5

4. Superficie dorsal de la cola con hileras de escamas agrandadas (Fig. 106) . . . . Chelydridae
Superficie dorsal de la cola sin hileras de escamas agrandadas. . . . . . . Kinosternidae (en parte)

5. Con una bisagra plastral presente, lóbulo anterior móvil 6
Sin bisagra plastral, plastrón fijo 7

6. Once escudos plastrales; carapacho y plastrón conectado por un puente (Fig. 105C) . . . .
. . . . Kinosternidae (en parte)
Doce escudos plastrales; carapacho y plastrón en contacto directo; sin puente (Fig. 105D)
. . . . Emydidae (en parte)

7. La cabeza y el cuello conspicuamente marcados con líneas o manchas color amarillo, anaran-
jado o rojo; carapacho con o sin manchas claras . . . . Emydidae (en parte)
Sin rayas o manchas en cabeza y cuello; carapacho uniformemente pardo, olivo o gris . . . .
. . . . Dermatemydidae

Family Cheloniidae
(Hard-shelled Sea Turtles)

These large marine turtles are highly adapted for an aquatic existence, and they rarely, if ever, come ashore other than to lay their eggs. The forelimbs are modified as flippers, and the carapace is generally low, broad, and heart or shield shaped in dorsal view. Representatives of this family range widely throughout the tropical and subtropical seas of the world, and individuals sometimes wander as far north as Alaska and the British Isles. Although most species generally inhabit shallow coastal waters, some undertake extraordinary long-distance migrations between their feeding and nesting grounds. Today this family is represented by six living species assigned to four genera, but the family includes many extinct forms, some of which are among the earliest known turtle fossils. Four species of hard-shelled sea turtles occur in the waters of the Yucatán Peninsula, representing each of the four living genera.

All species of sea turtles have suffered disastrous population declines at the hands of humans (Hildebrand, 1982:447), and this is certainly true of the populations off the coast of the Yucatán Peninsula (César Zurita et al., 1992; Nájera, 1990:29). The eggs of all sea turtle species are esteemed as food, as is the flesh of most species, especially the green turtle, *Chelonia mydas*. The hawksbill, *Eretmochelys imbricata*, is the source of tortoiseshell, and enormous numbers of individuals are harvested annually to supply the demand for that material. In addition, the skin of some species is used as leather, stuffed turtles are sold as curios, and oil from some species

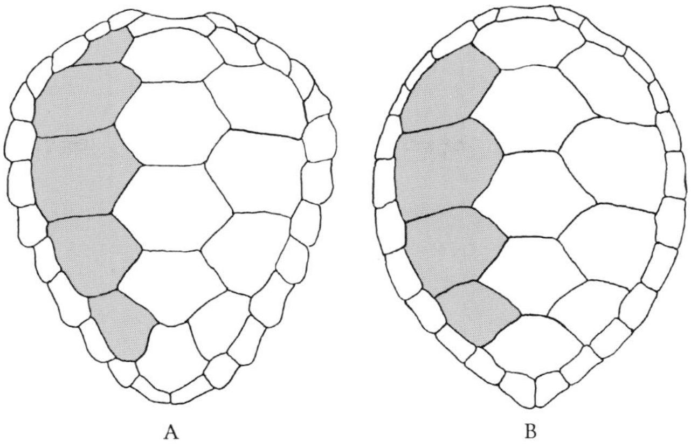

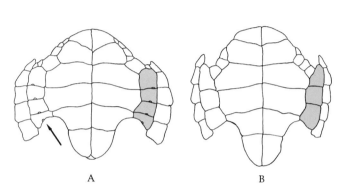

Fig. 107. Carapaces of sea turtles, showing numbers of pleural scutes (*shaded*). A, *Caretta caretta* with five pleural scutes. B, *Chelonia mydas* with four pleural scutes. Redrawn from Rebel, 1974, by permission of the University of Miami Press.

Fig. 108. Plastra of sea turtles showing numbers of inframarginal scutes and the presence or absence of inframarginal pores. A, *Lepidochelys kempii* with four inframarginal scutes (*shaded*), some with inframarginal pores (*arrow*). B, *Caretta caretta* with three inframarginal scutes (*shaded*), none with pores. Redrawn from Rebel, 1974, by permission of the University of Miami Press.

A   B

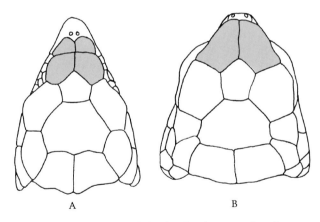

Fig. 109. Dorsal view of the heads of sea turtles showing prefrontal scales (*shaded*). A, *Eretmochelys imbricata* with two pairs of prefrontal scales. B, *Chelonia mydas* with one pair of prefrontal scales. Redrawn from Rebel, 1974, by permission of the University of Miami Press.

is used in the manufacture of cosmetics (Canin, 1989:27). Beachfront development has destroyed many of the nesting grounds of sea turtles. As a consequence, all species of sea turtles are seriously threatened. In 1973 sea turtles within Mexico's jurisdiction in the Gulf of Mexico were given com-

plete protection under Mexican law, and in May 1991 President Carlos Salinas de Gortari of Mexico afforded all marine turtles in Mexico protection by presidential decree. Thus, all members of this family (and the Dermochelyidae) are protected in Mexico. In 1992 the government of Belize made it unlawful to hunt hawksbill turtles and significantly shortened the hunting season for green and loggerhead turtles. This legislation was upgraded on 31 March 1993 to extend protection to all sea turtles of nesting size and to make it illegal for merchants to sell any product made from the shell of the hawksbill turtle. The legislation also placed restrictions on the number and size of *Dermatemys mawii* that can be harvested in Belize. Enforcing these regulations is difficult, however, and turtle populations continue to be threatened by clandestine and illegal slaughter of adults and poaching of eggs (Blanco-Casillo, 1990:185). Under no circumstances should any of these species be molested, nor should anyone contribute to their persecution by purchasing items derived from them.

Sea turtles have been the objects of intense study, partly because they are of commercial value and are endangered, but also because they are fascinating animals in their own right. Important summary works include those by Bjorndal (1982) and Frazier (1993), and the various proceedings of the Annual Workshop on Sea Turtle Biology and Conservation, published by the U.S. National Marine Fisheries Service.

Owing to their large adult size and the fact that they come ashore only to nest, sea turtles are poorly represented in museum collections. Specimen-based locality records are therefore few, and the distributions of the sea turtles in the waters surrounding the Yucatán Peninsula are poorly known. Locality records are generally based on skeletal remains, sight records, and literature citations.

Key to the Genera of the Family Cheloniidae

1. Five or more pleural scutes on each side (Fig. 107A) 2
   Four pleural scutes on each side (Fig. 107B) 3
2. Small sea turtles, carapace length less than 800 mm; four inframarginal scutes, some or all with pores (Fig. 108A) . . . . *Lepidochelys*
   Large sea turtles, carapace length more than 800 mm; three inframarginal scutes, none with pores (Fig. 108B) . . . . *Caretta*
3. Carapace scutes imbricate; two pairs of prefrontal scales (Fig. 109A); adult carapace length less than 1,000 mm . . . . *Eretmochelys*
   Carapace scutes not imbricate; one pair of prefrontal scales (Fig. 109B); adult carapace length greater than 1,000 mm. . . . . *Chelonia*

Clave para los Géneros de la Familia Cheloniidae

1. Cinco o más escudos pleurales en cada lado del cuerpo (Fig. 107A) 2
   Cuatro escudos pleurales en cada lado del cuerpo (Fig. 107B) 3
2. Tortugas marinas pequeñas, menores a 800 mm de largo del carapacho; cuatro escudos inframarginales, todos o algunos presentan poros (Fig. 108A) . . . . *Lepidochelys*
   Tortugas marinas grandes, mayores a los 800 mm de largo del carapacho; tres escudos inframarginales, sin poros (Fig. 108B) . . . . *Caretta*
3. Escudos del carapacho imbricados; dos pares de escudos prefrontales (Fig. 109A); adultos menores de 1,000 mm de largo del caparacho. . . . . *Eretmochelys*
   Escudos del carapacho sin imbricar; un par de escudos prefrontales (Fig. 109B); adultos mayores a los 1,000 mm de largo de carapacho . . . . *Chelonia*

Genus *Caretta* (Loggerhead Sea Turtle)

This genus contains a single extant species, the loggerhead (*Caretta caretta*). There are numerous fossil species, however, some of which lived 10 to 15 million years ago. *Caretta* is derived from the French *caret* (whence the Spanish "carey"), meaning "turtle" or "sea turtle."

Caretta caretta (Linnaeus)
(Figs. 104, 107A, 108B, 262, 263; Map 45)

Testudo caretta Linnaeus, 1758:197. TYPE: none designated. TYPE LOCALITY: Insulas Americanas; re-

stricted to the Bermuda Islands by H. M. Smith and Taylor (1950b:315) and to Bimini, Bahama Islands, by Schmidt (1953:107).

Loggerhead turtle; caguama, cahuama (Mexico).

DESCRIPTION This species is the largest member of the family Cheloniidae, and it is second in size only to *Dermochelys* among living turtles. The adults attain a carapace length of up to 2,300 mm and a probable mass of 540 kg (Pritchard, 1967:197). The carapace is heart shaped in dorsal aspect, and its posterior margin is weakly serrated (Figs. 104, 262). There are five pleural scutes on each side of the carapace and three inframarginals, all of which lack pores. The hatchlings and juveniles have a median keel and a pair of dorsolateral keels, all of which bear knobs; these become obscure in older individuals as the carapace becomes smoother. Young turtles have a pair of longitudinal ridges on the plastron, but these disappear with age. The head is unusually large and broad (Fig. 263), and the snout is pointed in dorsal view. There are enlarged scales on the leading and trailing edges of all four limbs, and each limb bears a pair of claws.

The carapace is brown or reddish brown, sometimes with an olive cast, and frequently yellowish or tan on the marginal scutes. The plastron is yellowish tan and distinctly lighter than the carapace. The dorsal surface of the head is dark brown or chestnut suffused with yellow or tan. The dorsal surfaces of the limbs are dark brown with light tan or yellow margins. The ventral surfaces of the appendages are light tan or yellow.

SIMILAR SPECIES *Caretta caretta* differs from *Chelonia* and *Eretomchelys* in possessing five or more pleural scutes on each side of the carapace rather than four. From *Lepidochelys* it differs in being much larger and in having three rather than four inframarginal scutes, none of which have pores.

DISTRIBUTION The loggerhead occurs throughout the tropical, subtropical, and temperate seas of the world, including the waters surrounding the Yucatán Peninsula (Map 45). It is said to nest in Belize (Ernst and Barbour, 1989:125) and on Isla

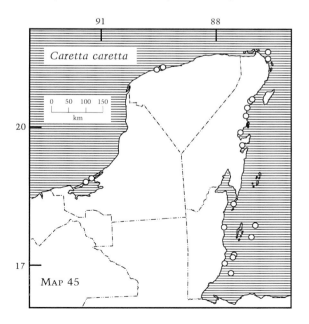

MAP 45

Contoy, Quintana Roo (H. M. Smith and Smith, 1979:306). In fact, *C. caretta* nests in large numbers on the beaches of Quintana Roo from Punta Allen to Isla Contoy, and more sparingly along the Yucatán and Campeche coasts to Isla del Carmen, Campeche (R. Byles, in litt.).

NATURAL HISTORY This turtle occurs in shallow coastal waters and bays, but it may also be found far out to sea, hundreds of kilometers from shore. It will enter rivers and wander considerable distances upstream, and there is a questionable record for this species from the Illinois River in Oklahoma (Carr, 1952:385).

A pugnacious temperament coupled with a large head and powerful jaws make the loggerhead a formidable adversary when cornered or otherwise molested. An article in the *New York Herald*, 3 September 1905, bore the headline "Big Turtle Victor over Five Men." The story, reprinted in full in Carr, 1952:389, and Pritchard, 1967:197–198, describes how five Connecticut fishermen in a rowboat attempted to recapture a large loggerhead that had escaped from its pen by tearing down the planks on the sides "as though they were toothpicks." The men speared the turtle, and a struggle of nearly an hour's duration ensued, during which the turtle very nearly succeeded in capsizing the boat. It crushed the oars in its jaws, battered the men with its flippers, and tore a long gash in the arm of one of the men. Eventually the turtle swam away, leaving the men to make their way back to port using the stumps of their oars as paddles and with one member of their party unconscious in the bottom of the boat.

Loggerheads are omnivorous. The diet includes a wide variety of marine invertebrates such as crabs, shrimp, squid, bivalve mollusks, and jellyfish as well as fish. The broad head and powerful jaws are well suited for crushing hard-shelled prey. They also eat various kinds of seaweed and turtle grass, but these items may be accidentally ingested (K. C. Dodd, pers. comm.).

Courtship and copulation take place offshore, often at a considerable distance from the nesting grounds. Nesting generally occurs in spring or early summer. The females crawl out onto the nesting beaches at night, usually (although not necessarily) at high tide, and deposit between 60 and 200 eggs in nests excavated in the sand. The incubation period is about 50 to 70 days, depending on the temperature. The hatchlings suffer high mortality at the hands of a variety of vertebrate and invertebrate predators (Dodd, 1988:table 21). Females may nest repeatedly during the reproductive season, at intervals of 12 to 15 days (Caldwell, 1962).

As is the case with many species of turtles, sex determination in *C. caretta* is temperature dependent. Eggs incubated at lower temperatures produce males, whereas those incubated at higher temperatures produce females (Mrosovsky and Yntema, 1981:271). The pivotal temperature (at which 50 percent of each sex is produced) is about 29C, according to data obtained from clutches from the East Coast of the United States (Mrosovsky, 1988:664). Mrosovsky and Provancha (1989:2536) reported a huge sex ratio bias favoring females (greater than 93 percent), determined from collections made throughout the summer nesting season in Florida, and warned that global warming could have serious adverse effects on sex ratios in this species.

SUBSPECIES Some herpetologists (e.g., H. M. Smith and Smith, 1979:297) recognize two subspecies, of which the nominate subspecies, *C. c. caretta*, would occur in the waters of the Yucatán Peninsula. Many others, however (e.g., Brongersma, 1961; Dodd, 1988, 1990b; Pritchard and Trebbau, 1984; Wermuth and Mertins, 1977), do not recognize subspecies.

ETYMOLOGY The specific name, *caretta*, is a tautonym of the generic name and is derived from the French *caret*.

COMMENT Although the flesh of this species is less esteemed than that of some other sea turtles, it is nonetheless consumed by the inhabitants of coastal Mexico, Central America, and the Caribbean. The eggs are very much sought after by humans and are eaten in large numbers. Such persecution in conjunction the destruction of nesting grounds to make way for beachfront houses and recreational facilities has drastically reduced loggerhead turtle populations. Although loggerheads once nested from New Jersey to southeast Brazil, now they nest predominantly in isolated or protected areas within the former nesting range (J. P. Ross, 1982:190).

Caretta caretta is listed as vulnerable in the IUCN Red Data Book (Groombridge, 1982:137) and is listed in Appendix 1 of the Convention on International Trade in Endangered Species. It is considered a threatened species under the United States Endangered Species Act.

The loggerhead has been the focus of many studies on various aspects of its natural history, and a substantial literature exists (see Dodd, 1987, for a bibliography of the loggerhead). Groombridge (1982) and Dodd (1988, 1990b) summarized information on *C. caretta* biology.

Locality Records *Belize*: Belize: Ambergris Cay, Rocky Point (D. Moll, 1985:156), Belize City (FMNH 4158), Long Cay, Lighthouse Reef (D. Moll, 1985:156), Northern Cay, Lighthouse Reef (D. Moll, 1985:156); Stann Creek: Carrie Bow Cay (D. Moll, 1985:156), Placentia Peninsula (D. Moll, 1985:156), South Water Cay (D. Moll, 1985:156); Toledo: Ranguana Cay (D. Moll, 1985:156). *Mexico*: Campeche: Isla Aguada (KU 71777); Isla del Carmen, Puerto Real (H. M. Smith and Smith, 1979:305); Quintana Roo: Akumal (Agardy and Hernández, 1989:199), Bahía de la Ascensión (Carranza, 1959:231), Bahía Espíritu Santo (Carranza, 1959:231), Boca Paila (FMNH 213654), Isla Contoy (Márquez, 1966), S end Isla Mujeres (FMNH 34645–46; KU 87852), Tulum (Himmelstein, 1980:26), X-Cacel (Agardy and Hernández, 1989:199); Yucatán: 1.6 mi E Chixulub (UU 9364–402, 9849), ca. 2 mi E Chixulub Puerto (CM 38956–57), Progreso (Ives, 1891:458).

Genus *Chelonia* (Green Sea Turtles)

This genus of sea turtles contains but two living species, although many more forms are known as fossils. The family is widely distributed throughout the tropical seas of the world, and one species occurs in the waters off the coast of the Yucatán Peninsula. *Chelonia* is derived from the Greek *chelon*, "tortoise" or "turtle."

Chelonia mydas (Linnaeus)
(Figs. 107B, 109B, 264; Map 46)

Testudo mydas Linnaeus, 1758:197. SYNTYPES: NRM 19, 26, 231 (three syntypes). TYPE LOCALITY: Insulas pelagi: insulam Adscensionis; restricted by Mertens and Müller (1928:23) to Ascension Island.

Green turtle; carey (Belize, Mexico); caguama, caguama negra, caguama prieta, parlama, tortuga blanca, tortuga verde (Mexico).

DESCRIPTION *Chelonia mydas* is a medium-sized sea turtle. The adults may attain a carapace length in excess of 1,500 mm, although today even a 1,200-mm specimen would be considered large. The carapace is heart shaped in dorsal aspect, rather low and broad, and its posterior margin is serrated (Fig. 264). There are four pleural scutes (Fig. 107B) and four inframarginals, none possessing pores. The scutes of the carapace are juxtaposed rather than imbricate, and the carapace of adults lacks a keel, although a median keel is present in hatchlings. In contrast with other sea turtles, the cutting edges of the lower jaws are serrated, and the inner surface of the upper jaw has distinct vertical ridges, presumably an adaptation to grazing on marine vegetation. There is a single pair of prefrontal scales (Fig. 109B). The tail in males is long and prehensile and ends in a flattened, keratinized nail. The males have a single strongly curved claw on the leading edge of each forelimb that is used to grasp the shell of the female during copulation (Carr, 1952:349).

The carapace is predominantly brownish above, sometimes with dark, wavy markings on the scutes. The dorsal surface of the head and appendages is brown, gray, or nearly black, and the scales on the dorsal and lateral surfaces of the head have light margins. The undersides of the limbs and tail are cream or yellowish. According to Ernst and Barbour (1972:207), the common name, "green turtle," refers to the fact that the fat of this species is greenish.

SIMILAR SPECIES *Chelonia mydas* differs from *Lepidochelys* and *Caretta* in possessing only four pleural scutes (Fig. 107) rather than five or more. The scutes of the *Eretmochelys* carapace are imbricate instead of juxtaposed, and *E. imbricata* has two pairs of prefrontal scutes rather than a single pair (Fig. 109).

DISTRIBUTION The green sea turtle is predominantly an animal of tropical waters, and it can be found throughout the Atlantic, Pacific, and Indian Oceans. Individuals are known to wander as far north as Alaska, however, and specimens are occasionally found off the British Isles, having apparently drifted across the Atlantic from North America. This species occurs throughout the Gulf of Mexico and the Caribbean and is known from coastal localities in Campeche, Yucatán, Quintana Roo, and Belize. It nests (or nested) on Islas Contoy, Mujeres, and Cozumel, Quintana Roo (H. M. Smith and Smith, 1979:271), and on Cayos Arcos, Arenas, Arrecife Alacrán, and Arrecife Triángulos on the Campeche Bank (Hildebrand, 1982:451) (Map 46).

NATURAL HISTORY *Chelonia mydas* typically inhabits relatively shallow coastal waters where

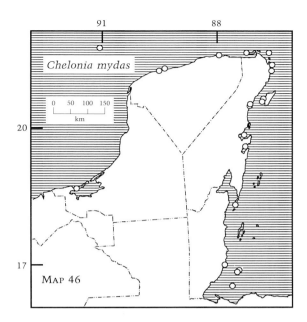

MAP 46

there is an abundance of the marine grasses that form a major component of its diet. Marine algae and various marine invertebrates are also consumed, but in lesser quantities, and captives readily accept fish and other kinds of meat. Nonetheless, the green turtle is primarily a vegetarian, and in this it is unique among sea turtles. In the Gulf of Mexico and the Caribbean Sea green turtles are most numerous in areas that have abundant eelgrass and many rocky holes, within which the turtles sleep at night (Carr, 1952:349). Especially important feeding grounds for this species are off the northwest and southeast coasts of the Yucatán Peninsula (Carr, 1965:81).

In contrast with some other sea turtles, especially *C. caretta*, the green sea turtle has a rather mild disposition, although individuals occasionally attempt to bite when first handled.

In the Caribbean, the Gulf of Mexico, and along the Central American coast, nesting generally takes place during the spring and summer months. Oviposition occurs at night. The females crawl up the nesting beach to a spot above the high-water mark and use their front flippers to excavate a large, shallow depression in the sand. The hind limbs are then used to excavate a smaller hole at the bottom of the depression, within which 100 to 150 eggs are deposited. Females usually breed every two or three years and are capable of ovipositing several times during a nesting season, at intervals of about two weeks. The incubation period is normally about six to eight weeks. For more than 30 years this species has been the focus of intense study at Tortuguero, Costa

Rica, by Archie Carr and his associates. Hirth (1988) studied nesting in first-time breeders at Tortuguero and found a positive correlation between clutch size and the size of the breeding adult, and a negative correlation between hatchling size and the size of the first-time breeder. Bjorndal and Carr (1989) determined a mean clutch size of 112 eggs for turtles at Tortuguero and showed both that clutch size and egg size are positively correlated with the female's body size, and that clutch size increases with the female's age.

The sex ratio of hatchling green turtles depends on the temperature at which the egg clutch was incubated. Eggs incubated at high temperatures produce mostly females, those incubated at lower temperatures produce mostly males (Mrosovsky, 1982).

SUBSPECIES   Two subspecies are commonly recognized, one in the Atlantic and another in the Pacific and Indian Oceans. According to this arrangement, the green turtles in the waters of the Yucatán Peninsula are *C. m. mydas.*

ETYMOLOGY   The specific name, *mydas*, is from the Greek *mydos*, "wetness" or "clamminess," apparently in reference to the aquatic nature of this species (H. M. Smith and Smith, 1979:266).

COMMENT   The flesh and eggs of the green turtle are highly prized foods, and hunters and egg poachers have severely reduced populations throughout the species' range (King, 1982:185). As early as 1820 green turtle numbers in the Cayman Islands had been so reduced that turtling ships were required to search the southern coast of Cuba for their quarry (Hirst, quoted in Lewis, 1940). Green turtles have become rare or have disappeared altogether from many localities where they were formerly numerous.

Chelonia mydas is listed as endangered in the IUCN Red Data Book (Groombridge, 1982:151) and is listed in Appendix 1 of the Convention on International Trade in Endangered Species. It is considered endangered or threatened under the United States Endangered Species Act.

Chelonia mydas was reviewed by H. M. Smith and Smith (1979), and information on its biology was summarized by Groombridge (1982).

Locality Records   Belize: Belize: Ambergris Cay (D. Moll, 1985:155); Stann Creek: Placentia Peninsula (D. Moll, 1985:156), Pompion Cay (D. Moll, 1985:156),

South Silk Cay (D. Moll, 1985:156), Northeast Cay (D. Moll, 1985:156). *Mexico:* Campeche: Campeche Bank (Carranza, 1959:230), Cayo Arcos (Carranza, 1959:230), Ciudad del Carmen (Parsons, 1962:35); Quintana Roo: Akumal (Agardy and Hernández, 1989:199), Bahía de la Ascensión (Carranza, 1959:231), Bahía Espíritu Santo (Carranza, 1959:231), Cancún (Carranza, 1959:231), Cozumel (Himmelstein, 1980:26), Cozumel, Playa Aventuras (MZCIQRO 58–65), Cozumel, 3.5 km N San Miguel (KU 71775), Isla Contoy (Carranza, 1959:231; Nájera, 1990:33), Isla Holbox (Nájera, 1990:33), Isla Mujeres (Himmelstein, 1980:26; UIMNH 86877–79), X-Cacel (Agardy and Hernández, 1989:199); Yucatán: Cayo Arenas (Carranza, 1959:230), 1.6 mi E Chicxulub (UU 9403–35), Isla Desterrada, Alacrán (MCZ 53127), Progreso (Ives, 1891:458), Río Lagartos (Nájera, 1990:33).

Genus *Eretmochelys*
(Hawksbill Sea Turtle)

This genus contains a single living species, the hawksbill. *Eretmochelys* is from the Greek *eretmon*, "oar," and *chelys*, "turtle" or "tortoise," presumably a reference to the paddle-shaped forelimbs.

Eretmochelys imbricata (Linnaeus)
(Figs. 109A, 265; Map 47)

Testudo imbricata Linnaeus, 1766:350. HOLOTYPE: probably ZMUU 130, *fide* H. M. Smith and Smith, 1979:280. TYPE LOCALITY: Mari Americano, Asiatico; restricted by H. M. Smith and Taylor (1950b:315) to Bermuda Islands, and by Schmidt (1953:106) to Belize, British Honduras.

Hawksbill turtle; tortuga carey (Mexico).

DESCRIPTION   This rather small sea turtle attains a maximum carapace length of a little less than 1,000 mm, although most specimens today are substantially smaller. There is pronounced sexual size dimorphism, with females growing larger than males. The carapace is heart shaped in young specimens but relatively long and narrow in older turtles (Fig. 265). The posterior margin of the carapace is serrated, and there are four pleural scutes on each side. The hatchlings have two longitudinal ridges on the plastron, but these disappear with age. The scutes of the carapace are strongly imbricate except in the very oldest specimens, in which they are juxtaposed. There is a median keel, especially evident on the posteriormost vertebral scutes. The four inframarginals on each side are not perforated by pores. There are two pairs of prefrontal scales. The head and snout are relatively narrow and elongate, and the upper jaw is decurved at the tip, vaguely resembling the beak of a hawk. The limbs bear enlarged scales on their leading and trailing edges, and there are two claws on each forelimb.

Hatchling hawksbill turtles are very dark—nearly black—except for the keel, the margins of the shell, and the edges of the appendages, all of which are light brown. The carapace of adults is predominantly brown with a "tortoiseshell" pattern of light yellow or cream markings. The plastron is predominantly yellow, but in young turtles it may have a few dark blotches. The scales on the dorsal surfaces of the head and limbs are brown, often with a reddish cast, and the margins of the scales are yellowish, cream, or tan. The chin, throat, and ventral surfaces of the limbs are yellow.

SIMILAR SPECIES *Eretmochelys* differs from *Lepidochelys* and *Caretta* in possessing four, rather than five or more, pleural scutes (Fig. 107) and in having strongly imbricate scutes on the carapace (in all but the very oldest individuals). The imbricate scutes distinguish *Eretmochelys* from *Chelonia* also, and it is further distinguished from *Chelonia* by having two pairs of prefrontal scales rather than a single pair (Fig. 109).

DISTRIBUTION The hawksbill occurs in subtropical and tropical portions of the Pacific, Atlantic, and Indian Oceans and throughout the Caribbean. In the Yucatán Peninsula it can be expected at any coastal locality, and its nesting distribution includes the beaches of southwestern Campeche and northeastern Yucatán (Carranza, 1959; Fuentes, 1967). It is found in greatest numbers on the Caribbean coast of the Yucatán Peninsula (Hildebrand, 1982:448; Meylan, 1989:105). Groombridge (1982:183) indicated that hawksbills nest in moderate numbers on the offshore cays of southern Belize, and D. Moll (1985:156) reported that five of eight nests found in Belize were in the Sapodilla Keys off the southern coast of Toledo District (Map 47).

NATURAL HISTORY The hawksbill inhabits shallow coastal waters. It is especially partial to rocky

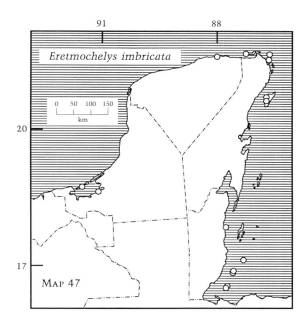

Eretmochelys imbricata

MAP 47

substrates and coral reefs but also occurs in areas with muddy bottoms. Individuals sometimes enter the lower reaches of streams.

This sea turtle is an omnivore, but it feeds predominantly on animals, including a variety of marine invertebrates and fishes. It specializes on encrusting organisms such as sponges, bryozoans, tunicates, mollusks, and algae, which it scrapes off reef faces (Mortimer, 1982:104), but it also eats jellyfish, including the Portuguese man-of-war. Some individuals may feed almost exclusively on sponges (Meylan, 1988).

This strictly aquatic turtle leaves the water only to lay eggs, which are deposited in nests excavated on a variety of beach types, including pocket beaches and beaches situated inside lagoons. The breeding season is protracted, spanning perhaps six to nine months, although in the Yucatán Peninsula the peak of reproduction is in June and July. Nesting occurs at night, usually at high tide. The clutch size ranges from about 50 to 200 eggs, and females are capable of breeding every three years. The incubation period is about eight weeks. The hatchlings and juveniles are apparently pelagic, but at a carapace length of about 230 to 250 mm they become benthic feeders in coastal habitats (Meylan, 1988:393).

SUBSPECIES Two subspecies of *E. imbricata* are commonly recognized on the basis of the configuration of the carapace and the coloration of the soft parts. The nominate race, *E. i. imbricata*, occurs in Atlantic and Caribbean waters, including the waters surrounding the Yucatán Peninsula. The other race, *E. i. bissa*, occurs in the Indo-Pacific oceans.

ETYMOLOGY   The specific name, *imbricata*, is the past participle of the Latin *imbrico*, "covered with tiles or scales," presumably in reference to the overlapping scutes on the carapace.

COMMENT   The hawksbill is the source of tortoiseshell, and it has long been exploited for that purpose. In addition, the eggs of this species are consumed in great numbers by humans. The hawksbill thus suffers tremendous mortality as a result of egg poaching and the continuing harvest of adults to satisfy the tortoiseshell trade. Hildebrand (1982:448) considered hawksbills to be the rarest marine turtles in the Gulf of Mexico, and their continued harvest has had a catastrophic effect on the species. In 1985, for example, 52.2 percent of the nests at Isla Aguada, Campeche, were lost, primarily to human poachers (Márquez et al., 1987). Meylan (1989:109) suggested that the harvest of hawksbills off the Caribbean coast of Honduras may have been 5,000 individuals in 1986. Unlike other species of sea turtles, the hawksbill has a diffuse nesting distribution, which makes it difficult for conservationists to establish protected areas. Every effort should be made to protect these turtles and their nests, and under no circumstances should one participate in their exploitation by purchasing items made of tortoiseshell.

This species is listed as endangered in the IUCN Red Data Book (Groombridge, 1982), and it appears in Appendix 1 of the Convention on International Trade in Endangered Species. It is considered endangered under the United States Endangered Species Act.

The systematics of *E. imbricata* was reviewed by H. M. Smith and Smith (1979), and information on the biology of this species was summarized by Groombridge (1982).

Locality Records   Belize: Belize: Belize City (FMNH 4159–60), Glover's Reef, Southwest Cay (D. Moll, 1985:156); Stann Creek: Pompion Cay (D. Moll, 1985:156); Toledo: Hunting Cay (D. Moll, 1985:156), Nicholas Cay (D. Moll, 1985:156), Ranguana Cay (D. Moll, 1985:156). *Mexico*: Campeche: Isla del Carmen (Strauch, 1890), Sama (H. M. Smith, 1938:21); Quintana Roo: Cozumel (Himmelstein, 1980:26), Cozumel, Playa Aventuras (MZCIQRO 66–69), Isla Contoy (UCM 16867), Isla Holbox (Nájera, 1990:33), N end Isla

Mujeres (KU 71774), Yucatán: Río Lagartos (Nájera, 1990:33, JCL photo).

Genus *Lepidochelys* (Ridley Sea Turtles)

Two species of small sea turtles, Kemp's ridley and the olive ridley, constitute the genus *Lepidochelys*, which is widely distributed in tropical and subtropical waters of the Atlantic, Indian, and Pacific Oceans. One species, *L. kempii*, nests on the coast of the Yucatán Peninsula and occupies its coastal waters. *Lepidochelys* is derived from the Greek *lepis*, "a scale," and *chelys*, "turtle" or "tortoise."

Lepidochelys kempii (Garman)
(Figs. 108A, 266; Map 48)

Thalassochelys kempii Garman, 1880:123. SYNTYPES: MCZ 46538–39 (two syntypes). TYPE LOCALITY: Gulf of Mexico; restricted to Key West, Monroe County, Florida, by H. M. Smith and Taylor (1950b:358).

Kemp's ridley sea turtle; lora, tortuga bastarda, tortuga de kemp, tortuga lora (Mexico).

DESCRIPTION   *Lepidochelys kempii* is the smallest of the sea turtles. The carapace length of adults averages about 600 to 650 mm, and there is apparently little or no sexual size dimorphism. The carapace is circular or heart shaped in dorsal aspect and bears a distinct median keel. In hatchlings and juveniles the keel has three to five knobs, but these disappear with age (Fig. 266). The posterior edge of the carapace is moderately serrated. There are four large inframarginal scales on each side, some with a musk gland pore at the posterior edge (Fig. 108A). The head is wide and the snout is rather pointed in dorsal aspect. The beak is hooked, and its cutting edge is unserrated. There are enlarged scales on the leading and trailing edges of the limbs, and each limb bears a pair of claws.

These turtles are predominantly gray or grayish green above, cream below. Hatchlings are dark brown to nearly black above and below and become lighter with age.

SIMILAR SPECIES   *Lepidochelys kempii* differs from *Chelonia* and *Eretmochelys* in possessing five or more, rather than four, pleural scutes on each side of the carapace. It differs from *C. caretta* in being smaller, in having four inframarginal scutes rather than three, and in possessing pores on the posterior margin of the inframarginal scutes (Fig. 108).

DISTRIBUTION   Kemp's ridley has a peculiar distribution. It is found throughout the Gulf of Mexico but apparently not in the Caribbean; and in the Atlantic Ocean it occurs between latitudes 18° and 35° N, including the waters off the British Isles and western Europe. The crustacean-rich banks of the Campeche-Tabasco area of the southern Gulf of Mexico are an important feeding ground for these turtles (Hildebrand, 1982:447; Byles, 1989:25), and there are confirmed records from the Mexican states of Campeche and Yucatán (Map 48). The major nesting site is in southern Tamaulipas, with secondary sites in Veracruz and Campeche (J. P. Ross et al., 1989). The species is known to have nested on the coast of southern Texas and on the west coast of Florida but presumably no longer does so.

NATURAL HISTORY   *Lepidochelys kempii* prefers relatively shallow waters, and in southern Florida it is partial to mangrove shorelines (Carr, 1952:401). This turtle is primarily carnivorous, feeding predominantly on crabs, especially those of the genera *Ovalipes* and *Callinectes* (Mortimer, 1982:104). Mollusks and plant material are also taken, and captives will eat fish.

In contrast with most other sea turtles, the females of this species usually come ashore to oviposit during the day. Nesting occurs from April through August, and females may lay as many as three clutches of eggs during a nesting season. Courtship and mating occur shortly before nesting. Nesting is generally synchronized, and large numbers of females emerge from the ocean at the same time, producing huge nesting aggregations called *arribadas*. These groups once numbered many thousands of individuals but are now reduced to a few hundred. The clutch size ranges from 42 to 167, and the incubation period is about 50 to 66 days (Casas-Andreu, 1978:149, 151).

ETYMOLOGY   The specific name, *kempii*, is a patronym that honors Richard M. Kemp, a Florida resident who supplied the type material on which Garman based his description.

COMMENT   Kemp's ridley is perhaps the rarest and most endangered of all sea turtles. The primary nesting site is near Rancho Nuevo, Tamaulipas. Hildebrand (1963) estimated the 1947 nesting population there to be about 42,000. By 1975 only a few hundred individuals were nesting there. This species is listed as endangered in the IUCN Red Data Book (Groombridge, 1982:201) and is considered endangered under the United States Endangered Species Act. It appears in Appendix 1 of the Convention on International Trade in Endangered Species.

Groombridge (1982), Pritchard and Márquez (1973), and H. M. Smith and Smith (1979) summarized information on the biology of *L. kempii.* R. V. Wilson and Zug (1991) summarized taxonomic and distribution information and the previous literature pertaining to this species. A volume edited by Caillouet and Landry (1989) summarizes current research on this endangered form.

Locality Records   Mexico: Campeche: Barra de San Pedro (Chávez, 1968:15), Campeche (Brongersma, 1968:440), Ciudad del Carmen (Chávez, 1968:15; Zwinenberg, 1977:181), bet. Ciudad del Carmen and Isla Aguada (Chávez, 1968:16), Diciplinas (Zwinenberg, 1977:182), Isla Aguada (Zwinenberg, 1977:181), bet. Isla Aguada and Bajamita (Chávez, 1968:16), Río San Pedro (Zwinenberg, 1977:182); Yucatán: Progreso (H. M. Smith and Smith, 1979:321).

Family Dermochelyidae
(Leatherback Sea Turtle)

This family contains but a single species, *Dermochelys coriacea*, the largest of all living turtles.

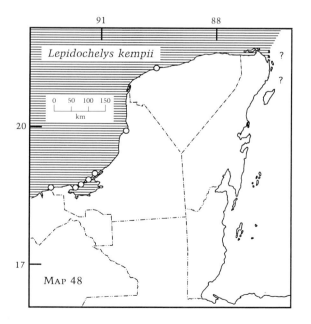

MAP 48

This strictly marine species occurs throughout the oceans of the world. The leatherback lacks many of the bones normally found in the carapaces and plastra of other turtles. In this and in other characters the leatherback is so anatomically divergent that it is occasionally placed in a separate suborder, the Athecae.

Genus *Dermochelys*

The leatherback is the sole member of this genus. *Dermochelys* is derived from the Greek *derma*, "skin" or "leather," and *chelys*, "tortoise," in reference to the leathery shell.

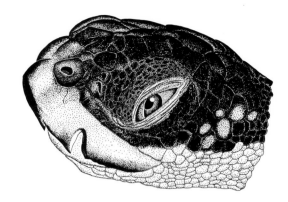

Fig. 110. Dorsolateral view of the head of a hatchling of *Dermochelys coriacea* (FAU, uncat.), Palm Beach Co., Fla. Note the distinctive maxillary cusp on the upper jaw.

Dermochelys coriacea (Vandelli)
(Figs. 110, 267; Map 49)

Testudo coriacea Vandelli, 1761. LECTOTYPE: ZMUP, unnumbered specimen, designated lectotype by Rhodin and Smith (1982:316). TYPE LOCALITY: Mari mediterraneo, Adriatico varius (= Mediterranean and Adriatic Seas); restricted to Palermo, Sicily, by H. M. Smith and Taylor (1950b:315); and to Laurentum, between Lido di Ostia and Tor Paterno, shore of the Tyrrhenian Sea, Italy, by Bour and Dubois (1984:359).

Leatherback turtle; trunk back (Belize); siete filos, tortuga laúd (Mexico).

DESCRIPTION This is the largest living turtle and one of the largest of all living reptiles. Pritchard (1971:10) reported a maximum carapace length of 1,800 mm for a sample of 192 nesting females in French Guiana and stated, "It is doubtful if a breeding leatherback could be much more than six feet (1.83 m) in carapace length." Carr (1952:446) reported a carapace length slightly in excess of 2,400 mm but could not ensure its validity because he was uncertain how the measurement had been made. The carapace is lyre shaped in dorsal view and tapers to a point posteriorly. The leatherback's carapace and plastron lack the keratinized scutes found in other turtles and are instead covered by a layer of leathery or rubbery skin (Fig. 267). There are seven longitudinal ridges on the carapace (hence the Spanish common name, *siete filos*) and five on the plastron. The skin is devoid of scales and claws, but immediately beneath the skin lie numerous mosaic bones, which may give the skin a knobbed appearance. The front flippers are comparatively long relative to those of other sea turtles, and they lack claws. The jaws are rather short, and there is a sharp, toothlike maxillary cusp or spine at the anterior margin of the upper jaw (Fig. 110).

The carapace and the dorsal surfaces of the head and appendages are dark brown or nearly black, sometimes with cream or yellowish spots. Young individuals tend to be more brightly colored that adults. In the young, the dorsal longitudinal ridges may be yellow, and the margin of the carapace and the edges of the flippers may also be yellow or cream.

SIMILAR SPECIES Its size and leathery carapace with seven longitudinal ridges distinguish this extraordinary animal from all other turtles.

DISTRIBUTION The leatherback occurs throughout the Atlantic, Pacific, and Indian Oceans, often at rather high latitudes, and in the Gulf of Mexico and the Caribbean Sea. In the Yucatán Peninsula it is said to nest on Arrecife Alacrán, Yucatán (Carranza, 1959), and it is known from several coastal localities in Campeche and Quintana Roo (Map 49).

NATURAL HISTORY Leatherbacks are pelagic animals, and they are infrequently encountered except on their nesting grounds.

They consume various seaweeds and a variety of marine invertebrates, but tunicates and jellyfish—and the fishes and crustaceans associated with jellyfish—are the major elements in the diet (Mortimer, 1982:104).

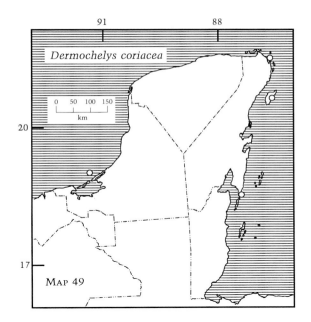

MAP 49

The females ascend the nesting beaches at night. Bacon (1973) described circling movements by some nesting females during the ascent crawl and noted that these were most likely to occur on cloudy moonlit nights. Bacon suggested that under conditions of changing illumination turtles may become disoriented, and he interpreted the movements as serving an orientation function.

Nesting females emit a variety of vocalizations, described as sighs or likened to the sound of a human belch by Mrosovsky (1972), who included audiospectrograms of the vocalizations.

SUBSPECIES   Two subspecies are usually recognized. The nominate form, *D. c. coricea*, occurs in the Atlantic Ocean, the Caribbean, and the Gulf of Mexico, including the waters off the Yucatán Peninsula. This race also occasionally enters the Mediterranean Sea. *Dermochelys coriacea schlegelii* is found in the Pacific and Indian Oceans.

ETYMOLOGY   The specific name, *coriacea*, comes from the Latin *corium*, "leather" or "skin," and the Latin suffix *-aceus*, "of" or "pertaining to," in reference to the leathery shell.

COMMENT   Throughout its range *D. coriacea* is hunted for its flesh and oil, and its eggs are universally prized. Carranza (1959:229) reported that leatherback flesh was used as shark bait by fishermen on the north coast of Yucatán. According to J. P. Ross (1982:192), populations of *Dermochelys*

have suffered serious declines. This species is listed as endangered in the IUCN Red Data Book (Groombridge, 1982:225) and is endangered under the United States Endangered Species Act. It appears in Appendix 1 of the Convention on International Trade of Endangered Species of Wild Flora and Fauna.

H. M. Smith and Smith (1979) reviewed the systematics of *D. coriacea*, and information on the biology of the species was summarized by Groombridge (1982) and Pritchard (1971).

Locality Records   Mexico: Campeche: 15 mi from Isla Aguada (Brainbridge and Pritchard, 1974:68); Quintana Roo: Isla Cozumel (Solórzano, 1963), Isla Mujeres (Solórzano, 1963), "off Xcalak" (McCoy, 1990:166).

Family Dermatemydidae
(Central American River Turtle)

This family comprises a single living genus and species, the Central American river turtle, *Dermatemys mawii*, and two extinct genera (Gaffney, 1979:236). Among living turtles the family is apparently most closely related to the mud turtles, Kinosternidae (Gaffney and Meylan, 1988:193).

Genus *Dermatemys*
(Central American River Turtle)

This genus, with its single species, is restricted to the lowlands of southern Mexico and northern Central America. *Dermatemys* derives from the Greek *dermatos*, the genitive of *derma*, "skin" or "leather," and *emys*, "freshwater tortoise."

Dermatemys mawii Gray
(Figs. 268, 269; Map 50)

Dermatemys mawii Gray, 1847:55. HOLOTYPE: BMNH 1947.3.4.12. TYPE LOCALITY: originally South America (in error, *fide* Stuart, 1963:47); restricted by H. M. Smith and Taylor (1950b:346) to Alvarado, Veracruz, Mexico.

Central American river turtle; hickety (Belize); tortuga blanca (Guatemala, Mexico); tortuga aplanada, tortuga plana (Mexico); nohoch ak (Lacandón Maya); suc aak, wau' (Yucatec Maya).

DESCRIPTION This very large aquatic turtle may attain a carapace length of about 650 mm and a mass in excess of 22 kg. The low, broad carapace is unicarinate in juveniles. The keel usually disappears with age, and the carapace assumes a smooth, leathery appearance, hence the generic name (Fig. 268). The posterior margin of the carapace is smooth, without serrations. The plastron is large, unhinged, and connected to the carapace by a broad bridge. The head is relatively small and flat, and the pointed snout is somewhat tubular and slightly upturned. There are no chin barbels. The toes are strongly webbed, and a series of enlarged scales fringes the outer margin of each foot. In males the tail is long and thick and extends well beyond the posterior margin of the carapace; in females the tail is much smaller, barely reaching the posterior margin of the carapace.

The carapace is uniform brown or dark olive, and the plastron is yellowish or cream, sometimes with dark suffusions of pigment, especially posteriorly. In males the dorsal surface of the head is yellowish, cream, or reddish brown, contrasting markedly with the olive gray lateral surfaces of the head (Fig. 269). In females the head is more or less uniform olive gray or brown, and the jaws and throat are yellowish cream. Juveniles have a gray or olive gray head with an indistinct yellowish orbital stripe. The dorsal surfaces of the appendages are gray or dark brown, and their ventral surfaces are cream or yellowish.

SIMILAR SPECIES Size alone will distinguish adults of *D. mawii* from all other freshwater turtles in the Yucatán Peninsula except *Chelydra serpentina*, which has a tricarinate carapace, a reduced cruciform plastron, and two series of enlarged scales on the dorsolateral surfaces of the tail.

DISTRIBUTION *Dermatemys mawii* occupies the Atlantic lowlands from southern Veracruz through northern Guatemala and Belize. It is absent from the northern portions of the Yucatán Peninsula (Map 50).

NATURAL HISTORY The Central American river turtle inhabits large streams, rivers, and freshwater lagoons; it occasionally enters brackish water as well, judging by a carapace from Belize that had barnacles attached to it (W. T. Allen and Neill, 1959:230). Its occurrence in brackish water was confirmed by D. Moll (1986:89), who observed spec-

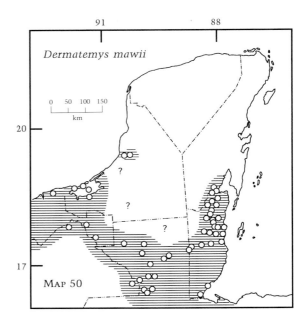

Map 50

imens in Corozal Bay. *Dermatemys mawii* seems to prefer clear water, and it is common in areas where it has not been subjected to intense hunting pressure. Although terrestrial locomotion is difficult for this thoroughly aquatic turtle, some such movement may occasionally occur, for Stuart (1935:56) found a specimen at La Libertad, Guatemala, in an aguada that subsequently became dry.

Dermatemys mawii is nocturnal and evidently feeds almost exclusively on plant material. Holman (1963:277) reported that the feces of a specimen from Veracruz contained only plant material, mostly aquatic grasses, and Alvarez del Toro et al. (1979:171) stated that fallen leaves and fruit are consumed in addition to aquatic vegetation. Vogt and Flores Villela (1992b:227) found that in the Lacandón of Chiapas, this species is almost exclusively herbivorous, consuming only trace amounts of animal material.

Dermatemys lays clutches of about 10 to 15 eggs, although Cope (1865:189) mentioned a clutch of 20. Holman (1963:277) reported that a captive laid 10 eggs between 25 August and 14 October. The eggs averaged 58.9 mm in length and had an average mass of 40.8 g. In Belize, mating occurs from mid-March through September, and nesting takes place from late September through December, with hatching in late May through July (Polisar, 1992:105). The females produce one to three clutches per year, with an average of about two clutches. The clutch size ranges from 2 to 20, with a mean of about 11 eggs (Polisar, 1992:49). In Tabasco, nesting occurs in

November and December (Cope, 1865:189). Alvarez del Toro et al. (1979:171) stated that *D. mawii* nests twice a year in Chiapas, in April and December; but H. M. Smith and Smith (1979:195) indicated that nesting occurs continuously from April to September. The nests are excavated very near the shoreline, for terrestrial locomotion is extremely difficult for these turtles. Nests are frequently exposed to inundation by rising water during the rainy season. *Dermatemys* is unusual in that its eggs remain viable when submerged for up to 27 days (Polisar, 1992:71).

Vogt and Flores-Villela (1992a) used field and laboratory data to determine that the eggs of *D. mawii* exhibit temperature-dependent sex determination, with lower incubation temperatures producing only males.

ETYMOLOGY   The specific name, *mawii*, is a patronym honoring Lieutenant Mawe of the British Royal Navy, who collected the type specimen in 1833.

COMMENT   The record from Uaxactún, El Petén (UMMZ 75598), is based on a carapace and plastron found in a burial urn at that archaeological site. Stuart (1958:19) suggested that the specimen was likely brought to Uaxactún and did not occur naturally in the Tikal-Uaxactún area. Similarly, the skeletal fragments of *Dermatemys* from kitchen middens at the archaeological site at Mayapán reported by Pollock and Ray (1957:648) were undoubtedly transported there.

Throughout its range the flesh and eggs of this species are esteemed as food, and the large carapace is often used as a feeding or watering trough; consequently, its numbers have been reduced in many areas. Flores-Villela and Gerez (1988:289) considered the species in danger of extinction in Mexico, and D. Moll (1986) documented serious declines in Belizean populations in areas near human population centers or otherwise accessible to human exploitation. Vogt and Flores Villela (1992b:228) recommended that populations in the Lacandón of Chiapas be protected and that hunting be prohibited during the nesting season.

Dermatemys mawii is listed as a vulnerable species in the IUCN Red Data Book (Groombridge, 1982:17) and as endangered under the United States Endangered Species Act. It appears in Appendix 2 of the Convention on International Trade in Endangered Species of Wild Flora and Fauna.

Dermatemys mawii was reviewed by Groombridge (1982), Iverson and Mittermeier (1980), and H. M. Smith and Smith (1979).

Locality Records   Belize: Belize: Belize City (UU 9813–38), Belize River above Burrell Boom (D. Moll, 1986:92), Belize River bet. Burrell Boom and Belize City (D. Moll, 1986:92), Belize River bet. Flowers Bank and St. Paul's Bank (UF 84769–71, 84774), lower Belize River watershed (UF 84778–82), Burrell Boom (W. T. Neill and Allen, 1959c:28; UF 84772–73, 84775–76), Cook's Lagoon (D. Moll, 1986:92), Jones Lagoon (D. Moll, 1986:92), Labouring Creek (D. Moll, 1986:92), Mussel Creek (D. Moll, 1986:92; UF 84783–84), New River Lagoon (D. Moll, 1986:92), Northern Lagoon, near Crooked Tree (D. Moll, 1986:92), Northern Lagoon, S Belize City (D. Moll, 1986:92), Rockstone Pond (UU 6435, 6624), Sibun River, S Belize (D. Moll, 1986:92), Southern Lagoon near Spanish Creek (D. Moll, 1986:92), Southern Lagoon near Gale's Point (D. Moll, 1986:92), Spanish Creek (UF 84785); Cayo: Macal River (D. Moll, 1986:92), Roaring Creek (D. Moll, 1986:92), Sibun River 3 mi above Hummingbird Hwy. (CM 107471), Succotz (KU 129754; UU 11219–24), 1 mi NW Succotz (UU 9811), Whitewater Lagoon (UF 84768); Corozal: Corozal Bay (D. Moll, 1986:92), Four Mile Lagoon (D. Moll, 1986:92), Progresso Lagoon (D. Moll, 1986:92), Río Hondo (UF 25048; D. Moll, 1986:92); Orange Walk: Chan Pine Ridge (MPM 8283), Honey Camp Lagoon (D. Moll, 1986:92), Lamanai (ROM H12727), Orange Walk (D. Moll, 1986:92), 2 mi N Orange Walk (UU 9449), Tower Hill (UU 9839–41); no specific locality (FMNH 4161–63, 4166, 4176); Toledo: Río Grande (D. Moll, 1986:92), Temash River (D. Moll, 1986:92). *Guatemala*: Alta Verapaz: Chinajá (Duellman, 1963:231); El Petén: Altar de Sacrificios (MCZ 85551), 16 km NNW Chinajá (KU 55983–84; MCZ 164925), Laguna Perdida (UMMZ 79127), Laguna Petenxil (UMMZ 79126), near La Libertad (UMMZ 75286), Paso de Caballo (UMMZ 79125), Remate (USNM 71419), Río San Pedro, 60 mi below El Paso (UMMZ 79128), Río de la Pasión above mouth of Río Santa Amelia (UMMZ 79129), Sayaxché (UCM 22178–82; UMMZ 79131; UU 11159–60), Seibal (AMNH 72607–9); no specific locality (USNM 71961). *Mexico*: Campeche: Balchacaj (H. M. Smith, 1938:20), 20 mi E mouth of Río Champotón (UMMZ 73123), Ciudad del Carmen (JBI), Ejido Uxmal (IHNHERP 505), Laguna de Términos (Gray, 1870), Río San Pedro 14 mi E Frontera (UU 9812), Yuncu (Gaige, 1936:303); Chiapas: Playas de Catazajá (UU 13349), Río Lacantún ca. 3 mi from mouth (CM 96058), Río Salinas (CM 117673, 117797–808); Quintana Roo: 6 km NE La Union (Bahena-Basave, 1995a:43); Tabasco: Emiliano Zapata (CM 62009; EAL 2961), Tenosique (USNM 108644).

Family Chelydridae (Snapping Turtles)

This small family contains two living genera, each with but a single species. They are large aquatic turtles with small cruciform plastra and strongly tricarinate carapaces. The family ranges from southern Canada southward to Colombia and Ecuador. One genus, *Chelydra*, occurs in the Yucatán Peninsula. Gaffney (1975) and Gaffney and Meylan (1988) included the monotypic Southeast Asian genus *Platysternon* in this family, but other herpetologists reject that arrangement (e.g., Ernst and Barbour, 1989; King and Burke, 1989).

Genus *Chelydra*

This New World genus contains only one living species, the snapping turtle of North and Central America. The genus was most recently reviewed by Ernst et al. (1988). *Chelydra* is the feminine form of the Greek *chelydros*, "water serpent."

Chelydra serpentina (Linnaeus)
(Figs. 105A, 106, 270, 271; Map 51)

Testudo serpentina Linnaeus, 1758:199. HOLO-TYPE: lost, *fide* Andersson, 1900:4, 23; but according to Iverson (1992:93) the holotype is NRM GA 49. TYPE LOCALITY: Habitat in calidis regionibus; restricted by H. M. Smith and Taylor (1950b:358) to New Orleans, Louisiana, and by Schmidt (1953:86) to the vicinity of New York City, New York.

Common American snapping turtle; sambodanga (Guatemala); chiquiguao, tortuga cocodrilo, tortuga lagarto, tortuga mordelona (Mexico); ruki'ak (Lacandón Maya).

DESCRIPTION This massive turtle may attain a carapace length of nearly 500 mm and a mass of 20 kg, although most individuals are about half that size (Fig. 270). The males are generally somewhat larger than the females (Ernst and Barbour, 1989:130). The carapace is tricarinate and rugose, and the vertebral and pleural scutes bear conspicuous knobs, especially posteriorly (in older turtles the keels and knobs may be obscure). The posterior margin of the carapace is strongly serrated. The plastron is reduced and cruciform, and it is attached to the carapace by a narrow bridge. The head is very large, and the snout is blunt and slightly protruding (Fig. 271). There are long, pointed tubercles on the neck and four barbels on the chin. The jaws are powerful and moderately hooked. The limbs are short and muscular, and the digits are extensively webbed. The long, thick tail bears two dorsolateral rows of enlarged scales (Fig. 106).

This is a predominantly brown turtle; its carapace ranges from tan to nearly black. Some individuals have a series of light radiating lines on each scute. The plastron is tan or yellowish and devoid of markings.

SIMILAR SPECIES The reduced, cruciform plastron distinguishes this species from all other turtles in the Yucatán Peninsula except *Staurotypus* and *Claudius*, and *C. serpentina* differs from both in having several rows of enlarged scales on the dorsolateral surfaces of the tail (Fig. 106), long, pointed tubercles on the neck, and a strongly serrated posterior margin on the carapace (Fig. 270).

DISTRIBUTION The snapping turtle occurs throughout much of North America east of the Rocky Mountains, from southern Canada to southern Texas. It is apparently absent from most of Mexico, but it occurs at low elevations from southern Veracruz, Tabasco, northern Chiapas, and Campeche through northern Guatemala and Belize, and thence southward through lower Central America to the Pacific coast of Colombia and Ecuador. This species occurs throughout the base of the Yucatán Peninsula (Map 51).

NATURAL HISTORY This large, highly aquatic turtle is apparently uncommon in the Yucatán Peninsula. It is found in rivers, lakes, sluggish streams, and forest pools, especially those with muddy bottoms, and is rarely encountered out of water. Although rather well studied in the temperate portions of its range, little of substance is known of its natural history in the Yucatán Peninsula. Alvarez del Toro (1983:36) reported that in Chiapas, oviposition occurs in April to June, and that 20 to 30 eggs are produced. *C. serpentina* exhibits temperature-dependent sex determination, with lower incubation temperatures producing predominantly or exclusively males (Vogt and Flores-Villela, 1992a).

Northern populations of these turtles are omnivorous. The diet includes a wide range of aquatic animals, invertebrate and vertebrate alike, along with many species of aquatic plants. Alvarez del Toro (1974:45) reported that *C. serpentina* preys

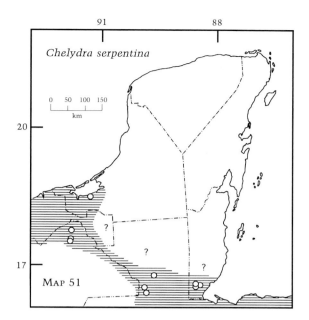

Maya site on Isla Cozumel, many hundreds of kilometers north of the present-day distribution of this species in the Yucatán Peninsula. Given the importance of turtles as food items and their role in Maya ritual (see "Ethnoherpetology in the Yucatán Peninsula," in this volume), the Cozumel record doubtless represents an instance of long-distance transport by humans.

Chelydra serpentina was reviewed by H. M. Smith and Smith (1979) and by Gibbons et al. (1988).

Locality Records Belize: Toledo: near Blue Creek Village (SGT photo), 1 mi W Salamanca (CM 105865), 0.5 mi W jct. Southern Hwy. and Punta Gorda–San Antonio Rd. (CM 105900). *Guatemala*: Alta Verapaz: Chinajá (Duellman, 1963:230); El Petén: 20 km NNW Chinajá (Duellman, 1963:230), Seibal (AMNH 71615). *Mexico*: Campeche: Balchacaj (FMNH 109496), no specific locality (Velasco, 1895:38); Chiapas: Catazajá (Alvarez del Toro, 1973), Palenque (USNM 46303, 51074), San Juanito (USNM 108643).

on hatchling crocodiles (*Crocodylus moreletii*). In turn, young snapping turtles are eaten by the indigo snake, *Drymarchon corais* (Ruthven, 1912:330). Snapping turtles have truly nasty dispositions and powerful jaws, and they should be handled with great care. They can strike with remarkable speed, and the bite can produce serious lacerations.

SUBSPECIES Gibbons et al. (1988) recognized four subspecies, of which *C. s. rossignonii* occurs in the Yucatán Peninsula.

ETYMOLOGY The specific name, *serpentina*, is Latin and means "serpentlike."

COMMENT Hamblin (1984:62) reported a shell fragment of *C. serpentina* from a Late Postclassic

Family Kinosternidae
(Mud and Musk Turtles)

This moderately large family ranges widely throughout the Americas, where it is represented by three genera, all of which occur in the Yucatán Peninsula. The two endemic Middle American genera, *Claudius* and *Staurotypus*, are sometimes treated as a separate family, the Staurotypidae, on the basis of chromosomal evidence (Bickham and Carr, 1983). Some herpetologists accept that arrangement (e.g., Flores-Villela, 1993:69; King and Burke, 1989), and others do not (Ernst and Barbour, 1989; Gaffney and Meylan, 1988).

Key to the Genera of the Family Kinosternidae

1. Plastron reduced in size, cruciform 2
   Plastron not reduced in size, not cruciform . . . . *Kinosternon*
2. Bridge attached to carapace by a ligament; plastron without hinge; adult carapace length less than 200 mm . . . . *Claudius*
   Bridge sutured directly to carapace; plastron movable, with a slight hinge; adult carapace length to 400 mm . . . . *Staurotypus*

Clave para los Géneros de la Familia Kinosternidae

1. Plastrón cruciforme, reducido en tamaño 2
   Plastrón no cruciforme, sin reducción en tamaño . . . . *Kinosternon*

2. Puente conectado al carapacho por medio de ligamentos; adultos menores a los 200 mm de largo de carapacho . . . . *Claudius*

Puente suturado directamente al carapacho; adultos hasta los 400 mm de largo de carapacho . . . . *Staurotypus*

Genus *Claudius*
(Narrow-bridged Musk Turtle)

This monotypic genus contains only the Middle American endemic species *Claudius angustatus*. *Claudius* is derived from the Latin *claudus*, "defective," perhaps in reference to the reduced size of the plastron.

Claudius angustatus Cope
(Figs. 272, 273; Map 52)

Claudius angustatus Cope, 1865:187. HOLOTYPE: USNM 6518, 6525 (parts of the same specimen, *fide* Iverson, 1986:132). TYPE LOCALITY: Tabasco, Mexico.

Narrow-bridged musk turtle; talmame, taiman (Mexico).

DESCRIPTION   This medium-sized turtle attains a maximum carapace length of approximately 170 mm. The males generally exceed the females in size by about 10 mm. The oval carapace is low and generally tricarinate, although the ridges may be obscure in older individuals (Fig. 272). The plastron is much reduced in size, cruciform, and lacks a movable hinge. The bridge is extremely narrow and is connected to the carapace by ligaments. The head is unusually large, the jaws are strongly hooked, and the upper jaws bear a pair of cusps (Fig. 273). There is a pair of barbels on the chin. The limbs are short and robust, and the digits are extensively webbed. The tail of the male is long, thick, and terminates in a keratinized spine.

The carapace is brown, yellowish brown, or nearly black, and the seams are darker. The plastron and bridge are yellow. In juveniles the scutes of the carapace may bear dark streaks and radiations. The head is yellowish brown to nearly black, and the jaws are lighter with dark streaks.

SIMILAR SPECIES   *Kinosternon* and *Staurotypus triporcatus* have extensive, hinged plastra. *Chelydra serpentina* is much larger, and the posterior margin of its carapace is strongly serrated (Fig. 270).

DISTRIBUTION   *Claudius angustatus* occurs at low elevations from southern Veracruz, Tabasco, and Campeche through northern Guatemala and northern Belize. Thus, it is restricted to the base of the Yucatán Peninsula, but it has not yet been recorded from southern Belize (Map 52).

NATURAL HISTORY   The narrow-bridged musk turtle inhabits slow-moving bodies of water such as swamps, marshes, ponds, and small streams, especially those with muddy bottoms. During the rainy season individuals may wander considerable distances, and specimens are occasionally encountered on roads during the day. Apparently they estivate during the dry season. Alvarez del Toro (1983:42) stated that individuals sequester themselves in the mud and are abroad only during the rainy season, and Cope (1865:188) said that they burrow into the soil to a depth of 2 or 3 feet. Duellman (1963:230) reported a specimen unearthed by a bulldozer in southern El Petén during the dry season.

These turtles are carnivorous. According to Holman (1963:278), a captive from Veracruz ate beef, skinned mice, and frogs. Alvarez del Toro (1982:42) reported that in Chiapas, this species feeds on snails and earthworms. According to Ernst and Barbour

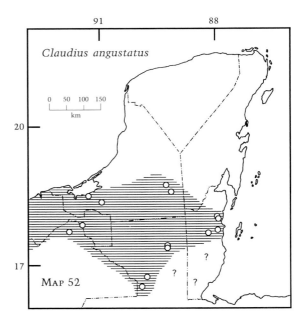

MAP 52

(1989:70) fishes, amphibians, and aquatic insects are also consumed.

Claudius angustatus is a pugnacious turtle, and newly captured individuals will attempt to bite at every opportunity. A turtle captured in Belize showed a distinctive defensive behavior, described by Dodd (1978:11). It leaned toward its adversary, keeping its head beneath its carapace. It maintained this posture by extending the front and hind limbs, and from this position directed several very quick upward biting lunges.

According to Pritchard (1979:588), oviposition occurs in November, during the dry season. The clutch size is two to eight eggs, and the incubation period is about four or five months (Ewert, 1979:356). The sex of *C. angustatus* is determined genetically; that is, the sex of the hatchlings does not depend on the incubation temperature (Vogt and Flores-Villela, 1992a).

In Chiapas, the flesh of *C. angustatus* is esteemed as food (Alvarez del Toro, 1983:42).

ETYMOLOGY   The specific name, *angustatus*, is from the Latin *angustare*, "to make narrow," presumably in reference to the narrow bridge between the plastron and carapace.

COMMENT   *Claudius angustatus* was reviewed by H. M. Smith and Smith (1979) and Iverson and Berry (1980).

Locality Records   Belize: Belize: 50 km NW Belize City (Dodd, 1978:11), near Hattieville (CM 91084), Rockstone Pond (UU 6437–38, 9751–55); Cayo: Beaver Dam Camp (UCM 25895); no specific locality (FMNH 4165). *Guatemala*: El Petén: 20 km NNW Chinajá (KU 55975), Sayaxché (UCM 22183), Tikal (UMMZ 117206–26), 3 km S Tikal (UMMZ 117203, 117204–5). *Mexico*: Campeche: Balchacaj (UMMZ 81922), Becan (UMMZ 76128), near Candelaria (JCL photo), Río Bec (UMMZ 76128); Chiapas: Catazajá (Alvarez del Toro, 1973); Tabasco: Emiliano Zapata (EAL 2959).

Genus *Staurotypus*
(Mexican Musk Turtles)

This small genus of strictly Middle American turtles occupies the Gulf and Caribbean lowlands from central Veracruz through the base of the Yucatán Peninsula to northern Honduras, and the Pacific slope from Oaxaca through El Salvador. Musk turtles prefer sluggish waterways such as lakes, marshes, and lagoons. Two species are referred to this genus, one of which occurs in the Yucatán Peninsula. *Staurotypus* derives from the Greek *stauros*, "cross," and *typos*, "shape," a reference to the cruciform plastron. Iverson (1985) summarized the literature on the genus *Staurotypus*.

Staurotypus triporcatus (Wiegmann)
(Fig. 274; Map 53)

Terrapene triporcata Wiegmann, 1828:364. HOLOTYPE: ZMB 127. TYPE LOCALITY: Río Alvarado, Veracruz, Mexico.

Mexican giant musk turtle; loggerhead, morocoy (Belize); guao, huau, tortuga tres lomos (Mexico); jolom kok (Yucatec Maya).

DESCRIPTION   This is the largest kinosternid in the Yucatán Peninsula. The adults may attain a carapace length of about 350 to 400 mm. The carapace is rather low and bears three very well developed longitudinal keels that remain distinct even in older animals. The posterior margin of the carapace lacks serrations, and the bridge is firmly sutured to the carapace. The plastron is reduced and cruciform but has a movable hinge. The head is large, and the jaws are powerful but only slightly hooked. There is one pair of barbels on the throat (Fig. 274). The limbs are short and muscular, and the digits are extensively webbed. The male has a long, thick tail; the female's tail is shorter and narrower.

The carapace is generally brown with lighter seams and dark brown streaks and radiations. The plastron is yellow or cream, sometimes with dark seams. The head and neck are olive, dark brown, or gray with contrasting light reticulation. The appendages are dark gray.

SIMILAR SPECIES   *Staurotypus triporcatus* differs from *Chelydra serpentina* in lacking a serrated posterior margin to the carapace. *Claudius angustatus* is smaller, has an extremely narrow bridge with a ligamentous attachment to the carapace, and lacks a plastral hinge. *Dermatemys* lacks the tricarinate carapace and cruciform plastron of *Staurotypus*. The species of *Kinosternon* are much smaller and have well-developed plastra.

DISTRIBUTION   This species occurs at low elevations on the Atlantic slope from central Veracruz south and eastward through northern Guatemala and Belize. It occupies the base of the Yucatán Pen-

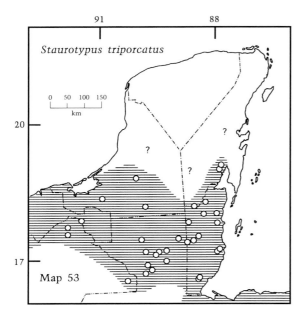

Map 53

Staurotypus triporcatus

occurs in November and December, but his report of clutch sizes ranging from 10 to 30 is questionable. The sex of *S. triporcatus* is genetically determined; that is the sex of the hatchlings does not depend on the incubation temperature (Vogt and Flores-Villela, 1992a).

Cope (1865:188) related the widespread belief, which he considered reliable, that "alligators" sometimes swallow *Staurotypus* whole and alive, and that the turtle then kills its captor by chewing its way out.

ETYMOLOGY The specific name, *triporcatus*, is from the Latin *tri*, "three" or "triple," and *porcatus*, "ridged," in reference to the tricarinate carapace.

COMMENT H. M. Smith and Smith (1979) and Iverson (1983b) reviewed and summarized information on *S. triporcatus*.

Locality Records Belize: Belize: Boom (W. T. Neill and Allen, 1959c:28), Missionary Lake Rd., 5.3 mi E jct. Northern Hwy. (CM 91073–76); Cayo: near Central Farm (CM 91085–91), Roaring Creek (W. T. Neill and Allen, 1959c:28), Rockstone Pond (UU 6400–10, 9774, 9778), 1 mi NW Succotz (UU 9773, 9775–77); Orange Walk: Gallon Jug (FMNH 69905), Lamanai (ROM H12726), Tower Hill (UU 9780); Stann Creek: Sittee River at Kendal (UU 9779), Sittee River Village (UU 9798–99); Toledo: ca. 2 mi SE Big Falls, Río Grande (CM 105898), ca. 0.5 mi W jct. Southern Hwy. and Punta Gorda–San Antonio Rd. (CM 105876–77); no specific locality (FMNH 4164). *Guatemala*: El Petén: Flores (UMMZ 79116–17; USNM 71417), S shore Lago Petén Itzá (UMMZ 79115), E end Lago Petén Itzá (UMMZ 79118), Laguna Eckibix (UMMZ 79119), Laguna de Zotz (UMMZ 79120), Paso de Caballo (UMMZ 79121, 79123–24), 1 km E Paso Subin (KU 68669), Río Homul ca. 20 mi E Tikal (UF 13481–84); no specific locality (USNM 71962). *Mexico*: Campeche: Laguna Chumpich (KU 75116–18), Laguna Petexbatun (AMNH 99920), Laguna Silvituc (EAL 2955; UU 9791–97), Pacaitún on Río Candelaria (FMNH 36604); Chiapas: Catazajá (Alvarez del Toro, 1973), vicinity of Palenque (UU 13531), Río Lacantún (CM 117810); Quintana Roo: Balneario Buena Vista (JRB photo), Lake Bacalar (LSUMZ 34666, 38938), 6 km NE La Unión (Bahena-Basave, 1995b:43); Tabasco: Emiliano Zapata (CM 96044; EAL 3330).

Genus *Kinosternon* (Mud Turtles)

This moderately small assemblage of New World turtles ranges from the eastern, central, and south-

insula northward to central Campeche and southern Quintana Roo. Although there are no specimen-based records north of Laguna Bacalar, J. R. Buskirk (in litt.) reported that this distinctive species is known by residents of Quintana Roo as far north as 60 km north of Felipe Carrillo Puerto (Map 53).

NATURAL HISTORY These large turtles inhabit slow-moving bodies of water such as lakes, marshes, and lagoons in large rivers. When disturbed they can be extremely aggressive. They bite viciously, and they are known to have actually driven people overboard. W. T. Neill and Allen (1959c:28) reported an incident in Belize concerning several residents who hauled an enraged loggerhead into their dugout and had to precipitously "take water." Holman (1963:278) remarked that in Veracruz these turtles are considered quite palatable, but the fishermen who capture them show great respect for their claws and powerful jaws.

In southern Veracruz, musk turtles consume a variety of aquatic invertebrates, especially mollusks, as well as large amounts of leaves, stems, seeds, and fruits (Vogt and Guzman, 1988). Pritchard (1979) reported that mud turtles (*Kinosternon acutum* and *K. leucostomum*) were included in the diet, and in Chiapas they eat snails (Alvarez del Toro, 1983:42).

Holman (1963:278) reported attempted copulation in captives on 29 September. In Chiapas, females produce clutches of 6 eggs (Alvarez del Toro, 1983:42). Ewert (1979) reported clutch sizes ranging from 3 to 6. Cope (1865:189) stated that oviposition

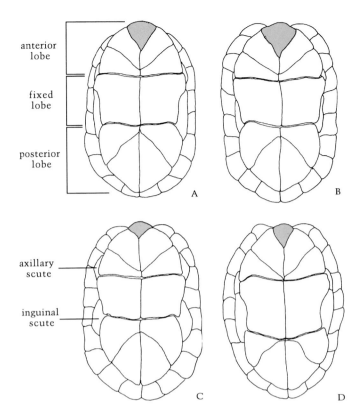

Fig. 111. Ventral views of the shells of the species of *Kinosternon* in the Yucatán Peninsula. *Kinosternon acutum* (A) and *K. creaseri* (B) with gular scutes (*shaded*) more than one-half the length of the anterior lobe of the plastron. *Kinosternon leucostomum* (C) and *K. scorpioides* (D) have gular scutes less than one-half the length of the anterior lobe of the plastron. Note that the axillary and inguinal scutes are in contact in *K. scorpioides*, and that in *K. creaseri* and *K. leucostomum* the anterior lobe of the plastron is longer than the fixed lobe.

western United States southward through mainland Mexico and lowland Central America to Bolivia and northern Argentina. Fifteen species are presently recognized, including some formerly placed in the genus *Sternotherus* (Ernst and Barbour, 1989:69). Four species of *Kinosternon* occur in the Yucatán Peninsula. They are small to medium-sized turtles with a maximum carapace length of about 200 mm. They typically have a rather high-domed carapace and a large hinged plastron. *Kinosternon* derives from the Greek *kineo*, "I move," and *sternon*, "breast" or "chest," in reference to the fact that the anterior lobe of the plastron can move relative to the middle lobe. Berry (1978) studied variation and systematics of the *K. scorpioides* and *K. leucostomum* complexes, and Iverson (1976) reviewed the *Kinosternon* of Belize.

Key to the Species of the Genus *Kinosternon*

1. Gular scute more than half the length of the anterior lobe of plastron (Fig. 111A,B) 2
   Gular scute less than half the length of the anterior lobe of plastron (Fig. 111C,D) 3
2. Anterior lobe of plastron equal to or less than length of fixed lobe (Fig. 111A); southern half of Yucatán Peninsula only (Map 54) . . . . *Kinosternon acutum*
   Anterior lobe of plastron longer than fixed lobe (Fig. 111B); northern half of Yucatán Peninsula only (Map 55) . . . . *Kinosternon creaseri*
3. Anterior lobe of plastron conspicuously longer than fixed lobe (Fig. 111C); never more than one median keel on carapace; light stripe on side of head and neck . . . .
   . . . . *Kinosternon leucostomum*
   Anterior lobe of plastron subequal to fixed lobe (Fig. 111D); usually three median keels on carapace; no light stripe on side of head or neck . . . . *Kinosternon scorpioides*

Clave para las Especies del Género *Kinosternon*

1. Escudo gular más largo que la mitad de la longitud del lóbulo anterior del plastrón (Fig. 111A,B)..2
   Escudo gular menor que la mitad de la longitud del lóbulo anterior del plastrón (Fig. 111C,D) 3

2. Lóbulo anterior del plastrón igual o menor que la longitud del lóbulo fijo (Fig. 111A); unicamente en la mitad sur de la Península de Yucatán (Mapa 54)...........*Kinosternon acutum*
   Lóbulo anterior del plastrón más largo que el lóbulo fijo (Fig. 111B); en la mitad norte de la Península de Yucatán (Mapa 55)................................*Kinosternon creaseri*

3. Lóbulo anterior del plastrón conspicuamente más largo que el lóbulo fijo (Fig. 111C); no mas de una sola quilla media en el carapacho; una línea clara a los lados de la cabeza y cuello ....
   ....*Kinosternon leucostomum*
   Lóbulo anterior del plastrón subigual al lóbulo fijo (Fig. 111D); usualmente tres quillas en la parte media del carapacho; sin una línea clara a los lados de la cabeza y cuello ....
   ....*Kinosternon scorpioides*

Kinosternon acutum (Gray)
(Figs. 111A, 275, 276; Map 54)

Kinosternon scorpioides acuta Gray, 1831b:34. HOLOTYPE: BMNH 1947.3.4.58. TYPE LOCALITY: believed by Schmidt (1941:488) to be Belize, but restricted by H. M. Smith and Taylor (1950b:347) to Cosamaloapan, Veracruz, Mexico.

Tabasco mud turtle; pochitoque (Guatemala); pochitoque jaquactero, casco, casquito (Mexico); nu putii (Yucatec Maya).

DESCRIPTION This medium-sized mud turtle attains a carapace length of up to 120 mm. The females are substantially longer than the males. The carapace is moderately high domed and has a median keel and a pair of weak dorsolateral keels, although these may be obscure, especially in older individuals (Fig. 275). The plastron has a double hinge, which allows the turtle to completely close the shell. The gular scute is more than half the length of the anterior lobe of the plastron, which in turn is equal to or slightly shorter than the fixed lobe (Fig. 111A). The posterior margin of the plastron is unnotched. The inguinal scute is much larger than the axillary scute, and the two are generally in contact or only narrowly separated. The males have a strongly hooked beak and a long, thick tail; the females have a relatively short tail. In both sexes the tail terminates in a keratinized spine.

The carapace of *K. acutum* is brown, dark brown, or nearly black, with dark seams. The plastron is yellow or yellowish brown, also with dark seams. The head, neck, and appendages are generally gray or yellowish with dark brown spots or vermicula-tions (Fig. 276). Yellow or reddish marks are usually present on the head, neck, and limbs.

SIMILAR SPECIES In the Yucatán Peninsula *K. acutum* is sympatric with *K. leucostomum* and *K. scorpioides*. It differs from both in having a gular scute longer than half the length of the anterior plastral lobe (Fig. 111A). *Kinosternon leucostomum* has a light stripe extending from the eye posteriorly onto the neck.

DISTRIBUTION *Kinosternon acutum* occurs at low elevations on the Atlantic slope from central Veracruz south and eastward through northern Guatemala to southern Quintana Roo and Belize. It probably occurs continuously through the base of the Yucatán Peninsula but apparently has not been recorded from southern Campeche or northwestern El Petén (Map 54).

NATURAL HISTORY This turtle is found in lakes, streams, and temporary bodies of water in the Gulf and Caribbean lowlands. Duellman (1963:230) found individuals in sluggish streams and forest pools in southern El Petén. Stuart (1935:55) described this species (as *K. berendtianum*) as very common in both forest and savanna habitats in the vicinity of La Libertad, El Petén, a week after the onset of the rainy season, although none were seen during the dry season.

According to Cope (1865:189), only a few eggs are produced, and nesting occurs in March and April.

ETYMOLOGY The specific name, *acutum*, is Latin for "pointed" or "acute," referring to the

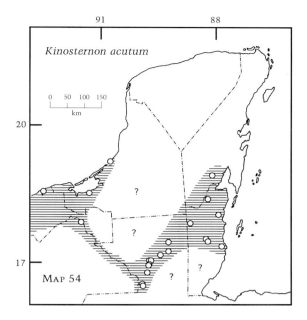

Map 54

Kinosternon acutum

pointed, unnotched posterior margin of the plastron.

COMMENT   H. M. Smith and Smith (1979) and Iverson (1980) reviewed *K. acutum*.

Locality Records Belize: Belize: Rockstone Pond (UU 6432–34, 9445–48); Cayo: 2 mi S Belmopan (CM 109018); Orange Walk: Gallon Jug (FMNH 69236–38), 2 mi N Orange Walk (UU 9449); Stann Creek: Melinda Forestry Station (MSU 4727), 50 mi NW Stann Creek (UF 30174). *Guatemala*: El Petén: 20 km NNW Chinajá (KU 55966, 55971–73), 30 km NNW Chinajá (Duellman, 1963:230), near La Libertad (UMMZ 75213), 0.75 mi W La Libertad (UMMZ 75217), 2.5 mi S La Libertad (UMMZ 75211), 5 mi S La Libertad (UMMZ 75218), 6 mi S La Libertad (UMMZ 75212), 8 mi S La Libertad (UMMZ 75219–22), W La Libertad (UMMZ 75214), NE La Libertad (UMMZ 75215–16), Remate (USNM 71418), San Benito (UMMZ 79113–14), near San Benito (UMMZ 79113), Sayaxché (UCM 22184–88), Tikal (UF 13485–86); no specific locality (BMNH 1864.2.19.1–2; USNM 71966). *Mexico*: Campeche: Balchacaj (UIMNH 19323–24), 43.8 km SW Champotón (UMRC 92-15); Quintana Roo: 13 mi NW Chetumal (BCB 11448); Tabasco: Emiliano Zapata (H. M. Smith and Smith, 1979:74), Frontera (USNM 6515).

Kinosternon creaseri Hartweg
(Figs. 111B, 277; Map 55)

Kinosternon creaseri Hartweg, 1934:1. HOLOTYPE: UMMZ 73090. TYPE LOCALITY: 1 mile south of the Hacienda, Chichén Itzá, Yucatán, Mexico.

Creaser's mud turtle; kok ak, xkokak, xtuk'is (Yucatec Maya).

DESCRIPTION   The males of this medium-sized mud turtle grow to about 125 mm in carapace length, the females to about 115 mm. The carapace is oval in dorsal aspect and moderately domed, and its posterior margin is smooth (Fig. 277). There is a weak median keel, but this may be obscure in older individuals. The plastron is double-hinged and unnotched posteriorly. The gular scute is more than half the length of the anterior plastral lobe, and the axillary and inguinal scutes are in narrow contact. The head is large, and the upper jaw is strongly hooked.

The carapace is dark brown or nearly black, and the plastron and bridge are yellowish with dark seams. The head, neck, and appendages are dark gray.

SIMILAR SPECIES   *Kinosternon creaseri* differs from its congeners, *K. leucostomum* and *K. scorpioides*, in having a gular scute that is more than one-half the length of the anterior lobe of the plastron (Fig. 111B). It is further distinguished from *K. leucostomum* in lacking light markings on the head and neck. It differs from *K. acutum* in having the anterior lobe of the plastron longer than the fixed lobe (Fig. 111A,B).

DISTRIBUTION   This species is endemic to the Yucatán Peninsula, where it is known from numerous localities in the Mexican states of Campeche, Quintana Roo, and Yucatán. It is apparently most abundant in eastern Yucatán and northern Quintana Roo and seems to avoid the dry northwest corner of the peninsula (Map 55).

NATURAL HISTORY   Although previously believed to be uncommon or even rare (Groombridge, 1982), *K. creaseri* is actually quite common in shallow temporary forest pools in Campeche, Yucatán, and especially in northern Quintana Roo (Iverson, 1988). Gaige (1936:304) wrote that a specimen was caught on a hook and line in a cenote near Chichén Itzá, but these turtles are more commonly found in temporary bodies of water. During the dry season they apparently estivate underground.

This pugnacious mud turtle is much more inclined to release its disagreeable musk and attempt to bite than to withdraw into its shell. Judging by their feces, mud turtles feed predominantly on

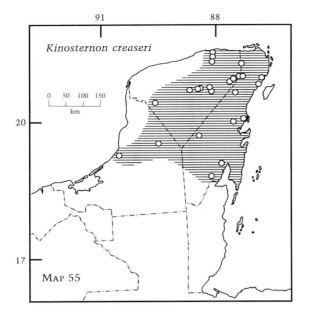

Kinosternon creaseri

MAP 55

aquatic invertebrates. Iverson (1988:288) stated that captives consumed only animal matter.

Little is known of their reproductive biology. Iverson (1988:288) found a copulating pair on 17 August, and he estimated that females attain reproductive maturity at a carapace length of 110 to 115 mm and an estimated age of 10 to 15 years. After dissecting a single female, Iverson (1988:289) suggested that females may produce multiple clutches, each consisting of single large egg. I found recent hatchlings in a forest pool near Cobá, Quintana Roo, in August.

ETYMOLOGY   The specific name, *creaseri*, is a patronym honoring Edwin P. Creaser, who collected the type specimen.

COMMENT   A specimen in the Museo de Zoología "Alfonso L. Herrera" in the Universidad Nacional Autónoma de Mexico (MZFC 409) is said to have come from between Teapa and Tenosique, Tabasco (Flores Villela et al., 1991:88). As that locality is far outside the known range of *K. creaseri*, the record requires confirmation.

Kinosternon creaseri is listed as rare in the IUCN Red Data Book (Groombridge, 1982:3).

This species was reviewed by Groombridge (1982), Iverson (1983a), and H. M. Smith and Smith (1979). Iverson's 1988 publication includes ecological and life history information on *K. creaseri*.

Locality Records Mexico: Campeche: 11 km S Champotón (KU 70928), Dzibalchén (KU 75644); Quintana

Roo: 4.6 km SE Cobá (JCL photo), 29.1 mi NE Felipe Carrillo Puerto (KU 157671), 3.8 km N Kantunil Kin (KU 171402), 13.4 mi SW Limones (KU 157670), Playa del Carmen (Himmelstein, 1980:25), Pueblo Nuevo X-Can (CM 40118–20; KU 70918–20; UU 9450), 1.5 km S, 7 km E Pueblo Nuevo X-Can (KU 70921–22; UU 9450), Vivienda de Platanal (FMNH 29131); Yucatán: 1.6 km SW Catzín (KU 171403), Chichén Itzá (FMNH 27270, 36605; MCZ 4121, 46501; UMMZ 73083–90, 73210, 81539–40), 1 mi S Chichén Itzá (UMMZ 73090), 1.5 mi S Libre Unión (UCM 29194), Pisté (KU 70923–27, 70929, 70931; UAZ 28839, 28843, 28846–47, 28849–50; UCM 16128, 18222–23), Santa Elena (JRB photo), Tekom (BMNH 1973.2505), 8 mi W Valladolid (UCM 45949), 20.5 km SW X-Can (EAL 2847).

Kinosternon leucostomum Duméril and Bibron
(Figs. 111C, 278, 279; Map 56)

Cinosternon leucostomum A. M. C. Duméril and Bibron, 1851:17, in A. M. C. Duméril and Duméril, 1851. LECTOTYPE: MNHNP 8311 (by restriction of type locality; see Stuart, 1963:49). TYPE LOCALITY: restricted to the Río Usumacinta, El Petén, Guatemala, by Schmidt (1941:488).

White-lipped mud turtle, white-faced mud turtle; swanka (Belize); pochitoque, tortuga de los pantanos (Guatemala, Mexico); casquito (Mexico); chan ak (Lacandón Maya); casco (Yucatec Maya).

DESCRIPTION   *Kinosternon leucostomum* is a medium-sized mud turtle. The adults average between 140 and 160 mm in carapace length, and males are generally larger than females (Ernst and Barbour, 1989:82). In comparison with other mud turtles, the carapace is rather low and flattened in lateral aspect, and it bears a single median keel, which may be obscure or absent in older individuals (Fig. 278). The length of the gular scute is usually much less than one-half the length of the anterior lobe of the plastron (Fig. 111C), which is generally longer than the fixed lobe. The posterior lobe of the plastron is unnotched, and in the majority of specimens the axillary and inguinal scutes do not meet (Fig. 111C).

The carapace is dark brown, and the plastron is usually yellow with dark seams, although in some specimens the plastron is nearly as dark as the carapace. The head and neck are dark brown. A broad, light stripe extends from the snout, over the eye, and onto the neck, although it may become obscure in older individuals. The jaws are light yellow or tan (Fig. 279).

The sexes are dimorphic in several respects. The males are larger and have large, muscular tails that terminate in a sharp, curved keratinized claw; the upper jaws are strongly hooked; and the plastron is slightly concave. In females the tail is much shorter, the upper jaw is less strongly hooked, and the plastron is flat or slightly convex.

SIMILAR SPECIES *Kinosternon scorpioides* has a higher, more domed carapace when seen in lateral view; the anterior and fixed lobes of the plastron are approximately equal in length (Fig. 111D), and it lacks a light stripe on the side of the head and neck. In *K. acutum* and *K. creaseri*, the length of the gular scute is more than one-half the length of the anterior plastral lobe (Fig. 111A,B).

DISTRIBUTION *Kinosternon leucostomum* occurs at low elevations from southern Veracruz south through Central America to Colombia and the Pacific lowlands of Ecuador. It is found through the base of the Yucatán Peninsula and as far north as southern Yucatán and central Quintana Roo. There is a single record, perhaps representing an isolated population, from northern Yucatán (Map 56).

NATURAL HISTORY White-lipped mud turtles inhabit lowland swamps, ponds, and streams, especially in forested areas. Duellman (1963:231) found them in small, sluggish streams and in syntopy with *K. acutum* on the forest floor in the forests of

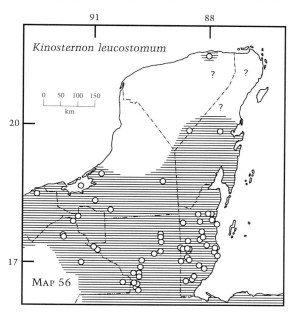

MAP 56

southern El Petén. Individuals often wander considerable distances from water. In the Choco of Colombia they enter brackish water (Medem, 1962). These turtles are usually nocturnal, although they have been observed crossing roads by day, and W. T. Neill and Allen (1959c:29) collected a specimen in Belize that was swimming on the sandy bottom of a stream by day.

The diet includes a variety of aquatic invertebrates and plants (Medem, 1962:284; E. O. Moll and Legler, 1971:89). Villa (1973:380) reported that in Nicaragua *K. leucostomum* feeds on dead fish and other carrion, and he reported one instance of predation on a black water snake, *Tretanorhinus nigroluteus*. In southern Veracruz this species is a generalist, feeding on a variety of vertebrate and invertebrate prey as well as seeds, fruits, leaves, and stems (Vogt and Guzman, 1988:39).

Little is known about the species' reproduction in the Yucatán Peninsula. In Panama and Colombia reproduction apparently occurs throughout the year and involves the production of multiple clutches. One to three eggs are laid in shallow nests in the forest floor or covered with leaf litter (Medem, 1962:284; E. O. Moll and Legler, 1971:90). Pritchard (1979:529) reported an incubation period of 126 to 148 days for eggs held under artificial conditions but at "normal" temperatures.

Vogt and Flores-Villela (1992a:268) studied the sex ratios produced from clutches incubated at various temperatures and concluded that *K. leucostomum* may be in the process of evolving genetically determined (rather than temperature-dependent) gender.

SUBSPECIES According to Berry (1978), two subspecies are recognized, of which the nominate form, *K. l. leucostomum*, occurs in the Yucatán Peninsula.

ETYMOLOGY The specific name, *leucostomum*, is from the Greek *leukon*, "white," and *stoma*, "mouth," in reference to the light pigmentation on the jaws.

COMMENT *Kinosternon leucostomum* was reviewed by H. M. Smith and Smith (1979) and by Berry (1978) as part of his review of the *K. leucostomum* complex.

Locality Records Belize: Belize: Belize City (BMNH 1973.2507; USNM 6548), Gomez Pond (CM 91093–96), mi 26 on Old Northern Hwy. (JBI photo), Rockstone Pond (UU 6139–43, 6533–58, 9472–73), 2 mi W Rockstone Pond (UU 9452–71), mi 42 on Western Hwy. (CM 109017); Cayo: Augustine (CM 105757–58; UMMZ 80705–8; UU 9478–92), 1.5 mi NE Augustine (UU 9474–77), ca. 3 mi S Belmopan (CM 112167–68), 7 mi E Belmopan (CM 111936), 4 mi SW Cayo (UMMZ 124748), 12 mi S Cayo (UMMZ 70462–64), near Central Farm (CM 91092), Chial (UU 9529–30), 31.4 mi S Georgeville (KU 157674), bet. Guacamallo Bridge and Chiquibul Branch (CM 112132), Hummingbird Hwy. in mountains (UMMZ 124749), Macal River at Guacamallo Bridge (CM 112134), near Millionario (CM 112133), Mountain Pine Ridge Rd., 36 to 49 mi S Belize-Cayo Rd. (UMMZ 124746), Mountain Pine Ridge Rd., 50 mi S Belize-Cayo Rd. (UMMZ 124747), Río Frio Cave (CM 105940), Río On (CM 105954–55), Succotz (UU 9531), Valentin (UMMZ 80703–4, 80727); Orange Walk: Gallon Jug (MCZ 71634), Lamanai (ROM H12724–25), Lemonal (JBI 523); Stann Creek: All Pines (CM 8489), Bokowina (BMNH 1973.2508; FMNH 49360), Middlesex (UCM 25896–902, 45197–204, 45396–401), Melinda Forestry Station (MSU 5728–30; UU 9493–519), 50 mi NW Stann Creek (UF 30373–77); Toledo: ca. 2 mi SE Big Falls, Río Grande (CM 105899), 1 mi N Bladen Bridge (CM 105928), 1 mi W Salamanca (CM 105862–64, 105871), 2.4 km W San Antonio (UF 87172), 0.5 mi S Swazey Bridge (CM 105937), Swazey Branch of Monkey River, near Punta Gorda Rd. (MCZ 71637–38), Waha Leaf Creek (MCZ 71635), 3 mi S Waha Leaf Lake (MCZ 71636); no specific locality (FMNH 4168; USNM 66890). *Guatemala*: Alta Verapaz: Chinajá (Duellman, 1963:231); El Petén: 7 km WNW Chinajá (KU 55970), 15 km NNW Chinajá (KU 55969), 20 km NNW Chinajá (KU 55967–68), 30 km NNW Chinajá (KU 59793–94), Desempeña (USNM 108605–7), near Flores (UMMZ 79111), Lago Petén Itzá (KU 171405), E end Lago Petén Itzá (UMMZ 79112), Laguneta Ixcoche (AMNH 99921), near La Libertad (UMMZ 75223–25), Piedras Negras (USNM 108604), 8 km S Río Tikal (AMNH 90363–64), San Juan Acul (AMNH 99922), Sayaxché (UCM 22189), 5 km E Sayaxché (UMRC 79-277), Sojio (AMNH 70019), Tikal (UF 13477–78, 13488; UMMZ 117227–40, 120342, 120454), Uaxactún (UMMZ 70465). *Mexico*: Campeche: Becan (UMMZ 76127), Laguna de Termino (Sclater, 1871), Pacaitún on Río Candelaria (FMNH 36607–8), Río Candelaria, 12 mi from Guatemala border (CM 37021–23), 11.5 km S Sabancuy (KU 171404), 15 km S Sabancuy (JCL photo); Chiapas: Laguna Ocotal (MCZ 53861), Palenque (USNM 108582–3), Río Lacantún, Pico do Oro (CM 117772), San Juanito (USNM 108584–87); Quintana Roo: 4 km NNE Felipe Carrillo Puerto (KU 70941); Tabasco: Emiliano Zapata (EAL 1639, 2956), 8.8 mi NE Emiliano Zapata (EAL 1636), 4 mi S Frontera (CM 39626), Río Tabasquillo, near Frontera (UU 9521–28); Yucatán: 9 mi SSE Dziuché (UU 9520), 13 mi S Río Lagartos (UCM 45951).

Kinosternon scorpioides (Linnaeus)
(Figs. 111D, 280; Map 57)

Testudo scorpioides, Linnaeus, 1766:352. TYPES: lost, *fide* King and Burke, 1989:65. TYPE LOCALITY: Surinam.

Scorpion mud turtle, red-cheeked mud turtle; casquito, casquito amarillo, pochitoque, tortuga de los pantanos (Mexico); nu putii (Yucatec Maya).

DESCRIPTION *Kinosternon scorpioides* is a moderately large mud turtle. The adults average between 155 and 175 mm in carapace length, and males are generally somewhat larger than females (Berry and Shine, 1980:186). The carapace is rather high and domed in lateral view and bears three keels that may become obscure or absent in older individuals (Fig. 280). The length of the gular scute is less than one-half the length of the anterior plastral lobe, which in turn is approximately the same length as the fixed plastral lobe (Fig. 111D). The axillary and inguinal scutes are generally in firm contact, and the posterior margin of the posterior plastral lobe is unnotched.

The carapace is variably light brown, tan, or yellowish, and the plastron is generally yellow with dark seams. The head is dark brown, usually with light reticulations and red or orange spots on the sides. The jaws are yellowish tan.

The sexes are strongly dimorphic in several respects other than size. The males have a long, muscular tail that terminates in a sharp, keratinized claw; the females have a much shorter tail. The upper jaw of males is strongly hooked; that of females is less so. Finally, the plastron of males is slightly concave, whereas that of females is flat or slightly convex.

SIMILAR SPECIES In *K. acutum* and *K. creaseri* the gular scute is greater than one-half the length of the anterior plastral lobe, whereas in *K. scorpioides* the gular scute is less than half the length of the anterior plastral lobe (cf. Fig. 111A,B,D). *Kinosternon leucostomum* has but a single keel on the carapace, possesses a light stripe on the side of the head and neck, and its inguinal and gular scutes are usually not in contact (Fig. 111C).

DISTRIBUTION This wide-ranging mud turtle occurs at low elevations on the Gulf and Caribbean slopes from southern Tamaulipas south through

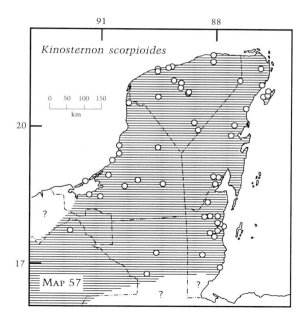

Map 57

Central America to northern Argentina and eastern and central Brazil. It occurs throughout most of the Yucatán Peninsula but is apparently not recorded from southern El Petén and southern Belize (Map 57).

NATURAL HISTORY Scorpion mud turtles occupy a variety of aquatic habitats, including ponds, streams, lakes, and slower-moving parts of rivers. They may be quite abundant locally. Himmelstein (1980:25) found a shallow pond on Isla Cozumel that contained 15 individuals. In northern Yucatán these turtles also inhabit cenotes (Duellman, 1965a:593). Turtles living in areas that dry up seasonally may bury themselves in the mud until the rains return (Ernst and Barbour, 1989:84). Duellman (1965a:592) described finding them on Isla Cozumel "buried in mud or dug in at the bases of clumps of cat-tails in a partly dried up marsh."

According to Vanzolini et al. (1980:140), in Brazil this species eats aquatic invertebrates, fish, amphibians, and plants. Himmelstein (1980:25) observed specimens on Cozumel eating aquatic vegetation.

In Chiapas, oviposition occurs in March and April (Alvarez del Toro, 1983:38). The females deposit about 10 eggs in shallow nests they excavate near the water.

SUBSPECIES This widely distributed species is highly variable geographically, and six subspecies are currently recognized (Ernst and Barbour,

1989:83). Of these, only *K. s. cruentatum* occurs in the Yucatán Peninsula.

ETYMOLOGY The specific name, *scorpioides*, comes from the Greek *skorpios*, "scorpion," and *-oides*, a contraction of the Greek *-o + eidos*, denoting likeness—hence "scorpion-like." The name presumably refers to the long, muscular tail of males, which terminates in a keratinized claw.

COMMENT Included within *K. scorpioides* is *K. cruentatum* Duméril and Bibron (1851), which has often been considered a full species. Legler (1965:621) implicitly included *K. cruentatum* in *K. scorpioides*, and Iverson (1976) followed that arrangement in his treatment of *Kinosternon* in Belize.

Kinosternon scorpioides was reviewed by H. M. Smith and Smith (1979) and by Berry (1978) as part of his review of the *K. scorpioides* complex.

Locality Records Belize: Belize: Belize City (FMNH 4426), near Belize City (CM 91098), 2 to 9 mi NW Belize City (UF 32624–26), 10 mi W Belize on Belize-Cayo Rd. (UMMZ 124745), Burrell Boom (CM 91097), Crooked Tree entrance at Northern Hwy. (CM 112130–31), ca. 2 mi E Hattieville (CM 105814), 10.3 km SE La Democracia (UF 87171), Rockstone Pond (UU 6559–89), Sand Hill (MSU 4731–33; UU 9640), 2 mi N, 1 mi E Sand Hill (UU 9582), mi 29.5 on Western Hwy. (CM 105994); Cayo: upper Raspaculo River basin (Stafford, 1991:14); Orange Walk: Lamanai (ROM H12723), Orange Walk Town (JBI 608; JBI photo); Stann Creek: Mango Creek (MCZ 71639–40, 71684); no specific locality (FMNH 4426–27; UF 24069–70). *Guatemala:* El Petén: near La Libertad (UMMZ 75189–90, 75192–99, 75200–10), San Andrés (UMMZ 75191). *Mexico:* Campeche: Balchacaj (FMNH 116488–89, 116491–93, 116496, 116498–500, 116506; UIMNH 19288–89, 19341–43), 53 mi SW Campeche (EAL 1205), Champotón (UMMZ 73091–106, 128379), 15.1 km NW Chekubúl (JCL photo), Dzibalchén (KU 75645–47), 7 mi W El Remate (TU 19782), Laguna Silvituc (KU 75114), Matamoros (FMNH 36606), 1 km SW Puerto Real (KU 71771), 8 km NE Río Candelaria on Hwy. 186 (JCL photo), 24.7 mi NE Sabancuy (LACM 61108; UMMZ 126439), 23 km W Xpujil (KU 75115); Chiapas: Catazajá (CM 117776); Quintana Roo: Agua Blanca (MCZ 53117), 10 mi N Chetumal (BCB 12777), 13 mi NW Chetumal (BCB 11450), Estación Santa Teresa, Sian Ka'an Reserve (MZCIQRO 56), Estero Franco, rd. to Río Hondo (MZCIQRO 50), 31.2 mi NE Felipe Carrillo Puerto (KU 157672), Isla Cozumel (CM 27580–81; Himmelstein, 1980:25; UMMZ 76142; USNM 13910, 13912–13), Isla Cozumel, 9 km SE San Miguel (UCM 12970), Cozumel,

10 km SW San Miguel (CM 41314), Cozumel, 6 km NE San Miguel (CM 41322–23), Cozumel, 7 mi SW San Miguel (CM 55806), Cozumel, 4.5 mi NE San Miguel (CM 55808), Cozumel, 3.5 km N San Miguel (KU 71770), Cozumel, 5 km N San Miguel (KU 70932–40), Cozumel, 14 to 14.5 km E San Miguel (CM 55809–10), Cozumel, 15 km from central Cozumel (CM 96021–25), Cozumel, 5 km S San Miguel (UF 24135, 24141), Cozumel, 6 km S San Miguel (UF 24136), Cozumel, 7 km S San Miguel (UF 24137–39), Cozumel, 9 km S San Miguel (UF 24140), Cozumel, 9 km SE San Miguel (UCM 12970), 0.5 mi E Presumida (UCM 48020), Pueblo Nuevo X-Can (UU 9563–80, 11874; AMNH 93244), 26 km SSW Puerto Juárez (LSUMZ 28300), 10 mi S, 5 mi W Puerto Morelos (UU 9539–62), Tulum (MZCIQRO 32), 32 km SW Vigía Chico (MZCIQRO 44); Yucatán: vicinity Izamal (UMMZ 81541–55), 12 mi S Izamal (UMMZ 81541–55), 1.5 mi S Libre Unión (UCM 16129–41, 47460–62), 1.6 mi S Libre Unión (UU 9583–639, 9642–47), 0.6 mi E, 1.5 mi S Libre Unión (UU 9532–38), 50 km S Mérida (UMMZ 81556–61), 18 mi SE Peto (BCB 11449), Progreso (USNM 6556), 1 mi S Progreso (UU 9581), Río Lagartos (UCM 45950), 13.4 mi S Río Lagartos (KU 157673), 13.5 mi S Río Lagartos (FMNH 157673), rd. to San Felipe, 1 km from road to Río Lagartos (UCM 39106–10), Telchac Puerto (FMNH 20629–30; UMMZ 76130–41), 3 km W Telchac Puerto (UMMZ 76130–41), 8 km N, 10 km W Tizimín (KU 75113).

Family Emydidae (Pond Turtles)

This largest turtle family is a predominantly Northern Hemispheric group of aquatic or semiaquatic turtles. In the New World the family ranges from southern Canada south through the United States, Mexico, and Central America to northern South America, through the Antilles, and discontinuously in Brazil and northern Argentina. In the Old World the family is found throughout much of Europe, North Africa, India, Southeast Asia, and the Indo-Malay Archipelago. Gaffney and Meylan (1988:202) elevated the emydid subfamily Batagurinae to family rank, although they recognized the nonmonophyletic nature of that taxon. Some systematists (e.g., Flores-Villela, 1993:69) accept that arrangement, whereas others (e.g., Ernst and Barbour, 1989:137) do not. The approximately 91 living species of emydid turtles (including those belonging to the Batagurinae) are grouped into 33 genera (Ernst and Barbour, 1989:136). In the Yucatán Peninsula the family is represented by 3 genera and 3 species.

Key to the Genera of the Family Emydidae

1. Carapace and plastron connected by a bridge (Fig. 105B); plastron fixed, lobes not movable 2
   Carapace and plastron in direct contact, without a bridge (Fig. 105D); plastron hinged, plastral lobes movable.. *Terrapene*
2. Aquatic or semiaquatic turtles with fully webbed digits; carapace marked with light ocelli with dark central spots.. *Trachemys*
   Terrestrial turtles with digits only slightly webbed; carapace without light ocelli with dark central spots .... *Rhinoclemmys*

Clave de los Géneros de la Familia Emydidae

1. Carapacho y plastrón conectados por un puente (Fig. 105B); plastrón modificado, los lóbulos no son movibles..2
   Carapacho y plastrón en contacto directo, sin un puente (Fig. 105D); plastrón charnelado, el lóbulo anterior es móvil............................... *Terrapene*
2. Tortugas acuáticas o semiacuáticas con dedos completamente palmeados; carapacho marcado con ocelos claros con manchas obscuras en el centro .... *Trachemys*
   Tortugas terrestres con los dedos sólo un poco palmeados; carapacho sin ocelos claros con manchas obscuras en el centro.. *Rhinoclemmys*

Genus *Rhinoclemmys*
(Neotropical Wood Turtles)

Members of this Neotropical genus are the sole representatives of the subfamily Batagurinae in the New World. The genus ranges from southern Sonora and southern Veracruz south to Ecuador and Brazil. Eight or nine living species are presently recognized, but only one occurs in the Yucatán Peninsula. *Rhinoclemmys* is derived from the Greek *rhinos*, "nose," and *klemmys*, "tortoise" or "turtle," in reference to the protuberant snout of some species. The genus *Rhinoclemmys* was revised by Ernst (1978), who also wrote a generic account of *Rhinoclemmys* (1981).

Rhinoclemmys areolata (Duméril and Bibron)
(Figs. 281, 282; Map 58)

Emys areolata A. M. C. Duméril and Bibron, 1851:10, in A. M. C. Duméril and Duméril, 1851. HOLOTYPE: MNHNP 9424. TYPE LOCALITY: Province du Petén, Guatemala; restricted by H. M. Smith and Taylor (1950b:318) to La Libertad, El Petén, Guatemala; corrected to Flores, El Petén, Guatemala, by Dunn and Stuart (1951:60).

Furrowed wood turtle; black-bellied turtle, black belly, aragagao (Belize); mojina (Guatemala, Mexico); kan ak (Lacandón Maya); chakpool (Yucatec Maya).

DESCRIPTION   This medium-sized turtle attains a carapace length of about 200 mm. The rather high carapace has a weak median keel, is wider posteriorly than anteriorly, and has a slightly serrated posterior margin (Fig. 281). The plastron is slightly notched posteriorly and turns up slightly at its anterior margin. The head is relatively small, and the neck is long. The digits are only slightly webbed, and the anterior surfaces of the forelimbs bear enlarged, heavily keratinized scales. In males the plastron is concave; in females it is flat. The tail is relatively longer in males than in females, and the vent is situated beyond the carapacial margin.

In adults the carapace is dark olive brown, tan, or black. Often the seams are darker, and there are usually indistinct suffusions of yellowish pigment. The juveniles have a small red or yellow spot at the center of each pleural scute. The plastron and bridge are yellowish. The head and neck are boldly marked with yellow or red spots and stripes, and the lower jaws and the throat are spotted with black (Fig. 282). The appendages are light tan or yellow spotted with darker pigment.

SIMILAR SPECIES   *Trachemys scripta* has yellow or orange stripes on the neck but differs from *R. areolata* in its larger size (to 600 mm), lower, wider carapace with a stronger median keel, and extensively webbed digits. *Kinosternon* and *Terrapene carolina* have hinged plastra.

DISTRIBUTION   *Rhinoclemmys areolata* is found at low elevations from southern Veracruz through Tabasco and northern Chiapas, through the Yucatán Peninsula, and possibly to eastern Honduras. It occurs throughout the Yucatán Peninsula (Map 58).

NATURAL HISTORY   Although predominantly inhabitants of savannas and other open situations, wood turtles also occur in forests and marshy areas, and some extrapeninsular populations are essentially aquatic (Pérez-Higareda and Smith, 1987:114). In the Yucatán Peninsula, however, this is a terrestrial form, and individuals are often abroad during the day, especially during the rainy season. Stuart (1935:56) found *R. areolata* abundant on the savannas of central El Petén, although many individuals were missing feet. This he attributed to the fires

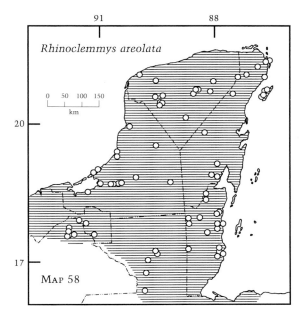

Map 58

that annually sweep across the savannas of that region, although it might also be the result of predation (C. H. Ernst, pers. comm.). Stuart also noted that natives hunted these turtles for food during an unusually dry winter.

Little is known of the diet of *R. areolata*, but Alvarez del Toro (1983:46) characterized it as omnivorous. Platt (1993:32) examined the feces of two specimens from northern Belize and found vegetable material, the remains of beetles and unidentified insects, and eggshells, possibly from *Trachemys scripta*.

According to Ernst and Barbour (1989:181), *R. areolata* produces elongate eggs with brittle shells. At the time of egg laying, the posterior margins of the female's carapace and plastron become flexible to allow passage of the eggs. For populations in western Tabasco, a single egg appears to constitute a clutch (Pérez-Higareda and Smith, 1988:263). The hatchlings have a carapace length of 52 to 55 mm.

In a defensive behavior described by Dodd (1978:11), a wood turtle leaned toward its adversary with the head and front legs hidden beneath the carapace and vigorously used its hind legs to maintain balance and change direction.

SUBSPECIES No subspecies are formally recognized, but Ernst (1978:118) noted that specimens from Isla Cozumel differ in several respects from other populations. Pérez-Higareda and Smith (1978) called attention to differences in morphology, color, ecology, and behavior among populations of *R. areolata*, and they tentatively identified (but did not formally recognize) three geographical units, two of which occur in the Yucatán Peninsula.

ETYMOLOGY The specific name, *areolata*, is derived from the Latin, *areola*, "a small open space," and the adjectival suffix *-ata*, in reference to the small, light spots present on the carapace of hatchlings.

COMMENT In the past this species was placed in the genera *Geoemyda* and *Callopsis*, and much of the earlier literature will be found under those names. H. M. Smith and Smith (1979:370–375) discussed the complicated nomenclatural history of the genus.

The record from Uaxactún, El Petén (UMMZ 75597), is based on a plastron removed from a burial urn at that archaeological site. The species probably never actually occurred in the heavily forested environs of Uaxactún (Stuart, 1958:19).

Rhinoclemmys areolata is listed as insufficiently known in the IUCN Red Data Book (Groombridge, 1982:53).

H. M. Smith and Smith (1979:383) reviewed this species and argued that it should be considered endangered in Mexico. Ernst (1980) also reviewed *R. areolata*, and Groombridge (1982) summarized information on its biology.

Locality Records Belize: Belize: Belize (BCB 13151; MCZ 136040; UCM 25900; USNM 6546), rd. to Corozalito, ca. 6 mi E Northern Hwy. (CM 105813, 105989), 1 km SW Hattieville (CM 91083), Rockstone Pond (UU 6144–45, 6439–532, 9760–64, 11227), 2 mi N, 1 mi E Sand Hill (UU 9766), 24 km S San Felipe (UF 87170); Cayo: near Augustine (JCL photo), 12 mi S Cayo (UMMZ 70461), mi 47 on Western Hwy. (CM 112185), no specific locality (UF 19167); Orange Walk: Gallon Jug (FMNH 69235), 8 mi N Gallon Jug (MCZ 71632), 1 mi N Gallon Jug (MCZ 71633), Orange Walk Town (USNM 194382), near Orange Walk Town (KU 157681–82), 6.4 mi S San Pablo (KU 157683), Boom (USNM 102894); Stann Creek: Freetown (CM 8516), Silk Grass (FMNH 49361), 7 mi W, 1 mi S Stann Creek (JLK 485), mi 42 on Southern Hwy. (CM 105938); no specific locality (USNM 59934). *Guatemala*: Alta Verapaz: Chinajá (Duellman, 1963:231); El Petén: Flores (UMMZ 79100; USNM 71416), La Libertad (USNM 71421–27), near La Libertad (UMMZ 75340–43, 75257–85), 12 km S La Libertad (AMNH 70018–20), near San Andrés (UMMZ 75244–54, 75256), Sayaxché (UCM 22190); no specific locality (USNM 71963–65). *Mexico*: Campeche: Balchacaj (FMNH 116490), 1.4 mi W Castamay (UMMZ 129704), Champotón (UMMZ 73114–21), 7.3 km S Champotón (EAL 2926), 48.5 mi SW Champotón (UU 9770), 72.8 km SW Champotón (EAL 2932), Dzibalchén (KU 75654–55), Escárcega (UCM 29176), 3 mi E Escárcega (UCM 29177), 5 mi W Escárcega (UCM 45955), Laguna Silvituc (KU 75119), Matamoros (FMNH 36602–3), Panlao (H. M. Smith, 1938:21), Hwy. 180 near jct. rd. to Sabancuy (AMNH 93241), 1 km E Xpujil (JCL photo); Chiapas: Catazajá (CM 117824), Palenque (USNM 108646), San Juanito (USNM 108647–48), 5 mi E Palenque (UMMZ 118297–301; USNM 108649–56), 3 km SW Palenque (EAL 3751), 13 mi N Palenque (BCB 17359); Quintana Roo: 7 mi N Bacalar (LSUMZ 33222), Calderitas (MZCIQRO 31), km 164, 13 mi NW Chetumal (BCB 13149–50), Chetumal-Tulum Hwy. (MZCIQRO 19), Cobá (FMNH 27268), Cozumel (CM 27579; FMNH 20631; Himmelstein, 1980:25; UIMNH 28004; UMMZ 76145–49), Cozumel, ca. 2 km W Cedral (CM 47957), Cozumel, ca. 3 mi W Cedral (CM 25432), Cozumel, 2 km N Cedral turnoff (CM 96019), Cozumel, Cedral (CM 96020), Cozumel, 2.5 km N San Miguel (KU 70945–57, 71772), Cozumel, 3.5 km N San Miguel (KU 70943–44, 70958–60), Cozumel, 3 mi N San Miguel (UCM 12403), Cozumel, San

Miguel (UCM 16148–57; UF 33120; UMMZ 78631–32), Cozumel, 3 mi S San Miguel (UMMZ 78633–38), Cozumel, 6 km NE San Miguel (CM 41313), Cozumel, 10 km SW San Miguel (CM 41319–21), Estación Santa Teresa, Sian Ka'an Reserve (MZCIQRO 55), Isla Mujeres (UMMZ 76144), bet. Leona Vicario and Puerto Juárez (UU 9772), Pueblo Nuevo X-Can (KU 70942, 70961; UU 9757–58), Puerto Morelos (UMMZ 76150), Rancho Las Vegas, 7 mi S Puerto Juárez (UU 9765), 2.1 mi S Vicente Guerrero (UU 9756), 3.3 mi E Xiatil (UU 9759); Tabasco: Emiliano Zapata (CM 62171; EAL 1643, 2960), 16 mi SE Emiliano Zapata (UMMZ 126702), 18 mi ESE Emiliano Zapata (UMMZ 129703), Tenosique (USNM 108645); Yucatán: Chichén Itzá (MCZ 26845; UMMZ 73107–11, 73113), 6 mi SW Chichén Itzá (UMMZ 73112), 1.6 mi S Libre Unión (UU 9767–68), Mayapán (Pollock and Ray, 1957:648), Mérida (EAL 1206; FMNH 153419–20), 60 km S Mérida (UMMZ 81566), 5 km S Muna (Dundee et al. 1986:40), 9.6 mi SE Muna (UMMZ 129706), 4 mi S Peto (LACM 113912), Pisté (KU 70962–64; UU 9771), near Pisté (UCM 16158), near Sisal (UU 9769), Tekom (FMNH 49362), Yokat (AMNH 38846); no specific locality (FMNH 153420; USNM 19279).

Genus *Terrapene* (Box Turtles)

This is a small genus of North American turtles with high-domed carapaces and hinged plastra. Although most species are terrestrial or semiaquatic, one is primarily aquatic. Representatives of the genus occur throughout the eastern, central, and southwestern United States and discontinuously through Mexico to Quintana Roo. Four living species are recognized, of which one occurs in the Yucatán Peninsula. *Terrapene* is derived from an Amerindian word meaning "a small turtle." Milstead (1969a) reviewed the genus and defined its species groups, and Ernst and McBreen (1991a) summarized information on the genus.

Terrapene carolina (Linnaeus)
(Figs. 105D, 283, 284; Map 59)

Testudo carolina Linnaeus, 1758:198. TYPE: Unknown. TYPE LOCALITY: Carolina; restricted by Schmidt (1953:93) to the vicinity of Charleston, South Carolina.

Common box turtle; tortuga de caja (Mexico).

DESCRIPTION These medium-sized turtles attain a carapace length of approximately 150 to 200 mm. The females are probably larger than the males. The domed carapace is rounded in dorsal aspect and usually has a distinct median keel on vertebral scutes 3 and 4, although this may be obscure in old animals (Fig. 283). The posterior margin of the carapace lacks serrations. The plastron may slightly exceed the carapace in length, and a single hinge divides it into anterior and posterior lobes, both of which are movable. The posterior lobe of males is slightly concave; that of females is flat. The carapace and plastron are sutured together directly; there is no bridge. The head is relatively small, and the upper jaw bears a moderately strong hook. The limbs are rather short and stout and bear heavy scutes. The tail of males is longer and thicker than that of females, and the vent extends beyond the posterior carpacial margin. There are four partly webbed toes on each hind foot.

The carapace is predominantly yellowish brown, tan, or olive, with darker seams and lighter blotches. The plastron is yellow with brown seams. The head and neck are usually yellowish tan with dark flecks (Fig. 284), but in some specimens the head is nearly white. The jaws are light tan or pinkish.

SIMILAR SPECIES *Rhinoclemmys areolata* and *Trachemys scripta* have lower carapaces and lack hinged plastra. The species of *Kinosternon* have lower, more oval carapaces and fully webbed digits, and they lack the yellowish carapace of *T. carolina*.

DISTRIBUTION This species occurs widely throughout the central and eastern United States and as isolated populations in Tamaulipas, San Luis Potosí, and Veracruz, and in the Yucatán Peninsula, where it is known from Campeche, Yucatán, and Quintana Roo (Map 59).

NATURAL HISTORY In the Yucatán Peninsula *T. carolina* inhabits both open and forested situations, although it appears to prefer the former. Individuals have been found in marshy areas, pastures, thorn forests, and tropical evergreen forest, but not in the tall mesic forests at the base of the peninsula. These turtles are terrestrial, although they may occasionally enter shallow water.

Little is known about their diet in the Yucatán Peninsula, but the northern races are omnivorous. Carr (1952:147) suggested an ontogenetic shift in diet, with the young being predominantly carnivorous and the adults largely herbivorous, but C. H. Ernst (pers. comm.) disagreed. A wide variety of invertebrates have been reported as prey items, and

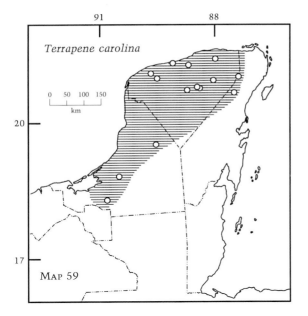

91 88

Terrapene carolina

0 50 100 150
km

20

17

MAP 59

vertebrates such as salamanders, frogs, snakes, lizards, other turtles, and small mammals are also taken when the opportunity arises.

Although nothing is known of reproduction in Yucatecan box turtles, the northern races breed during the spring, summer, or fall. Copulation is preceded by an elaborate courtship in which the male circles the female, biting and shoving her and titillating the sides of her carapace with the claws on his fingers. The female uses her hind limbs to excavate a nest into which she deposits two to seven eggs. The incubation period is highly variable. In temperate latitudes it lasts anywhere from 70 to 114 days, with an average of perhaps 87 to 89 days (Carr, 1952:146).

SUBSPECIES   The box turtles in the Yucatán Peninsula were formerly known as *T. mexicana*, a form said to be distinct from *T. carolina*, until Milstead (1967:176) analyzed fossil and Recent material and concluded that *T. mexicana* and *T. carolina* are conspecific. *Terrapene carolina* is represented in eastern Mexico by two subspecies, of which one, *T. c. yucatana* occurs in the Yucatán Peninsula. Ward (1980) suggested that the Yucatán populations may warrant full species status.

ETYMOLOGY   The specific name, *carolina*, is a toponym referring to the Carolinas, where the type material is believed to have originated.

COMMENT   This species was reviewed by Ernst

and McBreen (1991b), Milstead (1969), and H. M. Smith and Smith (1979).

Locality Records Mexico: Campeche: near Candelaria (JCL photo), Centenario (EAL 2953), Dzibalchén (KU 75657–59); Quintana Roo: Cobá (FMNH 27271), Pueblo Nuevo X-Can (UU 9809–10); Yucatán: Buctzotz (J. R. Buskirk, in litt.), Chichén Itzá (AMNH 38847; FMNH 27272–73; MCZ 9511–12; UMMZ 73122, 83291), 1.6 mi S Libre Unión (UU 9800–7), Mérida (UMMZ 76143), 7.5 mi NW Mérida (UU 9808), Pisté (KU 70970–73; UCM 16146–47), Santa Clara (MCZ 135051), 12 mi N Tizimín (UCM 45963–64), bet. Valladolid and Espita (JCL sight record).

Genus *Trachemys* (Slider Turtles)

As presently understood, this genus includes six species of predominantly aquatic, freshwater turtles. Representatives of the genus range across much of North America southward through Central America to Brazil and Argentina and are found on many Caribbean islands. One species occurs in the Yucatán Peninsula. Members of this genus have been placed variously in the genera *Pseudemys* and *Chrysemys*, but Seidel and Smith (1986) presented evidence supporting the recognition of *Trachemys*, which derives from the Greek *trachy*, "rough," and *emys*, "freshwater tortoise."

Trachemys scripta (Schoepf)
(Figs. 105B, 285; Map 60)

Testudo scripta Schoepf, 1792. TYPE: unknown. TYPE LOCALITY: unknown; designated as Charleston, South Carolina, by Schmidt (1953:102).

Common slider, ornate terrapin; bokatura, wayamu (Belize); hicotea, jicotea, tortuga de agua (Mexico); kan ak (Lacandón Maya); kaa nish (Yucatec Maya).

DESCRIPTION   This is a large turtle. A carapace length of about 600 mm is possible, although most specimens are much smaller. Middle American populations show little or no sexual size dimorphism, in contrast with populations in the United States, where males are substantially smaller than females. The carapace is oval in dorsal view, rather low, and may bear a weak median keel (Fig. 285). The posterior margin of the carapace is weakly serrated. The rigid plastron is attached to the carapace by a broad bridge (Fig. 105B), and the posterior margin of the plastron is slightly notched. The head is large, and the snout is slightly protuberant. The limbs are robust, and the digits are extensively webbed.

The carapace is brown or olive patterned with yellow lines and reticulations. Each pleural and vertebral scute generally has a light ocellus with a darker center. In juveniles the ocelli may be red. The head, neck, and limbs are greenish gray or brown with distinct yellow or orange stripes.

SIMILAR SPECIES *Rhinoclemmys areolata* has a higher, more domed carapace, and its digits are only slightly webbed. *Chelydra serpentina* and *Staurotypus triporcatus* have three well-developed keels on the carapace, whereas *T. scripta* has a weak median keel or no keel at all.

DISTRIBUTION *Trachemys scripta* has the widest geographical distribution of any nonmarine turtle. It ranges across the central and eastern United States and south through Mexico and Central America to Colombia and Venezuela. Disjunct populations occur in southeastern Brazil, Uruguay, and northern Argentina. The species occurs throughout the Yucatán Peninsula (Map 60).

NATURAL HISTORY This predominantly aquatic turtle is a common inhabitant of ponds, rivers, streams, lakes, and cenotes. Individuals occasion-

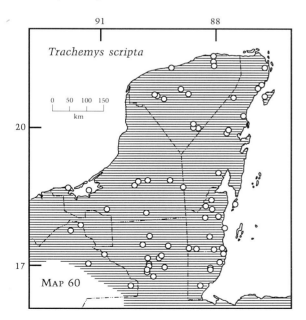

MAP 60

ally wander some distance from water, especially during the rainy season.

Probably more is known about the natural history of this species than any other turtle as a result of the work of E. O. Moll and Legler (1971) in Panama and of Gibbons and his co-workers (Gibbons, 1990) in the southeastern United States. The extent to which their findings can be applied to Yucatecan populations is open to question. Nonetheless, D. Moll and Moll (1990:161), in an overview of the biology of tropical populations, concluded that in terms of ecology, tropical subspecies of *T. scripta* are more similar to northern subspecies than to other species of tropical turtles. According to E. O. Moll and Legler (1971), nesting occurs during the dry season (December–May) in Panama, a pattern similar to that reported by Vogt (1990:163) for turtles in southeastern Mexico, where nesting takes place from late January through May. In Panama, females use communal nests, which are generally in open areas exposed to sunlight. Each female constructs a flask-shaped cavity about 150 mm deep into which she places 9 to 25 eggs. Females may produce one to six clutches per season. The eggs hatch in 71 to 83 days, and the hatchlings emerge from the nest early in the rainy season (May or June), as much as eight weeks after hatching. Females are mature at five to seven years of age and a plastral length of 240 mm. The sex of *T. scripta* hatchlings is determined by the temperature during incubation, with lower incubation temperatures producing predominantly or exclusively males (Vogt and Flores-Villela, 1992a).

Trachemys scripta is diurnal. The adults feed predominantly on aquatic vegetation, but sliders also consume animal material such as mollusks, insects, and fishes, especially as juveniles. In southern Veracruz they eat mainly leaves and stems, with lesser amounts of fish and shrimp rounding out the diet (Vogt and Guzman, 1988:41).

This species is commonly preyed on by crocodiles. Himmelstein (1980:26) described a specimen from Quintana Roo that had punctures on the carapace and plastron, suggesting attempted predation by a crocodile. On the other hand, Waldeck (quoted in Morelet, 1871:60) recounted the belief that crocodiles are themselves frequently killed by the *T. scripta* they ingest, because the turtles have a shell too hard to be crushed by the crocodile's jaws and a covering impervious to digestion. The hicotea "interferes with the monster's internal arrangements—so seriously, indeed, that the cayman [sic] soon pays the penalty of his greediness by death." Waldeck went on to say that he had often examined the bodies of defunct crocodiles and that he invariably found a living hicotea in their stomachs.

SUBSPECIES This species shows very pronounced geographic variation throughout its wide range, and as many as 14 subspecies have been recognized. According to Ernst (1990:62) and Legler (1990:88), the subspecies in the Yucatán Peninsula is *T. s. venusta*.

ETYMOLOGY The specific name, *scripta*, is from the Latin *scriptus*, "written," possibly in reference to the intricate pattern on the carapace in some races.

COMMENT This species has often been placed in the genera *Pseudemys* and *Chrysemys*, and much of the literature pertaining to it will be found under those names. Seidel and Smith (1986) presented evidence justifying recognition of the genus *Trachemys* and the placement of *scripta* within that genus.

Sliders are eaten by humans throughout the Yucatán Peninsula. Morelet (1871:59) stated that it was the most esteemed of all the turtles. As early as 1933 the species was in decline at Lago Petén Itzá, Guatemala, owing to overexploitation by humans (Stuart, 1935:56). The same applies in Alta Verapaz, where both the flesh and eggs are prized (Stuart, 1948:45).

The status of *T. scripta* in Mexico was reviewed by H. M. Smith and Smith (1979). The systematics, taxonomy, and geographic variation of the species as a whole were treated by Ernst (1990) and Legler (1990) (as *Pseudemys scripta*).

Locality Records Belize: Belize: Belize (FMNH 4173–75, 4428, 49363; USNM 55604–5), Maskall (W. T. Neill and Allen, 1959c:29), Missionary Lake Rd., 5.3 mi E jct. Northern Hwy. (CM 91077–80), 19.2 mi E Roaring Creek (KU 157676), Rockstone Pond (UU 6146–56, 6590–623, 9728–33), 2 mi W Rockstone Pond (UU 9722–27), S Thurton's Bank (USNM 51878); Cayo: ca. 3 mi S Georgeville (CM 91082), 1 mi NW Succotz (UU 9696); Corozal: Ambergris Cay, 17 km N, 6.5 km E San Pedro (CM 91100); Orange Walk: Chan Pine Ridge (MPM 8285–86), Kate's Lagoon (FMNH 49364), Lamanai (ROM H12728–30, H12731–32), 9 mi SE Orange Walk (UU 9695), Tower Hill (UU 9720); Stann Creek: 21.6 mi NW Mango Creek (KU 157675), Melinda Forest Station (UU 9697–98), 6.5 mi N, 1 mi W Melinda Forest Station (UU 9734), Middlesex (FMNH 4429;

UCM 25901, 45196), Sittee River Village (UU 9735–36); Toledo: ca. 0.5 mi W jct. Southern Hwy. and Punta Gorda–San Antonio Rd. (CM 105873–74), 2 mi S Waha Leaf Creek (MCZ 71642), 3 mi S Waha Leaf Creek (MCZ 71641); no specific locality (UF 24071). *Guatemala*: El Petén: Chuntuquí (USNM 71429), Flores (UMMZ 79101–2), Lago Petén (UMMZ 79101–2, 79110), Laguna Eckibix (UMMZ 79104), Laguna de Zotz (UMMZ 75230–31, 79105–7), near La Libertad (UMMZ 75226–29, 75232–39), 1 mi S La Libertad (UMMZ 79109), Paso de Caballo (UMMZ 79108), 1 km E Paso Subin (KU 55976), 5 mi S Piedras Negras (USNM 108670), 8.4 mi N Río de la Pasión (KU 157677), Seibal (AMNH 72606, 71614), Tikal (UF 13479, 13480; UMMZ 117241–43). *Mexico*: Campeche: 25 mi E Escárcega (UCM 29175), Laguna Chumpich (KU 75120–21), Laguna Chicancanab (Casas-Andreu, 1967), Laguna Silvituc (EAL 2954; KU 75122; UU 9694), Laguna de Términos (Gray, 1870), Río Candelaria, 12 mi from Guatemala border (CM 37019–20, 37686), 23.2 mi E Silvituc (KU 157678–79), 2 mi W Zacatal (UU 9705), Zoh Laguna (CM 45263); Chiapas: Catazajá (UU 12508), Laguna Ocotal (Shreve, 1957:242), Playas de Catazajá (UU 11353–54), Río Lacantún–Usumacinta region (Alvarez del Toro, 1960:48); Quintana Roo: Bacalar (MZCIQRO 27), Chunyaxché (Himmelstein, 1980:26), 4 km NNE Felipe Carrillo Puerto (KU 70967), 11 km NNE Felipe Carrillo Puerto (KU 70968), Isla Cozumel (Himmelstein, 1980:26; USNM 13908–9, 103707; UMMZ 76151–54), Lago Cobá (JCL photo; UMMZ 138349), Laguna Bacalar (UU 9721), Sian Ka'an Reserve (MZCIQRO 33), Puerto Morelos (UU 9737), 10 mi S, 5 mi W Puerto Morelos (UU 9714–19), Rancho Las Vegas, 2 mi S Puerto Juárez (UU 9706–13); Tabasco: Emiliano Zapata (CM 96052–54, 112796–812; EAL 2957; USNM 136612); Yucatán: 9 mi SSE Dziuché (UU 9699–701), 3 mi E Esmeralda (LACM 113907), 12 mi S Izamal (UMMZ 81562–64), 1.6 mi S Libre Unión (UU 9648–93, 12739), 0.6 mi E, 1.5 mi S Libre Unión (UU 9702–4), Mayapán (Pollock and Ray, 1957), 50 km S Mérida (UMMZ 81565), bet. Muna and Umán (Casas-Andreu, 1967), 29 mi SE Peto (H. M. Smith and Smith, 1979:499), 1.1 km S Río Lagartos (FMNH 171406), 13.4 mi S Río Lagartos (KU 157680), Telchac Puerto (UMMZ 76155–56), 12 mi N Tizimín (UCM 45956–62).

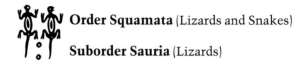

Order Squamata (Lizards and Snakes)

Suborder Sauria (Lizards)

With well over 3,000 living species, the saurians constitute the majority of contemporary reptiles. Lizards are found everywhere in the world except on some oceanic islands and at the highest latitudes. As a group, lizards are highly diverse. They range in size from the gigantic Komodo dragon, *Varanus komodoensis*, which attains a length of 3 m, to tiny *Sphaerodactylus* geckos no more than 3 cm in total length. Although lizards are typically rather generalized quadrupeds with long, often fragile tails, several lineages have independently evolved into serpentlike animals with elongated bodies and reduced limbs or no limbs at all. Most lizards are terrestrial, but many are arboreal, some are fossorial, and a few are semiaquatic and even marine. In general, lizards are carnivorous, but some feed predominantly on plant material, and some are omnivorous. The usual mode of reproduction is oviparity, but some species exhibit true viviparity, with a placental attachment between the embryo and the mother. At least 38 species of lizards exist as all-female parthenogenetic forms. The lizard fauna of the Yucatán Peninsula comprises 48 species belonging to 20 genera and 11 families.

IDENTIFICATION   In many cases lizards can be identified simply by comparing the specimen with the photographs and drawings provided here for each species. The location where the specimen was collected is important information, for some species can be eliminated from further consideration on the basis of their restricted distributions. In some cases it will be necessary to use the keys for a positive identification. The keys rely on external morphological features, especially the size, shape, and disposition of integumentary structures, particularly scales. A hand lens may be necessary to see some details. The size, shape, and ornamentation of lizard scales provide important clues to identification. Scales may be beadlike and nonoverlapping, in which case they are termed *granular*. Or they may

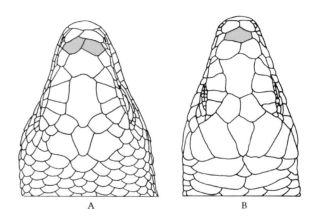

Fig. 112. Dorsal views of the heads of lizards. A, *Celestus* with paired frontonasal scales (*shaded*). Redrawn from Campbell and Camarillo, 1994, by permission of *Herpetologica*. B, *Eumeces* with a single frontonasal scale (*shaded*). Redrawn from Smith, 1946, by permission of Cornell University Press, copyright © 1946 by Comstock Publishing Company, Inc.

be flattened, smooth, and highly polished; these are termed *cycloid*. Scales that overlap are said to be *imbricate*, whereas those that do not overlap are termed *juxtaposed*. Enlarged conical scales are called *tubercles*, and skin that bears them is said to be *tuberculate*. Note whether or not the scales are keeled, and if the extent of keeling differs on different parts of the body. Compare the size and shape of the dorsal and ventral scales. The presence or absence of movable eyelids and the configuration of the pupil (round or vertically elliptical) are also useful characters. Some species have glandular structures on the ventral surfaces of the thighs (femoral pores) or in the vicinity of the anus (preanal pores). These are generally better developed in males than in females, and their presence or absence, number, and configuration can assist in identification.

Key to the Families of Lizards

1. Movable eyelids present 4
   Movable eyelids absent, the eye covered by a transparent spectacle 2
2. Five digits on the hand 3
   Four digits on the hand . . . . Gymnophthalmidae
3. Ventral scales juxtaposed, rectangular, and arranged in longitudinal rows . . . . . . Xantusiidae
   Ventral scales granular or imbricate . . . . Gekkonidae
4. Scales on dorsal surface of head enlarged, not granular; claws not situated within sheaths
   5
   Scales on dorsal surface of head granular; claws situated within sheaths . . . . . Eublepharidae

5. Scales on dorsum of body variable; ventral scales granular or imbricate, not rectangular
. . . . 6
   Scales on dorsum of body granular; ventral scales juxtaposed, rectangular, and arranged in
   longitudinal rows. . . . . Teiidae

6. Dorsal scales smooth, highly polished 10
   Dorsal scales granular, smooth, or keeled, but not highly polished 7

7. Femoral pores present (rudimentary in females) (Fig. 124D). 8
   Femoral pores absent 9

8. Scales of the vertebral row enlarged, forming a serrated crest, and/or tail bearing distinct
   whorls of enlarged spines, these separated by one or more interwhorls of small scales
   (Fig. 123). . . . . Iguanidae
   Scales of the vertebral row not enlarged; tail not bearing distinct whorls of enlarged spines
   separated by interwhorls of small scales . . . . Phrynosomatidae

9. Subdigital lamellae expanded; males with conspicuous throat fan (dewlap); no casque or
   crest on occipital region . . . . Polychrotidae
   Subdigital lamellae not expanded; males without throat fan; casque or crest present on
   occipital region (Figs. 119, 121). . . . . Corytophanidae

10. Paired frontonasal scales (Fig. 112A) . . . . Anguidae
    Single frontonasal scale (Fig. 112B) . . . . Scincidae

Clave para las Familias de Lagartijas

1. Con párpados movibles 4
   Sin párpados movibles, el ojo cubierto por una escama transparente 2

2. Cinco dedos en la mano 3
   Cuatro dedos en la mano . . . . Gymnophthalmidae

3. Escamas ventrales yuxtapuestas, rectangulares, y dispuestas en hileras longitudinales . . . . .
   . . . . Xantusiidae
   Escamas ventrales granulares o imbricadas. . . . . Gekkonidae

4. Escamas alargadas no granulares en la superficie dorsal de la cabeza; uñas no cubiertas por
   una vaina 5
   Escamas granulares en la superficie dorsal de la cabeza; uñas cubiertas por una vaina . . . . . .
   . . . . Eublepharidae

5. Escamas en el dorso del cuerpo variables; escamas ventrales granulares o imbricadas, no
   rectangulares 6
   Escamas granulares en el dorso del cuerpo; escamas ventrales yuxtapuestas, rectangulaes, y
   dispuestas en hileras longitudinales . . . . Teiidae

6. Escamas dorsales lisas, muy lustrosas 10
   Escamas dorsales granulares, lisas, o quilladas, pero no muy lustrosas. 7

7. Con poros femorales (rudimentarios en las hembras) (Fig. 124D). 8
   Sin poros femorales. 9

8. Escamas de la hilera vertebral alargadas, formando una cresta aserrada, y/o la cola con
   verticilos distintivos de espinas alargadas, los verticilos separados por una o más hileras de
   escamas pequeñas (Fig. 123) . . . . Iguanidae
   Escamas de la hilera vertebral no alargadas; cola sin verticilos distintivos de espinas alargadas que están separados por hileras de escamas pequeñas . . . . Phrynosomatidae

9. Lamelas subdigitales expandidas; machos con un abanico gular conspicuo; sin casco o cresta
   en la región occipital . . . . Polychrotidae
   Lamelas subdigitales no expandidas, machos sin abanico gular; con un casco o cresta en la
   región occipital (Figs. 119, 121). . . . . Corytophanidae

10. Un par de escamas frontonasales (Fig. 112A) . . . . Anguidae
    Una sola escama frontonasal (Fig. 112B) . . . . Scincidae

Family Eublepharidae

This moderately small family of apparently primitive lizards reaches its greatest diversity in the Old World, where it occurs in East and West Africa, southwestern and southeastern Asia, and the Indo-Australian Archipelago. In the New World, the family ranges from the southwestern United States south to Costa Rica. This assemblage has often been considered a subfamily within the Gekkonidae, but Kluge (1987) was able to diagnose the group on the basis of derived character states, and he therefore treated eublepharines as a family. Grismer (1988) provided further support for this arrangement and recognized five genera and 22 species, of which only one occurs in the Yucatán Peninsula.

Genus *Coleonyx* (Banded Geckos)

This genus of nocturnal, terrestrial geckos is restricted to North and Central America. They are small to medium in size, and their bodies are covered with granular scales, among which may be scattered enlarged tubercles. The distalmost digital scales are laterally compressed and enclose the claw, at least partially. The genus occurs at low to moderate elevations from the arid southwestern United States through Mexico and Central America to Panama. Seven living species are currently recognized (Grismer, 1988:455; Kluge, 1991:6), but only one occurs in the Yucatán Peninsula. Klauber (1945) reviewed the genus *Coleonyx*, Kluge (1962) studied the osteology of its members, Dixon (1970) summarized information on the genus, and Grismer (1983, 1988) and Kluge (1975) examined the relationships among the species. Dial and Grismer (1992) studied the evolution of three physiological attributes and the historical biogeography of the genus. *Coleonyx* is from the Greek *koleos*, "sheath," and *onyx*, "nail," "talon," or "claw," in reference to the sheathed claws of some species.

Coleonyx elegans Gray
(Figs. 113, 114B, 286–288; Map 61)

Coleonyx elegans Gray, 1845:163. HOLOTYPE: BMNH 1946.8.27.7. TYPE LOCALITY: Belize.

Yucatán banded gecko; escorpión, geco manchado, perrito, salamanquesa (Mexico); ix-hunpekin (Yucatec Maya).

DESCRIPTION   The adults of this attractive gecko attain a snout-vent length of about 108 mm, and the undamaged tail is approximately equal to the head and body in length. The limbs are rather long, slender, and delicate, and the digits terminate in claws that are partly recessed within sheaths (Fig. 114B). The eyes are large with vertically elliptical pupils (Fig. 287). Movable eyelids are present. The scales on the head and body are granular, with scattered enlarged tubercles. Seven to 13 preanal pores are present in males; these are rudimentary in females. Cloacal spurs are present, and a conspicuous post-anal swelling occurs in males.

The juvenile color pattern consists of a series of white transverse bands bordered in front and behind by dark brown or black; these extend the length of the body and tail. The interspaces are reddish brown, and the venter is immaculate cream. Occasional individuals are striped rather than banded (Fig. 286). In adult animals, blotches appear on the sides, and the bands become more irregular. Regenerated tails are speckled rather than banded.

SIMILAR SPECIES   All other geckos in the Yucatán Peninsula lack movable eyelids. *Lepidophyma flavimaculatum* and *L. mayae* are dark with yellow spots and lack movable eyelids.

DISTRIBUTION   *Coleonyx elegans* occurs at low elevations from southern Nayarit, Mexico, on the Pacific slope and Veracruz on the Atlantic slope, south through the Yucatán Peninsula, including

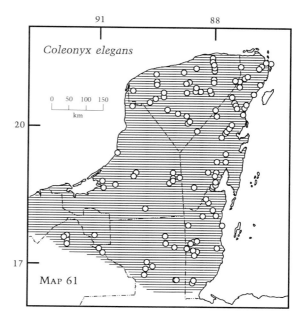

MAP 61

northern Guatemala and Belize. This species is pan-peninsular (Map 61).

NATURAL HISTORY   Banded geckos are largely nocturnal and terrestrial, although individuals are occasionally abroad during the day. Specimens have been found in caves, beneath surface debris, in rotting palm logs and stumps, within Maya ruins, and abroad on the forest floor at night. They are often found on roads at night. Stuart (1935:41) collected them on the savannas at La Libertad, El Petén, and suggested that they are active primarily during the rainy season.

Coleonyx elegans feeds on invertebrates, including spiders and insects. Gaige (1938:297) reported crickets in the stomachs of specimens from caves in western Yucatán, and Fugler and Webb (1957:108) found a large arachnid and the remains of beetles in the stomachs of specimens from Oaxaca.

These delicate lizards are graceful and catlike in their movements. When alarmed they inflate the throat and assume a stiff-legged posture with the body elevated well off the ground (Fig. 288).

Coleonyx elegans is capable of vocalization, although the role of vocal communication, if any, is unknown. When seized or otherwise provoked, these lizards emit a high-pitched, nasal squeak, with most of the acoustic energy concentrated at about 7,000 Hz (Fig. 113).

Like other members of the Eublepharidae, *C. elegans* is oviparous. Two females collected in Yucatán in April and August each contained two eggs (Duellman, 1965a:27). W. B. Davis and Dixon (1961:38) reported that females collected in June and July in Guerrero had two large ova ready to be deposited. Alvarez del Toro (1983:70) reported a clutch size of three or four eggs in Chiapas. Oviposition thus occurs during the rainy season, and more than a single clutch may be produced annually.

SUBSPECIES   According to Klauber (1945:191), this species is subdivided into two subspecies, of which the nominate form, *C. e. elegans*, occurs in the Yucatán Peninsula.

ETYMOLOGY   The specific name, *elegans*, is Latin meaning "elegant" or "fine," presumably in reference to the delicate form and attractive coloration of this species.

COMMENT   The vernacular name *escorpión* is commonly applied to many species of geckos in Mexico and Central America. In the case of *C. elegans*, the name may refer to the lizard's habit of curling its tail over its back when running. Many Yucatecans think that this harmless lizard is venomous and that it stings by throwing its tail, which is believed be a stinger (see the account of the *ixhunpekin* in "Ethnoherpetology in the Yucatán Peninsula," in this volume).

Coleonyx elegans was reviewed by Klauber (1945) as part of his revision of the genus *Coleonyx*. According to Dial and Grismer (1992), *C. elegans* and its closest relative, *C. mitratus*, exhibit the hypothesized ancestral physiological characteristics: low preferred body temperature, high evaporative water loss, and low standard metabolic rate.

Locality Records Belize: Belize: Belize (FMNH 4178), near Maskall (JCL photo), Rockstone Pond (AMNH 104418); Cayo: 6 mi ENE Augustine (LSUMZ 11451), Baking Pot (MCZ 18953), Benque Viejo (USNM 65132), 0.5 mi W Camalot (CM 105763), Central Farm (MCZ 71405–6), 4 km E Chial (CM 117244), 31.5 mi S Georgeville (KU 157084), San Luis (JCL sight record); Corozal: N edge Corozal Town (JLK 403), 2 mi N Corozal Town (JLK 400), 4 mi N Corozal Town (JLK 402), 6 mi N Corozal Town (JLK 401); Orange Walk: Gallon Jug (LSUMZ 8900), Lamanai (ROM H12754), Tower Hill (MPM 7498); Stann Creek: Stann Creek Valley (FMNH 49101); Toledo: Columbia Forest Reserve (MPM 8240), San Antonio (MCZ 71407–8). *Guatemala*: El Petén: N shore Lake Yaxhá (UTEP 6011), near La Libertad (UMMZ 75036), Piedras Negras (USNM 113069, 113073), 5 mi S Piedras Negras (USNM 113070–72), Poptún (UMMZ 117871), 1 km E Poptún (UMMZ 124364), Sayaxché (UCM 22192–95), Sojio (AMNH 69993–94), Tikal (KU 144922; UF 13493–97; UMMZ 117870, 120453), Toocog (Duellman, 1963:232), Uaxactún (AMNH 68525; KU 157085; UMMZ 70443; USNM 64908); no specific locality (USNM 71949–50,

Fig. 113. Defensive vocalization of *Coleonyx elegans*, recorded 9 August 1992, Calcehtok, Yucatán, Mexico.

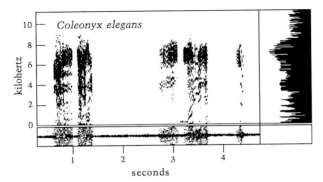

25106). *Mexico*: Campeche: Apazote (USNM 47795), Becan (UWZH 20551, 20556), Carretera Tankuche–San Mateo (IHNHERP 496), Champotón, Ejido Uxmal (IHNHERP 508), Encarnación (FMNH 123319–20; UIMNH 19534), 7.5 km W Escárcega (KU 70044), Laguna Chumpich (KU 74837), Tuxpeña Camp (UMMZ 73234), 8 km N Xpujil (KU 74838), 15 km N Xpujil (KU 74839), 20 km N Xpujil (KU 74840), 17 km E, 9 km N Xpujil (KU 74841–42); Chiapas: 13 mi S Palenque (LSUMZ 33142–46), 15.4 mi S Palenque (LSUMZ 38452), Palenque (EAL 3631; LSUMZ 33147), Palenque ruins (EAL 3327); Quintana Roo: 3.8 mi N Andrés Quintana Roo (KU 157094), vicinity of Bacalar (LSUMZ 33148), 1.7 mi S Bacalar (KU 157087), 10 mi W Bacalar (LSUMZ 33149–50), 15 km E Caobas (KU 74843), Chetumal (MZCIQRO 18), 1.6 mi N Chetumal (KU 157086), Chunyaxché (Himmelstein, 1980:27), Cobá (Himmelstein, 1980:27), 11 km SE Cobá (KU 171419–20), 21.5 km SE Cobá (KU 171422), 30.6 km SE Cobá (KU 171421), 5.2 mi NE Dziuché (KU 157095), Felipe Carrillo Puerto (UMMZ 113607–9), 10 km NNE Felipe Carrillo Puerto (KU 70050), 11.6 km N Felipe Carrillo Puerto (UMRC 80-39), 20.4 mi NE Felipe Carrillo Puerto (KU 157090), 17.5 km NE Felipe Carrillo Puerto (KU 171417), 42.8 km NE Felipe Carrillo Puerto (KU 171418), 45 km NW Felipe Carrillo Puerto (KU 171416), Isla Mujeres (UMMZ 78562), 7.5 km N Kantunil Kin (KU 171423), 3.3 mi N Limones (KU 157088), 13.7 mi N Limones (KU 157089), 10.4 km ESE Petcacab (JCL sight record), 10 mi N Playa del Carmen (LSUMZ 33153), 15.1 mi SW Playa del Carmen (KU 157091), Pueblo Nuevo X-Can (UCM 29145–47), near Pueblo Nuevo X-Can (UCM 29148–50), 10 km ENE Pueblo Nuevo X-Can (KU 70045), 11 km S Pueblo Nuevo X-Can (JCL photo), 17.5 km ENE Pueblo Nuevo X-Can (KU 70046–47), 32 km E Pueblo Nuevo X-Can (LSUMZ 28296), Puerto Juárez (Himmelstein, 1980:27), 9 km W Puerto Juárez (KU 70049), 21 km W Puerto Juárez (KU 70048), 15.8 mi S Tepich (KU 157093), Tulum (LSUMZ 33151–52), 1.4 mi NW Tulum (LSUMZ 38453), near Tulum (EAL 2875), 4 to 45 km NNW Tulum (CAS 154075–91), 1.5 mi S Yucatán–Quintana Roo border on Hwy. 295 (KU 157092); Tabasco: Tenosique (USNM 113074–75); Yucatán: 12.2 mi E Buctzotz (KU 157096), Calcehtok (JCL sight record; UMMZ 148118), 15 km E Celestún (JCL photo), Chichén Itzá (AMNH 38893; CM 36447; FMNH 49104, 123318, 123321; LSUMZ 28252, 28292; MCZ 26789–90; UMMZ 68200, 68697, 72870–72, 80814–15, 83285–86, 83928, 148901), 2.5 km E Chichén Itzá (KU 70056), Dzibilchaltún (FMNH 153448, 153450–53, 153455–59, 153461, 153464–66),

1.5 mi S Libre Unión (UCM 29153), Mayapán (FMNH 40667), Mérida (CM 44463–65; FMNH 153462), 6 km S Mérida (KU 70051), Oxkutzcab (UMMZ 80795–96), Peto (KU 157108), 11 mi SE Peto (BCB 12107–8), Pisté (KU 70052), 2 km N Pisté (KU 70053), 3 km N Pisté (KU 70054–55), 9.7 mi S Río Lagartos (KU 157098–99), 15 km S Río Lagartos (KU 157100), 2 km S Tecoh (KU 154648), 10 mi E Tekax (UCM 39111), Tekom (FMNH 49102–3), 1.8 mi W Temax (CAS 144213), near Tizimín (UMRC 78-31), 6 km N Tizimín (KU 74844–46), 12 mi N Tizimín (CM 40121; UCM 29151–52), 17.1 mi W Tizimín (KU 157097), 10.5 mi N Tizimín (KU 157101), 2.7 mi S Tizimín (KU 157102), 6.3 mi S Tizimín (KU 157103), 16.3 mi S Tizimín (KU 157104), 16.6 mi S Tizimín (KU 157105), 4.7 mi S Tizimín (KU 157106), 4 mi W Tunkás (KU 171414), 6.4 mi W Tunkás (KU 157107), 3.2 km NE Tunkás (KU 171415), 32 mi NE Uxmal (CAS 139695–96), 5 mi W Valladolid (CAS 114062), X-Can (CM 46902), Yucatán–Quintana Roo border on Hwy. 184 (JCL sight record).

Family Gekkonidae (Geckos)

The geckos are a large and cosmopolitan family of predominantly nocturnal lizards with spectacled eyes. Most have vertically elliptical pupils. They are small to medium sized and usually have a delicate integument covered with granular scales. The tail is extremely fragile and is a site of fat storage in many species. Some geckos are terrestrial, but most are arboreal, and their expanded subdigital lamellae, which allow them to cling to smooth vertical surfaces, reflect this. Preanal and femoral pores are present in the males of most species. Many geckos are capable of vocalization, and the calls function in courtship and territorial interactions. Geckos are oviparous and generally lay clutches of one or two eggs. At least three genera include parthenogenetic species. This family is essentially worldwide in its distribution save for the higher latitudes and some oceanic islands. Kluge (1967, 1976, 1982, 1983, 1987) published extensively on the phylogenetic relationships and classification of gekkonid lizards and their allies. Approximately 87 genera and about 761 species are currently recognized; 5 genera and 8 species occur in the Yucatán Peninsula.

Key to the Genera of the Family Gekkonidae

1. Subdigital lamellae divided, at least distally (Fig. 114A,C,D) 2
   Subdigital lamellae undivided (Fig. 114E,F) 3

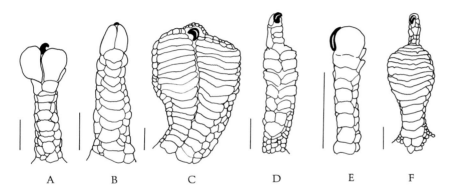

Fig. 114. Condition of subdigital lamellae in the genera of geckos in the Yucatán Peninsula. A, *Phyllodactylus*. B, *Coleonyx*. C, *Thecadactylus*. D, *Hemidactylus*. E, *Sphaerodactylus*. F, *Aristelliger*. Vertical line equals 5 mm.

2. Most subdigital lamellae divided (Fig. 114C,D) 4
   Only the distalmost subdigital lamellae divided (Fig. 114A); dorsum with enlarged tuberculate scales separated by granular scales . . . . *Phyllodactylus*

3. Digits asymmetrical, the claw situated laterally (Fig. 114E); diminutive lizards, adult SVL less than 35 mm . . . . *Sphaerodactylus*
   Digits 2–4 symmetrical, the claw situated medially (Fig. 114F); adult SVL much greater than 35 mm . . . . *Aristelliger*

4. Fifteen or more pairs of expanded subdigital lamellae (Fig. 114C) . . . . *Thecadactylus*
   Fewer than 15 pairs of expanded subdigital lamellae (Fig. 114D) . . . . *Hemidactylus*

Clave para los Géneros de la Familia Gekkonidae

1. Lamelas subdigitales divididas, por lo menos distalmente (Fig. 114A,C,D) 2
   Lamelas subdigitales sin dividir (Fig. 114E,F) 3

2. La mayoría de las lamelas subdigitales divididas (Fig. 114C,D) 4
   Solamente la lamela subdigital más distal dividida (Fig. 114A); dorso con escamas tuberculadas separadas por escamas granulares . . . . *Phyllodactylus*

3. Dedos asimétricos, la uña dispuesta lateralmente (Fig. 114E); lagartijas diminutas, adultos menores a los 35 mm de LHC . . . . *Sphaerodactylus*
   Dedos 2–4 simétricos, la uña dispuesta medialmente (Fig. 114F); adultos miden más de 35 mm de LHC . . . . *Aristelliger*

4. Quince o más pares de lamelas subdigitales expandidas (Fig. 114C) . . . . *Thecadactylus*
   Menos de quince pares de lamelas subdigitales expandidas (Fig. 114D) . . . . *Hemidactylus*

Genus *Sphaerodactylus* (Dwarf Geckos)

This essentially Neotropical genus is quite large. Some 80 species are known from the West Indies, plus another 10 from Middle America, 3 of which occur in the Yucatán Peninsula. These diminutive geckos are unique in having the claw of each digit displaced laterally by the expanded terminal subdigital lamella (Fig. 114E). Most *Sphaerodactylus* are secretive but not necessarily nocturnal. The females typically lay a single egg per clutch. *Sphaerodactylus* is from the Greek *sphaira*, "ball" or "sphere," and *daktylos*, "finger" or "toe," presumably in reference to the expanded lamella on the terminal phalanx of each digit.

Key to the Species of the Genus *Sphaerodactylus*

1. Dorsal scales smooth . . . . *Sphaerodactylus glaucus*
   Dorsal scales keeled 2

2. Midddorsal scales 38–50 in axilla-groin length; from coastal sites in northern Yucatán (Map 62) . . . . *Sphaerodactylus argus*
Middorsal scales 47–74 in axilla-groin length; low elevations in Chiapas, El Petén, Belize, and Isla Cozumel (Map 64) . . . . *Sphaerodactylus millepunctatus*

Clave para las Especies del Género *Sphaerodactylus*

1. Escamas dorsales lisas . . . . *Sphaerodactylus glaucus*
Escamas dorsales quilladas 2
2. Escamas mediodorsales 38–50 entre la axila-ingle; se distribuye en sitios costeros del norte de Yucatán (Mapa 62) . . . . *Sphaerodactyls argus*
Escamas mediodorsales 47–74 entre la axila-ingle; se distribuye a elevaciones bajas en Chiapas, El Petén, Belice, y la Isla Cozumel (Mapa 64) . . . . . *Sphaerodactylus millepunctatus*

Sphaerodactylus argus Gosse
(Figs. 115, 289; Map 62)

Sphaerodactylus argus Gosse, 1850:347. SYNTYPES: BMNH 1947.12.24.56 and 47.12.24.59. TYPE LOCALITY: Jamaica.

Oscillated gecko; bota la cola, gequillo, piconé, tira la cola (Mexico).

DESCRIPTION   This small gecko attains a maximum snout-vent length of only about 33 mm; females generally exceed males by about 2 mm. The head is distinct from the neck and slightly narrower than the body. The snout is rather narrow and pointed (Figs. 115, 289). The relatively large and protruding eyes are covered by a transparent spectacle, and the pupils are subcircular (Fig. 115B). The undamaged tail is approximately as long as the head and body. The limbs are short and rather stout, and the terminal lamella on each digit is expanded, resulting in lateral displacement of the claw. The scales on the dorsal surfaces of the body are keeled and slightly imbricate. The ventral scales are smooth and approximately twice the size of the dorsal scales. A small ocular spine is present above the eye (Fig. 115B). The supracaudal scales are smooth and strongly imbricate, and there is an enlarged median series of subcaudal scales (Fig. 115D).

The dorsum is generally gray or dark brown, and the tail often has a reddish cast. The ventral surfaces of the body, tail, and limbs are light gray or tan. Usually several narrow white or yellowish cream stripes originate on the top and sides of the head and extend onto the body. These are especially distinct in juveniles and may become broken up into a discontinuous series of small spots (ocelli) in older animals.

SIMILAR SPECIES   *Sphaerodactylus glaucus* has smooth dorsal scales instead of the keeled dorsals of *S. argus. Sphaerodactylus millepunctatus* has more dorsal scales than *S. argus* (47–74 in axilla-groin length vs. 38–50) and may have distinct dark suprapectoral and suprapelvic blotches, which are absent in *S. argus.*

DISTRIBUTION   This is a Caribbean form native to Jamaica, Cuba and its adjacent islets, and Isla San Andrés. It is also known from the Bahamas and Key West, Florida, and from scattered insular localities off the Caribbean coast of Nicaragua, Costa Rica, and Panama. In the Yucatán Peninsula the species is known only from three coastal localities in Yucatán, but it is likely present at other sites on the north coast of the peninsula (Map 62).

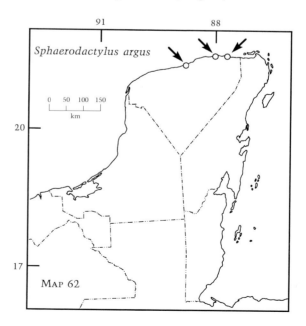

MAP 62

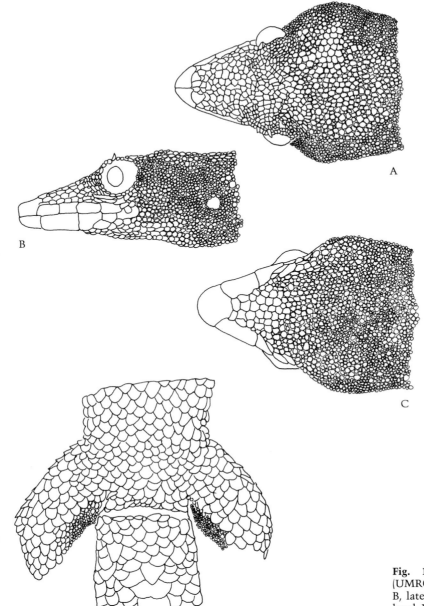

Fig. 115. *Sphaerodactylus argus* (UMRC 78-63), 25 mm SVL. A, dorsal; B, lateral; and C, ventral views of the head. D, ventral view of the thighs and vent region; Río Lagartos, Yucatán, Mexico.

NATURAL HISTORY   This secretive gecko is common at several sites along the north coast of the Yucatán Peninsula, where it has been found beneath fallen palm fronds, boards, and other surface debris in and around human habitations. It has also been taken from under loose bark on trees and fence posts and, occasionally, on the sides of buildings. These lizards feed on a variety of small invertebrates, predominantly insects.

Sphaerodactylus argus is oviparous. The eggs may be deposited under almost any kind of surface debris, and they have also been found in bromeliads (A. Schwartz and Henderson, 1991:468). Presumably only a single egg is produced per clutch, as is the case with other members of the genus.

SUBSPECIES   Two subspecies are currently recognized: *S. a. andresensis*, of Isla San Andrés, and the nominate subspecies, which occurs throughout the remainder of the geographic range of the species.

The populations in Yucatán are referable to the nominate subspecies, *S. a. argus*.

ETYMOLOGY   The specific name, *argus*, is after Argos, a giant from Greek mythology with a hundred shining eyes, in reference to the ocelli on the dorsum of some specimens.

COMMENT   These lizards were probably introduced into Yucatán by human agency, for the species is known only from edificarian situations there. J. C. Lee (1980:57) applied the name *S. lineolatus* to the populations along the north coast of the peninsula, but Harris and Kluge (1984:47) showed that those populations are actually *S. argus* and that they constitute the first record of this species from the mainland of Middle America.

Harris and Kluge (1984) reviewed *S. argus* as part of their revision of the Middle American species of *Sphaerodactylus*. Thomas (1975) treated the West Indian populations of this species.

Locality Records Mexico: Yucatán: Dzilam Bravo (KU 157140), Las Coloradas (JCL sight record), Río Lagartos (KU 157109–39; UMRC 78-63, 80-40).

Sphaerodactylus glaucus Cope
(Fig. 290; Map 63)

Sphaerodactylus glaucus Cope, 1865:192. SYNTYPES: USNM 6572, MCZ 13570. TYPE LOCALITY: near Mérida, Yucatán, Mexico.

Escorpión (Belize, Guatemala, Mexico); bota la cola, cuida casita, gequillo collarejo, piconé, tira la cola (Mexico); uyar tzotzok (Lacandón Maya).

DESCRIPTION   This is a tiny lizard, but medium sized for a *Sphaerodactylus*. The maximum snout-vent length for females is about 30 mm, for males about 29 mm. The head is distinct from the neck and slightly narrower than the body (Fig. 290). The eye is covered by a transparent spectacle, and the pupil is subcircular. The limbs are short and stocky, and the terminal lamella on each digit is expanded, resulting in lateral displacement of the claw. The undamaged tail is approximately as long as the head and body. The head and chin are covered with small granular scales, and there is a small ocular spine present over the eye. The scales on the dorsal surfaces of the body are flat, smooth, and imbricate, as are those on the venter, which are larger than the dorsals. This is the only *Sphaerodactylus* in the Yu-

catán Peninsula with smooth dorsal scales. The supracaudal scales are smooth and strongly imbricate; the subcaudal scales are also smooth, and the scales of the median subcaudal row are enlarged.

The color pattern of *S. glaucus* is highly variable. The ground color is generally tan or gray, sometimes with a brick reddish cast, and with fine or coarse dark spotting. There may be one or two dark collar bands, a dark nuchal spot, or a pair of nuchal ocelli. Paired ocelli are often present at the base of the tail, which frequently bears alternating light and dark rings, especially distally. The limbs often bear light or dark spots.

SIMILAR SPECIES   The other two species of *Sphaerodactylus* in the Yucatán Peninsula, *S. argus* and *S. millepunctatus*, have keeled dorsal scales.

DISTRIBUTION   This species occurs from Veracruz on the Atlantic slope and Oaxaca on the Pacific slope east through northern Guatemala to western Honduras. It probably occurs throughout the Yucatán Peninsula, although it is apparently unrecorded from the interior of the Mexican portion of the peninsula (Map 63).

NATURAL HISTORY   This secretive gecko occurs in virtually all peninsular habitats. Specimens are commonly encountered beneath surface debris associated with human habitations, beneath fallen palm fronds in coastal localities, and in forests under loose bark on standing trees and fallen logs. They are

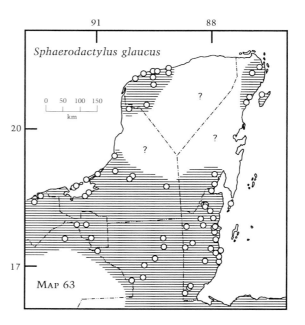

MAP 63

especially abundant in and around thatched houses. Like *S. argus* these tiny, inoffensive animals are greatly feared by many residents of the Yucatán Peninsula, who often refer to them as *escorpiones*.

Sphaerodactylus glaucus is oviparous, with a single egg produced per clutch. In Belize, W. T. Neill and Allen (1959c:33) collected an egg on 14 July that hatched on 18 August. In Tabasco, on 13 May, H. M. Smith (1949:34) found many adults and eggs under loose bark, indicating that these geckos nest communally.

ETYMOLOGY The specific name, *glaucus*, is from the Greek *glaukos*, meaning "silvery," "gleaming," "bluish green," or "gray."

COMMENT Harris and Kluge (1984) treated the biosystematics of *S. glaucus* as part of their review of the *Sphaerodactylus* of Middle America.

Locality Records Belize: Belize: Altun Ha (KU 171411), 14 mi ESE Belize City (CM 105695), Burrell Boom Rd., 3 mi W Northern Hwy. (CM 105793–95), bet. Ladyville and Sandhill (CM 90919–20), Lemonal Village (MPM 7503), Manatee (FMNH 5827), 1.5 mi N Stanley Airport (W. T. Neill and Allen, 1959c:33); Cayo: Ontario Village (= mi 59.5 on Western Hwy.) (CM 105991), Xunantunich (MCZ 61075, 61077); Corozal: Ambergris Cay, 22.5 km N, 14.5 km E San Pedro (CM 91110), S edge Corozal Town (JLK 410); Orange Walk: Gallon Jug (MCZ 71361), Lamanai (ROM H12709, H12715–21), Otro Benque (USNM 194119–20, 194949), Orange Walk Town (USNM 235737), Yo Creek (MPM 7611); Stann Creek: All Pines (CM 8493), Citrus Research Station (MPM 7504), E slope Cockscomb Mts. (CM 8484), Dangriga (RWV photo), Middlesex (UCM), Silk Grass (FMNH 49121), Stann Creek (Schmidt, 1941:489), 7 mi W, 1 mi S Stann Creek (JLK 411); Toledo: Blue Creek Cave (UMMZ 185918), Columbia Forest Reserve (MPM 8242), Dolores (JCL sight record); no specific locality (USNM 31338, 167761). *Guatemala*: El Petén: Altar de Sacrificios (AMNH 99901), Flores (UMMZ 79084–85), near La Libertad (UMMZ 75464), Piedras Negras (USNM 113085), Sayaxché (UCM 22196), Tikal (AMNH uncat.; UF 13498–500, 13695–700; UIMNH 52527; UMMZ 117874), Uaxactún (UMMZ 70447–50), no specific locality (USNM 25108–110). *Mexico*: Campeche: Apazote (USNM 47796), Balchacaj (FMNH 113487–504, 113506–9, 113511–17, 113519–22, 113524–34, 113537–39, 191033; UIMNH 19667–83; UMMZ 81926), Champotón (IHNHERP 507), Chuina, 46 km S Champotón (KU 74847), Ciudad del Carmen (FMNH 113505; UCM 20543–44; UIMNH 19684–86), 6 mi NNE Ciudad del Carmen (UIMNH 86922), Isla Aguada (UF uncat.), Los Coyos S of Isla Aguada across Laguna de Términos (UF uncat.), Ruinas Becan (KU 171412), near Sabancuy (JCL photo), Tankuche–El Remate (IHNHERP 500–502, 506), Tuxpeña Camp (UMMZ 73233); Chiapas: Palenque (EAL 2898); Quintana Roo: Akumal (Himmelstein, 1980:27), Lake Bacalar (LSUMZ 34775–76, 47712), Chetumal (USNM 194952), Cozumel (FMNH 153463), Cozumel, Cozumel (UMMZ 84352), 10 mi S Playa del Carmen (LSUMZ 47711, 47724), 4 km WSW Puerto Juárez (KU 70057), 35 km WSW Puerto Juárez (LSUMZ 28266); Tabasco: Balancán (MCZ 46200), Emiliano Zapata (EAL 3330; USNM 113095), Frontera (USNM 46694), 7 mi SW Frontera (UIMNH 86918–21), Tenosique (USNM 113087–95); Yucatán: Calcehtok (AMNH 38948–49), Dzibilchaltún (FMNH 153460), Mérida (CM 44462; FMNH 153437; MCZ 13570), Progreso (FMNH 113518, 113523, 113535–36, 113540), 2 mi E Progreso (TU 19500), Sisal (UMRC 80-41), 16.1 mi NE Sisal (KU 157142–46), Telchac (KU 157147), Telchac Puerto (JCL sight record).

Sphaerodactylus millepunctatus Hallowell (Map 64)

Sphaerodactylus millepunctatus Hallowell 1861: 480. SYNTYPES: USNM 6057a, 6057b, now lost; NEOTYPE designated by Harris and Kluge (1984:18): USNM 173053. TYPE LOCALITY: restricted by neotype designation to Río San Juan, Isla Mancarrón, Nicaragua (Harris and Kluge, 1984:17).

Spotted gecko; cuida casita, gequillo, piconé (Mexico).

DESCRIPTION The adults of this medium-sized sphaerodactyl range from about 24 to 31 mm in snout-vent length. The head is distinct from the neck and slightly narrower than the body. The snout is rather narrow and pointed in dorsal aspect. The eyes are large, protruding, and covered by a transparent spectacle. The pupils are subcircular. The undamaged tail is approximately as long as the head and body. The limbs are short and stocky, and the terminal lamella on each digit is expanded, resulting in lateral displacement of the claw. The head, chin, and dorsum are covered with small, granular, keeled scales, and there is a small ocular spine above the eye. The ventral scales are keeled and much larger than the dorsals. There is an enlarged median row of subcaudal scales.

Coloration is variable. The juveniles are light brown with a series of darker bands or paired crescents in the suprapectoral area, a dark suprapelvic spot, and dark bands on the distal portion of the tail. The adults are usually tan with numerous small dark and light spots.

SIMILAR SPECIES *Sphaerodactylus glaucus* has smooth dorsal scales, and *S. argus* is dark with longitudinal light lines or series of ocelli. *Sphaerodactylus millepunctatus* has more dorsal scales in the axilla-groin length than *S. argus* (47–74 vs. 38–50).

DISTRIBUTION The spotted gecko occurs at low elevations on the Atlantic slope from Oaxaca and on the Pacific slope from Nicaragua, south to northern Costa Rica. In the Yucatán Peninsula it is nearly restricted to the base of the peninsula, where it occurs in Chiapas, El Petén, and Belize. It is also known from Isla Cozumel, Quintana Roo (Map 64).

NATURAL HISTORY This secretive lizard is usually a forest dweller. Specimens have been found under surface debris and beneath loose bark on trees. However, Stuart (1958:20) found spotted geckos fairly common at Tikal, El Petén, mostly in the thatched roofs of houses.

Like other sphaerodactyls, this species is oviparous. Presumably a single egg is produced per clutch.

ETYMOLOGY The specific name, *millepunctatus*, is from the Latin *mille*, "thousand," and *punc-*

tatus, "spotted," in reference to the spotted pattern of many adults.

COMMENT The Yucatecan *Sphaerodactylus* with keeled dorsal scales were long known as *S. lineolatus*, but Harris and Kluge (1984:14) demonstrated that that name properly applies to lizards from lower Central America and Colombia, and that *S. millepunctatus* is the proper name for this form.

Locality Records Belize: Belize: Belize (Schmidt, 1941:489), 30.5 mi ESE Belize City (CM 109019–21), Burrell Boom Rd. at Belize River (CM 105796–98), Manatee (FMNH 4261); Cayo: Doyle's Delight (UMRC 89-45); Stann Creek: All Pines (Schmidt, 1941:489), E slope Cockscomb Mts. (CM 8484); no specific locality (FMNH 217114–18—part of 4261). *Guatemala*: El Petén: 15 km NW Chinajá (KU 59788), 1 mi W Ruinas Seibal (KU 157141), Piedras Negras (USNM 113084), Pueblo Nuevo S Flores (UMMZ 79083), Tikal (UMMZ 117873), Toocog (KU 55868), Uaxactún (MCZ 24497–500; UMMZ 70444–46). *Mexico*: Chiapas: Palenque (LACM 65133); Quintana Roo: Felipe Carrillo Puerto (MZFC 3497), Isla Cozumel (FMNH 153463; USNM 47644), Isla Cozumel, Punta Norte (MCZ 149565), Cozumel, San Miguel (UCM 16188–90; UMMZ 78564).

Genus *Aristelliger*

This genus of large and robust geckos is essentially West Indian in distribution. Of the six living species of *Aristelliger* presently recognized (Bauer and Russell, 1993a; Kluge, 1991:3), only one occurs in the Yucatán Peninsula. These are nocturnal and predominantly arboreal lizards. Their expanded subdigital lamellae are undivided, in contrast with those of the other large arboreal geckos in the Yucatán Peninsula (Fig. 114F). One or more digits on the hands and feet bear asymmetrical distal lamellae. Hecht (1947) provided a comprehensive treatment of the genus, studied the distribution of the living and fossil members (Hecht, 1951), and analyzed natural selection in scale characters of some *Aristelliger* species (Hecht, 1952). The most recent summary of information on *Aristelliger* is Bauer and Russell, 1993a. *Aristelliger* is derived from the Greek *ari-* a prefix denoting "excellence" or "goodness," and *stelliger*, Latin for "star bearing," possibly in reference to the punctate pattern of light dots on the head and dorsum of some species.

Map showing distribution of *Sphaerodactylus millepunctatus*. Scale bar: 0, 50, 100, 150 km. Latitude markers: 20, 17. Longitude markers: 91, 88. MAP 64

Aristelliger georgeensis (Bocourt)
(Figs. 114F, 291, 292; Map 65)

Idiodactylus georgeensis Bocourt, 1873:41. SYN-TYPES: MNHNP 2442 (four syntypes). TYPE LOCAL-ITY: l'île Saint-Georges, située à quelques milles de Belize (St. George Island, near Belize City, Belize).

St. George Island gecko; weatherman (Belize); escorpión, salamanquesa (Mexico).

DESCRIPTION *Aristelliger georgeensis* is a large, robust gecko. The males attain a snout-vent length of about 115 mm; the females are substantially smaller, reaching a maximum length of about 97 mm (Fig. 291). The eyes are covered by a transparent spectacle, the pupils are vertically elliptical with unscalloped margins, and the irises are coppery brown (Fig. 292). A small ocular spine is present over the eye. The head, chin, and dorsum are covered with small, weakly keeled granular scales. The scales on the venter are larger, smooth, and imbricate. There is a median row of enlarged subcaudals. The subdigital lamellae of digits 2–5 are expanded and undivided (Fig. 114F). On digit 1 the distalmost lamella adjacent to the claw is expanded, producing an asymmetry.

At night the dorsal coloration is gray, greenish gray, or tan, with indistinct darker markings. When brought into the light and during the day, the dorsal ground color is rich chocolate brown. The dorsal and lateral surfaces of the head are peppered with light bluish gray dots that extend posteriorly on the lateral surfaces of the body and become larger, forming a cream reticulum. The sutures of the labial scales bear distinct bluish gray spots. The dorsal surfaces of the appendages are covered with cream or gray spots against a brown background. The venter is a uniform yellowish cream, and the throat is darker with a few scattered light spots.

SIMILAR SPECIES *Aristelliger* is easily distinguished from the two species of *Hemidactylus* in the Yucatán Peninsula, from *Thecadactylus*, and from *Phyllodactylus* by its expanded but undivided subdigital lamellae (Fig. 114F).

DISTRIBUTION This Caribbean form occurs on Isla de Providencia, Isla Santa Catalina, and Isla San Andrés, and on Cayo Vivorillo, Honduras. In the Yucatán Peninsula it is known from numerous insular localities off the coast of Quintana Roo and

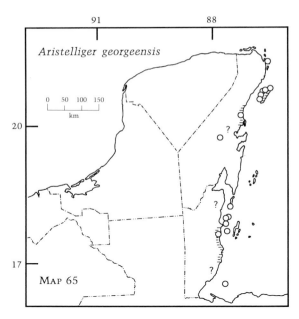

Belize and from a few scattered spots on the mainland coast (see Comment). Flores et al. (1991:93) recorded a specimen from Isla de la Concepción, Chiapas, but this record requires confirmation (Map 65).

NATURAL HISTORY These arboreal geckos are largely nocturnal. Specimens have been found at night on the trunks of coconut palms. During the day they can be found beneath surface debris at the base of palm trees. On many of the islands and cays off the coast of Quintana Roo and Belize this species is essentially a human commensal. On Cay Corker, for example, virtually every house has at least one *Aristelliger*, and they are common at night on the sides of houses near lights. At San Miguel on Isla Cozumel they are abundant on cinder-block walls, especially those with numerous crevices and holes. Himmelstein (1980:26) reported collecting a specimen during the day from a subterranean chamber in the Maya ruin at Chunyaxché.

Aristelliger georgeensis feeds on a variety of invertebrates and, apparently, other lizards. I found ants and beetles in the stomachs of specimens from Isla Cozumel, and several authors noted that *A. georgeensis* consumes anoline lizards (Dunn and Saxe, 1950:150; A. Schwartz and Henderson, 1991:362).

Like many other species of geckos, *A. georgeensis* produces a vocalization that has been described as a screech (A. Schwartz and Henderson, 1991:362) or a low chirp (Duellman, 1965a:593).

Aristelliger georgeensis is oviparous. Females collected on Cozumel in October contained enlarged ovarian follicles.

ETYMOLOGY   The specific name, *georgeensis*, is a toponym that refers to the type locality, St. George's Cay, approximately 15 km east-northeast of Belize City.

COMMENT   The interior record from Felipe Carrillo Puerto, Quintana Roo (UMMZ 113606), is anomalous, for this form is otherwise strictly insular or coastal, and subsequent intensive collecting in the Felipe Carrillo Puerto area by many herpetologists has failed to yield additional specimens. For many years the town of Felipe Carrillo Puerto was connected by narrow-gauge railroad to Vigía Chico, a small settlement on the coast at Bahía de la Ascensión, and I suggest that the specimen in question was transported from the coast to the interior through human agency.
Aristelliger georgeensis was reviewed by Bauer and Russell (1993b).

Locality Records Belize: Belize: Ambergris Cay, San Pedro (MPM 7793–95), Cay Bokel (MPM 7500–1), Cay Corker (MPM 8047–48), English Cay (MPM 7502), Manatee (FMNH 5628–29), Saint George's Cay (MNHNP 2442), Tom Owen Cay (FMNH 4451–52), S Water Cay (RWV photo). *Mexico*: Quintana Roo: Chunyaxché (Himmelstein, 1980:26), Cozumel (MCZ 67406; UF uncat.; UMMZ 84351, 148117), Cozumel, Punta Norte (MCZ 167271), N end Cozumel (KU 71761), Cozumel, San Miguel (CM 55813; UCM 16179–85; UMMZ 78557, 78559–61), Cozumel, 2.5 km N San Miguel (KU 70039), Cozumel, 3 km N San Miguel (KU 228744; UCM 12437–43), Cozumel, 3.5 km N San Miguel (KU 70038, 70040–43), Cozumel, 4 km S San Miguel (KU 228745–46), Cozumel, 8 km NE San Miguel (KU 228747), Cozumel, 18 km S San Miguel (KU 228748), Felipe Carrillo Puerto (UMMZ 113606), Isla Mujeres (UCM 16159–78), N end Isla Mujeres (KU 70027–37).

Genus *Hemidactylus*

This is a large genus of predominantly Old World geckos, several of which have been introduced and become widely distributed in the New World. Seventy-four species are currently recognized (Kluge, 1991:13–16). Two species occur in the Yucatán Peninsula. Both were introduced through human activities and remain closely tied to human habitations. *Hemidactylus* is from the Greek prefix *hemi-*, "half," and *daktylos*, "finger" or "toe," in reference to the divided subdigital lamellae.

Key to the Species of the Genus *Hemidactylus*

Dorsum with numerous keeled tuberculate scales . . . . *Hemidactylus turcicus*
Dorsum granular, with few tuberculate scales . . . . *Hemidactylus frenatus*

Clave para las Especies del Género *Hemidactylus*

Dorso con numerosas escamas tuberculadas quilladas . . . . *Hemidactylus turcicus*
Dorso granular, con pocas escamas tuberculadas . . . . *Hemidactylus frenatus*

Hemidactylus frenatus Schlegel
(Figs. 116, 293; Map 66)

Hemidactylus frenatus Schlegel, 1836:366, in A. M. C. Duméril and Bibron, 1836. HOLOTYPE: MNHNP 5135. TYPE LOCALITY: Java and Timor; restricted to Java by Loveridge (1947:127).

House gecko; cuija, escorpión (Mexico).

DESCRIPTION   Adult house geckos average 40 to 50 mm in snout-vent length. The undamaged tail is slightly longer than the head and body (Fig. 293). The eyes are covered by a transparent spectacle, and the pupils are vertically elliptical and have serrated edges. The head, chin, and body are covered with small granular scales, scattered among which are a few enlarged scales, some of which may be weakly keeled. The ventral scales are smooth, imbricate, and much larger than the granular dorsal scales. There is a median row of enlarged subcaudals. The lateral and dorsal surfaces of the tail are covered with small flat scales interrupted by whorls of enlarged, pointed tubercles, usually six per whorl. The whorls are separated by interwhorls of about eight rows of smooth, flat scales. Males have an unbroken series of approximately 30 femoral and preanal pores. The subdigital lamellae are expanded and divided.

The dorsum is light gray, tan, or brown with scattered small, dark spots. An indistinct dark stripe may extend from the eye, over the shoulder, onto the flanks, and along the lateral surface of the tail. The venter is pale cream or light tan and is devoid of pattern. At night, when these lizards are active, their color is much lighter than it is during the day.

SIMILAR SPECIES *Hemidactylus frenatus* differs from *H. turcicus* in possessing only a few smooth or weakly keeled dorsal tubercles scattered among the granular scales. *Phyllodactylus tuberculosus* and *P. insularis* have only a single pair of expanded subdigital lamellae (Fig. 114A).

DISTRIBUTION This species is widespread throughout the Old World tropics and subtropics and is discontinuously distributed in Middle America. In Mexico it is known from Guerrero, Veracruz, northern Chiapas, southwestern Campeche, Yucatán, and Quintana Roo. The distribution in the Yucatán Peninsula is highly discontinuous, reflecting

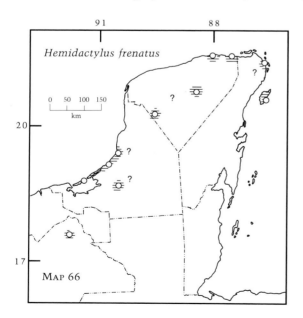

MAP 66

the house gecko's close association with humans and its tendency to be transported through human agency (Map 66).

NATURAL HISTORY As its common English name suggests, this species is closely tied to human habitations. It is currently expanding its range in the Yucatán Peninsula, where it is abundant at several localities. These nocturnal lizards often congregate on the walls of buildings near lights to capture their insect prey. During the day specimens have been found beneath surface debris and under loose bark on trees.

Hemidactylus frenatus is oviparous, with two eggs produced per clutch. In Java, Church (1962:262) found house geckos reproductively active throughout the year, although other herpetologists have found some suggestion of seasonality in reproductive activity farther to the north (Fukada, 1965:75). Church (1962:262) suggested the possibility of sperm storage in this species, and Murphy-Walker (1993) confirmed it by showing that females in Hawaii stored sperm for up to eight months, and that females isolated from males could produce as many as ten viable clutches.

Like many other geckos, these lizards are capable of vocalization. Marcellini (1974) studied acoustic behavior in San Luis Potosí and identified three functionally and bioacoustically distinct calls. The multiple chirp call, a *gack-gack-gack* suggestive of the barking of a small dog, was by far the most frequent. The call was given by both sexes, but most commonly by males and only by animals 45 mm or longer in snout-vent length. The call was usually given in aggressive interactions, and the number of chirps given increased as the air temperature increased. My analyses of recordings from Uxmal, Yucatán, indicate that acoustic energy is spread broadly across the frequency spectrum from about 2,000 to 5,000 Hz, with little harmonic structure (Fig. 116).

ETYMOLOGY The specific name, *frenatus*, is from the Latin *frenum*, "bridle" or "curb," and *-atus*, an adjectival suffix meaning "provided with"—thus "bridled."

COMMENT Although apparently unknown in the Yucatán Peninsula before 1980, house geckos are now abundant at several localities (Palenque, Chiapas; Escárcega and Sabancuy, Campeche; Punta Sam, Quintana Roo), and they are spreading rapidly

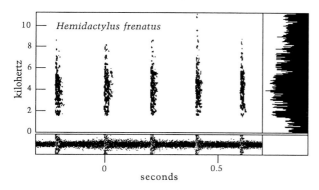

Fig. 116. Multiple chirp call of *Hemidactylus frenatus*, recorded 9 August 1992, Uxmal, Yucatán, Mexico.

throughout the northern portion of the peninsula, probably through human agency. In 1992 residents of Río Lagartos, on the northern coast of Yucatán, told me that they had first noticed house geckos approximately a year earlier.

Locality Records   Mexico: Campeche: Champotón (JCL sight record), 25 km NE Ciudad del Carmen (UMRC 80-42), Escárcega (UMRC 88-1), Sabancuy (JCL sight record), near Sabancuy (JCL sight record); Chiapas: Palenque (UMRC 91-21); Quintana Roo: 5 km N Puerto Juárez (JCL photo), Cozumel, Punta Chiqueros (JCL sight record); Yucatán: Chichén Itzá (JCL acoustic record), El Cuyo (JCL photo), Río Lagartos (JCL sight record), Uxmal (JCL acoustic record; JCL photo).

Hemidactylus turcicus (Linnaeus)
(Fig. 294; Map 67)

Lacerta turcica Linnaeus, 1758:202. TYPE: unknown, *fide* Smith and Taylor, 1950a:51. TYPE LOCALITY: Habitat in Oriente; restricted by Mertens and Müller (1940:24) to Turkey, and by H. M. Smith and Taylor (1950b:314) to Cairo, Egypt.

Mediterranean gecko; cuija, escorpión, geco pinto (Mexico).

DESCRIPTION   This is a medium-sized gecko with an average snout-vent length of 40 to 50 mm. The eyes are covered by a transparent spectacle, and the pupil is vertically elliptical. The dorsum is covered with small granular scales, embedded within which are 14 to 16 longitudinal rows of enlarged keeled tubercles (Fig. 294). There are 6 to 8 rows of keeled tubercles on the tail. The subdigital lamellae

are expanded and divided (Fig. 114D). The males have 3 to 10 preanal pores.

Coloration is somewhat variable but generally pale gray, pinkish tan, or brown, with numerous small, dark spots. The tubercles are usually whitish. These nocturnal lizards undergo a daily color change, being much lighter at night than during the period of daytime inactivity.

SIMILAR SPECIES   *Hemidactylus frenatus* lacks the rows of enlarged keeled tubercles characteristic of *H. turcicus*. Of the other tuberculate geckos in the Yucatán Peninsula, *Coleonyx elegans* has movable eyelids and sheathed claws, and *Phyllodactylus tuberculosus* and *P. insularis* have only the distal-most subdigital lamellae expanded (Fig. 114A).

DISTRIBUTION   *Hemidactylus turcicus* is widespread in the Mediterranean and the Middle East. In the New World it occurs throughout Florida and from central Texas and southern Louisiana south along the Gulf coast to Yucatán, where it is known from eastern Tabasco, northern Campeche, and northwestern Yucatán (Map 67).

NATURAL HISTORY   This common nocturnal gecko is essentially a human commensal. It feeds on invertebrates, especially insects (Saenz, 1993). Individuals are commonly seen at night on buildings, especially those with stone walls, and in Yucatán they seem especially partial to the walls of colonial period churches. During the day these lizards

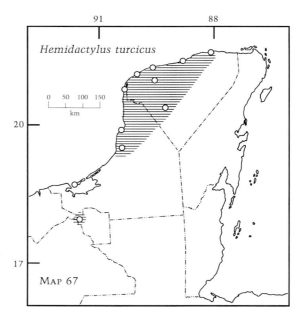

hide in the interstices of stone walls and beneath rocks, lumber, and other surface debris.

The Mediterranean gecko is oviparous. In Pakistan, hatchlings and females containing large eggs have been found in every month (Minton, 1966:85). In Texas, where this species has been introduced, breeding occurs over a four- or five-month period starting in March, and clutches of one or two eggs are laid beginning in April (Garrett and Barker, 1987:134).

ETYMOLOGY   The specific name, *turcicus*, is a toponym referring to Turkey, the probable type locality.

COMMENT   The restriction by H. M. Smith and Taylor (1950b:314) of the type locality to Cairo was rejected by W. T. Neill (1951:311) on the grounds that Linnaeus's selection of *turcicus* as the specific name clearly indicates the provenance of his material.

McCoy (1970a) summarized the available information on *H. turcicus*.

Locality Records   Mexico: Campeche: Campeche (UCM 18225–50, 45553–57), Ciudad del Carmen (CAS 14640–41; FMNH 106378–79, 106384, 106386,

110100, 110102, 110104–8, 110113, 110118–19, 110124–28, 110137, 110145, 112910, 112912; UIMNH 19584–94), San José Carpizo (UMMZ 99856); Tabasco: Emiliano Zapata (USNM 113034); Yucatán: Celestún (JCL photo; KU 157063–77), Dzilam Bravo (KU 157056–62), Mérida (UCM 18224, 39112), Oxkutzcab (KU 171407–10), Progreso (CAS 14639; FMNH 106377, 106380–83, 106385, 106387, 110101, 110103, 110109–12, 110114–17, 110120–23, 110129–36, 110138–44, 110146–49, 112906–9, 112911; MCZ 7039; UIMNH 19565–83), Río Lagartos (JCL photo), Sisal (JCL photo; KU 157078–83).

Genus *Phyllodactylus*
(Leaf-toed Geckos)

This genus of New World geckos comprises 56 species (Kluge, 1991:26–27), 2 of which occur in the Yucatán Peninsula. Leaf-toed geckos are distinguished from all other New World geckos by the terminal pair of subdigital lamellae, which are expanded to form two leaflike pads (Fig. 114A). *Phyllodactylus* comes from the Greek *phyllon*, "leaf," and *daktylos*, "finger" or "toe," in reference to the expanded terminal subdigital lamellae.

Key to the Species of the Genus *Phyllodactylus*

Sixteen or more longitudinal rows of enlarged dorsal tubercles; 30 or more enlarged paravertebral tubercles in axilla-groin length; insular only . . . . *Phyllodactylus insularis*

Fourteen or fewer longitudinal rows of enlarged dorsal tubercles; 22 or fewer enlarged paravertebral tubercles in axilla-groin length; insular and mainland . . . . *Phyllodactylus tuberculosus*

Clave para las Especies del Género *Phyllodactylus*

Dieciseis o más hileras longitudinales de tubérculos dorsales alargados; 30 o más tubérculos paravertebrales alargados entre la axila y la ingle; organismos unicamente insulares . . . . *Phyllodactylus insularis*

Catorce o menos hileras longitudinales de tubérculos dorsales alargados; 22 o menos tubérculos paravertebrales alargados entre la axila y la ingle; organismos insulares y continentales . . . . *Phyllodactylus tuberculosus*

Phyllodactylus insularis Dixon
(Fig. 295; Map 68)

Phyllodactylus insularis Dixon, 1960:9. HOLOTYPE: FMNH 34633. TYPE LOCALITY: Half Moon Cay, British Honduras.

Island leaf-toed gecko.

DESCRIPTION   The adults of this medium-sized gecko average between 55 and 65 mm in snout-vent length. The fragile, relatively short tail is approximately as long as the head and body. The head is moderately depressed and distinct from the neck (Fig. 295). The eyes are large and covered by a transparent spectacle, and the pupils are vertically elliptical with serrated edges. The limbs are slender, the hands and feet are pentadactyl, and the distalmost pair of subdigital lamellae is expanded to form a pair of terminal pads (Fig. 114A). There are 16 to 18 longitudinal rows of enlarged tubercles amid the small granular scales of the delicate skin on the dorsum. There are four enlarged postanal scales.

In specimens preserved in alcohol, the dorsal ground color is chocolate brown with indistinct undulating crossbands or spots of grayish white. In life these lizards undergo a diel color change. During the day they are dark grayish brown above with darker reticulations and light flecks. At night, when they are active, they become pale tan or gray with dark brown flecks. Generally a dark brown stripe extends from the snout, posteriorly through the eye, and onto the temporal region. The labial scales, the venter, and the ventral surfaces of the limbs and tail are yellowish cream. The iris is a metallic brown reticulum.

SIMILAR SPECIES *Phyllodactylus insularis* is very similar to *P. tuberculosus*, its presumed closest relative, which occurs on the mainland and on several cays off the coast of Belize, but differs in having smaller and more numerous dorsal tubercles, which are arranged in 16 to 18 longitudinal rows rather than 13 to 14 rows. *Phyllodactylus insularis* also has 30 or more paravertebral tubercles in the axilla-groin length rather than 22 or fewer.

DISTRIBUTION In the Yucatán Peninsula this species is known only from the type locality, a small cay at the southern end of Lighthouse Reef, approximately 72 km off the coast of central Belize. It can be expected to occur on other small cays on Lighthouse Reef and possibly in the nearby Turneffe Islands (Map 68). Dixon (1964) reported this species from the Bay Islands of Honduras, and Echternacht (1968:151) reported a specimen from Isla Guanaja, Honduras.

NATURAL HISTORY *Phyllodactylus insularis* is nocturnal. On the afternoon and evening of 23 August 1991, I found this species abundant on Half Moon Cay, Belize, beneath rocks at the bases of coconut palms and beneath logs. At night I found many individuals on the trunks of coconut palms

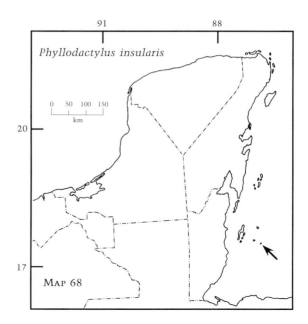

Phyllodactylus insularis

MAP 68

and on the ground amid fallen palm fronds. The bright reflection from their eyes rendered them very conspicuous in spite of their cryptic coloration. In general, subadults were found beneath surface objects, whereas adults were found almost exclusively on the trunks of palm trees, suggesting possible ecological segregation by age or size class.

These lizards presumably feed on small invertebrates, and captives readily accept a variety of insects. Nothing is known concerning reproduction. Presumably *P. insularis* is oviparous, as are other phyllodactyls.

ETYMOLOGY The specific name, *insularis*, is a Latin adjective meaning "of or belonging to an island; insular," in reference to the type locality.

Locality Records   Belize: Belize: Half Moon Cay (FMNH 34630–36; JCL photo).

Phyllodactylus tuberculosus Wiegmann (Fig. 296; Map 69)

Phyllodactylus tuberculosus Wiegmann, 1835: 241. SYNTYPES: ZMB 412 (two syntypes). TYPE LOCALITY: Californien; restricted by Dixon (1960:6) to the village of California, Nicaragua.

Leaf-toed gecko; mangrove gecko (Belize); cuija, escorpión, geco verrugoso, salamanquesa (Mexico).

DESCRIPTION The snout-vent length of *P. tuberculosus* adults averages between 55 and 65 mm (Fig.

296). The length of the relatively short tail is about equal to that of the head and body. The eyes are covered by a transparent spectacle, and the pupil is vertically elliptical with serrated edges. There is no ocular spine over the eye. The head and dorsum are covered with numerous keeled tubercles interspersed among small granular scales. The scales of the venter are smooth and imbricate. The dorsum of the undamaged tail is covered with keeled imbricate scales, and there is a median row of enlarged subcaudals. This species and its close relative, *P. insularis*, are unique among the geckos of the Yucatán Peninsula in having only the distalmost subdigital lamellae divided and conspicuously and abruptly enlarged (Fig. 114A).

These lizards are brown, tan, or gray above, with scattered small, dark brown spots and blotches. The venter and chin are immaculate yellowish cream or tan. The undamaged tail often has indistinct light and dark bands.

SIMILAR SPECIES *Phyllodactylus tuberculosus* is very similar to *P. insularis* but differs in possessing 22 or fewer paravertebral tubercles in the axilla-groin length rather than 30 or more, and in having 13 or 14 longitudinal rows of dorsal tubercles rather than the 16 to 18 found in *P. insularis*.

DISTRIBUTION This gecko occurs at low and moderate elevations from Sinaloa on the Pacific slope through western Guatemala to Costa Rica. In the Yucatán Peninsula it is known from several insular localities off the coast of Belize and from mainland coastal spots in Belize and Quintana Roo (Map 69).

NATURAL HISTORY This species is predominantly, though not invariably, nocturnal. J. R. Dixon (in litt.) observed diurnal activity within crevices in boulders and cliffs. Specimens have also been found in caves and beneath surface debris in forests. W. T. Neill and Allen (1959c:34) reported collecting specimens at night on a rotting log 2 miles west of Belize City, Belize. This species often occupies human habitations, where it hides by day in walls and thatch. Like many geckos, *P. tuberculosus* produces a vocalization. It has been described as sounding like a kiss (Alvarez del Toro, 1982:64).

Females with two oviductal eggs (one in each oviduct) and enlarged ovarian follicles were found in Sinaloa (Hoddenbach and Lannom, 1967:295), indicating that more than a single clutch is produced per season. At the Isthmus of Tehauntepec, Dixon (1964:104, 105) found females with mature oviductal eggs throughout the year, indicating continuous reproduction.

SUBSPECIES According to the most recent comprehensive treatment of this species (Dixon, 1964), *P. tuberculosus* exists as four subspecies, of which *P. t. ingeri* occurs along the east coast of the Yucatán Peninsula.

ETYMOLOGY The specific name, *tuberculosus*, is from the Latin *tubercul*, "tumor," "knob," or "hump," and *-osus*, a Latin suffix meaning "full of" or "rich in," presumably in reference to the abundant tubercles on the integument.

Locality Records Belize: Belize: Ambergris Cay, San Pedro (MPM 7796–98), Ambergris Cay, 22.5 km N, 14.5 km E San Pedro (CM 91111–12), Ambergris Cay, 5 km NNE San Pedro (CM 91125), Belize (FMNH 4449–50; KU 144921), 2 mi W Belize City (W. T. Neill and Allen, 1959c:34), small cay 5 mi E Belize City (USNM 306436), Cay Bokel (MPM 7499), Cay Corker (MPM 8049–50), Glover's Reef, Long Cay (UMMZ 145879), North River (Schmidt, 1941:490), North River Lagoon (USNM 52310), S Water Cay (RWV photo); Stann Creek: Rendezvous Cay (MCZ 66362), Stann Creek (Dixon, 1964:36). *Mexico*: Quintana Roo: Playa del Carmen (EAL 2864), Tulum (L. L. Grismer, pers. comm.).

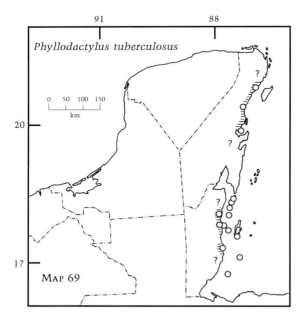

MAP 69

Genus *Thecadactylus*

The single species is widely distributed through tropical Mexico, Central America, the Lesser Antilles, and South America. *Thecadactylus* is derived from the Latin *thecatus*, "encased," and the Greek *dactylos*, "finger" or "toe," presumably in reference to the distal phalanges, which are surrounded by the expanded subdigital lamellae.

Thecadactylus rapicauda (Houttuyn)
(Figs. 114C, 297; Map 70)

Gekko rapicauda Houttuyn, 1782:322. HOLO-TYPE: originally in the private collection of Houttuyn; present location unknown, *fide* Stuart, 1963:58. TYPE LOCALITY: West Indies; restricted to Chichén Itzá, Yucatán, Mexico, by H. M. Smith and Taylor (1950b:352); rejected by Hoogmoed (1973:65), who restricted the type locality to Paramaribo, Surinam.

Turnip tail (Belize); escorpión (Guatemala, Mexico); geco patudo (Mexico).

DESCRIPTION This large gecko attains an average snout-vent length of about 90 to 100 mm. The undamaged tail is substantially shorter than the head and body and is constricted at its base. The tail is often grotesquely enlarged to accommodate stored fat, hence the common English name, "turnip tail." Postanal sacs and bones are present in some individuals (Hoogmoed, 1973:63). The head, chin, body, and dorsal surface of the tail are covered with small granular scales; the ventral scales are flat, smooth, imbricate, and larger than the dorsals. The eye is covered by a transparent spectacle, the pupil is vertically elliptical with scalloped edges, and one or two small ocular spines are present at the posterodorsal margin of the eye (Fig. 297). The proximal supracaudals are granular, becoming flattened posteriorly. The subcaudals are flat, juxtaposed, and about twice the size of the supracaudals. The subdigital lamellae are divided and greatly expanded. This is the only gekkonid in the Yucatán Peninsula with more than 12 divided subdigital lamellae on digit 4 of the hands and feet (Fig. 114C).

The dorsal ground color is brown, tan, or gray with a series of irregular dark blotches or bands, these sometimes arranged in the form of chevrons and extending onto the tail. Most specimens have a dark postocular stripe extending onto the shoulder. The labial scales are usually light tan, gray, or cream, and they contrast with the darker pigment on the lateral surfaces of the head. The chin and venter are light tan or gray, sometimes flecked, mottled, or suffused with darker pigment.

SIMILAR SPECIES *Aristelliger georgeensis* has undivided subdigital lamellae (Fig. 114F). The species of *Phyllodactylus* and *Hemidactylus* in the Yucatán Peninsula are smaller and have fewer than 12 divided subdigital lamellae on digit 4 of the hands and feet (Fig. 114A,D).

DISTRIBUTION *Thecadactylus rapicauda* occurs at low and moderate elevations from the Yucatán Peninsula into South America and the Lesser Antilles. Its distribution in the Yucatán Peninsula is discontinuous. The populations at the northern end of the peninsula are separated from those in Guatemala and Belize by a gap of several hundred kilometers (Map 70).

NATURAL HISTORY Turnip tails are primarily nocturnal and arboreal. By day they hide within the recesses of tree buttresses, beneath loose bark, and in the crevices of the stonework of Maya ruins. Maslin (1963a:7) reported that specimens were found in the thatch of dwellings in the vicinity of Chichén Itzá, Yucatán. Individuals in Surinam

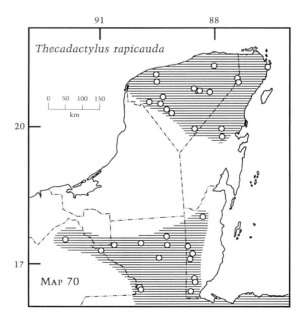

Thecadactylus rapicauda

0 50 100 150
km

MAP 70

were occasionally observed basking on tree trunks during the day (Hoogmoed, 1973:61), and Swanson (1945:212) found a specimen clinging to the wall of a building in Panama.

These carnivorous lizards feed on a wide variety of invertebrates, especially insects. Gaige (1938:297) reported snails, grasshoppers, and caterpillars in the stomachs of specimens from caves in western Yucatán. Stomach contents of lizards from Surinam included grasshoppers, cockroaches, beetles, termites, homopterans, caterpillars, and spiders (Hoogmoed, 1973:63). Duellman (1978:198) found that roaches formed 70 percent by volume of the stomach contents of lizards from the upper Amazon Basin of Ecuador; one specimen had consumed a scorpion.

Like many geckos, *T. rapicauda* is catlike and graceful in its movements. The soft skin is extremely delicate and easily damaged. Beebe (1944:157) described the vocalization of this species as "a high, rapidly reiterated chick-chick-chick or chack-chack-chack, fifteen or twenty times repeated, much like the note of some insect." M. L. Johnson (1946:108) described the vocalization emitted by a specimen from Trinidad as a batlike squeak. Very likely, the vocalizations help establish and maintain territories, although Beebe conjectured that the call might be used to attract the lizard's insect prey.

Thecadactylus rapicauda is oviparous. A single egg is produced per clutch. Beebe (1944:158) reported that a captive from British Guiana laid an egg in August, and Meyer (1966:174) reported that a female from northern Honduras contained a single egg on 1 July. Females with oviductal eggs have been found in May, June, and August in Amazonian Ecuador (Duellman, 1978:198).

ETYMOLOGY The specific name, *rapicauda*, is derived from the Latin *rapum*, "turnip," and *cauda*, "tail," in reference to the turniplike tail, which is often swollen with stored fat.

Locality Records Belize: Cayo: Thousand Foot Falls (CM 91010–11), Xunantunich (MCZ 61076, 66355); Orange Walk: Lamanai (ROM H12786); no specific locality (AMNH 46077); Toledo: Blue Creek (RWV photo), Crique Sarco (W. T. Neill and Allen, 1962:85), Gloria Camp, Columbia River Forest Reserve (USNM 319789). *Guatemala*: El Petén: 20 km NW Chinajá (KU 55865–66), 15 km NW Chinajá (KU 55867), El Repasto (UCM 22197), Flores (USNM 71411–12), Paso Caballos (FMNH 22212), Piedras Negras (USNM 113035–37), Tikal (AMNH uncat.; UF 13701–2; UMMZ 117872), Uaxactún (MCZ 24501, 38663). *Mexico*: Chiapas: 6.5 km SW Palenque (UTEP 12254); Quintana Roo: Cancún (MZCIQRO 42), Felipe Carrillo Puerto (UMMZ 133610), 10 mi N Felipe Carrillo Puerto (CAS 114057), Pueblo Nuevo X-Can (KU 70058), 1.5 km S, 1 km E Pueblo Nuevo X-Can (KU 70059); Yucatán: Chichén Itzá (FMNH 27298–99, 36453, 49109–12, 49114–17, 105185–88; KU 70061; LACM 114242; LSUMZ 28264–65, 28293–95, 28301; MCZ 7248, 18956–57; UIMNH 19664; UMMZ 68199, 68698–99, 76160, 80810–13, 83282–84, 83927; USNM 72743, 116709), Esmeralda (UMMZ 113550), Hacienda Chichén Itzá (UMMZ 72869), Dzibilchaltún (FMNH 153446–47, 153449, 153454), Grutas Balankanché (TCWC 57124), Mayapán (FMNH 40668–82), near Mérida (CM 93173), Oxkintok (AMNH 38860), Oxkutzcab (AMNH 38852; UMMZ 80792–94), Tekax (Gaige, 1938:297), Tekom (FMNH 49105–8), 6 mi N Tizimín (KU 74834–36), Xocempich (MCZ 52126), Yokat (AMNH 38853–59).

Family Corytophanidae

These distinctive Neotropical lizards range from southern Mexico south and eastward through Central America to northwestern South America. Corytophanids typically have laterally compressed bodies, long limbs and tails, and bony casques or integumentary crests on the occipital region. They are predominantly arboreal or semiarboreal inhabitants of lowland tropical forests. The family contains three genera, each of which is represented in the Yucatán Peninsula.

The three genera assigned to the family Corytophanidae were long known informally as "basiliscines" and placed within the family Iguanidae, but D. R. Frost and Etheridge (1989) partitioned the Iguanidae into several families and elevated the basiliscines to familial rank.

Key to the Genera of the Family Corytophanidae

1. Posterior region of skull not projecting backward as a horizontal casque; dorsal integumentary crest present on head (may be rudimentary in females) (Figs. 118–120) 2

Posterior region of skull projects backward as a horizontal casque (Figs. 121, 122A) . . . .
. . . . *Laemanctus*

2. Crest and gular flap serrated (Figs. 119, 120) . . . . *Corytophanes*
   Crest and gular flap smooth, not serrated (Fig. 118). . . . . *Basiliscus*

Clave para los Géneros de la Familia Corytophanidae

1. Región posterior del cráneo sin proyección como casco horizontal; cresta dorsal integumentaria presente en la cabeza (puede ser rudimentaria en las hembras) (Figs. 118–120)
   2
   Región posterior del cráneo proyectada hacia atrás como un casco horizontal (Figs. 121,122A)
   . . . . *Laemanctus*
2. Cresta y pliegue gular aserrados (Figs. 119, 120) . . . . *Corytophanes*
   Cresta y pliegue gular lisos, sin aserrar (Fig. 118) . . . . *Basiliscus*

Genus *Basiliscus* (Basilisks)

These medium-sized to large terrestrial or semiarboreal lizards are found in tropical America. The hind limbs are relatively large, and the tail is long and slender. The occipital region extends posteriorly and, in adult males, supports an integumentary crest. The genus occurs from Tamaulipas and Jalisco south and eastward through Central America to Ecuador, Venezuela, and Peru. There are four species of *Basiliscus*, but only one is found in the Yucatán Peninsula. *Basiliscus* is named after Basiliskos, a creature from Greek mythology with a crownlike crest, fiery breath, and a glance that could kill.

Basiliscus vittatus Wiegmann
(Figs. 117, 118, 298, 299; Map 71)

Basiliscus vittatus Wiegmann, 1828:373. SYN-TYPES: ZMB 549–51 (three syntypes, *fide* Taylor, 1969:iv). TYPE LOCALITY: Mexico; restricted by H. M. Smith and Taylor (1950b:351) to Veracruz, Veracruz, Mexico.

Striped basilisk; cock lizard, cock malakka (Belize); basilisco, basilisco rayado, pasarios, toloque, turipache (Mexico); torok (Lacandón Maya); tolok (Yucatec Maya).

DESCRIPTION The males of this large lizard average between 120 and 140 mm in snout-vent length; the females are substantially smaller. The hind limbs and digits are long and slender, and the scales bordering the subdigital lamellae of the toes

are enlarged, forming a fringe (Fig. 117). The exceptionally long, slender tail is nearly three times the length of the head and body. The head is relatively narrow, and the snout is pointed in dorsal aspect (Fig. 298). There is a distinct gular fold. Femoral pores are absent. The males possess a conspicuous integumentary crest; this is rudimentary in females and subadult males (Figs. 118, 298, 299). The scales on the appendages are imbricate and strongly keeled; those on the lateral surfaces of the body are smaller, more weakly keeled, and less heavily imbricate than those on the middorsal area. The ventrals are smooth or weakly keeled and conspicuously larger than the laterals. The scales of the

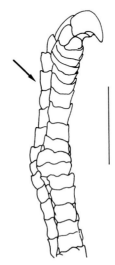

Fig. 117. Digit 3 of the foot of *Basiliscus vittatus* showing enlarged scales bordering the subdigital lamellae (*arrow*). Line equals 5 mm.

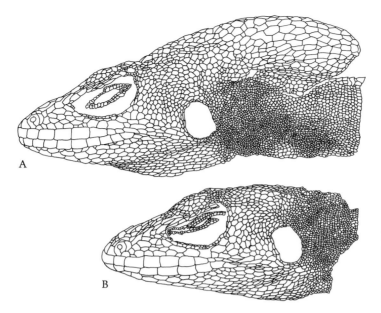

Fig. 118. Lateral views of the head of *Basiliscus vittatus*. A, male (UMRC 80-54), 126 mm SVL; Tizimín, Yucatán, Mexico. B, female (UMRC 80-4), 123 mm SVL; Uaxactún, El Petén, Guatemala.

vertebral row are enlarged and compressed laterally to produce a low crest that extends from the base of the head well onto the tail.

Striped basilisks are predominantly brown, olive brown, or tan above, with a series of about five dark brown or black bands that become indistinct posteriorly. The dorsal surfaces of the appendages are speckled or banded with dark pigment. A distinct yellow, yellow-green, or cream stripe extends from the posterior margin of the eye or the occipital region posteriorly along the dorsolateral surface of the body and becomes indistinct on the posterior third of the body. Another stripe originates on the side of the face, passes below the ear onto the neck, and terminates in the axillary region. The ventral surfaces of the body and appendages are light brown or gray, often mottled with dark markings. Adult males may have a suffusion of orange on the ventral surface of the body. In general, subadults are more brightly and distinctly patterned than older individuals, some of which may be very dark and nearly devoid of pattern.

SIMILAR SPECIES   The two species of *Corytophanes* in the Yucatán Peninsula have serrated crests and serrated gular flaps (Figs. 119, 120), whereas the crest of *B. vittatus* is smooth, and there is no serrated gular flap (Fig. 118). *Basiliscus* most closely resembles *Laemanctus*, but the two species of the latter genus have horizontal occipital casques (Figs. 121, 122A), are generally green, and lack the fringe of enlarged scales bordering the subdigital lamellae.

DISTRIBUTION   This species occurs at low and moderate elevations from Jalisco on the Pacific slope and Tamaulipas on the Atlantic slope, south and east through Central America to northern South America. In the Yucatán Peninsula *B. vittatus* is pan-peninsular (Map 71).

NATURAL HISTORY   *Basiliscus vittatus* is an abundant lizard in most habitats within the Yucatán Peninsula, especially areas adjacent to water. They are often seen darting across roads or scamper-

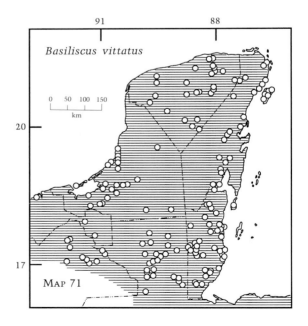

ing noisily through shrubbery or over the forest floor. Their long hind limbs enable basilisks to run very rapidly. At high speed the anterior portion of the body is elevated off the ground and the lizard becomes bipedal. The fringe of enlarged scales bordering the subdigital lamellae of the toes (Fig. 117) helps basilisks to run across the surface of water, a habit that has earned them the common Spanish names *pasarios* and *lagartija Jesu Cristo*. Laerm (1974) showed that juveniles can run faster on water than adults, and Hirth (1963) noted that Costa Rican juveniles are more partial to aquatic habitats than are adults.

These diurnal lizards are predominantly terrestrial, but they will ascend shrubs and small trees to a height of several meters. By day they are alert and wary, but at night they sleep perched conspicuously on vegetation and are vulnerable to capture. I removed a juvenile basilisk from the stomach of a nocturnal snake, *Imantodes cenchoa*, collected near Palenque, Chiapas. Gerhardt et al. (1993:350) reported that at Tikal this species is eaten by great black hawks, *Buteogallus urubitinga*.

Basilisks feed on a variety of invertebrates, especially insects. The juveniles are strictly carnivorous, whereas the adults also consume seeds, berries, and stems (Hirth, 1963).

Like other members of its genus, *B. vittatus* is oviparous. Stuart (1935:44) found a hatchling in El Petén in June, at the beginning of the rainy season; and Gaige (1936:296) collected a hatchling in Chichén Itzá, Yucatán, on 2 July. In Belize, W. T. Neill and Allen (1959c:37) found hatchlings abundant in July, whereas they had found none the previous April. Meyer (1966:175) reported clutches of six and seven eggs in females from northern Honduras collected on 23 June. According to Alvarez del Toro (1983:81), in Chiapas up to a dozen eggs are laid in April, May, or June and hatch during the rainy season. His estimate of clutch size seems high, however. Fitch (1970:27) examined a large series from throughout Central America and found gravid females in samples from February, March, April, June, July, and August, but none from September. The mean clutch size was 4.1, nearly identical to that determined by Hirth (1963:101) for lizards from Tortuguero, Costa Rica. His studies in the Atlantic lowlands of Costa Rica led Fitch (1973:92) to conclude that females become reproductive at about one year of age, and that at least four clutches of eggs are produced during the protracted breeding season at that locality.

ETYMOLOGY The specific name, *vittatus*, is Latin meaning "bound with a ribbon or strap." According to Lang (1989:122), the name refers to the crest carried by males, but more likely it refers to the distinct stripes on the side of the face.

COMMENT The available information on *B. vittatus* was summarized by Lang (1989) as part of his study of relationships among the basiliscines.

Locality Records Belize: Belize: Belize (CAS 39586; FMNH 4506, 4186, 4496–99, 4501–5, 4507–27, 49243–50; UMMZ 75043; USNM 24914–15, 26066, 26358, 51885–86, 56788–91), 2 mi NW Belize (UMMZ 75059), 3 mi W Belize (UMMZ 75041–42), 7.8 km W Belize City (CM 90966), 7 mi N Belize City (BCB 13591–92), 13.5 mi NW Belize City (KU 157291), 9 mi WSW Belize City (UF 73289), botanical station above Belize on river (FMNH 4528–29), 11 km SW Hattieville (CM 90907), Hummingbird Hershey Farm (CM 105829–30), bet. Ladyville and Sandhill (CM 90930, 90932, 90955–56), Lemonal (MPM 7692), Manatee (FMNH 6769–71, 218741–44), Maskalls (KU 157292), Missionary Lake Rd., 5.3 mi E jct. Northern Hwy. (CM 91056), 2.5 km S Sandhill (CM 105822); Cayo: Augustine (LSUMZ 11449; MCZ 71447; MPM 8199; UMMZ 80679; USNM 194955), Blancaneaux Lodge (CM 91009; JLK 419), Cayo (KU 144940; UMMZ 75056), 1 mi SW Cayo (UMMZ 124674), 4 mi SW Cayo (UMMZ 124675), 12 mi S Cayo (UMMZ 70425), Cocquercot (UMMZ 75057–58), Central Farm (MCZ 71415–16; MPM 7536), Chaa Creek (CM 105972), Georgetown (CM 90995–97), ca. 3 mi S Georgetown (CM 91054), 1.1 mi S Georgeville (KU 157286), 18.1 mi S Georgeville (KU 157283), 31.5 mi S Georgeville (KU 157284), Pine Ridge Rd., 36 mi S Western Hwy. (UMMZ 124672–73), Río On (KU 157285), 1 mi W San Ignacio (USNM 71374), upper Raspaculo River basin (Stafford, 1991:14), Xunantunich (MCZ 71448); Corozal: Ambergris Cay, 4.5 km N, 1 km E San Pedro (CM 91109), Ambergris Cay, 5 km NNE San Pedro (CM 91126), S edge Corozal Town (KU 157293–94); Orange Walk: Gallon Jug (MCZ 71417–46), Kate's Lagoon (FMNH 49258–61), Lamanai (ROM H12734–36, H12759), 20 mi SE Orange Walk Town (BCB 13590), Otro Benque (MPM 7537), Tower Hill (USNM 194086, 194935); Stann Creek: All Pines (CM 8491–92, 8494), Bokowina (FMNH 49251), Dangriga (RWV photo), Freetown (CM 8497–500, 8502–10), Mango Creek (MCZ 71458–63), 3 mi S, 14 mi W Mango Creek (LSUMZ 10291), Middlesex (FMNH 4530–31), 5.7 mi S Silk Grass (KU 157288–89), Southern Hwy. 10 mi SW Hummingbird Hwy. (UMMZ 124676), 0.3 mi NNW jct. Southern Hwy. and Hummingbird Hwy. (KU 157290), Stann Creek (FMNH 4532–35; KU 144941), 2 mi S Stann Creek (KU 157287; LSUMZ 11448), 17 mi W Stann Creek (JLK 418), Stann Creek Valley (FMNH 49252–57); Toledo: ca. 2 mi SE Big Falls, Río Grande (CM 105892, 105897), Bladen Branch of Monkey River (CM 105901), Blue Creek Village (UTA R-11058–61), Columbia Forestry Camp (USNM 243392), 28.2 mi NE Golden Stream (KU 157295), Medina Camp (MPM 7640–41), 1 mi W Salamanca (CM 105845–46, 105866), Monkey River, E Swazey Bridge (MCZ 71453–57), San Antonio (MCZ 71464–65; MPM 8264–66), ca. 4 mi S Swazey Bridge (CM 105934), 3 mi S Waha Leaf Creek (MCZ 71449–52); no specific locality (USNM 10289). *Guatemala*: El Petén: 4 km N Chinajá (KU 59592), 6 mi N Chuntuquí (USNM 71381), Desempeña (USNM 113498), El Paso (MCZ 38640, 38642; UMMZ 79068), Flores (UMMZ 79067; USNM 71410), near Flores (AMNH 72619–20), Lago Petén Itzá (AMNH 72627), Lago Petén Itzá, 3.6 mi W rd. to Tikal (KU 157315–16), Laguneta Ixcoche (AMNH 99911–12), La Libertad (USNM 71414), near La Libertad (UMMZ 75047–49, 75072–77), Las Cañas (CM 58239–54), Pacomon (USNM 71389), Paso Caballos (FMNH 21682), Piedras Negras (FMNH 115808, 115810, 115813, 115817, 115820–22, 115824–27, 115829, 115831–32, 115838–41, 124210–15, 171953–68; UIMNH 11581–627, 11752; USNM 113492–97), 5 mi S Piedras Negras (USNM 113499), Poptún (UMMZ 124344), near Poptún (UMMZ 117856–57), 4 mi N Poptún (KU 157306–9), 12.1 mi NW Poptún (KU 157310), Remate (UMMZ 75044–46, 75050, 75061, 75066, 75069–70; USNM 71430), 6.1 mi N Río de la Pasión (KU 157311), Sacluc (USNM 25111–14), San Andrés (UMMZ 75065), 2 km E Santa Elena (UMMZ 124345), Santa Rita (USNM 71386), Santa Teresa (UMMZ 75052–53, 75064), Sayaxché (KU 55795–97; UCM 22245–63), bet. Sayaxché and Subín (KU 57154), Seibal (AMNH 72610), 1 mi W Ruinas Seibal (KU 157312–14), Slaughter Island, in Lake Petén (USNM 71396–401), Tikal (UF 24577), Toocog (KU 59593), Tayasal (= Flores) (UMMZ 79066), Uaxactún (KU 157296–305; UMRC 78-54, 80-4), Yaxhá (UMMZ 75060), Zotz (UMMZ 75054); no specific locality (USNM 71806–14, 71952–53. *Mexico*: Campeche: Aguada Mocu (FMNH 36501), Balchacaj (FMNH 105828–29, 105833, 116417; UIMNH 20279–81), N of Carmen (MCZ 67407), 5 mi N Champotón (UCM 16193–95), Champotón (UMMZ 72980–73002), 3 mi S Champotón (UCM 29887), 11 km S Champotón (KU 70156), 6 km S Champotón (KU 70157), 5 km S Champotón (KU 70158–69), 13.5 mi SW Champotón (UCM 39136), 23 mi SW Champotón (BCB 13589), 41.1 mi S Champotón (UCM 18256), Chuina 46 km S Champotón (KU 74887–89), Ciudad del Carmen (UMMZ 83536), Dzibalchén (KU 75509–12), 69.3 mi NE Emiliano Zapata (EAL 1649), 79.9 km NE Emiliano Zapata (EAL 2917), Encarnación (FMNH 116406, 116408, 116410, 116412–16, 116419–28; UIMNH 20268–77),

5 mi W Escárcega (UCM 28570–72; UMMZ 123016), 7.5 km W Escárcega (KU 70170–72), 19.9 mi E Escárcega (KU 157317), 25 mi S Escárcega (UCM 28567–69), Laguna Alvarado, 65 km S Xpujil (KU 74894), Laguna Chumpich (KU 74883–86), Laguna Silvituc (FMNH 36490; KU 74890–93), Matamoros (FMNH 36419, 36502–4), Pacaitún (FMNH 36492–94), Pital (UIMNH 20278), 6 mi NE Sabancuy (UCM 39140), 24 mi E Sabancuy (UCM 39137–39), 24.7 mi NE Sabancuy (LACM 61911), Tres Brazos (FMNH 105827, 105831–32, 116407, 116418, 116429–31; UIMNH 20282–84), 3.8 mi S jct. Hwys 186 and 261 (KU 157318); Chiapas: bet. El Censo and Monte Libano (MCZ 53898), 42.1 km SE La Arena on rd. to Bonampak (KU 171521–22), Laguna Ocotal (MCZ 53867–71), Monte Libano (MCZ 53850), 7 km NW Ocosingo (UTEP 4697), Palenque, San Juancito (USNM 113483), Palenque (EAL 2897, 3337; FMNH 115807, 115816, 124219, 124221; USNM 113484–85), vicinity Palenque (LSUMZ 32967), 1 mi S Palenque (KU 94053–54), 3.8 mi SW Palenque (TCWC 58688), 10 to 15 mi S Palenque (LSUMZ 32972–79), Palenque ruins (EAL 2899; UIMNH 11330–38); Quintana Roo: 4.9 mi N Bacalar (KU 157319), Lake Bacalar (LSUMZ 32968–71), Chetumal (FMNH 49262), 6 mi W, 1 mi S Chetumal (UCM 28605), 82 km N Chetumal (UCM 39141), Chunyaxché (Himmelstein, 1980:27; MZFC 3396), Cobá (FMNH 27288–89), Cozumel (CM 27573; Himmelstein, 1980:27; MCZ 67407; UMMZ 78624), Cozumel, San Miguel (UCM 16202–8; UMMZ 78625–26), Cozumel, 2 km N San Miguel (UCM 12447–48), Cozumel, 3 km N San Miguel (UCM 12444–46), Cozumel, 3.5 km N San Miguel (KU 70185–89), Cozumel, 4 km N San Miguel (UCM 12449–50), Cozumel, 6 mi N San Miguel (UMMZ 78627), Cozumel, 3 mi S San Miguel (UMMZ 78628), Cozumel, 9 km S San Miguel (UCM 16209–11), Cozumel, 9 km SE San Miguel (UCM 12451–53), Cozumel, 10 km SW San Miguel (CM 40017), Cozumel, 2 km E San Miguel (UCM 20547), 4 km NNE Felipe Carrillo Puerto (KU 70180–82), 8.5 km NNE Felipe Carrillo Puerto (KU 70183), 1.6 mi S Felipe Carrillo Puerto (KU 157321), La Unión, rd. to Río Hondo (MZCIQRO 14), 20.4 km N Limones (EAL 2883), entrance rd. to Noh Bec (CM 45270–72), Playa del Carmen (Himmelstein, 1980:27; UCM 16196–201), Pueblo Nuevo X-Can (KU 70173–79; UCM 28581–84, 47401), Puerto Juárez (Himmelstein, 1980:27), Puerto Morelos (USNM 47566–67, 47648), 12.5 km S Puerto Morelos (EAL 2863), 65 km S Puerto Morelos (EAL 2868), 4 km WSW Puerto Juárez (KU 70184), 8.1 mi SW Vicente Guerrero (KU 157320), 5 mi inland from Vigía (UMMZ 78629); Tabasco: 12.2 km E Emiliano Zapata (EAL 2908), 7 mi SW Frontera (UIMNH 86963–68), Tenosique (USNM 113460–65); Yucatán: 9.1 mi E Buctzotz (KU 157325), Calcehtok (UMMZ 113553, 148954–56), Chichén Itzá (AMNH 38893–925; FMNH 27290–97, 36487–89, 36495, 36497, 36499–500, 116409, 116411; MCZ

7243, 165538–41; UIMNH 20296; UMMZ 68225, 68701–2, 72973–79, 73006, 80822–26), Dzibilchaltún (FMNH 153402–4), 3 mi E Esmeralda (LACM 113899–903), 3 mi NE Hunabchén (AMNH 38926), 1.5 mi S Libre Unión (UCM 16212–13, 28606), Mérida (CM 44467; FMNH 105825–26, 105830, 105834, 153401; MCZ 6268, 165697–711; UIMNH 20294–95; UMMZ 73004–5), Oxkutzcab (AMNH 38927), 15.8 km N Panabá (JCL photo), laberintos 3 km from Peto (MZFC 3172), Pisté (KU 70190–200; UCM 16214–19, 17028–32, 18257–70), 9.2 mi S Río Lagartos (KU 157328), 13.4 mi S Río Lagartos (KU 157329), 20 mi S Río Lagartos (UCM 39142), Saban (KU 157322), 2.3 mi S, 1.9 mi E Santa Rosa (KU 157323–24), bet. Tunkás and Sitilpich (KU 171520), 28 km E Sucopo (FMNH 36498), Tekom (FMNH 49263–64), Tizimín (UMRC 80-54), 6 km N Tizimín (KU 74895–901), 4.3 mi W Tizimín (KU 157326–27), 12 mi N Tizimín (CM 40124–25; UCM 28585–604), Valladolid (UCM 16220–23), 3.3 mi N Valladolid (UCM 16224), X-Can (UCM 18255), 16.2 km S Yaxcopoil (CM 45269), no specific locality (USNM 24863–64, 13905).

Genus *Corytophanes*

This is a small genus of strictly Neotropical lizards, all arboreal inhabitants of tropical forests. They have rather short, laterally compressed bodies, long tails, and long, slender limbs. In both sexes the occipital region of the skull is compressed laterally and projects posteriorly as an occipital crest. Members of the genus occur at low and moderate elevations from central Veracruz on the Gulf slope and the Isthmus of Tehauntepec on the Pacific slope southeastward to Colombia. The genus is unusual in containing both viviparous (*C. percarinatus*) and oviparous (*C. hernandezii*, *C. cristatus*) species. McCoy (1970b:101) recognized three species; two occur in the Yucatán Peninsula. *Corytophanes* is derived from the Greek *korys*, "helmet," and *phaneros*, "visible" or "evident," in reference to the occipital casque.

Key to the Species of the Genus *Corytophanes*

Occipital crest continuous with body crest (Fig. 119) . . . . *Corytophanes cristatus*
Occipital crest not continuous with body crest, interrupted at neck (Fig. 120) . . . .
. . . . *Corytophanes hernandezii*

Clave para las Especies del Género *Corytophanes*

La cresta occipital continua con la del cuerpo (Fig. 119) . . . . *Corytophanes cristatus*
La cresta occipital no es continua con la cresta del cuerpo, interrumpida en el cuello (Fig. 120)
. . . . *Corytophanes hernandezii*

Corytophanes cristatus (Merrem)
(Figs. 119, 300, 301; Map 72)

Agama cristata Merrem, 1821:50. TYPE: unknown, possibly a specimen that appeared as figure 4 in volume 1 of Seba, 1734 (*fide* Stuart, 1963:67). TYPE LOCALITY: Ceylon (in error); restricted to Orizaba, Veracruz, Mexico, by H. M. Smith and Taylor (1950b:349).

Helmeted basilisk; old man (Belize); piende jente, turipache selvatico (Mexico); xuxup torok (Lacandón Maya).

DESCRIPTION   This medium-sized, rather stocky lizard has a laterally compressed body (Fig. 300). The

adults average about 110 mm in snout-vent length. The long, slender tail is slightly compressed laterally and approximately 2 to 2.5 times the length of the head and body. The limbs and digits are long and slender. The head is relatively small, the eyes are large, and the irises are red or red-orange (Fig. 301). Both sexes have a deep frontal depression bordered by bony supraorbital ridges that converge posteriorly to form an occipital casque. A serrated flap of skin extends from the casque onto the dorsum, where it continues as a row of enlarged vertebral scales forming a middorsal crest that extends onto the base of the tail (Fig. 119). The lateral body scales are smaller, imbricate, and mostly smooth, with a few larger keeled scales scattered among them. The appendages, chin, and venter are covered with

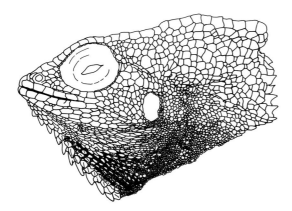

Fig. 119. Lateral view of the head of *Corytophanes cristatus* (FMNH 69227), 120 mm SVL; Gallon Jug, Orange Walk, Belize.

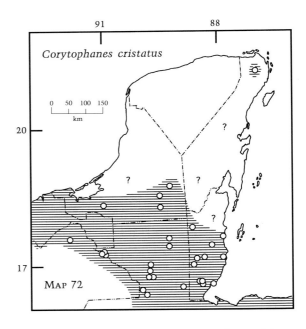

strongly keeled imbricate scales. A serrated median gular flap of skin extends from the chin to the gular fold.

The dorsal ground color is tan, brown, reddish brown, or greenish, with irregular darker spots or bands often forming a reticulum. There is often a light spot or bar in the shoulder region. The venter is lighter tan or cream, frequently with indistinct dark markings. These lizards are capable of rapidly changing color from green to olive brown to blackish (Taylor, 1956:166).

SIMILAR SPECIES *Corytophanes cristatus* differs from its congener, *C. hernandezii*, with which it is sympatric in the base of the Yucatán Peninsula, in having an uninterrupted dorsal crest (cf. Figs. 119, 120). Lizards of the genus *Laemanctus* have horizontal occipital casques and lack a serrated integumentary crest extending from the casque onto the dorsum of the body. The males of *Basiliscus vittatus* have an occipital crest, but it extends only to the nape of the neck and is not serrated (Fig. 118). *Basiliscus* also lacks the serrated gular flap present in *C. cristatus* (cf. Figs. 118, 119).

DISTRIBUTION This species is found at low and intermediate elevations on the Gulf and Caribbean slopes from central Veracruz to Colombia. In the Yucatán Peninsula it occurs through the base of the peninsula northward to southern Campeche. There is a single record for this species from northern Quintana Roo, at the northeast corner of the peninsula (Map 72).

NATURAL HISTORY These diurnal lizards inhabit primary and secondary forests, where they perch inconspicuously on tree trunks and lianas. In the Yucatán Peninsula they are uncommon, or at least they are not often seen. They rely on crypsis and stealth to avoid detection, and when pursued they are ungainly and awkward, often hopping bipedally in an attempt to escape (D. D. Davis, 1953:4). Their cryptic coloration makes them difficult to detect. They prey on a variety of invertebrates but specialize on extremely large arthropods, especially butterfly and beetle larvae, and katydids (R. M. Andrews, 1979:137). They are known to feed on small lizards of the genus *Anolis* (R. M. Andrews, 1983:410).

Corytophanes cristatus is oviparous. Ream (1964) reported that a captive female from Barro Colorado Island, Panama, laid six eggs on 5 February, of which only one hatched, this on 2 July. Sperm storage is indicated, as that female's last possible contact with a male was on the previous 21 August. Duellman (1963:235) reported that a female collected on 28 June in El Petén contained eight ova that averaged 11.1 mm in greatest diameter. Stuart (1958:22) found a juvenile at Tikal, El Petén, in early April. On 9 September, Taylor (1956:166) watched a female in Costa Rica deposit a clutch of six eggs in an excavation she had dug in the forest floor, and Bock (1987:35) reported that on 25 June a female in Costa Rica excavated a nest in the middle of a trail in wet tropical forest. The nest was about 95 mm deep and 50 mm in diameter, and it contained five eggs. Because the dorsal surface of the female's head was caked with soil, Bock suggested that the head had been used in nest construction. This idea is supported by Lazcano-Barrero and Góngora-Arones's (1993:68) observation that a female who deposited five eggs in a shallow nest in Chiapas on 27 July also had soil on the dorsal surface of her head. Fitch (1970:29) examined specimens from throughout the range of this species and concluded that breeding and oviposition occur during much of the year.

ETYMOLOGY The specific name, *cristatus*, is Latin meaning "crested," presumably in reference to the serrated middorsal crest.

COMMENT *Corytophanes cristatus* was treated taxonomically by McCoy (1970b), and information on this species was summarized by Lang (1989) as part of his study of relationships among the basiliscines.

Locality Records Belize: Belize: Manatee (FMNH 5826); Cayo: Caracol (CMM photo), Cohune Ridge (UMMZ 80678), 10 mi W, 5 mi N Middlesex (W. T. Neill and Allen, 1959c:39), upper Raspaculo River basin (Stafford, 1991:14); Orange Walk: Gallon Jug (FMNH 69226–28); Stann Creek: Silk Grass (FMNH 49240); Toledo: Blue Creek (RWV photo), 2 mi SW Big Falls, Río Grande (CM 105884), Punta Gorda (MPM 7303), San Miguel (MCZ 71362), 3 mi NE San Pedro Columbia (W. T. Neill, 1965:95). *Guatemala*: Alta Verapaz: Chinajá (Duellman, 1963:235); El Petén: 20 km NNW Chinajá (KU 55804), El Rosario Experimental Forest Station (JCL sight record), La Libertad (UMMZ 75037), Las Cañas (CM 58255–63), Piedras Negras (Smith and Taylor, 1950a:69), 5 mi S Piedras Negras (USNM 113170), Sayaxché (UCM 22264–66), Sojio (AMNH 69995), Tikal (MCZ 58769; UF 13489; UMMZ 117850–51), Uaxactún (UMMZ 70411); no specific locality (USNM 71816). *Mexico*: Campeche: Becan (UWZH 20545), Oxpemul (UMMZ 76123), Pacaitún (FMNH 36505), Pared de los Reyes (UMMZ 76124); Chiapas: near Palenque ruins (EAL 3032), across the river from Piedras Negras (USNM 113169); Quintana Roo: Reserva El Edén (COHECERN uncat.).

Corytophanes hernandezii (Wiegmann)
(Figs. 120, 302; Map 73)

Chamaeleopsis hernandezii Wiegmann, 1831, in Gray, in Griffith, *Cuvier's Animal Kingdom*, 9:45. SYNTYPES: ZMB 545–46 (three syntypes, *fide* Taylor, 1969:iv). TYPE LOCALITY: Mexico; restricted to Jalapa, Veracruz, Mexico, by H. M. Smith and Taylor (1950b:348).

Helmeted basilisk; old man (Belize), turipache de montaña (Mexico); xuxup torok (Lacandón Maya).

DESCRIPTION This medium-sized lizard is similar to *C. cristatus* in general size and shape (Fig. 302). The body is laterally compressed, and the limbs and toes are long and slender. The adults average roughly 100 mm in snout-vent length, and the long, laterally compressed tail is approximately 2.5 times as long as the head and body. The head is relatively small, and the eyes are large. The occipital portion of the skull projects posteriorly in the form of a laterally compressed occipital casque (Fig. 120). A large, sharp spine protrudes laterally from the temporal region, and a serrated flap of skin extends from the casque to the shoulders. The scales of the vertebral row are enlarged, forming a serrated middorsal crest extending from the shoulder region onto the base of the tail. The lateral body scales are weakly imbricate and generally smooth; those on the venter are somewhat larger than the laterals and strongly keeled. The scales on the limbs are strongly keeled and imbricate. Femoral pores are absent.

The dorsum is generally tan or olive, occasionally with a greenish or reddish cast, with scattered dark brown spots and blotches. On the side of the head, a broad, dark brown stripe extends from the loreal region to the tympanum, contrasting with the white supralabials and snout. The venter is more or less uniform gray.

SIMILAR SPECIES *Corytophanes hernandezii* differs from *C. cristatus* in having an interrupted dorsal crest (cf. Figs. 119, 120) and a large, sharp spine that extends laterally from the temporal region of the skull. The species of *Laemanctus* are predominantly green and have horizontally flattened cephalic casques. *Basiliscus vittatus* lacks a serrated median gular flap (Fig. 118).

Fig. **120**. Lateral view of the head of *Corytophanes hernandezii* (FMNH 27341), 85 mm SVL; Cobá, Quintana Roo, Mexico.

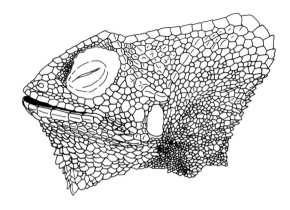

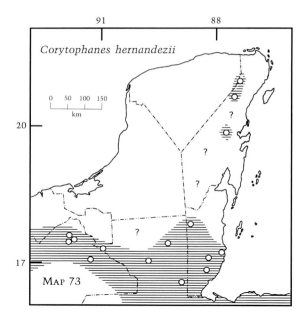

Corytophanes hernandezii

MAP 73

DISTRIBUTION *Corytophanes hernandezii* occurs at low and moderate elevations on the Gulf and Caribbean slopes from central Veracruz southeastward through northern Guatemala to Belize. It ranges through the base of the Yucatán Peninsula and extends northward, perhaps discontinuously, through the forests of Quintana Roo (Map 73).

NATURAL HISTORY These rather uncommon lizards are arboreal inhabitants of lowland tropical forests, where they perch inconspicuously on lianas, shrubs, and tree trunks, often less than a meter off the ground. Stuart (1958:22) found this species much more common in the dry forests at Tikal, El Petén, than *C. cristatus*. Apparently more tolerant of xeric conditions than its congener, *C. hernandezii* extends farther out into the dry north end of the Yucatán Peninsula. In color and configuration helmeted basilisks resemble dried leaves. They rely on crypsis and stealth rather than speed to avoid predators. They are watch-and-wait predators, and invertebrates, especially insects, are the prey.

Corytophanes hernandezii is oviparous. According to Alvarez del Toro (1983:84), females in Chiapas lay clutches of three or four eggs in May, June, or July. The eggs are placed in shallow excavations in leaf litter on the forest floor. Pérez-Higareda

(1981:72) reported that the female uses the dorsal surface of the head in excavating the nest. In El Petén, Stuart secured a hatchling in late May and a juvenile in mid-March (Stuart, 1935:44, 1958:22).

ETYMOLOGY The specific name, *hernandezii*, is a patronym that honors Francisco Hernández, Spanish explorer, physician to Philip of Spain, ethnographer, and naturalist, who traveled extensively in Mexico from 1570 to 1577.

COMMENT *Corytophanes hernandezii* was treated taxonomically by McCoy (1970b), and information on the species was summarized by Lang (1989) as part of his study of relationships among the basiliscines.

Locality Records *Belize*: Orange Walk: Gallon Jug (FMNH 69225; LSUMZ 8898); Stann Creek: Cockscomb Basin Wildlife Sanctuary (JCL photo), Silk Grass (FMNH 49239); Toledo: Bladen Branch of Monkey River (CM 105905, 105922). *Guatemala*: El Petén: La Libertad (UMMZ 75038–40), Las Cañas (CM 58255–63), Piedras Negras (UIMNH 20328; USNM 113165–67), Tikal (MCZ 58770; UF 13490; UMMZ 117852–55). *Mexico*: Chiapas: Laguna Ocotal (MCZ 53872–76), ca. 12 km S Palenque (JCL sight record), 13 mi SE Palenque (LSUMZ 34768), Palenque (FMNH 68382); Quintana Roo: Cobá (FMNH 27341), 8 mi NNE Felipe Carrillo Puerto (TCWC 58692), Pueblo Nuevo X-Can (KU 70201).

Genus *Laemanctus*

These exclusively Middle American lizards range from tropical Mexico to northern Honduras in lowland tropical forests. They are unique in that the occipital region of the skull extends posteriorly to form a horizontal bony casque. The genus *Laemanctus* was reviewed by Lang (1989) and McCoy (1968), both of whom recognized two species; both species occur in the Yucatán Peninsula. *Laemanctus* may derive from the Greek *laimos*, "neck," "throat," or "gullet," and *ankho*, a Greek verb meaning "to press tight, strangle." According to Lang (1989:141), the name refers to the tapered crowns of the marginal teeth.

Key to the Species of the Genus *Laemanctus*

Occipital region without a series of enlarged spines (Fig. 121); midddorsal scales not enlarged, no middorsal crest . . . . *Laemanctus longipes*

Occipital region with a series of enlarged spines (Fig. 122A,B); body scales of middorsal row enlarged and pointed, forming middorsal crest . . . . *Laemanctus serratus*

Clave para las Especies del Género *Laemanctus*

Región occipital sin una serie de espinas alargadas (Fig. 121); escamas mediodorsales del cuerpo sin alargar, no hay cresta mediodorsal . . . . *Laemanctus longipes*

Región occipital con una serie de espinas alargadas (Fig. 122A,B); escamas de la hilera medio-dorsal del cuerpo alargadas y punteadas, formando una cresta mediodorsal . . . .
. . . . *Laemanctus serratus*

Laemanctus longipes Wiegmann
(Figs. 121, 303, 304; Map 74)

Laemanctus longipes Wiegmann, 1834:46. HOLOTYPE: ZMB 494. TYPE LOCALITY: Jalapa, Veracruz, Mexico.

Casque-headed iguana; lemacto coludo (Mexico); xuxup torok (Lacandón Maya).

DESCRIPTION *Laemanctus longipes* is a moderately large lizard. The adults average 125 to 130 mm in snout-vent length, and the maximum length recorded is 150 mm (Ahl, 1930). The body is somewhat compressed laterally (Fig. 303). The long, slender tail is about 3.5 times the length of the head and body. The limbs and toes are extremely long and slender, and the subdigital lamellae are strongly keeled. Femoral pores are absent. The back of the skull is expanded and extends posteriorly in the form of a flat-topped cephalic casque (Figs. 121, 304). The dorsal and ventral body scales are imbricate and strongly keeled, as are those on the appendages. The middorsal scales are not conspicuously larger than the laterals.

The dorsum is predominantly bright green with a series of narrow, dark green bars that often alternate with black bars. The bars continue posteriorly onto the tail as dark rings against a light green back-

ground. The dorsal surface of the head is yellow-green, and the posterior margin of the casque is edged with black or dark brown. The lateral surfaces of the head are bright green. On each side, a narrow white, cream, or yellowish stripe originates on the supralabials and passes over the neck and onto the upper arm. The ventral surfaces are light green, and the iris is orange or yellowish brown.

SIMILAR SPECIES *Laemanctus longipes* differs from its congener, *L. serratus*, in lacking the enlarged conical scales on the posterior margin of the occipital casque and the vertebral row of enlarged scales. *Basiliscus vittatus* is predominantly brown or tan rather than green and lacks the flat-topped cephalic casque of *L. longipes*.

DISTRIBUTION This species occurs at low and moderate elevations from central Veracruz on the Gulf slope and the Isthmus of Tehauntepec on the

Fig. 121. Lateral view of the head of *Laemanctus longipes* (UF 33517), 99 mm SVL; Poptún, El Petén, Guatemala.

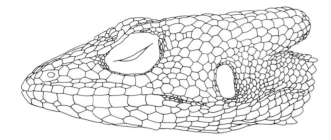

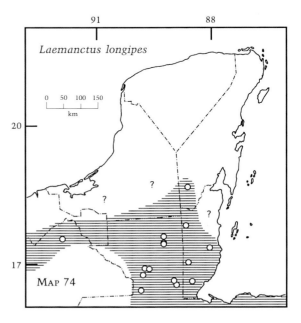

Pacific slope, south and east to northern Honduras. It occurs through the base of the Yucatán Peninsula to southern Quintana Roo (Map 74).

NATURAL HISTORY *Laemanctus longipes* is a rather uncommon arboreal inhabitant of lowland tropical forests. Duellman (1963:235) collected a specimen on a bush in humid forest in southern El Petén, and Stuart (1948:52) found this species in dense second growth in Alta Verapaz. *Laemanctus longipes* is apparently restricted to more mesic situations than those inhabited by *L. serratus*, which replaces it in the dry northern half of the Yucatán Peninsula. These lizards rely on stealth and their cryptic coloration to escape detection. They feed on invertebrates, especially insects.

Laemanctus longipes is oviparous. Duellman (1963:235) reported that a female collected on 28 June in southern El Petén contained four ova with an average length of 13.9 mm. He found a clutch of five eggs (average length 24.2 mm) in a rotting log in southern El Petén on 30 June that hatched on 30 August. The hatchlings had an average snout-vent length of 44 mm and an average tail length of 138 mm. McCoy (1968:676) reported a clutch size of three eggs. Thus, oviposition and hatching apparently occur during the rainy season, and clutch size ranges from three to five eggs.

SUBSPECIES Lang (1989) recognized three subspecies of *L. longipes*, of which only *L. l. deborrei* occurs in the Yucatán Peninsula.

ETYMOLOGY The specific name, *longipes*, is from the Latin *longus*, "long," and *pes*, "foot," reflecting what Wiegmann thought were unusually long feet in this species.

COMMENT *Laemanctus longipes* was reviewed by McCoy (1968) as part of his revision of the genus *Laemanctus*. The available information on this species was summarized by Lang (1989) as part of his study of relationships among the basiliscines.

Locality Records Belize: Cayo: Caracol (CMM photo); Orange Walk: Gallon Jug (W. T. Neill and Allen, 1959c:39); Stann Creek: Middlesex (FMNH 4488); Toledo: Columbia Forest Camp (MPM 8267). *Guatemala*: El Petén: 4 km N Chinajá (KU 59608), Las Cañas (CM 58264–66), S edge Poptún (UF 33517), Sayaxché (UCM 22267), Sojio (AMNH 70014), Tikal (UF 13492; UMMZ 117849), 2 km N Tikal (KU 157356), Toocog (KU 59609–13), Uaxactún (AMNH 68517). *Mexico*:

Chiapas: Palenque ruins (EAL 3644); Quintana Roo: 5 km E Caobas (KU 74911).

Laemanctus serratus Cope
(Figs. 122, 305; Map 75)

Laemanctus serratus Cope, 1864:176. HOLOTYPE: RMNH 2845. TYPE LOCALITY: Orizaba Valley, Mexico.

Serrated casque-headed iguana; lagartija de casco, lemacto coronado (Mexico); yaxtoloc (Yucatec Maya).

DESCRIPTION *Laemanctus serratus* is a moderately large lizard with an extremely long tail. The snout-vent length of adults averages about 120 to 130 mm, with a recorded maximum of 190 mm (Ahl, 1930). The body is moderately compressed laterally, and the tail is approximately 3.5 times the length of the head and body. The limbs and toes are long and slender, and the subdigital lamellae are strongly keeled. Femoral pores are absent (Fig. 122D). The relatively broad head is clearly distinct from the neck (Fig. 122A); its dorsal surface is flat, and the occipital region projects posteriorly as an occipital casque (Figs. 122B, 305). A series of enlarged conical spines borders the posterior margin of the casque (Fig. 122A,B). Virtually all the scales on the body and appendages are imbricate and strongly keeled. Those of the vertebral row are enlarged, forming a serrated middorsal crest.

These lizards are usually green but are capable of a rapid color change from green to brown. In the green phase, the ground color is light green with four to six (usually five) dark brown bands. The bands are most distinct in the middorsal area and tend to break up on the lateral surfaces of the body. The bands continue onto the tail, becoming indistinct posteriorly. The dorsal surfaces of the limbs are light green with indistinct, irregular brown bands and reticulations. Most specimens have a distinct white or cream spot immediately above and posterior to the insertion of the forelimbs. The ventral surface of the body is generally lighter green than the dorsum, with few if any darker markings. A conspicuous white or cream stripe extends from the axilla to the groin on the ventrolateral surfaces. The dorsal and lateral surfaces of the head are light green with a few small dark brown or black markings. The sutures of the supralabial scales bear dark brown or black spots. A distinct white stripe passes below each eye, extends posteriorly below the tym-

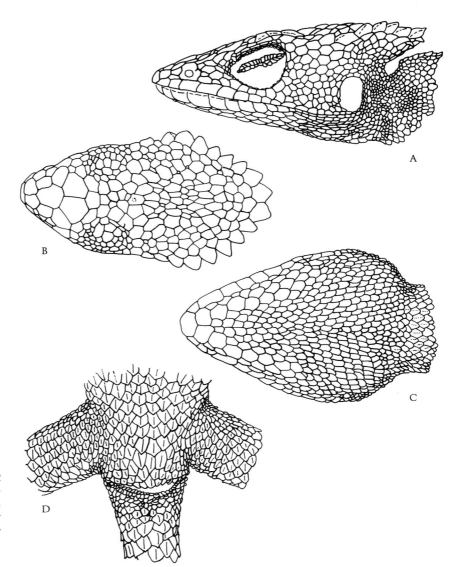

Fig. 122. *Laemanctus serratus* (UMRC 93-10), 115 mm SVL. A, lateral; B, dorsal; and C, ventral views of the head. D, ventral view of the thighs and vent region; Cristóbal Colón, Quintana Roo, Mexico.

panum onto the lateral surface of the neck, and is usually continuous with the ventrolateral stripe on the body. On the lateral surface of the head this stripe is usually bordered above by dark brown or black. In the brown phase the light green background color changes to light or medium tan.

SIMILAR SPECIES This species differs from *L. longipes* and *Basiliscus vittatus* in possessing enlarged conical scales on the occipital region (Fig. 122A,B) and a serrated dorsal crest.

DISTRIBUTION *Laemanctus serratus* occurs at low and moderate elevations on the Gulf slope from southern Tamaulipas and the Pacific slope from Oaxaca, south and eastward into the Yucatán Peninsula. The Yucatecan populations are apparently isolated from those to the south and east (Map 75).

NATURAL HISTORY These uncommon diurnal lizards are primarily arboreal inhabitants of lowland tropical forest. In the Yucatán Peninsula the species seems most abundant in the thorn and deciduous forests of the northwest. Individuals have been found perching low on the trunks of trees and on lianas. In southern Veracruz, Pérez-Higareda and Vogt (1985:143) found them on shrubs at heights of 1 to 2 m. They are occasionally seen running bipedally across roads. These lizards are rather slow and ungainly, and they rely on crypsis to avoid detection. They are watch-and-wait predators of invertebrates, primarily insects, although Martin (1958) reported that specimens from Tamaulipas consumed snails and a lizard (*Anolis*) as well, and Pérez-Higareda and Vogt (1985:143) found a frog of the genus *Eleutherodactylus* in the stomach of a specimen from southern Veracruz.

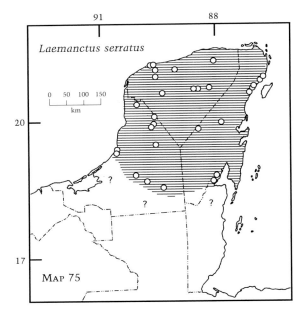

Like its congener, *L. serratus* is oviparous. According to Alvarez del Toro (1983:82), the nests are shallow excavations at the bases of trees, and the females deposit three or four eggs in June or July. Martin (1958:57) reported that females in Tamaulipas excavate their nests in mid-June, and hatchlings were observed in late August. The eggs are deposited beneath surface debris in southern Veracruz (Pérez-Higareda and Vogt, 1985:143). Of the four nests described by Pérez-Higareda and Vogt (1985:143), one contained seven eggs and three contained five eggs. The nests were discovered in May and June, and the eggs, which were incubated in the laboratory, hatched in August and September. The mean snout-vent length of the hatchlings was 40 mm; mean tail length was 80 mm. McCoy (1968:676) reported clutches of three to five eggs. In northern Campeche I found a specimen that contained four well-developed oviductal eggs in mid-May. Thus, clutch size ranges from three to seven, oviposition occurs in spring or early summer, and the hatchlings appear in late summer.

SUBSPECIES According to the review by Lang (1989), *L. serratus* exists as three subspecies, of which *L. s. alticoronatus* Cope, 1865 occurs in the Yucatán Peninsula.

ETYMOLOGY The specific name, *serratus*, is Latin for "saw shaped" or "serrated," a reference to the serrated middorsal crest.

COMMENT *Laemanctus serratus* was reviewed by McCoy (1968) as part of his revision of the genus *Laemanctus*. Lang (1989) summarized the available information on this species as part of his study of the relationships among the basiliscines.

Locality Records Belize: Corozal: 3 mi S Santa Elena (JLK 404). *Mexico:* Campeche: 3.6 km N Bolonchén de Rejón (UMRC 85-27), 5 mi S Bolonchén de Rejón (UCM 16191), Champotón (UMMZ 72931–33), 5 km S Champotón (KU 70265–68), Dzibalchén (KU 75532), 7 mi N Hopelchén (UCM 18271), near Nunkiní (JCL photo), Oxpemul (UMMZ 76122), Silvituc (MZFC 259), 63.2 km W Xpujil (UMRC 85-26); Quintana Roo: Cristóbal Colón (UMRC 93-10), 33.4 km N Felipe Carrillo Puerto (JCL 6792), Laguna Guerrero (MZCIQRO 17), Pino Suarez (UMRC 84-33), 7 mi N Playa del Carmen (CM 93169), 2 mi S Playa del Carmen (LSUMZ 33220), 5 mi S Playa del Carmen (LSUMZ 33221), 15.9 mi S Playa del Carmen (LSUMZ 38454–55), 10.6 km NW Pol-Yuc (UMRC 80-55), 1 mi E Puerto Morelos (UF uncat.); Yucatán: Cansahcab (AMNH 110037), Chichén Itzá (FMNH 36481–86; MCZ 7235; UCM 12797–98; UMMZ 72928–30, 80821, 83277; USNM 72742), 6.7 km E Chuburna Puerto (EAL 2945), Dzibilchaltún (FMNH 153398–400), Mayapán (FMNH 40705–6), Mérida (CM 44468; FMNH 40707; MCZ 6267), near Mérida (USNM 12283), Pisté (KU 70264; UCM 12799, 16192), 5 mi W Progreso (UIMNH 74465), 6 km N Tizimín (KU 74906–9), Tekom (FMNH 49265–70).

Family Iguanidae

Members of this moderately large family of predominantly New World lizards range from the southwestern United States through western and southern Mexico, and south and eastward through Central America to southern Brazil, northern Bolivia, Peru, and Ecuador. The family also occurs in the West Indies, the Galápagos Islands, and Fiji and Tonga. Iguanids are generally large, robust herbivores, at least as adults. They may be arboreal, semiarboreal, or terrestrial, and one species is semiaquatic. Of the eight genera presently assigned to the family Iguanidae, two occur in the Yucatán Peninsula.

The genera now included within the Iguanidae were long referred to informally as "iguanines" of the family Iguanidae (*sensu lato*). D. R. Frost and Etheridge (1989) elevated the iguanines to formal family rank and restricted the name Iguanidae to them.

Key to the Genera of the Family Iguanidae

Tail bearing distinct whorls of large spines (Fig. 123); no large circular scale below tympanum
....*Ctenosaura*
Tail without whorls of large spines; a large circular scale below tympanum (Fig. 125). . . . *Iguana*

Clave para los Géneros de la Familia Iguanidae

La cola con verticilos distintivos de espinas largas (Fig. 123); sin una escama circular en la mejilla
....*Ctenosaura*
La cola sin verticilos de espinas alargadas; con una escama circular grande en la mejilla (Fig. 125)
....*Iguana*

Genus *Ctenosaura* (Spiny-tailed Iguanas)

This is a moderately small group of medium-sized to very large diurnal lizards. The genus is confined to the New World tropics, and representatives occur in subarid to subhumid lowland habitats in Mexico and Central America. Most ctenosaurs are terrestrial or semiarboreal, but some, especially those formerly placed in the genus *Enyaliosaurus*, are primarily arboreal. As the common name suggests, the tails of these lizards bear whorls of enlarged spiny scales. When attacked, some species defend themselves by lashing the tail to and fro. Others seek refuge in hollow limbs or rock crevices and use the tail to block the opening. Ctenosaurs are generally omnivorous, feeding on fruits, flowers, and foliage as well as on small animals. Eleven species are presently recognized, including those formerly included within the genus *Enyaliosaurus* (de Queiroz, 1987). Two species occur in the Yucatán Peninsula. *Cteno-*

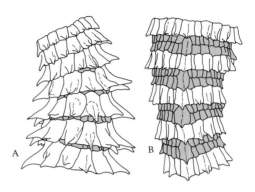

Fig. 123. Dorsal views of the proximal portions of tails of *Ctenosaura*. A, *C. defensor* showing whorls of heavy spines separated by one row of interwhorls (*shaded*). B, *C. similis* showing whorls of spines separated by two rows of interwhorls (*shaded*).

saura is from the Greek *ktenos*, "comb," and *sauros*, "lizard," in reference to the serrated dorsal crest seen especially in the males of many species.

Key to the Species of the Genus *Ctenosaura*

Tail dorsoventrally compressed; whorls of spines separated by no more than one interwhorl (Fig. 123A); adult SVL less than 175 mm; Yucatán and Campeche (Map 76) ....
....*Ctenosaura defensor*
Tail round in cross section, not dorsoventrally compressed; whorls of spines separated by more than one interwhorl (Fig. 123B); adult SVL greater than 175 mm; pan-peninsular ....
....*Ctenosaura similis*

Clave para las Especies del Género *Ctenosaura*

Cola comprimida en corte transversal; verticilos de espinas separadas por no más de una espira pequeña (Fig. 123A); adultos menos de 175 mm de LHC; organismos habitan en los estados de Campeche y Yucatán solamente (Mapa 76)............................*Ctenosaura defensor*

Cola redonda en corte transversal; verticilos de espinas separadas por más de una espira pequeña (Fig. 123B); adultos más de 175 mm de LHC; organismos habitan por todas partes de la Penísula de Yucatán . . . . *Ctenosaura similis*

Ctenosaura defensor (Cope)
(Figs. 123A, 124, 306, 307; Map 76)

Cachryx defensor Cope, 1866:124. SYNTYPES: USNM 12282 (three syntypes). TYPE LOCALITY: Yucatán; restricted to Chichén Itzá, Yucatán, Mexico, by H. M. Smith and Taylor (1950b:352).

Yucatán spiny-tailed iguana.

DESCRIPTION   The males of this medium-sized, robust lizard average between 120 and 140 mm in snout-vent length (Fig. 306). The females may be smaller, but size dimorphism has not been quantified. The body is moderately stout, the head is broad, and the snout is rounded in both dorsal and lateral aspects (Fig. 124A,B). The pupil is round, and the iris is red-orange (Fig. 307). The limbs are well developed, and the digits bear strong claws. The tail, which is about 85 percent as long as the head and body, is slightly flattened dorsoventrally and covered with whorls of large, heavy spines that are generally separated by a single row of interwhorls (Fig. 123A). The scales on the head and on the dorsal, lateral, and ventral surfaces of the body are generally smooth; the body scales are slightly imbricate. The scales of the vertebral row are enlarged and weakly keeled. Some scales on the dorsal surfaces of the limbs are enlarged and spiny, especially on the hind limbs. The males possess 6 to 10 femoral pores on the posteroventral surface of each thigh (Fig. 124D); in females these pores are rudimentary. A conspicuous gular fold is present (Fig. 124C).

These distinctive lizards are brightly colored. The head, neck, tail, and hind limbs are generally gray. The anterior half of the body is predominantly black dorsally, with the dark pigment arranged as large, irregular blotches or bands, scattered among which are light gray or tan spots. The posterior half of the body is predominantly red-orange. The dorsal surfaces of the forelimbs are black or gray with lighter spots. The hind limbs are gray. The chin and gular areas likewise are mostly gray but may exhibit considerable red-orange coloration, possibly serving a nuptial function. The black pigment on the body extends irregularly onto the venter, which is otherwise light gray. These lizards are capable of pronounced metachrosis—the gray areas become light powder blue—which, in combination with the contrasting red-orange and black dorsum, produces a striking effect.

SIMILAR SPECIES   *Ctenosaura similis*, which reaches a much larger size, also possesses whorls of enlarged spines on the tail, but the spines are less robust, the tail is rounded in cross section rather than dorsoventrally compressed, and the whorls of spines are separated by at least two interwhorls of smaller scales rather than one or no rows of interwhorls, as in *C. defensor* (Fig. 123).

DISTRIBUTION   This species is endemic to the Yucatán Peninsula, where it is known from the states of Campeche and Yucatán (Map 76).

NATURAL HISTORY   Very little is known about the natural history of *C. defensor*. Spiny-tailed iguanas live mainly in the xeric thorn forests of the northwestern portion of the Yucatán Peninsula, although they are also found in the tropical evergreen forests of northern Campeche (Duellman, 1965a:598). Cope (1866:124) thought their digits were too short for an arboreal lifestyle, and J. W. Bailey (1928:49) perpetuated the belief that they were terrestrial. Apparently, however, these lizards

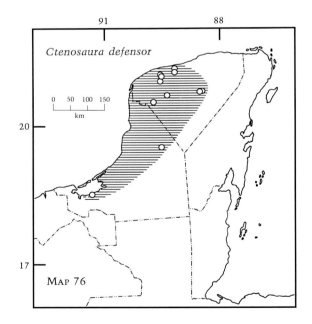

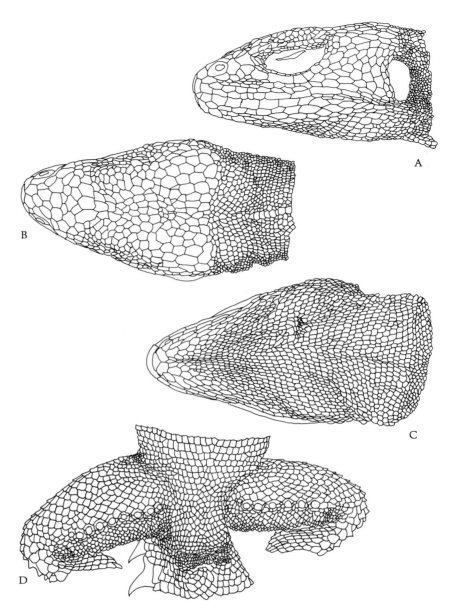

Fig. 124. *Ctenosaura defensor* (UMRC 89-38), 129 mm SVL. A, lateral; B, dorsal; and C, ventral views of the head. D, ventral view of the thighs and vent region; near Mérida, Yucatán, Mexico.

are predominantly arboreal and live in or near the hollow limbs of trees. According to C. J. McCoy (pers. comm.), in northern Yucatán these lizards are exceedingly wary. They perch near the openings of hollow limbs, into which they quickly disappear when startled. G. Köhler (in litt.), however, recently reported finding specimens inhabiting holes in limestone rocks in the vicinity of Telchaquillo and Tetiz, Yucatán, indicating that *C. defensor* may also be terrestrial. My observations on captives indicate that they enter hollow limbs headfirst, and the spiny tail blocks the entrance behind them. In this the behavior of *C. defensor* closely resembles

C. clarki of Michoacán (Duellman and Duellman, 1959), its closest relative (de Queiroz, 1987:898).

Little is known concerning reproduction in *C. defensor*, although it is presumably oviparous, as are other *Ctenosaura* species. According to G. Köhler (in litt.), native inhabitants of Yucatán state that this species produces clutches of two or three eggs. Pough (1973:839) considered this species to be herbivorous, and I found that captives will accept hibiscus blossoms. If spiny-tailed iguanas are like other ctenosaurs, they probably consume both plant and animal food, the latter primarily in the form of insects.

ETYMOLOGY The specific name, *defensor*, is Latin meaning "one who averts or repels" or "a thing which acts as a protection," presumably in reference to the whorls of heavy spines on the tail or the habit of blocking the entryway with the spines.

COMMENT This species was long placed in the genus *Enyaliosaurus*, but de Queiroz (1987) used cladistic analyses of morphological characters to determine that *Enyaliosaurus* should be included in *Ctenosaura*.

Köhler (1995:5) described *Ctenosaura alfredschmidti* from Pablo Garcia, Campeche. The new species is very similar to *C. defensor*, from which it is said to differ in several characters of scutellation.

Locality Records   Mexico: Campeche: Balchacaj (UIMNH 20327), Dzibalchén (KU 75528); Yucatán: 1 km S Calcetok (TU 19768), Chichén Itzá (MCZ 7095), Dzibilchaltún (FMNH 153414–15, 153427–29), Mayapán (FMNH 40708–15), Mérida (UCM 40095), 7 mi N Mérida (UF 41534), Pisté (CM 47213, 49894–902, 49904; KU 70261–62; UCM 16265, 40094, 41634), 7 mi N Telchac (UCM 28647), 3 mi S Telchac Puerto (UCM 28648–49); no specific locality (FMNH 153428–29; USNM 12282).

Ctenosaura similis (Gray)
(Figs. 123B, 308; Map 77)

Iguana (Ctenosaura) similis Gray, 1831b:38, in Griffith, ed., *Cuvier's Animal Kingdom*. HOLOTYPE: a dried skin in the "museum of Mr. Bell, London, England" (*fide* J. W. Bailey, 1928:32). TYPE LOCALITY: none given, but restricted to Tela, Honduras, Central America by J. W. Bailey (1928:32).

Spiny-tailed iguana, black iguana; wish-willy (Belize); garrobo, iguana de roca, iguana rayada (Mexico); hug (Lacandón Maya); huh, yholhuh, t'ol, yax ikil (Yucatec Maya).

DESCRIPTION Among lizards *Ctenosaura similis* is exceeded in size only by *Iguana iguana* in the Yucatán Peninsula. The males average about 340 to 350 mm in snout-vent length; the females are considerably smaller, about 275 mm (Fig. 308). In adults the tail is about 1.5 to 2 times as long as the head and body. The head is moderately distinct from the neck, and the limbs are robust and muscular. The scales on the dorsal surface of the body are relatively small, slightly imbricate, and weakly keeled; those on the dorsal surfaces of the appendages are somewhat larger and more heavily keeled.

The scales on the ventral surfaces of the body and appendages are smooth. Femoral pores are present in both sexes, but they are not well developed in females. Both sexes exhibit a vertebral row of enlarged spines beginning at the base of the head and continuing to the base of the tail. This dorsal crest is much larger in males. The tail bears whorls of enlarged, heavily keeled spiny scales. The whorls of spines are separated by paired interwhorls of smaller, more weakly keeled scales (Fig. 123B). In addition to pronounced sexual dimorphism in size, the males have relatively longer snouts and much more massive jaw musculature than females, features probably associated with male-male combat (Carothers, 1984:245; Gier, 1993).

Ctenosaurs undergo a dramatic ontogenetic color change (Fitch and Henderson, 1977:5). The hatchlings are pale grayish brown above with dark brown reticulations, but within a few months they become bright green, with or without darker markings. At about six months they begin to assume the adult color pattern, which consists of a series of dark dorsal bands against a tan or light gray background. These extend to the venter and continue onto the tail as a series of dark rings. The limbs are similarly banded with dark pigment; often they are very dark, nearly black. The head is generally tan, often with an orange cast. Reddish or orange spots are sometimes present on the dorsum.

SIMILAR SPECIES Size alone will distinguish the adults of this giant lizard from all others in the Yucatán Peninsula except *Iguana iguana*, which lacks enlarged whorls of spiny scales on the tail and has an enlarged circular scale below the tympanum. The green juveniles differ from the other bright green lizards of the Yucatán Peninsula, *Laemanctus* and *Anolis biporcatus*, in possessing a spiny tail. Adults of *C. defensor* are much smaller, their tails are dorsoventrally flattened, and the caudal whorls of spines are separated by no more than a single row of interwhorls (Fig. 123A).

DISTRIBUTION *Ctenosaura similis* is found at low and moderate elevations from southern Veracruz and Oaxaca south to Panama. The distribution in the Yucatán Peninsula appears to be discontinuous, with populations to the north and west isolated from those at the base of the peninsula (Map 77).

NATURAL HISTORY Spiny-tailed iguanas typically inhabit open, subarid habitats. In the Yucatán

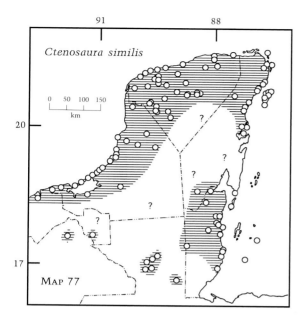

Ctenosaura similis

Map 77

clutch size ranges from 15 to 25 eggs (Alvarez del Toro, 1983:91). Lizards in western Nicaragua lay a single clutch of eggs, normally in February or March (Fitch and Henderson, 1978:490). The clutch size there averages about 43, with a recorded maximum of 88. The eggs are deposited within burrows in sandy open areas, and several females may use the same burrow system. A strong positive relationship exists between the female's size and the number of eggs she produces. The hatchlings generally appear in May, at about the onset of the rainy season, although Henderson (1973:29) reported that hatchlings appeared in mid-June in Belize. Duellman (1965a:599) noted that juveniles were common on Isla del Carmen and at Isla Aguada, Campeche, in early July and early June, respectively.

In addition to intense predation by humans (see Comment), this species is eaten by various saurophagous snakes (Henderson, 1982:75) and hawks (Himmelstein, 1980:28).

SUBSPECIES   Two subspecies are presently recognized (Etheridge, 1982:21); *C. s. similis* occurs in the Yucatán Peninsula.

ETYMOLOGY   The specific name, *similis*, is Latin meaning "like" or "resembling," possibly in reference to the fact that this species rather closely resembles some other members of the genus *Ctenosaura*.

COMMENT   Throughout much of southern Mexico and Central America, ctenosaurs are heavily exploited by humans as a source of food, just as they were by the pre-Colombian Maya of Yucatán (see "Ethnoherpetology in the Yucatán Peninsula"). Fitch and Henderson (1978) and Fitch et al. (1982) documented the marked decline in numbers throughout Central America as a result of overexploitation by humans and emphasized the urgent need for management practices to reverse the decline and ensure a sustained yield of these valuable and interesting reptiles.

Locality Records   Belize: Belize: Altun Ha (MPM 8063), Ambergris Cay, San Pedro (MCZ 71393–98), Belize (FMNH 4187, 4490–93, 49277–81; KU 144942), 12.8 mi NW Belize City (KU 157333), Glover's Reef (CM 8517), Glover's Reef, Middle Cay (FMNH 34612–16, 34619–22), Half Moon Cay (CM 4153–55, 7656–57; FMNH 34623; MCZ 61118), bet. Ladyville and Sandhill (CM 90921–23), Manatee (FMNH 5820), North River (USNM 56780); Cayo: Cocquercot

Peninsula they are especially common in open situations in thorn forest at the dry outer end of the peninsula. These lizards are often very common and conspicuous in and around areas of human activity (Henderson, 1973). Ctenosaurs perch on stone buildings, amid Maya ruins, on rock walls, and on rocky coastlines. They are frequently encountered lumbering across roads. They are diurnal and predominantly terrestrial or saxicolous, although they are also commonly found in trees. The juveniles, especially, ascend vegetation at night to sleep. At night and during the heat of the day, Costa Rican ctenosaurs occupy burrows in earth banks, beneath rocks and logs, or under buildings (J. Burger and Gochfeld, 1991:432).

Ctenosaura similis is unusual in undergoing an ontogenetic shift in diet. Although lizards of all ages consume plant matter, the juveniles take relatively larger amounts of animal protein, chiefly in the form of insects. J. W. Bailey (1928:34) found beetles and grasshoppers in the stomachs of some individuals, and Henderson (1973:30) reported predation on a skink (*Mabuya unimarginata*) in Belize. Fitch et al. (1971:399) observed a Costa Rican ctenosaur with a mastiff bat (*Eumops* sp.) in its jaws, and Fitch and Hackforth-Jones (1983:395) listed several species of rodents, birds, and lizards as prey items, as well as eggs of its own species. Ctenosaurs become predominantly herbivorous as they age (Iverson, 1982:61; Montanucci, 1968; Van Devender, 1982:170).

Ctenosaura similis is oviparous. In Chiapas,

(UMMZ 75026), San Ignacio (MCZ 152574); Corozal: San Pedro (USNM 204811); Orange Walk: Tower Hill (MPM 7538–39; USNM 194825–26); Stann Creek: Free Town (CM 8513), Mango Creek (MCZ 71399–404), Stann Creek (FMNH 4494–95), 2 mi S Stann Creek (KU 157330–32), no specific locality (USNM 24911, 26071). *Guatemala*: El Petén: Flores (UMMZ 79088), SE Flores (UMMZ 79087), near La Libertad (UMMZ 75027–29, 77447), Pacomon (USNM 71375–77), Poptún (UMMZ 117861), Sojio (AMNH 70015–16), Toocog (KU 55800–3, 55979, 90827), Tayasal (= Flores) (UMMZ 79086); no specific locality (USNM 71815). *Mexico*: Campeche: near Atasta (UIMNH 86986), Balchacaj (FMNH 105803, 105805, 105807–11, 105814–15, 105817, 108814; UIMNH 20252–58; UMMZ 81923), 12 mi W Campeche (BCB 11446), 29.7 mi S Campeche (UCM 18252–53), 53 mi SW Campeche (EAL 1198), Champotón (MCZ 53126; UMMZ 73009–12, 73021–24), 5 mi N Champotón (UCM 16229–30), 3 mi SW Champotón (LACM 75134), 5 km S Champotón (KU 70208–9, 71763), 6 km SW Champotón (KU 70210–21, 70260), 8.7 mi S Champotón (KU 157334–36), 6.3 km SW Champotón (CM 64686, 64688; EAL 2927–28), 8 km SW Champotón (CM 41312), 9 mi W Champotón (UCM 39144–46), 16 mi SW Champotón (UCM 39143), 30 km SW Champotón (EAL 2931), Ciudad del Carmen (FMNH 105802, 105806, 105812–13, 105816, 106151, 108813, 108816, 112260, 111518, 111522, 111527–29; UCM 20546; UIMNH 20259–67), 9 km E Ciudad del Carmen (CM 40012), 9 mi E Ciudad del Carmen (UCM 39155–56), Dzibalchén (KU 75514), 10 mi E Frontera, Tabasco (UIMNH 86988), 3 mi W Hopelchén (UCM 16231), 4 mi W Hopelchén (BCB 11447), Isla Aguada (KU 75515–27), 5 mi E Isla Aguada (UCM 39151–52), 9 mi NE Isla Aguada (UCM 39153), 10 mi E Isla Aguada (UCM 39154), Isla del Carmen, Puerto Real (UCM 45019–31), Isla del Carmen, 1 km SW Puerto Real (KU 70202–7, 70259), Isla del Carmen, 10 mi W Puerto Real (UCM 39150), 5 mi NE Sabancuy (UIMNH 86987), 24 mi E Sabancuy (UCM 39147–49), 24.7 mi NE Sabancuy (LACM 61930–31), 0.5 mi S Seybaplaya (EAL 1661), Tankuche-El Remate, 7 km (IHNHERP 462); Chiapas: Palenque (USNM 47593); Quintana Roo: Cobá (FMNH 27301), Culebra Cays, Bahía de la Ascención (UMMZ 78617–18, 78622–23), Isla Contoy (FMNH 34656, 34658–60; UCM 16233–38), Isla Cozumel (CM 27574, 27576, 27578; Himmelstein, 1980:27; USNM 47565, 78610), S end Cozumel (UMMZ 78611, 78614), Cozumel, San Miguel (UMMZ 78607–8, 78613, 78615), Cozumel, near San Miguel (UTEP 5957), Cozumel, 2 km N San Miguel (UCM 12767), Cozumel, 3 mi N San Miguel (UCM 12765–66), Cozumel, 3.5 km N San Miguel (KU 70231–33), Cozumel, 6 km N San Miguel (UCM 16241–45), Cozumel, 6 mi E San Miguel (UMMZ 78609, 78612), Cozumel, 9 km SE San Miguel (UCM 12768), Cozumel, 5 km S Cozumel (UCM 16239–40), Isla Mujeres (FMNH 34654–55, 34661; UCM 16248–54, 39160–61; UMMZ 78598–606), N end Isla Mujeres (KU 70225, 70230), S end Isla Mujeres (FMNH 34638, KU 70226), Isla Mujeres, Rancho Pirata (KU 70227–29), Kohunlich (MZFC 1998), La Glorieta, Sian Ka'an Reserve (MZCIQRO 20), Playa del Carmen (CM 64687; EAL 2866; UCM 16232), 2 mi S Playa del Carmen (LSUMZ 34040), Puerto Morelos (USNM 47647), 6 mi S Puerto Morelos (UCM 39162–63), 9.8 km S Puerto Morelos (EAL 2860), 12.5 km S Puerto Morelos (EAL 2862), Puerto Juárez (KU 70222–23; UCM 16246–47), 4 km WSW Puerto Juárez (KU 70224), Punta Allen (UMMZ 78616, 78619), Tulum (JCL photo), 2 km S Tulum (UMRC 84-93), Vigía (UMMZ 78620–21), Xcalak (KU 74902–3), Xel-Ha (JCL photo), no specific locality (USNM 13898, 47559–61); Tabasco: 7 mi SW Frontera (UIMNH 86985), Tenosique (UIMNH 36132, 52499–500); Yucatán: 5.1 mi W Buctzotz (KU 157338), 9.1 mi E Buctzotz (KU 157339), Calcehtok (UMMZ 113552, 148989–90), Cansahcab (AMNH 110036), 16.8 km E Celestún (Dundee et al. 1986:41), Chacmultún (JCL sight record), 3.4 km SW Chelem (EAL 2948), Chichén Itzá (AMNH 38929–31, 38949; FMNH 27300, 27302–4, 36454–66, 111512–14, 111517, 111525–26, 112258–59, 49241–42, 108814; MCZ 29239–40, 25989–94; UIMNH 20243–47; UMMZ 68227–28, 68703–4, 73007, 73013–20, 83121; USNM 47794, 47953–55, 47992–95), 7.8 km NW Chicxulub Puerto (EAL 2951), Chuburna Puerto (EAL 2947), 6.7 km E Chuburna Puerto (EAL 2940), Dzibilchaltún (FMNH 153412–13,), 0.7 mi E Dzibilchaltún (KU 157345–46), 1 mi W Dzibilchaltún (KU 157347; UMRC 80-85), 3.7 mi W Dzilam Bravo (KU 157342–43), El Cuyo (JCL sight record), 10.7 km E Izamal (KU 157344), 21 km W Kantunil (EAL 2844), 3.7 km SW Kinchil (Dundee et al., 1986:41), 1.5 mi S Libre Unión (UCM 16255–56, 28614–18), 2.5 km S Libre Unión (CM 40008), Mayapán (KU 157351; MCZ 54649), Mérida (FMNH 19431, 105804, 111524, 112257, 153479–80; KU 157337, 157352; MCZ 6270, 167158; UIMNH 20242, 20248; USNM 8220–21; UU 9296), 5 mi N Mérida (UCM 16257–58), 9 mi N Mérida (UCM 16259), 19 mi E Mérida (UCM 16260), 2.6 mi S Muna (UCM 18251), Oxkintok (AMNH 388943–44), Oxkutzcab (AMNH 38939–42), Pisté (KU 70234–55, 70257; UCM 12769–79, 17033, 18254), 0.5 mi S Pisté (UMMZ 73008), Progreso (FMNH 111511, 111519–21; UIMNH 20251), 5 mi W Progreso (UIMNH 86989–93), 1 mi E Río Lagartos (UCM 28613), 6 mi S Río Lagartos (UCM 28619–23), Sisal (KU 157340), 12.1 mi NE Sisal (KU 157341), 13 km WSW Sisal (KU 70258), 3 mi S Telchac (UCM 28638), 7 mi N Telchac (UCM 28639), 4 mi N Telchac (UCM 28640), 6 km N Tizimín (KU 74904–5), 12 mi N Tizimín (CM 40126–28; UCM 28624–33), 2 mi S Uxmal (AMNH 93256), Uxmal

(CAS 141874; CM 22755; JCL photo; KU 70256, 157348–50), no specific locality (USNM 24724–25, 24898).

Genus *Iguana*

These very large lizards are found throughout much of Mexico, Central America, and south to southern Brazil and Paraguay. Representatives also occur on coastal Caribbean islands and in the West Indies. Two species are recognized, of which one occurs in the Yucatán Peninsula. *Iguana* is derived from the Arawak *iwana*, meaning "lizard."

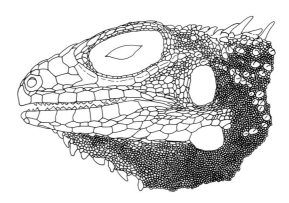

Fig. 125. Lateral view of the head of a juvenile *Iguana iguana*, 189 mm SVL.

Iguana iguana (Linnaeus)
(Figs. 125, 309, 310; Map 78)

Lacerta iguana Linnaeus, 1758:206. SYNTYPES: probably two syntypes, one in the Naturhistoriska Riksmuseet, Stockholm, and the other in the Gyllenborg collection in Uppsala (Hoogmoed, 1973:44). TYPE LOCALITY: In Indiis (= the Indies); restricted by Lazell (1973:7) to "Terre de Haut, Les Îles des Saintes, Departement de la Guadeloupe, French West Indies." Hoogmoed (1973:44, 152), however, noted that the specimens on which Linnaeus based his description were extant in Stockholm and Uppsala, and he restricted the type locality to "the confluence of the Coltica River and the Perica Creek, Surinam."

Green iguana; bamboo chicken, wayamaga (Belize); iguana ribera, iguana real (Mexico); yaax torok (Lacandón Maya); huh, yax-icil (Yucatec Maya).

DESCRIPTION   This is the largest lizard in the Yucatán Peninsula. Adult males average between 300 and 400 mm in snout-vent length; the females tend to be smaller, averaging about 100 mm less than males. The tail is extremely long, nearly three times the length of the head and body, and somewhat compressed laterally. The head is narrow and rather deep, the snout is rounded in dorsal view and truncated in lateral aspect (Fig. 309). The eyes are moderately large, and the pupils are vertically elliptical. The limbs are robust and powerful, and the digits bear large claws. The gular flap, which is especially conspicuous in adult males, bears enlarged triangular scales on the leading edge, giving a ser-

rated appearance. Beginning at the base of the head, a middorsal row of high, narrow scales extends the length of the body and onto the tail. The dorsal scales are small, juxtaposed, keeled, and larger than the lateral scales. The ventrals are smooth, imbricate, and larger than the dorsals. The dorsal surfaces of the limbs are covered with keeled imbricate scales; the ventral surfaces are smooth. The dorsal surfaces of the head are covered with enlarged, symmetrically arranged plates. A conspicuous enlarged circular scute on the side of the head ventral to the tympanum (Fig. 125) distinguishes this species from all other lizards in the Yucatán Peninsula. There is usually a series of enlarged spinose tubercles on the sides of the neck. About 18 to 20 femoral pores are present on the posteroventral surface of each thigh; these are larger in the males.

Iguanas change color as they age. Young individuals are bright green (Fig. 310), whereas older individuals—especially males—are greenish gray, tan, or brown, usually with an orange or orange-green head and a series of dark vertical bars on the sides of the body. The tail is distinctly marked with alternating light and dark bands of approximately equal width. The limbs and lower parts of the body are often suffused with orange.

SIMILAR SPECIES   *Ctenosaura similis*, the only species that approaches *Iguana* in size, is smaller, possesses whorls of enlarged spines on the tail (Fig. 123B), and lacks the enlarged circular scute on the side of the head seen in *Iguana* (Fig. 125). Adult ctenosaurs tend to be terrestrial, whereas adult iguanas are predominantly arboreal.

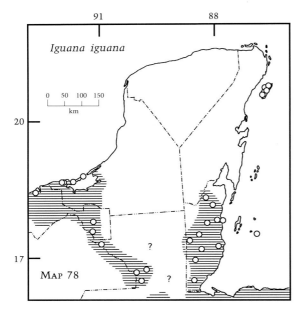

Iguana iguana

0 50 100 150
km

MAP 78

DISTRIBUTION The green iguana occurs at low elevations from Veracruz on the Atlantic slope and Sinaloa on the Pacific slope, south and eastward through Central America to tropical South America and on many Caribbean islands. This species occurs at the base of the Yucatán Peninsula from southwestern Campeche, eastern Tabasco, and El Petén to Belize. It is also known from Isla Cozumel and Quintana Roo, Mexico, and Half Moon Cay, Belize. Himmelstein (1980:28) said that he knew of reliable reports of I. iguana from mainland Quintana Roo, but I have found no documented records from that area (Map 78).

NATURAL HISTORY These large diurnal lizards are often associated with rivers and lakes. The adults perch conspicuously on branches overhanging the water. When disturbed they plunge in and disappear below the surface. They swim with limbs folded against the body, propelled largely by undulations of the tail.

In Belize, juvenile iguanas are often terrestrial, and there is a positive relationship between a lizard's size and the height at which it perches in the vegetation (Henderson, 1974b). Green iguanas are said to consume both plant and animal material as juveniles and then to become predominantly herbivorous as adults (e.g., Pough, 1973:841). Hoogmoed (1973:158) found only plant material in the stomachs of iguanas of all sizes from Surinam, however, and neither Iverson (1982:61) nor Van De-

vender (1982:171) found evidence of an ontogenetic shift from carnivory to herbivory.

Green iguanas are oviparous, and they are among the most fecund lizards in the New World. Rand (1984:115) reported a mean clutch size of 40.6 eggs in Panama, with a range of 9 to 71. The clutch size was positively correlated with the female's size. The females from Nicaragua studied by Fitch and Henderson (1977) laid fewer (mean = 30.5) and smaller eggs than Panamanian females of the same size. A large proportion of the females taken in western Nicaragua by Fitch and Henderson (1977:8) were gravid in January, February, and March. In Chiapas, breeding occurs in October and November, with oviposition in March and April (Alvarez del Toro, 1983:88–89). Thus, oviposition occurs during the dry season. The females construct nest burrows in sandy open areas such as stream banks. The nests are perhaps 1 to 2 m long and up to 0.5 m below the surface (Rand, 1968:558). Sometimes females form dense nesting aggregations, as at Slothia, Barro Colorado Island, Panama (Burghardt et al., 1977:689).

SUBSPECIES Two subspecies of Iguana were long recognized—I. i. rhinolopha, of northern Central America and Mexico, and the nominate subspecies, I. i. iguana, of lower Central America and South America—distinguished principally by the presence of enlarged, projecting scales on the snout in I. i. rhinolopha. Etheridge (1982:9) formally placed rhinolopha in the synonymy of iguana, however, because he found no consistent difference in this character among mainland populations of Iguana (Lazell, 1973:7).

ETYMOLOGY The specific name, iguana, is a tautonym of the generic name, which is derived from the Arawak iwana, meaning "lizard."

COMMENT This species is exploited extensively by humans as a source of animal protein, and its numbers have been substantially reduced throughout much of the range. Stuart (1948:53) noted the great reduction in numbers of green iguanas in the vicinity of human settlements in Alta Verapaz, and Fitch and Henderson (1978) and Fitch et al. (1982) documented other population declines in Middle America. In the late 1980s the Iguana Breeding Program at the Belize Zoo successfully released several hundred captive-bred iguanas into areas where numbers had been depleted.

Locality Records Belize: Belize: Belize (FMNH 4489; KU 144943–45), Boom (W. T. Neill and Allen, 1959c:40), Half Moon Cay (CM 4233, 7658; FMNH 34624; MCZ 61120), 8.5 mi W, 7.5 mi N Maskall (W. T. Neill and Allen, 1959c:40); Cayo: Chiquibul Branch, S Granos de Oro Camp (CM 112122), Coquercot (UMMZ 75026), Succotz (W. T. Neill and Allen, 1959c:40), upper Raspaculo River basin (Stafford, 1991:14); Orange Walk: near Orange Walk Town (MPM 8130); Stann Creek: 7 mi W, 1 mi S Stann Creek (JLK 509); Toledo: Crique Jute (MPM 8269), Las Lomitas (CM 105993). *Guatemala*: El Petén: Altar de Sacrificios (AMNH 99913), Arroyo Itzán (AMNH 99915), 16 km NNW Chinajá (KU 55978, 59882), Piedras Negras (UIMNH 11702–9; USNM 113505–12), Sayaxché (UCM 22243–44). *Mexico*: Campeche: near Atasta (JCL sight record; UIMNH 86996), 1.7 mi SW Carrillo Puerto (KU 15754–55), Ciudad del Carmen (FMNH 117783–86; MCZ 73904; UCM 20545), 25 km NE Ciudad del Carmen (KU 75529–31); Quintana Roo: Isla Cozumel (CM 27575, 27577; FMNH 749; USNM 13901–2), Cozumel (CM 27575, 27577; Himmelstein, 1980:28), Cozumel, Punta Moreno (UF uncat.), Cozumel, San Miguel (UMMZ 78596–97), Cozumel, 3.5 km N San Miguel (KU 70263), Cozumel, 6 mi E San Miguel (UMMZ 78595), Cozumel, 3 km W El Cedral (MCZ 141371); Tabasco: Balancán de Dominguez (JCL photo), 7 mi SW Frontera (UIMNH 86995), Tenosique (USNM 113500).

Family Phrynosomatidae

Nine genera of small to medium-sized diurnal lizards constitute this family, whose representatives range from southern Canada to Costa Rica. Most phrynosomatids live in open, semiarid habitats where they are typically terrestrial or saxicolous, although some species inhabit montane situations and a few species are arboreal. One phrynosomatid genus occurs in the Yucatán Peninsula.

The genera presently assigned to the Phrynosomatidae were long known informally as "sceloporines" until D. R. Frost and Etheridge (1989) elevated the group to family rank. The most recent analysis of relationships among phrynosomatid lizards is by Wiens (1993), who supported the monophyly of the *Sceloporus* group based on cladistic analysis of morphology, karyology, and behavior.

Genus *Sceloporus* (Spiny Lizards)

These small to medium-large lizards have heavily keeled—often spiny—dorsal, lateral, and caudal scales. Many species are terrestrial, some are saxicolous, and others are arboreal. Members of this genus inhabit a variety of habitats from sea level to high elevations, ranging from temperate North America throughout Mexico and Central America to Panama. Most species are oviparous, but viviparity has evolved independently several times (Shine, 1985). The most comprehensive treatment of the genus is H. M. Smith, 1939b. K. R. Larson and Tanner (1974) analyzed cranial osteology to infer the evolutionary history of the group (K. R. Larson and Tanner, 1975), and Hall (1973, 1980) and Cole (1971, 1978) studied the karyology of various species groups. Biochemical studies of Mexican *Sceloporus* include those by Sites and Davis (1989) and Sites et al. (1988). Recent hypotheses of phylogenetic relationships within the genus were summarized by Sites et al. (1992). The genus contains approximately 70 species, 5 of which occur in the Yucatán Peninsula. *Sceloporus*, is from the Greek *skelos*, "leg," and the Latin *porus*, "pore" or "passage," possibly in reference to the conspicuous femoral pores on males.

Key to the Species of the Genus *Sceloporus*

1. Postfemoral dermal pocket present 2
   No postfemoral dermal pocket 3
2. Venter of males with two large patches of purple or violet outlined in black; base of Yucatán Peninsula only (Map 83) . . . . *Sceloporus teapensis*
   Venter of males immaculate white or nearly so; coastal and insular in northern third of Yucatán Peninsula (Map 80) . . . . *Sceloporus cozumelae*
3. More than 22 femoral pores (total, both sides); venter of males immaculate or nearly so; adult SVL less than 65 mm . . . . *Sceloporus chrysostictus*

Fewer than 22 femoral pores; venter of males with two large bluish patches; adult SVL greater than 65 mm. 4

4. Distinct black nuchal collar bordered with white or yellow . . . . *Sceloporus serrifer*
   No distinct black nuchal collar. . . . . *Sceloporus lundelli*

Clave para las Especies del Género *Sceloporus*

1. Con una bolsa postfemoral 2
   Sin una bolsa postfemoral 3

2. El vientre de los machos con dos parches grandes de color morado o violeta delineados con negro; organismos que se distribuyen unicamente en la base de la Península de Yucatán (Mapa 83). . . . . *Sceloporus teapensis*
   El vientre de los machos inmaculado blanco, o casi blanco; organismos que se distribuyen en la costa e islas del tercio norte de la Península de Yucatán (Mapa 80) . . . . *Sceloporus cozumelae*

3. Más de 22 poros femorales; vientre de los machos inmaculado o casi blanco; adultos menores a 65 mm de LHC. . . . . *Sceloporus chrysostictus*
   Menos de 22 poros femorales (total de ambos lados); vientre de los machos con dos parches largos azulados; adultos mayores a 65 mm de LHC 4

4. Collar nucal distintivo color negro bordeado con blanco o amarillo . . . . . . *Sceloporus serrifer*
   Sin collar nucal distintivo . . . . *Sceloporus lundelli*

Sceloporus chrysostictus Cope
(Figs. 311, 312; Map 79)

Sceloporus chrysostictus Cope, 1866:125. SYN-TYPES: USNM 24865–66 (two syntypes), *fide* D. M. Cochran, 1961:134. TYPE LOCALITY: Yucatán, Mexico; restricted to Chichén Itzá, Yucatán, Mexico, by H. M. Smith and Taylor (1950b:352).

Yellow-spotted spiny lizard; lagartija escamosa (Mexico); merech (Yucatec Maya).

DESCRIPTION This rather small terrestrial lizard exhibits moderate sexual size dimorphism. The males average about 54 mm in snout-vent length, the females about 51 mm. The dorsal scales are imbricate, heavily keeled, and mucronate; those on the venter are smaller, imbricate, and smooth. The undamaged tail is roughly 1.4 times the head and body length. The limbs are well developed, the hands and feet are pentadactyl, and the digits terminate in strong claws. Twelve to 15 femoral pores are present on the posteroventral surface of each thigh; they are better developed and more conspicuous in males. Enlarged postanal scales are present in males.

Color and pattern vary ontogenetically and sexually. The females and subadult males are generally brown, tan, or gray above, with two rows of dark transverse bars or chevrons extending the length of the body and onto the tail, where they may coalesce to form bands. There may be a pair of indistinct light dorsolateral stripes that originate on the neck and extend to the base of the tail (Fig. 311). In both sexes the venter is immaculate white, cream, or yellow. The adult males generally have a pair of distinct yellow or cream dorsolateral stripes that contrast with the dark brown or gray dorsal ground color. The flanks of males are usually dark brown or nearly black with many scattered light spots, often of a pinkish or orange hue. Immediately above the insertion of the forelimbs there is a large, irregular black blotch (Fig. 312), usually smaller and less distinct in females. Reproductive females have a suffusion of red-orange pigment on the lips and shoulders.

SIMILAR SPECIES *Sceloporus cozumelae* and *S. teapensis* have a postfemoral dermal pocket and fewer (7–12 vs. 12–15) femoral pores on each thigh.

DISTRIBUTION This species is endemic to the Yucatán Peninsula, where it occurs from northern Guatemala and central Belize northward (Map 79).

NATURAL HISTORY *Sceloporus chrysostictus* is a diurnal lizard that is abundant in thorn forest, forest edge, and disturbed situations but shuns the

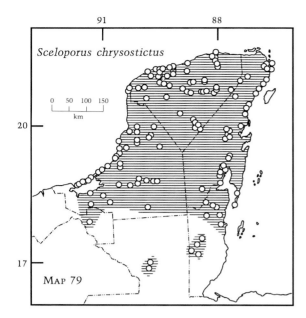

Sceloporus chrysostictus

0 50 100 150
km

MAP 79

deep shade of primary forest. Individuals are often seen darting across roads or heard scampering over the forest floor. They perch conspicuously on rock outcrops, logs, or the bases of trees and are unusually wary and difficult to capture (Maslin, 1963a:14; Penner, 1973:7). Penner (1970) studied their feeding habits in the vicinity of Progreso, Yucatán, and found that small invertebrates—mostly insects, but also spiders and mites—formed the largest part of the diet. In addition, cannibalism was reported by H. M. Smith and Fritts (1969:182).

Like most sceloporines, *S. chrysostictus* is oviparous. Fitch (1970:42) examined specimens from Campeche, Yucatán, and Quintana Roo and concluded that there is a relatively long reproductive period. A large proportion of females carry eggs during the winter and spring months. The number declines in July and then rises again in August and September. Individuals apparently are capable of producing multiple clutches within a breeding season. The average clutch size, 2.4, is remarkably small for a *Sceloporus*. In El Petén, the hatchlings appear in late May, coincident with the onset of the rainy season (Stuart, 1935:45). According to Fitch (1978:449), this species attains reproductive maturity within one year of birth.

ETYMOLOGY The specific name, *chrysostictus*, is from the Greek *chrysos*, "gold," and *stiktos*, "punctured," "dotted," or "dappled," presumably a reference to the yellow markings on males, which contrast strongly with their dark background color.

Locality Records Belize: Belize: Altun Ha (MPM 8064–65; USNM 194827–29), bet. Ladyville and Sandhill (CM 90924–27, 90931), 1 mi S Maskalls (KU 157357–62), Rockstone Pond (AMNH 104420), Kate's Lagoon (FMNH 49211–14); Cayo: ca. 2 mi W Belmopan (CM 105760–61), Blancaneaux Lodge (JLK 405–6), 12 mi S Cayo (UMMZ 70423–24), ca. 3 mi S Georgeville (CM 91018); Corozal: Ambergris Cay, 4.5 km N, 1 km E San Pedro (CM 91108); Orange Walk: Honey Camp (USNM 194903), Lamanai (ROM H12706, H12741, H12760–63, H12764, H13276–77), 20 mi SE Orange Walk Town (BCB 12788), Yo River (MPM 7614–15); no specific locality (USNM 57005). *Guatemala*: El Petén: near La Libertad (UMMZ 74957–69), Sojio (AMNH 70001). *Mexico*: Campeche: Balchacaj (FMNH 33521–22), 3 mi SW Bolonchén (UCM 28881–93, 88904–5), 5 mi E Campeche (UCM 16428), 36 mi E Campeche (UCM 16429), Candelaria (UCM 39209), 7.8 km SE Hwy. 186 on rd. to Candelaria (KU 171519), Champotón (UMMZ 72920–26), 5 mi N Champotón (UCM 16430–40), 41.1 mi S Champotón (UCM 18538–56), 9 mi W Champotón (UCM 39172), 9 mi SW Champotón (UCM 39173–76), 10.9 mi SW Champotón (UCM 39179–81), 13.5 mi SW Champotón (UCM 39183–85), 16 mi SW Champotón (UCM 39186–211), 16 mi W Champotón (UCM 39236–39), 5 km S Champotón (KU 70277–86), 8.7 mi S Champotón (KU 157363–64), 1.6 mi N Champotón (KU 157365–66), 6 km SW Champotón (KU 70287–91), 11 km S Champotón (KU 70292–93), 6.3 km SW Champotón (CM 64770; EAL 2929), 30 km SW Champotón (EAL 2930), 8.5 mi N Chencoyi (UCM 39170–71), Chuina (KU 74915–26), Ciudad del Carmen (FMNH 33516–20, 117241–42, 117244–46; UIMNH 20532–35), 6 mi NNE Ciudad del Carmen (UIMNH 87040–43), 12.3 mi ENE Ciudad del Carmen (KU 157367–72), Ciudad del Carmen (UCM 16427, 20752–54, 20755–59), 9 mi E Ciudad del Carmen (UCM 39281–88), 17 km E Ciudad del Carmen (CM 40007), 48 km N Concepción (KU 74913–14), Dzibalchén (KU 75544–56), Edzná ruins (KU 171509), 4.5 km N Edzná ruins (KU 171508), 5 mi W Escárcega (UCM 29107), 25 mi E Escárcega (UCM 28901–2, 29108–9), 40 mi E Escárcega (LSUMZ 33405–7), Grutas Xtacumbilxunán (CM 40135), 4.1 mi E Ich-Ek (LACM 61990), Isla Aguada (KU 75557–65), 15 mi W Isla Aguada (UCM 39253), 10 mi W Isla Aguada (UCM 39254), 10 mi E Isla Aguada (UCM 39255–260), 9 mi NE Isla Aguada (UCM 39261–80), 5–10 km NE Isla Aguada (UMRC 84-166), Isla del Carmen, Puerto Real (CM 38930; UCM 28865–80), Isla del Carmen, 1 km SW Puerto Real (KU 70269–76), 21.6 km E Ixbonil (EAL 2893), Laguna Chumpich (KU 74912), Laguna Silvituc (EAL 2895; KU 74927–31), 20 mi SW Lerma (UIMNH 87045), 24 mi E Sabancuy (UCM 39212–21), 6 mi NE Sabancuy (UCM 39204–52), 5 mi W Sabancuy 39222–24), 8.5 mi NE Sabancuy (UCM 39225–35), 4.8 km NE Sabancuy (KU 171515–18), 5 mi NE Sabancuy

(UIMNH 87044), 8.5 mi NE Sabancuy (UCM 36409), San José Carpizo (UMMZ 99857), 46 mi E Silvituc (UCM 28894–900), 52 mi E Silvituc (UCM 28903), 0.9 km E Silvituc (KU 171510–14), 9.4 km N Tenabo (EAL 2935), Tres Brazos (FMNH 33523–27, 117240, 117243); Quintana Roo: Akumal (Himmelstein, 1980:28), 4.9 mi N Bacalar (KU 157374), 7.1 mi S Bacalar (KU 157373), Lake Bacalar (LSUMZ 33409–12), Cancún (FMNH 34647–48), Chetumal (FMNH 49215–16), 32.3 mi N Chetumal (KU 157377–78), 82 km N Chetumal (UCM 39302), Chunyaxché (KU 171474–75), Cobá (KU 171470; JCL photo), 3 mi S Felipe Carrillo Puerto (UCM 28906–9), 3 mi NE Felipe Carrillo Puerto (CAS 141868), 8.5 km NE Felipe Carrillo Puerto (KU 171473), 4 km NNE Felipe Carrillo Puerto (KU 70337–41), 7 km NNE Felipe Carrillo Puerto (KU 70342), 11 km NNE Felipe Carrillo Puerto (KU 70343), 13.8 mi N Felipe Carrillo Puerto (KU 157376), Isla Mujeres (FMNH 34643–44; UMMZ 78565–66; UCM 16441–16454, 39291), S end Isla Mujeres (KU 70344–52), Isla Mujeres, Rancho Pirata (KU 70353–68), Kohunlich (LSUMZ 33408), 11.3 km N Limones (EAL 2884–86), 15.4 km N Limones (KU 171472), 30.7 km SW Limones (KU 171471), 3.3 mi N Limones (KU 157375), 5 mi S Las Palmas (km 106, S Felipe Carrillo Puerto) (UCM 39299–301), Playa del Carmen (UCM 16456–60), 24 km NNE Pueblo Nuevo X-Can (LSUMZ 28282–83), Pueblo Nuevo X-Can (KU 70294–319; UCM 28920–77), W edge Pueblo Nuevo X-Can (KU 157380), Puerto Juárez (KU 70320–22; UCM 16455), 1 km S Puerto Juárez (UCM 39293), 4 km WSW Puerto Juárez (KU 70323–36), 7 mi S Puerto Juárez (UCM 39295), 17.1 km S Puerto Juárez (EAL 2856–57), 65 km S Puerto Morelos (EAL 2869), Puerto Morelos (USNM 47628–29), 6 mi S Puerto Morelos (UCM 39296–98), Santa Cruz (probably Chan Santa Cruz = Felipe Carrillo Puerto) (UCM 18534–37), Tulum (Himmelstein, 1980:28), 5 mi inland from Vigía (UMMZ 78567–68), Xcalak (KU 74932), Xel-ha (JCL photo); Tabasco: 17.7 km E Emiliano Zapata (EAL 2909); Yucatán: Bella Flor (Dundee et al. 1986:41), 5.1 mi W Buctzotz (KU 157387), 22.1 km N Calkini (EAL 2938), N edge Celestún (KU 157385), 2 mi N Celestún (KU 157386), 3 mi E Chemax (CAS 141863–64), Chichén Itzá (AMNH 68973; FMNH 27339–40, 33494–95, 36526–28, 117251; JCL photo; MCZ 7117; TCWC 57127; UIMNH 20531; UMMZ 68203–213, 72906, 72908, 72910–18, 80867–75, 83117–20), 2 mi E Chichén Itzá (UCM 49605), 2 km E Chichén Itzá (KU 70444–45), 8.6 km E Chichén Itzá (EAL 2846), Hacienda Chichén Itzá (UMMZ 72896–900, 72902–5), 6.7 km E Churburna Puerto (EAL 2941), Dzibilchaltún (KU 157383; FMNH 153467–78, 153481–89, 153491–94), 1 mi W Dzibilchaltún (KU 157384), Dzilam de Bravo (AMNH 110039–41), 3 mi N Dzitás (UCM 39362), 7 mi N Dzitás (UCM 39358), 3 mi E Esmeralda (LACM 114032–40), Grutas Balankanché (TCWC 57123), 3 mi W Holca (UCM 39359–61), 12 mi S Izamal (UMMZ 80866), 12.3 mi E Izamal (KU 157382), 3.7 km SW Kinchil (TU 19808), 1.5 mi E Presumida (UCM 28910–19), 1.5 mi S Libre Unión (UCM 16461–68, 18566, 29046–51), Mayapán (FMNH 40685–89; UMRC 80-66, 84-95), Mérida (FMNH 33496, 117247), 5 mi N Mérida (UCM 16469–79), 9 mi N Mérida (UCM 12830–37), 7.1 km E Mérida (EAL 2840), 19 mi E Mérida (UCM 16480–92), 14 km N, 2 km E Mérida (UMMZ 72927), 8 mi SE Peto (UCM 39377–80), 18 mi SE Peto (BCB 12784), 29 mi SE Peto (BCB 12785), Pisté (FMNH 36529; KU 70369–442; UCM 12838–76, 16501–6, 17034–42, 18557–65; UMMZ 72919), 6.5 km W Pisté (KU 70443), Progreso (CAS 54639–40; FMNH 33488–93, 117248–50, 117252; MCZ 7124, 146939–41; UIMNH 20529–30; UMMZ 79471), 3 mi S Progreso (UCM 39331–55), 4 mi E Progreso (UCM 50754–56; UIMNH 87035), 5 mi W Progreso (UIMNH 87006–34), 2 km S Río Lagartos (KU 171476–77), 5 mi S Río Lagartos (UCM 28978–84), 6 mi S Río Lagartos (UCM 28985–90), 12 mi S Río Lagartos (UCM 39330), 4 km SE Río Lagartos (KU 171480–81), on beach across from Río Lagartos (UCM 39303–29), San Ignacio (MCZ 7240), 2.3 mi S, 1.9 mi E Santa Rosa (KU 157379), 1 mi W Sisal (UIMNH 87036), 3 km WSW Sisal (KU 70446–54), 5 mi SE Sisal (UIMNH 87037–39), 12 km E Sisal (UMRC 84-164), 12.5 km E Sisal (CM 45273), 8.3 km W Suma (KU 171479), 10 mi E Tekax (BCB 12789), 14 mi E Tekax (UCM 39374–76), Tekom (FMNH 49217–24), 2.4 mi N Telchac (UCM 29058–59), 4 mi N Telchac (UCM 29060–70), 6.6 mi S Telchac (CM 40131–34; UCM 29071–75, 29099–106), 7 mi N Telchac (UCM 29076–91), Telchac Puerto (UCM 29052–57; UMMZ 76159), 4 mi W Telchac Puerto (UCM 29092–98), 3 mi S Telchac Puerto (UCM 39356–57, 39363–73), 6 mi N Tizimín (KU 74933–49), 12 mi N Tizimín (UCM 28991–29045), bet. Tunkás and Sitilpech (KU 171478), Valladolid (UCM 16493–97), 3.3 mi N Valladolid (UCM 16498–500), 44 km N Campeche-Yucatán border (LSUMZ 28284); no specific locality (USNM 47630–31, 47640–42).

Sceloporus cozumelae Jones
(Figs. 126, 313; Map 80)

Sceloporus cozumelae Jones, 1927:1. HOLOTYPE: USNM 13904. TYPE LOCALITY: Isla Cozumel, Yucatán (= Quintana Roo), Mexico.

Cozumel spiny lizard; lagartija playera (Mexico); merech (Yucatec Maya).

DESCRIPTION *Sceloporus cozumelae* is a small terrestrial lizard with pronounced sexual size dimorphism. The males average about 51 mm in snout-vent length, the females about 46 mm. The

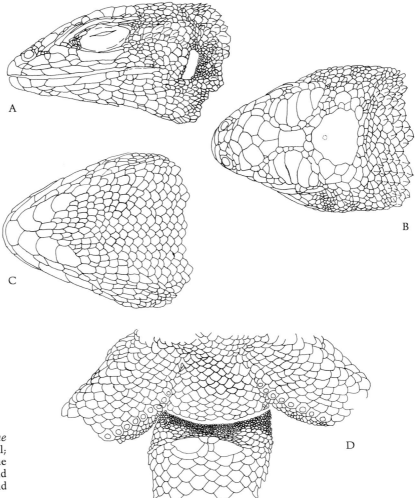

Fig. 126. *Sceloporus cozumelae* (UMRC 80-101), 53 mm SVL. A, lateral; B, dorsal; and C, ventral views of the head. D, ventral view of the thighs and vent region; between Progreso and Dzilam Bravo, Yucatán, Mexico.

dorsal scales are heavily keeled, imbricate, and mucronate (Fig. 126). The ventral scales are smaller than the dorsals, imbricate, and smooth. The limbs are well developed, the hands and feet are pentadactyl, and the digits terminate in strong claws. The undamaged tail is about a third longer than the snout-vent length. There are 6 to 10 femoral pores on the posteroventral surface of each thigh. The pores are well developed and conspicuous in males; in females they are rudimentary. The males possess a pair of enlarged postanal scales (Fig. 126D).

The color and pattern vary both ontogenetically and sexually. In general, these are rather pale lizards (Fig. 313). The females and young males typically have a brown or gray dorsal ground color with a light vertebral stripe and a pair of light dorsolateral stripes originating near the back of the head and extending the length of the body and onto the tail. Between the stripes there are usually two series of black chevron markings, these bordered posteriorly by white, light gray, or yellow. Reproductive females have a suffusion of red-orange on the lips and upper parts of the shoulders. In older, darker males, the dorsal pattern is obscure. The dorsal surfaces of the limbs are gray or brown with light and dark spots and bars. The venter is immaculate white in both sexes. Immediately above the insertion of the forelimbs there is a conspicuous black spot with a white or yellow border along the anterior margin; it is more distinct in males.

SIMILAR SPECIES *Sceloporus chrysostictus* lacks a postfemoral dermal pocket and has more (mean = 13) femoral pores on each thigh; *S. teapensis* occurs only at the base of the Yucatán Peninsula (Map 83), and the males have brightly colored venters.

DISTRIBUTION This species is endemic to the Yucatán Peninsula, where it is known from numerous coastal localities in Yucatán and Quintana Roo, and from Cozumel, Isla Contoy, and Isla Mujeres (Map 80).

NATURAL HISTORY This alert, swift-moving lizard is found on beaches and coastal strands; individuals are often seen darting among shrubs and low vegetation. Further inland this species appears to be replaced by *S. chrysostictus*, from which it differs in being much less wary and thus more easily approached (Penner, 1973). Diurnal and terrestrial, these watch-and-wait predators feed on insects and other small invertebrates. Penner (1970) studied the diet in the vicinity of Progreso, Yucatán, and found that lizards there consumed insects and isopod crustaceans.

Sceloporus cozumelae is oviparous, but little else is known of the reproduction of this Yucatecan endemic. The majority of the adult females collected by Maslin (1963a:13) during the summer months carried eggs. Gaige (1936:297) reported that two females from Yucatán each carried 5 eggs. According to Fitch (1978:447), however, the average number of eggs per female is only 1.8, the smallest clutch size of any *Sceloporus*. The presence of juveniles and subadults in a single sample suggests that breeding is prolonged, and females probably produce multiple clutches within a single breeding season. Fitch (1978:449) indicated that this species attains reproductive maturity within one year of hatching.

ETYMOLOGY The specific name, *cozumelae*, is a toponym that refers to Isla Cozumel, the type locality.

Locality Records *Mexico*: Quintana Roo: Cancún (López-Gonzales, 1991:105), Chiquila (JCL sight record), Cozumel (Himmelstein, 1980:28), Cozumel, San Miguel (UMMZ 78571), Cozumel, 3 km N San Miguel (UCM 12878–908), Cozumel, 3.5 km N San Miguel (KU 70478–88), Cozumel, 4 km N San Miguel (UCM 12909–23), Cozumel, 5 km N San Miguel (UCM 16622–25, 20760–61; UF 17558), Cozumel, 6 km N San Miguel (UCM 16626), Cozumel, 6 mi N San Miguel (UMMZ 78572), Cozumel, 3 mi S San Miguel (UMMZ 78573), Fraccionamiento La Vida (López-Gonzales, 1991:105), Isla Contoy (UCM 16617–21),

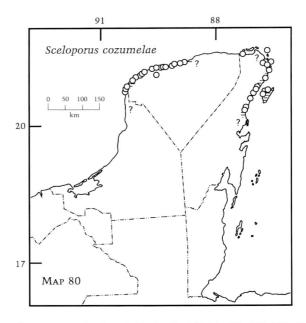

MAP 80

Isla Mujeres (UCM 16648–62, 39381–87; UF 17557; UMMZ 78569–70), S end Isla Mujeres (KU 70469–76), Petempich (López-Gonzales, 1991:105), Playa del Carmen (EAL 2865; Himmelstein, 1980:28; UCM 16605–16), km 91 on Hwy. 397 (López-Gonzales, 1991:105), 10 mi S Playa del Carmen (LSUMZ 33401–2), Puerto Aventuras (López-Gonzales, 1991:105), Puerto Juárez (JCL photo; KU 70455–68, 171434–53, 171759–60; UCM 16627–47), 1 mi SW Puerto Juárez (UCM 39388–92), 1 km S Puerto Juárez (UCM 39393–402), Puerto Morelos (AMNH 110042–43), Punta Maroma (López-Gonzales, 1991:105), Punta Nizuc (KU 171430–33), Punta Venado (López-Gonzales, 1991:105), Tulum ruins (AMNH 110044), 1.5 km S Tulum (KU 171428–29); no specific locality (USNM 47643); Yucatán: Celestún (KU 157436–40), 1 km N Celestún (UMRC 84-165), 4 km N Celestún (UMRC 84-161), 2 mi E Chicxulub Puerto (CM 38934), 5.4 km E Chicxulub Puerto (EAL 2949), 7.8 km NE Chicxulub Puerto (CM 64777–79; EAL 2952), bet. Chicxulub Puerto and Uaymitun (KU 171454–58), 6.7 km E Churburna Puerto (EAL 2944), Dzibilchaltún (FMNH 153490), Dzilam Bravo (Ives, 1891:459), Progreso (AMNH 38945; UIMNH 20590–92), near Progreso (UMMZ 72892–95; FMNH 33469–76, 106481–85; MCZ 7254, 146931–38), 2 mi E Progreso (TU 19501), 4 mi E Progreso (UIMNH 87046–49), 5 mi W Progreso (UIMNH 87050–90), bet. Progreso and Dzilam Bravo (UMRC 80-101), E edge Santa Clara (KU 157430–35), Sisal (JCL photo), SW edge Sisal (KU 157388–410), 1.6 km W Sisal (KU 171459–67; UIMNH 87091–97), 3 km WSW Sisal (KU 70489–503), 8 km WSW Sisal (KU 70504), 13 km WSW Sisal (KU 70505–14), 10 mi NE Sisal (KU 157411–14), 1.8 km S Sisal (CM 45274–76), Telchac Puerto (UMMZ 79470), 7.7 mi W Telchac Puerto (KU

157420–22), 4.6 mi E Telchac Puerto (KU 157423–29), 17.8 mi W Telchac Puerto (KU 157415–19).

Sceloporus lundelli Smith
(Figs. 127, 314; Map 81)

Sceloporus lundelli H. M. Smith, 1939b:66. HOLO-
TYPE: UMMZ 80674. TYPE LOCALITY: Cohune Ridge
(20 miles southeast of Benque Viejo), British Honduras.

Lundell's spiny lizard; largartija espinosa de Lundell (Mexico).

DESCRIPTION   The adults of this large, robust, and very spiny lizard average between 85 and 95 mm in snout-vent length (Fig. 314). Fitch (1978:446) reported significant sexual size dimorphism, with females averaging about 5 mm longer than males. The head is short and broad, and the snout is bluntly rounded in dorsal aspect (Fig. 127B). The body is rather stocky, and the limbs are short and robust. The scales on the dorsal surfaces of the body and appendages are large, heavily keeled, and mucro-nate. The ventral scales are smooth and smaller than the dorsals. Eight to 10 femoral pores are pres-ent on the posteroventral surface of each thigh (Fig. 127D), better developed in males than in females.

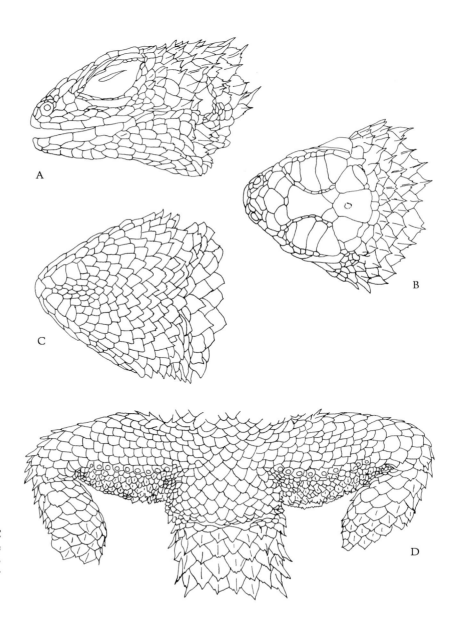

Fig. 127. *Sceloporus lundelli* (UMRC 89-41), 89 mm SVL. A, lateral; B, dorsal; and C, ventral views of the head. D, ventral view of the thighs and vent re-gion; Augustine, Cayo, Belize.

Sceloporus lundelli is predominantly gray. The dorsal pattern, if any, consists of a series of irregular, jagged dark brown or black transverse bars or spots that extend onto the tail. The anteriormost bar may form a narrow, indistinct nuchal collar. There may be a light interorbital bar on the dorsal surface of the head, and many specimens have a light spot on the parietal scale. A dark band is usually present on the posterior surface of the thigh of specimens from the base of the peninsula, but not on specimens from northern populations. Some individuals, especially those from the outer end of the peninsula, lack a dorsal pattern. In females the venter is immaculate bluish gray or cream. The adult males bear a pair of large, blue ventral patches, which may be continuous on the chest.

SIMILAR SPECIES   Their large size will distinguish the adults of this species from all others in the Yucatán Peninsula except *Sceloporus serrifer*, which is also similar in possessing very large and spiny dorsal scales. *Sceloporus serrifer* has a conspicuous black nuchal collar with a light border. *Sceloporus cozumelae* and *S. teapensis* possess postfemoral dermal pockets; *S. chrysostictus* is much less spinose and usually has more than 10 femoral pores on each thigh.

DISTRIBUTION   This species is endemic to the Yucatán Peninsula, where it occurs more or less continuously through the northwest portion of the peninsula. Southern populations, apparently disjunct, occur in El Petén and Belize (Map 81).

NATURAL HISTORY   *Sceloporus lundelli* is an arboreal, diurnal inhabitant of forests and forest edges. Individuals are typically seen on tree trunks, which they may ascend to a height of 20 m or more (Duellman, 1965a:603), but they have also been found on columnar cacti, and I have seen them on fences and on the sides of wooden buildings. At Balchacaj, Campeche, H. M. Smith (1939:71) found them both deep in heavily wooded areas and at the wood's edge. These lizards are alert, wary, and difficult to approach. They are watch-and-wait predators and presumably feed on a variety of invertebrates.

Fitch (1978:454) inferred viviparity for this species on the basis of its presumed close relationship to the viviparous *S. malachiticus*.

SUBSPECIES   Two subspecies are recognized: *S. l. lundelli*, which occurs through the base of the Yucatán Peninsula in southern Campeche, El Petén,

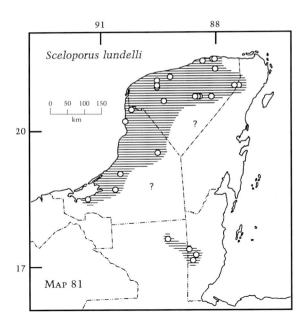

MAP 81

and Belize; and *S. l. gaigeae*, which is found on the more xeric outer end of the peninsula in Yucatán and northern Quintana Roo.

ETYMOLOGY   The specific name, *lundelli*, is a patronym honoring the collector of the type specimen, Cyrus Lundell, a botanist who studied the flora of the lowland Maya area under the auspices of the Carnegie Institute of Washington.

Locality Records   Belize: Cayo: Augustine (MPM 8198; UMRC 89-41), Cohune Ridge (UMMZ 80674), El Cayo (UMMZ 80675). *Guatemala*: El Petén: Uaxactún (AMNH 68518–20, 70937; MCZ 38665; UMMZ 70420–22). *Mexico*: Campeche: Balchacaj (FMNH 32061–62, 32088, 32123, 32257, 32778, 126888–91; UIMNH 27266–67; UMMZ 81906–8; USNM 138892), Chuina (KU 74950), Dzibalchén (KU 75569–75), 13 km W, 1 km N Escárcega (KU 70549), Jaina (USNM 46862), Tankuche–El Remate (IHNHERP 541); Quintana Roo: Pueblo Nuevo X-Can (KU 70535); Yucatán: Chichén Itzá (FMNH 27332–33, 36470–80; MCZ 7119, 29236, 53920; UMMZ 72880, 83113–16, 83926), Dzibilchaltún (FMNH 153390–91, 153395), Mayapán (FMNH 40696–703), Mérida (FMNH 31524, 32010, 40690–95; UIMNH 27265), 5 mi N Mérida (UCM 16666), Pisté (CM 49905, 49907–12; KU 70537–43; UCM 12947, 16667), 6.5 km W Pisté (KU 70536), Reserva Dzilam Bravo (UAYM uncat.), Río Lagartos (KU 171424–25), 1 mi E Río Lagartos (UCM 28707–20), San Ignacio (CM 38933), Tekom (FMNH 49225–34), 3 mi S Telchac (UCM 28739), 12 mi N Tizimín (UCM 28705–6), X-Can (UCM 18533); no specific locality (USNM 24875).

Sceloporus serrifer Cope
(Figs. 128, 315; Map 82)

Sceloporus serrifer Cope, 1866:124. HOLOTYPE: USNM 24868. TYPE LOCALITY: Yucatán; restricted by H. M. Smith and Taylor (1950b:352) to Mérida, Yucatán, Mexico.

Escamoso ocotero (Mexico).

DESCRIPTION This large, spiny *Sceloporus* averages between 80 and 90 mm in snout-vent length (Fig. 315). The fragile tail is only about 1.6 times the length of the head and body. The head is broad, distinct from the neck, and somewhat depressed. The snout is bluntly rounded in dorsal aspect (Fig. 128B). The body is moderately short and rounded in dorsal view, and the limbs are short and robust. Six to 11 femoral pores are present on the postero-ventral surface of each thigh (Fig. 128D); these are better developed in males than in females. The head is covered by a series of symmetrically arranged plates (Fig. 128B), whereas the dorsal surfaces of the body and the appendages are covered with large imbricate scales that are strongly keeled and mucronate. The ventral scales are smooth, imbricate, and conspicuously smaller than the dorsals.

The dorsum is yellowish tan or gray with about four indistinct, irregular, dark brown transverse bars, which are bordered posteriorly by light blue or

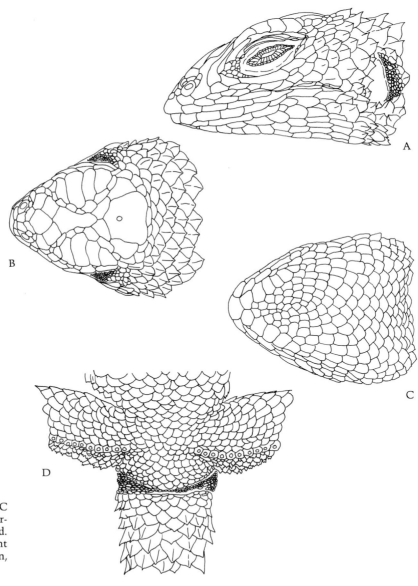

Fig. 128. *Sceloporus serrifer* (UMRC 79-308), 58 mm SVL. A, lateral; B, dorsal; and C, ventral views of the head. D, ventral view of the thighs and vent region; Ruinas Mayapán, Yucatán, Mexico.

gray. There is a distinct black or dark brown nuchal collar, narrow at the side of the neck and broadest in the middorsal area, bordered on both sides by light blue or gray. The dorsal surface of the head is dark brown or black with large white, yellow, or bluish spots. The dorsal surface of the tail has alternating dark and light bands, and the appendages are indistinctly banded with light and dark markings. In females the venter is immaculate bluish gray or tan, whereas in males the venter bears indistinct bluish patches.

SIMILAR SPECIES   The large size and spiny scales distinguish this species from all other *Sceloporus* except *S. lundelli*, which lacks the distinct black collar.

DISTRIBUTION   This species exists as a series of disjunct populations distributed at low and moderate elevations from southern Tamaulipas and eastern San Luis Potosí south and eastward on the Atlantic slope through Veracruz to Chiapas, northern Guatemala, Belize, and Yucatán. The populations at the base of the Yucatán Peninsula are apparently isolated from the northern populations (Map 82).

NATURAL HISTORY   *Sceloporus serrifer* is moderately common in the Yucatán Peninsula, where it occupies a variety of habitats ranging from tall mesic forests at the base of the peninsula, to low, arid thorn forests in northwestern Yucatán. In forested situations this species tends to occupy edge

habitats, and individuals are usually found on the trunks of large trees. In Yucatán they commonly occur on the rock walls bordering henequén fields and on Maya ruins. These diurnal lizards are alert, very wary, and difficult to approach.

In El Petén, Stuart (1935:45) saw "recently hatched" individuals in mid-May, before the onset of the rainy season; however, all members of the *torquatus* species group of *Sceloporus*, which includes *S. serrifer*, are believed to be viviparous (Fitch, 1970:49; Guillette et al., 1980:204).

ETYMOLOGY   The specific name, *serrifer*, derives from the Latin *serra*, "saw," and *-fer*, a suffix meaning "to bear" or "to carry," presumably in reference to the large spiny scales.

SUBSPECIES   Stuart (1970), recognized three subspecies, of which the nominate form, *S. s. serrifer*, occurs in the northern portion of the Yucatán Peninsula. Specimens from the base of the peninsula are intermediate between the other races, and Stuart was unable to assign them to any of the named subspecies. Olson (1987) considered *S. cyanogenys* of southern Texas and northern Mexico to be a subspecies of *S. serrifer*. According to McCoy (1990:165), the single known specimen from Belize is intermediate between *S. s. serrifer* of Yucatán and *S. s. prezygus* of southwestern Guatemala, the latter a form afforded specific status by some systematists (e.g., Axtell, 1960; Guillette et al., 1980:204).

Locality Records Belize: Cayo: Mountain Pine Ridge, Thousand-Foot Falls (CM 91003). *Guatemala*: El Petén: Desempeña (USNM 112340–41), El Repasto (UCM 22268–74), Piedras Negras (MCZ 46936; USNM 112326–39), Uaxactún (UMMZ 70420–22), Yaxchilán (JCL sight record), Zotz (UMMZ 74956). *Mexico*: Campeche: Balchacaj (FMNH 32304–5, 116591–92; UIMNH 21550); Tabasco: Tenosique (USNM 112342–43); Yucatán: 5.1 mi W Buctzotz (KU 157441–46), Calcehtok (UMMZ 113546), Chichén Itzá (FMNH 49235–38), Dzibilchaltún (FMNH 153392–94, 153396–97), 3.6 mi SW Hunucmá (KU 157447), 12 mi S Izamal (UMMZ 80865), Mayapán (UMRC 79-308, 84-96), Mérida (FMNH 19429–30, 32277–303, 116583–90, 116593–97, 116609–14; MCZ 6269; UIMNH 21551–58, 21616; UMMZ 72881–82), near Mérida (CM 93172), 1 mi N Mérida (UMMZ 72883–89), 9 km N Mérida (UCM 12936–46), 5 mi N Mérida (UCM 16773–16779), 14 km N, 2 km E Mérida (UMMZ 72890), Oxkintok (JCL photo), San Ignacio (CM 38932), Tekantó (Ives, 1891:459), 2.4 mi N Telchac (UCM 28690–91), 4 mi N Telchac (UCM 28692–94), 6.6 mi S

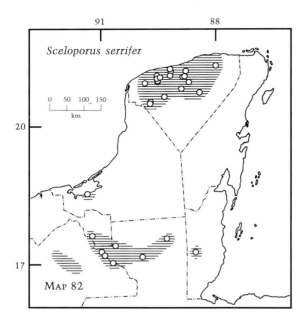

MAP 82

Telchac (UCM 28695–702, 29110), 7.1 km S Tepakan (KU 171426), 12 mi N Tizimín (CM 40144; UCM 28682–89, 28703–4), bet. Tunkás and Sitilpech (KU 171427).

Sceloporus teapensis Günther
(Figs. 129, 316, 317; Map 83)

Sceloporus teapensis Günther, 1890:75. SYN-TYPES: BMNH 1946.8.9.92–98. TYPE LOCALITY: Mexico, Teapa in Tabasco.

Rose-bellied lizard; escamoso variable (Mexico).

DESCRIPTION The males of this medium-sized *Sceloporus* average about 56 mm in snout-vent length. The females average about 52 mm, thus indicating a slight but significant sexual size dimorphism (based on specimens from Veracruz, Chiapas, and Oaxaca; see Fitch, 1978:444). The head is relatively narrow, and the snout is rather pointed in lateral aspect (Fig. 129A). The limbs are short and robust. The tail is moderately long and slender and about 1.6 times the head and body length. A post-femoral dermal pocket is present, and about 10 femoral pores are present on the posteroventral surface of each thigh (Fig. 129D). The pores are better

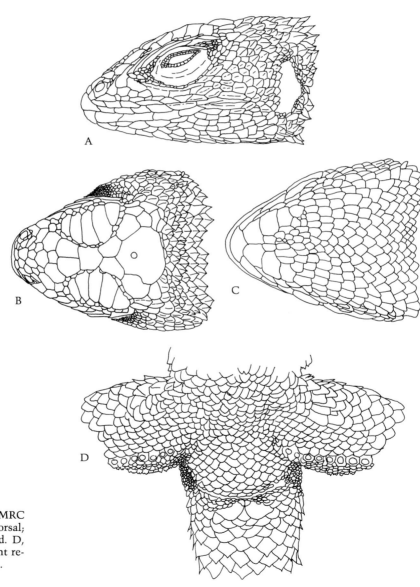

Fig. 129. *Sceloporus teapensis* (UMRC 78-26), 56 mm SVL. A, lateral; B, dorsal; and C, ventral views of the head. D, ventral view of the thighs and vent region; Poptún, El Petén, Guatemala.

developed and more conspicuous in males than in females. The dorsal surface of the head is covered with regularly arranged rugose plates. The dorsal surface of the body and the appendages is covered by large, heavily keeled, mucronate scales. The ventral scales are smooth and distinctly smaller than the dorsals.

This species exhibits pronounced ontogenetic and sexual variation in color and pattern. The females and subadult males tend to be predominantly tan or brown with two dorsal longitudinal rows of black or dark brown blotches, these bordered posteriorly with light gray (Fig. 316). These blotches begin on the neck and extend onto the tail, where they coalesce. The adult males are generally darker brown and have a pair of distinct cream or yellowish dorsolateral stripes extending from the neck onto the base of the tail (Fig. 317). The lateral surfaces of the body and the proximal segments of the limbs are dark brown, nearly black, with a suffusion of orange and a few small pale blue spots. Both sexes bear a conspicuous black spot on the side of the body immediately posterior to the insertion of the forelimb, although the spot is clearer in males. The anterior margin of this spot is bordered with light gray or cream. The adult males have a pair of large lavender patches on the venter that are bordered medially with dark purple or black, and which are separated along the midline by white or cream. In adult females the sides of the head and the labial scales are bright reddish orange.

SIMILAR SPECIES The only other *Sceloporus* in the Yucatán Peninsula that possesses a postfemoral dermal pocket is *S. cozumelae*, but it has much smaller dorsal scales, generally more than 15 femoral pores on each thigh, and the ventral surfaces of the males are not brightly colored.

DISTRIBUTION *Sceloporus teapensis* occurs at low elevations on the Atlantic slope from southern Veracruz and Oaxaca eastward through northern Guatemala and Belize. In the Yucatán Peninsula it ranges from northern Chiapas and eastern Tabasco through El Petén to Belize (Map 83).

NATURAL HISTORY Although these diurnal lizards occur throughout the base of the Yucatán Peninsula, they tend to avoid the deep shade of the forest, inhabiting instead such open situations as forest edges and savannas. Rose-bellied lizards are primarily terrestrial, and they can be found perching conspicuously on logs, rocks, or low on the

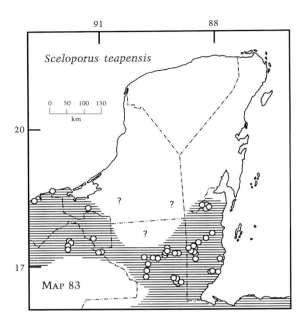

MAP 83

trunks of trees. They are primarily watch-and-wait predators that feed on small invertebrates, especially insects. Milstead (1969b) studied their feeding habits in coastal Veracruz in July and August and found that they consumed a variety of insects, but beetles were the major food item.

Sceloporus teapensis is oviparous. Stuart (1948:54) collected recently hatched young in late August in northern Alta Verapaz. Fitch (1985:26) reported a mean clutch size of 3.2 eggs in Veracruz, and Alvarez del Toro (1983:103) found the clutch size in Chiapas to be about 4. Ovigerous females were present there in every season, suggesting an extensive breeding season. According to Fitch (1978:449), they attain reproductive maturity within a year of hatching, and the females produce multiple clutches during a single breeding season.

SUBSPECIES In the most recent analysis of morphological variation in members of the *S. variabilis* complex, which includes *S. teapensis*, H. M. Smith et al. (1993) recognized no subspecies of *S. teapensis*.

ETYMOLOGY The specific name, *teapensis*, is a toponym that refers to Teapa, Tabasco, where the type series originated.

COMMENT The status of *S. teapensis* and its relation to *S. variabilis*, with which it is sometimes considered conspecific, is unclear. Cole (1978:8) reduced *S. teapensis* to the rank of a subspecies within *S. variabilis*, primarily on the basis of scale characters. Sites and Dixon (1982), who analyzed morphological variation, provided further support for that arrangement. H. M. Smith (1987:xlviii), however, disagreed, noting that *S. teapensis* lacks a subnasal scale and possesses a unique parietal peritoneal pigmentation. Mather and Sites (1985) treated *teapensis* as a subspecies of *S. variabilis*, and Sites et al. (1992:12) recognized the distinctiveness of *S. teapensis* but expressed uncertainty about its status as a full species. In the most recent review of this issue to date, based on morphological analysis, H. M. Smith et al. (1993) argued that *S. variablilis* and *S. teapensis* are separate species. While this issue is not yet fully resolved, Mendoza-Quijano et al. (1994) treats *S. teapensis* as a subspecies of *S. variabilis*, based on a recent electorphoretic analysis of isozymes.

Two specimens of *S. teapensis* (UF 17555–56) collected in 1961 by members of a University of Colorado field party bear the locality "Pisté, Yucatán, Mexico." As *S. teapensis* is otherwise unknown from the northern half of the Yucatán Peninsula, I consider the Pisté record erroneous.

Locality Records Belize: Belize: 30 mi W Belize City (CM 112104, 112197); Cayo: Augustine (LSUMZ 11771; MCZ 71307–81; UMMZ 80676–77), rd. to Augustine, 9 mi S Western Hwy. (NMSU 3068), Belmopan (CM 112095), Blancaneaux Lodge (CM 91007–8, 105952–53), 0.5 mi W Camalot (CM 105765–66), Central Farm (MCZ 71363), Chaa Creek (CM 105802), Georgetown (CM 91001), 1.1 mi S Georgeville (KU 157451), ca. 3 mi S Georgeville (CM 91017, 91019–20, 91023), Hidden Valley Falls (MCZ 152575), Little Vaqueros Creek at rd. to Augustine (NMSU 3070), Río On (CM 105951; KU 157450), San Luis (CM 105942; JCL photo; KU 157448–49), mi 62 on Western Hwy. (CM 112111), mi 32 on Western Hwy. (CM 112113), Xunantunich (KU 144946, 171505–7; MCZ 65376, 71364–69), near Xunantunich (CM 105959, 105982–83); Orange Walk: August Pine Ridge (USNM 194930), Guinea Grass Rd., ca. 4 mi S Northern Hwy. (CM 105740–41, 105754), Tower Hill (MPM 7540, 7724–25; USNM 194087), Otro Benque (USNM 194122); Stann Creek: Mango Creek (MCZ 71382–83), 13.2 mi SW Silk Grass (KU 157452); Toledo: 14 mi W Mango Creek (LSUMZ 11769), Swazey Branch of Monkey River (MCZ 71384–92). *Guatemala*: El Petén: 2.5 mi W El Cruce (KU 157460–61), 34.6 mi E El Cruce (KU 157468–69), Flores (AMNH 72628), near Flores (AMNH 72621), SE Flores (UMMZ 79073), near La Libertad (UMMZ 74976–77), 15 km SE La Libertad (KU 55805–35, 57162, 59711–14), 48.2 km W Melchor de Mencos (KU 171482), Piedras Negras (MCZ 46773–74; UIMNH 10831–55; USNM 112649–56, 112658–

73), Poptún (UMMZ 117859; UMRC 78-26), near Poptún (UMMZ 117858), 1 to 2 mi S Poptún (UMMZ 117860), 1 km W Poptún (UMMZ 124367), 2 km E Poptún (UMMZ 124369), 4 mi N Poptún (KU 157453–55), 9.9 mi NW Poptún (KU 157456), 12.1 mi NW Poptún (KU 157457–59), 18 km NW Poptún (UMMZ 125759), 15 km S Poptún (UMMZ 124368), Remate (UMMZ 74970–71; USMN 71408), 2.5 km N Remate (KU 171488–504), bet. Remate and Ixla (UMMZ 124371), 8.3 km SW San Benito (KU 171483–87), 3 km E Santa Elena (UMMZ 124365), 1 to 3 km S Santa Elena (UMMZ 124366), Sayaxché (UCM 22275), Sojio (AMNH 69996–98, 70000), Tikal (UTA R-22109), 3 mi S Tikal (KU 157463–67), 14.2 mi S Tikal (KU 157463), Zotz (UMMZ 74975); no specific locality (USNM 71842–63). *Mexico*: Campeche: 2 mi E Barra San Pedro y Pablo (AMNH 88871–72), Tres Brazos (FMNH 32011–13, 33515, 33563, 112001–4; UIMNH 21589); Chiapas: across the river from Piedras Negras (USNM 112674); San Juanito (USNM 112675–77, 112692–99); Palenque (UMMZ 172755; UMRC 85-22; UTEP 8015–16; USNM 112678–86), vicinity Palenque (FMNH 110562–66; LSUMZ 33403–4), Palenque ruins (UIMNH 11324–29), 10 mi S Palenque ruins (USNM 112687–91), 13 mi S Palenque (LSUMZ 33400); Tabasco: 5 mi W Frontera (UCM 39415–53), 7 mi SW Frontera (UIMNH 87382–99), Tenosique (USNM 112700–24).

Family Polychrotidae

This large family of New World lizards ranges from the southeastern United States through Middle America to southern Argentina. The family is also well represented in the Bahamas and in the Greater and Lesser Antilles. Polychrotids are typically rather slender lizards with long limbs and tails. They are predominantly diurnal and arboreal. The 11 genera included in this family were long known informally as "anoloids" in the family Iguanidae (*sensu lato*) until they were assigned familial rank by D. R. Frost and Etheridge (1989). One polychrotid genus occurs in the Yucatán Peninsula (but see below).

Genus *Anolis* (Anoles)

The genus *Anolis* is one of the largest of all vertebrate genera. There are about 300 species, and new forms are being described at the rate of several per year. Anoles are found from the southeastern

United States through Mexico and Central America to Bolivia and Paraguay. The genus is primarily Neotropical, with centers of diversity in the West Indies, Middle America, and Amazonian South America.

These are small to medium-sized lizards with small scales, relatively long hind limbs, rather slender bodies, and long, thin tails. The males generally have a well-developed throat fan, or dewlap, which is often brightly colored and is a signaling device in intraspecific social interactions. In some species the females have a small but functional dewlap as well. As a group anoles are arboreal, but semiarboreal, terrestrial, and even semiaquatic forms exist. The females typically produce multiple clutches, each consisting of a single egg.

This large and unwieldy assemblage of species has defied attempts at taxonomic partitioning. Guyer and Savage (1986) attempted a cladistic analysis of the anoles and advocated a taxonomy based on their results. Some herpetologists (e.g., Villa et al., 1988) accept their partitioning, which requires application of the name *Norops* to most of the *Anolis* in the Yucatán Peninsula, but E. E. Williams (1989) challenged the adequacy of their data, and their analytical procedures were criticized by Cannatella and de Queiroz (1989). Although Guyer and Savage (1992) offered a rejoinder to their critics, questions still remain concerning the monophyly of certain of their terminal taxa. Consequently, I retain the name *Anolis* for the 11 species of anoles in the Yucatán Peninsula, pending a definitive analysis of relationships within this group. *Anolis* derives from the West Indian *anoli*, "lizard."

The anoles of the Yucatán Peninsula can be exasperatingly difficult to identify, especially preserved specimens, which quickly assume a nondescript brown color that gives no hint of the bright colors and bold markings that may have characterized them in life. The collection location can eliminate some species from consideration, for two species are strictly insular and four are restricted to the base of the peninsula. Size differences will distinguish some species, and in most cases attention to anatomical detail will confirm a tentative identifica-

Fig. 131. Lateral view of segments of tails of *Anolis*. A, *A. cristatellus* showing enlarged supracaudal crest. B, *A. pentaprion* with unmodified supracaudal scales. C, *A. sagrei* showing enlarged supracaudal scales forming a serrated series.

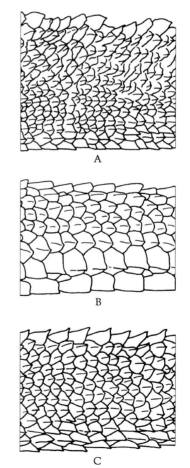

Fig. 130. Lateral views of the heads of *Anolis*. A, *A. cristatellus* showing oval tympanic opening. B, *A. allisoni* showing elongate tympanic opening.

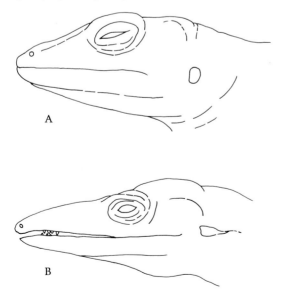

tion. The presence or absence of enlarged postanal scales in males, the relative size of dorsal and ventral scales, and the presence or absence of keels on the dorsal and ventral scales are important characters for anole identification.

The difficulty in constructing an identification key to anoles was best expressed by Stuart (1955:10), who, in introducing his key to Guatemalan anoles, wrote that "the worker who knows what species he has before him should experience few difficulties in its use."

Key to the Species of the Genus *Anolis*

1. Midventral scales at midbody smooth or only very weakly keeled 2
   Midventral scales at midbody strongly keeled 5

2. Small (adult SVL less than 50 mm), delicate, attenuate lizards; males with pale yellow dewlap . . . . *Anolis rodriguezii*
   Moderately large (adult SVL greater than 50 mm), robust lizards; dewlap of males not pale yellow 3

3. Ear opening oval, without a posterior longitudinal depression (Fig. 130A); color never green; mainland 4
   Ear opening elongate, posterior margin forming a longitudinal depression (Fig. 130B); color usually green; coastal islands of Belize (Map 84) . . . . *Anolis allisoni*

4. Supracaudal scales enlarged, forming a serrated crest (Fig. 131A); dewlap brown or tan, sometimes with red-orange or greenish cast; Isla Cozumel (Map 87) . . . . *Anolis cristatellus*
   Supracaudal scales not enlarged to form a serrated crest (Fig. 131B); dewlap red; mainland of Yucatán Peninsula (Map 89) . . . . *Anolis pentaprion*

5. Middorsal scales keeled 6
   Middorsal scales smooth. . . . . *Anolis capito*

6. Tail not laterally compressed; supracaudal scales not distinctly enlarged, no caudal crest 7
   Tail laterally compressed; supracaudal scales enlarged, keeled, forming a crest (Fig. 131C) . . . . *Anolis sagrei*

7. Middorsal scales equal to or only slightly larger than lateral scales. 8
   Eight to 10 rows of middorsal scales, these conspicuously and abruptly larger than lateral scales 10

8. Moderate to large lizards (adult SVL 50–90 mm); dewlap of males without blue or purple central spot. 9
   Small (adult SVL 30–40 mm) delicate, attenuate lizards; males with orange dewlap with blue or purple spot. . . . . *Anolis sericeus*

9. Fewer than eight supralabials to the middle of the eye; adult SVL 55 to 75 mm; dewlap of male red. . . . . *Anolis lemurinus*
   More than eight supralabials to the middle of the eye; adult SVL 85 to 95 mm; dewlap pink with bluish center . . . . *Anolis biporcatus*

10. Small (adult SVL less than 45 mm), stocky lizards; males with red dewlap, usually with purple spot. . . . . *Anolis uniformis*
    Larger (adult SVL greater than 50 mm); males with yellow-orange dewlap, without purple spot . . . . *Anolis tropidonotus*

Clave para las Especies del Género *Anolis*

1. Escamas medioventrales en la mitad del cuerpo lisas o muy poco quilladas 2
   Escamas medioventrales en la mitad del cuerpo fuertemente quilladas. 5

2. Organismos de tamaño pequeño (adultos menores a 50 mm de LHC), lagartijas delicadas; machos con un abanico gular de color amarillo pálido . . . . *Anolis rodriguezii*

Organismos moderadamente grandes (adultos mayores a 50 mm de LHC), lagartijas robustas, el abanico gular de los machos no es de color amarillo pálido 3

3. Abertura ótica oval, sin depresión posterior longitudinal (Fig. 130A); organismos nunca de color verde; se distribuyen en el continente 4
Abertura ótica elongada, margen posterior formando una depresión longitudinal (Fig. 130B); organismos usualmente de color verde; se distribuyen en las islas de la costa de Belice (Mapa 84) .... *Anolis allisoni*

4. Escamas supracaudales alargadas, formando una cresta aserrada (Fig. 131A); abanico gular pardo o bronceado, algunas veces con tonos rojo-anaranjados o verdosos; se distribuyen en la Isla Cozumel (Mapa 87) .... *Anolis cristatellus*
Escamas supracaudales no alargadas para formar una cresta aserrada (Fig. 131B); abanico gular rojo; en la Península de Yucatán .... *Anolis pentaprion*

5. Escamas mediodorsales quilladas 6
Escamas mediodorsales lisas .... *Anolis capito*

6. Cola no comprimida; escamas supracaudales sin alargarse distintivamente, sin cresta caudal. 7
Cola moderadamente comprimida; escamas supracaudales alargadas, quilladas, formado una cresta (Fig. 131C) .... *Anolis sagrei*

7. Escamas mediodorsales iguales, o sólo un poco más grandes que las escamas laterales 8
Ocho o diez hileras de escamas mediodorsales conspicua y notoriamente más largas que las escamas laterales. 10

8. Lagartijas grandes, adultos 50–90 mm de LHC, más robustas; el abanico gular de los machos sin una mancha central azul o morada 9
Lagartijas pequeñas, adultos 30–40 mm de LHC, cuerpo delgado, atenuado; machos con abanico gular anaranjado con una mancha azul o morada .... *Anolis sericeus*

9. Menos de ocho supralabiales a la altura del ojo, adultos 55–75 mm de LHC, abanico gular del macho color rojo .... *Anolis lemurinus*
Más de ocho supralabiales a la altura del ojo, adultos 85–95 mm de LHC, abanico gular rosa con el centro azuloso .... *Anolis biporcatus*

10. Lagartijas pequeñas, adultos menores a los 45 mm de LHC, robustas; machos con abanico gular rojo, usualmente con una mancha morada. .... *Anolis uniformis*
Lagartijas grandes, adultos mayores a 50 mm de LHC, machos con un abanico gular amarillo-anaranjado, sin una mancha morada .... *Anolis tropidonotus*

Anolis allisoni Barbour
(Figs. 130B, 318; Map 84)

Anolis allisoni Barbour, 1928:58. HOLOTYPE: MCZ 26725. TYPE LOCALITY: Coxen Hole, Ruatan (= Roatan), Bay Islands of Honduras.

Allison's anole.

DESCRIPTION   This is a moderately large, rather slender, long-snouted anole (Fig. 318). Sexual size dimorphism is apparently pronounced, for a series of seven males from Jobabo, Cuba (UMRC 54-127), averaged 82.5 mm in snout-vent length, while the single female of that series measured 65.5 mm. The head of adult males is relatively enormous, constituting approximately a third of the snout-vent length. The ear opening is elongate rather than oval,

and the posterior margin forms a longitudinal depression (Fig. 130B). The tail is long and slender and about 1.8 to 2 times the length of the head and body. The limbs are well developed, and the digits bear small, delicate claws and support expanded subdigital lamellae. The lateral body scales are small, slightly imbricate, and smooth or very weakly keeled. Toward the midline the scales are larger and more strongly keeled. The ventral scales are keeled and subequal to the middorsals. Conspicuous canthal and frontal ridges are present in adult males; these are less well developed in females and subadults.

Both sexes are normally green, but they are capable of changing rapidly to dark brown, the color they assume in preservative. Portions of the head and anterior portion of the body of males are often bluish during the green color phase. The dewlap is reddish in males; females do not have one.

SIMILAR SPECIES   The only other green anole in the Yucatán Peninsula is *A. biporcatus*, which has an oval external ear opening, a short, broad head, and does not occur in sympatry with *A. allisoni*. Of the other green lizards in the Yucatán Peninsula, juveniles of *Ctenosaura similis* have spiny tails, and the two species of *Laemanctus* have expanded occipital casques.

DISTRIBUTION   This is a West Indian species native to Cuba, the Bay Islands of Honduras, and Half Moon Cay off the coast of Belize (Map 84). There is a questionable record from Isla Cozumel, Quintana Roo (see Comment).

NATURAL HISTORY   These large and conspicuous anoles are common on Half Moon Cay, where I found individuals perching on the trunks of coconut palms at heights ranging from 1.5 m to 10 m or more. They are stealthy, wary, and difficult to approach. According to Ruibal (1964:486), they are common in the vicinity of human dwellings in central Cuba. The lizards perch head-downward on fence posts, houses, and the trunks of palm trees, generally at a height of 1.5 m or more. They are diurnal and arboreal, and they eat invertebrates, principally insects. Like other anoles, the females produce multiple clutches, each consisting of a single egg.

SUBSPECIES   Ruibal and Williams (1961:195) drew attention to the morphological differences be-

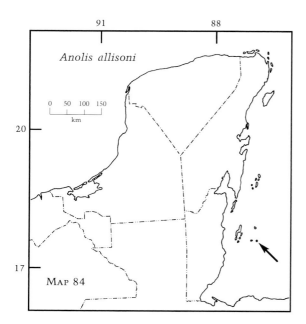

tween specimens from Cuba, Islas de la Bahía, and Half Moon Cay but declined to accord the populations subspecific status. Thus, no subspecies are presently recognized.

ETYMOLOGY   The specific name, *allisoni*, is a patronym that honors Allison V. Armous, Esq., under whose auspices Barbour visited the Bay Islands of Honduras, where the type specimen was secured.

COMMENT   A single subadult specimen, CM 34388, is said to be from Isla Cozumel, Quintana Roo. As no other specimens of this generally conspicuous and abundant lizard have been collected there, I consider its occurrence on Cozumel doubtful.

A species related to *Anolis allisoni*, *A. carolinensis*, has been recorded from Half Moon Cay based on a single specimen (UF 23924). I have examined this specimen and agree that it represents *A. carolinensis*. However, diligent search for this species on Half Moon Cay by me and others has failed to produce additional specimens of that species. Moreover, it is difficult to believe that two such closely related species could occur together on that tiny island. I suggest that if *A. carolinensis* ever occurred on Half Moon Cay, it is no longer present there.

Locality Records Belize: Belize: Half Moon Cay (CM 4156–57; FMNH 30541, 34628–29; JCL photo; MCZ 60983; UF 23924). *Mexico*: Quintana Roo: Isla Cozumel (CM 34388; see Comment).

Anolis biporcatus (Wiegmann)
(Figs. 319, 320; Map 85)

Dactyloa biporcata Wiegmann, 1834:47. HOLOTYPE: ZMB 524. TYPE LOCALITY: Mexico; restricted by H. M. Smith and Taylor (1950b:326) to Piedra Parada, Chiapas, Mexico.

Anolis verde, toloque (Mexico).

DESCRIPTION   This moderately large, robust anole is easily distinguished from all other mainland *Anolis* in the Yucatán Peninsula by its bright green color (Fig. 319), which fades to brown immediately after death. Males and females both average between 85 and 90 mm in snout-vent length and attain a maximum length of 105 mm. There is no sexual size dimorphism (Fitch 1976:4). The head is relatively long and narrow and is moderately distinct from the neck. The limbs are relatively short, and the digits bear expanded subdigital lamellae. The long, slender tail is about twice the length of the head and body. The middorsal scales are keeled and slightly larger than the laterals. The ventral scales are strongly keeled and twice the size of the middorsals. The scales on the dorsal surface of the head are keeled, and there is a shallow frontal depression.

In life, the head, body, and appendages of adults are bright green above, usually with scattered gray flecks and often with a darker green reticulum. The eyelids are yellow, and the irises are red-orange. The venter is gray or white. Juveniles may be gray-green (Fig. 320), and according to Stuart (1958:20) they possess a reticulate pattern. The dewlap of males is pinkish with a pale blue center, sometimes bordered with pale orange. The dewlap is rudimentary in females.

SIMILAR SPECIES   The large size and bright green color of the adults distinguishes them from all other mainland anoles in the Yucatán Peninsula. *Anolis biporcatus* differs from the other large green anole, *A. allisoni*, in lacking heavy frontal and canthal ridges and in having an oval ear opening. *Anolis lemurinus*, a smaller lizard, has fewer than eight supralabial scales from the rostrum to the middle of the eye.

DISTRIBUTION   *Anolis biporcatus* occurs at low and moderate elevations on the Atlantic slope from Chiapas south through lower Central America to northern South America. It ranges through the base of the Yucatán Peninsula from southern Campeche through El Petén and Belize (Map 85).

NATURAL HISTORY   These inhabitants of humid lowland forests perch on the trunks and limbs of large trees, often at considerable heights. In southern El Petén, Duellman (1963:233) found specimens in the tops of trees immediately after they were felled. At Tikal, El Petén, individuals have been found at night sleeping on palm fronds 2 to 3 m above the forest floor (E. Pérez Cruz, pers. comm.).

Anolis biporcatus is oviparous. Each clutch consists of single egg, and females can produce multiple clutches. Henderson (1972:240) reported that a captive female from Chiapas laid two eggs within seven hours on 7 March, suggesting the unlikely possibility that clutch size in this species is two. McCoy (1975) examined a series of specimens from southeastern Guatemala and found that there was never more than a single enlarged ovarian follicle in an ovary at any given time, and that no more than a single shelled oviductal egg was present in an oviduct. He concluded that clutch size was one, but that the interval between laying was short, for individuals with shelled oviducal eggs also had large unshelled eggs in the other oviduct.

This species is one of several in the genus *Anolis* known to vocalize. According to Myers (1971:27), it squeaks when handled.

SUBSPECIES   Of the two subspecies of *Anolis biporcatus* recognized by Williams (1966), the nominate form occurs in the Yucatán Peninsula.

ETYMOLOGY   The specific name, *biporcatus*, is from the Latin *porcatus*, "ridged," and *bi-*, a prefix meaning "two" or "twice."

COMMENT   Using correspondence from L. C. Stuart as evidence, Schmidt (1941:491) pointed out that previous workers had misapplied the name *A. biporcatus* to *A. bourgeaei* (now considered a geographic race of *A. lemurinus*), and that the name properly referred to the form known then as *A. copei*.

Locality Records   Belize: Cayo: Augustine (UMMZ 80682), Caracol (CMM photo), Cohune Ridge (UMMZ 80681), 8 mi S Georgeville (JLK 420), Guanacaste Park (RAL photo), Valentin (UMMZ 80683); Orange Walk: Chan Chich (CMM photo), Gallon Jug (FMNH 69229);

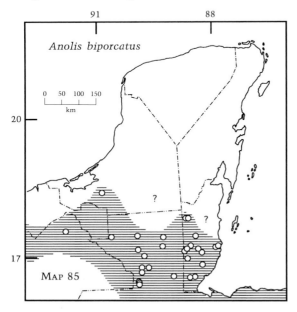

Anolis biporcatus

0 50 100 150
km

91   88

20

17

MAP 85

Stann Creek: Bokowina (FMNH 49205–8), Double Falls (FMNH 49209), Silk Grass (Schmidt, 1941:491); Toledo: ca. 2 mi SE Big Falls, ca. 8 km N Punta Gorda (UF 87173), Río Grande (CM 105882), Bladen Branch of Monkey River (CM 105907), Columbia Branch Camp (W. T. Neill, 1965:90), 1 mi W Salamanca (CM 105847). *Guatemala*: El Petén: 20 km NNW Chinajá (KU 55762–64), 17 km NNW Chinajá (KU 59458), 14 km NNW Chinajá (KU 59459), 30 km NNW Chinajá (KU 59497), El Paso de Caballo (UMMZ 79079), El Repasto (UCM), El Seibal (JCL sight record), Laguna Zotz (UMMZ 79078), near La Libertad (UMMZ 75178–81), Las Cañas (CM 58233–35), Remate (UMMZ 75177), Sayaxché (KU 55761; UCM 22198), 8 km S Sayaxché (MVZ 105202), Tikal (MCZ 58771; UF 13729–33; UMMZ 117843). *Mexico*: Campeche: Pacaitún (FMNH 36467–68); Chiapas: Zona Arqueológica Palenque (EAL 3636), 6.6 mi S Palenque (TCWC 58689).

Anolis capito (Peters)
(Figs. 321, 322; Map 86)

Anolis (Draconura) capito Peters, 1863a:142. TYPES: ZMB 4684 (originally two syntypes; lectotype, ZMB 4684; paratype, ZMB 36298, *fide* Stuart, 1963:61). TYPE LOCALITY: Costa Rica; restricted by H. M. Smith and Taylor (1950b:316) to Palmar, Costa Rica.

Big-headed anole; anolis jaspeado (Mexico).

DESCRIPTION *Anolis capito* is a large, broad-headed, stocky anole with long legs (Fig. 321). The adults average between 70 and 90 mm in snout-vent length, with the females generally exceeding the males by about 5 mm (Fitch, 1976:4). The long, slender tail is nearly twice as long as the head and body. The head is distinct from the neck, and the snout is rather blunt in dorsal aspect. The limbs are long and slender, and the digits bear expanded subdigital lamellae. The dorsal and lateral scales are subequal in size, smooth, flat, and juxtaposed. The ventrals are keeled and slightly imbricate. This is the only anole in the Yucatán Peninsula with keeled ventral scales and smooth dorsals. A deep frontal depression is present, and the scales on the dorsal surface of the head are keeled.

The dorsum is olive brown or tan with irregular dark streaks, spots, and bars. The females are polymorphic. Some have a broad, pale middorsal stripe (Fig. 322), whereas others have the mottled pattern of the males (Fig. 321). The dewlap of males is unusually small and is dull greenish yellow.

SIMILAR SPECIES The large size, broad, blunt head, and stocky body of adults distinguish this anole all others in the Yucatán Peninsula. Moreover, no other anole in the Yucatán Peninsula has keeled ventral scales and smooth dorsals.

DISTRIBUTION *Anolis capito* occurs at low and moderate elevations on the Atlantic slope from Tabasco to Panama. In the Yucatán Peninsula the species is restricted to the base of the peninsula in El Petén and Belize (Map 86).

NATURAL HISTORY This species occupies humid lowland forests, and individuals usually perch on the trunks of large trees at heights up to 10 m, although occasionally they are found on the ground near the bases of large trees (Fitch, 1975:41). The brown coloration of these diurnal lizards renders them inconspicuous against their usual background of bark and dead leaves, especially given their habit of pressing the body against the tree trunk (Duellman, 1963:233). They feed primarily on invertebrates, especially insects, although they also prey on other anoles (R. M. Andrews, 1983:410). In turn, they are preyed on by the blunt-headed tree snake, *Imantodes cenchoa* (Stuart, 1948:47).

Anolis capito is oviparous. The females produce multiple clutches of a single egg each. Fitch (1975:41) inferred that females deposited eggs in every month of the year in a Costa Rican rainforest.

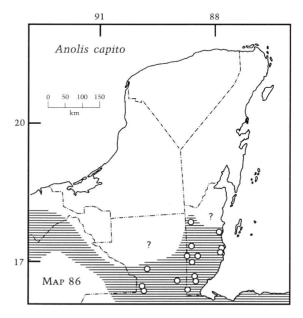

MAP 86

ETYMOLOGY The specific name, *capito*, is a Latin masculine adjective meaning "big headed," in reference to the large, broad head.

Locality Records   Belize: Belize: Manatee (MCZ 19320); Cayo: Caracol (CMM photo), Chiquibul Branch, S Granos de Oro Camp (CM 112127), McKinstrey's Farm (W. T. Neill and Allen, 1959c:35), Valentin (UMMZ 80683–87); Orange Walk: Chan Chich (CMM photo); Stann Creek: Bokowina (FMNH 49203), Silk Grass (FMNH 49204); Toledo: Blue Creek (RWV photo), Dolores (UMRC 90-12), Gloria Camp (USNM 319787–88). *Guatemala*: Alta Verapaz: Chinajá (Duellman, 1963:233); El Petén: 14 km NNW Chinajá (KU 59463), Las Cañas (CM 58236), Río de la Pasión bet. Sayaxché and Subín (KU 57152).

Anolis cristatellus Duméril and Bibron
(Figs. 130A, 131A, 323, 324; Map 87)

Anolis cristatellus A. M. C. Duméril and Bibron, 1837:143. SYNTYPES: MNHNP 2353, 2447 (two syntypes). TYPE LOCALITY: Martinique (in error, *fide* A. Schwartz and Thomas, 1975:75).

Crested anole.

DESCRIPTION Sexual size dimorphism is very pronounced in this moderately large, rather robust anole. The males average between 70 and 75 mm in snout-vent length (Fig. 324), and the females average about 20 to 25 mm less (Fig. 323). The undamaged tail is about twice the length of the head and body. The head is large, broad, and distinct from the neck. The limbs are robust, and the digits bear expanded subdigital lamellae. The scales on the dorsal surface of the body are small and granular, and those along the midline are slightly larger than the lateral scales. The ventral scales are smooth, slightly imbricate, and larger than the dorsal scales. The tail is compressed laterally, and the supracaudal scales are enlarged and flattened to produce a low, serrated crest that is especially visible in the males (Fig. 131A).

Generally these lizards are brown, tan, or gray with indistinct dark spots, bars, or chevrons. The females exhibit pattern polymorphism. Some have a distinct light vertebral stripe running the length of the body, and others have a dorsal pattern similar to that of the males. The males possess a large dewlap that is generally brown or tan, sometimes with a reddish orange or lime green cast. The small, rudimentary dewlap of the females bears only a trace of color.

SIMILAR SPECIES *Anolis sagrei* is similar in possessing a supracaudal crest, but it has keeled ventral scales and is smaller and less robust. *Anolis lemurinus* lacks a supracaudal crest, and the males have a red dewlap. *Anolis tropidonotus* has keeled ventrals and large, strongly keeled middorsal scales.

DISTRIBUTION *Anolis cristatellus* occurs naturally on Puerto Rico and the islands of the Puerto Rican Bank. It has been introduced into Florida, where it occurs at several localities in Dade County, and on the southern coast of the Dominican Republic (Fitch et al., 1989). In the Yucatán Peninsula it is known only from Isla Cozumel on the basis of a single specimen collected at the turn of the century (see Comment) (Map 87).

NATURAL HISTORY Nothing is known of the natural history of this species on Cozumel, if indeed it still exists there. Throughout its range on Puerto Rico and the adjacent islands, however, *A. cristatellus* is a very common in lowlands, and individuals perch conspicuously on tree trunks, fence posts, and the sides of buildings. These alert diurnal lizards feed primarily on insects and other invertebrates, but they occasionally consume other *Anolis* (A. Schwartz and Henderson, 1991:245). Like other anoles, *A. cristatellus* females lay but one egg per clutch and produce multiple clutches annually.

SUBSPECIES According to Heatwole (1976), two subspecies are recognizable: *A. c. wileyi*, on the Virgin Islands and the small islands east of Puerto

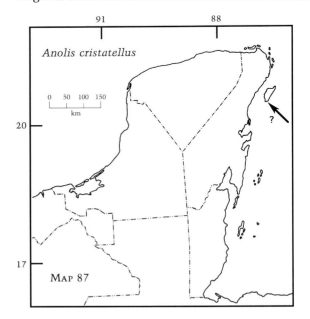

MAP 87

Rico; and the nominate subspecies, *A. c. cristatellus*, on Puerto Rico. The single known specimen of *A. cristatellus* from Cozumel has not been identified to subspecies.

ETYMOLOGY The specific name, *cristatellus*, is the diminutive form of the Latin adjective *cristatus*, "crested," presumably in reference to the conspicuous supracaudal crest on males from some populations.

COMMENT H. M. Smith (1939a:19) described *A. cozumelae* based on a specimen from Isla Cozumel, Quintana Roo, collected in 1899 by C. F. Millspaugh. This specimen (FMNH 751) is *A. cristatellus*, *fide* E. E. Williams (pers. comm.), a conclusion with which I concur, having examined the specimen. No additional specimens have ever been found on Cozumel, and the species' current existence there is doubtful.

Locality Record Mexico: Quintana Roo: Isla Cozumel (FMNH 751).

Anolis lemurinus (Cope)
(Fig. 325; Map 88)

Anolis (Gastrotropis) lemurinus Cope, 1861b:213. HOLOTYPE: originally ANSP, now apparently lost, *fide* Stuart, 1963:63. TYPE LOCALITY: Veragua, New Grenada (= Veragua, Panama).

Lagartija chipojo (Mexico).

DESCRIPTION *Anolis lemurinus* is a moderately large anole. The mean snout-vent length of a small series of males from Chichén Itzá, Yucatán, was 61.3 mm; females averaged 65.7 mm. Fitch (1976:4) reported snout-vent lengths of 67.0 and 69.6 mm for males and females, respectively, based on composite samples from southern Mexico and northern Central America. Thus, females apparently tend to be larger than males. The undamaged tail is long, slender, and more than twice the snout-vent length. The head is distinct from the neck in dorsal aspect, and the snout is moderately pointed (Fig. 325). The limbs are well developed and relatively long. The dorsal scales are small and keeled, and those on the middorsal area are only slightly larger than those on the lateral surfaces. The ventral scales are keeled and conspicuously larger than the dorsals. The enlarged supraorbital scales and the scales on the frontal depression are also keeled.

Like many anoles, these lizards can become darker or lighter depending on the temperature and their emotional state. Generally the dorsal ground color is brown, tan, or gray. Some specimens have a series of five or six dark brown blotches on the body and an additional several that extend onto the tail. In the middle of each of the light interspaces there is often a small, dark I- or hourglass-shaped spot. In other specimens a broad, irregular dark brown stripe extends from behind the eye, over the shoulder, and down the lateral surfaces of the body to the tail. Usually this stripe is bordered above and below by white or cream. The dorsal and lateral surfaces of the neck are usually marked with indistinct light stripes bordered by dark brown or black, and there is usually a dark interorbital bar on the dorsal surface of the head. The limbs bear indistinct dark spots and bars. The ventral surfaces are generally immaculate cream, tan, or gray. The males have a conspicuous red dewlap; the dewlap of females is rudimentary.

SIMILAR SPECIES *Anolis sagrei* has a series of enlarged supracaudal scales that form a serrated crest (Fig. 131C), and the males have enlarged postanal scales and a red-orange, orange, or yellowish dewlap. *Anolis tropidonotus* has an abruptly enlarged series of middorsal scales, and the males have a yellow-orange dewlap. *Anolis biporcatus* is larger, is usually green in life, and has more than eight supralabial scales to the middle of the eye and a pinkish dewlap with a bluish center.

DISTRIBUTION *Anolis lemurinus* occurs at low and moderate elevations from central Veracruz on the Atlantic slope and Chiapas on the Pacific slope, east and southward through Central America to Colombia. It is found throughout the Yucatán Peninsula except for the arid northwest corner (Map 88).

NATURAL HISTORY This anole is a common inhabitant of lowland forests, and individuals are frequently found perching low on the trunks or buttresses of trees, or can be heard scampering across the forest floor. They are diurnal and partial to shaded situations, where they watch and wait for their invertebrate prey.

Like other *Anolis*, this species is oviparous and lays but a single egg per clutch. Stuart (1948:49) reported that specimens from Alta Verapaz collected in early May had well-developed eggs in their bodies. Fitch (1970:25) examined a small sample from Guatemala and found that females collected in February and March lacked enlarged ova, whereas

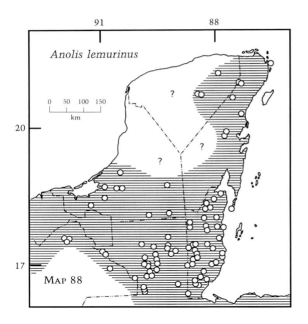

Map 88

all specimens collected in June were gravid, suggesting a seasonal breeding pattern.

SUBSPECIES   Two subspecies are presently recognized, of which *A. l. bourgeaei* occurs in the Yucatán Peninsula.

ETYMOLOGY   The specific name, *lemurinus*, is from the Latin *lemur*, meaning "shades" or "ghosts of the dead," and *-inus*, a adjectival suffix meaning "belonging to."

COMMENT   For many years the name *A. biporcatus* was applied to this species. Schmidt (1941:491), on the advice of L. C. Stuart, pointed out that the name *A. biporcatus* was properly applied to the large, arboreal green anole then known as *A. copei*, not to this taxon.

Locality Records   Belize: Belize: Altun Ha (USNM 194925), Belize (CM 90912, 90915–16), Belize, Fort George Hotel (USNM 194923), Burrel Boom Rd. at Belize River (CM 105778), Kate's Lagoon (FMNH 49200–2), Manatee (FMNH 5819), Missionary Lake Rd., 5.3 mi E jct. Northern Hwy. (CM 91055), North River (USNM 58171, 58173), north of Lemonal near Spanish Creek Lodge (MPM 7764), Lemonal (MPM 7765–67, 7769, 7774–75), Rockstone Pond (AMNH 104419); Cayo: Augustine (CM 105948–50; UMMZ 80697–99; LSUMZ 10283), Beaver Dam Creek (CM 109022–25), Blancaneaux Lodge (CM 109013), Blue Hole (CM 90992), Caracol (CMM photo), Central Farm (MCZ 71593), Chaa Creek (CM 105803–6, 105978–80),

Cohune Ridge (UMMZ 80695), Coquercot (UMMZ 80747), El Cayo (UF 24524–25), 0.5 mi S Georgeville (CM 105756), 3 mi S Georgeville (CM 91024), 4 mi S Georgeville (CM 105708–9), Macal River at Guacamallo Bridge (CM 112146), 3 mi S Millionario (UMMZ 124667), River Succotz (MPM 7528), 1 mi S Rockville (CM 111933), Valentin (UMMZ 80694), Xunantunich (CM 112108; KU 144929, 171631–32); Corozal: Ambergris Cay, 5 km NNE San Pedro (CM 91114); Orange Walk: Albion Island (USNM 194924), 8 mi N Gallon Jug (MCZ 71594–95), Gallon Jug (MCZ 71596–99; MPM 7645), near Guinea Grass (MPM 7770), Guinea Grass (MPM 7768; USNM 194917), Honey Camp (USNM 194927), Lamanai (ROM H12740, H12767, H12772, H12776), Orange Walk Town (USNM 194918), 20 mi SE Orange Walk Town (BCB 11717–20), Otro Benque (USNM 194954), Progresso Lagoon (MPM 7771–73), near Progresso Lagoon (USNM 194909–16), Tower Hill (MPM 7776; USNM 194921), Yo River (MPM 7612–13); Stann Creek: Freetown (CM 8495), 1 km W Mayflower Village (JLK 506), Middlesex (FMNH 4479–82), 4.4 mi S Silk Grass (KU 157163); Toledo: ca. 2 mi SE Big Falls, Río Grande (CM 105879–80, 105889–91), Bladen Branch of Monkey River (CM 105923), Blue Creek Village (UTA R-11044–55), Dolores (JCL sight record), 2.7 mi NE Golden Stream (KU 157164–65), near Jimmy Cut (CM 105855), W of Lubaantún ruins (MCZ 71600), 1 mi W Salamanca (CM 105848–51, 105859), 4 mi S Swazey Bridge (CM 105936). *Guatemala*: El Petén: Altar de Sacrificios (AMNH 99905–10), 4 km N Chinajá (KU 59518), 11 km NNW Chinajá (KU 55765), 16 km NNW Chinajá (KU 55768), 20 km NNW Chinajá (KU 55764, 55766–67, 55769), 30 km NNW Chinajá (KU 59519–20), Laguna Zotz (UMMZ 75141, 79078), near La Libertad (UMMZ 75122–27), 3 mi S La Libertad (MCZ 46306), 3 mi W La Libertad (MCZ 46307), 6 mi W La Libertad (MCZ 46308), 5 km SW La Libertad (KU 157177), Las Cañas (CM 58237–38), Pacomon (USNM 71390, 71393), Paso de los Caballos (UMMZ 79079), Piedras Negras (UCM 46231–66, 46272), 5 mi S Piedras Negras (UCM 46267–71), bet. Remate and Yaxhá (UMMZ 75175), San Andrés (UMMZ 75165), 2 km S Santa Elena (UMMZ 124376), Santa Rita (USNM 71388), Santa Teresa (UMMZ 75157–59), Sayaxché (KU 55770–77, UCM 22199–221), bet. Sayaxché and Subín (KU 57153), Seibal (AMNH 72612–16; KU 157170–71), 1 mi W Ruinas Seibal (KU 157172–73), Sojio (AMNH 70005, 70009–10), Tikal (KU 157174, 171630; UF 13742–72, 13802; UMMZ 117809–21), 3 mi SW Tikal (UMRC 78-25), 3 mi S Tikal (KU 157175–77), Toocog (KU 55778–82, 59521–22), Uaxactún (AMNH 68521; KU 157166–69; MCZ 24496, 38664; UMMZ 70426–33), Yaxhá (UMMZ 75151, 75176); no specific locality (USNM 71920, 71922–29, 71932–47). *Mexico*: Campeche: Becan (UMMZ 76121), Chuina (KU 74849–50, 74855–56), Ciudad del Carmen (UMMZ 83533–34), Encarnación (FMNH 113968, 114501-2), 5 mi W Escárcega (UMMZ 123014), 7.5 km W Escárcega (KU 70062, TCWC 58690), Laguna Chumpich (KU 74848), Laguna Alvarado (KU 74851), Matamoros (FMNH 36523, 36544), Pacaitún (FMNH 36520), Ruinas Becan (UMMZ 76121; UMRC 85-24), Tres Brazos (FMNH 113971, 124196-97); Chiapas: vicinity Bonampak (MZFC 486), Palenque ruins (UCM 46285-86; UIMNH 11322), 8 km W Palenque ruins (USNM 266270), San Juanito (UCM 46287); Quintana Roo: 3 km NW Chacchoben (CM 45285), Chunyaxché (KU 171526; MZFC 3394-95), Cobá (FMNH 27329), Felipe Carrillo Puerto (UCM 18429), 4 km NNE Felipe Carrillo Puerto (KU 70063), 17 km N Felipe Carrillo Puerto (AMNH 110035), Isla Mujeres (UCM 39114), 5 mi S Las Palmas (UCM 39113), Pueblo Nuevo X-Can (CM 45828; KU 70064-66), 1.5 km S, 6 km E Pueblo Nuevo X-Can (KU 70067); Tabasco: Tenosique (UCM 46298-307), near Tenosique (UCM 46297); Yucatán: Chichén Itzá (FMNH 27330-31, 36506-7, 36509-10, 36515-16, 49148, 49154-57, 49160-61, 82601-3; KU 70070; LSUMZ 28267; MCZ 7115, 26792-94, 57023-27; UMMZ 72861-64), 2 km E Chichén Itzá (KU 70068-69, 70154-55), Dzibilchaltún (FMNH 153443), 28 km E Sucupo (FMNH 36511-13).

Anolis pentaprion (Cope)
(Figs. 131B, 132; Map 89)

Anolis (Coccoessus) pentaprion Cope, 1862a:178. HOLOTYPE: formerly USNM, now lost, *fide* H. M. Smith and Taylor, 1950a:61. TYPE LOCALITY: New Granada, near the river Truando (= Truando River, Colombia).

Lichen anole.

DESCRIPTION   This is a medium-sized, distinctively patterned anole with short, stubby limbs and a short tail. In the Yucatán Peninsula, the adults average between 50 and 65 mm in snout-vent length, but size appears to vary geographically, for some populations from lower Central America average in excess of 70 mm, and the holotype of *A. pentaprion cristifer*, from the Pacific side of Chiapas, measures 72 mm (H. M. Smith, 1968:197). The males in a composite sample taken from throughout Middle America substantially exceeded the females in size (Fitch, 1976:4). The tail is only about 1.3 times as long as the head and body. The dorsal, lateral, and ventral scales are smooth and granular or conical, with those of the middorsal area slightly enlarged. The ventral scales are about twice the size of the dorsals. The scales on the dorsal surface of the head

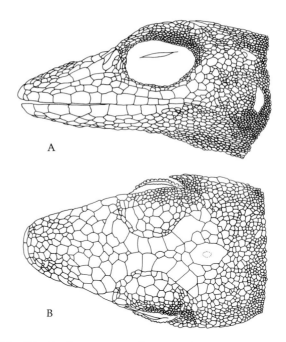

Fig. 132. *Anolis pentaprion* (UF 13773), 46 mm SVL. A, lateral; and B, dorsal views of the head; Tikal, El Petén, Guatemala.

are smooth, and there is a shallow frontal depression (Fig. 132B).

Anolis pentaprion is lichenose; that is, the dorsal pattern is an irregular dark gray, brown, or black reticulum within which are scattered light gray or tan or greenish spots. As described by Myers (1971:25) this species is capable of rapidly changing color to become pale ashy gray. The dewlap is usually red, reddish orange, or pinkish. It is present in both sexes but much better developed in males.

SIMILAR SPECIES   The distinctive lichenose pattern distinguishes this anole from others in the Yucatán Peninsula. In addition, other forest-dwelling anoles of similar size (*A. lemurinus*, *A. tropidonotus*) have keeled ventral and dorsal scales.

DISTRIBUTION   *Anolis pentaprion* occurs on both the Atlantic and Pacific slopes at the Isthmus of Tehauntepec and southward on the Caribbean slope through lower Central America to northwestern Colombia. It occurs through the base of the Yucatán Peninsula from northern Chiapas through El Petén to Belize (Map 89). There is a doubtful record from the state of Yucatán (see Comment).

NATURAL HISTORY   These arboreal lizards live on tree trunks in humid forests and forest edges.

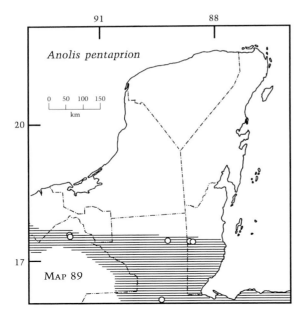

Anolis pentaprion

91   88

20

17

MAP 89

on the other, but he believed that the variation between populations was too slight to justify the recognition of subspecies.

ETYMOLOGY   The specific name, *pentaprion*, is from the Greek *penta-*, "five," and *prion*, "a saw," and refers to the keeled scales on the angulate tail of individuals from lower Central America.

COMMENT   Boulenger (1881) described *A. beckeri* from "Yucatán," and H. M. Smith and Taylor (1950b:351) restricted the type locality to Chichén Itzá, Yucatán. Barbour and Cole (1906:149) reported a specimen from Chichén Itzá that they described as "apparently typical, but in rather poor condition." In the ensuing 87 years no additional specimens have been found at Chichén Itzá—or anywhere else in the state of Yucatán. *A. p. beckeri* normally inhabits humid forests at the base of the Yucatán Peninsula. Thus, on both distributional and ecological grounds, I consider the Chichén Itzá record highly doubtful.

Locality Records   Belize: Cayo: San Ignacio (USNM 220398), Xunantunich (UMRC 93-19–20); no specific locality (FMNH 4483). *Guatemala*: El Petén: Tikal (UF 24616, 13773, 117822; UMMZ 117822). *Mexico*: Chiapas: Palenque (MCZ 93676–77; USNM 136491); San Juanito (UIMNH 37067–90; USNM 136492–516).

Anolis rodriguezii Bocourt
(Fig. 326; Map 90)

Anolis rodriguezii Bocourt, 1873:62. HOLOTYPE: MNHNP 2411. TYPE LOCALITY: a Panzos sur le Polochic (America Centrale) (= Panzos, Alta Verapaz, Guatemala).

Lagartija chipojo (Mexico); xtulub (Yucatec Maya).

DESCRIPTION   This small, delicate lizard averages between 40 and 45 mm in snout-vent length (Fig. 326). The long, slender tail is approximately 1.5 to 1.8 times as long as the head and body. There is little or no sexual size dimorphism (Fitch, 1976:4). The head is moderately narrow, and the snout is pointed in dorsal aspect. The limbs are rather long and slender, and the digits bear expanded subdigital lamellae. The middorsal scales are keeled and slightly larger than the lateral scales, which are granular. The ventral scales are smooth, slightly imbricate, and conspicuously larger than the dor-

They are uncommon, or at least infrequently encountered in the Yucatán Peninsula. Their lichenose pattern renders them inconspicuous against lichen-covered trunks and branches, however, and their behavior of clinging close to the surface makes them especially difficult to detect. They are diurnal and probably feed on insects and other small invertebrates.

The females produce multiple clutches of a single egg. H. M. Smith and Kerster (1955:201) collected a large series of hatchlings between 7 July and 2 August near Palenque, Chiapas, indicating that breeding occurs during the summer rainy season. All the specimens were taken from bromeliads, but no adults were found. According to J. R. Meyer (in litt.), a female of this species collected on 17 August at Xunantunich, Cayo District, laid one egg on 10 September and another on 15 October. These hatched on 20 October and around 15 November, respectively.

SUBSPECIES   Stuart (1955:20–21) called attention to the differences between populations from northern Central America and those from areas to the south, and three years later (Stuart, 1958:21) recognized the northern form (including the lizards in the Yucatán Peninsula) as subspecifically distinct, applying the name *A. p. beckeri*. Myers (1971) discussed the infraspecific taxonomy of this species, noting the differences between Honduran and Guatemala specimens, on the one hand, and those from lower Central America and Pacific Chiapas,

sals. The supraocular scales and the scales on the frontal depression are keeled. The males have enlarged postanal scales.

The dorsum is predominantly brown or tan with irregular and indistinct dark brown markings. The overall coloration can change from dark to light depending on the temperature and the emotional state of the animal. Often there is a middorsal series of dark I-or hourglass-shaped markings. The throat and labial scales are light cream or beige, and this contrasts sharply with the dark sides of the head. The venter is immaculate white, light gray, or cream. The males have a pale yellow dewlap, often with a hint of orange in the center. The dewlap is rudimentary or lacking in females.

SIMILAR SPECIES In size and shape *A. rodriguezii* most closely resembles *A. sericeus*, but differs in possessing smooth ventral scales and a yellow dewlap devoid of blue or purple. *Anolis uniformis* has abruptly enlarged middorsal scales and keeled ventrals, and the males have a reddish dewlap with a blue or purple spot.

DISTRIBUTION *Anolis rodriguezii* occurs at low elevations on the Atlantic slope from southern Veracruz throughout the Yucatán Peninsula to Honduras (Map 90).

NATURAL HISTORY These common diurnal anoles are found in a variety of forested situations, but most abundantly in seasonal dry forests and

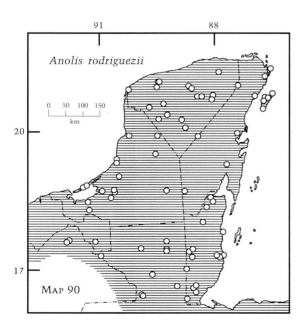

forest edges. They are often found perching on vegetation at heights of up to several meters, but they are sometimes encountered on the ground, in rock piles, and on the walls of Maya ruins. *Anolis rodriguezii* eats small invertebrates, especially insects and spiders.

There is no direct information on reproduction in this species, but it is surely oviparous, and the females probably lay multiple clutches of a single egg, the general pattern in *Anolis*.

ETYMOLOGY The specific name, *rodriguezii*, is a patronym honoring Juan Rodriguez, curator of the Museum of Zoology of Guatemala during the latter part of the nineteenth century.

COMMENT This form is the northern counterpart of *A. limifrons* of lower Central America, to which it is presumably closely related. Stuart (1948:50) relegated *A. rodriguezii* to subspecific rank within *A. limifrons*. Etheridge, who examined osteological features (1960:163, 167), placed *A. limifrons* and *A. rodriguezii* in different species series; and Fitch et al. (1976:119) argued persuasively for recognition of *A. rodriguezii* as a full species, noting that it differs from *A. limifrons* in habitat, body size, proportions, sexual dimorphism, dewlap color, and aggression display.

Locality Records *Belize*: Belize: Belize City (CM 90911), English Cay (MPM 7535), North River (USNM 58694); Cayo: Baking Pot (MCZ 18954), Blancaneaux Lodge (CM 91005–6), near El Cayo (UF 24518–19), Valentin (UMMZ 80688); Corozal: 2 mi SW Corozal (MCZ 71604–5), Progresso Lagoon (MPM 10780–82); Orange Walk: Lamanai (ROM H12769–70, H12775), Otro Benque (USNM 194919), Tower Hill (USNM 194920); Stann Creek: Dangriga (CM 112116), 7 mi W, 1 mi S Stann Creek (JLK 507), 14.75 mi W Stann Creek (JLK 407–8); Toledo: Blue Creek Village (UTA R-11043), Columbia Forest Reserve (MPM 8262), Dolores (UMRC 90-14), 1 mi W Salamanca (CM 105857, 105860–61). *Guatemala*: El Petén: 15 km NW Chinajá (KU 55790–91), 20 km NNW Chinajá (KU 55789), Paso Caballos (AMNH 72623), Piedras Negras (UCM 47408), Poptún (UMMZ 117831), Sojio (AMNH 69999, 70007), Tikal (KU 157180; UF 13774–75; UMMZ 117827–30), 3 mi S Tikal (KU 157181–82), Uaxactún (KU 157178–79); no specific locality (USNM 71921, 71931). *Mexico*: Campeche: Balchacaj (H. M. Smith, 1938:13), Becan (UWZH 20513, 20544), 5 mi E Campeche (UCM 22955), Champotón (UMMZ 72858–60), 5 km S Champotón (KU 70093–97), 21 km N Champotón (LSUMZ 28254), Chuina (KU 74857–67, 74870), 25 km NE Ciudad del Carmen (KU 75498), Dzibalchén

Caption for Map 90 (within image): 91 88 *Anolis rodriguezii* 0 50 100 150 km 20 17 MAP 90

(KU 75491–97), Encarnación (FMNH 112894–95, 112898–900, 112904), 7.5 km W Escárcega (KU 70098), 13 km W, 1 km N Escárcega (KU 70099), 24 km E, 20 km S Escárcega (USNM 224573), Isla del Carmen, Puerto Real (UCM 22954, 45018), Isla del Carmen, 1 km SW Puerto Real (KU 70071–92), Tres Brazos (FMNH 112893, 112896–97, 112902); Chiapas: Palenque (H. M. Smith and Taylor, 1950a:64); Quintana Roo: 15 km E Caobas (KU 74868), ca. 7 mi NW Circuito Benito Juárez (MCZ 149561), Cozumel (Himmelstein, 1980:27; MCZ 67409; UCM 47409–32), Cozumel, 3 km N Cozumel (UMMZ 84353), Cozumel, 4 km N San Miguel (UCM 12404), Cozumel, 3 mi N San Miguel (UCM 12423–29), Cozumel, San Miguel (UCM 22833–920; UMMZ 78575, 78577–78, 78580), Cozumel, vicinity San Miguel (UF 33510–15), S end Isla Cozumel (UMMZ 78579), Cozumel, 3.5 km N San Miguel (KU 70144–53), Cozumel, 4 km N San Miguel (KU 70143), Cozumel, 6 mi E San Miguel (UMMZ 78576), Cozumel, 3 mi S San Miguel (UMMZ 78574), Cozumel, 2 km E San Miguel (UCM 20548), Cozumel, Punta Norte (MCZ 149558–59), 3 mi E Esmeralda (LACM 114029–30), Isla Mujeres, Rancho Pirata (KU 70140), 5 km N Limones (KU 74869), Pueblo Nuevo X-Can (KU 70100–4), 17.1 km S Puerto Juárez (EAL 2854), near Puerto Morelos (CAS 114054), 2.3 mi S, 1 mi E Santa Rosa (KU 157508–12), 4.1 km SW Vigía Chico (UMRC 80-68), X-Caret (SDSNH 64454), no specific locality (USNM 17832, 47645); Tabasco: 1 mi E Teapa (UMMZ 119816), 4.5 mi N Teapa (UMMZ 119074); Yucatán: Calcehtok (AMNH 38947; UMMZ 113547), Catmís (FMNH 27336), 12 km N Celestún (UMRC 84-143), Chichén Itzá (FMNH 20637, 27335, 36531–40, 49145, 49147, 49149, 83036, 112903; MCZ 7116, 7251, 10929, 22066–68, 28744, 57393–94; UCM 12436; UMMZ 61755, 68201-2, 76161, 80876–82, 83924, 115071), vicinity Chichén Itzá (UMMZ 72854), Hacienda Chichén Itzá (UMMZ 72855–56), 1 km E Chichén Itzá (AMNH 110032–33; LSUMZ 28268), 1.5 km E Chichén Itzá (UMMZ 72857), 4 km E Chichén Itzá (LSUMZ 28255), 8.6 km E Chichén Itzá (EAL 2845), Citilpech (Ives, 1891:460), Dzibilchaltún (FMNH 153432–33, 153435–36, 153440, 153444–45), 1 mi W Dzibilchaltún (KU 157190), Grutas Balankanché (TCWC 57118–19), 12.3 mi E Izamal (KU 157189), 1.5 mi S Libre Unión (UCM 28670–71), Mérida (FMNH 112901), Oxkutzcab (AMNH 38862), Petectunich (JCL photo; UMRC 93-13), Pisté (FMNH 36530; KU 70105–9; UCM 12430–35, 18440–532, 22828–32, 22921–33), Ruinas Kabah (UMRC 80-67), Ruinas Mayapán (KU 157184–88; UMRC 93-12), Santa Rosa (KU 157508–512), Tekom (FMNH 49122–26; MCZ 57391–92), 12 mi N Tizimín (UCM 28668–69), bet. Tunkás and Sitilpech (KU 171525), Valladolid (AMNH 110034), X-Can (UCM 18419–20), no specific locality (FMNH 153432–33, 153435–36; USNM 6571, 10300–1).

Anolis sagrei Duméril and Bibron
(Figs. 131C, 327, 328; Map 91)

Anolis sagrei A. M. C. Duméril and Bibron, 1837:149. SYNTYPES: MNHNP 2430, 6797 (five syntypes). TYPE LOCALITY: Cuba; restricted by Ruibal (1964:490) to Havana, Havana Province, Cuba.

Brown anole; hu wa, cock maklala (Belize); lagartija chipojo, (Mexico); merech (Yucatec Maya).

DESCRIPTION The brown anole is a medium-sized, moderately robust lizard. Sexual size dimorphism is pronounced in this species. The males average between 55 and 60 mm in snout-vent length and reach a maximum of about 70 mm (Fig. 328). The much smaller females average 40 to 45 mm and attain a maximum size of about 57 mm (Fig. 327). Body size varies geographically throughout the extensive range of this species, with specimens from Middle America tending to be larger and more robust than those from elsewhere. The middorsal scales are enlarged and keeled, and the lateral scales are small and granular. The ventrals are keeled and conspicuously larger than the middorsals. The median supracaudal scales are enlarged, forming a keel that is especially conspicuous in males (Fig. 131C). The males have a pair of enlarged postanal scales.

The dorsal coloration is highly variable but generally brown or gray with darker spots, bars, or chevrons. The females are polymorphic. Some have a light vertebral stripe, and others have a pattern of chevrons, bars, and spots. The dewlap of males is yellow-orange to red-orange, and the scales of the dewlap often bear black pigment. The free edge of the dewlap is bordered with yellow or cream. In females the dewlap is small but functional and bears a trace of color.

SIMILAR SPECIES *Anolis lemurinus* has a shorter and broader head, longer legs, a red dewlap, and lacks a supracaudal keel and enlarged postanal scales. *Anolis tropidonotus* has 8 to 12 rows of abruptly enlarged middorsal scales and lacks a supracaudal keel. *Anolis pentaprion* has a lichenose dorsal pattern and smooth dorsal and ventral scales. *Anolis cristatellus* is larger, has smooth ventral scales, and the males have an orange dewlap with a greenish cast.

DISTRIBUTION This extraordinarily successful colonist is widespread in the western Caribbean,

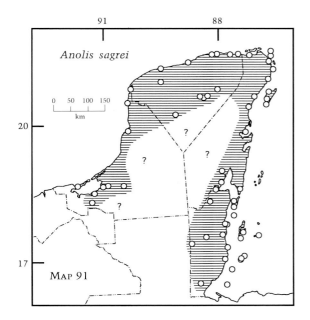

Anolis sagrei

0 50 100 150
km

MAP 91

the northern Bahamas, and the southern two-thirds of Florida. It is also established in Houston and New Orleans. On the mainland of Middle America it occurs at low elevations on the Atlantic slope from Tabasco through the Yucatán Peninsula to northern Honduras, including the Islas Bahías. *Anolis sagrei* has a discontinuous distribution in the Yucatán Peninsula, where it is generally associated with areas of human disturbance (Map 91).

NATURAL HISTORY This anole often perches conspicuously on rock walls, fence posts, and the sides of buildings. Throughout most of its Middle American range it is a human commensal, and it is rarely found far from areas of human disturbance. *Anolis sagrei* is easily transported through human agency, and the species is rapidly expanding its geographic distribution. Brown anoles are diurnal watch-and-wait predators that eat small invertebrates, especially insects. They are also known to consume other small anoles, including their own species (P. A. Cochran, 1989:70).

Anolis sagrei is oviparous. Sexton and Brown (1977) studied brown anole reproduction in Belize City and found that males and females were sexually mature at snout-vent lengths of 40 mm and 39 mm, respectively. The proportion of reproductively active lizards declined during the relatively dry winter months, but large males had enlarged testes regardless of the season. Thus, reproduction is seasonal, but the period of reproductive activity is

lengthy. Like other anoles, *A. sagrei* produces multiple clutches, each of a single egg. The minimum interovulation period, based on data obtained from captives from southern Florida, is about 10 days (J. C. Lee, unpubl. data).

SUBSPECIES Many subspecific names have been applied to various segments of this wide-ranging and highly variable species, although the validity of many is presently in doubt. The name *A. s. mayensis* Smith and Burger, 1949 has been applied to the lizards on the mainland of southern Mexico and northern Central America, and J. C. Lee (1992) demonstrated the morphological distinctness of these populations.

ETYMOLOGY The specific name, *sagrei*, is a patronym honoring Ramon de la Sagra, author of the *Historia física, política y natural de la isla de Cuba*, who collected a portion of the type material.

COMMENT Some confusion exists concerning the authorship of the name *A. sagrei*. Although most workers credit A. M. C. Duméril and Bibron, 1837, with the original description of this form, others (e.g., Fitzinger, 1843:17; Hoogmoed, 1973:29) recognize Cocteau as the author. The description by Duméril and Bibron appears in volume 4 of the *Erpétologie générale*, which was published in 1837. The description of *Anolis sagrei* is introduced on page 149 by a heading that reads: "19. L'ANOLIS DE LA SAGRA. *Anolis Sagrei*. Cocteau." At the end of Duméril and Bibron's account of *A. sagrei* is a synonymy that begins "*Anolis Sagrei*. Th. Coc. Hist. de l'île de Cub. par M. Ramon de la Sagra, part. Erpetol. tab. 10." Clearly, Duméril and Bibron recognized Cocteau as the author of the name *A. sagrei*. Elsewhere in that volume, however, they noted de la Sagra's volume dealing with reptiles and containing the description of *Anolis Sagrei* by Cocteau "non encore publies." It was not until the following year that Cocteau's descriptions of Cuban reptiles, including *A. sagrei*, were published. Thus, Duméril and Bibron's publication of the name has priority, notwithstanding the fact that Duméril and Bibron themselves explicitly credited Cocteau with the name.

Locality Records Belize: Belize: Belize (CM 90910, 90913–14, 91004; FMNH 4179–85, 4464–68, 49162–84; KU 144930–32, 144935–39; MCZ 119861–79, 121044–56; MPM 8052; NMSU 3055–64; ROM

H12774; UMMZ 75186–88), 1 mi NW Belize (UMMZ 75185), Belize, Fort George Hotel (USNM 194922), Belize, Yarbourough Cemetery (USNM 204805–6), Belize, Mopan Hotel (USNM 204807–10), Belize, St. John's College (UF 24540), Cay Bokel (MPM 7513, 7521, 7524), Cay Corker (MPM 8053–62), Glover's Reef (CM 8518–620, 8622–44), Glover's Reef, Long Cay (UMMZ 145878), Glover's Reef, Middle Cay (FMNH 34611, 34617–18), Glover's Reef, Southwest Cays (FMNH 34602–10), Half Moon Cay (FMNH 34653, 121049; MCZ 61106–7), Manatee (FMNH 5818, 56475–76; MCZ 19315–19; UMMZ 56475–76), Turneffe Island, Grant Point (FMNH 34625–26); Cayo: Belmopan (CM 91013), Benque Viejo (JCL sight record), Xunantunich (KU 144933–34); Corozal: Ambergris Cay, 2 to 3 mi S San Pedro (MCZ 71504–24), 5 km NNE San Pedro (CM 91115–19), Cash Kan Island (CM 91107), Cayo Iguano (CM 91103–6), Corozal (MCZ 71468–75, 71476–503), S edge Corozal Town (KU 157203–4), 2 mi S Corozal (MCZ 71466–67); Orange Walk: Orange Walk Town (MPM 8051; USNM 194926), Tower Hill (KU 157199–202; MPM 8174); Stann Creek: Mango Creek (MCZ 71566–92), Rendezvous Cay (MCZ 61108–13; MPM 7505–12, 7514–20, 7522–23, 7525–27), Stann Creek (FMNH 4469–77; UF 24541), 2 mi S Stann Creek (KU 157191–98), Tom Owen Cay (FMNH 4478); Toledo: Columbia Forest Reserve (MPM 8243–61); no specific locality (USNM 25104–5, 26070, 26072–73, 58290–92). *Mexico*: Campeche: Balchacaj (H. M. Smith, 1938:14), Campeche (KU 157205–7; UCM 18425–28; UMMZ 113549), Ciudad del Carmen (FMNH 116726–30, 116733–34, 116738–39, 124122–23; UCM 18272–417, 20551–750, 20185–21100, 45596), Encarnación (MCZ 54103), Escárcega (UMRC 88-2), Los Petenes, rumbo a Yaltún (IHNHERP 536, 539), Panlao (H. M. Smith, 1938:14), Tres Brazos (FMNH 75795); Quintana Roo: Akumal (JCL photo), Lake Bacalar (LSUMZ 33349), Cancún (Himmelstein, 1980:27), Chetumal (CM 54279–84; MCZ 96656–59, 100369–70), outskirts of Chetumal (AMNH 104520–21), Cozumel (CM 93196–98), Cozumel, Cedral (CM 40009), Cozumel, San Miguel (CM 55811, 55814, 55816, 55818; UCM 21451–520, 22951–53), S end Isla Cozumel (UMMZ 78583), Culebra Cays, Bahía de la Ascención (UMMZ 78584), Isla Contoy (UCM 21401–50), Isla Mujeres (UCM 21101–400, 39115–17, 22935–50; UMMZ 78581–82), N end Isla Mujeres (KU 70111–25), La Glorieta, Sian Ka'an Reserve (MZCIQRO 22), Puerto Juárez (MCZ 67410), Puerto Morelos (JCL sight record), Tulum (JCL sight record), Xcalak (KU 74871–75); Yucatán: Celestún (KU 157226–27; TU 19811), Chichén Itzá (H. M. Smith, 1938:3), 4 mi E Chichén Itzá (UCM 28656–63), Dzilam Bravo (KU 157214–25), Mérida (FMNH 116732, 116735, 116737, 116740; UCM 18423–24, 20550, 21521–26, 45419–30, 47433), Pisté (UCM 45597), Progreso (FMNH 116731, 116736), Río Lagartos (KU 157208–13; UCM 39118–33; UF 27615–777), Valladolid (JCL sight record).

Anolis sericeus Hallowell
(Figs. 329, 330; Map 92)

Anolis sericeus Hallowell, 1856:227. HOLOTYPE: originally ANSP, now apparently lost, *fide* Stuart, 1963:65. TYPE LOCALITY: El eucerso le Jalapa, Mexico (= Jalapa, Veracruz, Mexico).

Silky anole.

DESCRIPTION The males of this small, attenuate anole average about 46 mm in snout-vent length; the females are about 41 mm long (Figs. 329, 330). The head is rather narrow, and the snout is pointed in dorsal aspect. The tail is long and slender and roughly twice as long as the head and body. The limbs are slender, and the digits bear expanded subdigital lamellae. The dorsal scales are small and heavily keeled, and there are six to eight rows of somewhat enlarged middorsals. The ventrals are keeled and larger than the dorsals.

The dorsum is predominantly gray, brown, or bronze with indistinct dark reticulations and spots, especially on the limbs. The venter is pale yellow, cream, or white. The females exhibit pattern polymorphism. Some have a light vertebral stripe (Fig. 330); others closely resemble the males. The males have a yellow-orange to reddish dewlap with a blue or purple central spot. In females the dewlap is rudimentary and bears only a trace of color.

SIMILAR SPECIES *Anolis rodriguezii* has smooth ventral scales, and the males have a pale yellow dewlap. *Anolis uniformis* is short and stocky, its middorsal scales are abruptly enlarged relative to the lateral scales, and the males have a reddish dewlap with a purple spot. *Anolis sagrei* is larger and has a red or orange dewlap and a serrated supracaudal crest.

DISTRIBUTION This species is widespread at low and moderate elevations from Tamaulipas on the Atlantic slope and Oaxaca on the Pacific slope, through southeastern Mexico and Central America to northern Costa Rica. In the Yucatán Peninsula *A. sericeus* is pan-peninsular (Map 92).

NATURAL HISTORY These delicate anoles prefer open habitats such as savannas, forest edges, and

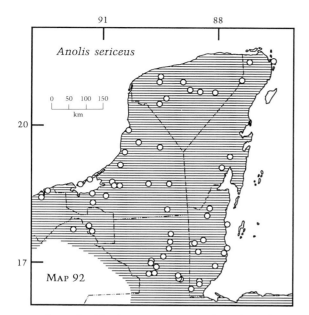

Anolis sericeus

0 50 100 150
km

20

17

MAP 92

areas disturbed by human activity, but they do penetrate forest habitats along roadsides. Generally they can be found perching on shrubs, bushes, and tufts of grass, although they are occasionally found on the ground. Like many other arboreal anoles, they flatten themselves against a stem, branch, or tree trunk when approached to render themselves inconspicuous. At night they sleep on leaves and grass stalks, and they can often be found in considerable numbers.

Fitch (1973:84) recorded body temperatures of this species in Guatemala and Mexico. All fell within a six-degree range, with an apparent preferred temperature between 32 and 33C, unusually high for an anole.

Henderson and Fitch (1975) studied structural habitat utilization by *A. sericeus* at two localities in Oaxaca and concluded that this widely distributed species can use a broad range of perch diameters. This versatility may contribute to the form's success.

Anolis sericeus is oviparous, and each clutch consists of a single egg. Fitch (1973:84; 1975:39) reported that reproduction was curtailed during the dry months of December through April on the seasonally dry Pacific slope from Costa Rica to Oaxaca.

ETYMOLOGY The specific name, *sericeus*, is Latin meaning "pertaining to silk," possibly in reference to the silky sheen on the dorsum.

COMMENT Populations of this form from the Yucatán Peninsula were long known as *A. ustus*

Cope. J. C. Lee (1980b) showed that *A. ustus* and *A. kidderi* Ruthven (type locality: Mérida, Yucatán) are indistinguishable from *A. sericeus*, a wideranging and variable form.

Information on *A. sericeus* was summarized by J. C. Lee (1980b).

Locality Records Belize: Belize: Belize City (FMNH 4259), North River (USNM 58476–78); Cayo: Augustine (CM 105945), El Cayo (UF 24520–23), 0.5 mi S Georgeville (CM 105696), Succoths (W. T. Neill and Allen, 1959c:35); Orange Walk: Guinea Grass (MPM 7534), Lamanai (ROM H12722), Tower Hill (MPM 7533); Stann Creek: Dangriga (RWV photo), 5.7 mi S Silk Grass (KU 157228–31); Toledo: Blue Creek Village (UTA R-11056–57), 2 km N Blue Creek Village (UF 87176), Dolores (UMRC 90-13), 14 mi W Mango Creek (LSUMZ 10284). *Guatemala*: El Petén: Caoba (KU 157254), S shore Lake Eckibix (UMMZ 79077), La Libertad (USNM 71413), near La Libertad (UMMZ 75080–83, 75086–88), 1.9 mi S La Libertad (KU 157252–53), 5 km SW La Libertad (KU 171553–67), Poptún (UMMZ 117842), 2 km E Poptún (UMMZ 124372, 124374), 6 km NW Poptún (UMMZ 124373), 12.1 mi NW Poptún (KU 157232), Sayaxché (KU 55793; UCM 22235–42), Seibal (AMNH 72611, 72617), 1 mi W Ruinas Seibal (KU 157233–51), Tikal (UF 13776–78; UMMZ 117823–26, 120124), Toocog (KU 59530), Uaxactún (AMNH 68522–24; UMMZ 70441–42); no specific locality (USNM 71917–19, 71930). *Mexico*: Campeche: Balchacaj (UMMZ 81927–28), Campeche (KU 157257), rd. to Candelaria, 7.8 km SE Hwy. 186 (KU 171551), 5 km W Champotón (KU 70127–32), Chuina (KU 74877–79, 74881), Ciudad del Carmen (H. M. Smith, 1938:14), Dzibalchén (KU 75503–8), 5 mi W Escárcega (UMMZ 123015), Isla Aguada (UF 33530), Isla del Carmen, 1 km SW Puerto Real (KU 70126), 8 km W La Cristalina (JCL photo), Laguna Alvarado (KU 74880), 10 km E Laguna Silvituc (KU 74876), 4.5 km N Ruinas Edzná (KU 171747), rd. to Sabancuy, 3.5 km N Hwy. 186 (KU 171529–50), Tres Brazos (H. M. Smith, 1938:14), Tuxpeña Camp (UMMZ 73232), 11.4 mi W Xpujil (KU 157255–56); Chiapas: Palenque (JCL photo); Quintana Roo: 4.9 mi N Bacalar (KU 157258), N end Isla Mujeres (KU 70141–42), 3.3 mi N Limones (KU 157259), Pueblo Nuevo X-Can (KU 70135; UCM 28674–76), 3.1 km N Solferino (KU 171552); Tabasco: 8 km E Emiliano Zapata (EAL 1640), 28.2 km SE Emiliano Zapata (KU 171567–76), Frontera (USNM 37748); Yucatán: Chichén Itzá (AMNH 38861; FMNH 27337, 36521–22, 36524, 49146, 203733–36; MCZ 7443; UMMZ 60209, 72851–53), Dzibilchaltún (FMNH 153434, 153438–39, 153441–42), 12.3 mi E Izamal (KU 157260–63), Mayapán (FMNH 40684), Mérida (UMMZ 72851), SE edge of Muna (KU 157264–65), Tekom (FMNH 49129–30, 49131), 12 mi N Tizimín (UCM 28664–67), 3.5 km E Yokdzonot (KU 70134); no specific locality (USNM 24860–62).

Anolis tropidonotus Peters
(Fig. 331; Map 93)

Anolis tropidonotus W. C. Peters, 1863a:135. TYPES: ZMB (originally two syntypes; lectotype, ZMB 382; paratype, ZMB 36299, *fide* Stuart, 1963:66). TYPE LOCALITY: Huanusco in Mexico (= Huatusco?), Veracruz, Mexico.

Greater scaly anole; anolis escamudo, lagartija chipojo (Mexico).

DESCRIPTION Sexual size dimorphism is pronounced in this medium-sized anole. The males average between 50 and 55 mm in snout-vent length, and females are about 10 mm shorter (Fitch, 1976:4). The head is rather narrow, and the snout is pointed in dorsal aspect. The limbs are moderately slender, and the digits bear subdigital lamellae that are only slightly expanded. The long, slender tail is about twice the length of the head and body. The dorsal scales are strongly keeled, with those of the 10 to 12 middorsal rows abruptly enlarged relative to the much smaller lateral scales. The ventral scales are also strongly keeled and are approximately equal to the middorsals in size. The scales of the dorsal surface of the head are strongly keeled, and there is a very shallow frontal depression.

These lizards are variable in color and pattern, but the ground color is generally brown, tan, or rusty (Fig. 331). The middorsal region of the body is often lighter than the lateral surfaces, and it may bear a series of dark markings, often arranged as pairs of triangles. The venter is generally light gray or tan and devoid of a pattern. The dewlap of males is rusty orange; that of females is rudimentary. The iris is yellowish orange.

SIMILAR SPECIES The abruptly enlarged, heavily keeled middorsal scales distinguish this species from all others in the Yucatán Peninsula except the much smaller *A. uniformis*, whose males have a reddish dewlap, usually with a purple spot, and whose females lack a dewlap. *Anolis uniformis* generally has seven or more supralabial scales to the middle of the eye, whereas *A. tropidonotus* generally has fewer than seven. The supraorbital semicircles are strongly differentiated in *A. tropidonotus* and weakly differentiated in *A. uniformis*.

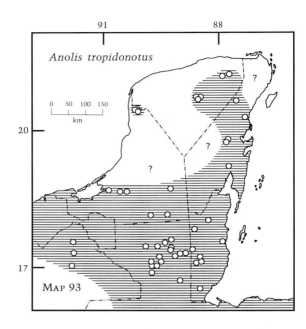

MAP 93

DISTRIBUTION *Anolis tropidonotus* occurs at low elevations on the Atlantic slope from Veracruz through northern Guatemala and Belize to Honduras and Nicaragua. It occurs continuously throughout the Yucatán Peninsula except in the arid northwest corner, where it is restricted to an area known locally as "Los Petenes" (Map 93).

NATURAL HISTORY This anole is a common diurnal inhabitant of shaded areas in primary and secondary forests, where individuals can often be observed running across the forest floor. When pursued, they sometimes dive under the leaf litter to escape. This species is predominantly terrestrial, as the slightly enlarged subdigital lamellae suggest, but the males especially may be found perching low in shrubs or on tree trunks or buttresses. They are watch-and-wait predators that feed on small invertebrates, especially insects.

Jackson (1973) studied this species in an upland pine forest in Honduras and estimated a population density of 33 to 36 adults per acre. Males had much larger home ranges than females, and males tended to perch higher than females, although none perched above 1.73 m.

Anolis tropidonotus is oviparous, producing multiple clutches of a single egg each. Jackson (1973:310) observed copulation on 28 May. All the males with snout-vent lengths greater than 40 mm that Jackson examined in late May had enlarged testes and turgid sperm ducts, and all the females 40 mm long or longer were reproductively mature, as indicated by the presence of yolked follicles. Jackson (1973:311) concluded that this species breeds at the beginning of the rainy season.

ETYMOLOGY   The specific name, *tropidonotus*, is from the Greek *tropos*, "a turn" or "change in manner," and *notus*, "the back," possibly referring to the strongly differentiated middorsal scales.

SUBSPECIES   According to Alvarez del Toro and Smith (1956), this species exists as two subspecies, of which *A. t. tropidonotus* occurs in the Yucatán Peninsula.

Locality Records   Belize: Belize: Manatee (Schmidt, 1941:492); Cayo: Augustine (CM 105946–47), Cohune Ridge (UMMZ 80693), Millionario (MPM 7531–32), 3 mi N Millionario (UMMZ 124666, 124669), Pine Ridge Rd., 36 mi S Western Hwy. (UMMZ 124664–65), Río Frio Cave (JCL photo), San Ignacio (USNM 75118); Orange Walk: Gallon Jug (MPM 7646–50), Lamanai (ROM H12771, H12773); Toledo: Columbia Forest Reserve (MPM 8241). *Guatemala*: El Petén: near El Paso de Caballo (UMMZ 79076), Flores (UMMZ 79075), La Libertad (Stuart, 1935:43), 6 mi N La Libertad (UMMZ 75092, 75098), Pacomon (USNM 71391), 10 km NW Poptún (UMMZ 124375), 12 mi E Remate (UMMZ 75099), 1 mi N Río Subín (UMMZ 75096), San Andrés (UMMZ 75090–91), W Santa Cruz (UMMZ 75089), Santa Rita (USNM 71387), Santa Teresa (UMMZ 75095, 75097, 76622), Saubich (USNM 71384–85), Tikal (KU 157274, 171524; MCZ 121113; UF 13779–801, 24617–22; UMMZ 117832–41, 117844–48), 3 mi SSW Tikal (UMRC 78-56), 3 mi S Tikal (KU 157275–81), Uaxactún (AMNH 70931; KU 157266–73, 157282; UMMZ 70434–40), Yaxhá (UMMZ 75093–94, 75100), 18 mi E Yaxhá (UMMZ 75101); no specific locality (USNM 71864–65, 71867–68, 71870–91, 71893–907, 71909–10, 71912–14, 71916). *Mexico*: Campeche: Becan (UMMZ 76120), Encarnación (H. M. Smith, 1938:14), 7.5 km W Escárcega (UMMZ 130239), Laguna Alvarado (KU 74853–54), Laguna Chumpich (KU74852), Matamoros (FMNH 36542; MCZ 57029), Tankuche–El Remate (IHNHERP 547–48); Chiapas: 30.7 km N Ocosingo (USNM 266280), Palenque ruins (EAL 3645; UCM 46672); Quintana Roo: Chunyaxché (KU 171523), Cobá (FMNH 27338; UMMZ 83921), Felipe Carrillo Puerto (MZFC 3374), 3 mi NE Felipe Carrillo Puerto (CAS 141867), 5 mi S Las Palmas (UCM 39134), 5 km N Limones (KU 74882); Yucatán: Chichén Itzá (FMNH 36541, 106894; MCZ 7036, 119960–61; UMMZ 72865–66), 6.5 mi W Chichén Itzá (UMMZ 72867), 4 mi SW Chichén Itzá (UMMZ 72868), Colubá (FMNH 36469), 28 km E Sucopo (FMNH 36469).

Anolis uniformis Cope
(Fig. 332; Map 94)

Anolis uniformis Cope, 1885b:392. SYNTYPES (24 syntypes): USNM 6774, 24734–48, 24750 (Guatemala), 24859 (Yucatán), MCZ 10933 (Guatemala). TYPE LOCALITY: Yucatán and Guatemala; restricted by H. M. Smith and Taylor (1950b:319) to 2 miles north of Santa Teresa, El Petén, Guatemala.

Lesser scaly anole; abaniquillo de selva (Mexico).

DESCRIPTION   This is the smallest anole in the Yucatán Peninsula. The short, stocky adults average about 37 mm in snout-vent length, and there is little or no sexual size dimorphism (Fitch, 1976:4). The undamaged tail is about 1.5 times the length of the head and body. The head is relatively blunt and moderately distinct from the body (Fig. 332). The limbs are short, and the digits bear subdigital lamellae that are only slightly expanded. The scales on the dorsal surface of the head and body are strongly keeled, and the medial 8 to 10 rows on the body are abruptly enlarged relative to the lateral scales. The scales on the supraorbital semicircles are little differentiated from those on the frontal depression. The ventral scales are also keeled, and the males have enlarged postanal scales.

The dorsal coloration is tan, brown, or reddish brown with a few indistinct darker markings. The limbs and tail may bear indistinct light spots and bars. Often there are several fine, yellowish vertical lines on the sides of the body. The venter is generally light tan or cream, sometimes with suffusions of dark pigment. The dewlap of males is reddish, rose, or purple, usually with a dark blue basal spot.

SIMILAR SPECIES   *Anolis tropidonotus* is similar in having several median rows of abruptly enlarged middorsal scales, but it is much larger, the males have an orange or yellowish dewlap, and the supraorbital semicircles are strongly differentiated. Moreover, the midventral and middorsal scales of *A. tropidonotus* are about equal in size, whereas the midventrals of *A. uniformis* are much smaller than the middorsals.

DISTRIBUTION   This species occurs at low elevations on the Atlantic slope from Chiapas through the base of the Yucatán Peninsula to Honduras. In the Yucatán Peninsula the species is known from numerous localities in Chiapas, El Petén, and Belize

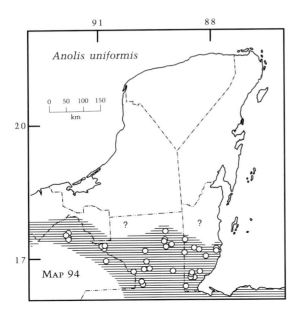

91 88

Anolis uniformis

0 50 100 150
km

20

17

MAP 94

(Map 94). There is a doubtful record from the state of Yucatán (see Comment).

NATURAL HISTORY These diminutive anoles inhabit the deep forest, where they are commonly encountered running or hopping across the forest floor during the day. They are generally terrestrial, although individuals are occasionally found low on the trunks or buttresses of trees. Stuart (1948:48) considered this species one of the most reliable indexes of virgin tall forest in Alta Verapaz. They prey on leaf litter invertebrates and are themselves eaten by various saurophagous snakes such as the blunt-headed tree snake, *Imantodes cenchoa* (Stuart, 1948:48).

Like other anoles, *A. uniformis* produces multiple clutches of a single egg. Stuart (1948:48) reported that females he collected in Alta Verapaz in mid-May contained well-developed eggs. In August, near Tikal, El Petén, I discovered a copulating pair beneath the bark of a standing tree, about 1.5 m above the ground. The females examined by J. A. Campbell et al. (1989) in southern Veracruz were sexually mature at a snout-vent length of 30 mm. Gravid females were present in every month for which specimens were available (March–October), but egg production peaked during the rainy months of summer and declined immediately before the onset of the dry season. Testes were largest at the end of the dry season.

ETYMOLOGY The specific name, *uniformis*, is a Latin adjective meaning "limited to a single kind; contained in a single form." It refers to the homogeneity of the scales on the dorsal surface of the head.

COMMENT Stuart (1948:48) relegated *A. uniformis* to subspecific status within *A. humilis* but emphasized the distinctness of specimens from Guatemala. Etheridge (1960:174), however, showed that *A. humilis* and *A. uniformis* differ in certain osteological features, and Meyer and Wilson (1971:107) formally restored *A. uniformis* to full species status on the basis of differences in morphology and dewlap color. Fitch (1976) treated the lizards in southern Mexico and northern Central America as specifically distinct from their close relatives to the south, noting that *A. humilis* males lack the blue or purple spot on the dewlap characteristic of *A. uniformis*. Echelle et al. (1978) provided behavioral evidence supporting the specific distinctness of *A. uniformis*.

A syntype of *A. uniformis* (USNM 24859) said to be from Yucatán (Cope, 1885b:392) is unequivocally this species, but the locality is doubtful, even allowing for the fact that in the past the name "Yucatán" was broadly and loosely applied to much of the Yucatán Peninsula. Although the specimen was collected by Arthur Schott, who made substantial collections of amphibians and reptiles in what is today the state of Yucatán, it is doubtful that USNM 24859 came from anywhere in the northern half of the Yucatán Peninsula, where the species is unknown and its occurrence is unexpected on ecological grounds.

W. T. Neill (in Henderson, 1976a:145) is said to have secured *A. uniformis* in Belize City sometime before 1963, whereas Henderson (1976a:145) found no evidence of this species in the city in 1970–1971. The peninsula on which Belize City rests is a low-lying mangrove swamp, habitat quite unsuitable for *A. uniformis*. If this species ever occurred in Belize City, it was doubtless brought there from elsewhere.

Locality Records Belize: Cayo: Caracol (CMM photo), 3 mi N Millionario (MCZ 71601; UMMZ 124668), Succoths (W. T. Neill and Allen, 1959c:35), Valentin (MCZ 46310; UMMZ 80689, 80991–92); Stann Creek: Bokowina (FMNH 49132–34, 49185–87), E slope Cockscomb Mts. (CM 8483), N slope Cockscomb Mts. (CM 8486), Dog Creek (FMNH 49135–36), Double Falls (FMNH 49142–44), Silk Grass (FMNH 49137–41,

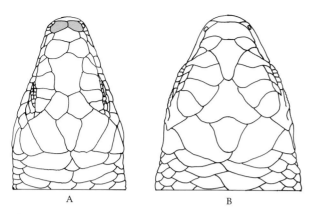

Fig. 133. Dorsal view of the heads of skinks. A, *Eumeces* showing presence of internasal scales (*shaded*). B, *Sphenomorphus* showing absence of internasal scales.

49188–99), 7 mi W, 1 mi S Stann Creek (JLK 409), 4 mi from Twelve-Mile Station (FMNH 4484–87); Toledo: ca. 2 mi SE Big Falls, Río Grande (CM 105893–94), Blue Creek Village (UTA R-11008–42), Dolores (JCL sight records), Gloria Camp (USNM 319770–72), 2.7 mi NE Golden Stream (KU 157148), 1 mi W Salamanca (CM 105853, 105867–70, 105872), San Pedro Columbia (MCZ 71602), 3 mi NE San Pedro Columbia (MCZ 71603), Unión Camp (USNM 319773). *Guatemala*: El Petén: Altar de Sacrificios (AMNH 99902–4), 4 km N Chinajá (KU 59515), 11 km NNW Chinajá (KU 55748), 15 km NW Chinajá (KU 55750–51, 55753–56, 59491–506), 20 km NNW Chinajá (KU 55747, 55749, 55752, 55757), Desempeña (UCM 46195–96), 6 mi N La Libertad (UMMZ 75098), Piedras Negras (UCM 46151–82, 46193–94, 46205–16), 5 mi S Piedras Negras (UCM 46183–92, 46197–204), 10 km NW Poptún (UMMZ 124375), 12 mi E Remate (UMMZ 75099), Sayaxché (KU 55760; UCM 22222), 1 mi W Ruinas Seibal (KU 157149–52), Santa Teresa (UMMZ 75095–97), Tikal (UF 13734–41; UMMZ 117844–48), 3 mi S Tikal (KU 157153–60), Uaxactún (AMNH 70932), Yaxhá (UMMZ 75105). *Mexico*: Chiapas: vicinity Bonampak (MZFC 487), Palenque (KU 94044–45; LSUMZ 33418; UCM 46219–26; MZFC 488), 13 mi S Palenque (LSUMZ 33416–17), 10 to 15 mi S Palenque (LSUMZ 33419–20, 33740–41), Palenque ruins (UIMNH 11323), San Juanito (UCM 46227–29), across river from Piedras Negras (UCM 46217–18). Yucatán: no specific locality (USNM 24859).

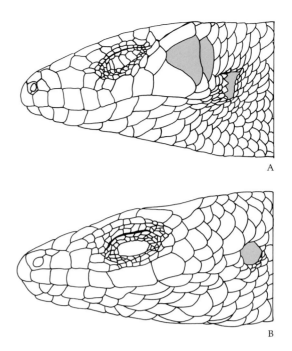

Fig. 134. Lateral view of the heads of skinks. A, *Eumeces* showing enlarged scales between eye and ear (*shaded*). B, *Mabuya* showing absence of enlarged scales between eye and ear.

Family Scincidae (Skinks)

This is a very large family of mostly diurnal lizards with more or less cylindrical, elongate bodies and relatively small, though often powerful, limbs. The body is usually covered with highly polished, imbricate cycloid scales. Femoral pores are absent. Most species are terrestrial, a few are arboreal, and at least one is semiaquatic. Several lineages within the family show a tendency toward limb reduction and a fossorial lifestyle. Some species have a translucent disk in the lower eyelid that permits vision while the eye is closed. Most skinks are oviparous, and the females of some species remain with their eggs until hatching occurs. Some species are viviparous.

This family is worldwide in distribution at latitudes below about 50°. More than 700 species are presently assigned to some 75 genera. Three genera and 4 species occur in the Yucatán Peninsula.

Key to the Genera of the Family Scincidae

1. Internasal scales present (Fig. 133A) 2
   Internasal scales absent (Fig. 133B) . . . . *Sphenomorphus*

2. Scales between eye and ear conspicuously enlarged relative to lateral scales (Fig. 134A); lower eyelid without undivided translucent disk . . . . *Eumeces*
Scales between eye and ear not conspicuously enlarged relative to lateral scales (Fig. 134B); lower eyelid with undivided translucent disk . . . . *Mabuya*

Clave para los Géneros de la Familia Scincidae

1. Con escamas internasales (Fig. 133A) 2
Sin escamas internasales (Fig. 133B) . . . . *Sphenomorphus*
2. Escamas entre el ojo y el oído conspicuamente alargadas con respecto a las escamas laterales (Fig. 134A); párpado inferior sin un disco translúcido sin dividir . . . . *Eumeces*
Escamas entre el ojo y el oído no alargadas conspicuamente con respecto a las escamas laterales (Fig. 134B); párpado inferior con un disco translúcido sin dividir . . . . *Mabuya*

Genus *Eumeces*

This large genus is confined to the Northern Hemisphere. Representatives are found in the New World, but the genus attains its greatest diversity in the Old World. Generally elongate and with relatively small limbs, these are typically terrestrial, diurnal insectivores. A few species are viviparous, but most are oviparous, and in some species the female attends the eggs. *Eumeces* is from the Greek *eu-*, "good," "well," "true," or "nice," and *mekos*, "length, height," presumably in reference to the attenuate form. The most recent comprehensive treatment of the genus is still Taylor, 1935. Approximately 60 species are presently recognized; 2 occur in the Yucatán Peninsula.

Key to the Species of the Genus *Eumeces*

Vertebral row of scales conspicuously larger than paravertebral rows (Fig. 135A) . . . .
. . . . *Eumeces schwartzei*
Vertebral row of scales not or only slightly larger than paravertebral rows (Fig. 135B) . . . .
. . . . *Eumeces sumichrasti*

Clave para las Especies del Género *Eumeces*

Hilera de escamas vertebrales conspicualmente más largas que las hileras paravertebrales (Fig. 135A) . . . . *Eumeces schwartzei*
Hilera de escamas vertebrales iguales o sólo un poco más largas que las hileras paravertebrales (Fig. 135B) . . . . *Eumeces sumichrasti*

Eumeces schwartzei Fischer
(Figs. 135A, 333; Map 95)

Eumeces schwartzei Fischer, 1884:3. SYNTYPES: originally three syntypes, two since destroyed; remaining type: ZMH 810 (*fide* Stuart, 1963:74). TYPE LOCALITY: einer kleinen Insel in der Laguna de Términos (Campeche bai) (a small island in Laguna de Términos, Campeche, Mexico).

Yucatán giant skink, Schwartze's skink; bek'ech (Yucatec Maya).

DESCRIPTION This distinctive lizard is the largest skink in the Yucatán Peninsula. The adults average about 110 to 115 mm in snout-vent length, and the undamaged tail is about 1.6 times the head and body length. The body is moderately elongate but relatively stout for a skink (Fig. 333). The limbs

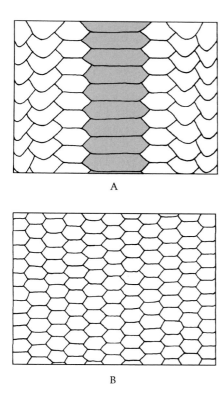

Fig. 135. Dorsal scale pattern in *Eumeces*. A, *E. schwartzei* showing enlarged vertebral and paravertebral scales. B, *E. sumichrasti* without enlarged vertebral and paravertebral scales.

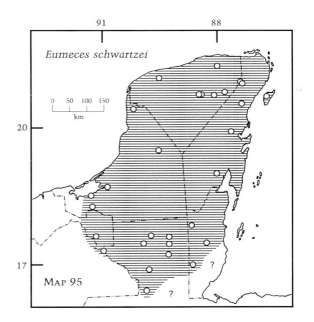

Eumeces schwartzei

Map 95

are well developed, pentadactyl, and do not overlap when adpressed. The head is only slightly distinct from the neck. The highly polished, imbricate scales appear to glisten. The scales of the vertebral and paravertebral rows are conspicuously larger than those of the lateral rows (Fig. 135A).

The color pattern is striking. Beginning at the rostrum there is a broad, dark brown stripe on the dorsal surface of the head that continues posteriorly onto the body. Bordering this are two light tan or cream stripes that begin at the rostrum, broaden posteriorly as they pass over the eyes, and extend onto the body, largely replacing the darker median stripe on the posterior third of the body. On the side of the head, a dark brown stripe begins at the nostril on each side and continues posteriorly through the eye and onto the body, where it breaks up into a series of dark and light spots. The posterior third of the body and the upper and lateral surfaces of the undamaged tail are covered with numerous quadrangular dark spots against a tan or yellowish back-

ground. The chin, throat, venter, and underside of the tail are cream or light tan.

SIMILAR SPECIES   *Ameiva* and *Cnemidophorus* have granular dorsal scales, rather than cycloid scales, and possess femoral pores. No other skink in the Yucatán Peninsula has the enlarged vertebral row of dorsal scales seen in *E. schwartzei* (Fig. 135A).

DISTRIBUTION   This species is endemic to the Yucatán Peninsula. It is probably pan-peninsular, although there are apparently no records from western Yucatán and western Campeche or from southern Belize (Map 95).

NATURAL HISTORY   Taylor (1935:101) presumed these lizards to be arboreal, but in fact they are terrestrial. They inhabit both dry deciduous and more mesic forests and are active on the forest floor by day, presumably foraging for invertebrates. Specimens have been found beneath surface debris, basking on the trunk of a fallen banana tree, and amid the stones of Maya ruins (Gaige, 1936:298). Alert and fast moving, they are difficult to capture, although they are caught and eaten by saurophagous snakes. Near Tizimín, Yucatán, I watched a subadult indigo snake (*Drymarchon corais*) consume a *Eumeces schwartzei*, and Blaney and Blaney (1978:92) found these skinks in the stomachs of coral snakes (*Micrurus diastema*) from Quintana Roo.

This species is presumably oviparous, but nothing specific is known about its reproduction.

ETYMOLOGY The specific name, *schwartzei*, is a patronym honoring E. W. E. Schwartze, of the Zoologische Gesellschaft of Hamburg.

Locality Records Belize: Cayo: ca. 3 mi S Belmopan (CM 112183), Caracol (CMM photo); Orange Walk: Gallon Jug (W. T. Neill, 1965:98). *Guatemala*: El Petén: 4 km N Chinajá (KU 59551), Piedras Negras (USNM 113603–6), El Paso (MCZ 38645), Chuntuquí (USNM 71380), Remate (USNM 71409), Sojio (AMNH 70012–13), Tikal (MCZ 55424; UF 13727; UMMZ 117862), Uaxactún (KU 157473–74; MCZ 24504); no specific locality (USNM 71948). *Mexico*: Campeche: Dzibalchén (KU 75586–87), Encarnación (FMNH 115681), Tankuche–El Remate (IHNHERP 433, 452, 458), Tres Brazos (H. M. Smith, 1938:17); Quintana Roo: 10 mi W Bacalar (LSUMZ 33345–46), 24.1 km SE Cobá (KU 171634), Cozumel (Himmelstein, 1980:29), 32 km NE Felipe Carrillo Puerto (MZCIQRO 23), Pueblo Nuevo X-Can (KU 70552; UCM 29144), 1.5 km S, 1 km E Pueblo Nuevo X-Can (KU 70553); Tabasco: Tenosique (H. M. Smith and Taylor, 1950a:162); Yucatán: Chichén Itzá (CM 36446; FMNH 27287; MCZ 29238; UMMZ 68226, 80816, 83278–79), Dzibilchaltún (FMNH 154584–90), Pisté (KU 70554–59; UCM 12780, 16846–47), Tekom (FMNH 49315), 12 mi N Tizimín (UCM 29143), 24.1 km E Valladolid (KU 171633).

Eumeces sumichrasti (Cope)
(Figs. 135B, 334; Map 96)

Plistodon sumichrasti Cope, 1866:321. HOLOTYPE: USNM 6601. TYPE LOCALITY: Orizava (in error); corrected by H. M. Smith and Taylor (1950a:164) to Potrero, Veracruz, Mexico ("en los encinales de Potrero, cerca de Córdoba a una altura de 590 metros").

Sumichrast's skink; eumeces listado (Mexico).

DESCRIPTION This species, the smaller of the two Yucatecan *Eumeces*, is nonetheless a moderately large skink, attaining a snout-vent length of at least 96 mm. The body is rather attenuate, and the relatively long limbs overlap when adpressed (Fig. 334). The head is narrow and scarcely distinct from the neck. The snout is pointed in dorsal aspect. The tail is about 1.8 times as long as the head and body. The dorsal surface of the head is covered with a series of enlarged, regularly arranged plates. The body and appendages are covered with the smooth, highly polished, imbricate scales characteristic of skinks. Femoral pores are absent, and there is no gular fold.

Eumeces sumichrasti changes markedly in color and pattern with age. The juveniles are dark brown or black with five yellow or cream stripes originating on the head and extending the length of the body and onto the base of the tail. The vertebral stripe bifurcates on the head at the level of the eyes and courses anteriorly to reunite on the snout. The tail is brilliant blue (Fig. 334). Older individuals lose the striped juvenile pattern and become olive gray or tan, although they may retain some blue on the tail. The chin and throat are cream or yellowish, and the abdomen is generally yellowish or bluish gray. According to Duellman (1963:236), the underside of the tail is orange.

SIMILAR SPECIES The striped pattern of juveniles vaguely resembles that of subadult *Cnemidophorus angusticeps*, but that species lacks a brilliant blue tail and has granular rather than smooth, highly polished dorsal scales. *Eumeces sumichrasti* lacks the enlarged paravertebral scales of *E. schwartzei* (Fig. 135), and its longer legs overlap when adpressed.

DISTRIBUTION Sumichrast's skink is found at low elevations on the Atlantic slope from central Veracruz south and eastward through northern Guatemala and Belize to Honduras. The species occurs through the base of the Yucatán Peninsula, and apparently isolated populations exist in the northeast corner (Map 96).

NATURAL HISTORY This species generally inhabits moist lowland forests, where individuals are occasionally seen running through the leaf litter or sunning on rotting logs or tree stumps. Others have been found beneath surface debris. *Eumeces sumichrasti* is primarily terrestrial, although individuals are occasionally found low on tree trunks or beneath the bark on standing trees. Stuart (1948:55) found them to be common in Alta Verapaz and frequently saw individuals in the grass along trails in second-growth forest. They are diurnal, rather secretive, alert, elusive, and difficult to capture. They feed primarily on insects but occasionally consume small lizards (Alvarez del Toro, 1983:110).

Taylor (1935:185) concluded that *E. sumichrasti*

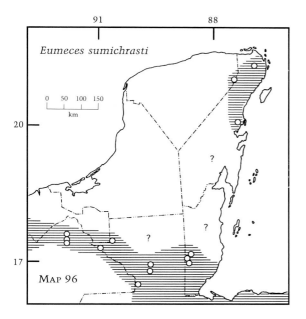

Map 96

is oviparous because a female he examined contained "ripe eggs" in the oviducts and he found no evidence of developing embryos.

ETYMOLOGY The specific name, *sumichrasti*, is a patronym that honors Francis Sumichrast, a Swiss naturalist who lived in Mexico between 1855 and 1882 and collected the type specimen.

Locality Records Belize: Cayo: Caracol (CMM photo), Cohune Ridge (UMMZ 80702), near Retiro (UMMZ 80701). *Guatemala*: El Petén: 20 km NNW Chinajá (Duellman, 1963:236), El Seibal (JCL sight record), El Repasto (UCM 22276), Piedras Negras (MCZ 46954; USNM 113609–12), Toocog (KU 55860). *Mexico*: Chiapas: Palenque ruins (UIMNH 11342), 10 mi S Palenque ruins (USNM 113613–15), 13 mi S Palenque (LSUMZ 33348); Quintana Roo: Reserva Biósfera Sian Ka'an (COHECERN uncat.), Reserva El Edén (COHECERN uncat.); Yucatán: X-Can (UCM 18618).

Genus *Mabuya*

This large genus of small to medium-sized skinks attains its greatest diversity in the Old World, and its representatives range throughout much of Africa, Madagascar, and southern Asia. In the New World, members of the genus occur in much of Mexico, Central and South America, Trinidad and Tobago, and the Lesser Antilles. Approximately 85 species are presently recognized, but only one oc-

curs in the Yucatán Peninsula. *Mabuya* is derived from the West Indian Spanish *mabuya*, "lizard."

Mabuya unimarginata (Cope)
(Figs. 134B, 335; Map 97)

Mabuia unimarginata Cope, 1862a:187. TYPE: presumably lost, *fide* Taylor, 1956:303. TYPE LOCALITY: Panama.

Esquinco, lagartija lisa, salamanquesa (Mexico); snake waiting boy (Belize); p'ik ron puch (Lacandón Maya); bek'ech (Yucatec Maya).

DESCRIPTION The males of this medium-sized, moderately slender skink average between 60 and 65 mm in snout-vent length; the females are significantly larger, averaging between 70 and 75 mm. The narrow head is scarcely distinct from the attenuate body (Fig. 335), and the snout is pointed in dorsal aspect. The limbs are relatively short and stout. The tail is long, slender, and rounded in cross section and about 1.7 to 1.9 times the length of the head and body. The head is covered with a series of regularly arranged smooth plates, and the body and appendages are covered with smooth, highly polished, imbricate scales characteristic of skinks. A translucent disk is present in the lower eyelid.

On each side of the predominantly brown dorsum a light gray or white lateral stripe originates at the tip of the snout, passes along the supralabial scales and through the ear, and then continues posteriorly on the lateral surface of the body to the groin. A second, less distinct, light dorsolateral stripe extends from above the eye posteriorly onto the body, where it becomes progressively more indistinct and ultimately disappears on the posterior third of the body. The lateral surface of the neck and body between the stripes is dark brown, in contrast with the lighter brown of the middorsal area. Occasional specimens have several obscure light stripes on the dorsum between the dorsolateral stripes. The dorsal stripes are obscure in older animals, which tend to be darker. The venter is generally gray, cream, or tan, and devoid of markings.

SIMILAR SPECIES The small brown skink *Sphenomorphus cherriei* most closely resembles *Mabuya*, but it is much smaller and lacks internasal scales (Fig. 133B) and distinct light dorsolateral stripes. *Gymnophthalmus speciosus* has only four digits on the hand and lacks movable eyelids. In the

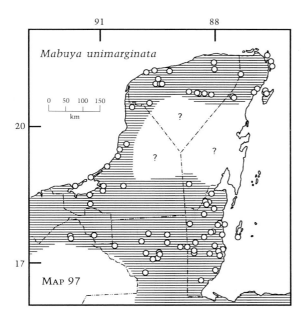

Map 97

two species of Yucatecan *Eumeces* the scales between the eye and ear are enlarged relative to the lateral scales, and there is no translucent disk in the lower eyelid. Lizards of the genera *Ameiva* and *Cnemidophorus* are similar in shape, but their dorsal scales are small and granular.

DISTRIBUTION *Mabuya unimarginata* is found at low and moderate elevations from central Mexico to lower Central America. It probably occurs throughout the Yucatán Peninsula, although it has not yet been taken in the central portion (Map 97).

NATURAL HISTORY This common arboreal and terrestrial skink occupies a variety of habitats within the Yucatán Peninsula, including savannas, thorn forests, and tall mesic forests. In forested areas it is partial to openings and edges. Specimens have been found in rock walls, in the stonework of Maya ruins, under loose bark on standing trees, and beneath logs, stones, and other surface debris, including that associated with human disturbance. Often individuals are seen basking with only the anterior portion of the body extending beyond a crevice or some other shelter. *Mabuya unimarginata* feeds on invertebrates, especially insects and spiders.

This is a viviparous species. Webb (1958:1312) examined a composite series from several Mexican states, including Campeche and Yucatán, and found that the females were reproductive at 62 mm snout-vent length, the males at 56 mm. The brood size ranged from four to six, with parturition occurring

in June and July. McCoy (1966:307) reported 6 to 9 uterine embryos (mean 7.2) in five females from Sayaxché, El Petén. The brood size ranges from four to seven in Chiapas (Alvarez del Toro, 1983:108).

ETYMOLOGY The specific name, *unimarginata*, is from the Latin *unus*, "one," *margo*, "edge or border," and the adjectival suffix *-ata*. Thus, the name is a feminine adjective meaning "enclosed with a border," presumably in reference to the narrow black band described by Cope (1862a:187) as having a bright yellow inferior border.

COMMENT The systematics of this species and its close relatives is not well understood. Several names have been applied to this wide-ranging and variable form, including *mabouya*, *alliacea*, *brachypoda*, and *unimarginata*. Webb (1958:1311) proposed applying the name *brachypoda* to all the members of the genus *Mabuya* occurring from Mexico to Costa Rica. Some herpetologists have accepted this arrangement (e.g., Flores-Villela, 1993:43; J. C. Lee, 1980a:61), but others (e.g., Savage, 1973; Savage and Villa, 1986:25; Villa et al., 1988:54) use the name *unimarginata*.

Locality Records Belize: Belize: Belize (FMNH 4190–95, 4457–58; KU 144947; USNM 25447, 58161–62), 29.5 mi W Belize City (CM 112177), 32 mi W Belize City (CM 112112), 1 mi W Burrell Boom Rd. on rd. to Double Head Cabbage (CM 105799), Cay Bokel (MPM 7549–50), bet. Ladyville and Sandhill (CM 90965), vicinity Parrot's Wood Biological Station (UF 79996); Cayo: Augustine (JCL photo), Belmopan (KU 157477; UTA R-11063), Blancaneaux Lodge (UF uncat.), 4 mi S Georgeville (CM 105699), Xunantunich (MCZ 71413–14); Corozal: Libertad Factory (MPM 8184); Orange Walk: Gallon Jug (MCZ 71409–10, 71412), Lamanai (ROM H12755–56), Otro Benque (USNM 194103–4), Tower Hill (MPM 7693), Yo River (MPM 7616); Stann Creek: 1.5 mi W Mango Creek (LSUMZ 10282), Middlesex (UCM 45194), near Silk Grass (JLK 510–11), 2 mi S Stann Creek (KU 157483), Dangriga (CM 105834–35), 1 mi W Dangriga (CM 105842), 7 mi W, 1 mi S Stann Creek (JLK 412, 414), 7 mi W Stann Creek (JLK 14.75 mi W Stann Creek (JLK 413), Stann Creek Valley (FMNH 49316–18); Toledo: ca. 2 mi SE Big Falls, Río Grande (CM 105896); no specific locality (USNM 26074, 31337). *Guatemala*: El Petén: 3 mi N Chuntuquí (USNM 71382), El Paso (MCZ 38646–47; UMMZ 79070), El Repasto (UCM 22278), Laguna de Zotz (UMMZ 75033, 79069), near La Libertad (UMMZ 75035), Pacomon (USNM 71392), Sacluc (USNM 25116), 2 km S Santa Elena (UMMZ 124363), Sayaxché

(UCM 22279–90), Slaughter Island, Lake Petén (USNM 71395), Tikal (UMMZ 117863–66, 149372), Uaxactún (AMNH 68527–32, 70933–35; UMMZ 70412–14), 16 mi E Yaxhá (UMMZ 75034); no specific locality (USNM 71951). *Mexico:* Campeche: Balchacaj (FMNH 103571, 104603, 117119, 117122–23, 117125–26; UIMNH 22586–87, 22590, 22593; UMMZ 81925), 29.7 mi S Campeche (UCM 18614), 6.9 mi N Champotón (EAL 1663), 4 km S Champotón (KU 70560), Ciudad del Carmen (UCM 16849–50, 20762–63), Encarnación (FMNH 103573, 104589, 117120; UIMNH 22591–92), Isla Aguada (KU 75588), 41.3 km NE Isla Aquada (EAL 2933), Matamoros (FMNH 36440–42), Panlao (H. M. Smith, 1938:16), Tankuche–El Remate (IHNHERP 436, 503), Tres Brazos (FMNH 103568, 104591, 104597, 104600, 117121, 117124, 117127; UIMNH 22588–89); Chiapas: Palenque (EAL 3632; USNM 113646–52), San Juanito (USNM 113653–55); Quintana Roo: 93 km W Chetumal (LSUMZ 28269), Cobá (FMNH 27305), SE edge Cobá (KU 171635), Isla Contoy (UCM 16852–53), Isla Cozumel, 2.5 km N San Miguel (KU 70562), Cozumel, 3.5 km N San Miguel (KU 70563–64), Cozumel, 9 km SE San Miguel (UCM 12800), Cozumel, 5 mi S San Miguel (UCM 16854–56), Isla Mujeres (FMNH 34639–42; UCM 16859–62; UMMZ 78594), S end Isla Mujeres (KU 70561), Playa del Carmen (UCM 16851), 5 mi S Playa del Carmen (LSUMZ 33344), Pueblo Nuevo X-can (UCM 29142); Tabasco: Tenosique (USNM 113640–44); Yucatán: Arrecife Alacrán, Isla Pérez (USNM 145307), Calcehtok (UMMZ 99882, 113548), Chichén Itzá (AMNH 38863–65; FMNH 27306–10, 36439, 49320–21; LACM 99756; LSUMZ 28281; MCZ 18958–59, 22069, 28746; UCM 12801; UMMZ 72873–77, 72879, 80817–19, 83280–81, 83925), 6.7 km E Churburna Puerto (CM 65371; EAL 2943), Dzibilchaltún (FMNH 154572–73), Grutas Balankanché (TCWC 57122), 1.5 mi S Libre Unión (UCM 18615), Mérida (CM 47214; FMNH 40683, 104602), 7.1 km E Mérida (EAL 2841), 13.6 mi E Mérida (KU 157475–76), Pisté (KU 70565–67; UCM 12802, 16863–65, 18616–17), Progreso (FMNH 103574), Tekom (FMNH 49319), 4 mi N Telchac (UCM 29140), 6 km N Tizimín (KU 74951), 12 mi N Tizimín (UCM 29141).

Genus *Sphenomorphus*

This is a large, wide-ranging, and morphologically heterogeneous assemblage of skinks whose taxonomy is poorly understood. All the species have pentadactyl limbs, although these may be somewhat reduced in size. The scales are smooth, imbricate, and cycloid in most forms. These are predominantly Old World lizards, ranging through Southeast Asia and the Indo-Malay Archipelago to northern and eastern Australia. Possibly three species occur in southern Mexico and Central America, one of which occurs in the Yucatán Peninsula. *Sphenomorphus* is derived from the Greek *sphen*, "wedge," and *morphe*, "form, shape," presumably in reference to the wedge-shaped heads of many species.

Sphenomorphus cherriei (Cope)
(Figs. 133B, 336; Map 98)

Mocoa cherriei Cope, 1893:340. HOLOTYPE: AMNH 9551 (incorrectly cited as AMNH 9531 in H. M. Smith and Taylor, 1950a:157). TYPE LOCALITY: Palmar, Costa Rica.

Ground skink; galliwasp (Belize); escincela parda (Mexico); tzotzok (Lacandón Maya).

DESCRIPTION   This is the smallest skink in the Yucatán Peninsula. The adults average between 50 and 55 mm in snout-vent length, and there is little if any sexual size dimorphism (Greene, 1969:55). The head is short, rather broad, and only slightly differentiated from the neck (Fig. 336). The snout is short and rounded in dorsal aspect. The body is elongate and round in cross section. The limbs are relatively short, and they overlap when adpressed in small individuals but not in larger animals. The relatively short tail is about 1.3 times as long as the head and body. The dorsal surface of the head is covered with large, symmetrical plates; internasal scales are absent (Fig. 133B). The body and appendages are covered with smooth, highly polished, imbricate scales, which give the skin a moist, glistening appearance. A translucent disk is present in the lower eyelid.

These lizards are rather nondescript brown above and light tan or cream below. The dorsal surface of the head and the middorsal region of the body are light brown. An irregular dark brown stripe originates on the snout and passes posteriorly through the eye, over the ear opening, and onto the anterior portion of the body, where it breaks up into an indistinct series of dark spots. The labial scales, the lateral surfaces of the head, and the anterior portion of the body are light cream or yellowish tan with scattered dark brown spots and blotches. The appendages are brown above, light tan or cream below.

SIMILAR SPECIES   The other brown skink in the Yucatán Peninsula, *Mabuya unimarginata*, has in-

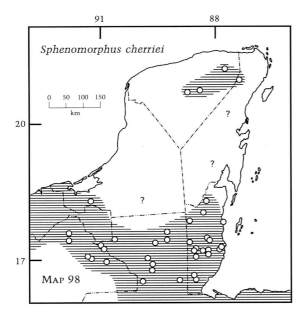

Sphenomorphus cherriei

0 50 100 150
km

Map 98

ternasal scales, is much larger, and usually has distinct light dorsal or dorsolateral stripes. *Gymnophthalmus* has four digits on the hand and lacks movable eyelids.

DISTRIBUTION *Sphenomorphus cherriei* occurs at low and moderate elevations from Tabasco on the Atlantic slope and Nicaragua on the Pacific slope, south to Panama. It occurs throughout the base of the Yucatán Peninsula from Chiapas through El Petén to Belize. Northern, apparently disjunct, populations are found in Yucatán and northern Quintana Roo (Map 98).

NATURAL HISTORY These diminutive skinks live in the leaf litter of lowland forests. They are terrestrial and diurnal and are often seen or heard running across the leafy substrate. They are quick, wary, and elusive, and thus are more often seen than captured. These tiny carnivores eat a variety of invertebrates.

Sphenomorphus cherriei is oviparous. Greene (1969:55) examined a composite sample from several localities in Central America and concluded that reproduction occurs at least from March through September. W. T. Neill and Allen (1959c:45) found a hatchling on 17 July in Belize. In the Atlantic lowlands of Costa Rica this species also breeds from October through February, indicating year-round breeding (Fitch, 1970:89). The clutch size ranges from 1 to 3 eggs, with a mean of about 2.3.

Fitch (1985:27) found geographic variation in clutch size, with animals from northern Guatemala averaging 2.8 eggs per clutch versus 2.2 for lizards from Costa Rica.

SUBSPECIES Stuart (1940:8) recognized two subspecies within the Yucatán Peninsula. The populations at the outer end of the peninsula in Yucatán and northern Quintana Roo are referred to *S. c. ixbaac*, and those in the base of the peninsula are referred to the nominate subspecies, *S. c. cherriei*.

ETYMOLOGY The specific name, *cherriei*, is a patronym that honors George K. Cherrie, a naturalist and officer of the Museo Nacional of San José, Costa Rica, in the latter part of the nineteenth century.

COMMENT *Sphenomorphus cherriei* has often been placed variously in the genera *Lygosoma*, *Leiolopisma*, and *Scincella*. A. E. Greer (1974:34) concluded that this species and its close relatives represent a New World offshoot of the *variegatus* species group of *Sphenomorphus*.

Stuart (1940) named *S. incertum* (type locality: Vocán Tajumulco, Guatemala), a high-elevation relative of *S. cherriei* that differs in having limbs that do not overlap when adpressed and fewer scale rows around midbody. Some specimens from the lowlands of the Yucatán Peninsula also have nonoverlapping adpressed limbs (e.g., USNM 194902, from Honey Camp, Orange Walk, Belize) and low midbody scale row counts, however, suggesting either that *S. incertum* co-occurs with *S. cherriei* in the Yucatán Peninsula, which is unlikely, or that a single wide-ranging, variable species is involved. Pending thorough and comprehensive analysis of variation in this complex, I tentatively accept the latter interpretation.

Locality Records Belize: Belize: Belize City (FMNH 4258); Cayo: Blancaneaux Lodge (CM 111935), near Blancaneaux Lodge (CM 91014–16), Caves Branch (CM 105800), Chiquibul Branch, S Granos de Oro Camp (CM 112129), Doyle's Delight (UMRC 89-49), Mountain Pine Ridge (MPM 7552), River On (MPM 7551, 7799–80), upper Raspaculo River basin (Stafford, 1991:14), Xunantunich (W. T. Neill and Allen, 1959c:45); Orange Walk: Gallon Jug (MPM 7652–53), Honey Camp (USNM 194902), Lamanai (ROM H12765–66, H12768); Stann Creek: Bokowina (FMNH 49323), Cockscomb Basin Wildlife Sanctuary (JCL photo), Double Falls (FMNH 49324–25), 10 mi W, 5 mi

N Middlesex (W. T. Neill and Allen, 1959c:45), N slope Cockscomb Mts. (CM 8487–88), Silk Grass (FMNH 49322), 7 mi W, 1 mi S Stann Creek (JLK 416–17, 512), 4 mi from Twelve-Mile Station (FMNH 4456); Toledo: Blue Creek Village (UTA R-11064–65). *Guatemala*: Alta Verapaz: Chinajá (Duellman, 1963:236); El Petén: 30 km NNW Chinajá (KU 59540), El Repasto (UCM 22277), La Libertad (Stuart, 1935:47), Las Cañas (CM 58271), Piedras Negras (MCZ 46956; UIMNH 10941; USNM 115155–63, 115168–70), 5 mi S Piedras Negras (USNM 115164–67, 115171–72), 1 mi W Ruinas Seibal (KU 157478–80), San Miguel (USNM 71379), Tikal (AMNH uncat.; UMMZ 117867), Toocog (KU 55859), Uaxactún (UMMZ 70413–14). *Mexico*: Campeche: Tres Brazos (H. M. Smith, 1938:17); Chiapas: vicinity Bonampak (MZFC 494), bet. El Censo and Laguna Ocotal (MCZ 53892), Laguna Ocotal (MCZ 53877–78), Palenque (UCM 49684–85; UIMNH 62352), 10 to 15 mi S Palenque (LSUMZ 33766–68), Palenque ruins (UIMNH 11339–41); Quintana Roo: 1.5 km S, 1 km E Pueblo Nuevo X-Can (KU 70568); Yucatán: Chichén Itzá (UMMZ 80820), Culubá, 28 km E Sucopó (FMNH 36438), 1.5 mi S Libre Unión (UCM 16848).

Family Gymnophthalmidae

Many of these small, attenuate lizards are semi-fossorial and show a tendency toward limb reduction. The family is restricted to the New World tropics and attains its greatest diversity in South America, but it also ranges northward through Central America to southern Mexico, and representatives are found in the Lesser Antilles. Twenty-nine genera and at least 130 species are presently recognized. Three genera have parthenogenetic representatives (Vrijenhoek et al., 1989:20). Only one species occurs in the Yucatán Peninsula.

The species in this family were once considered members of the family Teiidae, although their distinctiveness was recognized and they were known informally as "microteiids" (Ruibal, 1952:477). Presch (1983) used cladistic analysis of osteological, myological, dental, and hemipenial characters to determine that the microteiids represent an independent lineage. He therefore treated the microteiids as a separate family, the Gymnophthalmidae, and further suggested that teiids and gymnophthalmids may not even be sister taxa. Harris (1985) questioned the monophyly of the microteiids and provided morphological evidence supporting the monophyly of macroteiids and microteids (= Teiidae).

Genus *Gymnophthalmus*

These are small, slender lizards with cylindrical bodies and long, fragile tails. The limbs are short, and there are only four digits on each hand. The body is covered with large cycloid scales arranged in about 13 to 17 rows around midbody. Femoral pores are present. The ear openings are small, and the eyes are covered by transparent spectacles. This genus ranges from northern Central America to Argentina. There are six species, but only one occurs in the Yucatán Peninsula. One species, *G. underwoodi*, reproduces by means of parthenogenesis (L. M. Hardy et al., 1989). *Gymnophthalmus* is derived from the Greek *gymnos*, "naked" or "lightly clad," and *ophthalmos*, "the eye," in reference to the absence of movable eyelids.

Gymnophthalmus speciosus (Hallowell)
(Fig. 337; Map 99)

Blepharictisis speciosa Hallowell, 1861:484. HOLOTYPE: lost, *fide* J. A. Peters, 1967:23. TYPE LOCALITY: Nicaragua.

Lagartija dorada, salamanquesa (Mexico).

DESCRIPTION These small, slender lizards are superficially skinklike in general appearance (Fig. 337). The adults are about 40 mm in snout-vent length, and the undamaged tail is very long, nearly twice the length of the head and body. The only known specimen from the Yucatán Peninsula measures 43.5 mm in snout-vent length (McCoy, 1990:165). The scales on both the dorsum and the venter are large, highly polished, and imbricate, and the lateral scales are slightly smaller. The head is covered with a series of enlarged, smooth, symmetrically arranged plates. The limbs are rather small and weak, and they terminate in tiny claws. The eyes are small and covered by a transparent spectacle, and the pupils are round.

The dorsum, including the dorsal surface of the head, is generally tan, brown, or gray, often contrasting sharply with the darker sides. The venter ranges from light to dark gray; often each ventral scale is suffused with dark pigment. The tail, especially in younger individuals, is reddish orange and contrasts with the darker body. The chin is cream, yellow, or tan, often with dark spots.

SIMILAR SPECIES   No other lizard in the Yucatán Peninsula has only four digits on the hand. *Gymnophthalmus* superficially resembles *Sphenomorphus cherriei* but differs in having a transparent spectacle covering the eye.

DISTRIBUTION   *Gymnophthalmus speciosus* occurs at low to intermediate elevations from the Isthmus of Tehuantepec on the Pacific slope and from central Guatemala southward to northern South America and the Lesser Antilles. In the Yucatán Peninsula the species is known from a single specimen collected 3.2 km east of Carmelita in Orange Walk District (Map 99).

NATURAL HISTORY   Nothing is known about the ecology of *G. speciosus* in the Yucatán Peninsula, but elsewhere it is a secretive, diurnal, terrestrial inhabitant of forests and forest edges that seeks refuge beneath stones, logs, or in leaf litter. These diminutive lizards forage actively for small invertebrates, predominantly insects.

Gymnophthalmus speciosus is oviparous. In Chiapas oviposition occurs in March, and the adult females deposit clutches of 2 or 3 eggs in leaf litter (Alvarez del Toro, 1983:119). In Panama reproduction extends from late October through March (Telford, 1971). The clutch size there ranges from 1 to 4 (mean = 1.9), and females may produce up to three clutches per season. The hatchlings are 17 to 19 mm in snout-vent length and appear from February through May.

SUBSPECIES   Three subspecies are presently recognized, of which *G. s. birdi* occurs in the Yucatán Peninsula (McCoy, 1990:165).

ETYMOLOGY   The specific name, *speciosus*, is Latin meaning "showy" or "brilliant."

COMMENT   Biochemical, morphological, and karyological evidence led Cole et al. (1990) to conclude that *G. speciosus* is one of the ancestral species that gave rise, through hybridogenesis, to the

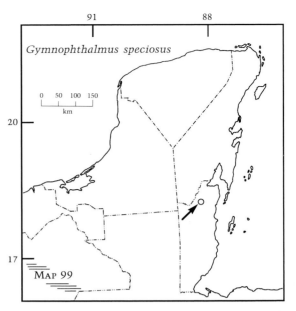

MAP 99

parthenogenetic populations of *G. underwoodi* in northern South America and the West Indies.

Locality Record Belize: Orange Walk: 2 mi E Carmelita (CM 105775).

Family Teiidae

This large family is restricted to the New World, where it attains its greatest diversity in the lowland tropics. The family ranges northward to temperate latitudes in Canada, however, and southward to about latitude 40 in South America. This morphologically diverse family includes both small insectivores and large cursorial predators of small mammals and birds. Teiids are usually somewhat attenuate with long tails and relatively small, but often powerful, limbs. They are primarily terrestrial, diurnal carnivores, and they rely on vision and chemosensory modalities to find their prey. Accordingly, most are active, fast-moving foragers. The family contains about nine genera and perhaps 70 species, of which two genera and 7 species occur in the Yucatán Peninsula.

Key to the Genera of the Family Teiidae

Scales of midgular region conspicuously enlarged (Figs. 138C, 139C); a single row of enlarged scales on dorsal surface of upper arm (Fig. 136A). . . . . *Ameiva*

Scales of midgular region not conspicuously enlarged (Figs. 141C, 142C); three or more rows of enlarged scales on dorsal surface of upper arm (Fig. 136B) . . . . *Cnemidophorus*

Clave para los Géneros de la Familia Teiidae

Escamas de la región mediogular conspicuamente alargadas (Figs. 138C, 139C); una sola hilera de escamas alargadas en la superficie dorsal del brazo (Fig. 136A) . . . . *Ameiva*

Escamas de la región mediogular no alragadas conspicuamente (Figs. 141C, 142C); tres o más hileras de escamas alargadas en la superficie dorsal del brazo (Fig. 136B) . . . . *Cnemidophorus*

Genus *Ameiva*

These large, diurnal macroteiids are terrestrial inhabitants of Neotropical lowlands. Most occupy open situations, but a few live in forests. Ameivas are moderately attenuate lizards with narrow heads, pointed snouts, and a conspicuous gular fold. The limbs are well developed and powerful, and the tail is long and slender. Femoral pores are present in both sexes but better developed in males. The genus ranges throughout Middle America and tropical South America and the West Indies. The most recent comprehensive taxonomic treatment of the genus is Barbour and Noble, 1915. Echternacht (1971) reviewed the Middle American species. About 15 species of *Ameiva* are presently recognized, of which 3 occur in the Yucatán Peninsula. *Ameiva* is an aboriginal name for a kind of lizard (Jaeger, 1944:13).

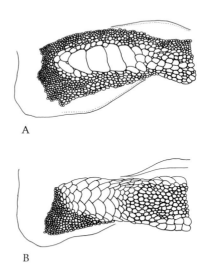

Fig. 136. Dorsal view of the upper arm of teiid lizards. A, *Ameiva* showing a single row of enlarged scales. B, *Cnemidophorus* showing more than a single row of enlarged scales.

Key to the Species of the Genus *Ameiva*

1. Scales of midgular region enlarged gradually (Fig. 139C); lateralmost row of ventral scales not conspicuously smaller than scales of midventral rows; no light vertebral stripe 2
   Scales of midgular region conspicuously and abruptly enlarged (Fig. 138C); lateralmost row of ventrals conspicuously smaller than scales of midventral rows; light vertebral stripe usually present . . . . *Ameiva festiva*
2. Adult SVL less than 90 mm; a pair of light dorsolateral stripes runs from the head to the base of the tail; northern Guatemala only (Map 100) . . . . *Ameiva chaitzami*
   Adult SVL greater than 90 mm; no light dorsolateral stripes on dorsum; pan-peninsular
   . . . . *Ameiva undulata*

Clave para las Especies del Género *Ameiva*

1. Escamas de la región mediogular alargadas gradualmente (Fig. 139C); las hileras más laterales de ventrales no son conspicuamente más pequeñas que las escamas en las hileras medioventrales; sin una línea vertebral clara 2
   Escamas de la región mediogular conspicua y abruptamente alargadas (Fig. 138C); las hileras más laterales de ventrales conspicuamente más pequeñas que las escamas de las hileras medioventrales; usualmente presentan una línea vertebral clara . . . . *Ameiva festiva*
2. Adultos menores a los 90 mm de LHC; un par de líneas claras dorsolaterales desde la cabeza hasta la base de la cola; habitan sólo en el norte de Guatemala (Mapa 100) . . . .
   . . . . *Ameiva chaitzami*

Ameiva chaitzami Stuart
(Fig. 137; Map 100)

Ameiva chaitzami Stuart, 1942:143. HOLOTYPE: UMMZ 90638 (listed as 90368 in type description). TYPE LOCALITY: along Cahabon-Languin trail about 2 km north of Finca Canihor, Alta Verapaz, Guatemala.

Chaitzam's ameiva.

DESCRIPTION This is the smallest *Ameiva* in the Yucatán Peninsula. The males attain a maximum snout-vent length of about 85 mm, the females reach 75 mm. This species is very similar to *A. undulata*, to which it is presumably closely related and which it resembles in being moderately elongate and having a pointed head that is somewhat distinct from the neck, and a long, slender tail. The dorsal scales are granular, and the ventrals are rectangular and arranged in longitudinal rows. The

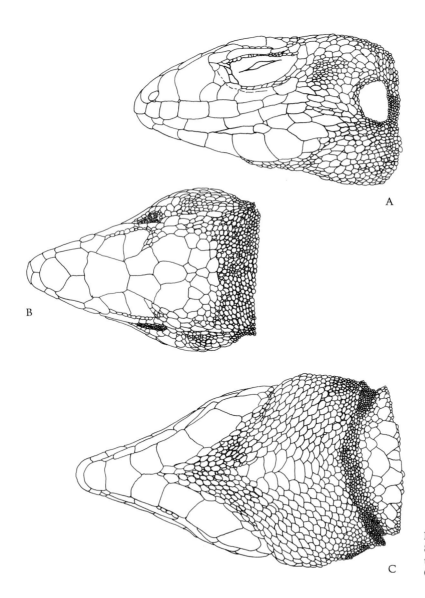

A

B

C

Fig. 137. *Ameiva chaitzami* (UMRC 89-52). A, lateral; B, dorsal; and C, ventral views of the head; near Comitán, Chiapas, Mexico.

dorsal surface of the head is covered with enlarged symmetrical plates (Fig. 137B). The tail is covered with whorls of rectangular scales that are keeled all along the tail except for those on the undersurface of the base of the tail, which are smooth. The limbs are well developed and pentadactyl. Femoral pores are present in both sexes but better developed in males.

The distinctive color pattern distinguishes this species from all other *Ameiva* in the Yucatán Peninsula. The middorsum is gray or grayish brown bordered laterally by narrow dorsolateral white or light gray stripes originating on the head and extending to the base of the tail or beyond. Between the light stripes on the dorsum there are often secondary stripes of velvety black, which also extend from the head onto the tail. A ventrolateral white stripe, often interrupted, is present on each side from the ear to the groin. The ventral surfaces are white, cream, or gray, without distinct markings.

SIMILAR SPECIES *Ameiva chaitzami* differs from the *Cnemidophorus* in the Yucatán Peninsula in possessing a single row of enlarged scales on the anterodorsal surface of the upper arm (*Cnemidophorus* species have more than one row). It is distinguished from the very similar *A. undulata* by its smaller size and distinct dorsolateral stripes. *Ameiva festiva* has abruptly (rather than gradually) enlarged midgular scales (cf. Figs. 137C, 138C) and a light vertebral stripe.

DISTRIBUTION This species is known only from eastern Chiapas and western and north-central Guatemala. In the Yucatán Peninsula it has been collected only on the pine savannas around Poptún, El Petén (Map 100).

NATURAL HISTORY This is an uncommon lizard. Echternacht remarked in 1971 that less was known about the biology of this species than any other Middle American *Ameiva* (Echternacht, 1971:63), and that observation still holds true today. In the Yucatán Peninsula these terrestrial, diurnal lizards are restricted to the pine savannas of central El Petén, where they occur in low population densities, possibly due to the periodic fires that characterize that vegetation type (Stuart, 1942; Stuart, in Echternacht, 1971). Stuart (1948:56) characterized *A. chaitzami* as an inhabitant of second growth in Alta Verapaz and commented on its ecological similarity to *A. u. hartwegi*.

Ameiva chaitzami is oviparous, but little else is known of its biology. Stuart (1942:144) noted that a specimen of *A. chaitzami* with a snout-vent length of 66 mm had "well formed eggs."

ETYMOLOGY The specific name, *chaitzami*, refers to Chaitzam, the mountain lord of Maya mythology who dominates the lower Cahabon Valley of Alta Verapaz.

COMMENT Echternacht (1971) reviewed *A. chaitzami* as part of his treatment of Middle American *Ameiva*.

Locality Records Guatemala: El Petén: 1 km N Poptún (UMMZ 124355), 2 km SW Poptún (UMMZ 124356), 2 km NE Poptún (UMMZ 124357), 4 mi N Poptún (KU 157501).

Ameiva festiva (Lichtenstein and von Mertens) (Figs. 138, 338; Map 101)

Cnemidophorus festivus Lichtenstein and von Mertens, 1856:13. LECTOTYPE: ZMB 881a (designated in Echternacht, 1971:26). TYPE LOCALITY: Veragoa (= Veraguas), Panama.

Lagartija parda (Mexico).

DESCRIPTION This medium-sized lizard attains a maximum snout-vent length of about 120 mm. The body is moderately elongate, the head is narrow, and the snout is pointed (Fig. 138A,B). The

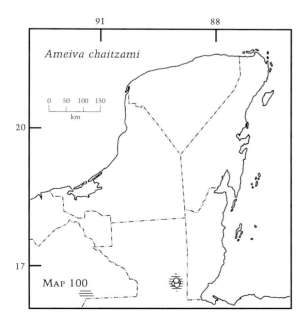

MAP 100

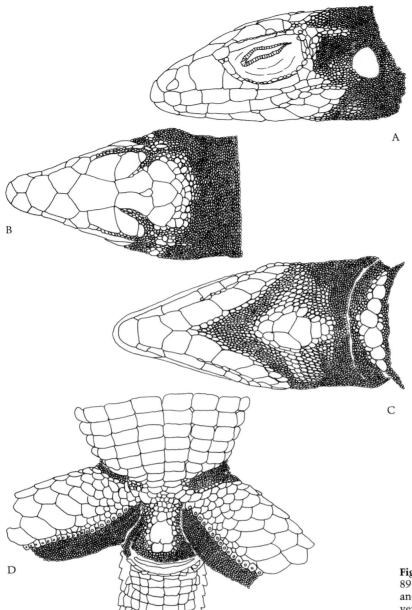

Fig. 138. *Ameiva festiva* (UMRC 89-39), 57 mm SVL. A, lateral; B, dorsal; and C, ventral views of the head. D, ventral view of thighs and vent region; El Rosario, El Petén, Guatemala.

pentadactyl limbs are well developed, and the undamaged tail is about twice the length of the head and body. The dorsal surface of the head is covered with large symmetrical plates (Fig. 138B). The scales on the dorsal surface of the body are granular, while those on the venter are enlarged, rectangular, and arranged in about eight longitudinal rows. The tail is covered with whorls of rectangular scales. These are keeled, except for those on the undersurface at the base of the tail. The scales of the midgular region are conspicuously and abruptly enlarged

(Fig. 138C). Femoral pores are present in both sexes but better developed in males (Fig. 138D).

This very attractive and colorful *Ameiva* is easily distinguished from all other teiids in the Yucatán Peninsula by the conspicuous light blue, white, or yellowish vertebral stripe that runs from the tip of the snout to the base of the tail (Fig. 338), although the stripe may be obscure in older individuals. The dorsal ground color is dark gray, brown, to nearly black, usually with two indistinct light paravertebral lines, the latter often discontinuous and broken up into spots. In hatchlings and juveniles the tail is bright blue. The venter is more or less uniform bluish gray.

SIMILAR SPECIES *Ameiva festiva* differs from all species of *Cnemidophorus* in the Yucatán Peninsula by possessing a single row of enlarged scales on the anterodorsal surface of the upper arm (*Cnemidophorus* species have more than one row). It differs from the other Yucatecan species of *Ameiva* in possessing a light vertebral stripe. Moreover, *A. chaitzami* is smaller and has a pair of light dorsolateral stripes on the dorsum, and *A. undulata* lacks abruptly enlarged midgular scales (cf. Figs. 138C, 139C).

DISTRIBUTION These lizards occur at low and moderate elevations on the Atlantic slope from the Isthmus of Tehauntepec through Central America to Colombia. In the Yucatán Peninsula the species occurs from northern Chiapas through El Petén and southern Belize (Map 101).

NATURAL HISTORY This is a terrestrial inhabitant of humid lowland forests, and individuals can frequently be found foraging actively on the forest floor for leaf litter invertebrates or sunning themselves in sunlit spots. Hillman (1969:480) found that grasshoppers and spiders predominated in the diet in Costa Rica, although he found two amphibians among the stomach contents of 21 specimens of *A. festiva*. In the Yucatán Peninsula this species tends to occupy deeper forest and more shaded situations than does *A. undulata*, a pattern also noted by Echternacht (1968:156) in northern Honduras. Stuart (1948:56) considered this an index species for virgin forest in Alta Verapaz. These lizards are alert, wary, and fast, though less so than the other species of *Ameiva* in the Yucatán Peninsula.

Ameiva festiva is oviparous. A juvenile with an umbilical scar was collected at Sayaxché, El Petén, on 14 March (Duellman, 1963:237). Duellman observed other juveniles at Chinajá, Alta Verapaz, in February and March and concluded that the young probably hatch early in the year. In Limon Province, Costa Rica, R. E. Smith (1968:238–239) reported essentially aseasonal reproduction and an average clutch size of 2.2 eggs. After examining samples from throughout the lowlands of Costa Rica, Fitch (1970:94) concluded that breeding occurs from January to at least September and possibly into November and December.

SUBSPECIES Of the four subspecies currently recognized, *A. f. edwardsii* occurs in the Yucatán Peninsula.

ETYMOLOGY The specific name, *festiva*, is from the Latin *festivus*, "gay, variegated with bright colors," presumably in reference to the bright color pattern.

COMMENT Echternacht (1971) reviewed *A. festiva* as part of his treatment of Middle American *Ameiva*.

Locality Records Belize: Belize: Cayo: upper Raspaculo River basin (Stafford, 1991:14), Río Frio Cave (CM 105808), Valentin (UMMZ 92372); Stann Creek: Bokowina (FMNH 49313–14), Middlesex (FMNH 4460), Silk Grass Creek State Forest (FMNH 4459); Toledo: Bladen Branch of Monkey River (CM 105908–9), Blue Creek Village (UTA R-11062), Dolores (JCL sight record), 1 mi E Swazey Branch of Monkey River (MCZ 71606–7). *Guatemala*: Alta Verapaz: Chinajá (Duellman, 1963:237); El Petén: 6 km NNW Chinajá (KU 55836), 11 km NNW Chinajá (KU 55837–38), 15 km NW Chinajá (KU 55851–56, 59567–73, 59883), El Repasto (UCM 22291–92), El Rosario (UMRC 89-39; JCL photo), Las Cañas (CM 58267–70), Pacomon (USNM 71394), Piedras Negras (FMNH 115429–43; UIMNH 11349–62), 2 km S Poptún (UMMZ 124360), 10 km NW Poptún (UMMZ 124361), 15 km S Poptún (UMMZ 124359), Remate (UMMZ 75000; USNM 71406), 20 mi E Remate (Stuart, 1935:11), Santa Cruz (UMMZ 74995), Santa Teresa (UMMZ 74997–98),

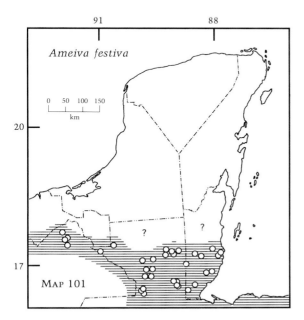

Ameiva festiva

0 50 100 150
km

20

17

MAP 101

1 mi W Ruinas Seibal (KU 157481), San Luis (CM 58267–70), Sayaxché (UCM 22293–316), 14.2 mi S Tikal (KU 157482), Toocog (KU 55840), 6 mi W Yaxhá (UMMZ 74996), S Zotz (UMMZ 74999); no specific locality (USNM 71817, 71823, 71826–27, 71829–31, 71836). *Mexico*: Chiapas: Palenque (USNM 133818–24), 10 to 15 mi S Palenque (LSUMZ 33390–93), Palenque ruins (KU 94107–8; UIMNH 11343), 16 mi NW Palenque (TCWC 21533).

Ameiva undulata (Wiegmann)
(Figs. 139, 339, 340; Map 102)

Cnemidophorus undulatus Wiegmann, 1834:27. SYNTYPES: ZMB 867–69 (three syntypes; 869 is missing, *fide* Taylor, 1969:iv). TYPE LOCALITY: Mexico; restricted to Tehauntepec, Oaxaca, Mexico, by H. M. Smith (1940:56).

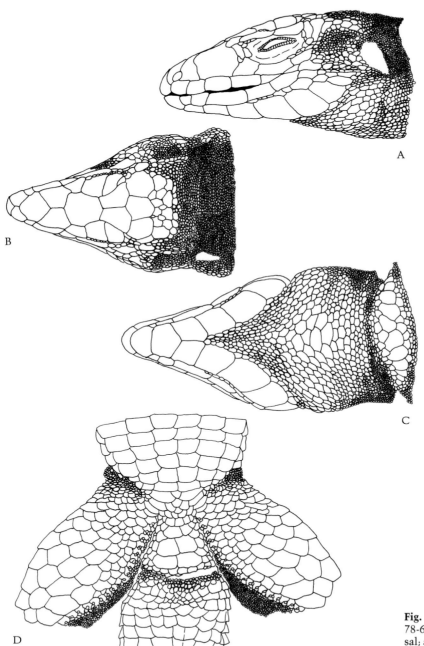

Fig. 139. *Ameiva undulata* (UMRC 78-61), 110 mm SVL. A, lateral; B, dorsal; and C, ventral views of the head. D, ventral view of thighs and vent region; Uaxactún, El Petén, Guatemala.

Lagartija metalica (Mexico); mechech (Lacandón Maya); kankalás (Yucatec Maya).

DESCRIPTION This is a medium-sized, moderately attenuate lizard, somewhat more robust than the preceding species of *Ameiva*. The head is rather narrow, though broader in males than in females. The snout is pointed (Fig. 139A,B), and the limbs are well developed and pentadactyl. The undamaged tail is long, slender, and more than twice the length of the head and body. Femoral pores are present in both sexes but better developed in males (Fig. 139D). The scales on the dorsal surface of the head are enlarged and symmetrical (Fig. 139B), and the midgular scales are only slightly and gradually enlarged (Fig. 139C). The scales on the dorsal surface of the body are granular. The ventral scales are enlarged, rectangular, and arranged in a series of longitudinal rows. The tail is covered with whorls of rectangular scales that are keeled except for those on the undersurface at the base of the tail.

The dorsal surface of the body and tail is predominantly rusty brown with scattered dark spots and flecks. The sides generally have a pattern of light turquoise blue markings; these are frequently arranged in the form of irregular vertical bars and extend onto the lateral surfaces of the tail. The venter is white, gray, or light blue. During the breeding season, males may exhibit a spectacular nuptial coloration in which the chin and labials become bright yellow, yellow-green, or orange (Figs. 339, 340).

SIMILAR SPECIES *Ameiva undulata* is distinguished from all species of *Cnemidophorus* in the Yucatán Peninsula by its single row of enlarged scales on the upper surface of the upper arm (*Cnemidophorus* species have more than one row; Fig. 136B). From *A. festiva* it differs in lacking abruptly enlarged midgular scales (cf. Figs. 138C, 139C) and a light vertebral stripe. It is larger than *A. chaitzami* and lacks that species' light dorsolateral stripes.

DISTRIBUTION *Ameiva undulata* occurs at low and moderate elevations from Tamaulipas on the Gulf slope, and Nayarit on the Pacific slope, south to northwestern Costa Rica. It is found throughout the Yucatán Peninsula (Map 102).

NATURAL HISTORY This active, terrestrial, diurnal teiid is one of the commonest and most conspicuous lizards in the Yucatán Peninsula. *Ameiva undulata* prefers open situations and forest edges and avoids the deep shade of tall humid forests, where it

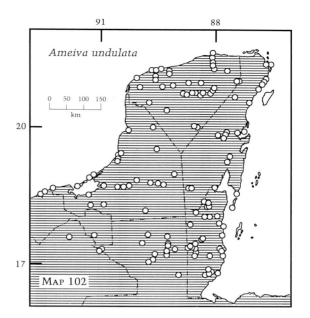

Ameiva undulata

MAP 102

appears to be replaced by *A. festiva*. Individuals often inhabit disturbed areas and are frequently seen darting across roads or encountered as they forage noisily through the leaf litter.

These carnivorous lizards feed predominantly on invertebrates, especially leaf litter insects. They are themselves the prey of several species of lizard-eating snakes, and E. O. Moll and Smith (1967:1) reported finding *A. undulata* in the stomach of a caecilian, *Dermophis mexicanus*, from Chiapas.

Ameiva undulata is oviparous. Gaige (1936:297) reported gravid females from Campeche and Yucatán in samples collected in June. Fitch (1970:95) found a mean clutch size of 5.3 for specimens from the vicinity of Pisté, Yucatán, and concluded that summer and fall constitute the breeding season at that location. Growth is rapid, and some individuals attain reproductive maturity within four months (Fitch 1985:10).

SUBSPECIES Two of the 12 named subspecies occur in the Yucatán Peninsula. *Ameiva undulata gaigeae* occurs throughout the northern portion of the Yucatán Peninsula and south to northern El Petén, where it is replaced by *A. u. hartwegi*, which occupies the base of the peninsula.

ETYMOLOGY The specific name, *undulata*, is Latin meaning "undulated, as if with waves."

COMMENT Echternacht (1971) reviewed *A. undulata* as part of his revision of Middle American *Ameiva*.

Locality Records   Belize: Belize: Altun Ha (KU 171677), Ambergris Cay, 2 mi N San Pedro (MCZ 71611), Ambergris Cay, 5 km NNE San Pedro (CM 91127), Belize City (CAS 39587; FMNH 4188–89, 4461–63, 49298–304), 11.7 mi W Belize City (KU 157485–87), Crooked Tree Village (CM 112198), Hummingbird Hershey Farm (CM 105831–32), bet. Ladyville and Sandhill (CM 90928), Manatee (FMNH 5821–22, 6766–68); Cayo: Augustine (KU 157484; MCZ 71622–24; MPM 8197), ca. 2 mi W Belmopan (CM 105759, 105762), 0.5 mi W Camalot (CM 105776), Central Farm (MCZ 71608–9), Chaa Creek (CM 105990), 4 mi S Georgeville (CM 105710), Macal River at Guacamallo Bridge (CM 112144–45), Over the Hill Camp (CM 90987), Pine Ridge Rd., 36 mi S Western Hwy. (UMMZ 124678), River Succotz (MPM 7547), San Ignacio (UMMZ 75012; USNM 71372–73), Xunantunich (MCZ 71619–21), near Xunantunich (CM 105960); Corozal: 0.5 mi N Corozal (MCZ 71610); Orange Walk: Albion Island (MPM 8270), Blue Creek Village (USNM 194951), Gallon Jug (MCZ 71612–17; MPM 7651, 7777–78), Guinea Grass Rd., 4.1 mi S Northern Hwy. (CM 105755), Kate's Lagoon (FMNH 49305–7), Lamanai (ROM H12757–58), Orange Walk (MCZ 71618), Tower Hill (MPM 7548, 10779); Stann Creek: Cockscomb Basin Wildlife Sanctuary (JCL sight record), Deep Creek, N Melinda Forest Station (CM 112120), Free Town (CM 8496), 14 mi W Mango Creek (LSUMZ 11765–66), Mango Creek (LSUMZ 11767–68; MCZ 71626–27), 7 mi W, 1 mi S Stann Creek (JLK 508); Toledo: Medina Camp (MPM 7642–44), 1 mi W Swazey Branch of Monkey River (MCZ 71629), 4 mi S Waha Leaf Creek (MCZ 71625); no specific locality (USNM 26069, 51897, 51880, 58373–75, 58377–78, 59936). *Guatemala*: El Petén: Arroyo El Chorro (AMNH 99916), Chuntuquí (Stuart, 1934:12), El Paso (MCZ 38644), 16.8 mi SW Flores (KU 157497–99), near La Libertad (UMMZ 75015–24), Nueva Aguada (USNM 71402), Paso Caballos (AMNH 72622), Piedras Negras (MCZ 66965; UIMNH 11363–93; USNM 129274–83), 12.1 mi N Poptún (KU 157496), Remate (USNM 71403–5, 71407, 75001–2), 1 km S Remate (UMMZ 124358), 2.5 km N Remate (KU 171678), Sacluc (USNM 25117), San Andrés (Stuart, 1934:12), Tikal (UF 13703–24; UMMZ 117875–81), 3 mi S Tikal (KU 157500), Uaxactún (AMNH 68507–16; KU 157488–95, UMRC 78-61); no specific locality (USNM 71383, 71818–21, 71828, 71834–35, 71837, 71841). *Mexico*: Campeche: Balchacaj (FMNH 106716–18, 106721; UIMNH 26167–69; UMMZ 81924), 2 mi E Barra San Pedro y Pablo (AMNH 88877), 3 mi SW Bolonchén (CM 40158–59; UCM 28176–207), 5 mi E Campeche (UCM 22373–74), Champotón (UMMZ 72956–57), 5 km S Champotón (KU 70569), 4.5 mi S Champotón (UCM 18568), 5 mi NE Champotón (UCM 22375–80; UIMNH 87513), 11 km S Champotón (KU 70570–74), Ciudad del Carmen (UMMZ 83535), Dzibalchén (KU 75589–98), Encarnación (FMNH 105290–93; UIMNH

27356), 6 km W Escárcega (KU 70575), 7.5 km W Escárcega (KU 70576–79; UMMZ 130237–38), 5 mi W Escárcega (UCM 28243–46), 6 mi W Escárcega (UCM 29886), 25 mi E Escárcega (UCM 28235–42), Isla Aguada (KU 75599–601), 5 mi E Isla Aguada (UCM 39481–82), Laguna Chumpich (KU 74952–55), Laguna Silvituc (FMNH 36444), Matamoros (FMNH 36445), Pacaitún (FMNH 36446), mouth Río San Pedro (CM 38937), 46 mi E Silvituc (CM 40156–57; UCM 28208–34), Tres Brazos (FMNH 106719, 115515–39; UIMNH 26172–75), 11.4 mi W Xpujil (KU 157502–3), 28.9 km W Xpujil (KU 171674), 32 km NE Xpujil (171675); Chiapas: across river from Piedras Negras (USNM 108600–1), Palenque (EAL 2900, 3325; UCM 49686; MZFC 491; USNM 133861–97; MCZ 66966), vicinity Palenque (LSUMZ 33388–89); Quintana Roo: Caobas (KU 74957), 3 km E Caobas (KU 74958), Cobá (Himmelstein, 1980:28; UMMZ 83945; UMRC 84-1), Culebra Cays, Bahía de la Ascención (UMMZ 78587), El Meco (FMNH 34650–51), 4 km NNE Felipe Carrillo Puerto (KU 70584, 70589–91), 7 km NE Felipe Carrillo Puerto (JCL photo), 1.6 mi S Felipe Carrillo Puerto (KU 157504–6), 17 mi W Felipe Carrillo Puerto (UCM 28348), Isla Mujeres (USNM 47651, 47568–70), Isla Mujeres, Rancho Pirata (KU 70585–88), La Vega (USNM 47649), 5 km N Limones (KU 74961), 15.4 km N Limones (KU 171676), Playa del Carmen (UCM 22384–87), 1.5 mi E Presumida (UCM 28345–47), Pueblo Nuevo X-Can (KU 70580–83; UCM 28341–44, 29885), Puerto Juárez (UCM 22381–83), Puerto Morelos (MZCIQRO 43), 6 mi S Puerto Morelos (UCM 39480), 12.5 km S Puerto Morelos (EAL 2861), 27.1 km NW Tulum (UMRC 84-85), 5 mi inland from Vigía (UMMZ 78586), Xcalak (KU 74959–60); Tabasco: Frontera (USNM 25091, 46659, 47453), Tenosique (UIMNH 34642–43; USNM 133898–919); Yucatán: 8.8 km W Bella Flor (TU 19809), Calcehtok (AMNH 38851), Chichén Itzá (AMNH 38848; FMNH 28281–92, 36443, 36448–49, 49311–12; MCZ 52171, 26796–800, 28387–90; UIMNH 26151; UMMZ 68215–24, 72934–47, 72951, 72954–55, 80847–64, 83289–90; USNM 47800, 244647), 2 km E Chichén Itzá (KU 70619, 70643–44), 3 mi SE Chichén Itzá (UCM 18569–757), 4 mi E Chichén Itzá (UCM 28339–40), 6.7 km E Chuburna Puerto (EAL 2946), 1 mi W Dzibilchaltún (KU 157507), 3 mi N Dzitás (UCM 39479), 5 km E Dziuché (CM 45366–68), 3 mi E Esmeralda (LACM 114021–25), 4.8 km E Kantunil (EAL 2842), 1.5 mi S Libre Unión (UCM 22388–90, 28333–38), 6 km S Mérida (KU 75196), 5 mi N Mérida (UCM 22391, 22395), 9 km N Mérida (UCM 12422), 19 mi E Mérida (UCM 22396–98), Oxkutzcab (AMNH 38850), Pisté (KU 70592–617, 70621–42; UCM 12408–21, 17049–59, 18576–91, 22399–471; UF 17551–52; UMMZ 72948–50, 72952), 2 mi N Pisté (UMMZ 72953), 6.5 km W Pisté (KU 70618), Progreso (FMNH 100030, 117409–412; MCZ 7118; UIMNH 27354–55; USNM 47650, 194614), 4 mi E Progreso (UIMNH 87514), Río Lagartos

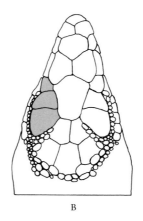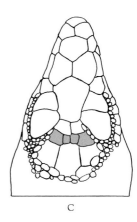

Fig. 140. Dorsal views of the heads of *Cnemidophorus*. A, *C. angusticeps* with four supraocular scales (*shaded*). B, *C. deppii* with three supraocular scales (*shaded*). C, *C. cozumela* with accessory scales (*shaded*) separating the frontoparietal scales from the parietal scales.

A   B   C

(CM 39817), on beach across from Río Lagartos (UCM 39474–77), 6 mi S Río Lagartos (UCM 28332), 3 km WSW Sisal (KU 70620), 28 km E Sucopo (FMNH 36447), Tekom (FMNH 49308–10), 4 mi N Telchac (UCM 28329), 7 mi N Telchac (UCM 28330–31), 3 mi S Telchac Puerto (UCM 39478), 6 km N Tizimín (KU 74962–66), 12 mi N Tizimín (UCM 28247–328), Tunkás (USNM 47799), Valladolid (UCM 22472–73), 2.3 mi N Valladolid (UCM 22474–78), X-Can (UCM 18567).

Genus *Cnemidophorus*
(Whiptails and Racerunners)

This is a moderately large genus of active, fast-moving lizards of open arid and subarid habitats.

All the species are diurnal and terrestrial, and all prey predominantly on invertebrates. At least 12 species exist as parthenogenetic (all-female) forms (Vrijenhoek et al., 1989:20). The genus occurs from the central United States through Mexico and Central America to northern Argentina. About 50 species are currently recognized (Cuellar and Wright, 1992:157). Four (or 5; see *C. cozumela*, Comment) species occur in the Yucatán Peninsula. The most recent summary of information on the genus *Cnemidophorus* is the volume edited by J. W. Wright and Vitt (1993). *Cnemidophorus* is from the Greek *knemidos*, "a legging," and *phoros*, "bearer," and can be translated as "wearing leg armor."

Key to the Species of the Genus *Cnemidophorus*

1. Normally three supraocular scales (Fig. 140B,C) 2
   Normally four supraocular scales (Fig. 140A) . . . . *Cnemidophorus angusticeps*

2. Frontoparietal scales separated from parietals by one or more accessory scales (Fig. 140C) 3
   Frontoparietal scales in contact with parietals (Fig. 140B) . . . . *Cnemidophorus deppii*

3. Dorsal pattern of indistinct paravertebral stripes, broken or obscure on posterior half of body; northeastern Quintana Roo only (Map 106) . . . . *Cnemidophorus rodecki*
   Dorsal pattern of four paravertebral stripes on each side continuous along body length; Campeche, Quintana Roo, El Petén, and Belize (Map 104) . . . . *Cnemidophorus cozumela*

Clave para las Especies del Género *Cnemidophorus*

1. Normalmente tres escamas supraoculares (Fig. 140B,C) 2
   Normalmente cuatro escamas supraoculares (Fig. 140A) . . . . . . *Cnemidophorus angusticeps*

2. Escamas frontoparietales separada de las parietales por una o más escamas accesorias (Fig. 140C) 3
   Escamas frontoparietales en contacto con las escamas parietales (Fig. 140B) . . . . *Cnemidophors deppii*

3. Patrón dorsal de líneas paravertebrales indistintas que son obscuras en la mitad posterior del cuerpo; habitan únicamente en el noreste de Quintana Roo (Mapa 106) . . . .
. . . . *Cnemidophorus rodecki*
Patrón dorsal de cuatro líneas paravertebrales en cada lado; habitan en Campeche, Quintana Roo, El Petén, y Belice (Mapa 104). . . . . *Cnemidophorus cozumela*

Cnemidophorus angusticeps Cope
(Figs. 140A, 141, 341; Map 103)

Cnemidophorus angusticeps Cope, 1878:95. LEC-TOTYPE: USNM 24876 (designated in Maslin and Secor, 1986:4–5). TYPE LOCALITY: Yucatán, Mexico; restricted by H. M. Smith and Taylor (1950b:351) to Chichén Itzá, Yucatán, Mexico.

Yucatán whiptail, narrow-headed whiptail; huico rayado, lagartija llanera (Mexico); ix kankalás (Yucatec Maya).

DESCRIPTION This medium-sized *Cnemidophorus* exhibits pronounced sexual dimorphism with respect to body measurements. Although size apparently varies geographically (Beargie and McCoy,

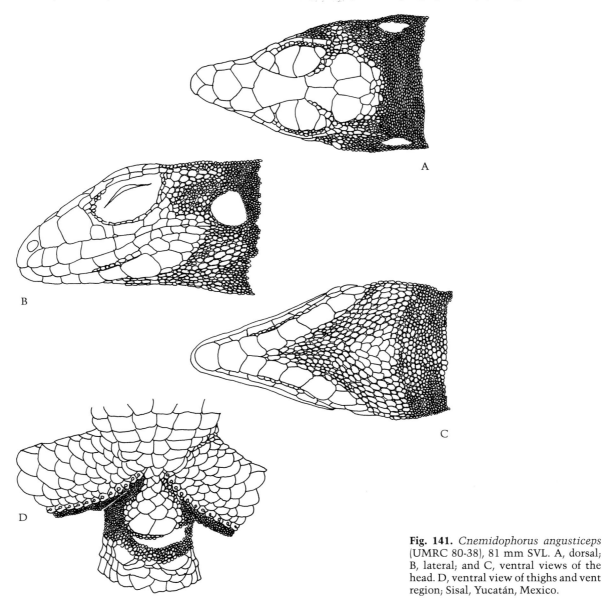

Fig. 141. *Cnemidophorus angusticeps* (UMRC 80-38), 81 mm SVL. A, dorsal; B, lateral; and C, ventral views of the head. D, ventral view of thighs and vent region; Sisal, Yucatán, Mexico.

1964), the males average between 80 and 85 mm in snout-vent length, and the females are generally 10 to 15 mm shorter. The long, thin tail is 2 to 2.5 times the length of the head and body. The body is rather elongate, and the limbs are short, robust, and muscular. The hands and feet are pentadactyl. In dorsal aspect the narrow head is slightly distinct from the neck, and it terminates in a rather pointed snout (Fig. 141A,B). The dorsal surface of the head is covered with enlarged symmetrical plates (Fig. 141A). The dorsal and lateral surfaces of the body are covered with small granular scales; the venter bears eight longitudinal rows of enlarged, slightly imbricate rectangular plates at midbody. The tail is covered with whorls of enlarged keeled scales. Femoral pores, 15 to 24 per thigh, are present in both sexes but better developed in males (Fig. 141D).

The dorsal pattern of adults typically consists of six cream or yellow stripes with intervening fields of reddish brown, dark brown, or nearly black. Some individuals are covered with light spots that obscure the stripes. There is pronounced ontogenetic variation in color pattern. The juveniles have six distinct dorsal stripes against a dark background. The stripes become less distinct with age, and light spots appear in between them. These may eventually coalesce to obscure the stripes on older individuals, producing a pattern of light spots and blotches against a dark background. This change is much more extensive in males than in females, which tend to retain distinct stripes. The tail and hind limbs of juveniles are bright reddish orange. The orange fades as the lizards mature, but adults are often reddish brown on the tail and hind limbs. In adults the lateral surfaces of the body are often barred or checkered with light markings against a dark background. The venter of males, even young ones, is more or less uniform black, bluish black, or mottled with dark pigment. The females are immaculate tan or light gray beneath.

SIMILAR SPECIES *Cnemidophorus angusticeps* differs from all species of *Ameiva* in possessing three or more rows of enlarged scales on the dorsal surface of the upper arm (*Ameiva* has one row; Fig. 136B). It differs from *C. cozumela* and *C. rodecki* in being larger and having six dorsal stripes, red on the hind limbs and tail, and, in adult males, black pigmentation on the venter. *Cnemidophorus deppii* has three rather than four supraocular scales.

DISTRIBUTION This species is endemic to the Yucatán Peninsula. It is more or less continuously

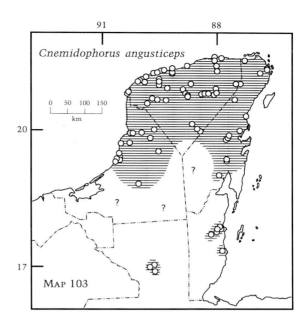

MAP 103

distributed throughout the northern half of the peninsula and occurs in the south as isolated populations on the savannas of El Petén and Belize (Map 103).

NATURAL HISTORY These wary, fast-moving lizards inhabit open situations such as savannas, roadsides, and forest edges. They are terrestrial and diurnal, and in many areas they are abundant. They are often seen actively foraging for their invertebrate prey in clearings or darting across roads. This is the only *Cnemidophorus* present throughout most of the Yucatán Peninsula.

Cnemidophorus angusticeps is oviparous, but little is known of its reproductive biology. Maslin (1963a:19) collected a large series in Yucatán during June and July, but only two specimens were juveniles. Gaige (1936:297) found gravid females in samples taken in June and July in Campeche and Yucatán. Presumably the females oviposit during the summer rainy season and the juveniles appear in late summer or early fall.

SUBSPECIES Beargie and McCoy (1962), the most recent reviewers of this species, recognized a northern subspecies, *C. a. angusticeps*, and a Guatemalan and Belizean form, *C. a. petenensis*.

ETYMOLOGY The specific name, *angusticeps*, derives from the Latin *angustus*, "narrow" or "small," and the adjectival suffix *-ceps*, "head," and presumably refers to Cope's observation of the "very narrow form of the parietal and interparietal plates" (Cope, 1878:95).

Locality Records Belize: Belize: 7.5 mi W, 2 mi N Belize City (W. T. Neill and Allen, 1959b:236), 1.5 mi S, 13 mi W Belize City (AMNH 126389–90, 126392), 18 mi W, 5.5 mi S Belize City (AMNH 126391), 4.5 mi N, 8 mi W Belize City (AMNH 126394), 12 mi W Belize City (UF 24532), 30 mi W Belize City (CM 112103, 112195–96), 2.5 mi S Boom (AMNH 126395), 7.5 mi S, 1 mi E Boom (AMNH 126393), bet. Ladyville and Sandhill (CM 90929), vicinity Parrot's Wood Biological Station (UF 79997–98), 2.5 km S Sandhill (CM 105815–21); Stann Creek: Melinda Forestry Station (Fugler, 1960:11). *Guatemala*: El Petén: 23.5 mi SW Flores (KU 157528), La Libertad (UCM 23926–37), near La Libertad (UMMZ 74980–94), Toocog (KU 58195–97). *Mexico*: Campeche: 3 mi SW Bolonchén (UCM 28367–70), 5 mi E Campeche (UCM 17563), 11 mi E Campeche (UCM 17564–66), 36 mi E Campeche (UCM 17567–70), 29.7 mi S Campeche (UCM 18599), Champotón (UMMZ 72963–64), 5 km S Champotón (KU 70645–49), 6 km SW Champotón (KU 70650–56), 7 mi SW Champotón (UCM 39483), 9 mi W Champotón (UIMNH 83758–64), 10.9 mi SW Champotón (UIMNH 83765), 11 km S Champotón (KU 70657), 8.7 mi S Champotón (KU 157513–14), 5 mi N Champotón (UCM 17572–92), 8.5 mi N Chencoyi (UIMNH 83766–69), Dzibalchén (KU 75602–6), 3 mi W Hopelchén (UCM 17571), 20 mi SW Lerma (UIMNH 87539), 2.9 mi S Seybaplaya (EAL 1662), 0.9 km E Silvituc (KU 171639–40); Quintana Roo: Bacalar (MZCIQRO 26, 30), S edge Chiquilá (JCL sight record), Cobá (FMNH 27311–12; Himmelstein, 1980:28; JCL photo; MCZ 149555–57), Chunyaxché (Himmelstein, 1980:28; KU 171642), Felipe Carrillo Puerto (UCM 18595–98), 4 km NNE Felipe Carrillo Puerto (KU 70673–78), 8.5 km NNE Felipe Carrillo Puerto (KU 70679–82), 13.8 mi N Felipe Carrillo Puerto (KU 157515), 40 mi S Felipe Carrillo Puerto (UIMNH 83775–79), La Glorieta, Sian Ka'an Reserve (MZCQRO 21), 15.4 km N Limones (KU 171641), 18.2 km N Limones (KU 171643), Pueblo Nuevo X-Can (KU 70658–72; LSUMZ 28261–62; UCM 28371–401), Puerto Juárez (Fritts, 1969:533), 1 km SW Puerto Juárez (UIMNH 83786–88), 20 mi W Puerto Juárez (USNM 244648), 5 mi inland from Vigía (UMMZ 78585); Yucatán: 22.1 km N Calkini (EAL 2937), Celestún (KU 157522), 1 km N Celestún (UMRC 84-167), 2 mi N Celestún (KU 157516–20), Chichén Itzá (AMNH 38877–91, 38946, 84518; FMNH 27313–21, 36451, 49294–95; MCZ 7253, 28756, 29237, 46945; TCWC 57128; UCM 12685–87; UIMNH 19779–80; UMMZ 68214; 68700, 72958–62, 72965–70, 72972, 80827–33, 80835–45, 83287–88; UMRC 79-307; USNM 47801), 4 mi E Chichén Itzá (UCM 28566), 1.5 mi E Chicxulub Puerto (CM 38938), 5.4 km E Chicxulub Puerto (EAL 2950), 4 km S Chocholá (EAL 2939), 6.7 km E Chuburna

Puerto (CM 65675–76; EAL 2942), Dzibilchaltún (FMNH 154575–82; KU 157527), Dzilam Bravo (KU 157526), 3 mi E Esmeralda (LACM 114026–28), Grutas Balankanché (TCWC 57120), 5 mi E Halacho (UIMNH 83770), 3 mi E Holca (UIMNH 83780–85), 12 mi S Izamal (UMMZ 80834), 4.8 km E Kantunil (EAL 2843), 2.5 km S Libre Unión (CM 45264), 1.5 mi S Libre Unión (UCM 17627–29, 28558–65), 10 km E Las Coloradas (UMRC 80-37), Mayapán (FMNH 40704), Mérida (CM 44466; FMNH 154574; UF uncat.), 5 mi N Mérida (UCM 17593–98), 9 km N Mérida (UCM 12566–70), 19 mi E Mérida (UCM 17599–626; UF 17553), 8 mi SE Peto (UIMNH 83771–74), Pisté (AMNH 84509–17; CAS 94042–49; KU 70683–710, 70712–37, 71768; UCM 12571–684, 12972, 17043–48, 17641–739, 18600–4; UF 17554; UMMZ 72971), 1.5 mi E Presumida (UCM 28402–8), Progreso (MCZ 7249; UIMNH 19777–78, 19781–82), 3 km S Progreso (UIMNH 83789–807), 4 mi E Progreso (UCM 28549–54; UIMNH 37536–38), 5 mi W Progreso (UIMNH 87527–35), Río Lagartos (UIMNH 83845), near Río Lagartos (UIMNH 83846–48), 1 mi E Río Lagartos (UCM 28555–56), 5 mi S Río Lagartos (UCM 28557), beach across from Río Lagartos (UIMNH 83814–44), Sisal (UMRC 80-38), 1 mi W Sisal (UIMNH 87524–25), 2.4 km W Sisal (KU 171637), 3 km WSW Sisal (KU 70738–57), 5 mi SE Sisal (UIMNH 87526), 13 km WSW Sisal (KU 70758–61), 10.2 km NE Sisal (KU 157523), 9.6 km S Sisal (KU 171638), Tekom (FMNH 49282, 49284–93), 3 mi S Telchac (UCM 28534–48; UIMNH 83808–13), 4 mi N Telchac (CM 40160–65; UCM 28461–508), 7 mi N Telchac (CM 40166–69; UCM 28509–33), Telchac Puerto (UCM 28451–60; UMMZ 76158; UMRC 85-23), 17.8 mi W Telchac Puerto (KU 157521), 3.4 mi N Temozón (KU 157524–25), 6 km N Tizimín (KU 74967–80), 12 mi N Tizimín (UCM 28409–50, 29667–69, 47452–56), Tunkás (Ives, 1891:459), Valladolid (UCM 17630–38), 3.3 mi N Valladolid (UCM 17639–40), X-Can (UCM 18592–94), 16.2 km S Yaxcopoil (CM 45265; KU 171636).

Cnemidophorus cozumela Gadow
(Figs. 142, 342; Map 104)

Cnemidophorus deppei cozumela Gadow, 1906: 316. SYNTYPES: BMNH 1951.1.8.24–27 (four syntypes); BMNH 1951.1.8.25 designated lectotype by Maslin and Secor (1986:11). TYPE LOCALITY: Isla Cozumel, Quintana Roo, Mexico.

Cozumel whiptail, huico (Mexico).

DESCRIPTION *Cnemidophorus cozumela* is a moderately slender, elongate lizard with a narrow head and a pointed snout (Fig. 142A,B). The

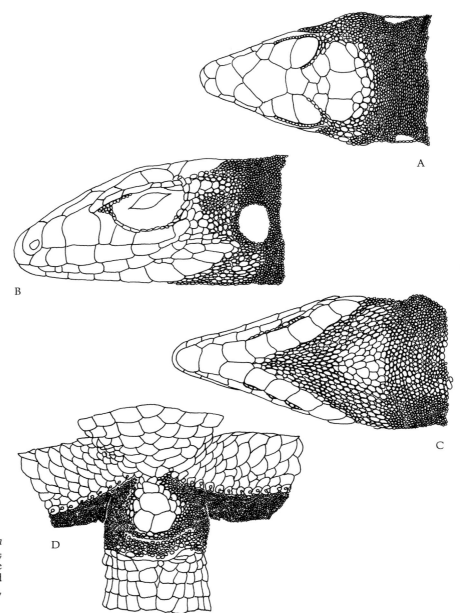

Fig. 142. *Cnemidophorus cozumela* (UMRC 80-36), 64 mm SVL. A, dorsal; B, lateral; and C, ventral views of the head. D, ventral view of the thighs and vent region; Santa Rosalia, Campeche, Mexico.

adults average between 65 and 70 mm in snout-vent length, and the slender tail is approximately twice the length of the head and body. The limbs are rather small but muscular, and the hands and feet are pentadactyl. The dorsal surface of the head is covered with enlarged symmetrical scales (Fig. 142A). The dorsum is covered with small granular scales. The ventral surface of the body bears eight rows of slightly overlapping rectangular scutes. Sixteen to 18 femoral pores are present on each thigh (Fig. 142D).

The dorsal coloration is grayish or tan. About four thin, light dorsolateral stripes originate on the side of the head and terminate in the groin region and on the base of the tail (Fig. 342). The medialmost stripe is usually indistinct, and the middorsal area is uniformly brown. The brown pigmentation between the dorsolateral stripes is darker than that on the middorsal area. The throat and the ventral surfaces of the body are immaculate light gray; the ventral surfaces of the limbs and tail are tan.

SIMILAR SPECIES   The Cozumel whiptail differs from all members of the genus *Ameiva* in possessing three or more rows of enlarged scales on the dorsal surface of the upper arm (*Ameiva* has one row; Fig. 136B). *Cnemidophorus angusticeps* usually has four (rather than three) supraocular scales (Fig. 140A,C) and has reddish hind limbs and tail. In *C. deppii* the frontoparietals and parietals are in contact, whereas in *C. cozumela* they are separated by one or more accessory scales (Fig. 140B,C). *Cnemidophorus rodecki* lacks dorsolateral stripes on the posterior third of the body.

DISTRIBUTION   This species, endemic to the Yucatán Peninsula and islands off its northeast coast, exhibits a highly discontinuous distribution. It has been recorded from coastal localities in southwestern Campeche and southern Quintana Roo, from islands at the northeast corner of the peninsula, and from interior localities in central El Petén and Belize (Map 104).

NATURAL HISTORY   These alert, active, terrestrial lizards inhabit open and disturbed areas such as beaches and savannas, where they can be seen darting about among the shrubs and bushes. They are strictly diurnal, emerging from their burrows by midmorning to forage for their invertebrate prey. In comparison with other *Cnemidophorus* they are unwary and can be approached rather closely, a characteristic they share with a few other parthenogenetic species of *Cnemidophorus* (e.g., A. H. Price, 1992). They are preyed on by hawks, for they have been found in the stomachs of buteos on Isla Cozumel.

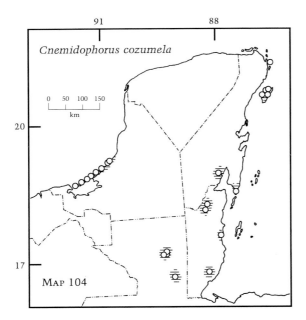

MAP 104

Cnemidophorus cozumela is parthenogenetic— that is, the species consists entirely of females— and, like other *Cnemidophorus*, oviparous. Maslin (1963a:18) found individuals with enlarged, nearly mature eggs in mid-June to mid-July, whereas animals taken at other times of the year had only slightly enlarged eggs. He suggested that there might be several clutches per season. I found gravid females in early October in Campeche, and I found hatchlings to be abundant in late October in the vicinity of El Remate, El Petén. Thus, the limited information available suggests a protracted breeding season, with oviposition throughout the rainy season and the hatchlings appearing in late summer and fall.

SUBSPECIES   Fritts (1969) recognized two subspecies (but see Comment). *Cnemidophorus cozumela maslini* occurs in southwestern Campeche and southern Quintana Roo, in El Petén, and in Belize; *C. c. cozumela* is found on Isla Cozumel.

ETYMOLOGY   The specific name, *cozumela*, is a toponym referring to Isla Cozumel, the type locality.

COMMENT   Like the other parthenogenetic *Cnemidophorus* species, *C. cozumela* arose as a consequence of hybridization between two bisexual species. Fritts (1969) used chromosomal evidence to show that the origin of *C. cozumela* likely involved hybridization between *C. deppii* and *C. angusticeps*, and he suggested that the two subspecies of *C. cozumela* represent independent hybridization events. Moritz et al. (1992) used mitochondrial DNA analysis to show that *C. angusticeps* is the maternal ancestor of both subspecies, but those authors found nothing to support an independent origin for the two subspecies.

H. L. Taylor and Cooley (1995) suggest elevating *C. c. maslini* to full species status on the basis of morphological evidence, a view endorsed by J. W. Wright (pers. comm.), who cited histocompatibility data (as yet unpublished).

Locality Records   Belize: Belize: Manatee (FMNH 5823); Orange Walk: Guinea Grass (MPM 7727), Tower Hill (MPM 7545–46, 7726, 7731); Toledo: ca. 4 mi S Swazey Bridge (CM 105935). *Guatemala*: El Petén: E end Lago Petén Itzá (KU 157554), 12.1 mi NW Poptún (KU 157531–33), 2.5 mi W El Cruce (KU 157534–35), Remate (UMMZ 74979), 2.5 mi N Remate (KU 171645–66), near Remate (UMMZ 124362); no specific locality (USNM 71822, 71824, 71832–33). *Mexico*:

Campeche: 10 mi SW Champotón (UIMNH 82621), 16 mi SW Champotón (UIMNH 82605–20), Ciudad del Carmen (UCM 15302–3, 16087), 25 km NE Ciudad del Carmen (KU 75613), 10 km N Isla Aguada (UMRC 84-168), 20 mi NE Isla Aguada (AMNH 93301), Isla del Carmen, 1 km SW Puerto Real (KU 70791–95, 70973), Sabancuy (JCL photo), near Sabancuy (JCL photo), Santa Rosalia (UMRC 80-36), 4.8 km NE Sabancuy (KU 171667–73), 15.3 km SW Sabancuy (JCL photo); Quintana Roo: Cozumel (BMNH 1951.1.8.24–27; CM 41324; Himmelstein, 1980:29; MCZ 67391; UF 17559–60; USNM 47653–55, 17830–31), N end Cozumel (KU 70796–802), Cozumel, San Miguel (UCM 15400–14, 15462–561), Cozumel, 3 mi N San Miguel (AMNH 89269; FMNH 131306; MCZ 67392–93), Cozumel, 3 km N San Miguel (UCM 12454–75), Cozumel, 3.5 km N San Miguel (KU 70762–90), Cozumel, 4 km N San Miguel (UCM 12476–500), Cozumel, 5 km S San Miguel (LACM 7716–17, UCM 15415–61), Cozumel, 9 km SE San Miguel (AMNH 89270; FMNH 131307; UCM 12501–32), Cozumel, 5 mi SE San Miguel (CAS 94032–41), Cozumel, 10 km SW San Miguel (CM 41317), Cozumel, Xpalbarco (MCZ 149564), Isla Mujeres (FMNH 131303–5; UMMZ 124531–33), Lake Bacalar (LSUMZ 33387), Xcalak (KU 74981–84).

Cnemidophorus deppii Wiegmann
(Fig. 143; Map 105)

Cnemidophorus deppii Wiegmann, 1834:28. HOLOTYPE: ZMB 882. TYPE LOCALITY: Mexico; restricted by H. M. Smith and Taylor (1950a:179) to Tehauntepec, Oaxaca, Mexico.

Black-bellied racerunner; lagartija verdiazul (Mexico).

DESCRIPTION This is a moderately attenuate lizard with short, muscular limbs. The males are generally somewhat larger than the females—70 to 80 mm in snout-vent length versus 65 to 75 mm. The fragile tail is long, slender, and about twice the length of the head and body. The head is rather narrow, and the snout is pointed in dorsal aspect (Fig. 143B). The dorsal surface of the head is covered with a series of smooth, regularly arranged plates (Fig. 143B). Small granular scales cover the dorsal surface of the body, and the venter bears eight rows of enlarged rectangular plates. The scales of the preanal region are enlarged (Fig. 143D), and a gular fold is present. Both sexes have about 18 to 22 femoral pores on the posteroventral surface of each thigh (Fig. 143D), but the pores are larger and more conspicuous in males.

The dorsal ground color is generally dark brown, gray, or black with eight thin yellow or cream paravertebral stripes. The stripes originate on the head and extend to the base of the tail. Six of the stripes continue onto the tail, where they coalesce and become obscure. Many specimens, especially juveniles and females, which have a more distinct dorsal pattern, also have a light vertebral stripe. The dorsal surfaces of the limbs are dark and spotted or irregularly striped with cream or gray. The striped pattern persists in older individuals, but it tends to become obscure with age. In particular, the lateralmost paravertebral stripes may become indistinct, and the light spots and stripes on the dorsal surfaces of the limbs may be replaced by uniformly dark coloration. With respect to ventral coloration, this species is sexually dichromatic. In the females the venter is more or less uniformly bluish gray. In the adult males, especially during the breeding season, the venter is bluish black; the dark pigment extends anteriorly beyond the gular fold and onto the throat. The lateralmost pair of ventral plates is usually lighter and may bear bluish gray spots.

SIMILAR SPECIES *Cnemidophorus deppii* differs from all members of the genus *Ameiva* in possessing several rows of enlarged scales on the dorsal surface of the upper arm (*Ameiva* has one row; Fig. 136A,B). *Cnemidophorus angusticeps* has four (rather than three) enlarged supraocular scales (Fig. 140A), and *C. cozumela* and *C. rodecki* have accessory scales between the frontoparietal and parietal scales (Fig. 140C).

DISTRIBUTION *Cnemidophorus deppii* occurs at low and moderate elevations on the Atlantic slope from northern Veracruz to extreme southwestern Campeche and through the interior valleys of Chiapas and central Guatemala to Honduras and El Salvador. On the Pacific slope this species ranges from Guerrero to Costa Rica. It barely enters the Yucatán Peninsula in southwestern Campeche, where it is known from Isla del Carmen (Map 105).

NATURAL HISTORY Black-bellied racerunners are diurnal, terrestrial inhabitants of open situations. As the name "racerunner" implies, they are alert and fast moving—and thus difficult to approach. In the Yucatán Peninsula they inhabit beaches and coconut plantations on Isla del Carmen. Like the other members of their genus, these lizards progress by a series of nervous, jerky move-

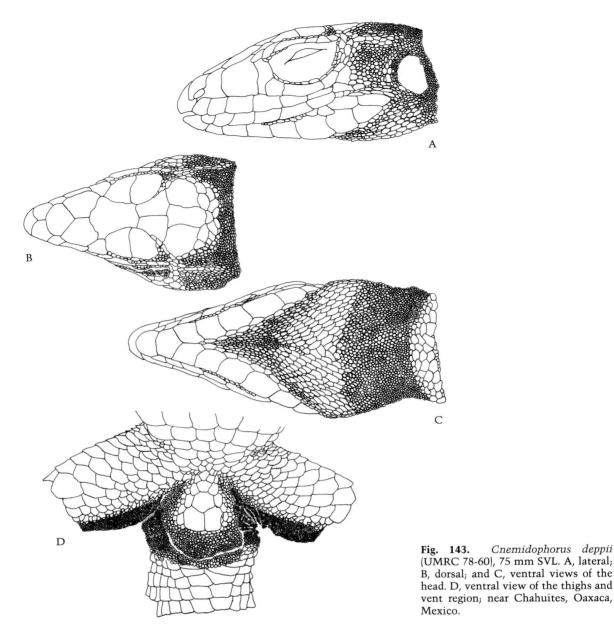

Fig. 143. *Cnemidophorus deppii* (UMRC 78-60), 75 mm SVL. A, lateral; B, dorsal; and C, ventral views of the head. D, ventral view of the thighs and vent region; near Chahuites, Oaxaca, Mexico.

ments. They actively forage for their prey, which Milstead (1969b) found to consist primarily of spiders, caterpillars, and adult butterflies in coastal Veracruz in July and August.

Cnemidophorus deppii is oviparous. W. B. Davis and Smith (1953:106) examined specimens from Morelos, Mexico, and suggested that clutch size ranges from 2 to 4. Fitch (1970:96) examined specimens from Nicaragua and Costa Rica and found gravid females in samples taken in June and July and a recently hatched specimen in mid-August. Kennedy (1968:94) observed copulation in this species in southern Veracruz on 12 June and found two ovarian eggs in a 66-mm female on 18 July.

SUBSPECIES   Maslin and Secor (1986:12–13) recognized three subspecies, of which *C. d. deppii* occurs in the Yucatán Peninsula. According to Harry L. Taylor (in litt.), the Isla del Carmen populations are sufficiently distinct morphologically to justify their recognition as a separate subspecies.

ETYMOLOGY   The specific name, *deppii*, is a patronym in honor of Ferdinand Deppe, a German who

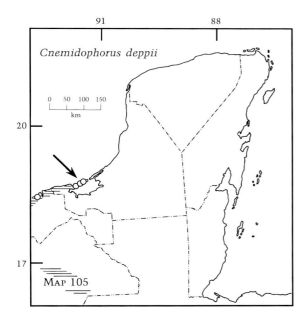

Map 105

Cnemidophorus deppii

collected Mexican amphibians and reptiles for Berlin and Vienna museums from 1824 to 1830.

COMMENT The most recent comprehensive review of the biosystematics of this species is Duellman and Wellman, 1960.

Locality Records Mexico: Campeche: Carmen Island (AMNH 102484; JCL photo), Ciudad del Carmen (FMNH 115281–98; UCM 16088–91, 16095–126, 18605–13; UIMNH 35976–86), Ciudad del Carmen, Laguna Azul (UCM 16092–94) 12.3 mi ENE Ciudad del Carmen (KU 157536–40), Isla del Carmen, 5 mi W Puerto Real (UCM 39485–87), 9 mi E Ciudad del Carmen (UCM 39488–509); Tabasco: 7 mi SW Frontera (UIMNH 87581).

Cnemidophorus rodecki McCoy and Maslin
(Fig. 343; Map 106)

Cnemidophorus cozumelus rodecki McCoy and Maslin, 1962:620. HOLOTYPE: UCM 15364. TYPE LOCALITY: Isla Mujeres, Quintana Roo, Mexico.

Rodeck's whiptail lizard; huico (Mexico).

DESCRIPTION The adults of this moderately small *Cnemidophorus* average about 65 mm in snout-vent length. The slender tail is about twice the length of the head and body. Like the other *Cnemidophorus* species, these are rather slender, attenuate lizards with relatively small but muscular limbs (Fig. 343). The head is narrow, the snout pointed. The head is covered with enlarged symmetrical plates. The dorsal surface of the body bears small granular scales, while the ventral scales are large, rectangular, slightly overlapping, and arranged in eight longitudinal rows at midbody. The tail is covered with whorls of enlarged keeled scales. There are 15 to 18 femoral pores on the posteroventral surface of each thigh.

Dorsally these lizards are olive tan, and the lateral surfaces of the head and throat and the ventral surfaces of the body are pale bluish gray. The undersurfaces of the tail and limbs are white. There are two pairs of thin, indistinct, broken white stripes on the sides of the body. These commence at the posterior margin of the tympanum, become progressively indistinct posteriorly, and disappear altogether on the posterior half of the body. In juveniles the lateral stripes are continuous from neck to groin, but they are interrupted even in young animals.

SIMILAR SPECIES *Cnemidophorus rodecki* differs from *Ameiva* in possessing three or more rows of enlarged scales on the dorsal surface of the upper arm (*Ameiva* has one row; Fig. 136A,B). It closely resembles *C. cozumela* but differs from it and all other *Cnemidophorus* in the Yucatán Peninsula in having a relatively unmarked dorsum with fewer and less distinct lateral stripes.

DISTRIBUTION This species, endemic to the Yucatán Peninsula, is known only from Islas Contoy and Mujeres and from the vicinity of Puerto Juárez on the adjacent mainland of Quintana Roo (Map 106).

NATURAL HISTORY *Cnemidophorus rodecki* is an active, fast-moving inhabitant of sandy beaches. McCoy and Maslin (1962) found it to be common in open, sandy habitats on Isla Mujeres and at Puerto Juárez, but uncommon on Isla Contoy, where dense vegetation renders the habitat unsuitable. This diurnal lizard preys on invertebrates.

Like *C. cozumela*, *C. rodecki* is a parthenogenetic species. It is surely oviparous, but virtually nothing is known of reproduction in this form.

ETYMOLOGY The specific name, *rodecki*, is a patronym honoring H. G. Rodeck, a member of the field party that collected the type material.

COMMENT McCoy and Maslin (1962) described this form as a subspecies of *C. cozumela*, but Fritts

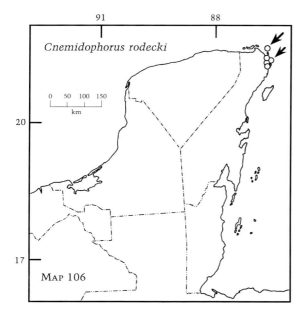

MAP 106

(1969) elevated *rodecki* to the rank of full species on the basis of consistent differences between the two forms in color pattern and scalation. Moritz et al. (1992) used mitochondrial DNA analysis to determine that this species arose as a result of hybridization between *C. angusticeps* and *C. deppii*, with the former being the maternal ancestor. Those authors also suggested that *C. rodecki* and *C. cozumela* arose from separate hybridization events.

Locality Records Mexico: Quintana Roo: Isla Contoy (UCM 15304), Isla Mujeres (AMNH 89266–68; CAS 94030–31; CM 40003; MCZ 67394–95; UCM 15305–49; UIMNH 52476–78, 82633–34, 82934–43; USNM 47652), Puerto Juárez (KU 70803–4; UCM 15371–95), 1 km S Puerto Juárez (UIMNH 82622–32), 5 km N Puerto Juárez (JCL photo), Punta Nizuc (KU 171644).

Family Xantusiidae (Night Lizards)

This is a small, morphologically homogeneous family of strictly New World lizards. Xantusiids have elongate bodies, relatively small limbs, and fragile tails. Femoral pores are present, although they are rudimentary in the females of some species. These lizards are superficially gekkolike because they lack

movable eyelids and have small granular scales on the dorsum, and sometimes tubercular scales as well. The venter is covered with large, juxtaposed rectangular scales. The pupils are vertically elliptical in some species, round in others. Night lizards are not necessarily nocturnal (e.g., J. C. Lee, 1974), but they are highly secretive, often hiding in rock crevices or decaying plants. Most species are terrestrial or saxicolous, but some are semiarboreal. So far as is known, all xantusiids are viviparous. One species is parthenogenetic, and another consists of bisexual and unisexual populations. Night lizards are predominantly carnivorous. They feed primarily on invertebrates, especially insects, but some species consume plant material as well.

The family is distributed throughout the southwestern United States and Mexico south through Central America to the Panamanian isthmus. One species occurs on Cuba. Savage (1963) defined the genera of xantusiid lizards, and Crother et al. (1986) provided a cladistic hypothesis of relationships among the genera, based primarily on morphology. Hedges et al. (1991) inferred the phylogentic relationships and biogeography of representatives of the three living genera based on mitochondrial DNA sequences. Of the approximately 20 living species currently recognized, 2 species, from a single genus, occur in the Yucatán Peninsula.

Genus *Lepidophyma*

This, the most widely distributed genus of xantusiid lizards, is also the largest. There are about 15 species, 2 of which occur in the Yucatán Peninsula. Bezy treated the systematics of the *Lepidophyma* of northeastern Mexico (1984) and Central America (1989). In general, these lizards occupy forest habitats at low and intermediate elevations from Tamaulipas and Michoacán south through Central America to Panama. The members of this genus lack movable eyelids. The eye is covered by a transparent spectacle, and the pupil is round. *Lepidophyma* is from the Greek *lepis*, "scale," and *phyma*, "swelling" or "tumor," presumably in reference to the numerous enlarged tubercles on the dorsum and tail in most species.

Key to the Species of the Genus *Lepidophyma*

Lateral tubercles arranged in 24 to 32 rows; postocular scales separated from second postorbital supralabial scale by two or more pretympanic scales (Fig. 144A) . . . . *Lepidophyma flavimaculatum*

Lateral tubercles arranged in 33 to 46 rows; postocular scales separated from second postorbital supralabial scale by no more than one pretympanic scale (Fig. 144B) . . . . . . *Lepidophyma mayae*

Clave para las Especies del Género *Lepidophyma*

Tubérculos laterales dispuestos en 24 a 32 hileras; escamas postoculares separadas desde la segunda escama postorbital por dos o más escamas pretimpánicas (Fig. 144A) . . . .
. . . . *Lepidophyma flavimaculatum*
Tubérculos laterales dispuestos en 33 a 46 hileras; escamas postoculares separadas desde la segunda escama postorbital y supralabial por no más de una escama pretimpánica (Fig. 144B)
. . . . *Lepidophyma mayae*

Lepidophyma flavimaculatum A. Duméril
(Figs. 144A, 344; Map 107)

Lepidophyma flavimaculatus A. H. A. Duméril, 1851:138, in A. M. C. Duméril and Duméril, 1851. HOLOTYPE: MNHNP 782. TYPE LOCALITY: Petén, Guatemala; restricted by H. M. Smith and Taylor (1950b:318) to Río de la Pasión.

Yellow-spotted night lizard; reina de culebra (Guatemala).

DESCRIPTION This is a medium-sized, rather elongate lizard. The adults average about 85 to 95 mm in snout-vent length, and the undamaged tail is approximately 1.3 times the length of the head and body. The eye is covered by a transparent spectacle, and the pupil is round (Fig. 144A). Dorsally, the head is covered by a series of enlarged symmetrical plates. The dorsal surface of the body and the chin are covered with small pointed scales. Irregular rows of enlarged pointed tubercles are scattered over the dorsum and on the sides. The venter is covered with 10 longitudinal rows of juxtaposed, smooth, rectangular plates. The males have 12 to 16 femoral pores on each thigh; the femoral pores of females are rudimentary. The dorsal and lateral surfaces of the tail bear whorls of enlarged tubercles separated by interwhorls of about four rows of smaller scales.

These lizards are typically dark gray or dark brown above with distinct yellowish or tan spots. The head is generally dark, but the upper and lower labials are boldly marked with dark bars against a lighter background (Fig. 344). The chin is tan or gray, often with a dark reticulum. The ventral scales are light tan or gray with dark pigment at their edges.

SIMILAR SPECIES *Lepidophyma flavimaculatum* differs from *L. mayae* in having fewer lateral

tubercle rows (24–32 vs. 33–46), a more distinctly spotted dorsum, and two or more pretympanic scales between the postocular scales and the second postorbital supralabial scale (Fig. 144A). *Coleonyx elegans* has movable eyelids and granular scales on the head. Lizards of the genera *Cnemidophorus* and *Ameiva* have movable eyelids and lack dorsal tubercles. *Gymnophthalmus speciosus* has only four digits on each hand.

DISTRIBUTION *Lepidophyma flavimaculatum* is found at low and moderate elevations on the At-

Fig. 144. Lateral views of the heads of *Lepidophyma*. A, *L. flavimaculatum* with more than one pretympanic scale (*shaded*) separating the postocular scales from the second postorbital supralabial scale. B, *L. mayae* with one pretympanic scale (*shaded*) separating the postocular scales from the second postorbital supralabial scale.

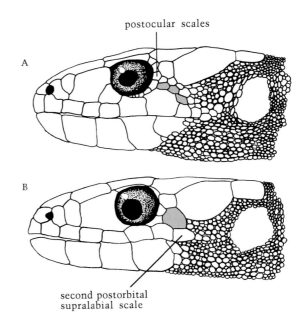

postocular scales

A

B

second postorbital
supralabial scale

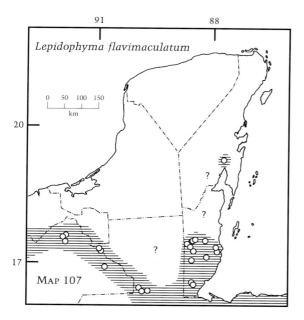

Lepidophyma flavimaculatum

MAP 107

lantic slope from Veracruz eastward through northern Guatemala, Belize, and northern Honduras. In lower Central America it occurs from southern Nicaragua through Costa Rica to the Panama Canal. In the Yucatán Peninsula it is known from northern Chiapas, El Petén, Belize, and southern Quintana Roo (Map 107).

NATURAL HISTORY This lizard is primarily a terrestrial forest dweller, although individuals are occasionally found on tree trunks or beneath the bark on standing trees. Specimens have been found beneath rocks and logs, under loose bark on fallen trees, in the crevices of Maya ruins, and in caves. Despite their English common name, they are at least occasionally diurnal. They feed on invertebrates, primarily insects. Slevin (1942:460) reported that termites were the principal food of animals from the vicinity of Quiriguá, Guatemala.

Like other xantusiids, *L. flavimaculatum* is viviparous, with a chorioallantoic placenta. Stuart (1948:55) reported that a female from Alta Verapaz contained six eggs on 29 March, and Duellman (1963) reported two "hatchlings" found on 28 June and 5 July in the forests of southern El Petén. A female from the Canal Zone, Panama, gave birth to five offspring (Telford and Campbell, 1970). According to the latter source and Bezy (1989:78), some populations of *L. flavimaculatum* in lower Central America are parthenogenetic.

ETYMOLOGY The specific name, *flavimaculatum*, is from the Latin *flavus*, "yellow," and *mac-*

ulata, "spotted," in reference to the yellow spots on the dorsum.

COMMENT In Alta Verapaz, the Maya call this species *reina de culebra* and hold it in high regard (Stuart, 1948:55).

Locality Records Belize: Cayo: Baking Pot (MCZ 18953), Chiquibul Branch, S Granos de Oro Camp (CM 112121), Georgetown (CM 90998), Mountain Pine Ridge (CM 117106), Ontario Village (CM 105964), 4.9 mi S San Ignacio (UF 73288), Xunantunich (KU 171679–80); Stann Creek: near Blue Hole (FMNH 4455), Bokowina (FMNH 49271–75), Double Falls (FMNH 49276), 4 mi from Twelve-Mile Station (FMNH 4453–54); Toledo: Blue Creek (RWV photo), 0.5 mi from Blue Creek Village (CM 117260), 2 km N Blue Creek Village (UF 87175). *Guatemala*: Alta Verapaz: Chinajá (Duellman, 1963:236); El Petén: ca. 15 km NW Chinajá (KU 55864, 59552), Desempeña (USNM 111484), Río de la Pasión, near Petén–Alta Verapaz border (UMMZ 79072), Piedras Negras (UIMNH 48875; USNM 111475–83). *Mexico*: Chiapas: vicinity Bonampak (MZFC 493), Palenque, San Juanito (USNM 111486–87), 10 to 15 mi S Palenque (LSUMZ 33379), vicinity Palenque (LSUMZ 33380), 9 mi S Palenque (LSUMZ 38456), Palenque ruins (EAL 3030–31); Quintana Roo: 6.6 km N Limones (UMRC 79-252).

Lepidophyma mayae Bezy
(Fig. 144B; Map 108)

Lepidophyma mayae Bezy, 1973:1. HOLOTYPE: KU 59554. TYPE LOCALITY: near Chinajá, elevation 140 m, Alta Verapaz, Guatemala.

Maya night lizard.

DESCRIPTION The adults of this apparently uncommon species probably average between 55 and 65 mm in snout-vent length. The body is moderately attenuate, and the head is rather narrow and only slightly distinct from the neck. The eye is covered by a transparent spectacle, and the pupil is round (Fig. 144B). A gular fold is present, and the snout is pointed in dorsal aspect. The tail is long, slender, and fragile, and about 1.4 times as long as the head and body. The limbs are well developed. The hands and feet are pentadactyl, and their digits terminate in strong, sharp claws. The head is covered by a series of regularly arranged plates, and the dorsum bears two paravertebral rows of enlarged tubercles surrounded by small granular scales. The lateral surfaces of the body support a nearly homogeneous field of tetrahedral tubercular scales. At midbody the venter is covered with ten longitudinal rows of large, rectangular juxtaposed plates. The tail bears whorls of enlarged tubercles separated by four or so interwhorls of smaller scales. Two of the interwhorls are generally incomplete across the ventral surface of the tail. There are 14 to 18 femoral pores on the posteroventral surface of each thigh; these are more conspicuous in males than in females.

The dorsum is predominantly dark brown or nearly black with dull brown mottling and several irregular rows of small, light tan or yellowish spots or flecks. The labial scales are dark brown or black and are barred at their sutures with cream or yellowish tan. The iris is dull reddish brown. The ventral surface of the body is yellowish tan with numerous small brown spots.

SIMILAR SPECIES *Lepidophyma mayae* differs from *Ameiva* and *Cnemidophorus* in lacking movable eyelids. *Gymnophthalmus* has only four digits on each hand and possesses enlarged cycloid scales on the dorsum. *Lepidophyma flavimaculatum* closely resembles *L. mayae*, with which it co-occurs, but it has fewer lateral tubercle rows (24–32 vs. 33–46), a more distinctly spotted dorsum, and more than one pretympanic scale between the postocular scales and the second postorbital supralabial scale (Fig. 144A).

DISTRIBUTION This species is known only from the type locality near the Alta Verapaz–El Petén border in Guatemala and the lower slopes of the Sierra de los Cuchumatanes and the Sierra Xucaneb

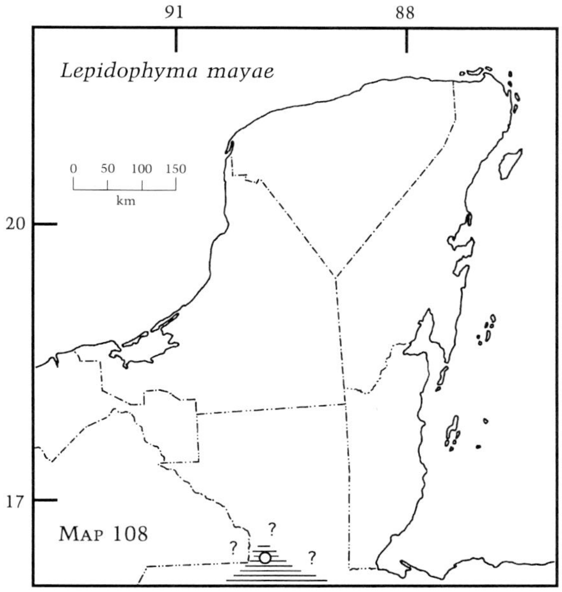

MAP 108

in the Departments of Huehuetenango and Alta Verapaz, respectively (Map 108). It may also occur at higher elevations in Alta Verapaz, if the specimen collected by Gustav Bernoulli in the 1870s and labeled "Vera Paz" originated in the vicinity of Cobán, as seems possible (Stuart, 1948:9). Although *L. mayae* has not yet been reported from Belize, its discovery there is expected.

NATURAL HISTORY In the Yucatán Peninsula, the Maya night lizard occupies the luxuriant humid forests at the border between the Guatemalan departments of Alta Verapaz and El Petén. The field notes of William E. Duellman, who collected the type series, indicate that all the specimens were taken in primary forest. Five of the seven specimens were taken from beneath logs or rocks, and two were abroad on the forest floor by day.

This species presumably feeds on small invertebrates, as do most other members of its genus. Likewise, it is probably viviparous, as are all xantusiids for which information is available.

ETYMOLOGY The specific name, *mayae*, refers to the indigenous inhabitants of the Department of El Petén, Guatemala.

Locality Records Guatemala: Alta Verapaz: Chinajá (KU 55863, 59554, 59556, 59558–59; LACM 75194–95).

Family Anguidae

Anguids are moderately to extremely attenuate lizards with relatively short limbs or none at all. The tail is long, slender, and fragile. Femoral pores are absent. Many species have a well-developed lateral groove on each side of the body, although the Yucatecan species does not. Anguids are diurnal and generally terrestrial or arboreal, but a few are fossorial. Most species feed primarily on invertebrates, but some species also eat small vertebrates. Oviparity is the predominant mode of reproduction, but some species are ovoviviparous (i.e., the eggs are retained within the body of the female until they hatch, and the young are thus brought forth alive). Some oviparous females tend their eggs. This family occurs throughout much of North, Central, and South America, the West Indies, Europe, North Africa, and southern Asia. About 10 genera and 78 species are currently recognized, but only 1 species occurs in the Yucatán Peninsula.

Genus *Celestus*

This rather small genus of skinklike lizards is restricted to Middle America and the West Indies. Twenty-two species are presently recognized, only one of which occurs in the Yucatán Peninsula. The generic distinctness of *Celestus* relative to the closely related genus *Diploglossus* has long been a matter of debate. Most taxonomists recognize *Celestus* (e.g., L. D. Wilson et al., 1986), although a few include the *Celestus* species within *Diploglossus* (e.g., J. A. Campbell and Camarillo, 1994). Pending a definitive analysis of relationships among these lizards, I retain the name *Celestus* for the single anguid found in the Yucatán Peninsula. *Celestus* derives from the Latin adjective *caelestis*, meaning "heavenly."

Celestus rozellae Smith
(Figs. 112A, 145; Map 109)

Celestus rozellae H. M. Smith, 1942c:372. HOLOTYPE: USNM 113526. TYPE LOCALITY: vicinity of Palenque, Chiapas, Mexico.

Galliwasp (Belize); celesto vientre verde (Mexico).

DESCRIPTION   This is a medium-sized, moderately attenuate, skinklike lizard. The adults probably average between 80 and 90 mm in snout-vent length; the maximum length recorded is 97 mm. The fragile tail is about 1.8 times the length of the head and body. The head is rather broad and somewhat depressed, and the snout is moderately pointed in dorsal aspect. The head is slightly distinct from the neck. There is no gular fold, and the ear opening is much smaller than the eye. The dorsal surface of the head is covered with enlarged symmetrical plates (Fig. 145B). The body and appendages are covered with smooth, highly polished cycloid scales, with those of the dorsum and venter subequal in size.

The dorsum of adults is brown or olive brown, slightly lighter on the head. Indistinct narrow, dark stripes are visible on the head and neck. The lateral surfaces of the neck and body bear a series of light bluish gray vertical bars about one scale row thick; often these are indistinct and broken. The middle of each ventral scale bears several fine lines of dark pigment, suggesting a series of longitudinal lines on the venter, which is otherwise light bluish gray. The color and pattern are brighter and more distinct

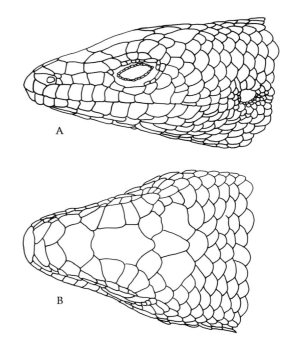

Fig. 145. Head of *Celestus rozellae* (KU 190853) in lateral (A), and dorsal (B) views; Los Amantes, Izabal, Guatemala.

in juveniles. H. M. Smith (1942c:373) described a juvenile from Piedras Negras, El Petén, as having light dorsolateral stripes that extended onto the head and were greenish in the temporal region and cream on the snout. There was a golden tint over most of the body. The lateral bars in this specimen were pale blue, and the ventral surface of the body was bright blue, lighter on the chin and limbs. Alvarez del Toro (1983:131) described juveniles from Chiapas as having metallic dorsolateral stripes, black vertical bars on the sides, and a bright orange tail.

SIMILAR SPECIES   Although superficially skinklike, *C. rozellae* differs from the Yucatecan species of *Eumeces* and from *Mabuya unimarginata* and *Sphenomorphus* in possessing a pair of frontonasal scales (cf. Figs. 112, 133). *Ameiva* and *Cnemidophorus* have granular rather than cycloid dorsal scales.

DISTRIBUTION   *Celestus rozellae* occurs at low elevations on the Atlantic slope from the Isthmus of Tehauntepec through El Petén to Belize (but see Comment). In the Yucatán Peninsula this species is known only from a few scattered localities in northern Chiapas, El Petén, and Belize (Map 109).

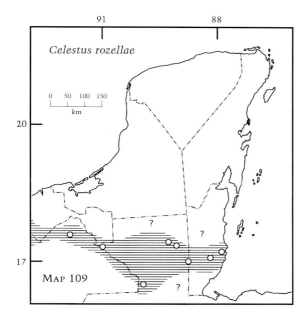

Celestus rozellae

MAP 109

NATURAL HISTORY This uncommon arboreal forest dweller is apparently restricted to the humid forests of the Atlantic lowlands. It lives at considerable heights, according to Alvarez del Toro (1983:131), although individuals can also be found on tree trunks near the ground and in thatched roofs. The holotype was found running rapidly up the trunk of a small tree near an open spot in a wooded area (H. M. Smith, 1942c:373), and Duellman (1963:237) obtained specimens in southern El Petén from trees. Henderson and Hoevers's (1975:32) characterization of *C. rozellae* as terrestrial is in error.

This species is viviparous. In Chiapas, broods of three to five young are born in May, June, or July (Alvarez del Toro, 1983:131).

ETYMOLOGY The specific name, *rozellae,* is a patronym honoring Rozella B. Smith, who collected the type specimen.

COMMENT According to Holman and Birkenholz (1963:144), a specimen of *C. rozellae* was taken at Chocola, Mazatenango, Guatemala, on the Pacific slope at about 890 m. J. A. Campbell and Camarillo (1994) examined the specimen (UIMNH 52157) and tentatively concluded that it is indeed *C. rozellae.* On both biogeographical and ecological grounds the record is anomalous, however, for this species is otherwise known only from low elevations on the Atlantic slope.

Celestus rozellae was treated by J. A. Campbell

and Camarillo (1994) as part of their review of the *Diploglossus* of Mexico and northern Central America.

Locality Records   Belize: Cayo: Valentin (UMMZ 80700); Stann Creek: Bokowina (Schmidt, 1941:495), E slope Cockscomb Mts. (CM 8482). *Guatemala:* El Petén: 20 km NNW Chinajá (Duellman, 1963:237), N shore Lake Yaxhá (UTEP 6022), Piedras Negras (USNM 113527), Tikal (JCL sight record; UF 13725–26; UMMZ 117868–69). *Mexico:* Chiapas: Palenque (USNM 113526).

Suborder Serpentes (Snakes)

All snakes are limbless, attenuate carnivores, yet in spite of their fundamental morphological similarity they have evolved to occupy a great variety of ecological settings. Although they are most diverse in the tropics, snakes occur throughout the world except at very high latitudes and on some oceanic islands. Most are surface dwellers, but some are fossorial and some are arboreal. One lineage has become completely marine, and many species are semiaquatic. In size, snakes range from tiny, blind burrowers no more than 100 mm long to giant constrictors that grow to nearly 10 m. Most snakes lay eggs, but many are live-bearers. At least one species is parthenogenetic.

Roughly 2,400 species of living snakes in some 420 genera are presently recognized. The evolutionary relationships among snakes are not well understood, however, and their higher classification is a matter of some controversy. Perhaps 11 living families of snakes can be recognized. Six families, 48 genera, and 73 species of snakes occur in the Yucatán Peninsula (see Table 1).

IDENTIFICATION Outwardly snakes represent extreme morphological simplification. In the course of evolution they have lost the movable eyelids, external ear openings, and limbs of their lizard ancestors. This reduction in complexity means that many species of snakes resemble one another rather closely, sometimes making identification difficult. Nonetheless, many of the species in the Yucatán Peninsula are distinctive in terms of color, pattern, size, and shape and can be readily identified by referring to the illustrations provided here. Identification can be facilitated by the distribution maps, for some species can be immediately eliminated on the basis

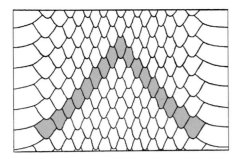

Fig. 146. Method of counting dorsal scales of snakes. In this example there are 17 rows of dorsal scales.

of their geographical distribution. To confirm or reject a tentative identification, compare the specimen with the description of that species in the species account and read the section on similar species.

It may be necessary to consult the identification keys, in which case careful attention to anatomical detail and a hand lens will be required. Note the size and general configuration of the snake. Size alone will often substantially narrow the range of possibilities. Shape, too, may be a helpful clue. Is the animal long and slender or thick and stocky? Is the body flattened from side to side (laterally compressed) or round in cross section? Is the head broad and distinct from the neck or little differentiated

from the neck? Look carefully for a deep loreal pit between the eye and the nostril (Fig. 150D). If a pit is present, treat the specimen with great care, for it is dangerously venomous.

Note whether the dorsal and ventral scales are the same size, and count the number of scale rows, for these tend to be relatively constant within species and thus are an important aid in identification. Figure 146 illustrates the method for counting scale rows. The number of scale rows at midbody should be compared with the number at a point about one head length anterior to the vent. Some species exhibit a reduction in the number of scale rows toward the posterior end, and others do not. Note whether the scales are smooth or have a ridge running down the middle; if the latter, the scales are said to be *keeled* (Fig. 147). Check the condition of the anal plate (Fig. 148). It may be undivided or divided, and this condition is generally constant within a species. Similarly, the condition of the subcaudal scales (divided or not) can be important in distinguishing species (Fig. 148). Under magnification, examine the trailing edge of the dorsal scales. Some species have a single apical pit at the apex of the scale; other species have a pair of such pits, and some have no apical pits at all (Fig. 147). The relative size of the eye, and especially the shape of

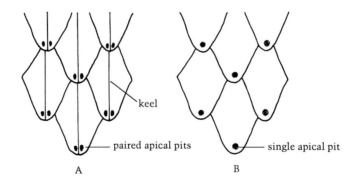

keel

paired apical pits

A

single apical pit

B

Fig. 147. Dorsal scales of snakes. A, keeled scales with paired apical pits. B, smooth scales with single apical pits.

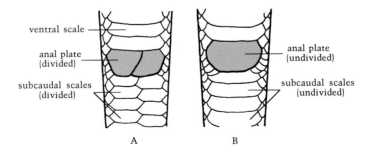

ventral scale

anal plate (divided)

subcaudal scales (divided)

anal plate (undivided)

subcaudal scales (undivided)

A

B

Fig. 148. Configuration of subcaudal scales and the condition of the anal plate (*shaded*) in snakes. A, anal plate and subcaudals divided. B, anal plate undivided (entire), subcaudals undivided.

the pupil, can be helpful characters. The pupils may be round, vertically elliptical, or somewhat in between, in which case they are said to be *subcircular*.

Note also the configuration of the scales on the head. The number, size, and shape of the head scales are important features. Figures 149 and 150 illustrate the typical pattern of head scales in several species and give the names of the scales.

Fig. 149. Dorsal views of the heads of snakes showing the configuration and terminology of head scales. A, *Boa constrictor*. B, *Symphimus mayae*. C, *Micrurus diastema*. D, *Atropoides nummifer*.

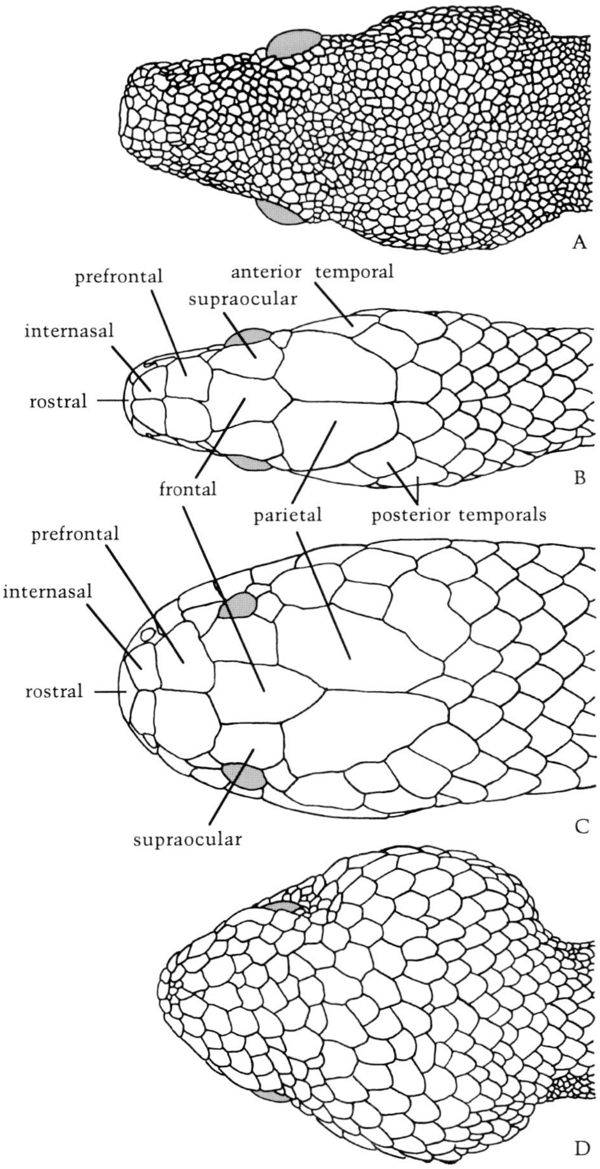

The habitat in which the snake was found and its behavior may help to identify it, for some species have restricted habitat requirements, and others exhibit distinctive behaviors. These characteristics are discussed in the section on natural history in each species account.

Finally, pay attention to color and color pattern. The number of stripes, bands, or blotches may be very helpful. Some snakes have distinctive ventral color patterns, so be sure to examine the underside of the specimen.

Fig. 150. Lateral views of the heads of snakes showing the configuration and terminology of head scales. A, *Boa constrictor*. B, *Symphimus mayae*. C, *Micrurus diastema*. D, *Atropoides nummifer*.

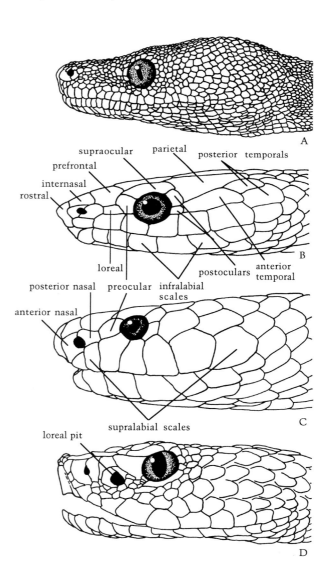

Key to the Families of Snakes

1. Ventral scales approximately equal to dorsal scales in size, not transversely elongated 2
   Ventral scales transversely elongated, distinctly larger than dorsal scales 3
2. Fourteen rows of scales at midbody; dorsal coloration predominantly brown or gray; ocular scale fused with a supralabial scale; no subocular scale (Fig. 151A) . . . . Leptotyphlopidae
   Eighteen rows of scales at midbody; dorsum pink (or occasionally white); ocular scale separate from the supralabial scales; subocular scale present (Fig. 151B) . . . . Typhlopidae
3. No pit in loreal region (Fig. 150A,B,C) 4
   Deep pit present in loreal region between the eye and the nostril (Fig. 150D) . . . . . . Viperidae
4. Dorsal surface of head covered with small, irregular scales (Fig. 149A); more than 50 rows of scales at midbody . . . . Boidae
   Dorsal surface of head covered with large, symmetrical scales (Fig. 149B,C); fewer than 50 rows of scales at midbody 5
5. Loreal scale absent (Fig. 150C), nonerectile fangs present on anterior portion of maxillary bone . . . . Elapidae
   Loreal scale present (Fig. 150B) or absent, no hollow fangs on anterior portion of maxillary bone . . . . Colubridae

Clave para las Familias de Serpientes

1. Escamas ventrales aproximadamente iguales a las escamas dorsales en tamaño, no elongadas tranversalmente 2
   Escamas ventrales transversalmente elongadas, distintivamente más largas que las escamas dorsales 3
2. Catorce hileras de escamas a la mitad del cuerpo; coloración dorsal predominantemente parda o gris; escama ocular fusionada con la escama supralabial; no hay escama subocular (Fig. 151A) . . . . Leptotyphlopidae
   Dieciocho hileras de escamas a la mitad del cuerpo; coloración dorsal rosa (ocasionalmente blanca); escama ocular separada de las escamas supralabiales; con una escama subocular (Fig. 151B) . . . . Typhlopidae
3. Sin una foceta en la región loreal (Fig. 150A,B,C) 4
   Con una foseta profunda presente en la región loreal entre el ojo y el nostrilo (Fig. 150D) . . . . Viperidae
4. Superficie dorsal de la cabeza cubierta con escamas pequeñas e irregulares (Fig. 149A); más de 50 hileras de escamas a la mitad del cuerpo . . . . Boidae
   Superficie dorsal de la cabeza cubierta con escamas largas y simétricas (Fig. 149B,C); menos de 50 hileras de escamas a la mitad del cuerpo 5
5. Sin escama loreal (Fig. 150A), colmillos no movibles en porción anterior del hueso maxilar . . . . Elapidae
   Con escama loreal (Fig. 150B) o sin ella, sin colmillos acanalados en porción anterior del hueso maxilar . . . . Colubridae

Family Typhlopidae (Blindsnakes)

These small, wormlike burrowers rarely exceed 400 mm in snout-vent length, although one species sometimes reaches twice that length. The head is blunt and rounded; the tail is short and terminates in a keratinized spine. The dorsal and ventral scales are subequal in size and smooth. The eyes are reduced and covered by an ocular scale that is not fused with a labial scale. This family is widely distributed throughout the New and Old World tropics, Eurasia, the Middle East, sub-Saharan Africa, Madagascar, and Australia.

Three genera and about 160 species are presently recognized. One genus occurs in the Yucatán Penin-

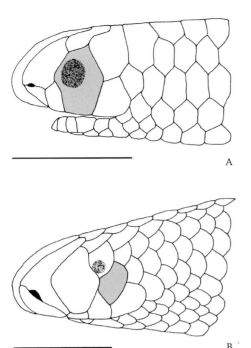

Fig. 151. Lateral views of the heads of leptotyphlopid and typhlopid snakes. A, *Leptotyphlops goudotii* showing fusion of the ocular scale with a supralabial scale (*shaded*). B, *Typhlops microstomus* showing presence of a subocular scale (*shaded*). Line equals 2 mm.

sula. I have chosen not to include *Ramphotyphlops*, even though Villa et al. (1988:85) listed *R. braminus* from Yucatán, citing Dixon and Hendricks, 1979, as their authority. I found no mention in Dixon and Hendricks, 1979, of *Ramphotyphlops* in the Yucatán Peninsula, nor do I know of any confirmed record for it within the peninsula. It is, however, known from Guatemala City and from several localities on the Pacific slope of Mexico. Given the facility with which this species is transported through human agency and its remarkable colonizing ability (owing in part to the fact that it is parthenogenetic), its eventual establishment in the Yucatán Peninsula is probable. In fact, the species may already occur on islands off the coast of Belize, for T. Garel (pers. comm.) informs me that a blindsnake resembling *Ramphotyphlops braminus* has been taken in the Turneffe Islands.

Genus *Typhlops*

These blind burrowing snakes are found throughout the world at tropical and subtropical latitudes.

Approximately 130 species are presently recognized, and one occurs in the Yucatán Peninsula. Thomas (1976) reviewed the Antillean species of *Typhlops*, and Dixon and Hendricks (1979) treated the Neotropical mainland forms. *Typhlops* is from the Greek *typhlos*, "blind," and *ops*, "eye" or "face," in reference to the degenerated eyes of members of this genus.

Typhlops microstomus Cope
(Fig. 151B, 345; Map 110)

Typhlops microstomus Cope, 1866:125. HOLO-TYPE: USNM 61064. TYPE LOCALITY: Yucatán, Mexico.

Yucatán blindsnake; culebra lumbricoide (Mexico).

DESCRIPTION These small, elongate snakes average about 270 mm in snout-vent length and attain a maximum of 366 mm (Fig. 345). The extremely short tail averages only about 10 percent of the snout-vent length. The eye is barely discernible beneath the ocular scale. The tail ends in a sharp, keratinized spine. There are 18 rows of scales at midbody and an average of 531 dorsal scales from the rostral to the tail spine (Dixon and Hendricks, 1979:21). This is the only New World typhlopid that possesses a subocular scale (Fig. 151B).

The coloration is normally uniform pink, for the integument is essentially devoid of pigment; however, E. W. Andrews (1937:365) stated that a live specimen from Chichén Itzá was pure white without any pink coloration.

SIMILAR SPECIES The only other snake in the Yucatán Peninsula with dorsals and ventrals that are the same size, *Leptotyphlops goudotii*, has a pigmented integument and 14 rows of scales at midbody, and its ocular scute is fused with a supralabial scale (Fig. 151A).

DISTRIBUTION *Typhlops microstomus* is endemic to the Yucatán Peninsula, where it is known from several localities in Yucatán and adjacent Quintana Roo. The scattered records from southern Campeche, Belize, and El Petén may represent isolated populations (Map 110).

NATURAL HISTORY This secretive burrower is apparently most common in the deciduous forests at

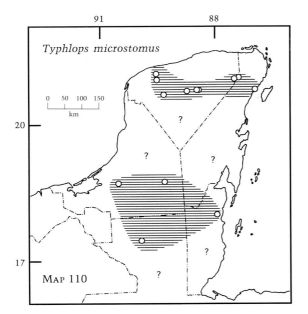

Map 110

Typhlops microstomus

7114; UMMZ 68244), Dzibilchaltún (FMNH 153526–28, 153590–95), Libre Unión (FMNH 36346), Mérida (FMNH 19416; USNM 6569), Pisté (CM 46903-4, 49555; KU 70815; UCM 41819), Telchaquillo (UWZH 20506), Tohil, 10 mi from Chichén Itzá (UMMZ 80797), X-Can (CM 46860, 47022–23); no specific locality (USNM 61064).

Family Leptotyphlopidae
(Slender Blindsnakes)

These tiny, slender, wormlike snakes are highly modified for a burrowing existence. Some species attain a snout-vent length in excess of 300 mm, but most are less than half that length. The eye is reduced in size and covered by an ocular scute that is fused to one of the supralabial scales (Fig. 151A). This family occurs from the southwestern United States to Argentina in the New World, and throughout the Middle East and North and sub-Saharan Africa in the Old World. Two genera and perhaps 95 to 100 living species are recognized. One genus occurs in the Yucatán Peninsula.

Genus *Leptotyphlops*

This genus ranges throughout the southwestern United States, most of Mexico, Central and South America, Africa, and southwestern Asia. Approximately 95 species are currently recognized, but only one occurs in the Yucatán Peninsula. *Leptotyphlops* is derived from the Greek *leptos*, "slender" or "thin," *typhlos*, "blind," and *ops*, "eye" or "face."

Leptotyphlops goudotii (Duméril and Bibron)
(Figs. 151A, 346; Map 111)

Stenostoma Goudotii A. M. C. Duméril and Bibron, 1844:330. HOLOTYPE: MNHNP 1068. TYPE LOCALITY: la vallée de la Magdeleine, à la Nouvelle-Grenade.

Slender blindsnake; agujilla, culebra lumbricoide (Mexico); u-kanil-beh (Yucatec Maya).

DESCRIPTION   This small, slender snake averages about 120 mm in snout-vent length. The tail is extremely short, only about 6 to 7 percent of the head and body length. The head and tail are bluntly

the north end of the Yucatán Peninsula, but little is known of its natural history. Specimens have been found beneath surface debris, and I removed a partly digested specimen from the stomach of a coral snake (*Micrurus diastema*). Meerman (1992b:26) found a specimen in Corozal District in a pit 1.6 m deep but could not exclude the possibility that the specimen had fallen into the pit from some lesser depth. *Typhlops microstomus* probably feeds on insects and their larvae, especially ants and termites. This species is presumably oviparous, as are the other members of the genus for which reproductive data are available.

ETYMOLOGY   The specific name, *microstomus*, is from the Greek *mikros*, "small," and *stoma*, "mouth," presumably in reference to what Cope thought was a relatively small mouth in these snakes.

COMMENT   The biosystematics of *T. microstomus* was reviewed by Dixon and Hendricks (1979) as part of their review of the mainland Neotropical forms of typhlopid snakes.

Locality Records   Belize: Belize: Altun Ha (ROM 10244); Corozal: Sarteneja (RMNH 25946). *Guatemala*: El Petén: El Paso (MCZ 38648). *Mexico*: Campeche: Escárcega (UCM 28119), km 143 on Hwy. 186 (UWZH 20550); Quintana Roo: 5.2 km S Playa del Carmen (UMRC 84-172), Pueblo Nuevo X-Can (CM 45287, 46816, 49016, 49086; UCM 40711–12, 40750, 41816–18); Yucatán: Chichén Itzá (FMNH 26975–76; MCZ

rounded, and the latter terminates in a small, sharp, keratinized spine (Fig. 346). The degenerated eyes are covered by scales and are visible as dark spots. The body scales are smooth, lack apical pits, and are arranged in 14 rows at midbody. The anal plate is undivided.

The dorsum is brown or silvery gray, and each dorsal and lateral scale has a light yellow or cream border, producing a striped appearance overall. There is a light spot on the snout and one at the tip of the tail. The ventral surface is light tan. The highly polished scales give this snake a metallic sheen.

SIMILAR SPECIES   The only other blind burrowing snake in the Yucatán Peninsula, *Typhlops microstomus*, differs from *L. goudotii* in being essentially devoid of pigmentation (and thus pink rather than brownish) and in possessing 18 rather than 14 rows of scales at midbody. Moreover, in *L. goudotii* the ocular scale is fused to a supralabial scale, whereas in *T. microstomus* the ocular and supralabial scales are distinct and separated by a subocular scale (Fig. 151A,B).

DISTRIBUTION   The slender blindsnake occurs at low elevations from Colima on the Pacific slope and the Isthmus of Tehauntepec on the Atlantic slope, southward through Central America to northern Colombia and Venezuela, and on many of the region's offshore islands. In the Yucatán Peninsula it is known from several localities in northern Yucatán and from Isla Cozumel, and there is one record from El Petén (Map 111).

NATURAL HISTORY   This secretive burrowing snake inhabits ant and termite nests and is occasionally found on the surface at night, especially following rains. Specimens have also been found beneath surface debris, especially in moist, sandy areas. Diurnal surface activity is suggested by the specimen (CM 41325) removed from the stomach of a hawk collected on Isla Cozumel.

These tiny insectivorous snakes prey on the workers, eggs, and larvae of the termites and ants with which they cohabit. According to Scott (1983b:406), in Costa Rica this species occasionally aggregates in small colonies.

Leptotyphlops goudotii is oviparous. In Chiapas, the females produce clutches of 8 to 12 eggs in June and July (Alvarez del Toro, 1983:147).

SUBSPECIES   Variation in the *L. albifrons* group is poorly understood, and the taxonomy of the group is

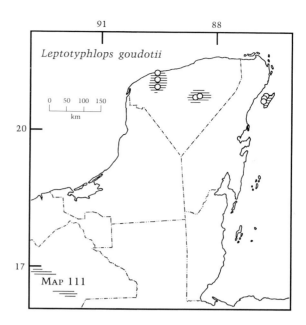

MAP 111

therefore uncertain. According to Orejas-Miranda (in J. A. Peters and Orejas-Miranda, 1970:169), this species consists of five subspecies, of which *L. g. phenops* occurs in the Yucatán Peninsula. L. D. Wilson and Hahn (1973) considered *phenops* a full species, but L. D. Wilson and Meyer (1985:20) provisionally accepted Orejas-Miranda's arrangement while stressing the need for a comprehensive study of variation in *L. goudotii*.

ETYMOLOGY   The specific name, *goudotii*, is a patronym honoring the French naturalist Goudot, who provided the type specimen.

Locality Records   Guatemala: El Petén: (UMMZ 117992). *Mexico*: Quintana Roo: Cozumel (CM 41325; Himmelstein, 1980:29), Cozumel, San Miguel (UMMZ 78639), Cozumel, 2.5 mi S San Miguel (UCM 16012), Cozumel, 12 km SW San Miguel (CM 41316); Yucatán: Chichén Itzá (FMNH 20606, 20616–18; MCZ 7113, 22060–62, 28747; UMMZ 68240–43, 73038, 80799, 80883–86), Dzibilchaltún (FMNH 153501, 153532–33, 153535–38, 153542–46, 153586–89, 153596), Mérida (CM 45286; UWZH 20557), Pisté (CM 46905, 47078–79, 49548–54), Progreso (USNM 194705–7).

Family Boidae (Boas)

Most boids are medium-sized to very large snakes, and the family includes the largest snake in the world, the anaconda, *Eunectes murinus* (about 10 m total length). Many species are arboreal, some are terrestrial, and a few are fossorial or semiaquatic. Most are powerful constrictors. Boids typically have many rows of smooth dorsal scales, and the ventral scales are transversely enlarged. Pelvic vestiges are present, and some species have external spurs at the base of the tail. These are generally better developed in males than in females. The family is circumtropical, and some species range into temperate latitudes. Eighteen genera and 60 species are presently recognized. One genus occurs in the Yucatán Peninsula.

Genus *Boa*

The genus *Boa* contains one living species, the boa constrictor of tropical America. *Boa* is Latin and refers to a kind of water serpent (Jaeger, 1944:32).

Boa constrictor (Linnaeus)
(Figs. 149A, 150A, 347; Map 112)

Boa constrictor Linnaeus, 1758:215. TYPE: unknown. TYPE LOCALITY: India (in error).

Imperial boa; owla, wanasai, wowia, wowla (Belize); boa (Guatemala, Mexico); mazacuata, mazacoatl (Mexico); och-can (Lacandón Maya, Yucatec Maya); k'axab yuk (Yucatec Maya).

DESCRIPTION   This is the longest and most massive snake in the Yucatán Peninsula. Elsewhere boa constrictors attain a length in excess of 5,000 mm, but in the Yucatán Peninsula the adults generally average between 1,500 and 2,000 mm in snout-vent length. The relatively short tail is about 15 to 20 percent of the head and body length. The head of this thick-bodied species is roughly triangular in dorsal aspect and distinct from the narrow neck, and the snout is truncate in dorsal view (Fig. 347). The eyes are small, and the pupils are vertically elliptical. The dorsal surface of the head is covered with numerous small scales (Fig. 149A). The dorsal scales on the body are smooth, lack apical pits, and are arranged in 55 to 80 rows at midbody. The anal plate is entire, and there is usually a pair of keratinized spurs at the base of the tail, better developed in males than in females.

The dorsal ground color is tan or gray with dark brown rectangular blotches or irregular dark brown bands, usually with lighter spots within them. The lateral surfaces of the body generally bear a series of dark spots with light centers. Posteriorly the spots and blotches may become reddish brown or nearly black. The dorsal surface of the head is tan or gray with a narrow, dark median stripe that originates on the snout and extends onto the body. A dark stripe originates on the lateral surface of the head at the level of the nostril and passes posteriorly through the lower half of the eye to beyond the angle of the jaws. The ventral surface of the body and tail is light tan, gray, or cream with irregular dark spots.

SIMILAR SPECIES   The adults of this distinctive species are unmistakable because of their great size. In addition, *B. constrictor* possesses a very large number of dorsal scale rows, far exceeding the number found on any other species of snake in the peninsula.

DISTRIBUTION   The boa constrictor occurs at low and moderate elevations from Tamaulipas on the Atlantic slope and Sonora on the Pacific slope south and eastward through southern Mexico and Central America to Argentina. It also occurs in the Lesser Antilles. It is found throughout the Yucatán Peninsula, including the islands off the coast of Belize (Map 112).

NATURAL HISTORY   This large, powerful snake is both terrestrial and arboreal. It is generally nocturnal, but individuals are sometimes found abroad during the day. It occurs in a variety of habitats, in-

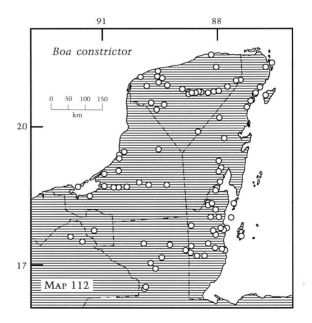

cluding beaches, savannas, mangrove swamps, second growth, and primary forest. Boas consume a variety of vertebrate prey such as lizards, birds, and mammals (including monkeys), and are in turn preyed on by ophiophagous snakes such as *Drymarchon corais* (Duellman, 1963:239), and by the great black hawk, *Buteogallus urubitinga* (Gerhardt et al., 1993:350). Boas are generally slow and deliberate in their movements, and they are quite variable in disposition. Some cannot be induced to bite, whereas others bite freely at any opportunity. Although boas are not venomous, large individuals can inflict a painful bite. The long, delicate teeth often break off and remain imbedded in the bite wound.

Boa constrictor is viviparous, and parturition evidently occurs during the summer rainy season. In Alta Verapaz, Stuart (1948:62) collected a specimen in April that contained 12 well-developed eggs. W. T. Neill (1962:242) reported litters of 16 and 12 born on 10 and 19 August, respectively, to females from Belize. I found newborn boas in August in Campeche; and Dundee et al. (1986:41) found juveniles with yolk in the gut in Yucatán on 10–12 July. The brood size ranges from 20 to 50 in Chiapas (Alvarez del Toro, 1960:148).

SUBSPECIES   J. A. Peters and Orejas-Miranda (1970:37) recognized eight subspecies, of which *B. c. imperator* supposedly occurs in the Yucatán Peninsula. On the other hand, L. D. Wilson and Meyer (1985:23) considered it inadvisable to recognize any subspecies given the rudimentary knowledge about geographic variation in *Boa constrictor*.

ETYMOLOGY   The specific name, *constrictor*, is modern Latin meaning "something that constricts," in reference to the method used by boas to subdue their prey.

COMMENT   *Boa constrictor* is listed in Appendix 2 of the Convention on International Trade in Endangered Species of Wild Flora and Fauna.

Locality Records   Belize: Belize: Altun Ha (MPM 7307), Belize City (FMNH 4255, 49365; UF 24624; USNM 26063), near Belize (UMMZ 74922), 3 km SW Belize City (CM 90990), 30 mi W Belize City (CM 112191), near Boom (W. T. Neill and Allen, 1959c:46), Cay Corker (MPM 7306), Cockroach Cay (MCZ 65582), Crooked Tree Village (CM 112089), bet. Stanley Airport and Belize City (W. T. Neill and Allen, 1959c:46), Turneffe Islands, Grand Point (FMNH

34627); Cayo: Augustine (MPM 7305, 8196), 11 mi W, 8 mi S Cayo (W. T. Neill and Allen, 1959c:46), Cocquercot (UMMZ 74926), bet. Roaring River and Blue Hole (CM 90991), San Ignacio (UMMZ 84345), 1 mi NW San Ignacio (USNM 71359), upper Raspaculo River basin (Stafford, 1991:14); Corozal: Ambergris Cay, 2 km W, 14 km N San Pedro (CM 94391), 0.25 mi N Corozal Town (JLK 464), 1 mi N Corozal Town (JLK 463); Orange Walk: Gallon Jug (MCZ 71669), 8.5 mi W, 7.5 mi N Maskall (W. T. Neill and Allen, 1959c:46), near Orange Walk (MPM 7782–86), just N Orange Walk Town (Dundee et al., 1986:42), Otro Benque (MPM 8123- 29), Tower Hill (MPM 7308, 7732); Stann Creek: Middlesex (UCM 25803, 30836–37), Stann Creek (UMMZ 124654), 4.4 mi W Stann Creek (JCL sight record); no specific locality (USNM 56693). *Guatemala*: El Petén: 15 km NW Chinajá (KU 55703), 19 km NNW Chinajá (KU 58166), 21 km NNW Chinajá (KU 58165), Fallabon (UMMZ 74923), Lago Petén Itzá, near Flores (UMMZ 79062), La Libertad (UMMZ 74924–25), Paso Caballos (MCZ 38581), Tikal (KU 157544; UF 13802-7; UMMZ 117963), Toocog (KU 55702); no specific locality (USNM 71781). *Mexico*: Campeche: Balchacaj (UIMNH 17563–64), Champotón (UMMZ 73069), 5 km S Champotón (KU 70817), Chuina (KU 74985), Ciudad del Carmen (UMMZ 83538–39), 17.1 km W Conhuas (JCL sight record), Dzibalchén (KU 75614), Encarnación (FMNH 106999), 7.5 km W Escárcega (KU 70818–19), 14.5 km W Escárcega (KU 70820), 2.1 km W Matamoros (JCL sight record), 3.8 km SE Sabancuy (JCL sight record), San José Carpizo (UMMZ 99896–97), Silvituc (MZFC 502), 7.5 mi W Xpujil (KU 157545); Chiapas: Palenque, San Juanito (USNM 111285–86), 6.7 mi E Penjamo (JCL sight record); Quintana Roo: Akumal (Himmelstein, 1980:29; UMRC 84-49), 0.3 mi N Akumal (LSUMZ 38575), 18 km N Akumal (EAL 2871), 7 mi N Bacalar (LSUMZ 38907), Chetumal (MCZ 53124), Cozumel (López-Gonzales, 1991:106), Felipe Carrillo Puerto (MZFC 3495), Isla Mujeres (FMNH 34657; MCZ 10306; UCM 16014), Hwy. 307, 29.3 km S of rd. to Majahual (JCL photo), 2.6 km S Noh Bec (UMRC 84-48), Ocum (MZCIQRO 24), Playa del Carmen (Himmelstein, 1980:29), 20 mi S Playa del Carmen (LSUMZ 34035), Pueblo Nuevo X- Can (CM 45691–93, 49111, 49142, 49148; KU 70821; UCM 28147, 40096-97, 47458), 13 km W Puerto Juárez (KU 70822), 23.4 mi S Tepich (KU 157546), Tulum (JCL sight record; UMRC 84-50), 18 km NNE Tulum (LSUMZ 28299); Tabasco: rd. to Tenosique, 10.9 km E Penjamo (KU 171682); Yucatán: Calcehtok (UMMZ 113542), Chichén Itzá (CM 37537; FMNH 26989–92, 36348, 49326; UMMZ 68708-9, 73068, 83938; USNM 46394), 3 km S Cooperativa (Dundee et al., 1986:41), Dzibilchaltún (UCM 20482), Kantunil (FMNH 36349), Kaua (LSUMZ 28242), 1.2 km SW Kinchil (Dundee et al., 1986:41), Libre Unión (FMNH 36350–51), 1.5 mi S

Libre Unión (UCM 16015), Mérida (CM 45694; EAL 1562; UCM 40098; USNM 6561, 11380), 24 km E Mérida (JCL photo), 2.5 mi SW Mocochá (KU 157547), 7.7 mi SW Mocochá (KU 157548), Pisté (CM 46906–8, 46978–81, 47080–85, 49556–72; KU 70823; UCM 40099–105), 1.6 km N Pisté (KU 70825), 5 km W Pisté (KU 70824), 3 mi S Progreso (UCM 39515), bet. Río Lagartos and San Felipe (JCL sight record), bet. Santa Elena and Uxmal (TU 19795–96), 3 km WSW Sisal (KU 77704), Tekom (FMNH 49327), 2.5 mi N Ticul (KU 157549), 12 mi N Tizimín (UCM 45448), 13 km E Valladolid (LSUMZ 28241), 34 mi NE Valladolid (BCB 11434), 1 mi E X-Can (UCM 47459), Yokdzonot (UMRC 84-90), near Yucatán–Quintana Roo border on Hwy. 184 (KU 171681).

Family Colubridae

This enormous assemblage includes nearly 80 percent of the living species of snakes. Eighty-two percent of the species of snakes found in the Yucatán Peninsula are colubrids. The distribution of the family encompasses that of the suborder Serpentes, and in terms of numbers of species and individuals this is the dominant family of snakes on all inhabited continents except Australia. Colubrids are present on many continental and oceanic islands, and they occur at higher elevations and latitudes than representatives of other snake families. The family is morphologically and ecologically very diverse. In the Yucatán Peninsula alone colubrid representatives include the small, secretive leaf litter inhabitant *Ninia sebae*, the aquatic fish-eating *Tretanorhinus nigroluteus*, slender arboreal forms such as *Imantodes* and *Oxybelis*, and the large, predominantly terrestrial *Masticophis mentovarius*, *Drymarchon corais*, and *Spilotes pullatus*, which attain total lengths in excess of 2 m.

Some colubrids possess enlarged teeth on the posterior portion of the maxillary bone. These fangs may or may not be grooved (McKinstry, 1983). Many of the rear-fanged species produce a mild to moderately virulent venom, and a few have been known to cause human fatalities. Some of the colubrids in the Yucatán Peninsula are rear-fanged, but none are likely to pose a serious threat to humans. Nonetheless, people's responses to venom vary, and a few snakes (e.g., *Conophis lineatus*, *Urotheca elapoides*) can deliver a bite that produces serious discomfort—and that is well worth avoiding.

Three major groups of colubrid snakes have long

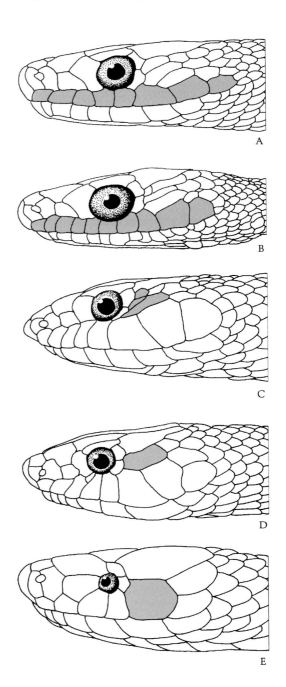

Fig. 152. Lateral views of the heads of colubrid snakes showing details of scutellation. A, *Senticolis triaspis* with eight supralabial scales (*shaded*), two of which border the eye. B, *Elaphe flavirufa* with more than eight supralabial scales (*shaded*), three of which border the eye. C, *Conophis lineatus* with more than one anterior temporal scale (*shaded*). D, *Coniophanes schmidti* with a single anterior temporal scale (*shaded*). E, *Geophis carinosus* with a supralabial scale (*shaded*) in contact with the parietal scale.

been recognized in the New World, but their monophyly is not firmly established, and relationships among and within the groups are yet to be fully elucidated. Cadle (1984a,b,c) analyzed the relationships among the xenodontines—the dominant Neotropical group of colubrids—using biochemical and immunological techniques. Sixty species of colubrids from 38 genera occur in the Yucatán Peninsula.

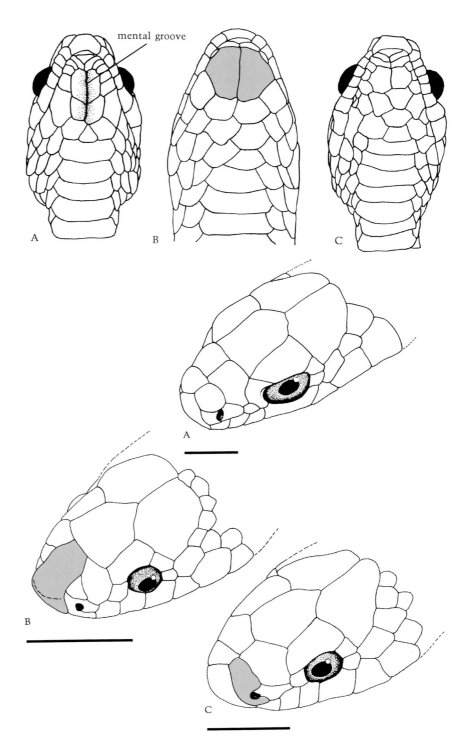

Fig. 153. Ventral views of the heads of colubrid snakes. A, *Sibon nebulata* showing presence of a mental groove. B, *Adelphicos quadrivirgatus* with enlarged chin shield (*shaded*). C, *Dipsas brevifacies* showing absence of a mental groove.

Fig. 154. Perspective views of the heads of colubrid snakes showing details of scutellation. A, *Spilotes pullatus* showing the normal colubrid configuration. B, *Ficimia publia* showing enlarged rostral scale (*shaded*) contacting the frontal scale and separating the internasal and prefrontal scales. C, *Stenorrhina freminvillei* showing fusion of internasal and nasal scales (*shaded*). Lines equal 0.5 cm.

Key to the Genera of the Family Colubridae

1. Scales of the vertebral and paravertebral rows at least weekly keeled....................2
   All dorsal scales smooth 22

2. Dorsal scales arranged in an even number of rows at midbody...................*Spilotes*
   Dorsal scales arranged in an odd number of rows at midbody..........................3

3. Twenty-one or more rows of dorsal scales at midbody 4
   Fewer than 21 rows of dorsal scales at midbody......................................9

4. Thirty-one or more rows of scales at midbody 5
   Fewer than 31 rows of scales at midbody..7

5. Dorsal and lateral scales heavily keeled ....*Nerodia* (part)
   Dorsal scales keeled, lateral scales smooth..6

6. Usually 8 supralabial scales, with 2 entering the orbit (Fig. 152A); usually more than 45
   blotches on the body...*Senticolis*
   Usually 9 or 10 supralabial scales, with 3 entering the orbit (Fig. 152B); usually fewer than 45
   blotches on the body ....*Elaphe*

7. Dorsal scales weakly keeled, lateral scales smooth; dorsal scales in 21 to 25 rows at
   midbody; anal plate entire...*Pseustes*
   Dorsal and lateral scales strongly keeled; anal plate divided.........................8

8. Dorsal scales in 21 rows at midbody.............................*Tretanorhinus* (part)
   Dorsal scales in 27 (rarely 25 or 31) rows at midbody.....................*Nerodia* (part)

9. Dorsal scales in 15 rows at midbody....................................*Leptophis*
   Dorsal scales in 17 or 19 rows at midbody..10

10. Dorsal scales in 17 rows at midbody..11
    Dorsal scales in 19 rows at midbody..14

11. Anal plate undivided 12
    Anal plate divided..17

12. At least one supralabial scale in contact with parietal scale (Fig. 152E)............*Geophis*
    Supralabial scales not in contact with parietal scale...............................13

13. Dorsal scales weakly keeled, lateral scales smooth.............................*Sibon*
    Dorsal and lateral scales heavily keeled ....*Dendrophidion* (part)

14. Dorsal scales keeled, lateral scales smooth.......................................15
    Dorsal and lateral scales keeled...16

15. Anal plate divided...*Tretanorhinus* (part)
    Anal plate entire ....*Pseustes*

16. Light nuchal collar (may be interrupted medially; see Fig. 174)...............*Ninia* (part)
    No light nuchal collar...*Thamnophis*

17. Dorsum predominantly red or reddish brown; light nuchal collar present ......*Ninia* (part)
    Dorsum not red or reddish brown; no light nuchal collar.............................18

18. Dorsal scales weakly keeled, lateral scales smooth................................19
    Dorsal and lateral scales heavily keeled..21

19. Small snakes, SVL less than 350 mm; pair of light postocular spots or stripes present
    (Fig. 177) ....*Rhadinaea*
    Larger snakes, SVL greater than 350 mm; no light postocular spots or stripes 20

20. Extremely slender snakes with narrow heads and acuminate snouts (Figs. 175, 176) ....
    ....*Oxybelis* (part)
    Not extremely slender, head not notably narrow, snout not acuminate ....*Drymobius*

21. Number of dorsal scale rows at midbody greater than at one head length anterior to vent
    ....*Dendrophidion* (part)
    Number of dorsal scale rows at midbody not greater than at one head length anterior to vent
    ....*Storeria*

Usually eight supralabials; two of which border eye; adults less than 1,200 mm SVL . . . .
. . . . *Coluber* (part)

45. Extremely slender snakes with narrow heads and acuminate snouts (Figs. 175, 176) . . . .
. . . . *Oxybelis* (part)
Not extremely slender, head not notably narrow, snout not acuminate. 46

46. Seven supralabial scales; single apical pit present on dorsal scales . . . . *Masticophis* (part)
Eight supralabials; no apical pits on dorsal scales . . . . *Coniophanes* (part)

47. Pattern of red, black, and yellow (or white) bands or rings, at least anteriorly. 48
Pattern of dark spots, blotches, or bands; or striped or monochrome 49

48. Bands present only on anterior portion of body; posterior portion with longitudinal rows of
dots . . . . *Scaphiodontophis*
Rings present all along body length . . . . *Urotheca*

49. Extremely slender snakes with broad heads and bulging eyes; more than 180 ventral scales
. . . . *Imantodes*
Moderately slender snakes, head not notably broad, eyes not bulging; fewer than 180 ventral
scales. . . . . *Amastridium*

Clave para los Géneros de la Familia Colubridae

1. Escamas quilladas, por lo menos débilmente, en las hileras vertebral y paravertebral 2
Todas las escamas dorsales lisas 22

2. Escamas dorsales dispuestas en hileras pares a mitad del cuerpo. . . . . *Spilotes*
Escamas dorsales dispuestas en hileras impares a mitad del cuerpo 3

3. Veintiún o más hileras de escamas sorsales a mitad del cuerpo 4
Menos de 21 hileras de escamas dorsales a mitad del cuerpo. 9

4. Treintaiún o más hileras de escamas dorsales a mitad del cuerpo 5
Menos de 31 hileras de escamas dorsales a mitad del cuerpo. 7

5. Escamas dorsales y laterales fuertemente quilladas . . . . *Nerodia* (en parte)
Escamas dorsales quilladas, escamas laterales lisas. 6

6. Usualmente 8 escamas supralabiales, 2 en contacto con la órbita (Fig. 152A); usualmente
más de 45 manchas en el cuerpo . . . . *Senticolis*
Usualmente 9 o 10 escamas supralabiales, 3 en contacto con la órbita (Fig. 152B); usualmente menos de 45 manchas en el cuerpo. . . . . *Elaphe*

7. Escamas dorsales débilmente quilladas, escamas laterales lisas; escamas dorsales en 21 o 25
hileras a mitad del cuerpo; placa anal completa . . . . *Pseustes*
Escamas dorsales y laterales fuertemente quilladas; placa anal dividida 8

8. Escamas dorsales en 21 hileras mediodorsales . . . . *Tretanorhinus* (en parte)
Escamas dorsales en 27 hileras a mitad del cuerpo (raramente 25 o 31) . . . *Nerodia* (en parte)

9. Escamas dorsales en 15 hileras a mitad del cuerpo. . . . . *Leptophis*
Escamas dorsales en 17 o 19 hileras a mitad del cuerpo 10

10. Escamas dorsales en 17 hileras a mitad del cuerpo 11
Escamas dorsales en 19 hileras a mitad del cuerpo 14

11. Placa anal sin dividir 12
Placa anal dividida 17

12. Por lo menos una escama supralabial en contacto con la escama parietal (Fig. 152E) . . . .
. . . . *Geophis*
Las escamas supralabiales no están en contacto con la escama parietal 13

13. Escamas dorsales débilmente quilladas, escamas laterales lisas . . . . *Sibon*
Escamas dorsales y laterales fuertemente quilladas . . . . *Dendrophidion* (en parte)

14. Escamas dorsales quilladas, escamas laterales lisas 15
Escamas dorsales y laterales quilladas 16

15. Placa anal dividida . . . . *Tretanorhinus* (en parte)
Placa anal completa. . . . . *Pseustes*

16. Con un collar nucal claro (puede estar interrumpido medialmente, Fig. 174) . . . .
    . . . . *Ninia* (en parte)
    Sin collar nucal claro. . . . . *Thamnophis*

17. Dorso predominantemente rojo o pardo rojizo; presentan collar nucal claro . . . .
    . . . . *Ninia* (en parte)
    Dorso ni rojo ni pardo rojizo; sin collar nucal claro 18

18. Escamas dorsales débilmente quilladas, escamas laterales lisas. 19
    Escamas dorsales y laterales fuertemente quilladas 21

19. Serpientes pequeñas, menores a 350 mm de LHC; con un par de manchas o rayas post-
    oculares claras (Fig. 177) . . . . *Rhadinaea*
    Serpientes grandes, mayores a 350 mm de LHC; sin manchas o líneas postoculares claras
    20

20. Serpientes extremadamente delgadas con cabeza angosta y hocico acuminado (Figs. 175,
    176) . . . . *Oxybelis* (en parte)
    Serpientes no muy delgadas, cabeza no muy angosta, hocico no muy acuminado . . . .
    . . . . *Drymobius*

21. Número de hileras de escamas dorsales a mitad del cuerpo mayor que a una cabeza de
    longitud antes de la cloaca. . . . . *Dendrophidion* (en parte)
    Número de hileras de escamas dorsales a mitad del cuerpo no mayor que a una cabeza de
    longitud antes de la cloaca . . . . *Storeria*

22. Escamas dorsales en 21 o más hileras a mitad del cuerpo. 23
    Escamas dorsales en menos de 21 hileras a mitad del cuerpo 25

23. Placa anal no dividida . . . . *Lampropeltis*
    Placa anal dividida 24

24. Pupila verticalmente elíptica; patrón de coloración dorsal en una serie de manchas obscuras,
    bandas, o puntos . . . . *Leptodeira*
    Pupila redonda; patrón de coloración dorsal de líneas claras u obscuras, o de un solo color
    . . . . *Coniophanes* (en parte)

25. Escamas dorsales en 19 hileras a mitad del cuerpo 26
    Escamas dorsales en menos de 19 hileras a mitad del cuerpo 30

26. Placa anal no divida 27
    Placa anal dividida 29

27. Patrón de coloración dorsal en una serie de bandas alternadas claras y obscuras . . . .
    . . . . *Oxyrhopus*
    Patrón de coloración dorsal sin bandas alternadas. 28

28. Patrón de coloración dorsal uniformemente negro, o rojo con una mancha obscura en el
    cuello, y un collar crema, blanco, o amarillo . . . . *Clelia* (en parte)
    Patrón dorsal de bandas irregulares pardas, manchas o manchones. . . . . *Xenodon*

29. Una sola escama temporal anterior (Fig. 152D) . . . . *Coniophanes* (en parte)
    Más de una escama temporal anterior (Fig. 152C) . . . . *Conophis*

30. Escamas dorsales en 17 hileras a mitad del cuerpo 37
    Escamas dorsales en 15 hileras a mitad del cuerpo 31

31. Placa anal no dividida. 32
    Placa anal dividida 33

32. Surco mental distintivo (Fig. 153A) . . . . *Sibon*
    Sin surco mental (Fig. 153C). . . . . *Dipsas*

33. Una escama subocular entre el ojo y las supralabiales (Fig. 158) . . . . *Coluber* (en parte)
    Sin escama subocular entre el ojo y las supralabiales 34

34. Escamas dorsales con un poro apical. . . . . *Symphimus*
    Escamas dorsales sin poro apical 35

35. Escudos gulares no grandemente expandidos; tercera infralabial no reducida o ausente 36
    Escudos gulares grandemente expandidos; tercera infralabial reducida o ausente (Fig. 153B)
    . . . . *Adelphicos*

Genus *Adelphicos*

This small, morphologically rather homogeneous group of semifossorial snakes is found only in southern Mexico and northern Central America. Most species inhabit pine-oak and cloud forests in the highlands of Chiapas and Guatemala. H. M. Smith (1942b) provided the first comprehensive review of the genus, and J. A. Campbell and Ford (1982) reviewed the species found in the highlands of Middle America. They recognized five species, and J. A. Campbell and Brodie (1988) brought the total to six with the description of *A. ibarrorum*. One species of

Adelphicos occurs in the Yucatán Peninsula. *Adelphicos* is from the Greek *adelphos*, "brother," and *-icos*, a suffix denoting relation—i.e., "brotherly."

Adelphicos quadrivirgatus Jan
(Figs. 153B, 155; Map 113)

Adelphicos quadrivirgatum Jan, 1862:18. TYPE: unknown, but presumably in the Milan Museum. TYPE LOCALITY: Mexico; restricted to Jicaltepec, Veracruz, Mexico, by H. M. Smith and Taylor (1950b:348).

Culebra zacatera (Mexico); tzinkan (Lacandón Maya).

DESCRIPTION   The adults of this small snake average between 280 and 300 mm in snout-vent length; the maximum length is about 320 mm. The tail is relatively short, approximately 15 to 20 percent of the head and body length. In dorsal view the small head is scarcely distinct from the neck and the snout is rather pointed (Fig. 155). The eyes are small and have round pupils. The dorsal scales are smooth, lack apical pits, and are arranged in 15 rows at midbody. The anterior chin shields are greatly enlarged, and the third infralabial scale is reduced or absent (Fig. 153B). The anal plate is divided.

The dorsal ground color is tan, yellowish tan, gray, or reddish, with a series of dark longitudinal stripes. The pair of dorsal-lateral stripes generally involves scale rows 4, 5, and 6, and the lateral stripes, which are typically less distinct, involve scale rows 1, 2, and 3. The ventral coloration is variable, ranging from immaculate tan or gray to heavily pigmented with dark spots and flecks. Some specimens have an indistinct median row of dark markings that become more distinct on the undersurface of the tail.

SIMILAR SPECIES   The various species of *Coniophanes* have more than 15 rows of scales at midbody. *Rhadinaea decorata* has weakly keeled dorsal scales, and *Geophis carinosis* has heavily keeled dorsal scales. *Tantilla* and *Tantillita* lack the greatly enlarged chin shields of *Adelphicos*.

DISTRIBUTION   *Adelphicos quadrivirgatus* occurs at low and moderate elevations on the Atlantic slope from central Veracruz through Guatemala and Belize to northern Honduras, and at moderate elevations on the Pacific slope in eastern Chiapas and

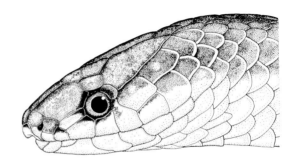

Fig. 155. Lateral view of the head of *Adelphicos quadrivirgatus* (FMNH 49359), 150 mm SVL; Silk Grass, Stann Creek, Belize.

western Guatemala. It occurs through the base of the Yucatán Peninsula (Map 113).

NATURAL HISTORY   This snake is a secretive inhabitant of humid forests at low and moderate elevations. Stuart (1948:78) considered this species a cloud forest and pine belt inhabitant in Alta Verapaz, and he reported finding specimens in the rubbish from sugarcane fields. H. M. Smith (1943:396) found a specimen in a rotting log near Palenque, Chiapas, and Stuart (1958:25) found one beneath rotting vegetation at the edge of the aguada at Tikal, El Petén. Landy et al. (1966:94) encountered this species in leaf litter from coffee fields and at the bases of large trees in Chiapas.

On coffee fincas in southern Chiapas and nearby Guatemala this species preys exclusively on earthworms (Seib, 1985a:27). Landy et al. (1966:94) also

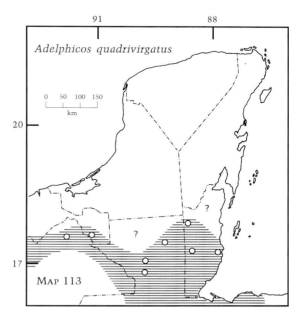

Map 113

found earthworms in the stomachs of specimens from Chiapas. These small snakes are themselves the prey of other snakes, including *Coniophanes fissidens* (Seib, 1985a:27) and the indigo snake, *Drymarchon corais* (Greene, 1975:479).

Adelphicos quadrivirgatus is oviparous. Pérez-Higareda and Smith (1989:5) found a clutch of three eggs in a termite nest in southern Veracruz in June. The termite nest was 1 to 1.5 m above the ground, and the eggs were about 10 cm from the surface of the nest. One of the three eggs hatched two weeks later. The hatchling measured 86 mm.

SUBSPECIES   Of the three subspecies recognized by J. A. Peters and Orejas-Miranda (1970:15), only *A. q. visoninus* occurs in the Yucatán Peninsula.

ETYMOLOGY   The specific name, *quadrivirgatus*, is from the Latin *quadrus*, "fourfold," and *virgatus*, "striped," in reference to the striped dorsum.

Locality Records Belize: Cayo: 16.1 km N Augustine (UF 60685); Orange Walk: Gallon Jug (FMNH 69230); Stann Creek: Silk Grass (FMNH 49359); no specific locality (USNM 24899). *Guatemala*: El Petén: La Libertad (UMMZ 74887, 117909), Sayaxché (UCM 22317), Tikal (UF 13809–10; UMMZ 117909). *Mexico*: Chiapas: Palenque, San Juanito (USNM 109706); Tabasco: Tenosique (H. M. Smith and Taylor, 1945:31).

Genus *Amastridrium*

This small genus of seemingly rare snakes is restricted to Middle America. Two species were long recognized, but Wilson and Meyer (1969) concluded that the genus is monotypic. *Amastridium* is from the Greek *master*, "searcher," and *-idium*, a diminutive suffix. L. D. Wilson (1988) suggested that Cope may have intended the *a-* to serve as an intensifier.

Amastridium veliferum Cope
(Fig. 348; Map 114)

Amastridium veliferum Cope, 1861a:370. HOLOTYPE: ANSP 3738. TYPE LOCALITY: Cocuyas de Veraguas, N Grenada (= Cocuyas, Panama).

Rusty-headed snake; culebra zacatera (Mexico).

DESCRIPTION   This is a small, moderately slender snake. The head is notably distinct from the neck, and the eyes are relatively small with round pupils (Fig. 348). The snout-vent length averages between 300 and 320 mm, and the tail is roughly 28 to 32 percent of the snout-vent length. The maximum total length recorded is 724 mm (L. D. Wilson, 1988b:449.1). The dorsal scales are smooth (males have supra-anal tubercles) and are arranged in 17 rows at midbody. Paired apical pits are present on the dorsal scales of the anterior third of the body but indistinct or absent posteriorly. The anal plate is divided.

The dorsal ground color is dark brown or gray with little or no pattern. Some specimens have a series of small white spots on scale row 5 every four to five scales. The venter is grayish brown, lighter anteriorly. The head is generally lighter brown or gray with a series of longitudinal dark lines on the dorsum and lateral surfaces posterior to the eye.

SIMILAR SPECIES   The species of *Dendrophidion* have heavily keeled dorsal scales, and the *Coniophanes* species sympatric with *Amastridium* have more than 17 rows of scales at midbody.

DISTRIBUTION   This species occurs on the Atlantic slope from Nuevo Leon and Tamaulipas and on the Pacific slope from Oaxaca through Chiapas, northern Guatemala, and Honduras, south to Panama. In the Yucatán Peninsula the species is restricted to the base of the peninsula (Map 114).

NATURAL HISTORY   This rare snake is apparently a terrestrial forest dweller. H. M. Smith (1943:397) mentioned a specimen from Chiapas that was found

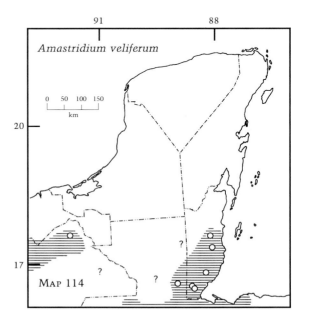

"hidden in gravel through (not over) which water trickled." At a Honduran cafetal, L. D. Wilson and Meyer (1969) collected two specimens that had fallen into pits dug in connection with road construction. *Amastridium veliferum* is diurnal, at least during some parts of the year, for Blaney and Blaney (1978b:692) found a specimen crawling in moist leaf litter during the morning hours in northern Chiapas. In southern Belize, S. G. Tilley (pers. comm.) found a specimen abroad during the day on the forest floor, and Hoevers and Henderson (1974:1) reported finding one "actively prowling inside of an empty hut at 1300 hrs."

Little is known of the diet. Martin (1955:178) reported frogs of the genus *Eleutherodactylus* in the stomachs of specimens from Tamaulipas, and Blaney and Blaney (1978b:692) found a small frog in the stomach of a specimen from northern Chiapas. Nothing is known about reproduction in *Amastridium*.

SUBSPECIES In their review of *Amastridium*, L. D. Wilson and Meyer (1969) considered the genus monotypic, although previous authors recognized a northern form, *A. sapperi*, and a southern one, *A. veliferum*. H. M. Smith (1971) and H. M. Smith and Smith (1976a) argued for subspecific recognition of the northern and southern segments, a treatment that was rejected by L. D. Wilson and Meyer (1985:30) and L. D. Wilson (1988b). If subspecies were recognized, the trinomial *A. s. sapperi* would apply to the snakes in the Yucatán Peninsula.

ETYMOLOGY The specific name, *veliferum*, is from the Latin *velifer*, meaning "carrying a sail" or "bearing a veil," perhaps in reference to the pattern on the head (L. D. Wilson, 1988b).

COMMENT *Amastridium veliferum* was reviewed by L. D. Wilson and Meyer (1969) and L. D. Wilson (1988b).

Locality Records *Belize*: Cayo: 15 mi E Belmopan (MCZ 150246); Stann Creek: Middlesex (UCM 30899); Toledo: Blue Creek Village (SGT photo), Columbia Forest Reserve (CM 105854), Medina Bank (MPM 6734). *Guatemala*: El Petén: Las Cañas (CM 58272). *Mexico*: Chiapas: 15 to 24 km SE Palenque (LSUMZ 33310), 21 km SE Palenque (LSUMZ 33311).

Genus *Clelia*

These large, smooth-scaled, predominantly ophiophagous snakes of the New World tropics range from southern Mexico to Amazonian South America. Enlarged, grooved fangs are present on the posterior margin of the maxillary bone. According to the most recent taxonomic arrangement, the genus has at least six species, two of which occur in the Yucatán Peninsula (J. R. Bailey, 1970). *Clelia* may derive from the Greek *kloios*, "collar," possibly in reference to the light nuchal band borne by juveniles of this genus.

Key to the Species of the Genus *Clelia*

Dorsal scales in 17 rows at midbody . . . . *Clelia scytalina*
Dorsal scales in 19 rows at midbody. . . . . *Clelia clelia*

Clave para las Especies del Género *Clelia*

Escamas dorsales en 17 hileras a mitad del cuerpo. . . . . *Clelia scytalina*
Escamas dorsales en 19 hileras a mitad del cuerpo . . . . *Clelia clelia*

Clelia clelia (Daudin)
(Fig. 156; Map 115)

Coluber clelia Daudin, 1803:330. SYNTYPES: originally two syntypes, now apparently lost, *fide* H. M. Smith and Taylor, 1945:36. TYPE LOCALITY: Surinam en Amérique.

Mussurana, zopilota (Belize); sumbadora (Guatemala); culebrera (Mexico).

DESCRIPTION This large snake attains a snout-vent length of at least 2,000 mm. The tail length is approximately 25 to 30 percent of the snout-vent length. The head is moderately distinct from the

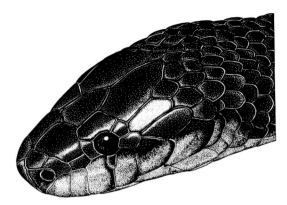

Fig. 156. Dorsolateral view of the head of *Clelia clelia*. Adapted from Lancini, 1986.

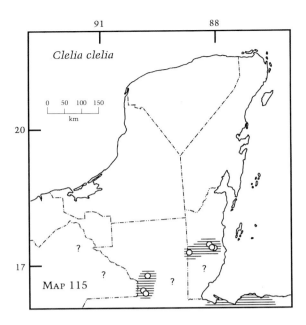

neck, the eyes are relatively small, and the pupils are subcircular (Fig. 156). The dorsal scales are smooth and are arranged in 19 rows at midbody; some bear weakly developed apical pits. The anal plate is undivided.

These snakes undergo a dramatic color change with age. The body and tail are bright red above in young snakes, and the scales are tipped with dark pigment on their trailing edges. The ventral coloration is immaculate white, cream, or light gray. The head and neck are black, and a broad white, cream, or yellow band runs across the posterior half of the head. In contrast, the adults are uniform black or dark gray above and white or light gray below, although dark pigment may extend onto the lateral edges of the ventral scales and the subcaudal scales may be suffused with dark pigment.

SIMILAR SPECIES *Clelia clelia* closely resembles its congener, *C. scytalina*, but differs in possessing 19 rather than 17 rows of dorsal scales at midbody. *Drymarchon corais* has 17 rows of dorsal scales at midbody and is generally tan or brown on the anterior half of the body. *Clelia clelia* juveniles closely resemble the red-bodied *Micrurus diastema* of Yucatán and northern Quintana Roo, but *Micrurus* lacks a loreal scale and has 15 rows of dorsal scales at midbody.

DISTRIBUTION *Clelia clelia* has a wide range in the New World tropics, but the details of its distribution in southeastern Mexico and northern Central America are obscure owing to confusion between this species and *C. scytalina* (H. M. Smith and Pérez-Higareda, 1989:8). *Clelia clelia* apparently occurs at low and moderate elevations on the Atlantic slope from northern Guatemala and Belize

southward through Central America to Uruguay and Argentina. In the Yucatán Peninsula it is known from Belize and southern El Petén (Map 115).

NATURAL HISTORY This large snake is a rare terrestrial inhabitant of humid lowland forests in the Yucatán Peninsula, where it is both diurnal and nocturnal. Duellman (1963:237) found a specimen in a pool of water in a forest in southern El Petén, W. T. Neill (1965:100) observed a specimen abroad by day on the forest floor in Belize, and I found a specimen crossing a road at night in Tabasco. *Clelia clelia* feeds on snakes, lizards, and mammals, and it is one of the few rear-fanged species that employ constriction as well as envenomation to subdue their prey. Scott (1983a:392) mentioned that in Costa Rica this species feeds on the fer-de-lance (*Bothrops asper*). Sexton and Heatwole (1965:40) found a *Cnemidophorus* lizard in the stomach of a specimen from Panama, and Duellman (1978:236) reported a snake (*Leimadophis reginae*), a lizard (*Ameiva ameiva*), and an unidentified rodent in the diet in the upper Amazon Basin of Ecuador.

Clelia clelia is oviparous. A female collected in El Petén contained 22 eggs (Duellman, 1963:237), and a female from the upper Amazon Basin of Ecuador collected in May had 20 immature ovarian eggs (Duellman 1978:236). Martínez and Cerdas (1986:12) described courtship, mating, and oviposition in captives from Costa Rica. A clutch of 10 eggs was produced in January, 47 days after copulation. The eggs averaged 61 mm long and 35 mm wide, and they hatched between 6 and 9 May after an incubation period of 117 to 120 days.

ETYMOLOGY The specific name, *clelia*, is a tautonym of the generic name, which may possibly derive from the Greek *kloios*, "collar," perhaps referring to the light nuchal collar of juveniles.

COMMENT *Clelia clelia* is listed in Appendix 2 of the Convention on International Trade in Endangered Species of Wild Flora and Fauna.

Locality Records Belize: Cayo: 6 mi SSE Cayo (W. T. Neill, 1965:100); Stann Creek: Middlesex (FMNH 4448), Sibun River at Hummingbird Hwy. (UF 24546), 23.9 mi W Stann Creek (KU 157550). *Guatemala*: El Petén: 15 km NNW Chinajá (KU 58167), 20 km NNW Chinajá (KU 55710), Sayaxché (UCM 22318).

Clelia scytalina (Cope)
(Fig. 157; Map 116)

Scolecophis scytalinus Cope, 1867:320. HOLOTYPE: USNM 6581. TYPE LOCALITY: near Tabasco, Mexico.

Mussurana (Belize).

DESCRIPTION This is a large, moderately slender snake. The adults probably average between 1 and 1.5 m in snout-vent length, but there are too few specimens from the Yucatán Peninsula to accurately estimate size there. The head is moderately distinct from the neck, the eyes are relatively small, and the pupils are subcircular (Fig. 157). The dorsal scales are smooth and arranged in 17 rows at midbody. The anal plate is undivided.

Like its congener, *C. scytalina* exhibits a dramatic ontogenetic change in color and pattern. The adults are shiny blue-black above and off-white below. The juveniles are uniformly pale red above with black pigment on the trailing edges of the dorsal scales. The venter is white. The snout is black, followed by a broad yellow band on the posterior surface of the head. This is followed by a black band that gradually merges with the red pigmentation on the neck.

SIMILAR SPECIES *Clelia scytalina* closely resembles its congener, *C. clelia*, but differs in possessing 17 rows of dorsal scales at midbody rather than 19. The juveniles may be mistaken for *Micrurus diastema* from the northern Yucatán Peninsula, which sometimes have a uniformly red body. *Micrurus diastema* has 15 rows of scales at midbody, however, and lacks a loreal scale.

DISTRIBUTION The distribution of this uncommon snake is apparently highly disjunct, although it is not well understood. It occurs at low elevations on the Atlantic slope in Veracruz, Tabasco, and Belize, and on the Pacific slope from Jalisco and Colima (H. M. Smith and Pérez-Higareda, 1989:8) to

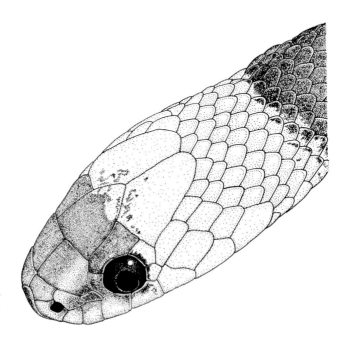

Fig. 157. Lateral view of the head of a juvenile *Clelia scytalina*, 480 mm SVL; Costa Rica.

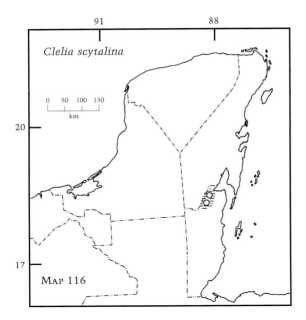

Map 116

Clelia scytalina

Genus *Coluber*

This large genus of nonvenomous snakes is restricted to the Northern Hemisphere, where it is well represented in both the Old World and the New. Representatives occur throughout most of the United States and Mexico, and south to northern Guatemala and Belize. In the Old World the genus ranges throughout central and southern Europe and the northern half of Africa, eastward through much of Asia and India to northern China and Korea. In general these are rather slender, quick-moving diurnal snakes of medium to large size. Schätti and Wilson (1986) recognized 34 living species, and many more fossil forms have been described. One species occurs in North and Central America, including the Yucatán Peninsula. *Coluber* is Latin for "snake" or "serpent."

Costa Rica. In the Yucatán Peninsula the species is known only from northern Belize (Map 116).

NATURAL HISTORY Nothing of substance is known concerning the natural history of this species. Hoevers and Henderson (1974:2) reported a specimen collected at night on the bank of the New River in Orange Walk District. Scott (1983a:392) mentioned that in Costa Rica this species occurs at higher elevations than *C. clelia*, but in the Yucatán Peninsula it appears to be a terrestrial inhabitant of lowland forests.

ETYMOLOGY The specific name, *scytalina*, is from the Greek diminutive of *skytale*, meaning "staff, club, cylinder"—or "a serpent of uniform roundness and thickness."

Locality Records Belize: Corozal: 2 mi N San Pablo (MPM 8183); Orange Walk: New River near Orange Walk Town (Hoevers and Henderson, 1974:2).

Coluber constrictor Linnaeus
(Fig. 158; Map 117)

Coluber constrictor Linnaeus, 1758:216. TYPE: none designated. TYPE LOCALITY: America septentrionale; restricted to Canada by Schmidt (1953:186).

Racer, Oaxaca racer.

DESCRIPTION The adults of this medium-sized, slender snake average between 450 and 500 mm in snout-vent length. The tail is long, approximately 35 to 40 percent of the head and body length. The head is moderately distinct from the neck, the eyes are large, and the pupils are round (Fig. 158). A small subocular scale is present below the preocular scale. There are usually 15 rows of smooth scales at midbody, and apical pits are present. The anal plate is divided.

This species exhibits marked ontogenetic variation in color pattern. The adults are a uniform greenish gray to olive above and yellowish to yel-

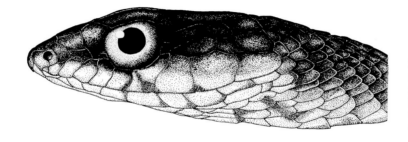

Fig. 158. Lateral view of the head of *Coluber constrictor* (CM 111932), 604 mm SVL; 6 mi S Belmopan, Cayo, Belize. Note the small subocular scale between the preocular and supralabial scales.

lowish green below, whereas the juveniles have a series of dark blotches against a lighter gray or olive background.

SIMILAR SPECIES   *Dryadophis melanolomus* lacks a small subocular scale below the preocular scale. *Masticophis mentovarius*, a larger snake, typically has seven supralabial scales and 17 rows of dorsal scales at midbody, whereas *C. constrictor* typically has eight supralabials and 15 rows of dorsal scales at midbody.

DISTRIBUTION   *Coluber constrictor* is widely distributed throughout North America from southern Canada and the northern tier of the United States south through much of Mexico to northern Guatemala and Belize. In the Yucatán Peninsula it is known from only a few records from the base of the peninsula (Map 117).

NATURAL HISTORY   Little is known of the habits of this species in the Yucatán Peninsula. Apparently it prefers savannas and other open habitats, for it is known from the La Libertad savannas of El Petén and the open parklike areas of the Mountain Pine Ridge in Belize. Presumably this form is diurnal, terrestrial, and, perhaps, semiarboreal, as it is elsewhere.

Nothing is known of the diet in the Yucatán Peninsula. Populations in southern Texas eat insects, lizards, frogs, and rodents (A. H. Wright and Wright, 1957:151).

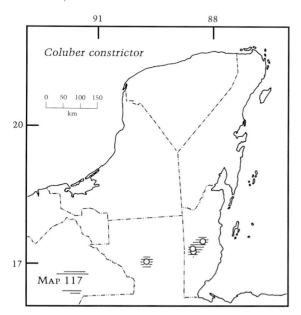

MAP 117

Coluber constrictor is oviparous. A specimen collected on 10 April near Augustine, Cayo District, contained 2 oviductal eggs (Hoevers and Henderson, 1974:2), far fewer than the average clutch size of this species at higher latitudes (5 to 16) (Fitch, 1970:127).

SUBSPECIES   L. D. Wilson (1978) recognized eight subspecies, of which only *C. c. oaxaca* occurs in the Yucatán Peninsula.

ETYMOLOGY   The specific name, *constrictor*, is Latin for "something that constricts," reflecting the mistaken notion that this species employs constriction to overpower its prey.

COMMENT   L. D. Wilson (1966) reviewed the Mexican populations of *C. constrictor* and the status of the species in northern Guatemala. The species as a whole is reviewed in L. D. Wilson, 1978.

Locality Records Belize: Cayo: just S Augustine (MPM 6735–36, 8186), 3 mi N, 2 mi E Augustine (JLK 484), 6 mi S Belmopan (CM 111932), rd. to Thousand Foot Falls (CM 105961). *Guatemala*: El Petén: 3 mi W La Libertad (UMMZ 75588).

Genus *Coniophanes*
(Black-striped Snakes)

These small to medium-sized snakes are terrestrial and largely nocturnal. They are rear-fanged and generally inoffensive, although a bite can produce local irritation and discomfort. This essentially Neotropical genus has 12 species distributed from southern Texas to Pacific Ecuador and Peru. Many, perhaps all, species of *Coniophanes* have fragile tails that are easily broken. Presumably this represents an antipredator strategy (Greene, 1973; Mendelson, 1991; Zug et al., 1979), and there is evidence that it is sometimes successful, for the tails of *Coniophanes* have been found in the stomachs of coral snakes (Schmidt, 1932:7). Six species of *Coniophanes* occur in the Yucatán Peninsula; two are endemic to the area. The most recent comprehensive taxonomic treatment of the genus is J. R. Bailey, 1939. McCoy (1969) reviewed the species of *Coniophanes* occurring in the Yucatán Peninsula. *Coniophanes* is from the Greek *konios*, "dusty," and *phanos*, "light," "bright," or "conspicuous."

Key to the Species of the Genus *Coniophanes*

1. Dorsal scales arranged in 17 rows at midbody . . . . *Coniophanes meridanus*
   Dorsal scales arranged in 19 or more rows at midbody 2
2. Dorsal scales arranged in 23 or more rows at midbody . . . . *Coniophanes schmidti*
   Dorsal scales arranged in fewer than 23 rows at midbody 3
3. Dorsal scales arranged in 19 rows at midbody. . . . . *Coniophanes imperialis*
   Dorsal scales arranged in 21 rows at midbody. 4
4. Each ventral scale with two large, dark, rounded spots at the lateral edges 5
   Ventral scales with small, dark dots or flecks, or immaculate; no large, dark, rounded spots
   . . . . *Coniophanes fissidens*
5. More than 150 ventral scales; chin scales spotted with dark pigment (Fig. 162) . . . .
   . . . . *Coniophanes quinquevittatus*
   Fewer than 150 ventral scales; chin scales not spotted, but edged with dark pigment (Fig. 159)
   . . . . *Coniophanes bipunctatus*

Clave para las Especies del Género *Coniophanes*

1. Escamas dorsales dispuestas en 17 hileras a mitad del cuerpo . . . . . . *Coniophanes meridanus*
   Escamas dorsales dispuestas en 19 o más hileras a mitad del cuerpo. 2
2. Escamas dorsales en 23 o más hileras a mitad del cuerpo . . . . *Coniophanes schmidti*
   Escamas dorsales en menos de 23 hileras a mitad del cuerpo. 3
3. Escamas dorsales en 19 hileras a mitad del cuerpo. . . . . *Coniophanes imperialis*
   Escamas dorsales en 21 hileras a mitad del cuerpo. 4
4. Cada escama ventral tiene dos manchas grandes, redondas, y obscuras en los extremos
   laterales 5
   Escamas ventrales con pequeñas manchas o puntos obscuros, o inmaculadas; sin manchas
   redondeadas grandes . . . . *Coniophanes fissidens*
5. Más de 150 escamas ventrales; escamas de la barba manchadas con un pigmento obscuro
   (Fig. 162). . . . . *Coniophanes quinquevittatus*
   Menos de 150 escamas ventrales; escamas de la barba sin manchas, pero los márgenes con un
   pigmento obscuro (Fig. 159). . . . . *Coniophanes bipunctatus*

Coniophanes bipunctatus (Günther)
(Fig. 159; Map 118)

Coronella bipunctata Günther, 1858:36. HOLO-
TYPE: BMNH 1946.1.9.58. TYPE LOCALITY: unknown, *fide* J. R. Bailey, 1939:24. Schmidt (1941:504)
suggested that the type probably came from Belize.

Two-spotted snake (Belize); culebra de agua, taba-
quilla (Mexico).

DESCRIPTION This medium-sized snake is large
for a *Coniophanes*, attaining an average snout-vent
length of between 500 and 550 mm and a tail length
approximately 35 to 40 percent of the snout-vent
length. The head is moderately distinct from the
neck, the eyes are relatively large, and the pupils are
round. The dorsal scales are smooth, lack apical

pits, and are usually arranged in 21 rows at midbody. The anal plate is divided.

The dorsal ground color is dark brown, sometimes with a reddish cast. There is a pair of dark
lateral stripes on scale rows 3, 4, and 5, and a dark
middorsal stripe on the vertebral row. The venter is
cream, tan, or yellowish orange, with a pair of dark
brown or black spots on each ventral scale.

SIMILAR SPECIES This species closely resembles
C. quinquevittatus, from which it differs in having fewer than 150 ventral scales and the chin and
throat scales bordered with dark pigment (Fig. 159)
rather than distinctly spotted.

DISTRIBUTION *Coniophanes bipunctatus* occurs at low elevations on the Atlantic slope from
southern Veracruz southward to Panama, includ-

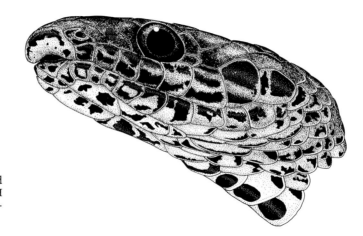

Fig. 159. Ventrolateral view of the head of *Coniophanes bipunctatus* (FMNH 36319), 303 mm SVL; Pacaitún, Campeche, Mexico.

ing the Bay Islands of Honduras. It is distributed through the base of the Yucatán Peninsula, extending northward in Quintana Roo. Apparently disjunct populations occur in northwestern Yucatán and northern Campeche (Map 118).

NATURAL HISTORY   In the Yucatán Peninsula this species is an uncommon inhabitant of moist lowland forests and, especially, swampy areas, but it has also been taken in the ciénega along the northwest coast of Yucatán. The holotype of *C. b. biseriatus*, collected in Palenque, was found in a grassy ravine under a log partially submerged in moist soil near the exit of a spring (H. M. Smith, 1940:60). H. M. Smith (1943:405) mentioned two specimens from Tenosique, Tabasco, that were obtained at night along a cart road shortly after a

heavy rain. Duellman (1963:238) found a specimen abroad during the day on the forest floor in Alta Verapaz. Little is known about what these snakes eat, but Alvarez del Toro (1983:157) suggested that the diet includes frogs.

Coniophanes bipunctatus is oviparous. H. M. Smith (1940:60) found a clutch of five eggs in a rotten stump on the bank of a stream in Chiapas on 20 July.

SUBSPECIES   H. M. Smith (1940:60) recognized two subspecies on the basis of color pattern and subcaudal scale counts. Specimens from central Veracruz to north-central Chiapas and western Campeche he assigned to *C. b. biseriatus*; all others he referred to the nominate subspecies, *C. b. bipunctatus*. Conant (1965:10) and L. D. Wilson and Meyer (1985:35) questioned the validity of this arrangement and pointed out that variation in this form is poorly understood.

ETYMOLOGY   The specific name, *bipunctatus*, is from the Latin *bi-*, "two," and *punctatus*, "spotted," in reference to the pair of bold dark spots on each ventral scale.

COMMENT   *Coniophanes bipunctatus* was reviewed by H. M. Smith in 1940, and by McCoy (1969) as part of his review of the *Coniophanes* of the Yucatán Peninsula.

Locality Records   Belize: Belize: Belize (KU 68905; USNM 24902, 26061, 55860), near Belize City (CM 109029), W Belize City (BCB 13410), 40 mi inland (BMNH 1924.2.18.9); Cayo: 3 mi W Georgeville (KU 157552), 31.4 mi S Georgeville (KU 157553); Orange Walk: Gallon Jug (AMNH 70929), Orange Walk (MPM 7309–10), 4 mi Orange Walk (UF 79995), Tower Hill

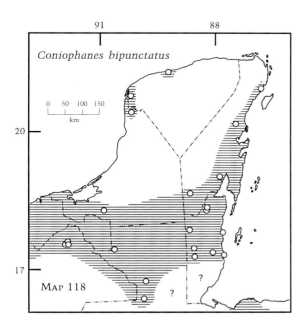

Coniophanes bipunctatus

MAP 118

(MPM 8182); Stann Creek: Middlesex (UCM 25715–16, 25843–44, 29956–57), Stann Creek (BMNH 1890.6.18.1, 1890.10.24.6, 1891.3.4.5); no specific locality (FMNH 4235–37; USNM 24902, 26061, 55860). *Guatemala*: Alta Verapaz: Chinajá (Duellman, 1963:238); El Petén: El Repasto (UCM 22319), Sayaxché (UCM 22320). *Mexico*: Campeche: Pacaitún (FMNH 36317–20), Tankuche–El Remate (IHNHERP 438); Chiapas: 5 km SW Palenque (EAL 3641), bet. Palenque and Palenque ruins (EAL 3324), San Juanito (USNM 108595, 109716–19); Quintana Roo: 68.3 km NE Felipe Carrillo Puerto (KU 171736), Laguna Chacanbacab (CM 45290), Lake Bacalar (LSUMZ 33236), 19 mi N Playa del Carmen (LSUMZ 33237); Yucatán: 13.9 km E Celestún (UMRC 79-304), 19.5 km E Chicxulub Puerto (CM 47956).

Coniophanes fissidens (Günther)
(Fig. 160; Map 119)

Coronella fissidens Günther, 1858:36. SYNTYPES: BMNH 1946.6.1.8.16–21, 1946.1.9.61, and 1946.1.3.2–3 (nine syntypes). TYPE LOCALITY: Mexico and America.

Culebra panza amarilla (Mexico).

DESCRIPTION This moderately small snake averages about 300 mm in snout-vent length, and the tail length is approximately 30 to 35 percent of the snout-vent length. There is little or no sexual dimorphism in body size, although males have slightly longer tails than females (Zug et al., 1979:5), a common condition in snakes. The head is slightly distinct from the neck in dorsal aspect, and the eyes are moderately small with round pupils (Fig. 160). The dorsal scales are smooth, lack apical pits, and are arranged in 21 rows at midbody. The anal plate is divided.

SIMILAR SPECIES *Coniophanes fissidens* most closely resembles *C. imperialis* but differs in possessing 21 rather than 19 rows of dorsal scales at midbody. It differs from *C. bipunctatus* and *C. quinquevittatus* in being smaller and lacking large paired blotches on the ventral scales. *Rhadinaea decorata* has 17 rows of dorsal scales at midbody, some of which are weakly keeled.

DISTRIBUTION *Coniophanes fissidens* occurs at low elevations on the Atlantic slope from southern Veracruz, and at low and moderate elevations on the Pacific slope from Oaxaca, east and south through Central America to Colombia and Ecuador. In the Yucatán Peninsula the species is known from northern Chiapas, El Petén, and Belize (Map 119).

NATURAL HISTORY This secretive, terrestrial snake hides in leaf litter and surface debris in humid lowland forests (Landy et al., 1966:94). The diet appears to be unusually broad. Seib (1985a,b) examined the stomach contents of preserved snakes from Chiapas and Guatemala and sampled live populations at three coffee fincas in southern Chiapas and adjacent Guatemala and found salamanders, frogs and their eggs, lizards, snakes, and reptile eggs. One juvenile had swallowed an earthworm, and another contained a lepidopteran larva. Among the snakes eaten were *Adelphicos quadrivirgatus*, *Ninia sebae*, and a conspecific. *Leptodactylus* frogs also form part of the diet (Minton and Smith, 1960:108; Landy et al., 1966:94).

Coniophanes fissidens is oviparous. Livezey and Peckham (1953:175) reported that a specimen from San Marco, Guatemala, collected in May contained two eggs. Zug et al. (1979) estimated that females attain sexual maturity at a snout-vent length of

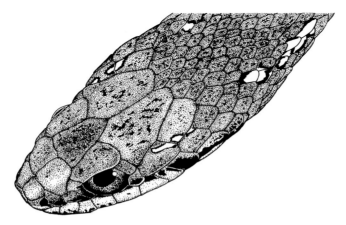

Fig. 160. Dorsolateral view of the head of *Coniophanes fissidens* (UMMZ 80710), 297 mm SVL; Cohune Ridge, Cayo, Belize.

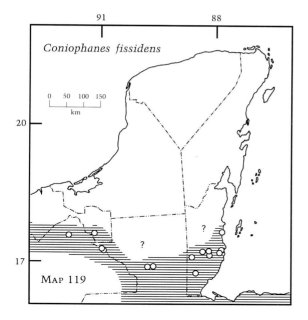

Coniophanes fissidens

MAP 119

about 250 mm and found that clutch size ranged from one to seven (mode = 3) in specimens from various parts of the range.

Like others of its genus, *C. fissidens* has a fragile tail, and individuals with incomplete tails are common (Mendelson, 1992). Zug et al. (1979) reported that 30 percent of the specimens in a sample comprising individuals from throughout the range had broken tails. Presumably the fragile tail represents an antipredator adaptation in which the snake is willing to sacrifice the part to save the whole (Greene, 1973).

SUBSPECIES   The most recent taxonomic treatment of this species is Fisher, 1969, which recognizes six subspecies. The nominate form, *C. f. fissidens*, occurs in the Yucatán Peninsula.

ETYMOLOGY   The specific name, *fissidens*, is derived from the Latin *fissio*, "a cleaving" or "split," and *dens*, "tooth."

Locality Records   Belize: Belize: Manatee (FMNH 5825); Cayo: Cohune Ridge (UMMZ 80710), upper Raspaculo River basin (Stafford, 1991:14); Stann Creek: Bokowina (Schmidt, 1941:504), Double Falls (FMNH 49331–32), N slope Cockscomb Mts. (CM 8485), Silk Grass (Schmidt, 1941:504); Toledo: Unión Camp, Columbia River Forest Reserve (USNM 319774). *Guatemala*: El Petén: 5 mi S Piedras Negras (USNM 109720–21), Piedras Negras (USNM 109722), Sojio (AMNH 69977–78), Toocog (KU 58123). *Mexico*: Chiapas: La-

guna Ocotal (MCZ 53880), Ruinas de Palenque (KU 94129); Tabasco: Tenosique (USNM 109783–84).

Coniophanes imperialis (Baird and Girard)
(Figs. 349, 350; Map 120)

Taeniophis imperialis Baird and Girard, 1859:23, in Baird, 1859. HOLOTYPE: USNM 2060. TYPE LOCALITY: given as Brownsville, Texas, but recorded as Matamoros, Tamaulipas, Mexico, in USNM catalog (D. M. Cochran, 1961:216).

Black-striped snake (Belize); vientre rojo (Guatemala, Mexico); culebra rayada (Mexico); yak'ik'kum (Lacandón Maya).

DESCRIPTION   This is a small to medium-sized, moderately slender snake (Figs. 349, 350). The average snout-vent length in adults is 250 to 300 mm. The tail is moderately long, about 45 percent of the head and body length. The head is slightly distinct from the neck in dorsal aspect, the eyes are moderately large, and the pupils are round. The dorsal scales are smooth, arranged in 19 rows at midbody, and lack apical pits. The anal plate is divided.

The dorsum is predominantly brown. The dark brown lateral surfaces of the body are separated from the lighter brown of the middorsal area by a thin, often indistinct, light line. A dark vertebral stripe usually runs the length of the body. This may be narrow and indistinct. The dorsal surface of the head is dark brown with a white or cream stripe that begins at the tip of the snout and passes through the upper edge of the eye and onto the temporal region. This stripe may be continuous with the light dorsolateral stripe on the body; more commonly it ends on the temporal scales, in which case there is usually a pair of distinct light spots at the base of the head between the terminus of the ocular stripe and the start of the light dorsolateral stripe. In some specimens these spots are continuous with the dorsolateral stripe. The rostrum, labials, chin, and venter are cream or light tan with scattered small dots and flecks of dark pigment. The ventral coloration may become orange, pinkish, or vermillion posteriorly. The dark pigment on the lateral surfaces of the body and tail extends onto the lateral edges of the ventrals and subcaudals.

SIMILAR SPECIES   Only two species of *Coniophanes—C. meridanus* and *C. fissidens*—are likely to be confused with *C. imperalis*. Of these, the for-

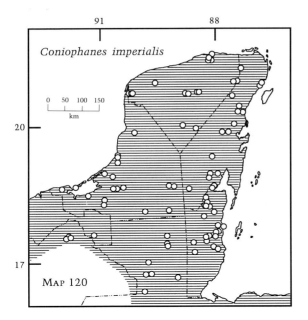

Coniophanes imperialis

MAP 120

mer has but 17 rows of scales at midbody, and the latter has 21 rows of scales at midbody. *Rhadinaea decorata* has 17 rows of scales at midbody, some of which are weakly keeled.

DISTRIBUTION *Coniophanes imperialis* occurs at low and moderate elevations on the Atlantic slope from southern Texas south and eastward through the Yucatán Peninsula to northern Honduras. It is found throughout the Yucatán Peninsula (Map 120).

NATURAL HISTORY This species, the most common *Coniophanes* in the Yucatán Peninsula, is terrestrial and primarily nocturnal. It occupies nearly all habitats within the peninsula. Specimens have been found beneath logs and other surface debris in forests and abroad during the day amid Maya ruins, and they are often encountered on roads at night. This species appears to persist in and around human habitations, for I found individuals beneath debris in yards and vacant lots in villages in Yucatán, and Henderson (1976a:145) reported a specimen found in the business area of Belize City. The adults of this rear-fanged snake are normally inoffensive and rarely bite, although juveniles occasionally do so. B. C. Brown (1939:109) reported that a bite caused burning, itching, swelling, and red discoloration in the region of the fang punctures, and that these symptoms persisted for two to three days. In addition to these symptoms I can personally attest that the bite of small specimens can produce a rather

intense throbbing pain and muscular stiffness that may persist for several days.

Little is known of this snake's diet in the Yucatán Peninsula. Henderson and Hoevers (1977b:352) found insects in the stomachs of specimens from northern Belize. A. H. Wright and Wright (1957:154) reported that captives ate toads. In Chiapas this species feeds on frogs and lizards (Alvarez del Toro, 1983:156), and I saw a specimen swallow a Stauffer's treefrog (*Scinax staufferi*) in Campeche.

Coniophanes imperialis is oviparous. Stuart (1958:24) reported finding a female containing 3 well-developed eggs at Tikal in mid-May. A specimen from Texas laid 5 eggs in early May (Werler, 1949:60). According to Alvarez del Toro (1983:156), in Chiapas this species lays about 10 eggs in the spring.

SUBSPECIES Three subspecies are presently recognized; *C. i. clavatus* occurs in the Yucatán Peninsula.

ETYMOLOGY The specific name, *imperialis*, is Latin for "imperial."

COMMENT McCoy (1969) reviewed *Coniophanes imperialis* as part of his treatment of the *Coniophanes* of the Yucatán Peninsula.

Locality Records Belize: Belize: Belize City (FMNH 4444–45), near Belize City (CM 109030), Belize River (UF 24550), Burrell Boom Rd. at Belize River (CM 105783–85), Grace Bank (UF 79992), 3 mi W Hattiesville (JLK 479), 6 mi SSW Hattiesville (AMNH 104043), near Maskall (JCL photo), Rabaurel Creek near Belize River (AMNH 71384); Cayo: Augustine (CM 105962), Blue Hole (CM 105956), Central Farm (MCZ 71670–71), mi 40 on Western Hwy. (MCZ 150247), mi 64 on Western Hwy. (JLK 481); Corozal: 6 mi N Corozal Town (JLK 480), San Pablo (MPM 7553); Orange Walk: Chan Pine Ridge (MPM 8147), Douglas (MPM 7695), Kate's Lagoon (Schmidt, 1941:505), Lamanai (ROM H12779, H12781), Hector's Creek (AMNH 70930, 71384), Orange Walk (MPM 7314), near Orange Walk (MPM 8148–49), Otro Benque (MPM 7316, 8181), Tower Hill (MPM 7311–13, 7315, 7317–18, 7694, 7733, 8280–81, 10783); Stann Creek: Middlesex (CM 48001–2; UCM 25727, 25734, 25741, 25845, 30840), 1 mi W Pamona (JLK 502), Stann Creek (USNM 50623), Stann Creek Valley (FMNH 49330); no specific locality (FMNH 4238–46; USNM 26064, 26355). *Guatemala*: Alta Verapaz: Chinajá (Duellman, 1963:238); El Petén: El Rosario (JCL sight record), Laguna Rompido (AMNH 99917), La Libertad (FMNH 43368–69; UMMZ 74889–92), 2 mi N Poptún (KU 157555), Sayaxché (UCM

22321–22), Tikal (MCZ 55425; UF 33496; UMMZ 117891–901, 120321; UMRC 89-43), 1.4 mi S Tikal (KU 157556), Uaxactún (UMMZ 70452), no specific locality (USNM 71783). *Mexico*: Campeche: 5 mi W Atasta (UIMNH 87649), Balchacaj (FMNH 105461–63; UIMNH 17610–11), Becan (UWZH 20495, 20516A, 20516B), Champotón (UMMZ 73067), 3.5 mi S Champotón (UCM 18619), 3.9 mi S Champotón (EAL 1659), 15 km S Champotón (KU 70826), 7 km SE Chekubúl (JCL sight record), 2 mi E Chencoyi (UIMNH 87650), Ciudad del Carmen (UCM 16026, 20765–68; UMMZ 83544–45), 79.9 km NE Emiliano Zapata (Tabasco) (EAL 2918), 5 mi W Escárcega (UCM 28120), 13 km W Escárcega (KU 70827), 14.5 km W Escárcega (KU 70828), Laguna Alvarado (KU 74987), Laguna Chumpich (KU 74986), Matamoros (FMNH 36326), Pacaitún (FMNH 36330), Plan de Ayala (JCL photo), 5.6 km SE Sabancuy (JCL sight record), 3.1 km W Xpujil (UMRC 85-16), 8.4 km E Xpujil (UMRC 85-43); Chiapas: Palenque (EAL 3747; UMMZ 126167), 4 km SW Palenque (EAL 3316), San Juanito (USNM 109785); Quintana Roo: Bacalar (LSUMZ 33211, 48401), 10 mi W Bacalar (LSUMZ 33212–15, 34767), 13 mi NW Chetumal (BCB 12295), Cobá (JCL sight record), 17.8 km N Felipe Carrillo Puerto (JCL 6802), 25 km NE Felipe Carrillo Puerto (KU 171738), 53.2 km NW Felipe Carrillo Puerto (JCL 6831), Laguna Chacanbacab (MCZ 53119), 4.5 km NNW Noh Bec (JCL sight record), 10 mi N Playa del Carmen (LSUMZ 33209), Pueblo Nuevo X-Can (CM 45695), 5.8 km S Puerto Morelos (EAL 2859), 20.5 km S Solferino (KU 171739), 4.7 mi S Tulum Pueblo (LSUMZ 38546), 5 mi W Tulum (LSUMZ 33210), 22 km NW Tulum (UMRC 84-46); Tabasco: Tenosique (H. M. Smith and Taylor, 1945:41); Yucatán: Catmís (FMNH 27002), near Catmís (E. W. Andrews, 1937:359), 7.9 km E Celestún (UMRC 84-4), 13 km E Celestún (JCL photo), 15.1 km E Celestún (UMRC 79-279), Chichén Itzá (Gaige, 1936:302), 5 km E Dziuché (CM 45289), Libre Unión (FMNH 36327), Mérida (FMNH 36328), 19.8 km N Panabá (JCL sight record), 22.9 km N Panabá (JCL sight record), 23.7 km N Panabá (JCL sight record), Pisté (CM 46982, 47086–87), Río Lagartos (JCL photo), 14.9 km S Río Lagartos (UMRC 84-2), X-Can (CM 47024), Yokdzonot (FMNH 36328).

Coniophanes meridanus Schmidt and Andrews
(Fig. 161; Map 121)

Coniophanes meridanus Schmidt and Andrews, 1936:179. HOLOTYPE: FMNH 19427. TYPE LOCALITY: Mérida, Yucatán, Mexico.

Culebra lisa peninsular (Mexico).

DESCRIPTION   This is a small to medium-sized, moderately slender snake. The adults average about 250 to 300 mm in snout-vent length; the tail length is about 60 percent of the head and body length. The head is slightly flattened and moderately distinct from the neck in dorsal aspect. The eyes are only moderately large, and the pupils are round (Fig. 161). The dorsal scales are smooth, arranged in 17 rows at midbody, and lack apical pits. The anal plate is divided.

The dorsum is predominantly brown or reddish tan. There may be an indistinct dark vertebral stripe approximately one scale row wide, and a ventrolateral dark stripe may be present on scale rows 3 and 4. These stripes are most distinct anteriorly and become indistinct or disappear altogether posteriorly. The dorsal and lateral surfaces of the head are dark brown. A light ocular stripe runs from the tip of the snout, through the upper edge of the eye, and onto the temporal scales. Some specimens have a pair of light nuchal spots. In others the spots are continuous with the light color of the chin and labial scales, forming a collar interrupted at the midline by dark pigment. The chin and ventral surfaces are light tan or reddish tan with a few small, dark spots anteriorly.

SIMILAR SPECIES   *Coniophanes meridanus* closely resembles *C. imperialis*, with which it is sympatric, but it has 17 rather than 19 rows of scales at midbody; *C. fissidens* has 21 rows of scales

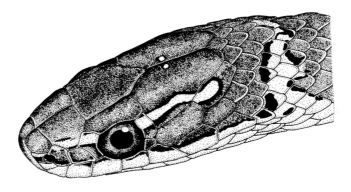

Fig. 161. Dorsolateral view of the head of *Coniophanes meridanus* (FMNH 153581), 218 mm SVL; Dzibilchaltún, Yucatán, Mexico.

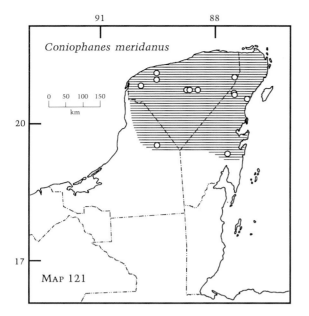

Coniophanes meridanus

MAP 121

at midbody, and its geographic distribution does not overlap that of *C. meridanus. Rhadinaea decorata* has weakly keeled dorsal scales; its geographic distribution does not overlap that of *C. meridanus*.

DISTRIBUTION   This species is endemic to the northern end of the Yucatán Peninsula, where it is known from several localities in Yucatán and northern Campeche and Quintana Roo (Map 121).

NATURAL HISTORY   Less is known about the biology of this species than any of the other *Coniophanes* in the Yucatán Peninsula. Apparently *C. meridanus* is a terrestrial and nocturnal inhabitant of thorn forest and tropical deciduous forest.

Nothing is known of reproduction in this species. It is presumably oviparous, like the other members of the genus *Coniophanes*.

ETYMOLOGY   The specific name, *meridanus*, is a toponym combining the name of the type locality, Mérida, and *-anus*, a Latin suffix meaning "belonging to."

COMMENT   *Coniophanes meridanus* was reviewed by McCoy (1969) as part of his treatment of the *Coniophanes* of the Yucatán Peninsula.

Locality Records Mexico: Campeche: Dzibalchén (KU 75618); Quintana Roo: Cobá (UMMZ 83942), 4.1 km SE Cobá (KU 171737), 15.6 km N jct. rd. to Noh Bec and Hwy. 307 (UMRC 84-94), 22 km NNW Tulum (CAS 154144); Yucatán: 6.1 km E Bella Flor

(UMRC 80-56), Dzibilchaltún (FMNH 153581), Mérida (FMNH 19427, 26998–27001), Pisté (CM 48023–24), X-Can (CM 48027).

Coniophanes quinquevittatus
(Duméril, Bibron, and Duméril)
(Fig. 162; Map 122)

Homalopsis quinque-vittatus A. M. C. Duméril, Bibron, and Duméril, 1854:975. HOLOTYPE: MNHNP 516. TYPE LOCALITY: unknown, but the type description mentions specimens from El Petén, Guatemala; H. M. Smith and Taylor (1950b:318) restricted the type locality to Flores, El Petén, Guatemala.

Five-lined snake; culebra punteada (Mexico).

DESCRIPTION   Adults of this snake average between 450 and 500 mm in snout-vent length; the tail length is 30 to 35 percent of the head and body length. The head is slightly distinct from the neck in dorsal aspect, the eyes are rather small and lie far forward on the head, and the pupils are round (Fig. 162). The dorsal scales are smooth and highly polished, lack apical pits, and are arranged in 21 rows at midbody. The anal plate is divided.

The dorsal pattern consists of a pair of lateral black stripes on scales rows 3, 4, and 5, and portions

Fig. 162. Frontal view of the head of *Coniophanes quinquevittatus* (UMRC 88-4), 405 mm SVL; 17.2 km NW Hunucmá, Yucatán, Mexico.

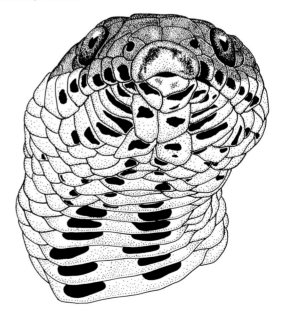

of rows 2 and 6. These stripes originate on the sides of the head and pass posteriorly onto the tail. They are bordered below by white, cream, or pale yellow on scale rows 1 and 2. The middorsal area between the lateral stripes is dark brown with a broad, indistinct dark vertebral stripe. The supralabial scales are light cream, and the anterior supralabials each have a bold dark spot. The infralabials and the scales on the chin and throat are white or cream and are boldly spotted with dark brown or black (Fig. 162). The venter is light tan or cream, and each ventral scale has a pair of large black spots. These spots may coalesce at the midline on the undersurface of the tail.

SIMILAR SPECIES *Coniphanes quinquevittatus* is similar to *C. bipunctatus*, which Conant (1965: 12) considered a sibling species, but has more than 150 ventral scales (*C. bipunctatus* has fewer than 150 ventrals). Moreover, the chin of *C. quinquevittatus* is boldly marked with distinct dark spots and flecks against a white, cream, or pale yellow background, whereas *C. bipunctatus* lacks distinct spots on the chin scales, which are instead edged with dark pigment, producing several indistinct parallel dark lines (Fig. 159).

DISTRIBUTION This species occurs at low elevations on the Atlantic slope from southern Veracruz eastward through Tabasco and northern Guatemala. The distribution in the Yucatán Peninsula, although very imperfectly known, appears to be highly disjunct. There are records from El Petén, northwestern Yucatán, and northern Campeche (Map 122).

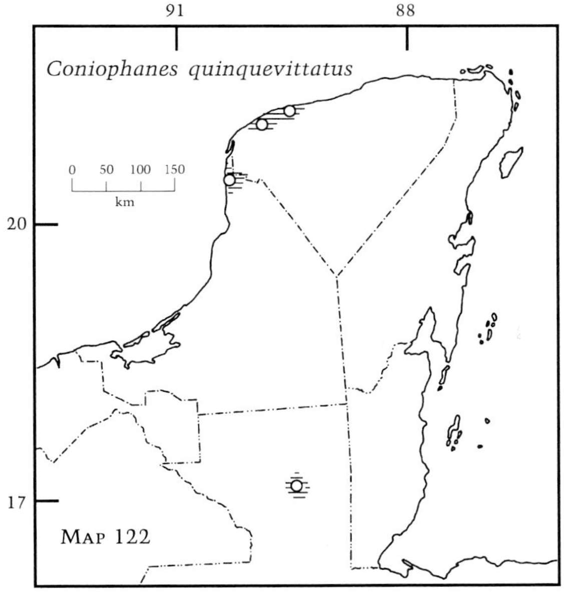

NATURAL HISTORY Little is known of the natural history of this apparently uncommon species. It is presumably semiaquatic, for individuals have been taken in marshy situations.

ETYMOLOGY The specific name, *quinquevittatus*, is derived from the Latin *quinque*, "five," and *vittatus*, "striped" or "bound with fillets," in reference to the striped dorsum of some specimens.

COMMENT McCoy (1969) reviewed *C. quinquevittatus* in his treatment of the *Coniophanes* of the Yucatán Peninsula.

Locality Records   *Guatemala*: El Petén: Flores (AMNH 74483; FMNH 43366–67; UMMZ 79060). *Mexico*: Campeche: Carretera El Remate–Isla Arena (IHNHERP 474); Yucatán: 17.2 km NW Hunucmá (UMRC 88-4), 1 mi S Progreso (CM 45288).

Coniophanes schmidti Bailey
(Figs. 152D, 351; Map 123)

Coniophanes schmidti J. R. Bailey, 1937:1. HOLOTYPE: UMMZ 73043. TYPE LOCALITY: Chichén Itzá, Yucatán, Mexico.

Schmidt's striped snake; culebra rayada (Mexico).

DESCRIPTION This is a medium-sized *Coniophanes*. The adults average about 400 mm in snout-vent length, and the tail length is approximately 65 to 70 percent of the head and body length. The head is moderately distinct from the neck, the eyes are rather small, and the pupils are round (Fig. 152D). The dorsal scales are smooth, lack apical pits, and are arranged in 23 to 27 rows at midbody. Supraanal tubercles are present in the males (Mahrdt, 1969:125). The anal plate is divided.

The dorsum is dark brown or black with a pair of narrow cream or yellow dorsolateral stripes that originate on the rostrum, pass through the dorsal surface of the eye, and extend to the tip of the tail. The cream or tan ventral coloration extends onto the lateral surfaces of the body. The dorsal and lateral surfaces of the head are dark brown. The chin, throat, and labial scales are cream or tan, usually peppered with dark pigment.

Coniophanes quinquevittatus

0 50 100 150
km

MAP 122

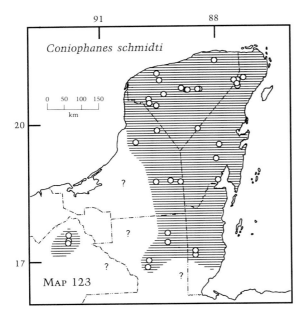

Coniophanes schmidti

0 50 100 150
km

MAP 123

SIMILAR SPECIES   In the Yucatán Peninsula, *C. schmidti* differs from all other members of its genus in possessing more (23–27) rows of dorsal scales at midbody. *Thamnophis proximus* has strongly keeled dorsal scales.

DISTRIBUTION   This Yucatecan endemic occurs from northern Chiapas and central El Petén northward. The species is probably pan-peninsular, but it is as yet unknown from western Campeche and northwestern El Petén (Map 123).

NATURAL HISTORY   These terrestrial, nocturnal, rear-fanged snakes inhabit lowland tropical forest. They are generally inoffensive and rarely bite. Nothing specific is known about their diet, but they probably feed mostly on frogs and lizards.

Like other *Coniophanes*, *C. schmidti* is oviparous. I collected a specimen from Campeche in June that contained four well-developed oviductal eggs.

ETYMOLOGY   The specific name, *schmidti*, is a patronym that honors Karl P. Schmidt, of the Field Museum of Natural History, Chicago.

COMMENT   This form has been treated variously as a subspecies of *C. piceivittis* (e.g., Werler and Smith, 1952; L. D. Wilson and Meyer, 1985:39) and as a full species (Stuart, 1963:92). It differs from *C. piceivittis* in having narrower dorsolateral stripes

that are 1 to 1.5 scale rows wide. W. T. Neill and Allen (1960:146) described a specimen from Belize that was intermediate between *C. schmidti* and *C. piceivittis* but declined to synonymize the former on the basis of a single specimen that was aberrant in some respects. In a recent review of the *C. piceivittis* species complex, Harrison (1993) concluded that *C. schmidti* merits full specific status.

McCoy (1969) reviewed *C. schmidti* in his treatment of the *Coniophanes* of the Yucatán Peninsula, and Harrison (1993) included the species in his taxonomic treatment of snakes of the *C. piceivittis* species group.

Locality Records Belize: Cayo: Augustine (W. T. Neill and Allen, 1960:145), Macal River at Guacamallo Bridge (CM 112148). *Guatemala:* El Petén: La Libertad (UMMZ 74893), Santa Teresa (UMMZ 74894), Sojio (AMNH 69980), Tikal (UF 13811; UMMZ 117901–2), 2.5 km N Uaxactún (KU 157557). *Mexico:* Campeche: Becan (UWZH 20503, 20507, 20514), Colonia López Mateos (UCM 28173), Ruinas Edzná (KU 101531), Santa Rosa Xtampak (JCL photo), 25.5 km E Xpujil (UMRC 84-13); Chiapas: Palenque ruins (SDSNH 45224), 18 km S Palenque (UMRC 85-15), 13 mi S Palenque (LSUMZ 33238–39); Quintana Roo: 1.2 km SE Cobá (KU 171735), Chetumal (MZCIQRO 08, 69), 20 mi S Felipe Carrillo Puerto (LSUMZ 33240), Petcacab (UMRC 84-86), Pueblo Nuevo X-Can (CM 45696; UCM 41635–36, 40106–11, 40714), 2.5 km S Pueblo Nuevo X-Can (UMRC 92-10), 12 km S Pueblo Nuevo X-Can (JCL photo), Tintal (UCM 40112–13); Yucatán: Calchetok (UMMZ 113543), Chichén Itzá (AMNH 38832; CM 38917; FMNH 20633, 36363, 36366, 36368; MCZ 22065; UMMZ 68706, 73039–43), Cholul (UTA R-28298), Dzibilchaltún (FMNH 153540–41, 153570–76), Kantunil (FMNH 36372), Libre Unión (FMNH 36365, 36370–71), Mayapán (FMNH 40726), Pisté (CM 46909–10, 46983, 48020–22; KU 70829–31; UCM 40114), 36.3 km S Río Lagartos (KU 171734), Uxmal (KU 171732), X-Can (CM 46861–62, 47025–27, 48025–26), Yokdzonot (FMNH 36364, 36367), near Yokdzonot (FMNH 36369), Hwy. 184 near Yucatán–Quintana Roo border (KU 171733).

Genus *Conophis* (Road Guarders)

The members of this small genus of exclusively Neotropical rear-fanged snakes are diurnal, terrestrial, fast-moving inhabitants of arid and semiarid areas of Mexico and Central America. The most recent comprehensive taxonomic treatment is Wellman, 1963, which recognizes three species; one of these occurs in the Yucatán Peninsula. *Conophis* is from the Greek *konos*, "cone" or "peak of a helmet," and *ophis*, "snake," presumably in reference to the rather pointed snout.

Conophis lineatus
(Duméril, Bibron, and Duméril)
(Figs. 152C, 352; Map 124)

Tomodon lineatum A. M. C. Duméril, Bibron, and Duméril, 1854:936. HOLOTYPE: MNHNP 3738. TYPE LOCALITY: Mexique; restricted by H. M. Smith and Taylor (1950b:351) to Veracruz, Veracruz, Mexico.

Many-lined snake (Belize); culebra rayada, guarda camino, sabanera (Mexico); tzinkan (Lacandón Maya); xulub-can (Yucatec Maya).

DESCRIPTION   This medium-sized, moderately stout snake attains a snout-vent length between 750 and 900 mm. The tail length is about 25 to 30 percent of the snout-vent length. The head is only slightly distinct from the neck in dorsal aspect, and the snout is pointed (Fig. 152C). The eyes are moderately small, and the pupils are round. The dorsal scales are smooth, lack apical pits, and are arranged in 19 rows at midbody. The anal plate is divided.

The color pattern of individuals from the Yucatán Peninsula varies geographically. Specimens from the northern portion of the peninsula have an immaculate pale gray to pale olive body, and the venter is white, cream, or pale yellow. A broad brown ocular stripe extends from the rostrum, through the eye, and onto the nape of the neck (Fig. 352). This stripe has a narrow dark brown or black border. Often a pair of thin, dark, broken paravertebral lines extends from the posterior margin of the parietal scales onto the neck. The labials are yellowish or cream with darker pigment at the sutures. Specimens from northern Guatemala and central and southern Belize have prominent dark brown or black dorsal stripes.

SIMILAR SPECIES   The various species of *Coniophanes* in the Yucatán Peninsula are striped, but only *C. imperialis* has 19 scale rows at midbody, and it has a single anterior temporal scale instead of the two or three seen in *Conophis*. The species of

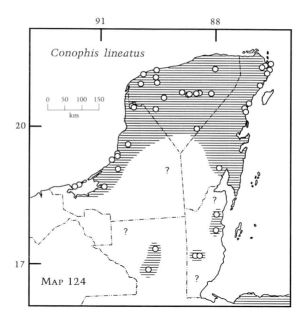

Stenorrhina differ from *Conophis* in having the internasal scales fused with the nasals and 17 rows of scales at midbody.

DISTRIBUTION   This species occurs at low and moderate elevations from central Veracruz on the Gulf slope and Chiapas on the Pacific slope, south and east through the Yucatán Peninsula and northern Honduras to Costa Rica. It appears to occur more or less continuously through the northern third of the Yucatán Peninsula and in isolated populations to the south in El Petén and Belize (Map 124).

NATURAL HISTORY   These active, fast-moving, diurnal snakes inhabit open situations such as savannas and beaches. They prey on vertebrates, especially lizards and other species of snakes, which they overcome with the aid of their large rear fangs and rather potent venom. Although probably not life threatening for humans, a bite can cause discomfort and considerable swelling. Wellman (1963:290) described the symptoms of several *Conophis* bites, which included localized burning and swelling. I was bitten on the base of the right thumb by an adult *C. lineatus*. The fang punctures bled copiously, and my entire hand and lower arm swelled noticeably within a few hours of the bite. Pain in the axillary lymph nodes followed. Several days passed before the swelling disappeared and I regained full use of the hand. Similar, although less dramatic, symptoms were reported by J. D. Johnson (1988) of a bite by the closely related *C. vittatus*. Johnson (1988) also showed that a case of envenomation ascribed by Cook (1984) to *Stenorrhina freminvillei* actually involved *C. lineatus*. W. T. Neill and Allen (1959c:56) commented on the difficulty of handling this snake without being bitten, even when the animal is held immediately behind the head in a firm grip. It can flex its head downward in such a way as to bring the fangs into close proximity to the holder's fingers.

Snakes of the genus *Conophis* feed predominantly on lizards, especially *Cnemidophorus*. Wellman (1963:290) saw a specimen of *C. lineatus* follow a lizard into a hole. Captives ate snakes of the genera *Thamnophis* and *Storeria*, toads, and hylid frogs (Mittleman, 1944:122). *Conophis lineatus* also consumes small mammals, for Wellman (1963:289) found a rodent in the stomach of a specimen from Chichén Itzá.

Conophis lineatus is oviparous. A specimen collected at Chichén Itzá (FMNH 20611) in May 1934 contained five well-formed eggs.

SUBSPECIES Wellman (1963:263) recognized three subspecies, of which two occur in the Yucatán Peninsula: *C. l. concolor*, an essentially unicolor form, occurs from northern Belize and southern Campeche northward; and *C. l. dunni*, a distinctly striped form, occupies the base of the peninsula.

ETYMOLOGY The specific name, *lineatus*, is Latin for "streaked, marked with lines," presumably in reference to the striped pattern of the nominate subspecies.

COMMENT According to Schmidt and Andrews (1936:178), the Yucatec Maya name means "horned snake" and refers to the fact that the lines of the head do not extend onto the body in the northern subspecies, thus they vaguely resemble horns.

Conophis lineatus was reviewed by Wellman (1963) as part of his revision of the genus *Conophis*.

Locality Records Belize: Belize: 1.5 mi S, 13 mi W Belize City (AMNH 126423), due W Chicago on Northern Hwy. (CM 105752); Cayo: near Augustine (MPM

7319), 10 mi E Augustine (W. T. Neill and Allen, 1960:147). *Guatemala*: El Petén: San Miguel (FMNH 43365), Sojio (AMNH 69969, 69986). *Mexico*: Campeche: 29.7 mi S Campeche (UCM 18620), Carmen Island (AMNH 102484), Champotón (UMMZ 73064–66), 3 mi S Champotón (UCM 28128), 16 mi W Champotón (UCM 39516), Chuina (KU 74990), Ciudad del Carmen (UCM 20769), Encarnación (FMNH 106462), Tankuche (IHNHERP 485), Tankuche–El Remate (IHNHERP 471); Quintana Roo: 5 mi N Bacalar (LSUMZ 33381), Cancún (López-Gonzales, 1991:106), Isla Mujeres (UCM 16027–28), 7 mi N Playa del Carmen (CM 93171), Petempich (López-Gonzales, 1991:106), Puerto Juárez (UCM 16029), 2 mi SW Puerto Juárez (BCB 11989), Tulum (LSUMZ 34101), near Tulum (JCL sight record), Xel-Ha (UMRC 92-13); Yucatán: Chichén Itzá (AMNH 38826, 38833; CM 36449–50; FMNH 20610–11, 20625, 26986–87, 36299–300, 36303–4, 36307, 36316; MCZ 7244, 28748; UMMZ 68236, 73060–62, 80806; USNM 46395), 10 km W Chichén Itzá (TU 19765), Dzibilchaltún (FMNH 153508, 153518, 153553, 153559), 3 mi E Esmeralda (LACM 113904), Kantunil (FMNH 36301, 36305–6, 36308–9, 36312–13), Libre Unión (FMNH 36302, 36310–11, 36314), Mayapán (FMNH 40720), vicinity Mérida (EAL 2962), Mérida (FMNH 19411–13, 153511; MCZ 142935; MZFC 3170; UMZH 20559), Pisté (CM 46911–16, 46984, 47088–95, 49573–91, 49822; KU 70832–36; UCM 16030–32, 18621, 28165, 41637), Progreso (FMNH 40721), 12.6 km S Sisal (TU 19804), 12.5 km E Sisal (CM 45291), Tekom (FMNH 49347), 6 km N Tizimín (KU 74988–89), Uxmal (KU 70837), Yokdzonot (FMNH 36315); no specific locality (FMNH 153559).

Genus *Dendrophidion* (Forest Racers)

These small to medium-sized, rather slender Neotropical snakes are generally terrestrial and diurnal. The genus occurs discontinuously from southern Veracruz through Central America to Bolivia and northern Brazil. Lieb (1988) recognized nine species, one of which was undescribed; two of these occur in the Yucatán Peninsula. *Dendrophidion* is from the Greek *dendron*, "tree" or "stick," and *ophidion*, the diminutive of *ophis*, "snake."

Key to the Species of the Genus *Dendrophidion*

Small snakes, adults generally less than 1 m total length; 111–128 subcaudals; first row of dorsal scales smooth or only weakly keeled . . . . *Dendrophidion vinitor*

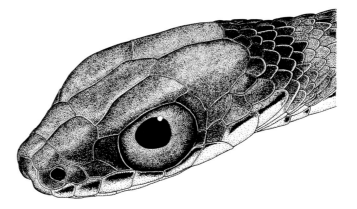

Fig. 163. Dorsolateral view of the head of *Dendrophidion nuchale* (CRE 8832), 380 mm SVL; 4 km S San Vito, Las Cruces, Costa Rica.

Medium-sized snakes, adults reaching at least 1.5 m total length; 132–163 subcaudals; first row of dorsal scales strongly keeled . . . . *Dendrophidion nuchale*

Clave para las Especies del Género *Dendrophidion*

Serpientes pequeñas, adultos menores a 1 m de largo total; 111–128 subcaudales; primera hilera de escamas dorsales lisas o solo débilmente quilladas . . . . *Dendrophidion vinitor*

Serpientes de mediano tamaño, los adultos alcanzan por lo menos los 1.5 m de largo total; 132–163 subcaudales; primera hilera de escamas dorsales fuertemente quilladas . . . .
. . . . *Dendrophidion nuchale*

Dendrophidion nuchale (W. Peters)
(Figs. 163, 353; Map 125)

Herpetodryas nuchalis W. C. Peters, 1863b:285. TYPES: two syntypes, formerly in the ZMB, now lost, *fide* Lieb, 1988:167. USNM 129579 designated neotype by Lieb (1988:167). TYPE LOCALITY: Camp Rafael Rangel, Aragua Province, Venezuela (by neotype designation).

Black-naped forest racer.

DESCRIPTION The adults of this medium-sized, moderately slender snake average between 650 and 750 mm in snout-vent length. The tail is long, about two-thirds the length of the head and body. The head is moderately distinct from the neck, and the snout is truncated in dorsal aspect. The eyes are large with round pupils (Fig. 163). There are 17 rows of strongly keeled scales at midbody. Apical pits are absent, and the anal plate is usually divided.

The dorsum is generally dark brown, gray, or greenish gray, with indistinct lighter bands, bars, or spots. In general, the anterior portion of the body is lighter than the posterior portion, and a dark nuchal collar is usually present. The pattern becomes ob-

scure in older individuals. The chin and labials are white or cream, contrasting with the dark head. The venter is white, cream, or gray with an extensive suffusion of dark pigment.

SIMILAR SPECIES *Dendrophidion vinitor* has fewer subcaudals (111–128 vs. 132–163 in *D. nuchale*), the first row of dorsal scales is smooth or only weakly keeled (strongly keeled in *D. nuchale*), and generally the anal plate is undivided. *Dryadophis melanolomus* has smooth dorsal scales with paired apical pits, whereas the dorsal scales are strongly keeled and lack apical pits in *D. nuchale*.

DISTRIBUTION This species occurs in Costa Rica, Panama, and on the Pacific slope of Colombia and Ecuador. Apparently, disjunct populations occupy northern Venezuela, northern Honduras, and Guatemala and Belize. In the Yucatán Peninsula the species is known from central Belize (Map 125).

NATURAL HISTORY This rare snake typically inhabits moist lowland forests in the Yucatán Peninsula. Nothing is known of its diet in the Yucatán Peninsula, but Lancini (1986:92) reported that in

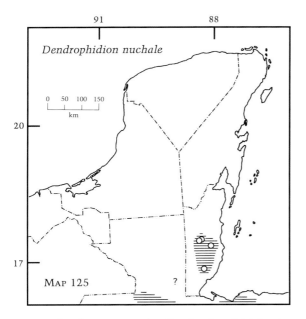

Dendrophidion nuchale

MAP 125

Venezuela this species (as *D. dendrophis*) feeds on lizards and rodents.

Dendrophidion nuchale is oviparous. McCoy (1970c:136) reported that a hatchling 425 mm in total length was taken on 17 August at Middlesex, Stann Creek District.

ETYMOLOGY The specific name, *nuchale*, is Latin and means "of the neck," in reference to the dark nuchal collar present in some specimens.

COMMENT Lieb (1988) reviewed the genus *Dendrophidion* and summarized the available information on *D. nuchale* (1991a).

Locality Records Belize: Cayo: 1.6 km W Baldy Subin (LSUMZ 8901), Dos Cuevas (LSUMZ 8902), Sibun Hill (LSUMZ 8903); Stann Creek: Middlesex (UCM 25708, 25794, 25805–6, 25846–47); Toledo: Bladen Nature Reserve (JAM photo).

Dendrophidion vinitor Smith
(Fig. 164; Map 126)

Dendrophidion vinitor H. M. Smith, 1941b:74. HOLOTYPE: USNM 110662. TYPE LOCALITY: Piedras Negras, Guatemala.

Barred forest racer; culebra barrada (Mexico); kuyun kan (Lacandón Maya).

DESCRIPTION These are small to medium-sized, rather slender snakes. The adults average 500 to 600 mm in snout-vent length, and the tail is approximately two-thirds the length of the head and body. The head is moderately distinct from the neck, and the snout is truncated in dorsal aspect. The eyes are large with round pupils (Fig. 164). There are 17 rows of scales at midbody; all are heavily keeled except those of the first row, which are smooth or only weakly keeled. Apical pits are absent, and the anal plate is usually undivided.

The dorsum is reddish brown or gray and bears a series of narrow, light vertical bars edged in black about one or two scales wide. These often meet mid-dorsally, producing a banded appearance, which becomes obscure in older individuals. The head is dark brown or gray above, and the chin and labials are white, cream, or yellowish, as is the median portion

Fig. 164. Dorsolateral view of the head of *Dendrophidion vinitor* (CRE 5099), 467 mm SVL; Costa Rica.

of the venter. The lateral margins of the ventrals and subcaudals are suffused with dark pigment.

SIMILAR SPECIES *Dendrophidion nuchale* has more subcaudal scales (130 or more vs. 111–128 in *D. vinitor*), usually has a divided anal plate (undivided in *D. vinitor*), and the first row of dorsal scales is heavily keeled (smooth or weakly keeled in *D. vinitor*). *Dryadophis melanolomus*, which is similar in appearance, has smooth dorsal scales with paired apical pits, whereas *D. vinitor* has strongly keeled dorsal scales without apical pits.

DISTRIBUTION *Dendrophidion vinitor* occurs from sea level to 1,300 m from southern Veracruz discontinuously through Central America to eastern Panama and adjacent Colombia. In the Yucatán Peninsula it is known with certainty only from the type locality, Piedras Negras, El Petén, and possibly from the vicinity of Flores (Map 126).

NATURAL HISTORY This rare snake is apparently a diurnal terrestrial inhabitant of lowland tropical forest.

ETYMOLOGY The specific name, *vinitor*, is from the Latin *vinea*, "vine." Although Lieb (1991b:1) translated the name as "vinedresser" and suggested an oblique reference to the forest habitat preferred by this species, H. M. Smith (in litt.) informed me that he intended the name to mean "a dweller in vines."

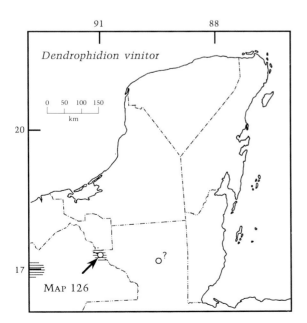

MAP 126

COMMENT This species is often confused with *D. nuchale*, and Lieb (1988) showed that specimens from Belize to which the name *vinitor* had been applied are actually *D. nuchale*. Lieb (1988, 1991b) reviewed *D. vinitor*.

Locality Records Guatemala: El Petén: vicinity Flores (Lieb, 1991b:1), Piedras Negras (USNM 110662).

Genus *Dipsas* (Thirst Snakes)

These harmless snakes are small to medium sized and have slender, laterally compressed bodies. Snail suckers are predominantly arboreal and are highly specialized morphologically for feeding on snails and slugs. They are crepuscular and nocturnal and have large, protruding eyes. Representatives of the genus *Dipsas* occur at low to moderate elevations throughout tropical Mexico and Central and South America. There are about 30 species of *Dipsas*; one occurs in the Yucatán Peninsula. J. A. Peters (1960) revised the genus *Dipsas* as part of his revision of the subfamily Dipsadinae. *Dipsas* refers to a venomous serpent from Greek mythology whose bite causes thirst.

Dipsas brevifacies (Cope)
(Figs. 153C, 354, 355; Map 127)

Tropidodipsas brevifacies Cope, 1866:127. HOLOTYPE: USNM 24886. TYPE LOCALITY: Yucatán, Mexico.

Short-faced snail sucker; snail-eating snake (Belize); chupa caracoles (Mexico).

DESCRIPTION These rather small snakes average about 370 mm in snout-vent length and reach a maximum of about 422 mm. The moderately long tail is 32 to 40 percent as long as the head and body, and males have relatively longer tails than females. The head is distinct from the neck, and the body is laterally compressed. The eyes are large and protruding, and the pupils are vertically elliptical. There is no mental groove (Fig. 153C). The dorsal scales are smooth and highly polished, lack apical pits, and are arranged in 15 rows at midbody. The anal plate is undivided.

The dorsal color pattern consists of a series of white, pink, or salmon rings alternating with shiny black rings, the latter usually two to three times the width of the former. The light nuchal ring does not extend anteriorly to below the eye. There is some suggestion of ontogenetic color change in this species, for the hatchlings and juveniles tend to have white bands (Fig. 355), whereas the light bands of older individuals are generally pink or salmon (Fig. 354).

SIMILAR SPECIES *Dipsas brevifacies* resembles *Sibon sartorii* and *S. fasciata* but differs from both in having smooth dorsal scales arranged in 15 rows at midbody, rather than weakly keeled dorsal scales in 17 rows at midbody.

DISTRIBUTION This species is endemic to the Yucatán Peninsula, where it is known from southern Campeche and central Belize northward through Quintana Roo and Yucatán (Map 127).

NATURAL HISTORY Snail suckers are rather common crepuscular and nocturnal snakes. They occupy the xeric thorn forests of northeastern Yucatán and the taller, more mesic forests on the east side of the peninsula. The slender, laterally compressed body suggests an arboreal lifestyle, but individuals are commonly encountered on roads at night, especially in eastern Yucatán and in Quintana Roo. These snakes are believed to feed exclusively on snails and slugs.

The short-faced snail sucker is oviparous, but little else is known about its reproductive biology. W. T. Neill (1962:239) collected a specimen in Be-

lize that he thought had hatched in middle or late September.

ETYMOLOGY The specific name, *brevifacies*, is from the Latin *brevis*, "short," and *facies*, "face."

COMMENT There is a single record for *D. brevifacies* from Ciudad del Carmen, Campeche (UMMZ 83541), far to the southwest of the other known locality records. The specimen was part of a collection of snakes purchased in 1937 by the University of Michigan from John Martin, the owner of several ranches in southwestern Campeche. All the specimens bear Ciudad del Carmen locality data, but there are no associated field notes (G. Schneider, in litt.). The collection includes such typical forest forms as *Imantodes cenchoa* and *Sibon nebulata*, species unlikely to inhabit the low, scrubby vegetation that characterizes the environs of Ciudad del Carmen. I suggest, therefore, that Ciudad del Carmen was simply the base of Martin's operations, and that many of his specimens, including the *D. brevifacies*, came from the interior of the state of Campeche.

Dipsas brevifacies was reviewed by J. A. Peters (1960) as part of his revision of the snakes of the subfamily Dipsadinae, and by Kofron (1982) as part of his treatment of the species of *Dipsas* in Mexico.

Locality Records Belize: Belize: 13 mi W, 1.5 mi S Belize City (W. T. Neill, 1962:239); Corozal: Santa Elena (Olson, 1986a:67); no specific locality (FMNH 4234). *Mexico*: Campeche: Becan (UWZH 20526), Ciudad del Carmen (UMMZ 83541); Quintana Roo: Cobá (CAS 154136; Himmelstein, 1980:29; JCL photo), 2 km SE Cobá (JCL photo), Felipe Carrillo Puerto (UMMZ 113556–57), 17.3 km NW Felipe Carrillo Puerto (JCL 6834), 14.8 km S Felipe Carrillo Puerto (JCL 6836), 18 mi NE Felipe Carrillo Puerto (KU 157559), 36.4 km N Felipe Carrillo Puerto (JCL 6808), 38.5 km NW Felipe Carrillo Puerto (JCL 6830), 82 km NNE Felipe Carrillo Puerto (LSUMZ 28247), 9.3 mi SW Limones (KU 157558), 3.9 km SW rd. to Noh Bec on Hwy. 307 (JCL sight record), 7.5 km SW rd. to Noh Bec on Hwy. 307 (JCL sight record), Playa del Carmen (Himmelstein, 1980:29), 0.5 mi S Playa del Carmen (LSUMZ 33232–34), 3.5 km S Playa del Carmen (JCL 6807), 3.1 mi SW Playa del Carmen (KU 157560), 9.5 mi S Playa del Carmen (LSUMZ 33235), 11 km S Playa del Carmen (UMRC 84-63), 15.5 km S Playa del Carmen (UMRC 84-62), Pueblo Nuevo X-Can (CM 45697–700, 49162; UCM 40620–23, 40738, 41638–42), 4.7 km S Pueblo Nuevo X-Can (UMRC 87-14), 6 mi E Pueblo Nuevo X-Can (UCM 28144), 14.2 km S Pueblo

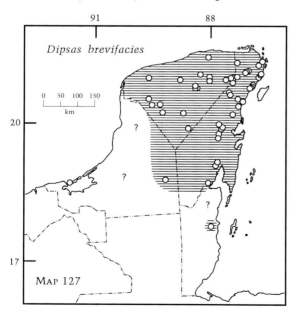

MAP 127

Nuevo X-Can (UMRC 84-64), Puerto Juárez (Himmelstein, 1980:29), 15 km W Puerto Juárez (KU 70838), 52 km SSW Puerto Juárez (AMNH 110045), 62 km SSW Puerto Juárez (AMNH 110046), 68 km SSW Puerto Juárez (LSUMZ 28246), 1 km S Puerto Morelos (AMNH 110047), 2 mi N Puerto Morelos (CAS 114074), 20 km N Puerto Morelos (CAS 154135), 14.2 km S Solferino (KU 171704), Tintal (UCM 41643–45), 8 km NW Tulum (MCZ 152579–80), 11.5 km S Tulum (JCL 6838), 19.4 km NW Tulum (UMRC 84-65); Yucatán: Balankanché (FMNH 153548), 0.7 km W Hwy. 180 on rd. to Calchetok (UMRC 87-14), 1.2 km S Calotmul (KU 171705), Chichén Itzá (FMNH 20634; UMMZ 73030), Sitilpech (ANSP 10129), bet. Cooperativa and Xul (TU 19755), Peto (CM 45310, Pisté (CM 46917, 46985–86, 49592–97; UCM 40624–25, 41646), 2.2 km N Pisté (KU 70839), 3 km N Pisté (KU 70840), 14.1 mi S Río Lagartos (KU 157562), 13.5 km S Santa Rosa (UMRC 84-66), 6.8 km N Temozon (UMRC 84-3), 2 km S Ticul (TU 19794), 17.2 mi W Tizimín (KU 157561), Ucu (JCL photo), Uxmal (MCZ 65454), near Uxmal (JCL photo), X-Can (CM 46817, 47028), 13 mi W X-Can (LSUMZ 28256), no specific locality (USNM 24886).

Genus *Dryadophis*

These moderately slender, fast-moving, diurnal snakes are found from southern Mexico through Central America to northern Argentina. About a dozen species are presently recognized. One species occurs in the Yucatán Peninsula. *Dryadophis* is from the Greek *dryas*, a deity or nymph of the woods, and *ophis*, meaning "snake" or "serpent."

Dryadophis melanolomus (Cope)
(Fig. 356; Map 128)

Masticophis melanolomus Cope, 1868:134. HOLOTYPE: USNM 24985. TYPE LOCALITY: Yucatán, Mexico.

Dryad snake (Belize); sumbadora (Guatemala); lagartijera olivacea (Mexico).

DESCRIPTION These are moderately large, terrestrial, racerlike snakes. The males attain a maximum snout-vent length of about 1,010 mm, the females about 980 mm. The tail is long, about 50 percent of the snout-vent length. The head is moderately distinct from the neck, the eyes are large, and the pupils are round (Fig. 356). The dorsal scales are smooth, arranged in 17 rows at midbody, and bear pairs of apical pits. The anal plate is divided.

The adults are dark brown or tan above, becoming lighter on the sides. Each dorsal scale is usually bordered narrowly by black. An indistinct dark stripe may be present on the scales of rows 2 and 3, especially on the posterior portion of the body and on the tail. The dorsal and lateral surfaces of the head are dark brown. The supralabials, chin, and anterior portion of the venter are immaculate yellowish cream, and the tan or brown of the lateral surface of the body extends onto the lateral surfaces of the ventral scales. Posteriorly the venter may become pinkish. Stuart (1941b:86) documented pronounced age-related variation in color pattern in some populations, especially those from the base of the Yucatán Peninsula. The juveniles have a dorsal pattern of narrow, light crossbands set against a dark brown, reddish brown, or gray ground color. In older individuals this banding is replaced by faint stripes, and eventually by a more or less uniform coloration.

SIMILAR SPECIES *Masticophis mentovarius*, a much larger snake, usually has seven supralabial scales and a single apical pit on the anterior middorsal scales, whereas *D. melanolomus* usually has nine supralabials and paired apical scale pits. *Drymarchon corais*, also a much larger snake, has eight supralabials and an undivided anal plate. *Symphimus mayae*, a smaller snake, has dorsal scales arranged in 15 rows at midbody. *Coluber constrictor* has a small subocular scale below the preocular scale (Fig. 158) and 15 rows of dorsal scales at midbody.

DISTRIBUTION This species is found at low and moderate elevations from Nayarit, Mexico, on the Pacific slope and Tamaulipas on the Atlantic slope south to Panama. It probably occurs throughout the Yucatán Peninsula, but there are apparently no records from southwestern Campeche (Map 128).

NATURAL HISTORY *Dryadophis melanolomus* is a largely terrestrial inhabitant of thorn forest, tropical deciduous and evergreen forests, and savannas. These alert, fast-moving, diurnal snakes are frequently seen darting across roads. As the Spanish name, *lagartijera olivacea*, suggests, they feed largely on lizards. Stuart (1948:66) found a *Sceloporus teapensis* in the stomach of a specimen from

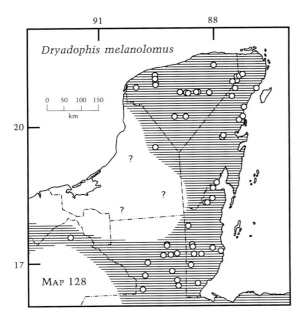

Dryadophis melanolomus

MAP 128

Alta Verapaz, and I observed *D. melanolomus* attempting to capture a lizard of that species in El Petén. Himmelstein (1980:29) saw a specimen swallow a *Cnemidophorus angusticeps* in Quintana Roo. Seib (1984, 1985a) studied the feeding ecology of *D. melanolomus* on three coffee fincas in southern Chiapas and adjacent Guatemala and examined the stomach contents of museum specimens from various localities in Chiapas and Guatemala. Lizards, especially *Anolis*, formed the bulk of the diet, with lesser numbers of anurans, snakes, reptile eggs, and small mammals also included. In Panama, Swanson (1945:214) observed a specimen with a mouse in its mouth, and Sexton and Heatwole (1965:40) found *Anolis limifrons* and *A. limifrons* eggs in the stomachs of Panamanian specimens. Although nonvenomous, these snakes bite freely if threatened.

Dryadophis melanolomus is oviparous. Stuart (1948:66) found well-formed eggs in a female collected in Alta Verapaz on 11 June. W. T. Neill (1965:101) found a juvenile in Belize that he believed had hatched in August. Censky and McCoy (1988) found specimens with mature ovarian follicles in nearly every month in Yucatán, yet the seasonal (November–January) appearance of posthatchlings argued against multiple annual cycles. They believed that the eggs are probably laid between August and November. The clutch size in Yucatán ranged from two to five (mean = 3.1). Censky and McCoy (1988) considered females to be mature at a snout-vent length of about 580 mm, and

they found a positive relationship between snout-vent length and clutch size.

SUBSPECIES   Five to seven subspecies are recognized on the basis of adult and juvenile coloration and ventral scale numbers (J. A. Peters and Orejas-Miranda, 1970:194; H. M. Smith, 1943; Stuart, 1941b:30). *Dryadophis m. melanolomus* occurs throughout most of the Yucatán Peninsula. It is replaced at the base by *D. m. laevis*. W. T. Neill (1965:100) believed that specimens from Belize were intermediate between *D. m. melanolomus* and *D. m. laevis*, an opinion endorsed by McCoy (1970c:136).

ETYMOLOGY   The specific name, *melanolomus*, derives from the Greek *melania*, "blackness," and *loma*, "fringe" or "border of a robe," presumably an allusion to the black border on the dorsal scales of the nominate subspecies.

COMMENT   This species is often placed in the genus *Mastigodryas*, and the appropriate genus name is a matter of ongoing debate. H. M. Smith (1963) proposed that *Mastigodryas* Amaral, 1934 be suppressed under the plenary powers of the International Commission on Zoological Nomenclature. H. M. Smith and Larson (1974) supported that proposal and argued for application of the name *Dryadophis* Stuart, 1939 because it is more widely known and because no one has established that the type species of *Mastigodryas* (*M. danieli*) is congeneric with *Dryadophis*. As of this writing no action has been taken on this request because Amaral (1964:13) pointed out that the type species of *Mastigodryas* is different from all *Dryadophis* in lacking apical pits and in possessing fewer subcaudal scales. Nonetheless, J. A. Peters and Orejas-Miranda (1970:190) synonymized the two genera and applied the earlier name, *Mastigodryas*, on the basis of priority. Some systematists (e.g., Villa et al., 1988; L. D. Wilson and Meyer, 1985) follow Smith and Larson and apply the name *Dryadophis*, while others (e.g., Scott 1983c:416) continue to use *Mastigodryas*. In summary, there are three possibilities: (1) *Mastigodryas* Amaral and *Dryadophis* Stuart are separate genera (Amaral's view), in which case *D. melanolomus* is the correct name for the species in the Yucatán Peninsula; (2) *M. danieli* is congeneric with *Dryadophis*, in which case the name *Mastigodryas* has priority (Peters and Orejas-Miranda's view); or (3) *M. danieli* is congeneric with *Dryadophis*, but the latter name should be applied owing to its wider currency (Smith and Larson's view). More recently, H. M. Smith and Pérez-Higareda (1986:53) pointed out that the morphological differences between *M. danieli* and the species of *Dryadophis* are more substantial than even Amaral realized, thereby strengthening the case for recognition of *Dryadophis* and *Mastigodryas* as separate genera.

Locality Records Belize: Cayo: Augustine (LSUMZ 8904; UMMZ 80714; W. T. Neill and Allen, 1959c:51), Caracol (CMM photo), Central Farm (MCZ 71672), 4 mi S Georgeville (CM 105713), upper Raspaculo River basin (Stafford, 1991:14); Corozal: 0.25 mi N Corozal Town (JLK 457), Progresso (MPM 7357); Orange Walk: Gallon Jug (LSUMZ 8899), Otro Benque (MPM 10785); Stann Creek: Middlesex (CM 48003; UCM 25804, 25848, 29959–60, 30838–39), Silk Grass (Schmidt, 1941:499); Toledo: ca. 2 mi SE Big Falls, Río Grande (CM 105886). *Guatemala*: Alta Verapaz: Chinajá (Duellman, 1963:238); El Petén: 6 km NNW Chinajá (KU 55709), 2.5 mi W El Cruce (KU 157597), 24.6 km E El Cruce (KU 171727), 36.5 mi E El Cruce (KU 157599), vicinity La Libertad (UMMZ 74897), Las Cañas (CM 58279), 3 km S Poptún (UMMZ 125761), Sayaxché (UCM 22323–25), Tikal (MCZ 55426; UF 13812–14), 3 mi S Tikal (KU 157598), km 74 on Flores-Poptún Rd. (AMNH uncat.). *Mexico*: Campeche: Dzibalchén (KU 75619–20); Chiapas: 4 km SE Palenque (EAL 3028); Quintana Roo: Chetumal (MCZ 53121; MZCIQRO 03, 05), Chunyaxché (Himmelstein, 1980:29), near Cobá (JCL photo), Felipe Carrillo Puerto (UMMZ 113563–64), 4 km NNE Felipe Carrillo Puerto (KU 70844–45), 80.4 km NE Felipe Carrillo Puerto (EAL 2878), 21 km S Kantunil Kin (JCL sight record), Macario Gómez (UMRC 92-9), 0.6 mi S Playa del Carmen (LSUMZ 38568), Pueblo Nuevo X-Can (CM 45712–21, 49077, 49121–22, 49124, 49130, 49144, 49149; KU 70843; UCM 28126, 40135–73, 41668–72), Tintal (UCM 40176–79, 41663–67), Tulum (López-Gonzales, 1991:106); Yucatán: 10.6 km W Bella Flor (TU 19807), Chichén Itzá (MCZ 26839–41; UMMZ 73076–78, 83292), Chichén Itzá–Valladolid trail (UMMZ 68233), Colonia Santa María (UMMZ 76164), Dzibilchaltún (FMNH 153568), Kantunil (FMNH 36081), Libre Unión (FMNH 36077, 36079, 36084–88, 36091–92, 36095), Mérida (FMNH 19426–27), 6 km S Mérida (KU 70841), 9 mi N Mérida (CM 45292), 9 mi W Nuevo Valladolid (UCM 16035), Peto (CM 45293), Pisté (CM 46918–25, 46987–94, 47096–100, 49598–628; KU 70842; UCM 40180–89, 41673–76), Popolná (UCM 40174–75), 10 km SE Tekax (TU 19788), Tekom (FMNH 49328), 12 mi N Tizimín (UCM 28125), X-Can (CM 46818–23, 46863–69, 47029–33), Yokdzonot (FMNH 36075, 36090, 36094, 36097); no specific locality (USNM 10302, 24985–86).

Genus *Drymarchon* (Indigo Snakes)

The genus *Drymarchon* contains a single wide-ranging species, *D. corais*, the indigo snake. The generic name is derived from the Greek *drymos*, "forest," and *archon*, "ruler," perhaps a reference to this snake's large size or ophiophagous habits.

Drymarchon corais (Boie)
(Fig. 357; Map 129)

Coluber corais Boie, 1827:537. TYPE: unknown. TYPE LOCALITY: America.

Black-tailed indigo snake; blacktail (Belize); cola sucia, culebra arroyera, reina de las culebras (Mexico); uka'ni'ha (Lacandón Maya); ek'uneil (Yucatec Maya).

DESCRIPTION This moderately stout snake, which attains a total length of nearly 3,000 mm, is second in size only to the boa constrictor in the Yucatán Peninsula. The head is distinct from the neck, and the eyes are fairly large with round pupils (Fig. 357). The dorsal scales are smooth and are arranged in 17 rows at midbody. Paired apical pits are present on some dorsal scales, especially posteriorly and on the tail. The anal plate is undivided.

The dorsal coloration is variable, but in general these snakes are olive brown to reddish tan anteriorly, darker posteriorly, and uniform black on the posterior third of the body and the tail. Usually there is an irregular diagonal black stripe on the neck and anterior portion of the body. Anteriorly the venter is uniform reddish tan or olive brown, becoming darker posteriorly. Often there are slivers of dark pigment on the lateral surfaces of the body and on the trailing edges of the ventral scales. The sutures of the fourth, fifth, sixth, and seventh supralabials are edged with black, as are the fourth, fifth, and sixth infralabials.

SIMILAR SPECIES Of the more or less unicolored racerlike snakes in the Yucatán Peninsula, *Masticophis mentovarius* is more slender, has a uniform tan dorsal coloration, and has one rather than two apical pits on the dorsal scales. *Dryadophis melanolomus* is much smaller, has a divided anal plate, and lacks the distinctive color pattern on the labial scales characteristic of *Drymarchon*.

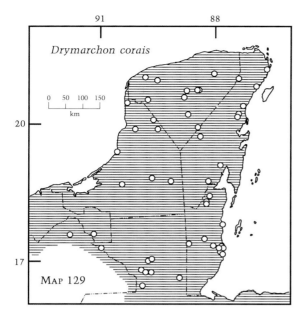

Drymarchon corais

MAP 129

DISTRIBUTION The black-tailed indigo snake occurs at low and moderate elevations on the Pacific slope from Sinaloa south, and on the Atlantic slope from the southern United States southward through Central America to northern Argentina. In the Yucatán Peninsula this species is pan-peninsular (Map 129).

NATURAL HISTORY This alert, fast-moving, diurnal snake occupies a variety of habitats in the Yucatán Peninsula, including savannas, mangroves, and thorn forests as well as the taller, wetter forests at the base of the peninsula. Although primarily terrestrial, it is often found in association with bodies of water. The diet includes a wide variety of vertebrate prey—birds, small mammals, fish, small turtles, frogs and toads, lizards, and other snakes, including venomous species. Duellman (1963:239) observed a *Drymarchon* in El Petén attempting to swallow a *Boa constrictor*. When captured, the *Drymarchon* was forced to regurgitate an adult *Atropoides nummifer*. Stuart (1948:67) found the tail of a *Urotheca elapoides* in the stomach of a *Drymarchon* from Alta Verapaz, and Greene (1975:479) captured a *Drymarchon* in southern Veracruz that regurgitated an *Adelphicos quadrivirgatus*. In Yucatán, I watched a subadult *D. corais* swallow a *Eumeces schwartzei*. Henderson and Hoevers (1977b:352) found *Bufo valliceps* in the stomach of a specimen from northern Belize. Gerhardt et al. (1993:350) reported that at Tikal, Guatemala, *Drymarchon* is preyed on by the great black hawk, *Buteogallus urubitinga*.

Drymarchon corais is oviparous. A specimen collected in early June in Alta Verapaz contained partly formed eggs (Stuart, 1948:67). At subtropical and temperate latitudes indigo snakes produce clutches ranging in size from 4 to 11 eggs (Fitch, 1970:130). A captive female that had been in isolation for four years and four months produced a clutch of 5 eggs, at least one of which was fertile, indicating a capacity for long-term sperm storage and delayed fertilization (Carson, 1945:225).

W. T. Neill and Allen (1959c:53) described a "combat dance" between two male *Drymarchon* at Cayo on 1 February. The snakes reared high into the air and pushed against each other. The same behavior was described for snakes from the United States (W. T. Allen and Neill, 1952:46).

SUBSPECIES Eight subspecies of this wide-ranging form are currently recognized; only one, *D. c. melanurus*, occurs in the Yucatán Peninsula.

ETYMOLOGY The specific name, *corais*, might derive from the Latin *cora*, "pupil of the eye."

Locality Records Belize: Belize: Belize (USNM 24913), outskirts of Belize (W. T. Neill and Allen, 1959c:53); Cayo: Cayo (W. T. Neill and Allen, 1959c:53), 4 km E Chial (CM 109016), ca. 3 mi S Belmopan (CM 112182); Corozal: Santa Cruz (MPM 7322); Orange Walk: Orange Walk (MPM 8175), Tower Hill (MPM 7320–21, 8145–46); Stann Creek: Bokowina (Schmidt, 1941:500), Freetown (CM 8511, 8514–15), Melinda Forestry Station (JLK 498), Middlesex (UCM 25861, 30841–42), Stann Creek (W. T. Neill and Allen, 1959c:53), 7.5 mi W Stann Creek (JLK 497); no specific locality (USNM 24913). *Guatemala*: El Petén: 15 km NNE Chinajá (KU 55701), El Paso (MCZ 38649), El Rosario (JCL sight record), La Libertad (UMMZ 74929), Pacomon (USNM 71371), Piedras Negras (USNM 110872–73), 2 mi E Poptún (UMMZ 124346), 6 km NW San Juan Acul (AMNH 99918), Sayaxché (KU 57149; UCM 22323–25). *Mexico*: Campeche: Champotón (EAL 3339), 3 mi E Chencoyi (UIMNH 87654), 4 km W, 2 km N El Remate (Dundee et al., 1986:42), 8 mi E Escárcega (LSUMZ 33357), 31 mi NNE Hopelchén (UMMZ 126162), López Mateos (EAL 2896), Santa Rosa Xtampak (JCL sight record), 46 mi E Silvituc (UCM 48305), Xpujil (R. W. Wade, pers. comm.); Chiapas: Palenque (USNM 110871); Quintana Roo: 7 mi N Bacalar (LSUMZ 33368), 65.6 km NNE Felipe Carrillo Puerto (UMRC 92-11), Othon Blanco (Dundee et al., 1986:42), Petempich (López-Gonzales, 1991:106), Playa del Carmen (Himmelstein, 1980:30), Pueblo Nuevo X-Can (CM 49128; UCM 40190–91), 140 km SSW Puerto Juárez (AMNH 110048), Tulum (López-

Gonzales, 1991:106), Ucum (R. W. Wade, pers. comm.); Tabasco: Tenosique (USNM 110870); Yucatán: Calcehtok (Dundee et al., 1986:42), 3 mi N Calotmul (UCM 39518), Chichén Itzá (AMNH 38838–40; UIMNH 17660; USNM 46393), 2 km E La Presumida (TU 19789), 1.5 mi S Libre Unión (UCM 28121), Mérida (H. M. Smith, 1938:7), Peto (CM 45294–95), Pisté (CM 46926, 47215–19, 49629–33; UCM 40192–93), 6 mi S Sisal (UIMNH 87655), 10 km SE Sotutá (Dundee et al., 1986:42), no specific locality (USNM 6554).

Genus *Drymobius* (Neotropical Racers)

This is a small genus of moderately slender, fast-moving, diurnal snakes. Representatives occur from southern Texas and Sonora south throughout Central America to Colombia and Peru. Four species were recognized by L. D. Wilson (1975a) in the most recent review of the genus. One species of *Drymobius* occurs in the Yucatán Peninsula. *Drymobius* is derived from the Greek *drymos*, "forest" or "oak wood," and *bios*, "life"—thus a forest-dwelling animal.

Drymobius margaritiferus (Schlegel)
(Figs. 358, 359; Map 130)

Herpetodryas margaritiferus Schlegel, 1837:184. HOLOTYPE: MNHNP 7309 (*fide* Stuart, 1963:97), but unknown *fide* L. D. Wilson (1974:172.1). TYPE LOCALITY: New Orleans (in error). H. M. Smith (1942c:383) suggested restriction to Veracruz, Mexico, and H. M. Smith and Taylor (1950b:347) further restricted the type locality to Córdoba, Veracruz, Mexico.

Speckled racer, green snake, guinea hen snake; speckled racer (Belize); petatilla, petatilla de pintas verdes, ranera (Guatemala, Mexico).

DESCRIPTION   These medium-sized, moderately slender racers have large eyes with round pupils. The head is moderately distinct from the neck. The adults average between 500 and 600 mm in snout-vent length, and the tail length is about 35 percent of the head and body length. The dorsal scales are weakly keeled, have apical pits, and are arranged in 17 rows at midbody. The anal plate is divided.

The dorsal color pattern distinguishes this snake from all other species in the Yucatán Peninsula. The dorsal scales are dark olive, brown, or black,

and each has a light yellow or yellow-orange center, this usually bordered by green or turquoise, especially anteriorly. The supracaudals are green or turquoise bordered by black. The venter is yellow or cream, with black on the trailing edges of the ventral scutes. Anteriorly the head is generally tan, becoming greenish posteriorly. The posterior margins of most of the scales on the head, including the supralabials, are outlined in black (Fig. 358). Often a dark temporal stripe forms an inverted V on the head, extending from the posteriormost supralabials and converging on the parietal scales (Fig. 359).

SIMILAR SPECIES   This distinctive snake can scarcely be confused with any other in the Yucatán Peninsula. When moving rapidly, the speckled racer appears greenish tan and might be mistaken for *Masticophis mentovarius* or *Dryadophis melanolomus*, both of which have smooth dorsal scales.

DISTRIBUTION   This wide-ranging species occurs at low, moderate, and intermediate elevations on the Pacific and Gulf slopes from southern Texas and Sonora south through Central America to northern Colombia. It is found throughout the Yucatán Peninsula (Map 130).

NATURAL HISTORY   Speckled racers are active, nervous, and diurnal. They inhabit both forested and open situations, and often frequent human settlements (Stuart, 1935:48). They move quickly and are generally terrestrial, and they are often found

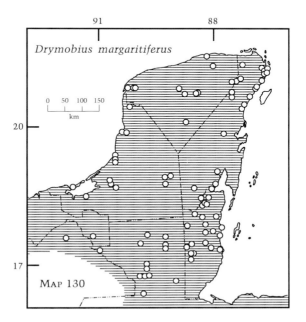

near bodies of water, where they feed primarily on frogs and toads. Duellman (1963:239) found *Bufo valliceps* and *Smilisca baudinii* in the stomachs of specimens from El Petén, Stuart (1935:48) reported *Rhinophrynus dorsalis* in a specimen from the savanna country of El Petén, and H. M. Smith (1943:424) found several species of *Eleutherodactylus* and two other leptodactylid frogs in the stomach of a specimen from El Petén. I found a *Rana berlandieri* in a specimen from Yucatán and saw a specimen from Stann Creek District swallow a *S. baudinii*. Henderson and Hoevers (1977b:352) found *B. valliceps*, *Hypopachus variolosus*, and *Leptodactylus* sp. in the stomachs of specimens from northern Belize. Seib (1984, 1985a) studied the diet of *D. margaritiferus* on three coffee fincas in southern Chiapas and adjacent Guatemala and augmented his data with stomach contents from preserved specimens from Chiapas and Guatemala. The diet in these areas consisted mostly of anurans, with occasional lizards, reptile eggs, and small mammals. Although nonvenomous, these snakes bite freely if provoked, and the bite bleeds copiously, suggesting the presence of an anticoagulant in the saliva, as conjectured by W. T. Neill and Allen (1959c:52). At Tikal, Guatemala, this species is preyed on by the great black hawk, *Buteogallus urubitinga* (Gerhardt et al., 1993:350).

Drymobius margaritiferus is oviparous. The breeding season is apparently protracted, and oviposition occurs throughout the rainy season. Gaige et al. (1937:18) reported that a gravid female collected in August contained fully developed eggs, and Stuart (1948:64) found females in Alta Verapaz with well-developed eggs in May and June. Werler (1949:59) reported a clutch of seven eggs laid on 22 April, two of which hatched on 9 June and 11 June. A hatchling collected on 15 October in Cayo District appeared to have hatched the preceding August (W. T. Neill, 1962:240). Solórzano and Cerdas (1987:75) reported that two females from Costa Rica produced clutches of five and four eggs on 29 March and 19 February, respectively, and that the incubation period ranged from 64 to 68 days.

SUBSPECIES L. D. Wilson (1975b:172.1) recognized four subspecies, of which only the nominate form, *D. m. margaritiferus*, occurs in the Yucatán Peninsula.

ETYMOLOGY The specific name, *margaritiferus*, comes from the Greek *margarites*, "pearl," and the

Latin *fero*, meaning "to bear"—thus "pearl bearing," in reference to the distinctive spotted pattern.

COMMENT L. D. Wilson (1975b) reviewed *D. margaritiferus*.

Locality Records Belize: Belize: Belize City (KU 94550), 20 mi W Belize City (BCB 11991), Lemonal (MPM 10788–89), vicinity Lucky Strike (UF 79990), Manatee (FMNH 3482); Cayo: 3 mi E Augustine (W. T. Neill, 1962:240), Central Farm (MCZ 71643), Chial (CM 112105), Cocquercot (UMMZ 74955), El Cayo (UMMZ 74954), Hummingbird Hwy. at Cave's Branch (LSUMZ 8905), Macal River at Guacamallo Bridge (CM 112149), Río Frio Cave (CM 105809), San Ignacio (UMMZ 74954), San Pastor (MPM 8207); Corozal: San Pablo (MPM 7738); S edge Corozal Town (JLK 472); Orange Walk: Blue Creek Village (MPM 8100, 8111), Chan Pine Ridge (MPM 7324), near Gallon Jug (MPM 7327), 0.5 mi N Gallon Jug (MCZ 71644–45), Lamanai (ROM H12737), Orange Walk (MPM 7323, 7326, 7328–29, 7605, 8109), Otro Benque (MPM 7325, 7736, 8105, 8112–22), Tower Hill (MPM 7389, 7734–35, 7737, 8101–4, 8106–8, 8110); Stann Creek: Melinda Forestry Station (JLK 486–87), Middlesex (FMNH 4442; UCM 25718–19, 25723, 25735, 25738, 25744, 25756, 25793, 25795–98, 25801–2, 25807, 25849–60, 29962, 30843–79); no specific locality (FMNH 4198–99; USNM 26353). *Guatemala*: Alta Verapaz: Chinajá (Duellman, 1963:239); El Petén: Chuntuquí (USNM 71363), El Rosario (JCL sight record), La Libertad (FMNH 43362–64; UMMZ 74931, 74933–53), Paso Caballos (MCZ 38586), Piedras Negras (USNM 110838), Poptún (UMMZ 117958), San Juan Acul, on Río de la Pasión (AMNH 99919), Santa Teresa (UMMZ 74932), Sayaxché (KU 57139; UCM 22328–35), Tikal (MCZ 55427; UF 13815–21; UMMZ 117954–57, 117959, 120319), 14.2 mi S Tikal (KU 157565), Uaxactún (FMNH 43361; KU 157563–64), no specific locality (USNM 71368). *Mexico*: Campeche: Balchacaj (UIMNH 17668), Becan (UMMZ 76125; UWZH 20515), Campeche (USNM 46454), 9.7 km E Castamay (EAL 2934), Champotón (UMMZ 73070–71), 11 km S Champotón (KU 70849), 24 km S Champotón (LSUMZ 28286), Ciudad del Carmen (UMMZ 83546–47), Escárcega (UCM 28123), 6 km N 18 de Marzo (EAL 3024), rd. to Sabancuy, 9.9 km N Hwy. 186 (KU 171726), Tankuche–El Remate (IHNHERP 464–65, 487), 32.1 km NE Xpujil (KU 171725), Zoh Laguna (CM 47955), no specific locality (USNM 46454); Chiapas: Palenque (USNM 110836); Quintana Roo: 1.3 mi N Bacalar (KU 157566), Cancún (López-Gonzales, 1991:106), Cobá (FMNH 26979–80; JCL photo; UMMZ 83943), 8.5 km N Cobá (UMRC 84-47), Chetumal (MCZ 53122), 4 km NNE Felipe Carrillo Puerto (KU 70846), 5.1 mi E Nicholas Bravo (R. W. Wade, pers. comm.), Petempich (López-Gonzales,

1991:106), Playa del Carmen (Himmelstein, 1980:30), Pueblo Nuevo X-Can (UCM 40194–207, 41687–88), 4 km WSW Puerto Juárez (KU 70848), 4.3 km S Puerto Juárez (KU 157567), Puerto Morelos (Himmelstein, 1980:30; USNM 46532), 24.1 km N Puerto Morelos (EAL 2858), Punta Maroma (López-Gonzales, 1991:106), Punta Venado (López-Gonzales, 1991:106), 3.3 km S Solferino (JCL sight record), Tintal (UCM 40208–17, 41677–86), Tulum (LSUMZ 33354), 10.6 km NW Tulum (JCL 6799), Xcopen (MCZ 9576–78); Tabasco: Tenosique (USNM 110835); Yucatán: 22.4 km W Bella Flor (UMRC 84-146), 6.1 km E Celestún (TU 19805), 20 km E Celestún (TU 19761, 19799), Chichén Itzá (MCZ 26829–33; USNM 46572), 5 km NW Dziuché (KU 70847), 12 mi S Izamal (UMMZ 80802–3), 1.5 mi S Libre Unión (UCM 16034), Pisté (CM 46995, 47101, 49634; UCM 40218), bet. Río Lagartos and San Felipe (UMRC 92-8), 12 mi N Tizimín (UCM 28124), X-Can (CM 46870).

Genus *Elaphe* (Rat Snakes)

Rat snakes are powerful constrictors that prey predominantly on small mammals and birds. Some species are terrestrial, but many have a propensity to climb, and individuals are occasionally found in trees at considerable heights. As a group, these are attractive snakes, typically with bold patterns of blotches or stripes. The genus *Elaphe* is predominantly Northern Hemispheric, with representatives in North America, Europe, and Asia. In the New World the genus ranges throughout the eastern United States southward through Mexico and Central America to Nicaragua. Nearly 50 living species are presently recognized, one of which occurs in the Yucatán Peninsula. *Elaphe* derives from the Greek *elaphos*, "deer" or "stag," perhaps in reference to the branched markings on the head and neck of some species, which resemble the antlers of a deer.

Elaphe flavirufa (Cope)
(Figs. 152B, 165, 360; Map 131)

Coluber flavirufus Cope, 1867:319. HOLOTYPE: USNM 6566. TYPE LOCALITY: Yucatán, Mexico; Izamal, Yucatán, Mexico, according to D. M. Cochran (1961:165).

Tropical rat snake; ratonera manchada (Mexico); chuc choc (Yucatec Maya).

DESCRIPTION The tropical rat snake may reach a snout-vent length of about 1,300 mm. The relatively short tail is approximately 20 percent of the snout-vent length. The head is distinct from the neck and roughly triangular in dorsal view. The eyes are unusually large for an *Elaphe*, and the pupils are round (Fig. 165). The middorsal scales are keeled, and those on the lateral surface of the body are smooth. Paired apical pits are present on the dorsal scales, and the number of dorsal scale rows at midbody varies from 27 to 31. The ventral scales are angulate, and the anal plate is divided.

The dorsal ground color of juvenile and young adult specimens is light tan or yellowish tan with a series of brown or reddish brown blotches edged with dark brown or black. Many of the adjacent blotches coalesce, producing an irregular zigzag pattern. On the lateral surfaces of the body a series of smaller blotches alternates with those on the dorsum. The dorsal surface of the head is tan or gray, usually with a median dark, lance-shaped mark on the frontal and parietal scales. A thin, broken dark stripe extends from the supraocular scale along the lateral margins of the parietals onto the temporal

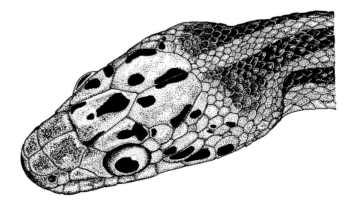

Fig. 165. Dorsolateral view of the head of *Elaphe flavirufa* (UMRC 84-89), 453 mm SVL; 6.9 km W Yokdzonot, Yucatán, Mexico.

region of the head. There is a dark postocular stripe. A pair of dark stripes originates on the posterior surface of the head and passes posteriorly, merging with the first dorsal blotch. The ventral surfaces of the body and tail are yellowish, cream, or tan, with or without squarish dark brown blotches. Large individuals tend to be darker with a grayish ground color and dark brown or nearly black dorsal markings (Fig. 360).

SIMILAR SPECIES *Elaphe flavirufa* most closely resembles *Senticolis triaspis*, from which it differs in having larger eyes and 9 or 10, rather than 8, supralabials (Fig. 152A,B). *Pseustes poecilonotus* lacks the lance-shaped mark on the dorsal surface of the head and possesses an undivided anal plate. *Leptodeira frenata* has smooth scales and vertically elliptical pupils.

DISTRIBUTION This species occurs at low elevations on the Atlantic slope from southern Tamaulipas to northern Honduras, and on Corn Island, Nicaragua. It also occurs on the Pacific slope in Chiapas. *Elaphe flavirufa* may occur throughout the Yucatán Peninsula, but it has not yet been recorded from western El Petén (Map 131).

NATURAL HISTORY *Elaphe flavirufa* inhabits both humid lowland forests and the seasonally dry forests at the northern end of the Yucatán Peninsula. It appears to be most common in northern Quintana Roo. In my experience it is nocturnal, and

all of Duellman's (1965:607) specimens were obtained at night. This rat snake is both terrestrial and arboreal.

The tropical rat snake feeds on small mammals, as its common names suggest, but very little information is available concerning the diet in the Yucatán Peninsula. A specimen from Chichén Itzá in the University of Michigan Museum of Zoology (UMMZ 73072) contained the remains of a bird.

Little is known of reproduction in this species. It is doubtless oviparous, like the other members of the genus *Elaphe*.

SUBSPECIES Dowling (1952) recognized four subspecies of *E. flavirufa*, two of which occur in the Yucatán Peninsula. The nominate subspecies, *E. f. flavirufa*, occurs through the base of the Yucatán Peninsula and has more than 31 body blotches, whereas *E. f. phaescens* occurs at the dry outer end of the peninsula and has fewer than 32 body blotches (Dowling, 1952:13). L. D. Wilson and Meyer (1985:49) questioned Dowling's arrangement, however, noting that variation among the various forms is clinal. Some taxonomists (e.g., Flores Villela et al., 1991:181; H. M. Smith and Taylor, 1966:21) consider *E. f. phaescens* a full species.

ETYMOLOGY The specific name, *flavirufa*, is derived from the Latin *flavus*, "yellow," and *rufus*, "reddish," in reference to the yellow ground color and brick red dorsal blotches on young individuals.

Locality Records Belize: Cayo: Caracol (CMM photo), Central Farm (MCZ 71673); Orange Walk: 10 mi S Orange Walk Town (JLK 500). *Guatemala*: El Petén: Tikal (UF 13822–24; UMMZ 126424). *Mexico*: Campeche: Carretera El Remate–Isla Arena, km 2 (IHNHERP 470), Tuxpeña Camp (UMMZ 73224), no specific locality (USNM 14848); Quintana Roo: Cancún (López-Gonzales, 1991:106), 21.6 km N Felipe Carrillo Puerto (JCL 6795), Playa del Carmen (López-Gonzales, 1991:106), 2.4 mi SW Playa del Carmen (KU 157568), 2.5 mi N Playa del Carmen (LSUMZ 38603), 7 mi N Playa del Carmen (LSUMZ 33159), 11.4 km S Playa del Carmen (JCL 6794), 21.7 km S Playa del Carmen (JCL 6839), 8 km W Puerto Juárez (KU 70850–51), 12 mi W Puerto Juárez (UCM 39519), 34.1 km SW Puerto Juárez (EAL 2851), Puerto Morelos (López-Gonzales, 1991:106), 6.7 km NE Puerto Morelos (KU 171718), 8 km SW Puerto Morelos (MZFC 3399), Punta Maroma (López-Gonzales, 1991:106), Punta Venado (López-Gonzales, 1991:106), Tulum (López-Gonzales, 1991:106), 4.9 km NW Tulum (UMRC 84-58), 24.5 km S Tulum (JCL 6796), km 92 on rd. bet. Tulum and Felipe

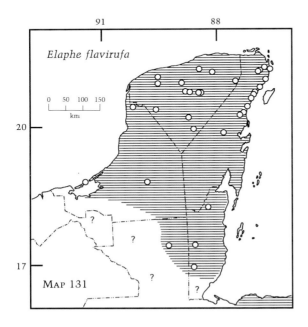

Elaphe flavirufa

MAP 131

Carrillo Puerto (MCZ 152722); Yucatán: 16.4 mi E Buctzotz (KU 157570), Chichén Itzá (KU 70852; MCZ 29241; UMMZ 73072–74), Dzibilchaltún (FMNH 153563, 153565, 153580), Izamal (USNM 6566), 10.6 mi E Kantunil (KU 157569), Laguna Chicankanab (MCZ 53118), vicinity Mérida (EAL 3022), Peto (UMRC 80-81), Pisté (CM 49635–36; UCM 16036), 9.1 mi W Tizimín (KU 157571), Uxmal (TU 19760), X-Can (CM 47034), 6.9 km W Yokdzonot (UMRC 84-89).

Genus *Ficimia* (Hooknosed Snakes)

This genus comprises seven species of small, rather stocky snakes with upturned snouts and short tails. They occur at low and moderate elevations from the southern United States southward through Mexico to Guatemala, Belize, and northern Honduras. Hooknosed snakes are nocturnal and fossorial, and most feed predominantly on spiders. The genus is unusual because the females of some species possess hemipenes. A single species of *Ficimia* occurs in the Yucatán Peninsula. The most recent review of this genus is L. M. Hardy, 1975. According to Hardy (in litt.), *Ficimia* comes from the Latin *ficus*, "fig" or "fig tree," and the Greek *mia* or *myia*, "fly." Perhaps the type specimen was found near a fig tree where small flies were attracted to decaying vegetation.

Ficimia publia Cope
(Figs. 154B, 166, 361, 362; Map 132)

Ficimia publia Cope, 1866:126. LECTOTYPE: USNM 16428 (designated in L. M. Hardy, 1975:135). TYPE LOCALITY: Yucatán, Mexico; restricted by H. M. Smith and Taylor (1950b:352) to Chichén Itzá, Yucatán, but that restriction rejected by L. M. Hardy (1975:134).

Yucatán hooked-nosed snake; barber pole (Belize); naricilla manchada (Mexico); kani'ha (Lacandón Maya); xoc-mis (Yucatec Maya).

DESCRIPTION This is a small, rather stocky snake with a short tail and a short, broad head only slightly distinct from the neck. The adults are about 230 to 280 mm in snout-vent length. The tail length is about 15 to 20 percent of the head and body length. The eyes are small, and the pupils are round. This is the only species in the Yucatán Peninsula with a conspicuously pointed, upturned rostral scale (Fig. 166) that is in broad contact with the frontal scale and separates the internasals (Fig. 154B). The dorsal scales are smooth, have a single apical pit, and are arranged in 17 rows at midbody. The anal plate is undivided.

The dorsal color and pattern are quite variable. The ground color is tan, brown, reddish brown, or gray with a series of dark brown or gray middorsal blotches, often with lighter centers and edged with black (Figs. 361, 362). The lateral surfaces of the body and tail are covered with irregular small spots and blotches. The dorsal surface of the head is generally tan, brown, or gray with indistinct darker markings. Many specimens have a dark subocular spot on the supralabials below the eye. The chin and venter are usually immaculate white, cream, or tan, although in some specimens the lateral blotches extend onto the lateral surfaces of the ventral scales.

SIMILAR SPECIES No other snake in the Yucatán Peninsula has a conspicuously pointed, upturned rostral scale contacting the frontal and separating the internasals. *Stenorrhina* species may have a slightly upturned rostrum, but their internasals are fused with the anterior nasal scales (Fig. 154C) and are not separated by the rostral scale.

DISTRIBUTION *Ficimia publia* occurs at low elevations from northern Veracruz, Morelos, and

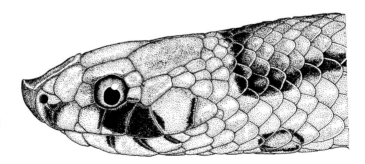

Fig. 166. Lateral view of the head of *Ficimia publia* (UMRC 85-17), 230 mm SVL; Uxmal, Yucatán, Mexico.

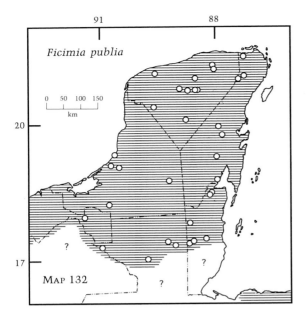

Ficimia publia

MAP 132

meaning "common," "ordinary," "vulgar," or "general" (L. M. Hardy, 1980:254.2).

COMMENT   L. M. Hardy (1975) reviewed *F. publia* as part of his revision of the genus *Ficimia* and in a later publication summarized the available information on this species (Hardy, 1980).

Locality Records   Belize: Belize: Rockville Quarry (UF 79991); Cayo: vicinity Baking Pot (W. T. Neill, 1965:104), 2.5 mi S Belmopan (JLK 490), Cayo (MSU 6010H); Corozal: Libertad Factory (MPM 7554), 16 mi N Orange Walk (JLK 489); Orange Walk: Gallon Jug (FMNH 69232; MCZ 71666–68). *Guatemala*: El Petén: N shore Lake Yaxhá (UTEP 6021), 4 mi N La Libertad (UMMZ 74888), Piedras Negras (USNM 110295), Tikal (UF 13825–26; UMMZ 117917; UMRC 79-275). *Mexico*: Campeche: Becan (UWZH 20495, 20540, 20549), 11.2 km SW Champotón (JCL sight record), Chuina (KU 74992), near Sabancuy (JCL photo), San Enrique, Río Candelaria (FMNH 36100); Quintana Roo: Chetumal (MCZ 53123), 2.9 km S Chiquilá (KU 171695), Felipe Carrillo Puerto (UMMZ 113569–70), 19.3 km N Noh Bec (UMRC 84-41), Pino Suarez (UMRC 84-40), Pueblo Nuevo X-Can (UCM 40232–35, 41697–98), Tintal (UCM 40236, 41698); Tabasco: 37.3 mi E Catazajá (LSUMZ 38291); Yucatán: Catmís (FMNH 26993), Chichén Itzá (CM 36448; FMNH 20623, 20635; MCZ 7120, 28754–55; UMMZ 83931), Dzibilchaltún (FMNH 153512), Libre Unión (FMNH 36256), Pisté (CM 46927–29, 47109, 49648–51; KU 70859; UCM 40237, 41699), 39.7 km S Río Lagartos (KU 171696), near Tizimín (JCL photo), 9.7 km NE Tunkás (KU 171697), Uxmal (UMRC 85-17), Yokdzonot (FMNH 36260).

Guerrero southeastward through the Yucatán Peninsula and Guatemala to northern Honduras. It probably occurs throughout the Yucatán Peninsula, but I have found no records from southern El Petén or southern Belize (Map 132).

NATURAL HISTORY   These small, secretive snakes are moderately common in the Yucatán Peninsula, where they occur in virtually all habitats. They are terrestrial, largely nocturnal, and completely innocuous. H. M. Smith (1943:429) found specimens abroad at night along trails in the tall forest at Piedras Negras, Guatemala. I found individuals crossing roads at night in thorn forest and tropical deciduous forest. They feed primarily on spiders.

Ficimia publia is oviparous. A. E. Greer (1966) reported that a female from Belize contained two large eggs.

SUBSPECIES   As many as three subspecies of *F. publia* have been recognized, including *F. p. wolffsohni*, described by W. T. Neill (1965) from Belize, and the nominate form, *F. p. publia*, which occurs elsewhere in the Yucatán Peninsula. L. M. Hardy (1975:148) analyzed morphological variation, however, and concluded that no subspecies should be recognized.

ETYMOLOGY   The specific name, *publia*, is from the Latin *publ*, "public," "state," or "people," and the suffix *-ia*, "of" or "belonging to," apparently

Genus *Geophis* (Earth Snakes)

This moderately large assemblage of small burrowing snakes is distributed from northern Mexico to Colombia. Members of the genus exhibit many morphological features associated with burrowing, including a narrow head, a short tail, a long, pointed snout, a narrow gape, and a reduced number of head shields.

The most recent comprehensive treatment of the genus *Geophis* is by Downs (1967), who recognized 33 species but acknowledged that many forms were poorly known at that time and would likely be relegated to subspecific status when more material had been acquired. One species of *Geophis* occurs in the Yucatán Peninsula. *Geophis* derives from the Greek geo, "earth," and *ophis*, "snake," in reference to the burrowing habits of these snakes.

Geophis carinosus Stuart
(Fig. 152E; Map 133)

Geophis carinosus Stuart, 1941a:3. HOLOTYPE: UMMZ 89082. TYPE LOCALITY: Finca San Francisco, 27 km northeast of Nebaj, El Quiche, Guatemala.

Keeled earth snake; minadora carinada (Mexico).

DESCRIPTION This small, rather thick-bodied snake averages between 160 and 180 mm in snout-vent length. The tail is about 35 to 40 percent as long as the head and body. The head is bluntly rounded in dorsal aspect and scarcely distinct from the neck. The eyes are small, and the pupils are round. The dorsal scales are arranged in 17 rows at midbody and lack apical pits. The dorsal scales are keeled, except for the first scale row, which is normally smooth. The anal plate is undivided. There is no enlarged supraocular scale, and the parietal scales are in broad contact with a supralabial scale (Fig. 152E).

The dorsum is uniform tan or brown. The venter is cream or tan, and each ventral scale has a brown anterior border. The infralabials, chin, and throat are mottled with brown and white.

SIMILAR SPECIES The other small burrowing snakes in the Yucatán Peninsula, *Typhlops* and *Lep-*

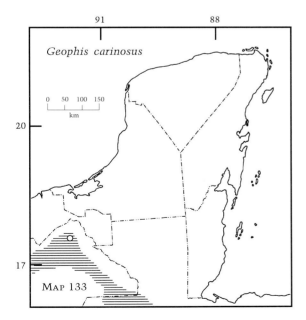

MAP 133

totyphlops, have degenerate eyes, and their ventral scales are the same size as their dorsals. No other colubrid snake in the Yucatán Peninsula lacks an enlarged supraocular scale; nor are the parietal and supralabial scales in contact in any other Yucatecan colubrid (Fig. 152E).

DISTRIBUTION *Geophis carinosus* occurs at low and moderate elevations on the Atlantic slope of Chiapas and Guatemala. In the Yucatán Peninsula it is known only from the vicinity of Palenque (Map 133).

NATURAL HISTORY The natural history of this species in the Yucatán Peninsula is poorly known. Stuart (1941a:4) found the type specimen abroad at night on a trail in a coffee grove. It is probably secretive and fossorial. Other members of the genus *Geophis* are said to feed on earthworms (Bogert and Porter, 1966; J. A. Campbell et al., 1983), on arthropods, slugs, and earthworms (J. A. Campbell and Murphy, 1977), and on earthworms and leeches (Seib, 1985a), but nothing is known specifically about the diet of *G. carinosus*.

Presumably *G. carinosus* is oviparous, as are the other species of *Geophis* for which information on reproduction is available (Bogert and Porter, 1966; J. A. Campbell et al., 1983).

ETYMOLOGY The specific name, *carinosus*, is from the Latin *carina*, "keel," and *-osus*, a suffix meaning "full of, augmented, prone to," in reference to the keeled dorsal scales present in this form but not in other members of the genus *Geophis*, which typically have smooth scales.

COMMENT Downs (1967:81) reviewed *G. carinosus* as part of his revision of the genus *Geophis*.

Locality Record Mexico: Chiapas: Palenque ruins (EAL 3326).

Genus *Imantodes*
(Blunt-headed Vine Snakes)

These unusually slender and elongate snakes of tropical America are highly specialized for an arboreal existence, although specimens are not infrequently found on the ground. Rear-fanged but inoffensive and harmless to humans, these snakes feed primarily on lizards and frogs. They are crepuscular and nocturnal. The genus occurs at low to intermediate elevations from tropical Mexico to Argentina and Paraguay. Zweifel (1959) reviewed the *Imantodes* of western Mexico, Myers (1982) treated the Panamanian species, and Savage and Scott (1987) reviewed the forms occurring in Costa Rica. Six species are recognized, of which three occur in the Yucatán Peninsula. *Imantodes* is derived from the Greek *himantos*, the genitive of *himas*, "leather strap" or "thong," and the suffix *-odes*, "like," in reference to the extremely attenuate body form.

Key to the Species of the Genus *Imantodes*

1. Scales of the vertebral row not or only slightly enlarged (Fig. 167B). 2
   Scales of the vertebral row abruptly and conspicuously enlarged (Fig. 167A) . . . .
   . . . . *Imantodes cenchoa*

2. Dorsal color pattern of dark brown or reddish brown blotches against a tan background, the blotches distinct and unbroken laterally; more than 240 ventral scales . . . .
   . . . . *Imantodes tenuissimus*
   Dorsal color pattern of dark brown blotches with lighter centers, the blotches edged with white and often continuous, posteriorly often broken on the sides (Fig. 167B); fewer than 240 ventral scales . . . . *Imantodes gemmistratus*

Clave para las Especies del Género *Imantodes*

1. Escamas de la hilera vertebral levemente o no alargadas (Fig. 167B) 2
   Escamas de la hilera vertebral alargadas abrupta y conspicuamente (Fig. 167A) . . . .
   . . . . *Imantodes cenchoa*

2. Patrón dorsal de coloración pardo obscuro, o con manchas pardo rojizas sobre un fondo moreno, las manchas son distintivas y sin interumpirse lateralmente; más de 240 escamas ventrales. . . . . *Imantodes tenuissimus*
   Patrón dorsal de coloración parda con manchas con los centros claros, las manchas con márgenes blancos y usualmente continuos; a menudo las manchas se fragmentan en los lados posteriormente (Fig. 167B); menos de 240 escamas ventrales . . . .
   . . . . *Imantodes gemmistratus*

Imantodes cenchoa (Linnaeus)
(Figs. 167A, 168, 363; Map 134)

Coluber cenchoa Linnaeus, 1758:226. TYPE: unknown. TYPE LOCALITY: America.

Blunt-headed tree snake (Belize); bejuquilla, cordelilla manchada (Guatemala, Mexico); k'aaxche kan (Lacandón Maya); zac ak can (Yucatec Maya).

DESCRIPTION   This is the largest of the three *Imantodes* species in the Yucatán Peninsula (Fig. 363). The adults may exceed 850 mm in snout-vent length, although the average is probably between 600 and 700 mm. The tail is long, about 40 to 45 percent of the snout-vent length. This is an extremely attenuate snake with a blunt head that is very distinct from the narrow neck (Fig. 168). The eyes are large and bulging, and the pupils are ver-

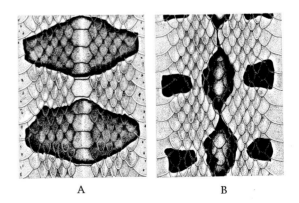

Fig. 167. Middorsal views of *Imantodes*. A, *I. cenchoa* showing the conspicuously enlarged scales of the vertebral scale row. B, *I. gemmistratus* showing slightly enlarged scales of the vertebral scale row.

A   B

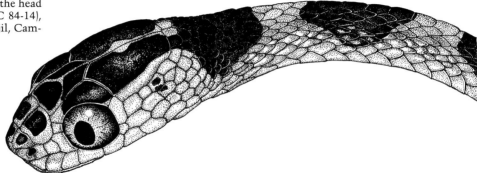

Fig. 168. Dorsolateral view of the head of *Imantodes cenchoa* (UMRC 84-14), 450 mm SVL; 27.8 km E. Xpujil, Campeche, Mexico.

tically elliptical. This is the only Yucatecan *Imantodes* with conspicuously enlarged vertebral scales (Fig. 167A). The dorsal scales are smooth, lack apical pits, and are arranged in 17 rows at midbody. The anal plate is divided.

The dorsal color pattern is a series of dark brown bands, often edged with black, against a light tan background. The venter is tan or cream with small brown flecks.

SIMILAR SPECIES   *Imantodes tenuissimus* is similar in color and pattern, but it is smaller and the scales of the vertebral row are not conspicuously enlarged.

DISTRIBUTION   *Imantodes cenchoa* occurs at low and moderate elevations in Mexico from Chiapas on the Pacific slope and Tamaulipas on the Atlantic slope, through Central America to Argentina and Paraguay. In the Yucatán Peninsula this species

occurs from southern Campeche through El Petén and Belize, and north through Quintana Roo (Map 134). It is apparently absent from the northwest portion of the peninsula, where it is replaced by *I. tenuissimus*.

NATURAL HISTORY   Blunt-headed tree snakes are nocturnal and crepuscular inhabitants of primary and secondary forests, where they forage for lizards and frogs on the outer tips of tree branches. Stuart (1948:80) found *Anolis capito* and *A. uniformis* in the stomachs of snakes from Alta Verapaz. Duellman (1978:245) reported only lizards in the stomachs of specimens from eastern Ecuador. I found a small *Basiliscus vittatus* in the stomach of a specimen from the vicinity of Palenque, and Landy et al. (1966:96) found an *Anolis* and reptile eggs in the stomach of one from Vocán Tacaná, Chiapas. Although they spend most of their time in the trees, these snakes are occasionally terrestrial and are sometimes found on roads at night. By day they hide in bromeliads and other arboreal vegetation (Henderson and Nickerson, 1976:206).

Imantodes cenchoa is oviparous. Stuart (1948:80) found females carrying well-formed eggs in late April and mid-June in Alta Verapaz. Zug et al. (1979) examined samples from throughout the range and concluded that females attain reproductive maturity at a snout-vent length of about 620 mm and an estimated age of approximately two years. The clutch size in these specimens ranged from one to three, with a mean of two eggs. Fitch (1970:152) suggested a protracted breeding season for this species in Amazonia, and Duellman (1978:245) reported gravid females collected in March, June, July, and November in Amazonian Ecuador. Three of his females contained two eggs and one had one egg. Thus, clutch size evidently ranges from one to three, but the data are insufficient to delineate a breeding season in the Yucatán Peninsula.

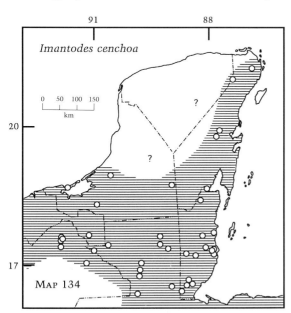

Imantodes cenchoa

0 50 100 150
km

MAP 134

SUBSPECIES   H. M. Smith (1942c:385) recognized three subspecies of *I. cenchoa* on the basis of color pattern and applied the name *I. c. leucomelas* to the populations in Mexico and Guatemala.

ETYMOLOGY   The specific name, *cenchoa*, may derive from the Greek *kenchros*, "millet," or "anything in small grains," also "a kind of snake with bead-like protuberances" (Jaeger, 1944:44), perhaps in reference to the small lateral spots seen in some specimens.

Locality Records Belize: Belize: 16 km SE Hattieville (CM 90988); Cayo: Augustine (MPM 8205), 34 mi W Belize City (CM 112097), San Pastor (MPM 8206), upper Raspaculo River basin (Stafford, 1991:14); Corozal: Corozal (MPM 7739); Orange Walk: 4 mi N Orange Walk (JLK 491–92); Stann Creek: Double Falls (Schmidt, 1941:505), Melinda Forestry Station (JLK 493), Middlesex (UCM 30880), Silk Grass (FMNH 49350), 10 mi W Stann Creek (JLK 465), 7 mi W Stann Creek (JLK 494); Toledo: Blue Creek (RWV photo), Dolores (UMRC 90-15), ca. 2 mi SE Big Falls, Río Grande (CM 105885), Unión Camp, Columbia River Forest Reserve (USNM 319775). *Guatemala*: Alta Verapaz: Chinajá (Duellman, 1963:239); El Petén: N shore Lake Yaxhá (UTEP 6009–10), La Libertad (AMNH 69990; UMMZ 74869–71), Las Cañas (CM 58274), Piedras Negras (USNM 110549), El Repasto (UCM 22336), Sayaxché (UCM 22337–38), Sojio (AMNH 69973–74), Tikal (UMMZ 117918–22), near Tikal (JCL photo), Uaxactún (AMNH 68526). *Mexico*: Campeche: Chuina (KU 74993), Ciudad del Carmen (UMMZ 83543), Pacaitún on Río Candelaria (FMNH 36244), 27.8 km E Xpujil (UMRC 84-14); Chiapas: Laguna Ocotal (MCZ 53881), ca. 15 km N Ocosingo (JCL sight record), Palenque (EAL 3031; KU 94132; USNM 110535–37), 8.2 mi S Palenque (LSUMZ 38542), 10 mi S Palenque (LSUMZ 33154–56), 13 mi S Palenque (LSUMZ 33157–58), 14.6 km S Palenque (USNM 266284), Palenque ruins (UIMNH 11344); Quintana Roo: Felipe Carrillo Puerto

(UMMZ 113573), 11.9 mi NE Felipe Carrillo Puerto (KU 157572), Pueblo Nuevo X-Can (LSUMZ 28260; UCM 40238), 13.2 mi SW Puerto Juárez (KU 157573); Tabasco: Tenosique (USNM 110548).

Imantodes gemmistratus (Cope)
(Figs. 167B, 169, 364; Map 135)

Himantodes gemmistratus Cope, 1860:264. HOLOTYPE: lost, *fide* H. M. Smith and Taylor, 1945:75. TYPE LOCALITY: near Izalco, El Salvador.

Bejuquillo, cordelilla escamuda (Mexico); k'aax-che kan (Lacandón Maya).

DESCRIPTION   This is a slender snake, but relatively stout for an *Imantodes* (Fig. 364). The adults average about 400 mm in snout-vent length, and the tail is about 35 to 40 percent of the head and body length. The body is laterally compressed, the head is moderately distinct from the neck, and the eyes, although large, are smaller and less protruding than the eyes of the other two *Imantodes* in the Yucatán Peninsula (Fig. 169). The pupils are vertically elliptical. The dorsal scales are smooth, lack apical pits, and are in 17 rows at midbody. The anal plate is divided.

The dorsal color pattern consists of a series of dark brown blotches with lighter centers set against a tan to gray background. The blotches are usually edged in black and extend laterally onto the ventral scales. Posteriorly the blotches become broken on the sides (Fig. 167B). The venter is tan or light gray, often peppered with tiny dark spots.

SIMILAR SPECIES   *Imantodes gemmistratus* differs from *I. cenchoa* in lacking conspicuously enlarged scales on the vertebral row (Fig. 167B) and

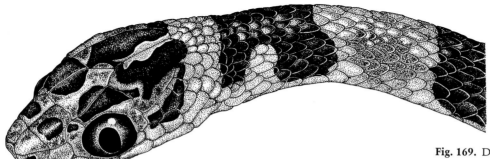

Fig. 169. Dorsolateral view of the head of *Imantodes gemmistratus* (UMRC 79-303), 401 mm SVL; 3.2 km W Kinchil, Yucatán, Mexico.

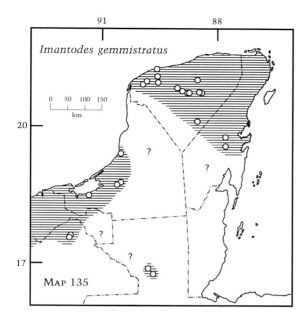

Map 135

from *I. tenuissimus* in having fewer than 240 ventral scales. *Sibon dimidiata* is similarly slender and elongate, but it has 15 rather than 17 rows of scales at midbody and an undivided anal plate.

DISTRIBUTION   This species occurs at low and moderate elevations in Mexico from Sonora on the Pacific slope and Veracruz on the Atlantic slope south to Colombia. It may occur throughout the Yucatán Peninsula, although it has not been recorded from north-central Campeche, southern Quintana Roo, or Belize (Map 135).

NATURAL HISTORY   *Imantodes gemmistratus* is crepuscular and nocturnal. Specimens of this predominantly arboreal snake can be found beneath loose bark on standing trees and within bromeliads (H. M. Smith, 1943:435), and sometimes under ground debris. They are occasionally encountered on roads at night. They feed predominantly on lizards, especially anoles. Myers (1982:30), reporting on Panamanian and Colombian snakes, found only *Anolis* in the stomachs of *I. gemmistratus*. Henderson and Nickerson (1976) noted that captives ate anoles and frequently entered water.

This is an oviparous snake. Myers (1982:30) found a clutch size of two eggs in each of three Panamanian females, but a Costa Rican specimen of *Imantodes*, possibly *I. gemmistratus*, contained six eggs.

SUBSPECIES   The taxonomy of this species is presently unstable. As many as six subspecies of *I.*

gemmistratus have been recognized (e.g., J. A. Peters and Oreja-Miranda, 1970:134), although Yingling (1972) recognized only two. Savage and Scott (1987:124) called attention to the distinctiveness of the Yucatecan populations, to which the trinomial *I. g. splendidus* has long been applied.

ETYMOLOGY   The specific name, *gemmistratus*, is derived from the Latin *gemma*, "bud" or "gem," and *stratus*, "paved"—thus "paved with gems."

Locality Records   Guatemala: El Petén: El Rosario (JCL sight record), Sojio (AMNH 69965, 69975). *Mexico*: Campeche: Balchacaj (UMMZ 81920–21), Ejido Ulumal (IHNHERP 429), 1.6 mi N Escárcega (KU 157574), 4 mi W Escárcega (LSUMZ 34765); Chiapas: Palenque (USNM 110522–27), bet. Palenque and Palenque ruins (EAL 3323); Quintana Roo: Felipe Carrillo Puerto (UMMZ 113572), 16.9 mi S Felipe Carrillo Puerto (KU 157575); Yucatán: Chichén Itzá (FMNH 20601–2; UMMZ 73033, 80936), Dzibilchaltún (FMNH 153577), 25.1 km NE Dziuché (UMRC 80-57), 24.7 km NE Dziuché (JCL photo), 2 km W Hunucmá (UMRC 84-163), Kantunil (FMNH 36249), 3.2 km W Kinchil (UMRC 79-303), Libre Unión (FMNH 36239–40, 36242), Mérida (Schmidt and Andrews, 1936:177), Pisté (CM 46930, 49652), 9.1 km NE Tunkás (KU 171699), Yokdzonot (FMNH 36241, 36243), 1.3 mi W Xocchel (KU 157576).

Imantodes tenuissimus (Cope)
(Fig. 170; Map 136)

Himantodes tenuissimus Cope, 1867:317. HOLOTYPE: USNM 6563. TYPE LOCALITY: Yucatán, Mexico.

Yucatán blunt-headed tree snake; bejuquilla, cordelilla, culebra nocturna (Mexico); katzim (Yucatec Maya).

DESCRIPTION   As the species name suggests, this is an extremely slender snake. The adults average between 475 and 525 mm in snout-vent length, with a maximum of about 600 mm. The tail is about 45 percent as long as the head and body. The body is laterally compressed, and the head is blunt and very distinct from the narrow neck (Fig. 170). The eyes are large and bulging, and the pupils are vertically elliptical. The dorsal scales are smooth, lack apical pits, and are arranged in 17 rows at midbody. The anal plate is divided.

The dorsal color pattern consists of distinct brown or reddish brown unbroken blotches against

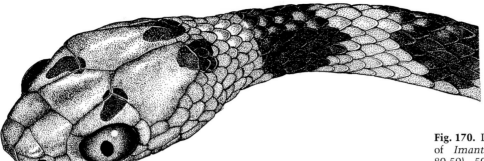

Fig. 170. Dorsolateral view of the head of *Imantodes tenuissimus* (UMRC 80-59), 508 mm SVL; 14.4 km NE Dziuché, Yucatán, Mexico.

a light tan background. The blotches are widest middorsally, then narrow laterally and extend onto the ventral scales. The venter is cream or tan with a few tiny dark spots.

SIMILAR SPECIES   This species closely resembles the larger *I. cenchoa,* from which it differs in lacking a conspicuously enlarged vertebral scale row.

DISTRIBUTION   *Imantodes tenuissimus* is endemic to the Yucatán Peninsula, where it is known from several localities in Quintana Roo and Yucatán, and from one in Campeche (Map 136). An unconfirmed record from Prussia, Chiapas, is doubtful.

NATURAL HISTORY   This nocturnal snake inhabits the deciduous forests of Yucatán and the taller, more mesic forests of neighboring Quintana Roo.

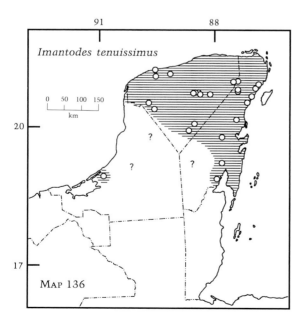

MAP 136

Imantodes tenuissimus is predominantly arboreal (although individuals have been found on roads at night) and probably eats lizards and frogs. Schmidt and Andrews (1936:177) described defensive behavior in an individual from Chichén Itzá in which the specimen rolled itself up into a ball on the end of a twig and would not unroll itself, even when it was touched.

Imantodes tenuissimus is oviparous. A specimen from Telantunich, Yucatán (FMNH 26971), contained three well-formed eggs.

ETYMOLOGY   The specific name, *tenuissimus,* is from the Latin *tenuis,* "thin," "narrow," or "slender," and *-issimus,* a superlative suffix denoting "very much" or "most," in reference to the extremely attenuate body form.

Locality Records Mexico: Campeche: 13.7 km SE Sabancuy (UMRC 91-14); Quintana Roo: 20.9 km N Bacalar (EAL 2887), 9 mi N Chetumal (BCB 12196), Felipe Carrillo Puerto (UMMZ 113589), ca. 70 km NNE Felipe Carrillo Puerto (AMNH 110049), Playa del Carmen (López-Gonzales, 1991:106), 9.6 km NE Playa del Carmen (KU 171700), Pueblo Nuevo X-Can (CM 45722–24, 45741, 49084, 49161; UCM 40239–40, 40724, 41700–2), 30.6 km S Pueblo Nuevo X-Can (JCL 6816), 31.9 km S Pueblo Nuevo X-Can (JCL 6815), Punta Venado (López-Gonzales, 1991:106), Reserva Biósfera Sian Ka'an (COHECERN uncat.), 16.3 km NW Tulum (JCL 6798); Yucatán: Chichén Itzá (FMNH 20612, 20622, 20638; MCZ 7239), 3 mi SE Chichén Itzá (UCM 18624), Dzibilchaltún (FMNH 153506), 14.4 km NE Dziuché (UMRC 80-59), bet. Muna and Opichén (TU 19824), Pisté (CM 46931, 46999, 47110–11, 49653–61; KU 70860; LSUMZ 44992; UCM 40241), 2.5 km W Pisté (KU 70861), Progreso (MCZ 7245), 2.7 km S Tekom (UMRC 84-38), Telantunich (FMNH 26971), 23.7 km S Telchac Puerto (KU 171698), bet. Uxmal and Santa Elena (TU 20663), X-Can (CM 46828, 47038); no specific locality (USNM 6563, 24889).

Genus *Lampropeltis* (King Snakes)

This is a strictly New World genus of nonvenomous, moderately large constrictors with smooth, highly polished scales. *Lampropeltis* ranges from southern Canada southward through Central America to northwestern South America. It is predominantly a North American assemblage, however, and only one of the 16 species is found in tropical Mexico and Central and South America. *Lampropeltis* is from the Greek *lampros*, "shining" or "beautiful," and *pelte*, "shield," presumably in reference to the polished scales characteristic of members of this genus.

Lampropeltis triangulum (Lacépède)
(Fig. 365; Map 137)

Coluber triangulum Lacépède, 1788:86. TYPE: unknown, *fide* K. L. Williams, 1988:53. TYPE LOCALITY: America; restricted to the vicinity of New York City, New York, by Schmidt (1953).

Tropical kingsnake, tropical milk snake; bead and coral (Belize); coralillo, coralillo falso (Guatemala, Mexico); culebra pinta, culebra real escarlata (Mexico); kuyun kan (Lacandón Maya).

DESCRIPTION This is a large and distinctive snake. Elsewhere in the range the males attain a snout-vent length of nearly 1.7 m, and the substantially shorter females reach about 1.1 m. In the Yucatán Peninsula the males reach a maximum snout-vent length of about 1.5 m, and the females about 1.05 m, although most specimens are substantially smaller. The tail is relatively short, usually about 13 to 15 percent of the head and body length, and males generally have relatively longer tails than females. The head is moderately distinct from the neck in dorsal aspect, the eyes are medium-large, the pupils are round, and the irises generally have some gold pigment. The dorsal surface of the head bears the typical colubrid configuration of symmetrical shields. The dorsal scales are smooth, highly polished, bear a pair of apical pits on their trailing edges, and are arranged in 21 rows at midbody. The anal plate is undivided.

The dorsal coloration usually consists of a series of relatively broad red rings bordered by black rings, which in turn are bordered by yellow, orange, or cream rings (Fig. 365). The scales of the yellow and red rings are tipped with black. In some specimens

the anterior half of the head is black; in others the snout is black but a yellow or white band passes between the eyes and the nostrils. Some specimens from Yucatán (e.g., UMMZ 76162) lack the yellow and black rings and are entirely red, except that the red scales are tipped with black.

SIMILAR SPECIES This snake superficially resembles the venomous coral snakes, *Micrurus*, with which it broadly co-occurs in the Yucatán Peninsula. The two species are probably members of a Batesian mimicry complex (Greene and McDiarmid, 1981). In the Yucatán Peninsula, coral snakes usually differ from their mimics in having the red and yellow rings in contact rather than separated by black rings, in lacking a loreal scale, and in having relatively much smaller eyes. Moreover, coral snakes have 15 rows of scales at midbody, whereas *L. triangulum* has 21. *Urotheca elapoides* is a smaller, more slender snake with a much longer tail. It has a divided anal plate, dorsal scales arranged in 17 rows at midbody, and red rings bordered by yellow rings rather than by black ones.

DISTRIBUTION *Lampropeltis triangulum* has one of the most extensive distributions of any snake in the New World. It occurs from southern Ontario and Quebec south through most of the United States east of the Rocky Mountains. It is found throughout most of mainland Mexico and Central America to South America, where is occurs in west-

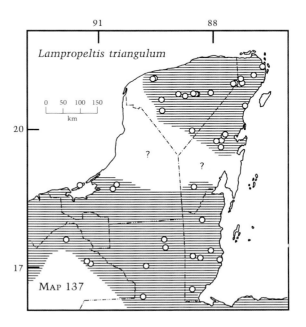

ern Ecuador and Colombia and in northern Venezuela. In the Yucatán Peninsula this species is probably pan-peninsular, but is has not yet been found in the central portion of the peninsula (Map 137).

NATURAL HISTORY   Tropical king snakes are moderately common terrestrial forest dwellers. They are largely noctural and hide beneath logs, rocks, and other surface debris during the day, although Duellman (1963:240) found an individual on the forest floor during the day. They feed on lizards, small snakes, frogs, and small mammals, but in the Yucatán Peninsula small mammals apparently predominate. Stuart (1948:70) found a shrew in the stomach of a specimen from Alta Verapaz. Gerhardt et al. (1993:350) reported that at Tikal, Guatemala, this species is preyed on by the great black hawk, *Buteogallus urubitinga*.

Lampropeltis triangulum is oviparous. Not much information is available concerning its reproductive biology in the Yucatán Peninsula, but Kardon (1979) reported that a captive female *L. t. polyzona* produced 5 eggs that hatched on 17 and 18 September. Werler (1951:44) reported that a clutch of 5 eggs laid on 5 June hatched on 24 and 25 July, and another clutch of 5 eggs laid on 21 July hatched on 26 and 28 August. Fitch (1970:137), who summarized data for this species from throughout its extensive range, reported the clutch size as ranging from 5 to 16, with an average of 10.2 eggs.

SUBSPECIES   K. L. Williams (1988) recognized 25 subspecies, 3 of which occur in the Yucatán Peninsula. *Lampropeltis triangulum blanchardi* occurs in the northern half of the peninsula and is replaced in El Petén and Belize by *L. t. abnorma*. The third subspecies, *L. t. polyzona*, enters the Yucatán Peninsula in eastern Tabasco and northern Chiapas.

ETYMOLOGY   The specific name, *triangulum*, is from the Latin *tri*, "three," and *angulus*, "angle."

COMMENT   K. L. Williams (1988) treated the biosystematics of *L. triangulum* in his comprehensive monograph on the species.

Locality Records   *Belize*: Cayo: Augustine (MPM 8185), upper Raspaculo River basin (Stafford, 1991:14); Orange Walk: Lamanai (ROM H12733); Stann Creek: Middlesex (CM 48004; UCM 30889), Regalia (W. T. Neill and Allen, 1961a:47); Toledo: Blue Creek Village

(UTA R-12340); no specific locality (FMNH 4200). *Guatemala*: Alta Verapaz: Chinajá (KU 57156); El Petén: La Libertad (FMNH 43370), vicinity of La Libertad (UMMZ 74927–28), Tikal (FMNH 204524; JCL photo; MCZ 58767–68; UF 13827–32), Uaxactún (KU 157578); no specific locality (USNM 25132). *Mexico*: Campeche: 22 mi NE Ciudad del Carmen (UMMZ 124659), 7.5 km W Escárcega (UMMZ 130236), 7.1 mi N Escárcega (KU 157579); Chiapas: Laguna Ocotal (MCZ 53879), Monte Libano (MCZ 53849), Palenque ruins (EAL 3033); Quintana Roo: 69 km W Chetumal (LSUMZ 28251), Colonia Santa María (UMMZ 76162), Felipe Carrillo Puerto (UMMZ 113590), 3.7 mi NE Felipe Carrillo Puerto (KU 157580), 7.9 km W Felipe Carrillo Puerto (KU 171714), 14.4 km NW Felipe Carrillo Puerto (UMRC 89-50), 18 to 28 mi S Felipe Carrillo Puerto (LSUMZ 38689), 3.5 mi E Pueblo Nuevo X-Can (UCM 28130), 6 mi E Pueblo Nuevo X-Can (UCM 28131), Pueblo Nuevo X-Can (CM 45725–31, 49059; UCM 40242–43, 40725–28, 41703–6), 11 km ENE Pueblo Nuevo X-Can (KU 70862), Puerto Juárez (Himmelstein, 1980:30), Tintal (UCM 40244–45), 18 km NNW Tulum (CAS 150334); Yucatán: Chichén Itzá (AMNH 58291; MCZ 7122, 7252, 28753, 29242; UMMZ 68238–39, 73029), Dzibilchaltún (FMNH 153502–3), 1.6 mi W Dzibilchaltún (KU 157577), 1 mi N Esmeralda (LACM 113905), Kantunil (FMNH), Pisté (CM 46932, 47112, 49662–64; UCM 40246, 41707), 9 km W Pisté (KU 70863), 4 km S Ticul (TU 19757), Valladolid (UCM 47400), Valladolid trail (UMMZ 68238), X-Can (CM 46829–30, 47039), Yokdzonot (FMNH 36210).

Genus *Leptodeira* (Cat-eyed Snakes)

This genus of mildly venomous rear-fanged snakes is essentially Neotropical in distribution. All are moderately slender snakes with broad heads, large eyes, and vertically elliptical pupils. Most are arboreal and nocturnal, although individuals are not infrequently encountered on the ground. The genus ranges from southern Texas and Sonora south through Central America to northern Argentina and Paraguay. The most recent comprehensive taxonomic treatment of the genus is Duellman, 1958a. Nine species are currently recognized, of which two occur in the Yucatán Peninsula. *Leptodeira* is from the Greek *leptos*, "slender" or "thin," and *deire*, "neck" or "throat," probably a reference to the relatively narrow neck.

Key to the Species of the Genus *Leptodeira*

More than 190 ventral scales . . . . *Leptodeira septentrionalis*

Fewer than 190 ventral scales . . . . *Leptodeira frenata*

Clave para las Especies del Género *Leptodeira*

Más de 190 escamas ventrales . . . . *Leptodeira septentrionalis*

Menos de 190 escamas ventrales . . . . *Leptodeira frenata*

Leptodeira frenata (Cope)
(Fig. 366; Map 138)

Sibon frenatum Cope, 1886:184, in Farrari-Pérez, 1886. HOLOTYPE: originally number 298 in the collection of the Geographical Exploring Commission of Mexico, now lost. TYPE LOCALITY: Jalapa, Veracruz, Mexico.

Cat-eyed snake, cohune tommygoff (Belize); culebra nocturna, falsa nauyaca (Mexico); chac-kokob (Yucatec Maya).

DESCRIPTION   The adults of this medium-sized snake average about 450 mm in snout-vent length, with the tail roughly 30 percent as long as the head and body. The head is rather broad, flat, and distinct from the neck (Fig. 366). The eyes are large, and the pupils are vertically elliptical. The dorsal scales are smooth, arranged in 21 rows at midbody, and bear a pair of apical pits. The anal plate is normally divided.

The dorsal ground color is light brown or tan, often pinkish, with a series of dark brown blotches, these generally widest dorsally and narrowing on the sides, where they alternate with dark lateral spots. The head is generally light brown or tan with a conspicuous postocular stripe that is continuous with the first dorsal blotch. The labial scales are light brown, usually with darker pigment at their margins. The chin and venter are immaculate cream or tan, except where the dorsal blotches extend onto the lateral margins of the ventral scales.

SIMILAR SPECIES   *Elaphe flavirufa*, *Pseustes poecilonotus*, and *Senticolis triaspis* have round pupils and keeled middorsal scales. *Leptodeira septentrionalis* is more slender and has more than 190 ventral scales.

DISTRIBUTION   *Leptodeira frenata* occurs at low and moderate elevations on the Atlantic slope from Veracruz southeastward through northern Guatemala and Belize. In the Yucatán Peninsula it is probably pan-peninsular, although it is yet to be found in southern El Petén or southernmost Belize (Map 138).

NATURAL HISTORY   *Leptodeira frenata* is a terrestrial and arboreal inhabitant of humid lowland forests. On Isla Cozumel it is common around human habitations. I have found specimens beneath logs, under the bark on fallen trees, beneath driftwood on the beach, and in cinder-block walls. They have also been taken from bromeliads during the dry season (Duellman, 1958a:62; H. M. Smith,

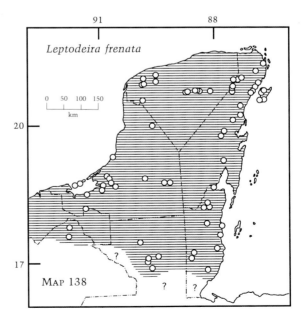

1943:442). Stuart (1935:53) encountered specimens near watering holes in northern Guatemala. They feed largely on frogs, toads, and lizards. Barbour and Cole (1906:150) reported a *Ctenosaura similis* in the stomach of a specimen from Chichén Itzá, and another specimen from Chichén Itzá (UMMZ 73027) contained a *Triprion petasatus*. A specimen I collected in western Campeche contained an adult *Anolis lemurinus*, and Gaige (1936:302) reported a partially digested *Anolis* in the stomach of a specimen from Tuxpeña, Campeche. Henderson and Hoevers (1977b:352) found *Bufo valliceps*, *Smilisca*, and *Sceloporus* in the stomachs of specimens from northern Belize.

When disturbed, *L. frenata* flattens the body and head. The head takes on a triangular shape, giving the snake a sinister viperlike aspect. Although rear-fanged, this snake generally does not bite and is essentially harmless to humans.

Leptodeira frenata is oviparous. Stuart (1935:53) found seven mature eggs in a female collected on 19 April in La Libertad, El Petén. Himmelstein (1980:30) described a female from Isla Cozumel that contained three well-developed eggs in February.

SUBSPECIES According to Duellman (1959:58), this species exists as three subspecies, of which *L. f. yucatanensis* occurs in the northern portion of the peninsula, and *L. f. malleisi* occurs to the south in El Petén and Belize and along the east coast of the peninsula in Quintana Roo.

ETYMOLOGY The specific name, *frenata*, is from the Latin *frenum*, "bridle" or "curb," and *-atum*, a Latin suffix meaning "provided with."

COMMENT *Leptodeira frenata* was reviewed by Duellman (1959) as part of his revision of the genus *Leptodeira*.

Locality Records Belize: Belize: Belize (FMNH 4446–47; UMMZ 124650), Lemonal (MPM 7696–97), Manatee River (FMNH 3481); Cayo: Augustine (UMMZ 80718), Cohune Ridge (UMMZ 80715–16); Corozal: S edge Corozal Town (JLK 471); Orange Walk: Guinea Grass (MPM 7606), Kate's Lagoon (FMNH 49343), Otro Benque (MPM 7741), Tower Hill (MPM 7330–39, 7555–58, 7698, 7740, 7742–44, 8141–42); Stann Creek: Stann Creek Valley (Schmidt, 1941:497); Toledo: 5.1 mi E Monkey River (KU 157581); no specific locality (FMNH 4248–49; MCZ 66977; USNM 125348). *Guatemala*: El Petén: Flores (FMNH 43374), La Esperanza (UTA R-26105), La Libertad (AMNH 69989, 69991;

FMNH 43371–73; UMMZ 74881–86), near La Libertad (MCZ 46512), Paso Caballos (MCZ 38588–89), Toocog (KU 55714). *Mexico*: Campeche: Balchacaj (UMMZ 81919), Becan (UWZH 20518), 3 mi SW Bolonchén (UCM 28174), 38.5 mi NE Catazajá (LSUMZ 38200), 12 mi WSW Champotón (UCM 39520), 3.6 km SE Chekubúl (UMRC 92-12), Chicanná (UWZH 20554), 8 km ENE Ciudad del Carmen (KU 70865), Encarnación (H. M. Smith, 1938:18), 7.5 km W Escárcega (KU 70864), Isla del Carmen (AMNH 103203), Pital (FMNH 105480), 3.5 km SE Sabancuy (UMRC 91-4), 23.3 km SE Sabancuy (JCL sight record), Tuxpeña Camp (UMMZ 73229–30), rd. to Sabancuy 12.1 km N Hwy. 186 (UMRC 91-3); Chiapas: Palenque (USNM 111258–60), 19.1 km N Palenque (EAL 2902); Quintana Roo: Chunyaxché (Himmelstein, 1980:30), 10 km N Cobá (CAS 154140), 19 km N Cobá (UMRC 87-13), 28.3 km N Cobá (UMRC 87-12), Colonia Santa María (UMMZ 76169), Felipe Carrillo Puerto (UMMZ 113561–62), 11 km NNE Felipe Carrillo Puerto (KU 70867–68), 70.6 km NE Felipe Carrillo Puerto (EAL 2879), near Río Hondo (AMNH 68611), Isla Cozumel (AMNH 102188; CM 93195, 93199–200; Himmelstein, 1980:30; UMMZ 76170), Cozumel, San Miguel (UMMZ 78641–42), Cozumel, 3 mi S San Miguel (UMMZ 78640), Cozumel, 5 km NE Punta Celerain (JCL photo), Cozumel, San Miguel (JCL photo), Cozumel, 1.5 mi N San Miguel (UCM 16039), Cozumel, 2 mi N San Miguel (UCM 16040–41), Cozumel, 3.5 km N San Miguel (KU 70866), 3.3 mi N Limones (KU 157582–83), Playa del Carmen (Himmelstein, 1980:30), 5 mi N Playa del Carmen (LSUMZ 33320), 9.3 mi S Playa del Carmen (LSUMZ 38541), 17.6 mi SW Playa del Carmen (KU 157584), Pueblo Nuevo X-Can (CM 45733–34, 49073, 49095; UCM 40260–64, 40731–33), Puerto Juárez (Himmelstein, 1980:30; UCM 40266), Tintal (UCM 40265), 5 mi W Tulum (LSUMZ 33319); Yucatán: Balankanché (FMNH 153550), 4.1 km E Bella Flor (UMRC 79-263), 22.1 km N Calkiní (EAL 2936), Chichén Itzá (AMNH 7867–71; FMNH 545, 20604; MCZ 7242, 46889; UMMZ 68230, 73027–28, 75589; USNM 46397), 2 mi E Chichén Itzá (UCM 49854), Dzibilchaltún (FMNH 153520–21), 1.8 mi NE Kinchil (KU 157585), Libre Unión (FMNH 36359), Mérida (FMNH 19421, UTA R-4470), Pisté (CM 46940–41, 47113, 49665–69; KU 70869; UCM 41709), Tekom (FMNH 49344), X-Can (CM 46831), Yokdzonot (FMNH 36360, 36362); no specific locality (USNM 46566).

Leptodeira septentrionalis (Kennicott)
(Fig. 367; Map 139)

Dipsas septentrionalis Kennicott, 1859:16, in Baird, 1859. SYNTYPES: USNM 4267, 4273, 2288 (now 131739). TYPE LOCALITY: Matamoras, Tamaulipas, Mexico, and Brownsville, Texas; restricted by

H. M. Smith and Taylor (1950b:361) to Brownsville, Texas.

Cat-eyed snake, cohune tommygoff (Belize); nauyaca (Guatemala); culebra destenida, culebra nocturna, falsa nauyaca (Mexico); kuyun kan (Lacandón Maya); box-kokob (Yucatec Maya).

DESCRIPTION This moderately long, slender snake attains a maximum snout-vent length of about 800 mm. The tail length is approximately 25 to 35 percent of the head and body length. The body is slightly compressed laterally, and the head is broad and quite distinct from the neck (Fig. 367). The eyes are large and somewhat protruding, and the pupils are vertically elliptical. The dorsal scales are smooth, lack apical pits, and are arranged in 21 to 25 (usually 23) rows at midbody. The anal plate is divided.

The dorsal ground color is tan or light brown, sometimes with an orange cast, or grayish. There is a middorsal series of dark brown or black transverse blotches. These may be lighter at their centers and are sometimes broken, forming staggered pairs of dark spots. The lateral surfaces of the body may bear small dark spots that alternate with the middorsal blotches. The dorsal surface of the head is tan or grayish, usually with a dark median stripe that originates at the posterior margin of the parietal scales and extends onto the nape of the neck. A dark postocular stripe is present. The ventral surfaces of the body and tail are immaculate tan or grayish.

SIMILAR SPECIES *Leptodeira septentrionalis* differs from *Imantodes* and *Sibon* in possessing more than 17 rows of scales at midbody. It differs from its congener, *L. frenata*, in being more slender and possessing more than 190 ventral scales.

DISTRIBUTION *Leptodeira septentrionalis* has a very wide geographical distribution. It is found at low and moderate elevations on the Atlantic slope from southern Texas and on the Pacific slope from Sinaloa, southward to Peru. It probably occurs throughout the Yucatán Peninsula, although there are apparently no records from northern Campeche or western Yucatán (Map 139).

NATURAL HISTORY This snake is a nocturnal, arboreal inhabitant of humid lowland forests, where individuals have been found in bromeliads, in the axils of palm fronds, and foraging at heights of 10 m

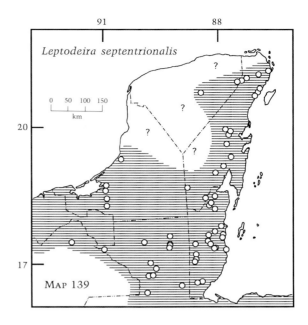

MAP 139

Leptodeira septentrionalis

or more. They are not exclusively arboreal, however, for individuals are sometimes found on roads at night, and Stuart (1958:27) found a specimen beneath a log at the edge of the aguada at Tikal, Guatemala. These snakes are especially common in the vicinity of frog choruses, where they feed not only on frogs but also on the eggs of such leaf-breeding species as *Agalychnis callidryas* (Duellman, 1963:240) and *A. moreletii* (H. M. Smith, 1943:439). A specimen from Chichén Itzá contained the remains of a *Smilisca baudinii* in its stomach (Schmidt and Andrews, 1936:175), and Stuart (1948:81) observed *L. septentrionalis* in the act of swallowing a *Hyla loquax*. I observed individuals consuming *Smilisca* in Campeche. Henderson and Hoevers (1977b:352) found *Bufo valliceps*, *Smilisca*, and *Scinax staufferi* in the stomachs of specimens from northern Belize, and a specimen from Tikal contained an *Elaphe flavirufa*. R. Allen and Neill (1959:232) wrote that this species also consumes small lizards, and Ditmars (1939:238) mentioned that captives ate young mice. Although rear-fanged, these snakes are inoffensive and can rarely be induced to bite.

Leptodeira septentrionalis is oviparous. W. T. Neill (1962:239) estimated that a hatchling collected in Belize had emerged in August. Haines (1940) reported that a captive obtained in 1934 from a bunch of bananas "presumably from Central America" laid 7 eggs in March 1936, 6 in May 1938, 11 in March 1939, and 13 in May 1940. At least 5 of the latter 13 eggs were fertile. The fact that this specimen had been held in isolation since its capture indicates that *L. septentrionalis* is capable of long-term sperm storage and delayed fertilization. Ditmars (1939) mentioned that a captive deposited a clutch of 12 eggs.

SUBSPECIES Four subspecies were recognized by Duellman (1958a), and Shannon and Humphrey (1963:262) recognized an additional subspecies. Of these, *L. s. polysticta* occurs in the Yucatán Peninsula.

ETYMOLOGY The specific name, *septentrionalis*, is Latin meaning "northern," presumably in reference to the fact that this species has the northernmost geographical distribution of all the *Leptodeira*.

COMMENT Duellman (1958a) reviewed *L. septentrionalis* as part of his revision of the genus *Leptodeira*.

Locality Records Belize: Belize: 17 mi W, 7 mi S Belize City (AMNH 126426), Manatee (Schmidt, 1941:505), Northern Lagoon (BMNH 1845.8.5.24), mi 42 on Western Hwy. (MCZ 147419), 3 mi E Sandhill (CM 91002), Spanish Creek (CM 109028); Cayo: Augustine (AMNH 126427), ca. 3. mi S Belmopan (CM 112165–66), 31.4 km SE Belmopan (UTA R-11066), Central Farm (MCZ 71674–75), Cohune Ridge (UMMZ 80717), Hummingbird Hwy., 10 mi S Belize-Cayo Rd. (UMMZ 124648), 3 mi from Millionario Camp (UMMZ 124649); Corozal: Santa Cruz (MPM 8143); Orange Walk: 20 mi SE Orange Walk (BCB 14350–53), Otro Benque (MPM 8179), Tower Hill (MPM 7340–43, 7345–47, 7699–701, 7745–47, 8144, 8180); Stann Creek: Middlesex (UCM 25711, 25742–43, 25799, 25870, 29969), 3 mi W Middlesex (JLK 505), Stann Creek (USNM 26058); Toledo: ca. 2 mi SE Big Falls, Río Grande (CM 105887–88), Blue Creek Village (UTA R-11067); no specific locality (BMNH 1924.2.18.8; FMNH 4250–53, 21705). *Guatemala:* Alta Verapaz: Chinajá (Duellman, 1963:240); El Petén: La Libertad (FMNH 43375–76; UMMZ 74872–80), Las Cañas (CM 58277–78), Paso Caballos (MCZ 38590), Piedras Negras (USNM 111227), Sayaxché (UCM 22339), 6.3 mi W Seibal (KU 157586), Tikal (AMNH uncat.; JCL photo; MCZ 55428, 58761, 77584; UF

13833–37; UMMZ 115661, 115664–66, 115668–69, 120323, 126422), 2 km SW Tikal (UMMZ 115662–63), 3 mi S Tikal (KU 157587–90), Toocog (KU 58084–91), Uaxactún (AMNH 70943); no specific locality (USNM 71788–90). *Mexico:* Campeche: 6.9 mi S Champotón (EAL 1658), Encarnación (UIMNH 17789), 30 mi SW Escárcega (LSUMZ 33315), Pacaitún on Río Candelaria (FMNH 36324), Pital (FMNH 105444); Chiapas: 10 to 15 mi S Palenque (LSUMZ 33313–14); Quintana Roo: 10 mi W Bacalar (LSUMZ 33317–18, 34768), 1.7 km N Cancún Airport (UMRC 84-91), Colonia Santa María (UMMZ 76168), Felipe Carrillo Puerto (UMMZ 113559–600), 3.3 km NE Felipe Carrillo Puerto (KU 171723), 13.3 km NE Felipe Carrillo Puerto (KU 171722, 171724), 15 mi S Felipe Carrillo Puerto (LSUMZ 33316), 22.7 km N Felipe Carrillo Puerto (JCL photo), Hwy. 307, 1.8 km S rd. to Majahual (UMRC 92-14), Laguna Chacanbacab (MCZ 53120), 14.4 km N jct. Hwy. 307 and rd. to Noh Bec (UMRC 84-92), Playa del Carmen (López-Gonzales, 1991:106), 3.3 mi SW Playa del Carmen (KU 157591), Pueblo Nuevo X-Can (CM 45732, 49129; UCM 40247–56, 40729, 40730), Punta Venado (López-Gonzales, 1991:106), Tintal (UCM 40257–59, 41708), Xcopen (MCZ 9496); Yucatán: Chichén Itzá (FMNH 20620; MCZ 26838; UMMZ 73036), X-Can (CM 47040).

Genus *Leptophis* (Tree Snakes)

These are medium-sized to large racerlike snakes with slender bodies, moderately elongate heads, and large eyes. All possess rear ungrooved fangs and mildly toxic venom, but they do not constitute a threat to humans. They are arboreal or semiarboreal, diurnal, and swift. Representatives of this genus occur at low and intermediate elevations from Tamaulipas on the Atlantic slope and Sinaloa and Chihuahua on the Pacific slope south through Central America to southern Brazil and Argentina. There are seven species, two of which occur in the Yucatán Peninsula. Oliver (1948) published the most recent comprehensive taxonomic treatment of the genus (as *Thalerophis*). *Leptophis* is from the Greek *leptos*, "slender," "thin," or "small," and *ophis*, "snake."

Key to the Species of the Genus *Leptophis*

Loreal scale absent (Fig. 171) . . . . *Leptophis ahaetulla*
Loreal scale present (Fig. 172) . . . . *Leptophis mexicanus*

Clave para las Especies del Género *Leptophis*

Sin escama loreal (Fig. 171) . . . . *Leptophis ahaetulla*

Con escama loreal (Fig. 172) . . . . *Leptophis mexicanus*

Leptophis ahaetulla (Linnaeus)
(Figs. 171, 368; Map 140)

Coluber ahaetulla Linnaeus, 1758:225. TYPE: unknown. TYPE LOCALITY: Asia-America.

Green tree snake, green tommygoff (Belize); ranera verde (Mexico); rerek cho (Lacandón Maya); chayilcan (Yucatec Maya).

DESCRIPTION This very large, slender, bright green snake is unmistakable. The males may reach a total length of 2,250 mm, of which about 800 mm is tail. The females are smaller, about 1,900 mm in total length (Oliver, 1948:190). The head is distinct from the neck, the eyes are large with yellow irises, and the pupils are round (Fig. 368). There are 15 rows of dorsal scales at midbody. The scales of the middorsum are keeled, and the lateral scales are smooth. A single apical pit is present on the dorsal scales, the anal plate is divided, and there is no loreal scale (Fig. 171).

This species is bright green above and lighter green below (blue in preservative). The scales of the head and dorsum are finely edged in black. The keels of the middorsal scales are black, producing a series of thin, parallel black lines. The skin between the scales is yellow and is arranged as a series of indistinct yellow chevrons on the anterior two-thirds of the body. The head is uniform green, and Yucatecan populations lack the black postocular stripe that characterizes this species elsewhere.

SIMILAR SPECIES The only other large bright green snake in the Yucatán Peninsula, *Oxybelis fulgidus*, has a narrow, attenuate head, and its dorsal scales are arranged in 17 rows at midbody.

DISTRIBUTION This extremely widespread and variable species occurs from Veracruz on the Atlantic slope and the Isthmus of Tehauntepec on the Pacific slope south through Central America to Brazil and Argentina. It is found throughout the base of the Yucatán Peninsula and extends northward on the east side, apparently avoiding the dry northwest corner (Map 140).

NATURAL HISTORY *Leptophis ahaetulla* is an alert, active, diurnal snake that typically inhabits clearings, second growth, and forest edges as well as primary forest. It is mainly arboreal, and individuals may ascend trees to considerable heights. In southern El Petén, Duellman (1963:241) obtained specimens from trees right after they were felled. Speci-

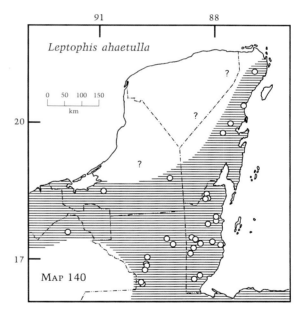

MAP 140

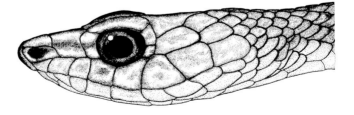

Fig. 171. Lateral view of the head of *Leptophis ahaetulla* (UMRC 85-25), 992 mm SVL; 35 km NE Felipe Carrillo Puerto, Quintana Roo, Mexico.

mens are sometimes encountered on the ground, however, where they have been observed foraging (Beebe, 1946:32). They feed primarily on frogs, as the Spanish name *ranera* suggests, but lizards, snakes, birds, and bird eggs have also been reported to form part of the diet (Oliver, 1948:255). Sexton and Heatwole (1965:41) observed a specimen stalking an *Anolis limifrons* in Panama.

Leptophis ahaetulla is oviparous. According to Oliver (1947:5), who examined a series from Iquitos, Peru, gravid females were present in samples from every month (no specimens were available for April, September, and October). Sexton and Heatwole (1965:41) captured a gravid female in Panama on 27 July that contained three eggs. Duellman (1978:249) reported two gravid females from Amazonian Ecuador; one contained one egg, the other three eggs. Duellman (1978:249) also described a composite clutch of eggs found in a bamboo cavity about 12 m above the ground. The nest contained eggs of *L. ahaetulla* and *Leptodeira*. The *Leptophis* eggs hatched in two groups approximately five weeks apart, indicating that two clutches had been laid more than a month apart.

SUBSPECIES   This widespread form exhibits pronounced geographic variation in scutellation and color pattern, and as many as a dozen subspecies have been recognized (J. A. Peters and Orejas-Miranda, 1970:162). *Leptophis ahaetulla praestans* occurs in the Yucatán Peninsula.

ETYMOLOGY   The specific name, *ahaetulla*, is a Singhalese word meaning "eyeplucker," and it is applied to several green arboreal snakes of Sri Lanka (Oliver, 1948:167).

COMMENT   *Leptophis ahaetulla* was reviewed by Oliver (1948) as part of his revision of the genus *Leptophis* (as *Thalerophis*).

Locality Records   Belize: Belize: Pork Bank (W. T. Neill and Allen, 1959c:53), mi 23 on Northern Hwy. (MPM 7349); Cayo: Augustine (JLK 470), Central Farm (MCZ 71648), Cocquercot (UMMZ 74905), Cohune Ridge (UMMZ 80713), 8.2 mi S Georgeville (KU 157592), Hidden Valley (CMM photo); Orange Walk: 9 mi N Orange Walk (MPM 10790), Otro Benque (MPM 8178), Tower Hill (MPM 7348, 7749–52); Stann Creek: 4 mi W Dangriga (CM 112117), Middlesex (UCM 25709); Toledo: Blue Creek Village (UTA R-11068–69, R-12685), ca. 2 mi SE Big Falls, Río Grande (CM 105883). *Guatemala*: El Petén: 13 km NNW Chinajá (KU 57161), 20 km NNW Chinajá (KU 55716), La Lib-

ertad (UMMZ 74904, 79053), 12 km S La Libertad (AMNH 69988), Nueva Agua (USNM 71366), Santa Teresa (UMMZ 74851), Sayaxché (UCM 22340), Tikal (UF 13838; UMMZ 124341–42). *Mexico*: Campeche: 38 km S 18 de Marzo (EAL 3026), Xkanha District (AMNH 7861), near Xpujil (UMRC 78-86); Chiapas: Ruinas de Palenque (KU 94133); Quintana Roo: Colonia Santa María (UMMZ 76165), Felipe Carrillo Puerto (UMMZ 113571), 35 km NE Felipe Carrillo Puerto (UMRC 85-25), 0.7 mi S Tulum (LSUMZ 38599).

Leptophis mexicanus
Duméril, Bibron, and Duméril
(Figs. 172, 369, 370; Map 141)

Leptophis mexicanus A. M. C. Duméril, Bibron, and Duméril, 1854:536. COTYPES: MNHNP 3453, 3455. TYPE LOCALITY: Mexique.

Mexican green tree snake; green-headed tree snake, green head (Belize); bejuquillo (Guatemala); ranera, ranera bronceada (Mexico); yakikun (Lacandón Maya); k'ok'okan (Yucatec Maya).

DESCRIPTION   The males of this slender, medium-sized snake attain a snout-vent length of about 880 mm and a tail length of approximately 500 mm. The females may be slightly smaller, and they have shorter tails (Oliver, 1948:190). The head is moderately elongate, the eyes are large, and the pupils are round (Fig. 172). There are 15 rows of dorsal scales at midbody. The middorsals are keeled, and the lateral scales are weakly keeled or smooth, especially those of the first scale row. Unpaired apical pits are present on the dorsal scales, and the anal plate is normally divided.

The distinctive color pattern distinguishes this species from all other snakes in the Yucatán Peninsula. The head and neck are bluish green dorsally (Fig. 369, 370). A black stripe extends from the rostrum, through the eye, and posteriorly on the lateral scales, which are bright green edged in black. The middorsal scales are yellowish tan or bronze, hence the Spanish name *ranera bronceada*. The chin, labial scales, and venter are immaculate white or cream. Specimens from the Turneffe Islands of Belize have a very faint postocular stripe and an emerald green dorsum devoid of markings (Henderson, 1976b).

SIMILAR SPECIES   *Leptophis mexicanus* differs from the larger *L. ahaetulla* in possessing a loreal scale (cf. Figs. 171, 172). Its greenish head distin-

Fig. 172. Lateral view of the head of *Leptophis mexicanus* (UMRC 85-20), 706 mm SVL; 2.1 km N Chekubúl, Campeche, Mexico.

guishes this species from all other slender racerlike snakes in the Yucatán Peninsula.

DISTRIBUTION *Leptophis mexicanus* occurs at low and moderate elevations from Tamaulipas on the Atlantic slope and the Isthmus of Tehuantepec on the Pacific slope to Costa Rica. It is found throughout the Yucatán Peninsula, including on some islands off the coast of Belize (Map 141).

NATURAL HISTORY This is a common arboreal and terrestrial inhabitant of forest edges and second growth. Individuals sometimes inhabit dried-up bromeliads (H. M. Smith, 1941e:39), and I found them hidden at the base of palm fronds 2 m above the ground. Nervous and fast moving, these diurnal snakes feed on a variety of vertebrates, especially frogs, and also, less frequently, lizards and small snakes. Stuart (1935:50) observed a specimen attempting to capture a *Triprion petasatus* on the savannas of El Petén, and he removed a *Bolitoglossa rufescens* and a *Hyla loquax* from the stomach of a specimen from Alta Verapaz (Stuart, 1948:67). Oliver (1948:255) recorded hylid frogs and *Thecadactylus rapicauda* as prey items. A specimen from El Petén had ingested a *Smilisca baudinii* (Duell-

man, 1963:241), and one from Honduras regurgitated the remains of a bird egg (Meyer, 1966:178). On Cay Bokel, Belize, this species was observed pursuing *Anolis sagrei* (Hoevers and Henderson, 1974:3). Henderson (1976a:144) found *A. sagrei* in the stomach of a snake from the vicinity of Belize City. Henderson and Hoevers (1977b:352) reported an unidentified hylid frog in the stomach of a specimen from northern Belize and said (1977b:353) that *L. mexicanus* also eats *Phrynohyas venulosa* and *Ninia sebae*. Henderson et al. (1977:231) added *Bufo valliceps* to the diet and noted that captives accepted a variety of frogs and lizards. Frogs, especially *Smilisca baudinii*, predominated in a series of specimens from Yucatán, but tadpoles, *Anolis*, and bird eggs were also among the stomach contents (Henderson, 1982:75).

Leptophis mexicanus is oviparous. A female containing nine fully formed eggs was collected on 4 June in Alta Verapaz (Stuart, 1948:67). In Yucatán, this species breeds from March or April through late October or early November; the clutch size ranges from two to six eggs; and females become reproductive at a snout-vent length of about 542 mm and about 18 months of age (Censky and McCoy, 1988).

SUBSPECIES Henderson (1976b) recognized four subspecies based on color pattern and scutellation. Two subspecies occur on the mainland of the Yucatán Peninsula: the nominate form, *L. m. mexicanus*, at the base of the Yucatán Peninsula, and *L. m. yucatanensis* at the north end. Henderson (1976b) described *L. m. hoeversi* from Big Cay Bokel, Turneffe Islands, Belize.

ETYMOLOGY The specific name, *mexicanus*, is a toponym referring to Mexico, the type locality.

COMMENT Oliver (1948) reviewed *Leptophis mexicanus* as part of his revision of the genus *Leptophis* (as *Thalerophis*).

Locality Records Belize: Belize: Belize (FMNH 49352; KU 144949, 150672; USNM 24907, 26056, 26356, 65149), 7.8 mi W Belize City (KU 157593), Cay Bokel (MPM 6737–39), Lemonal (MPM 7702), Manatee

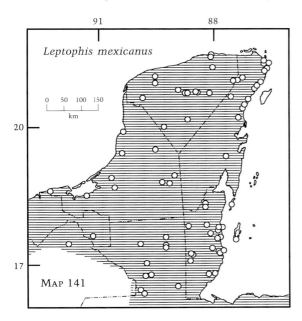

91   88

Leptophis mexicanus

0   50   100   150
km

20

17

MAP 141

(FMNH 5633, 6931), Manatee River (FMNH 3479), Stanley Field (MCZ 66356–58); Cayo: 37.5 mi W Belize City (CM 112192), Cohune Ridge (UMMZ 80709), ca. 3 km W Thousand Foot Falls (CM 90994), Thousand Foot Falls (CM 91012); Corozal: Ambergris Cay, 17 km N, 6.5 km E San Pedro (CM 91099); Orange Walk: Gallon Jug (FMNH 69231; MCZ 71649–50), Orange Walk (MPM 7354), Tower Hill (MPM 7350–53, 7607, 7703, 8131–34, 8138, 10791); Stann Creek: Dangriga (RWV photo), 1.3 km SW Dangriga turnoff on Southern Hwy. (UTA R-11070), Mango Creek (MCZ 71651), Middlesex (CM 48005–8; UCM 25707, 25712, 25720, 25724–25, 25790–92, 25808, 25862–68, 29972–77, 30881–84), 6 mi W Stann Creek (JLK 461–62), 7 mi W, 1 mi S Stann Creek (JLK 488); Toledo: 13 mi W Mango Creek (LSUMZ 8906); no specific locality (FMNH 4219–27; USNM 24907, 26056, 56149). *Guatemala*: Alta Verapaz: Chinajá (Duellman, 1963:241); El Petén: 15 km NW Chinajá (KU 55715), El Paso (MCZ 38650), El Rosario (JCL sight record), La Libertad (FMNH 43381–83; UMMZ 74850, 74852–58), Las Cañas (CM 58275–76), Sayaxché (KU 57140, 57146–48; UCM 22341–51), Tikal (AMNH uncat.; MCZ 140186; UF 13839–40; UMMZ 120320), 0.6 mi S Tikal (KU 157595), 3 mi S Tikal (KU 157594), Uaxactún (UMMZ 70454–56); no specific locality (USNM 71364–65, 71782). *Mexico*: Campeche: Balchacaj (FMNH 103233, 103235; UIMNH 17829), Campeche (JCL sight record), 2.1 km N Chekubúl (UMRC 85-20), Dzibalchén (KU 75624–26), 7.5 km W Escárcega (KU 70870–71), San José Carpizo (UMMZ 99888), 46 mi E Silvituc (Colonia López Mateos) (UCM 28132), 26 mi W Xicalango (BCB 11990), 33 km NE Xpujil (CM 47954); Chiapas: 10 mi S Palenque (LSUMZ 33384); Quintana Roo: Akumal (Himmelstein, 1980:30), Cancún (Himmelstein, 1980:30), 1.7 km N Cancún Airport (UMRC 84-91), Cobá (UMMZ 83940–41), Hwy. 307, 14.4 km N jct. rd. to Noh Bec (UMRC 84-92), Isla Mujeres (FMNH 34637), Playa del Carmen (Himmelstein, 1980:30), 7 mi N Playa del Carmen (CM 93170), Pueblo Nuevo X-Can (CM 45736–40, 49060, 49063, 49075, 49078, 49108, 49112, 49140, 49158; UCM 38133, 40267–307, 41714–18), Puerto Juárez (Himmelstein, 1980:30), 5 km N Puerto Juárez (JCL photo), Puerto Morelos (López-Gonzales, 1991:160), Tintal (UCM 40308–12, 40314–18, 41710–13), Tulum (Himmelstein, 1980:30; LSUMZ 33385), 4.8 mi NW Tulum (LSUMZ 38571), 18.9 mi SW Tulum (KU 157596); Tabasco: Tenosique (USNM 110553); Yucatán: Chichén Itzá (CM 36451; MCZ 15550, 22063–64; TCWC 57126; UMMZ 73035, 46567), Dzibilchaltún (FMNH 153498), 4.6 mi N Halacho (LSUMZ 38572), Kantunil (FMNH 36436), Libre Unión (FMNH 36434), Mérida (FMNH 36435), 6 mi S Peto (LACM 113911), Pisté (CM 46933–39, 47000, 47114–24, 49670–88; KU 70872–77, 71769; UCM 16044–46, 40319–28, 41719–21), Río Lagartos (UCM 28134), 3 mi S Río Lagartos (UCM 39521), 5 mi S Sisal (UIMNH 87664), Tekom (FMNH 49351), 6 km N Tizimín (KU 74994), X-Can (CM 46832, 46875–76, 47041), Xkichmook (FMNH 40746), Yokdzonot (FMNH 36433, 36437; UIMNH 39962).

Genus *Masticophis* (Whipsnakes)

These fast-moving, diurnal snakes are moderately large to large, with slender bodies, narrow, elongate heads, and large eyes. As a group, whipsnakes tend to occupy arid and subarid open habitats. Most are terrestrial or semiarboreal. The genus ranges throughout the southern half of the United States and south through most of Mexico and much of Central America. Disjunct populations occur in Colombia and Venezuela. Eight species are presently recognized, of which one occurs in the Yucatán Peninsula. *Masticophis* is derived from the Greek *mastix*, "whip," and *ophis*, "snake," in reference to the attenuate body form and braided appearance of the scales of some species. The most recent review of this genus is by L. D. Wilson (1973).

Masticophis mentovarius
(Duméril, Bibron, and Duméril)
(Figs. 371, 372; Map 142)

Coryphodon mento-varius A. M. C. Duméril, Bibron, and Duméril, 1854:187. SYNTYPES: MNHNP 3199, 3331. TYPE LOCALITY: Mexique; restricted to Tehuantepec, Oaxaca, by H. M. Smith and Taylor (1950b:340).

Tropical whipsnake; Central American whipsnake (Belize); chirrionera, corredora gris, sabanera (Mexico).

DESCRIPTION This large, robust whipsnake is alert, fast, and terrestrial. Individuals attain a snout-vent length of at least 1,886 mm (J. D. Johnson, 1977). The tail length is 30 to 35 percent of the snout-vent length. The head is rather elongate and moderately distinct from the neck in dorsal aspect. The eyes are large with yellowish irises and round pupils (Fig. 371). There are generally seven supralabial scales; those immediately below the eye are fused. The dorsal scales are smooth, arranged in 17 rows at midbody, and have a single apical pit on the middorsal scales, especially those on the anterior third of the body. The anal plate is normally divided.

The dorsum of adults is uniform brown, tan, or gray with little or no indication of pattern, although individual dorsal scales may have an indistinct smudge of dark pigment on the trailing edge. The dorsal surface of the head is tan, reddish tan, or gray, and the chin and infralabials are usually cream or tan with darker flecks or spots. The supralabials are generally marked with cream on their inferior borders and along their sutures, and there is a cream spot on the preocular scale. The juveniles are also predominantly gray or tan, but they have a pair of thin cream or white stripes on the lateral surfaces of the neck and on the anterior portion of the body (Fig. 372).

SIMILAR SPECIES *Masticophis mentovarius* differs from the smaller *Dryadophis* in usually possessing seven rather than nine supralabials, and in having single apical pits on the dorsal scales rather than paired apical pits. The much smaller *Symphimus mayae* has 15 rather than 17 dorsal scale rows at midbody. *Coluber constrictor* has 15 rows of dorsal scales at midbody, and normally has eight supralabials rather than seven. *Drymarchon corais* has paired rather than single apical pits on the dorsal scales and bold, dark markings on the supralabials.

DISTRIBUTION *Masticophis mentovarius* occurs at low, moderate, and intermediate elevations on the Pacific and Atlantic slopes from Sonora and San Luis Potosí, respectively, south and eastward through the Yucatán Peninsula to Costa Rica. Apparently disjunct populations occur in Panama, northern Colombia, and Venezuela. The species is probably found throughout the Yucatán Peninsula, although there are no records from central Campeche or southern Quintana Roo (Map 142).

NATURAL HISTORY The tropical whipsnake inhabits open situations such as savannas, beaches, and the edges of deciduous forests. It has also been collected in mangrove swamps. It is predominantly terrestrial, but individuals are occasionally found in shrubs and trees. Like others of its genus, this species is rather nervous and will bite freely when threatened. It feeds on lizards and small mammals. I observed a juvenile capture a *Sceloporus cozumelae* in Quintana Roo, and Alvarez del Toro (1983:162) said that this species consumes lizards, especially *Cnemidophorus*, in Chiapas. Henderson and Hoevers (1977b:352) found small mammals in the stom-

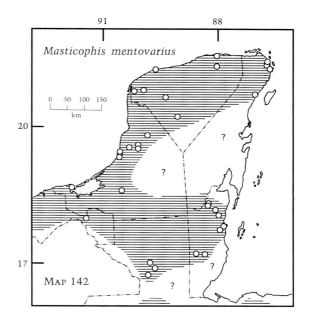

MAP 142

achs of specimens from northern Belize, and Weyer (1990:31) indicated that *M. mentovarius* also feeds on small snakes in Belize. In turn, these snakes are preyed on by the great black hawk, *Buteogallus urubitinga* (Gerhardt et al., 1993:350).

Masticophis mentovarius is oviparous and apparently lays its eggs during the spring. A captive from Alvarado, Veracruz, deposited 17 eggs between 23 and 25 March (Werler, 1951:41). In Chiapas, females produce clutches of around 20 eggs in the spring (Alvarez del Toro, 1983:163). Two females from Veracruz captured on 23 March contained 16 and about 30 eggs, and another female observed on the same day appeared to have recently oviposited (Minton and Minton, 1991:101).

SUBSPECIES Of the five subspecies recognized by J. D. Johnson (1977), only the nominate form, *M. m. mentovarius*, occurs in the Yucatán Peninsula.

ETYMOLOGY The specific name, *mentovarius*, is from the Latin *mentum*, "chin," and *varius*, "different, changing, varying," which, according to J. D. Johnson (1982:295.1) refers to the spots on the chin of the nominate subspecies.

COMMENT *Masticophis mentovarius* was reviewed by J. D. Johnson (1977, 1982).

Locality Records Belize: Belize: 0.4 mi W Belize City (W. T. Neill and Allen, 1959c:54), Hattieville (UCM

25869), 16.1 km NW Maskall (KU 171712), mi 41–42 on Northern Hwy. (MPM 7803); Cayo: Mountain Pine Ridge (MPM 8200), upper Raspaculo River basin (Stafford, 1991:14); Orange Walk: Orange Walk (MPM 7355, 7801–2), near Orange Walk (MPM 7804), Tower Hill (MPM 7356). *Guatemala*: El Petén: La Libertad (UMMZ 74930), Sayaxché (UCM 22352), Toocog (KU 55717). *Mexico*: Campeche: 34.6 mi S Campeche (UCM 18622), Champotón (UMMZ 73044), rd. to Cayal, 0.3 km N rd. to Champotón (KU 171711), 4 km S Champotón (JCL photo), 18 km S Escárcega (EAL 3338), 14 km S Hool (UMRC 90-11), 15 mi W Hopelchén (AMNH 93343), Xicalango (UCM 45432); Chiapas: 10.3 mi E Tabasco-Chiapas border (LSUMZ 33374); Quintana Roo: Cancún (López-Gonzales, 1991:106), 1 km S Puerto Juárez (UCM 39522), 5 km N Puerto Juárez (JCL photo), Punta Venado (López-Gonzales, 1991:106); Yucatán: 10 km W Bella Flor (TU 19807), Carretera Chelem–Chuburna (IHNHERP 587), 11.8 km E Celestún (UMRC 84-15), Mayapán (FMNH 40748), 10 km SE Tekax (Dundee et al. 1986:44), 12 mi N Tizimín (UCM 28145), ca. 5 km S Río Lagartos (MCZ 152671).

Genus *Nerodia*
(New World Water Snakes)

Members of the genus *Nerodia* are generally large, heavy-bodied, semiaquatic snakes. They are nonvenomous, but most species do not hesitate to bite if provoked, and many release a foul-smelling musk from glands at the base of the tail when they are handled. The genus is restricted to North America, where it ranges from the eastern and central United States to southeastern Mexico. Nine species are presently recognized, of which one enters the Yucatán Peninsula at its western periphery. Before 1977, members of this genus were placed in the genus *Natrix*. Rossman and Eberle (1977) revived the name *Nerodia* for the North American species previously assigned to *Natrix*. *Nerodia* is derived from the Greek *neros*, "a swimmer," and *-odes*, "like," presumably a reference to the semiaquatic habits of these snakes.

Nerodia rhombifer (Hallowell)
(Fig. 173; Map 143)

Tropidonotus rhombifer Hallowell, 1852:177. HOLOTYPE: ANSP 5047. TYPE LOCALITY: the Arkansas River and its tributaries near the northern boundary of the Creek Nation; restricted by H. M. Smith and Taylor (1950b:360) to Tulsa, Tulsa County; and by Conant (1969:56) to Arkansas River between Keystone and Tulsa, Tulsa County, Oklahoma.

Diamondback water snake.

DESCRIPTION These heavy-bodied snakes attain a snout-vent length of about 1,200 mm. The females are substantially larger than the males. The short tail is about 25 percent of the head and body length. The head is broad, flattened, and distinct from the neck. The eyes are moderately large and situated high on the head, and the pupils are round (Fig. 173). The dorsal scales are heavily keeled and are usually arranged in 23 to 27 rows at midbody. Paired apical pits are present on some dorsal scales. The anal plate is divided, as are most of the subcaudal scales.

The dorsal ground color is generally brown or olive brown with a series of black or very dark brown middorsal blotches arranged in a chainlike pattern. These blotches may be solid, or their interiors may be invaded by lighter coloration. There is a lateral series of dark markings that are invaded to a variable extent by the lighter ground color. The venter is yellowish with dark greenish gray or black markings. The iris is reddish brown.

SIMILAR SPECIES Of the other semiaquatic or aquatic snakes with which *Nerodia* might be confused, *Tretanorhinus nigroluteus* has fewer than 23 rows of dorsal scales at midbody. *Coniophanes quinquevittatus* usually has 21 rows of dorsal scales at midbody and dorsal stripes. The two species of *Thamnophis* in the Yucatán Peninsula are slenderer than *Nerodia* and possess no more than 19 rows of scales at midbody.

DISTRIBUTION The diamondback water snake ranges throughout the central United States from Iowa, Illinois, and Indiana south through the Gulf lowlands of Mexico to Tabasco, northern Chiapas,

Fig. 173. Lateral view of the head of *Nerodia rhombifer* (UMRC 78-167), 338 mm SVL; 41 km S Tampico, Veracruz, Mexico.

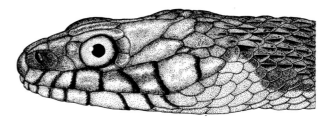

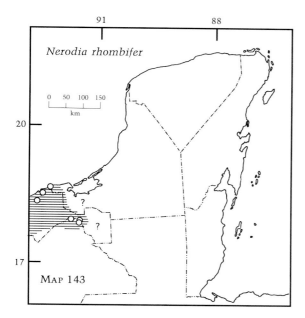

Map 143

and westernmost Campeche. Thus it enters the Yucatán Peninsula only in the southwest corner (Map 143).

NATURAL HISTORY   The diamondback water snake inhabits ponds, lakes, streams, and sloughs. In the Yucatán Peninsula this semiaquatic snake occurs in wetlands on the Usumacinta-Grijalva floodplain. Manjarrez and Macias-Garcia (1991) studied the feeding ecology of *N. rhombifer* in southern Veracruz and found that the diet consisted almost exclusively of fish. There was a positive relationship between body size and the size of ingested prey; that is, the adult snakes took larger species of fish than the juveniles. In temperate and subtropical latitudes these snakes also consume frogs, toads, crayfish, and young turtles (A. H. Wright and Wright, 1957:502). The Veracruz snakes were primarily nocturnal, but elsewhere in the range individuals are sometimes seen during the daytime sunning themselves on shrubs overhanging water. These nonvenomous snakes have a rather nasty disposition, and they do not hesitate to bite when molested. Nonetheless, they are preyed on by wading birds, for two specimens were removed from the stomach of a common egret (*Casmerodius albus*) in southern Veracruz (Conant, 1969:78).

Nerodia rhombifer is viviparous. Little is known of its reproductive habits in the Yucatán Peninsula, but Fitch's (1970:162) review of the species in the United States reports birth dates from 5 August to 2 October and brood sizes ranging from 14 to 62.

SUBSPECIES   Of the three Mexican subspecies recognized by Conant (1969), *N. r. werleri* occurs in the Yucatán Peninsula.

ETYMOLOGY   The specific name, *rhombifer*, is from the Greek *rhombos*, "rhombus," and the Latin *fero*, "to bear," in reference to the diamond-shaped dorsal blotches.

COMMENT   Although the specific name for the diamondback water snake has long been spelled *rhombifera*, D. R. Frost and Collins (1988:73) noted that the correct orthography for the specific name is *rhombifer*. Conant (1969) treated the biosystematics of *N. rhombifer*, and McAllister (1985) summarized the available information on the species.

Locality Records Mexico: Campeche: ca. 15 mi S Boca San Pedro on Río San Pedro y San Pablo (AMNH 85073); Chiapas: Playas, within 35 mi of Palenque (AMNH 99656), Tabasco: Emiliano Zapata (USNM 110511), 20 mi SW Frontera (BCB 11646), near Frontera on rd. to Playa Miramar (UTEP 13989–91), S side Río Usumacinta at Emiliano Zapata (EAL 3025).

Genus *Ninia* (Coffee Snakes)

Members of the genus *Ninia* are small, semifossorial inhabitants of Neotropical forests, where they often constitute an important component of the leaf litter herpetofauna. Representatives of the genus range from southern Mexico to northern South America. The genus was briefly reviewed by W. L. Burger and Werler (1954). Eight species were once recognized (J. A. Peters and Orejas-Miranda, 1970:221), but Scott (1969) considered three of these conspecific, an arrangement that was later formalized by Savage and Lahanas (1991). Two of the six species of *Ninia* occur in the Yucatan Peninsula. *Ninia* probably was named after Nina, the Greek goddess of the sea depths; the ending -*ia* denotes "quality of" or "state of being."

Key to the Species of the Genus *Ninia*

Dorsum predominantly red, red-orange, or brown; head black with yellow nuchal collar; ventral scales immaculate or with scattered dark flecks . . . . *Ninia sebae*

Dorsum dark brown, gray, or black; ventral scales with bold, dark markings; yellow nuchal collar usually present . . . . *Ninia diademata*

Clave para las Especies del Género *Ninia*

Dorso predominantemente rojo, rojo-anaranjado, o pardo; cabeza negra con un collar nucal amarillo; escamas ventrales inmaculadas o con flecos obscuros esparcidos . . . . *Ninia sebae*

Dorso pardo obscuro, gris, o negro; escamas ventrales con marcas obscuras conspicuas; un collar nucal amarillo usualmente presente . . . . *Ninia diademata*

Ninia diademata Baird and Girard
(Fig. 174; Map 144)

Ninia diademata Baird and Girard, 1853:49. HOLOTYPE: USMN 12122. TYPE LOCALITY: Orizaba, Mexico (= Orizaba, Veracruz, Mexico).

Ring-necked coffee snake; dormilona de collar (Mexico).

DESCRIPTION This small snake averages between about 250 and 270 mm in snout-vent length, and the tail is about 20 to 25 percent as long as the head and body. The head is slightly distinct from the neck in dorsal view (Fig. 174). The eyes are moderately small, and the pupils are round. The dorsal scales are heavily keeled, striated, and ar-

Fig. 174. Dorsal view of the head of *Ninia diademata* (EAL 3637), 204 mm SVL; 3 km SW Palenque, Chiapas, Mexico.

ranged in 19 rows at midbody. The anal plate is usually undivided. During the breeding season nuptial tubercles are present on the chin and snout in males.

The dorsum is predominantly dark gray or black with a light yellow or cream collar that begins at the posterior margin of the parietal scales and is often interrupted medially by black pigment (Fig. 174). The collar is continuous with the light coloration of the labial scales and chin. Each dorsal scale in rows 1, 2, and 3 has a light spot. The venter is gray with a median row of bold black spots and dark pigment on the lateral surfaces of each ventral scale.

SIMILAR SPECIES No other snake in the Yucatán Peninsula combines a dark dorsum, light nuchal collar, and boldly spotted venter. The other snakes with dark bodies and a light nuchal collar are *Tantilla moesta*, *T. cuniculator*, and *T. schistosa*, all of which have smooth dorsal scales arranged in 15 rows at midbody.

DISTRIBUTION *Ninia diademata* occurs at low and moderate elevations on the Atlantic slope from San Luis Potosí and the Pacific slope from Oaxaca, eastward through Guatemala and Belize to northern Honduras. Its distribution in the Yucatán Peninsula is imperfectly known but appears to be discontinuous from northern Chiapas through El Petén to Belize (Map 144).

NATURAL HISTORY This is a secretive, nocturnal inhabitant of humid forests. Individuals hide during the day in the leaf litter and beneath surface debris, including rotting corozo palm logs. H. M. Smith (1943:456) found a specimen abroad at night along a trail through the high forest of Piedras Negras, Guatemala. Although apparently abundant elsewhere (W. L. Burger and Werler, 1954:646), *N. diademata* is uncommon in the Yucatán Peninsula, where it feeds predominantly on mollusks. Taylor

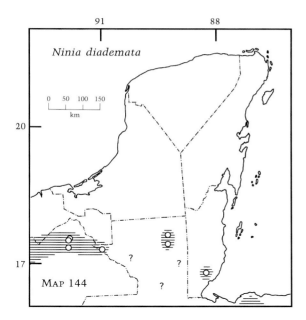

Map 144

91   88

Ninia diademata

0 50 100 150
km

20

17

(1949:195) found small slugs in the stomachs of specimens from San Luis Potosí. Seib (1985a) conducted a six-year study of the diet of this species on coffee fincas in southern Chiapas and adjacent Guatemala and found that *N. diademata* there fed exclusively on snails and slugs.

When disturbed, this harmless snake flattens its body, hides its head beneath its body, and elevates its tail in an upright spiral (Greene, 1975:481).

Nothing is known of reproduction in this species, but it is presumably oviparous, as are other *Ninia* for which reproductive data are available.

SUBSPECIES   In the most recent review, W. L. Burger and Werler (1954) recognized four subspecies of *N. diademata*, of which *N. d. nietoi* occurs in the Yucatán Peninsula; but L. D. Wilson and Meyer (1985:73) questioned the utility of recognizing subspecies in this form.

ETYMOLOGY   The specific name, *diademata*, is a Latin adjective meaning "crowned" or "wearing a diadem," in reference to the light nuchal collar.

COMMENT   *Ninia diademata* was reviewed by W. L. Burger and Werler (1954). L. D. Wilson and Meyer (1985) summarized information on Honduran populations.

Locality Records Belize: Toledo: 2.7 mi NE Golden Stream (KU 157600). *Guatemala*: El Petén: Piedras Negras (USNM 109807), Tikal (UMMZ 117912), Uaxactún (MCZ 24937). *Mexico*: Chiapas: Palenque ruins

(EAL 3029), 3 km SW Palenque (EAL 3637), 10 to 15 mi S Palenque (LSUMZ 33294).

Ninia sebae (Duméril, Bibron, and Duméril)
(Figs. 373, 374; Map 145)

Streptophorus sebae A. M. C. Duméril, Bibron, and Duméril, 1854:515. HOLOTYPE: MNHNP 3778. TYPE LOCALITY: Mexique; restricted by Schmidt and Andrews (1936:170) to the state of Veracruz, Mexico; and by H. M. Smith and Taylor (1950b:351) to Veracruz, Veracruz, Mexico.

Red coffee snake; bead and coral (Belize); dormilona (Mexico); kuyun kan (Lacandón Maya); chac-ib-can (Yucatec Maya).

DESCRIPTION   The adults of *N. sebae* average between 220 and 270 mm in snout-vent length, and the short tail is approximately 15 to 25 percent of the head and body length. The head is slightly distinct from the neck when seen in dorsal aspect, and the eyes are rather small with round pupils. The dorsal scales are heavily keeled, lack apical pits, bear longitudinal striations, and are arranged in 19 (rarely 17) rows at midbody. The anal plate is usually undivided.

This species exhibits substantial geographic variation in color and pattern. The predominant dorsal coloration is red, red-orange, or reddish brown. The dorsal surface of the head is black, bordered behind by a yellow or cream nuchal collar of varying width, which is in turn bordered by a black blotch also of varying width. The yellow nuchal collar extends onto the throat and chin. The venter is immaculate cream, light gray, or pinkish. Specimens from the base of the Yucatán Peninsula tend to have a series of narrow black bands with thin yellow borders (Fig. 374). Often these bands are offset at the midline, producing a staggered arrangement. At the outer end of the Yucatán Peninsula these snakes generally have fewer and smaller dark bands, and often the dark pigment is reduced to mere spots or dots (Fig. 373). Some specimens are uniformly red except for the black head and the nuchal pattern.

SIMILAR SPECIES   No other snake in the Yucatán Peninsula combines a predominantly red body, black head, and heavily keeled dorsal scales. Banded individuals may vaguely resemble coral snakes (*Micrurus*) or their mimics (*Urotheca, Lampropeltis, Scaphiodontophis*), but *Ninia*'s heavily keeled dorsal scales readily distinguish it from those species.

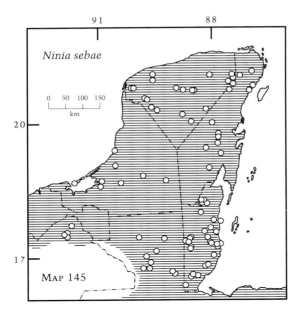

Map 145

DISTRIBUTION This species occurs at low and moderate elevations on the Atlantic slope from Veracruz and the Pacific slope from Oaxaca, south and eastward through Central America to Costa Rica. It is found throughout the Yucatán Peninsula (Map 145).

NATURAL HISTORY *Ninia sebae* is common in a variety of habitats in the Yucatán Peninsula, including forests, savannas, and agricultural areas. It is terrestrial, secretive, and largely nocturnal, although H. M. Smith (1938:19) found specimens abroad during the morning daylight hours in Campeche. Individuals are often found beneath surface debris, especially the leaf litter of coffee groves, hence the English common name, "red coffee snake." This species is frequently encountered on roads at night, and specimens have also been found beneath fallen palm fronds, in and under rotting logs, and in the stomachs of coral snakes.

These harmless, inoffensive snakes do not bite. When threatened, they flatten the body and head dorsoventrally, giving an impression of greater size. Greene (1975:481) described a defensive display given by snakes from the region of Los Tuxtlas in southern Veracruz in which the anterior third or half of the body was flattened and elevated vertically. He suggested that this head display might mimic the tail display of coral snakes (Greene, 1973). Henderson and Hoevers (1977a) described similar behavior in a specimen from northern Belize.

In Veracruz, these snakes eat earthworms, slugs, and snails (Greene, 1975:479), and on coffee fincas in southern Chiapas they feed predominantly on earthworms and leeches, and occasionally on mollusks (Seib, 1985a:98). Landry et al. (1966) reported that a specimen from Chiapas had eaten a caecilian.

Ninia sebae is oviparous, and oviposition apparently occurs during the summer months. The males develop breeding tubercles on the chin during the breeding season. Stuart (1948:77) estimated that in Alta Verapaz, sexual maturity is attained at a snout-vent length of about 250 mm, but Greene (1975:480) found a gravid female in southern Veracruz that was only 223 mm. According to Alvarez del Toro (1983:179), *N. sebae* produces clutches of three or four eggs in Chiapas; W. L. Burger and Werler (1954:647) reported a range of two to four eggs per clutch in the same area. Greene (1975:480) reported clutches of one, two, and three eggs laid between 28 August and 6 September in southern Veracruz. The incubation period for those clutches ranged from 75 to 79 days. Gaige (1936:298) found gravid females in Yucatán in mid-July; Meyer (1966:179) found a specimen in northern Honduras on 21 July that contained three eggs; and Stuart (1958:24) found juveniles in El Petén in mid-March and early April that presumably had hatched the previous summer. Thus, in southeastern Mexico and northern Central America, clutch size ranges from one to four, and oviposition occurs during the summer rainy season.

SUBSPECIES In the most recent comprehensive review of this species, Schmidt and Rand (1957) recognized four subspecies on the basis of color pattern and scutellation. In their scheme, the nominate form, *N. s. sebae*, occurs at the base of the Yucatán Peninsula, and *N. s. morleyi* replaces it at the other end in the Mexican states of Campeche, Yucatán, and Quintana Roo. L. D. Wilson and Meyer (1985:75) found the color pattern in Honduran snakes to be so variable as to preclude the recognition of subspecies in Honduras, however, and they questioned the validity of Schmidt and Rand's subspecies.

ETYMOLOGY The specific name, *sebae*, is a patronym honoring Albertus Seba, a German (later Dutch) naturalist of the seventeenth and eighteenth centuries whose collection of natural history objects formed the nucleus of the Russian national collection. The plates illustrating his four-volume *Locupletissimi rerum naturalium thesauri* served as the types for the original descriptions of many amphibians and reptiles.

COMMENT Geographic variation in *N. sebae* was reviewed by Schmidt and Rand (1957).

The Maya of Yucatán believe that the bite of this snake can be fatal (Pacheco-Cruz, 1919:34), possibly because they confuse this species with *Micrurus diastema*, which may be uniformly red in the northeastern portion of the Yucatán Peninsula. Roys (1931:331) suggested that the Yucatec name, *chac-ib-can*, should be translated as "red-bean-snake," perhaps in reference to the two dark spots on the head and neck.

Locality Records Belize: Belize: Belize City (FMNH 49333, 49339), Burrell Boom Rd. at Belize River (CM 105779–80), 11 km SW Hattieville (CM 90993), Manatee River (FMNH 7008–22), Missionary Lake Rd., 5.3 mi E jct. Northern Hwy. (CM 91057–58, 91081), Tropical Park (MPM 8271–72); Cayo: Baking Pot (KU 144950–52; MCZ 18951), Cayo (FMNH 109776), Central Farm (MCZ 71654–59), Chaa Creek (CM 105807, 105973–77), 4 km E Chial (CM 105984–87, 109014–15), 1 mi W Cotton Tree (CM 105801), 3 mi S Georgeville (CM 91022), Mountain Pine Ridge, Río On (MPM 7704), 50 mi S Belize-Cayo Rd. on Mountain Pine Ridge Rd. (UMMZ 124656), 2.6 mi W San Ignacio (UF 79993), 0.5 mi N Soccotz (UF 24548); Orange Walk: Guinea Grass (MPM 7707), Guinea Grass Rd., ca. 4 mi S Northern Hwy. (CM 105738, 105742–46), Guinea Grass Rd., ca. 4.1 mi S Northern Hwy. (CM 105747–48), Lamanai (ROM H12777, H12783), 20 mi SE Orange Walk (BCB 12179–80), Tower Hill (MPM 7358–62, 7705–6, 7753–54, 10784), near Tower Hill (MPM 8177), Yo Creek (MPM 7559); Stann Creek: Bokowina (FMNH 49334), Hummingbird Hwy., 31 mi NW Stann Creek (UF 24547), Middlesex (CM 48011–15; UCM 25713–14, 25746, 25751–55, 25800, 25871–73, 29981–83), 4 to 5 mi E Middlesex (CM 112193), Silk Grass (FMNH 49335–36), Stann Creek (USNM 26062), 7 mi W, 1 mi S Stann Creek (JLK 477, 495–96), 14.75 mi W Stann Creek (JLK 478), 30 mi SW Stann Creek (UMMZ 124657), Stann Creek Valley (FMNH 49337–38; MPM 7780–81); Toledo: ca. 2 mi SE Big Falls, Río Grande (CM 105881), 0.9 m. S Bladen Bridge (JCL photo), Blue Creek (RWV photo), Dolores (JCL sight record), 0.75 mi E Swazey Bridge, Monkey River (MCZ 71660), San Antonio (MCZ 71661), San Pedro (MCZ 71662); no specific locality (USNM 56433–34). *Guatemala*: El Petén: El Paso (MCZ 38651–52), La Libertad (FMNH 43377–79; UMMZ 74898–903), Paso Caballos (MCZ 38584–85), Poptún (UMMZ 124348), 10 km NW Poptún (UMMZ 124347), Sacluc (USNM 24909–10, 25118–31), Santa Elena (UMRC 79-273), Sayaxché (UCM 22353–55), Seibal (AMNH 72618), Tikal (MCZ 55429, 58766; UF 13841–43; UMMZ 117910–11), Toocog (KU 58113). *Mexico*: Campeche: Becan (UWZH 20521), Champotón (UMMZ 73050–55), Chuina (KU 74995), Ciudad del Carmen (UMMZ 83540), Encarna-

ción (FMNH 105199–201; UIMNH 18674), Matamoros (FMNH 36222), Pital (UIMNH 18675), Tuxpeña Camp (UMMZ 73231); Chiapas: Palenque (EAL 3634), 8 km S Palenque (JCL photo), 3 km S jct. rd. to Nututun and Palenque ruins (EAL 3328), 16 mi NW Palenque (TCWC 21542), San Juanito (USNM 109874–75); Quintana Roo: 10 mi W Bacalar (LSUMZ), 44 mi SE Chunhuhub (LSUMZ 38290), 7.4 km N Cobá (JCL photo), 36.1 km N Cobá (UMRC 87-9), Colonia Santa María (UMMZ 76166), Felipe Carrillo Puerto (UMMZ 113591–99), 1 mi S Felipe Carrillo Puerto (KU 157601), 7.3 mi S Felipe Carrillo Puerto (KU 157602), 20 mi S Felipe Carrillo Puerto (LSUMZ 33300), Hwy. 307, 6.9 km N of rd. to Noh Bec (UMRC 84-54), Playa del Carmen (Himmelstein, 1980:30), 3.4 mi S Playa del Carmen (LSUMZ 38567), Pueblo Nuevo X-Can (CM 45297, 45735, 49132, 49151; UCM 40329–36, 41723–24), 13.4 km S Pueblo Nuevo X-Can (UMRC 84-55), 35.9 mi S Tepich (KU 157603), Tihosuco (UMRC 84-56), Tintal (UCM 41722); Yucatán: 14.3 km E Celestún (UMRC 84-142), 15.2 km E Celestún (UMRC 84-149), Chichén Itzá (CM 23933; FMNH 20619; MCZ 7122, 26801–23; UCM 12965–66; UIMNH 41519; UMMZ 68231–32, 73045–48, 90669; USNM 46569), Dzibilchaltún (FMNH 153539, 153583–84), 6.2 mi NE Dziuché (KU 157604), Kantunil (FMNH 36212, 36214–15, 36220, 36236), Mérida (CM 44473; FMNH 20607–8, 19419–20, 19422, 19434, 153585; MZFC 43–44; UWZH 20560), Oxkintok (UMRC 92-7), bet. Oxkintok and Calcehtok (UMRC 92-6), Peto (CM 45298–300), Pisté (CM 46942–44, 47125–30, 49689–700; UCM 16052, 40338–49, 41725), Popolná (UCM 40337), Santa Elena (JCL photo), bet. Sayil and Labná (TU 19766), 11.6 mi S Tizimín (KU 157605), X-Can (CM 46833–34), Yokdzonot (FMNH 36218–19, 36221, 36227, 36231, 36237–38); no specific locality (USNM 12459, 24893–96, 164264, 164830).

Genus *Oxybelis* (Tropical Vine Snakes)

These are extremely slender, vinelike snakes with narrow, elongate heads and long snouts. They are rear-fanged and mildly venomous. Although they pose no serious threat to humans, large individuals should nonetheless be handled carefully. Vine snakes are diurnal and largely arboreal. The genus occurs at low to intermediate elevations from southern Arizona through tropical Mexico and Central America to Brazil, Bolivia, and Peru. Five species are recognized, two of which occur in the Yucatán Peninsula. A bibliography for the genus can be found in Keiser, 1992. *Oxybelis* is from the Greek adjective *oxybeles*, "sharp pointed," in reference to the sharp, attenuate snout.

Key to the Species of the Genus *Oxybelis*

Bright green snakes (bluish in preservative); a pair of white or yellow stripes present on lateral edges of ventral scales . . . . *Oxybelis fulgidus*

Brown or tan snakes, often with small, dark brown spots; no light stripes on lateral edges of ventral scales. . . . . *Oxybelis aeneus*

Clave para las Especies del Género *Oxybelis*

Color verde brillante (azuloso en conservador); un par de líneas blancas o amarillas en los extremos laterales de las escamas ventrales. . . . . *Oxybelis fulgidus*

Color pardo o moreno, a menudo con pequeñas manchas obscuras; sin líneas claras en los márgenes laterales de las escamas ventrales. . . . . *Oxybelis aeneus*

Oxybelis aeneus (Wagler)
(Figs. 175, 375; Map 146)

Dryinus aeneus Wagler, 1824:12, in Spix, 1824. HOLOTYPE: ZSM 2645/0. TYPE LOCALITY: near Ega, Brazil (= Tefe), "on the south bank of the Amazon River near the junction of the Río Teffe, almost in the center of the state of Amazonas."

Neotropical vine snake; gray vine snake, tie tie snake (Belize); bejuca, bejuquilla parda (Mexico); k'oche kan (Lacandón Maya); xtab-choyil (Yucatec Maya).

DESCRIPTION This is an unusually slender snake (Fig. 375) with an elongated head and pointed snout (Fig. 175). The adults average perhaps 700 mm in snout-vent length and attain a maximum of about 1,000 mm. Females may average larger than males (Henderson, 1974a:22). The tail is about 60 to 70 percent as long as the head and body. The eyes are moderately large with round pupils. The dorsal scales are smooth or weakly keeled, arranged in 17 rows at midbody, and lack apical pits. The anal plate is normally divided.

The dorsal color is light tan, brown, reddish brown, or gray, often with small, dark brown spots extending onto the dorsal surface of the head. The upper and lower labials and throat are white or yellowish, and there is a black eye stripe. The venter is light tan or gray, without conspicuous markings.

SIMILAR SPECIES The only other attenuate snake with a narrow, elongate head in the Yucatán Peninsula is *O. fulgidus*, which is bright green. *Symphimus mayae* is stouter, has 15 rows of smooth scales at midbody, and does not have a narrow head and pointed snout.

DISTRIBUTION This species occurs at low and moderate elevations from southern Arizona south along both the Atlantic and Pacific slopes in Mexico, through Central America, and south at least to southern Brazil and central Bolivia. *Oxybelis aeneus* probably occurs throughout the Yucatán Peninsula, although it is not recorded from southern Campeche (Map 146).

NATURAL HISTORY Vinelike in appearance, as its English common name suggests, this rear-fanged snake is not dangerous to humans, although its bite can cause irritation. *Oxybelis aeneus* is a diurnal, arboreal inhabitant of thorn forest, second growth, and forest edges, where it forages for lizards, especially *Anolis*. Himmelstein (1980:31) observed an individual stalking an *Anolis* in Quintana Roo, and H. M. Smith and Grant (1958:211) found *Gymnophthalmus speciosus* and *Cnemidophorus lemniscatus* in the stomachs of *O. aeneus* from Panama. L. D. Wilson and Cruz Díaz (1993:18) found *A. allisoni* in the stomach of a specimen from Cayos Cochinos, Honduras. The stomach contents of a series

Fig. 175. Lateral view of the head of *Oxybelis aeneus* (UMRC 78-58), 678 mm SVL; Chiapas, Mexico.

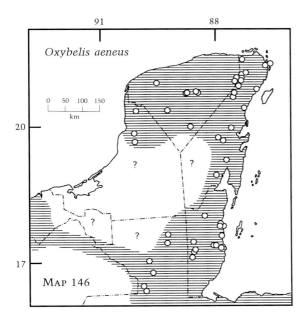

Oxybelis aeneus

0 50 100 150
km

MAP 146

of *O. aeneus* from Yucatán contained exclusively lizards, with *Anolis* predominating (Henderson, 1982:75). In addition to lizards, vine snakes occasionally consume insects, frogs, birds, and small mammals (Keiser, 1967). Henderson (1974a) studied the ecology of *O. aeneus* in Belize and found that females grew more slowly than males but attained a larger size. Henderson and Nickerson (1977), who studied behavior in captives, found that horizontal movements by *O. aeneus* were extremely limited, but that vertical movements were common. These snakes apparently sleep at night at the distal tips of branches, where they assume a characteristic loose-coiled, head-down posture.

Although predominantly arboreal, vine snakes are occasionally found on the ground. When startled, they usually remain motionless, often with the tongue extended and the tongue tips adpressed. This tongue-thrusting behavior was described by both Kennedy (1965) and Keiser (1975:131), who concluded that its purpose might be to disrupt the outline of the snake, making it more cryptic; or it might facilitate olfactory contact with the environment without attracting undue attention. When threatened, vine snakes assume an S-shaped coil, open the mouth to reveal the blue-black lining of the oral cavity, and strike repeatedly but weakly. Crimmins (1937:233) reported that a bite from an *Oxybelis* from Coahuila, Mexico, caused slight local swelling, itching, and redness. Based on the locality, the snake was likely *O. aeneus*.

Oxybelis aeneus is oviparous. Sexton and Heat-

wole (1965:40) found four eggs in a depression in leaf litter on 1 July in Panama. Three of the eggs hatched on 13 July, and the hatchlings ranged from 22.6 to 22.9 mm in snout-vent length. In Yucatán, the reproductive activity of females is restricted to a 12- to 13-week period from March to May (Censky and McCoy, 1988). Three to five eggs (mean = 3.6) are laid and hatch during the summer rainy season. In June 1974 I found a specimen on the Pacific slope of Chiapas that contained five well-formed oviductal eggs.

SUBSPECIES Keiser (1974) studied variation in this species throughout its extensive range and concluded that no subspecies should be recognized.

ETYMOLOGY The specific name, *aeneus*, is Latin for "bronze" or "copper," presumably in reference to the brown color of this species.

COMMENT Keiser (1974) reviewed *Oxybelis aeneus* and summarized the available information on this species (1982).

Locality Records Belize: Belize: Belize (FMNH 4443; KU 144953–54), 5.3 mi NE Belize City (KU 157606), 1.5 km N Ladyville (CM 91060), Manatee (FMNH 5632), Stanley Field (MCZ 66359–60); Cayo: Augustine (UMMZ 80711), Central Farm (MCZ 71652), Cohune Ridge (UMMZ 80712), Mountain Pine Ridge (MPM 8201–2), near Privassion Creek (W. T. Neill and Allen, 1959c:56); Orange Walk: Lamanai (ROM H12780); Stann Creek: Melinda Forestry Station (JLK 503), Middlesex (UCM 25875), Mullins River Rd., 3.5 mi N Hummingbird Hwy. (JLK 504), Stann Creek Valley (FMNH 49353); no specific locality (FMNH 4209–11; USNM 55905). *Guatemala*: Alta Verapaz: Chinajá (Duellman, 1963:241); El Petén: 20 km NNW Chinajá (KU 55720), El Rosario (JCL sight record), La Libertad (FMNH 43380; UMMZ 74908), Tikal (UMMZ 117953), Uaxactún (USNM 64907). *Mexico*: Campeche: 11.5 km W Chencoyi (JCL sight record), 7.6 mi N Ruinas Edzná (KU 157607), bet. Nunkiní and Santa Cruz (TU 19790); Quintana Roo: SE edge Cobá (KU 171707), 4.6 km N Cobá (UMRC 84-52), 8.5 mi S Felipe Carrillo Puerto (KU 157609), 17 km W Felipe Carrillo Puerto (CM 45306), 39.1 km NE Felipe Carrillo Puerto (EAL 2881), Isla Mujeres (FMNH 34652), 3.5 km S Kantunil Kin (KU 171709), 8.8 mi N Limones (KU 157608), Playa del Carmen (Himmelstein, 1980:31), Pueblo Nuevo X-Can (CM 45742–68, 49054, 49074, 49079, 49082, 49085, 49088, 49092, 49101, 49103–4, 49110, 49113, 49118, 49145, 49147; UCM 40373–453, 41746–68), 6.6 km S Pueblo Nuevo X-Can (JCL 6818),

11.4 km S Pueblo Nuevo X-Can (JCL 6820), 12.9 km S Pueblo Nuevo X-Can (JCL 6817), 36.9 km S Pueblo Nuevo X-Can (JCL 6814), Puerto Juárez (Himmelstein, 1980:31), rd. to Reforma, 18.3 km NE Hwy. 307 (KU 171710), 5.4 km N Solferino (KU 171708), Tintal (UCM 40454–72, 41744–45), Tulum (Himmelstein, 1980:31; LSUMZ 33355); Yucatán: Chichén Itzá (FMNH 20615; LACM 103647; LSUMZ 38573; MCZ 7870, 26827–28; UMMZ 73034; USNM 46565, 46573), Libre Unión (FMNH 36140, 36148, 36151–52, 36154, 36161, 36165), Mérida (FMNH 40744), Oxkutzcab (AMNH 38841), Pisté (CM 46945, 47001, 47131–38, 49701–19; KU 70878; UCM 12967, 40478–82), 4.3 km S Polinkin (UMRC 84-53), Popolná (UCM 40473–77), X-Can (CM 46835–39, 46877, 47042–43), Yokdzonot (FMNH 36139, 36141–47, 36150, 36153, 36155–60, 36162–63).

Oxybelis fulgidus (Daudin)
(Figs. 176, 376; Map 147)

Coluber fulgidus Daudin, 1803:352. HOLOTYPE: MNHNP, not definitely identifiable, *fide* Stuart, 1963:109. TYPE LOCALITY: Port-au-Prince, Saint Domingue (presumably in error); Schmidt (1941:506) suggested restriction to Surinam.

Green vine snake; bejuquilla verde, culebra verde arbórea (Guatemala, Mexico); yaaxkan k'ix (Lacandón Maya); chayilcan (Yucatec Maya).

DESCRIPTION   *Oxybelis fulgidus* is a large, slender, bright green snake with a narrow, elongate head and a pointed snout (Fig. 176). Individuals may exceed 1,500 mm in snout-vent length. The tail is about 50 to 60 percent of the head and body length. The eyes are moderately large, and the pupils are round. The dorsal scales are weakly keeled, lack apical pits, and are arranged in 17 rows at midbody. The anal plate is divided.

The dorsum is uniformly green above, and the upper and lower labials and chin are lighter green or cream (Fig. 376). A dark green or black eye stripe is usually present. A pair of white, cream, or yellow stripes extends the length of the body on the lateral edges of the ventral scales.

SIMILAR SPECIES   The only other bright green snake in the Yucatán Peninsula, *Leptophis ahaetulla*, has a blunt snout and dorsal scales arranged in 15 rows.

DISTRIBUTION   *Oxybelis fulgidus* occurs at low and intermediate elevations on the Atlantic and Pacific slopes from the Isthmus of Tehuantepec through Central America to Argentina. It probably occurs throughout the Yucatán Peninsula, although it has not yet been recorded from southern Campeche (Map 147).

NATURAL HISTORY   Green vine snakes are predominantly arboreal and moderately common inhabitants of second growth and forest edges. They feed on a variety of vertebrate prey, including lizards (Swanson, 1945:214), birds (H. M. Smith, 1943:458; Stuart, 1948:82), and small mammals. Henderson (1982:75) examined the stomach contents of a series of *O. fulgidus* from Yucatán and found that lizards of several species predominated in the diet, and that warblers were also eaten. In Belize, *O. fulgidus* is known to prey on the clay-colored robin, *Turdus grayi* (K. Duplouy, photo). Conners (1989:73) reported that captives ate *Anolis* lizards and mice. Prey animals are overpowered with the aid of a mild venom injected through the large rear fangs. Gerhardt et al. (1993:350) reported that at Tikal, Guatemala, this species is preyed on by the great black hawk, *Buteogallus urubitinga*.

When startled, these snakes extend the tongue and remain motionless for long periods. Green vine snakes will bite when handled, and although this species is probably not dangerous to humans, the bite has been known to cause local pain and swelling (J. A. Campbell and Lamar, 1989:295). People's responses to envenomation vary, of course, and large individuals should be handled carefully.

This species is oviparous. Stuart (1948:82) found

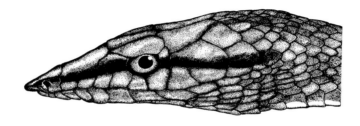

Fig. 176. Lateral view of the head of *Oxybelis fulgidus*, 1,295 mm SVL; Costa Rica.

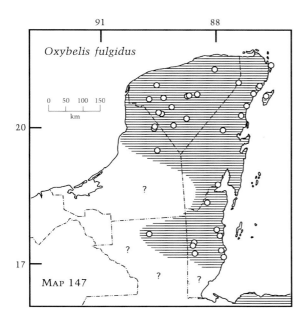

Oxybelis fulgidus

0 50 100 150
km

91   88

20

17

MAP 147

gravid females in mid-April in Alta Verapaz. Conners (1989:73) reported that a captive produced a clutch of 10 eggs on or around 19 May; 2 eggs hatched on 22 August, and another hatched on 23 August. The mean snout-vent length of the three hatchlings was 235 mm.

ETYMOLOGY The specific name, *fulgidus*, is a Latin adjective meaning "shining."

Locality Records Belize: Belize: 11 km SW Hattieville (CM 90954), Manatee River (FMNH 3478); Cayo: Central Farm (MCZ 71653), Chaa Creek (CM 105971), Río Frio Cave (MPM 8203); Corozal: mi 56–57 on Northern Hwy. (MPM 7755); Orange Walk: Orange Walk (MPM 8135–37); Stann Creek: Freetown (CM 8501), jct. Hummingbird and Southern Hwys. (JLK 475); no specific locality (FMNH 4207–8). *Guatemala:* El Petén: Chuntuquí (USNM 71362). *Mexico:* Campeche: 2 mi S Bolonchén de Rejon (UIMNH 87666), 3 km NE Crucero (KU 70879), Dzibalchén (KU 75628); Quintana Roo: Chetumal (MZCIQRO 12), 33.4 km N Felipe Carrillo Puerto (JCL 6800), Isla Cozumel (López-Gonzales, 1991:106), Isla Mujeres (UCM 16053–54), Playa del Carmen (López-Gonzales, 1991:106), 4 mi S Playa del Carmen (LSUMZ 33356), 8.8 km NE Playa del Carmen (KU 171706), 15.8 km N Playa del Carmen (JCL 5412), Pueblo Nuevo X-Can (CM 45769–70, 49123; UCM 40483–84, 41769–71), Punta Venado (López-Gonzales, 1991:106), 13.5 km N Tulum (JCL 6822), 20.8 km S Tulum (JCL 6827); Yucatán: Labná (Ives, 1891:460), Libre Unión (FMNH 36189), 15 km NE Maxcanú (TU 19802), Mayapán (FMNH 40747), S edge Mérida (KU 157610), Peto (CM 45307–9), Pisté

(CM 46946–50, 47002–3, 47139–41, 49720–30; UCM 47063, 40485), 4 km S Salvador Alvarado (TU 19762), 6 km N Santa Elena (Dundee et al., 1986:44), 0.5 km W Teabo (Dundee et al., 1986:44), 6 km N Tizimín (KU 74996), 10 km E Uxmal (TU 19763), Yokdzonot (FMNH 36190, 36193).

Genus *Oxyrhopus*

These moderately slender rear-fanged Neotropical snakes range from southern Mexico to Peru and southeastern Brazil. The genus comprises roughly a dozen species, of which one occurs in the Yucatán Peninsula. *Oxyrhopus* may derive from the Greek *oxyrropos,* an adjective meaning "turning quickly."

Oxyrhopus petola (Linnaeus)
(Fig. 377; Map 148)

Coluber petola Linnaeus, 1758:225. TYPE: unknown. TYPE LOCALITY: Africa (in error).

Red-banded snake; bead and coral (Belize); kuyun kan (Lacandón Maya).

DESCRIPTION This moderately slender snake attains a snout-vent length somewhat in excess of 600 mm, and males are generally larger than females (Duellman, 1979:254). The tail is about 35 to 40 percent of the snout-vent length. The head is distinct from the neck and somewhat triangular in dorsal aspect. The eyes are relatively small, and the pupils are vertically elliptical. There are 19 rows of smooth scales at midbody, and the anterior dorsal scales bear a pair of apical pits. The anal scale is undivided.

The color and pattern change with age. In adults, the dorsal coloration of the body and tail typically consists of broad alternating bands of black and red or red-orange (Fig. 377). The bands are approximately equal in width, and there is a narrow yellow or cream nuchal band that extends onto the labial scales and is continuous with the light coloration on the chin and venter. The dorsal surface of the head is black. The venter is essentially immaculate cream or yellowish, although posteriorly the dorsal coloration may extend onto the ventral scales. The juveniles have yellowish bands rather than red or orange ones, and these become red or red-orange as the snake grows older, at which time the red bands may be edged with yellow. Large individuals tend to have dark red bands and to have an orange rather than a yellowish nuchal band.

SIMILAR SPECIES *Oxyrhopus petola* differs from *Sibon fasciata* and *S. sartorii* in having light and dark bands that are approximately equal in width, and in possessing smooth rather than weakly keeled middorsal scales, which are arranged in 19 rather than 17 rows. *Dipsas brevifacies* has 15 rows of middorsal scales, and its dark rings are much broader than the light ones. The species of *Micrurus* differ from *Oxyrhopus* in lacking a loreal scale and having small eyes with round pupils and 15 rows of middorsal scales. Moreover, the *Micrurus* in the Yucatán Peninsula usually have black rings bordered by yellow rings. *Lampropeltis* has 21 rather than 19 rows of middorsal scales, and *Urotheca* and *Scaphiodontophis* have 17 rows of middorsal scales.

DISTRIBUTION *Oxyrhopus petola* occurs at low and moderate elevations on the Atlantic slope from Veracruz to Bolivia and northern Brazil, and on the Pacific slope from Costa Rica to Ecuador. In the Yucatán Peninsula this species is known from northern Chiapas, El Petén, and adjacent Belize (Map 148).

NATURAL HISTORY These uncommon, terrestrial snakes inhabit humid lowland forests in the Yucatán Peninsula. They appear to be predomi-

nantly nocturnal, and they prey primarily on lizards and snakes, which they overpower by means of their rear fangs and (presumably) weak venom. Duellman (1979:255) found the lizards *Kentropyx pelviceps* and *Prionodactylus manicatus* in the stomachs of specimens from Amazonian Ecuador.

Oxyrhopus petola is oviparous. Fitch (1970:154) reported clutch sizes ranging from 5 to 10 (mean = 7.3) for snakes collected in March, September, and November from the vicinity of Iquitos, Peru. Test et al. (1966:43) stated that a female from Estada Aragua, Venezuela, laid 7 eggs on 1 and 2 June, 2 of which hatched on 1 and 2 September.

SUBSPECIES Of the three subspecies recognized by J. R. Bailey (1970:234), *O. p. sebae* occurs in the Yucatán Peninsula.

ETYMOLOGY The specific name, *petola*, may derive from the Latin adjective *paetula*, meaning "squinting slightly" or "leering."

Locality Records Belize: Belize: 30.5 mi ESE Belize City (CM 109026); Cayo: Augustine (W. T. Neill and Allen, 1959c:55; JLK 460), 9.0 km SE Belmopan (UTA R-11071), Central Farm (MCZ 71678). *Guatemala*: El Petén: 17 mi W Melchor (KU 157611), Paso de los Caballos (UMMZ 79062), San Pedro River (MCZ 38657), Sojio (AMNH 69984), Tikal (MCZ 55430; UMMZ 117916), 8.7 km S Tikal (UMRC 89-42). *Mexico*: Chiapas: 10 to 15 mi S Palenque (LSUMZ 33309).

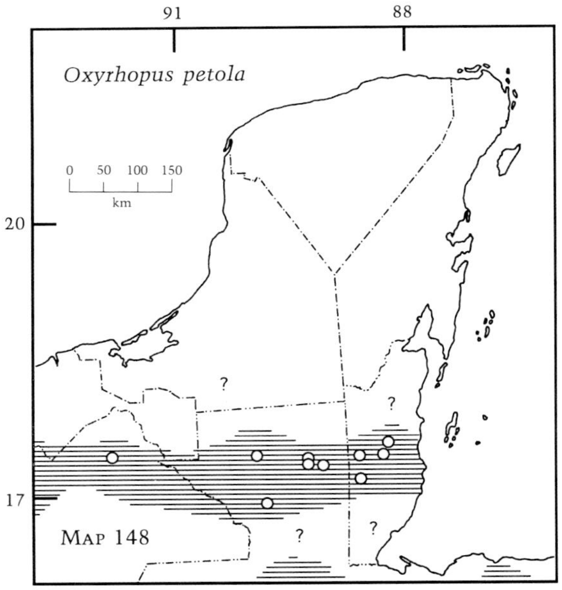

MAP 148

Genus *Pseustes* (Puffing Snakes)

These large snakes may exceed 2,000 mm in total length. Representatives of the genus occur from southeastern Mexico through Central America to Bolivia and Brazil. Of the four species recognized, one occurs in the Yucatán Peninsula. *Pseustes* is Greek for "liar" or "cheat."

Pseustes poecilonotus (Günther)
(Fig. 378; Map 149)

Spilotes poecilonotus Günther, 1858:100. SYNTYPES: BMNH 1946.1.7.41 (two syntypes). TYPE LOCALITY: Honduras or Mexico. Boulenger (1894:20) recognized the Honduran specimen as the type; Schmidt (1941:499) suggested that the Honduran specimen may actually have come from Belize.

Brown tree snake; puffer (Belize); sumbadora (Guatemala); culebra manchada, pajarera (Mexico); chair (Lacandón Maya).

DESCRIPTION This is one of the larger snakes in the Yucatán Peninsula. The adults may attain a snout-vent length of 1,500 mm, although most range between 750 and 1,000 mm. The length of the tail is about 40 percent of the snout-vent length. In dorsal aspect the snout is bluntly rounded and the head is moderately distinct from the neck (Fig. 378). The eyes are large with round pupils. The middorsal scales are keeled, and the lateral scales are smooth. Paired apical pits are present on some dorsal scales, and the number of dorsal scale rows at midbody varies from 19 to 25. The ventral scales are angulate, and the anal plate is undivided.

There is pronounced ontogenetic variation in color and pattern. The dorsal ground color of subadults and young adults is generally tan, with a series of narrow, dark brown transverse blotches on the body. These blotches have light tan centers and are outlined in dark brown or black. They extend onto the lateral surfaces of the body and the lateral margins of the ventral scales. Often the blotches assume a crescent shape or an inverted V, especially on the anterior third of the body. The ventral surfaces of the body and tail are tan or cream and finely speckled with brown. Some specimens have a few small, dark brown spots on the chin and throat. The dorsal surface of the head is tan, usually with three darker spots, one on the posterior margin of the frontal scale and one on each parietal. There is an indistinct postorbital stripe, and the iris is cream above and darker below. Large adults tend to be predominantly dark brown, olive brown, or nearly black above, with or without pale spots on the dorsal scales.

SIMILAR SPECIES Subadult *P. poecilonotus* superficially resemble *Elaphe flavirufa* and *Senticolis triaspis* but differ in possessing fewer than 31 rows of dorsal scales and having an undivided anal plate. From *Leptodeira frenata* they differ in having keeled middorsal scales and round pupils. The adults of *Pseustes poecilonotus* may resemble *Spilotes pullatus*, but that species has dorsal scales arranged in an even number of rows at midbody.

DISTRIBUTION The brown tree snake occurs at low and moderate elevations on the Atlantic slope from San Luis Potosí to Bolivia and Brazil, and on

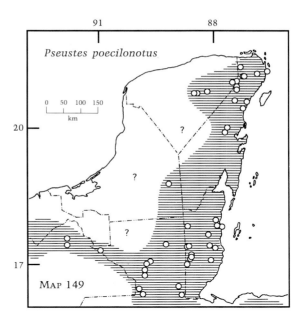

MAP 149

the Pacific slope from Oaxaca to lower Central America. It occurs through the base of the Yucatán Peninsula and northward through Quintana Roo, apparently avoiding much of the drier western portion of the peninsula (Map 149).

NATURAL HISTORY *Pseustes poecilonotus* is a moderately common inhabitant of humid lowland forests and savannas, where it is both terrestrial and arboreal. I found individuals on the forest floor in Quintana Roo and in a small tree on the savannas of El Petén. Duellman (1963:243) found them on the forest floor and on low bushes in southern El Petén. Stuart (1958:26) recorded a specimen at Tikal, El Petén, taken from a rotting palm 5 feet above the ground.

When threatened, this harmless snake may exhibit a series of defensive behaviors that increase in intensity (Rand and Ortleb, 1969). Low-intensity defensive behavior involves lateral compression of the body followed by a flattening of the head and inflation of the lung. The latter activity increases the dorsoventral dimension of the anterior portion of the body, making the snake appear larger. This may be followed by mouth gaping and, finally, a strike. Rand and Ortleb (1969:48) suggested that these behaviors increase the snake's resemblance to a pitviper.

In Chiapas, this species feeds on birds, hence its Spanish common name, *pajarera* (Alvarez del Toro, 1983:192). A specimen from Panama had eaten bird eggs (Sexton and Heatwole, 1965:41).

SUBSPECIES The extensive distribution of this form combined with the pronounced ontogenetic variation in coloration that it exhibits have made the recognition of subspecies problematic. J. A. Peters and Orejas-Miranda (1970:257) recognized four subspecies, of which only the nominate form, *P. p. poecilonotus*, occurs in the Yucatán Peninsula.

ETYMOLOGY The specific name, *poecilonotus* is from the Greek *poikilos*, "variegated, many colored," and *notos*, "the back," presumably in reference to the variegated dorsal pattern of some individuals.

Locality Records   Belize: Belize: Belize City (CM 117108), bet. Ladyville and Sandhill (CM 90953), mi 28–29 on Northern Hwy. (MPM 7708); Cayo: Augustine (MPM 8190), Beaver Dam Creek (CM 112119), Macal River at Guacamallo Bridge (CM 112147), 5 mi E Melchor (Guatemala) (UF 51679), Vaquero, Mountain Pine Ridge (UMMZ 80720), Valentin (UMMZ 80719), Xunantunich (CM 112109); Orange Walk: near Gallon Jug (MPM 7363); Stann Creek: Cockscomb Basin Wildlife Preserve (CMM photo), 5 mi NW Middlesex (JLK 468), 29 mi W Stann Creek (JLK 467). *Guatemala*: Alta Verapaz: Chinajá (Duellman, 1963:243); El Petén: 20 km NNW Chinajá (KU 55721), 16.8 mi SW Flores (KU 157613), La Libertad (UMMZ 74912–13), Las Cañas (CM 58280–81), Piedras Negras (USNM 110517–20), 23.4 mi SE San Luis (KU 157612), Sayaxché (UCM 22358), Sojio (AMNH 69971), Tikal (MCZ 55431; UF 13845–46; UMMZ 117929). *Mexico*: Campeche: Becan (UWZH 20502); Chiapas: Palenque (USNM 110516), 10 to 15 mi S Palenque (LSUMZ 33323); Quintana Roo: Cancún (López-Gonzales, 1991:106), 12.2 km SE Cobá (UMRC 84-42), 2 mi W Cristóbal Colón (UCM 22970), 12.7 km NE Felipe Carrillo Puerto (KU 171720), 23.8 km NE Felipe Carrillo Puerto (KU 171721), 4 km W, 11 km S Puerto Juárez (UCM 28136), Pueblo Nuevo X-Can (CM 45771–75, 49067, 49080; UCM 40686–91, 41772–77), 8.2 km S Pueblo Nuevo X-Can (UMRC 84-12), 15.4 km S Pueblo Nuevo X-Can (UMRC 84-11), bet. Pueblo Nuevo X-Can and Leona Vicario (UMRC 79-272), 17.6 km S Solferino (UMRC 79-271), Tintal (UCM 40492), Tulum (LSUMZ 33322), 26.3 km NW Tulum (JCL 6812); Yucatán: Chichén Itzá (MCZ 26844; UMMZ 73035, 80805, 83936–37), Pisté (CM 46952–54, 49732–33; UCM 40493–94), 10 mi W Valladolid (LSUMZ 38576), X-Can (CM 46840–43, 46879, 47044).

Genus *Rhadinaea*
(Graceful Brown Snakes)

This genus of small to medium-sized terrestrial snakes is predominantly Neotropical in distribu-

tion, ranging from the southeastern United States to northern Argentina. Most species are brown with darker longitudinal stripes. The posteriormost maxillary teeth are generally enlarged, and in at least one species the maxillary teeth are grooved. The most recent revision of the genus is Myers, 1974, which recognizes about 45 species. That number was reduced by 7 with the reallocation of the *lateristriga* group of *Rhadinaea* to *Urotheca* by Savage and Crother (1989:343). Only 1 species of *Rhadinaea* occurs in the Yucatán Peninsula. *Rhadinaea* is from the Greek *rhadinos*, meaning "slender," "slim," or "slight," or possibly "graceful," and *-ea*, a Latin generic ending.

Rhadinaea decorata (Günther)
(Figs. 177, 379; Map 150)

Coronella decorata Günther, 1858:35. SYNTYPES: BMNH 1946.1.9.3–4 (two syntypes); BMNH 1946.1.9.4 was designated the lectotype by Myers (1974:68). TYPE LOCALITY: Mexico.

Hojarasquera (Mexico); tzinkan (Lacandón Maya).

DESCRIPTION This is a small, moderately slender brown snake with a pair of light dorsolateral stripes bordered below by a thin black line (Fig. 379). The maximum snout-vent length is about 265 mm for males and about 280 mm for females, but most are smaller. The relatively long tail is approximately 40 percent of the head and body length. The head is rather narrow and only slightly distinct from the neck in dorsal aspect. The eyes are relatively large, and the pupils are round. The dorsal scales are weakly keeled and arranged in 17 rows at midbody. Apical pits may be present on the dorsal scales of the neck region. The anal plate is normally divided.

The dorsum is brown, with the sides of the body darker than the middorsal area. Separating the dorsal and lateral surfaces is a light cream or white stripe bordered below by a thin black line. Often there is a vague dark middorsal line, which becomes obscure posteriorly. These snakes are distinctive in having a conspicuous light postocular spot on the lateral edge of the parietal scales (Fig. 177). The spot is white, cream, or tan and is bordered with black. A similar spot is generally present at the nape of the neck between the temporal scales and the beginning of the light dorsolateral stripe. The dorsal and lateral surfaces of the head are brown, with the

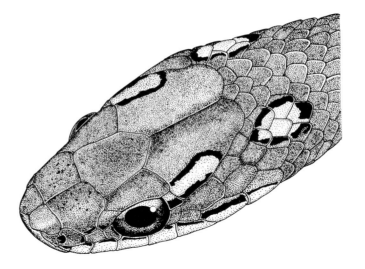

Fig. 177. Dorsolateral view of the head of *Rhadinaea decorata* (UMMZ 126432), 225 mm SVL; Tikal, El Petén, Guatemala.

brown pigment extending to the upper portion of the supralabials and bordered by a thin black line. The lower portion of the supralabials is white or cream, and the infralabials and chin are also white, with or without a few small, dark spots. The throat and the anterior portion of the venter may be cream, yellowish, or orange, becoming reddish orange posteriorly.

SIMILAR SPECIES In the Yucatán Peninsula *R. decorata* is most similar to *Coniophanes imperialis*, but the latter has 19 middorsal scale rows rather than 17. *Coniophanes meridanus* has 17 rows of middorsal scales, but it does not overlap geographically with *R. decorata* (cf. Maps 121, 150).

DISTRIBUTION *Rhadinaea decorata* ranges widely at low to moderate elevations on the Atlantic slope of Mexico from southern San Luis Potosí through the Isthmus of Tehauntepec, south and westward through Central America to Ecuador. In the Yucatán Peninsula this species is known from northern Chiapas, El Petén, and southern Belize (Map 150).

NATURAL HISTORY Although moderately common elsewhere in its range, this snake is rare in the Yucatán Peninsula, and virtually nothing is known concerning its natural history there. In the Lacandón region of Chiapas I found a specimen crossing a road in the afternoon. Myers (1974:76) reported that this species is a diurnal inhabitant of the forest floor in Panama, and he found specimens prowling there by day; other specimens were found beneath surface

debris. H. M. Smith (1943:463) reported *Bolitoglossa rufescens* in the stomach of a specimen from Veracruz. According to Scott (1983c:416), this species feeds on frogs and is oviparous.

SUBSPECIES Myers (1974) analyzed variation in scutellation, color pattern, dentition, and hemipenial morphology and concluded that no subspecies should be recognized in spite of the wide geographical distribution of this species.

ETYMOLOGY The specific name, *decorata*, is Latin meaning "adorned" or "decorated," in reference to the light markings on the head.

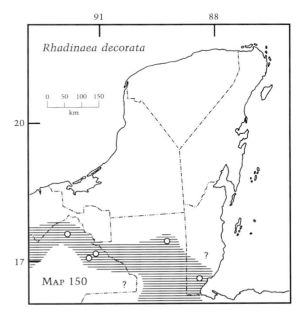

COMMENT *Rhadinaea decorata* was reviewed by Myers as part of his revision of the genus *Rhadinaea*.

Locality Records Belize: Toledo: Big Falls, Río Grande (MCZ 151476). *Guatemala*: El Petén: Tikal (UMMZ 126432). *Mexico*: Chiapas: bet. El Censo and Monte Libano (MCZ 53899), Palenque ruins (UIMNH 11345), San Cristóbal de Colón, on rd. to Bonampak (KU 171731).

Genus *Scaphiodontophis*
(Shovel-toothed Snakes)

This genus was erected by Taylor and Smith (1943) to accommodate a small assemblage of Neotropical snakes with peculiar spatulate, hinged teeth. Representatives of the genus range from northeastern Mexico to northern South America. They possess long, fragile tails and feed almost exclusively on hard-bodied lizards, predominantly skinks. The most recent comprehensive systematic treatment of the genus (Morgan, 1973) recognizes two species, one of which occurs in the Yucatán Peninsula. *Scaphiodontophis* is derived from the Greek *scaphis*, "shovel," *odonto-*, an adjectival prefix referring to "teeth," and *ophis*, "snake," in reference to the shovel-shaped teeth.

Scaphiodontophis annulatus
(Duméril, Bibron, and Duméril)
(Fig. 380; Map 151)

Enicognathus annulatus A. M. C. Duméril, Bibron, and Duméril, 1854:335. HOLOTYPE: MNHNP 7283. TYPE LOCALITY: Cobán (Haute-Vera-Paz) (= Cobán, Alta Verapaz, Guatemala).

Shovel-toothed snake; double snake (Belize); culebra añadida (Mexico); kuyun kan (Lacandón Maya).

DESCRIPTION The adults of this medium-sized, moderately slender snake average between 250 and 300 mm in snout-vent length. The tail is extremely long, roughly 40 to 50 percent of the head and body length. The head is slightly distinct from the neck, the eyes are rather large, and the pupils are round (Fig. 380). The dorsal scales are smooth, arranged in 17 rows at midbody, and lack apical pits. The anal plate is divided.

The anterior portion of the body bears a series of narrow yellow or white bands bordered by black bands and separated by broad red interspaces, the scales of which are black-tipped. In some specimens the pattern of bands extends the length of the body and tail, but more typically the posterior portion of the body and the tail are uniformly brown or grayish, with three longitudinal rows of small, dark spots producing an indistinct striped pattern. Thus, the anterior portion of the body resembles the ringed pattern of a coral snake, whereas the posterior portion is nondescript brown or gray, hence the Belizean name "double snake." The ventral surfaces of the body and tail are cream or yellowish, with a suffusion of darker pigment on the lateral edges of the ventral scales.

SIMILAR SPECIES Typical specimens from the Yucatán Peninsula are unique in combining a coral snake–like pattern on the anterior portion of the body with a drab unicolor posterior. Specimens that are banded along the entire length of the body can be distinguished from *Micrurus* by their 17 rather than 15 rows of scales at midbody, and by their loreal scale. *Scaphiodontophis* differs from both *Micrurus* and *Urotheca* in having yellow or white bands bordered by black ones, rather than black rings bordered by yellow or white rings. *Lampropeltis*, a larger, more robust snake, has 21 rows of scales at midbody.

DISTRIBUTION *Scaphiodontophis annulatus* occurs at low and moderate elevations from Tamaulipas on the Atlantic slope and the Isthmus of Tehauntepec on the Pacific slope, east and southward through Central America at least to Colombia. It occurs at the base of the Yucatán Peninsula, and disjunct populations apparently exist at the outer end of the peninsula in Yucatán and Quintana Roo (Map 151).

NATURAL HISTORY Throughout its range this uncommon snake is primarily an inhabitant of humid lowland forests, although it also occupies the subhumid forests at the northern end of the Yucatán Peninsula. It is found in leaf litter and is probably also fossorial, for W. T. Neill and Allen (1959c:47) reported a specimen in Belize unearthed by a bulldozer. This is a secretive snake, but specimens have been observed abroad during the day. Shovel-toothed snakes are rather quick in their movements, and nervous, but they are inoffensive and seldom if ever bite.

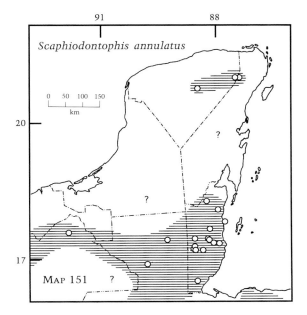

Scaphiodontophis annulatus

MAP 151

Like several other genera of snakes (e.g., *Coniophanes* and *Urotheca*), *Scaphiodontophis* have fragile, easily broken tails, and individuals with incomplete tails are common. J. W. Wright (quoted in Henderson, 1984:185–186) reported tail thrashing in *S. annulatus*. In this behavior the anterior ringed portion of the body is elevated and held motionless while the unicolor posterior portion of the body and tail undulates and thrashes in the bushes. This behavior, coupled with the fragile tail, is most likely a strategy to induce predators to attack the tail and leave the head alone (Greene, 1973).

Shovel-toothed snakes have a relatively restricted diet. They prey predominantly on hard-bodied lizards, especially *Sphenomorphus* skinks, although captives also may accept *Anolis* lizards. Each tooth has a connective tissue hinge at its base that allows the tooth to fold backward, facilitating the manipulation of hard-bodied prey (Savitzky, 1981). Alvarez del Toro (1983:152) and Henderson (1984:185) remarked on the astonishing rapidity with which these snakes subdue and swallow their lizard prey. Henderson (1984:185) reported a mean handling time of 7.73 seconds for six feeding trials involving *Sphenomorphus*, with a minimum time of 2.8 seconds.

Scaphiodontophis annulatus is oviparous, and the eggs are laid during the summer rainy season. Alvarez del Toro and Smith (1958:16) reported a clutch of 4 eggs laid on 16 June in Chiapas; these hatched on 15 August. W. F. Pyburn (quoted in Henderson, 1984:186) found 3 eggs beneath a rotting log

in southern Veracruz, one of which hatched on 12 October. According to Alvarez del Toro (1983:153), the clutch size in Chiapas is generally 6 to 10 eggs.

ETYMOLOGY The specific name, *annulatus*, is Latin meaning "ringed," in reference to the pattern seen on at least the anterior portion of the body.

Locality Records Belize: Belize: near Altun Ha (JCL sight record), Belize (Schmidt, 1941:497), 31 mi WSW Belize City (JCL photo); Cayo: 2.5 mi E Augustine (JLK 469), 3 to 10 mi S Belmopan (CM 105939), 1.5 mi S, 1 mi E Caves Branch and Hummingbird Hwy. (W. T. Neill and Allen, 1959c:47), Central Farm (MCZ 71679), Mountain Pine Ridge (MPM 7728–29), Río Frio Cave (CM 105810), upper Raspaculo River basin (Stafford, 1991:14); Orange Walk: Tower Hill (MPM 10786); Stann Creek: Middlesex (UCM 25745, 25747, 25788–89, 29988–89), Stann Creek Valley (Schmidt, 1941:497); Toledo: 12 mi W Punta Gorda (UF 79994). *Guatemala*: El Petén: Sojio (AMNH 69979), Tikal (AMNH uncat.; UMMZ 117903). *Mexico*: Chiapas: Palenque (EAL 3633); Quintana Roo: Pueblo Nuevo X-Can (CM 45776–77); Yucatán: Pisté (KU 70884), X-Can (CM 47046).

Genus *Senticolis*

This genus was erected in 1987 by Dowling and Fries to accommodate a single species, *Senticolis triaspis*, the Neotropical ratsnake. Information on the genus was summarized by R. M. Price (1991). *Senticolis* derives from the Latin *sentis*, "thorn" or "bramble," and *colis*, "penis," in reference to the heavy basal spines on the hemipenis.

Senticolis triaspis (Cope)
(Fig. 152A, 381; Map 152)

Coluber triaspis Cope, 1866:128. HOLOTYPE: USNM 24903. TYPE LOCALITY: Belize; restricted by H. M. Smith and Taylor (1950b:316) to the town of that name, but that restriction was considered doubtful by R. Allen and Neill (1959:229).

Neotropical ratsnake; ratonera oliva (Mexico); yegrukicho'rerek (Lacandón Maya).

DESCRIPTION This is a medium-sized snake. The adults attain a maximum snout-vent length of about 1,000 mm, and females grow substantially larger than males (Censky and McCoy, 1988). The tail length is approximately 25 to 35 percent of the snout-vent length. The head is moderately narrow and distinct from the neck. The eyes are relatively small, and the pupils are round (Fig. 152A). The middorsal scales are weakly keeled, and the lateral scales are smooth. Paired apical pits are present on some dorsal scales, but they may be indistinct. The number of dorsal scale rows at midbody is quite variable, ranging from 29 to 39. The ventral scales are angulate, and the anal plate is normally divided.

Senticolis triaspis juveniles are blotched, but there is geographic variation in the extent to which the blotching persists in adults. Specimens from central El Petén and northward retain the blotched pattern as adults. They generally have a gray or light olive green dorsum, often with a yellowish cast, and a series of dark olive or brown blotches is present on the dorsum. The blotches are generally rectangular and outlined in dark brown or black. A lateral series of smaller blotches alternates with the dorsal ones. A dark transverse crescent is usually present on the dorsal surface of the head anterior to the eyes, and a dark median frontoparietal band with a light central opening is usually present as well. An indistinct postocular stripe may also be present, and the chin and the labial scales are white or cream. The venter is predominantly cream, white, or light gray, but the dorsal ground color extends onto the lateral surfaces of the ventral scales, and indistinct dark smudges may be present, especially posteriorly. Specimens from the base of the Yucatán Peninsula tend to lose the blotched juvenile pattern as they grow older and have a uniformly tan or reddish tan dorsum.

SIMILAR SPECIES *Senticolis triaspis* most closely resembles *Elaphe flavirufa*, from which it differs in usually possessing eight supralabials, two of which enter the orbit, rather than nine supralabial scales, three of which enter the orbit. Further, *S. triaspis* generally has more than 45 blotches on the body, whereas *E. flavirufa* usually has fewer than 45. *Pseustes poecilonotus* has fewer than 31 rows of scales at midbody and an undivided anal plate. The species of *Leptodeira* have smooth dorsal scales and vertically elliptical pupils.

DISTRIBUTION *Senticolis triaspis* occurs at low and moderate elevations from Tamaulipas on the Atlantic slope and Arizona on the Pacific slope, south to Costa Rica. It probably occurs throughout the Yucatán Peninsula, but there are apparently

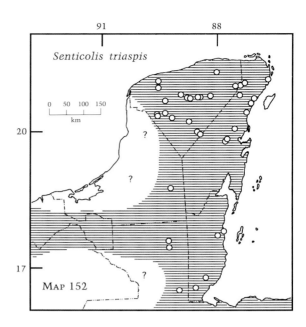

MAP 152

no records from northern and western Campeche (Map 152).

NATURAL HISTORY Neotropical ratsnakes are primarily terrestrial and nocturnal. They inhabit the deciduous thorn forests of northern Yucatán as well as the taller, wetter forests to the east and south. They are constrictors, and they prey primarily on small mammals, as the Spanish common name, *ratonera oliva*, suggests. The remains of a shrew were found in the stomach of a specimen from Yucatán (Schmidt and Andrews, 1936:173), Dowling (1960:56) reported mammal hair in the stomach of a specimen from Guerrero, and Duellman (1958b:11) found a house mouse (*Mus musculus*) in the stomach of a specimen from Colima, Mexico. Meyer (1966:178) observed a specimen in a Honduran cave in the act of constricting a bat, and R. M. Price (1991:525.3) indicated that birds are also eaten.

Senticolis triaspis is oviparous. In Yucatán, reproduction apparently continues throughout the year. Dowling (1960) reported two oviductal eggs in a female collected in October at Chichén Itzá; and Censky and McCoy (1988) found specimens with enlarged ovarian follicles in March and November, with oviductal eggs in September, and with stretched oviducts in November and February. The clutch size in these specimens ranged from three to seven (mean 4.8) and showed no covariation with female body size.

SUBSPECIES Of the three subspecies recognized by R. M. Price (1991), *S. t. triaspis* occurs in the northern and central portions of the Yucatán Peninsula, *S. t. mutabilis* occurs at the base of the peninsula, and *S. t. intermedius* may occur in the Lacandón region of Chiapas (R. M. Price, 1991:1). McCoy (1990:165) suggested intergradation between *triaspis* and *mutabilis* in central Belize and northern Honduras.

ETYMOLOGY The specific name, *triaspis*, comes from the Greek *treis*, "three," and *aspis*, "shield," perhaps referring to the three elongate anterior temporal scales that are usually present.

COMMENT Before 1987 this species was placed in the genus *Elaphe*. In 1987, however, Dowling and Fries erected the genus *Senticolis*, with *triaspis* its sole member, based primarily on anatomical peculiarities of the hemipenes.

Senticolis triaspis was reviewed by Dowling (1960) and R. M. Price (1991).

Locality Records Belize: Belize: Belize City (USNM 24903), Rockville Quarry (Gracy Bank) (McCoy, 1990:165); Toledo: Blue Creek Village (CM photo 33025.42), Bladen Nature Reserve (JAM photo). *Guatemala*: El Petén: Las Cañas (CM 58273), Tikal (Stuart, 1958:26), Uaxactún (USNM 64906). *Mexico*: Campeche: Becan (UWZH 20517); Chiapas: bet. Palenque and Chajul (MZFC 3106); Quintana Roo: Felipe Carrillo Puerto (CAS 141869; UMMZ 113600–5), 3.9 km NE Felipe Carrillo Puerto (KU 171717), 4 km NNE Felipe Carrillo Puerto (KU 70853), 54 km NNE Felipe Carrillo Puerto (LSUMZ 28248), 13.7 mi S Playa del Carmen (LSUMZ 38604), Pueblo Nuevo X-Can (CM 45701–2, 45704–11, 49070, 49081, 49094, 49102, 49125, 49137, 49168; UCM 40219–26, 40718–23, 40739, 41689–94), 30.6 km S Pueblo Nuevo X-Can (JCL 6821), 36 km N Puerto Morelos (CAS 154148), Tintal (UCM 40227–28), Tulum Ruins (MCZ 147418), 29.2 km NW Tulum (JCL 6799); Yucatán: Chichén Itzá (FMNH 20624, 153525; MCZ 7250, 29241, 28751–52; UMMZ 68234–35, 83283, 83929–30; USNM 46398, 46574–77, 46579), 3 km N Kikil (KU 171716), Dzibil-

chaltún (FMNH 153500, 153517, 153522–24), 3 mi E Esmeralda (LACM 114041), Kantunil (FMNH 36113, 36120, 36126–27, 36130), Libre Unión (FMNH 36105, 36109, 36134–35, 36138), Mayapán (FMNH 40722), Mérida (AMNH 7866, 101059; CM 44469; FMNH 19428, 20603; MZFC 854; UCM 40229, 41695; UWZH 20558), Peto (CM 45296, 45703), Pisté (CM 46996–98, 47102–8, 49637–47; KU 70854–58; UCM 17061, 40230–31), 3 km S Ticul (TU 19797), bet. Uxmal and Santa Elena (TU 19758), 1 km S Uxmal (TU 19759), 11 mi W Valladolid (BCB 12255), 1 km W Yotholin (TU 19823), X-Can (CM 46824–27, 46871–74, 47036–37), near Yucatán–Quintana Roo border on Hwy. 184 (KU 171715), Yokdzonot (FMNH 36107, 36114–15, 36117, 36122, 36125, 36128–29, 36131, 36136), no specific locality (FMNH 7007).

Genus *Sibon* (Snail-eating Snakes)

This strictly Neotropical genus contains 10 species of predominantly arboreal, gastropod mollusk-eating snakes of small to medium size. The common name, snail sucker, refers to the ability of these animals (and those of the related genus *Dipsas*) to extract snails from their shells. To accomplish this, the snout is pressed against the margin of the shell opening, and the lower jaws are inserted between the body of the snail and the shell. They are extended far forward, then retracted, prying the snail free. Specializations for feeding on snails and slugs include reorientation of the jaw bones and associated muscles in order to allow a secure grip on the slimy prey. The genus occurs at low and moderate elevations from southern Mexico through Central America to northern South America. Five species are found in the Yucatán Peninsula. The genus *Sibon* was reviewed by J. A. Peters (1960) as part of his revision of snakes of the subfamily Dipsadinae. More recently the genus was redefined and its species groups reviewed by Kofron (1985, 1987, 1988, 1990). *Sibon* may derive from the Latin noun *sibonis*, a kind of hunting spear.

Key to the Snakes of the Genus *Sibon*

1. Anteriormost pair of infralabials in contact medially behind the mental shield (Fig. 178A) . . . 2
   Anteriormost pair of infralabials separated by an azygous scale (Fig. 178B) 4
2. Dorsal scales in 17 rows, weakly keeled; apical pits present; dorsal pattern of distinct light rings alternating with dark rings 3

Dorsal scales in 15 rows, smooth, lacking pits; dorsal pattern of indistinct dark blotches or bands against a gray background . . . . *Sibon nebulata*

3. Nuchal band extending anteriorly on supralabials to beyond the eye; light rings of yellow, orange, or red-orange alternating with black rings . . . . *Sibon sartorii*

Nuchal band not extending anteriorly on supralabials to beyond the eye; light rings white, tan, or gray alternating with dark brown or black rings . . . . *Sibon fasciata*

4. Dorsal pattern a series of small, dark brown spots against a tan background; 143–162 ventrals . . . . *Sibon sanniola*

Pattern variable, often light brown or orange blotches or bands against a gray or brown background; 160–206 ventrals . . . . *Sibon dimidiata*

Clave para las Especies del Género *Sibon*

1. El par más anterior de labiales inferiores en contacto en la región media detrás de los escudos mentales (Fig. 178A) 2

El par más anterior de labiales inferiores separado por una escama áziga (Fig. 178B) 4

2. Escamas dorsales en 17 hileras, débilmente quilladas; poros apicales presentes en las escamas; patrón de coloración dorsal consistente de anillos claros distintivos, alternando con anillos obscuros 3

Escamas dorsales en 15 hileras, lisas, sin poros apicales; patrón de coloración dorsal consistente de manchas obscuras y/o bandas sobre un fondo gris . . . . *Sibon nebulata*

3. Banda nucal que se extiende anteriormente sobre las supralabiales a través del ojo; anillos claros, amarillos, anaranjados, o rojo-anaranjados alternando con anillos negros . . . . *Sibon sartorii*

Banda nucal que no se extiende anteriormente sobre las supralabiales a través del ojo; anillos claros o blancos, morenos, o grises alternando con anillos pardo obscuros o negros . . . . *Sibon fasciata*

4. Patrón dorsal en una serie de pequeñas manchas pardo obscuro sobre un fondo moreno; 143–162 ventrales . . . . *Sibon sanniola*

Patrón variable, a menudo manchas o bandas pardo claro o anaranjado sobre un fondo gris o pardo; 160–206 ventrales . . . . *Sibon dimidiata*

Sibon dimidiata (Günther)
(Figs. 178B, 179, 382; Map 153)

Leptognathus dimidiatus Günther, 1872:31. HOLOTYPE: BMNH 1946.1.20.97. TYPE LOCALITY: Mexico.

Slender snail sucker; cordel negro (Mexico); kosche kan (Lacandón Maya).

DESCRIPTION This extremely slender *Sibon* is reminiscent of an *Imantodes*. The adults may attain a snout-vent length of about 500 mm. The tail is long, about 50 percent of the snout-vent length. The head is very distinct from the neck, and the body is laterally compressed. The eyes are large and protruding with subcircular pupils (Fig. 179). The dorsal scales are smooth, lack apical pits, and are arranged in 15 rows. The anal plate is undivided.

The dorsal color pattern is variable but usually consists of a series of brown blotches that are most often edged in black. The blotches are lighter at their centers, and they extend onto the ventral scales, where they contrast strongly with the light gray, tan, or creamy white venter. The interspaces are bright orange along the middorsum. The dorsal surface of the head is dark with a symmetrical pattern of irregular light spots. The labial scales and throat are cream with dark spots. According to Mc-Coy (1990:166), the hatchlings have black dorsal bands that contrast strongly with the cream interspaces and a vivid orange middorsum (Fig. 382).

SIMILAR SPECIES *Sibon dimidiata* most closely resembles members of the genus *Imantodes* but differs in having 15 rather than 17 rows of dorsal scales at midbody and an undivided anal scale. *Sibon dimidiata* differs from *S. nebulata* in possessing an azygous scale that separates the first pair of infralabial scales (Fig. 178A,B).

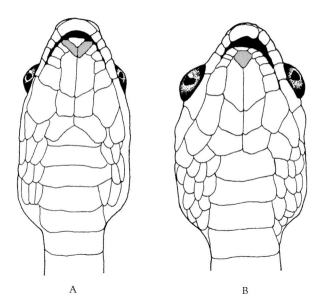

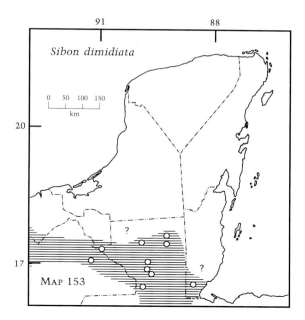

Fig. 178. Ventral views of the heads of (A) *Sibon nebulata* and (B) *S. dimidiata*, showing the first pair of infralabial scales in contact (A, *shaded*) and separated by an azygous scale (B, *shaded*).

DISTRIBUTION This species occurs at low, moderate, and intermediate elevations on the Pacific slope of Guatemala, and from Veracruz on the Atlantic slope south through northern Guatemala to Costa Rica. In the Yucatán Peninsula it is known only from northern Guatemala and southern Belize (Map 153).

NATURAL HISTORY *Sibon dimidiata* is uncommon in the Yucatán Peninsula. It is an arboreal and nocturnal inhabitant of humid lowland forests, where specimens have been found in bromeliads, at the bases of palm fronds, and on low vegetation at night. H. M. Smith (1943:470) found specimens beneath loose bark on fallen trees at Piedras Negras, Guatemala. Presumably these snakes feed on snails and slugs, but there is no specific information on the diet in the Yucatán Peninsula.

Sibon dimidiata is oviparous. McCoy (1990:166)

reported that a female from Toledo District produced a clutch of two eggs.

SUBSPECIES J. A. Peters (1960) recognized two subspecies, largely on the basis of dorsal color pattern. According to his scheme, the nominate subspecies, *S. d. dimidiata*, occurs in the Yucatán Peninsula. L. D. Wilson and Meyer (1985:91), however, declined to recognize subspecies because the color pattern may exhibit ontogenetic variation and Honduran specimens do not fit Peters's subspecific scheme. Likewise, Kofron (1990) considered *S. dimidiata* monotypic.

ETYMOLOGY The specific name, *dimidiata*, comes from the Latin *dimidiatus*, "divided" or "halved," possibly in reference to the mental groove dividing the lower jaw, in contrast with the condition in some related genera.

COMMENT *Sibon dimidiata* was reviewed in 1960 by J. A. Peters as part of his revision of the

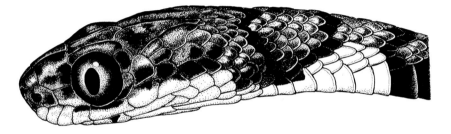

Fig. 179. Lateral view of the head of *Sibon dimidiata* (CRE 3812), 375 mm SVL; 4 km S San Vito de Java, Puntarenas, Costa Rica.

subfamily Dipsadinae, and more recently by Kofron (1990).

Locality Records Belize: Toledo: Blue Creek Village (RWV photo). *Guatemala*: El Petén: 20 km NNW Chinajá (KU 55723–24), vicinity El Rosario (JCL sight record), La Libertad (UMMZ 74895–96), Paso Caballos (MCZ 38592), Piedras Negras (UIMNH 18753; USNM 109903–6), Sojio (AMNH 69976), Tikal (UMMZ 117912), Uaxactún (MCZ 38666), Yalpemech (FMNH 40885). *Mexico*: Chiapas: Laguna Ocotal (MCZ 53882).

Sibon fasciata (Günther)
(Fig. 180; Map 154)

Tropidodipsas fasciata Günther, 1858:181. SYNTYPES: there are five syntypes in the BMNH, but only three belong to this species, *fide* Boulenger, 1894:295, 297; and Günther, 1894:139. LECTOTYPE: BMNH 1946.1.23.66, *fide* Kofron, 1987:211. TYPE LOCALITY: Central America, by lectotype designation; restricted by H. M. Smith and Taylor (1950b:352) to Chichén Itzá, but Kofron (1987:214) argued against that restriction.

Banded snail sucker; culebra anillada (Mexico); kuyun kan (Lacandón Maya).

DESCRIPTION This moderately slender snake may reach a snout-vent length of about 550 mm. The tail is about 30 to 35 percent of the snout-vent length. The head is distinct from the neck, the protruding eyes are relatively small for a *Sibon*, and the pupils are subcircular-elliptical (Fig. 180). The body is moderately compressed laterally. The dorsal scales are weakly keeled and arranged in 17 rows. Paired apical pits are generally present on the dorsal scales. The anal plate is undivided.

The color pattern consists of white or gray rings alternating with dark brown or black ones, the former much narrower than the latter. The light rings are generally two or three scales wide at the vertebral row and expand to six or seven scales wide laterally. The anterior portion of the head is dark brown or black, and there is a light nuchal collar, suffused with darker pigment, that is continuous with the light pigmentation of the throat.

SIMILAR SPECIES *Sibon sartorii* has pink, orange, or reddish orange light rings and a nuchal band that extends beyond the eye; it usually has eight or more infralabial scales, whereas *S. fasciata* usually has seven. *Dipsas brevifacies* has smooth dorsal scales that lack apical pits and are arranged in 15 rows at midbody.

DISTRIBUTION *Sibon fasciata* occurs at low and moderate elevations in Mexico from Guerrero on the Pacific slope and Veracruz on the Atlantic slope to Guatemala and the Yucatán Peninsula. This species is probably rather widely distributed throughout the northern half of the peninsula, but there are too few records to accurately delineate the pattern of distribution. It is known from eastern Campeche, Yucatán, and central Quintana Roo (Map 154).

NATURAL HISTORY The banded snail sucker is uncommon in the Yucatán Peninsula, where it is a nocturnal and crepuscular inhabitant of tropical deciduous and tropical evergreen forests. The protruding eyes and moderate lateral compression of the body suggest an arboreal lifestyle, and specimens have been found in hollow logs and limbs, including some several meters above the ground. Occasionally specimens are found on roads at night. Although nonvenomous, banded snail suckers are said to bite freely when provoked (Alvarez del Toro, 1983:184). This species feeds predominantly on snails, although Kofron (1987:216) reported an earthworm in the stomach of one specimen.

Sibon fasciata is presumably oviparous, like other species of the genus. A specimen from the

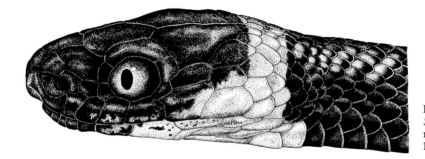

Fig. 180. Lateral view of the head of *Sibon fasciata* (UMRC 79-305), 380 mm SVL; 17.4 km W Felipe Carrillo Puerto, Quintana Roo, Mexico.

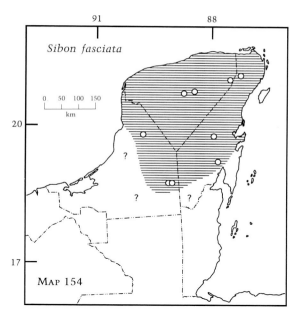

Sibon fasciata

0 50 100 150
km

20

?

17

Map 154

Isthmus of Tehauntepec had six corpora lutea (Kofron, 1987:216).

ETYMOLOGY   The specific name, *fasciata*, is from the Latin *fascia*, "a band," in reference to the banded pattern.

SUBSPECIES   J. A. Peters and Orejas-Miranda (1970:312) recognized three subspecies, only two of which were recognized by Kofron (1987). According to the latter, the nominate subspecies, *S. f. fasciata*, occurs in the Yucatán Peninsula.

COMMENT   This species was known as *Tropidodipsas fasciata* until Kofron (1985) placed *Tropidodipsas* in the synonymy of *Sibon* on the basis of cranial osteology. *Sibon fasciata* was reviewed by Kofron (1987).

Locality Records Mexico: Campeche: Becan (UWZH 20519), 11 km W Hopelchén (KU 75635), 1.2 km W Ixbonil (EAL 2894); Quintana Roo: 17.4 km W Felipe

Carrillo Puerto (UMRC 79-305), Hwy. 307, 4.8 km S rd. to Majahual (UMRC 92-5), Tintal (UCM 41791); Yucatán: Chichén Itzá (FMNH 36194), X-Can (CM 46849), Yokdzonot (FMNH 36195).

Sibon nebulata (Linnaeus)
(Figs. 178A, 181; Map 155)

Coluber nebulatus Linnaeus, 1758:222. TYPE: originally in the Museum Adolphi Friderici Regis, now in the Naturhistoriska Riksmuseet Stockholm (lectotype designated in Andersson, 1899:19). TYPE LOCALITY: Africa (in error, *fide* H. M. Smith and Taylor, 1945:126); restricted by H. M. Smith and Taylor (1950b:349) to Jicaltepec, Veracruz, Mexico; given as America by Stuart (1963:116).

Speckled snail sucker; culebra jaspeada (Mexico).

DESCRIPTION   The adults of this medium-sized *Sibon* average about 500 mm in snout-vent length. The tail is about 35 to 40 percent of the snout-vent length. The body is moderately slender and laterally compressed. The head is distinctly wider than the neck, the eyes are large and somewhat protruding, and the pupils are subcircular (Fig. 181). The dorsal scales are smooth, in 15 rows, and lack apical pits. The vertebral row is slightly enlarged, and the anal plate is undivided. The anteriormost pair of lower labials is in broad contact behind the mental shield (Fig. 178A).

The labial scales and chin shields have large black spots. The dorsal pattern is variable. Often it consists of a series of irregular black blotches, bands, or both against a gray or purplish background. The bands are speckled with white, especially laterally. The venter is white, cream, or pink, with strongly contrasting black check marks.

SIMILAR SPECIES   The juveniles of *Elaphe flavirufa* and *Senticolis triaspis* have keeled dorsal

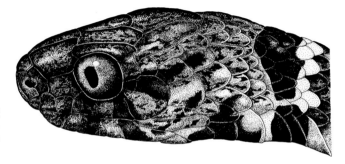

Fig. 181. Lateral view of the head of *Sibon nebulata* (UMRC 84-37), 468 mm SVL; 14.2 km S Santa Rosa, Quintana Roo, Mexico.

scales and round pupils. *Sibon dimidiata* possesses an azygous scale separating the first pair of infralabial scales (Fig. 178B).

DISTRIBUTION This species is widespread at low and moderate elevations from Nayarit on the Pacific slope and Veracruz on the Atlantic slope, south through the lowlands of Central America and into northern South America. In the Yucatán Peninsula it ranges from Isla del Carmen, Campeche, through the base of the peninsula, and northward through Belize and Quintana Roo. It is apparently absent from the northwest corner of the peninsula (Map 155).

NATURAL HISTORY *Sibon nebulata* is moderately uncommon in the Yucatán Peninsula. It is a secretive and nocturnal snake that generally inhabits deciduous forest, tropical evergreen forest, and rainforest. It tends to be arboreal but may also be found beneath rotting logs and other surface debris, and individuals are occasionally seen abroad at night on the forest floor and on roads. Stuart (1958:28) considered it to be both arboreal and terrestrial at Tikal, and he noted that all the juveniles he captured apparently came from beneath surface debris or leaf litter, whereas adults were found in trees. Although it may be moderately common locally, *S. nebulata* is not frequently encountered owing to its arboreality and its retiring and nocturnal habits. Like other members of the genus *Sibon*, *S. nebulata* apparently feeds exclusively on snails and slugs.

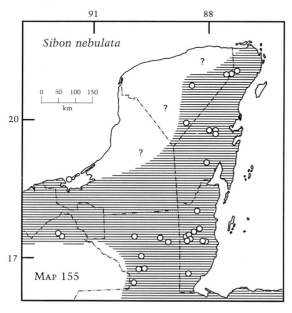

MAP 155

Sibon nebulata is oviparous. Stuart (1958:28) found recently hatched individuals at Tikal between mid-March and mid-April.

SUBSPECIES J. A. Peters (1960:199) recognized four subspecies, but Kofron (1990:218) was not certain that all were valid. If Peters's subspecies of *S. nebulata* are recognized, the nominate form, *S. n. nebulata*, occurs in the Yucatán Peninsula.

ETYMOLOGY The specific name, *nebulata*, is an adjective formed from the Latin *nebula*, "cloud"—hence "cloudy," presumably in reference to the dorsal color pattern.

COMMENT *Sibon nebulata* was reviewed by J. A. Peters (1960) as part of his revision of the subfamily Dipsadinae. The most recent treatment was by Kofron (1990).

Locality Records *Belize*: Belize: mi 37 on Western Hwy. (MCZ 150248); Cayo: Baking Pot (W. T. Neill, 1965:109), Belize-Cayo Rd., 5 mi SW Hummingbird Hwy. (UMMZ 124653), Central Farm (MCZ 71680), Chaa Creek (CM 105981), 9.3 mi S Georgeville (KU 157614), mi 31 on Hummingbird Hwy. (JLK 482), ca. 1 mi E San Antonio (CM 112106), mi 47 on Western Hwy. (CM 112184); Orange Walk: Lamanai (ROM H12784); Stann Creek: Middlesex (CM 48016; UCM 25717, 25721, 25739, 25876, 29990, 30890), 3 mi W Middlesex (JLK 483), Toledo: Unión Camp, Columbia River Forest Reserve (USNM 319778). *Guatemala*: El Petén: 20 km NNW Chinajá (KU 55725), El Paso (MCZ 38654–55), El Rosario (JCL sight record), N shore Lake Yaxhá (UTEP 6020), La Libertad (UMMZ 74895–96), Paso Caballos (MCZ 38593), Sayaxché (UCM 22359), Tikal (MCZ 58764; UF 13847; UMMZ 117930–43). *Mexico*: Campeche: Ciudad del Carmen (UMMZ 83542); Chiapas: 6.5 km SW Palenque (UTEP 12231), 10 mi S Palenque (LSUMZ 33370); Quintana Roo: Felipe Carrillo Puerto (UMMZ 113558), 6.8 mi S Felipe Carrillo Puerto (KU 157615), 17 mi W Felipe Carrillo Puerto (UCM 28171), Hwy 307 9.7 mi N Andrés Quintana Roo (KU 157616), Pueblo Nuevo X-Can (CM 49156; UCM 40502), Tintal (UCM 41782); Yucatán: Chichén Itzá (UMMZ 73026), 14.2 km S Santa Rosa (UMRC 84-37), X-Can (CM 46880).

Sibon sanniola (Cope)
(Figs. 182, 383, 384; Map 156)

Mesopeltis sanniolus Cope, 1867:318. HOLOTYPE: USNM 6564. TYPE LOCALITY: Yucatán; restricted by H. M. Smith and Taylor (1950b:352) to Chichén Itzá, Yucatán, Mexico.

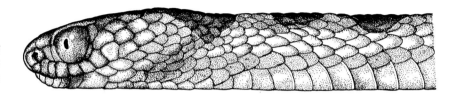

Fig. 182. Lateral view of the head of *Sibon sanniola* (UMRC 84-97), 281 mm SVL; 11.4 km SE Cobá, Quintana Roo, Mexico.

Pygmy snail sucker; culebrita (Mexico).

DESCRIPTION This diminutive snake is the smallest of the snail suckers in the Yucatán Peninsula. Individuals rarely exceed 320 mm in snout-vent length. The moderately long tail averages about 35 to 40 percent of the snout-vent length. The head is moderately distinct from the neck, the eyes are very large and protruding, and the pupils are subcircular (Fig. 182). An azygous scale separates the first pair of infralabial scales. The dorsal scales are smooth, lack apical pits, and are in 15 rows. The anal plate is undivided.

The dorsal color pattern is variable (Figs. 383, 384) but usually consists of a series of small brown blotches against a tan background; in some specimens the blotches coalesce to produce a zigzag pattern. Often there is a series of indistinct lateral blotches that may extend onto the ventral scales. In specimens from Belize and El Petén, the dorsal and lateral blotches fuse, producing distinct crossbands. A distinct nuchal blotch extends anteriorly onto the parietal scales and may extend laterally onto the ventrals. The venter is tan, often peppered with tiny brown spots or, occasionally, with indistinct tan check marks.

SIMILAR SPECIES Its small size and relatively enormous eyes distinguish this snake from all other adult snakes in the Yucatán Peninsula. *Sibon sanniola* differs from all *Sibon* in the Yucatán Peninsula except *S. dimidiata* in possessing an azygous scale that separates the anteriormost infralabial scales (Fig. 178B). It differs from *S. dimidiata*, with which it is allopatric, in having 143 to 162 rather than 160 to 206 ventral scales.

DISTRIBUTION *Sibon sanniola* is endemic to the Yucatán Peninsula, where is it known from northern Campeche and throughout Yucatán and Quintana Roo. There are several records from Belize and one from El Petén (Map 156).

NATURAL HISTORY This inoffensive, secretive, terrestrial snake is crepuscular and nocturnal. In Quintana Roo it is one of the snakes most likely to be encountered on roads at night, especially in tall forests. *Sibon sanniola* apparently feeds exclusively on snails and slugs.

Sibon sanniola is oviparous. A specimen collected on 22 June at Chichén Itzá contained three large eggs (Gaige, 1936:301). W. T. Neill (1962:239) thought that a specimen from Belize collected in early November had probably hatched in late September. In northern Yucatán and Quintana Roo the clutch size is two to five eggs (Kofron, 1983). The eggs are laid during the rainy season, between June and September, and hatch in October and November.

ETYMOLOGY The specific name, *sanniola*, comes from the Latin *sannio*, "one who mimics," "clown," "buffoon," and -*ola*, a Latin diminutive suffix.

COMMENT Although Henderson et al. (1977) described *S. neilli* from Belize, Kofron (1985) considered it a subspecies of *S. sanniola*, and McCoy (1986) confirmed its subspecific status. This species was reviewed most recently by Kofron (1990).

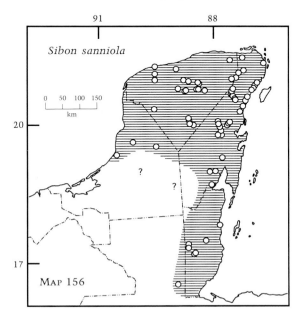

MAP 156

Locality Records Belize: Belize: vicinity Belize City (MPM 8929); Cayo: Augustine (JLK 476), near Augustine (MPM 8208), Chaa Creek (CM 105981), 8 km SSE Belmopan (Olson, 1986b:67), Xunantunich (MCZ 56994); Corozal: 0.5 mi S Santa Elena (JLK 466); no specific locality (FMNH 4247). *Guatemala*: El Petén: Las Cañas (CM 58282). *Mexico*: Campeche: 5 km S Champotón (KU 70885), Dzibalchén (KU 75630), 8.5 km W Ruinas Edzná (KU 171694); Quintana Roo: Lake Bacalar (LSUMZ 33186), 10 mi W Bacalar (LSUMZ 33185), 6.8 km SSW Chiquilá (UMRC 79-296), Chunyaxché (Himmelstein, 1980:31), Cobá (Himmelstein, 1980:31), 3.1 km SE Cobá (UMRC 87-5), 7.8 km SE Cobá (KU 171686), 9.3 km SE Cobá (KU 171687), 9.4 km SE Cobá (KU 171688), 10.8 km SE Cobá (KU 171689–90), 11.4 km SE Cobá (UMRC 84-97), 14.5 km SE Cobá (UMRC 87-6), 17.2 km SE Cobá (KU 171691), 16.8 km N Cobá (UMRC 87-8), 17.9 km N Cobá (UMRC 87-7), Felipe Carrillo Puerto (JCL 5414; UMMZ 113584–88; MZFC 3412), 1.7 mi S Felipe Carrillo Puerto (KU 157618), 5.4 km N Felipe Carrillo Puerto (JCL 5413), 5.7 km N Felipe Carrillo Puerto (JCL 6810), 6.1 km W Felipe Carrillo Puerto (KU 171683), 23.1 km N Felipe Carrillo Puerto (JCL 6809), 24.3 km N Felipe Carrillo Puerto (JCL 5415), 27.9 mi NE Felipe Carrillo Puerto (KU 157619), 31 km NE Felipe Carrillo Puerto (AMNH 110053), 33 km NE Felipe Carrillo Puerto (AMNH 110051), 38.6 km NE Felipe Carrillo Puerto (KU 171684), 44.9 km N Felipe Carrillo Puerto (JCL 5416), 49.6 km NE Felipe Carrillo Puerto (KU 171685), 9.7 km S Kantunil Kin (KU 171692), 9.6 mi N Limones (KU 157617), Playa del Carmen (Himmelstein, 1980:31; LSUMZ 33193), 2 mi S Playa del Carmen (LSUMZ 33194, 34766), 6.4 km N Playa del Carmen (JCL 6824), 5 mi S Playa del Carmen (LSUMZ 33195–97), 8 mi S Playa del Carmen (LSUMZ 33198), 11.4 mi SW Playa del Carmen (KU 157620), 16.5 mi S Playa del Carmen (LSUMZ 38566), 7 mi N Playa del Carmen (LSUMZ 33192), 8 mi N Playa del Carmen (LSUMZ 33191), 9 mi N Playa del Carmen (LSUMZ 33187–90), Pueblo Nuevo X-Can (CM 45778–85, 49056, 49062, 49136, 49154, 49159, 49163; UCM 28163, 40115–26, 40715–17, 41652–57), 30.5 km S Pueblo Nuevo X-Can (JCL sight record), Puerto Juárez (Himmelstein, 1980:31), 115 km SSE Puerto Juárez (AMNH 110052), 35.3 mi S Tepich (KU 157621), Tintal (UCM 40127, 41647–51), Tulum (AMNH 110054), 15.4 km N Tulum (JCL 6825), 29.9 km NW Tulum (UMRC 84-81); Yucatán: 6.6 km NE Cansahcab (KU 171693), Chichén Itzá (FMNH 20609, 20613; MCZ 7241, 7246, 26842; UMMZ 68707, 73031–32, 83294, 83932; USNM 46568), 1 km W Chichén Itzá (KU 70888), 1.8 km N Colonia Yucatán (UMRC 92-4), Dzibilchaltún (FMNH 153499, 153505, 153507, 153529, 153560–62, 153564, 153578–79, 153582), 1.5 km S Dzitás (KU 70887), bet. Dzitás and Quintana Roo (UMRC 79-295), 3 mi E Esmeralda (LACM 122910), 14.7 mi E Izamal (KU 157622), 3 km W Kaua (TCWC 57116), 3.1 km W Kaua (TCWC 57117), Kantunil (J. A. Peters, 1960:189), Libre Unión (J. A. Peters, 1960:189), Mérida (FMNH 19424), Pisté (CM 46955–56, 46958, 47004, 47142–48, 49734–56; UCM 17060, 18625–26, 40128–34, 41658–62), Progreso (J. A. Peters, 1960:189), 3 km S Santa Elena (TU 19767), Santa Rosa (UMRC 84-82), 1.5 km S Santa Rosa (UMRC 84-78), 6.2 km S Santa Rosa (UMRC 84-84), 9 km N Santa Rosa (UMRC 84-79, 84-80, 84-83), 15 km N Santa Rosa (UMRC 84-77), 5.5 mi W Tunkás (KU 157623), X-Can (CM 46844–45, 46881–83), Yokdzonot (J. A. Peters, 1960:189).

Sibon sartorii (Cope)
(Figs. 183, 385; Map 157)

Tropidodipsas sartorii Cope, 1863:100. HOLOTYPE: originally in USNM, now lost. TYPE LOCALITY: Mirador, Vera Cruz, Mexico.

Sartorius's snail sucker; coralillo (Belize, Guatemala, Mexico); coralillo falso (Mexico, Guatemala); culebra negrinaranja (Mexico); kuyun kan (Lacandón Maya).

DESCRIPTION This rather stout *Sibon* attains an average snout-vent length of about 450 mm. The tail length is about 20 to 30 percent of the head and body length. The head is broad and moderately distinct from the neck. The eyes are relatively small in comparison with most other snail suckers, and the pupils are subcircular (Fig. 183). The dorsal scales are weakly keeled, bear apical pits, and are arranged in 17 rows at midbody. The anal scale is undivided.

The color pattern consists of narrow white, yellow, orange, or reddish orange rings alternating with much wider black rings (Fig. 385). The scales of the light rings are often tipped with dark pigment on their trailing edges. A distinct light nuchal band extends forward on the side of the head to beyond the eye (Fig. 183). The color pattern changes with age. The light rings are white, cream, or yellowish in young snakes and become yellow-orange, orange, or reddish orange as the animal matures.

SIMILAR SPECIES *Dipsas brevifacies* has 15 rows of dorsal scales that are smooth and lack apical pits. The much less common *S. fasciata* is slenderer and has white or gray rings rather than yellow, orange,

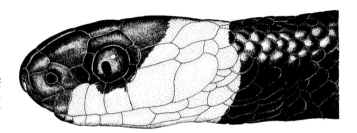

Fig. 183. Lateral view of the head of *Sibon sartorii* (UMRC 85-18), 497 mm SVL; Nicholas Bravo, Campeche, Mexico.

or reddish orange rings, and its nuchal band does not extend beyond the eye anteriorly (cf. Figs. 180, 183).

DISTRIBUTION *Sibon sartorii* occurs at low and moderate elevations from San Luis Potosí on the Atlantic slope and Chiapas on the Pacific slope through Guatemala. This species probably occurs throughout the Yucatán Peninsula, but there are apparently no records from northern Campeche (Map 157).

NATURAL HISTORY This common terrestrial snake is nocturnal and crepuscular. It is often encountered on roads at night, especially in the forested regions of eastern Yucatán and Quintana Roo. Its movements are quick and nervous, much like those of a coral snake, but it is harmless and completely inoffensive. *Sibon sartorii* apparently feeds exclusively on snails and slugs. Gaige (1938:298) reported only snails in the stomachs of two specimens from western Yucatán, and Seib (1985a), who studied the feeding ecology of this species on coffee

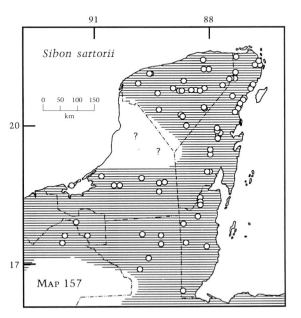

MAP 157

fincas in southern Chiapas and adjacent Guatemala, found only snails and slugs. My examination of stomach contents of specimens from Chiapas, Quintana Roo, and Yucatán likewise revealed only slugs and snails. Dundee et al. (1986:44) found a slug in the stomach of a specimen from Yucatán. *Sibon sartorii* is in turn eaten by the coral snake (*Micrurus diastema*), for specimens have been found in the stomachs of coral snakes from Ciudad del Carmen and Oxpemul, Campeche.

Sibon sartorii is presumably oviparous. During the breeding season males develop breeding tubercles on the chin and snout (Stuart, 1948:74).

SUBSPECIES J. A. Peters and Orejas-Miranda (1970:312) recognized three subspecies, defined primarily on the basis of color pattern. In a more recent review, Kofron (1988) recognized two subspecies, of which the nominate form, *S. s. sartorii*, occurs in the Yucatán Peninsula.

ETYMOLOGY The specific name, *sartorii*, is a patronym honoring Charles Sartorius, who collected specimens in Veracruz in the middle of the nineteenth century and secured the type specimen.

COMMENT This species was placed in the genus *Tropidodipsas* until Kofron (1985) put that genus in the synonymy of *Sibon* on the basis of cranial osteology. *Sibon sartorii* was reviewed by Kofron (1988).

Locality Records Belize: Cayo: Central Farm (MCZ 71682); Corozal: San Pablo (MPM 7609); Orange Walk: Gallon Jug (CMM photo; FMNH 69233), Lamanai (ROM H12785), near Orange Walk (MPM 7378), Tower Hill (MPM 7377, 7379, 7761); Stann Creek: Middlesex (CM 48019; UCM 25879, 30896–97); Toledo: Dolores (JCL sight record). *Guatemala*: El Petén: Chuntuquí (USNM 71361), 10.8 km SW Flores (KU 157634), 7.5 mi N Río de la Pasíon (KU 157635), Tikal (UF 13851; UMMZ 117923, 117925), Uaxactún (UMMZ 70457–58). *Mexico*: Campeche: Becan (UWZH 20553), 1.5 km

N Chekubúl (UMRC 80-58), Ciudad del Carmen (UMMZ 125681), near Escárcega (JCL photo), 5 km E Francisco Escárcega (UTEP 3934), Nicholas Bravo (UMRC 85-18), Oxpemul (UMMZ 125680), Tuxpeña Camp (UMMZ 73225-27), 19 km W Xpujil (KU 74998), km 143 on Hwy. 186 (UWZH 20541); Chiapas: 5 km NW Palenque (EAL 3027), 10 to 15 mi S Palenque (LSUMZ 33303); Quintana Roo: 1.4 km N Akumal (UMRC 84-68, 84-74), 2.8 km S Akumal (UMRC 84-67), 8 mi W Bacalar (LSUMZ 33308), 10 mi W Bacalar (LSUMZ 33307), 10.9 km S Cancún Airport (UMRC 84-73), 7 km SSW Chiquilá (UMRC 79-268), 13 km SE Cobá (KU 171703), Felipe Carrillo Puerto (UMMZ 113582), 1 km NE Felipe Carrillo Puerto (MZFC 3373), 2.8 km NW Felipe Carrillo Puerto (JCL 6823), 5.4 km S Felipe Carrillo Puerto (JCL 6837), 7.4 km N Felipe Carrillo Puerto (JCL 6835), 10 mi N Felipe Carrillo Puerto (LSUMZ 38560), 14.6 km NE Felipe Carrillo Puerto (KU 171701), 13 km NE Felipe Carrillo Puerto (KU 171702), 10.3 km SSW Kantunil Kin (UMRC 79-269), La Unión, rd. to Río Hondo (MZCIQRO 49), 8.4 km N Noh Bec (UMRC 84-70), 19 km N Noh Bec (UMRC 84-69), Playa del Carmen (Himmelstein, 1980:31), 1 mi S Playa del Carmen (LSUMZ 38565), 2 mi S Playa del Carmen (LSUMZ 33304-5), 2.2 mi S Playa del Carmen (LSUMZ 38564), Pueblo Nuevo X-Can (CM 45313-14, 45800-1; UCM 40626-38, 49109, 49150), 1.5 km S, 1 km E Pueblo Nuevo X-Can (KU 70900), 3.8 km W Pueblo Nuevo X-Can (UMRC 87-10), 7 km W Pueblo Nuevo X-Can (JCL 6819), 27 km S Pueblo Nuevo X-Can (JCL photo), Puerto Juárez (Himmelstein, 1980:31), 18.4 km SW Puerto Juárez (EAL 2853), Tulum (LSUMZ 33306), 4 mi S Tulum ruins (LSUMZ 38562), 2 mi S Tulum ruins (LSUMZ 38563), 3.7 km N Tulum (UMRC 84-72), 3.8 mi S Tulum Pueblo (LSUMZ 38561), 4.7 mi S Tulum Pueblo (LSUMZ 38545), 15.9 km N Tulum (JCL 5417), 21.3 km S Tulum (JCL 6803), 82.6 km N Tulum (JCL 5418), 83.1 km N Tulum (JCL 5419), 3.5 km N X-Caret (UMRC 84-75); Tabasco: Emiliano Zapata (USNM 109907), Tenosique (USNM 109908); Yucatán: Balankanché (FMNH 153547), Catzín (CM 45315), Chichén Itzá (FMNH 36196, 36199-200, 36202; MCZ 17082; UMMZ 73037; UTA R-4471), Dzibilchaltún (FMNH 40729, 153495-97, 153549), 1 mi W Dzibilchaltún (TU 19756), 2 km W Ebtún (LSUMZ 28243), Kantunil (FMNH 36198), 4 km E Kaua (LSUMZ 28244), 2.8 mi NE Kinchil (KU 157640), Libre Unión (FMNH 36201), Loltún Cave (UMMZ 80801), Mayapán (FMNH 40730-33), 4.4 km N Panabá (JCL sight record), Peto (KU 74999), 10 km SE Peto (KU 75000), Pisté (CM 47008, 47158-62, 49819-21; UCM 40639), 8.2 km S Santa Rosa (UMRC 84-71), Tizimín (JCL photo), 10.8 mi W Tizimín (KU 157636), 3.2 mi W Tunkás (KU 157639), Ucu (JCL sight record), X-Can (CM 46850, 46887-88, 47054-59), Yokdzonot (FMNH 36197), 5.7 mi N Yucatán–Quintana Roo border on Hwy. 295 (KU

157638), 5.9 mi N Yucatán–Quintana Roo border on Hwy. 295 (KU 157637).

Genus *Spilotes* (Tropical Rat Snakes)

This genus comprises a single wide-ranging species. *Spilotes* is from the Greek *spilotos*, "soiled" or "dirty," presumably in reference to the dark color of these snakes.

Spilotes pullatus (Linnaeus)
(Figs. 154A, 386; Map 158)

Coluber pullatus Linnaeus, 1758:225. TYPE: unknown; originally in the Drottningholmense, now in the Royal Museum in Stockholm (*fide* Andersson, 1899:23). TYPE LOCALITY: Asia (in error).

Tropical rat snake; bocotora clapansaya, monkey snake, thunder and lightning snake (Belize); culebra mico (Guatemala); voladora (Mexico); chair (Lacandón Maya).

DESCRIPTION *Spilotes pullatus* is one of the largest snakes in the Yucatán Peninsula. Individuals commonly attain snout-vent lengths in excess of 2,000 mm. The tail length is about 30 to 35 percent of the head and body length. It is a moderately slender snake with a somewhat laterally compressed body. In dorsal aspect the head is distinct from the neck and the snout is rounded. The eyes are large with very dark brown or black irises, and the pupils are round. The middorsal scales are keeled, and the lateral scales are smooth. The dorsal scales are arranged in an even number of rows (usually 18) at midbody, and at least some bear paired apical pits. The anal plate is normally undivided.

This is a black snake boldly marked with irregular bars, chevrons, and spots of yellow or cream (Fig. 386). The head is yellow, cream, or light tan with varying amounts of black on the dorsal surface. There is usually a black band across the posterior portion of the parietal scales that narrows as it extends to the lip. The labial scales and those on the chin and snout are generally edged with black. The ventral surfaces of the body and tail are yellow with black spots or semilunar markings, especially on the lateral surfaces of the ventral scales. On the undersurface of the tail, dark pigment may form an irregular median stripe. The color pattern exhibits some ontogenetic change (W. T. Neill and Allen, 1960:152). The juveniles tend to be black with well-defined yellow crossbands. The extent of the yellow coloration increases with age such that snakes may appear to be black with yellow markings, or the reverse.

SIMILAR SPECIES   Large, dark *Pseustes poecilonotus* superficially resemble *S. pullatus* but differ in possessing an odd number of dorsal scale rows at midbody. *Elaphe flavirufa* and *Senticolis triaspis* generally have 29 or more rows of dorsal scales at midbody.

DISTRIBUTION   *Spilotes pullatus* has a very wide range. It occurs at low and moderate elevations on the Atlantic slope from San Luis Potosí to Peru, Bolivia, and Brazil; and on the Pacific slope from Oaxaca to lower Central America. It occurs throughout the Yucatán Peninsula (Map 158).

NATURAL HISTORY   This large and distinctively marked snake is moderately common in the Yucatán Peninsula. It is terrestrial and arboreal, and it occurs in a variety of habitats, including forested areas and savannas as well as mangrove swamps. It is capable of moving very rapidly through shrubs and trees, almost giving the appearance of flying, hence the Spanish common name *voladora*. W. T. Neill and Allen (1959c:52) characterized this species as abundant in black mangrove forest near Belize City and described how, at Xunantunich, Cayo

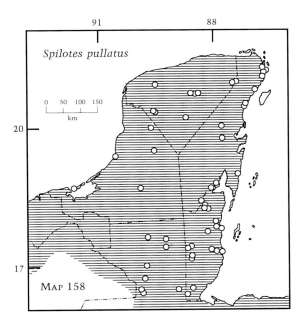

District, it sought refuge in ant nests when disturbed. Although it is nonvenomous, this snake will laterally compress the neck and anterior portion of the body (Fig. 386) and strike repeatedly when threatened. Gerhardt et al. (1993:350) reported that at Tikal, Guatemala, this species is preyed on by the great black hawk, *Buteogallus urubitinga*.

W. T. Neill (1962:240) suggested that *S. pullatus* feeds on birds and small mammals, a conjecture partly verified by Henderson and Hoevers (1977b:352), who found small mammals in the stomachs of two specimens from northern Belize. In Chiapas this species feeds predominantly on birds (Alvarez del Toro, 1983:186). According to Weyer (1990:30), rats, birds, and bird eggs are major food items in Belize. Sexton and Heatwole (1965:42) found the remains of a small mammal in the stomach of a specimen from Panama.

Spilotes pullatus is oviparous. W. T. Neill (1962:240) estimated that a hatchling from Cayo District with a slightly healed umbilical scar had hatched in August. McCoy (1970c:137) reported three hatchlings collected during the first three weeks of August at Middlesex, Stann Creek District. In Quintana Roo, Himmelstein (1980:31) found a female that contained eight well-developed eggs.

SUBSPECIES   J. A. Peters and Orejas-Miranda (1970:283) recognized five subspecies of *S. pullatus*, distinguished largely on the basis of color pattern. They applied the name *S. p. mexicanus* to the snakes in the Yucatán Peninsula, but the ontogenetic and geographic variation in color pattern in Yucatecan populations is so great as to preclude subspecific recognition.

ETYMOLOGY   The specific name, *pullatus*, is Latin meaning "clothed in a black robe," presumably in reference to the extensive black pigmentation.

Locality Records   Belize: Belize: outskirts of Belize City (W. T. Neill and Allen, 1959c:52), 19 mi N Belize City (JLK 499), bet. Ladyville and Sandhill (CM 90951–52); Cayo: Central Farm (FMNH 210074; MCZ 71681), Cocquercot (UMMZ 74906–7), Guacamallo Crossing (W. T. Neill, 1962:240), mi 40 on Hummingbird Hwy. (CM 112107), Mountain Pine Ridge (MPM 8210), ca. 2 mi W of turnoff to Thousand Foot Falls (CM 105812), Xunantunich (W. T. Neill and Allen, 1959c:52); Corozal: Santa Elena (W. T. Neill and Allen, 1959c:53). Orange Walk: Kate's Lagoon (FMNH 49366), Orange Walk (MPM 7367, 8171–72); Tower Hill (MPM 7364–66, 7368–69, 7756–58, 8166, 8169); Stann Creek: Dangriga (CM 105833), Middlesex (CM 48017–18; UCM 25757, 25877–78, 25881, 29993, 30891–95); Toledo: near Blue Creek (MPM 8173), Dolores (JCL sight record); no specific locality (FMNH 4205–6). *Guatemala*: El Petén: 7 km NNW Chinajá (KU 55726), 8 km NNW Chinajá (KU 55727), 20 km NNW Chinajá (KU 55729), Chuntuquí (USNM 71360), La Libertad (UMRC 79-306), Las Cañas (CM 58283), Sayaxché (KU 57150; UCM 22360–63), Tikal (UF 13848; UMMZ 117960–62), Uaxactún (JCL sight record); no specific locality (USNM 71791–92). *Mexico*: Campeche: 2 mi S Bolonchén (UCM 18628), Champotón (UMMZ 73080), Ciudad del Carmen (UMMZ 83548), 78 km E Escárcega (KU 74997), Dzibalchén (KU 75631); Quintana Roo: Cancún (Himmelstein, 1980:31; López-Gonzales, 1991:106), 11.5 km N Cancún Airport (UMRC 84-61), Chetumal (MCZ 53125; MZCIQRO 09, 15), 4 km N Chetumal (MZCIQRO 06), Felipe Carrillo Puerto (UMMZ 113581), 43.9 km N Felipe Carrillo Puerto (JCL 6793), 1 km W Mahahual (JCL photo), Petempich (López-Gonzales, 1991:106), Playa del Carmen (Himmelstein, 1980:31), near Pueblo Nuevo X-Can (UCM 28137–38), Pueblo Nuevo X-Can (CM 45795, 49131; UCM 41783), 6.7 km W Puerto Juárez (KU 70890), 7.7 km NW Tulum (UMRC 84-100), 16.2 km NW Tulum

(JCL 6792), Xcopen (MCZ 9573), Xtocmoc (LACM 113906); Yucatán: Chichén Itzá (UMMZ 68237, 73079, 83939; UMRC 84-16), Mérida (FMNH 19423), Peto (CM 45311), Pisté (CM 46959–61, 47005, 47150–55, 49799–804; KU 70889; UCM 16058, 40503), 5 mi E Pisté (UTA R-4472), Uxmal (UCM 18627; USNM 238379), 2 mi N Uxmal (UIMNH 87670), X-Can (CM 47049).

Genus *Stenorrhina*
(Scorpion-eating Snakes)

Two species constitute this genus of strictly Neotropical snakes. Representatives occur at low and moderate elevations from Guerrero on the Pacific slope and Veracruz on the Atlantic slope, southward through Central America to Colombia, Venezuela, and Ecuador. Both species of *Stenorrhina* occur in the Yucatán Peninsula. These snakes are mildly venomous and have enlarged, grooved fangs on the posterior portion of the maxillary bone. They are, however, inoffensive and to my knowledge have never been known to bite. *Stenorrhina* is from the Greek adjective *stenorrhinos*, "with a narrow nose."

Key to the Species of the Genus *Stenorrhina*

Dorsal pattern mottled, banded, or unicolor; usually fewer than 160 ventral scales; base of the Yucatán Peninsula (Map 159) . . . . *Stenorrhina degenhardtii*

Dorsal pattern unicolor or striped; more than 160 ventral scales; widely distributed throughout the Yucatán Peninsula (Map 160) . . . . *Stenorrhina freminvillei*

Clave para las Especies del Género *Stenorrhina*

Patrón de coloración dorsal de manchas, motas, o bandas, o de un solo color; menos de 160 ventrales; habitan en la base de la Península de Yucatán (Mapa 159) . . . . *Stenorrhina degenhardtii*

Patrón de coloración dorsal de un solo color o bandeado; más de 160 ventrales; organismos panpeninsulares (Mapa 160) . . . . *Stenorrhina freminvillei*

Stenorrhina degenhardtii (Berthold)
(Map 159)

Calamaria degenhardtii Berthold, 1846:18. HOLOTYPE: ZFMK 44/256. TYPE LOCALITY: Popayan, Colombia.

Degenhardt's scorpion-eating snake; alacranera de Degenhardt (Mexico).

DESCRIPTION The adults of this medium-sized, moderately stout snake average perhaps 500 to 550 mm in snout-vent length and reach a maximum of 757 mm. Too few specimens are known from the Yucatán Peninsula, however, to reliably estimate the adults' size there. The tail is short, generally about 15 percent of the snout-vent length. The head is only slightly distinct from the neck, the eyes are small, and the pupils are round. The internasal scales are fused with the anterior nasal scales. The dorsal scales are smooth, lack apical pits, and are arranged in 17 rows at midbody. The anal plate is divided.

The dorsal coloration is generally olive brown or gray with a series of indistinct dark brown blotches or bands, which in older individuals may be obscure. The labials, chin, and venter are usually cream, and the ventral scales may bear a series of median dark spots, forming a midventral stripe.

SIMILAR SPECIES *Stenorrhina degenhardtii* most closely resembles its congener, *S. freminvillei*, but differs in usually possessing fewer than 160 ventral scales and in sometimes having a banded dorsum rather than stripes or a uniform color. *Conophis lineatus* has 19 rows of scales at midbody.

DISTRIBUTION This species occurs at low to moderate elevations on the Atlantic slope from southern Veracruz southward to Venezuela, and on the Pacific slope from Honduras to Ecuador. It is known in the Yucatán Peninsula from a few records from Chiapas and El Petén (Map 159).

NATURAL HISTORY Little is known of the natural history of this uncommon species. It is a terrestrial and semifossorial inhabitant of humid lowland forests and savannas. It appears to be predominantly nocturnal, and its diet consists largely of spiders. Duellman (1963:244) found a large spider in the

stomach of a specimen from northern Alta Verapaz, and Sexton and Heatwole (1965:41) found a spider and an orthopteran in the stomach of a specimen from Panama.

Stenorrhina degenhardtii is probably oviparous, like its congener, but nothing specific is known concerning reproduction in this species.

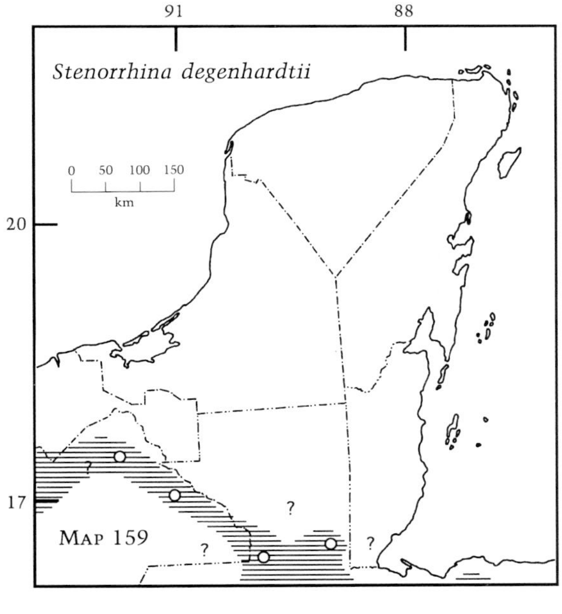

SUBSPECIES As many as three geographic segments of *S. degenhardtii* have been recognized as subspecies, based on color and pattern, but some systematists (e.g., Duellman, 1963; Stuart, 1963; and L. D. Wilson and Meyer, 1985) refuse to recognize subspecies because the species is so variable. The most recent review of this species is by J. D. Johnson (unpubl. MS), who believes that no subspecies should be recognized (J. D. Johnson, in litt.). If subspecies are recognized, the name *S. d. mexicana* applies to the snakes in the Yucatán Peninsula.

ETYMOLOGY The specific name, *degenhardtii*, is a patronym honoring a Mr. Degenhardt, who secured herpetological specimens in Colombia in the middle part of the nineteenth century and collected the type specimen.

Locality Records Guatemala: Alta Verapaz: Chinajá (Duellman, 1963:243); El Petén: Las Cañas (CM 58284). *Mexico*: Chiapas: 42.1 km SE La Arena on rd. to Bonampak (KU 171730); 10 to 15 mi S Palenque (LSUMZ 33876).

Stenorrhina freminvillei
(Duméril, Bibron, and Duméril)
(Figs. 154C, 184, 387; Map 160)

Stenorrhina freminvillii A. M. C. Duméril, Bibron, and Duméril, 1854:868. HOLOTYPE: MNHNP 4816. TYPE LOCALITY: Mexique. The restriction to Totolapam, Oaxaca, Mexico, by H. M. Smith and Taylor (1950b:341) was considered unjustified by L. D. Wilson and Meyer (1985:99).

Scorpion-eating snake; culebra alacranera (Mexico); tzinkan (Lacandón Maya); sikil-can (Yucatec Maya).

DESCRIPTION This is a rather stout, medium-sized snake (Fig. 387). In Yucatán, the males attain a snout-vent length of 714 mm; the smaller females are up to 681 mm (Censky and McCoy, 1988). The

Stenorrhina degenhardtii

0 50 100 150
km

MAP 159

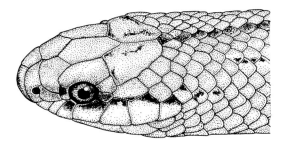

Fig. 184. Dorsolateral view of the head of *Stenorrhina freminvillei* (UMRC 91-2), 365 mm SVL; 25 km SE Sabancuy, Campeche, Mexico.

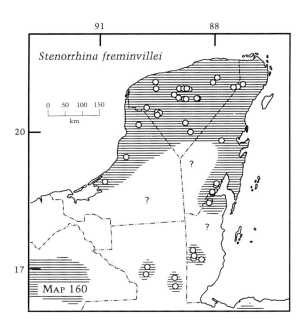

tail is short, about 15 percent of the snout-vent length. The head is scarcely distinct from the neck, the eyes are rather small, and the pupils are round (Fig. 184). The dorsal scales are smooth, lack apical pits, and are arranged in 17 rows at midbody. The anal plate is divided. The internasal scales are fused with the anterior nasal scales (Fig. 154C).

Color and color pattern vary within and among localities. Snakes from the northern end of the Yucatán Peninsula are generally a uniform light brown, tan, orange, or gray above, with the dorsal scales tipped with dark brown or black pigment on their trailing edges. Specimens from the base of the peninsula and as far north as central Campeche often have a distinctly striped pattern consisting of a vertebral stripe, a lateral stripe on scale rows 3 and 4, and sometimes a less distinct paravertebral stripe on scale row 6. These stripes are usually most distinct anteriorly and become indistinct posteriorly. The ventral surfaces of the body are generally yellow, cream, or white, and there is often an indistinct median subcaudal stripe.

SIMILAR SPECIES *Stenorrhina degenhardtii* usually has fewer than 160 ventral scales, a dorsal pattern of blotches or bands, and is restricted to the base of the Yucatán Peninsula. The smaller *Ficimia publia* has an upturned rostral scale, and its internasals are not fused to the anterior nasal scales (Fig. 154B). *Conophis lineatus* has 19 rows of scales at midbody, and its internasals are not fused to the anterior nasal scales (Fig. 152C).

DISTRIBUTION *Stenorrhina freminvillei* occurs at low, moderate, and intermediate elevations on the Atlantic slope from the Isthmus of Tehauntepec and on the Pacific slope from Guerrero to lower Central America. This species probably occurs throughout the Yucatán Peninsula, but it has not yet been recorded from southern Campeche and southern Quintana Roo (Map 160).

NATURAL HISTORY This is a moderately common terrestrial and fossorial inhabitant of the Yucatán Peninsula. Specimens are occasionally found abroad during the day, but the species is generally nocturnal. Stuart (1935:54) found specimens beneath logs near aguadas in the savanna region of La Libertad, El Petén. In the northern portions of the Yucatán Peninsula the species is common in thorn forests and on savannas, but apparently heavily forested regions are avoided. They feed on invertebrates, especially spiders and scorpions, as the Spanish common name, *culebra alacranera*, suggests. These snakes are rear-fanged, but they are generally inoffensive and, in my experience, cannot be induced to bite. A case of envenomation that occurred near Tulum, Quintana Roo, was mistakenly ascribed to this species (Cook, 1984), but J. D. Johnson (1988) showed that the offender was actually *Conophis lineatus*.

Stenorrhina freminvillei is oviparous. Stuart (1935:54) found females with four to six fully developed eggs in April at La Libertad. According to Censky and McCoy (1988), females oviposit in Yucatán during the dry season, from October to April; the clutch size ranges from 5 to 19 (mean = 11.6), and hatchlings have been collected in March and April.

SUBSPECIES Although several subspecies have been described, Stuart (1963:117) argued against recognizing any, based on the high degree of intrapopulational variation in the characters supposedly diagnostic of the various subspecies.

ETYMOLOGY The specific name, *freminvillei*, is a patronym that honors "M. le capitaine de fregate de *Freminville*," who provided the type specimen.

Locality Records Belize: Belize: 4 km E Chial (CM 105712); Cayo: Augustine (AMNH 126437), Blancaneaux Lodge (UF uncat.), 4 mi S Georgeville (CM 105698, 105712), Mountain Pine Ridge Rd., 36 mi S Belize-Cayo Rd. (UMMZ 124663), upper Raspaculo River basin (Stafford, 1991:16; Corozal: S edge Corozal Town (JLK 459), 3 mi N Corozal Town (JLK 458; UTEP 9363–64), Santa Clara, 7.8 mi N San Pablo (KU 157624), Santa Cruz (MPM 8140, 8176); no specific locality (FMNH 4218). *Guatemala*: El Petén: 2 km SE Dolores (UMMZ 124351), La Libertad (Stuart, 1935:17), Poptún (UMMZ 117913–14, 120318), Sojio (AMNH 69968, 69970, 69982); no specific locality (USNM 71370). *Mexico*: Campeche: 25 km SE Sabancuy (UMRC 91-2), San José Carpizo (UMMZ 99325), 6 mi NE Tenabo (UTA R-4469); Quintana Roo: 4 km N Chetumal (MZCIQRO 10), 8 km NNE Chetumal (CM 40011), 2.3 km N Felipe Carrillo Puerto (UMRC 84-88), Pueblo Nuevo X-Can (CM 40011, 45796–99, 49053, 49057, 49064, 49066, 49069, 49072, 49083, 49105, 49114–15, 49117, 49119–20, 49127, 49138–39, 49152–53, 49155, 49157, 49167, 49169; UCM 40504–48, 50556–609, 41784–89), Tintal (UCM 40610–11); Yucatán: Calcehtok (AMNH 38828–29; UMMZ 113544–45), S edge Calotmul (KU 171728), Chichén Itzá (AMNH 38827; MCZ 7037, 29243; UCM 12969; UMMZ 68229, 83295–96; USNM 46396, 46563, 46564), Dzibilchaltún (FMNH 153504, 153509–10, 153551–52, 153554–56), Holactun (UMRC 88-6), Izamal (KU 157627), 9 mi E Izamal (KU 157626), Kantunil (FMNH 36007, 36019, 36050, 36054, 36058, 36060, 36065, 36070), Libre Unión (FMNH 36011, 36013–14, 36017–18, 36021–23, 36025, 36029, 36031–32, 36038, 36043–45, 36051–52, 36064, 36069, 36071), Mérida (CM 44470–72; FMNH 19414, 153557–58; UCM 45817; UMMZ 73059), 7.7 mi SE Muna (KU 157631), 12.3 mi SE Muna (KU 157630), 15.2 mi W Peto (KU 157628), Pisté (CM 45312, 46962–64, 47006–7, 47156–57, 49757–98; KU 70892; UCM 17062, 40612–16), 4 km S Santa Rosa (UMRC 84-87), bet. Ticul and Santa Elena (TU 19764), 11.9 km E Tizimín (KU 171729), 3.1 mi W Tunkás (KU 157629), 4.7 mi W Tunkás (KU 157625), X-Can (CM 46884, 47050–53), Yokdzonot (FMNH 36009, 36015–16, 36024, 36026–28, 36030, 36033–36, 36039–40, 36046–49, 36055–57, 36059, 36061–62, 36068).

Genus *Storeria*
(Brown Snakes, Red-bellied Snakes)

This genus includes two species of small, secretive, terrestrial snakes. *Storeria* is essentially a North American genus, ranging from southern Canada to Honduras, with one species probably entering the Yucatán Peninsula. The most recent comprehensive treatment of the genus is Trapido, 1944. *Storeria* honors D. H. Storer, a nineteenth-century Massachusetts naturalist and zoological commissioner of that state.

Storeria dekayi (Holbrook)
(Fig. 185; Map 161)

Coluber Dekayi Holbrook, "1836" [probably 1839]:121. LECTOTYPE: ANSP 5832 (designated in Trapido, 1944:47). TYPE LOCALITY: Massachusetts, New York, Michigan, and Louisiana; restricted to Massachusetts by Trapido (1944:47), and to Cambridge, Massachusetts, by Schmidt (1953:165), but Adler (1976:xxxiii) argued persuasively that the type specimen is from the northern coast of Long Island, New York.

Tropical brown snake.

DESCRIPTION This small, moderately slender snake probably does not exceed 400 mm in snout-vent length, although so few specimens are known from the immediate vicinity of the Yucatán Peninsula that size cannot be reliably estimated. Judging from specimens collected elsewhere, the tail is short, about 22 to 35 percent of the head and body length. The head is moderately distinct from the neck, and the eyes are medium sized with round pupils (Fig. 185). There are normally seven supralabial scales, and no loreal scale. The dorsal scales are heavily keeled, lack apical pits, and are arranged in 17 rows at midbody. The anal plate is divided.

The dorsum is generally pale brown or gray with a variable pattern of small, dark dots. There is usually a horizontal dark line through the anterior temporal scale. The venter is light tan or gray, often with scattered spots, especially along the margins of the ventral scutes.

SIMILAR SPECIES The species of *Thamnophis* found in the Yucatán Peninsula have 19 or more

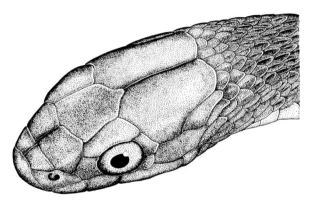

Fig. 185. Dorsolateral view of the head of *Storeria dekayi* (FMNH 21796), 227 mm SVL; Subirana Valley, Yoro, Honduras.

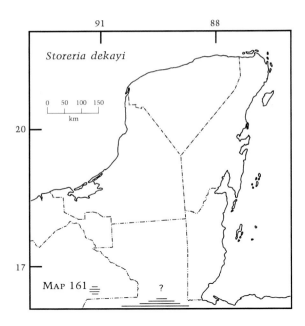

rows of scales at midbody, rather than 17. The other small, predominantly brown snakes in the Yucatán Peninsula such as *Symphimus*, *Tantilla*, and *Coniophanes* lack heavy keels on the dorsal scales.

DISTRIBUTION This wide-ranging form occurs from southern Canada throughout the eastern half of the United States, and south along the Gulf slope to Veracruz and Oaxaca. An apparently disjunct subspecies occurs from eastern Chiapas through central Guatemala and into western Honduras. This species is marginal in the Yucatán Peninsula, possibly entering at the very base of the peninsula near the Alta Verapaz–El Petén border (Map 161).

NATURAL HISTORY The tropical brown snake, rare and poorly known in the Yucatán Peninsula, was characterized by Stuart (1948:63) as an inhabitant of the tropical zone in Alta Verapaz. Presumably it is a secretive terrestrial snake that hides beneath surface debris and is active at night, like its northern relatives. At temperate latitudes this species feeds on earthworms, slugs, insects, fish, and treefrogs (A. H. Wright and Wright, 1957:702).

Storeria dekayi is viviparous, but little is known of reproduction in the populations in and adjacent to the Yucatán Peninsula. Stuart (1948:63) reported that a specimen from Alta Verapaz collected on 27 March contained well-formed eggs. At temperate latitudes this species produces broods of 3 to 24 young, usually during the summer months (A. H. Wright and Wright, 1957:701).

SUBSPECIES Christman (1982:306.1) recognized eight subspecies. The isolated Central American

subspecies that occurs in the Yucatán Peninsula is *S. d. tropica*.

ETYMOLOGY The specific name, *dekayi*, is a patronym that honors James Edward De Kay, a nineteenth-century New York naturalist who provided the specimen illustrated in volume 1 of Holbrook's *North American Herpetology*.

COMMENT Stuart (1963:117) considered this species (as *S. tropica*) to be an element of the herpetofauna of El Petén. The type locality for *S. tropica* is simply "Petén, Guatemala," which, as Stuart (1934:5) noted, at one time included more territory than it does at present. I know of no specific locality from the Yucatán Peninsula where this snake has been found; however, it definitely occurs immediately to the south, in Alta Verapaz, and very likely extends into El Petén.

Christman (1982) reviewed the biosystematics of *S. dekayi*.

Genus *Symphimus*

Two species constitute this genus of small, diurnal, Neotropical colubrid snakes. The geographical distribution of the genus is disjunct, with one species endemic to the Yucatán Peninsula and the other restricted to the west coast of Mexico. *Symphimus* is from the Greek *syn-*, "together," and *phimos*, "a muzzle"—or "that which stops up an opening."

Symphimus mayae (Gaige)
(Figs. 149B, 150B, 186, 388; Map 162)

Eurypholis mayae Gaige, 1936:300. HOLOTYPE: UMMZ 73082. TYPE LOCALITY: Dzitás, Yucatán, Mexico.

Yucatán white-lipped snake; culebra Maya (Mexico)

DESCRIPTION This is a medium-sized, moderately slender snake, rather racerlike in general appearance (Fig. 388). The head is somewhat elongate and fairly distinct from the neck in dorsal aspect. The adults average 450 to 500 mm in snout-vent length, and the tail is long, about 60 percent of the head and body length. The eyes are moderately large with round pupils (Fig. 186). The dorsal scales are smooth and arranged in 15 rows at midbody. A single apical pit is present on most dorsal scales, especially on the posterior surface of the body. The anal scale is divided.

The dorsum is grayish tan. A slightly darker but indistinct vertebral stripe about four scale rows wide extends the length of the body. The bases of the dorsal scales are yellowish orange, but this coloration is not normally apparent unless the skin is stretched. On each side a thin, dark, indistinct lateral stripe runs the length of the body on scale rows 3 and 4. The dorsal surface of the head is tan, and the supralabial and infralabial scales are immaculate cream. The venter is predominantly tan or gray, and each ventral scute bears a pair of indistinct small, dark marks.

SIMILAR SPECIES The racerlike snakes of the genera *Coluber*, *Masticophis*, and *Dryadophis* are similar to *Symphimus*, but they are larger, and all have more than 15 rows of scales at midbody.

DISTRIBUTION *Symphimus mayae* is endemic to the Yucatán Peninsula, where it is known from the Mexican states of Yucatán and Quintana Roo. It can be expected to occur in neighboring Campeche, and there are two records from Belize, where a disjunct population may occur (Map 162).

NATURAL HISTORY Little is known of the biology of this Yucatecan endemic. It is diurnal and

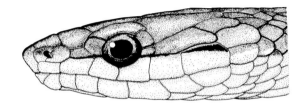

Fig. 186. Lateral view of the head of *Symphimus mayae* (UMRC 80-53), 490 mm SVL; between Cobá and Pueblo Nuevo X-Can, Quintana Roo, Mexico.

apparently both terrestrial and arboreal. Individuals have been found on roads, but Gaige (1936:301) reported that the type specimen "dropped on a truck from a tree overhanging the Dzitás–Chichén Itzá road." *Symphimus mayae* is known both from deciduous thorn forests and from the more mesic forests on the eastern side of the peninsula. Rossman and Schaefer (1974:10) reported that the stomachs of four specimens from Yokdzonot, Yucatán, contained the remains of insects, especially grasshoppers, katydids, and crickets.

These snakes are probably oviparous.

ETYMOLOGY The specific name, *mayae*, refers to the indigenous people of the Yucatán Peninsula.

COMMENT This species was long referred to the genus *Opheodrys*. When Gaige (1936) described *Eurypholis* (= *Opheodrys*) *mayae*, she noted its similarity to *Symphimus leucostomus* Cope, and Rossman and Schaefer (1974) showed that on the basis of

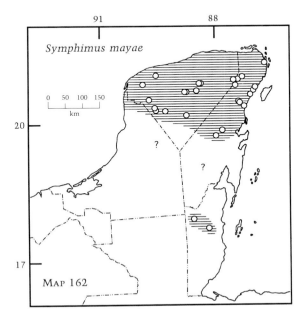

Symphimus mayae

MAP 162

cranial osteology this species properly belongs to the genus *Symphimus*.

Locality Records Belize: Belize: 28.5 mi WSW Belize City (UMRC 93-18), Orange Walk: Río Bravo Research Station (UMRC 94-11). *Mexico*: Quintana Roo: 12.2 km N Akumal (UMRC 84-59), bet. Cobá and Pueblo Nuevo X-Can (UMRC 80-53), 28.5 km SE Cobá (UMRC 87-11), 21.1 km N Felipe Carrillo Puerto (JCL 6832), 23 km W Felipe Carrillo Puerto (CM 45301), La Vega (USNM 46531), 2 mi S Playa del Carmen (LSUMZ 33312), Pueblo Nuevo X-Can (CM 45786–90, 45792–94, 49065, 49116, 49166; UCM 28146, 40350–66, 40734–37, 41729–41; LSUMZ 27779), 65 km S Puerto Morelos (EAL 2867), Tintal (UCM 40367, 41726–28), Tulum (López-Gonzales, 1991:106), 14.1 km NW Tulum (JCL 6811), 26 km NNE Tulum (LSUMZ 28254); Yucatán: Chichén Itzá (AMNH 64560; UMMZ 83297), Dzibilchaltún (FMNH 153519, 153566), Dzitás (UMMZ 73082), 0.7 mi NE Kinchil (JCL sight record), Labná (MZFC 3171), Libre Unión (FMNH 36389), 3 km E Opichén (TU 19786), Pisté (CM 45302–5, 46965, 47149, 49805–9, 49812–17; LSUMZ 37780; UCM 18623, 40368–372, 41742–43), 3 km S Santa Elena (TU 19785), 6.4 mi N Uxmal (KU 157632), X-Can (CM 46846–48, 46885–86, 47047–48), Yokdzonot (FMNH 36383, 36386–88, 36390–91, 36393–94).

Genus *Tantilla* (Centipede Snakes)

These small, secretive, smooth-scaled snakes are terrestrial or fossorial and apparently largely nocturnal. Although they are rear-fanged, their small size and retiring habits make them essentially harmless to humans. They feed predominantly on centipedes and beetle larvae. *Tantilla* is one of the largest colubrid genera. L. D. Wilson (1982a), who provided the most recent comprehensive treatment of the Central American species and a key to all members of the genus, recognized 48 species. The genus, which is restricted to the New World, ranges from the southern United States through Mexico and Central America to northern Argentina. So far as is known, all members of the genus are oviparous and produce clutches of one, two, or three eggs (Fitch 1970:156). Three species occur in the Yucatán Peninsula, two of which are endemic. *Tantilla* is derived from the Latin *tantillum*, "so small a thing," alluding to the small size of these snakes.

Key to the Species of the Genus *Tantilla*

1. Dorsal and ventral coloration uniform dark brown or black . . . . *Tantilla moesta*
   Dorsum brown or tan; venter distinctly lighter than dorsum 2
2. Pale lateral stripe present on dorsal scale rows 3 and 4; El Petén and northern Belize northward . . . . *Tantilla cuniculator*
   No pale lateral stripe; El Petén and central Belize southward . . . . *Tantilla schistosa*

Clave para las Especies del Género *Tantilla*

1. Coloración dorsal y ventral de color uniforme pardo obscura o negro . . . . *Tantilla moesta*
   Coloración dorsal parda o morena; coloración ventral distintivamente más clara que la coloración dorsal 2
2. Con una línea lateral pálida en las tercera y cuarta hileras de escamas dorsales; habitan en El Petén y norte de Belice hacia el norte . . . . *Tantilla cuniculator*
   Sin una línea lateral pálida en las tercera y cuarta hileras de escamas dorsales; habitan en El Petén y centro de Belice hacia el sur . . . . *Tantilla schistosa*

Tantilla cuniculator Smith
(Fig. 187; Map 163)

Tantilla moesta cuniculator Smith, 1939a:32. HOLOTYPE: FMNH 19408. TYPE LOCALITY: Mérida, Yucatán, Mexico.

Yucatán centipede snake.

DESCRIPTION *Tantilla cuniculator* is a small, dark brown snake with a light nuchal collar. The maximum snout-vent length is about 155 mm, and the tail length is about 20 to 25 percent of the snout-

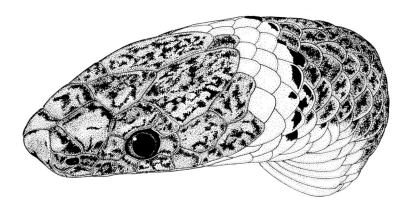

Fig. 187. Dorsolateral view of the head of *Tantilla cuniculator* (UMRC 84-162), 154 mm SVL; 1 km N Celestún, Yucatán, Mexico.

vent length. The head is slightly distinct from the neck in dorsal aspect, the eyes are moderately small, and the pupils are round (Fig. 187). The dorsal scales are smooth, arranged in 15 rows throughout, and lack apical pits. The anal plate is divided.

The dark brown dorsal coloration becomes lighter on the first two rows of scales. Usually there is no indication of a light vertebral stripe, although one may be barely discernible on the anterior portion of the body on some specimens. The nuchal collar is pale yellow, yellow-orange, or tan and covers the posterior end of the parietal scales and two or three middorsal scales. There is usually a light postorbital spot, and often a thin, pale lateral stripe on dorsal scale rows 3 and 4, this becoming indistinct posteriorly. The venter is reddish orange or cream.

SIMILAR SPECIES   Of the other species of *Tantilla* in the Yucatán Peninsula, *T. moesta* is a uniform dark brown or black dorsally and ventrally, and *T. schistosa* lacks the pale stripe on dorsal scale rows 3 and 4 and enters the Yucatán Peninsula only at the base of the peninsula, whereas *T. cuniculator* occurs principally in the northern two-thirds of the peninsula (cf. Maps 163, 165).

DISTRIBUTION   This species is endemic to the Yucatán Peninsula, where it is known from Yucatán, northern Quintana Roo, northern El Petén, and northern Belize (Map 163).

NATURAL HISTORY   Little is known about the habits of this uncommon snake. It is apparently a secretive fossorial or terrestrial inhabitant of thorn and tropical evergreen forests. Specimens have been found beneath surface debris and abroad at night.

Presumably *T. cuniculator* is oviparous, but nothing is known of its reproductive biology.

ETYMOLOGY   The specific name, *cuniculator*, is a Latin noun meaning "miner," after this snake's fossorial habits.

COMMENT   L. D. Wilson (1982a) summarized information on *T. cuniculator* as part of his review of Central American *Tantilla* and later (L. D. Wilson, 1988) reviewed the species.

Locality Records   Belize: Orange Walk: Tower Hill (MPM 7608). *Guatemala*: El Petén: Tikal (L. D. Wilson, 1982a:37). *Mexico*: Quintana Roo: 2.6 km SE Cobá (UMRC 79-274), 9.7 km SE Cobá (KU 171745), 3.5 mi N Felipe Carrillo Puerto (TCWC 58691), Pueblo Nuevo X-Can (LSUMZ 28599), 1.3 km S Pueblo Nuevo X-Can (UMRC 84-39); Yucatán: 1 km N Celestún (UMRC 84-162), Mérida (FMNH 19408; MCZ 53940), Pisté (KU 70895; UCM 40619).

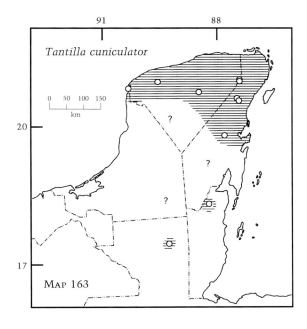

Tantilla moesta (Günther)
(Figs. 188, 389; Map 164)

Homalocranium moestum Günther, 1863:352. HOLOTYPE: BMNH 1946.1.9.74. TYPE LOCALITY: El Petén, Guatemala; restricted by H. M. Smith and Taylor (1950b:318) to Flores, El Petén, Guatemala.

Blackbelly centipede snake.

DESCRIPTION   This distinctive snake, which attains a maximum snout-vent length of about 490 mm, is the largest *Tantilla* in the Yucatán Peninsula. The tail length is about 20 to 25 percent of the snout-vent length. The head is slightly distinct from the neck in dorsal aspect, the eyes are moderately small, and the pupils are round (Fig. 188). The dorsal scales are smooth, arranged in 15 rows throughout, and lack apical pits. The anal plate is usually divided.

These snakes have a uniform dark brown or black dorsum and venter (Fig. 389). The conspicuous pale nuchal band may extend anteriorly on the lateral surfaces of the head to below the eyes and posteriorly onto two to seven of the dorsal scales beyond the parietals.

SIMILAR SPECIES   No other snake in the Yucatán Peninsula combines a uniform dark brown or black dorsum and venter with a conspicuous light nuchal band. *Tantilla cuniculator* and *T. schistosa* have light nuchal collars but are smaller and distinctly lighter beneath. *Ninia diademata* has heavily keeled dorsal scales.

DISTRIBUTION   This species is endemic to the Yucatán Peninsula and occurs more or less continuously through northern Yucatán south to central Quintana Roo. The several records from El Petén may represent an isolated popuation (Map 164). Although not yet recorded from Belize and Campeche, it very likely occurs there.

NATURAL HISTORY   *Tantilla moesta* is secretive, terrestrial, and largely nocturnal. Specimens have been taken in both thorn forest and tropical evergreen forest. Stuart (1958:28) reported a specimen found beneath a log in the forest at Tikal, El Petén, and I found specimens abroad at night in the tropical evergreen forests of Quintana Roo.

Presumably *T. moesta* is oviparous, but nothing is known of its reproductive biology.

ETYMOLOGY   The specific name, *moesta*, comes from the Latin *moestus*, "sad" or "sorrowful," perhaps an allusion to this snake's somber coloration.

COMMENT   L. D. Wilson (1982a) summarized the available information on *T. moesta* and later reviewed the species (Wilson, 1988).

Locality Records   Guatemala: El Petén: Flores (UMMZ 79058–59), Paso Caballos (MCZ 38591), Tikal (AMNH uncat.; MCZ 55432; UMMZ 117904). *Mex-*

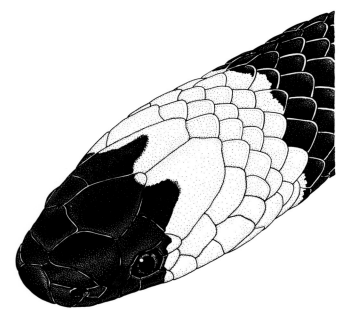

Fig. 188. Dorsolateral view of the head of *Tantilla moesta* (UMRC 89-51), 198 mm SVL; 14 km SE Cobá, Quintana Roo, Mexico.

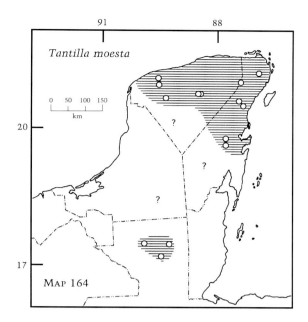

Tantilla moesta

0 50 100 150
km

20

?

?

?

17

MAP 164

ico: Quintana Roo: 14 km SE Cobá (UMRC 89-51), 33.2 km SE Cobá (KU 171713), Felipe Carrillo Puerto (UMMZ 113583), 18 mi S Felipe Carrillo Puerto (LSUMZ 33299), Pueblo Nuevo X-Can (UCM 40617), 25 mi W Puerto Juárez (USNM 157815); Yucatán: Chichén Itzá (FMNH 36321), Dzibilchaltún (FMNH 153515), Mayapán (FMNH 40716), Mérida (FMNH 19406–8, 20605; USNM 6565), Pisté (UCM 40618); no specific locality (USNM 24883).

Tantilla schistosa (Bocourt)
(Fig. 189; Map 165)

Homalocranion schistosum Bocourt, 1883:584.
LECTOTYPE: MNHNP 1883-506 (designated in H. M. Smith, 1942a). TYPE LOCALITY: Alta Verapaz, Guatemala (by lectotype designation).

DESCRIPTION The maximum snout-vent length of this small snake is about 245 mm, and the tail length is about 20 to 25 percent of that. The head is slightly distinct from the neck in dorsal aspect, the eyes are moderately small, and the pupils are round (Fig. 189). The dorsal scales are smooth, arranged in 15 rows throughout, and lack apical pits. The anal scale is divided.

Tantilla schistosa is dark brown, tan, or olive with a pale, sometimes indistinct, nuchal collar. Most specimens have no dorsal pattern, but a thin, pale vertebral stripe is discernible in some. The pale nuchal collar begins on the posterior portion of the parietals and extends one or two middorsal scales beyond them. Some specimens bear a pale postocular spot. The venter is immaculate cream or reddish orange.

SIMILAR SPECIES *Tantilla schistosa* differs from *Tantillita canula* in normally possessing a light nuchal collar, although this is occasionally obscure. *Tantillita canula* has fewer than 115 ventral scales, whereas *T. schistosa* has more than 115. *Tantilla moesta* has a dark brown or black venter and dorsum. *Tantilla cuniculator* has a light stripe on scale rows 3 and 4 and is restricted to the northern two-thirds of the Yucatán Peninsula, whereas *T. schistosa* generally lacks a lateral stripe and enters the Yucatán Peninsula only at its base.

DISTRIBUTION This species occurs at low, mod-

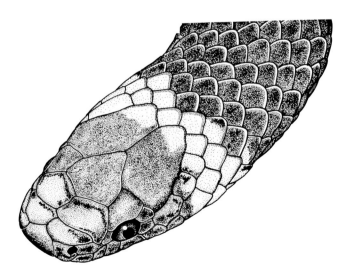

Fig. 189. Dorsolateral view of the head of *Tantilla schistosa* (CRE 4507), 177 mm SVL; Costa Rica.

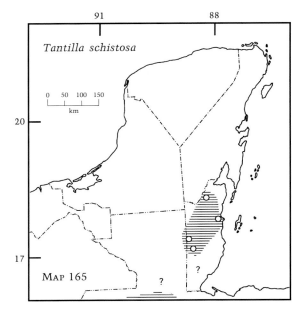

Tantilla schistosa

MAP 165

centipedes and to a much lesser extent on insect larvae.

Presumably *T. schistosa* is oviparous. Stuart (1948:83) reported that two juveniles "not many days old" were collected on 25 June in Alta Verapaz.

ETYMOLOGY The specific name, *schistosa*, is from the Greek *schistos*, "divided" or "cleft," and the Latin termination *-osa*, "full of," "augmented," or "prone to," possibly in reference to the contrast between the dark head and body and the light nuchal collar.

COMMENT *Tantilla schistosa* was reviewed by L. D. Wilson (1982a) as part of his treatment of Central American *Tantilla*. He published a summary of the available information on this species in 1987.

Locality Records Belize: Belize: bet. Hattieville and Burrell Boom (CM 105823); Cayo: near Augustine (MPM 8204), Xunantunich (MCZ 56993); Orange Walk: Tower Hill (MPM 7608); no specific locality (MPM 8209).

erate, and intermediate elevations on the Gulf slope from central Veracruz and the Pacific slope from Oaxaca, through Central America to Panama. In the Yucatán Peninsula it is known only from Belize, although its presence in neighboring El Petén is a virtual certainty (Map 165).

NATURAL HISTORY These secretive, terrestrial snakes are probably largely nocturnal, although Shannon (1951:482) reported a specimen abroad in late afternoon in Oaxaca. They generally inhabitant humid forests. A series of specimens was secured from beneath decaying rubbish in coffee groves in Alta Verapaz (Stuart, 1948:83). Seib (1985a) found that snakes from coffee fincas in southern Chiapas and neighboring Guatemala fed predominantly on

Genus *Tantillita*

This small genus of poorly known snakes is restricted to southeastern Mexico and northern Central America. Apparently closely allied to *Tantilla*, the genus contains three species, two of which occur in the Yucatán Peninsula. *Tantillita* is derived from the Latin *tantillum*, "so small a thing," and the diminutive suffix *-ita*. The genus *Tantillita* was reviewed by L. D. Wilson (1988d).

Key to the Species of the Genus *Tantillita*

Light vertebral stripe present; light areas present on snout and dorsal surface of head . . . . *Tantillita canula*

No light vertebral stripe; head uniform brown, no light areas on snout or dorsal surface of head . . . . *Tantillita lintoni*

Clave para los Especies del Género *Tantillita*

Con una línea vertebral pálida; con áreas pálidas en el hocico y superficie de la cabeza . . . . *Tantillita canula*

Sin una línea vertebral pálida; color de la cabeza café uniforme, sin áreas pálidas en el hocico y superficie de la cabeza. . . . . *Tantillita lintoni*

Tantillita canula (Cope)
(Fig. 190; Map 166)

Tantilla canula Cope, 1876:144. SYNTYPES: USNM 24881–82. TYPE LOCALITY: Yucatán, Mexico.

Yucatán dwarf short-tailed snake.

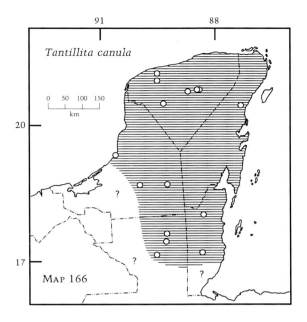

DESCRIPTION   The maximum snout-vent length of this small, nondescript snake is about 145 mm. The tail is about 20 percent of the head and body length. The head is slightly distinct from the neck in dorsal aspect, the eyes are moderately small, and the pupils are round (Fig. 190). The dorsal scales are smooth, lack apical pits, and are arranged in 15 rows throughout. The anal plate is divided.

This brown or tan snake is devoid of any dorsal pattern save for a thin, light vertebral stripe present in most specimens. The dorsal coloration on the head is slightly darker than that on the body, and there are usually small light spots on the snout and parietal scales. The venter is immaculate cream.

SIMILAR SPECIES   *Tantillita canula* differs from all *Tantilla* in the Yucatán Peninsula in lacking a light nuchal collar or band. Although *Tantilla schistosa* may have an indistinct nuchal collar, it also has more than 115 ventral scales (*T. cannula* has fewer than 115) and lacks indistinct light markings on the head. *Tantillita canula* differs from *T. lintoni* in having light markings on the snout and parietal scales and (usually) a thin, light vertebral stripe.

DISTRIBUTION   This species is endemic to the Yucatán Peninsula, where it is known from north-ern El Petén northward (Map 166). L. D. Wilson (1982a:29) suspected that the type of *Homalocranium breve* Günther (= *Tantilla brevis*) was actually *T. canula*. The type specimen of *H. breve* was probably collected somewhere along the Belize River (W. T. Neill and Allen, 1961b:91), thus establishing the occurrence of *T. canula* in Belize, where it is now known from two localities.

NATURAL HISTORY   These uncommon snakes are terrestrial, secretive, and probably nocturnal. Specimens have been found beneath surface debris in thorn forest and tropical evergreen forest. L. D. Wilson (1982a:27) found one beneath a board in Pisté, Yucatán.

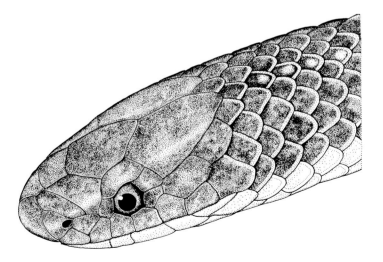

Fig. 190. Dorsolateral view of the head of *Tantillita canula* (ROM H12707), 134 mm SVL; Lamanai, Orange Walk District, Belize.

Presumably *T. canula* is oviparous, but nothing is known of its reproductive biology.

ETYMOLOGY The specific name, *canula*, derives from the Latin *cannula*, the diminutive of *canna*, "tube," "reed," or "tunnel."

COMMENT As discussed by Van Devender and Cole (1977) and L. D. Wilson (1982a), *T. canula* has been confused with *T. lintoni* and *Tantilla brevis*, the latter a form of uncertain status. According to L. D. Wilson (1982a:27), specimens identified by Stuart (1958:27–28) as intermediate between *Tantilla canula* (now *Tantillita canula*) and *T. brevis* are actually *Tantillita lintoni*. H. M. Smith et al. (1993) placed *Tantilla canula* in the genus *Tantillita* because it lacks enlarged grooved teeth on the posterior portion of the maxilla.

L. D. Wilson (1982a) summarized the available information on *Tantillita canula* (as *Tantilla canula*) and reviewed its biosystematics (1988a).

Locality Records Belize: Cayo: upper Raspaculo River basin (Stafford, 1991:16); Orange Walk: Lamanai (ROM H12707, H12782). *Guatemala*: El Petén: near Flores (UF 47802), Tikal (MCZ 58765; UF 13849), Uaxactún (AMNH 70936; MCZ 24930–36). *Mexico*: Campeche: Becan (UWZH 20511, 20520, 20527, 20546), Centenario near Silvituc (LSUMZ 28597), 6 km SW Champotón (KU 70894); Quintana Roo: 5 mi W Tulum (LSUMZ 33302); Yucatán: Chichén Itzá (MCZ 31949), Dzibilchaltún (FMNH 153513–14, 153516, 153530–31, 153534, 153567), Libre Unión (FMNH 36409–10), Mérida (Flores et al., 1991:204; MZFC 940; USNM 194824), Pisté (CM 49818, 28598), Ticul (AMNH 110055); no specific locality (USNM 24880–82).

Tantillita lintoni (Smith)
(Fig. 191; Map 167)

Tantilla lintoni H. M. Smith, 1940:61. HOLOTYPE: USNM 108603. TYPE LOCALITY: Piedras Negras, Guatemala, some 45 miles by trail from Tenosique, Tabasco, Mexico, on the bank of the Usumacinta River.

DESCRIPTION The adults of this tiny snake average between 125 and 135 mm in snout-vent length. The tail is about 40 percent of the snout-vent length. In dorsal aspect the snout is rounded and the head is only slightly distinct from the neck. The eyes are relatively large, and the pupils are round (Fig. 191). The dorsal scales are smooth, lack apical pits, and are arranged in 15 rows at midbody. The anal plate is divided, and there is no loreal scale.

The dorsum is uniform brown, and the venter is immaculate white, cream, or yellowish cream.

SIMILAR SPECIES This species closely resembles its congener, *T. canula*, with which it is often confused. *Tantillita lintoni* differs in lacking any indication of a light vertebral stripe and in possessing a uniformly brown head without the light markings seen in *T. canula*.

DISTRIBUTION This species ranges from southern Veracruz through northern Guatemala to Honduras. In the Yucatán Peninsula it has been recorded from El Petén and southern Belize (Map 167).

NATURAL HISTORY This seemingly rare and secretive snake inhabits humid lowland forests at ele-

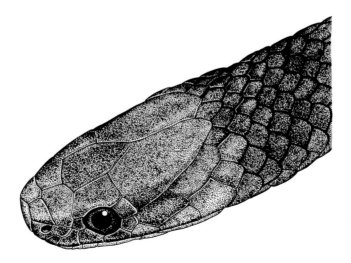

Fig. 191. Dorsolateral view of the head of *Tantillita lintoni* (UMRC 89-48), 124 mm SVL; Tikal, El Petén, Guatemala.

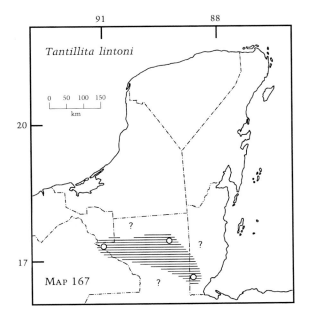

Tantillita lintoni

vations from sea level to about 350 m. At Tikal, El Petén, I observed a specimen abroad at dusk on the landing strip. H. M. Smith (1940:62) found the type specimen moving among leaves on the ground at night in heavy forest.

Nothing is known about the diet or reproductive biology of this species.

SUBSPECIES Two subspecies, distinguishable by color pattern, are presently recognized. *Tantillita lintoni rozellae* occurs in southern Veracruz, and

the nominate subspecies, *T. l. lintoni*, occurs in northern Guatemala, southern Belize, and northern Honduras.

ETYMOLOGY The specific name, *lintoni*, is a patronym in honor of Linton P. Satterthwaite, an archaeologist at Piedras Negras who facilitated H. M. Smith's work there.

COMMENT *Tantillita lintoni* was reviewed by L. D. Wilson (1988d:455.2).

Locality Records Belize: Toledo: 3 km N San José (UMRC 92-23). *Guatemala*: El Petén: Piedras Negras (USNM 108603), Tikal (UF 13850; UMMZ 117905–8; UMRC 89-48); no specific locality (USNM 71787).

Genus *Thamnophis*
(Garter and Ribbon Snakes)

This is a moderately large genus of predominantly North American snakes, and its representatives range from central Canada to Costa Rica. Most are slender and semiaquatic, usually with a dorsal pattern of light stripes against a darker background. All are viviparous. Twenty-two living species are presently recognized, two of which occur in the Yucatán Peninsula. *Thamnophis* is from the Greek *thamnos*, "shrub," and *ophis*, "snake."

Key to the Species of the Genus *Thamnophis*

Light crescent present immediately behind last supralabial scale; large, dark blotch present at nape of neck . . . . *Thamnophis marcianus*

No light crescent present immediately behind last supralabial scale; no dark blotch at nape of neck . . . . *Thamnophis proximus*

Clave para las Especies del Género *Thamnophis*

Con una mancha clara en forma de media luna inmediatamente detrás de la última escama supralabial; con una mancha grande y obscura en la nuca . . . . *Thamnophis marcianus*

Sin una mancha clara en forma de media luna inmediatamente detrás de la última escama supralabial; sin una mancha obscura en la nuca . . . . *Thamnophis proximus*

Thamnophis marcianus (Baird and Girard)
(Fig. 390; Map 168)

Eutainia marciana Baird and Girard, 1853:36.
HOLOTYPE: USNM 844. TYPE LOCALITY: Red River,

Arkansas; restricted to vicinity of Slough Creek, east of Hollister, Tillman County, Oklahoma, by Mittleman (1949:243).

Checkered garter snake, Marcy's garter snake,

FAMILY COLUBRIDAE   381

Central American garter snake; pine ridge tommygoff (Belize); cantil de agua, culebra de agua (Mexico).

DESCRIPTION   This is a moderately slender snake, but somewhat thick bodied for a *Thamnophis* (Fig. 390). The adults average 350 to 400 mm in snout-vent length. The long, slender tail is 24 to 27 percent of the head and body length. The head is cylindrical and only slightly distinct from the neck. The eyes are large with round pupils. The dorsal scales are strongly keeled, usually arranged in 19 rows at midbody, and lack apical pits. The anal plate is undivided. Adult males may possess small tubercles on the chin scales and on the prefrontal and internasal scales (A. G. Smith, 1946:106).

The dorsal ground color is generally brown or tan with alternating dark blotches on the lateral surfaces of the body. There is a light vertebral stripe one to three scale rows wide and a weakly differentiated lateral stripe. The stripes may be interrupted by the intrusion of the lateral blotches, and occasional specimens (e.g., USNM 46549) lack stripes altogether. The color pattern on the head is distinctive. The sutures between the supralabial scales are boldly marked with dark pigment, and there is a conspicuous light crescent immediately posterior to the last supralabial scale and immediately anterior to a broad, dark nuchal band. The venter is generally cream; it may be immaculate, or it may bear two rows of small, rounded spots.

SIMILAR SPECIES   In the Yucatán Peninsula *T. proximus* most closely resembles *T. marcianus* but differs in being more slender and in lacking the distinctive head markings of *T. marcianus*.

DISTRIBUTION   This species ranges at low and moderate elevations throughout the southwestern United States and northern Mexico, and on the Pacific slope at the Isthmus of Tehauntepec. On the Atlantic slope it ranges from northern Chiapas and eastern Tabasco through the Yucatán Peninsula southward to Costa Rica. Its range in the Yucatán Peninsula is imperfectly understood. It appears to be widely but discontinuously distributed throughout the peninsula in scattered localities in Chiapas, Yucatán, and Quintana Roo, and in north-central Belize (Map 168).

NATURAL HISTORY   This is an uncommon garter snake in the Yucatán Peninsula, where it is gener-

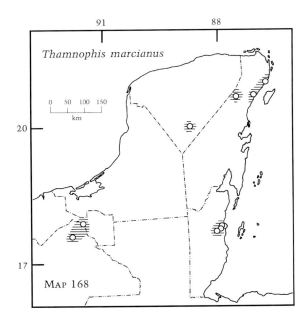

ally found in marshes, swamps, and at the edges of lakes and ponds. W. T. Neill and Allen (1959a:224) secured a specimen that had been unearthed by a bulldozer in pine-palmetto savanna in Belize.

Virtually nothing is known concerning the diet of this species in the Yucatán Peninsula, but in Texas *T. marcianus* feeds predominantly on frogs, toads, tadpoles, and earthworms, and to a lesser extent on fish and salamanders (Fouquette, 1954:177).

Thamnophis marcianus is viviparous, and parturition apparently takes place during the summer rainy season. In Belize, newborn individuals have been found in July and August, and Weyer (1990:34) reported a brood of 10 young born to a captive on 28 June. Wright and Wright (1957:804) recorded brood sizes of 12, 16, and 18 born to snakes collected in Texas, and the parturition dates ranged from 24 July to 2 August.

SUBSPECIES   In the most recent comprehensive systematic treatment of *T. marcianus*, Rossman (1971) recognized three subspecies, of which *T. m. praeocularis* occurs in the Yucatán Peninsula.

ETYMOLOGY   The specific name, *marcianus*, is a patronym honoring Randolph B. Marcy, a participant in the exploration of the Red River in Texas and Oklahoma who collected the type specimen in 1852.

COMMENT   *Thamnophis marcianus* was most recently reviewed by Rossman (1971).

Locality Records   Belize: Belize: Belize (MNHNP 1172), British Airport Camp (MPM 7759), Burrel Boom (KU 144955), Tropical Park (MPM 8273), 24 mi W, 11.5 mi S Belize City (AMNH 126438); Cayo: Hidden Valley Falls (FD photo). *Mexico*: Chiapas: Palenque (USNM 108597); Quintana Roo: Cobá (JCL sight record), 17 mi W Playa del Carmen (LSUMZ 33374), Puerto Morelos (López-Gonzales, 1991:106; USNM 46528–29); Tabasco: Emiliano Zapata (USNM 46549); Yucatán: Catmís (FMNH 26994).

Thamnophis proximus (Say)
(Fig. 391; Map 169)

Coluber proximus Say, 1823:187, in James, 1823. TYPE: lost, *fide* H. M. Smith and Taylor, 1945:166. TYPE LOCALITY: stone quarry on west side of Missouri River, 3 miles above the mouth of Boyers River; restated as "approximately 3 mi ENE Fort Calhoune, Washington County, Nebraska," by Rossman (1963:109).

Central American ribbon snake (Belize); culebra de agua, culebra palustre (Mexico).

DESCRIPTION   This striped snake is medium sized, slender, and semiaquatic. The average snout-vent length is about 350 to 400 mm, and the tail length is about 35 percent of the snout-vent length. The head is elongate and moderately distinct from the neck; the eyes are large with round pupils. The dorsal scales are strongly keeled, arranged in 19 rows at midbody, and lack apical pits. The anal plate is undivided.

The dorsal ground color is generally olive green. A conspicuous light yellow or yellowish green vertebral stripe is present, beginning at the posterior margin of the parietal scales and extending the length of the body, becoming indistinct on the tail (Fig. 391). A light yellow or yellowish green lateral stripe is present on scale rows 3 and 4. The ventral scales are yellowish green, often with a yellowish orange blush, especially on the anterior portion of the venter. The light yellow-green or yellow-orange of the venter extends onto the labial scales. The chin and throat are usually immaculate white, contrasting with the labial scales. The dorsal and lateral surfaces of the head are dark brown or olive. The iris is yellow-orange.

SIMILAR SPECIES   No other distinctly striped snake in the Yucatán Peninsula possesses 19 rows of strongly keeled dorsal scales at midbody. The striped species of *Coniophanes* and *Tantilla* have smooth dorsal scales. *Leptophis mexicanus* has 15 rows of dorsal scales at midbody. *Thamnophis marcianus* has alternating dark spots between the dorsal and lateral stripes, dark pigment on the sutures of the supralabial scales, and a conspicuous light crescent immediately posterior to the last supralabial scale.

DISTRIBUTION   *Thamnnophis proximus* is widely distributed through the central United States from Wisconsin and Michigan southward, at low, moderate, and intermediate elevations along the Gulf and Atlantic slopes of Mexico and Central America, and on the Pacific slope from Guerrero to Costa Rica. It occurs throughout the base of the Yucatán Peninsula, northward through Quintana Roo, and along the north coast of Yucatán but is apparently unknown from the interior of the peninsula (Map 169).

NATURAL HISTORY   These semiaquatic snakes are moderately common in the Yucatán Peninsula, but they are rarely found far from permanent fresh water such as marshes, aguadas, and cenotes. They are essentially terrestrial, although I found them coiled in emergent vegetation half a meter above the surface of the water. Ribbon snakes may be active day or night. Little is known of the diet in the Yucatán Peninsula, although Weyer (1990:34) mentioned frogs, tadpoles, and small fish in the diet of

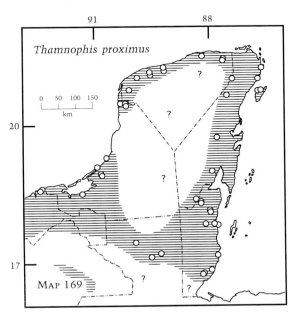

specimens from Belize. Himmelstein (1980:31) described a specimen from Isla Cozumel that regurgitated a *Smilisca baudinii*, and Manjarrez and Macias-Garcia (1992:61) found *Leptodactylus melanonotus* and *Bufo valliceps* in the stomachs of specimens from southern Veracruz. In Texas, frogs and toads form the bulk of the diet, and fish, salamanders, and birds are occasionally consumed (Fouquette, 1954:183).

Beyond the fact that these snakes are viviparous, little is known of their reproductive biology in the Yucatán Peninsula. W. T. Neill (1962:240) reported that a specimen collected in Belize on 10 April gave birth to six young on 3 July. Tinkle (1957) studied reproduction in a Louisiana population and found that nearly 90 percent of the females collected from April to July were gravid, that the average brood size was 13, and that females exhibited a positive correlation between snout-vent length and brood size.

An unusual instance of predation on *T. proximus* was reported by Manjarrez and Macias-Garcia (1992:61), who observed a giant water bug (Belostomatidae) capture and kill an adult female of this species in southern Veracruz.

SUBSPECIES   Of the six subspecies recognized by Rossman (1970), the Central American race, *T. p. rutiloris*, occurs in the Yucatán Peninsula.

COMMENT   Rossman (1962) demonstrated the validity of *T. proximus* and reviewed the species as part of his revision of the *sauritus* group of *Thamnophis* (Rossman, 1963). The most recent summary of information on this species is Rossman, 1970.

ETYMOLOGY   The specific name, *proximus*, is Latin for "the nearest, next to."

Locality Records Belize: Belize: Belize City: (AMNH 126439; FMNH 4441; KU 144956–57; UF 24549), 28 mi N Belize City (BCB 12300), Bermudian Landing (MPM 7560), Maskalls (W. T. Neill, 1962:240), Stanley Field (MCZ 66361); Orange Walk: near Orange Walk (MPM 7371–76), Tower Hill (MPM 7709); Stann Creek: All Pines (CM 8490), Mango Creek (MCZ 71646); Toledo: Deep River Bank (MPM 7370), Monkey River 1 mi E Bladen Bridge (MCZ 71647); no specific locality (FMNH 4228–33; USNM 26060, 26357, 59937). *Guatemala*: El Petén: El Paso (MCZ 38656), El Remate (FMNH 43360), Flores (FMNH 43359), Paso Caballos (MCZ 38582), W edge San Benito (UMMZ 124353). *Mexico*: Campeche: Balchacaj (FMNH 99651–52, 99654–69; UIMNH 18908–17), 38 mi SW Champotón (BCB 12299), El Remate, extreme NW tip

of state (TU 19803), 15.5 km SE Sabancuy (JCL photo), 16.9 km SE Sabancuy (JCL photo), 19.1 km SE Sabancuy (JCL sight record), 20 mi E Sabancuy (UCM 39524), Tankuche–El Remate (IHNHERP 434, 437, 439, 444, 447, 449, 454), Tankuche–El Remate, km 8 (IHNHERP 477), Tankuche–Punta Arena, km 19 (IHNHERP 494), 41 mi W Xicalango (BCB 12301); Quintana Roo: S edge Cancún (UMRC 84-45), Cobá (FMNH 26972; MCZ 149500), Cozumel (AMNH 102189; CM 40010; Himmelstein, 1980:31; MCZ 145375), Cozumel, Xpalbarco (MCZ 149567), Cozumel, 3.5 km N San Miguel (KU 70896), Cozumel, 6 km NE San Miguel (CM 41316), 3 mi S Felipe Carrillo Puerto (UCM 28127), Lake Bacalar (LSUMZ 33229–30), Pueblo Nuevo X-Can (UCM 41790), Puerto Morelos (MCZ 145376; UCM 39525–26; USNM 46530), Xcopen (MCZ 10766–68); Tabasco: 10 mi E Frontera (UIMNH 87706), bet. Frontera and Barra de San Pedro on Hwy. 180 (UTEP 13984–88); Yucatán: 22.5 km N Chunchucmil (TU 19806), 21.2 km N Colonia Yucatán (JCL sight record), 21.7 km N Colonia Yucatán (UMRC 92-3), 17 km S El Cuyo (JCL sight record), 17 km N Mérida (MCZ 53912), 22.3 km N Panabá (JCL sight record), La Ciénega, S of Progreso (UMMZ 80807–9), Progreso (H. M. Smith, 1938:5), 5.4 mi SE Sisal (KU 157633), Telchac (UMMZ 76163), 1.8 km S Telchac Puerto (KU 171719).

Genus *Tretanorhinus*
(Middle American Swamp Snakes)

Four species of aquatic Neotropical snakes constitute the genus *Tretanorhinus*. Representatives occur in the Antilles and from southern Mexico through Central America to northern South America. One species occurs in the Yucatán Peninsula. *Tretanorhinus* is derived from the Greek *tretos*, "pierced," and *rhinos*, "nose," presumably in reference to the slitlike nostrils of these aquatic snakes.

Tretanorhinus nigroluteus Cope
(Figs. 192, 392; Map 170)

Tretanorhinus nigroluteus Cope, 1861c:298.
HOLOTYPE: USNM 5568. TYPE LOCALITY: Greytown, Nicaragua (in error; probably Aspinwall, Panama, *fide* Dunn, 1939:216).

Black water snake, orangebelly swamp snake; cativo (Belize); buceadora, nauyaca de agua (Mexico); kon kon kan (Lacandón Maya).

DESCRIPTION   The adults of this medium-sized, moderately stout snake average between 350 and

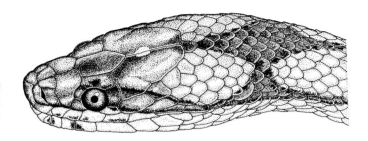

Fig. 192. Lateral view of the head of *Tretanorhinus nigroluteus* (UMRC 92-22), 320 mm SVL; Sarteneja, Corozal, Belize.

400 mm in snout-vent length (Fig. 392). The tail is approximately 40 to 45 percent of the head and body length. The rather long, narrow head is slightly distinct from the neck. The relatively small eyes are situated high on the head, and the nostrils are directed upward and are slitlike, features reflecting the aquatic habits of these snakes (Fig. 192). The pupils are round. *Tretanorhinus nigroluteus* is unusual in possessing a variable number of loreal scales, ranging from none to two. The number of dorsal scale rows is variable, too, but most specimens have 19 or 21 scale rows at midbody. The middorsal scales are keeled and lack apical pits, but the extent of keeling on the dorsal scales is variable. In some specimens the scales on the lateral surfaces of the body are smooth, whereas in others all dorsal scales are heavily keeled. The anal plate is divided.

In color and pattern this species is also quite variable. Some specimens are olive or grayish brown with a double row of small, rounded, dark brown or gray blotches. Others have a dorsal pattern of dark gray or brown bands against a lighter gray or brown background. In still others the dorsum may be nearly uniform dark gray. Most specimens have a dark stripe that originates on the rostrum and passes posteriorly through the eye and onto the body. A light lateral stripe is usually present involving some combination of scale rows 2, 3, and (sometimes) 4. The stripe is generally cream or light gray, but W. T. Neill and Allen (1959c:49) described the stripe in a juvenile from Belize as scarlet. The venter may be uniformly dark; light with scattered streaks, spots, and bars; or, like the specimen described by Neill and Allen, scarlet. In some specimens a dark midventral stripe is evident on the posterior half of the body and the tail.

SIMILAR SPECIES *Nerodia rhombifer*, a much larger snake, has 25 to 31 scale rows at midbody. The semiaquatic species of *Coniophanes* in the Yucatán Peninsula, *C. bipunctatus* and *C. quinquevittatus*, have two rows of bold dark spots on the ventral surface of the body.

DISTRIBUTION *Tretanorhinus nigroluteus* occurs at low elevations on the Atlantic slope from Tabasco eastward through northern Guatemala, Belize, and extreme southern Quintana Roo, Mexico, south to northern South America. In the Yucatán Peninsula this species occurs in southern Campeche, southern Quintana Roo, El Petén, and Belize (Map 170).

NATURAL HISTORY This nocturnal and crepuscular aquatic snake is rarely found far from water. It appears to be partial to shallow, slow-moving water, especially where aquatic vegetation is abundant (Villa, 1970). Individuals have been found in or near streams in humid lowland forests and in the sluggish oxbows of larger rivers, as well as in swamps, where they hide in aquatic vegetation. Black water snakes also inhabit mangrove swamps, according to Barbour and Amaral (1924:132), and J. R. Meyer (pers. comm.) secured a specimen said to have been killed by a fisherman "swimming under surface of sea, in Chetumal Bay, 1–200 yards from shore of Sartenaja Village, Corozal District, Belize." They

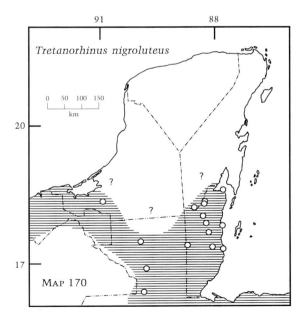

MAP 170

eat fish, tadpoles, and frogs. In northern Belize, Henderson and Hoevers (1977b:351) observed an individual "anchored to aquatic vegetation where it ambushed fish." This snake is itself prey for some species of wading birds, for Conant (1965:34) noted that a specimen was removed from the stomach of a bittern in Honduras. Villa (1973:380) reported an instance of predation by the turtle *Kinosternon leucostomum.*

Tretanorhinus nigroluteus is oviparous. W. T. Neill (1962:240) reported a juvenile with a trace of an umbilical scar collected in April in northern Belize.

SUBSPECIES Although several geographical segments of *T. nigroluteus* have been recognized as subspecies (e.g., J. A. Peters and Orejas-Miranda, 1970:306; Villa, 1969), L. D. Wilson and Hahn (1973:133) concluded that subspecies were unwarranted given the discordant nature of geographical variation in this species. If a trinomial were applied to the populations in the Yucatán Peninsula, it would be *T. n. lateralis.*

ETYMOLOGY The specific name, *nigroluteus,* is from the Latin *niger,* "dark" or "black," and *luteus,* "muddy" or "golden yellow," presumably in reference to the color pattern of some individuals.

Locality Records Belize: Belize: Belize (USNM 26057, 56369), mi 35.5 on Western Hwy. (MCZ 147421), Lemonal (MPM 7711); Cayo: Cayo at Belize River (UF 24623); Corozal: 100 to 200 yd offshore, Sarteneja (UMRC 92-22); Orange Walk: Lamanai (ROM H12738), New River (MPM 7710, 7760), near Orange Walk (MPM 7390), Orange Walk (MPM 8066–99), Tower Hill (MPM 8139); Stann Creek: Dangriga (RWV photo), Middlesex (UCM 30898). *Guatemala*: Alta Verapaz: Chinajá (Duellman, 1963:244); El Petén: Arroyo Subín (UMMZ 79056), Laguna Yalac (UMMZ 79055), Paso Caballos (MCZ 38583; UMMZ 79054). *Mexico*: Campeche: Pacaitún on Río Candelaria (FMNH 36352–58); Quintana Roo: 3 km NE La Union (Bahena-Basave, 1995d:47).

Genus *Urotheca* (False Coral Snakes)

As presently conceived, the genus *Urotheca* contains nine species and ranges from Tamaulipas and Oaxaca south through Central America to Ecuador. One species occurs in the Yucatán Peninsula. These are small to medium-sized snakes. Some bear bright red, yellow (or white), and black bands or rings, and these are most certainly mimics of the highly venomous coral snakes, *Micrurus.* Others are nondescript brown, often with light stripes, but all have unusually long, fragile tails, enlarged fangs on the posterior portion of the maxillary bone, and a deep pocket on the asulcate surface of the hemipenis at the base of the capitulum. The genus *Urotheca* was revived by Savage and Crother (1989), who placed the genus *Pliocercus* and members of the *lateristriga* group of *Rhadinaea* within it. Although it is followed here, this arrangement has not received unanimous acceptance (e.g., Flores-Villela, 1993:68). *Urotheca* is from the Greek *oura,* "tail," and *theke,* "a case" (for something).

Urotheca elapoides (Cope)
(Figs. 193, 393; Map 171)

Pliocercus elapoides Cope, 1860:253. SYNTYPES: ANSP 3810–13. TYPE LOCALITY: near Jalapa, Mexico.

False coral; bead and coral, coral falso (Belize); coral, coralillo (Guatemala, Mexico); kuyun kan (Lacandón Maya).

DESCRIPTION This is a moderately small, rather slender snake with an unusually long and fragile tail. The adults average between 300 and 350 mm in snout-vent length, and the tail length is about 60 to 70 percent of the head and body length. The head is distinct from the neck in dorsal aspect, the eyes are medium sized, and the pupils are round (Fig. 193). The dorsal scales are smooth, lack apical pits, and are arranged in 17 rows at midbody. The anal plate is divided.

Urotheca elapoides exhibits enormous geographic variation in color and pattern. In the Yucatán Peninsula individuals are usually brightly colored with red rings alternating with black rings bordered with yellow (Fig. 393). The scales of the yellow and red rings are tipped with black. The anterior portion of the head is generally black, but the inferior border of the rostral scale and the chin and labial scales are usually yellow and are continuous with a yellow band across the parietal scales.

SIMILAR SPECIES *Urotheca elapoides* closely resembles certain venomous coral snakes (*Micrurus*),

Fig. 193. Dorsolateral view of the head of *Urotheca elapoides* (USNM 319777), 230 mm SVL; Union Camp, Columbia Forest Reserve, Toledo, Belize.

with which it is sympatric throughout virtually its entire range. This resemblance is probably Batesian mimicry (Greene and McDiarmid, 1981). In contrast with *Micrurus*, however, *U. elapoides* possesses a loreal scale, has dorsal scales arranged in 17 rather than 15 rows at midbody, and has relatively large eyes (cf. Figs. 193, 194). *Lampropeltis triangulum* is larger, has red and yellow rings separated by black rings, and possesses 21 rows of dorsal scales at midbody. *Scaphiodontophis* has bright bands on the anterior portion of the body, but in Yucatecan specimens the posterior portion of the body is brown.

DISTRIBUTION *Urotheca elapoides* occurs at low and moderate elevations on the Atlantic slope from Tamaulipas and on the Pacific slope from Oaxaca, south and eastward through the Yucatán Peninsula to western Honduras and El Salvador. It appears to occur continuously through the base of the Yucatán Peninsula and in isolated populations at the outer end of the peninsula in the states of Yucatán and Quintana Roo (Map 171).

NATURAL HISTORY This nocturnal snake, uncommon in the Yucatán Peninsula, apparently inhabits lowland forests, where specimens have been found abroad at night on the forest floor and on roads. The diet includes the salamanders *Bolitoglossa dofleini* (Stuart, 1948:18) and *B. mexicana* (Duellman, 1963:242). Seib (1985a) studied the diet of *U. elapoides* on coffee fincas in southern Chiapas

and adjacent Guatemala and examined the stomach contents of museum specimens from Chiapas and Guatemala. Among the prey items he discovered were frogs of the genus *Eleutherodactylus*, salamanders of the genus *Bolitoglossa*, and amphibian eggs.

A large proportion of museum specimens of *Urotheca* have incomplete tails (Savage and Crother, 1989:359). The unusually long, fragile tail may be displayed to predators, which take the tail while the

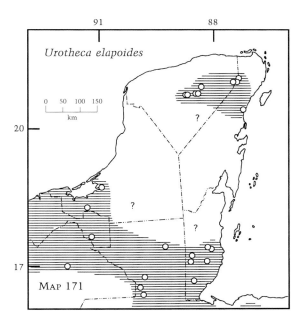

MAP 171

rest of the snake escapes. Greene (1973:144) described tail displays in snakes, including *U. elapoides*, and suggested such an antipredator function. The survival value of such behavior is clear, for Stuart (1948:67) reported finding the tail of a *U. elapoides* in the stomach of an indigo snake (*Drymarchon corais*) from Alta Verapaz.

False coral snakes have enlarged, ungrooved fangs on the posterior margin of the maxillary bone. They are generally docile and disinclined to bite, but they will bite. Seib (1980), who was bitten on the finger by a small individual, experienced immediate searing pain, swelling in the finger and hand, and swollen and tender axillary lymph nodes. After about six hours the pain was nearly intolerable and came in waves of about two minutes' duration, about a minute apart. Five days after the bite, the skin of the hand was nearly black and remained so for about 24 hours. A painful ache continued in the finger for about three weeks, and total recovery took about six weeks. Obviously these snakes should be handled with caution.

SUBSPECIES Many subspecific names have been applied to geographical segments of this highly variable species. L. D. Wilson and Meyer (1985:81) questioned the validity of the named subspecies, and Savage and Crother (1989) recognized no subspecies of *U. elapoides*.

ETYMOLOGY The specific name, *elapoides*, is derived from the Greek *elops*, a kind of serpent, and *-oides* a contraction denoting "likeness." The name presumably refers to this snake's resemblance to members of the genus *Micrurus* of the family Elapidae.

COMMENT This species was long placed in the genus *Pliocercus*, and much of the literature on it will be found under that name. Savage and Crother (1989) revived the generic name *Urotheca*, assigned the species of *Pliocercus* and certain species of *Rhadinaea* to it, and placed *P. andrewsi* in the synonymy of *U. elapoides*.

Locality Records *Belize*: Cayo: Augustine (MPM 8189), 7 mi SSW Guacamallo Crossing (TU 18529), Sibun Hill (TU 18530), mi 62 on Western Hwy. (CM 117107); Stann Creek: vicinity Arthur's Seat (UF 79989), Double Falls (FMNH 72471), Middlesex (UCM 25748, 25889, 30888); Toledo: Union Camp, Columbia River Forest Reserve (USNM 319776–77). *Guatemala*: Alta Verapaz: Chinajá (Duellman, 1963:242); El Petén:

Río San Roman (Duellman, 1963:242), Sayaxché (UCM 22356–57), Tikal (UF 13844). *Mexico*: Campeche: Encarnación (FMNH 100274), Tres Brazos (FMNH 100273); Chiapas: 2 mi SE Ocosingo (UTEP 9518); Tabasco: Tenosique (USNM 110767); Quintana Roo: 19.6 km S Kantunil Kin (UMRC 80-44), Pueblo Nuevo X-Can (CM 45802, 49097, 49141; UCM 40683, 40685, 40692), Tulum (CAS 154138); Yucatán: Chichén Itzá (MCZ 26843), Libre Unión (FMNH 36323), Pisté (CM 46951, 49731; KU 70881), Popolá (UCM 40698), X-Can (CM 46878, 47045), Yokdzonot (MCZ 46796).

Genus *Xenodon*
(False Fer-de-lances)

This genus includes a small assemblage of medium-sized, rather stout-bodied snakes that range from southern Mexico to Argentina. Six species are presently referred to this genus; one occurs in the Yucatán Peninsula. *Xenodon* derives from the Greek *xenos*, "stranger," and *odous*, "tooth," in reference to the several enlarged teeth on the posterior margin of the maxillary bone that contrast with the much smaller anterior teeth.

Xenodon rabdocephalus (Wied)
(Fig. 394; Map 172)

Coluber rhabdocephalus Wied, 1824:668. TYPE: unknown. TYPE LOCALITY: Brazil; further restricted by Wied (1825) to Bahía, Brazil.

Barba amarilla (Guatemala); culebra engañosa (Mexico); hanag rum (Lacandón Maya).

DESCRIPTION The adults of this medium-sized, rather thick-bodied snake average 650 to 700 mm in snout-vent length. The short tail is about 18 to 20 percent as long as the head and body. The head is distinct from the neck in dorsal aspect, the eyes are large, and the pupils are round. The dorsal scales are smooth and are arranged in 19 rows at midbody. A single apical pit is present on the dorsal scales. The anal plate is undivided.

The dorsal ground color is tan or gray with irregular transverse dark brown bands (Fig. 394). The bands are usually edged with black, and the interspaces are bordered with white or cream. The dorsal surface of the head is brown, and there is a light interobital bar or inverted V at the level of the eyes. A light band originates above each eye and passes posterolaterally onto the neck. Coloration of the ventral surface of the body and tail is variable. In some specimens the venter is dark brown or gray with irregular light marks on the lateral margins of the ventral scales. In others the ventral surfaces are light tan, yellowish, or gray with dark blotches or a suffusion of dark pigment.

SIMILAR SPECIES *Xenodon rabdocephalus* superficially resembles *Bothrops asper*, from which it differs in possessing a round pupil and smooth dorsal scales and lacking a loreal pit.

DISTRIBUTION *Xenodon rabdocephalus* has an extensive distribution. It is found at low and moderate elevations on the Atlantic slope from Veracruz and the Pacific slope from Guerrero, southward through Central America to Amazonian South America. It occurs through the base of the Yucatán Peninsula and northward through Quintana Roo (Map 172).

NATURAL HISTORY This species inhabits moist lowland forests. It is terrestrial, both diurnal and nocturnal, and feeds primarily on frogs and toads. Near Tikal, El Petén, I observed an individual swallowing a *Bufo valliceps* at midday. In turn, these snakes are preyed on by the great black hawk, *Buteogallus urubitinga* (Gerhardt et al., 1993:350). Stuart (1935:51) described snakes of this species as sluggish, but I have not found them to be so. When disturbed, these rather nervous snakes flatten the head and anterior portion of the body and make quick, jerky movements. There is a superficial resem-

blance to the fer-de-lance (*Bothrops asper*), perhaps an instance of Batesian mimicry. Stuart (1935:51) wrote that the natives in the vicinity of La Libertad, El Petén, confused the two, applying the name *barba amarilla* to both.

Nothing is known concerning reproduction in this species in the Yucatán Peninsula, but it is presumably oviparous, like other members of the genus.

Swanson (1945:213) described a Panamanian specimen that exhibited voluntary bleeding at the mouth when it was captured.

SUBSPECIES Two subspecies were recognized in the past on the basis of their nonoverlapping numbers of ventral scales (J. A. Peters and Orejas-Miranda, 1970:324; H. M. Smith, 1940:59). The name *X. r. mexicanus* was applied to snakes ranging from Veracruz to Guatemala, and *X. r. rabdocephalus* to the form ranging from Nicaragua to South America. L. D. Wilson and Meyer (1985:110) synonymized the two forms after finding intermediate specimens from Honduras.

ETYMOLOGY The specific name, *rabdocephalus*, is from the Greek *rhabdos*, "rod," and *kephale*, "head."

Locality Records Belize: Belize: Belize City (FMNH 4257); Cayo: Central Farm (MCZ 71683), Mountain Pine Ridge Rd., 36 mi S Belize-Cayo Rd. (UMMZ 124655); Orange Walk: Kate's Lagoon (FMNH 49349); Stann Creek: Middlesex (UCM 25740, 25880, 29995), Silk Grass (FMNH 49348). *Guatemala*: Alta Verapaz: Chinajá (Duellman, 1963:244); El Petén: 18 km NNW Chinajá (KU 55732), El Paso (MCZ 38653), El Rosario (JCL sight record), La Libertad (UMMZ 74919–21), Paso Caballos (MCZ 38587; UMMZ 79057), Piedras Negras (USNM 108596), Santo Toribio (AMNH 69992), Sayaxché (UCM 22364), Tikal (AMNH uncat.; MCZ 55433, 58762–63; UF 13852–53; UMMZ 117926–28, 118254, 120314–15), 4 mi S Tikal (KU 157641); no specific locality (USNM 71785–86). *Mexico*: Quintana Roo: Felipe Carrillo Puerto (UMMZ 113580), 14 mi E Leona Vicario (UCM 39527).

Family Elapidae
(Coral Snakes, Cobras, and Their Allies)

The hollow fangs of these venomous snakes are attached to the front of a relatively immobile maxillary bone. This family includes the dangerously venomous cobras, kraits, mambas, and sea snakes,

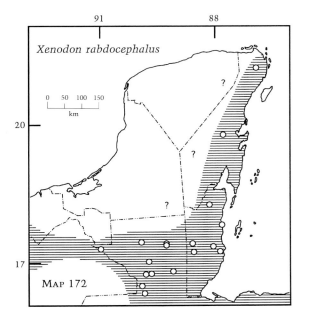

MAP 172

and many human fatalities each year are attributable to the bites of elapid snakes. In the New World the family ranges from the southern United States through Central America to northern Argentina and Uruguay. In the Old World elapids are found throughout much of Africa, India, Southeast Asia, the Indo-Malay Archipelago, and Australia. The family contains about 250 species in approximately 60 genera. One genus occurs in the Yucatán Peninsula.

Genus *Micrurus* (Coral Snakes)

Coral snakes are rather slender, semifossorial snakes with small eyes and cylindrical bodies. Most are brilliantly colored with some combination of red, yellow, and black rings, and many species serve as models for harmless and not-so-harmless mimics (Greene and McDiarmid, 1981). Most coral snakes feed on lizards and especially snakes, which they overpower with the aid of their potent neurotoxic venom. Several species of secretive snakes previously unknown to science have been discovered in the stomachs of coral snakes (e.g., Schmidt, 1932:8). Although less dangerous than the pitvipers, coral snakes are nonetheless capable of delivering a very serious bite, and human fatalities have been recorded (Minton and Minton, 1969). The genus ranges from the southeastern United States to Argentina but exhibits the greatest diversity in the tropics. There are approximately 50 species of coral snakes in the genus *Micrurus*, of which 3 occur in the Yucatán Peninsula. *Micrurus* derives from the Greek *mikros*, "small," and *oura*, "tail," which aptly describes the relatively short tail of members of this genus.

Key to the Species of the Genus *Micrurus*

1. Snout usually with light spot; males lack supra-anal tubercles; red scales tipped with black or not..2
   Snout uniform black; supra-anal tubercles present in adult males; red scales tipped with black; Belize and adjacent Guatemala only (Map 175) .... *Micrurus nigrocinctus*
2. Black tail rings 1.5 to 2 times as wide as the yellow rings dividing them; red scales heavily tipped with black; pan-peninsular .... *Micrurus diastema*
   Black tail rings less than 1.5 times as wide as the yellow rings dividing them; red scales without black pigment or lightly tipped with black; Belize and adjacent Guatemala only (Map 174) .... *Micrurus hippocrepis*

Clave para las Especies del Género *Micrurus*

1. Hocico usualmente con una mancha clara; sin tubérculos supra-anales en los machos; las escamas rojas pueden tener o no la punta negra 2
   Hocico uniformemente negro; con tubérculos supra-anales en machos adultos; escamas rojas con la punta negra; habitan en Belice y Guatemala adyacente únciamente (Mapa 175) ....
   .... *Micrurus nigrocinctus*
2. Con anillos negros en la cola de 1.5 a 2 veces el ancho de los anillos amarillos que los separan; escamas rojas con las puntas de color negro; organismos pan-peninsulares ....
   .... *Micrurus diastema*
   Con anillos negros en la cola de menos de 1.5 veces el ancho de los anillos amarillos que los separan; escamas rojas sin pigmento negro, o ligeramente manchadas de negro en la punta; habita en Belice y Guatemala adyacente únicamente (Mapa 174) ...... *Micrurus hippocrepis*

Micrurus diastema
(Duméril, Bibron, and Duméril)
(Figs. 194, 395, 396; Map 173)

Elaps diastema A. M. C. Duméril, Bibron, and Duméril, 1854:1222. HOLOTYPE: MNHNP E337/3.

TYPE LOCALITY: Mexique; restricted by H. M. Smith and Taylor (1950b:328) to Colima, Colima, Mexico (presumably in error, *fide* Roze, 1967).

Many-ringed coral snake; bead and coral (Belize); coral, coralillo (Guatemala, Mexico); coralillo anillado (Mexico); kuyun kan (Lacandón Maya); chac ib can, kalam (Yucatec Maya).

DESCRIPTION These medium-sized, moderately slender snakes average between 550 and 650 mm in snout-vent length, although some individuals attain a snout-vent length in excess of a meter. The tail is relatively short, about 15 to 20 percent of the head and body length, and somewhat longer in males than in females. The head is slightly distinct from the neck in dorsal aspect, the eyes are small, and the pupil is subcircular (Fig. 194). There is no loreal scale. The dorsal scales are smooth and arranged in 15 rows at midbody. There are no apical pits on the scales, and the anal plate is divided.

These snakes typically have a color pattern of red rings alternating with black rings bordered by yellow rings (Fig. 395). The scales of the red rings are tipped with black pigment. The anterior half of the head is generally black, although the rostrum may bear a light spot. The chin and labial scales are usually yellow and are continuous with a yellow nuchal collar. This species is extremely variable in color pattern. In the northeastern portion of the peninsula the number of black and yellow body rings tends to be reduced, and the red rings thus predominate (Fig. 396). In extreme examples the body is uniformly red, the tail bears yellow and black rings, and the head is black with a yellow nuchal collar.

SIMILAR SPECIES *Lampropeltis triangulum* has 21 rows of dorsal scales at midbody, a loreal scale, and red and yellow rings separated by black rings. *Urotheca elapoides* has 17 rows of dorsal scales at midbody, a loreal scale, and relatively larger eyes (cf. Figs. 193, 194). *Micrurus nigrocinctus* closely resembles *M. diastema*, but the males of *M. nigrocinctus* have supra-anal tubercles, and where the two species co-occur in Belize *M. nigrocinctus* has a completely black snout. Where *M. diastema* co-occurs with *M. hippocrepis* it has black tail rings 1.5 to 2 times the width of the yellow rings, and *M. hippocrepis* has black and yellow tail rings that are approximately equal in width.

DISTRIBUTION *Micrurus diastema* occurs at low and moderate elevations on the Atlantic slope from central Veracruz and Oaxaca south and eastward through northern Guatemala and Belize to western Honduras. It is found essentially throughout the Yucatán Peninsula, although it has yet to be recorded from southernmost Belize (Map 173).

NATURAL HISTORY This is the common coral snake of the Yucatán Peninsula. It is terrestrial and secretive and occurs in virtually all habitats but is commonest in forested areas, especially the taller forests on the eastern side of the peninsula and to the south. Duellman (1963:244) found specimens in

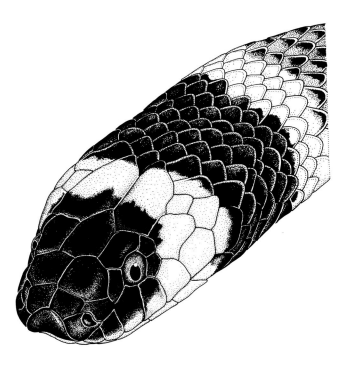

Fig. 194. Dorsolateral view of the head of *Micrurus diastema* (UMRC 84-5), 657 mm SVL; between Labná and Oxkutzcab, Yucatán, Mexico.

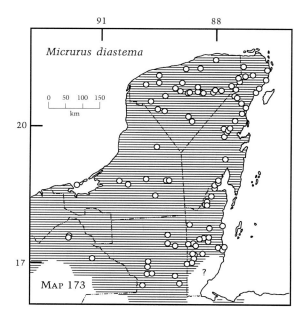

Micrurus diastema

0 50 100 150
km

91

88

20

17

Map 173

?

the leaf litter of the forest at Chinajá and Sayaxché, El Petén. Individuals are frequently encountered crossing roads at night, but W. T. Neill and Allen (1959c:56–57) reported finding specimens abroad during the day in Belize, including one swimming across a creek. Dundee et al. (1986:46) found an individual abroad at 11:00 A.M. in northern Quintana Roo, and I found specimens at Uxmal, Yucatán, and near El Seibal, El Petén, that were out during the day. These snakes use quick, rather jerky movements, giving the impression of nervousness. Some individuals are docile and disinclined to bite, but others bite viciously when disturbed.

Coral snakes prey predominantly on snakes, and to a lesser extent on lizards. A specimen from the vicinity of Balankanché, Yucatán, had a *Coniophanes* in its stomach, and another from near Playa del Carmen, Quintana Roo, contained an adult *Typhlops microstomus*. *Sibon sartorii* were taken from the stomachs of *M. diastema* from Oxpemul and Ciudad del Carmen, Campeche. Blaney and Blaney (1978a) reported *Eumeces schwartzei* in the diet of this species in Quintana Roo. Seib (1985a) studied feeding ecology on coffee fincas in southern Chiapas and Guatemala and found that *M. diastema* fed exclusively on snakes, especially *Ninia sebae*. Seib (1985a:128) also documented an instance of cannibalism in this species.

Like the other members of its genus, *M. diastema* is oviparous. Stuart (1948:85) found a female with well-formed eggs on 4 April in Alta Verapaz, suggesting oviposition during the summer rainy sea-

son. W. T. Neill (1962:241), however, found a juvenile in Belize on 14 July that might have hatched in late January or early February; on the other hand, it might have hatched in late October or early November and then entered a period of inactivity during the winter dry season.

SUBSPECIES Owing to great geographical variation in this species, especially in color pattern, as many as seven geographical segments of *M. diastema* have been recognized as subspecies. Fraser (1973), who provided the most comprehensive analysis of variation in this species, concluded that no subspecies should be recognized. Blaney and Blaney (1979), however, distinguished two subspecies in the Yucatán Peninsula on the basis of color pattern: *M. d. alienus*, a form with relatively few black rings on the body, at the north end of the peninsula; and *M. d. sapperi*, with more numerous black rings, in the central and southern portions of the peninsula. J. A. Campbell and Lamar (1989:106) accepted this arrangement but noted the difficulty of recognizing subspecies of *M. diastema* on the basis of anything other than geographical distribution.

ETYMOLOGY The specific name, *diastema*, is Greek and means "a natural space in the body," more specifically, a gap between two teeth.

COMMENT Bahena-Basave (1995cc:46) reported *Micrurus browni* from southern Quintana Roo, on the basis of five specimens collected in the vicinity of La Union. Given the enormous variation seen in *M. diastema* and the fact that *M. browni* is otherwise restricted to the Pacific versant and the highlands of Mexico and Guatemala, occurrence of *M. browni* in the Caribbean lowlands of Quintana Roo seems doubtful. *Micrurus diastema* was reviewed by Fraser (1973), and the available information on this species was summarized by J. A. Campbell and Lamar (1989).

Locality Records Belize: Belize: Belize City (FMNH 4254; USNM 24906, 56611), Tropical Park (MPM 8274); Cayo: Augustine (CM 105944), 9.6 mi S Augustine (KU 157642), Belmopan (CM 90989), 1.2 mi S Blancaneaux Lodge (CM 105711), Caracol (CMM photo), Central Farm (MCZ 71676–77; MPM 8188), 4 km E Chial (CM 112110), Chiquibul Branch, S Granos de Oro Camp (CM 112126), Coquercot (UMMZ 74911), ca. 6 mi S Georgeville (CM 105963), mi 47 on Hummingbird Hwy. (CM 112118), 1.3 mi S Little Vaqueros Creek (UF 79988), Macal River at Guacamallo Bridge

(CM 112150), Mountain Pine Ridge (MPM 8187; W. T. Neill and Allen, 1959c:56), Roaring Creek (FMNH 71534), upper Raspaculo River basin (Stafford, 1991:16), Valentin (UMMZ 80721), Western Hwy. at Beaver Dam Creek (W. T. Neill and Allen, 1959c:56), Xunantunich (W. T. Neill and Allen, 1959c:56); Corozal: Corozal Island (Schmidt, 1941:507), S edge Corozal Town (JLK 474), Santa Cruz (MPM 7383), 0.5 mi S Santa Elena (JLK 473); Orange Walk: Chan Pine Ridge (MPM 8282), Gallon Jug (W. T. Neill, 1965:111), near Orange Walk (MPM 7712, 10787), Tower Hill (MPM 7380, 7382, 7713–14); Stann Creek: 62 mi from Punta Gorda (MPM 7381), Silk Grass (Schmidt, 1941:507), Stann Creek Valley (FMNH 49355–56); no specific locality (FMNH 4201-4; MCZ 53941; USNM 24905, 56611). *Guatemala*: El Petén: 20 km NNW Chinajá (KU 55718–19), 12 km S La Libertad (AMNH 69983), La Libertad (FMNH 43384; UMMZ 74909–10), Las Cañas (CM 58285), Parque Nacional de Yaxhá (UTEP 9955), 7 mi NW Poptún (KU 157643), Sayaxché (KU 57141; UCM 22365–66), 1 mi W Seibal (KU 157644), Tikal (MCZ 55434–35, 152579; UF 13854; UIMNH 52526; UMMZ 117882–90, 120522), Uaxactún (AMNH 69983; MCZ 32300; UMMZ 70453); no specific locality (USNM 71784). *Mexico*: Campeche: Becan (UWZH 20555), Ciudad del Carmen (UMMZ 83537), Dzibalchén (KU 75636), 10.8 mi N Escárcega (KU 157645), 18 mi E Escárcega (UCM 28149), Oxpemul (UMMZ 76126), 46 mi E Silvituc (UCM 28148), Tuxpeña Camp (UMMZ 73228); Chiapas: Laguna Ocotal (MCZ 53883–85), Palenque (EAL 3635; USNM 46392), 0.5 km NE Palenque ruins (JCL sight record); Quintana Roo: 10.8 km N Akumal (EAL 2873), 1.1 km S Cancún Airport (JCL 6826), Chetumal (MZCIQRO 11), 4 km N Chetumal (MZCIQRO 07), Cobá (FMNH 26974; TLB 16707; UMMZ 76126, 83944), 3 km E Cobá (UMRC 84-7), 3.7 km SE Cobá (UMRC 79-262), Felipe Carrillo Puerto (UMMZ 113565–68), 8.2 mi NE Felipe Carrillo Puerto (KU 157647), 17.9 mi N Felipe Carrillo Puerto (KU 157649), 24.3 km NE Felipe Carrillo Puerto (KU 171744), 28.1 mi NE Felipe Carrillo Puerto (KU 157648), 64.6 km NE Felipe Carrillo Puerto (KU 171743), 8.5 km NNW Kantunil Kin (UMRC 79-261), 18.9 km S Kantunil Kin (UMRC 80-43), 8.9 mi N Limones (KU 157646), Playa del Carmen (Himmelstein, 1980:31; López-Gonzales, 1991:106), 5.2 km S Playa del Carmen (UMRC 84-34), 16.5 km S Playa del Carmen (JCL 6840), Pueblo Nuevo X-Can (CM 45803–11, 49055, 49090–91, 49093, 49098–99, 49107, 49134, 49143; TU 19754; UCM 28150, 40677–82, 40684, 40686–91, 40693–97, 40744–49, 41812–13), 52 km SW Puerto Juárez (AMNH 110056), Puerto Morelos (López-Gonzales, 1991:106), Punta Venado (López-Gonzales, 1991:106), Tintal (UCM 40699–706, 41808–11, 41911), near Tulum (EAL 2876), 15.7 km S Tulum (JCL 6804), 19.7 km NW Tulum (UMRC 84-57), bet. X-Can and Cobá, km 47 (TU 19754); Yucatán: 11.4 mi E Buctzotz (KU 157651), Catzín (CM 45316–17), Chichén Itzá (AMNH 7865, 38825, 49200, 49220; CM 40178; FMNH 20628, 19409–10, 152313; MCZ 7247, 26835, 26837, 28749, 31871; UMMZ 73057–58; USNM 46562), Dzibilchaltún (FMNH 152313–15), 10.6 mi S Dzilam Bravo (KU 157653), Grutas Balankanché (UMRC 84-6), near Hoctún (UF 33492), 3.6 mi SW Hunucmá (KU 157654), Izamal (USNM 260844), Kantunil (FMNH 36416, 36423, 36430), bet. Labná and Oxkutzcab (UMRC 84-5), Libre Unión (FMNH 34425, 36411, 36421), Mayapán (FMNH 40719), Mérida (FMNH 19409–10, 20628), 2 km E Opichén (TU 19753), Peto (CM 45318), 11.7 mi W Peto (KU 157656), 11.9 mi W Peto (KU 157655), Pisté (CM 46966–69, 47009–13, 47163–67, 49823–33; UCM 40707–10, 41814–15), 11.7 km N Pisté (KU 70902), Popolná (UCM 40698), 14.1 mi S Río Lagartos (KU 157652), Tekom (FMNH 49354), Uxmal (JCL sight record), 1 km N Uxmal (TU 19752), Valladolid (MCZ 31874), 12 mi W Valladolid (KU 157650), X-Can (CM 46851–54, 46889–92, 47060–63; UCM 28150), Yokdzonot (FMNH 36414, 36418–19, 36426, 36428, 36431–32); no specific locality (USNM 24890–92).

Micrurus hippocrepis (Peters)
(Map 174)

Elaps hippocrepis Peters, 1861b:925. HOLOTYPE: ZMB 4065. TYPE LOCALITY: Santo Tomás de Guatemala (= Puerto Matias de Galvez, Guatemala).

Maya coral snake; bead and coral (Belize); coral, coralillo (Belize, Guatemala).

DESCRIPTION This rather small coral snake averages between 400 and 450 mm in snout-vent length. The tail is about 15 to 20 percent of the snout-vent length. This species exhibits sexual size dimorphism, with females being substantially larger than males (J. A. Campbell and Lamar, 1989:119). The head is slightly distinct from the neck, the eyes are small, and the pupils are subcircular. There is no loreal scale. The dorsal scales are smooth, lack apical pits, and are arranged in 15 rows at midbody. The anal plate is divided.

The color pattern on the body consists of a series of black rings narrowly edged with yellow and separated by broader red rings. Some black rings may be interrupted by yellow along the dorsal midline. The red scales have little or no black pigment on them. The snout is typically yellow, although in some specimens it may be black. The black head cap is bordered by a yellow band across the posterior portion of the head, itself bordered by a black nuchal band. The tail bears alternating rings of black and yellow that are approximately equal in width.

SIMILAR SPECIES *Micrurus hippocrepis* differs from the false coral snakes such as *Lampropeltis* and *Urotheca* in possessing 15 rows of dorsal scales at midbody, lacking a loreal scale, and having much smaller eyes. *Micrurus nigrocinctus* has a uniform black snout and has black pigment on the red scales. Where *M. diastema* co-occurs with *M. hippocrepis* it has black pigment on the red scales, and its black tail rings are 1.5 to 2 times the width of the yellow rings that separate them, whereas the yellow and black tail rings of *M. hippocrepis* are approximately equal in width.

DISTRIBUTION *Micrurus hippocrepis* is known only from Cayo and Stann Creek Districts, Belize, and eastern Guatemala. Documentation of its occurrence in the foothills of the Maya Mountains in Toledo District can be expected (Map 174).

NATURAL HISTORY Little is known of the natural history of this uncommon and secretive snake. It is probably nocturnal much of the time, although J. A. Campbell and Lamar (1989:120) reported finding active animals during the day. In Belize it has been taken in the citrus groves of the Upper Stann Creek Valley at Middlesex, in the Mountain Pine Ridge, and from beneath a rotting log in the humid forest of the Cockscomb Basin Wildlife Sanctuary. Like most other *Micrurus*, this is a quick-moving

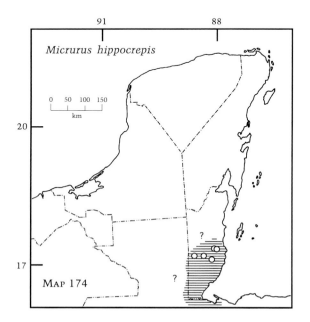

MAP 174

snake that progresses with nervous, jerky movements. It probably feeds on snakes and lizards, as do many species of *Micrurus*.

Micrurus hippocrepis is probably oviparous, like the other members of its genus, but specific details of its reproductive biology are unknown.

ETYMOLOGY The specific name, *hippocrepis*, may derive from the Greek *hippos*, "horse," and *crepis*, which refers to a kind of man's boot or half boot. The name might be loosely translated as "horseshoe," perhaps referring somehow to the snake's markings.

COMMENT The status of this form is not well understood. The enormous geographic variation seen in *M. diastema* encompasses that of *M. hippocrepis*; moreover, the two share a similar karyotype (Gutiérrez et al., 1988:110). W. T. Neill and Allen (1959c:57) suggested that the characteristic absence of melanin from the red scales of *M. hippocrepis* may be a consequence of ontogenetic loss of dark pigment. They thus suggest, by implication, that specimens of *M. hippocrepis* are merely old individuals of *M. diastema*.

Information on this species was summarized by J. A. Campbell and Lamar (1989).

Locality Records Belize: Cayo: Mountain Pine Ridge, Río On (MPM 7679), upper Raspaculo River basin (Stafford, 1991:16); Stann Creek: Cockscomb Basin Wildlife Sanctuary (UMRC 91-18), Middlesex (CM 48010), near Middlesex (MPM 7384); no specific locality (USNM 24906).

Micrurus nigrocinctus (Girard)
(Fig. 195; Map 175)

Elaps nigrocinctus Girard, 1854:226. SYNTYPES: USNM 7347 (two syntypes). TYPE LOCALITY: Taboga, Bay of Panama.

Central American coral snake; coral, coralillo, bead and coral (Belize).

DESCRIPTION This medium-sized coral snake may attain a total length slightly in excess of 1,000 mm. The tail is relatively short, about 15 percent of the head and body length. The head is only slightly distinct from the neck in dorsal aspect. The snout is rounded, the eyes are small, and the pupils are subcircular (Fig. 195). The dorsal scales are smooth, lack apical pits, and are arranged in 15 rows at mid-

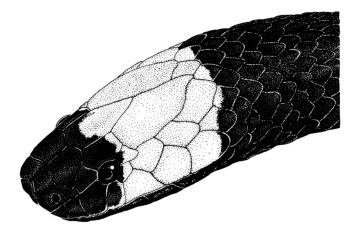

Fig. 195. Dorsolateral view of the head of *Micrurus nigrocinctus* (UMRC 89-18), 504 mm SVL; Honduras.

body. Supra-anal tubercles are present in adult males, and the anal plate is divided.

The color pattern on the body consists of a series of black rings bordered by narrow yellow rings and separated by broad red rings. The black snout is followed by a broad yellow ring across the posterior half of the head. This is bordered posteriorly by a black nape ring. The tail has three to eight black rings that are approximately equal to the yellow rings in width. The trailing edges of the red scales are heavily marked with black.

SIMILAR SPECIES *Micrurus nigrocinctus* differs from the various false coral snakes in lacking a loreal scale and possessing fewer than 17 rows of dorsal scales at midbody. In Belize, it differs from *M. diastema* and *M. hippocrepis* in possessing fewer than 30 black body rings and by the presence of supra-anal tubercles in males. Where it co-occurs with *M. nigrocinctus*, *M. diastema* has heavier, more uniform black pigment on the red scales. In Belize both *M. diastema* and *M. hippocrepis* usually have a yellow spot on the snout.

DISTRIBUTION *Micrurus nigrocinctus* occurs at low and moderate elevations on the Pacific slope from Chiapas and on the Atlantic slope from Belize through Central America to northern South America. In the Yucatán Peninsula this species is known only from Belize (Map 175).

NATURAL HISTORY This is a secretive, predominantly nocturnal coral snake that often hides in leaf litter. Nonetheless, specimens have been observed abroad during the day. In Chiapas, Schmidt and Smith (1943:28) observed a specimen at night crawling through bushes at a height of about 3 m. Smith

and Grant (1958:214) reported snakes, including other coral snakes, in the diet of *M. nigrocinctus* from Panama. Seib (1985a) studied the feeding habits of this species on coffee fincas in southern Chiapas and neighboring Guatemala and found the diet to consist exclusively of snakes, especially the genera *Adelphicos*, *Coniophanes*, *Geophis*, and *Ninia*. Greene and Seib (1983:406) summarized several published accounts involving 28 specimens of *M. nigrocinctus* from numerous localities and reported a caecilian, reptile eggs, and snakes in the diet.

Micrurus nigrocinctus is presumably oviparous, as are the other species of *Micrurus* for which data are available.

SUBSPECIES Numerous subspecies of this highly variable and wide-ranging species have been recog-

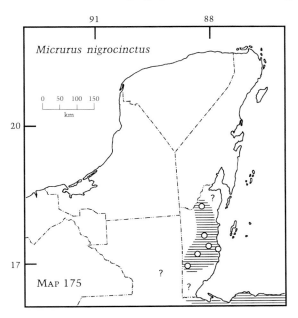

nized (Roze, 1967:38–40, 1982:306), but L. D. Wilson and Meyer (1972) recognized no subspecific taxa in Honduras, and Savage and Vial (1974) reached a similar conclusion with respect to this species in Costa Rica. If subspecies are recognized, the name *M. n. divaricatus* applies to the populations in Belize and northern Honduras.

ETYMOLOGY The specific name, *nigrocinctus*, is from the Latin *niger*, "dark" or "black," and *cinctus*, "banded," in reference to the black rings encircling the body.

COMMENT Information on the biology of *M. nigrocinctus* was summarized by Greene and Seib (1983), and the species was reviewed by J. A. Campbell and Lamar (1989).

Locality Records Belize: Belize: mi 39 on Western Hwy. (MCZ 152577); Cayo: Caracol (CMM photo), upper Raspaculo River basin (Stafford, 1991:16); Orange Walk: Guinea Grass Rd. ca. 4 mi S Northern Hwy. (CM 105735); Stann Creek: Middlesex (UCM 25710, 25722, 25726, 25749–50, 25809, 25885–88, 25890–94, 29979–80, 30885–87; CM 48010), Stann Creek (USNM 24906).

Family Viperidae (Vipers and Pitvipers)

Members of this large and widespread family have short, rotatable maxillary bones, each of which bears one or two enlarged, caniculate fangs. Their venoms are generally hemotoxins. Some vipers attain relatively enormous size (e.g., *Lachesis muta*, *Bothrops asper*) and are among the most dangerous of all venomous snakes. Viperids are typically nocturnal, heavy bodied, and terrestrial, but some are moderately slender and arboreal. Most species feed predominantly on vertebrates, at least as adults, and most are viviparous. The family is found everywhere in the world except Australia, most oceanic islands, and the higher latitudes. Relationships within the Viperidae are not well understood, although Cadle (1992) provided intriguing immunological evidence supporting the existence of several distinct lineages. Nearly 200 living species are recognized, grouped into approximately 28 genera. Six genera and 7 species of viperids occur in the Yucatán Peninsula.

Key to the Genera of the Family Viperidae

1. No rattle at tip of tail 2
   Rattle present at tip of tail . . . . *Crotalus*
2. Dorsal surface of head covered by small, irregular scales (Fig. 196B,C) 3
   Dorsal surface of head covered with enlarged, symmetrical plates (Fig. 196A) . . . *Agkistrodon*
3. Rostral scale not much wider than high; rostrum not upturned (Fig. 197A,C) 4
   Rostral scale much higher than wide; rostrum upturned (Fig. 197B) . . . . *Porthidium*
4. Supraoculars not bordered by enlarged, upward-projecting scales 5
   Supraoculars bordered by several enlarged, upward-projecting scales (Fig. 197C) . . . .
   . . . . *Bothriechis*
5. Subcaudal scales mostly divided . . . . *Bothrops*
   Subcaudal scales mostly undivided . . . . *Atropoides*

Clave para los Géneros de la Familia Viperidae

1. Sin cascabel en la punta de la cola 2
   Con cascabel en la punta de la cola . . . . *Crotalus*
2. Superficie dorsal de la cabeza cubierta por escamas pequeñas e irregulares (Fig. 196B,C) 3
   Superficie dorsal de la cabeza cubierta con placas alargadas y simétricas (Fig. 196A) . . . .
   . . . . *Agkistrodon*
3. Escama rostral no tan ancha como alta; rostrum no proyectado hacia arriba (Fig. 197A,C)
   4
   Escama rostral mucho más alta que ancha; rostrum proyectado hacia arriba (Fig. 197B) . . . . . .
   . . . . *Porthidium*

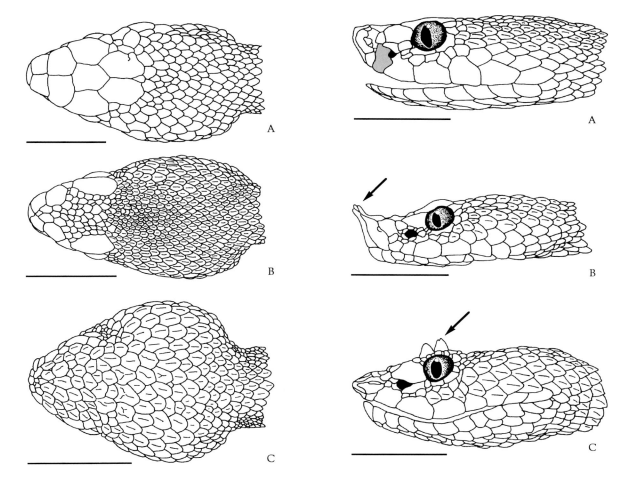

Fig. 196. Dorsal views of the heads of pitvipers. A, *Agkistrodon bilineatus* showing large symmetrical shields covering the dorsal surface of the head. *Bothrops asper* (B) and *Atropoides nummifer* (C) have numerous small scales covering the dorsal surface of the head. Line equals 1 cm.

Fig. 197. Lateral views of the heads of pitvipers. A, *Bothrops asper*, in which the second supralabial (*shaded*) enters the loreal pit; note the unmodified rostral and supraocular scales. B, *Porthidium nasutum* with upturned rostrum (*arrow*). C, *Bothriechis schlegelii* with enlarged, spinelike superciliary scales (*arrow*). Line equals 1 cm.

4. Las supraoculares sin escamas alargadas que las bordeen 5
   Las supraoculares bordeadas por varias escamas alargadas, proyectadas hacia arriba (Fig. 197C) . . . . *Bothriechis*
5. La mayoría de escamas subcaudales divididas . . . . *Bothrops*
   La mayoría de escamas subcaudales sin dividir . . . . *Atropoides*

Genus *Agkistrodon*
(Cottonmouths, Copperheads, and Their Allies)

This genus of pitvipers is exclusively a Northern Hemispheric group. The three New World species range collectively throughout the eastern United States southward through Mexico to Costa Rica. In the Old World, seven species are distributed from the vicinity of the Caspian Sea and northern India eastward through China to Japan. In the Yucatán Peninsula the genus is represented by one species, *Agkistrodon bilineatus*, the cantil. Gloyd and Conant (1990) provided an exhaustive summary of information on the genus *Agkistrodon*. Knight et al. (1992), who studied the evolution and systematics of the genus using molecular techniques, demonstrated the monophyly of the New World *Agkistro-*

don and supported the recognition of Old World *Agkistrodon* as a separate genus, *Gloydius*. *Agkistrodon* is derived from the Greek *ankistron*, "fishhook," and *odon*, "tooth," in reference to the fangs of the type species, *A. mokasen*.

Agkistrodon bilineatus (Günther)
(Figs. 196A, 198, 397; Map 176)

Ancistrodon bilineatus Günther 1863:364. HOLO-TYPE: BMNH 64.1.26.396. TYPE LOCALITY: Pacific coast of Guatemala.

Yucatecan cantil; cantil, cantil de agua, víbora pinta (Mexico); uolpoch (Yucatec Maya).

DESCRIPTION The adults of this medium-sized, stout-bodied pitviper average perhaps 500 to 600 mm in snout-vent length in the Yucatán Peninsula and reach a maximum of about 730 mm. The short tail is about 22 to 26 percent of the snout-vent length, and longer in males than in females. The head is depressed and roughly triangular in dorsal aspect and distinct from the neck. The pupils are vertically elliptical, and there is a deep loreal pit between the eye and the nostril (Fig. 198). The dorsal surface of the head is covered with enlarged, symmetrical shields (Fig. 196A). There are 23 (rarely 25) rows of dorsal scales at midbody, many of which bear a pair of apical pits. The dorsal scales are keeled, except for those of the first, and sometimes the second, scale rows. The anal plate and the proximal subcaudal scales are undivided, whereas the distal subcaudals are divided. The tip of the tail ends in a terminal spine that is deflected downward.

The dorsal ground color is tan, brown, or reddish brown with a series of 12 to 18 dark brown transverse bands (Fig. 397). The bands are lighter at their centers, and the scales at the borders of the bands are flecked with black and white. The dorsal surface of the head is a uniform dark brown. A thin white or cream stripe originates at the rostrum and passes posteriorly over and through the eye and then angles posteroventrally onto the base of the neck. Another light stripe, generally broader, originates at the rostrum and passes downward and posteriorly below the nostril and the loreal pit and then onto the upper labial scales. This stripe becomes irregular at the angle of the jaws and then merges with the light pigment on the lateral margins of the ventral scales. A vertical light line edged with black bisects the rostral scale and extends onto the mental. The chin is dark brown with numerous light spots, flecks, and short lines edged with black. The venter is brown, and the dark brown dorsal bands extend onto the lateral surfaces of the ventral scales. Numerous flecks of white bordered by dark brown or black are scattered over the ventral scales. According to L. E. Dieckman, of St. John's College, Belize (quoted in Gloyd and Conant, 1990:83), a specimen from Orange Walk Town had a bright green tail. Elsewhere in the range juveniles have yellowish tails.

SIMILAR SPECIES In addition to the distinctive facial pattern, *A. bilineatus* is the only pitviper in the Yucatán Peninsula that has large, symmetrical plates on the dorsal surface of the head (Fig. 196A).

DISTRIBUTION This species occurs at low and moderate elevations on the Pacific slope from Sonora south to northern Costa Rica. It occurs discontinuously on the Atlantic slope in Tamaulipas, San Luis Potosí, and Nuevo Leon, and in the Yucatán Peninsula, where it known from several localities in Yucatán, Campeche, northern Quintana Roo, and northern Belize (Map 176).

NATURAL HISTORY This snake is nocturnal, terrestrial, and, in the Yucatán Peninsula, uncommon. The Yucatecan cantil is primarily an inhabitant of deciduous and thorn forests, although there are a few records from the tall forests of Quintana Roo, and Hoevers and Henderson (1974:3) reported two

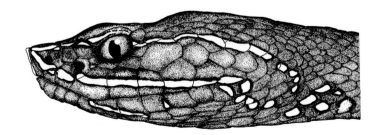

Fig. 198. Lateral view of the head of *Agkistrodon bilineatus* (UMRC 88-3), 388 mm SVL; 20 km ESE Mérida, Yucatán, Mexico.

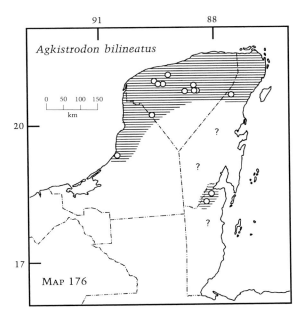

MAP 176

specimens "taken in a wet area near Santa Cruz" near Corozal Town, Belize.

Agkistrodon bilineatus is a dangerously venomous snake that is widely feared by the native people of Yucatán. It is believed to be capable of prodigious jumps and to deliver venom both through its bite and with its tail, which is thought to act as a stinger (see the account of the *uolpoch* in "Ethnoherpetology in the Yucatán Peninsula," in this volume). Gaige (1936:303) reported that a woman from Motul, Yucatán, died a few hours after being bitten by an *A. bilineatus* (UMMZ 73056).

Little information is available on the feeding habits of this species in the Yucatán Peninsula. Hoevers and Henderson (1974:4) reported a rodent in the stomach of a specimen from northern Belize, and I found a specimen in Yucatán with the remains of a small mammal in its stomach. Elsewhere this species consumes a wide variety of vertebrate prey, including snakes, amphibians, and fishes (Gloyd and Conant, 1990:78). Juvenile cantils attract their prey, which consists of small insectivorous vertebrates such as frogs and lizards, by elevating and wiggling the tail, which E. R. Allen (1949:226) described as bright yellow with a gray tip, "giving an unmistakable appearance of a yellow caterpillar with a head."

Agkistrodon bilineatus is viviparous. According to Alvarez del Toro (1983:204), the brood size is 12 to 20 in Chiapas. E. R. Allen (1949:225) reported that a specimen from Mexico gave birth to a brood of 8 on 5 July 1948. Hoevers and Henderson (1974:4)

reported on a specimen from northern Belize that contained 12 oviductal eggs.

SUBSPECIES In the most recent comprehensive review of variation in *A. bilineatus*, Gloyd and Conant (1990:59) recognized four subspecies, of which *A. b. russeolus* occurs within, and is restricted to, the Yucatán Peninsula.

ETYMOLOGY The specific name, *bilineatus*, derives from the Latin prefix *bi-*, "two" or "twice," and *lineatus*, "streaked," "marked with lines," in reference to the distinct facial pattern.

Likewise, the common name *cantil* derives from the Tzeltal Mayan words *kan*, "yellow," and *tlil*, "lips," also in reference to the striking facial pattern (Corzo, 1978:38).

COMMENT Gloyd and Conant (1990:63–64) pointed out that after the original description by Günther, the holotype of *A. bilineatus* (BMNH 64.1.26.396) was confused with a specimen from Belize (BMNH 1946.1.19.97); the latter was incorrectly cited as the holotype by several authors.

Agkistrodon bilineatus was reviewed by Gloyd and Conant (1990) as part of their monographic treatment of the genus *Agkistrodon*, and the species was treated thoroughly by J. A. Campbell and Lamar (1989).

Locality Records Belize: Corozal: Santa Cruz (Hoevers and Henderson, 1974:3); Orange Walk: Orange Walk Town (MPM 21173); no specific locality (BMNH 1946.1.19.97; FMNH 4196). *Mexico*: Campeche: 5 km S Champotón (KU 70903); Quintana Roo: Cobá (KU 206242); Yucatán: Chichén Itzá (UMMZ 83934), Libre Unión (FMNH 36253), Mérida (FMNH 19425), 20 km ESE Mérida (UMRC 88-3), Motul (UMMZ 73056), Pisté (CM 47014, 47168–69, 49834–37; KU 70904; UCM 40640–41, 41792), 11.7 km N Pisté (KU 70905), ca. 20 km SW Santa Elena (JCL photo), Tekik de Regil (UMRC 84-114).

Genus *Atropoides* (Jumping Vipers)

The three species that form this small genus of pitvipers collectively range from San Luis Potosí on the Atlantic slope and Oaxaca on the Pacific slope to Panama. All are stout-bodied, terrestrial forms that occur at low and moderate elevations. One species of *Atropoides* occurs in the Yucatán Peninsula. The members of the genus *Atropoides* were formerly placed in the genus *Porthidium*, and before that in the genus *Bothrops*. Werman (1992) used cladistic analysis of biochemical and morphological data to conclude that the jumping vipers constitute a monophyletic group, and he therefore erected the genus *Atropoides* to accommodate the three species. At the time of this writing Dwight Lawson, of the University of Texas at Arlington, is studying the relationships among the members of the genus. *Atropoides* is named after the Greek goddess Atropos, who cuts the thread of life; the suffix *-oides* means "similar to" or "having the nature of."

Atropoides nummifer (Rüppell)
(Figs. 150D, 196C, 398; Map 177)

Atropos nummifer Rüppell 1845:313. HOLOTYPE: SMF 21196. TYPE LOCALITY: unknown. W. L. Burger (1950:62) suggested restriction to Teapa, Tabasco, Mexico.

Jumping pitviper; jumping tommygoff (Belize); brazo de piedra (Guatemala); nauyaca saltadora (Mexico); uol pooch (Yucatec Maya).

DESCRIPTION   This extremely thick-bodied pitviper averages about 400 to 600 mm in snout-vent length. The tail is short, approximately 10 to 15 percent of the head and body length. The head is broad and distinct from the neck in dorsal aspect, and the snout is bluntly rounded (Fig. 196C). The eyes are relatively small, and the pupils are vertically elliptical. There is a deep loreal pit situated on the side of the head between the eye and the nostril (Fig. 150D). The dorsal scales are arranged in 23 to 31 rows and are heavily keeled, producing a rugose appearance. Apical pits are lacking. The subcaudals and anal plate are undivided.

The dorsal ground color is tan or gray with a series of dark brown or black middorsal diamond-shaped blotches (Fig. 398). A series of dark lateral blotches may or may not coalesce with the middorsal series. The dorsal surface of the head is dark brown or gray, and the lateral surfaces are lighter and bear a distinct dark postocular stripe. The ventral coloration is cream or tan, and some specimens have bold markings of brown or black squares; in others the venter is devoid of dark markings. In juveniles the tip of the tail is yellow (W. T. Neill, 1960:114), suggesting use as a caudal lure to attract frogs and lizards.

SIMILAR SPECIES   Owing to its short, thick body this viper is not likely to be confused with any other. In the Yucatán Peninsula the species of *Porthidium* are smaller and have upturned rostral scales (Fig. 197B). *Bothrops asper* is much larger and slenderer, and it has divided subcaudal scales, whereas the majority of the subcaudals are undivided in *A. nummifer*.

DISTRIBUTION   The jumping viper occurs at low, moderate, and intermediate elevations on the Atlantic slope from San Luis Potosí south and eastward to Panama, on the Pacific slope from Oaxaca to El Salvador, and in Costa Rica and Panama. The species is restricted to the base of the Yucatán Peninsula in El Petén and Belize (Map 177).

NATURAL HISTORY   This snake is a terrestrial inhabitant of primary forest. W. T. Neill (1962:243) characterized the jumping viper in Belize as a rainforest and jungle form. Stuart (1935:55) reported a specimen from the high bush of central El Petén, and Duellman (1963:245) found specimens on the forest floor in southern El Petén. In Chiapas, juveniles have been found in trees at heights of up to 3 m (Alvarez del Toro, 1983:209).

According to Alvarez del Toro (1983:209), the jumping viper feeds on rodents, and captives accept mice. March (cited in Picado, 1931:67) stated that newborns in Costa Rica fed on grasshoppers and crickets. The yellow tail tip of young individuals probably serves as a lure to attract frogs and lizards, likely prey of juveniles. *Atropoides nummifer* is preyed on by *Drymarchon corais*, for Duellman

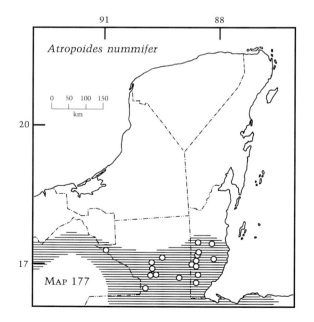

(1963:239) found the remains of one in the stomach of a *Drymarchon* in southern El Petén. Gerhardt et al. (1993:350) reported that at Tikal, Guatemala, *Atropoides nummifer* is preyed on by the great black hawk, *Buteogallus urubitinga*. Chiszar (1989) noted that the predatory strike of the jumping viper differs from that of most terrestrial vipers in that the prey is held in the jaws rather than released, and that a fold of skin covers the pit and partially covers the eye during such episodes, presumably protecting these delicate sensory organs during the prey's death struggle.

This dangerously venomous snake is reputed to be able to strike great distances and to be able to launch itself into the air, hence the English common name. In fact, jumping vipers, like most other vipers, are capable of striking about one-half their own body length. They do, however, exhibit a dramatic defensive mouth-gape behavior when threatened. According to J. A. Campbell and Lamar (1989:324) this species may possess a relatively weak venom, for several victims of snakebite in Guatemala and Honduras suffered localized pain and swelling but recovered completely within a few days.

This species is viviparous, and parturition occurs during the summer rainy season. W. T. Neill (1962:243) found juveniles in August and September in Belize that he estimated had been born in August. Rokosky (1941:267) reported that a 530-mm female from Honduras gave birth to 21 young on 17 July at the Chicago Zoological Park. A second female, measuring 670 mm and also from Honduras, gave birth to 17 young on 25 July. This female died the following day and was found to contain six additional offspring. The average total length of the two broods was 178 and 202 mm, respectively. Broods of 5 to 27 have been recorded for snakes from Costa Rica (Picado, 1931:67).

SUBSPECIES As discussed by L. D. Wilson and Meyer (1985:123–124), the relationships among the various geographical segments of this species are poorly understood, and its infraspecific taxonomy is thus confused. Perhaps three subspecies can be recognized, of which *A. n. mexicanum* occurs in the Yucatán Peninsula.

ETYMOLOGY The specific name, *nummifer*, may derive from the Latin *nummus*, "a piece of money," "a coin," and *-fer*, a suffix meaning "bearing," perhaps in reference to the dorsal pattern of blotches.

COMMENT Information on *A. nummifer* was summarized by J. A. Campbell and Lamar (1989).

Locality Records   Belize: Cayo: Augustine (AMNH 126443), Caracol (CMM photo), Central Farm (MCZ 71665), Cohune Ridge (UMMZ 80724), N side Mountain Pine Ridge (AMNH 126446–47), Mountain Pine Ridge (MPM 8192–93), Dry Creek at Hummingbird Hwy. (AMNH 126448), Valentin (UMMZ 80723); Stann Creek: Double Falls (FMNH 49357); Toledo: near Esperanza (UMMZ 80722), 1 mi W Salamanca (CM 105852). *Guatemala*: El Petén: 15 km NW Chinajá (KU 55707, 58104), El Rosario (JCL sight record), La Libertad (USNM 25133), near La Libertad (UMMZ 74916), Piedras Negras (MCZ 46861; UIMNH 40711; USNM 110426, 110428), ca. 9 km NW Poptún (UMMZ 124354), Sacluc (USNM 25133), Sayaxché (KU 55706), Sojio (AMNH 69985), Yalpemech (FMNH 40884).

Genus *Bothriechis* (Palm Pitvipers)

This is a moderately small genus of slender, mostly arboreal New World pitvipers. Most members of the genus are montane forms, and all but one of the seven species are restricted to Middle America. Only the wide-ranging *B. schlegelii*, the only *Bothriechis* found in the Yucatán Peninsula, occurs north of the Isthmus of Tehauntepec and south of Panama. For many years the palm pitvipers were placed in the genus *Bothrops*, and much of the early literature on these snakes will be found under that generic name. Burger (1971) partitioned the genus *Bothrops* into five genera and applied the name *Bothriechis* for the predominantly Central American arboreal forms. This arrangement was followed by Campbell and Lamar (1989), and Werman (1992) provided support for this classificaiton based on a cladistic analysis of biochemical and morphological data. Crother et al. (1992) examined the historical biogeography of the genus and its phylogenetic relationships. *Bothriechis* is from the Greek *bothros*, "hole" or "trench," and *echis*, "viper," presumably a reference to the infrared heat receptor pits that perforate the loreal region.

Bothriechis schlegelii (Berthold)
(Figs. 197C, 199, 399; Map 178)

Trigonocephalus schlegelii Berthold 1846:13. HOLOTYPE: ZFMK 121/261. TYPE LOCALITY: Popayan Province, Colombia.

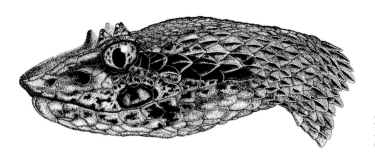

Fig. 199. Lateral view of the head of *Bothriechis schlegelii*, 415 mm SVL; Costa Rica.

Eyelash palm pitviper; eyelash viper, green tommygoff, horned palm viper (Belize); víbora del árbol (Guatemala); nauyaca cornuda, nauyaca de pestanas (Mexico).

DESCRIPTION   This moderately small viper can be immediately distinguished from all other snakes in the Yucatán Peninsula on the basis of the enlarged, upward-projecting superciliary scales bordering the supraocular scales (Figs. 197C, 199). Large specimens may exceed 800 mm in total length, but the average is between 500 and 600 mm. These are rather slender snakes, with a head that is distinct from the neck and roughly triangular in dorsal aspect. The eyes are relatively small, the pupils are vertically elliptical, and there is a deep loreal pit between the eye and the nostril. The dorsal scales are heavily keeled, lack apical pits, and are arranged in 21 to 25 (usually 23) rows. The temporal scales and those on the dorsal surface of the head are also keeled. Most of the subcaudal scales are undivided, and the anal plate is entire.

This species is highly variable in color and pattern both throughout its range and within local populations. In southeastern Mexico and northern Central America the dorsal ground color of most specimens is predominantly greenish gray with brown, tan, or rusty blotches (Fig. 399). The blotches may be arranged in two paravertebral series, which are often offset, producing a staggered pattern. The blotches are generally lighter at their centers and outlined in dark brown or black. There is a series of small, dark spots on the lateral surfaces of the body, and these may extend onto the lateral surfaces of the ventral scales. A distinct dark postorbital stripe is present, and the iris is yellow or yellowish orange.

SIMILAR SPECIES   The "eyelashes"—enlarged superciliary scales bordering the supraocular scales (Figs. 197C, 199)—distinguish this snake from all others in the Yucatán Peninsula.

DISTRIBUTION   *Bothriechis schlegelii* occurs at low elevations on the Atlantic slope from northern Chiapas and northern Guatemala and Belize through Central America to Pacific Colombia, Ecuador, and extreme northwestern Venezuela. It is known from several localities in northern Chiapas, El Petén, and Belize in the base of the Yucatán Peninsula (Map 178).

NATURAL HISTORY   The eyelash viper, an arboreal form with a prehensile tail, is rare in the Yucatán Peninsula. Duellman (1963:245) reported finding one in the thatched roof of a house in El Petén, but they are more typically found in forest settings. Specimens are occasionally found sunning themselves on leaves or branches, but usually they are active at night.

In Chiapas eyelash vipers feed on *Anolis* lizards, frogs, and mice (Alvarez del Toro, 1983:212). The stomach of a specimen from El Petén contained the

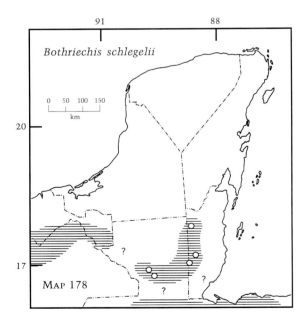

remains of a small mammal (Duellman, 1963:245), and captives readily accept mice. The adaptive significance of the enlarged scales bordering the supraocular scales is uncertain, but Cohen and Myers (1970:575) suggested that they protect the eyes from abrasion as the animal crawls through vegetation.

Although it is a relatively small snake, *B. schlegelii* has especially potent venom (Minton and Minton, 1969:217), and three to six people die each year in Costa Rica after being bitten (Seifert, 1983:385). Most of the bites sustained by humans are on the upper parts of the body because the snakes are in trees or shrubs when they are encountered. When disturbed, the eyelash viper assumes a defensive posture with the mouth agape.

Nothing is known of the reproductive biology of this species in the Yucatán Peninsula. Picado (1931:79) reported a brood of 18 born to a female from Costa Rica. Antonio (1980) observed mating and reproduction in captives from Honduras. Copulation occurred late on the evening of 24 February, and parturition was on 9 August, after a gestation period of 166 days. Four infertile eggs and 20 live neonates were produced. The snakes averaged 198 mm in snout-vent length and had an average tail length of 34 mm. The young snakes accepted frogs of the genera *Eleutherodactylus* and *Hyla* as food and used their brightly colored tails as lures, confirming W. T. Neill's suggestion (1960:184) that *B. schlegelii* exhibits caudal luring behavior.

SUBSPECIES   Taylor (1954) described *Bothrops schlegelii supraciliaris* on the basis of a single specimen from Costa Rica. Stuart (1963:131) considered *supraciliaris* specifically distinct, but L. D. Wilson and Meyer (1982) concluded that the Costa Rican specimen is really a slightly aberrant *B. schlegelii*, a view confirmed by Werman (1984:485), who concluded that *B. s. supraciliaris* is not a valid subspecies. Thus, no subspecies of *Bothriechis schlegelii* are presently recognized.

ETYMOLOGY   The specific name, *schlegelii*, is a patronym honoring Hermann Schlegel, a nineteenth-century naturalist who wrote extensively on reptiles and amphibians.

COMMENT   Information on *B. schlegelii* was summarized by J. A. Campbell and Lamar (1989), and the relationship of this species to other members of the genus *Bothriechis* was examined by Crother et al. (1992).

Locality Records Belize: Cayo: Chiquibul Forest Reserve (MPM 191), Valentin (UMMZ 80725); Orange Walk: Gallon Jug (FMNH 69234). *Guatemala*: El Petén: El Rosario (JCL sight record), Paso Subín (KU 58105).

Genus *Bothrops* (Lanceheads)

This genus of New World pitvipers comprises 31 living species, most of which inhabit the lowland tropics of South America. On the mainland only *B. asper* occurs north of Colombia, and thus only that species occurs in the Yucatán Peninsula. Lanceheads are predominantly terrestrial, although some do climb, especially as juveniles. Members of the genus *Bothrops* are very venomous, and some reach relatively enormous size, in excess of 2,000 mm. Throughout the New World tropics many deaths are attributable to these formidable animals each year. *Bothrops* derives from the Greek *bothros*, "hole" or "trench," and *ops*, "eye," "face," or "countenance," presumably referring to the deep loreal pit present in members of this genus.

Bothrops asper (Garman)
(Figs. 196B, 197A, 400; Map 179)

Trigonocephalus asper Garman, 1884:124. HOLOTYPE: MCZ 2718. TYPE LOCALITY: Obispo, Panama.

Terciopelo, fer-de-lance; yellow-jaw tommygoff (Belize); cantil devanador (Guatemala); barba amarilla, cola blanca, cola de hueso, cuatro narices, nauyaca real, víbora de sangre (Mexico); kum cokoo, taxinchan (Yucatec Maya).

DESCRIPTION   The fer-de-lance, the largest and most dangerous of the venomous snakes in the Yucatán Peninsula, may attain a total length in excess of 2,000 mm; fortunately, most individuals are substantially smaller. The head is roughly triangular in dorsal aspect and is distinct from the neck (Fig. 400). The eyes are moderately large, and the pupils are vertically elliptical. There is a deep loreal pit between the eye and the nostril. The second supralabial scale (lacunolabial) forms the anterior margin of the loreal pit (Fig. 197A). The interorbital scales are small, keeled, and disposed irregularly over the dorsal surface of the head. The number of rows of dorsal scales at midbody varies from 25 to 29. The dorsal scales are heavily keeled and lack apical pits.

The anal plate is undivided, and most of the subcaudal scales are divided.

Color and pattern vary considerably within and among populations. In the Yucatán Peninsula the dorsal ground color is usually tan, brown, or gray, sometimes with a pinkish cast. The head is generally uniform dark gray or brown above, whereas the chin, loreal region, and labial scales are lighter, usually with a distinct yellowish suffusion. There is a distinct dark postocular stripe, usually with a light border along its upper margin. On the body the dorsal pattern consists of two series of triangular dark blotches arranged with their apices pointing toward the midline and their bases oriented ventrally. These blotches may be situated opposite one another, thus producing an hourglass pattern, or they may be staggered, giving a zigzag appearance. The blotches are generally lighter at their centers, and they often have light borders. Darker patches of scales may be embedded within the blotches, especially at the apices. Alternating with the blotches are lighter interspaces that often have indistinct darker spots. The venter is cream or grayish with a suffusion of darker pigment. An irregular series of dark lateral spots extends onto the lateral surfaces of the ventral scales. In juveniles the tip of the tail is yellowish or yellowish orange, suggesting its use as a caudal lure. W. L. Burger and Smith (1950:431) reported that the yellow tail is present only in males.

SIMILAR SPECIES   The adults of *B. asper* can be distinguished from all other rattleless pitvipers in the Yucatán Peninsula by their size alone. Small specimens differ from members of the genera *Atropoides* and *Porthidium* in possessing divided subcaudal scales and a lacunolabial scale (Fig. 197A). *Xenodon rabdocephalus*, a possible mimic of *B. asper*, has a round pupil, lacks a loreal pit, and has smooth dorsal scales that are arranged in 19 rows at midbody.

DISTRIBUTION   *Bothrops asper* is found at low and moderate elevations on the Atlantic slope from Tamaulipas southward through Central America to Ecuador, Colombia, and Venezuela. An apparently disjunct population occurs on the Pacific slope of Chiapas and Guatemala. This species is widespread in the Yucatán Peninsula everywhere but in the arid northwest corner (but see Comment) (Map 179).

NATURAL HISTORY   The fer-de-lance is typically terrestrial, although individuals, especially juve-

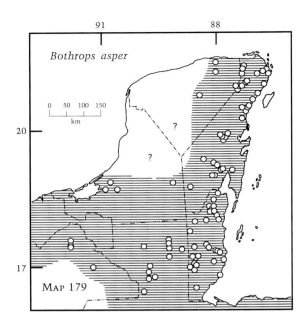

Map 179

niles, are occasionally found in trees. This species is common in the eastern and southern portions of the Yucatán Peninsula, where it is frequently encountered in and around human habitations, milpas, and second-growth vegetation in addition to primary forest.

Large size, an excitable disposition, and a propensity to live near humans all combine to make this an extremely dangerous snake, and many human fatalities are attributable to this formidable animal each year in Middle America. The bite can cause intense pain, swelling and edema, discoloration and blisters on the affected area, severe headache, and gastrointestinal hemorrhage and vomiting, as I can personally attest. Colwell (1985) gave an especially entertaining account of *B. asper* envenomation, and D. L. Hardy (1994a,b) summarized a number of case histories of *B. asper* bites (including mine). In my experience fer-de-lances show great variation in temperament. Some are sluggish and lethargic; others are quickly aroused, move rapidly, and strike viciously.

The adults of *B. asper* feed predominantly on birds and small mammals, but Stuart (1948:87) found the remains of a skink (*Sphenomorphus cherriei*) as well as mammalian remains in the stomachs of specimens from Alta Verapaz. Henderson and Hoevers (1977b:352) found a mammal in the stomach of a specimen from northern Belize, and Sexton and Heatwole (1965:42) found *Anolis limifrons* and mammal hair in the stomachs of Panamanian specimens. W. L. Burger and Smith (1950:432) reported that a young captive *B. asper* killed and attempted to swallow a young timber rattlesnake (*Crotalus horridus*). Another young *B. asper* attempted unsuccessfully to swallow a littermate, and, failing that, swallowed a *Storeria dekayi* instead. Juveniles also consume small frogs, and Greene (1992:112) found a centipede in the stomach of a juvenile from Colombia. This information suggests a shift in diet from invertebrates and small vertebrates (frogs, lizards, and snakes) in juveniles to birds and mammals in adults.

Bothrops asper is viviparous. W. T. Neill (1962:243) estimated that a juvenile collected on 4 November in Cayo District had been born the preceding August. Solórzano and Cerdas (1989) studied reproduction in this species on both the Atlantic and Pacific slopes in Costa Rica. Snakes from both slopes produced broods of 5 to 86 young. Pacific slope snakes mated between September and November, with parturition occurring between April and June. Snakes from the Atlantic slope mated in March and gave birth between September and November. Females became reproductive at a snout-vent length of about 1.1 m, males at about 1 m.

SUBSPECIES Some herpetologists recognize the snakes in Mexico, Central America, and portions of northern South America as a subspecies of *Bothrops atrox* (see Comment).

ETYMOLOGY The specific name, *asper*, is Latin meaning "rough, thorny," perhaps in reference to the heavily keeled scales on the dorsum.

COMMENT The taxonomic status of this species and its close relative *B. atrox* of South America is uncertain and confused. Some systematists treat the two as subspecies of a single species (e.g., Klemmer, 1963), some decline to recognize even a subspecific distinction between the two (Villa, 1984b; L. D. Wilson and Meyer, 1985), and still others regard the two forms as specifically distinct (J. A. Campbell and Lamar, 1989). Markezich and Taphorn (1993) advocated conspecificity based on morphology and color pattern of specimens from western Venezuela, but they were unwilling to synonymize the two species without having more information about variation in other populations. Only additional investigation will resolve the issue.

A record of *B. asper* from Mérida, Yucatán (FMNH 36166), is based on a specimen from a collection assembled by Eunice Blackburn of the Colegio Americana, Mérida, and deposited at the Field Museum in 1934. I suggest that the specimen actually origi-

nated elsewhere, as there are apparently no other confirmed records of this species from the arid northwest corner of the Yucatán Peninsula.

Information on the biology of *B. asper* was summarized by J. A. Campbell and Lamar (1989).

Locality Records Belize: Belize: Rockstone Pond (UU 9297–98), mi 32 on Northern Hwy. (MPM 10792); Cayo: Augustine (CM 105958; W. T. Neill, 1962:243; MPM 7716–17), near Augustine (MPM 8195), 5 mi ENE Augustine (LSUMZ 11640), 0.4 mi S Belmopan (KU 157657), 10 mi S Belmopan (CM 114642), Caracol (CMM photo), 20 mi S Cayo (MCZ 61074), Central Farm (MCZ 71663), Macal River at Guacamallo Bridge (CM 112151–52), 3 mi from Millionario Camp (UMMZ 124662), Valentin (UMMZ 80726); Corozal: Cerro Maya, across bay from Corozal (JLK 501), near Corozal (MPM 8159–61), Santa Cruz (MPM 7387); Orange Walk: Cinderella Town (MPM 8150), 8 mi SW Gallon Jug (MCZ 71664), Kate's Lagoon (FMNH 49358), Lamanai (ROM H12778), Orange Walk (MPM 7610), Río Bravo Management Area, N Gallon Jug (UF 79987), San Estevan (MPM 7386), Tower Hill (MPM 7385), near Tower Hill (MPM 8151–58), mi 40 on Northern Hwy. (MPM 7762); Stann Creek: Cockscomb Range W of Kendall (CM 105992), Freetown (CM S 8512), near Mango Creek (MPM 7715), Middlesex (CM 47997–8000; UCM 25882–84, 29952–53, 30833–35), 4 mi E Middlesex (JLK 454), 10 mi W Stann Creek (JLK 456), 15 mi W Stann Creek (JLK 455); Toledo: Blue Creek Village (UTA R-11072). *Guatemala*: El Petén: 15 km NW Chinajá (KU 55704), 4 km from El Cruce (AMNH uncat.), El Rosario (JCL sight record), La Libertad (UMMZ 74914–15, 79065), 6 km from Naranjo on Flores-Melchor Rd. (AMNH uncat.), Paso Caballos (FMNH 22211; MCZ 38594; UMMZ 79064), Sayaxché (KU 57138), Sojio (AMNH 69972), Tikal (MCZ 58759–60; UF 13856–65; UMMZ 117946–52, 117964–65, 118252–53, 120316–17, 126423, UTA R-22226), Uaxactún (FMNH 23796; UMMZ 70459–60) 8 mi S Uaxactún (KU 157658); no specific locality (USNM 71780). *Mexico*: Campeche: ca. 19 km E Cayal (UTA R-16961), Encarnación (FMNH 105314–18; UIMNH 40716–18), 5 mi W Escárcega (UCM 28151), rd. to Sabancuy, 10.4 km N Hwy. 186 (UMRC 85-21), 8 km N Xpujil (KU 75001), Campeche–Quintana Roo border (AMNH 7860); Chiapas: Laguna Ocotal (MCZ 53886), Palenque (KU 94137; MZFC 35; USNM 110430), 10 mi S Palenque (LSUMZ 33217), 13 mi S Palenque (LSUMZ 33216); Quintana Roo: 7 mi W Bacalar (LSUMZ 33219), 10 mi W Bacalar (LSUMZ 33218), Cancún (López-Gonzales, 1991:106), 39.2 km N Cobá (UMRC 87-15), 64 km N Chetumal (CAS 114058), 86 km W Chetumal (KU 75002–3), 41.5 mi SE Chunhuhub (LSUMZ 40498), Chunyaxché (Himmelstein, 1980:32), Felipe Carrillo Puerto (UMMZ 113574–79), 5 km NE Felipe Carrillo Puerto (KU 171742), 7.8 km N Felipe Carrillo Puerto

(JCL photo), 8.2 mi NE Felipe Carrillo Puerto (KU 157660), 17.4 km NW Felipe Carrillo Puerto (JCL 6829), 17.9 mi NE Felipe Carrillo Puerto (KU 157659), 18.4 km NW Felipe Carrillo Puerto (JCL 6832), 19.3 km N Felipe Carrillo Puerto (JCL 6828), Hwy. 307, 5.5 km S rd. to Majahual (JCL sight record), Kantunil Kin (JCL photo), 3.5 km W Kantunil Kin (JCL sight record), 17.7 km NW Kantunil Kin (UMRC 79-270), 22.5 km N Kantunil Kin (KU 171758), 5.9 km NE Leona Vicario (EAL 2850), 5 mi S Los Palmas (UCM 39528), 40 km NW Majahual (MZCIQRO 25), 2.4 km W Noh Bec (UMRC 84-36), Playa del Carmen (Himmelstein, 1980:31), 28.5 km S Playa del Carmen (JCL 6806), 12.2 km ESE Petcacab (JCL sight record), Pueblo Nuevo X-Can (CM 45812–21, 49058, 49089, 49100, 49106, 49126, 49133, 49164, 49170; KU 70906; LSUMZ 28263; UCM 28152, 28157, 40642–46, 40740–41, 41795–96), 2 km E Pueblo Nuevo X-Can (LSUMZ 28259), 4 mi E Pueblo Nuevo X-Can (UCM 28153), 2 km W Pueblo Nuevo X-Can (LSUMZ 28258), 12 mi E Pueblo Nuevo X-Can (UCM 28154), 17.5 km ENE Pueblo Nuevo X-Can (KU 70907), Puerto Juárez (Himmelstein, 1980:32), 9 km W Puerto Juárez (KU 70908), Puerto Morelos (Himmelstein, 1980:32; López-Gonzales, 1991:106), Punto Venado (López-Gonzales, 1991:106), Río Hondo (CM 16802), 12.1 mi S Río Lagartos (KU 157663), Tintal (UCM 40647, 41793–94), 6 km N Tizimín (KU 75004), vicinity Tulum (LSUMZ 38663), 9.1 km NW Tulum (UMRC 84-35), 12 km NE Tulum (CAS 150329), 16 km NE Tulum (CAS 150330), 8.1 mi SW Vicente Guerrero (KU 157661); Yucatán: Chichén Itzá (MCZ 26834), X-Can (CM 46855–59, 46893–97, 47064–74), 3 km W X-Can (LSUMZ 28257), 2.5 mi E X-Can (UCM 28156), 4 mi E X-Can (UCM 28155).

Genus *Crotalus* (Rattlesnakes)

This is a moderately large genus of strictly New World pitvipers. All but one of the 26 species are restricted to North America, and the genus is most diverse on and adjacent to the Mexican Plateau. One species occurs in the Yucatán Peninsula. The definitive work on rattlesnakes is by Klauber (1956, 1972). J. A. Campbell and Lamar (1989) treated the Latin American species of *Crotalus*, a name derived from the Greek *krotalon*, "a rattle."

Crotalus durissus Linnaeus
(Fig. 401; Map 180)

Crotalus durissus Linnaeus 1758:214. TYPE: lost, *fide* Klauber, 1956:31. TYPE LOCALITY: America; restricted to Jalapa, Veracruz, Mexico, by H. M. Smith

and Taylor (1950b:348), but that restriction questioned by Klauber (1956:31).

Tropical rattlesnake; rattlesnake (Belize); cascabel (Guatemala, Mexico); cascabel tropical, culebra de hueso, víbora de cascabel, víbora real (Mexico); ahau-can, tzabcan (Yucatec Maya).

DESCRIPTION This is a very large, heavy-bodied, and extremely dangerous snake (Fig. 401). The males may attain a snout-vent length of 1,600 mm; the females reach 1,555 mm. The head is broad, roughly triangular in dorsal aspect, and distinct from the neck. There is a deep pit between the eye and the nostril. The eyes are moderately large with vertically elliptical pupils. The dorsal scales are tuberculate and heavily keeled, producing an extremely rugose appearance. They are arranged in 27 to 31 (usually 29) rows at midbody and lack apical pits. Tropical rattlesnakes have a pronounced spinal ridge that is most conspicuous on the anterior portions of large individuals. The anal plate and most of the subcaudals are undivided. The tail terminates in a keratinized rattle.

The dorsal ground color is tan, yellowish, or grayish, with a middorsal series of dark brown diamond-shaped blotches. The blotches have lighter centers and are bordered with white or cream. Dark brown triangular markings are present on the lateral surfaces of the body. These markings are also bordered with white or cream and may coalesce with the dorsal blotches. Posteriorly the dorsal pattern becomes obscure, and the tail is generally a uniform brown or gray. The dorsal surface of the head is tan or gray with irregular dark brown markings on the supraocular and prefrontal scales. A pair of dark brown stripes, each approximately two scales wide, originates at the level of the supraocular scales and passes posteriorly onto the anterior portion of the body. The chin and the ventral surface of the body are immaculate cream, tan, or gray. The subcaudal scales are darker brown or gray.

SIMILAR SPECIES This distinctive snake can scarcely be confused with any other, for it is the only one in the Yucatán Peninsula with a rattle. In addition, no other snake in the Yucatán Peninsula combines a dorsal pattern of diamond-shaped blotches on the body with a pair of stripes on the head and neck.

DISTRIBUTION *Crotalus durissus* has the most extensive geographical distribution of any rattle-

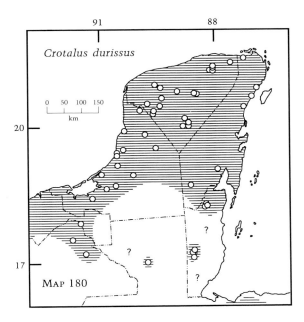

Crotalus durissus

MAP 180

snake. In Middle America it occurs at low and moderate elevations on the Atlantic slope in Tamaulipas and Nuevo Leon, and from central Veracruz south and eastward through the Yucatán Peninsula to northern Honduras. On the Pacific slope it occurs from Michoacán east and southward to Costa Rica. The tropical rattlesnake is widely distributed in South America as well, occurring as far south as central Argentina. The species occurs through the northern portion of the Yucatán Peninsula and as isolated populations in northern Guatemala and central Belize (Map 180).

NATURAL HISTORY   Although there are a few records from the tall forests of Quintana Roo, the *tzabcan* is most commonly encountered in thorn forests and savannas, and most of the records are from the northwestern portion of the peninsula (Map 180). J. C. Lee (1980a:30) conjectured that *Bothrops asper* might outcompete *C. durissus* in the mesic forests on the eastern side of the Yucatán Peninsula, although the two species are sympatric in southwestern Campeche, eastern Yucatán, and northern Quintana Roo. In El Petén and neighboring Belize this rattlesnake is apparently restricted to savanna habitats (Fugler, 1960:12; Stuart, 1935:55). Despite Armstrong and Murphy's (1979:15) assertion to the contrary, in the Yucatán Peninsula this is not a rainforest form.

The tropical rattlesnake is terrestrial and may be diurnal, crepuscular, or nocturnal, depending on the season. During the cooler months of the dry sea-

son individuals are generally encountered abroad during the day, whereas during the warmer months of the rainy season activity tends to be crepuscular and nocturnal.

Large size and an unpredictable disposition (Armstrong and Murphy, 1979:15) make this an extremely dangerous snake. It is quite capable of delivering a life-threatening bite; indeed, many fatalities in Central and South America are attributable to this formidable animal. J. A. Campbell and Lamar (1989:345) reported a mortality rate of 72 percent for untreated bites of *C. d. terrificus* in Brazil. Although the different clinical symptoms of envenomation by different subspecies suggest geographic variation in the chemical composition of the venom, all races of *C. durissus* should be considered extremely dangerous and treated accordingly.

The defensive posture is spectacular. When threatened, this snake elevates the anterior third of the body vertically off the ground and throws the neck into a hairpin curve with the head facing the adversary.

Although little is known about the diet in the Yucatán Peninsula, the tropical rattlesnake appears to prey predominantly on rodents. Klauber (1956:591) reported mammal remains in the stomachs of 13 specimens from the Yucatán Peninsula, and captives readily accept mice and rats. In other parts of the range this species is known to occasionally consume birds and lizards.

Like other *Crotalus*, *C. durissus* is viviparous. Armstrong and Murphy (1979:15) described courtship observed in captives from Yucatán. Copulation occurred on 2 January, and a brood of 21 young was produced on 31 August. Those authors reported other parturition dates of 2 and 3 August, and I observed newborn rattlesnakes in Yucatán and Quintana Roo in late August and early September. Dundee et al. (1986:47) noted a recently born specimen taken on 17 July in northwestern Yucatán. W. T. Neill (1962:242) reported an average total length at birth of 315 mm.

SUBSPECIES   J. A. Campbell and Lamar (1989:344) recognized 14 subspecies of this wide-ranging rattlesnake, whereas J. R. McCranie (1993) recognized 12 subspecies. Only *C. d. tzabcan* occurs in the Yucatán Peninsula.

ETYMOLOGY   The specific name, *durissus*, is from the Latin *durus*, "hard," and *issimus*, a superlative suffix denoting "very much, most."

COMMENT   Information on *C. durissus* was summarized by J. A. Campbell and Lamar (1989) and by J. R. McCranie (1993).

Locality Records   Belize: Cayo: Augustine Forestry Station (Fugler, 1960:12), 6 mi ENE Augustine (LSUMZ 11639), 3 mi S Blancaneaux Lodge (CM 105811), N side Mountain Pine Ridge (W. T. Neill, 1962:242), Mountain Pine Ridge Rd., 12.7 mi S Belize-Cayo Rd. (UMMZ 124661), 2 mi S San Luis (CM 105957); Orange Walk: August Pine Ridge (UF 83820), near Guinea Grass (MPM 8162–65), near Otro Benque (MPM 7763), Tower Hill (MPM 7388). *Guatemala*: El Petén: La Libertad (UMMZ 74917–18). *Mexico*: Campeche: Campeche (H. M. Smith, 1938:20), 1 mi N Champotón (UMMZ 73081), 5 km S Champotón (KU 70911–13), 30.9 mi S Champotón (EAL 1655), Dzibalchén (KU 75639–41), 6 km W Escárcega (KU 70914), 14 mi W Hopelchén (AMNH 93374), near Mamantel (JCL sight record), 6 mi W Río Candelaria (UCM 39529), 3.9 km S Sabancuy (JCL sight record), 5 mi S Sabancuy (UCM 18630), San José Carpizo (UMMZ 99835–36), Yohaltun, near Apazote (USNM 46399–400), 3.7 mi S Campeche-Yucatán border on Hwy. 261 (KU 157666); Chiapas: 12 mi SE Palenque (KU 94141), 10.9 km SE Penjamo on rd. to Bonampak (KU 171740); Quintana Roo: 7 mi N Bacalar (LSUMZ 46890–920), 86 km W Chetumal (KU 75005), 3.4 km S Chiquilá (JCL sight record), Paamul (Himmelstein, 1980:32), 3.2 km N Playa del Carmen (JCL 6812), 4 km N Tulum (CAS 154141); Tabasco: Emiliano Zapata (H. M. Smith, 1943:413); Yucatán: Calcaná (CM 45827), Calcehtok (AMNH 38837), Catmís (FMNH 26973), Chichén Itzá (AMNH 7863–64; FMNH 49367; MCZ 7125, 28750, 29244; UMMZ 83935; USNM 46570), 1.3 km N Colonia Yucatán (JCL sight record), Kantunil (FMNH 36167–69; UIMNH 39960), Mayapán (FMNH 40728), Mérida (Izamal) (USNM 6557), 15 mi SW Mérida (KU 159589), Peto (CM 45321), 24 km S Peto (UMMZ 113541), Pisté (CM 46973–77, 47019–21, 47195–212, 49878–93; KU 70915–17; UCM 16681, 40671–76), bet. Santa Elena and Kabah ruins (TU 19798), 8 km N, 10 km W Tizimín (KU 75006), 6 km N Tizimín (KU 75642), 8.2 mi N Tizimín (KU 157669), 12 mi N Tizimín (CM 40176), Uxmal (KU 158547–48; LACM 104859; UTA R-6732–35, 6802, 7647, 7676–77), Yokat (AMNH 38835–36).

Genus *Porthidium* (Hognosed Pitvipers)

Snakes of the genus *Porthidium* are generally small to medium-sized pitvipers with moderately stout bodies and short tails. The rostral scale is higher than wide, producing the upturned snout that gives this group its common name. This predominantly Middle American assemblage includes eight species distributed from San Luis Potosí and Colima southward through Central America to northern South America. Two species of hognosed pitvipers occur in the Yucatán Peninsula. All the species in the genus are treated in J. A. Campbell and Lamar, 1989. *Porthidium* comes from the Greek *portheo*, "to destroy" or "ravage," and *-idium*, a Latin diminutive suffix, presumably in reference to the small size but destructive capabilities of these snakes.

Key to the Species of the Genus *Porthidium*

Rostrum approximately twice as high as wide (Fig. 197B); usually 23 rows of dorsal scales at midbody; base of the Yucatán Peninsula (Map 181) . . . . *Porthidium nasutum*

Rostrum less than twice as high as wide; usually 25 rows of dorsal scales at midbody; northern third of Yucatán Peninsula (Map 182) . . . . *Porthidium yucatanicum*

Clave para las Especies del Género *Porthidium*

Rostrum aproximadamente dos veces más largo que ancho (Fig. 197B); usualmente con 23 hileras de escamas dorsales a la mitad del cuerpo; habitan en la base de la Península de Yucatán (Mapa 181) . . . . *Porthidium nasutum*

Rostrum menos dos veces más largo que ancho; usualmente 25 hileras de escamas dorsales a la mitad del cuerpo; habitan en el tercio norte de la Península de Yucatán (Mapa 182) . . . . *Porthidium yucatanicum*

Porthidium nasutum (Bocourt)
(Figs. 197B, 402; Map 181)

Bothrops nasutus Bocourt 1868:202. HOLOTYPE: MNHNP 1592. TYPE LOCALITY: a Pansos, sur les bords du Polochic (Guatemala).

Rainforest hognosed pitviper; xalpate de palo (Guatemala); nauyaca chatilla (Mexico); ek shush (Yucatec Maya).

DESCRIPTION This small, stout pitviper differs from all others in the Yucatán Peninsula in having a conspicuously upturned snout that is at least twice as high as wide (Fig. 197B). The adult females average about 315 mm in snout-vent length, whereas the considerably smaller males average only 255 mm (Porras et al., 1981). The head is broad, roughly triangular in dorsal aspect, and very distinct from the neck. The eyes are moderately large, and the pupil is vertically elliptical (Fig. 402). The dorsal scales are heavily keeled, lack apical pits, and are usually arranged in 23 rows at midbody. The anal plate is usually entire, and the subcaudals are mostly undivided.

The color and pattern are highly variable. In general, the juveniles are more brightly colored than the adults. Individuals are generally light to dark brown or gray above with a series of dark blotches down the dorsum, these often partly outlined in white. The right and left halves of the blotches are often offset at the midline, producing a zigzag pattern. The blotches become indistinct on the lateral surfaces of the body, where they may extend onto the lateral margins of the ventrals or may be replaced by a separate series of lateral blotches. Most specimens have a thin, pale vertebral stripe, although this becomes obscure in older specimens. The chin and venter are suffused with dark pigment. The head is usually dark, often uniformly so, but sometimes has a light postocular and/or subocular stripe, the latter extending onto the lower jaw. In juveniles the tip of the tail is yellowish white (W. T. Neill, 1960:113–114).

SIMILAR SPECIES *Porthidium yucatanicum* most closely resembles *P. nasutum*, but its rostrum is only slightly upturned, and its rostral scale is less than twice as high as wide. *Atropoides nummifer* is larger and heavier bodied and lacks an upturned rostrum. *Bothrops asper* lacks the upturned rostrum, has divided subcaudals, and the second supralabial enters the loreal pit.

DISTRIBUTION *Porthidium nasutum* occurs at low elevations on the Atlantic slope from at least northern Chiapas through northern Guatemala and Honduras, through lower Central America, and onto the Pacific slope of Colombia and Ecuador. In the Yucatán Peninsula the species is restricted to the base of the peninsula, where it is known from El Petén and Belize (Map 181).

NATURAL HISTORY Hognosed pitvipers live primarily in humid forests, where they are generally nocturnal and terrestrial. Specimens are occasionally found on low shrubs, and I once found a juvenile coiled on an inclined tree trunk 1.5 m above the ground near Tikal, El Petén. More frequently they are found beneath surface debris, in hollow logs and stumps, and within the crumbling walls of Maya ruins. According to Alvarez del Toro (1983), hognosed pitvipers feed on *Anolis* lizards and mice. Porras et al. (1981:91) reported that captives ate frogs, *Anolis*, mice, and one another. The juveniles may use the yellowish white tail as a lure to attract lizards and frogs (W. T. Neill, 1960:113–114). Newborn captives in Costa Rica ate earthworms (Picado, 1931:71). Its small size notwithstanding, the bite of this species has caused human fatalities (Daniel, 1949). Gerhardt et al. (1993:350) reported that at Tikal, Guatemala, this species is preyed on by the great black hawk, *Buteogallus urubitinga*.

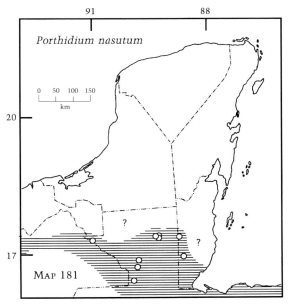

MAP 181

Porthidium nasutum is viviparous. Picado (1931:71) reported a brood of 18 born to a specimen from Costa Rica, and Porras et al. (1981:91) noted that a female from Costa Rica gave birth to 14 young in September 1967.

ETYMOLOGY The specific name, *nasutum*, is a Latin adjective meaning "large nosed."

COMMENT According to Porras et al. (1981:88), the presence of this species in Belize has not been confirmed. The specimen reported by W. T. Neill (1965) was described too vaguely to be verifiably *P. nasutum*. Neill supposed that Schmidt's (1941:509) record of *P. yucatanicum* from Benque Viejo was really *P. nasutum*. McCranie and Porras (1978:108) examined the specimen (USNM 61781), which consists of only a head, and concluded that it is in fact *P. yucatanicum*, but Porras et al. (1981:88) questioned that conclusion. J. A. Campbell and Lamar (1989:36) and McCoy and Censky (1992:218) also doubted the presence of *P. yucatanicum* in Belize. In any event, Carolyn M. Miller's photos of *P. nasutum* from Caracol, Cayo District, firmly establish the presence of this species in Belize.

Porras et al. (1981) reviewed the biosystematics of *P. nasutum*, and L. D. Wilson and McCranie (1984) summarized the available information on the species.

Locality Records Belize: Cayo: Benque Viejo (USNM 61781), Caracol (CMM photo). *Guatemala*: El Petén: 12 km NW Chinajá (KU 55705), Piedras Negras (USNM 110415), Sayaxché (UCM 22367), Sojio (AMNH 69966–67, 69987), Tikal (AMNH uncat.; MCZ 55436–37; UF 13866, 13868–69; UMMZ 117944), ca. 1 mi N Tikal (FD photo, 8.4 mi S Tikal (KU 157664), 3 mi S Tikal (KU 157665), 4 km SE Tikal (AMNH 100410). *Mexico*: Chiapas: Lake Miramar (USNM 136966–67).

Porthidium yucatanicum (Smith)
(Fig. 403; Map 182)

Trimeresurus yucatanicus Smith 1941a:62. HOLOTYPE: USNM 46571. TYPE LOCALITY: Chichén Itzá, Yucatán, Mexico.

Yucatán hognosed pitviper; víbora (Mexico), chaccam (Yucatec).

DESCRIPTION This snake, the smallest pitviper in the Yucatán Peninsula, exhibits pronounced sexual size dimorphism. Mature females average 462 mm in snout-vent length, whereas mature males average only 368 mm (McCoy and Censky, 1992:219). The tail length is roughly 12 to 15 percent of the snout-vent length, and males have longer tails than females. This is a moderately stout snake (Fig. 403). The head is roughly triangular in dorsal view and distinct from the neck. In lateral view the rostrum is upturned and the rostral scale is distinctly higher than wide. The moderately small eyes have vertically elliptical pupils. A deep pit perforates the loreal region between the eye and the nostril. The dorsal scales are heavily keeled, usually arranged in 25 or 27 rows at midbody, and lack apical pits. The anal plate and subcaudal scales are undivided.

The dorsal ground color is gray or tan, often with an orange or reddish cast, and there is a series of broad, dark brown blotches that are narrowly edged with black and have light centers. A very thin orange or yellow vertebral stripe is usually present bisecting the dorsal blotches, the halves of which are offset, producing a staggered pattern. The tip of the tail is pale yellow in juveniles (Fig. 403). The dorsal surface of the head is tan or gray, usually with a few indistinct dark markings. The lower labial scales have several light spots. The venter is yellowish tan with a variable amount of dark pigmentation.

SIMILAR SPECIES *Porthidium yucatanicum* rather closely resembles *P. nasutum*, which replaces it at the base of the Yucatán Peninsula. The rostral scale of *P. nasutum* is approximately twice as high as wide, however, whereas in *P. yucatanicum* it is less than twice as high as wide. In addition, *P. yucatanicum* usually has 25 rather than 23 rows of dorsal scales at midbody.

DISTRIBUTION This species is endemic to the Yucatán Peninsula, where it is known from numerous localities in the Mexican states of Quintana Roo and Yucatán, and from Campeche (Map 182).

NATURAL HISTORY This small hognosed pitviper is a moderately common inhabitant of thorn forest, tropical deciduous forest, and tropical evergreen forest. It is terrestrial and predominantly nocturnal, although in Quintana Roo I found a juvenile coiled on the forest floor by day. The diet apparently consists exclusively of vertebrates. Duellman (1965a:611) reported a lizard (*Sceloporus chrysostictus*) in the stomach of a specimen from Pisté, Yucatán. McCoy and Censky (1992:218) found that the lizards *S. chrysostictus* and *Coleonyx elegans* were

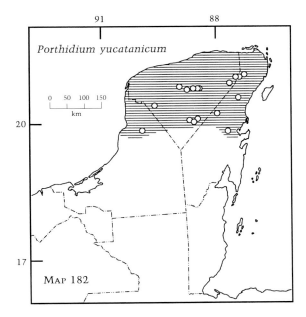

Porthidium yucatanicum

MAP 182

the most common prey items in the stomachs of snakes from Pisté and Pueblo Nuevo X-Can, Quintana Roo; other prey items included a frog (*Leptodactylus labialis*), a blindsnake (*Leptotyphlops goudotii*), small mammals, and a bird. McCoy and Censky (1992:219) suggested an ontogenetic shift in diet, with juveniles taking lizards and frogs, and larger individuals incorporating small mammals and birds into the diet. Juveniles possess yellow tails (Fig. 403), which probably function as caudal lures to attract lizards and frogs.

Porthidium yucatanicum is viviparous. According to McCoy and Censky (1992), the females attain sexual maturity at a minimum snout-vent length of 410 mm, and the males are mature at 328 mm. Reproduction is seasonal. Copulation probably occurs in January or February, and ovulation is in

March and April. Parturition occurs between late June and mid-August. The brood size ranges from 4 to 10, with a mean of 6.9.

ETYMOLOGY The specific name, *yucatanicum*, is a toponym referring to Yucatán, where the type specimen originated.

COMMENT A specimen from Benque Viejo, Belize, has variously been identified by herpetologists as *P. yucatanicum* and *P. nasutum*. On ecological and distributional grounds it is most likely the latter species, but the issue has yet to be resolved (see *P. nasutum*, Comment).

Porthidium yucatanicum was reviewed by J. A. Campbell and Lamar (1989), and McCoy and Censky (1992) summarized information on the biology of this species.

Locality Records Mexico: Campeche: ca. 19 km E Cayal (UTA R-16960); Quintana Roo: 21 km SE Cobá (JCL photo), 3 mi NE Felipe Carrillo Puerto (CAS 143255), Pueblo Nuevo X-Can (CM 45319–20, 45322–26, 49052, 49071, 49087, 49096, 49135, 49146, 49160, 49165; UCM 40648–60, 40742–43, 41800–4), 16.8 mi S Tepich (KU 157667), Tintal (UCM 41797–99); Yucatán: 3.1 km E Catzín (KU 171741), Chichén Itzá (CM 22756; FMNH 20621, 20626, 36176–79; UMMZ 83933; USNM 46571), 20.8 mi NE Dziuché (KU 157668), Kantunil (FMNH 36170, 36172, 36181, 36183–84, 36186), Libre Unión (FMNH 36174, 36185), Pisté (CM 46970–72, 47015–18, 47170–94, 49838–77; KU 70909–10; UCM 12960, 18629, 40661–70, 41805–6), 0.5 km W Santa Rosa, near Quintana Roo (TU 19787), 1.7 km S Santa Rosa (UMRC 84-44), 4.8 km S Santa Rosa (UMRC 84-43), Uxmal (UF 32851), X-Can (CM 46898–901, 47075–77), Yokdzonot (FMNH 36171, 36173, 36175, 36180, 36182, 36187–88); no specific locality (FMNH 544).

Ethnoherpetology in the Yucatán Peninsula

Amphibians and reptiles featured prominently in the thought, mythology, and religion of the ancient Maya. Serpents are ubiquitous in virtually all aspects of Maya artistic expression, but turtles, crocodiles, lizards, frogs, and toads also appear frequently and in varied contexts. Indeed, it is an unusual codex page, carved monument, glyph panel, or funerary ceramic that does not have herpetological imagery represented somewhere. But apart from their symbolic importance, amphibians and reptiles were also of practical significance to the ancient Maya. They were food, they provided raw materials for the manufacture of various items, and they may have been a source of psychoactive chemicals used in religious rituals.

This chapter is not a comprehensive treatise on Yucatecan ethnoherpetology—such a treatment is well beyond the scope of this book. Indeed, a thorough consideration of even one aspect of the topic—the role of the serpent in Maya religion and mythology, for example—would require a monograph. Instead I offer a necessarily brief overview of the subject, illuminated by specific examples designed to illustrate the richness and diversity of Maya thought as applied to amphibians and reptiles. This chapter offers a very different perspective from that in the preceding pages, where the drier facts of identification and distribution predominate. Here we will consider the herpetofauna from the perspective of a people who interacted—and whose descendants continue to interact—with their natural environment on an intimate survival basis.

Information on the roles of amphibians and reptiles in the secular and religious life of the Maya

comes from four sources. First, there is evidence from "dirt" archaeology. In particular there are the representations of amphibians and reptiles in Maya paintings, ceramics, stuccoes, stelae, monuments, and other carved objects. In addition there are the remains of the animals themselves, retrieved by archaeozoologists and ethnozoologists from caches, burials, and middens. Second, we have the records of the early Spanish chroniclers. Diego de Landa's *Relación de las cosas de Yucatán*, written in 1566, is an especially useful source. Third, there are accounts written by the Maya themselves, including the four surviving Maya codices that date from before the Conquest. Also available are the colonial-period accounts recorded by literate Maya scribes under the direction and encouragement of Spanish clergy (e.g., *Popol Vuh*, the *Books of Chilam Balam*, and the *Rituals of the Bacabs*). Fourth, the present-day inhabitants of the Yucatán Peninsula, the lineal descendants of the ancient Maya, have much to tell us. Their personal testimony concerning their beliefs about the natural world and the roles of amphibians and reptiles in it constitutes a link with remote generations, albeit an increasingly tenuous one contaminated, distorted, and in some cases obliterated by allocthonous influences. I have for several years recorded conversations and interviews with the rural Maya concerning their beliefs about amphibians and reptiles and the role of these animals in their mythology. These narratives augment and illuminate the anthropological record and ethnological studies, and, for me, animate and personalize the subject.

The following discussion is divided into two major sections. The first treats the role of amphibians and reptiles in the secular life of the Maya. The second concerns religious, ritual, and mythological aspects of Yucatecan ethnoherpetology. This dichotomy is completely artificial, for it exists purely as an organizational device. In fact, the distinction between the secular and the religious is frequently difficult or impossible to maintain. For example, animals that are consumed as food may also have medicinal properties, may serve as items of ritual sacrifice, and may be important in religious symbolism. For the Maya themselves, who drew no sharp distinction between the animate and the inanimate, and for whom virtually every detail of daily life had its religious aspect, my distinction between the secular and the religious would be meaningless.

Amphibians and Reptiles in the Secular Life of the Maya

Food

Evidence both circumstantial and direct indicates that the ancient Maya consumed amphibians and reptiles, which may have become an increasingly important source of animal protein during Late Classic times (ca. 600–900 A.D.). Ecological factors, including declining agricultural production during the Late Classic period, have been implicated as important elements contributing to the collapse of the Classic Maya in the southern lowlands (e.g., Lowe, 1985). A burgeoning population coupled with a deteriorating agricultural base would obviously impel a search for alternative sources of food. The accelerated deforestation required to meet increasing demands for crop production would have reduced game animals, and in the absence of large domestic animals, which the Maya never possessed, smaller animals such as amphibians and reptiles would likely have been incorporated into the diet. In their analysis of the vertebrate remains at Dzibilchaltún, Wing and Steadman (1980:328) found evidence of a decline in the consumption of large animals such as deer and an increase in the consumption of smaller animals such as chachalacas and spiny-tailed iguanas. These authors concluded that the large human population (estimated at 40,000) at Dzibilchaltún "must have placed a severe strain on the local large animal species." Saul's examination of the skeletal remains at Altar de Sacrificios, El Petén, revealed relatively

high levels of malnutrition, including lesions suggestive of iron deficiency, indicating "the presence of disorders that would depress population energy levels" (Saul, 1972:72).

Paleozoological investigation at several sites has confirmed the presence of reptiles in the diet of Classic and Post-classic Maya. Mercer (1896), searching for evidence of paleolithic humans in caves in the Puuc region of Yucatán, found the bones of turtles and lizards associated with Maya artifacts, suggesting their presence in the diet of the ancients, although ritual use cannot be excluded in this case. Turtle remains are especially common at archaeological sites throughout the lowland Maya area, from Cozumel to Lubaantún, and from Altar de Sacrificios to Dzibilchaltún. Often the remains show signs of burning, suggesting that the turtles were cooked and eaten. Pollock and Ray (1957:648) found remains of *Dermatemys mawii* at Mayapán, far to the north of that turtle's present-day distribution. Because the remains were associated with dwellings, the obvious conclusion is that the turtles were food items. Pohl (1985:142) documented consumption of turtles at Seibal, El Petén, and suggested that the distribution of turtle and deer bones at that Classic site reflects the priority access to animal protein enjoyed by the Maya elite. The same was evidently true at Altun Ha, Belize, where virtually all of the vertebrate remains were associated with one very large palace midden (Pendergast, 1977; Pohl, 1990:167). Wing (1974:186) found abundant sea turtle remains in a Maya midden on Cancún, and Post-classic house mounds and middens on Cozumel contained the bones of both marine (Cheloniidae) and freshwater turtles, especially *Rhinoclemmys areolata*, *Trachemys scripta*, and *Kinosternon* sp. (Hamblin, 1984:60).

The contexts in which the turtle remains were found suggest multiple uses. Remains recovered from house mounds indicate that turtles were eaten. Some were found in burials and in ceremonial contexts, however, indicating that turtles also played a role in the ceremonial life of the Cozumel Maya. Two species of iguanas, *Ctenosaura* and *Iguana*, were common at the Cozumel sites, which also yielded the remains of several crocodiles (Hamblin, 1984:60). A similar assemblage of turtles, iguanas, and crocodiles was uncovered at Selin Farm, a Classic site on the coast of northern Honduras (Healy, 1983). Olsen (1972:245) found crocodile and turtle remains at Altar de Sacrificios, and Wing (1975:382) reported remains of turtles, crocodiles, and iguanas at Lubaantún in southern Belize. Wing and Steadman (1980:328) reported remains of spiny-tailed iguanas, various freshwater turtles, and the green turtle (*Chelonia mydas*) from Dzibilchaltún in northern Yucatán. The latter species must have been transported inland a minimum of about 20 km.

Historical sources report that the Maya hunted several species of reptiles for food during colonial times. In his fifth letter to Charles V, written in 1525, Cortés recounted how, in the vicinity of what was probably Lago Macanché, El Petén, his men captured Indian hunters with "some iguanas, which are large lizards found in the Islands" (Pagden, 1986:377). In the *Relación de las cosas de Yucatán*, Diego de Landa recounted how the Indians caught iguanas with lassos as the lizards lay on trees or in their holes. Concerning turtles, Landa said, "There are turtles of great size, much larger than immense shields, of excellent eating, and satisfying" (Gates, 1937:99). The Chontal text, written early in the seventeenth century, describes how the Maya of Tabasco and southwestern Campeche hunted iguanas (Scholes and Roys, 1968:30, 404).

Contemporary studies confirm the role of amphibians and reptiles in the diet of the Maya, for today the Lacandón Maya regularly consume several species of amphibians and reptiles, especially the larger turtles and lizards (Góngora-Arones, 1987:15). Even smaller lizards such as *Ameiva undulata* and *Corytophanes* are eaten, as is at least one species of snake, *Boa constrictor*. The Maya eat several species of frogs but avoid toads (*Bufo*), at least as food items. Indeed, consumption of amphibians appears to be uncommon among the Maya, although Roys (1931:292) reported that they ate *uo* (*Rhinophrynus dorsalis*), and Juan Briceño de la Cruz (pers. comm.), of Becan, Campeche, told me that the legs of the frog *Rana berlandieri* are eaten by the inhabitants of southern Campeche. The children of the contemporary Kekchi Maya of southern Belize consume a wide variety of the small animals, including insects and lizards, that they encounter in the course of their daily activities (R. R. Wilk, pers. comm.). Today, many rural Maya eat the iguanas *Iguana iguana* and *Ctenosaura similis* as well as their eggs, which are high in calories and unusually rich in calcium and vitamin A (Pohl, 1990:160).

Several species of freshwater turtles are commonly consumed, especially *Dermatemys mawii*, *Staurotypus triporcatus*, and *Trachemys scripta*. On occasion, rattlesnakes are eaten—but with an interesting proviso, according to the following account by Arturo Canché of Kanek, western Yucatán (pers. comm.):

Only the rattlesnake is eaten, not the other snakes. There is a way to prepare rattlesnake meat, but if you eat rattlesnake you can't have anything sweet, you can't have coffee with sugar because you can be poisoned. You have to wait a long time before you can eat anything sweet. You can suck on sour orange or lemon, but without sugar. If you have sugar after eating rattlesnake you will get sick. When they cook it, they remove the head because all the poison is in the head.

Snake remains are generally rare at archaeological sites, but those that do occur are usually from large species, suggesting their use as food. For example, the boa constrictor and the large colubrid snakes *Drymarchon corais* and *Spilotes pullatus* are known from Tikal (H. Moholy-Nagy, pers. comm.), and these three species plus *Masticophis* are known from the Preclassic site at Cuello, in northern Belize (Wing and Scudder, 1991:86). Olsen (1978:173) reported a rattlesnake vertebra from El Seibal, and rattlesnake remains were found at Tikal (S. J. Scudder, pers. comm.). Whether the rattlesnakes served as food or as ceremonial objects is unknown, but their presence is significant, for rattlesnakes do not occur in the heavy forest that now characterizes the vegetation at El Seibal and Tikal. Similarly, the remains of *Agkistrodon bilineatus* from the Classic period at Tikal (H. Moholy-Nagy, in litt.) are from an area substantially beyond the present-day range of this species. Most likely, the snakes were transported to the sites. The rattlesnakes may have come from the nearby savanna region of central El Petén, where they do occur today.

Medicinal Uses

Remarkable curative powers are attributed by the contemporary Maya to some species of amphibians and reptiles. Thompson (1963:78) reported that in southern Belize the Maya regard the fat of the iguana (*Iguana iguana*) as a potent curative for many ailments, and the skin secretions of some species of frogs and toads are used throughout the Maya area to cure sores and infected wounds. Two contemporary accounts, one from Yucatán and the other from Belize, illustrate this belief. First, Arturo Canché said:

Some frogs, either the yellow ones [*Hyla micro-cephala*?] or the smallest, are used to cure sores. The frogs have very little blood, they have resin. Their whole back is pure resin. So if there is a disease such as sores that won't heal, then you pierce its back, the resin comes out. You put the resin on the sore because it gets rid of all the germs. Every sore produced by the body has its germ. Well, it can be cured with the frog resin.

Aurora García, of San Antonio, Cayo District, related the following treatment for infected wounds:

There is a certain kind of toad, they don't grow very large. It is red [probably *Hypopachus vari-olosus* or the red morph of *Bufo valliceps*] and they say that they get it for when they have a wound that won't heal, when the flesh is already rotten—we call it in Spanish *gangrenar*, which means "to not have a cure." We use the little frogs and rub it over the wound nine times. Then you have to go and enclose the frog in something and see if it dies. If the frog dies then you will get cured.

The blood of certain kinds of turtles is believed to be useful in treating various sores and infections. Again, Arturo Canché explained:

There are people who have cracks all around their feet. Then they look for those big turtles that they call *tokac*. They cut off its head, they put all the warm blood on the foot where it's cracked, because the blood is a drying agent. After eight days it's scabbed over. Little by little, little by little, until one's foot is back to normal. When you start to walk it will crack and bleed. Then you look for that turtle, cut its throat, gather the blood, and you bathe the whole foot in the blood. Then after it has been scabbing for eight days, there's new skin. Then it's healed.

Turtle blood is also used to cure whooping cough, according to Francisco Itzá, of Cobá, Quintana Roo, who spoke from personal experience. According to him, the turtle is placed on its back and decapitated, and the fresh blood is swallowed by the person suffering from whooping cough. The flesh is cooked and eaten as well, and it is said that the patient normally recovers within six days.

According to Juan Briceño de la Cruz, the fat of various species of turtles is effective in preventing sunburn if applied to the skin before exposure to the sun.

Another treatment effective against a variety of ailments involves use of the *cocan*, the teeth of a snake. According to Baqueiro Lopez (1983:60), when the fangs of the rattlesnake are used to make small punctures in the skin, the evil—the *mal viento*—is allowed to escape, thus effecting a cure. The rattles cure headache when they are passed nine times over the temples of the patient. Isauro Tuyuc May, of Xlapac, Yucatán, related the belief that rattlesnake fat is beneficial for curing cancer: "When the infection is in the early stages, not very advanced, then you get a rattlesnake, kill it, cook it, and eat it. Because the fat is so fine, it makes the infection break loose and disappear. It appears in the place where it broke off, but everything that's infected goes out because the rattlesnake fat cuts it out once and for all."

Rattlesnake fat is also applied as a topical ointment to treat insect stings and bites. Consumption of rattlesnake flesh is believed to alleviate a variety of symptoms, including those of arthritis. Juan Briceño de la Cruz told me that the flesh may be cooked and eaten as a part of the diet. Alternatively, the flesh can be dried, pulverized, and taken in a drink.

Miscellaneous Uses

The Classic Maya used turtle carapaces to make percussion instruments, or so the famous murals at Bonampak, Chiapas, suggest. In the murals, which commemorate a great military victory, richly adorned Maya royalty celebrate, entertained by an orchestra including a musician playing a turtle carapace struck by antlers (Coe, 1987:104; Ivan-off, 1973:79).

A crocodile mandible from Altar de Sacrifícios, El Petén, shows clear evidence of having been worked by humans, and the two crocodile teeth with holes drilled through them also found at that site (Olsen, 1972:245) might have served an ornamental function. Wing and Steadman (1980:328) reported a drilled crocodile tooth recovered from the ruins of Dzibilchaltún that may have served as an ornament.

Crocodile Attack and Snakebite

Although reptiles provide both food and medicine to the Maya, a few species sometimes constitute a threat to human life. In what is surely the first European account of a human fatality due to crocodile attack in Yucatán, Landa reported in the *Relación de las cosas de Yucatán* that "there are many fierce alligators which . . . will swallow any kind of strange thing; to my own knowledge one killed one of our monastery Indians while he was bathing in a lake." Landa further related how the friars used a small dog as bait to capture the offending animal, inside of which they found "the half of the man, with the dog" (Gates, 1937:99). Landa did not distinguish between the two species of *Crocodylus* in Yucatán, but his description of the nesting habits ("they lay them [the eggs] in a large hole in the sand very near the water") and the behavior of the hatchlings ("they wait for a wave of the sea striking close to them") clearly indicate that his descriptions apply to *C. acutus*.

A much greater danger is posed by venomous snakes, which are not uncommon in the lowland Maya area. Three snakes—the *tzabcan* (*Crotalus durissus*), the *taxinchan* (*Bothrops apser*), and the *uolpoch* (*Agkistrodon bilineatus*)—clearly commanded the attention and respect of the ancient Maya, as they do among the Maya today. Page 24 of the Madrid Codex (pagination follows T. A. Lee, 1985) shows a deity bedeviled by snakes, one of which is biting the god's nose while another bites his hand. Page 40 of that same document clearly shows a rattlesnake with its fangs embedded in the foot of a hapless Maya hunter (Fig. 200). In his *Relación* Landa wrote that "the diversity of snakes or serpents is great, of many colors and not harmful, except for two kinds of very poisonous ones, much larger than those we have here in Spain; one of which they call *taxinchan*. There are also others very large and very poisonous, with rattles in their tails" (Gates, 1937:100).

The taxinchan, or fer-de-lance, is indeed a formidable snake. Its bite causes hemolysis, hemorrhage, and, frequently, death. With respect to this species, Herrara (quoted in Morelet, 1871:61) stated that "there is in Chiapa [*sic*] great brown vipers resembling decayed wood. One of which having bitten a horse, the animal immediately perspired blood from every pore and did not survive it more than a day." The Maya of Yucatán say that "when it bites a person, it causes him to exude blood from every pore like a bloody sweat, and if no remedy is applied, he will die in a day" (Roys, 1931:339). An unpublished post-Conquest manuscript, "Yerbas y hechicerías del Yucatán," advises that the taxin-

Fig. 200. Maya hunter bitten on the foot by a rattlesnake; from the Madrid Codex, page 40. Modified from Lee, 1985.

chan "is of four varieties according to its color. Hence some of the young resemble the mother and others are different. They are poisonous in various degrees, since the different varieties interbreed, and those (of mixed breed) are the worst" (Roys, 1931:339).

Although smaller than the fer-de-lance, the uolpoch, or cantil, is considered by many contemporary Maya to be the most dangerous of all Yucatecan snakes (Pacheco-Cruz, 1919:33). It is thought to be very intelligent and to have the habit of following people (Isauro Tuyuc May, pers. comm.). Many believe that it can bite and sting with its tail simultaneously, as the following account by Arturo Canché reveals:

The uolpoch—in Spanish it's called *víbora pinta*—doesn't grow very long, but it is rather thick. It can bite with its mouth and its tail. It has a stinger, and it can jump as much as five meters. When you are sleeping in a hammock it will form a coil to reach you. If it reaches your shoulder, then it'll bite your shoulder and your rib, in two places. If it reaches your foot then it'll bite here and there, in two places. That's how he bit my father. Where he was bitten on the foot it looked like the leg of a bull, that size. It got swollen, he was bitten here and there by the same viper. When it jumped, the stinger got him in his foot and the two fangs here in his leg, both. He couldn't move for twenty-four hours. He was given medicine and in a month he was walking, but he was very weak. He didn't lose his leg, thank goodness, but he was disabled for six months.

At a very early age Maya boys are taken by

their fathers to help at the milpa, where they are taught to avoid ants and venomous snakes (Blom, 1944). The Maya invoke the gods to protect them against snakebite. For example, Tozzer (1907:175) recounted this Lacandón prayer offered for the welfare of a son:

Guard my son, my father, let any evil cease, let fever cease. Do not injure him by letting evil trample him underfoot. Do not injure him by letting fever trample him underfoot. *Do not injure him by letting a serpent bite my son.* Do not injure him by sending death. He is playing, my son. When he is grown up he will give you an offering of posol, he will give you an offering of copal. When he is grown up he will give you an offering of tortillas. When he is grown up he will give you an offering of bark-cloth fillets. When he is grown up he will sacrifice to you. (Emphasis added.)

In a similar vein is a prayer collected by Thompson (1930:45) in southern Belize. It was given in preparation for felling the forest to clear a milpa:

O god, my father, my mother, lord of the hills and valleys, spirit of the forest treat me well. I am about to do as has always been done. Now I am about to make my offering to you that you may know that I am molesting your heart. Suffer it. I am going to destroy your beauty, I am going to work you in order that I may live. Suffer no animal to pursue me, *suffer not the snake*, or scorpion, or wasp to bite me. Do not allow a falling tree to hit me, nor axe or machete to cut me. With all my heart I am going to work you. (Emphasis added.)

Treatment of snakebite involved ritual incantations, according to a sixteenth-century report: "Formerly, in the time when they were pagans, they attempted to cure themselves of this [snake] poisoning by means of spells and enchantments." Moreover, the powerful Maya sorcerers "had their books for charming and enchanting them [the snakes]. With a few words which they recited they charmed and tamed poisonous serpents; they caught them and held them in their hands without their doing any injury" (*Relaciones de Yucatán*, quoted in Roys, 1931:xxi). Snake handling persists today among the Quiche Maya of the Guatemalan highlands. In *la danza de la culebra*, men dressed as women handle live snakes during a ritual dance related to fertility and penance (Peterson, 1990:122).

Various plants were commonly used to treat snakebite. Among these was guaco (*Aristolochis* spp.), which, according to Morelet (1871:87), was used by the Maya in the vicinity of Palenque as an antidote to the bite of *Bothrops asper*. Morelet (1871:87) also reported the belief that the *arum* plant would cause the fangs of venomous snakes to fall out simply by its touch. Contemporary Maya use contrayerba (*Bouvardia* spp.) to treat snakebite, as the following account, related by Serapio Canultep of Punta Laguna, Quintana Roo, reveals:

The *bujón* is a large black snake, and if you get close to snakes like the bujón, they expel the poison, like smoke, like the wind, that's how it comes out. One day, my uncle and I were felling trees to prepare the milpa, and my uncle says, "Listen, there's a big snake there." I went over to see, but I was telling him—after he had already killed the snake—that he shouldn't touch it because sometimes the snake, when it's dying, it expels the poison like the wind, like a spray. That's what happened to my uncle. In about 20 minutes the poison was already inside and he had welts all over, even in his eyes and lips. They turned black, and were bleeding, even from the mouth. In Chemax, my village, lived many of my father's brothers and grandparents, and people who could cure any snakebite. Well it took us about two days on horseback to get to Chemax. When we arrived my uncle couldn't get off of the horse because his body was completely swollen. My grandfather is the best herb medicine doctor. He knows the herbs for snakebite. When one knows about that, one can prepare it and one's life can depend on it. There were no doctors a long time ago. You had to help your neighbor. And so my grandfather was able to cure my uncle. The herb used to cure snakebite is the contrayerba. You mix it with another type, the *chuyai*, and you take the two types and mix them together with lemon juice and grind it up and put it where the bite is, and you wash it very well with cotton, remove it, and put the herb on the bite. And in two days the swollen part is fine, the swelling is gone. That's the medicine for snakes. It works for *cuatro nariz* bites.

Although today some rural Maya recognize that certain species are harmless or even beneficial, the prevailing attitude toward snakes is fear, and they are generally killed at every opportunity. Armando Mian, of Santa Elena, Yucatán, exemplifies this attitude: "Everyone is afraid of snakes. The person who is not afraid of them is rare. And they kill all the snakes that they see, because snakes are the devil."

The snake as a personification of the devil doubtless reflects Christian influence, but the view that snakes possess great power and, at times, a decidedly sinister aspect is also characteristically Maya. Some contemporary Maya view snakes as carriers of sickness sent by sorcerers. One species, called *hoonob*, is said to be so dangerous that if it crawls over one's hat or sandals, death will result when the garment is later worn (Redfield and Rojas, 1971:178). In ancient times aspiring *hechiceros* (sorcerers) were obliged to endure an initiation, designed to increase their powers, that required them to sit naked on an anthill and summon forth the great master of sorcery, who would appear as a giant serpent. The serpent would lick the body of the aspirant, then swallow him alive. A few minutes later the apprentice sorcerer would emerge from the vent of the serpent, having passed through the digestive system intact (Baqueiro López, 1983:54).

One particularly fearsome snake is the mythical *chayilcan*, which is merely one aspect or manifestation of a malevolent entity called the *kakasbal*. In his book *El alma misteriosa del Mayab*, Rosado Vega (1957:78) described the chayilcan and its capacity to do evil:

Chayilcan is the mysterious old serpent, many hundreds of years old, a centenarian many times over. And it is in her that the evil spirit is infused. When this happens she is not a serpent although she resembles one . . . it is the kakasbal. Beware of her when you hear her prolonged hissing in the night . . . when you see her—magnificent and soft in color and beauty, for she doesn't lose her splendor with age—like a wide emerald ribbon sliding out from underneath the rugged, brambly ground, or from the mouth of the cenotes, or uncoiling languidly at the foot of a tree. . . . This is what happened. The milpero's body lay in the milpa. It was bloodless like an empty thing. And dry as if all the moisture in his body had evaporated. Someone had sucked out all his blood. It was the chayilcan, it was the chayilcan. I saw her last night when I was alone in my cabana. The green serpent passed quickly by the door of my house and disappeared right away. But at that moment a horrible man with the skin of a snake and claws on his hands and feet rose out of the place where she had disappeared. It was the kakasbal, and I ran until I reached and climbed a tree whose green, hard fruit I could use to throw at the monster. . . . People came to my aid, but the evil one laughed and told

us to go to the milpa to pick up my husband's body, and then she immediately turned back into the chayilcan and, hissing, slithered away . . . she had killed my husband and had sucked all of his blood. It is good for those of you who are listening to know that the mysterious transmutation of the kakasbal into the green snake, hundreds of years old, occurs at nightfall and on cold nights, and that blood is her favorite substance.

In addition to its serpentine aspect, the kakasbal can also assume the form of a horrible bird that enters homes at night and hovers over sleeping infants and children. Its wingbeats produce an evil wind that enters their mouths, causing death. Sometimes the kakasbal manifests itself as a cold, evil wind. Another demon, or a different manifestation of the kakasbal, is the *x-tabai*, which dwells in the forest, especially in the vicinity of the ceiba tree. She frequently takes the form of a beautiful woman with long hair who entices young men to follow her into the bush. Once there, she transforms into the chayilcan and asphyxiates her victim by inserting the tip of her tail into his nostrils (Redfield and Rojas, 1971:122).

The chayilcan is usually described as a green snake. Only two green snakes occur in the Yucatán Peninsula and could thus have served as models: *Leptophis ahaetulla* (Fig. 366) and *Oxybelis fulgidus* (Fig. 374). In some accounts the chayilcan is said to seek out nursing women in order to suck the mother's milk and kill the woman, her infant, or both by inserting her bifurcated tail into their nostrils and asphyxiating them. Males, however, are not exempt from the chayilcan's attack. Macario Cach, of San Simon, Yucatán, related the belief that if the snake is female, it will attack a man. The belief that snakes will nurse at the breasts of pregnant or lactating women is widespread throughout Mexico, and various species of snakes are implicated. One, the *ek'uneil* (*Drymarchon corais*), has a dirty tail and is said (correctly) to feed on other snakes. It is also believed to fly and to attack nursing women by coiling around them and inserting its bifurcated tail into their nostrils, and then to nurse at their breasts (Baqueiro Lopez, 1983:42). Armando Mian described the *ochcan* (*Boa constrictor*) as the species involved:

The ochcan catches mice and hens and all that. It goes into a town and climbs into the thatched houses looking for mice. But once it is in the house, they say that the ochcan will suck at the woman's breast. In those days there was no electric current and you worked with candlelight. Well, the ochcan was sucking at the breast of the woman even though the baby was crying, until the husband lit candles and saw then that the snake was sucking at the woman's breast.

Although there are no venomous lizards in the Yucatán Peninsula, several species are widely believed to be venomous or otherwise capable of doing harm. In Yucatán, as elsewhere in Mexico and Central America, various species of geckos are termed *escorpion* and are thought to deliver venom by throwing the tail (hence the vernacular names *bota la cola* and *tira la cola*).

In Yucatán, a lizard called *ix-hunpekin* (probably *Coleonyx elegans*) is believed to "not only attack with the mouth and also with the tail, but by biting the shadow of a person's head they produce a headache so severe that it will be fatal if not immediately cured" (Pacheco-Cruz, 1919:32). The ix-hunpekin is "so poisonous that when it touches a person, even the garment, without biting or stinging, it kills completely and in a brief time" (Roys, 1931:333). With respect to this lizard, Arturo Canché said: "When the ix-hunpekin reaches the shadow of your head it throws its tail. After ten minutes have passed you will have a headache, your head will start to hurt. But we also have some plants called ix-hunpekin which are a secret medicine that we have. You grind that up and put it on your head and the headache goes away."

Pacheco-Cruz (1919:32–33) described the plant used to cure the pain caused by the ix-hunpekin as similar to the henequén but smaller, and with poorly developed spines. A leaf of the plant is placed in hot coals, roasted, and then split into halves. Tobacco and salt are added to the leaf, which is then ground with bitter anise. If anise is not available, urine can be substituted. The material is applied directly to the affected area and tied into place. More than a single application may be necessary to relieve the suffering.

The brightly colored males of *Ameiva undulata* are believed to be so brilliant that merely gazing on them can cause a severe headache, according to my informant Francisco Itzá. Another lizard considered dangerous by the Yucatec Maya is the *yaxtoloc* (*Laemanctus serratus*), which is believed to be capable of delivering a bite that is very slow to heal. Arturo Canché explained: "The green lizard here bites. When they bite you it takes a long time to heal. Something like a pimple or sore [*grano*] is

formed. Matter will get inside the bite and stay in the bite. If you don't squeeze it at that moment it will stay in the bite and form a lump. It is very dangerous."

Amphibians and Reptiles in Maya Religion and Mythology

Creation Myths

Although anthropologists have recorded a variety of creation myths among the various Maya peoples, many of the stories have fundamental features in common. Often the accounts speak of several (usually three) separate creation events in which gods produce humanlike beings but, finding them defective, destroy them or allow them to persist as monkeys. Only the products of the third creation are pleasing to the gods and are allowed to live and populate the world. Generally, these first humans are formed from maize dough. In the version of the Cakchiquel Maya of the Guatemalan highlands, blood of the tapir and the serpent is the mucilage used to bind together this primeval dough (Recinos, 1953:47). Thus, as in the Judeo-Christian tradition, serpents also feature in the Maya version of creation, but here they are viewed in a considerably more positive light.

In the *Books of Chilam Balam*, the colonial-period prophecy texts attributed to the mythical Jaguar Priests of Yucatán, a version of creation involves the crocodile (Sayer-Lauçanno, 1987:51):

> I speak to you now
> of Oxlahun-Ti-Ku,
> god of the thirteen heavens
> and of Bolon-Ti-Ku,
> god of the nine hells
> of how they created
> the world and all life
> and then destroyed it again
> by washing the world in water
> and of how Oxlahan-Ti-Ku
> slit the throat
> of the great earth crocodile,
> Itzám-Cab-Ain, and with his body
> formed the Petén, land of the Mayas.

Another common theme involves two (occasionally three) brothers, sometimes presented as twins, and an old woman—often their grandmother—who plays something of an adversarial role. The brothers experience a series of adventures and endure various trials, including a harrowing descent into the Maya underworld, Xibalba, before eventually assuming their duties as celestial bodies—the sun, the moon, or Venus, depending on the version. In the *Popol Vuh* of the Quiche Maya, these "Hero Twins" are summoned by their grandmother, who sends them the message that they must present themselves before the evil lords of Xibalba. The message is initially carried by a louse, which is swallowed by a toad, which in turn is consumed by a snake, and the snake by a bird of prey. The message arrives when the bird regurgitates the snake, which regurgitates the toad, which still has the louse in its mouth (Tedlock, 1985:131–132).

A seemingly related story from the Mopan Maya of southern Belize involves three boys and their grandmother, XKitza. The boys rely on a toad and a large crested lizard to spy on their grandmother, whom they suspect of conspiring against them, together with her lover, a giant monster. Warned by their herpetological allies of her intention to kill them, the boys circumvent her attempts and instead kill her with an arrow (Thompson, 1930:120–23).

This is a widespread story, with variants known beyond the Maya area. In the version of the Mazastec-Popoloca of southern Mexico, the old woman, enraged at being tricked by the boys, treads on the toad, which explains why toads today are flat (I. W. Johnson and Johnson, 1939).

Linda Schele proposed a synthesis linking the creation myth accounts of the *Popol Vuh* with astronomical movements of the Milky Way and various constellations (see the summary in Wertime and Schuster, 1993). In this view, the Milky Way represented the canoe of life, propelled by paddler gods (Fig. 201), which transported the Maize God, or First Father, to his birthplace, the place of creation. First Father entered the world when he emerged from the cracked carapace of a turtle (Fig. 202). Subsequently, First Father raised the sky and created the World Tree, which took the form of a giant crocodile, situated at the center of the cosmos.

Cosmological Beliefs of the Maya

In common with other Middle American peoples, the Classic and Post-classic Maya evidently conceived of the world as the back of a huge reptilian monster—often depicted as saurian or crocodilian, but sometimes represented as a giant turtle—floating in an enormous body of water. This concept of an earth monster with reptilian features was developed extensively by Thompson (1930, 1970), who identified the monster as Itzamná (literally, "Iguana House"). This deity existed as several distinct manifestations, celestial and terrestrial, and had several names, some of which can be roughly translated as "Iguana Earth" or "Iguana Earth Crocodile." Like some other major gods, Itzamná existed in quadruplicate. Each Itzám formed one of the four sides of the Iguana House, and each was associated with one of the four cardinal directions. This concept of a deity with multiple aspects finds parallels in other religions, of course, including the Christian Trinity. Thompson considered Itzamná the most important of the numerous gods of the Maya pantheon, which included deities for each day of the Maya twenty-day "month," the *uinal*. According to some sources, the crocodile god, Itzám Cab Ain, was associated with the first of the twenty days, and Ahau Can, the rattlesnake god, was associated with the fourth (Edmonson, 1986:32).

Some Mayanists today believe that Thompson overemphasized the importance of Itzamná (N. M. Hellmuth, pers. comm.). Nonetheless, monstrous creatures with decidedly saurian or crocodilian features abound in Classic Maya art. For example, altar

Fig. 201. Scene incised on bone; burial 116, Tikal, Guatemala. Redrawn from Schele and Miller, 1986, by permission of the Kimball Art Museum, Fort Worth, Texas.

Fig. 202. Scene from a funerary plate from El Petén, Guatemala, or southern Campeche, Mexico. Modified from Coe, 1987.

41 at Copan, Honduras, shows a two-headed, quadrupedal reptile (Fig. 203) with a human face emerging from its jaws. Moreover, as noted above, the crocodile is prominent in some Maya creation myths contained in the *Books of Chilam Balam* (e.g., Sawyer-Lauçanno, 1987:51).

Overarching the earth was the sky, represented by a serpent, the sky serpent, bearing the signs of various celestial bodies. The association between the sky and the serpent may stem from the fact that in Cholan Maya the word for "sky," *caan*, is a homonym for the word *snake* (Coe, 1987:165; Schele and Freidel, 1990:52), although the fact that the sky is sometimes symbolized as a two-headed serpent among Andean peoples casts some doubt on that explanation (E. P. Benson, in litt.).

Beneath the earth and sky lay Xibalba ("Place of Fright"), the Maya underworld populated by nine evil gods. Maya kings could communicate with the inhabitants of this otherworldly realm by means of

Fig. 203. Bicephalic reptilian monster; altar 41, Copan, Honduras. Redrawn from Schele and Miller, 1986, by permission of the Kimball Art Museum, Fort Worth, Texas.

ritual and sacrifice. When they died, they themselves passed over into Xibalba, where they had to overcome the lords of the underworld, just as the Hero Twins had done before them.

A particularly clear representation of the descent into Xibalba—and one containing vivid herpetological imagery—appears on four incised bones from a burial at Tikal. Several related scenes show a Maya lord seated in a canoe along with a menagerie of animals. Two gods are paddling, one fore and one aft (Fig. 201). Among the animals is a lizard with large vertebral spines and an enlarged circular scale on the side of its head that clearly identify it as *Iguana iguana*. In one scene the canoe progresses horizontally, but in two others the canoe and its passengers are seen plunging beneath the surface of the water. Schele and Miller (1986:270) interpreted this canoe trip as a metaphor for the passage of a Tikal ruler through life and his subsequent entrance into the afterworld as the canoe sinks below the surface.

In the Maya pantheon, the wife, consort, or female aspect of Itzamná is Ix-Chel, the moon goddess or the goddess of healing, sewing, and birthing, who is often associated with serpents. In the Dresden Codex, for example, she is frequently depicted wearing a coiled serpent headdress (Fig. 204). The following account, related by Aurora García, illustrates the mythological association between Ix-Chel and snakes, in this case the rattlesnake (*Crotalus durissus*):

Fig. 204. Two representations of Ix-Chel with naturalistic serpent headdress; from the Dresden Codex, pages 20 and 22.

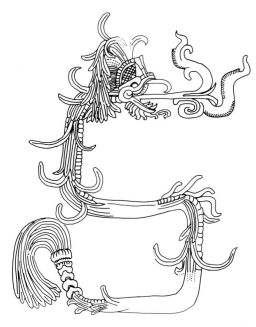

Fig. 205. Fantastically stylized feathered serpent; Chichén Itzá, Yucatán, Mexico. Redrawn from Spinden, 1913, by permission of Dover Publications.

Ix-Chel is the wife of Itzamná. She is the goddess of embroidery and is also the midwife. The rattlesnake is where Ix-Chel gets the patterns for sewing. One day the other gods asked her to go to the leaf-cutter ants because it was from their hole that the serpent would emerge. And the serpent came out and licked Ix-Chel all over her body nine times. And then afterward, the serpent lay flat so that the goddess could pick out all the designs she wanted from the snake's pattern. After that she cut off the little rattles and then she went home. So now and then when she forgets the patterns, she can rattle the rattle, and the snake will come back to remind her of the patterns.

The Snake in Maya Art

Perhaps no other natural motif is more characteristic of Maya art than the snake. Virtually all cultures accord snakes an important position in their folklore and mythology, but in few if any cultures is the influence of the snake so pervasive and its appearance so ubiquitous.

Spinden (1913) was the first to analyze the role of snakes in Maya art in a thorough and systematic way. He showed that representations of snakes ranged from the realistic and anatomically correct to highly modified, elaborate forms that incorporated speech scrolls, feathers, various sorts of undulating lines, glyphs, and such anthropomorphic elements as nose and ear plugs. In their most extreme, fantastic, and stylized forms, the snakes become so

elaborate that they are difficult to recognize as serpents (Fig. 205).

A partial explanation for the frequent occurrence of snakes in Maya art, Spinden felt, lay in the form of the serpent, whose long and undulating body contains possibilities for artistic development lacking in other animals. Certainly the effect of the fluid, undulating lines of the serpents that adorn the west façade of the so-called Nunnery Quadrangle at Uxmal could not have been achieved using any other animal's form.

But an explanation based merely on the aesthetic properties of the serpentine form cannot, by itself, adequately account for the prominence of the serpent motif in Maya art. Perhaps an additional factor is the fact that snakes periodically shed their skins and thus serve as symbols of regeneration and renewal (E. P. Benson, in litt.).

Objects incorporating serpents apparently signified power and rulership. Two objects in particular, the so-called manikin scepter and the ceremonial bar, are likely to exhibit serpentine elements and to appear in the hands of high-ranking individuals. The manikin scepter is a small object that combines the head and body of a serpent, which serves as a handle, with a small, grotesque figure (Fig. 206). The figure often has a flared or flamelike upper tooth and is said to represent god GII of the Palen-

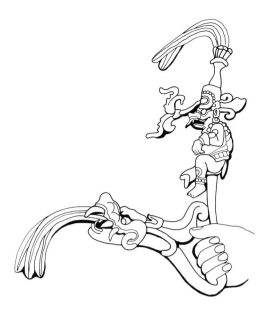

Fig. 206. Manikin scepter; Quiriguá, Guatemala. Redrawn from Spinden, 1913, by permission of Dover Publications.

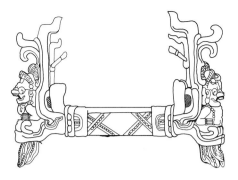

Fig. 207. Rigid ceremonial bar in the form of a two-headed serpent; stela N, Copan, Honduras. Redrawn from Spinden, 1913, by permission of Dover Publications.

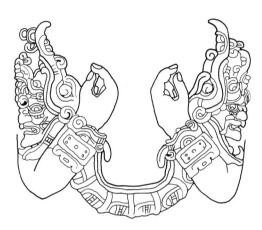

Fig. 208. Flexible ceremonial bar in the form of a two-headed serpent cradled in the arms of a ruler; stela P, Copán, Honduras. Redrawn from Spinden, 1913, by permission of Dover Publications.

que triad (Schele and Miller, 1986:49). This god is also known as the flare god or the serpent-footed god (Schele and Freidel, 1990:414) because the serpent is usually an extension of the god itself, growing out of one of the god's legs.

The ceremonial bar, which often appears cradled in the arms of a ruler or other person of high rank, generally takes the form of a two-headed serpent with open jaws. It may be rigid (Fig. 207) or flexible (Fig. 208). A human face or a grotesque representation of a god is usually seen emerging from the gaping jaws. This motif—the human or humanlike face emerging from reptilian jaws—is a very common element of Maya art and was considered by Spinden to be perhaps its "most striking and original feature" (Spinden, 1913:35). The motif is by no means limited to snakes; the two-headed reptilian monster on altar D at Copan was mentioned previously. In fact, at many of the archaeological sites in the Chenes and Río Bec regions of southwestern and southern Campeche, access to the interior of certain ceremonial buildings requires passage through broad doorways that represent the gaping jaws of various kinds of monstrous cosmic reptiles (Fig. 209), sometimes Itzamná, sometimes a serpent creature. The association between rulers, gods, and serpents is also evident in the costumes worn by the Maya and their gods. Serpents frequently adorn the elaborate headdresses worn by the Maya elite—as, for example, the headdress of Lord Great Skull, seen

in lintel 14 of Yaxchilán (Fig. 210)—and they appear as elements in the costumes of the gods as well. As mentioned above, the goddess Ix-Chel is portrayed wearing a realistic snake as a headdress in the Dresden Codex (Fig. 204). At El Seibal, stela 13, the so-called stela of the seven serpents, shows a male figure with a serpent knotted at his waist and wearing an apron from which six other serpents emerge (Fig. 211). The *Chilam Balam* of Chumayel speaks of the ritual seating of a new Jaguar Priest, who is dressed in robes of jaguar and rattlesnake skin (Edmonson, 1986:22).

The Yucatecan rattlesnake, *Crotalus durissus tzabcan* (*tzabcan* means "rattlesnake" in Yucatec Maya), unquestionably served as the model and inspiration for many ophidian depictions. Rattles are clearly evident at the ends of the tails of some snake carvings at Chichén Itzá, and the wall of the re-

Fig. 209. Entrance to a building requiring passage through the jaws of a cosmic reptilian monster; Chicanná, Campeche, Mexico.

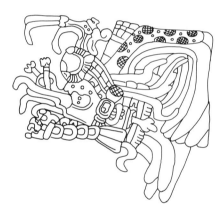

Fig. 210. Detail of lintel 14, Yaxchilán, Chiapas, Mexico, showing a snake as a component of a headdress. Redrawn from Schele and Miller, 1986, by permission of the Kimball Art Museum, Fort Worth, Texas.

Fig. 211. The stela of the seven serpents; stela 13, El Seibal, Guatemala. Redrawn from figure 31 by James Porter in Graham, 1990. Copyright 1990 by the President and Fellows of Harvard College.

stored ball court at Uxmal has embedded within it the feathered tail of a rattlesnake (Fig. 212). This formidable animal, which is capable of delivering a life-threatening bite, must have been as widely feared by the ancient Maya as it is today. The Mexican anthropologist José Díaz-Bolio (1971) contended that the Maya calendar and virtually all aspects of Maya art, architecture, astronomy, and mathematics were inspired by properties of the tropical rattlesnake. For example, he saw in the

Fig. 212. Feathered rattlesnake tail; wall of the ball court, Uxmal, Yucatán, Mexico.

Fig. 213. Viper depicted in the Dresden Codex.

Fig. 214. Detail from a polychrome vase. An old god dances with a realistic serpent, perhaps a boa constrictor; Altar de Sacrificios, Guatemala. Modified from Coe, 1987.

rhomboid pattern of the rattlesnake's skin the geometric basis for Maya temple pyramids and vaulted ceilings, the proportions of the Maya face and body, and a geometric representation of the movements of celestial bodies.

Snakes other than rattlesnakes are frequently represented in Maya art, but the stylization makes it difficult or impossible to associate them with known species. In some cases, however, an informed conjecture can be offered. For example, page 36 of the Dresden Codex (Fig. 213) shows a thick-bodied snake, somewhat stylized but devoid of rattles and with front fangs. Those characteristics apply to several Yucatecan pitvipers, but the uolpoch (*Agkistrodon bilineatus*) has a particularly sinister reputation among the present-day Maya, as discussed above. Moreover, in the codex representation a dark line that passes from the snout backward through the eye, dividing the face into upper and lower light portions, is vaguely similar to the distinct light stripes on the face of the uolpoch. Finally, the tip of the tail is dark, contrasting sharply with the light color of the head and body. In young individuals of *A. bilineatus* the tip of the tail contrasts strongly with the coloration of the body and functions as a caudal lure (see species account for *Agkistrodon bilineatus*).

Very large snakes with dorsal patterns of dark blotches are frequently represented in Maya art, and these can plausibly be interpreted as boa constrictors, ochcan. For example, a mid-eighth-century funerary vase from Altar de Sacrificios shows an old god, possibly god L of the underworld (Coe, 1987:124), dancing with a snake that bears a strong resemblance to the boa both in color pattern and in the configuration of the head and body (Fig. 214).

Amphibians and Reptiles in the Ceremonial Life of the Maya

Amphibians Frogs and toads are associated with water and the water-earth transition in the mythologies of many cultures (Cirlot, 1971:114). Frogs are often important in rituals invoking rainfall, and this is certainly the case among the Maya in the Yucatán Peninsula, where rainfall is highly seasonal and often unpredictable and crop failure as a consequence of inadequate rainfall is always a possibility, especially in the arid northwest portion of the peninsula. For the ancient Maya, the decision of when to initiate the planting cycle was critical, and they made astronomical calculations and consulted the calendar in order to determine the most propitious time to plant.

The aboveground activity of frogs and toads is closely coupled with the seasonal rainfall pattern in the Yucatán Peninsula. As the first heavy rains of May or June fall, marking the onset of the rainy season, huge breeding aggregations of frogs and toads suddenly appear, and their vocalizations fill the spring and summer nights. Quite naturally, frogs and toads came to be viewed as helpers, messengers, or musicians of the *chacs*, the rain gods. In general there were four chacs, or four manifestations of chac, one for each cardinal direction, and each with its own associated color. During the dry season frogs are likely to be found in cenotes and caves, places where the chacs were also believed to go.

The contemporary Maya of Yucatán and Quintana Roo still perform a ceremony, the *ch'a chaac*, to propitiate the chacs and bring the rains. Redfield and Rojas (1971:142) described this rain ceremony as performed by the Maya of Chan Kom, Yucatán. It is a ritual that was also known to Landa and is presumably of great antiquity. At one point in the ceremony four boys are tied to the legs of a rectangular altar. The boys impersonate frogs or toads, mimicking their vocalizations and acting as associates of the *kunku-chaac*, the chief of the rain gods. Arturo Canché provided additional details of this ritual. According to him, frogs and toads represent the *anunciadores* of the rainy season, and two kinds are imitated, each by two boys. One species is the *wowoc* (*Rhinophrynus dorsalis*), which says *wo, wo, wo, wo*. The other is the *totmuch* (*Bufo marinus*), which says *to, to, to, to*.

Frogs appear frequently in the pages of the Madrid Codex, usually in connection with rain deities or in contexts involving rain imagery. For example, several long-nosed deities are depicted on page 17 with a plumed serpent, a turtle, and a frog, all of which are associated with rain imagery (Fig. 215). Page 31 shows a long-nosed rain deity with four frogs, each associated with water.

Associated with archaeological sites throughout the lowland Maya area are large, flask-shaped, subterranean chambers called *chultúns*. These served primarily to accumulate and store water, and in the arid northwest portion of the Yucatán Peninsula they were waterproofed with several layers of plaster and surrounded by a contoured catchment platform. Frogs and toads would have been attracted to these water cisterns, especially during the dry season, further strengthening their association with water. Sometimes this association was made explicit by the Maya: a stucco frog fixed to the inside wall of a chultún was discovered at Sayil, Yucatán, in the late 1980s (A. Delgado and J. Casanova, pers. comm.).

In addition to serving as harbingers of rain or helpers of the rain gods, frogs were associated with agriculture. The Madrid Codex, for example, shows a frog sowing seeds and making furrows with a planting stick. Frogs were also sometimes considered bearers of corn, which they brought here from another world, as the following account, related by Aurora García, reveals:

> You have the rains, there is a heavy rain, and they say that they [the frogs] come from the sky, you know, that is a story. And they say that whenever they fall down if you see where they fall down then you can go and cut them in half so that their intestines can come out, and then you can see only green corn grains there, inside the frog's intestines. They say that the frogs come from another world, and that they only eat green corn. That is why when they come here, the frogs have green corn in their intestines.

The frog in question is probably the uo (*Rhinophrynus dorsalis*), whose Maya name is an onomatopoeic rendering of its vocalization (see the species account for *Rhinophrynus*). The uo is associated with the rain cult of the Yucatec Maya, and its call is believed to announce the rains. Uo is also the name of the second of the eighteen months of the Maya "vague year," which falls at the height of the rainy season.

The skeletal remains of the toads *Bufo valliceps*

Fig. 215. Page 17 from the Madrid Codex. Snakes, turtles, and frogs are associated with rain imagery. Modified from Lee, 1985.

and, especially, *B. marinus* have been found at Maya sites widely separated in space and time. For example, Post-classic burials on Cozumel contain large numbers of *B. marinus* bones (Hamblin, 1984:51). Olson (1978:173) reported a *B. marinus* in a Late Classic burial at Seibal, and the bones of both species were found in a burial chamber at Mayapán, presumably of Post-classic age (Pollock and Ray, 1957:649). Likewise, Wing and Steadman (1980:328) reported *B. marinus* in a burial at Dzibilchaltún in northern Yucatán. Moreover, toads and toadlike animals appear frequently in Maya art. Furst (1974:154) described small Maya bowls representing toads with large parotoid glands.

Dobkin de Rios (1974) offered an intriguing explanation for the ubiquity of the toad motif and the common occurrence of toad remains at Maya archaeological sites. She pointed out that the skin of most amphibians is rich in glands that produce toxic alkaloids. These glands are especially plentiful in toads, where they are densely concentrated in the "warts" and the parotoid glands at the nape of the neck. The toxins produced by the parotoid glands, in particular two classes of toxic cardiac glycosides—bufogenin and bufotoxin—affect the adrenal system and may have dangerous effects on the human cardiovascular system. Indeed, ingestion of these toxins has been known to cause human fatalities (see the species account for *B. marinus*). Bufotenin, also produced by the parotoid glands, is said to have hallucinatory properties as well, but the evidence on this point is equivocal. Fabing and Hawkins (1956:886) reported hallucinogenic effects reminiscent of LSD or mescaline when bufotenin was injected into humans, and LaBarre (1970:146) considered it a "violently hallucinogenic drug." Some later studies failed to elicit hallucinogenic activity, however, even at higher doses (Schultes and Hoffman, 1973:90). Nonetheless, as Hamblin (1984:54) noted, the indole alkaloid 5-hydroxy-N,N-dimethyltryptamine, an active compound in bufotenin, is grouped by some pharmacologists with such known hallucinogens as psilocybin and LSD (Rech and Moore, 1971). Moreover, the same compound is found in the plant *Anadenanthera peregrina*, from which natives of Amazonia and the West Indies prepare a hallucinogenic snuff used to bring about mystical states in religious ceremonies (Hamblin, 1984:54; Schultes and Hoffmann, 1973:89). Reports from San Francisco, Calif., and Australia provide strong supporting evidence for the psychoactive properties of bufotenin. Authorities in those areas reported that people in search of altered states of consciousness boil *B. marinus* and consume the liquid for its supposed hallucinogenic effects. Alternatively, the skin can be dried, ground, and smoked in order to obtain the same effect. Sometimes people ingest the skin secretions directly by licking live toads (*Miami Herald*, 31 January 1990).

According to Dobkin de Rios, the hallucinogenic properties of bufotenin account, at least in part, for the importance ascribed to toads by the ancient Maya. She suggested that the Maya used bufotenin to bring about altered states of consciousness in connection with religious activities. Other Mayanists were reluctant to accept Dobkin de Ríos's thesis (e.g., Proskouriakoff, 1974; Thompson, 1974), even though Coe (1971:74) had offered a similar explanation for the abundance of *B. marinus* remains in Olmec rubbish heaps at San Lorenzo in southern Veracruz. Evidence of ritualistic use of psychoactive materials, possibly including the skin secretions of frogs and toads (e.g., Carneiro, 1970:340; Furst, 1972:43, 1974:154), by the ancient peoples to the north and south of the Maya area is incontrovertible, however, and the suggestion that the Classic Maya elite may have practiced ritual enemas in which hallucinogenic substances were administered lends credence to her assertion.

At least one colonial report supports the idea that toads were used in the preparation of a ritual drink. According to Thompson (1958:225), the seventeenth-century Dominican friar Thomas Gage stated that the Pokomam Maya of highland Guatemala produced a fermented drink called *chicha* and that "in some places they have put in a live toad, and closed up the jar for a fortnight or a month, till all that they have put in be thoroughly steeped, the toad consumed, and the drink well strengthened." According to Gage the resultant noxious brew "stinketh most filthily, and certainly is the cause of many Indians' death, especially where they use the toad's poison with it." According to Robert M. Carmack (cited in Furst, 1972:44), the practice of steeping toads in fermenting chicha is still practiced among the Quiche Maya of the Guatemalan highlands.

Despite the considerable circumstantial evidence that *B. marinus* was a source of hallucinogenic compounds for the ancient Maya, W. B. Davis and Weil (1992) pointed out that hallucinatory properties have yet to be unambiguously demonstrated for any of the skin secretions that toad produces. Moreover, they argued, bufotenin is relatively incapable of crossing the blood-brain barrier, and the toxic compounds also present in the secretions would seem to preclude its use as a ritual intoxicant. Instead, they advanced the intriguing alternative hypothesis that the hallucinogenic toad of the Maya might be another species of *Bufo*, the Sonoran Desert toad, *B. alvarius*, whose skin secretions are definitely known to contain powerful hallucinogens (Davis and Weil, 1992:56). *Bufo alvarius* occurs only in the Sonoran Desert of northwestern Mexico and the southwestern United States, far from the Maya area. Extensive trade routes connected northwestern Mexico with much of Mesoamerica, however, and the movement of toad secretions, if not of the toads themselves, is a distinct possibility.

Reptiles Turtles were evidently of mythical or religious importance to the Maya, for Landa reported that they were used in sacrifices. The House of the Turtles at Uxmal has a series of realistic turtles carved in stone (possibly *Rhinoclemys areolata* or *Trachemys scripta*) adorning the exterior surface of its upper walls (Fig. 216). Moreover, turtles were associated with certain celestial bodies; for example, some stars of the constellation Gemini were called *ac* (turtle) (Coe, 1987:178).

Stone carvings and clay models found at Mayapán

Fig. 216. Detail from the Casa de las Tortugas, Uxmal, Yucatán, Mexico, showing a realistic turtle.

may indicate that turtles played an important part in the ceremonial life of the Maya there. Pollock and Ray (1957:648, 649) reported finding shells of *Terrapene carolina* and *Trachemys scripta* that had been cut or drilled, suggesting use as ornaments or ceremonial objects. The remains of *Dermatemys mawii* and *Rhinoclemmys areolata* found in burial urns at Uaxactún (Stuart, 1958:19) suggest a religious function for those species, which today do not occur in the immediate area. The sarcophagus portrait of Pacal, the great ruler of Palenque from 615 to 683 A.D., shows him wearing a turtle pectoral, identified by Merle Green Robertson as *Staurotypus triporcatus* (E. P. Benson, in litt.).

The turtle as earth monster was discussed above. Related to this idea is a scene on a funerary plate from northern Guatemala that depicts the surface of the earth as the carapace of a giant turtle. A human figure is emerging from a deep crack in the earth/carapace. According to Coe (1987:168), the figure represents First Father, or the maize god, Hun Hunahpu, resurrected by his sons, the Hero Twins, Hunahpu and Xbalanque (Fig. 202).

Turtles are still viewed by some contemporary Maya as having special properties. Aurora García, for example, said that "turtles are special for us because they say that it is a sacred animal. And they say that it has about thirteen lives. That is why it is special, because even though you kill it you can see the meat still jumping. They're alive, they don't die, even when you eat it." According to Redfield and Rojas (1971:207), in Yucatán turtles are respected, even revered, by the contemporary Maya, and the village *H-menob* (shaman priests) advise that they

should never be killed. As protection against sickness, Maya mothers often hang the cross-shaped plastron of turtles around their childen's necks.

Apart from their use as food and curatives, lizards seem to have been important in Maya ritual primarily as sacrificial items. Landa reported that lizards (probably *Ctenosaura* and *Iguana*) were sacrificed, and lizards often appear in the codices as ceremonial offerings. The same may be true for crocodiles, for their bones sometimes appear in the ruins of high-status public places such as ball courts and plazas (Pohl, 1990:163).

In spite of snakes' frequent appearance in Maya iconography, their remains are uncommon in the middens, caches, and burials of Maya archaeological sites. Their delicate skeletons and loosely articulated skulls are unlikely to be preserved, and snakes are presumably underrepresented in the archaeological record for that reason. As I mentioned earlier, a rattlesnake vertebra was uncovered at El Seibal, although the significance of its occurrence there is unclear. The remains of a colubrid snake, possibly *Lampropeltis triangulum*, found in a burial at Dzibilchaltún (Wing and Steadman, 1980:328) suggest a ceremonial role for at least some snakes, however. Vertebrae of unidentified viperids (possibly *Crotalus durissus* or *Bothrops asper*) found at Tikal show clear signs of having been altered and polished, and perhaps were strung on a cord and worn as a necklace (S. J. Scudder, in litt.).

The Vision Serpent Some contemporary Mayanists (e.g., Schele and Freidel, 1990; Schele and Miller, 1986) believe that hallucinatory visions were central to Maya ritual because they provided a link with long-departed ancestors or gods. The visions were called forth during altered states of consciousness induced by ingesting hallucinogenic materials, as discussed above, and by autosacrificial bloodletting. In Maya art, these visions often take the form of a serpent, known as the hallucinatory serpent of autosacrifice and bloodletting (Robicsek and Hales, 1982:46), or simply the vision serpent (Schele and Miller, 1986:46). The body of the vision serpent is often smooth, and details of scutellation and pattern are apparent—as, for example, on Yaxchilán lintel 25 (Fig. 217). In other representations the vision serpent is feathered. Sometimes it is represented as two-headed, with a head at each end of the body. Usually the snout is long and bulbous, and a head emerging from the gaping jaws represents the person or deity being contacted in the ritual. Often

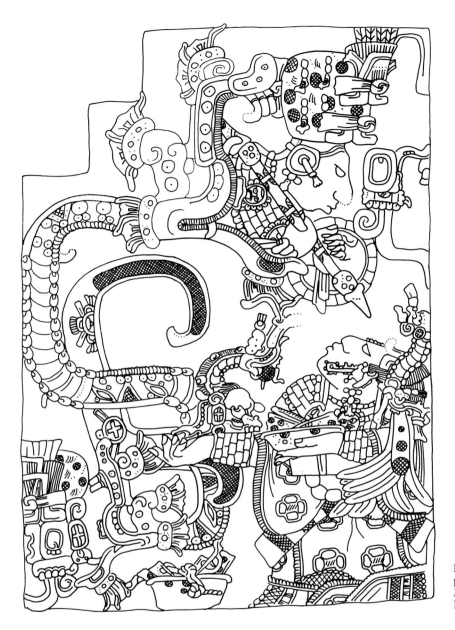

the serpent is rearing up above the priest who called forth the vision.

Epilogue

It is said that the *Books of Chilam Balam* foretold the Spanish Conquest and the subjugation of the Maya. In the texts, the Jaguar Priests speak also of the future and of redemption, and once more the serpent appears, this time as metaphor for the Maya themselves and all that they have endured. Rosado Vega (1957) characterized this aspect of the prophecies:

What is to come will occur just as what happened in the past had to take place, because as our downfall was predicted, so has our future redemption been foretold.

According to tradition, before the *Chilam* foretold of the conquest . . . the entire body of the rattlesnake was covered with rattles that sounded like music, and the rattlesnake decreased the number of rattles to avoid being heard as much, because today only its tail is covered with rattles, the others are concealed, and today their sound produces fear. . . . Everything passes and everything returns. The new day will come . . . it will come as I predict, for the spirits who watch over us speak through me. As long as the ceibas are standing in the forest, and as long as the caves in the soil of the Mayab are open, wait for the new day because it must come. Then you will see strange things, but above all you will see these things of which I speak. You will see the rattlesnake joyfully shake all the rattles on its entire body, for it will reveal the ones that are hidden today . . .

because with that sound which will be heard from one end of this land to the other, it is the rattlesnake who will summon all Maya to convene on that day . . . wait . . . wait . . . wait, the rattlesnake will shake all its rattles and they will be heard in every corner of the Mayab. That prophecy which is yet to be fulfilled, is the one that all Maya await, and it will be fulfilled in due time. That is why the Maya turn pale when they hear the sound of the rattles of the green snake, because the Maya know that the rattlesnake is polishing its rattles more frequently in order to be ready.

Gazetteer

Listed below are localities in the Yucatán Peninsula where herpetological specimens have been collected or that provide points of reference in relation to important collecting stations. Most of the place-names mentioned in this book will be found here, including many of those given in the locality records that accompany each species account. Localities are listed alphabetically by country, by political subdivisions within countries (Belizean district, Guatemalan department, Mexican state), and alphabetically by locality within political subdivisions. Latitude and longitude are given to the nearest degree, and distances are straight-line distances. Each locality is numbered to correspond with its position on the accompanying map for each political subdivision (Maps 183–188).

Many place-names in the Yucatán Peninsula have variant spellings, and the names of many localities have changed with time. Moreover, boundaries between political subdivisions within the peninsula have fluctuated historically such that some localities have shifted jurisdiction. A particularly dramatic example of shifting state boundaries involves the borders between the Mexican states of Campeche, Quintana Roo, and Yucatán. Before 1968 the boundary between Campeche and Quintana Roo lay nearly 50 km to the west of its present location, and the apex of the Yucatán triangle lay farther to the north. Today the border between Campeche and Quintana Roo is essentially a northward extension of the boundary between Belize and Guatemala, and the apex of the Yucatán triangle lies farther south and east (Dundee, 1985:6). The practical effect is that Campeche and Yucatán have gained territory at the expense of Quintana Roo, and several important collecting localities formerly in Quintana Roo presently lie in southern Yucatán. Such names are cross-referenced and can thus be found under either state.

For localities with variant spellings, I first give the spelling that appears to be in most frequent and current use, followed by the lesser-used variants. If a name has been changed, I first give the name in current usage, followed by the older name(s) in parentheses. My decisions concerning preferred names and spellings are based on my own familiarity with the localities and on usage determined by recent maps and gazetteers.

I somewhat arbitrarily characterize *cities* as population centers that have in excess of 30,000 permanent inhabitants and a decidedly urban aspect, including a diversified economy, large-scale public works, and multiple social strata. *Towns* are smaller permanent assemblages, with between 1,000 and 30,000 inhabitants, a simpler economy, less social stratification, and smaller-scale public works. *Villages* are areas permanently occupied by fewer than 1,000 inhabitants. They are rural in nature and have a simplified economy based typically on agriculture, fishing, or forestry. *Camps* are ephemeral or seasonally occupied locations, usually associated with lumbering or the harvest of chicle. Many were abandoned long ago and no longer exist as recognizable entities. I use the term *settlement* in a purposely ambiguous way to designate localities of uncertain status.

Belize (Map 183)

Belize District

1. Altun Ha (Rockstone Pond). 17° 46′ N, 88° 22′ W; an archaeological site in northern Belize District on the Old Northern Highway. Corozal palms, deciduous forest, and cultivated fields surround the site.

2. Ambergris Cay. 18° 03′ N, 87° 56′ W (approx.), sea level; a large cay approximately 20 to 30 km off the coast of Corozal and Belize Districts.

3. Belize City. 17° 30′ N, 88° 12′ W, sea level; the principal city of Belize, situated on a small peninsula jutting into the Caribbean Sea. Much of the surrounding area is mangrove swamp.

4. Bermudian Landing. 17° 33′ N, 88° 31′ W; a town in western Belize District on the Belize River, approx-

imately 37 km WNW of Belize City.

5. Burrell Boom (Boom, Boom Town, Burrel's Town). 17° 34′ N, 88° 24′ W; a town amid agricultural fields and pastures in central Belize District on the Belize River, approximately 24 km WNW of Belize City.

6. Cay Bokel. 17° 10′ N, 87° 54′ W, sea level; a small cay at the southern end of the Turneffe Islands, approximately 48 km SE of Belize City.

7. Cay Chapel. 17° 42′ N, 88° 03′ W, sea level; a small cay approximately 25 km NE of Belize City.

8. Cay Corker. 17° 46′ N, 88° 02′ W, sea level; a cay approximately 10 km NE of Belize City.

Cayo Iguano. *See* Iguana Cay

9. Churchyard. 17° 18′ N, 88° 33′ W; a town in western Belize District, approximately 45 km SW of Belize City.

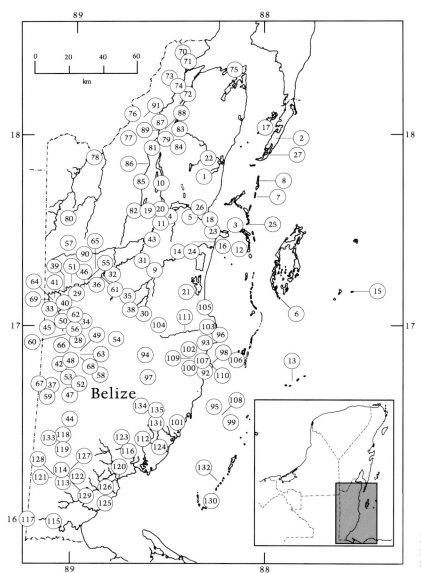

MAP 183. Gazetteer map of Belize. The numbers correspond to locality entries in the Gazetteer.

10. Crooked Tree. 17° 45′ N, 88° 32′ W; a town on the Northern Lagoon in northwestern Belize District, approximately 49 km NW of Belize City.

11. Double Head Cabbage. 17° 33′ N, 88° 33′ W; a village in western Belize District, approximately 40 km W of Belize City.

12. English Cay. 17° 20′ N, 88° 03′ W; a cay approximately 10 km SE of Belize City.

13. Glover's Reef. 16° 49′ N, 87° 48′ W; a cluster of cays approximately 40 km ESE of Dangriga.

14. Gracy Rock, Gracie Rock. 17° 23′ N, 88° 26′ W; a rocky promontory overlooking the Sibun River, approximately 25 km SW of Belize City. The surrounding vegetation is savanna with scattered palms, pines, and patches of scrub.

15. Half Moon Cay. 17° 12′ N, 87° 32′ W, sea level; a small cay near the southern end of Lighthouse Reef, approximately 75 km ESE of Belize City. The island supports open stands of coconut palms and a dense tangle of low trees.

16. Hattieville. 17° 28′ N, 88° 23′ W; a village in east-central Belize District on the Western Highway, approximately 22 km WSW of Belize City.

17. Iguana Cay (Cayo Iguano). 18° 04′ N, 87° 58′ W; a small cay off the coast of Corozal District, approximately 16 km NNW of San Pedro, Ambergris Cay.

18. Ladyville. 17° 33′ N, 88° 17′ W; a village on the Northern Highway in eastern Belize District, approximately 14 km NE of Belize City.

19. Lemonal (Lemonal Village). 17° 37′ N, 88° 36′ W; a settlement on Spanish Creek in western Belize District, approximately 55 km WNW of Belize City.

20. Lime Walk. 17° 38′ N, 88° 29′ W; a village on the Belize River in central Belize District, approximately 35 km WNW of Belize City.

21. Manatee River. 17° 14′ N, 88° 22′ W; a river in eastern Belize District that flows predominantly eastward into the Southern Lagoon.

22. Maskall, Maskalls. 17° 53′ N, 88° 19′ W; a town on the Northern River in northern Belize District, approximately 35 km SE of Orange Walk Town.

23. Philip Goldson International Airport. 17° 32′ N, 88° 18′ W; the international airport of Belize, situated approximately 13 km WNW of Belize City.

Rockstone Pond. *See* Altun Ha

24. Rockville. 17° 24′ N, 88° 27′ W; a town in east-central Belize District, approximately 31 km WSW of Belize City.

25. Saint George's Cay. 17° 33′ N, 88° 04′ W; a small cay approximately 10 km ENE of Belize City.

26. Sand Hill. 17° 38′ N, 88° 22′ W; a town on the Northern Highway in eastern Belize District, approximately 25 km NW of Belize City.

27. San Pedro. 17° 56′ N, 87° 57′ W; the principal town on Ambergris Cay.

Stanley Airport. *See* Philip Goldson International Airport

Cayo District

28. Augustine, Augustin (San Augustine). 16° 58′ N, 88° 59′ W, elev. 460 m; the district forestry camp in the Mountain Pine Ridge in south-central Cayo District. The camp is situated in pine parkland with gallery forest and tropical broadleaf forest nearby.

29. Baking Pot. 17° 12′ N, 89° 01′ W; a settlement near the Western Highway in western Cayo District, approximately 14 km ENE of San Ignacio.

30. Baldy Sibun. 17° 00′ N, 88° 43′ W; a settlement in western Cayo District.

31. Beaver Dam Creek. 17° 22′ N, 88° 38′ W; a tributary of Labouring Creek in northeastern Cayo District. It flows in a northerly direction, intersecting the Western Highway approximately 14 km ENE of Roaring Creek.

32. Belmopan. 17° 15′ N, 88° 47′ W; the capital of Belize. Formerly tropical broadleaf forest, the area is now largely edificarian and second-growth vegetation.

33. Benque Viejo (Benque Viejo del Carmen). 17° 05′ N, 89° 08′ W; a town on the Western Highway in westernmost Cayo District, at the Guatemalan border. The surrounding vegetation is largely pastures and cultivated fields.

34. Blancaneau. 17° 03′ N, 88° 58′ W; formerly a settlement in the Mountain Pine Ridge, now abandoned. The habitat is pine parkland.

35. Blue Hole. 17° 08′ N, 88° 42′ W; a national park on the Southern Highway situated in tropical rainforest.

36. Camalot. 17° 15′ N, 88° 49′ W; a village on the Western Highway in western Cayo District, approximately 3 km WSW of Roaring Creek.

37. Caracol. 16° 56′ N, 89° 07′ W; an archaeological site in western Cayo District in tropical rainforest.

38. Cave's Branch. 17° 14′ N, 88° 35′ W; a tributary of the Sibun River, flowing generally northeast in eastern Cayo District.

Cayo. *See* San Ignacio

39. Central Farm. 17° 12′ N, 89° 01′ W; an agricultural station at Baking Pot, Cayo District. *See* Baking Pot.

40. Chaa Creek. 17° 05′ N, 89° 07′ W; a resort (formerly a farm) overlooking a branch of the Mopan River in western Cayo District.

41. Chial. 17° 06′ N, 89° 07′ W; a settlement on the Western Highway in western Cayo District, approximately 7 km SW of San Ignacio.

42. Cohune Ridge. 16° 49′ N, 88° 37′ W; a small settlement or camp in southwestern Cayo District. Tropical rainforest and corozo palms characterize the surrounding vegetation.

43. Coquericot, Cocquericot. 17° 27′ N, 88° 37′ W; a small settlement on Beaver Dam Creek in western Cayo District, approximately 26 km NNE of Belmopan.

44. Doyle's Delight. 16° 30′ N, 89° 00′ W (approx.), elev. 1,160 m; a collecting station in the Maya Mountains in southern Cayo District. The surrounding vegetation is montane forest.

45. El Arenal (Arenal). 17° 02′ N, 89° 09′ W; a settlement in northern Cayo District on the Mopan River.

46. Georgeville. 17° 11′ N, 89° 01′ W; a town on the Western Highway in central Cayo District.

47. Granos de Oro Camp, Grano de Oro Camp. 16° 38′ N, 89° 01′ W; a camp situated on the Vaca Plateau, approximately 35 km SSW of Augustine.

48. Guacamallo Bridge. 16° 52′ N, 89° 02′ W; a crossing on the Macal River in southern Cayo District. The surrounding vegetation is tropical rainforest.

49. Little Vaqueros Creek. 17° 03′ N, 88° 59′ W; a small stream in the Mountain Pine Ridge of central Cayo District, approximately 2.5 km N of Augustine. The surrounding vegetation is pine parkland with broadleaf gallery forest.

50. Macal River. 16° 52′ N, 89° 01′ W; a river in western Cayo District that flows predominantly south to north into the Belize River.

51. McKinstry's Farm. 17° 10′ N, 89° 05′ W; a farm in western Cayo District near the Western Highway. The surrounding vegetation is pasture and cultivated fields, with scattered remnants of tropical rainforest.

52. Millionario. 16° 45′ N, 88° 59′ W; a camp on the Vaca Plateau in southern Cayo District, approximately 25 km SSW of Augustine. The vegetation in the vicinity is predominantly tropical rainforest.

53. Mountain Cow. 16° 47′ N, 88° 59′ W, elev. 215 m; an archaeological site in southwestern Cayo District situated in tropical rainforest.

54. Mountain Pine Ridge. 16° 53′ N, 88° 55′ W (approx.); a region on the northwest slopes of the Maya Mountains in south-central Cayo District. The vegetation is pine parkland with broadleaf gallery forest.

55. Ontario (Ontario Village). 17° 13′ N, 88° 53′ W; a settlement in western Cayo District on the Western Highway, approximately 13 km WSW of Roaring Creek.

56. Privassion Creek, Privacion Creek (Río Privación). 17° 02′ N, 89° 01′ W, elev. 340 m; a predominantly westward-flowing creek in the Mountain Pine Ridge in south-central Cayo District.

57. Ramonal. 17° 25′ N, 89° 09′ W; a camp in northwestern Cayo District situated in tropical rainforest.

58. Raspaculo Branch. 16° 47′ N, 88° 50′ W (approx.); a tributary of the Macal River that drains the northwest flank of the Maya Mountains.

59. Retiro. 16° 44′ N, 89° 09′ W, elev. 215 m; a small settlement or camp in the southwest corner of Cayo District situated in tropical rainforest.

60. Río Frio Cave. 17° 00′ N, 89° 03′ W, elev. 460 m; a system of caves near Augustine in the Mountain Pine Ridge. The surrounding vegetation is pine parkland and tropical rainforest. *See* Augustine.

61. Roaring Creek. 17° 13′ N, 88° 46′ W; a village on the Western Highway in central Cayo District.

62. San Antonio. 17° 05′ N, 89° 01′ W; a town in central Cayo District. Milpas, pastures, and remnants of tropical moist forest surround the settlement. *See* San Antonio, Toledo District.

San Augustine, San Augustin. *See* Augustine
San José Succotz. *See* Soccoths

63. San Luis. 17° 03′ N, 88° 59′ W; a sawmill and small settlement on Vaqueros Creek in the Mountain Pine Ridge of central Cayo District, now abandoned. Pine parkland and scattered patches of broadleaf forest characterize the surrounding vegetation.

64. Soccoths, Soccotz, Socotz, Succoths, Tzokotz, (San José Soccotz, San José Succotz). 17° 06′ N, 89° 07′ W; a town on the southeast bank of the Belize River, on the Western Highway near the Guatemalan border in western Cayo District.

65. Spanish Lookout. 17° 13′ N, 88° 59′ W; a settlement in west-central Cayo District, approximately 12 km NNE of San Ignacio.

Tzokotz. *See* Soccoths

66. Vaca Plateau. 16° 45′ N, 89° 10′ W (approx.); a plateau lying in southwestern Cayo District, northwest of the Maya Mountains, with an elevation generally between 600 and 700 m. The vegetation is predominantly tropical rainforest.

67. Valentin. 16° 47′ N, 89° 09′ W; a camp in southwestern Cayo District at the Guatemalan border. The surrounding vegetation is tropical rainforest.

68. Vaqueros Creek. 17° 03′ N, 88° 59′ W; a stream flowing through the pine parkland of the Mountain Pine Ridge of central Cayo District.

69. Xunantunich. 17° 05′ N, 89° 08′ W; an archaeological site overlooking the Belize River in western Cayo District, near the Guatamalan border. Second-growth forest and remnants of tropical rainforest characterize the surrounding vegetation.

Corozal District

70. Chan Chen. 18° 26′ N, 88° 27′ W; a village in northern Corozal District, approximately 8 km NW of Corozal.

71. Corozal (Corozal Town). 18° 24′ N, 88° 24′ W; a town in northern Corozal District on Bahía Chetumal.

72. Progresso Lagoon. 18° 13′ N, 88° 26′ W (approx.); a long, narrow lagoon in central Corozal District.

73. Santa Clara. 18° 18′ N, 88° 30′ W; a town in northwestern Corozal District, approximately 18 km SW of Corozal.

74. Santa Cruz. 18° 16′ N, 88° 28′ W; a town on the New River in northern Corozal District, approximately 18 km SSE of Corozal.

75. Sarteneja. 18° 22′ N, 88° 10′ W; sea level, a vil-

Fig. 218. *Dermophis mexicanus*, a specimen at the University of Texas at Arlington. Photo by R. W. Van Devender.

Fig. 219. *Bolitoglossa dofleini*, Honduras.

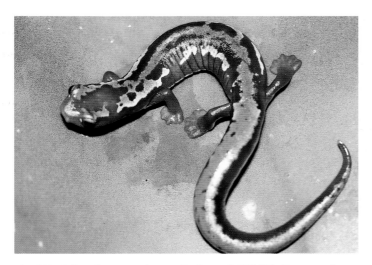

Fig. 220. *Bolitoglossa mexicana*, Cockscomb Wildlife Preserve, Stann Creek, Belize. Photo by Carol Farneti.

Fig. 221. Detail of the head of *Bolitoglossa mexicana*, Cayo, Belize. Photo by Robert A. Lubeck.

Fig. 222. *Bolitoglossa rufescens*, Blue Creek, Toledo, Belize. Photo by R. W. Van Devender.

Fig. 223. *Bolitoglossa yucatana*, 14.6 km SE Cobá, Quintana Roo, Mexico.

Fig. 224. *Rhinophrynus dorsalis*, Plan de Ayala, Campeche, Mexico.

Fig. 225. *Eleutherodactylus alfredi*, Cuautlapan, Veracruz, Mexico. Photo by Roy W. McDiarmid.

Fig. 226. *Eleutherodactylus chac*, Blue Creek, Toledo, Belize. Photo by R. W. Van Devender.

Fig. 227. *Eleutherodactylus rhodopis*, Sierra de Los Tuxtlas, Veracruz, Mexico. Photo by Richard C. Vogt.

Fig. 228. *Eleutherodactylus rugulosus* (gray morph), Palenque, Chiapas, Mexico.

Fig. 229. *Eleutherodactylus rugulosus* (reddish morph), Palenque, Chiapas, Mexico.

Fig. 230. *Eleutherodactylus yucatanensis*, near Cobá, Quintana Roo, Mexico.

Fig. 231. *Leptodactylus labialis*, Kinchel, Yucatán, Mexico.

Fig. 232. *Leptodactylus labialis*, near Palenque, Chiapas, Mexico.

Fig. 233. *Leptodactylus melanonotus*, 17 km SE Sabancuy, Campeche, Mexico.

Fig. 234. *Physalaemus pustulosus*, 6.8 km S Chekubúl, Campeche, Mexico.

Fig. 235. *Bufo marinus*, Chekubúl, Yucatán, Mexico.

Fig. 236. Amplectant pair of *Bufo valliceps*, 5.4 km E Bella Flor, Yucatán, Mexico.

Fig. 237. Vocalizing male of *Bufo valliceps* showing the single subgular vocal sac, 5.4 km E Bella Flor, Yucatán, Mexico.

Fig. 238. *Agalychnis callidryas*, 15 km S Palenque, Chiapas, Mexico.

Fig. 239. *Agalychnis moreletii*, Caracol, Cayo, Belize. Photo by Carolyn M. Miller.

Fig. 240. *Hyla ebraccata*, Blue Hole, Cayo, Belize.

Fig. 241. Amplectant pair of *Hyla loquax*, 78 km ESE Villahermosa, Tabasco, Mexico.

Fig. 242. *Hyla microcephala*, Cayo, Belize. Photo by Robert A. Lubeck.

Fig. 243. *Hyla picta*, near Blue Hole, Cayo, Belize.

Fig. 244. *Hyla valancifer*, 2 km E, 2.4 km S Purulhá, Baja Verapaz, Guatemala. Photo by Jonathan A. Campbell.

Fig. 245. *Phrynohyas venulosa*, 7.9 km N Felipe Carrillo Puerto, Quintana Roo, Mexico.

Fig. 246. Calling male of *Phrynohyas venulosa* showing paired lateral vocal sacs, Plan de Ayala, Campeche, Mexico.

Fig. 247. *Scinax staufferi*, Cayo, Belize. Photo by Carolyn M. Miller.

Fig. 248. Amplectant pair of *Smilisca baudinii*, Oxholom, Yucatán, Mexico.

Fig. 249. Calling male of *Smilisca baudinii* showing paired subgular vocal sacs, Oxholom, Yucatán, Mexico.

Fig. 250. Amplectant pair of *Smilisca cyanosticta*, Sierra de los Tuxtlas, Veracruz, Mexico. Photo by Richard C. Vogt.

Fig. 251. *Smilisca cyanosticta*, Puente Natural, Cayo, Belize. Photo by Carolyn M. Miller.

Fig. 252. Female *Triprion petasatus* clasped simultaneously by two males, 5.4 km E Bella Flor, Yucatán, Mexico.

Fig. 253. *Hyalinobatrachium fleischmanni*, 6.9 km N Ocosingo, Chiapas, Mexico.

Fig. 254. *Gastrophryne elegans*, Tikal, El Petén, Guatemala.

Fig. 255. *Hypopachus variolosus*, Cobá, Quintana Roo, Mexico.

Fig. 256. *Rana berlandieri*, near Escárcega, Campeche, Mexico.

Fig. 257. *Rana berlandieri*, San Luis, Cayo, Belize.

Fig. 258. Subadult *Rana juliani*, San Luis, Cayo, Belize.

Fig. 259. *Rana vaillanti*, Cockscomb Wildlife Sanctuary, Stann Creek, Belize.

Fig. 260. *Crocodylus acutus*, Broward Co., Fla. Photo by Paul Moler.

Fig. 261. *Crocodylus moreletii*, near Maskalls, Belize, Belize.

Fig. 262. *Caretta caretta*. Photo by Anne Heimann.

Fig. 263. Detail of the head of *Caretta caretta*, Fla. Photo by Tom Smoyer.

Fig. 264. *Chelonia mydas*, Fla. Photo by Anne Heimann.

Fig. 265. *Eretmochelys imbricata*, near Mona Island, Puerto Rico. Photo by Anne Heimann.

Fig. 266. *Lepidochelys kempii*, Fla. Photo by Anne Heimann.

Fig. 267. Nesting female *Dermochelys coriacea* on St. Croix, Virgin Islands. Photo by Anne Heimann.

Fig. 268. *Dermatemys mawii*, Veracruz, Mexico. Photo by John B. Iverson.

Fig. 269. Detail of the head of *Dermatemys mawii*, Lacandón, Chiapas, Mexico. Photo by John B. Iverson.

Fig. 270. Adult *Chelydra serpentina* showing serrated posterior margin of carapace, Blue Creek, Toledo, Belize. Photo by Stephen G. Tilley.

Fig. 271. Detail of the head of a juvenile *Chelydra serpentina*, Toledo District, Belize. Photo by R. W. Van Devender.

Fig. 272. Adult *Claudius angustatus*, near Candelaria, Campeche, Mexico.

Fig. 273. Detail of the head of *Claudius angustatus* showing strongly hooked upper jaw, near Candelaria, Campeche, Mexico.

Fig. 274. Detail of the head of *Staurotypus triporcatus* showing barbels on the chin and slightly hooked upper jaw, Veracruz, Mexico. Photo by R. W. Van Devender.

Fig. 275. Adult female *Kinosternon acutum*, of unknown provenance. Photo by John B. Iverson.

Fig. 276. Detail of the head of a female *Kinosternon acutum*, of unknown provenance. Photo by John B. Iverson.

Fig. 277. *Kinosternon creaseri*, 21.9 km NNE Playa del Carmen, Quintana Roo, Mexico. Photo by John B. Iverson.

Fig. 278. *Kinosternon leucostomum*, mi 26 on Old Northern Hwy., Belize, Belize. Photo by John B. Iverson.

Fig. 279. Detail of the head of *Kinosternon leucostomum*, mi 26 on Old Northern Hwy., Belize, Belize. Photo by John B. Iverson.

Fig. 280. Male *Kinosternon scorpioides*, Orange Walk Town, Orange Walk, Belize. Photo by John B. Iverson.

Fig. 281. *Rhinoclemmys areolata*, near Augustine, Cayo, Belize.

Fig. 282. Detail of the head of *Rhinoclemmys areolata*, 1 km E Xpujil, Campeche, Mexico.

Fig. 283. *Terrapene carolina*, near Candelaria, Campeche, Mexico.

Fig. 284. Detail of the head of *Terrapene carolina*, near Candelaria, Campeche, Mexico.

Fig. 285. *Trachemys scripta*, Cobá, Quintana Roo, Mexico.

Fig. 286. Juvenile *Coleonyx elegans* (striped morph), 11 km S Pueblo Nuevo X-Can, Quintana Roo, Mexico.

Fig. 287. An adult *Coleonyx elegans* showing movable eyelids and vertically elliptical pupil, near Uxmal, Yucatán, Mexico.

Fig. 288. *Coleonyx elegans* showing stiff-legged defensive posture, 15 km E Celestún, Yucatán, Mexico.

Fig. 289. *Sphaerodactylus argus*, Río Lagartos, Yucatán, Mexico.

Fig. 290. *Sphaerodactylus glaucus*, Sabancuy, Campeche, Mexico.

Fig. 291. *Aristelliger georgeensis*, San Miguel, Isla Cozumel, Quintana Roo, Mexico.

Fig. 292. Head of *Aristelliger georgeensis* showing details of scutellation and the vertically elliptical pupil, San Miguel, Isla Cozumel, Quintana Roo, Mexico.

Fig. 293. *Hemidactylus frenatus*, Escárcega, Campeche, Mexico.

Fig. 294. *Hemidactylus turcicus*, Sisal, Yucatán, Mexico.

Fig. 295. *Phyllodactylus insularis*, Half Moon Cay, Belize, Belize.

Fig. 296. *Phyllodactylus tuberculosus*, S Water Cay, Belize, Belize. Photo by R. W. Van Devender.

Fig. 297. *Thecadactylus rapicauda*, Blue Creek, Toledo, Belize. Photo by R. W. Van Devender.

Fig. 298. Head of a male *Basiliscus vittatus* showing details of scutellation and the integumentary crest, Mountain Pine Ridge, Cayo, Belize.

Fig. 299. Head of a female *Basiliscus vittatus* showing details of scutellation and the rudimentary crest, near Tizimín, Yucatán, Mexico.

Fig. 300. *Corytophanes cristatus*, Honduras.

Fig. 301. Head of *Corytophanes cristatus* showing details of scutellation and the orange iris, Honduras.

Fig. 302. *Corytophanes hernandezii*, Cockscomb Wildlife Sanctuary, Stann Creek, Belize.

Fig. 303. *Laemanctus longipes*, Caracol, Cayo, Belize. Photo by Carolyn M. Miller.

Fig. 304. Head of *Laemanctus longipes* showing details of scutellation and the cephalic casque, Caracol, Cayo, Belize. Photo by Carolyn M. Miller.

Fig. 305. *Laemanctus serratus* showing enlarged spines on the border of the cephalic casque and the enlarged, sawtoothed vertebral scales, near Nunkiní, Campeche, Mexico.

Fig. 306. *Ctenosaura defensor*, near Mérida, Yucatán, Mexico.

Fig. 307. Head of *Ctenosaura defensor* showing details of scutellation, near Mérida, Yucatán, Mexico.

Fig. 308. An adult male *Ctenosaura similis*. A female is visible in the background (*lower left*), Ruinas Xel-Ha, Quintana Roo, Mexico.

Fig. 309. *Iguana iguana*, photographed at the Belize Zoo.

Fig. 310. Juvenile *Iguana iguana* from Belize. Photo by Robert A. Lubeck.

Fig. 311. Female *Sceloporus chrysostictus,* Chichén Itzá, Yucatán, Mexico.

Fig. 312. Male *Sceloporus chrysostictus,* Ruinas Xel-Ha, Quintana Roo, Mexico.

Fig. 313. *Sceloporus cozumelae*, Puerto Juárez, Quintana Roo, Mexico.

Fig. 314. *Sceloporus lundelli*, Augustine, Cayo, Belize.

Fig. 315. *Sceloporus serrifer*, Ruinas Oxkintok, Yucatán, Mexico.

Fig. 316. Female *Sceloporus teapensis*, Palenque, Chiapas, Mexico.

Fig. 317. Male *Sceloporus teapensis*, Palenque, Chiapas, Mexico. Photo by Alan H. Savitzky.

Fig. 318. *Anolis allisoni*, Half Moon Cay, Cayo, Belize.

Fig. 319. *Anolis biporcatus*, Chan Chich, Orange Walk, Belize. Photo by Carolyn M. Miller.

Fig. 320. Juvenile *Anolis biporcatus*, Guanacaste National Park, Cayo, Belize. Photo by Robert A. Lubeck.

Fig. 321. *Anolis capito*, Caracol, Cayo, Belize. Photo by Carolyn M. Miller.

Fig. 322. Female *Anolis capito* showing the striped pattern characteristic of some females of this species, Caracol, Cayo, Belize. Photo by Carolyn M. Miller.

Fig. 323. Female *Anolis cristatellus*, Miami, Dade Co., Fla.

Fig. 324. Male *Anolis cristatellus*. The nuchal crest is normally erected only during courtship and in aggressive displays; note the supracaudal crest; Miami, Dade Co., Fla.

Fig. 325. *Anolis lemurinus*, Chaa Creek, Cayo, Belize.

Fig. 326. *Anolis rodriguezii*, Petectunich, Yucatán, Mexico.

Fig. 327. Female *Anolis sagrei*, Miami, Dade Co., Fla.

Fig. 328. Male *Anolis sagrei*, Akumal, Quintana Roo, Mexico.

Fig. 329. *Anolis sericeus*, Palenque, Chiapas, Mexico.

Fig. 330. Female *Anolis sericeus* showing the striped color pattern characteristic of some females of this species, 8 km E La Cristalina, Campeche, Mexico.

Fig. 331. *Anolis tropidonotus*, Río Frio Cave, Cayo, Belize.

Fig. 332. *Anolis uniformis*, Caracol, Cayo, Belize. Photo by Carolyn M. Miller.

Fig. 333. *Eumeces schwartzei*, Caracol, Cayo, Belize. Photo by Carolyn M. Miller.

Fig. 334. *Eumeces sumichrasti*, Caracol, Cayo, Belize. The blue coloration of the tail disappears with age. Photo by Carolyn M. Miller.

Fig. 335. *Mabuya unimarginata*, Augustine, Cayo, Belize.

Fig. 336. *Sphenomorphus cherriei*, Blue Creek, Toledo, Belize. Photo by R. W. Van Devender.

Fig. 337. *Gymnophthalmus speciosus*, Costa Rica. Photo by R. W. Van Devender.

Fig. 338. Juvenile *Ameiva festiva* showing the bright coloration and bluish tail characteristic of subadults, El Rosario, El Petén, Guatemala.

Fig. 339. Male *Ameiva undulata* showing nuptial coloration on the head and throat, 7 km NE Felipe Carrillo Puerto, Quintana Roo, Mexico.

Fig. 340. Male *Ameiva undulata* showing nuptial coloration on the head, throat, and neck, Campeche, Mexico. Photo by Alan H. Savitzky.

Fig. 341. *Cnemidophorus angusticeps*, Cobá, Quintana Roo, Mexico.

Fig. 342. *Cnemidophorus cozumela*, 15.3 km SW Sabancuy, Campeche, Mexico.

Fig. 343. *Cnemidophorus rodecki*, Quintana Roo, Mexico.

Fig. 344. *Lepidophyma flavimaculatum*, Blue Creek, Toledo, Belize. Photo by R. W. Van Devender.

Fig. 345. *Typhlops microstomus*, Belize. Photo by Frederick W. Dodd.

Fig. 346. *Leptotyphlops goudotii*, Isla Cozumel, Quintana Roo, Mexico. Photo by Jeffrey Himmelstein.

Fig. 347. *Boa constrictor*, 24 km E Mérida, Yucatán, Mexico.

Fig. 348. *Amastridium veliferum*, Blue Creek, Toledo, Belize. Photo by Stephen G. Tilley.

Fig. 349. *Coniophanes imperialis*, Río Lagartos, Yucatán, Mexico.

Fig. 350. *Coniophanes imperialis*, Tikal, El Petén, Guatemala.

Fig. 351. *Coniophanes schmidti*, 12 km S Pueblo Nuevo X-Can, Quintana Roo, Mexico.

Fig. 352. *Conophis lineatus*, Xel-Ha, Quintana Roo, Mexico.

Fig. 353. *Dendrophidion nuchale*, Bladen Nature Reserve, Toledo, Belize. Photo by Jacob A. Marlin.

Fig. 354. *Dipsas brevifacies*, 2 km SE Cobá, Quintana Roo, Mexico.

Fig. 355. Juvenile *Dipsas brevifacies*, near Uxmal, Yucatán, Mexico.

Fig. 356. *Dryadophis melanolomus*, Cobá, Quintana Roo, Mexico.

Fig. 357. *Drymarchon corais*, 65.6 km NNE Felipe Carrillo Puerto, Quintana Roo, Mexico.

Fig. 358. *Drymobius margaritiferus*, Cobá, Quintana Roo, Mexico.

Fig. 359. Juvenile *Drymobius margaritiferus*, Cobá, Quintana Roo, Mexico.

Fig. 360. *Elaphe flavirufa*, Quintana Roo, Mexico. Photo by R. W. Van Devender.

Fig. 361. *Ficimia publia* (reddish morph), near Sabancuy, Campeche, Mexico.

Fig. 362. *Ficimia publia* (gray morph), Tizimín, Yucatán, Mexico.

Fig. 363. *Imantodes cenchoa*, Tikal, El Petén, Guatemala.

Fig. 364. *Imantodes gemmistratus*, 24.7 km NE Dziuché, Yucatán, Mexico.

Fig. 365. *Lampropeltis triangulum*, 14.4 km NW Felipe Carrillo Puerto, Quintana Roo, Mexico.

Fig. 366. *Leptodeira frenata*, Isla Cozumel, Quintana Roo, Mexico.

Fig. 367. *Leptodeira septentrionalis*, 22.7 km N Felipe Carrillo Puerto, Quintana Roo, Mexico.

Fig. 368. *Leptophis ahaetulla*, 35 km NE Felipe Carrillo Puerto, Quintana Roo, Mexico.

Fig. 369. *Leptophis mexicanus*, 2.1 km N Chekubúl, Campeche, Mexico.

Fig. 370. Detail of the head of *Leptophis mexicanus*, Cayo District, Belize. Photo by Robert A. Lubeck.

Fig. 371. *Masticophis mentovarius*, 4 km S Champotón, Campeche, Mexico.

Fig. 372. Juvenile *Masticophis mentovarius*, Punta Sam, Quintana Roo, Mexico.

Fig. 373. *Ninia sebae* showing the predominantly red dorsum of specimens from the northern portions of the Yucatán Peninsula, Santa Elena, Yucatán, Mexico.

Fig. 374. *Ninia sebae* showing the dorsal pattern of dark markings characteristic of specimens from the base of the Yucatán Peninsula, 8 km S Palenque, Chiapas, Mexico.

Fig. 375. *Oxybelis aeneus,* Finca La Pacífica, Guanacaste, Costa Rica. Photo by R. W. Van Devender.

Fig. 376. *Oxybelis fulgidus,* Sarteneja, Corozal, Belize.

Fig. 377. *Oxyrhopus petola*, 8.7 km S Tikal, El Petén, Guatemala.

Fig. 378. *Pseustes poecilonotus,* Pueblo Nuevo X-Can, Quintana Roo, Mexico.

Fig. 379. *Rhadinaea decorata*, Comadre, Limón, Costa Rica. Photo by R. W. Van Devender.

Fig. 380. *Scaphiodontophis annulatus*, 50 km WSW Belize City, Belize, Belize.

Fig. 381. *Senticolis triaspis*, Bladen Nature Reserve, Toledo, Belize. Photo by Jacob A. Marlin.

Fig. 382. A hatchling *Sibon dimidiata*, Blue Creek, Toledo, Belize. Photo by R. W. Van Devender.

Fig. 383. *Sibon sanniola*, near Cobá, Quintana Roo, Mexico.

Fig. 384. *Sibon sanniola*, Cayo District, Belize. Photo by Robert A. Lubeck.

Fig. 385. *Sibon sartorii*, Tizimín, Yucatán, Mexico.

Fig. 386. *Spilotes pullatus* showing defensive behavior involving lateral compression of the neck and anterior portion of the body, 1 km W Mahahual, Quintana Roo, Mexico.

Fig. 387. *Stenorrhina freminvillei*, 1 km E Los Angeles, Guanacaste, Costa Rica. Photo by Norman J. Scott.

Fig. 388. *Symphimus mayae*, km 33, between Tulum and Cobá, Quintana Roo, Mexico. Photo by William W. Lamar.

Fig. 389. *Tantilla moesta*, 14 km SE Cobá, Quintana Roo, Mexico.

Fig. 390. *Thamnophis marcianus*, Hidden Valley Falls, Cayo, Belize. Photo by Frederick W. Dodd.

Fig. 391. *Thamnophis proximus*, 15.5 km S Sabancuy, Campeche, Mexico.

Fig. 392. *Tretanorhinus nigroluteus*, Dangriga, Stann Creek, Belize. Photo by R. W. Van Devender.

Fig. 393. *Urotheca elapoides*, 19.6 km S Kantunilkin, Quintana Roo, Mexico. Note the close resemblance to *Micrurus diastema* (Fig. 395) from the same locality.

Fig. 394. Juvenile *Xenodon rabdocephalus*, Cayo District, Belize. Note the close resemblance to *Bothrops asper* (Fig. 400).

Fig. 395. *Micrurus diastema* showing the reduced number of black and yellow rings characteristic of specimens from the northeastern portion of the Yucatán Peninsula, 18.9 km S Kantunilkin, Quintana Roo, Mexico.

Fig. 396. *Micrurus diastema* showing the pattern characteristic of specimens from the base of the Yucatán Peninsula, Izabal, Guatemala. Photo by Jonathan A. Campbell.

Fig. 397. *Agkistrodon bilineatus*, 20 km ESE Mérida, Yucatán, Mexico.

Fig. 398. *Atropoides nummifer*, Caracol, Cayo, Belize. Photo by Carolyn M. Miller.

Fig. 399. *Bothriechis schlegelii*, specimen from Costa Rica photographed at the Belize Zoo.

Fig. 400. Juvenile *Bothrops asper*, 50 km WSW Belize City, Belize, Belize.

Fig. 401. *Crotalus durissus*, 50 km WSW Belize City, Belize, Belize.

Fig. 402. *Porthidium nasutum*, 1 mi N Tikal, El Petén, Guatemala. Photo by Frederick W. Dodd.

Fig. 403. *Porthidium yucatanicum*, 21 km SE Cobá, Quintana Roo, Mexico. Note the pale yellow tail tip, which probably serves as a caudal lure.

lage on the coast of Bahía Chetumal in northern Corozal District.

Orange Walk District

76. Albion Island. 18° 10' N, 88° 40' W; an island at the Mexican border bounded by branches of the Río Hondo in northwestern Orange Walk District.

77. August Pine Ridge. 17° 59' N, 88° 43' W; a village in western Orange Walk District, approximately 21 km SW of Orange Walk Town.

78. Blue Creek Village. 17° 53' N, 88° 54' W; a village in northwestern Orange Walk District, approximately 40 km SW of Orange Walk Town, near the Mexican border. *See* Blue Creek, Toledo District.

79. Carmelita. 18° 02' N, 88° 23' W; a settlement in northern Orange Walk District, approximately 6 km SSE of Orange Walk Town.

80. Gallon Jug. 17° 33' N, 89° 01' W, elev. 60 m; a settlement at the railroad terminus in southwestern Orange Walk District; formerly an important logging center and now an area for ecotourism. The vegetation is predominantly tropical rainforest.

81. Guinea Grass. 17° 57' N, 88° 36' W; a village in southern Orange Walk District, approximately 15 km SSW of Orange Walk.

82. Hill Bank. 17° 35' N, 88° 42' W; a small settlement in southern Orange Walk District located at the southern end of the New River Lagoon.

83. Honey Camp. 18° 02' N, 88° 28' W; a camp in northern Orange Walk District, approximately 12 km ESE of Orange Walk.

84. Kate's Lagoon, Skate's Lagoon. 17° 59' N, 88° 28' W; a lake in northern Orange Walk District, approximately 16 km SE of Orange Walk.

85. Lamanai (Indian Church). 17° 46' N, 88° 40' W; an archaeological site and village on the New River Lagoon in southern Orange Walk District, approximately 36 km SSW of Orange Walk.

86. New River. 18° 22' N, 88° 24' W (approx.); a river flowing in a predominantly northerly direction through northern Orange Walk and Corozal Districts, emptying into Corozal Bay.

87. Orange Walk (Orange Walk Town). 18° 06' N, 88° 33' W; a town on the New River in northern Orange Walk District situated in an area of intense sugarcane agriculture, with scattered patches of deciduous forest.

88. Otro Benque. 18° 06' N, 88° 33' W; a locality on the New River in the vicinity of Orange Walk Town.

Skate's Lagoon. *See* Kate's Lagoon

89. Tower Hill. 18° 02' N, 88° 33' W; a settlement and sugarcane center on the New River in Northern Orange Walk District, approximately 7 km S of Orange Walk Town.

90. Yalbac. 17° 22' N, 88° 56' W; a camp in southernmost Orange Walk District, on Yalbac Creek, at the base of the base of the Yalbac Hills, approximately 21 km NW of Roaring Creek.

91. Yo Creek. 18° 05' N, 88° 39' W; a settlement and minor archaeological site in northern Orange Walk District, approximately 8 km W of Orange Walk.

Stann Creek District

92. All Pines. 16° 47' N, 88° 18' W; a village near the Caribbean coast in eastern Stann Creek District. The surrounding vegetation is predominantly pine savanna.

93. Bocawina, Bokowina. 16° 54' N, 88° 23' W; a village in east-central Stann Creek District.

94. Cockscomb Mountains (Cockscomb Range). 16° 48' N, 88° 37' W (approx.); a west-projecting spur of the Maya Mountains in western Stann Creek District. Much of the area supports tropical rainforest and montane forest.

95. Crawl Cay. 16° 36' N, 88° 13' W, sea level; a small cay approximately 15 km off the coast of southern Stann Creek District.

96. Dangriga (Stann Creek, Stann Creek Town). 16° 88' N, 88° 13' W; the administrative capital of Stann Creek District, situated on the Caribbean coast at the mouth of Stann Creek.

97. Double Fall, Double Falls. 16° 42' N, 88° 38' W; formed by Double Fall Creek, a tributary of the Swasey Branch of the Monkey River. The falls are situated in southernmost Stann Creek District. The surrounding vegetation is tropical rainforest.

98. Freetown. 16° 50' N, 88° 18' W; a village on the Sittee River, approximately 18 km SSW of Dangriga.

99. Hatchet Cay. 16° 28' N, 88° 04' W; a small cay approximately 40 km off the coast of northern Toledo District.

100. Kendal, Kendall. 16° 48' N, 88° 23' W; a village on the Southern Highway in northeastern Stann Creek District, approximately 23 km SW of Dangriga.

101. Mango Creek. 16° 33' N, 88° 24' W; a village on Mango Creek in southernmost Stann Creek District, approximately 2 km inland from the Caribbean coast.

102. Mayflower Village (Mayflower Camp). 16° 56' N, 88° 22' W; a settlement and minor archaeological site in northern Stann Creek District, approximately 7 km NNW of Silk Grass.

103. Melinda Forestry Camp. 17° 00' N, 88° 18' W; a forestry station in the lower Stann Creek Valley in northeastern Stann Creek District, approximately 12 km WNW of Dangriga.

104. Middlesex. 17° 02' N, 88° 31' W; a village in the upper Stann Creek Valley. Citrus is cultivated extensively on the valley floor and on the lower slopes of the surrounding hills. Remnants of tropical rainforest are at higher elevations.

105. Mullins River. 17° 07' N, 88° 18' W; a village on the Mullins River near the Caribbean coast in north-

eastern Stann Creek District, approximately 18 km NNW of Dangriga.

106. Ragged Cay. 16° 51' N, 88° 08' W; a cay approximately 25 km ESE of Dangriga.

107. Regalia. 16° 48' N, 88° 18' W; a settlement in northern Stann Creek District, approximately 20 km SSW of Dangriga.

108. Rendezvous Cay. 16° 33' N, 88° 06' W; a cay approximately 40 km SE of Dangriga.

109. Silk Grass. 16° 54' N, 88° 21' W; a village in eastern Stann Creek District. The surrounding vegetation is predominantly pine savanna.

110. Sittee. 16° 50' N, 88° 17' W; a village on the Sittee River near the Caribbean coast, approximately 18 km SSW of Dangriga.

Stann Creek. *See* Dangriga

111. Stann Creek Valley. 17° 00' N, 88° 25' W (approx.); the valley of Stann Creek in northern Stann Creek District. The valley supports extensive citrus cultivation.

Toledo District

112. Bladen Branch. 16° 24' N, 88° 33' W (approx.); a southern tributary of the Monkey River draining the southeastern flanks of the Maya Mountains in northern Toledo District.

113. Blue Creek. 16° 12' N, 89° 03' W; a village and minor archaeological site on Blue Creek in southern Toledo District, approximately 27 km WNW of Punta Gorda.

114. Columbia Branch Camp. 16° 18' N, 89° 01' W; a camp on the Columbia Branch of the Río Grande in southern Toledo District, approximately 7 km N of San Antonio.

115. Crique Sarco. 15° 58' N, 89° 04' W; a settlement on the Temash River in southern Toledo District, approximately 8 km N of the Guatemalan border.

116. Deep River. 16° 17' N, 88° 39' W; a river draining the southeast flanks of the Maya Mountains in central Toledo District.

117. Dolores. 15° 59' N, 89° 13' W; a Kekchi Maya village in southern Toledo District, approximately 1 km E of the Guatemalan border. The surrounding vegetation is predominantly tropical rainforest with scattered farm plots.

118. Esperanza (Esperanza Camp). 16° 26' N, 89° 03' W; a camp in northwestern Toledo District on the southeast flank of the Maya Mountains, near Little Quartz Ridge. Vegetation in the area is tropical rainforest.

119. Gloria Camp. 16° 22' N, 89° 10' W, elev. about 680 m; a camp on the southwest slope of the Maya Mountains, Toledo District. The vegetation is tropical rainforest.

120. Golden Stream. 16° 14' N, 88° 44' W (approx.); a river draining the southeast flanks of the Maya Mountains and entering the Gulf of Honduras at Port Honduras.

121. Little Quartz Ridge. 16° 24' N, 89° 06' W (approx.); a formation in the southwestern portion of the Maya Mountains in northwestern Toledo District. The vegetation is tropical rainforest.

122. Lubaantún. 16° 17' N, 88° 58' W; an archaeological site in southern Toledo District, approximately 25 km NW of Punta Gorda.

123. Medina Bank. 16° 27' N, 88° 45' W; a settlement on the Southern Highway in southeastern Toledo District.

124. Monkey River. 16° 22' N, 88° 29' W (approx.); a river draining the southeast flanks of the Maya Mountains in northeastern Toledo District. It consists of a northern tributary, the Swasey Branch; a middle tributary, the Trio Branch; and a southern tributary, the Bladen Branch. The river flows in a southeasterly direction and enters the Caribbean Sea at Monkey River Town.

125. Punta Gorda. 16° 07' N, 88° 48' W; a town that is the administrative capital of Toledo District, on the Gulf of Honduras.

126. Río Grande, Río Grand. 16° 08' N, 88° 44' W; a river draining the southeastern slopes of the Maya Mountains and flowing into the Gulf of Honduras.

127. Salamanca (Salamanca Forestry Camp). 16° 16' N, 89° 03' W; a forestry camp in southern Toledo District, approximately 31 km NW of Punta Gorda.

128. San Antonio. 16° 15' N, 89° 02' W; a village in southern Toledo District, approximately 28 km NW of Punta Gorda. *See* San Antonio, Cayo District.

129. San Pedro Columbia (San Pedro). 16° 17' N, 88° 58' W; a village in south-central Toledo District on the Columbia Branch of the Río Grande, approximately 25 km NW of Punta Gorda.

130. Sapodilla Cays. 16° 07' N, 88° 16' W (approx.); a cluster of cays in the Gulf of Honduras, approximately 38 km SE of Monkey River Town, Toledo District.

131. Swasey Branch. 16° 24' N, 88° 33' W (approx.); a northern tributary of the Monkey River, draining the southeast flanks of the Maya Mountains in northern Toledo District.

132. Tom Owen Cay. 16° 12' N, 88° 13' W; a small cay in the Gulf of Honduras, approximately 34 km SE of Monkey River Town, Toledo District.

133. Unión Camp. 16° 23' N, 89° 08' W, elev. about 700 m; a camp on the southeast slope of the Maya Mountains in southern Toledo District. The vegetation is tropical rainforest.

134. Waha Leaf Camp. 16° 35' N, 88° 38' W; a camp near Waha Leaf Creek, in northern Toledo District.

135. Waha Leaf Creek. 16° 34' N, 88° 23' W (approx.); a tributary of the Bladen Branch of the Monkey

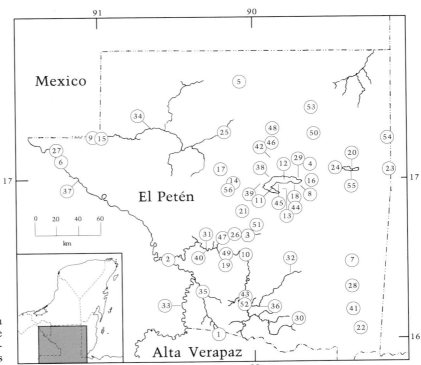

MAP 184. Gazetteer map of northern Guatemala showing localities in the Departments of Alta Verapaz and El Petén. The numbers correspond to entries in the Gazetteer.

River, draining the southeastern flanks of the Maya Mountains in northern Toledo District.

Guatemala (Map 184)

Department of Alta Verapaz

1. Chinajá. 16° 04′ N, 90° 15′ W, elev. 140 m; a small settlement and camp of the Ohio Oil Company situated in tropical rainforest in northernmost Alta Verapaz, near the El Petén border.

Department of El Petén

2. Altar de Sacrificios (Altar de los Sacrificios). 16° 28′ N, 90° 32′ W; an archaeological site on the Río de la Pasión in southeastern El Petén. The vegetation is predominantly tropical rainforest.

3. Arroyo Subín. 16° 38′ N, 90° 12′ W (approx.); a river in central El Petén flowing westward and then south into the Río de la Pasión.

Bocamonte, Boca del Monte. *See* Pacomon

4. Caoba. 17° 02′ N, 89° 40′ W; a village near the east end of Lago Petén Itzá on the road to Tikal. The surrounding vegetation is predominantly second growth and cultivated fields with remnants of tropical evergreen forest.

Ceibal. *See* El Seibal

5. Chuntuquí, Chuntunquí, Chantuouí, Chantuquí. 17° 31′ N, 90° 09′ W; a settlement in northwestern El Petén in tropical evergreen forest.

6. Desempeño, Desempeña (El Desempeño). 17° 07′ N, 91° 13′ W; a settlement on the Río Usumacinta, approximately 7 km upstream (SE) from Piedras Negras, in westernmost El Petén. The surrounding vegetation is tropical rainforest.

7. Dolores. 16′ 31 N, 89° 25′ W; a village on the Poptún-Flores road in southeastern El Petén. Pine savanna and gallery forest characterize the surrounding vegetation. *See* Dolores, Toledo District, Belize.

8. El Cruce. 17° 00′ N, 89° 42′ W; the intersection of the Benque Viejo–Flores road and the road to Tikal, at the east end of Lago Petén Itzá. The vegetation is predominantly second growth and cultivated fields with remnants of tropical evergreen forest.

9. El Repasto. 17° 13′ N, 91° 04′ W; a camp on the Río San Pedro in western El Petén, near the Mexican border.

10. El Seibal, El Ceibal, Seibal. 16° 33′ N, 90° 03′ W; an archaeological site near the southern shore of the Río de la Pasión. Tropical rainforest, stands of corozo palms, milpas, and second-growth forest surround the site.

Fallabon. *See* Melchor de Mencos

11. Flores (Tayasal). 16° 56′ N, 89° 53′ W; a town and the administrative capital of the Department of El

Petén, situated on an island in Lago Petén Itzá.

Lago Macanché. *See* Laguna Macanché

12. Lago Petén Itzá (Lago Petén). 16° 59′ N, 89° 50′ W (approx.); a large lake in central El Petén, approximately 30 km in length and averaging about 3.5 km in width.

13. Laguna de Eckixil (Laguna Exequil, Laguna Eckisil). 16° 55′ N, 89° 48′ W; a lake near the south shore of Lago Petén Itzá in central El Petén.

14. Laguna de Zotz, Laguna de Sotz. 16° 59′ N, 90° 09′ W; a lake in central El Petén, approximately 30 km W of Lago Petén Itzá.

15. Laguna El Repasto. 17° 12′ N, 91° 01′ W; a lake near the Río San Pedro in westernmost El Petén, near the Mexican border.

16. Laguna Macanché (Laguneta Macanché). 16° 58′ N, 89° 38′ W; a lake in central El Petén, approximately 8 km E of the east end of Lago Petén Itzá.

17. Laguna Perdida. 17° 05′ N, 90° 13′ W; a lake and camp in northwest El Petén.

18. Laguna Petenxil, Laguna Petenchel. 16° 55′ N, 89° 50′ W; a small lake approximately 20 km E of Flores.

19. Laguna Petexbatún, Laguna Petexbatúm. 16° 27′ N, 90° 13′ W; a lake in southwestern El Petén, approximately 10 km S of Sayaxché.

20. Laguna Yaxhá, Laguna Yaxjá, Laguna Yaxá. 17° 06′ N, 89° 23′ W; a lake just north of the Benque Viejo–Flores road in eastern El Petén.

Laguneta Macanché. *See* Laguna Macanché

21. La Libertad. 16° 47′ N, 90° 07′ W, elev. 170 m; a town in the savanna region of central El Petén, approximately 25 km SW of Flores. Nanze savanna with gallery forest, secondary growth, and occasional patches of hardwood forest characterize the vegetation.

22. Las Cañas. 16° 06′ N, 89° 22′ W, elev. 107 m; a small settlement in southeastern El Petén near the Belize border, approximately 18 km SE of San Luis.

23. Melchor de Mencos (Fallabon, Plancha de Piedra). 17° 04′ N, 89° 10′ W; a town on the Río Mopan on the Benque Viejo–Flores road, near the Belize border.

24. Nueva Aguada. 17° 04′ N, 89° 32′ W; a camp approximately 10 km W of the west end of Laguna Yaxhá in east-central El Petén.

Pacomon. An unknown site at which Henry Malleis collected in 1923. Stuart (1934:4) suggested that Malleis was referring to the camp named Bocamonte, which lies at the edge of the savanna country about 20 km SW of Flores.

25. Paso de los Caballos (Paso de Caballos, Paso Caballos). 17° 15′ N, 90° 16′ W; a village on the Río San Pedro in northeastern El Petén.

26. Paso Subín (Paso de Subín). 16° 38′ N, 90° 12′ W, elev. 90° m; a village on the Arroyo Subín, approximately 10 km SSW of La Libertad. Milpas, pastures, and second-growth forest characterize the vegetation.

27. Piedras Negras. 17° 12′ N, 91° 15′ W; an archae-ological site on the Río Usumacinta in westernmost El Petén. Rainforest surrounds the site.

Plancha de Piedra. *See* Melchor de Mencos

28. Poptún. 16° 21′ N, 89° 26′ W, elev. 140 m; a town in pine savanna in southeastern El Petén, approximately 83 km SE of Flores.

29. Remate, Ramate (El Remate, El Ramate). 17° 00′ N, 89° 42′ W; a village at the east end of Lago Petén Itzá, not to be confused with El Remate, at 17° 30′ N, 90° 18′ W, in northwestern El Petén. Milpas, second growth, and remnants of tropical evergreen forest characterize the surrounding vegetation.

30. Riachuelo Machaquila. 16° 08′ N, 89° 45′ W (approx.); a river in southern El Petén that flows westward into the Río de la Pasión through tropical rainforest.

31. Río de la Pasión. 16° 28′ N, 90° 33′ W (approx.); a large river in southwestern El Petén flowing northward and then westward into the Río Usumacinta. Much of the area drained by the Río de la Pasión supports tropical rainforest.

32. Río Machaquila. 16° 25′ N, 89° 45′ W (approx.); a river in southern El Petén flowing predominantly west and southwest to join the Río Santa Amelia before entering the Río de la Pasión. Much of the drainage is covered with tropical rainforest.

33. Río Salinas. 16° 13′ N, 90° 26′ W (approx.); a major north-flowing tributary of the Río Usumacinta. It forms a portion of the international boundary between Mexico and Guatemala.

34. Río San Pedro. 17° 16′ N, 90° 43′ W (approx.); a river in northwestern El Petén that flows westward into Tabasco, Mexico. The vegetation in the drainage of the Río San Pedro is predominantly tropical evergreen forest.

35. Río San Román. 16° 21′ N, 90° 22′ W (approx.), elev. 110 m; a river in southwestern El Petén that flows north and northwest into the Río Salinas. The surrounding vegetation is predominantly tropical rainforest.

36. Río Santa Amelia. 16° 13′ N, 90° 01′ W (approx.); a tributary of the Río Machaquila in southern El Petén. Tropical rainforest covers most of the area drained by the Río Santa Amelia.

37. Río Usumacinta. 16° 55′ N, 91° 03′ W (approx.); the largest river in Middle America. It flows in a predominantly northwesterly direction and forms a portion of the international boundary between Guatemala and Mexico, and, in Mexico, part of the border between the states of Chiapas and Tabasco.

38. San Andrés. 16° 58′ N, 89° 55′ W; a village on the north shore of Lago Petén Itzá in central El Petén.

39. San Benito. 16° 55′ N, 89° 54′ W, elev. 90 m; a village on the west shore of Lago Petén Itzá in central El Petén.

40. San Juan Acul. 16° 33′ N, 90° 17′ W; a village on the Río de la Pasión, approximately 12 km WNW

of Sayaxché. The surrounding vegetation is predominantly tropical rainforest.

41. San Luis. 16° 14′ N, 89° 27′ W, elev. 135 m; a town on the Poptún-Flores road in southeastern El Petén, approximately 16 km S of Poptún.

42. San Miguel. 17° 09′ N, 89° 53′ W; a camp in central El Petén, approximately 17 km N of San Andrés. The surrounding vegetation is tropical evergreen forest.

43. Santa Amelia. 16° 15′ N, 90° 02′ W; a village on the Río de la Pasión in southern El Petén, approximately 33 km SE of Sayaxché. The surrounding vegetation is predominantly tropical rainforest.

44. Santa Ana. 16° 48′ N, 89° 50′ W; a town on the Poptún-Flores road in central El Petén, approximately 16 km SE of Flores.

Santa Cruz. A camp whose exact location is unknown. Stuart, 1934:4, locates it about 6 miles east of Yaxhá; however, the map accompanying Stuart, 1935, indicates a camp of that name approximately 25 km WSW of Uaxactún, and the gazetteer for Guatemala published by the U.S. Department of the Interior (1965) indicates a Santa Cruz at approximately that latitude and longitude. Stuart's 1935 map shows no Santa Cruz anywhere in the vicinity of Yaxhá. Six miles east of Yaxhá would presumably be on the Benque Viejo–Remate trail, at that time the principal overland route into El Petén from Belize. Both Henry Malleis and Stuart traversed that trail, making collections en route, the former in 1923 and the latter in 1933. Malleis, however, also secured specimens in the vicinity of Chuntuquí, northwest of Lago Petén Itzá, and he may possibly have collected in the vicinity of Santa Cruz at 17° 19′ N, 89° 45′ W.

45. Santa Elena. 16° 55′ N, 89° 54′ W; a village on the south shore of Lago Petén Itzá in central El Petén, now the site of an international airport.

46. Santa Rita. 17° 14′ N, 89° 58′ W; a camp in north-central El Petén, approximately 35 km N of San Andrés. The vegetation is predominantly tropical evergreen forest.

47. Santa Teresa. 16° 41′ N, 90° 10′ W; a camp on Arroyo Subín, approximately 5 km W of Paso Subín, in southwestern El Petén.

48. Saubich. A collecting locality in north-central El Petén mentioned by Henry Malleis. Stuart (1934:4) said that Saubich does not exist and suggested that the name applies to Sacchich, a locality approximately 52 km N of San Andrés, thus at approximately 17° 27′ N, 89° 54′ W.

49. Sayaxché. 16° 31′ N, 90° 10′ W, elev. 80 m; a town on the south bank of the Río de la Pasión in southwestern El Petén. Vegetation in the vicinity of the town is second-growth forest, milpas, and pastures with remnants of tropical rainforest.

Seibal. *See* El Seibal

Sojio. *See* Toocog

Sos. *See* Zotz

Sotz. *See* Zotz

Subín. *See* Paso Subín

Tayasal. The principal city of the Itzá Maya, who were conquered by the Spanish in 1697. The present city of Flores was built on the ruins of Tayasal. *See* Flores.

50. Tikal. 17° 20′ N, 89° 39′ W; an archaeological site and village in northeastern El Petén, now a part of Tikal National Park. The vegetation is tropical evergreen forest.

51. Toocog (The Ohio Oil Company of Guatemala), Sojio. 16° 41′ N, 90° 02′ W, elev. 140 m; an oil camp and small settlement approximately 15 km SE of Flores. The vegetation is savanna at the edge of broadleaf forest.

52. Tres Islas. 16° 12′ N, 90° 01′ W; a settlement and archaeological site on the Río de la Pasión in southern El Petén, approximately 40 km SSE of Sayaxché. The surrounding vegetation is tropical rainforest.

53. Uaxactún. 17° 24′ N, 89° 39′ W; an archaeological site and small settlement in northeastern El Petén. The surrounding vegetation is tropical evergreen forest, second growth, and milpas.

54. Yaloch. 17° 19′ N, 89° 11′ W; a camp and archaeological site near the Belize border in easternmost El Petén, approximately 20 km NNW of San Ignacio, Belize.

55. Yaxhá, Yaxja. 17° 06′ N, 89° 23′ W; a village on the south shore of Laguna Yaxhá, just north of the Benque Viejo–Flores road in eastern El Petén.

56. Zotz, Sotz, Sos, El Sos. 16° 59′ N, 90° 09′ W; a camp on the west side of Laguna de Zotz in central El Petén, approximately 25 km WNW of Flores.

Mexico

Campeche (Map 185)

1. Apazote. 18° 55′ N, 90° 22′ W, elev. 90° m; a ranch in west-central Campeche, approximately 50 km NE of Escárcega, in tropical evergreen forest and savanna.

2. Atasta. 18° 38′ N, 92° 04′ W; a town in southwestern Campeche situated on the north shore of Laguna de Atasta on Hwy. 180, approximately 27 km W of Ciudad del Carmen.

3. Balakbal. 18° 53′ N, 89° 35′ W; a camp and archaeological site in southeastern Campeche, approximately 70 km NNE of Tikal, Guatemala. The vegetation is tropical evergreen forest.

4. Balchacaj, Balchacah. 18° 25′ N, 91° 30′ W; an hacienda near the mouth of the Río Chumpán, on the southern shore of Laguna de Términos, southwestern Campeche. The area is low and swampy with scattered hammocks.

5. Becan. 18° 31′ N, 89° 25′ W, elev. 250 m; an archaeological site in southeastern Campeche. For-

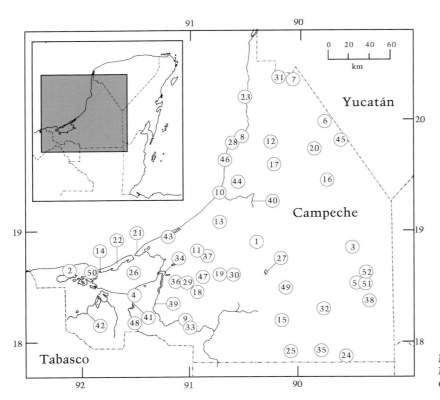

MAP 185. Gazetteer map of Campeche, Mexico. The numbers correspond to locality entries in the Gazetteer.

merly tropical evergreen forest, now milpas, pastures, second growth, and remnant forest.

6. Bolonchén, Bolonchén de Rejón, Bolonchén de Ticul. 20° 00′ N, 89° 49′ W, elev. 80 m; a town on Hwy. 261 in northern Campeche, situated in tropical deciduous forest.

7. Calkiní. 20° 22′ N, 90° 03′ W; a town in northernmost Campeche, near the Yucatán border, situated in thorn forest.

8. Campeche. 19° 51′ N, 90° 32′ W, sea level; the capital city of the state of Campeche, on the Gulf of Mexico. The vegetation inland from the city is tropical deciduous forest.

9. Candelaria. 18° 11′ N, 91° 03′ W; a village on the Río Candelaria in southwestern Campeche. Pastures, cultivated fields, and second-growth vegetation characterize the surrounding vegetation.

10. Champotón. 19° 21′ N, 90° 43′ W, sea level; a town on the Gulf of Mexico at the mouth of the Río Champotón. Coconut plantations predominate along the coast, with tropical deciduous forest inland.

11. Chekubúl. 18° 51′ N, 90° 58′ W; a village on the Sabancuy-Escárcega road in southwestern Campeche. The surrounding countryside is pastures, marshes, and open forest.

12. Chencoyi. 19° 48′ N, 90° 14′ W; a village in northern Campeche, approximately 35 km ESE of Champeche, situated in tropical deciduous forest.

13. Chuina. 18° 58′ N, 90° 41′ W, elev. 65 m; a village approximately 45 km S of Champotón. The surrounding vegetation is tropical deciduous forest and savannas.

14. Ciudad del Carmen (Laguna). 18° 38′ N, 91° 50′ W, sea level; a town at the southwest end of Isla del Carmen, in the mouth of Laguna de Términos, southwestern Campeche. Coconut plantations and low shrubs grow in the vicinity of the town.

15. Concepción. 18° 13′ N, 90° 04′ W, elev. 65 m; a village in southeastern Campeche situated in tropical evergreen forest.

16. Dzibalchén. 19° 24′ N, 89° 45′ W, elev. 100 m; a town in north-central Campeche situated in tropical deciduous forest.

17. Edzná, Etzná. 19° 35′ N, 90° 15′ W; an archaeological site in western Campeche situated amid cultivated fields and second-growth forest.

18. Encarnación. 18° 29′ N, 90° 57′ W; an hacienda in southwest Campeche. The surrounding area consists of cultivated and abandoned fields, pastures, and tall forest.

19. Escárcega, Francisco Escárcega. 18° 37′ N, 90° 44′ W, elev. 65 m; a town in southwestern Campeche at the intersection of Hwys. 186 and 261. Formerly surrounded by tropical evergreen forest, the area is now cultivated fields, pastures, and second growth.

20. Hopelchén. 19° 45′ N, 89° 51′ W, elev. 80 m; a

town in northern Campeche on Hwy. 261 situated in tropical deciduous forest.

21. Isla Aguada. 18° 48' N, 91° 31' W, sea level; a town at the tip of a small peninsula extending southwest into the Laguna de Términos. Coconut plantations, scrubby beach vegetation, and mangroves surround the town.

22. Isla del Carmen. 18° 43' N, 91° 41' W, sea level to 2 m; an island in the mouth of Laguna de Términos, in southwestern Campeche. Coconut palms and scrubby dune vegetation cover much of the island, with mangrove swamp along the coast.

23. Jaina. 20° 13' N, 90° 28' W, sea level; a small island and archaeological site immediately off the coast of Campeche, approximately 45 km N of the city of Campeche.

Laguna. *See* Ciudad del Carmen

24. Laguna Alvarado. 17° 51' N, 89° 33' W, elev. 150 m; a lake situated in tropical evergreen forest in southern Campeche, approximately 10 km N of the Guatemalan border.

25. Laguna Chumpich. 17° 59' N, 90° 03' W, elev. 150 m; a lake in southern Campeche situated in tropical evergreen forest.

26. Laguna de Términos, La Laguna. 18° 40' N, 91° 30' W (approx.); a large embayment in southwestern Campeche that is continuous with the Gulf of Mexico; Isla del Carmen lies at its mouth.

27. Laguna Silvituc, Laguna Cilvituk (Laguna Noh). 18° 40' N, 90° 15' W, elev. 60 m; a lake and village in south-central Campeche. Pastures, cultivated fields, and tropical evergreen forest surround the lake.

28. Lerma. 19° 48' N, 90° 36' W, sea level; a town on the Gulf of Mexico approximately 10 km SW of Campeche on Hwy. 180. Tropical deciduous forest occurs inland.

29. Mamantel. 18° 33' N, 91° 05' W; a village in southwestern Campeche on the Río Mamantel, approximately 35 km WSW of Escárcega. Pastures, wetlands, and cultivated fields characterize the surrounding vegetation.

30. Matamoros, Escárcega de Matamoros. 18° 35' N, 90° 38' W, elev. 65 m; a village a few kilometers east of Escárcega, formerly surrounded by tropical evergreen forest, now by pastures, cultivated fields, and second-growth scrub.

Noh Laguna. *See* Laguna Silvituc

31. Nunkiní. 20° 20' N, 90° 11' W; a town in northern Campeche situated in tropical deciduous forest, approximately 70 km NNE of Campeche.

32. Oxpemul. 18° 18' N, 89° 48' W; a camp and archaeological site in southeastern Campeche, approximately 45 km SW of Xpujil. The surrounding vegetation is tropical evergreen forest.

33. Pacaitún, Pacaytún. 18° 13' N, 91° 05' W; a village on the Río Candelaria in southwestern Campeche.

34. Panlao, Paulau. 18° 37' N, 91° 16' W; a settlement on a small island in Laguna de Panlao at the eastern end of Laguna de Términos.

35. Pared de los Reyes. 17° 59' N, 89° 48' W; an archaeological site in southeastern Campeche, approximately 70 km SW of Xpujil. The surrounding vegetation is tropical evergreen forest.

36. Pital. 18° 33' N, 91° 08' W; a village in southwestern Campeche, approximately 42 km WSW of Escárcega. Pastures, cultivated fields, and remnant tropical evergreen forest characterize the surrounding vegetation.

37. Plan de Ayala. 18° 45' N, 90° 59' W; a village on the road between Sabancuy and Escárcega in southwestern Campeche. Savannas, wetlands, pastures, and patches of open forest are found in the vicinity of the village.

38. Río Bec. 18° 23' N, 89° 18' W; an archaeological site in southern Campeche situated in tropical evergreen forest, approximately 17 km SSE of Xpujil.

39. Río Candelaria. 18° 15' N, 91° 15' W (approx.); a river in southwestern Campeche that flows predominantly northwest, then north into Laguna de Términos, which it enters at Laguna de Panlao.

40. Río Champotón. 19° 19' N, 90° 35' W (approx.); a river in western Campeche, and the northernmost river of any consequence in the Yucatán Peninsula. It flows in a generally west-northwesterly direction, entering the Bahía de Campeche at the town of Champotón.

41. Río Chumpán, Río Champán. 18° 15' N, 91° 32' W (approx.); a river in southwestern Campeche that flows northward into Laguna de Términos, which it enters at Boca de Balchacah.

42. Río Palizada. 18° 20' N, 91° 55' W (approx.); a river in southwestern Campeche that flows in a generally northeasterly direction into Laguna de Términos.

43. Sabancuy. 18° 58' N, 91° 11' W; a town on the *estero* (estuary) near the Gulf coast, approximately 67 km SW of Champotón. Coconut plantations grow along the coast, and scrub forest, pastures, and marshy areas characterize the surrounding countryside.

44. San José Carpizo. 19° 28' N, 90° 33' W; a town in northern Campeche, approximately 21 km NE of Champotón, situated in tropical deciduous forest.

45. Santa Rosa Xtampak. 19° 47' N, 89° 36' W; an archaeological site in northeastern Campeche, approximately 25 km SE of Bolonchén de Rejón. The site is situated among rolling hills and tropical deciduous forest, with cultivated fields in the vicinity. *See* Santa Rosa, Yucatán.

46. Seybaplaya. 19° 39' N, 90° 40' W; a town on the Gulf of Mexico, approximately 23 km SW of Campeche. Rocky shoreline alternates with narrow sandy beaches.

47. Treinta y Seis. 18° 38' N, 90° 58' W, elev. 65 m; a village in southwestern Campeche near the intersec-

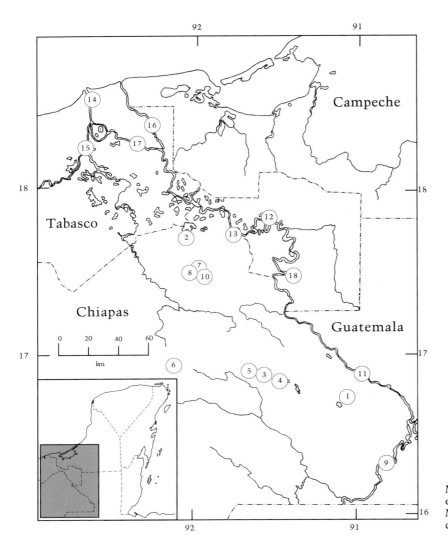

MAP 186. Gazetteer map of northeastern Chiapas and eastern Tabasco, Mexico. The numbers correspond to locality entries in the Gazetteer.

tion of Hwy. 186 and the road to Sabancuy. The vegetation, formerly tropical evergreen forest, is now pastures, cultivated fields, and second growth.

48. Tres Brazos. 18° 11′ N, 91° 31′ W; a village on the Río Chumpán, approximately 10 km N of the Tabasco border. Wetlands, pastures, and remnant stands of tropical evergreen forest characterize the vegetation.

49. Tuxpeña Camp, La Tuxpeña. 18° 27′ N, 90° 04′ W; a camp in south-central Campeche, approximately 65 km ESE of Escárcega, in tropical evergreen forest.

50. Xicalango. 18° 38′ N, 91° 53′ W; a town and archaeological site on Punta Xicalango at the west end of Laguna de Términos.

51. Xpujil, Xpuhil. 18° 30′ N, 89° 24′ W, elev. 250 m; an archaeological site and village in eastern Campeche on Hwy. 186. Milpas and second-growth forest are in the immediate vicinity, and tropical evergreen forest characterizes the outlying areas.

52. Zoh Laguna, Zoh-Laguna. 18° 36′ N, 89° 24′ W; a village and sawmill in southeastern Campeche, approximately 10 km N of Xpujil. The surrounding vegetaton is tropical evergreen forest.

Chiapas (Map 186)

1. Bonampak. 16° 44′ N, 91° 05′ W; an archaeological site in the Lacandón region of eastern Chiapas situated in tropical rainforest.

2. Catazajá. 17° 44′ N, 92° 02′ W; a town in northern Chiapas on Laguna Catazajá, approximately 97 km ESE of Villahermosa, Tabasco. Pastures, cultivated fields, and remnants of tropical rainforest characterize the surrounding area.

3. El Censo. 16° 54′ N, 91° 33′ W, elev. 700 m; a village in northeastern Chiapas, approximately 9 km SE of Monte Libano. Vegetation in the vicinity is tropical rainforest.

Laguna Catazajá. *See* Catazajá

4. Laguna Ocotal. 16° 49′ N, 91° 27′ W, elev. 950 m; a lake in La Selva Lacandona, eastern Chiapas. Tropical evergreen and pine forests characterize the surrounding vegetation.

5. Monte Libano. 16° 57′ N, 91° 36′ W, elev. 600 m; a village in northeastern Chiapas, approximately 50 km E of Ocosingo.

6. Ocosingo. 16° 57′ N, 92° 07′ W, elev. 850 m; a town in the central Chiapan highlands. Pine-oak forest characterizes the nearby vegetation.

7. Palenque, Palenque Pueblo. 17° 31′ N, 91° 59′ W, elev. 250 m; a town in northern Chiapas, approximately 7 km NE of the archaeological site of Palenque. The vegetation was originally tropical rainforest and is now pastures, cultivated fields, and some second-growth forest. *See* Palenque ruins.

8. Palenque ruins. 17° 29′ N, 92° 01′ W; an archaeological site in northern Chiapas, approximately 7 km SW of the town of Palenque. The surrounding vegetation is largely tropical rainforest. *See* Palenque.

Playas de Catazajá. *See* Catazajá

9. Río Lacantún, Río Lacantúm. 16° 20′ N, 90° 45′ W (approx.); a tributary of the Usumacinta in eastern Chiapas that flows eastward and then northeast into the Usumacinta. Throughout much of the Lacantún drainage the vegetation is tropical rainforest.

10. San Juanito. 17° 31′ N, 91° 58′ W; a ranch approximately 1.6 km ESE of the town of Palenque. The vegetation consists of pastures, cultivated fields, and remnants of tropical rainforest.

11. Yaxchilán. 16° 54′ N, 90° 59′ W; an archaeological site on the Río Usumacinta in eastern Chiapas, approximately 115 km W of Flores, El Petén, Guatemala. The site is situated in tropical rainforest.

Quintana Roo (Map 187)

1. Akumal, Acumal. 20° 25′ N, 87° 18′ W, sea level; a village and resort on the Caribbean coast approximately 22 km NE of Tulum. Low dune vegetation and mangroves characterize the area.

2. Bacalar. 18° 43′ N, 88° 27′ W, sea level; a village in southern Quintana Roo on Laguna de Bacalar. The surrounding vegetation is transitional between trop-

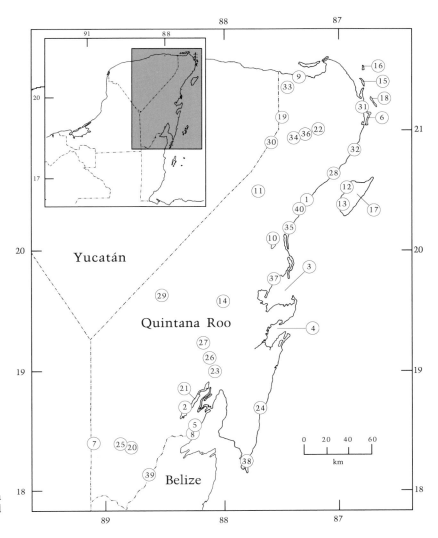

MAP 187. Gazetteer map of Quintana Roo, Mexico. The numbers correspond to locality entries in the Gazetteer.

ical deciduous and tropical evergreen forest. *See* Laguna de Bacalar.

3. Bahía de la Ascensión (Bahía Emiliano Zapata). 19° 43′ N, 87° 35′ W (approx.); a large bay on the Caribbean coast. Mangrove swamp lines much of the shoreline.

4. Bahía Espíritu Santo (Bahía Venustiano Carranza). 19° 20′ N, 87° 35′ W (approx.); a large bay on the Caribbean coast. Mangrove swamp lines much of the shoreline.

5. Calderitas, Calderita. 18° 33′ N, 88° 15′ W, sea level; a village approximately 7 km N of Chetumal amid tropical deciduous forest and cultivated fields.

6. Cancún, Isla Cancún. 21° 05′ N, 86° 46′ W, sea level; a small, sandy island immediately off the northeastern coast of the Yucatán Peninsula; also the town on the mainland immediately across from Isla Cancún. Formerly the vegetation was coconut plantations, scrubby dune vegetation, and mangroves, but the area is now an international tourist resort.

7. Caobas. 18° 27′ N, 89° 06′ W, elev. 175 m; an ejido and lake in western Quintana Roo approximately 3 km S of Hwy. 186, formerly in tropical evergreen forest, now pastures, cultivated fields, and second growth.

Chan Santa Cruz. *See* Felipe Carrillo Puerto

8. Chetumal (Playa Obispo). 18° 30′ N, 88° 18′ W, sea level; the capital city of the state of Quintana Roo, situated on Bahía Chetumal. The surrounding vegetation is tropical deciduous forest.

9. Chiquilá, Chinquilá. 21° 29′ N, 87° 23′ W, sea level; a small fishing village on the northern coast of Quintana Roo near the Yucatán border. There is low dune vegetation in the immediate vicinity of the village, with mangroves and scrub vegetation farther inland.

10. Chunyaxché (Muyil). 20° 05′ N, 87° 37′ W, elev. 5 m; an archaeological site near Laguna Chunyaxché in eastern Quintana Roo. The surrounding vegetation is tropical evergreen forest and cultivated fields.

11. Cobá. 20° 34′ N, 87° 35′ W; an archaeological site and village in northern Quintana Roo near the Yucatán border. Lakes and tropical evergreen forest characterize the site.

12. Cozumel, San Miguel de Cozumel, San Miguel. 20° 31′ N, 86° 55′ W, sea level to 5 m; the principal city on Isla Cozumel, situated on the northwest coast. Tropical deciduous forest and some mangroves characterize the surrounding vegetation. *See* Isla Cozumel.

Dziuché. *See* Dziuché, Yucatán

13. El Cedral. 20° 20′ N, 86° 59′ W, elev. 5 m; a village and archaeological site on Cozumel, in the south-central part of the island. Tropical deciduous forest surrounds the site.

Esmeralda, Esmeraldas. *See* Esmeralda, Yucatán

14. Felipe Carrillo Puerto (Santa Cruz de Bravo, Chan Santa Cruz). 19° 35′ N, 88° 02′ W, elev. 30 m; a town in central Quintana Roo, formerly in dense tropical evergreen forest, now amid cultivated fields, second-growth forest, and remnants of tropical evergreen forest.

15. Isla Blanca. 21° 24′ N, 86° 49′ W, sea level; a small, sandy island at the northeast corner of Quintana Roo.

16. Isla Contoy. 21° 29′ N, 86° 48′ W, sea level; a small island at the northeast corner of Quintana Roo. Low, scrubby vegetation covers much of the island.

17. Isla Cozumel. 20° 27′ N, 86° 53′ W (approx.), sea level to ca. 10 m; a large island approximately 18 km off the northeast coast of the Yucatán Peninsula. The vegetation is predominantly tropical deciduous forest with some large trees and scattered palms.

18. Isla Mujeres. 21° 15′ N, 86° 48′ W, sea level to about 30 m; a small island approximately 4 km off the northeast coast of the Yucatán Peninsula. Coconut groves, scrub vegetation, and rocky coastlines characterize the island.

19. Kantunilkin, Kantunil Kin. 21° 09′ N, 87° 36′ W; a town in northern Quintana Roo, approximately 70 km W of Puerto Juárez, surrounded by pastures, cultivated fields, and remnants of tropical deciduous forest.

20. Kohunlich. 18° 24′ N, 88° 47′ W; an archaeological site in southern Quintana Roo, approximately 55 km WSW of Chetumal. The site is situated in tropical evergreen forest with extensive tracts of corozo palms.

La Esmeralda. *See* Esmeralda, Yucatán

21. Laguna de Bacalar (Lago Bacalar). 18° 43′ N, 88° 22′ W (approx.), sea level; a large lake in southern Quintana Roo that parallels Bahía Chetumal. The surrounding vegetation is transitional between tropical deciduous forest and tropical evergreen forest.

Laguna Chichancanab. *See* Laguna Chichancanab, Yucatán

Laguna Chunyaxché. *See* Chunyaxché

La Presumida. *See* Presumida, Yucatán

La Vega. 21° 05′ N, 86° 46′ W; formerly a small village on the mainland opposite Isla Cancún, now incorporated into the urban sprawl of Cancún. *See* Cancún.

22. Leona Vicario. 21° 00′ N, 87° 11′ W; a town in northern Quintana Roo on Hwy. 180, approximately 43 km WSW of Puerto Juárez. The surrounding vegetation was tropical evergreen forest but is now second growth, pastures, and cultivated fields.

23. Limones. 18° 59′ N, 88° 10′ W, elev. 15 m; a village in southern Quintana Roo on Hwy. 307. The nearby vegetation was tropical evergreen forest but is now pastures, cultivated fields, and second-growth vegetation.

24. Majahual. 18° 42′ N, 87° 43′ W, sea level; a fishing village on the Caribbean coast of Quintana Roo, approximately 65 km NE of Chetumal. Coconut palms and scrubby beach vegetation characterize the surrounding vegetation, with mangroves inland.

Muyil. *See* Chunyaxché

25. Nicholas Bravo. 18° 28′ N, 88° 56′ W; a village in southern Quintana Roo on Hwy. 186, approximately

67 km W of Chetumal. Formerly tropical evergreen forest, now pastures, cultivated fields, and second-growth forest.

26. Nohbec. 19° 05′ N, 88° 11′ W; a town and archaeological site near Laguna Nohbec, approximately 50 km SSW of Felipe Carrillo Puerto, in southern Quintana Roo. The vegetation was tropical evergreen forest but is now pastures, cultivated fields, and second-growth forest.

27. Petcacab. 19° 17′ N, 88° 14′ W; a town in central Quintana Roo, approximately 35 km SSW of Felipe Carrillo Puerto. The vegetation, formerly tropical evergreen forest, consists of pastures, cultivated fields, and second growth.

28. Playa del Carmen. 20° 37′ N, 87° 04′ W; a town on the Caribbean coast of northern Quintana Roo, approximately 1 km SE of Hwy. 307. Coconut palms and low dune vegetation are in the immediate vicinity of the town, with mangrove swamp inland.

Playa Obispo. *See* Chetumal

29. Polyuc, Pol-Yuc. 19° 36′ N, 88° 37′ W; a village in north-central Quintana Roo on Hwy. 184, approximately 53 km W of Felipe Carrillo Puerto. The surrounding vegetation is open forest and wetlands.

Presumida. *See* Presumida, Yucatán

30. Pueblo Nuevo X-Can, Nuevo X-Can, Nuevo XCan. 20° 52′ N, 87° 36′ N, elev. 10 m; a town near the Yucatán border on Hwy. 180. The vegetation was tropical evergreen forest but is now cultivated fields, secondary growth, and scattered patches of forest.

31. Puerto Juárez. 21° 10′ N, 86° 49′ W, sea level; a port and town at the northeast corner of the Yucatán Peninsula now undergoing rapid development. Coconut groves, sandy beaches with scrubby dune vegetation, and mangroves inland characterize the vegetation.

32. Puerto Morelos. 20° 50′ N, 86° 52′ W; a town on the Caribbean coast of northern Quintana Roo on Hwy. 307, approximately 42 km SSW of Puerto Juárez. Low dune vegetation and mangroves surround the town.

San Miguel. *See* Cozumel

Santa Cruz de Bravo. *See* Felipe Carrillo Puerto

Santa Rosa. *See* Santa Rosa, Yucatán; and Santa Rosa Xtampak, Campeche

33. Solferino. 21° 22′ N, 87° 34′ W; a village in northern Quintana Roo near the Yucatán border. The surrounding vegetation is thorn forest, cultivated fields, and pastures.

34. Tintal, El Tintal. 20° 54′ N, 87° 28′ W; a village in northern Quintana Roo on Hwy. 180. Cultivated fields, second-growth scrub, and scattered stands of taller trees characterize the surrounding vegetation.

35. Tulum. 20° 12′ N, 87° 26′ W, sea level to 10 m; an archaeological site and village on bluffs overlooking the Caribbean Sea. The area, formerly dense tropical evergreen forest and mangrove, is now a manicured park with scrub forest and mangroves adjacent.

36. Vicente Guerrero. 20° 59′ N, 87° 20′ W; a town in northern Quintana Roo near the Yucatán border, approximately 20 km ENE of Pueblo Nuevo X-Can.

37. Vigía Chico. 19° 46′ N, 87° 35′ W, sea level; a small settlement, formerly a small town, on the Caribbean coast at Bahía de la Acensión, approximately 52 km ENE of Felipe Carrillo Puerto. Mangrove swamp characterizes the area.

38. Xcalak. 18° 16′ N, 87° 49′ W, sea level; a village and archaeological site on the Caribbean coast in southeastern-most Quintana Roo. Coconut groves and mangroves surround the village.

39. Xcopen. 18° 11′ N, 88° 42′ W; a village in southern Quintana Roo on the Río Hondo at the Belize border, approximately 55 km SW of Chetumal.

40. Xel-Ha. 20° 21′ N, 87° 19′ W, sea level; an archaeological site and rocky cove on the Caribbean coast of central Quintana Roo.

Tabasco (Map 186)

12. Balancán (Balancán de Domingues). 17° 48′ N, 91° 32′ W; a village in eastern Tabasco surrounded by pastures, cultivated fields, and remnants of tropical rainforest.

13. Emiliano Zapata (Montecristo, Monte Cristo). 17° 45′ N, 91° 46′ W, elev. 60 m; a town on the Río Usumacinta in eastern Tabasco surrounded by pastures, cultivated fields, savannas, and remnants of tropical rainforest.

14. Frontera. 18° 32′ N, 92° 38′ W, sea level; a town in northern Tabasco on Hwy. 180 at the Río Grijalva.

Montecristo. *See* Emiliano Zapata

15. Río Grijalva. 18° 15′ N, 92° 40′ W (approx.); a large river draining much of western Tabasco. In Tabasco it flows generally northward, joining the Río Usumacinta before entering the Gulf of Mexico.

16. Río San Pedro y San Pablo. 18° 30′ N, 92° 25′ W (approx.); a large river in eastern Tabasco that flows northwestward and forms a portion of the border with Campeche. It enters the Gulf of Mexico at San Pedro.

17. Río Usumacinta. 18° 20′ N, 92° 25′ W (approx.); the largest river in Middle America. In Tabasco it flows in a generally northwesterly direction, forming a portion of the border with Chiapas and joining the Río Grijalva before entering the Gulf of Mexico. *See* Río Usumacinta, El Petén, Guatemala.

18. Tenosique (Tenosique de Pino Suárez). 17° 29′ N, 91° 26′ W, elev. 60 m; a town in eastern Tabasco on the Río Usumacinta. The countryside consists of pastures, cultivated fields, and remnants of tropical rainforest.

Yucatán (Map 188)

1. Acancéh. 20° 49′ N, 89° 27′ W; an archaeological site and town in northwestern Yucatán, approx-

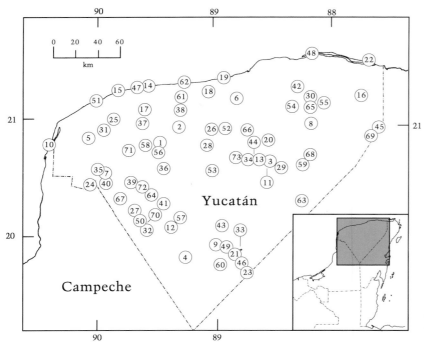

MAP 188. Gazetteer map of Yucatán, Mexico. The numbers correspond to locality entries in the Gazetteer.

imately 22 km SE of Mérida. Thorn forest, milpas, and henequén fields characterize the surrounding vegetation.

2. Aké. 20° 56′ N, 89° 18′ W; a town and archaeological site in central Yucatán situated amid henequén fields and thorn forest.

3. Balankanché. 20° 42′ N, 88° 29′ W, elev. 10 m; a cave and archaeological site approximately 6 km E of Chichén Itzá, in thorn forest.

4. Becanchén. 19° 54′ N, 89° 21′ W; a town in southern Yucatán, approximately 56 km SW of Peto. Cultivated fields and tropical deciduous forest surround the town.

5. Bella Flor. 20° 53′ N, 90° 04′ W; a village in northwestern Yucatán, approximately 40 km WSW of Mérida, surrounded by thorn forest, pastures, and cultivated fields.

6. Buctzotz, Buctzot. 21° 12′ N, 88° 47′ W; a settlement centered on an henequén hacienda in north-central Yucatán. Active and abandoned henequén fields and thorn forest characterize the surrounding vegetation.

7. Calcehtok, Cacehtok. 20° 34′ N, 89° 55′ W; a village in southwestern Yucatán situated in thorn forest.

8. Calotmul. 21° 01′ N, 88° 11′ W; a town in eastern Yucatán, approximately 39 km N of Valladolid on Hwy. 295. The surrounding vegetation was tropical evergreen forest but is now pastures, cultivated fields, and second-growth forest.

9. Catmís. 19° 58′ N, 88° 58′ W; a village in southern Yucatán, approximately 17 km S of Peto. Rem-

nants of tropical evergreen forest, pastures, and cultivated fields characterize the countryside.

10. Celestún. 20° 52′ N, 90° 24′ W; a fishing village on the northwest coast of Yucatán. Coconut plantations, low dune vegetation, mangroves, and thorn forest surround the village.

11. Cenote Seco. 20° 41′ N, 88° 33′ W, elev. 10 m; a small cenote approximately 2 km E of Chichén Itzá, featuring mesic plants such as figs and elephant ears, surrounded by thorn forest.

12. Chacmultún. 20° 08′ N, 89° 21′ W; an archaeological site in southwestern Yucatán in the Sierrita de Ticul. The site is surrounded by dense thorn forest and scattered cultivated fields.

13. Chichén Itzá. 20° 41′ N, 88° 34′ W, elev. 10 m; an archaeological site in east-central Yucatán on Hwy. 180. The surrounding vegetation is thorn forest.

14. Chicxulub Puerto. 21° 17′ N, 89° 31′ W, sea level; a town on the northern coast of Yucatán, approximately 6 km E of Progreso. Low, scrubby vegetation lies immediately behind the beach, with thorn forest inland.

15. Chuburna (Chuburna Puerto). 21° 15′ N, 89° 49′ W; a town on the northern coast of Yucatán, approximately 12 km WSW of Progreso. Low dune vegetation is present immediately behind the beach, with thorn forest inland.

16. Colonia Yucatán. 21° 15′ N, 87° 43′ W; a town in northeastern Yucatán, approximately 45 km ENE of Tizimín. Pastures, cultivated fields, and remnants of tropical evergreen forest surround the town.

17. Dzibilchaltún, Dzibichaltún. 21° 02′ N, 89° 34′ W, elev. 5 m; an archaeological site in northwestern Yucatán, approximately 13 km N of Mérida, situated amid henequén fields and thorn forest.

18. Dzidzantún. 21° 15′ N, 89° 03′ W; a town in northern Yucatán situated in thorn forest and henequén fields.

19. Dzilám Bravo, Dzilám de Bravo (Dzilám, Dzilán, Silán). 21° 24′ N, 88° 53′ W; a village on the north coast of Yucatán. Low dune vegetation and coconut palms surround the village, with mangrove swamp and thorn forest inland.

20. Dzitás. 20° 50′ N, 88° 26′ W, elev. 10 m; a town in east-central Yucatán, approximately 18 km NNE of Chichén Itzá, surrounded by milpas and thorn forest.

21. Dziuché. 19° 53′ N, 88° 49′ W, elev. 40 m; a town in southern Yucatán on Hwy. 184, approximately 28 km SSE of Peto. Pastures, cultivated fields, and remnant forest characterize the countryside.

22. El Cuyo (Cuyo). 21° 31′ N, 87° 41′ W, sea level; a fishing village on the northeast coast of Yucatán, approximately 65 km NE of Tizimín.

23. Esmeralda, Esmeraldas (La Esmeralda). 19° 45′ N, 88° 45′ W, elev. 40 m; a settlement and lake in southern Yucatán (formerly in Quintana Roo) situated in forest that is transitional between tropical deciduous and tropical evergreen, with cultivated fields and pastures.

24. Halachó. 20° 29′ N, 90° 05′ W; a town in western Yucatán near the Campeche border, approximately 72 km SW of Mérida, situated amid cultivated fields and thorn forest.

25. Hunucmá. 21° 01′ N, 89° 52′ W; a town in western Yucatán, approximately 28 km WNW of Mérida, situated amid thorn forest, milpas, and henequén fields.

26. Izamal. 20° 57′ N, 89° 02′ W; a town in central Yucatán, approximately 60 km E of Mérida, situated in thorn forest, henequén fields, and milpas.

27. Kabah. 20° 15′ N, 89° 40′ W; an archaeological site in extreme southwestern Yucatán on Hwy. 261 situated in thorn forest.

28. Kantunil. 20° 48′ N, 89° 02′ W; a town in central Yucatán on Hwy. 180, approximately 61 km ESE of Mérida. Thorn forest, pastures, and cultivated fields surround the town.

29. Kaua. 20° 37′ N, 88° 25′ W; a village in central Yucatán on Hwy. 180, approximately 20 km ESE of Chichén Itzá. Thorn forest and cultivated fields surround the village.

30. Kikíl. 21° 12′ N, 88° 09′ W, elev. 8 m; a village in eastern Yucatán, approximately 7 km NW of Tizimín. Pastures, cultivated fields, and tropical deciduous forest characterize the surrounding vegetation.

31. Kinchil. 20° 55′ N, 89° 57′ W; a town in western Yucatán on Hwy. 261, approximately 31 km WSW of Mérida, amid thorn forest and henequén plantations.

32. Labná. 20° 09′ N, 89° 35′ W; an archaeological site in southwestern Yucatán, approximately 92 km S of Mérida, situated in dense thorn forest.

33. Laguna Chichancanab, Chignancanab, Chicnancanab, Chicnankanab, Chinchancanab. 19° 51′ N, 88° 46′ W (approx.); a large lake in southern Yucatán (formerly in Quintana Roo). Vegetation in the vicinity of the lake is remnant tropical evergreen forest, with pastures and cultivated fields.

34. Libre Unión. 20° 42′ N, 88° 49′ W; a village in central Yucatán on Hwy. 180, approximately 22 km W of Chichén Itzá. The surrounding vegetation is thorn forest, pastures, cultivated fields, and second-growth scrub.

35. Maxcanú. 20° 36′ N, 90° 00′ W; a town in western Yucatán near the Campeche border, approximately 58 km SW of Mérida, situated amid thorn forest and cultivated fields.

36. Mayapán. 20° 28′ N, 89° 28′ W; an archaeological site in western Yucatán, approximately 44 km ESE of Mérida, situated in henequén fields and thorn forest.

37. Mérida (Tiho). 20° 58′ N, 89° 35′ W, elev. 10 m; the capital city of Yucatán, situated in the northwestern portion of the state. Henequén haciendas and thorn forest surround the city.

38. Motul. 21° 06′ N, 89° 17′ W; a town in western Yucatán, approximately 37 km ENE of Mérida. The surrounding vegetation is thorn forest with active and abandoned henequén fields.

39. Muna (Muna de Leopoldo). 20° 29′ N, 89° 42′ W, elev. 20 m; a town in southwestern Yucatán, approximately 55 km S of Mérida, near the Sierrita de Ticul. Thorn forest and cultivated fields surround the town.

40. Oxkintok. 20° 34′ N, 89° 55′ W; an archaeological site in western Yucatán, approximately 55 km SW of Mérida, situated amid cultivated fields, pastures, and thorn forest.

41. Oxkutzcab. 20° 18′ N, 89° 25′ W; a town in western Yucatán at the base of the Sierrita de Ticul, approximately 75 km SSE of Mérida. Thorn forest, cultivated fields, and citrus groves surround the town.

42. Panabá. 21° 18′ N, 88° 17′ W; a town in northeastern Yucatán, approximately 24 km NW of Tizimín. Pastures, remnants of forest, and cultivated fields surround the town.

43. Peto. 20° 07′ N, 88° 57′ W, elev. 30 m; a town in south-central Yucatán, approximately 118 km SE of Mérida, surrounded by cultivated fields, pastures, and tropical deciduous forest.

44. Pisté. 20° 42′ N, 88° 35′ W, elev. 10 m; a town on Hwy. 180 in east-central Yucatán, approximately 5 km NW of Chichén Itzá, situated in thorn forest.

45. Popolná, Poponá. 20° 59′ N, 87° 32′ W; a town in eastern Yucatán, approximately 16 km NNE of X-Can, situated amid pastures, cultivated fields, and remnants of tropical evergreen forest.

46. Presumida (La Presumida). 19° 48′ N, 88° 44′ W; a town in southern Yucatán (formerly Quintana Roo),

approximately 8 km NW of the Quintana Roo border on Hwy. 184. The town is surrounded by cultivated fields, pastures, and forest transitional between thorn forest and tropical evergreen forest.

47. Progreso. 21° 17' N, 89° 40' W, sea level; a town on the northwest coast of Yucatán, approximately 31 km N of Mérida. Progreso is the principal port of the state. Coconut groves, low dune vegetation, and mangroves characterize the surrounding vegetation.

48. Río Lagartos. 21° 36' N, 88° 10' W, sea level; a town on the northeast coast of Yucatán, approximately 95 km N of Valladolid. Scattered coconut palms and low dune vegetation surround the town, with mangrove swamp and thorn forest inland.

Sací. *See* Valladolid

49. Santa Rosa. 19° 57' N, 88° 53' W, elev. 30 m; a settlement and hacienda in southern Yucatán, approximately 18 km SSE of Peto. Pastures, cultivated fields, and remnant forest characterize the countryside. *See* Santa Rosa Xtampak, Campeche.

50. Sayil. 20° 10' N, 89° 39' W; an archaeological site in southwestern Yucatán, approximately 87 km S of Mérida, situated in thorn forest.

Silan. *See* Dzilám Bravo

51. Sisal. 21° 10' N, 90° 00' W, sea level; a town on the northwest coast of Yucatán, approximately 46 km NW of Mérida. Low, scrubby dune vegetation surrounds the town.

52. Sitilpech. 20° 56' N, 88° 58' W; a town in central Yucatán, approximately 6 km E of Izamal, situated in thorn forest.

53. Sotutá. 20° 36' N, 89° 01' W; a town in central Yucatán, approximately 75 km SE of Mérida, situated in thorn forest with cultivated fields.

54. Sucilá. 21° 09' N, 88° 19' W; a town in eastern Yucatán, approximately 16 km W of Tizimín. Pastures, cultivated fields, and patches of second-growth forest surround the town.

55. Sucopó. 21° 10' N, 88° 04' W; a village in eastern Yucatán, approximately 9 km ENE of Tizimín.

56. Tecoh. 20° 46' N, 89° 27' W; a town in western Yucatán, approximately 31 km SSE of Mérida. Thorn forest, milpas, and henequén plantations characterize the surrounding vegetation.

57. Tekax, Tekax de Alvaro Obregon. 20° 12' N, 89° 17' W; a town on Hwy. 184 in western Yucatán, approximately 92 km SSE of Mérida, at the base of the Sierrita de Ticul. Thorn forest and cultivated fields surround the town.

58. Tekik (Tekik de Regil). 20° 47' N, 89° 36' W; a town and henequén hacienda situated in thorn forest and henequén fields, approximately 19 km SSE of Mérida.

59. Tekom. 20° 36' N, 88° 16' W; a town in eastern Yucatán, approximately 9 km SW of Valladolid, situated amid cultivated fields, second growth, and remnants of tropical deciduous forest.

60. Telantunich. 19° 48' N, 88° 55' W; an archaeological site in southern Yucatán, approximately 35 km S of Peto. The area consists of pastures, cultivated fields, and remnants of tropical evergreen forest.

61. Telchac. 21° 12' N, 89° 16' W; a town in northern Yucatán on Hwy. 172, approximately 42 km NE of Mérida, situated in thorn forest.

62. Telchac Puerto. 21° 21' N, 89° 16' W, sea level; a town on the north coast of Yucatán, approximately 40 km ENE of Progreso. Coconut groves, scrubby dune vegetation, and thorn forest characterize the immediate vicinity.

63. Tepich. 20° 18' N, 88° 12' W; a town in eastern Yucatán near the Quintana Roo border on Hwy. 295, approximately 47 km S of Valladolid. Pastures and second-growth scrub now characterize the vegetation, which was once tropical evergreen forest.

64. Ticul. 20° 24' N, 89° 32' W; a town in western Yucatán at the base of the Sierrita de Ticul. Cultivated fields, thorn forest, and citrus groves characterize the surrounding vegetation.

Tiho. *See* Mérida

65. Tizimín. 21° 09' N, 88° 08' W, elev. 8 m; a town in northeastern Yucatán on Hwy. 295, approximately 50 km N of Valladolid, surrounded by pastures, cultivated fields, and remnants of forest.

66. Tunkas. 20° 54' N, 88° 45' W; a town in east-central Yucatán, approximately 27 km E of Izamal. The surrounding vegetation is thorn forest with milpas and pastures.

67. Uxmal. 20° 23' N, 89° 46' W, elev. 70 m; an archaeological site in southwestern Yucatán on Hwy. 261, approximately 68 km SSW of Mérida. The surrounding vegetation is milpas and thorn forest.

68. Valladolid (Sací). 20° 41' N, 88° 12' W; the principal city of eastern Yucatán. Cultivated fields, pastures, and second-growth vegetation surround the town, which was once situated in a transitional area between tropical deciduous and tropical evergreen forest.

69. X-Can, XCan. 20° 50' N, 87° 43' W; a town in easternmost Yucatán on Hwy. 180, approximately 2 km W of the Quintana Roo border. The vegetation, formerly tropical evergreen forest, is now cultivated fields and second growth.

70. Xlapak. 20° 10' N, 89° 37' W; an archaeological site in southwestern Yucatán, approximately 30 km SSE of Muna, in dense thorn forest.

71. Yaxcopoil. 20° 44' N, 89° 44' W; a settlement and henequén hacienda in western Yucatán, approximately 29 km SSW of Mérida on Hwy. 261, now a tourist attraction, situated amid thorn forest and cultivated fields.

72. Yokat. 20° 25' N, 89° 36' W; a town in southwestern Yucatán, approximately 7 km NW of Ticul on Hwy. 184. Cultivated fields and thorn forest characterize the surrounding vegetation.

73. Yokdzonot. 20° 41' N, 88° 41' W, elev. 10 m; a town in central Yucatán on Hwy. 180, approximately 17 km W of Chichén Itzá. The surrounding vegetation is thorn forest and cultivated fields.

Glossary

Successful use of the identification keys in this book and full understanding and appreciation of the species accounts requires some knowledge of the technical words and specialized terminology of herpetology. These are listed and defined below. Some terms have multiple meanings, and others may be used in different ways by different people. The definitions that follow give the meaning of a term as used in this book. The treatment is neither exhaustive nor definitive, for this is not a comprehensive dictionary of herpetology. A more thorough treatment of herpetological words and terms is given in J. A. Peters, 1964.

Abdomen *n* Generally, the ventral area of the body of vertebrates lying between the pectoral and pelvic appendages. Specifically, the cavity lying posterior to the lungs.

Abdominal *adj* Of or pertaining to the abdomen.

Abdominal scute *n* In turtles, one of a pair of plastral scutes bordered anteriorly by the pectoral scute and posteriorly by the femoral scute.

Acuminate *adj* Tapering to a sharp point, pointed; for example, the tails of some tadpoles (e.g., *Hyla picta*, Fig. 74) are acuminate.

Adpress *v* To press closely against the body. The number of costal grooves that lie between the adpressed forelimb and hindlimb is a useful character in salamander identification.

Allantois *n* One of four extraembryonic membranes found in amniotes. During development the allantois stores nitrogenous wastes.

Allopatric *adj* Of or pertaining to geographic distributions that do not overlap.

Allopatry *n* The condition (or circumstance) in which two or more geographic distributions do not overlap. Populations whose geographic distributions do not overlap are said to be allopatric.

Amniote *n* Any vertebrate in which an amnion is present in the egg or placenta. Reptiles, birds, and mammals are amniotes.

Amplectant *adj* Of or pertaining to amplexus.

Amplexus *n* The sexual embrace or clasping of (normally) a female anuran by a male. In most species of frogs amplexus is axillary; that is, the male clasps the female in the axilla (Fig. 241). A few species (e.g., *Rhinophrynus dorsalis*) exhibit inguinal amplexus, in which the male clasps the female around the pelvis.

Anal *adj* Of or pertaining to the anus, and, by traditional, to the cloaca of squamates.

Anal plate *n* In snakes, the enlarged transverse scale that covers the vent. It may be entire (= single, undivided) or divided (Fig. 148).

Anal scute *n* In turtles, one of a pair of plastral scutes forming the posteriormost margin of the plastron and bordered anteriorly by the femoral scute.

Annular *adj* Of or pertaining to an annulus.

Annular groove *n* A groove in the integument of caecilians that borders and defines an annulus. Dermal scales are present in the annular grooves of some species of caecilians.

Annulus (pl. **annuli**) *n* A ring or ringlike structure or marking. The body segments of caecilians are termed *annuli*. Primary annuli are defined by annular grooves that completely encircle the body; secondary annuli are defined by annular grooves that incompletely encircle the body.

Anterior *adj* The anatomical direction pertaining to or toward the front (head) end. Synonyms: cranial, rostral.

Anterior temporal scale *See* Temporal scale

Anteroventral *adj* A position intermediate between anterior and ventral. For example, the mouths of many species of tadpoles (e.g., *Agalychnis moreletii*, Fig. 63) are oriented forward and downward and are thus said to be anteroventral.

Anura *n* The order of amphibians that contains frogs and toads.

Anuran *adj* Of or pertaining to the Anura or to members of that order.

Anus *n* The posterior opening of the digestive tract (when that tract is separate from the urogenital tract).

Apical *adj* Of, at, or constituting the apex.

Apical pit *n* A tiny depression in the dorsal surface of an epidermal scale, near the trailing edge. Apical pits are characteristic of some lizards and snakes and are thought to serve a tactile function. They may be single or paired, and their presence or absence is useful in identification (Fig. 147). Synonym: scale pit.

Arboreal *adj* Living in trees.

Assortative mating *n* Mating in which individuals similar to one another by some criterion (e.g., size) mate with one another more frequently than would be expected by chance.

Asulcate *adj* Lacking a sulcus (q.v.). For example, the surface of the hemipenis of snakes that lies opposite the sulcus spermaticus is termed the asulcate surface.

Attenuate *adj* Elongate, slender, or thin.

Axilla *n* The posterior angle formed with the body by insertion of the forelimbs.

Axilla-groin length *n* The straight-line distance between the point of insertion of the forelimb and the point of insertion of the hind limb. The number of dorsal scales within the axilla-groin length is a useful character in lizard identification.

Axillary *adj* Of or pertaining to the axilla.

Axillary amplexus *See* Amplexus

Axillary membrane *n* A thin sheet of skin connecting the posterior margin of the upper arm to the axillary region of the body in anurans. *Hyla loquax* has a well-developed axillary membrane (Fig. 32).

Axillary scute *n* In turtles, one of a pair of scutes lying at the axillary notch. In some species (e.g., *Kinosternon scorpioides*) the axillary scute may be in contact with the inguinal scute (Fig. 111D).

Azygous *adj* Unpaired. The term is usually applied to the unpaired, median head scales of snake and lizards. In *Sibon dimidiata*, for example, the first pair of infralabial scales are separated by an azygous scale (Fig. 178B).

Barbel *n* A thin, fleshy protuberance, usually on the head or neck. The term is applied to the series of structures around the mouth of the tadpole of *Rhinophrynus dorsalis* (Fig. 39), and to structures on the chin of some turtles (e.g., *Chelydra* and *Staurotypus*, Fig. 274).

Basal *adj* At or pertaining to the base. Anurans whose interdigital webbing is restricted to the base of the digits are said to have basal webbing.

Beak *See* Jaw sheaths

Bridge *n* That portion of the shell in turtles that connects the carapace and plastron. In some species (e.g., *Terrapene carolina*) the carapace and plastron are in direct contact and there is no bridge.

Buccopharyngeal *adj* Of or pertaining to the combined oral (= buccal) and pharyngeal cavities.

Canthal *adj* Of or pertaining to the canthus rostralis, or that region of the head.

Canthal scale *n* Any of a series of scales lying on the canthal ridge.

Canthus rostralis *n* The angle (when present) between the top of the head and the side of the snout that forms a ridge extending from the tip of the snout to the eye.

Capitulum *n* The head or headlike structure at the apex of the hemipenis of snakes. A capitulum is present when the apical region of the hemipenis is clearly separated from the basal portion by a distinct groove.

Carapace *n* The upper portion of the shell of turtles, generally composed of bony elements on which are superimposed keratinized scutes.

Carapace length *n* A measurement used to index size in turtles. It is the straight-line length along the midline from the anterior margin of the nuchal scute to the posterior margin of the supracaudal scute.

Casque *n* A bony, helmetlike projection of the skull as seen in some lizards (e.g., *Laemanctus*, Figs. 121, 122). Also, the condition in which there is proliferation of the dermal roofing bones of the skull, producing a "casqued," or helmeted, appearance, as seen in frogs of the genus *Triprion* (Figs. 88, 252).

Caudal *adj* Of or pertaining to the tail.

Cephalic *adj* Of or pertaining to the head.

Chemosensory *adj* Of or pertaining to taste, olfaction, or the related function of the vomeronasal (= Jacobson's) organ.

Chin shield *n* Any of several paired, elongate scales on the lower jaw of snakes.

Chorioallantoic *adj* Of or pertaining to the chorion and the allantois collectively; for example, lizards of the genus *Lepidophyma* have a chorioallantoic placenta.

Chorion *n* The outermost of the extraembryonic membranes of amniotes.

Clade *n* Any group that contains all the descendants of a common ancestor; i.e., a monophyletic group.

Cladistic *adj* Of or pertaining to cladistics, the systematic methodology that infers evolutionary relationships among organisms soley on the basis of shared derived characters.

Cloaca *n* The common chamber that receives the contents of the digestive, excretory, and reproductive systems; it communicates to the outside through the vent.

Cloacal spur *n* One of a pair of projections at the base of the tail, immediately behind the vent, in certain lizards (e.g., *Coleonyx elegans*). The spur is the outward manifestation of an underlying cloacal bone.

Commensal *adj, n* Pertaining to, or a member of, a commensalistic association. For example, in the Yucatán Peninsula, *Anolis sagrei* is primarily a human commensal.

Commensalism *n* An association between two species in which one benefits and the other neither benefits nor is harmed.

Conical *adj* Resembling or shaped like a cone. The scales of some species of lizards (e.g., certain dorsal scales of *Anolis pentaprion*) are conical.

Conspecific *n, adj* A member of the same species, or pertaining to such a member (cf. Heterospecific).

Co-ossified *adj* The condition in which the integument is fused to the underlying bones. The skin on the dorsal surface of the head of *Triprion petasatus*, for example, is co-ossified with certain cranial bones.

Cornified *adj* Covered by or impregnated with keratin.

Cosmopolitan *adj* Occurring worldwide.

Costal *adj* Of or pertaining to a rib, and by extension the sides, as in the costal (= pleural) scutes of a turtle.

Costal fold *n* A fold in the integument of salamanders that lies between costal grooves and corresponds to a body segment (Fig. 27).

Costal groove *n* A groove or trough in the integument of salamanders that borders and defines a costal fold (Fig. 27). The number of costal grooves is an important character in salamander identification.

Cotype *n* One of a pair of specimens that constitutes the type series of a taxon.

Cranial *adj* 1. Of or pertaining to the skull. 2. Anterior.

Cranial crest *n* An elevated, bony ridge on the dorsal surface of the head of some species of toads (Bufonidae, Fig. 54). The configuration of the cranial crests is a useful characteristic in anuran identification.

Crepuscular *adj* Active under conditions of dim illumination, such as at dawn and dusk.

Cruciform *adj* Having the shape of a cross. The plastron of *Chelydra serpentina* (Fig. 105A) is cruciform.

Crypsis *n* The condition of being cryptic.

Cryptic *adj* Difficult to detect, especially visually, owing to an animal's resemblance to its surroundings.

Cryptic species *n* Species that are essentially indistinguishable morphologically but can be shown to be specifically distinct.

Cursorial *adj* Of or pertaining to running; specialized for running.

Cutaneous *adj* Of or pertaining to the skin.

Denticle *n* One of a series of keratinized, toothlike structures surrounding the mouths of some tadpoles (Fig. 35). Such structures are sometimes called *teeth*.

Depressed *adj* Flattened in a horizontal plane.

Dermis *n* The inner layer of the skin, generally consisting of connective tissue fibers, nerves, blood vessels, and dermal derivatives such as osteoderms.

Dewlap 1. *n* A midventral fold of skin lying in the throat region of certain lizards. The dewlap is often supported by elements of the hyoid apparatus and may be raised or lowered. It is often brightly colored and is used in displays associated with courtship and territorial defense. The dewlap is especially well developed in males of the genus *Anolis*. Synonym: throat fan. 2. *v* The act of displaying the dewlap. More generally, the posturing by some herpetologists that occurs (especially) at scientific meetings.

Dextral *adj* Of or pertaining to the right side. For example, the vent tube of tadpoles is dextral when it opens to the right of the ventral midline.

Dichromatism *n* Two colors. Species in which the sexes are of different colors are said to exhibit sexual dichromatism.

Diel *adj* Of or pertaining to the 24-hour day. A diel cycle, for example, has a period of approximately 24 hours.

Digit *n* A finger or toe.

Dimorphism *n* Two morphologies. Species in which the sexes differ in morphology (e.g., members of one sex are larger than members of the other) are said to exhibit sexual dimorphism.

Direct development *n* In salamanders and anurans, embryonic development that is completed within the egg, there being no free-living larval stage.

Disk *n* A flat, circular, platelike structure. The tips of the digits of some anurans (e.g., many hylids) are expanded to form adhesive disks (Fig. 31).

Distal *adj* Situated away from the base or point of attachment of a structure. The expanded disks at the tips of the digits of hylid frogs are distal to the phalanges at the base of the digits, for example.

Dominant frequency *n* In bioacoustics, the frequency within which the greatest amount of acoustic energy is concentrated.

Dorsal *adj* Of or pertaining to the upper surface of the body or of a structure.

Dorsolateral *adj* A position that is intermediate between dorsal and lateral. For example, the eyes of the tadpoles of many species are dorsolateral in position.

Dorsolateral fold *n* One of a pair of longitudinal folds or ridges in the skin on the dorsolateral surface of the body of some anurans (e.g., *Rana berlandieri*).

Dorsum *n* The upper surface of the body or of a structure.

Ectothermic *adj* Of or pertaining to ectothermy, the condition in which body temperature is determined largely by heat sources external to the animal. Animals that exhibit ectothermy are called *ectotherms*.

Edificarian *adj* Of or pertaining to human habitation.

Emarginate *adj* Of or pertaining to a margin that is indented, notched, or scalloped (e.g., the expanded toe disks of some species of *Eleutherodactylus*, Fig. 41).

Endemic 1. *adj* Restricted or peculiar to a given area or region. 2. *n* An organism that is so restricted. Many species of amphibians and reptiles are endemic to the Yucatán Peninsula.

Epidermis *n* The superficial layer of the skin, generally consisting of an outer dead, keratinized layer and several living cell layers, together with epidermal derivatives such as exocrine glands, epidermal scales, and claws.

Estivate *v* To be in estivation.

Estivation *n* Inactivity or dormancy during periods of heat, drought, or both. Also spelled *aestivation*.

Face mask *n* Dark pigmentation on the sides of the head, usually extending from the snout and including the eye. The term is often applied with regard to frogs and toads.

Femoral *adj* Of or pertaining to the femur or femora.

Femoral pore *n* One of a series of openings on the posteroventral surface of the thighs of some species of lizards (e.g., *Ctenosaura defensor*, Fig. 124D). The pores, which are generally better developed in males than in females, are the apertures through which the secretions of exocrine glands are released.

Femoral scute *n* In turtles, one of a pair of plastral scutes bordered anteriorly by the abdominal scute and posteriorly by the anal scute.

Femur (pl. **femora**) *n* An endochondral long bone in the proximal segment of the hind limb of vertebrates; the thigh bone.

Fossorial *adj* Pertaining to burrowing or digging; thus, often applied to organisms that live underground.

Frontal *adj* Of or pertaining to the frontal area of the head, which lies on the dorsal surface approximately between and anterior to the eyes.

Frontal depression *n* A depression on the dorsal surface of the head of lizards, especially those of the genus *Anolis*, lying between and anterior to the eyes.

Frontal scale *n* A large, unpaired scale on the dorsal surface of the head of snakes (Fig. 149).

Frontonasal scale *n* A scale (or scales) on the dorsal surface of the head of lizards and turtles that lies between the internasals, prefrontals, and loreals.

Frontoparietal *n* A dermal roofing bone in the skull of anurans formed by fusion of the frontal and parietal bones.

Frontoparietal scale *n* A scale (or scales) lying between the frontal and the parietal scales of some lizards (e.g., *Cnemidophorus*, Fig. 140C).

Fundamental frequency *n* In bioacoustics, the first (i.e., lowest frequency) harmonic.

Gametogenesis *n* Gamete formation; the series of cell divisions by which eggs or sperm are formed.

Generic *adj* Of or pertaining to a genus.

Genus (pl. **genera**) *n* A taxonomic category below the level of the family and above the level of the species.

Gestation *n* The period of time during which developing young are retained within the oviduct or uterus of the mother of a viviparous species.

Glandular ridge *n* A narrow, elevated ridge of glandular skin, usually on the dorsal surface of the body, as seen in some species of frogs.

Globose *adj* Rounded, ball-shaped (e.g., the bodies of some species of tadpoles).

Granular *adj* Possessing granules; for example, the skin on the dorsal surface of the body of *Eleutherodactylus rugulosus* is granular.

Granule *n* A small, rounded elevation on the skin of some frogs.

Groin *n* The angle formed with the body by the anterior surface of the hind limb at its insertion.

Gular *adj* Of or pertaining to the ventral surface of the throat or neck.

Gular flap *n* A midventral flap of skin found in some lizards (e.g., *Iguana iguana*).

Gular fold *n* A transverse fold of skin found in the gular region of some salamanders (Fig. 27) and lizards (Fig. 139C).

Gular scute *n* Usually the anteriormost pair of epidermal scutes on the plastron of turtles, lying immediately anterior to the humeral scutes. In members of the Kinosternidae the gular is an unpaired, median scute lying at the anterior margin of the plastron (Fig. 111).

Harmonic *n* In bioacoustics, a frequency within which acoustic energy is concentrated.

Hatchling *n* Newly hatched (cf. Neonate).

Heliothermic *adj* Term that describes ectothermic organisms that rely on direct solar radiation to elevate the body temperature.

Hemipenis (pl. **hemipenes**) *n* One of the paired copulatory organs of male snakes and lizards. The configuration of the hemipenes is useful in identification and classification.

Herbivorous *adj* Of or pertaining to herbivory—feeding on plants. Animals that practice herbivory are termed *herbivores*.

Heterospecific *adj* Belonging to different species. *Sceloporus serrifer* and *S. teapensis* are heterospecific, for example (cf. Conspecific).

Holarctic *adj* Of or pertaining to the temperate and Arctic regions of the Northern Hemisphere; includes the Nearctic and Palearctic realms.

Holotype *n* The single specimen designated by the author of a taxon as the exemplar of that taxon. In the eighteenth century, published illustrations occasionally served as the holotypes for original descriptions.

Humeral *adj* Of or pertaining to the humerus or humeri.

Humeral scute *n* In turtles, one of a pair of plastral scutes bordered anteriorly by the gular scute and posteriorly by the abdominal scute.

Humerus (pl. **humeri**) *n* An endochondral bone that forms the skeletal support of the upper arm in tetrapods.

Imbricate *adj* Overlapping, as when the distal portion of one scale overlaps the proximal portion of the next scale. The scales of snakes and of many species of lizards are imbricate (cf. Juxtaposed).

Infralabial *n* One of a series of epidermal scales bordering the lower lip of snakes and lizards. They are numbered from anterior to posterior, and their number and configuration are useful characters in identification.

Inframarginal scute *n* In turtles, any one of several (usually two) epidermal scutes lying between the marginals of the carapace and the adjacent plastral scutes.

Infraspecific *adj* Of or pertaining to a taxonomic category below the level of the species. Synonym: subspecific.

Inguinal *adj* Of or pertaining to the groin region of the body.

Inguinal amplexus *See* Amplexus

Inguinal scute *n* In turtles, one of a pair of plastral scutes lying at the inguinal notch immediately behind the inframarginal and abdominal scutes. In some species (e.g., *Kinosternon scorpioides*) the inguinal scute is typically in contact with the axillary scute (Fig. 111D).

Inner tarsal tubercle *n* A tubercle on the inner, or medial, side of the tarsus in certain species of frogs (e.g., *Eleutherodactylus rhodopis*).

Insular *adj* Of or pertaining to islands. Organisms that occur on islands (e.g., *Phyllodactylus insularis*) are said to be insular.

Integument *n* Skin. It consists of an outer layer, the epidermis, and an inner layer, the dermis.

Integumentary *adj* Of or pertaining to the integument.

Intercalary cartilage *n* A small cartilage lying between the last (ultimate) and the second to last (penultimate) phalanges in the digits of some frogs (e.g., those of the family Hylidae).

Intercalated *adj* Inserted. For example, the small groups of irregular caudal scales in *Crocodylus moreletii* are intercalated between the regular whorls of scales (Fig. 102B).

Internasal *n* One of the two or more scales lying between the nasal scales in lizards and snakes.

Interorbital *adj* Of or pertaining to the area on the dorsal surface of the head between the eyes.

Interorbital bar *n* A bar-shaped marking on the dorsal surface of the head between the eyes, especially in frogs.

Interwhorl *n* A ring of small scales encircling the tail of lizards and alternating with whorls of enlarged scales, as in *Ctenosaura* (Fig. 123).

Jaw sheaths *n* The keratinized sheaths that cover the upper and lower jaws of some tadpoles (Fig. 35).

Juxtaposed *adj* Placed side by side; for example, the ventral scales of lizards of the genus *Ameiva*.

Karyology *n* The subdiscipline within genetics concerned with the study of karyotypes.

Karyotype *n* The appearance, number, size, and shape of chromosomes.

Keel *n* A raised, ridgelike process. The term is usually applied to the scales of those reptiles in which there is a median ridge running down the long axis of the scale (Fig. 147). The scales of snakes of the genera *Thamnophis* and *Nerodia* are keeled.

Keratin *n* A hard protein, impermeable to water, found in the epidermis of vertebrates and comprising the bulk of the epidermal scales of reptiles.

Labial *adj* Of or pertaining to the lips, or the region of the lips.

Labial scale *n* Any of a series of scales bordering the upper or lower margin of the jaw. *See* Infralabial; Supralabial scale.

Labial papillae *n* The small, fleshy projections that surround the oral disk in the tadpoles of many species of anurans (Fig. 35). The labial papillae may completely surround the oral disk, or they may be discontinuous anteriorly, posteriorly, or both.

Labial shelf *n* A bony, shelflike projection along the upper lip of some anurans (e.g., *Triprion petasatus*, Fig. 88).

Lamella (pl. **lamellae**) *n* One of a series of flat, overlapping plates. The term is usually applied to the scales on the undersurface of the digits of lizards, termed *sub-*

digital lamellae. Often the lamellae are expanded, as in most lizards of the genus *Anolis* and many species of geckos (Fig. 114).

Lateral *adj* Of or pertaining to the side of the body or a structure; the opposite of medial. The tails of some reptiles are laterally compressed, meaning that they are flattened from side to side.

Lectotype *n* One of a series of syntypes designated by an author, subsequent to publication of the original description, to serve as the type specimen.

Lichenose *adj* Resembling a lichen. A color pattern in which an irregular dark reticulum encloses patches of pale color. *Anolis pentaprion* has a lichenose dorsal color pattern.

Loreal *adj* Of or pertaining to the lateral surface of the head between the eye and the nostril.

Loreal pit *n* The external opening to the infrared heat receptors (pit organs) in the loreal region of pitvipers (Fig. 150D).

Loreal scale *n* One or more scales in the loreal region of snakes (Fig. 150B) and lizards.

Maxillary bone *n* One of a pair of marginal dermal bones at the anterior end of the skull of amphibians and reptiles. The maxillary bones often bear teeth and are the largest elements of the maxillary arch.

Maxillary cusp *n* A sharp, toothlike structure on the anterior margin of the upper jaw in *Dermochelys coriacea* (Fig. 110).

Medial *adj* Of or pertaining to the midline; the opposite of lateral.

Mental *adj* Of or pertaining to the chin or the chin region.

Mental gland *n* A gland in the chin region of some male salamanders; its secretions are sexually stimulating to female salamanders.

Mental groove *n* A median groove lying between the chin shields in the lower jaw of most snakes (Fig. 153A).

Mental scale *n* The unpaired median scale at the anterior margin of the lower jaw.

Mesic *adj* Moderately moist.

Mesoptychial scales *n* In lizards, the scales in the throat region that lie immediately anterior to the gular fold.

Metachrosis *n* Color change; the ability to change color. Lizards such as *Laemanctus serratus* and *Anolis biporcatus*, for example, are capable of pronounced, rapid metachrosis.

Metatarsal tubercle *n* An elevated, thickened bump on the skin of the metatarsus of anurans (Fig. 31). The size, shape, and position of the tubercles are useful identification characters. Often there are inner and outer metatarsal tubercles, situated near the medial and the lateral margins of the metatarsus, respectively.

Metatarsus *n* The sole of the foot; specifically, the portion of the foot supported by the metatarsal bones and extending from the heel to the base of the digits.

Middorsal *adj* The portion of the dorsal surface of the body that lies along the midline. The number of middorsal scales in the axilla-groin length is a useful character in lizard identification.

Midventral *adj* The portion of the ventral surface of the body that lies along the midline.

Monophyletic *adj* A term describing any group that includes a common ancestor and all its descendents.

Monotypic *adj* A term used to describe a genus that contains only a single species or a species that contain no subspecies; thus, having only a single included taxon.

Morphological *adj* Of or pertaining to morphology.

Morphology *n* 1. The form of an organism, especially considered as a whole. 2. The subdiscipline within biology that is concerned with the study of form, including gross anatomy.

Mosaic bone *n* One of many small bony plates embedded in the dermis of *Dermochelys coriacea*.

Mucronate *adj* Bearing a projecting spine on the trailing edge, as in certain scales in some species of lizards (e.g., *Sceloporus serrifer*, Fig. 128A).

Naris (pl. **nares**) *n* A nasal opening, usually paired. Nares that open to the outside are usually termed *external nares*, or *nostrils*, whereas those that open into the pharynx are *internal nares*, or *choanae*.

Nasal scale *n* In squamates, a scale perforated by or bordering the external naris. Lizards have one nasal scale on each side; snakes may have a single nasal on each side, or each scale may be divided, in which case an anterior and a posterior nasal scale may be recognized (Fig. 150C).

Nasolabial groove *n* A narrow trough, running from the upper margin of the lip to the external naris, that conducts chemicals to the vomeronasal organ. It is characteristic of members of the salamander family Plethodontidae.

Neonate *n* Newly born or hatched.

Neotropical *adj* Of or pertaining to the Neotropics.

Neotropics *n* The New World tropics. Also, the biogeographic realm that includes tropical Mexico, the West Indies, and all of Central America and South America.

Nocturnal *adj* Active at night.

Nominal *adj* Named. Any named taxon is a nominal form, regardless of its validity.

Nominate *adj* A subspecies that includes the population from which the type specimen of a polytypic species originated, and which thus bears the specific name as the trinomial. For example, *Dryadophis melanolomus melanolomus* is the nominate subspecies of *Dryadophis melanolomus*.

Nomenclatural *adj* Of or pertaining to nomenclature.

Nomenclature *n* The branch of systematics that is concerned with naming organisms.

Note repetition rate *n* In anuran vocalization, the number of repetitions of a note within a call per unit time.

Nuchal *adj* Of or pertaining to the dorsal surface of the neck or the neck region.

Nuchal bone *n* In turtles, the anteriormost unpaired bony element in the carapace lying along the dorsal midline.

Nuchal scute *n* In turtles, the anteriormost epidermal scute in the carapace. It lies in the midline immediately anterior to the first vertebral scute. Synonym: cervical.

Nuptial excrescence *n* A thick, roughened pad on the skin of sexually active male anurans, usually on the thumb. Synonym: nuptial pad.

Nuptial pad *See* Nuptial excrescence

Occipital *adj* Of or pertaining to the posterior portion of the skull or to the occipital bones surrounding the foramen magnum.

Ocellus (pl. **ocelli**) *n* An eyelike structure or pattern element. More generally, any rounded spot.

Ocular *adj* Of or pertaining to the eye.

Ocular scale *n* A scale that covers the eye in some species of snakes (e.g., *Leptotyphlops goudotii* and *Typhlops microstomus*, Fig. 151).

Ocular spine *n* A small, pointed integumentary structure over the eye of certain lizards (e.g., some *Sphaerodactylus*, Fig. 115A).

Omnivorous *adj* Feeding on both plants and animals.

Ontogenetic *adj* Of or pertaining to ontogeny; often used to describe differences (ontogentic changes) that occur as an organism matures. For example, juveniles of the skink *Eumeces sumichrasti* have blue tails, but the color disappears as the lizard approaches maturity.

Ontogeny *n* The developmental history of an individual from fertilization until death.

Ophiophagous *adj* Literally, "snake-eating"; an organism that includes snakes in its diet (e.g., the snake *Lampropeltis triangulum*).

Oral disk *n* In tadpoles, the area surrounding the mouth and supporting the various mouthparts such as the jaw sheaths, denticles, and labial papillae (Fig. 35).

Oral papilla *n* A small, fleshy, pimplelike projection of skin in the region of the mouth. In many tadpoles, the mouthparts are surrounded by numerous oral papillae whose extent and position are useful characters in identification (Fig. 35).

Osteological *adj* Of or pertaining to bone or to the skeleton.

Ovarian egg *n* An egg still within the ovary.

Oviductal egg *n* An egg within the oviduct. Some authors prefer the term *oviducal*.

Ovigerous *adj* Containing fertilized eggs. Synonym: gravid.

Oviparity *n* The type of reproduction in which eggs are deposited outside the body (i.e., "egg-laying"). *See* Viviparity.

Oviparous *adj* Of or pertaining to oviparity.

Oviposit *v* To lay eggs; the placement of eggs, as in a nest.

Oviposition *n* The act of laying eggs.

Ovoid *adj* Shaped like an oval. The bodies of same species of tadpoles appear ovoid when seen in lateral view (e.g., *Triprion petasatus*, Fig. 89).

Ovum (pl. **ova**) *n* Egg.

Palpebral membrane *n* The transparent eyelid of anurans. It may be clear, as in most species of *Hyla*, or reticulate, as in *Agalychnis callidryas* (Fig. 59).

Papilla *n* A small, fleshy projection.

Paratype *n* Any specimen or specimens of the type series not designated as holotype.

Paravertebral *adj* Of or pertaining to an area immediately lateral to the dorsal midline. Scales that are immediately lateral to the vertebral scale row are paravertebral.

Parietal peritoneum *n* The lining of the coelomic cavity. The pigmentation of the parietal peritonium is of taxonmic importance in some groups of lizards and snakes.

Parietal scale *n* 1. In lizards, one or more scales on the dorsal surface of the head lying posterior to the frontoparietal scales. 2. In snakes, one of a pair of large scales on the dorsal surface of the head lying immediately posterior to the frontal scale (Fig. 149B).

Parotoid gland *n* A large glandular structure situated behind the eye and extending onto the neck and shoulder. It is especially well developed in toads of the genus *Bufo* (Fig. 54). The term *parotid* is sometimes applied, incorrectly, to this gland, but that term properly refers to the large salivary gland of mammals.

Parthenogenesis *n* Mode of reproduction involving formation of a new individual from an unfertilizaed egg. Some species of amphibians and reptiles (e.g., *Cnemidophorus cozumela* and *C. rodecki*) reproduce by means of parthenogenesis and exist as all-female species.

Parthenogenetic *adj* Of or pertaining to parthenogenesis.

Parturition *n* The act of bringing forth young; birth.

Patronym *n* A scientific name formed from the given name or surname of a person. For example, *Coniophanes schmidti* is named after Karl P. Schmidt, and the specific name is thus a patronym.

Pectoral *adj* Of or pertaining to the chest; thus, also pertaining to the forelimb girdle.

Pectoral scute *n* In turtles, one of a pair of plastral scutes bordered anteriorly by the humeral scute and posteriorly by the abdominal scute.

Pelagic *adj* Of or pertaining to the open ocean.

Pelvic *adj* Of or pertaining to the hip; thus, also pertaining to the hind limb girdle.

Pentadactyl *adj* Bearing five digits. The hands and feet of most lizards are pentadactyl.

Phalanx (pl. **phalanges**) *n* One of several bones in each finger or toe.

Phragmosis *n* A behavior in which a sequestered animal uses a portion of its body to seal or otherwise plug an entrance or hole. *Triprion petasatus* uses the dorsal surface of its head to plug the opening to its daytime retreat.

Pitviper *n* Any venomous snake of the subfamily Crotalinae (e.g., rattlesnakes). Pitvipers are so named for the deep loreal pit that lies between the eye and the nostril (Fig. 150D) and houses a heat-receptive organ.

Plastral *adj* Of or pertaining to the plastron.

Plastral hinge *n* A transverse, movable articulation be-

tween components of the plastron of certain turtles. Species possessing hinged plastra may have a single hinge dividing the plastron into two movable lobes (as in *Terrapene carolina*) or anterior and posterior hinges that divide the plastron into three lobes, of which the anterior and posterior are capable of moving relative to the fixed middle lobe (e.g., *Kinosternon*, Fig. 111).

Plastron (pl. **plastra**) *n* The ventral portion of the shell of turtles, generally consisting of bony elements on which are superimposed keratinized scutes.

Pleural scute *n* In turtles, any of several epidermal scutes covering the ribs in the carapace. The number of pleural scutes is a useful character in identification.

Polymorphic *adj* Of or pertaining to polymorphism; an organism that exhibits polymorphism.

Polymorphism *n* The existence of more than a single distinct morphological type within a population. For example, the females of many species of *Anolis* exhibit pattern polymorphism in that some possess a distinct vertebral stripe whereas others lack the stripe (cf. Figs. 321, 322).

Polytypic *adj* Of or pertaining to any taxon containing two or more immediately subordinate taxa.

Polytypic species *n* Any species consisting of two or more geographic variants (subspecies).

Postanal *adj* Of or pertaining to the region immediately posterior to the anus.

Postanal bone *n* One of a pair of bones lying within the postanal sac; characteristic of some species of gekkonid and eublepharid lizards, among others.

Postanal sac *n* One of a pair of invaginations lying immediately behind the vent in some lizards (e.g., certain gekkonids and eublepharids).

Postanal scale *n* One of a pair of enlarged scales lying immediately posterior to the vent, characteristic of the males of some species of lizards (Fig. 126D).

Posterior *adj* Pertaining to the rear or caudal end of the body or of a structure.

Postfemoral *adj* Of or pertaining to the posterior surface or region of the femur.

Postfemoral dermal pocket *n* An invagination in the skin on the posterior surface of the femur at its point of insertion, characteristic of some species of lizards (e.g., *Sceloporus cozumelae*, *S. teapensis*).

Postocular *adj* Of or pertaining to the region immediately behind the eye. Many snakes (e.g., *Bothriechis schlegelii*, Fig. 199) have a postocular stripe.

Postocular scale *n* In snakes and lizards, a scale or scales bounding the posterior margin of the eye.

Preanal *adj* Of or pertaining to the region immediately anterior to the anus or vent.

Preanal pore *n* The opening of an exocrine gland situated in the preanal region. The males of the lizard *Coleonyx elegans* have preanal pores.

Prefrontal scale *n* One of a pair (or more) of epidermal scutes on the dorsal surface of the head of snakes (Fig. 149B), lizards, and turtles (Fig. 109). The prefrontal scales lie immediately anterior to the frontal scale.

Premaxillary bone *n* One of a pair of dermal bones at the anterior end of the skull in amphibians and reptiles. The premaxillary bones, which often bear teeth, constitute the anteriormost portion of the maxillary arch.

Prenasal bone *n* An unpaired dermal bone lying anterior to the premaxillary bones in *Triprion petasatus*.

Preocular scale *n* In lizards and snakes, the scale or scales lying immediately anterior to the eye and forming its anterior border.

Prepollex *n* A small skeletal element on the inner side of digit 1 (the pollix) of the hand of some anurans.

Prevomer *n* The name some authors prefer for a pair of dermal bones lying in the skull immediately posterior to the premaxillary bones. *See* Vomer.

Primary annulus *See* Annulus

Primary note *n* The longer of two or more notes in an anuran call sequence. For example, the advertisement call of *Hyla ebraccata* (Fig. 68) consists of a primary note followed by a series of secondary notes.

Proximal *adj* Situated near or toward the point of attachment. The phalanges at the base of a digit lie proximal to those at the tip of the digit, for example.

Pulse *n* In bioacoustics, the distinct pulsations of sound that constitute a note, often apparent as vertical marks on an audiospectrogram (e.g., in the vocalization of *Bufo valliceps*, Fig. 58).

Pulse rate *n* In bioacoustics, the number of pulses per unit time, usually expressed as pulses per second.

Pustulate *adj* Bearing pustules. A term applied to the skin of some anurans (e.g., *Physalaemus pustulosus*).

Pustule *n* A small wart or excrescence on the skin of amphibians.

Quadruped *n* A four-footed animal.

Race *See* Subspecies

Rear-fanged *adj* A term applied to snakes in which one or more teeth at or near the posterior end of the maxillary bone are enlarged to form fangs. Such snakes may be venomous to varying degrees, and the fangs bear grooves for the conduction of venom. Synonym: opisthoglyphous.

Reticulate *adj* With respect to color pattern, having the appearance of a net or mesh; netlike.

Rostral *adj* Of or pertaining to the snout; anterior.

Rostral scale *n* In snakes and lizards, an unpaired scale at the tip of the snout that divides the supralabial series (Fig. 149C).

Rostrum *n* The snout.

Rugose *adj* Rough, wrinkled, or folded.

Saxicolous *adj* Dwelling on or among rocks.

Scale pit *See* Apical pit

Scute *n* A large, flat scale. The term is often applied to the transverse scales on the ventral surface of most snakes and to the epidermal covering of the shell of turtles. Some authors prefer the term *lamina* when referring to turtles. Synonym: plate.

Seam *n* The boundary between two epidermal scutes on the shell of a turtle.

Seat patch *n* In anurans, a trianglar area of skin surrounding the vent, generally darkly pigmented and contrasting with the lighter coloration of the adjacent skin.

Secondary annulus *See* Annulus

Secondary note *n* In anuran vocalization, one or more notes that follow a primary note. Secondary notes are of shorter duration than the primary note. The advertisement call of *Hyla ebraccata* (Fig. 68) consists of a primary note followed by several secondary notes.

Serrated *adj* Possessing a linear series of scales that give a sawtoothed appearance, as in the supracaudal scales of males of *Anolis sagrei* and *A. cristatellus* (Fig. 131A,C).

Sexual dichromatism *n* Within a species, a difference between the sexes with respect to coloration. For example, in some lizard species the males are brightly colored and the females are drab.

Sexual dimorphism *n* Within a species, a morphological difference between the sexes. For example, in many species of anurans the females are substantially larger than the males.

Sinistral *adj* Of or pertaining to the left side. Spiracles that open on the left side of the body in tadpoles are sinistral.

Sister species *n* Two species that shared a common ancestor more recently than either did with any other species. Sister species are each other's closest cladistic relatives.

Snout-vent length *n* The straight-line distance from the tip of the snout to the posterior margin of the vent; abbreviated SVL.

Spectacle *n* The immovable, transparent covering of the eye of snakes and some lizards, formed by the fusion of the eyelids.

Spinose *adj* Replete with spines.

Spiracle *n* In tadpoles, an opening from the gill chamber to the outside. The number of spiracles and their position are important characters in identification (Fig. 34).

Squamate *n* Any member of the order Squamata, the taxon containing snakes, lizards, and amphisbaenians.

Subarticular tubercle *n* In anurans, any tubercle that lies immediately below the point of articulation of adjacent phalanges (Fig. 31).

Subcaudal *adj* Of or pertaining to the inferior surface of the tail.

Subcaudal scale *n* One of a series of epidermal scales on the undersurface of the tail of reptiles.

Subdigital *adj* Of or pertaining to the inferior surface of a digit; for example, the wide scales on the undersurface of the digits of lizards are termed subdigital lamellae.

Subgular *adj* Of or pertaining to the area below the gular region. Thus, when inflated, the vocal sacs of males of some species of anurans are subgular in position (e.g., Fig. 237).

Sublingual fold *n* A fold of skin below the tongue in certain species of salamanders (e.g., those of the genus *Oedipina*).

Subnasal scale *n* A scale lying immediately below the nasal scale, characteristic of some members of the genus *Sceloporus* (e.g., populations of *S. teapensis* in the Yucatán Peninsula).

Subocular *adj* Of or pertaining to the region immediately below the eye.

Subocular scale *n* In snakes and lizards, one or more scales bordering the inferior margin of the eye (or the preocular scale) and lying immediately above the supralabial scales (Fig. 158).

Subspecies *n* A geographic subdivision within a species that is afforded nomenclatural recognition. For example, the tropical rattlesnake, *Crotalus durissus*, exists as several subspecies, of which *C. d. tzabcan* occurs in the Yucatan Peninsula. Synonym: race.

Sulcate *adj* Possessing a sulcus.

Sulcus *n* A shallow groove, generally open on one side. For example, the semen canal on the surface of the hemipenis of snakes is termed the *sulcus spermaticus*.

Supernumerary tubercle *n* In anurans, a tubercle on the hand or foot that does not lie immediately below a point of articulation between phalanges; thus, a tubercle on the palmar or plantar surface other than a subarticular tubercle (Fig. 31).

Supra-anal tubercle *n* One of a group of small, rounded bumps on the dorsal scales above the vent in some species of snakes (e.g., *Micrurus nigrocinctus*), apparently found only in males.

Supracaudal *adj* Of or pertaining to the superior (upper) surface of the tail.

Supralabial *adj* Of or pertaining to the region immediately above the upper margin of the jaw.

Supralabial scale *n* One of a series of scales bordering the upper margin of the jaw, numbered from anterior to posterior. The number of supralabial scales is an important character in snake and lizard identification.

Supraocular *adj* Of or pertaining to the region immediately above the eye.

Supraocular scale *n* 1. One of a group of scales occupying the supraorbital region in lizards. 2. One of a pair of enlarged scales lying immediately above the eye in some snakes (Fig. 149B). Synonym: supraorbital.

Supraorbital *See* Supraocular

Supraorbital semicircle *n* An arc of small scales bordering the enlarged supraorbital scales of some lizards, especially those of the genus *Anolis*.

Supratympanic fold *n* A fold of skin lying above the tympanum in some frogs and toads. Its presence or absence is a useful identifying character for some species.

Supratympanic stripe *n* A stripe lying above the tympanic membrane in some anurans (e.g., *Smilisca cyanosticta*).

Suture *n* The border, line, or groove between two adjacent parts, especially used with respect to abutting bones, as in the shell of turtles.

Sympatric *adj* Having geographic distributions that overlap. *See* Sympatry.

Sympatry *n* An area of overlapping geographic distributions. Species whose geographic distributions overlap are said to occur in sympatry (cf. Allopatry).

Syntopic *adj* Occurring at the same place. The term implies at least the potential for biotic interaction and thus a more intimate association than that implied by the term *sympatric*.

Syntopy *n* The condition in which members of different species occur at the same place.

Syntype *n* Any member of the type series studied by the author of a taxon who did not designate a single type specimen, or holotype.

Tarsal fold *n* A fold of skin running along the tarsus in some species of frogs and toads. Its presence or absence is a useful character in anuran identification.

Tarsus *n* The hind limb segment lying between the tibia and fibula and the metatarsal bones; the ankle. In anurans, the tarsus is elongate and may bear a tarsal fold, tarsal tubercles, or both.

Tautonym *n* A scientific name in which the generic and specific names are the same (e.g., *Caretta caretta*).

Taxonomy *n* The subdiscipline within systematic biology that is concerned with classification and the application of scientific names.

Temperature-dependent sex determination. *n* A condition exhibited by many species of turtles and crocodilians in which the incubation temperature determines the sex of the hatchlings. Typically, lower temperatures produce a preponderance of males, and higher temperatures produce a preponderance of females.

Temporal *adj* Of or pertaining to the temporal region, which lies behind the orbit in the skull of vertebrates.

Temporal scale *n* A scale or scales in the temporal region of the head of snakes and lizards. Temporal scales lie posterior to the postocular scales, below the parietal scales, and above the supralabial scales. Those in contact with the postocular scales are *anterior temporals*, those lying behind the anterior temporals are *posterior temporals*. The number of temporals is a useful character in snake identification (Figs. 150, 152C,D).

Tentacle *n* In caecilians, a fleshy, protrusible structure situated in a groove or canal in the maxillary bone. The tentacle apparently serves a chemosensory function.

Tentacular opening *n* In caecilians, the opening between the nostril and the eye through which the tentacle is protruded. The position of the opening relative to the nostril and eye is an important distinguishing character for some species.

Terminal *adj* An anatomical position pertaining to the end of a structure. For example, in tadpoles, the mouth is terminal if it opens at the anterior end of the head.

Terminus *n* End.

Terrestrial *adj* Living on the ground.

Tetrapod. *n* Any four-footed animal; thus, by extension, any member of the group that includes amphibians, reptiles, birds, and mammals, regardless of the presence or absence of four feet.

Tibia *n* An endochondral bone in the lower leg of vertebrates; sometimes used to refer to the hind limb segment between the knee and the ankle. The term *shank* is sometimes used as a synonym.

Titillate *v* In turtles, courtship behavior in which a male fans or gently taps the female, especially in the vicinity of her head. Titillation involves tactile stimulation of the female by means of rapid vibratory movements of the male's forelimb claws.

Toponym *n* The species (= trivial) portion of a scientific name based on a region or locality; for example, the lizard *Cnemidophorus cozumela* is named for the island of Cozumel.

Tricarinate *adj* Having three keels; usually applied to turtles having three longitudinal keels on the carapace, such as *Chelydra serpentina*.

Trinomial *n* A scientific name consisting of three parts, the third part being the subspecific name (e.g., *Conophis lineatus concolor*).

Truncate *adj* Flattened or appearing cut off; generally applied to appendages or extremities that terminate abruptly rather than tapering. The snout of *Smilisca cyanosticta* is truncate in lateral view.

Tubercle *n* A small, rounded bump on the skin of some amphibians and reptiles.

Tuberculate *adj* Bearing tubercles; as, for example, the skin of the gecko *Hemidactylus tuberculosus*.

Tympanum *n* The membrane covering the external opening of the middle ear; the eardrum. Synonym: tympanic membrane.

Type locality *n* The place where the holotype (or lectotype) originated.

Unicarinate *adj* Having only a single (usually median) keel; as exhibited, for example, by the carapace of the turtle *Kinosternon leucostomum*.

Vent *n* The cloacal aperture. The posterior opening through which the products of the digestive, reproductive, and excretory systems pass.

Venter *n* The lower surface of the body.

Ventral *adj* 1. Of or pertaining to the lower surface of the body or of a structure. 2. The direction or position toward the lower surface of the body.

Ventral disk *n* A portion of the abdomen that is demarcated by a circular fold of skin, the presence or absence of which is of taxonomic importance; *Leptodactylus labialis*, for example, has a ventral disk.

Ventrolateral *adj* A position intermediate between ventral and lateral. The spiracle of some tadpoles is ventrolateral in position (Fig. 34B).

Vent tube *n* A tube of skin surrounding the vent aperture of tadpoles. The tube may open at the ventral midline (medial) or to the right of the ventral midline (dextral) (Fig. 37).

Vermiculate *adj* A color pattern consisting of wavy irregular lines or streaks; resembling worms or the tracks of worms.

Vermiform *adj* Wormlike, extremely elongate (e.g., the tadpole of *Hyalinobatrachium fleischmanni*, Fig. 92).

Vertebral *adj* Of or pertaining to a vertebra or the vertebral column.

Vertebral scute *n* In turtles, any of a series of unpaired epidermal scutes lying along the dorsal midline of the carapace.

Vertebral stripe *n* A longitudinal middorsal stripe.

Viscera (sing. **viscus**) *n* Collectively, all of the soft internal organs of an animal.

Viviparity *n* Reproduction in which development occurs within the oviduct or uterus and the young are brought forth alive (i.e., live-bearing). Includes *ovoviviparity*, in which eggs are retained within the body until they hatch and the embryo receives most nutrients from ovarian provisioning (= lecithotrophy); *placental viviparity*, in which the developing embryo receives maternal sustenance via a placental connection (= matrotrophy); and *aplacental viviparity*, in which the embryo receives continuing maternal sustenance by a means other than a placental attachment.

Viviparous *adj* Of or pertaining to viviparity.

Vocal sac *n* A ventral outpocketing of the oral cavity in male anurans that serves to amplify vibrations of the vocal cords.

Vocal slit *n* In male anurans, one of a pair of slitlike valves in the floor of the mouth through which air passes between the buccal cavity and the the vocal sac(s).

Vomer *n* Paired dermal bones immediately posterior to the premaxillary bones in the roof of the mouth of vertebrates (Fig. 28). Those of amphibians and reptiles are perhaps not homologous with the vomer of mammals, in which case the name *prevomer* would apply. *See* Prevomer.

Vomerine teeth *n* Teeth borne on the vomer of amphibians. Sometimes called *prevomerine teeth*, reflecting the uncertain homology of that bone with the vomer of mammals. The number of teeth and their position on the bone are important characters in salamander identification (Fig. 28).

Wart *n* A rounded, elevated bump on the skin of certain anurans, especially those of the family Bufonidae. Warts are larger than pustules, although some authors do not distinguish between the two.

Whorl *n* A ring of scales encircling the tail of a lizard or crocodilian. Usually refers to alternating series of scales that differ in size, shape, or both. The tails of *Ctenosaura* (Fig. 123) are covered with whorls of scales, for example.

Xeric *adj* Arid, lacking in moisture.

Xiphicercal *adj* Drawn out as a fine filament. The tails of some tadpoles (e.g., *Hyla microcephala*, Fig. 72) are xiphicercal.

Literature Cited

Abercrombie, C. L., III, D. Davidson, C. A. Hope, and D. E. Scott. 1980. Status of Morelet's crocodile, *Crocodylus moreleti*, in Belize. Biol. Conserv. 17:103–113.

Adler, K. 1976. New genera and species described in Holbrook's *North American Herpetology*. *In*: John Edwards Holbrook, North American herpetology. Reprint by the Society for the Study of Amphibians and Reptiles, Oxford, Ohio, pp. xxix-xliii.

Adler, K. 1989. Herpetologists of the past. *In*: K. Adler (ed.), Contributions to the history of herpetology, pp. 5–141. Society for the Study of Amphibians and Reptiles, Oxford, Ohio.

Agardy, T., and R. G. Hernandez. 1989. Biology and conservation of sea turtles nesting in Quintana Roo, Mexico, during 1988. *In*: A. S. Eckert, K. L. Eckert, and T. H. Richardson (comps.), Proceedings of the Ninth Annual Workshop on Sea Turtle Conservation and Biology, pp. 199–200. NOAA Technical Memorandum NMFS-SEFC-232. National Oceanic and Atmospheric Administration, Washington, D.C.

Aguilar, M. X. 1994. Efecto de la temperatura de incubación sobre la determinación del sexo en *Crocodylus acutus* y *C. moreletii*. Tesis de Maestría en Ciencias. Facultad de Ciencias, Universidad Nacional Autónoma de México, Mexico City.

Ahl, E. 1930. Reptilia (Kriechetiere). Tabulae Biol. 6:625–715.

Alexander, T. R. 1964 [1965]. Observations on the feeding behavior of *Bufo marinus* (Linne). Herpetologica 20:255–259.

Allen, E. R. 1949. Observations on the feeding habits of the juvenile cantil. Copeia 1949:225–226.

Allen, R., and W. T. Neill. 1952. The indigo snake. Fla. Wildl. 6:44–47.

Allen, R., and W. T. Neill. 1956. Effect of marine toad toxins on man. Herpetologica 12:150–151.

Allen, R., and W. T. Neill. 1959. Doubtful locality records in British Honduras. Herpetologica 15:227–233.

Altig, R. 1970. A key to the tadpoles of the continental United States and Canada. Herpetologica 26:180–207.

Altig, R. 1987. Key to the anuran tadpoles of Mexico. Southwest. Nat. 32:75–84.

Altig, R., and R. A. Brandon. 1971. Generic key and synopses for free-living larvae and tadpoles of Mexican amphibians. Tulane Stud. Zool. Bot. 17:10–15.

Alvarez del Toro, M. 1960. Reptiles de Chiapas. Instituto Zoológico del Estado, Tuxtla Gutiérrez, Chiapas, Mexico. 204 pp.

Alvarez del Toro, M. 1973. Los reptiles de Chiapas. 2nd ed. Gobierno del Estado, Tuxtla Gutiérrez, Chiapas, Mexico. 178 pp.

Alvarez del Toro, M. 1974. Los Crocodylia de México (estudio comparativo). Instituto Mexicano de Recursos Naturales Renovables, Mexico City. ix + 70 pp.

Alvarez del Toro, M. 1983 [dated 1982]. Los reptiles de Chiapas. 3rd ed. Instituto de Historia Natural, Tuxtla Gutiérrez, Chiapas, Mexico. 248 pp.

Alvarez del Toro, M., R. A. Mittermeier, and J. B. Iverson. 1979. River turtle in danger. Oryx 15:170–173.

Alvarez del Toro, M., and H. M. Smith. 1956. Notulae herpetologicae Chiapasiae I. Herpetologica 12:3–17.

Alvarez del Toro, M., and H. M. Smith. 1958. Notulae herpetologicae Chiapasiae II. Herpetologica 14:15–17.

Amaral, A. do. 1964. Comment on the proposal to substitute the generic name *Dryadophis* Stuart, 1939, for *Mastigodryas* Amaral, 1934. Bull. Zool. Nomencl. 21:13.

Andersson, L. G. 1899. Catalogue of Linnean type-specimens of snakes in the Royal Museum in Stockholm. Handl. Svenska Vet. Akad. 24:1–35.

Andersson, L. G. 1900. Catalogue of Linnean type-specimens of Linnaeus's Reptilia in the Royal Museum in Stockholm. Handl. Svenska Vet. Akad. 26:1–29.

Andrews, E. W. 1937. Notes on snakes from the Yucatán Peninsula. Field Mus. Nat. Hist. Zool. Ser. 20:355–359.

Andrews, R. M. 1979. The lizard *Corytophanes cristatus*:

An extreme "sit-and-wait" predator. Biotropica 11:136–139.

Andrews, R. M. 1983. *Norops polylepis. In*: D. H. Jansen (ed.), A Costa Rican natural history, pp. 409–410. University of Chicago Press, Chicago. xi + 816 pp.

Antonio, F. B. 1980. Mating behavior and reproduction of the eyelash viper (*Bothrops schlegeli*) in captivity. Herpetologica 36:231–233.

Armstrong, B. L., and J. B. Murphy. 1979. The natural history of Mexican rattlesnakes. Univ. Kans. Publ. Mus. Nat. Hist. Spec. Publ. 5. vii + 88 pp.

Axtell, R. W. 1960. The rediscovery of *Sceloporus prezygous* Smith in Chiapas, Mexico, with a re-evaluation of its relationships. Tex. J. Sci. 12:232–239.

Bacon, P. R. 1973. The orientation circle in the beach ascent crawl of the leatherback turtle, *Dermochelys coriacea*, in Trinidad. Herpetologica 29:343–348.

Bacon, P. R., F. Berry, K. Bjorndal, H. Hirth, L. Ogren, and M. Weber (eds.). 1984. Proceedings of the Western Atlantic Turtle Symposium. University of Miami Press, Miami, Fla. Vol. 1, 306 pp.; vol. 2, 318 pp.; vol. 3., 514 pp.

Bahena-Basave, H. 1994. Los reptiles de la Unión, sur del estado de Quintana Roo y algunos aspectos de sus hábitos alimenticios. Thesis, Universidad Nacional Autónoma de México, Campus Iztacala. ii + 57 pp.

Bahena-Basave, H. 1995a. *Dermatemys mawii* (Central American river turtle): Geographic distribution. Herpetol. Rev. 26:43.

Bahena-Basave, H. 1995b. *Staurotypus triporcatus* (Mexican giant mud turtle): Geographic distribution. Herpetol. Rev. 26:43.

Bahena-Basave, H. 1995c. *Micrurus browni* (Brown's coral snake): Geographic distribution. Herpetol. Rev. 26:46.

Bahena-Basave, H. 1995d. *Tretanorhinus nigroluteus* (orangebelly swamp snake): Geographic distribution. Herpetol. Rev. 26:47.

Bailey, J. R. 1937. New forms of *Coniophanes* Hollowell, and the status of *Dromicus clavatus* Peters. Occas. Pap. Mus. Zool. Univ. Mich. 362:1–6.

Bailey, J. R. 1939. A systematic study of the snakes of the genus *Coniophanes*. Pap. Mich. Acad. Sci. Arts Lett. 24:1–48.

Bailey, J. R. 1970. *Clelia. In*: J. A. Peters and B. Orejas-Miranda (eds.), Catalogue of the Neotropical Squamata. Part 1: Snakes, pp. 62–64. Bull. U.S. Natl. Mus., no. 297. viii + 347 pp.

Bailey, J. W. 1928. A revision of the lizards of the genus *Ctenosaura*. Proc. U.S. Natl. Mus. 73:1–58.

Baird, S. F. 1859. Reptiles of the boundary. United States and Mexican boundary survey, under the order of Lieut. Col. W. H. Emory, Major First Cavalry, and United States Commissioner. Vol. 2, pt. 2, pp. 1–35.

Baird, S. F., and C. Girard. 1853. Catalogue of North American reptiles in the museum of the Smithsonian Institution. Part 1: Serpents. U.S. Government Printing Office, Washington, D.C. xvi + 172 pp.

Baqueiro López, O. 1983. Magia, mitos y supersticiones entre los Mayas. Maldonado Editores, Mérida, Yucatán, Mexico. 76 pp.

Barbour, T. 1928. Reptiles from the Bay Islands. Proc. New Engl. Zool. Club 10:55–61.

Barbour, T., and A. D. Amaral. 1924. Notes on some Central American snakes. Occas. Pap. Bost. Soc. Nat. Hist. 5:129–132.

Barbour, T., and L. J. Cole. 1906. Vertebrata from Yucatán. Reptilia, Amphibia, Pisces. Bull. Mus. Comp. Zool. Harv. Univ. 50:146–159.

Barbour, T., and G. K. Noble. 1915. A revision of the lizard genus *Ameiva*. Bull. Mus. Comp. Zool. Harv. Univ. 59:417–479.

Barrera, A. 1963. La península de Yucatán como provincia biótica. Rev. Soc. Mex. Hist. Nat. 24:71–105.

Bauer, A. M., and A. P. Russell. 1993a. *Aristelliger*. Cat. Am. Amphib. Reptiles 565.1–565.4.

Bauer, A. M., and A. P. Russell. 1993b. *Aristelliger georgeensis*. Cat. Am. Amphib. Reptiles 568.1–568.2.

Beargie, K., and C. J. McCoy. 1964. Variation and relationships of the teiid lizard *Cnemidophorus angusticeps*. Copeia 1964:561–570.

Beebe, W. 1944. Field notes on the lizards of Kartabo, British Guiana, and Caripito, Venezuela. Part 1: Gekkonidae. Zoologica 29:145–160.

Beebe, W. 1946. Field notes on the snakes of Kartabo, British Guiana, and Caripito, Venezuela. Zoologica 31:11–52.

Berry, J. F. 1978. Variation and systematics in the *Kinosternon scorpioides* and *K. leucostomum* complexes (Reptilia: Testudines: Kinosternidae) of Mexico and Central America. Ph.D. dissertation, University of Utah, Salt Lake City.

Berry, J. F., and R. Shine. 1980. Sexual size dimorphism and sexual selection in turtles (order Testudines). Oecologia 44:185–191.

Berthold, A. A. 1846. Über verschiedene neue oder seltene Reptilien aus New Granada und Crustacien aus China. Abh. Ges. Wiss. Gött. 3:3–32.

Bezy, R. L. 1973. A new species of the genus *Lepidophyma* (Reptilia: Xantusiidae) from Guatemala. Los Ang. Cty. Mus. Contrib. Sci. 239:1–7.

Bezy, R. L. 1984. Systematics of xantusiid lizards of the genus *Lepidophyma* in northeastern Mexico. Los Ang. Cty. Contrib. Sci. 349:1–16.

Bezy, R. L. 1989. Morphological differentiation in unisexual and bisexual xantusiid lizards of the genus *Lepidophyma* in Central America. Herpetol. Monogr. 3:61–80.

Bickham, J. W., and J. Carr. 1983. Taxonomy and phylogeny of the higher categories of cryptodiran turtles based on a cladistic analysis of chromosomal data. Copeia 1983:918–932.

Bjorndal, K. A. (ed.). 1982. Biology and conservation of sea turtles. Smithsonian Institution Press, Washington, D.C. 583 pp.

Bjorndal, K. A., and A. Carr. 1989. Variation in clutch size and egg size in the green turtle nesting population at Tortuguero, Costa Rica. Herpetologica 45:181–189.

Blair, W. F. 1972. Evolution in the genus *Bufo*. University of Texas Press, Austin. viii + 459 pp.

Blanco-Casillo, Y. 1990. Mexican war to protect sea turtles. *In*: T. H. Richardson, J. I. Richardson, and M. Donnelly (comps.), Proceedings of the Tenth Annual Workshop on Sea Turtle Biology and Conservation, pp. 185–188. NOAA Technical Memorandum NMFS-SEFC-278. National Oceanic and Atmospheric Administration, Washington, D.C.

Blaney, R. M., and P. K. Blaney. 1978a. Notes on three species of *Micrurus* (Serpentes: Elapidae). Herpetol. Rev. 9:92.

Blaney, R. M., and P. K. Blaney. 1978b. Additional specimens of *Amastridium veliferum* Cope (Serpentes: Colubridae) from Chiapas, Mexico. Southwest. Nat. 23:692.

Blaney, R. M., and P. K. Blaney. 1979. Variation in the coral snake, *Micrurus diastema*, in Quintana Roo, Mexico. Herpetologica 35:276–278.

Blom, F. 1944. La vida de los Mayas. Biblioteca Enciclopédica Popular. Secretaría de Educación Pública, Mexico City.

Bock, B. C. 1987. *Corytophanes cristatus*: Nesting. Herpetol. Rev. 18:35.

Bocourt, M. F. 1868. Descriptions de quelques crotaliens nouveaux appartenant au genre *Bothrops*, recueillis dans le Guatemala. Ann. Sci. Nat. Paris (5)10:201–202.

Bocourt, M. F. 1873–1897. Études sur les reptiles. *In*: Mission scientifique au Mexique et dans l'Amérique Centrale—Recherches zoologiques. Paris, Imprimerie Impériale. Vols. 2–15, pp. 33–860.

Boettger, O. 1893. Ein neuer Laubfrosch aus Costa Rica. Ber. Senckenb. Naturforsch. Ges. 1892–1893:251–252.

Bogert, C. M., and A. P. Porter. 1966. The differential characteristics of the Mexican snakes related to *Geophis dubius* (Peters). Am. Mus. Novit. 2277:1–19.

Boie, F. 1827. Bemerkungen über Merrem's Versuch eines Systems der Amphibien. Isis von Oken 20:508–566.

Boulenger, G. A. 1881. Description of a new species of *Anolis* from Yucatán. Proc. Zool. Soc. Lond. 1881:921–922.

Boulenger, G. A. 1882. Catalogue of the Batrachia Gradientia s. Ecaudata in the collection of the British Museum. 2nd ed. Taylor and Francis, London. xvi + 503 pp.

Boulenger, G. A. 1894. Catalogue of the snakes in the British Museum (Natural History). Vol. 2, pp. 1–382. Taylor and Francis, London.

Boulenger, G. A. 1898. Fourth report on additions to the batrachian collection in the Natural History Museum. Proc. Zool. Soc. Lond. 1898:473–482.

Bour, R., and A. Dubois. 1984 [dated 1983]. Nomenclatural availability of *Testudo coriacea* Vandelli, 1761: A case against a rigid application of the rules to old, well-known zoological works. J. Herpetol. 17:356–361.

Brainbridge, J. S., Jr., and P. C. H. Pritchard. 1974. The world's largest sea turtles remain a reptilian mystery. Smithsonian 5:64–73.

Brame, A. H., Jr. 1968. Systematics and evolution of the Mesoamerican salamander genus *Oedipina*. J. Herpetol. 1-2:1–64.

Brazaitis, P. 1973 [1974]. The identification of living crocodilians. Zoologica 58 (Fall 1973):59–101.

Brocchi, P. 1877. Sur quelques batraciens raniformes et bufoniformes de l'Amérique Centrale. Bull. Soc. Philomath. Paris (7)1:175–179.

Brocchi, P. 1881–1883. Études des batraciens de l'Amérique Centrale. *In*: Mission scientifique au Mexique et dans l'Amérique Centrale, Recherches zoologiques. Paris, Imprimerie Impériale.

Brodie, E. D., Jr., and J. A. Campbell. 1993. A new salamander of the genus *Oedipina* (Caudata: Plethodontidae) from the Pacific versant of Guatemala. Herpetologica 49:259–265.

Brongersma, L. D. 1961. Notes upon some sea turtles. Zool. Verh. (Leiden) 51:1–46.

Brongersma, L. D. 1968. Miscellaneous notes on turtles I. Proc. K. Ned. Akad. Wet. Ser. C, Biol. Med. Sci. 71:439–442.

Brown, B. C. 1937. Notes on *Coniophanes imperialis* (Baird). Copeia 1937:234.

Brown, B. C. 1939. The effect of *Coniophanes* poisoning in man. Copeia 1939:109.

Brown, K. M., and O. J. Sexton. 1973. Stimulation of reproductive activity of female *Anolis sagrei* by moisture. Physiol. Zool. 46:168–172.

Burger, J., and M. Gochfeld. 1991. Burrow site selection by black iguana (*Ctenosaura similis*) at Palo Verde, Costa Rica. J. Herpetol. 25:430–435.

Burger, W. L. 1950. A preliminary study of the subspecies of the jumping viper, *Bothrops nummifer*. Bull. Chic. Acad. Sci. 9:59–67.

Burger, W. L., and P. W. Smith. 1950. The coloration of the tail tip of young fer-de-lances: Sexual dimorphism rather than adaptive coloration. Science 112:431–433.

Burger, W. L., and J. E. Werler. 1954. The subspecies of the ring-necked coffee snake, *Ninia diademata*, and a short biological and taxonomic account of the genus. Univ. Kans. Sci. Bull. 36:643–672.

Burghardt, G. M., H. W. Greene, and A. S. Rand. 1977. Social behavior in hatchling green iguanas: Life in a reptile rookery. Science 195:689–691.

Burghardt, G. M., and A. S. Rand (eds.). 1982. Iguanas of the world. Their behavior, ecology, and conservation. Noyes Publications, Park Ridge, N.J. xix + 472 pp.

Buskirk, J. R. 1993. Yucatan box turtle, *Terrapene carolina yucatana*. Tortuga Gaz. 29:1–4.

Byles, R. A. 1989. Satellite telemetry of Kemp's ridley sea turtle, *Lepidochelys kempi*, in the Gulf of Mexico. *In*: S. A. Eckert, K. L. Eckert, and T. H. Richardson (comps.), Proceedings of the Ninth Annual Workshop on Sea Turtle Conservation and Biology, pp. 25–26. NOAA Technical Memorandum NMFS-SEFC-232. National Oceanic and Atmospheric Administration, Washington, D.C.

Cadle, J. E. 1984a. Molecular systematics of Neotropical xenodontine snakes. I. South American xenodontines. Herpetologica 40:8–20.

Cadle, J. E. 1984b. Molecular systematics of Neotropical

xenodontine snakes. II. Central American xenodontines. Herpetologica 40:21–30.

Cadle, J. E. 1984c. Molecular systematics of Neotropical xenodontine snakes. III. Overview of xenodontine phylogeny and the history of New World snakes. Copeia 1984:641–652.

Caillouet, C. W., Jr., and A. M. Landry, Jr. (eds.). 1989. Proceedings of the First International Symposium on Kemp's Ridley Sea Turtle Biology, Conservation, and Management. Special Publication of the Sea Grant College Program, Texas A & M University, TAMU-SG-89-105. v + 260 pp.

Caldwell, D. K. 1962. Comments on the nesting behavior of Atlantic loggerhead sea turtles, based primarily on tagging returns. Q. J. Fla. Acad. Sci. 25:287–302.

Campbell, H. W. 1972. Preliminary report: Status investigations of Morelet's crocodile in Mexico. Zoologica 57:135–136.

Campbell, J. A., and E. D. Brodie, Jr. 1988. A new colubrid snake of the genus *Adelphicos* from Guatemala. Herpetologica 44:416–422.

Campbell, J. A., and J. L. Camarillo R. 1994. A new lizard of the genus *Diploglossus* (Anguidae: Diploglossinae) from Mexico, with a review of the Mexican and northern Central American species. Herpetologica 50:193–209.

Campbell, J. A., and L. S. Ford. 1982. Phylogenetic relationships of the colubrid snakes of the genus *Adelphicos* in the highlands of Middle America. Occas. Pap. Mus. Nat. Hist. Univ. Kans. 100:1–22.

Campbell, J. A., L. S. Ford, and J. P. Karges. 1983. Resurrection of *Geophis anocularis* Dunn with comments on its relationships and natural history. Trans. Kans. Acad. Sci. 86:38–47.

Campbell, J. A., D. R. Formanowicz, and P. B. Medley. 1989. The reproductive cycle of *Norops uniformis* (Sauria: Iguanidae) in Veracruz, Mexico. Biotropica 21:237–243.

Campbell, J. A., D. M. Hillis, and W. W. Lamar. 1989. A new lizard of the genus *Norops* (Sauria: Iguanidae) from the cloud forest of Hidalgo, Mexico. Herpetologica 45:232–242.

Campbell, J. A., and W. W. Lamar. 1989. The venomous reptiles of Latin America. Cornell University Press, Ithaca. xii + 425 pp.

Campbell, J. A., and J. B. Murphy. 1977. A new species of *Geophis* (Reptilia, Serpentes, Colubridae) from the Sierra de Coalcomán, Michoacán, Mexico. J. Herpetol. 11:397–403.

Campbell, J. A., J. M. Savage, and J. R. Meyer. 1994. A new species of *Eleutherodactylus* (Anura: Leptodactylidae) of the *rugulosus* group from Guatemala and Belize. Herpetologica 50:412–419.

Campbell, J. A., and J. P. Vannini. 1989. Distribution of amphibians and reptiles in Guatemala and Belize. Proc. West. Found. Vertebr. Zool. 4:1–21.

Canin, J. 1989. International trade in sea turtle products. *In*: S. A. Eckert, K. L. Eckert, and T. H. Richardson (comps.), Proceedings of the Ninth Annual Workshop on Sea Turtle Conservation and Biology, pp. 27–29.

NOAA Technical Memorandum NMFS-SEFC-232. National Oceanic and Atmospheric Administration, Washington, D.C.

Cannatella, D. C., and K. de Queiroz. 1989. Phylogentic systematics of the anoles: Is a new taxonomy warranted? Syst. Zool. 38:57–69.

Carneiro, R. L. 1970. Hunting and hunting magic among the Amahuaca of the Peruvian montaña. Ethnology 9:331–341.

Carothers, J. H. 1984. Sexual selection and sexual dimorphism in some herbivorous lizards. Am. Nat. 124:244–254.

Carr, A. 1952. Handbook of turtles. Cornell University Press, Ithaca. Reprinted 1995, Comstock Classic Handbooks, Cornell University Press. xv + 542 pp.

Carr, A. 1965. The navigation of the green turtle. Sci. Am. 212:78–86.

Carr, A. F., Jr., A. Meylan, J. Mortimer, K. Bjorndal, and T. Carr. 1982. Surveys of sea turtle populations and habitats in the western Atlantic. NOAA Technical Memorandum NMFS-SEFC-91. National Oceanic and Atmospheric Administration, Washington, D.C. 91 pp.

Carranza, J. 1959. Pesca y recursos pesqueros. Tortugas. *In*: Enrique Beltrán (ed.), Los recursos naturales del sureste y su aprovechamiento, pp. 227–238. Instituto Mexicano de Recursos Naturales Renovables, Mexico City.

Carson, H. L. 1945. Delayed fertilization in a captive indigo snake. Copeia 1945:222–225.

Casas-Andreu, G. 1967. Contribución al conocimiento de las tortugas dulceacuícolas de México. Universidad Nacional Autónoma de México, Mexico City. vii + 96 pp.

Casas-Andreu, G. 1978. Análisis de la anidación de las tortugas marinas del género *Lepidochelys* en México. An. Centro Cienc. del Mar Limnol. Univ. Nac. Autón. Méx. 5:141–158.

Casas-Andreu, G., and M. Guzman A. 1970. Estado actual de las investigaciones sobre cocodrilos Mexicanos. Bol. Inst. Nac. Inv. Biol. Pesqueras, Ser. Divulgación 3:15–20.

Casas-Andreu, G., and C. J. McCoy. 1987. Anfibios y reptiles de México. 2nd ed. Editorial Limusa, Mexico City. 87 pp.

Catesby, M. 1743. The natural history of Carolina, Florida, and the Bahama Islands: Containing the figures of birds, beasts, fishes, serpents, insects and plants, etc. Revised by Mr. Edwards. W. Innys, London. Vol. 2. iv + 100 pp.

Catesby, M. 1754. The natural history of Carolina, Florida and the Bahama Islands: Containing the figures of birds, beasts, fishes, serpents, insects and plants, etc. Revised by Mr. Edwards, C. Marsh, T. Wilcox, and B. Stichall. London. Vol. 2. iv + 100 pp.

Censky, E. J., and C. J. McCoy. 1988. Female reproductive cycles of five species of snakes (Reptilia: Colubridae) from the Yucatán Peninsula. Biotropica 20:326–333.

César Zurita, G., J. A. César-Dachary, and E. Suárez. 1992. Aspectos históricos de la pesquería de las tortugas marinas en las costas del mar Caribe mexicano. Publ. Soc. Herpetol. Mex. 1:75–81.

Chávez, H. 1968. Marcado y recaptura de individuos de tortuga lora, *Lepidochelys kempi* (Garman). Inst. Nac. Invest. Biol. Pesq. Bol. Prog. Nac. Marc. Tort. Mar. 19:1–28.

Chiszar, D. 1989. The predatory strike of the jumping viper (*Porthidium nummifer*). Copeia 1989:1037–1039.

Christman, S. P. 1982. *Storeria dekayi*. Cat. Am. Amphib. Reptiles 306.1–306.4.

Church, G. 1962. The reproductive cycles of the Javanese house geckos *Cosymbotus platyurus*, *Hemidactylus frenatus*, and *Peropus mutilatus*. Copeia 1962:262–269.

Cirlot, J. E. 1971. A dictionary of symbols. 2nd ed. Dorset Press, New York. lv + 419 pp.

Clark, M. 1981. Instinto parental y comportamiento sexual de *Centrolenella fleischmanni* (Anura, Centrolenidae). Trabajo de graduación [senior thesis], Escuela de Biologia, Facultad de Ciencias Naturales y Farmacia, Universidad de Panama, Panama.

Cochran, D. M. 1961. Type specimens of reptiles and amphibians in the U.S. National Museum. Bull. U.S. Natl. Mus., no. 220. xv + 291 pp.

Cochran, P. A. 1989. *Anolis sagrei* (brown anole): Behavior. Herpetol. Rev. 20:70.

Coe, M. D. 1971. The shadow of the Olmecs. Horizon 13:67–74.

Coe, M. D. 1987. The Maya. 4th ed. Thames and Hudson, London. 200 pp.

Cohen, A. C., and B. C. Myres. 1970. The function of the horns (supraocular scales) in the sidewinder rattlesnake, *Crotalus cerastes*, with comments on other horned snakes. Copeia 1970:574–575.

Cole, C. J. 1971. Karyotypes of the five monotypic species groups of lizards in the genus *Sceloporus*. Am. Mus. Novit. 2450:1–17.

Cole, C. J. 1978. Karyotypes and systematics of the lizards in the *variabilis*, *jalapae*, and *scalaris* species groups of the genus *Sceloporus*. Am. Mus. Novit. 2653:1–13.

Cole, C. J., H. C. Dessauer, C. R. Townsend, and M. G. Arnold. 1990. Unisexual lizards of the genus *Gymnophthalmus* (Reptilia: Teiidae) in the Neotropics: Genetics, origin, and systematics. Am. Mus. Novit. 2994:1–29.

Colwell, R. K. 1985. A bite to remember. Nat. Hist. 94:2–8.

Conant, R. 1965. Miscellaneous notes and comments on toads, lizards, and snakes from Mexico. Am. Mus. Novit. 2205:1–38.

Conant, R. 1969. A review of the water snakes of the genus *Natrix* in Mexico. Bull. Am. Mus. Nat. Hist. 142:1–140.

Conners, J. S. 1989. *Oxybelis fulgidus* (green vine snake): Reproduction. Herpetol. Rev. 20:73.

Cook, D. G. 1984. A case of envenomation by the Neotropical colubrid snake *Stenorrhina freminvillei*. Toxicon 22:823–827.

Cope, E. D. 1860. Catalogue of the Colubridae in the museum of the Academy of Natural Sciences of Philadelphia, with notes and descriptions of new species. Part 2. Proc. Acad. Nat. Sci. Phila. 12:241–266.

Cope, E. D. 1861a. Descriptions of reptiles from tropical America and Asia. Proc. Acad. Nat. Sci. Phila. 12:368–374.

Cope, E. D. 1861b. Notes and descriptions of anoles. Proc. Acad. Nat. Sci. Phila. 13:208–215.

Cope, E. D. 1861c. Contributions to the ophiology of lower California, Mexico and Central America. Proc. Acad. Nat. Sci. Phila. 13:292–306.

Cope, E. D. 1862a. Contributions to Neotropical saurology. Proc. Acad. Nat. Sci. Phila. 14:176–188.

Cope, E. D. 1862b. Catalogue of the reptiles obtained during the explorations of the Parana, Paraguay, Vermejo and Uraguay Rivers, by Capt. Thos. J. Page, U.S.N., and of those procured by Lieut. N. Michler, U.S. Top. Eng., commander of the expedition conducting the survey of the Atrato River. Proc. Acad. Nat. Sci. Phila. 14:346–359.

Cope, E. D. 1863. Descriptions of new American Squamata in the museum of the Smithsonian Institution, Washington. Proc. Acad. Nat. Sci. Phila. 15:100–106.

Cope, E. D. 1864. Contributions to the herpetology of tropical America. Proc. Acad. Nat. Sci. Phila. 16:166–183.

Cope, E. D. 1865. Third contribution to the herpetology of tropical America. Proc. Acad. Nat. Sci. Phila. 17:185–198.

Cope, E. D. 1866. Fourth contribution to the herpetology of tropical America. Proc. Acad. Nat. Sci. Phila. 18:123–132.

Cope, E. D. 1867. Fifth contribution to the herpetology of tropical America. Proc. Acad. Nat. Sci. Phila. 18:317–323.

Cope, E. D. 1868. An examination of the Reptilia and Batrachia obtained by the Orton expedition to Ecuador and the upper Amazon, with notes on other species. Proc. Acad. Nat. Sci. Phila. 20:96–140.

Cope, E. D. 1869. A review of the species of Plethodontidae and Desmognathidae. Proc. Acad. Nat. Sci. Phila. 21:93–118.

Cope, E. D. 1870. Seventh contribution to the herpetology of tropical America. Proc. Am. Philos. Soc. 11:147–169.

Cope, E. D. 1874. Description of some species of reptiles obtained by Dr. John F. Bransford, assistant surgeon United States Navy, while attached to the Nicaraguan surveying expedition in 1873. Proc. Acad. Nat. Sci. Phila. 26:64–72.

Cope, E. D. 1876. On the Batrachia and Reptilia of Costa Rica. J. Acad. Nat. Sci. Phila. (2)8:93–154.

Cope, E. D. 1878. Tenth contribution to the herpetology of tropical America. Proc. Am. Philos. Soc. 17:85–98.

Cope, E. D. 1879. Eleventh contribution to the herpetology of tropical America. Proc. Am. Philos. Soc. 18:261–277.

Cope, E. D. 1885a [dated 1884]. Twelfth contribution to the herpetology of tropical America. Proc. Am. Philos. Soc. 22:167–194.

Cope, E. D. 1885b. A contribution to the herpetology of Mexico. Proc. Am. Philos. Soc. 22:379–404.

Cope, E. D. 1886. Thirteenth contribution to the herpetology of tropical America. Proc. Am. Philos. Soc. 23:271–287.

Cope, E. D. 1893. Second addition to the knowledge of the Batrachia and Reptilia of Costa Rica. Proc. Am. Philos. Soc. 31:333–347.

Cope, E. D. 1900. The crocodilians, lizards, and snakes of North America. Rep. U.S. Nat. Hist. Mus. 1898:153–1294.

Corzo, E. C. 1978 [dated 1980]. Palabras de origen indígena en el español de Chiapas. Costa-Amic Editores, Mexico City. 326 pp.

Crimmins, M. L. 1937. A case of Oxybelis poisoning in man. Copeia 1937:233.

Crother, B. I., J. A. Campbell, and D. M. Hillis. 1992. Phylogeny and historical biogeography of the palm-pitvipers, genus Bothriechis: Biochemicial and morphological evidence. In: J. A. Campbell and E. D. Brodie, Jr. (eds.), Biology of the pitvipers, pp. 1–20. Selva Press, Tyler, Tex.

Crother, B. I., M. M. Miyamoto, and W. F. Presch. 1986. Phylogeny and biogeography of the lizard family Xantusiidae. Syst. Zool. 35:37–45.

Cuellar, O., and J. W. Wright. 1992. Isogenicity in the unisexual lizard Cnemidophorus velox. C. R. Soc. Biogeogr. 68:157–160.

Cuvier, G. 1807. Sur les différentes espèces de crocodiles vivants et sur leurs caractères distinctifs. Ann. Mus. Natl. Hist. Nat. (Paris) 10:8–66.

Daniel, H. 1949. Las serpientes en Colombia. Rev. Fac. Natl. Mus. Agron. (Medellín) 10:301–333.

Daudin, F. M. 1803. Histoire naturelle, générale et particulière des reptiles. Paris. Vol. 6. 447 pp.

Davidson, E. H., and B. R. Hough. 1969. Synchronous oogenesis in Engystomops pustulosus, a Neotropic anuran suitable for laboratory studies: Localization in the embryo of RNA synthesized at the lampbrush stage. J. Exp. Zool. 172:25–48.

Davis, D. D. 1953. Behavior of the lizard Corytophanes cristatus. Fieldiana Zool. 35:1–8.

Davis, W. B., and J. R. Dixon. 1961. Reptiles (exclusive of snakes) of the Chilpancingo region, Mexico. Proc. Biol. Soc. Wash. 74:37–56.

Davis, W. B., and J. R. Dixon. 1964. Amphibians of the Chilpancingo region, Mexico. Herpetologica 20:225–233.

Davis, W. B., and H. M. Smith. 1953. Lizards and turtles of the Mexican state of Morelos. Herpetologica 9:100–108.

de Queiroz, K. 1987. A new spiny-tailed iguana from Honduras, with comments on relationships within Ctenosaura (Squamata: Iguania). Copeia 1987:892–902.

Dial, B. E., and L. L. Grismer. 1992. Phylogenetic analysis of physiological-ecological character evolution in the lizard genus Coleonyx and its implications for historical biogeographic reconstruction. Syst. Biol. 41:178–195.

Díaz-Bolio, J. 1971. Instructive guide to the ruins of Uxmal. Area Maya, Mérida, Yucatán, Mexico. 82 pp.

Dioscoro, S. R. 1952. Preliminary notes on the giant toad, Bufo marinus (Linn.), in the Philippine Islands. Copeia 1952:281–282.

Ditmars, R. L. 1939. Field book of North American snakes. Doubleday, Doran, New York. xii + 305 pp.

Dixon, J. R. 1960. The discovery of Phyllodactylus tuberculosus (Reptilia: Sauria) in Central America, the resurrection of P. xanti, and description of a new gecko from British Honduras. Herpetologica 16:1–11.

Dixon, J. R. 1964. The systematics and distribution of lizards of the genus Phyllodactylus in North and Central America. Sci. Bull. N.M. State Univ. Res. Cent., no. 64–1. 139 pp.

Dixon, J. R. 1970. Coleonyx. Cat. Am. Amphib. Reptiles 95.1–95.2.

Dixon, J. R., and F. S. Hendricks. 1979. The wormsnakes (family Typhlopidae) of the Neotropics, exclusive of the Antilles. Zool. Verh. (Leiden) 173:1–39.

Dobkin de Rios, M. 1974. The influence of psychotropic flora and fauna on Maya religion. Curr. Anthropol. 15(2):147–152.

Dodd, C. K., Jr. 1978. A note on the defensive posturing of turtles from Belize, Central America. Herpetol. Rev. 9:11–12.

Dodd, C. K., Jr. 1987. A bibliography of the loggerhead sea turtle, Caretta caretta (Linnaeus, 1758). U.S. Fish Wildl. Serv. Endang. Species Rep. 16:1–64.

Dodd, C. K., Jr. 1988. Synopsis of the biological data on the loggerhead sea turtle, Caretta caretta (Linnaeus, 1758). U.S. Fish Wildl. Serv. Biol. Rep. 88, no. 14. vii + 110 pp.

Dodd, C. K., Jr. 1990a. Caretta. Cat. Am. Amphib. Reptiles 482.1–482.2.

Dodd, C. K., Jr. 1990b. Caretta caretta. Cat. Am. Amphib. Reptiles 483.1–483.7.

Dodds, C. T. 1923. A note on Bufo marinus. Copeia 1923:5–6.

Dowling, H. G. 1952. A taxonomic study of the ratsnakes, genus Elaphe Fitzinger. II. The subspecies of Elaphe flavirufa (Cope). Occas. Pap. Mus. Zool. Univ. Mich. 540:1–14.

Dowling, H. G. 1960. A taxonomic study of the ratsnakes, genus Elaphe Fitzinger. VII. The triaspis section. Zoologica 45:53–80.

Dowling, H. G., and I. Fries. 1987. A taxonomic study of the ratsnakes. VIII. A proposed new genus for Elaphe triaspis (Cope). Herpetologica 43:200–207.

Downie, J. R. 1988. Functions of the foam in the foam-nesting leptodactylid Physalaemus pustulosus. Herpetol. J. 1:302–307.

Downie, J. R. 1990. Functions of the foam in foam-nesting leptodactylids: Anti-predator effects of Physalaemus pustulosus foam. Herpetol. J. 1:501–503.

Downs, F. L. 1967. Intrageneric relationships among colubrid snakes of the genus Geophis Wagler. Misc. Publ. Mus. Zool. Univ. Mich., no. 131. 193 pp.

Dubois, A., and W. R. Heyer. 1992. Leptodactylus labialis, the valid name for the American white-lipped frog (Amphibia: Leptodactylidae). Copeia 1992:584–585.

Ducey, P. K., E. D. Brodie, Jr., and E. A. Baness. 1993. Salamander tail autotomy and snake predation: Role of antipredator behavior and toxicity for three Neotropical *Bolitoglossa* (Caudata: Plethodontidae). Biotropica 25:344–349.

Duellman, W. E. 1956. The frogs of the hylid genus *Phrynohyas* Fitzinger, 1843. Misc. Publ. Mus. Zool. Univ. Mich., no. 96. 47 pp.

Duellman, W. E. 1958a. A monographic study of the colubrid snake genus *Leptodeira*. Bull. Am. Mus. Nat. Hist. 114:5–152.

Duellman, W. E. 1958b. A preliminary analysis of the herpetofauna of Colima, Mexico. Occas. Pap. Mus. Zool. Univ. Mich. 589:1–22.

Duellman, W. E. 1960. A distributional study of the amphibians of the Isthmus of Tehauntepec, Mexico. Univ. Kans. Publ. Mus. Nat. Hist. 13:19–72.

Duellman, W. E. 1963. Amphibians and reptiles of the rainforests of southern El Petén, Guatemala. Univ. Kans. Publ. Mus. Nat. Hist. 15:205–249.

Duellman, W. E. 1965a. Amphibians and reptiles from the Yucatán Peninsula, Mexico. Univ. Kans. Publ. Mus. Nat. Hist. 15:577–614.

Duellman, W. E. 1965b. A biogeographic account of the herpetofauna of Michoacán, Mexico. Univ. Kans. Publ. Mus. Nat. Hist. 15:627–709.

Duellman, W. E. 1968a. *Smilisca*. Cat. Am. Amphib. Reptiles 58.1–58.2.

Duellman, W. E. 1968b. *Smilisca baudinii*. Cat. Am. Amphib. Reptiles 59.1–59.2.

Duellman, W. E. 1968c. *Smilisca cyanosticta*. Cat. Am. Amphib. Reptiles 60.1–60.2.

Duellman, W. E. 1970. The hylid frogs of Middle America. Univ. Kans. Mus. Nat. Hist. Monogr. 1:1–753.

Duellman, W. E. 1971a. The burrowing toad, *Rhinophrynus dorsalis*, on the Caribbean lowlands of Central America. Herpetologica 27:55–56.

Duellman, W. E. 1971b. A taxonomic review of South American hylid frogs, genus *Phrynohyas*. Occas. Pap. Mus. Nat. Hist. Univ. Kans. 4:1–21.

Duellman, W. E. 1978. The biology of an equatorial herpetofauna in Amazonian Ecuador. Univ. Kans. Mus. Nat. Hist. Misc. Publ. 65. 352 pp.

Duellman, W. E. 1993. Amphibian species of the world: Additions and corrections. Mus. Nat. Hist. Univ. Kans. Spec. Publ. 21. iii + 372 pp.

Duellman, W. E., and D. Cannatella. 1984. Leptodactylid frogs of the *Physalaemus pustulosus* group. Copeia 1984:902–921.

Duellman, W. E., and A. S. Duellman. 1959. Variation, distribution, and ecology of the iguanid lizard *Enyaliosaurus clarki* of Michoacán, Mexico. Occas. Pap. Mus. Zool. Univ. Mich. 598:1–10.

Duellman, W. E., and M. J. Fouquette, Jr. 1968. Middle American hylid frogs of the *Hyla microcephala* group. Univ. Kans. Publ. Mus. Nat. Hist. 17:517–557.

Duellman, W. E., and L. T. Klaas. 1964. The biology of the hylid frog *Triprion petasatus*. Copeia 1964:308–321.

Duellman, W. E., and L. Trueb. 1966. Neotropical hylid frogs, genus *Smilisca*. Univ. Kans. Publ. Mus. Nat. Hist. 17:281–375.

Duellman, W. E., and L. Trueb. 1986. Biology of amphibians. McGraw-Hill, New York. xvii + 670 pp.

Duellman, W. E., and J. B. Tulecke. 1960. The distribution, variation, and life history of the frog *Cochranella viridissima* in Mexico. Am. Midl. Nat. 63:392–397.

Duellman, W. E., and J. Wellman. 1960. A systematic study of the lizards of the *deppei* group (genus *Cnemidophorus*) in Mexico and Guatemala. Misc. Publ. Mus. Zool. Univ. Mich., no. 111. 80 pp.

Duellman, W. E., and J. Wiens. 1992. The status of the hylid frog genus *Ololygon* and the recognition of *Scinax* Wagler, 1830. Occas. Pap. Mus. Nat. Hist. Univ. Kans. 151:1–23.

Dugès, A. 1889. Francisco Hernández. La Naturaleza 1:282–288.

Duméril, A. H. A. 1853. Mémoire sur les batraciens anoures de la famille des Hylaeformes ou rainettes, comprenant la description d'un genre nouveau et de onze espèces nouvelles. Ann. Sci. Nat. (3)19:135–179.

Duméril, A. M. C., and G. Bibron. 1834–1844. Erpétologie générale, ou Histoire naturelle complète des reptiles. Librairie Encyclopédique de Roret, Paris. Vols. 1–6, 8.

Duméril, A. M. C., G. Bibron, and A. H. A. Duméril. 1854. Erpétologie générale, ou Histoire naturelle complète des reptiles. Librairie Encyclopédique de Roret, Paris. Vol. 7, pt. 1, 780 pp., pt. 2, xii + 785 pp.; vol. 9, xx + 440 pp.

Duméril, A. M. C., and A. H. A. Duméril. 1851. Catalogue méthodique de la collection des reptiles du Muséum d'Histoire Naturelle. Gide and Boudry, Paris. iv + 224 pp.

Dundee, H. A. 1985. A geographic dilemma in the Yucatán Peninsula of Mexico. Assoc. Syst. Collect. Newsl. 13:6.

Dundee, H. A., and E. A. Liner. 1985a. *Phrynohyas venulosa* (veined treefrog): Food. Herpetol. Rev. 16:109.

Dundee, H. A., and E. A. Liner. 1985b. *Phrynohyas venulosa* (veined treefrog): Reproduction and size. Herpetol. Rev. 16:109.

Dundee, H. A., D. A. White, and V. Rico-Gray. 1986. Observations on the distribution and biology of some Yucatán Peninsula amphibians and reptiles. Bull. Md. Herpetol. Soc. 22:37–50.

Dunn, E. R. 1926. The salamanders of the family Plethodontidae. Southward Press, Portland, Me. viii + 441 pp.

Dunn, E. R. 1939. Mainland form of the snake genus *Tretanorhinus*. Copeia 1939:212–217.

Dunn, E. R., and L. H. Saxe, Jr. 1950. Results of the Catherwood-Chapin West Indies expedition. 1948. Part V. Amphibians and Reptiles of San Andrés and Providencia. Proc. Acad. Nat. Sci. Phila. 52:141–165.

Dunn, E. R., and L. C. Stuart. 1951. Comments on some recent restrictions of type localities of certain South and Central American amphibians and reptiles. Copeia 1951:59–61.

Easteal, S. *Bufo marinus*. Cat. Am. Amphib. Reptiles 395.1–395.4.

Echelle, A. F., A. A. Echelle, and H. S. Fitch. 1978. Behavioral evidence for species status of *Anolis uniformis*. Herpetologica 34:205–207.

Echternacht, A. C. 1968. Distributional and ecological notes on some reptiles from northern Honduras. Herpetologica 24:151–158.

Echternacht, A. C. 1971. Middle American lizards of the genus *Ameiva* (Teiidae) with emphasis on geographic variation. Univ. Kans. Mus. Nat. Hist. Misc. Publ. 55. 86 pp.

Edmonson, M. S. 1986. Heaven born Merida and its destiny. The book of Chilam Balam of Chumayel. University of Texas Press, Austin. viii + 309 pp.

Ernst, C. H. 1978. A revision of the Neotropical turtle genus *Callopsis* (Testudines: Emydidae: Batagurinae). Herpetologica 34:113–134.

Ernst, C. H. 1980. *Rhinoclemmys areolata* (Duméril and Bibron). Cat. Am. Amphib. Reptiles 251.1–251.2.

Ernst, C. H. 1981. *Rhinoclemmys* Fitzinger. Cat. Am. Amphib. Reptiles 274.1–274.2.

Ernst, C. H. 1990. Systematics, taxonomy, variation, and geographic distribution of the slider turtle. *In*: J. W. Gibbons (ed.), Life history and ecology of the slider turtle, pp. 57–67. Smithsonian Institution Press, Washington, D.C.

Ernst, C. H., and R. W. Barbour. 1972. Turtles of the United States. University Press of Kentucky, Lexington. 347 pp.

Ernst, C. H., and R. W. Barbour. 1989. Turtles of the world. Smithsonian Institution Press, Washington, D.C. xii + 313 pp.

Ernst, C. H., J. W. Gibbons, and S. S. Novak. 1988. *Chelydra*. Cat. Am. Amphib. Reptiles 419.1–419.4.

Ernst, C. H., and J. F. McBreen. 1991a. *Terrapene*. Cat. Am. Amphib. Reptiles 511.1–511.6.

Ernst, C. H., and J. F. McBreen. 1991b. *Terrapene carolina*. Cat. Am. Amphib. Reptiles 512.1–512.13.

Eschscholtz, J. F. 1829–1833. Zoologischer Atlas, enthaltend Abbildungen und Beschreibunger neuer Thierarten, wahrend des Flottcapitains von Kotzebue zweiter Reise aus dem West, auf der Russisch-Kaiserlich Kriegsschlupp Predpriaetie in den Jahren 1823–1826. G. Reimer, Berlin.

Estes, R., K. de Queiroz, and J. Gauthier. 1988. Phylogenetic relationships within Squamata. *In*: R. Estes and G. Pregill (eds.), Phylogentic relationships of the lizard families, essays commemorating Charles L. Camp, pp. 119–281. Stanford University Press, Stanford.

Etheridge, R. E. 1960. The relationships of the anoles (Reptilia: Sauria: Iguanidae): An interpretation based on skeletal morphology. Ph.D. dissertation, University of Michigan, Ann Arbor. 236 pp.

Etheridge, R. E. 1982. Checklist of the iguanine and Malagasy iguanid lizards. *In*: G. M. Burghardt and A. S. Rand (eds.), Iguanas of the world. Their behavior, ecology, and conservation, pp. 7–37. Noyes Publications, Park Ridge, N.J.

Etheridge, R. E., and K. de Queiroz. 1988. A phylogeny of Iguanidae. *In*: R. Estes and G. Pregill (eds.), Phylogenetic relationships of the lizard families, essays commemorating Charles L. Camp, pp. 283–367. Stanford University Press, Stanford.

Ewert, M. A. 1979. The embryo and its egg: Development and natural history. *In*: M. Harless and H. Morlock (eds.), Turtles: Perspectives and research, pp. 333–413. Wiley-Interscience, New York.

Fabing, H. D., and J. R. Hawkins. 1956. Intravenous injection of bufotenine in the human being. Science 123:886–887.

Feder, M. E., J. F. Lynch, H. B. Shaffer, and D. B. Wake. 1982. Field body temperatures of tropical and temperate zone salamanders. Smithson. Herpetol. Infor. Ser. 52:1–23.

Ferrari-Perez, F. 1886. Catalogue of the animals collected by the geographical and exploring commission of Mexico. III. Reptiles. Proc. U.S. Natl. Mus. 1886:182–199.

Firschein, I. L. 1951. Rediscovery of the broad-headed frog *Eleutherodactylus laticeps* (Duméril) of Mexico. Copeia 1951:268–274.

Firschein, I. L., and H. M. Smith. 1956. A new fringe-limbed *Hyla* (Amphibia: Anura) from a new faunal district of Mexico. Herpetologica 12:17–21.

Fischer, J. G. 1884. Herpetologische Bemerkungen. Abh. Natur. Ver. Hamburg 8:3–11.

Fisher, C. B. 1969. A systematic revision of the species *Coniophanes fissidens* (Günther) (Serpentes, Colubridae). M.S. thesis, Northwestern State College, Natchitoches, La. 65 pp.

Fitch, H. S. 1970. Reproductive cycles in lizards and snakes. Univ. Kans. Mus. Nat. Hist. Misc. Publ. 52. 247 pp.

Fitch, H. S. 1973. A field study of Costa Rican lizards. Univ. Kans. Sci. Bull. 50:39–126.

Fitch, H. S. 1975. Sympatry and interrelationships in Costa Rican anoles. Occas. Pap. Mus. Nat. Hist. Univ. Kans. 40:1–60.

Fitch, H. S. 1976. Sexual size differences in the mainland anoles. Occas. Pap. Mus. Nat. Hist. Univ. Kans. 50:1–21.

Fitch, H. S. 1978. Sexual size differences in the genus *Sceloporus*. Univ. Kans. Sci. Bull. 51:441–461.

Fitch, H. S. 1985. Variation in clutch and litter size in New World reptiles. Univ. Kans. Mus. Nat. Hist. Misc. Publ. 76. 76 pp.

Fitch, H. S., A. F. Echelle, and A. A. Echelle. 1976. Field observations on rare or little known mainland anoles. Univ. Kans. Sci. Bull. 51:91–128.

Fitch, H. S., A. V. Fitch, and C. W. Fitch. 1971. Ecological notes on some common lizards of southern Mexico and Central America. Southwest. Nat. 15:398–399.

Fitch, H. S., and J. Hackforth-Jones. 1983. *Ctenosaura similis*. *In*: D. Janzen (ed.), Costa Rican natural history, pp. 394–396. University of Chicago Press, Chicago.

Fitch, H. S., and R. W. Henderson. 1977. Age and sex differences, reproduction and conservation of *Iguana iguana*. Milw. Public Mus. Contrib. Biol. Geol. 13:1–21.

Fitch, H. S., and R. W. Henderson. 1978. Ecology and exploitation of *Ctenosaura similis*. Univ. Kans. Sci. Bull. 51:483–500.

Fitch, H. S., R. W. Henderson, and H. Guarisco. 1989. Aspects of the ecology of an introduced anole: *Anolis cristatellus* in the Dominican Republic. Amphib.-Reptilia 10:307–320.

Fitch, H. S., R. W. Henderson, and D. M. Hillis. 1982. Exploitation of iguanas in Central America. *In*: G. M. Burghardt and A. S. Rand (eds.), Iguanas of the world. Their behavior, ecology, and conservation, pp. 397–417. Noyes Publications, Park Ridge, N.J.

Fitzinger, L. 1843. Systema reptilium. Apud Braumuller et Seidel Bibliopolas. vi + 106 pp.

Flores-Villela, O. 1993. Herpetofauna Mexicana. Carnegie Mus. Nat. Hist. Spec. Publ. 17. iv + 73 pp.

Flores Villela, O., E. H. Garcia, and A. N. Montes de Oca. 1991. Catálogo de anfibios y reptiles del Museo de Zoologia, Facultad de Ciencias, Universidad Nacional Autónoma de Mexico. Universidad Nacional Autónoma de México, Mexico City. 222 pp.

Flores Villela, O., and P. Gerez. 1988. Conservación en México: Síntesis sobre vertebrados terrestres, vegetación y uso del suelo. Instituto Nacional de Investigacions sobre Recursos Bióticos, Xalapa, Veracruz, Mexico. xiv + 302 pp.

Foster, M. S., and R. W. McDiarmid. 1983. *Rhinophrynus dorsalis*. *In*: Janzen, D. H. (ed.), A Costa Rican natural history, pp. 419–420. University of Chicago Press, Chicago.

Fouquette, M. J., Jr. 1954. Food competition among four sympatric species of garter snakes, genus *Thamnophis*. Tex. J. Sci. 6:172–188.

Fouquette, M. J., Jr. 1969. *Rhinophrynus dorsalis*. Cat. Am. Amphib. Reptiles 78.1–78.2.

Fouquette, M. J., Jr., and A. J. Delahoussaye. 1977. Sperm morphology in the *Hyla rubra* group (Amphibia, Anura, Hylidae), and its bearing on generic status. J. Herpetol. 11:387–396.

Fouquette, M. J., Jr., and D. A. Rossman. 1963. Noteworthy records of Mexican amphibians and reptiles in the Florida State Museum and the Texas Natural History Collection. Herpetologica 19:185–201.

Fowler, H. W. 1913. Amphibians and reptiles from Ecuador, Venezuela, and Yucatán. Proc. Acad. Nat. Sci. Phila. 65:153–176.

Fraser, D. F. 1973. Variation in the coral snake, *Micrurus diastema*. Copeia 1973:1–17.

Frazier, J. (ed.). 1993. Memorias del IV taller regional sobre programas de conservación de tortugas marinas en la Península de Yucatán. Universidad Autónoma de Yucatán, Mérida, Yucatán, Mexico. iii + 211 pp.

Frazier, J., and E. Rodriguez. 1992. The marine turtle situation in the Yucatán Peninsula: The need for a regional action plan. *In*: M. Salmon and J. Wyneken (comps.), Proceedings of the Eleventh Annual Workshop on Sea Turtle Biology and Conservation, pp. 45–48. NOAA Technical Memorandum NMFS-SEFSC-302. National Oceanic and Atmospheric Administration, Washington, D.C.

Freidel, D., L. Schele, and J. Parker. 1993. Maya cosmos: Three thousand years on the shaman's path. William Morrow, New York. 543 pp.

Fritts, T. H. 1969. The systematics of the parthenogenetic lizards of the *Cnemidophorus cozumela* complex. Copeia 1969:519–535.

Frost, D. R. 1985. Amphibian species of the world, a taxomonic and geographic reference. Association of Systematics Collections and Allen Press, Lawrence, Kans. v + 732 pp.

Frost, D. R., and J. T. Collins. 1988. Nomenclatural notes on reptiles of the United States. Herpetol. Rev. 19:73–74.

Frost, D. R., and R. E. Etheridge. 1989. A phylogenetic analysis and taxonomy of Iguanian lizards (Reptila: Squamata). Univ. Kans. Mus. Nat. Hist. Misc. Publ. 81. 65 pp.

Frost, J. S. 1982. Functional genetic similarity between geographically separated populations of Mexican leopard frogs (*Rana pipiens* complex). Syst. Zool. 31:57–67.

Fuentes, C. D. 1967. Perspectivas de cultivo de tortugas marinas en el Caribe mexicano. Inst. Nac. Invest. Biol. Pesq. Bol. Prog. Nac. Marc. Tort. Mar. 1:1–9.

Fugler, C. M. 1960. New herpetological records for British Honduras. Tex. J. Sci 12:8–13.

Fugler, C. M., and R. G. Webb. 1957. Some noteworthy reptiles and amphibians from the states of Oaxaca and Veracruz. Herpetologica 13:103–108.

Fukada, H. 1965. Breeding habits of some Japanese reptiles (critical review). Bull. Kyoto Gakugei Univ., Ser. B, 27:65–82.

Funkhouser, A. 1957. A review of the Neotropical treefrogs of the genus *Phyllomedusa*. Occas. Pap. Nat. Hist. Mus. Stanford Univ. 5:1–90.

Furst, P. T. 1972. Symbolism and psychopharmacology: The toad as earth mother in Indian America. *In*: J. L. King and N. C. Tejero (eds.), Religion in Mesoamerica, pp. 37–45. XII Mesa Redonda, Sociedad Mexicana de Antropología, Mexico.

Furst, P. T. 1974. Comments (on Dobkin de Rios, 1974). Curr. Anthropol. 15:154.

Gadow, H. 1906. A contribution to the study of evolution based upon Mexican species of *Cnemidophorus*. Proc. Zool. Soc. Lond. 1:277–375.

Gaffney, E. S. 1975. Phylogeny of the chelydrid turtles: A study of shared derived characters in the skull. Fieldiana Geol. 33:157–178.

Gaffney, E. S. 1979. Comparative cranial morphology of Recent and fossil turtles. Bull. Am. Mus. Nat. Hist. 164:65–376.

Gaffney, E. S., and P. A. Meylan. 1988. A phylogeny of turtles. *In*: M. J. Benton (ed.), The phylogeny and classification of tetrapods. Vol. 1: Amphibians, reptiles, birds, pp. 157–219. Clarendon Press, Oxford.

Gaige, H. T. 1936. Some reptiles and amphibians from Yucatán and Campeche, Mexico. Carnegie Inst. Wash. Publ. 457:289–305.

Gaige, H. T. 1938. Some reptilian records from caves of Yucatán. Carnegie Inst. Wash. Publ. 491:155–157.

Gaige, H. T., N. Hartweg, and L. C. Stuart. 1937. Notes on a collection of amphibians and reptiles from eastern Nicaragua. Occas. Pap. Mus. Zool. Univ. Mich. 357:1–18.

Gaige, H. T., and L. C. Stuart. 1934. A new *Hyla* from Guatemala. Occas. Pap. Mus. Zool. Univ. Mich. 281:1–3.

García Téllez, N., and J. Golubov Figueroa. 1992. Tortugas marinas en la porción central reserva de la biosfera Sian Ka'an, pp. 1–7. Amigos de Sian Ka'an.

Garel, T., and S. Matola. 1996. A field guide to the snakes of Belize. In press.

Garman, S. 1880. On certain species of Chelonioidae. Bull. Mus. Comp. Zool. Harv. Univ. 6:123–126.

Garman, S. 1884 [dated 1883]. The reptiles and batrachians of North America. Mem. Mus. Comp. Zool. 8:1–185.

Garrett, J. M., and D. G. Barker. 1987. A field guide to reptiles and amphibians of Texas. Texas Monthly Press, Austin. xi + 225 pp.

Gates, W. 1937. Yucatán before and after the conquest. The Maya Society, Baltimore. 162 pp.

Gerhardt, R. P., P. M. Harris, and M. A. Vásquez Marroquin. 1993. Food habits of nesting great black hawks in Tikal National Park, Guatemala. Biotropica 25:349–352.

Gibbons, J. W. (ed.). 1990. Life history and ecology of the slider turtle. Smithsonian Institution Press, Washington, D.C. xiv + 268 pp.

Gibbons, J. W., S. S. Novak, and C. H. Ernst. 1988. *Chelydra serpentina*. Cat. Am. Amphib. Reptiles 420.1–420.4.

Gier, P. J. 1993. The mating system and sexual selection in *Ctenosaura similis*. Paper presented at the joint annual meeting of the American Society of Ichthyologists and Herpetologists and the Herpetologists' League, University of Texas, Austin, 27 May–2 June 1993.

Girard, C. 1854. Abstract of a report to Lieut. James M. Gillis, U.S.N., upon the reptiles collected during the U.S.N. astronomical expedition to Chili. Proc. Acad. Nat. Sci. Phila. 7:226.

Gloyd, H. K., and R. Conant. 1990. Snakes of the *Agkistrodon* complex: A monographic review. Society for the Study of Amphibians and Reptiles, Oxford, Ohio. vi + 614 pp.

Goldman, E. A. 1951. Biological investigations in Mexico. Smithson. Misc. Collect., no. 115. xiii + 476 pp.

Goldman, E. A., and R. T. Moore. 1945. The biotic provinces of Mexico. J. Mammal. 26:347–360.

Góngora-Arones, E. 1987. Etnozoología lacandona: La herpetofauna de Lacanjá-Chansayab. Cuad. Divulgación, Instituto Nacional de Investigaciones sobre Recursos Bióticos 31:1–31.

Gosner, K. L. 1960. A simplified table for staging anuran embryos and larvae with notes on identification. Herpetologica 16:183–190.

Gosse, P. H. 1850. Descriptions of a new genus and six new species of saurian reptiles. Ann. Mag. Nat. Hist. (2)6:344–348.

Graham, J. A. 1990. Monumental sculpture and hieroglyphic inscriptions. In: G. R. Willey (ed.), Excavations at Seibal. Mem. Peabody Mus. Archaeol. Ethnol. Harv. Univ. 17, no. 1.

Gray, J. E. 1831a. A synopsis of the species of the class Reptilia. Anim. Kingdom 9:1–110.

Gray, J. E. 1831b. Synoposis Reptililium, or short descriptions of the species of reptiles. Part 1: Cataphracta. Tortoises, crocodiles, and enaliosaurians. Treuttel, Wurtz, London. viii + 85 pp.

Gray, J. E. 1845. Description of a new genus of night lizards from Belize. Ann. Mag. Nat. Hist. (1)16:162–163.

Gray, J. E. 1847. Description of a new genus of Emydae. Proc. Zool. Soc. Lond. 1847:55–56.

Gray, J. E. 1870. On the family Dermatemyidae, and a description of a living species in the gardens of the society. Proc. Zool. Soc. Lond. 1870:711–716.

Greding, E. J., Jr. 1972. Call specificity and hybrid compatibility between *Rana pipiens* and three other *Rana* species in Central America. Copeia 1972:383–385.

Greding, E. J., Jr. 1976. Call of the tropical American frog *Rana palmipes* Spix (Amphibia, Anura, Ranidae). J. Herpetol. 10:263–264.

Greene, H. W. 1969. Reproduction in a Middle American skink, *Leiolopisma cherriei* (Cope). Herpetologica 25:55–56.

Greene, H. W. 1973. Defensive tail display by snakes and amphisbaenians. J. Herpetol. 7:143–161.

Greene, H. W. 1975. Ecological observations on the red coffee snake, *Ninia sebae*, in southern Veracruz, Mexico. Am. Midl. Nat. 93:478–484.

Greene, H. W. 1992. The ecological and behavioral context for pitviper evolution. In: J. A. Campbell and E. D. Brodie, Jr. (eds.), Biology of the pitvipers, pp. 107–117. Selva Press, Tyler, Tex.

Greene, H. W., and R. W. McDiarmid. 1981. Coral snake mimicry: Does it occur? Science 213:1207–1213.

Greene, H. W., and R. L. Seib. 1983. *Micrurus nigrocinctus* (coral, coral snake, coralillo). In: D. H. Janzen (ed.), Costa Rican natural history, pp. 406–408. University of Chicago Press, Chicago.

Greer, A. E. 1966. Viviparity and oviparity in the snake genera *Conopsis*, *Toluca*, *Gyalopion* and *Ficimia*, with comments on *Tomodon* and *Helicops*. Copeia 1966:371–373.

Greer, A. E. 1974. The generic relationships of the scincid lizard genus *Leiolopisma* and its relatives. Aust. J. Zool., supp. ser., 31:1–67.

Greer, B. J., and K. D. Wells. 1980. Territorial and reproductive behavior of the tropical American frog *Centrolenella fleischmanni*. Herpetologica 36:318–326.

Grismer, L. L. 1983. A reevaluation of the North American gekkonid genus *Anarbylus* Murphy and its cladistic relationships to *Coleonyx* Gray. Herpetologica 39:394–399.

Grismer, L. L. 1988. Phylogeny, taxonomy, classification, and the biogeography of eublepharid geckos. In: R. Estes and G. Pregill (eds.), Phylogentic relationships of the lizard families, essays commemorating Charles L. Camp, pp. 369–469. Stanford University Press, Stanford.

Gronovius, L. Tl. 1756. Museum ichthyologici tomus secundus sistens piscium indigenorum & nonnullorum exoticorum, quorum maxima pars in Museo Laurentii Theodorii Gronovii, J. U. D. adservatur, nec non quorundam in aliis Museis observtorum descriptiones. Accedunt nonnullorum exoticorum Piscium icones aeri incisae et Amphibiorum Animalium Historia Zoologica. Th. Haak, Leiden. viii + 88 pp.

Groombridge, B. 1982. The IUCN Amphibia-Reptilia red data book: Testudines, Crocodylia, Rhynchocephalia. International Union for the Conservation of Nature and Natural Resources, Gland, Switzerland. Pt. 1. xliii + 426 pp.

Groombridge, B. 1987. The distribution and status of world crocodilians. *In*: G. J. W. Webb, S. C. Manolis, and P. J. Whitehead (eds.), Wildlife management: Crocodiles and alligators, pp. 9–21. Surrey Beatty and Sons, Sydney.

Guillette, L. J., Jr., R. E. Jones, K. T. Fitzgerald, and H. M. Smith. 1980. Evolution of viviparity in the lizard genus *Sceloporus*. Herpetologica 36:201–215.

Günther, A. C. L. G. 1858. Catalogue of colubrine snakes in the collection of the British Museum. London, British Museum (Natural History). xvi + 281 pp.

Günther, A. C. L. G. 1863. Third account of the snakes in the collection of the British Museum. Ann. Mag. Nat. Hist. (3)12:348–365.

Günther, A. C. L. G. 1872. Seventh account of new species of snakes in the collection of the British Museum. Ann. Mag. Nat. Hist. (4)9:13–37.

Günther, A. C. L. G. 1890. Reptilia and Batrachia. *In*: F. D. Godman and O. Salvin (eds.), Biologia Centrali-Americana, pp. 57–80. R. H. Porter, and Dulau & Company, London. 326 pp.

Günther, A. C. L. G. 1901. Reptilia and Batrachia. *In*: F. D. Godman and O. Salvin (eds.), Biologia Centrali-Americana, pp. 269–292. R. H. Porter, and Dulau & Company, London. 326 pp.

Gutiérrez, J. M., A. Solórzano, L. Cerdas, and J. P. Vannini. 1988. Karyotypes of five species of coral snakes (*Micrurus*). J. Herpetol. 22:109–112.

Guyer, C., and J. M. Savage. 1986. Cladistic relationships among anoles (Sauria: Iguanidae). Syst. Zool. 35:509–531.

Guyer, C., and J. M. Savage. 1992. Anole systematics revisited. Syst. Biol. 41:89–110.

Haines, T. P. 1940. Delayed fertilization in *Leptodeira annulata polysticta*. Copeia 1940:116–118.

Hall, W. P. 1973. Comparative population cytogenetics, speciation, and evolution of the crevice-dwelling species of *Sceloporus* (Sauria, Iguanidae). Ph.D. dissertation, Harvard University, Cambridge.

Hall, W. P. 1980. Chromosomes, speciation, and evolution of Mexican iguanid lizards. Natl. Geogr. Res. 12:309–329.

Hallowell, E. 1852. Descriptions of new species of reptiles inhabiting North America. Proc. Acad. Nat. Sci. Phila. 6:177–182.

Hallowell, E. 1856. Notes on the reptiles in the collection of the Academy of Natural Sciences of Philadelphia. Proc. Acad. Nat. Sci. Phila. 8:221–237.

Hallowell, E. 1861. Report upon the Reptilia of the North Pacific exploring expedition, under command of Capt. John Rogers, U.S.N. Proc. Acad. Nat. Sci. Phila. 12:480–510.

Hamblin, N. 1984. Animal use by the Cozumel Maya. University of Arizona Press, Tucson. 206 pp.

Hardy, D. L. 1994a. *Bothrops asper* (Viperidae) snakebite and field researchers in Middle America. Biotropica 26:198–207.

Hardy, D. L. 1994b. Snakebite and field biologists in Mexico and Central America: Report on ten cases with recommendations for field management. Herpetol. Nat. Hist. 2:67–82.

Hardy, L. M. 1975. A systematic revision of the colubrid snake genus *Ficimia*. J. Herpetol. 9:133–168.

Hardy, L. M. 1980. *Ficimia publia*. Cat. Am. Amphib. Reptiles 254.1–254.2.

Hardy, L. M., C. J. Cole, and C. R. Townsend. 1989. Parthenogenetic reproduction in the Neotropical unisexual lizard *Gymnophthalmus underwoodi* (Reptilia: Teiidae). J. Morphol. 201:215–234.

Harris, D. M. 1985. Infralingual plicae: Support for Boulenger's Teiidae (Sauria). Copeia 1985:560–565.

Harris, D. M., and A. G. Kluge. 1984. The *Sphaerodactylus* (Sauria: Gekkonidae) of Middle America. Occas. Pap. Mus. Zool. Univ. Mich. 706:1–59.

Harrison, C. R. 1993. A taxonomic revision of the snakes of the *Coniophanes piceivittis* species group. M.S. thesis, University of Texas, El Paso. xi + 65 pp.

Hartweg, N. 1934. Description of a new kinosternid from the Yucatán. Occas. Pap. Mus. Zool. Univ. Mich. 277:1–2.

Hartweg, N., and J. A. Oliver. 1940. A contribution to the herpetology of the Isthmus of Tehauntepec IV. Misc. Publ. Mus. Zool. Univ. Mich., no. 47. 31 pp.

Hayes, M. P. 1991. A study of clutch attendance in the Neotropical frog *Centrolenella fleischmanni* (Anura: Centrolenidae). Ph.D. dissertation, University of Miami, Miami. 239 pp.

Healy, P. F. 1983. The paleoecology of the Selin Site (H-CN-5): Department of Colon, Honduras. *In*: R. M. Leventhal and A. L. Kolata (eds.), Civilization in the ancient Americas, essays in honor of Gordon R. Willey. University of New Mexico Press, Las Cruces. xiv + 487 pp.

Heatwole, H. 1976. Herpetogeography of Puerto Rico. VII. Geographic variation in the *Anolis cristatellus* complex in Puerto Rico and the Virgin Islands. Occas. Pap. Mus. Nat. Hist. Univ. Kans. 46:1–18.

Hecht, M. K. 1947. A revision of the lizards of the genus *Aristelliger*, with further evidence as to the zoogeography of the fauna of the Greater Antilles. M.S. thesis, Cornell University, Ithaca. 62 pp.

Hecht, M. K. 1951. Fossil lizards of the West Indian genus *Aristelliger* (Gekkonidae). Am. Mus. Novit. 1538:1–33.

Hecht, M. K. 1952. Natural selection in the lizard genus *Aristelliger*. Evolution 6:112–124.

Hedges, S. B. 1989. Evolution and biogeography of West Indian frogs of the genus *Eleutherodactylus*: Slow-evolving loci and the major groups. *In*: C. A. Woods (ed.), Biogeography of the West Indies: Past, present, and future, pp. 305–370. Sandhill Crane Press, Gainesville, Fla.

Hedges, S. B., R. L. Bezy, and L. R. Maxson. 1991. Phylogenetic relationships and biogeography of xantusiid lizards, inferred from mitochondrial DNA sequences. Mol. Biol. Evol. 8:767–780.

Hedges, S. B., R. A. Nussbaum, and L. R. Maxson. 1993. Caecilian phylogeny and biogeography inferred from mitochondrial DNA sequences of the 12S rRNA and 16S rRNA genes. Herpetol. Monogr. 7:64–76.

Henderson, R. W. 1972. Notes on the reproduction of a giant anole, *Anolis biporcatus* (Sauria, Iguanidae). J. Herpetol. 6:239–240.

Henderson, R. W. 1973. Ethoecological observations of *Ctenosaura similis* (Sauria: Iguanidae) in British Honduras. J. Herpetol. 7:27–33.

Henderson, R. W. 1974a. Aspects of the ecology of the Neotropical vine snake, *Oxybelis aeneus* Wagler. Herpetologica 30:19–24.

Henderson, R. W. 1974b. Aspects of the ecology of the juvenile common iguana (*Iguana iguana*). Herpetologica 30:327–332.

Henderson, R. W. 1976a. Notes on reptiles in the Belize City, Belize (British Honduras), area. J. Herpetol. 10:143–146.

Henderson, R. W. 1976b. A new insular subspecies of the colubrid snake *Leptophis mexicanus* (Reptilia, Serpentes, Colubridae) from Belize. J. Herpetol. 10:329–331.

Henderson, R. W. 1978. Notes on *Agkistrodon bilineatus* (Reptilia, Serpentes, Viperidae) in Belize. J. Herpetol. 12:412–13.

Henderson, R. W. 1982. Trophic relationships and foraging strategies of some New World tree snakes (*Leptophis, Oxybelis, Uromacer*). Amphib.-Reptilia 3:71–80.

Henderson, R. W. 1984. *Scaphiodontophis* (Serpentes: Colubridae): Natural history and test of a mimicry-related hypothesis. *In*: R. A. Seigel, L. E. Hunt, J. L. Knight, L. Malaret, and N. L. Zuschiag (eds.), Vertebrate ecology and systematics—a tribute to Henry S. Fitch, pp. 185–194. Museum of Natural History, University of Kansas, Lawrence.

Henderson, R. W., and M. H. Binder. 1980. The ecology and behavior of vine snakes (*Ahaetulla, Oxybelis, Thelotornis, Uromacer*): A review. Milw. Public Mus. Contrib. Biol. Geol. 37:1–38.

Henderson, R. W., and H. S. Fitch. 1975. A comparative study of the structural and climatic habitats of *Anolis sericeus* (Reptilia: Iguanidae) and its syntopic congeners at four localities in southern Mexico. Herpetologica 31:459–471.

Henderson, R. W., and L. G. Hoevers. 1975. A checklist and key to the amphibians and reptiles of Belize, Central America. Milw. Public Mus. Contrib. Biol. Geol. 5:1–63.

Henderson, R. W., and L. G. Hoevers. 1977a. The head-neck display of *Ninia s. sebae* (Reptilia, Serpentes, Colubridae) in northern Belize. J. Herpetol. 11:106–108.

Henderson, R. W., and L. G. Hoevers. 1977b. The seasonal incidence of snakes at a locality in northern Belize. Copeia 1977:349–355.

Henderson, R. W., L. G. Hoevers, and L. D. Wilson. 1977. A new species of *Sibon* (Reptilia, Serpentes, Colubridae) from Belize, Central America. J. Herpetol. 11:77–79.

Henderson, R. W., and M. A. Nickerson. 1976. Observations on the behavioral ecology of three species of *Imantodes* (Reptilia, Serpentes, Colubridae). J. Herpetol. 10:205–210.

Henderson, R. W., and M. A. Nickerson. 1977. Observations on the feeding behaviour and movements of the snakes *Oxybelis aeneus* and *O. fulgidus*. Br. J. Herpetol. 5:663–667.

Henderson, R. W., M. A. Nickerson, and L. G. Hoevers. 1977. Observations and comments on the feeding behavior of *Leptophis* (Reptilia, Serpentes, Colubridae). J. Herpetol. 11:231–232.

Heyer, R. W. 1969a. Studies on the genus *Leptodactylus* (Amphibia, Leptodactylidae). III. A redefinition of the genus *Leptodactylus* and a description of a new genus of leptodactylid frogs. Contrib. Sci. (Los Ang.) 155:1–14.

Heyer, R. W. 1969b. The adaptive ecology of the species groups of the genus *Leptodactylus* (Amphibia: Leptodactylidae). Evolution 23:421–28.

Heyer, R. W. 1970. Studies on the frogs of the genus *Leptodactylus* (Amphibia: Leptodactylidae). IV. Biosystematics of the melanonotus group. Los Ang. Cty. Mus. Contrib. Sci. 191:1–48.

Heyer, R. W. 1971. *Leptodactylus labialis*. Cat. Am. Amphib. Reptiles 104.1–104.3.

Heyer, R. W. 1973. Relationships of the *marmoratus* species group (Amphibia; Leptodactylidae) within the subfamily Leptodactylinae. Los Ang. Cty. Mus. Contrib. Sci. 253:1–46.

Heyer, R. W. 1978. Systematics of the *fuscus* group of the frog genus *Leptodactylus* (Amphibia, Leptodactylidae). Nat. Hist. Mus. Los Ang. Cty. Sci. Bull. 29:1–85.

Heyer, R. W. 1979. Systematics of the *pentadactylus* species group of the frog genus *Leptodactylus* (Amphibia: Leptodactylidae). Smithson. Contrib. Zool. 301:1–43.

Heyer, R. W., and A. S. Rand. 1977. Foam nest construction in the leptodactylid frogs *Leptodactylus pentadactylus* and *Physalaemus pustulosus* (Amphibia, Anura, Leptodactylidae). J. Herpetol. 11:225–28.

Hildebrand, H. H. 1963. Hallazgo del área de anidación de la tortuga marina "lora," *Lepidochelys kempi* (Garman), en la costa occidental del Golfo de México. Ciencia (Mex. City) 22:105–112.

Hildebrand, H. H. 1982. A historical review of the status of sea turtle populations in the western Gulf of Mexico. *In*: K. Bjorndal (ed.), Biology and conservation of sea turtles, pp. 447–453. Smithsonian Institution Press, Washington, D.C.

Hillis, D. M. 1981. Premating isolating mechanisms among three species of the *Rana pipiens* complex in Texas and southern Oklahoma. Copeia 1981:312–319.

472   LITERATURE CITED

Hillis, D. M., and R. de Sa. 1988. Phylogeny and taxonomy of the *Rana palmipes* group (Salientia: Ranidae). Herpetol. Monogr. 2:1–26.

Hillis, D. M., J. S. Frost, and D. A. Wright. 1983. Phylogeny and biogeography of the *Rana pipiens* complex: A biochemical evaluation. Syst. Zool. 32:132–143.

Hillman, P. E. 1969. Habitat specificity in three sympatric species of *Ameiva* (Reptilia: Teiidae). Ecology 50:476–481.

Himmelstein, J. 1980. Observations and distributions of amphibians and reptiles in the state of Quintana Roo, Mexico. Bull. N.Y. Herpetol. Soc. 16(2):18–34.

Hirth, H. F. 1963. The ecology of two lizards on a tropical beach. Ecol. Monogr. 33:80–112.

Hirth, H. F. 1988. Intrapopulation reproductive traits of green turtles (*Chelonia mydas*) at Tortuguero, Costa Rica. Biotropica 20:322–325.

Hoddenbach, G. A., and J. R. Lannom, Jr. 1967. Notes on the natural history of the Mexico gecko, *Phyllodactylus tuberculosus*. Herpetologica 23:293–296.

Hoevers, L. G., and R. W. Henderson. 1974. Additions to the herpetofauna of Belize (British Honduras). Milw. Public Mus. Contrib. Biol. Geol. 2:1–6.

Holbrook, J. E. 1836 [probably 1839]. North American herpetology; or, a description of the reptiles inhabiting the United States. J. Dobson, Philadelphia. Vol. 1. viii + 132 pp.

Holbrook, J. E. 1838. North American herpetology; or, a description of the reptiles inhabiting the United States. J. Dobson, Philadelphia. Vol. 2. iv + 125 pp.

Holman, J. A. 1963. Observations on dermatemyid and stuarotypine turtles from Veracruz, Mexico. Herpetologica 19:277–279.

Hoogmoed, M. S. 1973. Notes on the herpetofauna of Surinam. IV. The lizards and amphisbaenians of Surinam. Biogeographica 4. v + 419 pp.

Houttuyn, M. 1782. Het Onderscheid der Salamanderen van de Haagdissen in't algemeeneen, en van de Gekkoos in't byzonder. Verh. Genootsch. Wet. Vlissing 9:304–336.

Hunt, R. H. 1975. Maternal behavior in the Morelet's crocodile, *Crocodylus moreleti*. Copeia 1975:763–764.

Hunt, R. H. 1977. Aggressive behavior by adult Morelet's crocodiles toward young. Herpetologica 33:195–201.

Ivanoff, P. 1973. Monuments of civilization: Maya. Grosset and Dunlap, New York. 191 pp.

Iverson, J. B. 1976. The genus *Kinosternon* in Belize (Testudines: Kinosternidae). Herpetologica 32:258–262.

Iverson, J. B. 1980. *Kinosternon acutum*. Cat. Am. Amphib. Reptiles 261.1–261.2.

Iverson, J. B. 1982. Adaptations to herbivory in iguanine lizards. *In*: G. M. Burghardt and A. S. Rand (eds.), Iguanas of the world. Their behavior, ecology, and conservation, pp. 60–78. Noyes Publications, Park Ridge, N.J.

Iverson, J. B. 1983a. *Kinosternon creaseri*. Cat. Am. Amphib. Reptiles 312.1–312.2.

Iverson, J. B. 1983b. *Staurotypus triporcatus* (Wiegmann). Cat. Am. Amphib. Reptiles 328.1–328.2.

Iverson, J. B. 1985. *Staurotypus*. Cat. Am. Amphib. Reptiles 362.1–362.2.

Iverson, J. B. 1986. A checklist with distribution maps of the turtles of the world. Paust Printing, Richmond, Ind. viii + 283 pp.

Iverson, J. B. 1988. Distribution and status of Creaser's mud turtle, *Kinosternon creaseri*. Herpetol. J. 1:285–291.

Iverson, J. B. 1992. A revised checklist with distribution maps of the turtles of the world. Privately printed. Richmond, Ind. xiii + 363 pp.

Iverson, J. B., and J. F. Berry. 1980. *Claudius. Claudius angustatus*. Cat. Am. Amphib. Reptiles 236.1–236.2.

Iverson, J. B., and R. A. Mittermeier. 1980. *Dermatemys. Dermatemys mawii*. Cat. Am. Amphib. Reptiles 237.1–237.4.

Ives, J. E. 1891. Reptiles and batrachians from northern Yucatán and Mexico. Proc. Acad. Nat. Sci. Phila. 53:458–463.

Jackson, J. F. 1973. Notes on the population biology of *Anolis tropidonotus* in a Honduran highland pine forest. J. Herpetol. 7:309–311.

Jacobson, S. K. 1985. Reproductive behavior and male mating success in two species of glass frogs (Centrolenidae). Herpetologica 41:396–404.

Jaeger, E. C. 1944. A source-book of biological names and terms. Charles C. Thomas, Springfield, Ill. xxvi + 256 pp.

Jan, G. 1862. Prodromo dell'iconografia generale degli ofidi. Part 2, v. gruppo: Calamaridae. Milan. xii + 76 pp.

Janzen, D. H. 1962. Injury caused by toxic secretions of *Phrynohyas spilomma* Cope. Copeia 1962:651.

Johnson, I. W., and J. B. Johnson. 1939. Un cuento mazateco-popoloca. RMEA (Mexico) 3:217–226.

Johnson, J. D. 1977. The taxonomy and distribution of the Neotropical whipsnake. *Masticophis mentovarius* (Reptilia, Serpentes, Colubridae). J. Herpetol. 11:287–309.

Johnson, J. D. 1982. *Masticophis mentovarius*. Cat. Am. Amphib. Reptiles 295.1–295.4.

Johnson, J. D. 1988. Comments on the report of envenomation by the colubrid snake *Stenorrhina freminvillei*. Toxicon 26:519–521.

Johnson, J. D. 1989. A biogeographic analysis of the herpetofauna of northwestern nuclear Central America. Milw. Public Mus. Contrib. Biol. Geol. 76:1–66.

Johnson, M. L. 1946. Herpetological notes from Trinidad. Copeia 1946:108.

Jones, J. P. 1927. Descriptions of two new scelopori. Occas. Pap. Mus. Zool. Univ. Mich. 186:1–7.

Kardon, A. 1979. A note on captive reproduction in three Mexican milk snakes. Int. Zoo Yearb. 19:94–96.

Keiser, E. D., Jr. 1967. A monographic study of the Neotropical vine snake, *Oxybelis aeneus* (Wagler). Ph.D. dissertation, Louisiana State University, Baton Rouge. 157 pp.

Keiser, E. D., Jr. 1974. A systematic study of the Neotropical vine snake, *Oxybelis aeneus* (Wagler). Bull. Tex. Mem. Mus. 22:1–51.

Keiser, E. D., Jr. 1975. Observations on tongue extension of vine snakes (genus *Oxybelis*) with suggested behavioral hypotheses. Herpetologica 31:131–133.

Keiser, E. D., Jr. 1982. *Oxybelis aeneus*. Cat. Am. Amphib. Reptiles 305.1–305.4.

Keiser, E. D., Jr. 1991. Bibliography of the genus *Oxybelis* Wagler (Serpentes: Colubridae). Smithson. Herpetol. Info. Ser. 80:1–45.

Kellogg, R. 1932. Mexican tailless amphibians in the United States National Museum. Bull. U.S. Natl. Mus., no. 160. 224 pp.

Kennedy, J. P. 1965. Notes on the habitat and behavior of a snake, *Oxybelis aeneus* Wagler, in Veracruz. Southwest. Nat. 10:136–139.

Kennedy, J. P. 1968. Observations on the ecology and behavior of *Cnemidophorus guttatus* and *Cnemidophorus deppei* (Sauria, Teiidae) in southern Veracruz. J. Herpetol. 2:87–96.

King, F. W. 1982. Historical review of the decline of the green turtle and the hawksbill. *In*: K. Bjorndal (ed.), Biology and conservation of sea turtles, pp. 183–188. Smithsonian Institution Press, Washington, D.C.

King, F. W., and R. L. Burke. 1989. Crocodilian, tuatara, and turtle species of the world, a taxonomic and geographic reference. Association of Systematics Collections, Washington, D.C. xxii + 216 pp.

King, F. W., H. W. Campbell, and P. E. Moler. 1982. Review of the status of the American crocodile. Proc. Fifth Working Meeting of the Crocodile Specialist Group of the Species Survival Commission of the IUCN convened at the Florida State Museum. International Union for the Conservation of Nature and Natural Resources, Gland, Switzerland.

Klauber, L. M. 1945. The geckos of the genus *Coleonyx* with descriptions of new subspecies. Trans. San Diego Soc. Nat. Hist. 10:311–393.

Klauber, L. M. 1956. Rattlesnakes: Their habits, life histories, and influence on mankind. 2 vols. University of California Press, Berkeley. 1476 pp. 2nd ed. 1972, 1533 pp.

Klemmer, J. 1963. Liste der rezenten Giftschlangen: Elapidae, Hydropheidae, Viperidae and Crotalidae. *In*: Die Giftschlangen der Erde, pp. 254–464. N. G. Ewert Universitäts- und Verlagsbuchhandlung, Marburg/Lahn.

Kluge, A. G. 1962. Comparative osteology of the eublepharid lizard genus *Coleonyx* Gray. J. Morphol. 110:299–332.

Kluge, A. G. 1967. Higher taxonomic categories of gekkonid lizards and their evolution. Bull. Am. Mus. Nat. Hist. 135:1–59.

Kluge, A. G. 1975. Phylogenetic relationships and evolutionary trends in the eublepharine lizard genus *Coleonyx*. Copeia 1975:24–35.

Kluge, A. G. 1976. A reinvestigation of the abdominal musculature of gekkonoid lizards and its bearing on their phylogenetic relationships. Herpetologica 32:295–298.

Kluge, A. G. 1982. Cloacal bones and sacs as evidence of gekkonoid lizard relationships. Herpetologica 38:348–355.

Kluge, A. G. 1983. Cladistic relationships among gekkonid lizards. Copeia 1983:465–475.

Kluge, A. G. 1987. Cladistic relationships in the Gekkonoidea (Squamata, Sauria). Misc. Publ. Mus. Zool. Univ. Mich., no. 173. 54 pp.

Kluge, A. G. 1991. Checklist of gekkonoid lizards. Smithson. Herpetol. Info. Ser. 85:1–35.

Knight, A., L. D. Densmore III, and E. D. Rael. 1992. Molecular systematics of the *Agkistrodon* complex. *In*: J. A. Campbell and E. D. Brodie, Jr. (eds.), Biology of the pitvipers, pp. 49–69. Selva Press, Tyler, Tex.

Kofron, C. P. 1982. A review of the Mexican snail-eating snakes *Dipsas brevifacies* and *Dipsas gaigeae*. J. Herpetol. 16:270–286.

Kofron, C. P. 1983. Female reproductive cycle of the Neotropical snail-eating snake *Sibon sanniola* in northern Yucatán, Mexico. Copeia 1983:963–969.

Kofron, C. P. 1985. Systematics of the Neotropical gastropod-eating snake genera *Tropidodipsas* and *Sibon*. J. Herpetol. 19:84–92.

Kofron, C. P. 1987. Systematics of Neotropical gastropod-eating snakes: The *fasciata* group of the genus *Sibon*. J. Herpetol. 21:210–225.

Kofron, C. P. 1988. Systematics of Neotropical gastropod-eating snakes: The *sartorii* group of the genus *Sibon*. Amphib.-Reptilia 9:145–168.

Kofron, C. P. 1990. Systematics of Neotropical gastropod-eating snakes: The *dimidiata* group of the genus *Sibon*, with comments on the *nebulata* group. Amphib.-Reptilia 11:207–223.

Köhler, G. 1995. Eine neue Art der Gattung *Ctenosaura* (Sauria: Iguanidae) aus dem südlichen Campeche, Mexico. Salamandra 31:1–14.

LaBarre, W. 1970. The ghost dance: Origins of religion. Doubleday, Garden City, N.Y.

Lacépède, B. G. E. 1788. Histoire naturelle des quadrupèdes ovipares et des serpens. Acad. R. Sci. (Paris) 1:1–651.

Laerm, J. 1974. A functional analysis of morphological variation and differential niche utilization in basilisk lizards. Ecology 55:404–411.

Lancini, A. R. 1986. Serpientes de Venezuela. 2nd ed. Gráficas Armitano, Caracas. 262 pp.

Landy, M. J., D. A. Langebartel, E. O. Moll, and H. M. Smith. 1966. A collection of snakes from Vocan Tacana, Chiapas, Mexico. J. Ohio Herpetol. Soc. 5:93–101.

Lang, M. 1989. Phylogenetic and biogeographic patterns of basiliscine iguanians (Reptilia: Squamata: "Iguanidae"). Bonn. Zool. Monogr. 28:1–172.

Langebartel, D. A. 1953. The reptiles and amphibians. *In*: R. T. Hatt, H. I. Fisher, D. A. Langebartel, and G. W. Brainerd, Faunal and archeological researches in Yucatán caves, pp. 91–108. Cranbrook Inst. Sci. Bull. 33:1–119.

Langebartal, D. A., and P. W. Smith. 1959. Noteworthy records of amphibians and reptiles from eastern Mexico. Herpetologica 15:27–29.

Larson, A. 1983. A molecular phylogentic perspective on the origins of a lowland tropical salamander fauna. I. Phylogentic inferences from protein comparisons. Herpetologica 39:85–99.

Larson, K. R., and W. W. Tanner. 1974. Numeric analysis of the lizard genus *Sceloporus* with special reference to cranial osteology. Great Basin Nat. 34:1–41.

Larson, K. R., and W. W. Tanner. 1975. Evolution of the sceloporine lizards (Iguanidae). Great Basin Nat. 35:1–20.

Laurenti, J. N. 1768. Specimen medicum, exhibens synopsin reptilium emedatum cum experimentis circa venena et antidota reptilum austriacorum. Vienna. 214 pp.

Lazcano-Barrero, M. A. 1984. Granja piloto para la explotación comercial y conservación de los cocodrilos. Memorias Primeras Reunion Regional de Ecologia Sureste, Tuxtla Gutiérrez, pp. 113–119.

Lazcano-Barrero, M. A. 1992a. First record of *Bolitoglossa mulleri* (Caudata: Plethodontidae) from Mexico. Southwest. Nat. 37:315–316.

Lazcano-Barrero, M. A. 1992b. *Bolitoglossa mulleri*. Cat. Am. Amphib. Reptiles 533.1–533.2.

Lazcano-Barrero, M. A., O. A. Flores-Villela, M. Benarbid-Nisenbaum, J. A. Hernández-Gómez, M. P. Chávez-Peón, and A. Cabrera-Aldave. 1988. Estudios y conservación de los anfibios y reptiles de México: Una propuesta. Cuad. Divulgación, Instituto Nacional de Investigaciones sobre Recursos Bióticos 25:1–44.

Lazcano-Barrero, M. A., and E. Gongóra-Arones. 1993. Observation and review of the nesting and egg-laying of *Corytophanes cristatus* (Iguanidae). Bull. Md. Herpetol. Soc. 29:67–75.

Lazell, J. D., Jr. 1973. The lizard genus *Iguana* in the Lesser Antilles. Bull. Mus. Comp. Zool. Harv. Univ. 145:1–28.

Legler, J. M. 1965. A new species of turtle, genus *Kinosternon*, from Central America. Univ. Kans. Publ. Mus. Nat. Hist. 15:615–625.

Legler, J. M. 1990. The genus *Pseudemys* in Mesoamerica: Taxonomy, distribution, and origins. *In*: J. W. Gibbons (ed.), Life history and ecology of the slider turtle, pp. 82–105. Smithsonian Institution Press, Washington, D.C.

Lee, J. C. 1974. The diel activity cycle of the lizard *Xantusia henshawi*. Copeia 1974:934–940.

Lee, J. C. 1976. *Rana maculata* Brocchi, an addition to the herpetofauna of Belize. Herpetologica 32:211–214.

Lee, J. C. 1980a. An ecogeographic analysis of the herpetofauna of the Yucatán Peninsula. Univ. Kans. Mus. Nat. Hist. Misc. Publ. 67. 75 pp.

Lee, J. C. 1980b. Variation and systematics of the *Anolis sericeus* complex (Sauria: Iguanidae). Copeia 1980:310–320.

Lee, J. C. 1986. Is the large-male mating advantage in anurans an epiphenomenon? Oecologia 69:207–212.

Lee, J. C. 1992. *Anolis sagrei* in Florida: Phenetics of a colonizing species. III. West Indian and Middle American comparisons. Copeia 1992:942–954.

Lee, J. C. 1993. Geographic variation in size and shape of Neotropical frogs: A precipitation gradient analysis. Occas. Pap. Mus. Nat. Hist. Univ. Kans. 163:1–20.

Lee, J. C., and M. L. Crump. 1981. Morphological correlates of male mating success in *Triprion petasatus* and *Hyla marmorata* (Anura: Hylidae). Oecologia 50:153–157.

Lee, J. C., and M. A. Salzburg. 1989. Mating success and pairing patterns in *Bufo valliceps* (Anura: Bufonidae). Southwest. Nat. 34:155–157.

Lee, R. C. 1969. Observing the tortuga blanca (*Dermatemys mawi*). J. Int. Turt. Tort. Soc. 3:32–34.

Lee, T. A., Jr. 1985. Los códices Mayas. Universidad Autónoma de Chiapas, Mexico. 213 pp.

Leon, J. R. 1969. The systematics of the frogs of the *Hyla rubra* group in Middle America. Univ. Kans. Publ. Mus. Nat. Hist. 18:505–545.

Leviton, A., R. H. Gibbs, Jr., E. Head, and C. E. Dawson. 1985. Standards in herpetology and ichthyology. Part 1: Standard codes for institutional resource collections in herpetology and ichthyology. Copeia 1985:802–832.

Lewis, C. B. 1940. The Cayman Islands and marine turtles. Bull. Inst. Jam. Sci. Ser. 2:56–65.

Lichtenstein, H., and E. Von Martens. 1856. Nomenclator reptilium et amphibiorum musei zoologici berolinensis. Königl. Akad. Wissensch., Berlin. iv + 48 pp.

Lieb, C. S. 1988. Systematic status of the Neotropical snakes *Dendrophidion dendrophis* and *D. nuchalis* (Colubridae). Herpetologica 44:162–175.

Lieb, C. S. 1991a. *Dendrophidion nuchale*. Cat. Am. Amphib. Reptiles 520.1–520.2.

Lieb, C. S. 1991b. *Dendrophidion vinitor*. Cat. Am. Amphib. Reptiles 522.1–522.2.

Linnaeus, C. 1758. Systema naturae per regna tria naturae, secundum classes, ordines, genera, species cum characteribus, differentiis, synonymis, locis. 10th ed. L. Salvius, Stockholm. Vol. 1. iv + 826 pp.

Linnaeus, C. 1766. Systema naturae per regna tria naturae, secundum classes, ordines, genera, species cum characteribus, differentiis, synonymis, locis. 12th ed. L. Salvius, Stockholm. Vol. 1. 532 pp.

Livezey, R. L., and R. S. Peckham. 1953. Some snakes from San Marcos, Guatemala. Herpetologica 8:175–177.

López-Gonzalez, C. A. 1991. Estudio prospectivo de los vertebrados terrestres del corredor turístico Cancún-Tulum, Quintana Roo, México. Tesis, Escuela Nacional de Estudios Profesionales, Iztacala, Universidad Nacional Autónoma de México. vi + 127 pp.

Loveridge, A. 1947. Revision of the African lizards of the family Gekkonidae. Bull. Mus. Comp. Zool. 98:1–469.

Lowe, J. W. G. 1985. The dynamics of apocalypse, a systems simulation of the classic Maya collapse. University of New Mexico Press, Las Cruces. vii + 275 pp.

Lundell, C. L. 1934. Preliminary sketch of the phytogeography of the Yucatán Peninsula. *In*: Contributions to American Archaeology, vol. 2, no. 12, pp. 257–321. Carnegie Institution, Washington, D.C.

Lynch, J. D. 1965a. Two new species of *Eleutherodactylus* from Mexico (Amphibia: Leptodactylidae). Herpetologica 20:246–252.

Lynch, J. D. 1965b. A review of the *rugulosus* group of

Eleutherodactylus in northern Central America. Herpetologica 21:102–113.

Lynch, J. D. 1970a. A taxonomic revision of the leptodactylid frog genus *Syrrhophus* Cope. Univ. Kans. Publ. Mus. Nat. Hist. 20:1–45.

Lynch, J. D. 1970b. Systematic status of the American leptodactylid frog genera *Engystomops*, *Eupemphix*, and *Physalaemus*. Copeia 1970:488–496.

Lynch, J. D. 1971. Evolutionary relationships, osteology, and zoogeography of leptodactyloid frogs. Univ. Kans. Mus. Nat. Hist. Misc. Publ. 53. 238 pp.

Lynch, J. D. 1991. Three replacement names for preoccupied names in the genus *Eleutherodactylus* (Amphibia: Leptodactylidae). Copeia 1991:1138.

Mahrdt, C. 1969. First record of the snake *Coniophanes schmidti* from the state of Chiapas, Mexico. Herpetologica 25:125.

Manjarrez, J., and C. Macias-Garcia. 1991. Feeding ecology of *Nerodia rhombifera* in a Veracruz swamp. J. Herpetol. 25:499–502.

Manjarrez, J., and C. Macias-Garcia. 1992. *Thamnophis proximus rutiloris*. Herpetol. Rev. 23:61–62.

Marcellini, D. L. 1974. Acoustic behavior of the gekkonid lizard *Hemidactylus frenatus*. Herpetologica 30:44–52.

Markezich, A. L., and D. C. Taphorn. 1993. A variational analysis of populations of *Bothrops* (Serpentes: Viperidae) from western Venezuela. J. Herpetol. 27:248–254.

Márquez, R. 1966. Lista de tortugas marinas marcadas por la Estación de Biología Pesquera de El Sauzal, B.C. Bol. Prog. Nac. Marc. Tort. Mar. 1:1–4.

Márquez, R., A. Villanueva, R. Bravo, and E. Sánchez. 1987. Abundancia y distribución de tortugas marinas durante la temporada de anidación 1985, 1986 en Isla Aguada, Campeche. Final report, Consejo Nacional de Ciencia y Tecnología, Clave PCEBNA-021204.

Martin, P. S. 1955. Herpetological records from the Gómez Farías region of southwestern Tamaulipas, Mexico. Copeia 1955:173–180.

Martin, P. S. 1958. A biogeography of reptiles and amphibians in the Gómez Farías region, Tamaulipas, Mexico. Misc. Publ. Mus. Zool. Univ. Mich., no. 101. 102 pp.

Martínez, S., and L. Cerdas. 1986. Captive reproduction of the mussurana, *Clelia clelia* (Daudin), from Costa Rica. Herpetol. Rev. 17:12–13.

Maslin, T. P. 1963a. Notes on a collection of herpetozoa from the Yucatán Peninsula of Mexico. Univ. Colo. Stud. Ser. Biol. 9:1–20.

Maslin, T. P. 1963b. Notes on some anuran tadpoles from Yucatán, Mexico. Herpetologica 19:122–128.

Maslin, T. P., and D. M. Secoy. 1986. A checklist of the lizard genus *Cnemidophorus* (Teiidae). Contrib. Zool. Univ. Colo. Mus. 1:1–60.

Mather, C. M., and J. W. Sites. 1985. *Sceloporus variabilis*. Cat. Am. Amphib. Reptiles 373.1–373.3.

McAllister, C. T. 1985. *Nerodia rhombifera*. Cat. Am. Amphib. Reptiles 376.1–376.4.

McCarthy, T. J. 1982. A note on reproduction in *Laemanctus longipes* in Belize. Caribb. J. Sci. 18:133–136.

McCoy, C. J., Jr. 1966. Additions to the herpetofauna of southern El Petén, Guatemala. Herpetologica 22:306–308.

McCoy, C. J., Jr. 1968. A review of the genus *Laemanctus*. Copeia 1968:665–678.

McCoy, C. J., Jr. 1969. Snakes of the genus *Coniophanes* from the Yucatán Peninsula, Mexico. Copeia 1969:847–849.

McCoy, C. J., Jr. 1970a. *Hemidactylus turcicus*. Cat. Am. Amphib. Reptiles 87.1–87.2.

McCoy, C. J., Jr. 1970b. *Corytophanes*. *In*: J. A. Peters and R. Donoso-Barros, Catalogue of the Neotropical squamata. II. Lizards and amphisbaenians, p. 101. Smithsonian Institution Press, Washington, D.C. viii + 293 pp.

McCoy, C. J., Jr. 1970c. The snake fauna of Middlesex, British Honduras. J. Herpetol. 3–4:135–140.

McCoy, C. J., Jr. 1975. Reproduction in Guatemalan *Anolis biporcatus* (Sauria: Iguanidae). Herpetologica 31:65–66.

McCoy, C. J., Jr. 1986. Results of the Carnegie Museum of Natural History expeditions to Belize. I. Systematic status and geographic distribution of *Sibon neilli* (Reptilia, Serpentes). Ann. Carnegie Mus. 55:117–123.

McCoy, C. J., Jr. 1990. Additions to the herpetofauna of Belize, Central America. Caribb. J. Sci. 26:164–166.

McCoy, C. J., Jr., and E. J. Censky. 1992. Biology of the Yucatán hognosed pitviper, *Porthidium yucatanicum*. *In*: J. A. Campbell and E. D. Brodie, Jr. (eds.), Biology of the pitvipers, pp. 217–222. Selva Press, Tyler, Tex.

McCoy, C. J., Jr., E. J. Censky, and R. W. Van Devender. 1986. Distribution records for amphibians and reptiles in Belize, Central America. Herpetol. Rev. 17:28–29.

McCoy, C. J., Jr., and T. P. Maslin. 1962. A revision of the teiid lizard *Cnemidophorus cozumelus* and the recognition of a new race, *Cnemidophorus cozumelus rodecki*. Copeia 1962:620–627.

McCoy, C. J., Jr., and P. H. Miller. 1964. *Eumeces sumichrasti* (Reptilia: Scincidae) in Quintana Roo, Mexico. Herpetologica 19:224.

McCranie, J. R. 1993. *Crotalus durissus*. Cat. Am. Amphib. Reptiles 577.1–577.11.

McCranie, J. R., and L. Porras. 1978. Geographical distribution: *Bothrops yucatanicus*. Herpetol. Rev. 9:108.

McDiarmid, R. W. 1968. Populational variation in the frog genus *Phrynohyas* Fitzinger in Middle America. Los Ang. Cty. Mus. Contrib. Sci. 134:1–25.

McDiarmid, R. W., and K. Adler. 1974. Notes on territorial and vocal behavior of Neotropical frogs of the genus *Centrolenella*. Herpetologica 30:75–78.

McDiarmid, R. W., and M. S. Foster. 1975. Unusual sites for two Neotropical tadpoles. J. Herpetol. 9:264–265.

McDiarmid, R. W., and R. D. Worthington. 1970. Concerning the reproductive habits of tropical plethodontid salamanders. Herpetologica 26:57–70.

McKinstry, D. M. 1983. Morphological evidence of toxic saliva in colubrid snakes: A checklist of world genera. Herpetol. Rev. 14:12–15.

Medem, F. 1962. La distribución geográfica y ecología de

los Crocodylia y Testudinata en el Departamento del Choco. Rev. Acad. Colomb. Cien. Exactas Fis. Nat. 11:279–303.

Meerman, J. C. 1992a. The status of crocodiles in the eastern Corozal District. J. Belize Nat. Hist. Soc. 1:1–5.

Meerman, J. C. 1992b. A new snake for Belize. J. Belize Nat. Hist. Soc. 1:26–27.

Meerman, J. C. 1993. Checklist of the reptiles and amphibians of the Shipstern Nature Reserve. Occas. Pap. Belize Nat. Hist. Soc. 2:65–69.

Mendelson, J. R. 1991. Tail breakage in *Coniophanes fissidens* and other tropical colubrids. Paper presented at the joint annual meeting of the Society for the Study of Amphibians and Reptiles and the Herpetologists' League, Pennsylvania State University, 6–11 August 1991.

Mendelson, J. R. 1992. Frequency of tail breakage in *Coniophanes fissidens* (Serpentes: Colubridae). Herpetologica 48:448–455.

Mendelson, J. R. 1993. An evaluation of the systematics of the *Bufo valliceps* group: USA, Mexico, and Guatemala. Paper presented at the joint annual meeting of the American Society of Ichthyologists and Herpetologists and the Herpetologists' League, University of Texas, Austin, 27 May–2 June 1993.

Mendelson, J. R., III. 1994. A new species of toad (Anura: Bufonidae) from the lowlands of eastern Guatemala. Occas. Pap. Mus. Nat. Hist. Univ. Kans. 166:1–21.

Mendoza-Quijano, F., O. Flores-Villela, and J. W. Sites. 1994. Genetic variation and distribution of the lizards of the *variabilis* group of the genus *Sceloporus*. Paper presented at the joint annual meeting of the Herpetologists' League and the Society for the Study of Amphibians and Reptiles, University of Georgia, Athens, 28 July–1 August 1994.

Mercer, H. C. 1896. The hill-caves of Yucatán, a search for evidence of man's antiquity in the caverns of Central America. J. B. Lippincott, Philadelphia. 183 pp.

Merrem, B. 1821. Versuch eines Systems der Amphibien. Tentamen systematis amphibiorum. Marburg. xv + 191 pp.

Mertens, R. 1952. Die Amphibien und Reptilien von El Salvador. Abh. Senckenb. Naturforsch. Ges. 487:1–120.

Mertens, R., and L. Müller. 1928. Liste der Amphibien und Reptilien Europas. Abh. Senckenb. Naturforsch. Ges. 41:1–62.

Mertens, R., and L. Müller. 1940. Die Amphibien und Reptilien Europas. Abh. Senckenb. Naturforsch. Ges. 451:1–56.

Meyer, J. R. 1966. Records and observations on some amphibians and reptiles from Honduras. Herpetologica 22:172–181.

Meyer, J. R., and L. D. Wilson. 1971. Taxonomic studies and notes on some Honduran amphibians and reptiles. Bull. South. Calif. Acad. Sci. 70:106–114.

Meyer, J. R., and L. D. Wilson. 1973. A distributional checklist of the turtles, crocodilians, and lizards of Honduras. Los Ang. Cty. Mus. Contrib. Sci. 244:1–39.

Meylan, A. 1988. Spongivory in hawksbill turtles: A diet of glass. Science 239:393–395.

Meylan, A. 1989. Status report of the hawksbill turtle. *In*: L. Ogren, F. Berry, K. Bjorndal, H. Kumpf, R. Mast, G. Medina, H. Reichart, and R. Witham (eds.), Proceedings of the Second Western Atlantic Turtle Symposium, pp. 101–115. NOAA Technical Memorandum NMFS-SEDC-226. National Oceanic and Atmospheric Administration, Washington, D.C.

Miller, B. W., and C. M. Miller. 1992. Distributional notes and new species records for birds in Belize. Occas. Pap. Belize Nat. Hist. Soc. 1:6–25.

Milstead, W. W. 1967. Fossil box turtles (*Terrapene*) from central North America, and box turtles of eastern Mexico. Copeia 1967:168–179.

Milstead, W. W. 1969a. Studies on the evolution of box turtles (genus *Terrapene*). Bull. Fla. State Mus. Biol. Sci. 14:1–108.

Milstead, W. W. 1969b. Studies on beach lizards in Veracruz, Mexico. Herpetologica 25:140–146.

Minton, S. A., Jr. 1966. A contribution to the herpetology of West Pakistan. Bull. Am. Mus. Nat. Hist. 134:27–184.

Minton, S. A., Jr., and M. R. Minton. 1969. Venomous reptiles. New York, Charles Scribner's Sons.

Minton, S. A., Jr., and M. R. Minton. 1991. *Masticophis mentovarius* (Neotropical whipsnake): Reproduction. Herpetol. Rev. 22:100–101.

Minton, S. A., Jr., and H. M. Smith. 1960. A new subspecies of *Coniophanes fissidens* and notes on Central American amphibians and reptiles. Herpetologica 16:103–111.

Mittleman, M. B. 1944. Feeding habits of a Central American opisthoglyph snake. Copeia 1944:122.

Mittleman, M. B. 1949. Geographic variation in Marcy's garter snake, *Thamnophis marcianus* (Baird and Girard). Bull. Chic. Acad. Sci. 8:235–249.

Miyamoto, M. M. 1983. Frogs of the *Eleutherodactylus rugulosus* group: A cladistic study of allozyme, morphological, and karyological data. Syst. Zool. 32:109–124.

Miyamoto, M. M., and J. H. Cane. 1980a. Behavioral observations of noncalling males in Costa Rican *Hyla ebraccata*. Biotropica 12:225–227.

Miyamoto, M. M., and J. H. Cane. 1980b. Notes on the reproductive behavior of a Costa Rican population of *Hyla ebraccata*. Copeia 1980:928–930.

Moll, D. 1985. The marine turtles of Belize. Oryx 19:144–157.

Moll, D. 1986. The distribution, status, and level of exploitation of the freshwater turtle *Dermatemys mawei* in Belize, Central America. Biol. Conserv. 35:87–96.

Moll, D., and E. O. Moll. 1990. The slider turtle in the Neotropics: Adaptation of a temperate species to a tropical environment. *In*: J. W. Gibbons (ed.), Life history and ecology of the slider turtle, pp. 152–161. Smithsonian Institution Press, Washington, D.C.

Moll, E. O., and J. M. Legler. 1971. The life history of a Neotropical slider turtle, *Pseudemys scripta* (Schoepff), in Panama. Bull. Los Ang. Cty. Mus. Nat. Hist. 11:1–102.

Moll, E. O., and H. M. Smith. 1967. Lizards in the diet of an American caecilian. Chic. Acad. Sci. Nat. Hist. Misc. 187:1–2.

Montanucci, R. R. 1968. Comparative dentition in four iguanid lizards. Herpetologica 24:305–315.

Morelet, A. 1871. Travels in Central America. Leypoldt, Holt, and Williams, New York. xvii + 430 pp.

Morfín, M. 1918. Informe rendido a la Secretaría de Fomento referente a la fauna del territoria de Quintana Roo. *In*: P. C. Sánchez and S. Toscano, Informe rendido por la Comisión Geográfico-Exploradora de Quintana Roo al C. Secretaría de Fomento, México, pp. 40–48. Mexico City.

Morgan, E. C. 1973. Snakes of the subfamily Sibynophiinae. Ph.D. dissertation, University of Southwestern Louisiana, Lafayette. 205 pp.

Moritz, C., J. W. Wright, V. Singh, and W. M. Brown. 1992. Mitochondrial DNA analyses and the origin and relative age of parthenogenetic *Cnemidophorus*. V. The *cozumela* species group. Herpetologica 48:417–424.

Mortimer, J. A. 1982. Feeding ecology of sea turtles. *In*: K. Bjorndal (ed.), Biology and conservation of sea turtles, pp. 103–109. Smithsonian Institution Press, Washington, D.C.

Mrosovsky, N. 1972. Spectrographs of the sounds of leatherback turtles. Herpetologica 28:256–258.

Mrosovsky, N. 1982. Sex ratio bias in hatchling sea turtles from artificially incubated eggs. Biol. Conserv. 23:309–314.

Mrosovsky, N. 1988. Pivotal temperatures for loggerhead turtles (*Caretta caretta*) from northern and southern nesting beaches. Can. J. Zool. 66:661–669.

Mrosovsky, N., and J. Provancha. 1989. Sex ratios of loggerhead sea turtles hatching on a Florida beach. Can. J. Zool. 67:2533–2539.

Mrosovsky, N., and C. L. Yntema. 1981. Temperature dependence of sexual differentiation in sea turtles: Implications for conservation. Biol. Conserv. 18:271–280.

Müller, L., and W. Hellmich. 1936. Amphibien und Reptilien. I. Amphibia, Chelonia, Loricata. Wissenschaftliche Ergebnisse der Deutschen Gran Chaco-Expedition. xvi + 120 pp.

Müller, P. 1973. The dispersal centers of terrestrial vertebrates in the Neotropical realm. W. Junk, The Hague. 244 pp.

Murphy-Walker, S. 1993. Oviductal sperm storage potential in *Hemidactylus frenatus* lizards (family Gekkonidae). Paper presented at the joint annual meeting of the American Society of Ichthyologists and Herpetologists and the Herpetologists' League, University of Texas, Austin, 27 May–2 June 1993.

Myers, C. W. 1971. Central American lizards related to *Anolis pentaprion*: Two new species from the Cordillera de Talamanca. Am. Mus. Novit. 2471:1–40.

Myers, C. W. 1974. The systematics of *Rhadinaea* (Colubridae), a genus of New World snakes. Bull. Am. Mus. Nat. Hist. 153:1–262.

Myers, C. W. 1982. Blunt-headed vine snakes (*Imantodes*) in Panama, including a new species and other revisionary notes. Am. Mus. Novit. 2738:1–50.

Nájera, J. J. D. 1990. Nesting of three species of sea turtle in the northeast coast of the Yucatán Peninsula. *In*: T. H. Richardson, J. I. Richardson, and M. Donnelly (comps.), Proceedings of the Tenth Annual Workshop on Sea Turtle Biology and Conservation, pp. 29–33. NOAA Technical Memorandum NMFS-SEFC-278. National Oceanic and Atmospheric Administration, Washington, D.C.

Neill, W. E., and J. C. Grubb 1971. Arboreal habits of *Bufo valliceps* in central Texas. Copeia 1971:347–348.

Neill, W. T. 1951. The type locality of the Mediterranean gecko, *Hemidactylus t. turcicus* (Linnaeus). Copeia 1951:311.

Neill, W. T. 1960. The caudal lure of various juvenile snakes. Q. J. Fla. Acad. Sci. 23:173–200.

Neill, W. T. 1962. The reproductive cycle of snakes in a tropical region, British Honduras. Q. J. Fla. Acad. Sci. 25:234–253.

Neill, W. T. 1965. New and noteworthy amphibians and reptiles from British Honduras. Bull. Fla. State Mus. Biol. Sci. 9:77–130.

Neill, W. T., and R. Allen. 1959a. The rediscovery of *Thamnophis praeocularis* (Bocourt) in British Honduras. Herpetologica 15:223–227.

Neill, W. T., and R. Allen. 1959b. Additions to the British Honduras herpetofaunal list. Herpetologica 15:235–240.

Neill, W. T., and R. Allen. 1959c. Studies on the amphibians and reptiles of British Honduras. Publ. Res. Div. Ross Allen's Reptile Inst. 2(1):1–76.

Neill, W. T., and R. Allen. 1960. Noteworthy snakes from British Honduras. Herpetologica 16:146–162.

Neill, W. T., and R. Allen. 1961a. Further studies on the herpetology of British Honduras. Herpetologica 17:38–52.

Neill, W. T., and R. Allen. 1961b. Colubrid snakes (*Tantilla, Thamnophis, Tropidodipsas*) from British Honduras and nearby areas. Herpetologica 17:90–98.

Neill, W. T., and R. Allen. 1962. Reptiles of the Cambridge expedition to British Honduras, 1959–60. Herpetologica 18:79–91.

Nelson, C. E. 1972a. Systematic studies of the North American microhylid genus *Gastrophryne*. J. Herpetol. 6:111–137.

Nelson, C. E. 1972b. *Gastrophryne elegans*. Cat. Am. Amphib. Reptiles 121.1–121.2.

Nelson, C. E. 1973a. Systematics of the Middle American upland populations of *Hypopachus* (Anura: Microhylidae). Herpetologica 29:6–17.

Nelson, C. E. 1973b. *Gastrophryne*. Cat. Am. Amphib. Reptiles 134.1–134.2.

Nelson, C. E. 1974. Further studies on the systematics of *Hypopachus* (Anura: Microhylidae). Herpetologica 30:250–275.

Nelson, C. E., and R. Altig. 1972. Tadpoles of the micro-hylids *Gastrophryne elegans* and *G. usta*. Herpeto-logica 28:381–383.

Noble, G. K. 1918. The amphibians and reptiles collected by the American Museum expedition to Nicaragua in 1916. Bull. Am. Mus. Nat. Hist. 38:311–347.

Nussbaum, R. A. 1988. On the status of *Copeotyphlinus syntremus*, *Gymnopis oligozona*, and *Minascaecilia sartoria* (Gymnophiona, Caeciliidae): A comedy of errors. Copeia 1988:921–928.

Nussbaum, R. A., and M. Wilkinson. 1989. On the classification and phylogeny of caecilians (Amphibia: Gymnophiona), a critical review. Herpetol. Monogr. 3:1–42.

Oliver, J. A. 1947. The seasonal incidence of snakes. Am. Mus. Novit. 1363:1–14.

Oliver, J. A. 1948. The relationships and zoogeography of the genus *Thalerophis* Oliver. Bull. Am. Mus. Nat. Hist. 92:157–280.

Olsen, S. J. 1972. Animal remains from Altar de Sacrificios. *In*: G. R. Willey (ed.), The artifacts of Altar de Sacrificios, pp. 243–246. Pap. Peabody Mus. Harv. Univ. 64, no. 1.

Olsen, S. J. 1978. Vertebrate faunal remains. *In*: G. R. Willey (ed.), Excavations at Seibal. Mem. Peabody Mus. Archaeol. Ethnol. Harv. Univ. 14, nos. 1–3.

Olson, R. E. 1984. *Centrolenella fleischmanni*. Herpetol. Rev. 15:76.

Olson, R. E. 1986a. *Dipsas brevifacies*. Herpetol. Rev. 17:67.

Olson, R. E. 1986b. *Sibon sanniola*. Herpetol. Rev. 17:67.

Olson, R. E. 1987. Taxonomic revision of the lizards *Sceloporus serrifer* and *cyanogenys* of the Gulf Coastal Plain. Bull. Md. Herpetol. Soc. 23:158–167.

Pace, A. E. 1974. Systematics and biological studies of the leopard frogs (*Rana pipiens* complex) of the United States. Misc. Publ. Mus. Zool. Univ. Mich., no. 148. 140 pp.

Pacheco-Cruz, S. 1919. Léxico de la fauna Yucateca. Mérida, Yucatán, Mexico. 76 pp.

Pagden, A. 1986. Hernán Cortés, letters from Mexico. Yale University Press, New Haven. 563 pp.

Parker, T. A., III, B. K. Holst, L. H. Emmons, and J. R. Meyer. 1993. A biological assessment of the Columbia River Forest Reserve, Toledo District, Belize. Conserv. Int. Rapid Assess. Progr. Work. Pap. 3:1–81.

Parsons, J. J. 1962. The green turtle and man. University of Florida Press, Gainesville. x + 126 pp.

Pearse, A. S. 1945. La fauna. *In*: Enciclopedia Yucatanense, vol. 1, pp. 109–271. Gobierno de Yucatán, Mérida.

Pearse, A. S., and collaborators. 1938. Fauna of the caves of Yucatán. Carnegie Inst. Wash. Publ. 491:1–304.

Pendergast, D. M. 1977. Commentary. *In*: E. Benson (ed.), The sea in the precolumbian world, pp. 55–56. Dumbarton Oaks, Washington, D.C. vii + 188 pp.

Penner, J. E. 1970. The ecology and behavior of two lizards of the genus *Sceloporus* (Iguanidae) from Yucatán, Mexico. M.S. thesis, University of Oklahoma. viii + 66 pp.

Penner, J. 1973. Habitat preferences of *Sceloporus chrysostictus* and *Sceloporus cozumelae* in the vicinity of Progreso, Yucatán, Mexico. Bull. Md. Herpetol. Soc. 9:6–7.

Pérez-Higareda, G. 1980. Notes on nesting of *Crocodylus moreleti* in southern Veracruz, Mexico. Bull. Md. Herpetol. Soc. 16:52–53.

Pérez-Higareda, G. 1981. Nesting and incubation times in *Corytophanes hernandezi* (Lacertilia: Iguanidae). Bull. Md. Herpetol. Soc. 17:71–73.

Pérez-Higareda, G. 1985. A new subspecies of the genus *Tantilla* from southern Veracruz, Mexico (Serpentes: Colubridae). Bull. Md. Herpetol. Soc. 21:38–40.

Pérez-Higareda, G., A. Rangel-Rangel, and H. M. Smith. 1989. The courtship and behavior of Morelet's crocodile (*Crocodylus moreleti*) in southern Veracruz, Mexico. Bull. Chic. Herpetol. Soc. 24:131–132.

Pérez-Higareda, G., A. Rangel-Rangel, and H. M. Smith. 1990. Maximum sizes of Morelet's and American crocodiles. Bull. Md. Herpetol. Soc. 27:34–37.

Pérez-Higareda, G., A. Rangel-Rangel, H. M. Smith, and D. Chiszar. 1989. Comments on the food and feeding habits of Morelet's crocodile. Copeia 1989:1039–1041.

Pérez-Higareda, G., and H. M. Smith. 1989. Termite nest incubation of the eggs of the Mexican snake *Adelphicos quadrivirgatus*. Herpetol. Rev. 20:5–6.

Pérez-Higareda, G., and R. C. Vogt. 1985. A new subspecies of arboreal lizard, genus *Laemanctus*, from the mountainous region of Los Tuxtlas, Veracruz, Mexico (Lacertilia, Iguanidae). Bull. Md. Herpetol. Soc. 21:139–144.

Peters, J. A. 1953. Snakes and lizards from Quintana Roo, Mexico. Lloydia 16:227–232.

Peters, J. A. 1960. The snakes of the subfamily Dipsadinae. Misc. Publ. Mus. Zool. Univ. Mich., no. 114. 224 pp.

Peters, J. A. 1964. Dictionary of herpetology. Hafner, New York. vii + 392 pp.

Peters, J. A. 1967. The lizards of Ecuador, a check list and key. Proc. U.S. Natl. Mus. 119:1–49.

Peters, J. A., and R. Donoso-Barros. 1970. Catalogue of the Neotropical Squamata. Part II: Lizards and amphisbaenians. Bull. U.S. Natl. Mus., no. 298. viii + 293 pp.

Peters, J. A., and B. Orejas-Miranda. 1970. Catalogue of the Neotropical Squamata. Part I: Snakes. Bull. U.S. Natl. Mus., no. 297. viii + 347 pp.

Peters, W. C. 1861a. Über eine Sammlung von Schlangen aus Huanusco in Mexico welche das Königl. zoologische Museum kürzlich von Dr. Hille erworden hat. Monatsber. Akad. Wiss. Berl. 1861:460–462.

Peters, W. C. 1861b. Über neue Schlangen des Königl. zoologischen Museums. Monatsber. Akad. Wiss. Berl. 1861:922–925.

Peters, W. C. 1863a. Über einige neue Arten der Saurier-Gattung *Anolis*. Monatsber. Akad. Wiss. Berl. 1863:135–149.

Peters, W. C. 1863b. Über einige neue oder weniger bekannte Schlangenarten des Zoologischen Museums zu Berlin. Monatsber. Akad. Wiss. Berl. 1863:273–289.

Peters, W. C. 1874. Über neue Amphibien (*Gymnopis, Siphonops, Polypedates, Rhacophorus, Hyla, Cyclodes*,

Euprepes, Clemmys). Monatsber. Königl. Akad. Wiss. Berl. 1874:616–624.

Peters, W. C. 1882. Eine neue Art der urodelen Batrachier, *Oedipus yucatanus,* aus Yucatán (Centralamerica). Sber. Ges. Naturforsch. Freunde Berl. 1882:137–138.

Peterson, J. F. 1990. Precolumbian flora and fauna, continuity of plant and animal themes in Mesoamerican art. Mengei International Museum of World Folk Art, San Diego. 148 pp.

Picado, T. C. 1931. Serpientes venenosas de Costa Rica: Seroterapía anti-ofídica. Sauter, Arias, San José, Costa Rica. 219 pp.

Platt, S. 1992. Morelet's crocodile studies. IUCN Crocodile Specialist Group Newsl. 11:7.

Platt, S. 1993. *Rhinoclemmys areolata* (furrowed wood turtle): Diet. Herpetol. Rev. 24:32.

Platz, J. E. 1991. *Rana berlandieri.* Cat. Am. Amphib. Reptiles 508.1–508.4.

Pohl, M. D. 1983. Maya ritual faunas: Vertebrate remains from burials, caches, caves, and cenotes in the Maya lowlands. *In*: R. M. Leventhal and A. L. Kolata (eds.), Civilization in the ancient Americas, essays in honor of Gordon R. Willey, pp. 55–103. University of New Mexico Press, Las Cruces. xiv + 487 pp.

Pohl, M. D. 1985. The privileges of Maya elites: Prehistoric vertebrate fauna from Seibal. *In*: M. Pohl (ed.), Prehistoric lowland Maya environment and subsistence economy, pp. 133–145. Pap. Peabody Mus. Archaeol. Ethnol. Harv. Univ. 77. x + 209 pp.

Pohl, M. D. 1990. The ethnozoology of the Maya: Faunal remains from five sites in Petén, Guatemala. *In*: G. R. Willey (ed.), Excavations at Seibal, pp. 141–174. Mem. Peabody Mus. Archaeol. Ethnol. 17, nos. 1–4.

Polisar, J. 1992. Reproductive biology and exploitation of the Central American river turtle *Dermatemys mawii* in Belize. M.S. thesis, University of Florida. xiv + 179 pp.

Pollock, H. E. D., and C. E. Ray. 1957. Notes on vertebrate animal remains from Mayapán. Carnegie Inst. Rep. 41:633–656. Department of Archaeology, Carnegie Institute, Washington, D.C.

Pooley, A. C., T. Hines, and J. Shield. Attacks on humans. *In*: C. A. Ross and S. Garnett (eds.), Crocodiles and alligators, pp. 172–187. Facts on File, New York. 240 pp.

Porras, L., J. R. McCranie, and L. D. Wilson. 1981. The systematics and distribution of the hognose viper *Bothrops nasuta* Bocourt (Serpentes: Viperidae). Tulane Stud. Zool. 22:85–107.

Porter, K. R. 1962. Mating calls and noteworthy collections of some Mexican amphibians. Herpetologica 18:165–171.

Porter, K. R. 1970. *Bufo valliceps.* Cat. Am. Amphib. Reptiles 94.1–94.4.

Pough, F. H. 1973. Lizard energetics and diet. Ecology 54:837–844.

Powell, J. H., Jr. 1965. The status of *Crocodylus moreleti* in Yucatán. IUCN Bull., n.s., 16:6.

Presch, W. 1983. The lizard family Teiidae: Is it a monophyletic group? Zool. J. Linn. Soc. 77:189–197.

Price, A. H. 1992. Comparative behavior in lizards of the genus *Cnemidophorus* (Teiidae), with comments on the evolution of parthenogenesis in reptiles. Copeia 1992:323–331.

Price, R. M. 1991. *Senticolis.* Cat. Am. Amphib. Reptiles 525.1–525.4.

Pritchard, P. C. H. 1971. The leatherback or leathery turtle *Dermochelys coriacea.* IUCN Monogr. 1:1–39.

Pritchard, P. C. H. 1976. Living turtles of the world. T. F. H. Publishing, Jersey City, N.J. 288 pp.

Pritchard, P. C. H. 1979. Encyclopedia of turtles. T. F. H. Publishing, Neptune, N.J. 895 pp.

Pritchard, P. C. H., and R. Márquez. 1973. Kemp's ridley turtle or Atlantic ridley (*Lepidochelys kempi*). IUCN Monogr. 2, Marine Turtle Ser. 30 pp.

Proskouriakoff, T. 1974. Comments (on Dobkin de Rios, 1974). Curr. Anthropol. 15(2):159.

Pyburn, W. F. 1964. Breeding behavior of the leaf-frog, *Phyllomedusa callidryas,* in southern Veracruz. Yearb. Am. Phil. Soc. 1964:291–294.

Pyburn, W. F. 1966. Breeding activity, larvae and relationship of the treefrog *Hyla phaeota cyanosticta.* Southwest. Nat. 11:1–18.

Pyburn, W. F. 1967. Breeding and larval development of the hylid frog *Phrynohyas spilomma* in southern Veracruz, Mexico. Herpetologica 23:184–194.

Pyburn, W. F. 1970. Breeding behavior of the leaf-frogs *Phyllomedusa callidryas* and *Phyllomedusa dacnicolor* in Mexico. Copeia 1970:209–218.

Rand, A. S. 1968. A nesting aggregation of iguanas. Copeia 1968:552–561.

Rand, A. S. 1983. *Physalaemus pustulosus. In*: D. H. Janzen (ed.), Costa Rican natural history, pp. 412–415. University of Chicago Press, Chicago.

Rand, A. S. 1984. Clutch size in *Iguana iguana* in central Panama. *In*: R. A. Seigel, L. E. Hunt, J. L. Knight, L. Malaret, and N. L. Zuschlag (eds.), Vertebrate ecology and systematics—a tribute to Henry S. Fitch, pp. 115–122. Univ. Kansas Mus. Nat. Hist. Allen Press, Lawrence.

Rand, A. S., and E. P. Ortleb. 1969. Defensive display in the colubrid snake *Pseustes poecilonotus shropshirei.* Herpetologica 25:46–48.

Rand, A. S., and M. J. Ryan. 1981. The adaptive significance of a complex vocal repertoire in a Neotropical frog. Z. Tierpsychol. 57:209–214.

Ream, C. H. 1964. Notes on the behavior and egg laying of *Corythophanes cristatus.* Herpetologica 20:239–242.

Rebel, T. P. 1974. Sea turtles and the turtle industry of the West Indies, Florida, and the Gulf of Mexico. Rev. ed. University of Miami Press, Coral Gables. 250 pp.

Rech, R. H., and K. E. Moore. 1971. An introduction to psychopharmacology. Raven Press, New York. xii + 353 pp.

Recinos, A. 1953. The annals of the Cakchequels and title of the lords of Totonicapan. University of Oklahoma Press, Norman. ix + 217 pp.

Redfield, R., and A. V. Rojas. 1971. Chan Kom: A Maya village. University of Chicago Press, Chicago. x + 236 pp.

Rhodin, A. G., and H. M. Smith. 1982. The original authorship of *Dermochelys coriacea*. J. Herpetol. 16:316–317.

Richardson, T. H., J. I. Richardson, and M. Donnelly (comps.). 1990. Proceedings of the Tenth Annual Workshop on Sea Turtle Biology and Conservation. NOAA Technical Memorandum NMFS-SEFC-278. National Oceanic and Atmospheric Administration, Washington, D.C. 286 pp.

Roberts, W. E. 1994. Explosive breeding aggregations and parachuting in a Neotropical frog, *Agalychnis saltator*. J. Herpetol. 28:193–199.

Robicsek, F., and D. M. Hales. 1982. Maya ceramic vases from the classic period. Delmar Printing Company, Charlotte, N.C. xv + 63 pp.

Rokosky, E. J. 1941. Notes on new-born jumping vipers, *Bothrops nummifera*. Copeia 1941:267.

Rosado Vega, L. 1957. El alma misteriosa del Mayab. 2nd ed. Ediciones Botas, Mexico City. 258 pp.

Ross, C. A. 1987. *Crocodylus moreletii*. Cat. Am. Amphib. Reptiles 407.1–407.3.

Ross, C. A., and W. E. Magnusson. 1989. Living crocodilians. *In*: C. A. Ross and S. Garnet (eds.), Crocodiles and alligators, pp. 58–73. Facts on File, New York. 240 pp.

Ross, C. A., and F. D. Ross. 1974. Caudal scalation of Central American *Crocodylus*. Proc. Biol. Soc. Wash. 87(21):231–234.

Ross, C. A., and F. D. Ross. 1987. Identity of *Crocodylus mexicanus* Bocourt, 1869 (Reptilia: Crocodylidae). Proc. Biol. Soc. Wash. 100:713–716.

Ross, F. D., and G. C. Mayer. 1983. On the dorsal armor of the Crocodilia. *In*: A. G. Rhodin and K. Miyata (eds.), Advances in herpetology and evolutionary biology—essays in honor of Ernest E. Williams, pp. 305–331. Harvard University Press, Cambridge.

Ross, J. P. 1982. Historical decline of loggerhead, ridley, and leatherback sea turtles. *In*: K. Bjorndal (ed.), Biology and conservation of sea turtles, pp. 189–195. Smithsonian Institution Press, Washington, D.C.

Ross, J. P., S. Beavers, D. Mundell, and M. S. Amoss. 1989. The status of Kemp's ridley. Center for Marine Conservation, Washington, D.C.

Rossman, D. A. 1962. *Thamnophis proximus* (Say), a valid species of garter snake. Copeia 1962:741–748.

Rossman, D. A. 1963. The colubrid snake genus *Thamnophis*: A revision of the *Sauritus* group. Bull. Fla. State Mus. 7:99–178.

Rossman, D. A. 1970. *Thamnophis proximus*. Cat. Am. Amphib. Reptiles 98.1–98.3.

Rossman, D. A. 1971. Systematics of the Neotropical populations of *Thamnophis marcianus* (Serpentes: Colubridae). Occas. Pap. Mus. Zool. La. State Univ. 41:1–13.

Rossman, D. A., and W. G. Eberle. 1977. Partition of the genus *Natrix*, with preliminary observations on evolutionary trends in natricine snakes. Herpetologica 33:34–43.

Rossman, D. A., and G. C. Schaefer. 1974. Generic status of *Opheodrys mayae*, a colubrid snake endemic to the Yucatán Peninsula. Occas. Pap. Mus. Zool. La. State Univ. 45:1–12.

Rostand, J. 1962. The substance of man. Doubleday, Garden City, N.Y. 298 pp.

Roys, R. L. 1931. The ethno-botany of the Maya. Middle American Research Series, no. 2. xxiv + 359 pp.

Roze, J. 1967. A checklist of the New World venomous coral snakes (Elapidae), with descriptions of new forms. Am. Mus. Novit. 2287:1–60.

Roze, J. 1982. New World coral snakes (Elapidae): A taxonomic and biological summary. Mem. Inst. Butantan (São Paulo) 46:305–338.

Ruibal, R. 1952. Revisionary studies of some South American Teiidae. Bull. Mus. Comp. Zool. 106:477–529.

Ruibal, R. 1964. An annotated checklist and key to the anoline lizards of Cuba. Bull. Mus. Comp. Zool. Harv. Univ. 130:473–520.

Ruibal, R., and E. E. Williams. 1961. Two sympatric Cuban anoles of the *carolinensis* group. Bull. Mus. Comp. Zool. 125:183–208.

Ruiz-Carranza, P. M., and J. D. Lynch. 1991. Ranas Centrolenidae de Colombia. I. Propuesta de una nueva clasificación genérica. Lozania 57:1–30.

Rüppell, E. 1845. Verzeichniss der in dem Museum der Senckenbergischen Gesellschaft aufgestellten Sammlung. Amphibien. Mus. Senckenb. 3:293–316.

Ruthven, A. G. 1912. The amphibians and reptiles collected by the University of Michigan–Walker expeditions in southern Vera Cruz, Mexico. Zool. Jahrb. Abt. Allg. Zool. 32:295–332.

Ryan, M. J. 1985. The Tungara frog, a study in sexual selection and communication. University of Chicago Press, Chicago. xv + 230 pp.

Saenz, D. 1993. Dietary overview of *Hemidactylus turcicus* with possible implications of food partitioning. Paper presented at the joint annual meeting of the American Society of Ichthyologists and Herpetologists and the Herpetologists' League, University of Texas, Austin, 27 May–2 June 1993.

Sanders, O. 1973. A new leopard frog (*Rana berlandieri brownorum*) from southern Mexico. J. Herpetol. 7:87–92.

Sanderson, I. T. 1941. Living treasure. Viking Press, New York. 290 pp.

Saul, F. P. 1972. The human skeletal remains of Altar de Sacrificios, an osteobiographic analysis. Pap. Peabody Mus. Archaeol. Ethnol. Harv. Univ. 63, no. 2. ix + 123 pp.

Savage, J. M. 1963. Studies on the lizard family Xantusiidae. IV. The genera. Los Ang. Cty. Mus. Contrib. Sci. 71:1–38.

Savage, J. M. 1973. A preliminary handlist of the herpetofauna of Costa Rica. University Graphics, Los Angeles. 17 pp.

Savage, J. M. 1975. Systematics and distribution of the Mexican and Central American stream frogs related to *Eleutherodactylus rugulosus*. Copeia 1975:254–306.

Savage, J. M. 1987. Systematics and distribution of the Mexican and Central American rainfrogs of the *Eleutherodactylus gollmeri* group (Amphibia: Leptodactylidae). Fieldiana Zool., n.s., 33:1–57.

Savage, J. M., and B. I. Crother. 1989. The status of *Plio-*

cercus and *Urotheca* (Serpentes: Colubridae), with a review of included species of coral snake mimics. Zool. J. Linn. Soc. 95:335–362.

Savage, J. M., and R. W. Heyer. 1967. Variation and distribution in the tree-frog genus *Phyllomedusa* in Costa Rica, Central America. Beitr. Neotrop. Fauna 5:111–131.

Savage, J. M., and R. W. Heyer. 1969. The tree-frogs (family Hylidae) of Costa Rica: Diagnosis and distribution. Rev. Biol. Trop. 16:1–127.

Savage, J. M., and P. N. Lahanas. 1991. On the species of the colubrid snake genus *Ninia* in Costa Rica and western Panama. Herpetologica 47:37–53.

Savage, J. M., and N. J. Scott. 1987. The *Imantodes* (Serpentes: Colubridae) of Costa Rica: Two or three species? Rev. Biol. Trop. 33:107–132.

Savage, J. M., and J. L. Vial. 1974. The venomous coral snakes (genus *Micrurus*) of Costa Rica. Rev. Biol. Trop. 21:295–349.

Savage, J. M., and J. Villa. 1986. Herpetofauna of Costa Rica. Contributions to Herpetology 3. Society for the Study of Amphibians and Reptiles, Oxford, Ohio. viii + 207 pp.

Savage, J. M., and M. H. Wake. 1972. Geographic variation and systematics of the Middle American caecilians, genera *Dermophis* and *Gymnopis*. Copeia 1972:680–695.

Savitzky, A. H. 1981. Hinged teeth in snakes: An adaptation for swallowing hard-bodied prey. Science 212:346–349.

Sawyer-Lauçanno, C. 1987. The destruction of the jaguar. Poems from the books of Chilam Balam. City Lights Books, San Francisco. vi + 59 pp.

Say, T. 1823. *In*: E. James, Account of an expedition from Pittsburgh to the Rocky Mountains, performed in the years 1819, 1820, vol. 1. Longman, Hurst, Rees, Ovme, and Brown, London. 344 pp. [Reference taken from Cat. Am. Amphib. Reptiles.]

Schätti, B., and L. D. Wilson. 1986. *Coluber*. Cat. Am. Amphib. Reptiles 399.1–399.4.

Schele, L., and D. Freidel. 1990. A forest of kings. William Morrow, New York. 542 pp.

Schele, L., and M. E. Miller. 1986. The blood of kings. George Braziller, New York. xii + 335 pp.

Schlegel, H. 1837. Essai sur la physionomie des serpens. Amsterdam. Vol. 2. 606 pp.

Schmidt, K. P. 1924. Notes on Central American crocodiles. Field Mus. Nat. Hist. Publ. Zool. Ser. 12:79–92.

Schmidt, K. P. 1932. Stomach contents of some American coral snakes, with description of a new species of *Geophis*. Copeia 1932:6–9.

Schmidt, K. P. 1933. New reptiles and amphibians from Honduras. Field Mus. Nat. Hist. Publ. Zool. Ser. 20:15–22.

Schmidt, K. P. 1936. Guatemalan salamanders of the genus *Oedipus*. Field Mus. Nat. Hist. Publ. Zool. Ser. 20:135–166.

Schmidt, K. P. 1941. The amphibians and reptiles of British Honduras. Field Mus. Nat. Hist. Publ. Zool. Ser. 22:475–510.

Schmidt, K. P. 1953. A check list of North American amphibians and reptiles. 6th ed. American Society of Ichthyologists and Herpetologists, Chicago. viii + 280 pp.

Schmidt, K. P. 1955. Herpetology. *In*: A century of progress in the natural sciences 1853–1953. California Academy of Sciences, San Francisco. x + 807 pp.

Schmidt, K. P., and E. W. Andrews. 1936. Notes on snakes from Yucatán. Field Mus. Nat. Hist. Publ. Zool. Ser. 20:167–187.

Schmidt, K. P., and A. S. Rand. 1957. Geographic variation in the Central American colubrine snake *Ninia sebae*. Fieldiana Zool. 39:73–84.

Schmidt, K. P., and H. M. Smith. 1943. Notes on coral snakes from Mexico. Field Mus. Nat. Hist. Publ. Zool. Ser. 29:25–31.

Schoepf, J. D. 1792–1801. Historia Testudinum Iconibus Illustrata. J. J. Palm, Erlangen. xii + 136 pp.

Scholes, F. V., and R. L. Roys. 1968. The Chontal Indians of Acalan-Tixchel. University of Oklahoma Press, Norman. xii + 565 pp.

Schultes, R. E., and A. Hoffman. 1973. The botany and chemistry of hallucinogens. Charles C. Thomas, Springfield, Ill.

Schwartz, A., and R. W. Henderson. 1991. Amphibians and reptiles of the West Indies. University Presses of Florida, Gainesville. xvi + 720 pp.

Schwartz, A., and R. Thomas. 1975. A checklist of West Indian amphibians and reptiles. Carnegie Mus. Nat. Hist. Spec. Publ. 1. 216 pp.

Schwartz, J. J. 1986. Male calling behavior and female choice in the Neotropical treefrog *Hyla microcephala*. Ethology 73:116–127.

Schwartz, J. J., and K. D. Wells. 1984. Interspecific acoustic interactions of the Neotropical treefrog *Hyla ebraccata*. Behav. Ecol. Sociobiol. 14:211–224.

Schwartz, J. J., and K. D. Wells. 1985. Intra- and interspecific vocal behavior of the Neotropical treefrog *Hyla microcephala*. Copeia 1985:27–38.

Sclater, P. L. 1871. Notes on rare or little-known animals now or lately living in the society's gardens. Proc. Zool. Soc. Lond. 1871:743–749.

Scott, N. J., Jr. 1969. A zoogeographic analysis of the snakes of Costa Rica. Ph.D. dissertation, University of Southern California. xiv + 390 pp.

Scott, N. J., Jr. 1976. Abundance and diversity of the herpetofauna of tropical forest litter. Biotropica 8:41–58.

Scott, N. J. 1983a. *Clelia clelia*. *In*: D. H. Janzen (ed.), Costa Rican natural history, p. 392. University of Chicago Press, Chicago. xi + 816 pp.

Scott, N. J. 1983b. *Leptotyphlops goudotii*. *In*: D. H. Janzen (ed.), Costa Rican natural history, p. 406. University of Chicago Press, Chicago. xi + 816 pp.

Scott, N. J. 1983c. *Rhadinaea decorata*. *In*: D. H. Janzen (ed.), Costa Rican natural history, p. 416. University of Chicago Press, Chicago.

Seba, A. 1734–1765. Locupletissimi rerum naturalium thesauri accurata descriptio et iconibus artificiossimis expressio, per universam physices historiam. Amsterdam.

Seib, R. L. 1980. Human envenomation from the bite of an

aglyphous false coral snake, *Pliocercus elapoides* (Serpentes: Colubridae). Toxicon 18:399–401.

Seib, R. L. 1984. Prey use in three syntopic Neotropical racers. J. Herpetol. 18:412–420.

Seib, R. L. 1985a. Feeding ecology and organization of Neotropical snake faunas. Ph.D. dissertation, University of California, Berkeley. 229 pp.

Seib, R. L. 1985b. Europhagy in a tropical snake, *Coniophanes fissidens*. Biotropica 17:57–64.

Seibert, E. A., H. B. Lillywhite, and R. Wassersug. 1974. Cranial coossification in frogs: Relationship to rate of evaporative water loss. Physiol. Zool. 47:261–265.

Seidel, M. E., and H. M. Smith. 1986. *Chrysemys, Pseudemys, Trachemys* (Testudines: Emydidae): Did Agassiz have it right? Herpetologica 42:242–248.

Seifert, R. P. 1983. *Bothrops schlegelii*. *In*: D. H. Janzen (ed.), Costa Rican natural history, pp. 384–385. University of Chicago Press, Chicago.

Sexton, O. J., and K. M. Brown. 1977. The reproductive cycle of an iguanid lizard, *Anolis sagrei*, from Belize. J. Nat. Hist. 11:241–250.

Sexton, O. J., and H. Heatwole. 1965. Life history notes on some Panamanian snakes. Caribb. J. Sci. 5:39–43.

Shannon, F. A. 1951. Notes on a herpetological collection from Oaxaca and other localities in Mexico. Proc. U.S. Natl. Mus. 101:465–484.

Shannon, F. A., and F. L. Humphrey. 1963. Remarks on *Leptodeira* and *Pseudoleptodeira* from the west coast of Mexico. Herpetologica 19:262–269.

Shattuck, G. C., et al. 1933. The peninsula of Yucatán; medical, biological, meteorological and sociological studies. Carnegie Institute, Washington, D.C. xvii + 576 pp.

Shine, R. 1985. The evolution of viviparity in reptiles: An ecological analysis. *In*: C. Gans and F. Billet (eds.), Biology of the Reptilia, vol. 15, pp. 605–694. Academic Press, New York.

Shreve, B. 1957. Reptiles and amphibians from the selva Lacandona. *In*: R. A. Paynter (ed.), Biological investigations in the selva Lacandona, Chiapas, Mexico. Bull. Mus. Comp. Zool. 116:193–298.

Sites, J. W., Jr., J. W. Archie, C. J. Cole, and O. Flores Villela. 1992. A review of phylogentic hypotheses for lizards of the genus *Sceloporus* (Phrynosomatidae): Implications for ecological and evolutionary studies. Bull. Am. Mus. Nat. Hist. 213:1–110.

Sites, J. W., Jr., J. L. Camarillo, A. Gonzales, F. Mendoza, L. Javier, M. Mancilla, and G. Lara-Gongora. 1988. Allozyme variation and genetic divergence within and between three chromosome races of the *Sceloporus grammicus* complex (Sauria, Iguanidae) in central Mexico. Herpetologica 44:297–307.

Sites, J. W., Jr., and S. K. Davis. 1989. Phylogenetic relationships and variability within and among six chromosome races of *Sceloporus grammicus* (Iguanidae) based on nuclear and mitochondrial markers. Evolution 43:296–317.

Sites, J. W., Jr., and J. R. Dixon. 1982. Geographic variation in *Sceloporus variabilis* and its relationship to *S. teapensis* (Sauria: Iguanidae). Copeia 1982:12–27.

Slevin, J. R. 1942. Notes on a collection of reptiles and amphibians from Guatemala. II. Lizards. Proc. Calif. Acad. Sci. (4)23(31):453–462.

Smith, A. G. 1946. Notes on the secondary sex characters of *Thamnophis ruthveni*. Copeia 1946:106.

Smith, H. M. 1938. Notes on reptiles and amphibians from Yucatán and Campeche, Mexico. Occas. Pap. Mus. Zool. Univ. Mich. 388:1–22.

Smith, H. M. 1939a. Notes on Mexican reptiles and amphibians. Field Mus. Nat. Hist. Publ. Zool. Ser. 24:15–35.

Smith, H. M. 1939b. The Mexican and Central American lizards of the genus *Sceloporus*. Field Mus. Nat. Hist. Publ. Zool. Ser. 26:1–397.

Smith, H. M. 1940. Descriptions of new lizards and snakes from Mexico and Guatemala. Proc. Biol. Soc. Wash. 53:55–64.

Smith, H. M. 1941a. Notes on Mexican snakes of the genus *Trimeresurus*. Zoologica 26:61–64.

Smith, H. M. 1941b. A new name for the Mexican snakes of the genus *Dendrophidion*. Proc. Biol. Soc. Wash. 54:73–76.

Smith, H. M. 1941c. A new genus of Central American snakes related to *Tantilla*. J. Wash. Acad. Sci. 31:115–117.

Smith, H. M. 1941d. A review of the subspecies of the indigo snake (*Drymarchon corais*). J. Wash. Acad. Sci. 31:466–481.

Smith, H. M. 1941e. Snakes, frogs and bromelias. Chic. Nat. 4:35–43.

Smith, H. M. 1942a. A résumé of Mexican snakes of the genus *Tantilla*. Zoologica 27:33–42.

Smith, H. M. 1942b. A review of the snake genus *Adelphicos*. Proc. Rochester Acad. Sci. 8:175–195.

Smith, H. M. 1942c. Mexican herpetology miscellany. Proc. U.S. Natl. Mus. 92:349–395.

Smith, H. M. 1943. Summary of the collections of snakes and crocodilians made in Mexico under the Walter Rathbone Bacon Traveling Scholarship. Proc. U.S. Natl. Mus. 93:393–504.

Smith, H. M. 1946. Handbook of lizards. Comstock Publishing Associates, Ithaca. Reprinted 1995, Comstock Classic Handbooks, Cornell University Press, Ithaca. xxi + 557 pp.

Smith, H. M. 1949. Miscellaneous notes on Mexican lizards. J. Wash. Acad. Sci. 39:34–43.

Smith, H. M. 1951. The identity of *Hyla underwoodi* Auctorum of Mexico. Herpetologica 7:184–190.

Smith, H. M. 1953. A new subspecies of the treefrog *Hyla phaeota* Cope of Central America. Herpetologica 8:150–152.

Smith, H. M. 1959. Herpetozoa from Guatemala I. Herpetologica 15:210–216.

Smith, H. M. 1963. *Dryadophis* Stuart, 1939 (Reptilia, Serpentes): Proposed validation under the plenary powers. Bull. Zool. Nomencl. 20:230.

Smith, H. M. 1968. A new pentaprionid anole (Reptila: Lacertilia) from Pacific slopes of Mexico. Trans. Kans. Acad. Sci. 71:195–200.

Smith, H. M. 1969. The first herpetology of Mexico. Southwest. Herpetol. Soc. 3:1–16.

Smith, H. M. 1971. The snake genus *Amastridium* in Oaxaca, Mexico. Great Basin Nat. 31:254–255.

Smith, H. M. 1987. Current nomenclature for the names and material cited in Günther's Reptilia and Batrachia volume of the *Biologia Centrali-Americana. In*: Introduction to *The Biologia Centrali-Americana, Reptilia and Batrachia*. Facsimile reprint by the Society for the Study of Amphibians and Reptiles, Oxford, Ohio, pp. xxiii-l.

Smith, H. M., and W. L. Burger. 1949. A new subspecies of *Anolis sagrei* from the Atlantic coast of tropical America. An. Inst. Biol. Univ. Mex. 20:407–410.

Smith, H. M., O. Flores Viella, and D. Chiszar. 1993. The generic allocation of *Tantilla canula* (Reptilia: Serpentes). Bull. Md. Herpetol. Soc. 29:126–129.

Smith, H. M., and T. H. Fritts. 1969. Cannibalism in the lizard *Sceloporus chrysostictus*. J. Herpetol. 3(3–4):182–83.

Smith, H. M., and C. Grant. 1958. New and noteworthy snakes from Panama. Herpetologica 14:207–215.

Smith, H. M., and H. W. Kerster. 1955. New and noteworthy Mexican lizards of the genus *Anolis*. Herpetologica 11:193–201.

Smith, H. M., and K. R. Larson. 1974. The nominal snake genera *Mastigodryas* Amaral, 1934, and *Dryadophis* Stuart, 1939. Great Basin Nat. 33:276.

Smith, H. M., and G. Pérez-Higareda. 1986. The proper name for the southern Atlantic coast subspecies in Mexico of the lagartijera, *Dryadophis* (Reptilia: Serpentes). Bull. Md. Herpetol. Soc. 22:51–55.

Smith, H. M., and G. Pérez-Higareda. 1989. The distribution of the snake *Clelia scytalina* in Mexico. Bull. Chic. Herpetol. Soc. 24:8.

Smith, H. M., G. Pérez-Higareda, and D. Chiszar. 1993. A review of the members of the *Sceloporus variabilis* lizard complex. Bull. Md. Herpetol. Soc. 29:85–125.

Smith, H. M., and R. B. Smith. 1971. Synopsis of the herpetofauna of Mexico. Vol. 1: Analysis of the literature of the Mexican axolotl. Eric Lundberg, Augusta, W.V.

Smith, H. M., and R. B. Smith. 1973. Synopsis of the herpetofauna of Mexico. Vol. 2: Analysis of the literature exclusive of the Mexican axolotl. John Johnson, North Bennington, Vt.

Smith, H. M., and R. B. Smith. 1976a. Synopsis of the herpetofauna of Mexico. Vol. 3: Source analysis and index for Mexican reptiles. John Johnson, North Bennington, Vt.

Smith, H. M., and R. B. Smith. 1976b. Synopsis of the herpetofauna of Mexico. Vol. 4: Source analysis and index for Mexican amphibians. John Johnson, North Bennington, Vt.

Smith, H. M., and R. B. Smith. 1977. Synopsis of the herpetofauna of Mexico. Vol. 5: Guide to Mexican amphisbaenians and crocodilians. Bibliographic addendum 2. John Johnson, North Bennington, Vt.

Smith, H. M., and R. B. Smith. 1979. Synopsis of the herpetofauna of Mexico. Vol. 6: Guide to Mexican turtles. Bibliographic addendum 3. John Johnson, North Bennington, Vt.

Smith, H. M., and E. H. Taylor. 1945. An annotated checklist and key to the snakes of Mexico. Bull. U.S. Natl. Mus., no. 187. iv + 239 pp.

Smith, H. M., and E. H. Taylor. 1948. An annotated checklist and key to the Amphibia of Mexico. Bull. U.S. Natl. Mus., no. 194. iv + 118 pp.

Smith, H. M., and E. H. Taylor. 1950a. An annotated checklist and key to the reptiles of Mexico exclusive of the snakes. Bull. U.S. Natl. Mus., no. 199. v + 255 pp.

Smith, H. M., and E. H. Taylor. 1950b. Type localities of Mexican reptiles and amphibians. Univ. Kans. Sci. Bull. 33(8):313–380.

Smith, H. M., and E. H. Taylor. 1966. Herpetology of Mexico. Annotated checklists and keys to the amphibians and reptiles. A reprint of bulletins 187, 194, and 199 of the U.S. National Museum, with a list of subsequent taxonomic innovations. Eric Lundberg, Ashton, Md.

Smith, R. E. 1968. Studies on reproduction in Costa Rican *Ameiva festiva* and *Ameiva quadrilineata* (Sauria: Teiidae). Copeia 1968:236–239.

Solórzano, A. 1963. Prospección acerca de las tortugas marinas de México. Trab. Div., Inst. Nac. Invest. Biol.-Pesq. 6:1–12.

Solórzano, A., and L. Cerdas. 1987. *Drymobius margaritiferus* (speckled racer): Reproduction. Herpetol. Rev. 18:75–76.

Solórzano, A., and L. Cerdas. 1989. Reproductive biology and distribution of the terciopelo, *Bothrops asper* Garmen (Serpentes: Viperidae) in Costa Rica. Herpetologica 1989:444–450.

Spinden, H. J. 1913. A study of Maya art. Mem. Peabody Mus. Archaeol. Ethnol. 6. xxvi + 285 pp.

Spix, J. B. 1824. Serpentum Brasiliensium species novae, ou histoire naturelle des espèces nouvelles de serpens, recueillies et observées pendant le voyage dans l'intérieur du Brésil dans les années 1817, 1818, 1819, 1820. Publiée par Jean de Spix. Écrite d'après les notes du voyageur par Jean Wagler. Munich. 75 pp.

Stafford, P. J. 1991. Amphibians and reptiles of the joint services scientific expedition to the upper Raspaculo, Belize, 1991. Br. Herpetol. Soc. Bull. 38:10–17.

Stafford, P. J. 1994. *Gymnopis syntrema* (Cope); an addition to the herpetofauna of Belize. Caribb. J. Sci. 30:277–278.

Starrett, P. H. 1960. Descriptions of tadpoles of Middle American frogs. Misc. Publ. Mus. Zool. Univ. Mich., no. 110. 37 pp.

Starrett, P. H., and J. M. Savage. 1973. The systematic status and distribution of Costa Rican glass-frogs, genus *Centrolenella* (family Centrolenidae), with description of a new species. Bull. South. Calif. Acad. Sci. 72:57–78.

Stejneger, L. 1907. Herpetology of Japan and adjacent territory. Bull. U.S. Natl. Mus., no. 58. 577 pp.

Strauch, A. 1890. Bemerkungen über die Schildkrötensammlung in zoologischen Museum der kaiserlichen Akademie der Wissenschaften zu St. Petersburg. Mem. Acad. Imp. Sci. St. Petersb. 38:1–127.

Stuart, L. C. 1934. A contribution to a knowledge of the

herpetological fauna of El Petén, Guatemala. Occas. Pap. Mus. Zool. Univ. Mich. 292:1–18.

Stuart, L. C. 1935. A contribution to a knowledge of the herpetofauna of a portion of the savanna region of central Petén, Guatemala. Misc. Publ. Mus. Zool. Univ. Mich., no. 29. 56 pp.

Stuart, L. C. 1937. Some further notes on the amphibians and reptiles of the Petén forest of northern Guatemala. Copeia 1937:67–70.

Stuart, L. C. 1940. Notes on the "Lampropholus" group of Middle American *Lygosoma* (Scincidae) with descriptions of two new forms. Occas. Pap. Mus. Zool. Univ. Mich. 421:1–16.

Stuart, L. C. 1941a. Some new snakes from Guatemala. Occas. Pap. Mus. Zool. Univ. Mich. 452:1–7.

Stuart, L. C. 1941b. Studies of Neotropical Colubridae. VIII. A revision of the genus *Dryadophis* Stuart, 1939. Misc. Publ. Mus. Zool. Univ. Mich., no. 49. 106 pp.

Stuart, L. C. 1942. Comments on the *undulata* group of *Ameiva* (Sauria). Proc. Biol. Soc. Wash. 55:143–150.

Stuart, L. C. 1943a. Taxonomic and geographic comments on Guatemalan salamanders of the genus *Oedipus*. Misc. Publ. Mus. Zool. Univ. Mich., no. 56. 33 pp.

Stuart, L. C. 1943b. Comments on the herpetofauna of the Sierra de los Cuchumatanes of Guatemala. Occas. Pap. Mus. Zool. Univ. Mich. 471:1–28.

Stuart, L. C. 1948. The amphibians and reptiles of Alta Verapaz Guatemala. Misc. Publ. Mus. Zool. Univ. Mich., no. 69. 109 pp.

Stuart, L. C. 1955. A brief review of the Guatemalan lizards of the genus *Anolis*. Misc. Publ. Mus. Zool. Univ. Mich., no. 91. 31 pp.

Stuart, L. C. 1958. A study of the herpetofauna of the Uaxactun-Tikal area of northern El Petén, Guatemala. Contrib. Lab. Vertebr. Biol. Univ. Mich. 75:1–30.

Stuart, L. C. 1961. Some observations on the natural history of tadpoles of *Rhinophrynus dorsalis* Duméril and Bibron. Herpetologica 17:73–79.

Stuart, L. C. 1963. A checklist of the herpetofauna of Guatemala. Misc. Publ. Mus. Zool. Univ. Mich., no. 122. 150 pp.

Stuart, L. C. 1970. A brief review of the races of *Sceloporus serrifer* Cope with special reference to *Sceloporus serrifer prezygus* Smith. Herpetologica 26:141–149.

Swanson, P. L. 1945. Herpetological notes from Panama. Copeia 1945:210–216.

Taylor, E. H. 1935. A taxonomic study of the cosmopolitan scincoid lizards of the genus *Eumeces* with an account of the distribution and relationships of its species. Univ. Kans. Sci. Bull. 36(14):1–643.

Taylor, E. H. 1939. On North American snakes of the genus *Leptotyphlops*. Copeia 1939:1–7.

Taylor, E. H. 1949. A preliminary account of the herpetology of the state of San Luis Potosí, Mexico. Univ. Kans. Sci. Bull. 33:169–215.

Taylor, E. H. 1956. A review of the lizards of Costa Rica. Univ. Kans. Sci. Bull. 38(1):1–322.

Taylor, E. H. 1968. The caecilians of the world. University of Kansas Press, Lawrence. viii + 848 pp.

Taylor, E. H. 1969. Wiegmann and the herpetology of

Mexico. Introduction to A. F. A. Wiegman, *Herpetologia Mexicana*. Facsimile reprint no. 23, by the Society for the Study of Amphibians and Reptiles, Oxford, Ohio, pp. iii-vi.

Taylor, E. H., and H. M. Smith. 1943. A review of American sibynophine snakes, with a proposal of a new genus. Univ. Kans. Sci. Bull. 29(2):301–336.

Taylor, E. H., and H. M. Smith. 1945. Summary of the collections of amphibians made in Mexico under the Walter Rathbone Bacon Traveling Scholarship. Proc. U.S. Natl. Mus. 95:521–613.

Taylor, H. L., and C. R. Cooley. 1995. A multivariate analysis of morphological variation among parthenogenetic teiid lizards of the *Cnemidophorus cozumela* complex. Herpetologica 5:67–76.

Tedlock, D. 1985. Popol Vuh. Simon and Schuster, New York. 380 pp.

Telford, S. R., Jr. 1971. Reproductive patterns and relative abundance of two microteiid lizard species in Panama. Copeia 1971:670–675.

Telford, S. R., Jr., and H. W. Campbell. 1970. Ecological observations on an all female population of the lizard *Lepidophyma flavimaculatum* (Xantusiidae) in Panama. Copeia 1970:379–381.

Test, F. H., O. J. Sexton, and H. Heatwole. 1966. Reptiles of Rancho Grande and vicinity, Estado Aragua, Venezuela. Misc. Publ. Mus. Zool. Univ. Mich., no. 128. 63 pp.

Thomas, R. 1975. The *argus* group of West Indian *Sphaerodactylus* (Sauria: Gekkonidae). Herpetologica 31:177–195.

Thomas, R. 1976. Systematics of Antillean snakes of the genus *Typhlops* (Serpentes: Typhlopidae). Ph.D. dissertation, Louisiana State University, Baton Rouge. 288 pp.

Thompson, J. E. S. 1930. Ethnology of the Mayas of southern and central British Honduras. Field Mus. Nat. Hist. Anthropol. Ser. 17:31–213.

Thompson, J. E. S. (ed.). 1958. Thomas Gage's travels in the New World. University of Oklahoma Press, Norman. li + 379 pp.

Thompson, J. E. S. 1963. Maya archeologist. University of Oklahoma Press, Norman. xvii + 284 pp.

Thompson, J. E. S. 1970. Maya history and religion. University of Oklahoma Press, Norman. xxxii + 415 pp.

Thompson, J. E. S. 1972. A commentary on the Dresden Codex, a Maya hieroglyphic book. American Philosophical Society, Philadelphia. 156 pp.

Thompson, J. E. S. 1974. Comments (on Dobkin de Rios, 1974). Curr. Anthropol. 15(2):160.

Thorbjarnarson, J. B. 1992. Crocodiles: An action plan for their conservation. International Union for the Conservation of Nature and Natural Resources, Gland, Switzerland. 136 pp.

Thurow, G. R., and H. J. Gould. 1977. Sound production in a caecilian. Herpetologica 33:234–237.

Tinkle, D. W. 1957. Ecology, maturation and reproduction of *Thamnophis sauritus proximus*. Ecology 38:69–77.

Towle, K. G. 1989. Observation of the American crocodile (*Crocodylus acutus*) in Quintana Roo, Mexico. M.S. thesis, York University, Ontario, Canada. 105 pp.

Tozzer, A. M. 1907. A comparative study of the Mayas and the Lacandones. Macmillan, New York. xx + 195 pp.

Trapido, H. 1944. The snakes of the genus *Storeria*. Am. Midl. Nat. 31:1–84.

Trueb, L. 1970. The evolutionary relationships of casque-headed treefrogs with co-ossified skulls (family Hylidae). Univ. Kans. Publ. Mus. Nat. Hist. 18:547–716.

Vandelli, D. 1761. Epistola de holothurio, et testudine coriacea ad celeberrinum Carolum Linnaeum equitem naturae curiosum Discoridum II. Consatti, Patavii (Padova). 12 pp.

Van Devender, R. W. 1982. Growth and ecology of the spiny-tail and green iguanas in Costa Rica, with comments on the evolution of herbivory and large body size. *In*: G. M. Burghardt and A. S. Rand (eds.), Iguanas of the world. Their behavior, ecology, and conservation, pp. 162–183. Noyes Publications, Park Ridge, N.J.

Van Devender, R. W., and C. J. Cole. 1977. Notes on a colubrid snake, *Tantilla vermiformis*, from Central America. Am. Mus. Novit. 2625:1–12.

Vanzolini, P. E. 1986. Addenda and corrigenda to the *Catalogue of Neotropical Squamata*. Smithson. Herpetol. Info. Ser. 70:1–25.

Vanzolini, P. E., A. M. M. Ramos-Costa, and L. J. Vitt. 1980. Repteis das caatingas. Academia Brasileira de Ciencias, Rio de Janeiro. 161 pp.

Velasco, A. L. 1895. Geografía y estadística del estado de Campeche. *In*: Geographía y estadística de la República Mexicana. Secretaría de Fomento, Mexico City. Vol. 16. 140 pp.

Velasco, A. L. 1898. Geografía y estadística del estado de Chiapas. *In*: Geografía y Estadística del la República Mexicana. Secretaría de Fomento, Mexico City. Vol. 20. 164 pp.

Villa, J. 1969. Two new insular subspecies of the natricid snake *Tretanorhinus nigroluteus* Cope from Honduras and Nicaragua. J. Herpetol. 3:145–150.

Villa, J. 1970. Notas sobre la historia natural de la serpiente de los pantanos, *Tretanorhinus nigroluteus*. Rev. Biol. Trop. 17:97–104.

Villa, J. 1973. A snake in the diet of a kinosternid turtle. J. Herpetol. 7:380–381.

Villa, J. 1977. A symbiotic relationship between frog (Amphibia, Anura, Centrolenidae) and fly larvae (Drosphilidae). J. Herpetol. 11:317–322.

Villa, J. 1984a. Biology of a Neotropical glass frog, *Centrolenella fleischmanni* (Boettger), with special reference to its frogfly associates. Milw. Public Mus. Contrib. Biol. Geol. 55:1–60.

Villa, J. 1984b. The venomous snakes of Nicaragua: A synopsis. Milw. Public Mus. Contrib. Biol. Geol. 59:1–41.

Villa, J., L. D. Wilson, and J. D. Johnson. 1988. Middle American herpetology. University of Missouri Press, Columbia. xxxvi + 132 pp.

Vogt, R. C. 1990. Reproductive parameters of *Trachemys scripta venusta* in southern Mexico. *In*: J. W. Gibbons (ed.), Life history and ecology of the slider turtle, pp. 162–168. Smithsonian Institution Press, Washington, D.C.

Vogt, R. C., and O. F. Flores-Villela. 1992a. Effects of incubation temperature on sex determination in a community of Neotropical freshwater turtles in southern Mexico. Herpetologica 48:265–270.

Vogt, R. C., and O. F. Flores Villela. 1992b. Aspectos de la ecología de la tortuga blanca (*Dermatemys mawii*) en la reserva de la Biósfera Montes Azules. *In*: M. A. Vázquez Sánchez and M. A. Ramos (eds.), Reserva de la Biósfera Montes Azules, Selva Lacandona: Investigación para su conservación, pp. 221–231. Centro de Estudios para la Conservación de los Recursos Naturales, A.C. San Cristóbal de las Casas, Chiapas, Mexico.

Vogt, R. C., and S. Guzman G. 1988. Food partitioning in a Neotropical freshwater turtle community. Copeia 1988:37–47.

Volpe, E. P., and S. M. Harvey. 1958. Hybridization and larval development in *Rana palmipes* Spix. Copeia 1958:197–207.

Vrijenhoek, R. C., R. M. Dawley, C. J. Cole, and J. P. Bogart. 1989. A list of the known unisexual vertebrates. *In*: R. M. Dawley and J. P. Bogart (eds.), Evolution and ecology of unisexual vertebrates. Bull. N.Y. State Mus. 466:19–23.

Wade, D., and A. T. Weil. 1992. Identity of a New World psychoactive toad. Ancient Mesoameria 3:51–59.

Wagler, J. 1824. Serpentum brasiliensium species novae, ou histoire naturelle des espèces nouvelles de serpens, recueillies et observées pendant le voyage dans l'intérieur du Brésil; dans les années 1817, 1818, 1819, 1820. Publiée par Jean de Spix, Franc. Seraph. Hubschmanni, Monachii. vii + 75 pp.

Wagner, W. E., Jr., and B. K. Sullivan. 1992. Chorus organization in the Gulf Coast toad (*Bufo valliceps*): Male and female behavior and the opportunity for sexual selection. Copeia 1992:647–658.

Wake, D. B., and P. Elias. 1983. New genera and a new species of Central American salamanders, with a review of the tropical genera (Amphibia, Caudata, Plethodontidae). Los Ang. Cty. Mus. Contrib. Sci. 345:1–19.

Wake, D. B., and J. D. Johnson. 1989. A new genus and species of plethodontid salamander from Chiapas, Mexico. Los Ang. Cty. Mus. Contrib. Sci. 411:1–10.

Wake, D. B., and J. F. Lynch. 1976. The distribution, ecology, and evolutionary history of plethodontid salamanders in tropical America. Nat. Hist. Mus. Los Ang. Cty. Sci. Bull. 25:1–65.

Wake, M. H. 1977. The reproductive biology of caecilians: An evolutionary perspective. *In*: D. H. Taylor and S. I. Guttman (eds.), The reproductive biology of amphibians, pp. 73–101. Plenum Press, New York.

Wake, M. H. 1980. Reproduction, growth, and population structure of the Central American caecilian *Dermophis mexicanus*. Herpetologica 36:244–256.

Wake, M. H., and J. A. Campbell. 1983. A new genus and species of caecilian from the Sierra de las Minas of Guatemala. Copeia 1983:857–863.

Walters, V. 1953. Notes on reptiles and amphibians from El Vocan de Chiriqui, Panama. Copeia 1953:125–127.

Ward, J. P. 1980. Comparative cranial morphology of the freshwater turtle subfamily Emydinae: An analysis of the feeding mechanisms and systematics. Ph.D. dissertation, North Carolina State University, Raleigh.

Webb, R. G. 1958. The status of the Mexican lizards of the genus *Mabuya*. Univ. Kans. Sci. Bull. 38:1303–1313.

Weins, J. J. 1993. Phylogenetic relationships of phrynosomatid lizards and monophyly of the *Sceloporus* group. Copeia 1993:287–299.

Wellman, J. 1963. A revision of snakes of the genus *Conophis* (family Colubridae) from Middle America. Univ. Kans. Publ. Mus. Nat. Hist. 15(6):251–295.

Wells, K. D. 1977. The social behavior of anuran amphibians. Anim. Behav. 25:666–693.

Wells, K. D. 1988. The effect of social interactions on anuran vocal behavior. *In*: B. Fritzsch, M. J. Ryan, W. Wilczynski, T. E. Hetterington, and W. Walkowiala (eds.), The evolution of the amphibian auditory system, pp. 433–454. John Wiley and Sons, New York.

Wells, K. D., and M. Bard. 1987. Vocal communication in a Neotropical treefrog, *Hyla ebraccata*: Response of females to advertisement and aggressive calls. Behavior 101:200–210.

Wells, K. D., and B. J. Greer. 1981. Vocal responses to conspecific calls in a Neotropical hylid frog, *Hyla ebraccata*. Copeia 1981:615–624.

Wells, K. D., and J. J. Schwartz. 1984. Vocal communication in a Neotropical treefrog, *Hyla ebraccata*: Aggressive calls. Behavior 91:128–145.

Werler, J. E. 1949. Eggs and young of several Texas and Mexican snakes. Herpetologica 5:59–60.

Werler, J. E. 1951. Miscellaneous notes on the eggs and young of Texan and Mexican reptiles. Zoologica 36:37–48.

Werler, J. E., and H. M. Smith. 1952. Notes on a collection of reptiles and amphibians from Mexico, 1951–1952. Tex. J. Sci. 4:551–573.

Werman, S. D. 1984. The taxonomic status of *Bothrops superciliaris* Taylor. J. Herpetol. 18:484–486.

Werman, S. D. 1992. Phylogenetic relationships of Central and South American pitvipers of the genus *Bothrops* (*sensu lato*): Cladistic analyses of biochemical and anatomical characters. *In*: J. A. Campbell and E. D. Brodie, Jr. (eds.), Biology of the pitvipers, pp. 21–40. Selva Press, Tyler, Tex.

Wermuth, H., and R. Mertens. 1977. Liste der rezenten Amphibien und Reptilien. Testudines, Crocodylia, Rhynchocephalia. Das Tierreich 100. W. de Gruyter, Berlin. xxvii + 174 pp.

Werner, F. 1903. Über Reptilien und Batrachier aus Guatemala und China in der zoologischen Staats-Sammlung in München nebst einem Anhang über seltene Formen aus anderen Gebieten. Abh. Bayer Akad. Wiss. Math.-Phys. Kl. 22:343–384.

Wertime, R. A., and A. M. H. Schuster. 1993. Written in the stars. Archaeology 46:26–35.

Weyer, D. 1990. Snakes of Belize. Belize Audubon Society, Angelus Press. 54 pp.

Wied-Neuwied, M. 1824. Verzeichniss der Amphibien, welche im zweiten Bande der Naturgeschichte Brasiliens vom Prinz Max von Neuwied werden beschrieben werden. Isis von Oken 6:662–674.

Wiegmann, A. F. A. 1828. Beyträge zur Amphibienkunde. Isis von Oken 21:364–383.

Wiegmann, A. F. A. 1833. Herpetologische Beyträge. 1. Über die mexicanischen Kröten nebst Bemerkungen über ihnen verwandte Arten anderer Weltgegenden. Isis von Oken 26:651–662.

Wiegmann, A. F. A. 1834. Herpetologica Mexicana, seu descriptio amphibiorum novae hispaniae . . . pars prima. C. G. Luderitz, Berlin. vi + 54 pp.

Wiegmann, A. F. A. 1835. Amphibien. *In*: F. G. F. Meyen, Beiträge zur Zoologie, gesammelt auf ein Reise um die Erde. Nova Acta Acad. Caesar Leop.-Carol. (Halle) 17:183–188, 268a-268d.

Wiens, J. L. 1993. Phylogenetic relationships of phrynosomatid lizards and monophyly of the *Sceloporus* group. Copeia 1993:287–299.

Williams, E. E. 1966. South American anoles: *Anolis biporcatus* and *Anolis fraseri* (Sauria, Iguanidae) compared. Breviora 239:1–14.

Williams, E. E. 1989. A critique of Guyer and Savage (1986): Cladistic relationships among anoles (Sauria: Iguanidae): Are the data available to reclassify the anoles? *In*: C. A. Woods (ed.), Biogeography of the West Indies, pp. 433–478. Sandhill Crane Press, Gainesville, Fla. xvii + 878 pp.

Williams, K. L. 1988. Systematics and natural history of the American milk snake. 2nd ed. Milwaukee Public Museum, Milwaukee. x + 176 pp.

Wilson, L. D. 1966. The range of the Rio Grande racer in Mexico and the status of *Coluber oaxaca* (Jan). Herpetologica 22:42–47.

Wilson, L. D. 1973. *Masticophis*. Cat. Am. Amphib. Reptiles 144.1–144.2.

Wilson, L. D. 1975a. *Drymobius*. Cat. Am. Amphib. Reptiles 170.1–170.2.

Wilson, L. D. 1975b. *Drymobius margaritiferus*. Cat. Am. Amphib. Reptiles 172.1–172.2.

Wilson, L. D. 1978. *Coluber constrictor*. Cat. Am. Amphib. Reptiles 218.1–218.4.

Wilson, L. D. 1982a. A review of the colubrid snakes of the genus *Tantilla* of Central America. Milw. Public Mus. Contrib. Biol. Geol. 52:1–77.

Wilson, L. D. 1982b. *Tantilla* Cat. Am. Amphib. Reptiles 307.1–307.4.

Wilson, L. D. 1987. *Tantilla schistosa*. Cat. Am. Amphib. Reptiles 409.1–409.2.

Wilson, L. D. 1988a. *Tantilla canula* Cat. Am. Amphib. Reptiles 434:1.

Wilson, L. D. 1988b. *Amastridium. Amastridium veliferum*. Cat. Am. Amphib. Reptiles 449.1–449.3.

Wilson, L. D. 1988c. *Tantilla moesta*. Cat. Am. Amphib. Reptiles 454.1.

Wilson, L. D. 1988d. *Tantillita, T. brevissima, T. lintoni*. Cat. Am. Amphib. Reptiles 455.1–455.2.

Wilson, L. D., and G. A. Cruz Díaz. 1993. The herpetofauna of the Cayos Cochinos, Honduras. Herpetol. Nat. Hist. 1:13–23.

Wilson, L. D., and D. E. Hahn. 1973. The herpetofauna of the Islas de la Bahía, Honduras. Bull. Fla. State Mus. 17:93–150.

Wilson, L. D., and J. R. McCranie. 1984. *Bothrops nasuta*. Cat. Am. Amphib. Reptiles 349.1–349.2.

Wilson, L. D., J. R. McCranie, and K. L. Williams. 1985. Two new species of fringe-limbed hylid frogs from nuclear Middle America. Herpetologica 41:141–150.

Wilson, L. D., J. R. McCranie, and K. L. Williams. 1986. The identity of the crocodile of Lago de Yojoa, Honduras. J. Herpetol. 20:87–88.

Wilson, L. D., and J. R. Meyer. 1969. A review of the colubrid snake genus *Amastridium*. Bull. South. Calif. Acad. Sci. 68:145–159.

Wilson, L. D., and J. R. Meyer. 1972. The coral snake *Micrurus nigrocinctus* in Honduras (Serpentes: Elapidae). Bull. South. Calif. Acad. Sci. 71:139–145.

Wilson, L. D., and J. R. Meyer. 1982. The snakes of Honduras. Milwaukee Public Museum, Milwaukee. 159 pp.

Wilson, L. D., and J. R. Meyer. 1985. The snakes of Honduras. 2nd ed. Milwaukee Public Museum, Milwaukee. x + 150 pp.

Wilson, L. D., L. Porras, and J. R. McCranie. 1986. Distributional and taxonomic comments on some members of the Honduran herpetofauna. Milw. Public Mus. Contrib. Biol. Geol. 66:1–18.

Wilson, R. V., and G. R. Zug. 1991. *Lepidochelys kempii*. Cat. Am. Amphib. Reptiles 509.1–509.8.

Wing, E. S. 1974. Vertebrate faunal remains. *In*: E. W. Andrews IV et al., Excavation of an early shell midden on Isla Cancún, Quintana Roo, Mexico, pp. 186–188. Middle American Research Institute Publication 21. Tulane University, New Orleans.

Wing, E. S. 1975. Animal remains from Lubaantún. *In*: N. Hammond (ed.), Lubaantún a classic Maya realm, pp. 379–383. Peabody Mus. Archaeol. Ethnol. Harvard Univ., Peabody Mus. Monogr. 2. xvii + 428 pp.

Wing, E. S., and S. J. Scudder. 1991. The exploitation of animals. *In*: N. Hammond (ed.), Cuello, an early Maya community in Belize, pp. 84–97. Cambridge University Press, Cambridge.

Wing, E. S., and D. Steadman. 1980. Vertebrate faunal remains from Dzibilchaltún. *In*: E. W. Andrews IV and E. W. V. Andrews (eds.), Excavations at Dzibilchaltún, Yucatán, Mexico, pp. 326–331. Middle American Research Institute Publication 48. Tulane University, New Orleans.

Wright, A. H., and A. A. Wright. 1957. Handbook of snakes of the United States and Canada. 2 vols. Comstock Publishing Associates, Ithaca. Reprinted 1994, Comstock Classic Handbooks, Cornell University Press, Ithaca. 1105 pp.

Wright, J. W., and L. J. Vitt (eds.). 1993. Biology of whiptail lizards (genus *Cnemidophorus*). Oklahoma Museum of Natural History and the University of Oklahoma Press, Norman. xiv + 417 pp.

Wright, N. P. 1973. A guide to Mexican amphibians and reptiles. 3rd ed. Minutiae Mexicana, Mexico. 112 pp.

Yingling, R. P. 1972. A review of the colubrid snake *Imantodes gemmistratus*. M.S. thesis, San Diego State University. 87 pp.

Yntema, C. L., and N. Mrosovsky. 1982. Critical periods and pivotal temperatures for sexual differentiation in loggerhead sea turtles. Can. J. Zool. 60:1012–1016.

Zug, G. R., S. B. Hedges, and S. Sunkel. 1979. Variation in reproductive parameters of three Neotropical snakes, *Coniophanes fissidens*, *Dipsas catesbyi*, and *Imantodes cenchoa*. Smithson. Contrib. Zool. 300:1–20.

Zug, G. R., E. Lindgren, and J. R. Pippet. 1975. Distribution and ecology of the marine toad, *Bufo marinus*, in Papua New Guinea. Pac. Sci. 29:31–50.

Zug, G. R., and P. B. Zug. 1979. The marine toad, *Bufo marinus*: A natural history resume of native populations. Smithson. Contrib. Zool. 284:1–58.

Zweifel, R. G. 1959. Snakes of the genus *Imantodes* in western Mexico. Am. Mus. Novit. 1961:1–18.

Zweifel, R. G. 1964. Life history of *Phrynohyas venulosa* (Salientia: Hylidae) in Panama. Copeia 1964:201–208.

Zwinenberg, A. J. 1977. Kemp's ridley, *Lepidochelys kempii* (Garman, 1880), undoubtedly the most endangered marine turtle today (with notes on the current status of *Lepidochelys olivacia*). Bull. Md. Herpetol. Soc. 13:170–192.

Subject Index

Citations of material in the black-and-white figures, the maps, and the table are designated by "f," "m," and "t," respectively, following their page numbers. Citations of material in the color photos is by figure number. Figs. 1–24 follow page 20, and Figs. 218–403 follow page 436.

Palenque (Chiapas), 22, 47, 184, 234, 299, 323, 417, 422–423, 429, 444m, 445
Palenque triad, 422–423
parthenogenesis
    in *Cnemidophorus*, 25
    in *Cnemidophorus cozumela*, 266
    in *Cnemidophorus rodecki*, 269
    in *Ramphotyphlops braminus*, 279
Pearse, A. S., 20, 21
Pérez Cruz, Enrique, 27
Peters, J. A., 24
Peters, Wilhelm Carl Hartwig, 18–19
phragmosis in *Triprion petasatus*, 114
physiography, 7–8
Piedras Negras (El Petén), 22, 322, 342, 359, 439m, 440
Platt, Steven, 27
plumed serpent, 422f.205, 426
Poliser, John, 27
Popol Vuh, 412, 420
Porras, Louis, 26

rainfall, amount and seasonality, 8
ramonal, 14
Ramón de la Sagra, 237
rattlesnake god. *See* Ahau Can
Relación de las cosas de Yucatán, 412, 414, 416
reproduction. *See under* "*Natural History*" *in individual species accounts*
reptiles, general characteristics, 129
Rick, Anne Meachem, 22
Ricketson, Oliver G., Jr., 21
Río Bec region (Campeche), 423
Rituals of the Bacabs, 412

salamanders
    body temperature, 42, 44
    general characteristics, 37
    identification, 37–38
    nasolabial groove in plethodontids, 38
Salvin, Osbert, 18
Sanderson, Ivan T., 23
Satterthwaite, Linton P., 381
Savage, Jay M., 66
savanna
    nanze, 14
    pine, 14
Schiede, Christian, 17
Schmidt, Karl Patterson, 23, 28, 306
Schoepf, J. D., 17
Schott, Arthur, 20
sea turtles, conservation status, 138
Seba, Albertus, 17, 344
Seibal (El Petén), 314, 414, 423, 427, 429, 439, 439m
serpent-footed god, 423
Sierrita de Ticul (Yucatán), 2m, 7
Sites, Jack W., 26
sky serpent, 421
Smith, Hobart M., 21, 22, 28,
Smith, Rozella B., 22, 275
Smithe, Frank B., 21
Smithson, James, 19
snake bite
    among ancient Maya, 416, 416f

symptoms of bite by
    Agkistrodon bilineatus, 399
    Atropoides nummifer, 401
    Bothriechis schlegelii, 403
    Bothrops asper, 404
    Coniophanes imperialis, 302
    Conophis lineatus, 284, 307
    Crotalus durissus, 407
    Drymobius margaritiferus, 318
    Oxybelis aeneus, 347
    Oxybelis fulgidus, 348
    Porthidium nasutum, 409
    Urotheca elapoides, 284, 388
    treatment among Maya, 417
snakes
    general characteristics, 275
    identification, 275–278
    Maya belief in dangers of, 417–418
    Maya belief in medicinal properties, 415
    in Maya diet, 414
    in Maya iconography, 412, 416f, 421–422, 422f–425f, 427f, 430f
    mimicry in, 329, 343, 354, 387, 389, 404
    remains recovered from archaeological sites, 429
Sordelli, Ferdinand, 19
species diversity of herpetofauna, 15
spiracles of tadpoles, 50–51, 50f.34
Stanton, W. A., 23
Steyermark, Julian, 21
Stuart, Laurence C., 21, 23, 28
subspecies, recognition, 5

tadpoles
    configuration of tail, 51, 51f.38
    identification, 50–53
    mouthparts, 50f.35, 51, 51f.36
    position of eye, 51
    position of vent tube, 51, 51f.37
    spiracles, 50–51, 50f.34
taxinchan, 416
taxonomic composition of herpetofauna, 15, 15t
Taylor, Edward H., 22
Taylor, Harry L., 26
temperature-dependent sex determination
    in crocodilians, 133, 135
    in turtles, 142, 144, 151, 152, 169
temperatures of Yucatán Peninsula, 8
Thompson, Edward H., 20
Thompson, Frederick G., 25
Tikal (El Petén), 21, 22, 56, 181, 193, 196, 228, 291, 302, 333, 351, 362, 376, 381, 389, 409, 414, 421, 429, 439m, 441
toads
    association with rain, 426
    general characteristics, 47
    as helpers of chacs, 426
    identification, 47–49
    Maya belief in medicinal properties, 415
    in Maya ceremony, 426
    in Maya iconography, 412, 427
    in Maya religion and mythology, 426
    remains found at archaeological sites, 426–427
    as sources of hallucinogens, 428
    vocal sacs, 49; Fig. 237

Towle, Kenneth, 26
turtles
    conservation status of sea turtles, 138
    in diet of Maya, 413–414
    as earth monster, 420, 421f.202, 429
    general characteristics, 136
    identification, 136–138
    incubation temperature of eggs, 141, 144, 151, 155, 156, 161, 169
    Maya belief in medicinal properties, 415
    in Maya iconography, 412, 415, 420, 421f.202, 427
    as Maya musical instruments, 415
    in Maya religion and mythology, 413, 428
    as Maya sacrificial items, 428
    remains recovered from Maya archaeological sites, 413–414
    temperature-dependent sex determination, 142, 144, 151, 152, 169
tzabcan, 416, 416f, 423

Uaxactún (El Petén), 21, 151, 166, 429, 439m, 441
uinal, 420
uolpoch, 416, 425
Uxmal (Yucatán), 422, 424, 428, 448m, 450

Vaca Plateau (Belize), 7, 434m, 436
Vaillant, Leon-Louis, 19, 128
Vandelli, D., 17
van der Schalie, Henry, 21
Van Tyne, Josselyn, 21, 23
vegetation of Yucatán Peninsula, 9–10; Figs. 1–4, 7–14, 21–24
Velasco, Alfonso Luis, 20
vent tube, position in tadpoles, 51, 51f.37
Victoria Peak (Belize), 7
vision serpent, 429, 430f
Vitt, Laurie J., 25
vocalization
    by frogs and toads, *see individual species accounts*
    by lizards, 174, 174f, 182, 184, 185f, 228
vocal sacs in frogs and toads, 49; Figs. 237, 246, 249
Vogt, Richard C., 26
von Sack, Graf, 17

Waldeck, Jean-Fréderic, 169–170
Welling, Edward, 25
Wellman, John, 24
wetland, 13; Fig. 21
Wiegmann, Arend Friedrich August, 17
Wilson, Larry David, 26
Wolffsohn, Anthony, 24

Xbalanque, 421f.202, 429. *See also* Hero Twins
Xibalba, 420, 421
x-tabai, 418
Xunantunich (Belize), 24, 234, 434m, 436

Yaxchilán (Chiapas), 423, 429, 444m, 445
yaxtoloc, 419
Yucatán Peninsula, definition, 1

Taxonomic Index

Page numbers in boldface indicate the location of the detailed discussion of the taxon. Citations of material in the black-and-white figures and maps are designated by "f" and "m," respectively, following their page numbers. Citations of material in the color photos is by figure number. Figs. 1–24 follow page 20, and Figs. 218–403 follow page 436.

Mabuya (cont.)
  unimarginata, 12, 207, 243f.134, **247–249**, 248m; Fig. 335
Manilkara zapota, 9
Masticophis, 287, 289, **338**, 414
  melanolomus, 313. See also Dryadophis melanolomus
  mentovarius, 18, 284, **338–340**, 339m; Figs. 371, 372
Mastigodryas, 314, 315. See also Dryadophis
  danieli, 314, 315
  melanolomus, 314. See also D. melanolomus
mazacoatl, mazacuata, 282. See also Boa constrictor
mechech, 259. See also Ameiva undulata
merech, 212, 214, 236. See also Anolis sagrei, Sceloporus chrysostictus, S. cozumelae
Mesopeltis sanniolus, 362
Microhylidae, 49, 50, **117**
Micrurus, 386, 388, **390**, 394
  diastema, 14, 18, 246, 277f, 280, 345, 365, **390–393**, 391f, 392m; Figs. 395, 396
    alienus, 392
    sapperi, 392
  hippocrepis, 19, 390, **393–394**, 394m
  nigrocinctus, 19, 390, **394–396**, 395f,m
    divaricatus, 396
Mimosa albida, 10
Minascaecilia sartoria, 37. See also Gymnopis syntrema
Mocoa cherriei, 249. See also Sphenomorphus cherriei
mojina, 165. See also Rhinoclemmys areolata
much, 76, 79. See also Bufo marinus, B. valliceps
Mus musculus, 356
mussurana, 293, 295. See also Clelia clelia, C. scytalina

naricilla manchada, 321. See also Ficimia publia
Natrix, 340. See also Nerodia
nauyaca, 333. See also Leptodeira septentrionalis
  de agua, 384. See also Tretanorhinus nigroluteus
  chatilla, 409. See also Porthidium nasutum
  cornuda, 402. See also Bothriechis schlegelii
  de pestanas, 402. See also Bothriechis schlegelii
  real, 403. See also Bothrops asper
  saltadora, 400. See also Atropoides nummifer
Nerodia, 286, 288, **340**
  rhombifer, 13, 15, **340–341**, 340f, 341m
    werleri, 341
  rhombifera, 341
nim li compopó, 76. See also Bufo marinus
Ninia, 286, 289, **341**, 343, 395
  diademata, 14, 19, **342–343**, 342f, 343m
    nietoi, 343
  sebae, 18, 284, 300, 337, 342, **343–345**, 344m; Figs. 373, 374
    morleyi, 344
    sebae, 344
nohoch ak, 149. See also Dermatemys mawii

Norops, 224. See also Anolis
nu putii, 158, 162. See also Kinosternon acutum, K. scorpioides

och-can, ochcan, 282, 418. See also Boa constrictor
Oedipina, 39, **46**
  elongata, **46–47**, 46f, 47m
Oedipus
  elongatus, 46. See also Oedipina elongata
  rufescens, 43. See also Bolitoglossa rufescens
old man, 195, 197. See also Corytophanes cristatus, C. hernandezii
Ololygon, 104, 106. See also Scinax
Opheodrys mayae, 373. See also Symphimus mayae
Orbignya cohune, 9, 13
ornate terrapin, 168. See also Terrapene carolina
Ovalipes, 147
owla, 282. See also Boa constrictor
Oxybelis, 25, 284, 286, 289, **345**, 346, 347
  aeneus, **346–348**, 346f, 347m; Fig. 375
  fulgidus, 346, **348–349**, 348f, 349m, 418; Fig. 376
Oxyrhopus, 287, 289, **349**
  petola, **349–350**, 350m; Fig. 377
  sebae, 350

pajarera, 351. See also Pseustes poecilonotus
Paludicola pustulosa, 73. See also Physalaemus pustulosus
parlama, 142. See also Chelonia mydas
pasarios, 191. See also Basiliscus vittatus
perito, 173. See also Coleonyx elegans
petatilla, petatilla de pintas verdes, 317. See also Drymobius margaritiferus
Pharyngodon petasatus, 112. See also Triprion petasatus
Phrynohyas, 83, **101**
  venulosa, 4, 17, 48, 49, 52, 53, 83, **101–104**, 101f, 102f,m, 337; Figs. 245, 246
Phrynosomatidae, 172, **211**
Phyllodactylus, 23, 176, **186**
  insularis, 23, **186–188**, 187m; Fig. 295
  tuberculosus, 186, **187–188**, 188m; Fig. 296
    ingeri, 188
Phyllomedusa, 84
Physalaemus, 57, **73**
  pustulosus, 47, 52, 53, **73–75**, 74f, 75m; Fig. 234
piconé, 177. See also Sphaerodactylus argus
piende jente, 195. See also Corytophanes cristatus
p'ik ron puch, 247. See also Mabuya unimarginata
Pinus
  caribaea, 14
  oocarpa, 9
Piper, 9
pitviper
  hognosed, 408. See also Porthidium
    rainforest, 409. See also P. nasutum
    Yucatán, 410. See also P. yucatanicum
  jumping, 400. See also Atropoides nummifer
  palm, 401. See also Bothriechis
    eyelash, 402. See also B. schlegelii

Platysternon, 152
Plethodontidae, **38**
Pliocercus, 386, 388. See also Urotheca
  andrewsi, 388
  elapoides, 386. See also Urotheca elapoides
pochitoque, 158, 160, 162. See also Kinosternon acutum, K. leucostomum, K. scorpioides
  jaquactero, 158. See also K. acutum
Podocarpus guatemalensis, 9
Polychrotidae, 172, **223**
Porthidium, 396, 400, **408**
  nasutum, 397f.197, 408, **409–410**, 409m, 411; Fig. 402
  yucatanicum, 22, 25, 408, **410–411**, 411m; Fig. 403
Prionodactylus manicatus, 350
Pseudemys, 168. See also Trachemys
Pseustes, 286, 288, **350**
  poecilonotus, 14, 17, **350–352**, 351m; Fig. 378
puffer, 351. See also Pseustes poecilonotus

quech yaax, 84, 87. See also Agalychnis callidryas, A. moreletii
Quercus, 9

racer, 296. See also Coluber constrictor
  barred forest, 310. See also Dendrophidion vinitor
  black-naped forest, 309. See also D. nuchale
  Oaxaca, 296. See also C. constrictor
  speckled, 317. See also Drymobius margaritiferus
racerunner, black-bellied, 267. See also Cnemidophorus deppii
ramón, 9, 14
Ramphotyphlops braminus, 279
rana
  arbórea, 84, 87, 101, 107, 112. See also Agalychnis callidryas, A. moreletii, Phrynohyas venulosa, Smilisca baudinii, Triprion petasatus
  arborícola, 93, 95, 97. See also Hyla loquax, H. microcephala, H. picta
  arborícola mexicana, 107. See also Smilisca baudinii
  cavernícola de cabeza ancha, 61. See also Eleutherodactylus laticeps
  leopardo, 122. See also Rana berlandieri
  manglera, 119. See also Hypopachus variolosus
  verde, 84, 126. See also Agalychnis callidryas, Rana vaillanti
Rana, **121**
  berlandieri, 13, 48f.30, 52, 53, 121, **122–125**, 122f, 123f,m, 318, 414; Figs. 256, 257
    brownorum, 123, 124
  juliani, 13, 52, 54, 121, 122, **125–126**, 125f, 126m; Fig. 258
  maculata, 126
  palmipes, 126, 127
  sierramadrensis, 126
  vaillanti, 19, 52, 54, 121, 122, **126–128**, 127f,m; Fig. 259
  venulosa, 101
ranera, 317, 336. See also Drymobius margaritiferus, Leptophis mexicanus
  bronceada, 336. See also L. mexicanus
  verde, 335. See also L. ahaetulla
Ranidae, 49, 50, **121**

ranita, 64, 95, 97. See also *Eleutherodac-tylus rhodopis, Hyla microcephala, H. picta*

boquita, 54. See also *Rhinophrynus dorsalis*

hojarasca, 68, 71. See also *Leptodactylus labialis, L. melanonotus*

verde, 115. See also *Hyalinobatrachium fleischmanni*

ratonera

manchada, 319. See also *Elaphe flavirufa*

oliva, 355. See also *Senticolis triaspis*

reina

de culebra, 271, 272. See also *Lepidophyma flavimaculatum*

de las culebras, 315. See also *Drymarchon corais*

Reptilia, **129**

rerek, 95, 97, 107. See also *Hyla microcephala, H. picta, Smilisca baudinii*

cho, 335. See also *Leptophis ahaetulla*

Rhadinaea, 286, 289, **352**, 386, 388

decorata, **352–354**, 353f,m; Fig. 379

lateristriga, 386

Rhinoclemmys, 164, **165**

areolata, 18, **165–67**, 165m, 413, 428, 429; Figs. 281, 282

Rhinophrynidae, 49, **54**

Rhinophrynus, **54**

dorsalis, 14, 18, 49, 52, 53, **54–56**, 55f,m, 318, 414; Fig. 224

Rhizophora mengale, 11

Rhynchocephalia, 129

ruki'ak, 152. See also *Chelydra serpentina*

Sabal, 9

sabanera, 307, 338. See also *Conophis lineatus, Masticophis mentovarius*

Saccharum officinarum, 12

salamander

Doflein's, 40. See also *Bolitoglossa dofleini*

lungless, 38. *See also* Plethodontidae

Müller's, 42. See also *B. mulleri*

rufescent, 43. See also *B. rufescens*

Yucatán, 44. See also *B. yucatana*

salamandra de Yucatán, 44. See also *Bolitoglossa yucatana*

salamanquesa, 41, 42, 44, 173, 182, 187, 247, 251. See also *Aristelliger georgeensis, Bolitoglossa mexicana, B. mulleri, B. yucatana, Coleonyx elegans, Gymnophthalmus speciosus, Mabuya unimarginata, Phyllodactylus tuberculosus*

sambodanga, 152. See also *Chelydra serpentina*

sapito, 118. See also *Gastrophryne elegans*

sapo

borracho, 54. See also *Rhinophrynus dorsalis*

común, 79. See also *Bufo valliceps*

grande, 76. See also *B. marinus*

marino, 76. See also *B. marinus*

Scaphiodontophis, 18, **354–355**, 355m; Fig. 380

annulatus, 18, **354–355**, 355m; Fig. 380

Sceloporus, 4, **211**, 332

chrysostictus, 12, 19, 211, **212–214**, 213m, 410; Figs. 311, 312

cozumelae, 12, 11, 211, 212, **214–217**, 215f, 216m, 339; Fig. 313

cyanogenys, 220

lundelli, 23, 121, **217–218**, 217f, 218m; Fig. 314

gaigeae, 218

lundelli, 218

malachiticus, 218

serrifer, 12, 19, 212, **219–221**, 219f, 220m; Fig. 315

prezygus, 220

serrifer, 220

teapensis, 211–212, **221–223**, 221f, 222m; Figs. 316, 317

torquatus, 220

variabilis, 222, 223

Scinax, 83, **104**, 106

staufferi, 12, 13, 53, 54, **104–106**, 104f, 105f,m, 302, 333; Fig. 247

staufferi, 105

Scincella, 250

Scincidae, 172, **243**

Scolecophis scytalinus, 295. See also *Clelia scytalina*

Senticolis, 286, 288, **355**

triaspis, 19, 284f, **355–357**, 356m; Fig. 381

intermedius, 357

mutabilis, 357

triaspis, 357

Sibon, 286, 288, **357**

dimidiata, **358–360**, 359f,m; Fig. 382

fasciata, 17, 358, **360–361**, 360f, 361m

frenatum, 331

nebulata, 285f.153, 312, 358, 359f.178, **361–362**, 361f, 362m

neilli, 363

sanniola, 358, **362–364**, 363f,m; Figs. 383, 384

neilli, 363

sartorii, 358, **364–366**, 365f,m, 392; Fig. 385

siete filos, 148. See also *Dermochelys coriacea*

sikil-can, 369. See also *Stenorrhina freminvillei*

Siphonops

mexicanus, 35. See also *Dermophis mexicanus*

syntremus, 36. See also *Gymnopis syntremus*

skink, 243. See also *Eumeces*, Scincidae

ground, 249. See also *Sphenomorphus cherriei*

Schwartze's or Yucatán giant, 244. See also *E. schwartzei*

Sumichrast's, 246. See also *E. sumichrasti*

slider, common, 168. See also *Trachemys scripta*

Smilisca, 83, **106**, 332, 333

baudinii, 4, 13, 18, 49, 53, 54, **107–110**, 107f, 108f, 109m, 333, 337, 384; Figs. 248, 249

cyanosticta, 22, 53, 54, 107f, **110–112**, 111f, 112m; Figs. 250, 251

snail sucker

banded, 360. See also *Sibon fasciata*

pygmy, 363. See also *S. sanniola*

Sartorius', 364. See also *S. sartorii*

short-faced, 311. See also *Dipsas brevifacies*

slender, 358. See also *S. dimidiata*

speckled, 361. See also *S. nebulata*

snake

black-striped, 301. See also *Coniophanes imperialis*

black water, 384. See also *Tretanorhinus nigroluteus*

blindsnake, 278. *See also* Leptotyphlopidae

slender, 280. See also *Leptotyphlops goudotii*

brown, 371. See also *Storeria*

tropical, 371. See also *S. dekayi*

cat-eyed, 330, 331, 333. See also *Leptodeira*

coffee

red, 343. See also *Ninia sebae*

ring-necked, 342. See also *N. diademata*

coral, 19, 280, 297, 344, 354, 365. See also *Micrurus*

Central American, 394. See also *M. nigrocinctus*

many-ringed, 390. See also *M. diastema*

Maya, 393. See also *M. hippocrepis*

diamondback water, 340. See also *Nerodia rhombifer*

double, 354. See also *Scaphiodontophis annulatus*

dryad, 313. See also *Dryadophis melanolomus*

five-lined, 304. See also *Coniophanes quinquevittatus*

garter, 381. See also *Thamnophis*

Central American, checkered, or Marcy's, 381–382. See also *T. marcianus*

green or guinea hen, 317. See also *Drymobius margaritiferus*

hooknosed, Yucatán, 321. See also *Ficimia publia*

indigo, black-tailed, 315. See also *Drymarchon corais*

kingsnake, tropical, 329. See also *Lampropeltis triangulum*

many-lined, 307. See also *Conophis lineatus*

milk, tropical, 329. See also *Lampropeltis triangulum*

monkey, 366. See also *Spilotes pullatus*

rat

Neotropical, 355. See also *Senticolis triaspis*

tropical, 319. See also *Elaphe flavirufa*

rattlesnake, 16, 405, 414, 415, 416, 420, 421, 423, 424, 425, 430, 431. See also *Crotalus*

Neotropical, 406. See also *C. durissus*

red-banded, 349. See also *Oxyrhopus petola*

red-bellied, 371. See also *Storeria*

ribbon, 381. See also *Thamnophis*

Central American, 383. See also *T. proximus*

shovel-tooth, 354. See also *Scaphiodontophis annulatus*

snail-eating, 311. See also *Dipsas brevifacies*

thunder and lightning, 366. See also *Spilotes pullatus*

tie tie, 346. See also *Oxybelis aeneus*

tree

blunt-headed, 324. See also *Imantodes*

brown, 351. See also *Pseustes poecilonotus*

green, 335. See also *Leptophis ahaetulla*

Yucatán blunt-headed, 327. See also *I. tenuissimus*